The SAGE
Handbook of
Hospitality
Management

The SAGE
Handbook of
Hospitality
Management

Edited by

Bob Brotherton and
Roy C. Wood

Los Angeles • London • New Delhi • Singapore

First Published 2008

SAGE Publications Ltd
1 Oliver's Yard
55 City Road
London EC1Y 1SP

SAGE Publications Inc.
2455 Teller Road
Thousand Oaks, California 91320

SAGE Publications India Pvt Ltd
B 1/I 1 Mohan Cooperative Industrial Area
Mathura Road
New Delhi 110 044

SAGE Publications Asia-Pacific Pte Ltd
33 Pekin Street #02-01
Far East Square
Singapore 048763

Library of Congress Control Number: 2007933009

British Library Cataloguing in Publication data

A catalogue record for this book is available from
the British Library

ISBN 978-1-4129-0025-6

Typeset by CEPHA Imaging Pvt. Ltd., Bangalore, India
Printed in Great Britain by The Cromwell Press Ltd,
Trowbridge, Wiltshire
Printed on paper from sustainable resources

Contents

Tables

Figures

Contributors

Helen Atkinson is Principal Lecturer at the School of Service Management in the University of Brighton, UK. She has a background in Hospitality Management, a BA (Hons) Accounting and Finance and is a qualified Management Accountant with CIMA. She has an MBA from Henley Management College and has lectured, researched and published in the area of hospitality accounting since 1989 and is currently on the education committee of BAHA (the British Association of Hospitality Accountants). Her research interests include; strategic management accounting; performance management; strategy implementation in the hospitality and service industries and approaches to budgeting in hotels. She has published in journals and text books.

Clayton Barrows is Professor of Hospitality Management at the University of New Hampshire, USA. He has worked in the hospitality industry and hospitality education in North America for 25 years, most recently at the University of Guelph, Canada. His areas of expertise are food and beverage management and private club management. He has published numerous articles in both of these areas in such journals as the *Journal of Foodservice Business Research* and the *International Journal of Contemporary Hospitality Management*. Additionally, he has co-authored four books relating to the hospitality industry. He is editor of the *International Journal of Hospitality and Tourism Administration*, a Haworth Press publication.

Paul Beals, PhD, is Visiting Professor at France's IMHI-ESSEC Business School, where he is responsible for MBA courses in finance and hotel real estate. For more than 25 years, Beals's academic research and consulting have been concentrated in hotel-industry development and financing, asset management, and management contracts. He is the editor, along with Greg Denton, of *Hotel Asset Management: Principles and Practices*, published in 2004 by the Educational Institute of the American Hotel and Lodging Association. In addition to two other books he has written more than 50 book chapters and articles, primarily in the area of hotel finance and investments, which have appeared in *The Cornell Hotel and Restaurant Administration Quarterly*, *Journal of Real Estate Finance*, *Real Estate Review*, *Journal of Hospitality Financial Management*, *Journal of Retail and Leisure Property*, *L'Hôtel Revue*, and *Le Monde*. A member of Phi Beta Kappa, the Hospitality Asset Managers Association (HAMA), and the Cornell Hotel Society, he has earned master's and doctorate degrees from Cornell University.

John Bowen is the Dean of the Conrad N. Hilton College of Hotel and Restaurant Management at the University of Houston, USA. John has presented marketing courses and seminars in Asia, Australia, Central America, Europe, Mexico and South America. He has published over 100 articles on marketing. John is a co-author of *Marketing for Hospitality and Tourism*, the leading hospitality marketing text worldwide. It is currently published in eight languages. He is also the co-author of *Restaurant Marketing for Owners and Managers*. John has won numerous awards for both his teaching and research. John's industry experience was in the area of food and beverage. He worked in hotels, freestanding restaurants and as the corporate food and beverage manager for a hotel management company.

Bob Brotherton, PhD, was, until 2004, a Principal Lecturer in Hospitality Management at the Manchester Metropolitan University, UK, where he held positions of Director of undergraduate, and latterly postgraduate, Hospitality and Tourism programs. Prior to this he was a Reader in Hospitality Management at Blackpool and the Fylde College. He has published numerous articles in peer-reviewed journals, presented papers at international conferences, undertaken consultancy assignments in the UK and other countries, acted as an external examiner to numerous universities in the UK and overseas, and has produced three edited texts relating to the hospitality industry. He is presently semi-retired and living in Southern Spain, where he is currently writing a new textbook on research methods for hospitality and tourism students.

Judi Brownell is a professor of organizational communication and Dean of Students at the School of Hotel Administration, Cornell University, USA. She has served as the Associate Dean for Academic Affairs and as the Richard J. and Monene P. Bradley Director for Graduate Studies. Professor Brownell teaches graduate and undergraduate courses in organizational behavior, leadership, management communication, and human resources and has also instructed courses in Asia and Europe. She participates regularly in the School's executive education programs and has designed and conducted training seminars for a wide range of hospitality, educational, high-technology, and other work organizations. Current research projects include the career challenges women hospitality leaders confront, and the competencies associated with career development in the hospitality industry. Dr. Brownell is author of several textbooks, including *Listening: Principles, Attitudes, and Skills* (Allyn and Bacon, 2006), and *Organizational Communication and Behavior: Communicating for Improved Performance* (Holt, Rinehart, and Winston, 1991). She is currently co-authoring an organizational behavior text for hospitality managers, and has published over eighty articles in refereed discipline and hospitality industry journals.

Eliza Ching-Yick Tse is a professor of School of Hotel and Tourism Management and the Director of Hotel Management Services at The Chinese University of Hong Kong. She was also a faculty member at the Virginia Polytechnic Institute and State University, USA where she received her PhD degree. Dr. Tse has published numerous articles in top refereed journals and proceedings. Her primary research interests are in the areas of strategic management, information technology, and market analysis. In addition to co-authoring *Strategic Management in the Hospitality Industry*, she also has been a chapter contributor to a number of books. Dr. Tse is the editor of the *Journal of the International Academy of Hospitality Research* and she serves on the editorial board for *Cornell Hotel and Restaurant Administration Quarterly* and *Asia Pacific Journal of Tourism Research*. She was the past President for ApacCHRIE chapter and she has just been elected as the Director of Marketing for the International Council on the Hotel, Institutional and Education Board.

Julia Christensen Hughes is professor in the School of Hospitality and Tourism Management, College of Management and Economics, at the University of Guelph in Ontario, Canada, where she teaches strategic human resource management. Julia is also President of the Society for Teaching and Learning in Higher Education (STLHE), a national association of academics committed to the enhancement of teaching and learning in higher education. Julia's research interests include strategic and universal HRM, HRM issues unique to resort communities, empowerment, motivation and workforce diversity. She holds an MBA and PhD in Organizational Behavior from York University's Schulich School of Business and a BComm from the University of Guelph.

Robert Christie-Mill is a professor in the School of Hotel, Restaurant and Tourism Management in the Daniels College of Business at the University of Denver, USA. He holds a PhD and an MBA from Michigan State University and a BA from the University of Strathclyde's Scottish Hotel School. He has worked for Trust House Forte, Canadian Pacific, McTavish's Kitchens and Inter-Continental Hotel Corporation. He is author/co-author of *The Tourism System, Tourism: The International Business, Managing for Productivity in the Hospitality Industry, Restaurant Management: Customers, Operations and Employees, Resorts: Management and Operation* and *Managing the Lodging Operation*. Most are in multiple editions and have been translated into Korean,

Portuguese, Indonesian, and Chinese. He has been a chapter contributor to an additional five books in the areas of marketing and hospitality operations, and he has scores of refereed and non-refereed articles in academic journals in addition to trade press articles.

Dan Connolly, PhD, is an assistant professor of information technology and electronic commerce at the University of Denver's Daniels College of Business, USA, with a dual appointment in the School of Hotel, Restaurant and Tourism Management and in the Department of Information Technology and Electronic Commerce. His teaching, research, and consulting are in the areas of information technology strategy and electronic commerce. Dr. Connolly has authored or co-authored numerous publications, including a book entitled *Technology Strategies for the Hospitality Industry* (Pearson Prentice Hall, 2005), and routinely presents his work at industry and professional conferences and symposiums around the world. He is a founding father and advisor to Hotel Technology Next Generation (HTNG), a board member for the Hotel Information Technology Association (HITA), and vice-chairman of the American Hotel and Lodging Association's Technology Committee. Before joining the faculty at the University of Denver, Dr. Connolly spent nearly eight years working for Marriott International at its corporate headquarters and served on the faculties of Cornell University, Michigan State University, Virginia Tech, and Concord College, where he taught graduate and undergraduate courses in information technology, strategic management, finance, and hospitality administration. Dr. Connolly earned his Ph.D from Virginia Polytechnic Institute and State University, his MBA from American University, and his BS from Cornell University.

Yuksel Ekinci, MSc, MA, PhD, is a senior lecturer at the University of Surrey, UK. He set up and managed his own business (King Hotel) prior to starting his career in international hospitality companies (Hilton, Grand Hotel Trabya, Istanbul). Yuksel enjoys working with people who have different backgrounds in industry and academia. To this end, he completed joint consultancy projects for private sector companies (e.g., Compass, OCi, IBM, Marketpoint, UK) and the public sector agencies (EU, MRC) relating to customer satisfaction, brand loyalty, CRM and quantitative data analysis. Yuksel has published more than 25 refereed journal articles on service quality, customer satisfaction and services branding and presented research papers at international conferences such as EMAC, CHRIE, TTRA, and EIRASS. He is a member of the editorial review board for *Journal of Travel Research*, *Journal of Retailing and Consumer Services*, *Tourism Analysis*, *Advances in Tourism and Recreation Research*, *Anatolia and e-Tourism Review*.

Cathy A. Enz is The Lewis G. Schaeneman Professor of Innovation at the School of Hotel Administration at Cornell University, USA, where she also serves as the associate dean for industry research and affairs. Dr. Enz has published over seventy journal articles, book chapters, and three books in the area of strategic management and organization studies. Her book, *American Lodging Excellence: The Key to Best Practices in the U.S. Lodging Industry* was the winner of an excellence award from the American Hotel and Lodging Association. In addition to teaching competitive strategy and innovation courses she presents in numerous executive programs in Europe, Asia, and Central America, and consults extensively in North America.

Arnaud Frapin-Beaugé is a graduate of The Scottish Hotel School at the University of Strathclyde and has a Masters degree from the University of Perugia and Postgraduate Certificate in Advanced Academic Practice. He has many years experience working in hotels in Front of House departments, in positions such as Night Manager, Reservation Manager and Reception Manager and has been teaching since 2000 in Swiss hotel schools. He is currently Senior Lecturer at the International Hotel Management Institute (IMI) Luzern since 2002 teaching front office, accommodation management, marketing and tourism subjects.

Donald Getz, PhD, is a professor at the University of Queensland, Australia and School of Tourism, Haskayne School of Business, University of Calgary, and a visiting professor at the University of Goteborg, who teaches, conducts research and consults in the fields of tourism, hospitality and event management, with specific interests in destination and resort management, events, small and family businesses, and wine consumption and tourism. He has authored a general text entitled *Event Management and Event Tourism*, now in its second edition (2005) and recently completed the book *Event Studies: Theory, Research and Policy for Planned Events* (2007). Some of his current research concerns the relationship between involvement in sports and lifestyle elements and event-related travel. He has also co-authored the book *The Family Business in Tourism and Hospitality* (with Jack Carlsen and Alison Morrison, 2005), *Explore Wine Tourism* (2000), and co-edited (with Stephen Page) *The Business of Rural Tourism*.

Yvonne Guerrier is Professor of Organization Studies and Dean of the School of Business and Social Sciences at Roehampton University, London. She is author or editor of several books and numerous refereed articles on work in the hospitality industry, and is particularly interested in the work of customer service staff and in managers and their careers.

Mark G. Haley, CHTP is a Prism Partner overseeing the firm's Technology practice. Services include strategy development, needs analysis, system selection, specification development and more. Relevant technologies include customer relationship management, Internet applications, property management, central reservations and global distribution systems, and all aspects of hotel voice and data communications. He speaks frequently at hospitality industry conferences and has written numerous articles and handbooks on hospitality technology. Haley has been consulting since 1997, having founded High Touch Technologies after spending 15 years with ITT Sheraton. He started at Sheraton at the front desk and left as the director of property technology after assuming a number of positions of increasing responsibility at every level of the corporation. Mark Haley is currently the chairman of the American Hotel and Lodging Association's Technology Committee and a member of the Hospitality Financial and Technology Professional's (HFTP) Northeast Region's Board of Directors. He is a graduate of the University of Virginia and the University of Denver's School of Hotel, Restaurant, and Tourism Management.

Jeffrey S. Harrison is the W. David Robbins Chair of Strategic Management in the Robins School of Business at the University of Richmond. Prior to his current appointment, he served on the faculty at Cornell University. Dr. Harrison's research interests include strategic management and business ethics, with particular expertise in the areas of mergers and acquisitions, diversification, strategic alliances and stakeholder management. Much of his work has been published in prestigious academic journals such as *Academy of Management Journal*, *Strategic Management Journal*, and *Journal of Business Ethics*. He has authored or co-authored six books and worked as a consultant or trainer for a wide range of companies.

Giri Jogaratnam, PhD, is Professor of Hotel and Restaurant Management at Eastern Michigan University (EMU). Most recently, Dr. Jogaratnam spent two years at the Hong Kong Polytechnic University before returning to EMU. He has published in premier peer-reviewed journals including *Journal of Hospitality and Tourism Research*, *Cornell Hotel and Restaurant Administration Quarterly*, *International Journal of Hospitality Management*, *Journal of Travel and Tourism Marketing*, *Journal of Vacation Marketing*, *Tourism Management*, and *International Journal of Contemporary Hospitality Management*. He has also been recognized by his academic peers for research excellence. Most recently he received the Article of the Year Award – from the *Journal of Hospitality and Tourism Research* (2003). He also received the Best Paper Award at the International Society of Travel and Tourism Educators (ISTTE) Annual Conference in 2005.

Novie Johan is a graduate of the MBA Program at the School of Hospitality and Tourism Management from the University of Guelph. She is currently working as a Course Developer and Research Assistant focusing on training, education and marketing in the Hospitality and Tourism Industry. She has international experience with travel agents, airlines, hotels and restaurants in Indonesia, Switzerland, USA and Canada. She is a member of the Travel and Tourism Research Association (TTRA) and Pacific Asia Travel Association (PATA). She is also an assistant to the editor of *International Journal of Hospitality and Tourism Association* (IJHTA), a Haworth Press publication.

Peter Jones, PhD, is the ITCA Professor of Production and Operations Management, and formerly the Forte Professor of Hotel Management at the University of Surrey. He is the author or editor of nine textbooks and over 30 refereed journal articles, and has presented at conferences in thirteen countries on five continents. His research has focused on the application of operations management theory to the hospitality industry. He has a doctorate from the University of Surrey and an MBA from London Business School.

Tracy Jones is a senior lecturer in the Department of Leisure, Tourism and Hospitality at the University of Gloucestershire. She worked in various sectors of the industry before joining Oxford Brookes University to complete her HCIMA professional qualifications, being awarded the Greene Belfield-Smith Award for achieving the highest marks nationally in the financial management examination. She remained at Oxford Brookes, completing a BSc (Hons) in Hotel and Catering Management and an MPhil for her research into the financial and operational information needs of managers. Her main teaching areas are applied finance and accounting. Her research, for a PhD, is concerned with hotel budgeting practices. She has published her work in a number of journals and books, as well as presenting research at conferences.

Conrad Lashley CMBII, is professor and Director of the Centre for Leisure Retailing at Nottingham Business School, Nottingham Trent University, UK. He has undertaken a cluster of commercial research projects for firms in the licensed retail sector, and has published extensively about licensed retailing in the UK. His clients include J D Wetherspoon, Everard's Brewery, Greene King, The Publican, and the British Institute of Innkeeping. He is currently Chair of the panel of judges for the BII's national training awards, an annual event which celebrates training excellence in licensed retailing.

Andrew Lockwood, PhD, is the Forte Professor of Management and Deputy Head of the School of Management at the University of Surrey, where he teaches undergraduate and postgraduate courses in international hospitality management, operations management, and operations analysis. He has developed and taught short courses for the hospitality industry in the UK, Bali, Bulgaria, Crete, Cyprus, Ireland, and Mauritius. He also has extensive experience of hospitality education, having taught from craft to masters degree levels. He has been external examiner at a number of higher education institutions and was a member of the HEFCE review panel on Hospitality Management Education in 1997/8 and specialist advisor to the RAE on hospitality research in 1996/7. He has written or edited ten books and over 100 articles, chapters and conference papers on the management of hospitality operations. His longstanding research interests lie in the fields of service quality management, hospitality education and managerial activity in the hospitality industry. He is Chair of the HCIMA's quality working group and was instrumental in devising their Hospitality Assured programme.

Michael Riley is Professor of Organizational Behavior at the School of Management University of Surrey, Guildford, UK where he is Director of Postgraduate Research Studies. He studied labor economics, industrial relations and manpower planning at the University of Sussex, UK and was later awarded a doctorate at the University of Essex, UK. He became an academic after a career in human resource management in the hospitality industry. His work over two decades centers upon tourism employment issues, labor markets and human resource management and occasionally on aspects of consumer behavior in tourism.

Udo A. Schlentrich is a professor and Director of the Rosenberg International Center of Franchising in the Whittemore School of Business and Economics, University of New Hampshire, USA and a member of the board of the Educational Foundation of the International Franchise Association. He is a graduate of the Lausanne Hotel Management School, Cornell University, and holds his PhD from Strathclyde University. Schlentrich is engaged in advancing the field of franchising and hospitality marketing through applied research, teaching and outreach. Prior to embarking on his educational career, Schlentrich held CEO and senior board level positions with leading American and international hospitality organizations such as Hilton International, Loew's, Stakis, Omni International, Preferred

Hotels and Steigenberger. He is a regular consultant for international hospitality and investor groups.

Constantinos Verginis is a senior manager (Real Estate and Hospitality Consulting) with Deloitte and Touche (Middle East) based in Dubai, United Arab Emirates. Prior to this he was an Assistant Professor at the Emirates Academy of Hospitality Management, Dubai, teaching accounting and finance. Costas completed his doctorate with the University of Strathclyde, Scotland, in the area of real estate (hotel) finance. Dr. Verginis has worked for a number of years with a number of international hotel operators in Greece, Cyprus, Switzerland, and the UK. He began his teaching career at The Scottish Hotel School, University of Strathclyde. With Roy C. Wood he is the co-editor of *Accommodation Management: Perspectives for the International Hotel Industry* and has co-authored several journal articles and conference papers in the field of hospitality management.

Kate Walsh is an assistant professor of Management at Cornell University's School of Hotel Administration. She received her PhD from Carroll's School of Management at Boston College. Her primary research is in the area of services, specifically the influence of professional career management on outcomes for service firms. Dr. Walsh also conducts research examining the role of human capital investments on organizational performance. Her work has appeared in a number of outlets including *Organization Science, Journal of Applied Behavioral Science, Learning Organization, International Journal of Hospitality Management, Trends in Organizational Behavior* and the *Cornell Hotel and Restaurant Administration Quarterly*.

Roy C. Wood FHEA, FIH was, until 2003, Professor of Hospitality Management at The Scottish Hotel School, University of Strathclyde, Glasgow, which he originally joined as a lecturer in 1984. In 2001 he took a leave of absence to become Principal and Managing Director of IMI Institute of Hotel and Tourism Management in Luzern, Switzerland, a private school. In July 2006 Dr Wood moved to The Oberoi Group, one of the world's leading hotel companies, as Dean of the Oberoi Centre of Learning and Development, the company's corporate management training centre, where he remained until April 2008. He is currently employed by the Dhadabai Group in Bahrain as Chief Operating Officer of the Gulf Hospitality and Tourism Education Company, the largest private sector provider of hospitality training and education in the Middle East. Dr Wood is the author, co-author, editor or co-editor of 15 books and over 60 research papers in refereed journals as well as numerous other publications. He is a member of the Hong Kong Council for Accreditation of Academic and Vocational Qualifications (for tourism and hospitality subjects), and holds or has held numerous visiting academic appointments in universities in Europe and Asia. He is a Fellow of both the UK Higher Education Academy (formerly the UK Institute for Learning and Teaching) and the UK Institute of Hospitality.

Larry Yu, PhD, is an associate professor in the Department of Tourism and Hospitality Management, School of Business and Public Management, at the George Washington University at Washington, DC. He currently serves as the Chair of the Department. His teaching and research interest focuses on international tourism and hospitality development and management. He is the author of *The International Hospitality Business: Management and Operations*. He consults with international hotel companies, government agencies and international organizations, such as Choice Hotels International, Mandarin Oriental Hotels and InterContinental Hotels, US government agencies and the World Bank Group. He has worked on numerous tourism and hospitality projects in Africa, Asia and North America. He is also a visiting professor at Shanghai Institute of Tourism in Shanghai, China.

Editorial Introduction

Bob Brotherton and Roy C. Wood

INTRODUCTION

The commissioning of this *Handbook* imposed a responsibility to produce a volume on the 'state of the art' of hospitality management, a not unproblematic task. As we shall discuss in this Introduction, the whole area of 'hospitality management' is volatile, complex, controversial and increasingly and frequently contested – contested within the subject area itself, although there are those who would be reluctant to accept this view, and within the wider academy. This means that, as editors, we have had to make some difficult decisions. The most important and obvious of these has been to ensure that through the commissioning of contributions to this volume we have included critical reviews of the key thematic areas that comprise 'hospitality management' and represent, though not exhaustively, a map of the field of the subject area as it currently is. We recognize that there is a real world of hospitality education and research with researchers involved in exploring and elaborating different facets of hospitality management with considerable expertise. As in this educational community in general, not all the contributors to this volume would necessarily view the wider subject of hospitality management as ideologically or conceptually problematic. Indeed, it is perhaps important to note that insofar as the field of hospitality management *is* contested within the subject, this phenomenon or trend is, so far, largely British in origin and execution. Accordingly, in our editorial capacity, we have not sought to impose an overall ideological or particular, critical, perspective on contributors to the volume but rather have confined these to parts of this Introduction and our opening chapter, thereby seeking to represent the diversity of assumptions, themes and perspectives that contribute to the study of hospitality management.

The main purpose of this Introduction is to evaluate critically the evolution and status of 'hospitality management' as a subject. We do this, first, by briefly examining some of the general definitions in circulation and, second, elaborating in greater detail their implications for hospitality management research and education. Following this is a summary overview of the development and current forms of the hospitality industry and a thumbnail mapping of the principal subject areas that contribute to the study of the industry and management within it, the purpose of which is to provide a grounded understanding of the contributions to this volume.

DEFINING 'HOSPITALITY' AND 'HOSPITALITY MANAGEMENT'

In the first chapter of this *Handbook*, we explore in detail the concept of hospitality and touch upon the nature of 'hospitality management'. Our more prosaic intention here, and the sections that follow is, as signaled in our opening remarks, to critically explore issues attendant on the development of the subject that 'is' hospitality management.

Perhaps one of the fundamental philosophical questions faced by hospitality management researchers is 'What is Hospitality?' As Wood (1999), Taylor and Edgar (1999) and Brotherton (1998, 1999) point out, the term, let alone the concept, of hospitality is defined and used by many hospitality management researchers in a variety of often quite indistinct and frequently unsatisfactory ways. Precisely what different researchers mean when they use the term 'hospitality' is rarely clearly defined. It is equally unclear as to where the boundaries of hospitality are drawn in relation to 'near neighbors' such as tourism and leisure (Brotherton, 1989), or the structural and behavioral characteristics of other service industries. A parallel lack of conceptual clarity exists in use of the term 'hospitality management'. Outside of the United States, 'hospitality management' is a label only comparatively recently employed to refer to the management of those activities associated with the 'hospitality industry', itself a term with problems of boundary definition but one which is normally taken to embrace hotels, restaurants and other forms of business activity concerned with the provision of food, beverages and lodging. The increasingly widespread adoption of the term 'hospitality management' to describe a variety of occupational roles and intellectual and vocational practices associated with this industry sector is equally characterized in use by fluidity and lack of precision.

In the UK and elsewhere 'hospitality management' has come to replace more precise but limited labels such as 'hotel and catering management'. It has been a creeping change, the historical roots of which are unclear. A partial explanation may be found in changes within the industry itself which has become more diverse in terms of the range of variant operations that have developed in the food service and accommodation sectors in the last 30 years and have rendered 'hotel and catering management' inadequate to describing this diversity. This said, as labels go 'hospitality management' can hardly be regarded as much of an improvement. In rejecting the extreme of limiting precision it embraces an almost meaningless amorphousness. Although the term appears to have originated and been most widely adopted in the USA, here other more precise terms are also in use to describe specific sectors of the hospitality industry such as 'food service industry' and 'lodging industry'.

Perhaps the most depressing aspect of terminological and definitional questions over 'hospitality', the 'hospitality industry' and 'hospitality management' is that they have figured in debates in the academic literature for at least 20 years or more without any evidence of closure or general agreement. In the 1980s commentators such as Nailon (1982) and Slattery (1983) raised similar questions and Cassee (1983: xvi) ventured: 'What we need is a sound theory of hospitality based on research'. Middleton (1983: 51) pointed out that: 'There is a definitional problem from the term "hospitality industry"' and 'It may be surprising that,

in the 1980s, one must contemplate educational programs for the hospitality industry without agreement on what the industry comprises'. More recently, Jones (1996: 6–7) has suggested that: 'there is certainly no commonly shared paradigm of what we mean by "hospitality"... Reference to the research literature would indicate that there has been little or no discussion of what we mean by hospitality ... I would propose that the idea of hospitality research exists more in form than in substance'. Similarly, Taylor and Edgar (1996: 215, 218), in reflecting on the (then) current state of development of hospitality management research contended that 'An essential first step ... is to decide what the scope of hospitality research should be [and] if academic research in hospitality is to develop *satisfactorily* it is our view that it must do so within a coherent framework' (emphasis in original). Olsen (2001: 96) tends to support these views. In reviewing progress in hospitality research over the last 70 years, he suggests that early research efforts in the 1940s and 1950s, were contextual, descriptive and prescriptive with a primary emphasis on 'how to' with research 'driven more by serendipity than strategy' and that the prevailing view was 'anything was better than nothing at all'. The next phase (1960s–1980s) he terms 'imitation and borrowing' where hospitality researchers turned to other disciplines for conceptual and theoretical inspiration in order to apply theoretical insights developed elsewhere to hospitality. However, as Olsen correctly argues, this 'imitate and borrow' activity rarely involved any serious and credible attempts to 'validate the application of these theories in the context of the hospitality industry' (Olsen, 2001: 96).

Nevertheless, following exhortations from a number of scholars (Edgar and Umbreit, 1988; Lewis, 1988; Littlejohn, 1990; Evans, 1992) for the hospitality management research community to raise the profile and importance of hospitality management research Olsen (2001) argues that more recently there has been progress in hospitality research and the general quality of research activity and outputs have improved, albeit at a slower rate than desired. However, he adds the codicil that a great deal of this research work is essentially of a repackaged nature, and, in a depressing vein concludes that: 'for a field that has been a viable academic pursuit for almost a complete century, the body of knowledge is nowhere near defined. There appears to be no common understanding of what should be in this body of knowledge and almost no work that has addressed this problem. Scholars seem to be content in replicating the work of others or continually looking inwardly' (Olsen, 2001: 103). This view is shared by Lynn (2002) who, in an editorial for the *Cornell Hotel and Restaurant Administration Quarterly*, argues that the prevalence of descriptive research evident in the papers submitted for publication in that journal is less than helpful for managers in the industry, with most based on existing wisdom and practice and doubtfully valid. He makes a plea for researchers to 'submit manuscripts that report the results of correlational studies and experiments designed to identify the causes of outcomes that industry practitioners care about'. Equally, these kinds of problems are apparently not unheard of in related subject areas. In culinary arts according to Hegarty and Maloney (1998: 345) 'There is no agreed knowledge base for culinary arts/hospitality' and Robert Christie Mill, in Chapter 3 of this volume, touches on similar issues in the leisure and tourism field.

Given that debates over the definition of the hospitality (and wider tourism) industry have a long history and are still current, adoption of the term 'hospitality management' appears as little more than a flag of convenience. It has certainly achieved little in terms of refining understanding of the industry, or the concepts and practices that underpin it, and to which it is meant to be addressed. There are, however, other ways in which the tendency to favor the term 'hospitality management' can be explained. Its veritable vagueness can be seen as a cloak of (relative) respectability that encourages avoidance of snobbish reactions to the negative connotations of alternatives. In the UK at least, the term 'catering' would be one such alternative. Adoption of the term 'hospitality management' arguably goes some small way to body swerving the variably pejorative societal stereotyping of certain kinds of service jobs and occupations including, of course, many in the hospitality industry. In a world where the term 'McJob', derived from a highly emotional and prejudicial interpretation of employment in the world's largest fast food chain, has become a generalized term for low paid, low skill employment, it is perhaps unsurprising that the hospitality industry and hospitality educators have adopted a softer and less distinct label to hide behind. The old but still frequently encountered joke (in all its variations) 'How do you open a conversation with a graduate in hospitality management who

you meet socially?' (answer: 'A Big Mac, fries and a strawberry shake please') gives – if the pun can be forgiven – a further flavor of the kind of sentimental reactions encountered by those involved at all levels of the hospitality industry.

Of course, none of this excuses or explains the almost willful tendency to obscurantism embodied in the term 'hospitality management'. As we have noted elsewhere (Brotherton and Wood, 2000) and touch upon again in Chapter 1, the most common response to defining hospitality management has been to see it as coterminous with the hospitality industry. In the UK, a 1998 study, *Review of Hospitality Management*, commissioned by a key public body, the Higher Education Funding Council for England (HEFCE, 1998: 2), defined hospitality management as 'having a core which addresses the management of food, beverages and/or accommodation in a service context'. This is an unsatisfactory and evasive response that reflects an essentially *post hoc* approach to a term that has gained currency with little thought or justification. It requires no great genius to understand that hotel management is about the management of hotels, and by the same standards of linguistic pedantry, hospitality management should be about the management of hospitality. As King (1995: 220) points out, 'Effective management of hospitality in any type of organization must begin with a clearly understood definition of what hospitality is'. A response of 'bravo' seems appropriate to this remark but it is not advice that has been especially heeded. Indeed, even predominantly American terms such as 'lodging management' and 'food service industry (management)' are, like 'hospitality management', generalized evasions that obfuscate rather than illuminate.

Hospitality management then is an 'accidental' term generally delimited in meaning to describing the management of various sectors of the hospitality industry. Its essential circularity is demonstrated semantically in that 'hospitality' is what the hospitality industry offers and hospitality management is the management of what is offered, which is hospitality – *quod erat demonstrandum*. This position itself reflects an often noted and criticized (but still remarkably current) assumption that there is something unique about the hospitality industry that requires a special response in terms of adaptive management models, and more importantly, dedicated educational provision and (more bizarrely) unique research methodologies. In the early days of the growth of the field, it is this notion perhaps more than any other that underpinned the development of research orientations and activity, as well as educational provision and practice, thereby justifying a more detailed consideration of each.

HOSPITALITY MANAGEMENT RESEARCH

As Wood (1999) points out, the view that the hospitality industry is imbued with unique properties implies a need for particular epistemological and methodological configurations to be developed and adopted in order that its characteristics and activities may be effectively researched. The hospitality management education and research community has been content to promulgate this notion to both the wider academic and hospitality practitioner communities with which it interfaces. More importantly, its acceptance *within* that community has led to a dangerous insularity and severely limited the epistemological and methodological development of hospitality management research. Furthermore, Wood (1999) claims that a major consequence of hospitality management researchers accepting the 'uniqueness' issue on the one hand, whilst simultaneously seeking to emulate the dominant epistemology and methods of research traditions in the natural sciences on the other is both epistemologically and ontologically illogical. Positivistic, quantitatively oriented studies invariably strip the phenomenon from its context in the interests of enhancing external validity and generalizability, and are seen as important components within a research strategy ultimately designed to seek legitimacy and credibility for the 'discipline' of hospitality. Thus, contemporary hospitality management research *per se* does not have a complete epistemology because it is dominated by a primary concern with methodological priorities rather than conceptual development, a feature that inhibits the creation of a coherent body of theory to guide empirical research.

Taylor and Edgar (1999) refer to this phenomenon as 'conceptual malnutrition', and argue that philosophical questions are not resolved by additional empirical enquiry but by sound reasoning based on fundamental beliefs and logic. Hence, they propose that hospitality management research needs to develop appropriate 'enquiry paradigms' which not only address the implementation aspects of research, i.e. methodological questions, but which also focus more strongly on the methodological drivers of epistemology and ontology constituting the strategic aspects of research design. In common with Jones (1996) and Brotherton (1999b), they argue that hospitality management research will continue to be plagued by a significant vagueness concerning its objectives and scope, suggesting in the words of Shaw and Nightingale (1995) that it will never progress beyond being a 'scholarship of application' which simply adopts epistemological stances, conceptual frameworks, and methodological techniques developed in other disciplines or fields of enquiry.

Why should this be so? The absence of a common research paradigm or paradigms within the hospitality field cannot be explained only by the self-delusional notion of hospitality's uniqueness. Given that research activity tends to be the domain of universities, comparatively few university hotel schools across the globe began with a research mission. Rather, as hospitality management education has matured and been incorporated into the academy, research has increasingly become a requisite for survival. Initially, such research started from a low base because, for the most part, university-level hotel schools were not constituted originally as research centers, including in the United States where perhaps the majority of faculty in university hotel schools were rarely qualified beyond master's degree level (Barrows, 1999). There was thus little in the way of either research by faculty or the operation of doctoral programs to produce future researchers. As the area was, and is, focused on the management of organizations in the hospitality industry it is unsurprising that then as now, hotel schools comprise faculty of many different interests (even where the majority have some formal credentials in hospitality management). The pressure to publish when combined with a sense of the 'uniqueness' of hospitality, but no discernable tradition of theoretical or conceptual development to support the notion, has meant that quite naturally the research active have turned to the concepts, philosophies and methods of the disciplines and subjects that inform their interests.

This has meant that in terms of published research output, the 'field' of hospitality research appears to be, and is, highly fragmented, a fact reflected in the growth of academic journals within the field. Prior to the establishment of the *International Journal of Hospitality Management* (IJHM) in 1982, the only recognizably international outlet for hospitality research was the *Cornell Hotel and Restaurant Administration Quarterly* and this was, and remains, more of a house magazine for that university's hotel school (Losekoot, Verginis and Wood, 2001). The IJHM has been joined over the years by a number of other publications purporting to cater for the general field of 'hospitality management' but what is striking about these is precisely the fact that they contain an enormous diversity of discipline-based papers that reflect little common understanding of the nature of hospitality, hospitality management or the hospitality industry. More recently, as has been the case in the parallel field of tourism, there has been a tendency to greater specialization, with journals devoted to specific topics 'within' hospitality management, for cxample, human resources, food production and hospitality education. Even here, however, such journals tend to act as a repository of diverse theory-light papers that demonstrate little of any shared sense of intellectual coherence.

Given the inherent difficulties involved in resolving the type of philosophical issues and questions noted above it is perhaps not surprising that much hospitality research lacks shared conceptual and theoretical schema and that many hospitality management researchers have instead tended to concentrate their attention on methodological, or perhaps more accurately, method concerns. However, there is evidence of a less than rigorous attention to detail in methodological applications (Jones, 1996; Brotherton, 1999b) and numerous examples of the paucity of methodological thought given to research projects by hospitality management researchers (Brotherton, 1999c). The dominant approach taken to hospitality management research, especially in the USA, is one of a quantitative nature, based on a positivistic philosophy that in terms of its ultimate expression in hospitality research shows a serious bias towards survey instruments. Jones (1998) in the editorial of a special edition of the *International Journal of Hospitality Management* devoted to the 'state of play' in hospitality research, reviewed publications across a range of specialisms and indicated that out of some 664 articles cited, 307 (46%) were classified as conceptual in nature and 357 (54%) as empirical. Furthermore,

within the latter category 223 (62%) used quantitative methodologies and 134 (38%) qualitative. In a similar vein Elsworth, Yoon and Bai (1999) report on an analysis of the content of 145 papers published in the *Hospitality Research Journal* (more recently renamed the *Journal of Hospitality and Tourism Research*) between 1990 and 1996. This showed that 26% of these employed conceptual and 59% empirical, survey, methods with other empirical methods rarely featuring. Elsworth et al. (1999) found that quantitative methodologies dominated, with 100 of the 145 papers using some form of statistical analysis. However, they also note that this analysis was frequently of a descriptive nature and not always correctly employed in supporting the conclusions derived from it, a deficiency also identified by Fyall and Thomas (1999) who lament the lack of technical competency in quantitative data analysis found in many hospitality research studies, and Hampton (1999) in relation to qualitative data analysis employed in such studies. The topics most frequently researched in these papers were human resource management, followed by marketing and operations management, a feature also reported by Jones (1998). In their analysis of papers published in the areas of hospitality systems and technology, Kirk and Pine (1998) concluded that approximately one third were conceptual in nature and that amongst the empirical papers the vast majority used quantitative approaches and methods. Bowen and Sparks (1998) in their review of hospitality marketing research, where empirical studies also tended to dominate, pointedly comment on the question of poor, or non-existent, use of empirical data analysis to develop greater conceptual and theoretical insights either generally or in relation to the hospitality industry.

In hospitality research generally then, and even in the use of survey instruments, a lack of methodological sophistication is evident. Lucas (1999) stresses the importance of methodological rigor for survey design in order to minimize error and bias and maximize the validity and reliability of the empirical data collected. She also points to one of the major Achilles heels frequently encountered in hospitality management survey research; sampling. Lucas (1999) identifies the enormous sampling frame, selection, access, and size variations to be found in much contemporary hospitality management research, the implications of which are often ignored by researchers who proceed to utilize statistical tests designed for large N studies on very small samples. In addition, as Brotherton points out (1999d) such sampling deficiencies are further found in the 'comparative' hospitality management research literature where the use of small and potentially unrepresentative samples is rife.

Methodological issues of measurement are also frequently problematic. Buttle (1999) comments that the hospitality management research literature is characterized by a virtual absence of researchers developing innovative measures related to the specific, contingent characteristics of the hospitality environments being researched. The predominant *modus operandi* is for hospitality management researchers to either adopt, often unquestioningly, or adapt, often inadequately, operational definitions and measures previously developed in studies of other organizational environments, invariably with a lack of consideration given to matters of contingency and validation. As Buttle (1999) remarks, current practices amongst hospitality management researchers in this respect are characterized by a general lack of concern for the integrity of the empirical data collected in many research projects. In short, the fundamentally important task of validating the measurement instrument is generally less than adequately dealt with by many hospitality management researchers. Again, Brotherton (1999d) notes that this problem is also endemic within comparative hospitality management research where, especially in cross-national/cultural studies, there is inadequate attention paid to the development of valid measurement instruments and procedures, invariably generating doubts about the validity and robustness of the comparisons made.

Despite the apparently widespread adoption of a positivistic orientation within the hospitality management research community, Jones (1999) observes that, paradoxically, utilization of the 'ultimate' positivist methodology, experimental research, is conspicuously absent in the literature. Though it is found in some areas of hospitality research (e.g. food science, nutrition, food and beverage product evaluation), it is not a commonly adopted methodology elsewhere. Other researchers, who deal with occupationally or industrially specific subjects in psychology, marketing, operational and systems research, routinely adopt experimental methodologies as a matter of course. It is possible that the absence of such methodologies from academic hospitality research relates to the absence of competence in such approaches. Alternatively, it may be that there exists a perception that experimental research is more difficult to design and conduct than questionnaire surveys, and/or is an inappropriate choice for the research questions being explored. The latter would of course be justifiable, the former misinformed, for, as Jones (1999) indicates, in industry, experimentation is frequently adopted as a preferred research method. Test marketing, new product concept evaluations, pilot implementations of new methods and procedures, and menu innovations are all routinely investigated by true and/or quasi-experiments in the real world. It would appear that academic researchers do not share their practitioner colleagues' enthusiasm for experimentation an avoidance that Jones (1999), perhaps bordering on overstating the case, argues is unfortunate as the deployment of experimental method(s) may help to strengthen the conceptual and technical aspects of hospitality management research in general.

A popular alternative to the survey instrument in hospitality research is the case study which also, however, reveals a tendency to methodological over-simplification (Brotherton, 1999e). Typical difficulties include researchers providing poor rationales for the selection of cases in the first place and apparently encountering problems in being able to define and delimit the case(s) under investigation. Researchers also exhibit a tendency to ignore specific, contingent aspects of their case in attempts to conduct cross-sectional, variable-oriented, survey-type studies to demonstrate the external validity and generalizability of the results. In other words, a tool that lends itself to qualitative research approaches tends to revert to crude positivistic 'survey' roots. This is a serious irony for, as Brotherton (1999d) argues, the potential value of qualitative case study research for exploring the 'uniqueness', or otherwise, of the phenomenon–context nexus is considerable. Similarly, although methodological and data source/type triangulation, is often claimed to be a particular methodological strength of the case study approach (Stake, 1994; Yin, 1994), it would appear to be largely absent from this type of research.

It would be mistaken to argue that these issues have gone unrecognized in the hospitality management research community but the extent of discussion is not as great as it should be.

A common response to methodological limitations has been to argue for a combination of pragmatism and practicality in research. Lashley (1999) highlights the practical orientation and purported real-world value of action research and stresses the importance of viewing theory and practice as symbiotic partners. However, action research presents significant methodological problems for hospitality management and other researchers alike as its design and conduct conflicts with the dominant, positivistic tradition. As Lashley (1999) comments, action research is essentially anti-positivistic in philosophy, as it emphasizes a constructionist and interpretative philosophical stance and places researcher involvement and reflection at the heart of its design and implementation. It is thus unsurprising that Lashley notes that action research has not been widely adopted in hospitality management. Once again this may be seen as another irony: on the one hand, hospitality management researchers make constant reference to the 'uniqueness' of hospitality and hospitality research, whether this is justified or not, whilst on the other they would appear to be rejecting methodological choices which have a greater potential to confirm or disconfirm such contentions. This paradox Lashley (1999), Brotherton (1999d; 1999e), Hemmington (1999) and Jauncey (1999) all record in relation to action, case study, comparative, and participative observation research respectively.

Consequences: the research politics of higher education

It is perhaps important at this point to note we are not arguing that there is no hospitality research of any quality, although there is, as in the academy as a whole, a great deal which *is* of poor quality. The assumption of the uniqueness of 'hospitality', the 'hospitality industry' and 'hospitality management' has been, as we have argued and will argue again in this Introduction, not only largely responsible for a significant failure of sophistication in hospitality research but also for a decline in the credibility of hospitality management education more generally (see also Wood, 2007). As we indicated at the start of this Introduction, hospitality management within the academy enjoys an ambiguous position for a variety of reasons, not least the perceived (lack of) quality of research output. The growing obsession with research as a performance measure in higher education, not least in the English-speaking world, represents a significant threat to the future of hospitality management education in traditional higher education establishments, and thus to hospitality research. In the UK, where there is a periodic national 'research assessment exercise' (RAE) based on peer review and bearing on the allocation of public monies to higher education institutions, the panel responsible for evaluating hospitality research (in fact the panel responsible for reviewing all business and management subjects) in 2002 wrote in their final report:

> Hospitality is less mature as a sub-area, and there is little work of international quality, with around half rated at below national level. Much of the output published in hospitality journals comprises conceptual work, extended literature reviews, and reports of small pilot studies. The sub-area relies heavily on theory developed in the management field, with only application to the hospitality industry, and in some cases work lags a number of years behind theory development in mainstream management (http://www.hero.ac.uk/rae/overview/docs/UoA43.pdf).

It is difficult for any objective observer to demur from the superficial factual content of these comments. However, the statement is perhaps more important for its profound and submerged judgemental ignorance of the factors that lend its broad sentiments veracity, an ignorance that might be considered alarming in itself, but is more so because it is itself intended to represent a coherently intelligent platform on which policy will be based. It may be legitimate to criticize 'conceptual work' although given the prevailing model of knowledge generation in universities this implied criticism is presumably a terminological infelicity that has crept into the report, rather than a reflection of panel members' grasp on reality.

The panel's comment that the 'sub-area relies heavily on theory developed in the management field, with only application to the hospitality industry' is, as we have seen, resonant of concerns *within* the field. Yet at the same time, there is an implicit notion in these remarks that hospitality research should rely on 'something else' (its own body of theory?), a notion then apparently contradicted by the somewhat paradoxical observation of a time lag in the application of management theory to the subject. Either the panel producing the report fell for, and accepted, the wider ideological notion that hospitality management is in someway intellectually distinct from management *per se* or it is implying that hospitality management should rely on other sources of theoretical inspiration. Whatever the case, such comments are suggestive that in contending with the nature of hospitality research the panel experienced some of the difficulties in comprehending the nature and scope of the field that we have so far mentioned. Nevertheless, such ignorance is apparently no impediment to policy making and the general consequences that perceived failings in research have had for university level hospitality education overall are evident to describe. At its simplest, supposed delinquencies in research output and quality have been used as a stick to beat hospitality education (and indeed, in the UK at least, other subjects as well) without regard to wider achievements in educational processes more generally. It is to hospitality education more generally that we now turn our attention.

HOSPITALITY MANAGEMENT EDUCATION

Hospitality management has experienced debates similar to those in other fields about whether it is a 'discipline' (and rather more importantly an 'academic' discipline) or a subject, or a field of study. Similarly, there have been intermittent reflections on whether hospitality is a multidisciplinary subject or an interdisciplinary one, a fact reflected upon in this volume by Riley (Chapter 5). As we noted above, use of the terms 'hospitality' and 'hospitality management' is problematic and there is some mileage in definitional debates, not least in terms of circumscribing and defining what it is we are talking about when we speak of 'hospitality management'. Such debates should not, however, be driven to the point of sterility, and in educational terms, the niceties of the nature of the educational process should not obscure the main drivers that forge and sustain educational practice.

The root of much higher-level hospitality education is in vocational programs designed to train front-line workers such as chefs, cooks and waiting staff. This does not universally hold true however. The two oldest and arguably still most reputable (in at least the sense that few in the global industry cannot have

heard of them) hotel management schools in the world are Lausanne in Switzerland (established 1893) and the School of Hotel Administration of Cornell University (1922, USA). More or less from their beginnings, put simplistically, these schools focused on how best to manage hotels, and have provided models that many have sought to replicate, few successfully. Both these establishments, being pioneers, enjoyed substantial industry support at their inception, Lausanne from the Swiss Hoteliers' Association and Cornell from the American Hotel Association for whom the request for a hospitality management program originated (Barrows, 1999) but both embodied and developed different traditions. For many years (but only coming many years after its creation) Cornell represented the principal global focus for, and source of, hotel school based hospitality research, to be joined by other US establishments in due time. In other parts of the English-speaking world, hospitality education rarely figured in universities or at degree level. In Britain, The Scottish Hotel School, established in Glasgow in 1944 was a courageous attempt to fuse emerging theoretical treatments of management with the practical emphasis of schools such as Lausanne (Gee, 1994), whose focus, far from being research, was the practical education of hoteliers in Switzerland and, eventually, beyond.

According to Barrows (1999: 10) at the end of the last millennium, four-year university programs in hospitality management in the USA numbered around 175, the majority having been started during the 1970s and 1980s. He attributes this growth to the growth and consolidation of the hospitality industry itself and the concomitant demand for greater numbers of professionally qualified managers. Prior to this, around 10 to 12 hospitality management programs dominated American provision at university level. A similar situation prevailed in the UK (Gee, 1994). In the 1960s, Britain had only three university level hotel management-type schools at Strathclyde University in Glasgow (of which The Scottish Hotel School had become a part), Surrey University near London (the University itself was forged from a College of Advanced Technology that housed a reputable hotel school) and Cardiff University in Wales. Significantly, Strathclyde and Surrey universities were 'new' in the 1960s and further degree level development of hospitality education took place from the 1970s onwards in the Polytechnics created by the 1964–1970 Labour governments. These polytechnics were not intended principally as research, but teaching, institutions but they themselves became 'new' universities from 1992.

Cornell and Lausanne Hotel Schools represent the two basic models of hospitality education on which all other schools, whether in the public or private sector, are to a greater or lesser degree, modeled. In the anglophone world for the most part, the Cornell model has come to dominate, at least in the sense of hospitality management schools forming part of established (mainly public) higher education institutions. In Australia and New Zealand, as in the UK, for example, a significant proportion of hospitality education is to be found in the state university sector in institutions that were originally established as polytechnic-like vocational colleges and have been since 'upgraded' to university status. In these countries there are (relatively) few private schools of hospitality. In America, provision of hospitality education is distributed across the diverse range of institutional provision – private and public (land grant) universities, community colleges and the like. Elsewhere, hospitality education has been more or less firmly excluded from the 'state' university (though not necessarily higher education) sector, viewed firmly as a subject to be taught in vocational colleges (whether private or public). In some countries, Malaysia being a fair example, higher education level private colleges with a vocational bent have become the dominant mode of provision for hospitality education. In others, for instance India, there is a vibrant 'mixed economy' of public and private sector institutions (a useful if uneven collection of papers on the parallel area of tourism education gives some useful insights into the plurality of these systems, see Airey and Tribe, 2005).

The key point, however, is that where hospitality education forms part of a 'traditional' university sector, hospitality schools have faced, as we noted earlier, university expectations in terms of research output. Although Lausanne now enjoys the status of an applied technical university institute within Switzerland and undertakes research of a kind, in the 'Lausanne model' the emphasis on research output is absent or limited with, instead, the educative and training process being emphasized in these essentially 'teaching' institutions. This has been the approach adopted by most private schools of hotel management, not least in Switzerland, where there is possibly the highest concentration of such establishments and where, it is worth noting in passing, the term 'hospitality' has been most actively excluded from the names of these schools. It is also the case that current growth in hospitality education tends, globally, to be in the private sector and based on the 'Lausanne model'. University hotel schools, especially in the English-speaking world, are currently fairing less well. There are five broad categories of reason for this. The first we have already dealt with at some length – the perceived (lack of) quality of hospitality research. The other four are closely related. They are: the career status of the hospitality industry; the expense of providing hospitality education; the nature of industry support; and institutionalized snobbery.

Career status of the hospitality industry

Middle-class students, who are the principal beneficiaries of higher education in most advanced industrial societies, do not necessarily see the hospitality industry as offering the social status, working conditions or rewards commensurate with their class position, making recruitment to hospitality courses somewhat volatile. Even in times of 'boom' recruitment, as in the UK in the early to mid-1990s, there is evidence of high wastage of hospitality graduates from the industry after a relatively short period. A positive 'spin' on this is that hospitality courses furnish students with transferable skills valued by employers in other industrial sectors. Whilst this may be true, it diverts attention from the variably poor conditions of employment in the industry, especially in terms of work-life balance, and the fact that in certain countries at least, the hospitality industry has a poor record of accomplishment in developing graduates. Several studies over the years, one of the more notable being Riley and Turam's (1988), have pointed out that in terms of career development, graduates enjoy no preferment advantages compared with non-graduates entering the sector.

Expense of provision

Secondly here is the expense of providing hospitality education in universities and other more traditional (and largely state-supported) institutes of higher education. For much of the history of hospitality education, the view has been taken by educators (and is still taken by many) and often endorsed by employers, that to ensure the credibility of programs and enhance graduates' career opportunities, a strong practical component to such programs is a necessity, manifest most usually in the requirement for at least a training restaurant and kitchen as part of a school's provision of facilities. Commentators external to the industry have seen this aspect of hospitality programs, together with the usual requirement for students to complete relevant internships, as part of an industry pre-entry socialization process designed to instill the peculiarities of the sector's culture (e.g. Mars, Bryant and Mitchell, 1979). However, as the economic circumstances of higher education have tightened in many countries, the justification for this type of provision has become more difficult to sustain. Although alternative models have always existed (for example, practical training acquired during (a) internships rather than in school; (b) in school but through service training in another 'mainstream' university facility such as a faculty dining room; and (c) in the training facilities of another establishment such as a vocational or technical college, 'in-house' facilities have been an unusually cherished element of hotel schools. This is now changing in many places, notably in the UK, where these alternative models receive favorable consideration (Dutton and Farbrother, 2005) although with uncertain concern for the views of the industry and the career prospects of graduates.

Industry support

Hospitality management is not the only area where poor research performance and declining student interest in pursuing the subject has been used as a pretext for downsizing or eradicating programs and schools. However, as we shall shortly argue, comments like those of the UK research assessment panel discussed earlier reflect a deeper, snobbish, ambivalence to the field in traditional higher education that appears to be intent on choking the child to death before it reaches adulthood. Before moving to this topic however, it is important to discuss another significant reason why university level hospitality education has been, and remains,

so vulnerable. This is to do with the fact that whilst often unloved by the rest of the academic community, it also fails in the affections of the industry it is intended to support.

In what is believed to be (perhaps not entirely accurately) the most diverse national 'system' in terms of the mix of private and state institutions, that of the United States, the culture of educational and industry philanthropy and engagement with higher education is perceived as more developed than elsewhere. Industry involvement in the USA and elsewhere can be in terms of informal support or more formal arrangements including endowments for faculty positions, research and more prosaic but no less important 'bricks and mortar' projects and in his review of this topic, Barrows (1999) remains optimistic that general industry support that has been forthcoming in the USA will continue. In the UK, where the higher education infrastructure is almost universally funded from general taxation there is a feeling in industry generally that, through this mechanism, 'dues have been paid' and further subventions are unnecessary. In hospitality, there has been a persistent unease in the relationship between education and industry, the latter feeling that university graduates in hospitality are ill equipped with the practical skills the sector requires. For the reasons outlined earlier, conformity to the intellectual ambitions of universities has made it problematic for hotel schools to justify an emphasis on these practical skills. The situation has not been aided in the UK by a culture of generalized indifference and laughably unreasonable approach by industry to the payment of new graduates (although it must be added that those who stay the course frequently achieve higher rewards sooner than contemporaries in many other sectors).

Institutionalized snobbery

The final reason why hospitality education fares poorly in the university sector is rather more emotional and one we have already touched upon – pure and simple snobbery in the sense of looking down upon those perceived as inferior in social position. Although the quality of this snobbery varies considerably in the English-speaking world (and elsewhere) the historical associations of hospitality with (domestic) service, servants, servility and servitude continue to persist. There can be no reasonably well-attuned hospitality academic who has not encountered the astonishment of the uninitiated in comments of the 'You teach students to be waiters – in a university?' kind. Such attitudes are also, naturally, to be found in universities themselves, despite the fragility of much of what passes for 'knowledge' in the late (or post-) modern academy and which, naturally, attracts little reflection from academicians themselves. Some hospitality educators have recently sought to counter intellectually hostile snobbery by arguing that 'hospitality management' should mutate to 'hospitality studies' (Lashley, 2003), predicated on the view that the pervasive nature of hospitality in society should be understood in terms of sociological dimensions with hospitality management as one manifestation of the phenomenon. This kind of strategy has a whiff of desperation about it and, whilst superficially attractive, is quite possibly too little and too late a response to a situation where, arguably, for hospitality education in universities, the pass has been sold (Wood, 2004a). In 2000, the UK's then Chief Inspector of Schools, Chris Woodhead, criticized 'Mickey Mouse' university courses, which he identified as including, *inter alia*, golf course management. When the UK chief inspector of schools (in 2000) and the government minister responsible for universities (in 2003) can both complain of 'Mickey Mouse' courses then one must seriously doubt if rationality is likely to be much use as a weapon of persuasion (http://news.bbc.co.uk/1/hi/education/878600.stm; http://news.bbc.co.uk/1/hi/education/2655127.stm).

THE FUTURE OF 'HOSPITALITY' RESEARCH AND EDUCATION

The pessimism of our commentary so far should not disguise the fact that both the quantity, and to a certain extent the sophistication, of hospitality management research has expanded greatly over the last two decades (Lundberg, 1997), a fact to which this volume is testimony. This is a significant achievement for the hospitality management research community and should be recognized. Despite many conflicting pressures hospitality management researchers have proved to be a determined and resilient body of people in their quest to expand and raise the profile of what is still, a fact often forgotten,

an emergent area of enquiry. In arguing thus, we make no bones about the fact that one aim of *this* enterprise is a sense of pride in what hospitality research and education has achieved. We believe that both the study and practice of hospitality management research and education, however it may be circumscribed, is no less meritorious an intellectual activity than any other form of management or academic study. If this sounds defensive it is because we believe that such a defense is necessary but in the educational and research arena at least it is one that should address the concerns of those who judge the hospitality industry and its associated institutions in terms of 'Mickey Mouse jobs' and, at the risk of overextending the metaphor, 'Donald Duck ideas'. In short, it is necessary to be both honest and realistic about the field's limitations, the purpose of this section of the discussion.

The future of hospitality management research

Although the general profile of hospitality management research today is far more encouraging than it was two decades ago, it is necessary to take stock of the benefits obtained thus far from the quantitative growth that has occurred. Indeed, it may well be that rather than seeking to continue in the same way the hospitality management research community should pause, reflect, consolidate and capitalize on the gains made to date to develop systematic strategies for the future (Olsen, 2001). This demands discourse and debate relating to a number of key issues.

First, there is still some justifiable argument over what constitutes hospitality *per se*, the nature of hospitality management, and the boundaries of the hospitality industry. Historically, many researchers as, have we have argued, sought to avoid these crucial considerations by either, implicitly or explicitly, regarding the hotel/lodging and catering/foodservice industry and its management as being synonymous with the hospitality industry and hospitality management. Alternatively, they have sought refuge in the view that the hospitality industry is merely a sub-set of the wider service sector, and that hospitality management is a branch of service operations management. However, at the same time there has also been a strong tendency for hospitality management researchers to claim that hospitality is at the very least different and, in more extreme views, unique.

Whilst these may, or may not, be defensible assertions the main point is that the field has basic unresolved dilemmas to which insufficient attention has been paid. These include conceptual and methodological eclecticism where this is based on dubiously valid importations and customizations from other disciplines and fields of enquiry; and inadequate epistemological, conceptual and/or methodological development within hospitality management research. The essentially retroactive approach to defining 'hospitality management' noted in the opening comments of this Introduction (and elaborated further in Chapter 1) raises fundamental questions about the nature of hospitality that have barely been addressed. There are times when a certain amount of intellectual 'navel gazing' is necessary and the absence of this activity in sufficient quantity and quality in the hospitality field has arguably led to proliferation without reflection. More importantly, whereas as previously suggested, there are limits to the usefulness of pursuing definitional precision, the widespread adoption of the term 'hospitality management' has done little to communicate clarity about its scope to external audiences. In addition to its amorphous qualities noted earlier the term, even in its delimited form, referring to the activities involved in managing elements of the hospitality industry, assumes a degree of industry and sectoral homogeneity that is at odds with reality. This is so whether discussing the unity of general organizational models (see, for example, Guerrier's comments on the diversity of such forms in Chapter 11) or business models (for example the increasing tendency of many sub-sectors of the industry to adopt 'retail' business models rather than more traditional hospitality ones, see for example Lashley, 2000).

Second here, there is a general need for hospitality management researchers to improve the level of professional 'craft' applied to their research. Some, but by no means all, hospitality management researchers do not come from strong disciplinary backgrounds and/or have not received sufficient research training. This is often reflected in poor methodological choices, under-utilization of generic extant literature, inadequate operationalization of existing concepts and validation of associated measures when transferred into hospitality management,

a relative paucity of new concept and/or measurement development, and the production of unreliable generalizations. It is also seen in the widespread adoption of epistemological and methodological stances based on those dominant in the natural and physical sciences, which are apparently seen by many to offer the best chance for hospitality management research to attain credibility and legitimacy. Essentially this is a quality issue. If hospitality management research is to reach beyond its own relatively small community and be taken seriously by external audiences, then it must build greater confidence among such constituencies. Any increase in confidence is likely to be directly related to the value and robustness of research design, conduct and validity and usefulness. Research activity in, and output from, established disciplines and fields is generally accepted as legitimate because its supporters and recipients alike have confidence in the credibility of its basic design and implementation processes. In addition, confidence in such research is invariably enhanced by a perception, justified or otherwise, that these research communities have well-developed, rigorous internal quality assurance/control procedures that establish and maintain high standards. The research community in hospitality has yet to convince others it possesses such procedures and this is a matter that requires urgent discourse and action.

Third, given that most of the research effort conducted to date in many sub-areas of hospitality management is fragmented and characterized by gaps and imbalances across these sub-areas, there is a need for researchers operating within each of the specialist areas to establish both an enhanced level of internal coherence and determine the future agenda of those fields. At present there is a general lack of organization, vision, and leadership within these areas arising from their eclectic evolution and an uncritical importation on an almost epidemic scale of perspectives, models, instruments and techniques from their 'base disciplines' (Olsen, 2001). Thus, there is considerable scope for leading researchers to stimulate the required debate amongst their colleagues, and to initiate the process of determining priorities and setting agendas for both the individual specialism *per se* and its sub-sets. Such agendas and priorities will need to reflect not only the principal themes in relation to the more substantive research issues but also those concerning the development of appropriate conceptual, methodological, and technical innovations.

Fourth, many authors suggest there is a need for a greater emphasis to be placed on research of an inter/multi-disciplinary and/or comparative nature, and that conducted through cross-national/cultural teams. The general view appears to be that much extant hospitality research literature could have been sounder and more persuasive, and similar research might be in the future, if such approaches were to be adopted. Inter/multi-disciplinary research arguably promotes philosophical and methodological dialog between members of research teams that help to generate more innovative and robust approaches to research questions (Brookes, Roper and Hampton, 1999; Roper and Brookes, 1999). Similarly, the use of cross-national/cultural research teams may help to reduce the degree of such bias found in many contemporary studies, bringing new insights, especially to those researched within the international arena. This said the ideas underpinning these views are not uncontroversial as Riley (Chapter 5) outlines. There is a danger that, if loosely conceived, these approaches assume the characteristics of the worst kind of pragmatism in coming to acquire the quality of a panacea for the ills of hospitality research. Nevertheless, comparative research in the broadest sense is acquiring some momentum in hospitality management and, for good or ill, is likely to be influential in the future development of the field.

Finally, there is a need for the hospitality management research community as a whole to engage in more substantive, agenda setting, conceptual research, in short to engage with many of the themes discussed here. The priority given in hospitality research to method over theory remains, encouraged by a 'publish or perish' research culture that emphasizes micro-quantitative precision over qualitative reflection and is still motivated to a certain degree by the desire to be 'relevant' to the industry the field serves. Underlying these trends is an occasionally discernible intolerance of those who raise critical questions of a theoretical, conceptual and methodological nature: strong and entrenched views too often substitute for openness and engagement. Unlike in many other areas of intellectual enquiry there is an absence of distinctive schools of thought and conceptual and theoretical positions (save those

touched upon here). The emphasis on method, on pragmatism, appears at times to reflect a fear of contamination by nasty intellectualism, a fear reinforced by a narrowly defined desire for 'relevance'.

Yet within business and management studies generally, theoretical and conceptual development has not always impeded originality in the conduct and findings of research. Indeed, most established disciplines and fields of enquiry generally exhibit pluralistic tendencies and sub-divisions based on soundly articulated schools of thought that stimulate debate within and between the advocates of the various schools. Such debate, ranging from the ideological to the technical aspects of research, tends to provide a major stimulus for advancement. In this sense, and despite its historical origins, there is a good case for hospitality management to adopt a *more*, rather than a less, abstract and theoretical approach to its subject matter. It is pragmatism for pragmatism's sake that has led to the current parlous state of hospitality management within the academy, an inability to answer the question 'What is your subject about?'. Development (and tolerance) of theoretical diversity and different schools of thought within hospitality management research may ultimately help individuals in this community to establish a clearer, more coherent, and definitive, critical mass of research within each particular school and across the field of enquiry as a whole. The danger here, of course, is that internal fragmentation occurs without overall coherence as different camps battle for dominance across the field as a whole. In short, it does not remove the need for a thorough and systematic critique of what has gone before and what exists now. If hospitality management research is to progress, develop legitimacy, and evolve into a credible field of enquiry the research community must engage in greater reflective practice, extend theoretical and conceptual development and enhance its skills base in terms of research competence. In many respects hospitality management research in aggregate has arrived at its current point by accident. It exhibits considerable progress in some areas but significantly less in others, and has a fragmented profile. Though considerably advanced on 20 or even 10 years ago, especially in terms of the volume of output, it now faces a watershed and, as we hope to have shown in this discussion, necessary and fundamental choices in philosophy and approach.

The future of hospitality management education

Hospitality management education is in trouble although some remain optimistic about its future (see for example the contribution of Barrows and Johan to this volume, Chapter 6). As with hospitality research, underpinning these difficulties is the historical tendency for educators to advocate the separateness of hospitality education within the academy on the grounds of its uniqueness and the uniqueness of the hospitality industry. The problem with this position is that there is an implied intellectual duty to consider why, within institutes of higher education, hospitality management should be justified as a distinct field of study as opposed to other specialized forms of management, a question often evaded in the past, or at best dealt with in an inconsistent manner. Contemporarily, it is arguably reasonable to advocate continuing evasion by simply asserting that we have to deal with hospitality management in higher education in Everest-like fashion, because it is there. However, that hospitality management has enjoyed, and continues to enjoy, a somewhat uneasy place within the academy effectively closes out this option. As we have argued, for many within the academic hospitality community, let alone external audiences, the study of hospitality management is both contentious and contested. Ignoring such contention in an ostrich-like manner will not make such criticism go away. Nor will excessive proselytizing about the global economic significance of the industry (a characteristic of many lobbying groups, for example the World Travel and Tourism Council) persuade many of the legitimacy of a view of the industry as unique or as requiring special separate forms of education to support it.

In short and in reality, it is increasingly difficult, if not impossible to justify the proposition that hospitality management is a distinct field of study within higher education. This is at least in part because the 'distinctiveness' argument that has colored the development of hospitality management education and that research has come to be perceived as of variably weak quality. Over a number of decades, hospitality educators have been fighting for intra-institutional autonomy off the back of insubstantial and largely phony arguments. In parts of the academy others are taking this view. One result has been the end to many separate schools of hotel management within universities, their programs absorbed into (usually) business schools or disappearing altogether. This is certainly the UK experience but even a casual review of university web sites in other parts of the anglophone world reveals similar processes at work (including in the USA where Barrows (1999), attributes the phenomenon to declining rolls throughout the early 1990s, but in this volume sees a North American resurgence, see Chapter 6).

We examined earlier some of the reasons for the fragility of hospitality education. It certainly seems that many of the current changes in the configuration of higher educational provision are due largely (at the university level in the English-speaking world at least) to perceptions that hospitality educators have singly failed to deliver in terms of satisfying the main performance criteria for success within the university system: research. Certainly, for hospitality management education, the 'Cornell model' appears to be under threat, at least where universities are, as in the UK, principally state funded institutions. Private hospitality schools, colleges and institutes in contrast appear to be thriving although the evidence is somewhat sketchy (a useful indicator of the rise of the private sector can be found by scrutinizing www.hotelschool.com although as with all such listings, it is useful only as an indicator of trends in size and scope, rather than quality). Is then the future of hospitality management education private?

There are a number of good reasons to think that it might be, and some to suggest that it ought to be. First, private schools have a significant advantage over those located in traditional higher education sectors in that they are normally free to focus on the educative process and have no research mission. Resources can therefore be directed towards those practical as well as theoretical aspects of education valued, or perceived to be valued, by employers, without the need to explain, excuse or apologize. Two routine objections to such a philosophy are that (a) education should not be about providing cannon fodder for employers and (b) that research activity is essential to maintaining a rich and developing curriculum and a learning and teaching culture. The first of these is such a piece of obvious academic cant that it is somewhat surprising to find it still in such wide circulation. Employment is not the only purpose of education but it is one that tends, ultimately, to interest students most and explains why private hotel management schools appear to be thriving. The second view is, admittedly, more problematic for the private sector. It has been readily embraced by hospitality academics in traditional higher education institutions but for reasons we have already explored, has achieved little in garnering respect and support for hospitality management education. A more persuasive counter to the view is that hospitality education survived for many years without a significant research culture and one might infer that this was because it was perceived to be meeting the needs of the industry it serves. Insofar as one can differentiate research from scholarship (the latter we take to mean being routinely well informed about one's subject and developments within it) there is no *de facto* reason why the absence of conventional research activity should debilitate curricula or the culture of learning and teaching.

Second here, it can be argued that private schools by definition, in charging a fee, are in a stronger position to attract only those students who are likely to be seriously motivated to join and remain with the industry upon graduation. We alluded earlier to the apparently high drop out rates from the industry of those educated in traditional higher education institutions. Evidence for retention in the industry of private school graduates is almost non-existent and it is here that a deficiency in knowledge might be usefully addressed by meaningful research. Apart from genuine ignorance, a further objection to this second point is that the quality assurance of private schools across the globe is at best inconsistent and at worst erratic, making it problematic to assess the quality of inputs, outputs and endurance. It must be conceded that there is much in such an objection. In Switzerland where, at the time of writing, there are around 30 (mainly English speaking) private schools of hotel management, there are evident variations in quality. The Swiss Hotel Schools' Association (Association Suisse d'Ecole Hotelier or ASEH) established as a membership organization for the 'best' institutions has apparently failed in this regard. The first five years of the twenty-first century saw the voluntary departure of three of the globally most respected schools – Lausanne, Glion and Les Roches – over concerns about the uneven quality of ASEH membership. This is perhaps unsurprising as an inspection of the ASEH membership criteria reveals not a recognizable quality assurance system, but a list of benchmarking criteria (www.aseh.ch).

After more than a century of non-involvement in the regulation of private schools, the Swiss Federal Government is now seeking consensus on implementation of an official recognition scheme although it is unclear as to whether, given the highly devolved nature of the Swiss political system, the will exists to implement such a scheme.

Diverse opinions as to the nature and purpose of education are always politically and ideologically informed. In hospitality management, private education has always been an option and, while the last two to three decades have seen, across the globe, expansion and contraction in both public and private provision, three factors suggest that at present, the smart money would be on the eventual dominance of the latter. The first factor here is the problem of the credibility faced, rightly or wrongly, by publicly provided hospitality education within the academy, combined with the relative indifference of the industry to such education. The second factor is the inability of the public sector to meet demand for hospitality education, especially in developing and less-developed countries. Though the US, UK, Australia and Switzerland remain popular destinations for the modestly well-off middle classes of such countries (and not just in hospitality management) the numbers of those modestly well-off are growing. This not only stimulates supply locally, but also as the perceived quality of such supply improves the competitive advantage and attractiveness of overseas provision declines, especially in cost terms. A final consideration in understanding why private hospitality education may be increasingly favored relates not to supply, but to the twin influences of demand and credentialism. The growth of the international and national hospitality industries (we consider this distinction further in the next section) is most dynamic in the less-developed and developing world and the demand for labor is arguably increasing, not because of expansion alone, but also because of high wastage rates, a phenomenon familiar in the West, conventionally defined. Many of these societies also place considerable emphasis upon the importance of formal educational credentials, even for access to relatively modest labor market positions. The demand for educational courses directed towards growth industries is stimulated accordingly but most easily met by the private sector. This raises important issues of quality and the comparability of courses, issues which those in conventional academic institutions, with their sense of often *faux* superiority, are all too eager to highlight. However, the idea that education is a market made up of many differing kinds and quality of offers is becoming increasingly well established and the notion of the comparability of qualifications and the places where they were earned does not appear to greatly concern, at least in hospitality, either students or employers as consumers.

MAPPING THE FIELD OF HOSPITALITY MANAGEMENT

The nature of the discussion in the first part of this chapter necessitated an attempt at a certain degree of analytic introspection. Our objective in what follows is more prosaic: it is to circumscribe the field of hospitality management more in terms of its component elements and in so doing to introduce the content of this volume. In order fully to appreciate the diversity of themes and subjects/disciplines that contribute to hospitality management some insight into the development, nature and scope of the hospitality industry is appropriate in establishing the challenges that analysis faces.

Evolution and current form of the hospitality industry

The contemporary hospitality industry, or perhaps more correctly the international hospitality industry and numerous national hospitality industries (particularly in the developed economies), is a very different animal today than it was in the past. Historically, hospitality industries in different countries have emerged from varying degrees of domestic or institutionally based provision. Historically and in modern times, hospitality has been provided to both travelers (strangers), kin and people known, but not related to, the provider (others), for a variety of reasons; including those of superstition and fear, religious duty or social obligation (Gray and Ligouri, 1980). However, virtually all commentators agree that the forms of early, non-commercial hospitality and the varieties of commercial hospitality that have evolved over time, were stimulated by developments in transportation, trade and destinations (Van Hoof, McDonald, Yu and Vallen, 1996; Lane and Dupre, 1997;

Powers and Barrows, 1999; Dittmer, 2002). This is certainly true in relation to hospitality provision predicated upon people traveling away from their normal place of residence, what may be referred to as travel and/or tourism related hospitality provision, undertaken for either leisure or business reasons, but is only a partial explanation of the development of the hospitality industry or hospitality industries.

It is axiomatic that the existence of, and changes over time to, major travel and trade routes, technologies and destination types, in addition to general, societal change in relation to economic development and social norms, have conspired to influence the emergence of commercial hospitality provision over the ages, and still do so. Yet this remains at best a partial explanation of the driving forces lying behind the evolution of the industry and, as such, cannot account for the emergence, development and evolution of the totality of the hospitality industry. For example, a substantial part of the hospitality industries in many countries is not travel or tourism determined or dependent. Many 'local' hospitality businesses, even though they may benefit to varying degrees from travel and tourism related business exist primarily to serve the local hospitality market and came into being for this purpose (Wood, 1997; Brotherton, 2003). This is less true of hotels, for obvious reasons, but it is certainly true for many restaurants, cafés, public houses, bars, and businesses such as contract foodservice operators. For such businesses, demand derived from travel and tourism is incidental rather than central to their existence. Therefore, any explanation of where, why and in what form commercial hospitality exists must take into account temporal factors; spatial influences; politico-legal influences on business establishment and operation; and the economic and social organization of societies. In respect of the latter, the degree of urbanization, and the volume of economic surplus in the form of discretionary income available to the population both generally and locally is of particular significance (Brotherton, 2002, 2006).

In general, the influence of factors such as travel, trade and transportation have usually received a rather naïve treatment in the hospitality industry literature. There is invariably an unquestioned assumption that changes in the location and forms of commercial hospitality provision over time are contingent upon prior changes in the spatial, economic and technological aspects of these three influences, whether they arise indigenously or are imported from overseas (Litteljohn, 2000). While such antecedents have influenced the evolution of the hospitality industry to accept such a linear cause–effect relationship as an adequate explanation for how and why the industry has evolved, it is a negligent view in the extreme. Indeed, as Brotherton (2006) points out, the evolution of the industry is far more likely to be determined by a dialectical process wherein the forces from the past, the present, and those expected to prevail in the future, act dynamically to not only determine present, but also future, industry configurations. He argues that past forces act to 'push' the industry into present configurations and that current conditions, and expectations of future conditions, interact to influence prevailing industry structures and conditions. This interplay of conservative and innovative forces thus gives rise to combinational outcomes that may lead the industry towards expansion and development, consolidation or retrenchment.

As the industry has evolved over time this evolution has, in general, followed patterns and vectors similar to other industries, both in manufacturing and service. This is to be expected as the hospitality industry does not exist and operate in a vacuum. It has, and continues to be, influenced by the same general forces and processes of economic, social, technological and industrial development as other industries, whether at national or global level. The contemporary structure and behavior of the hospitality industry is influenced by changing views of industrial organization, the operations of capital and investment markets and managerial thinking and corporate behavior in the same way as vehicle manufacturing, banking or retailing industries are. Because of the industry's *modus operandi,* it has, at least to some extent, not been subject to the imperatives of these forces in totality, or in the same manner, and therefore has not evolved in such a homogeneous fashion as other industries. That said, and in common with other industries, there has been a general move to greater scope and scale, and increasing levels of concentration and dominance amongst leading companies in some sectors of the industry (Go, 1999; Litteljohn, 1999). This is most notably in the hotel and contract foodservice sector (Haywood and Wilson, 2003; Litteljohn, 2003), and to a lesser extent in the restaurant sector (Ball and Roberts, 2003). On the other hand, because many hospitality enterprises are 'local' and not 'global' many national hospitality industries comprise a high proportion of small, fragmented, owner-operated companies (Brotherton, 2003). Conversely, at the international or global level, the hospitality industry tends to be dominated by large international corporations which, in turn, are extending their market reach and power through branding and the economies of scope and scale as Larry Yu points out in Chapter 2 of this volume.

Indeed, as Brotherton (2003) has argued, these dualities of domestic and international/global, markets create difficulties for any attempt to define and delimit national and international hospitality industries. There is a divide between, on the one hand, the enormous number of small, independent, owner-operated hospitality businesses, and on the other, companies who do not always own the property assets but operate global brands through management contracts and franchising. Neither extreme can be regarded as entirely belonging to a national hospitality industry or the international hospitality industry *per se* as they both engage with domestic and international markets. Thus, to establish a dividing line to differentiate between a given domestic hospitality industry and the international hospitality industry is extremely problematic, both conceptually and practically.

One way forward on this might be the development of a type of 'exposure index' to establish the extent to which different hospitality organizations are exposed to, and dependent upon, the vagaries of the world economy in general and international travel volumes, both business and leisure motivated, in particular (Brotherton, 2003). At one extreme, it would not be difficult to establish that small, local hospitality businesses in many locations could be regarded as virtually immune to such macro-influences as they exist to serve the local community with little, or no, contact with international travelers. At the other, it may also be possible, where the vast majority of a company's business is derived from international travel, to classify certain international hotel companies as essentially belonging to the international hospitality industry, rather than having one foot in this category and another in a particular domestic hospitality industry. The problem, of course, is not the extremes but the middle ground. It is here that more work needs to be done to establish reasonable criteria and procedures to enable a logical distinction to be made between those regarded as belonging to the international hospitality industry and those who should more properly be classified as belonging to a particular domestic hospitality industry.

That the hospitality industry, whether viewed domestically or internationally, has grown significantly over the last two to three decades in particular and that it is a major employer and value creator across the globe is indisputable (Tse and Olsen, 1999). Larry Yu cogently argues in this volume (Chapter 2) that this growth has occurred in line with general economic development and the explosion in world travel and tourism. It has been facilitated, on the demand side of the equation, by a greater propensity for travel, and a greater ability to realize this propensity in the form of increased time and income availability. At the macro-level, a key influence has been greater political openness, i.e. the reduction or removal of travel restrictions (inbound and outbound) in countries previously more politically closed. On the supply side airline deregulation and 'open skies' policies have led to the establishment of low-cost, or budget, airlines which have dramatically cut ticket prices, particularly for domestic and short-haul routes. Further, the desire to develop tourism industries as a route to economic development in general, but particularly in emergent economies, and innovative practices on the part of destination and hospitality industry managers have all contributed to this growth.

On this last point, hospitality enterprises have begun to explore and utilize alternative strategies to finance their international expansion plans (see Paul Beal's analysis of this in Chapter 16) in ways designed to control the risk endemic in such ventures. They use market entry strategies, such as management contracts and franchising, in a similar manner to spread ownership/investment and operator risks, but they have also developed new or, at the very least, new variations on old forms of provision to reflect and stimulate changing market and consumer trends. This can be seen, for example, in the significant development of the Meetings, Incentive, Conventions and Exhibitions (MICE) sector of the industry as analyzed by Schlentrich in Chapter 18. It is also evident in the move to capitalize upon people's desire for real estate or property ownership, in varying forms such as timeshares or condominiums, in relation to their recreational and vacational activities as noted in Robert Christie Mill's observations on resort development in Chapter 20. Beyond these

examples, more creative approaches to cruising are becoming evident, as is the utilization of the 'all-inclusive' concept in many destinations and hotels. With the growth predicted in the leisure and international travel markets over the coming decades and the industry's track record of innovation the future for the international hospitality industry looks bright, albeit one that is highly susceptible to unexpected exogenous shocks, as has been seen in the recent past in the form of terrorist attacks and natural disasters.

Core subjects and themes

As with the hospitality industry, and as we have noted, hospitality management is a broad and diverse field characterized both by the application of 'generic' business disciplines and specialisms to the hospitality case and certain preoccupations with eliciting the uniqueness aspects of the case through such applications. It is also an enterprise characterized by fragmentation, eclecticism and a lack of methodological sophistication, or at least pluralism, in terms of the range of methodological choices hospitality management researchers have made, the type of research conducted (conceptual versus empirical), and the coverage and coherence of the research effort in relation to particular specialisms and their sub-areas. Having briefly reviewed some of the main features of the development of the industry, we now turn to a summary of those dominant research strands in the extant literature that constitute the core of contributions to this volume.

These are presented in three sections. The first details several of those areas in hospitality management on which we have already touched. To summarize, in Chapter 1, Brotherton and Wood review the current debates about the definition and meaning of hospitality and hospitality management. In Chapter 2, Larry Yu examines the development of the international hospitality industry whereas Robert Christie Mill's Chapter 3 develops more generally the relationships between hospitality, tourism, leisure and recreation, both as subjects and economic and social activities. In Chapter 4 Brownell and Walsh tackle a subject that has not figured extensively in this Introduction – the significance of gender in analyzing the hospitality industry. Gender figures prominently in several sub-disciplinary areas of hospitality research, notably organizational studies and human resource management. However, Mazurkiewicz's (1983) seminal paper on gender and social consumption in hotels apart, there is remarkably little literature dedicated to gender questions in hospitality in their own right. Brownell and Walsh focus on the role of women as workers and consumers in the hospitality industry. In employment, women have dominated the workforce of many national hospitality industries for a very long time but few reach the highest levels of the industry. As consumers of hospitality, women are becoming more significant in their own right rather than, *pace* Mazurkiewicz, as appendages to male consumption. Brownell and Walsh offer valuable and fascinating insights into these neglected themes in hospitality research. Chapter 5 by Michael Riley returns us to many of the matters discussed earlier in this Introduction in his critique of hospitality management research and, in particular, the concepts of multi- and inter-disciplinarity in such research, concepts of which he is highly skeptical. Chapter 6, by Clayton Barrows and Novie Johan offers a far more upbeat review of the state of hospitality management education than has been essayed in this discussion, both these final chapters in the first section then offering useful alternative views or correctives to the concerns of the Editors.

Parts Two and Three of the *Handbook* are perhaps more traditional in conception than the first, focusing respectively on generic and specialized management functions in the hospitality industry. Generic functions we have taken to include strategic management, operations management, innovation and entrepreneurship, financial management, organization studies, human resource management, marketing, service quality and information technology. The fields of innovation and entrepreneurship, and of real estate management, are perhaps two of the most neglected areas of hospitality research and management. Both have a claim to be at least as important as strategic management, yet in the area of entrepreneurship and innovation, there has been remarkably little systematic research of any range, entrepreneurship being consistently associated with the small business sector of the hospitality industry. Given that small businesses dominate the hospitality industry this is understandable and relevant but as Enz and Harrison show in Chapter 9, there is a broader picture to be discerned in examining the relationship between entrepreneurship and innovation.

Specialized functions include real estate management; accommodation and facilities management; meetings, incentives, conferences/conventions and exhibitions (MICE) sector management; food and beverage management (including food production and service systems); licensed retail management; flight catering; resort management; and events management. These specialized functions are 'specialized' in different senses. We have already suggested that the relative neglect of real estate management in the hospitality field is difficult to understand. This is not simply because of the property implications of obtaining and running hospitality businesses, but because it arguably underpins most other areas of 'functional management', and not least finance. It stands to gain importance in the years ahead and it is not unrealistic to assume that it may well come to be considered a 'generic' rather than specialized function. Subjects like accommodation and facilities management and food and beverage management/food production and service systems are specialized in the sense that they effectively define the 'distinctiveness' of hospitality management, addressed as they are to the industry's core products. The other fields included under this heading really evidence the extent to which specialized industry sectors have called into being the need for combinations of distinctive skills and technologies drawing from across other hospitality and, indeed, non-hospitality sectors. Flight catering and licensed retail management are significant, and specialized, sub-sectors of the industry. The first requires the precise combination of such skills with advanced food technology and sophisticated distribution systems. The second demonstrates how what was originally, and remains, a socially and politically sensitive area – the provision of alcohol in public places – has mutated beyond recognition as a result of sectoral innovation underpinned by various 'rational' management systems. The MICE; resorts; and event (or events) management sectors represent perhaps the three most important emerging sub-sectors of modern hospitality markets, and the last two at least, because of their significance, have brought forth their own specialized educational qualifications in some parts of the world. The MICE sector might, perhaps, be viewed as a 'trans-industry' phenomenon since meetings, incentives, conventions and exhibitions are held in many different physical locations, and make use of diverse types of hospitality business for food, accommodation and other facilities.

Each contribution to these two sections offers a thorough review of the principal themes, issues and research underpinning the relevant subject. By way of an introduction to the major themes covered, as well as the relationships between them, the following discussion continues the scene-setting process with brief vignettes of the areas covered.

Strategic management

In the current curricula of business studies courses, strategy and strategic management have assumed in the last 20 years an increasingly important role, often acquiring a 'capstone' status in such programs, posited as a way of integrating other forms of management learning. In hospitality management curricula, strategy and strategic planning and management have historically been more contentious in terms of whether they should be included in programs below postgraduate level. The 'against' school has contended that strategy is dealt with by senior management/executives and, because the primary purpose of undergraduate hospitality management education is the production of graduates who are immediately employable in terms of operational competence, the inclusion of strategic management effectively crowds out more relevant subjects at this level. The 'for' school have, of course, argued the reverse. Their argument has been along the lines that undergraduates should not only be trained to be operationally competent, important though this is, but have some capacity to cope with tomorrow as well as today. In this view, operational decisions at a unit level are taken within an overall corporate strategic context and, furthermore, many sub-organizational units are increasingly becoming centers of strategic thinking, planning and management in their own right (i.e. strategic business units, SBUs), putting strategy at the heart of unit management decision making.

Thankfully, it would appear that, the 'for' school has prevailed in this debate and at least one module on strategy is now probably a universal feature on most final year hospitality management undergraduate programs. Both the hospitality management curricula/teaching and research emphasis has tended to reflect the changing emphases evident in industry and strategy academia in general. Over the last half-century or so this has evolved from a primary concern with formal strategic planning, through one more focused on the development and management of strategy to achieve sustainable competitive advantage (Mintzberg, 1994), to one that, in an increasingly turbulent and fast-moving world, sees strategy as a revolutionary rather than evolutionary endeavor (Hamel, 1996). In many senses the emphasis has moved from a pre-eminent concern with the structural and process element of strategic planning and management to the more cognitive and creative focus of strategic thinking, reflecting the greater emphasis now given, in both academia and industry, to innovative and entrepreneurial skills. This, in turn, is a reflection of new competitive imperatives that demand not only improved organizational performance in relation to the competitive status quo for basic survival purposes, but different business models to transform the competitive landscape into one where the innovator can achieve dominance (Olsen, West and Tse, 1998).

As noted earlier in this Introduction, much of the early, and some would argue the contemporary, strategic management teaching and research focus has tended to be of a 'borrower and applier' nature, theories and models developed in other industrial sectors being assessed with respect to their applicability to the hospitality industry, in some cases without actually conducting any empirical investigation (Olsen and Roper, 1998). However, as Tse and Jogaratnam argue in Chapter 7 here, more recent empirical approaches to theory testing and building have been evident within which the multi-faceted dimensions of strategy and strategic management, contingency, performance, competitive methods and core competencies have been investigated. Interestingly, there has been greater use of case study methodologies in a considerable amount of this work in an attempt to produce more in-depth analyses. This reflects the use of the case study medium more generally within strategic management teaching over the years and constitutes a rare example of teaching informing research!

That said the contemporary picture in the strategic management field related to the hospitality industry is far from complete or mature. Not only is there a relative dearth of strategic management research in service industries *per se* compared with that existing on manufacturing industry, this is even more pronounced in the case of the hospitality industry. Hence, the 'borrower and applier' focus, noted above, followed by relatively limited and episodic empirical forays to establish theory in the context of hospitality. Best categorized as well-intentioned, resource-limited, spasmodic and producing some outcomes of value, the strategic hospitality management field is one that requires much greater sustained research effort, of more critical mass, to investigate the key issues through comparative and longitudinal studies. There are examples of hospitality companies regarded as innovators, leaders and business model changers. Most obvious is McDonald's who changed the face of the fast-food, low-cost eating out industry, but others in different sectors have been pioneers (for example, in the UK, of low-cost and budget lodging hotel brands such as Travel Inns) and radically redrawn industry configurations and competitive conditions. There has been a distinct lack of research on such organizations to identify why and how they achieved this and thus became leaders in their field. Similarly, there seems to have been little appetite amongst researchers to conduct comparative studies between the best and worst performers in the same sector of hospitality business, and following similar strategies, to identify why there should be such a variation in performance. It is to the causal rather than the descriptive that the focus of research effort in this field needs to shift in the future.

Operations management

Operations management, in conjunction with food and beverage and accommodation management, is widely regarded as the 'holy trinity' of hospitality management curricula as these three fields concentrate on what many regard as the 'core' hospitality products of food, drink, accommodation and the infrastructure and processes designed to present and deliver these to the customer. Hospitality Operations Management (HOM) is essentially a sector specific subset of Service Operations Management (SOM) that, in turn is a sub-set of the generic Production and Operations Management (POM) field. However, as Jones and Lockwood (1998) note, this relationship is not always recognized or utilized by analysts of hospitality operations management where research is not strongly rooted in, or linked to, the large body of generic operations management literature. Most of this research output is of a characteristically isolationist kind, researchers taking the view that hospitality operations are different from other types of operations with the consequence that the

use and application of theoretical insights from wider SOM and POM research environments are largely inappropriate. Jones and Lockwood (1998), Lockwood and Ingram (1999) and Jones (1999b) argue that because of this, much hospitality operations management research is empirically interesting but frequently conceptually weak, an observation that echoes Taylor and Edgar's (1999) earlier noted comment that hospitality management research suffers from 'conceptual malnutrition'.

This is, of course, a fallacy and a road to disaster for hospitality management *per se* as well as hospitality operations management as Jones and Lockwood argue in their contribution to this text (Chapter 8). That there are some differences between hospitality, other service and manufacturing environments is true (Bowen and Ford, 2004), but these are not fundamental or as significant as many 'isolationist' proponents would claim. Indeed, there is no substantial or systematic body of comparative research evidence to support such claims. If the proponents of this view truly believe it to be correct then it is time for them to produce the research evidence to support this. In a slightly wider context, one of the major reasons for the persistence of the 'unique' standpoint has been the adoption of a 'protectionist' policy on the part of many hospitality management academics. As experience is now confirming, hospitality researchers and educators have historically sought to maintain this mystique as a mechanism for maintaining independence and survival and to avoid hospitality management programs being absorbed into related vocational subjects within educational institutions (e.g. tourism and generic business and management). As we suggested earlier, this policy has largely failed in many institutions, damaging the reputation of both hospitality management research generally, and that undertaken in the hospitality operations field because research evidence to support claims of 'difference' has not been produced, and it is highly unlikely it ever will be.

As Jones and Lockwood (1998, 1999 and in Chapter 8 here) consistently point out, hospitality operations management research embraces a wide range of topic areas, some of which are also addressed by marketing, human resource management, finance and quality research agendas. These include, *inter alia*, process types, design and layout, capacity and production planning, materials and inventory management, productivity and workforce management, quality management, yield and revenue management, strategy, service encounters and queuing, property and asset management. Given the inclusive nature of 'operations' this is not surprising, but the breadth of areas encompassed by hospitality operations management researchers creates a diversity that may well have inhibited the development of a more focused research effort, thereby limiting the degree of maturity in research output that might have been expected by now. In view of this the call made by Jones and Lockwood, previously (1998) and in this volume, for hospitality operations management researchers to ground future research in established generic POM theory, empirically test existing models, and to use and develop more robust methodologies remains apposite.

Financial and real estate management

In common with generic, and more sector-specific, business-related education, financial and managerial accounting modules are normally included in the core components of hospitality programs. Hotels, restaurants and other forms of commercial hospitality provision are businesses and, as such, managers of these businesses need to understand financial fundamentals in order to survive and prosper. Indeed, the cases of failed hospitality businesses, even those with a sound underlying concept, are legion, often because the owners and/or operators did not have the necessary financial acumen to ensure that, as businesses, they were financially viable. The financial basis of hospitality businesses is therefore as critically important, perhaps even more so, than the 'softer' more behavioral elements more usually associated with the notion of hospitality.

As both Atkinson and Jones (Chapter 10) and Beals (Chapter 16) in this volume highlight, the hospitality industry is not composed of homogeneous entities. Rather, it is diverse with many types of enterprises where the hospitality product is multi-faceted, e.g. hotels, and there is often a separation of ownership and operational control (for example in enterprises operated on a management contract basis). These features generate a challenging environment for management not least in the financial aspects of the managerial function. Not surprisingly, from curricula, teaching and research perspectives, much of the focus and content of these activities has been, and largely continues to be, centered on operational performance, because, in curricula

and teaching terms, the primary focus resides in developing students to be operationally competent and employable upon graduation. Thus, financial modules tend to concentrate on the financial techniques and skills operational managers require to manage hospitality businesses, or sub-units within such businesses. Similarly, and as a direct consequence of this, it is equally unsurprising that most of the financial research work conducted within the context of the hospitality industry has also had a strong operational performance focus. Given that in operational terms, financial planning, budgeting, cost control, pricing and revenue generation, and the measurement of financial performance are invariably central to business and managerial success it is to be expected that research effort will tend to concentrate on these areas as both Atkinson and Jones (Chapter 10), and Harris and Brander-Brown (1998) confirm.

However, as Atkinson and Jones note in their contribution here, the quality of this research in many cases leaves much to be desired, a view shared by others in the field (Harris and Brander-Brown, 1998; Barlow, 1999). Barlow (1999: 252) goes so far as to comment that the body of generic accounting and financial management research is 'light-years ahead of much of the work done related to the hospitality industry' and that there is a need not only for more research *per se* in this field, but more of an interdisciplinary nature. In a slightly different vein Harris and Brander-Brown (1998: 174) comment that their review of research in this field indicates some considerable enthusiasm on the part of accounting and financial management researchers to explore a range of topics and publish. Unfortunately, they also note that much of this research is not of the highest quality but is characterized by 'poor research design and inadequate methodologies' that 'result in simplistic and superficial findings, adding little to the knowledge base'. They add that 'it is apparent that much of the research and development to date has been isolated and fragmented'. More recently, the volume of research effort and publication has increased but as Atkinson and Jones note here, this remains largely fragmented and isolated from the mainstream. It would appear that one of the major problems in the hospitality financial accounting/management research field is not only relevance and quality but also a lack of a critical mass of researchers and research output.

One example of the operational bias of hospitality accounting and finance research is reflected in Beals' contribution to this volume (Chapter 16, see also Beals and Denton, 2004). Beals indicates that focus upon the financial aspects of operational performance largely, though not totally, ignores other financial issues of real estate investment and asset management. As Beals notes, investors in hospitality assets and hospitality operators have differing time-horizons and views of what is important in terms of operational performance and investment return, and these views frequently conflict. Although there is a body of research work relating to the financial appraisal of investment decisions (see Harris and Brander-Brown, 1998; Barlow, 1999), much of this focuses on investment return, associated with what may be termed operational investments rather than property or real estate as an asset class. However, real estate financing and investments are seen largely as a matter of strategy, and one not directly and immediately relevant to hospitality management graduates and unit level management. For this and other reasons (such as lack of space in already crowded curricula and institutions not having the necessary teaching expertise for this dimension) real estate financing and investment tend not to figure as discrete topics in hospitality programs. Where they are included, it is often as part of other modules, even though, as we suggested earlier, real estate management is a core element of strategy in the hospitality industry.

Organizational studies and human resource management

Within the hospitality field, organizational studies or behavior (OB) and human resource management (HRM) research almost certainly represents the single largest, most consistent and richest field of research endeavor, a fact captured in the contributions of Guerrier (Chapter 11) and Christenson Hughes (Chapter 12) to this *Handbook*. That OB (or organization studies as Guerrier here prefers) and HRM have faired well in hospitality research is perhaps unsurprising given the recurring cliché that hospitality is a 'people' industry, an assertion that nevertheless overlooks the aforementioned observation by Beals (Chapter 16) that this ignores the significant investment in land, property and utilities that underpins it. Equally unsurprising given the

slow development of hospitality management within higher education is that most early research into OB and HRM in hospitality was not conducted by 'hospitality academics'. Wood's surveys of the literature (Wood, 1992, 1994b, 1997) show that prior to the 1990s, there was little (or at least little of any significant quality or quantity) OB and HRM research in hospitality from within the field. The majority of contributions came from social scientists making forays into studying the industry, an industry that was, implicitly at least, often depicted, usually sympathetically, as pathologically 'abnormal'. This trend has continued into the twenty-first century with an important change in tone, however. Sympathy and empathy have become unfashionable, replaced by a more cynical and aggressive perspective on service industries and service work in general, and in hospitality and related industries in particular, not least signaled in the fact that neologisms such as 'McJobs' and 'Disneyfication' have passed into the English language as terms (mainly) of snobbish abuse, or at least insensitivity. Often, analysis combines with much hand-wringing over the decline of dignity in employment supposedly represented by the expansion of services, an attitude that conveniently ignores the less appealing aspects of employment in other sectors, notably extractive and manufacturing industries. The 'romance of labor' (or perhaps 'romancing' is more accurate) is alive and well in the employment research of the increasing number of bourgeois academics who have belatedly turned their attention to services.

One might infer from Guerrier's wide-ranging contribution to this volume (Chapter 11) that a possible reason for these trends is that research into service organizations and cultures *in general* from within mainstream OB research is a comparatively recent phenomenon, as it is in HRM. One is reminded of the old joke about English buses: you wait at the bus stop for several hours for a bus that does not come, and then three buses come along at the same time. After years of neglect of service work and service industries, mainstream researchers in OB and HRM now appear in increasing numbers to desire to rectify this deficiency as quickly as possible. Of course, hospitality is not the only industry of choice for the attentions of contemporary OB and HRM researchers. Indeed, one is struck by the extent to which many 'external' research interventions still have the character of slightly exotic expeditions off the beaten track. Ironically, the arguable exception to this is a number of ethnographically informed studies of hospitality work in recent years that might have been expected to exhibit the tendency to exoticism reflected in earlier studies, for example Mars and Nicod's (1984) analysis of the 'tribe' of waiters.

One instance of where hospitality *has* been centrally 'showcased' in mainstream OB and HRM is undoubtedly in Ritzer's initial starting point for his crusade against 'McDonaldization'. The McDonaldization idea has created a bandwagon onto which many mainstream OB and HRM researchers have jumped despite the profound unoriginality of Ritzer's thesis (Wood, 1998). Yet even here, and despite the object case chosen by Ritzer, the main trend has been to seek elaboration and exemplification of his ideas in service industries other than hospitality.

Undoubtedly, in the early days of research into OB and HRM in hospitality, many research contributions by mainstream social scientists provided a necessary uncovering of essentially novel information. Subsequently built upon by others, more recently the building project appears to have stumbled a little. Many studies by contributors 'external' to hospitality management and education have elaborated new examples of existing concepts but conceptual development itself has been patchier and the creation of genuinely new knowledge and insight rather more infrequent. Hospitality researchers have tended to confine themselves to small-scale studies, also often replicatory in character and relying on low power methodologies. In other words, well-established furrows are being overplowed. To some extent, this state of affairs can be attributed – at least in the case of 'mainstream' researchers – to the essentially interventionist tradition of which they are a part. In other words, for these researchers the hospitality industry is one amongst many to capture their interest and provide a vehicle for the exploration of specific theories, themes and concepts. In hospitality management education and research, OB and HRM is just one possible area of management inquiry giving scholarly output an inevitable flavor of piecemeal incompleteness.

The contributions on OB and HRM to this *Handbook* both indicate the importance of gaining an overview of the theoretical, conceptual and empirical state of the fields. Guerrier's sensitive and thoughtful contribution on organization studies (Chapter 11) gives a subtle insight into these questions but also

indicates many of the tensions that exist, conceptually, in generating a coherent research agenda. Christensen Hughes' magisterial contribution on human resource management (Chapter 12) shows that by a fair, critical and systematic application of current concepts and frameworks, it is possible to generate a reasoned contextual analysis both of what is known, what might reasonably be inferred from what is known, and what gaps in knowledge need to be addressed. The defining feature of both contributions is that they take an 'outside-in' approach, that is, the main reference point in each case is the mainstream of their discipline and how it has dealt or can deal with the case of hospitality work and employment.

Marketing and service quality

Marketing and service quality are dealt with in separate chapters within this volume (see Bowen, Chapter 13, and Ekinci, Chapter 14) because, although closely related in many respects, they are not automatic bedfellows. Quality is an issue also considered by strategists, operations managers, accountants and human relations specialists. However, it does have something of a natural affinity with marketing because of its focus on notions of customer satisfaction and value, hence its inclusion with marketing in this section.

A central, core subject in hospitality management curricula for some considerable time, marketing, in common with its more generic manifestation, has attracted a significant amount of interest from researchers. In their review of the hospitality marketing literature Bowen and Sparks (1998) found that approximately one-third of the articles they surveyed were conceptual in nature and two-thirds were empirical, with more than half of the latter type focused on consumer behavior and market segmentation. Their study suggested that these relative proportions had moved in favor of empirical work compared to an earlier review that found a more even distribution of conceptual and empirical studies (Crawford-Welch and McCleary, 1992). Although Bowen and Sparks' (1998) analysis found some aspects of the marketing field to have received quite significant attention from hospitality marketing researchers (in addition to the two areas mentioned above, conceptual and empirical research into hospitality products, pricing promotion and distribution was prominent) certain aspects of the field were underdeveloped and represented. For example, internal marketing, personal selling and database marketing received scant attention, unlike in generic marketing research.

This has arguably changed in the years since that review. As Bowen suggests here (Chapter 13) technological developments, particularly those associated with information and communication technologies, have re-focused hospitality marketing researchers' attention on database marketing, data warehousing and mining, customer relationship management and electronic distribution channels (see also O'Connor and Piccoli, 2003). In conjunction with this, 'quality' researchers have developed an increasing focus on the relationship between quality, customer satisfaction and loyalty as Ekinci (Chapter 14) observes. In this respect the service quality research agenda in general, and that associated with hospitality, has moved from a concern 20 years ago with identifying the attributes and characteristics of service quality, invariably from a production/delivery perspective, to one more concerned with how consumers evaluate or judge service quality and how this can be measured (Johns, 1999). The main problems it has faced in doing so have been the development of robust constructs and dimensions, metrics based on these (see for example Buttle, 1996) and the selection of an appropriate comparison standard (Ekinci, 2003). In addition, service quality has had, and still does have to some extent, something of an identity crisis in terms of where it belongs in hospitality management curricula and research. As noted earlier it appears, in both contexts, within a range of more established fields, though it would appear to be migrating more towards the marketing field than others as its emphasis shifts towards a closer relationship with customer satisfaction, loyalty and repeat business.

Marketing and quality assurance are both also central to understanding important emergent markets and business activities. As noted earlier, currently important in this respect are the MICE sector (meetings, incentives, conferences/conventions and exhibitions); event or events management; and resorts. At first glance, these three areas appear very different but, while there are differences, they represent examples of a similar phenomenon, namely the bundling or combination of different products and services into a greater whole. Udo Schlentrich (Chapter 18) gives a clear view of the importance of MICE business to the hospitality industry, his own research over a

long period highlighting how an increasingly 'macro' business relies very much on the micro-management of a combination of interpersonal, marketing and quality matters relating to the service offer, with customer loyalty and satisfaction being key success factors in the segment. Resorts are becoming an increasingly important hospitality product combining accommodation, foodservice, leisure, recreational and other amenities. Robert Christie Mill (Chapter 23) highlights the real estate aspects of the growth of resorts. The variety of service and quality offers encompassed by the resort concept goes a considerable way to explaining their growth in popularity. In Chapter 24, Don Getz reviews the emerging field of event management. The higher education courses in this area springing up all over the world reflect the extent to which all those activities that fall under the 'events' umbrella – for example, festivals and sporting competitions – have developed in recent years from relatively self-contained phenomena to huge business concerns with implications that reach far beyond the event itself, to communities and regional and national economic well-being. All three sectors indicate the increasing complexity of the hospitality industry, giving some insight into the equally greater complexity of skills that are, and will be, required for its future management. Just as importantly, to a great extent all three are in some respects reliant upon the creation of desirable 'experiences' that people wish to buy, placing marketing and service quality issues at the heart of their offering.

Information technology

Information (and communication) technologies, systems and management are becoming increasingly important to the operation, and some would argue ultimate success, of hospitality enterprises, whether they are global corporations or localized businesses. The inexorable march of technological advancement has stung an industry that has been historically rather slow, compared with others, to recognize and utilize the operational and competitive advantages offered by such technologies because of its relatively insular nature and belief that, at its heart, hospitality is essentially a human relations exercise to deliver products created by traditional craftspeople. As we have seen, this view still exerts a strong restraining influence in many quarters of the industry but it has been losing its strength in general for some time, and particularly over the last couple of decades. Given the reductions in cost, greater ease of use and the impact of the Internet there is now no doubt that IT and associated technologies are important strategic levers for small and large hospitality companies alike (Frew, 2000; O'Connor and Piccoli, 2003).

Not only has the view that hospitality is unique, as compared with other forms of economic endeavor, engendered attitudes amongst industry practitioners that can be described as skeptical, and sometimes downright resistant to a view that IT should be endemic to hospitality businesses, but this has also been reflected in hospitality management curricula. Such curricula have historically, and even more contemporarily, tended to follow 'what the industry has said it needs/wants' from the graduates being developed as its future managers (Geller, 1984). Hence, industrial advisory panels and committees have not strongly advocated the role of IT knowledge and skills to educational institutions. Because of this, and the associated costs of provision, hospitality management education institutions in general have been relieved that they have not been required to invest in specialist IT equipment and teaching skills. This has meant that, with perhaps a few exceptions, IT modules on hospitality management programs have been either sparse in existence or viewed as something useful but not critical to the hospitality managerial role. Where IT applications, such as property and restaurant management systems (PMS/RMS) and electronic point of sale systems (EPOS) have been integrated into accommodation and food and beverage management modules it has normally been on the advice of industry advisers and on the grounds of their use in operations. Thus 'creeping' IT in the hospitality curriculum has come from operational demands and the desire to have 'operationally competent' graduates even where companies use different systems that require specific training.

However, as Connolly and Hales point out in this volume (Chapter 15) times are changing and future hospitality managers will require a far more substantial knowledge of the role IT already plays, and can play in business development. Of particular importance will be knowledge of how IT and related technologies can be used creatively to enhance the customers' experience and add value to the organization (Olsen, 1999; Olsen and Connolly, 2000) and constitute a source of 'strategic enablement'

(Nyheim, McFadden and Connolly, 2005) to achieve wider competitive advantage (Siguaw, Enz and Namasivayam, 2000). The view of the nature and role of IT within hospitality businesses is changing because the industry is being forced to change. So, too, is the focus of research effort. It is moving away from a historical concern with applications, through systems development to more emphasis on how such technology can be used to improve, enhance and extend core business practices in hospitality companies, in some cases because the technology itself has made past practices redundant or reduced their revenue generating ability (Nyheim, McFadden and Connolly, 2005). It is becoming less eclectic than in the past (Baker, Sussmann and Welch, 1999) and more focused on the strategic, operational and customer enhancement improvements it can facilitate in an increasingly crowded and competitive marketplace.

Accommodation and facilities management

The contribution to this volume on accommodation management by Frapin-Beaugé, Verginis and Wood (Chapter 17) is a perhaps unusual one. Accommodation is, in most hotels, recognized as the principal source of revenue and it is on hotels that this contribution focuses, although within the hospitality industry there are many alternatives to hotel accommodation. However, the traditional, operations-biased approach to accommodation management teaching in hospitality management has favored an emphasis on two areas – front office management and housekeeping (and, additionally in certain curricula, hotel engineering). Though in practice each of these contains a human, 'service', element, they are essentially technique- and skill-oriented and not the ideal focus for scrutiny in a volume such as this. This remark hints at another important observation in respect of accommodation management in hospitality – the area has virtually no research tradition of any kind, the majority of writing on the subject dealing prosaically with systems and procedures relating to design, construction and maintenance.

Chapter 17, then, focuses on the relationship between accommodation management in hotels and the concept of facilities management. Facilities management is, like hospitality, a young (actually younger) emerging specialized field that is experiencing similar problems of identity and credibility to those facing hospitality and described earlier in this Introduction – the parallels are in fact instructive (de Bruijn, van Wezel and Wood, 2001). This rather gratuitous reason for the combination of the two areas is not the principal reason for the comparison however. Rather, the term facilities management, like hospitality management has become something of a catch-all term and one increasingly adopted in a wide variety of organizations, including those in the hospitality industry. A central purpose of the discussion in this volume is to utilize certain aspects of the comparison between the two to explore whether there are any grounds for supposing that a more abstract, conceptual approach to the management of hospitality accommodation may yield not only useful analytic generalizations about the field but also contribute more effectively to accommodation management.

Food and beverage management

Together with the management of accommodation and facilities, food and beverage management is the significant defining element in hospitality education and practice that lends hospitality management its distinctiveness in terms of that which is additional to a general business curriculum (Wood, 2000, 2007). The food and beverage component of hospitality management course curricula invariably include both practical and theoretical elements. The practical component of food and beverage management normally entails students spending some time in hotel school training kitchens and restaurants learning how to prepare and serve food for restaurant service. This model of food and beverage education is globally familiar; training and operations oriented; principally based on a hotel fine-dining model; and potentially expensive in terms of the plant and facilities required. The operational (despite the 'food and beverage *management*' label) emphasis of food and beverage education is, of course, meant to establish credibility with employers in terms of the knowledge required for managing the industry's core products. As we noted earlier in this Introduction, it has long been observed that these specialist areas, supported by industrial internships (principally in operative roles) act as a form of pre-entry socialization to the industry, instilling a view of hospitality management as short-term and operations-centered (Mars, Bryant and Mitchell, 1979).

Food and beverage management research and scholarship has hitherto generally reflected this operational bias though, unlike with accommodation management, there is, in addition to the many manuals and texts on the operational management of food and beverage facilities, at least some evidence of additional analytic traditions, even though again, the range of literature is piecemeal and fragmented. These include, as noted earlier, work on the operations management aspects of food and beverage systems, an area that subsumes a reasonably healthy sub-literature on food production and service systems. In addition there are sectoral surveys of the foodservice industry and commentaries on gastronomy aimed specifically at the hospitality industry. Given the operational significance of the area, there has been more evidence of cross-subject fertilization. Thus, there are strong affiliations between food and beverage management and financial control and this has led to exploration of other linkages, for example with marketing and decision analysis (most notably with the development of the Boston Consultancy Group matrix in the context of 'menu engineering' and similar models of product positioning, performance and life cycles). One of the more productive areas of research has been to contextualize food and beverage management more widely within generic business, philosophic and other social scientific scholarship.

In the true isolationist tradition of hospitality management, this last strand of research has thus far had little impact on the field though it constitutes a reservoir of underlying vibrancy, which, if tapped, is promising for the future (see Wood, 2000, 2004b, 2007). A problem is, however, that intellectual isolationism is not the only cause of the limited scope of food and beverage management research. The operationally, training oriented model of food and beverage education with its emphasis on credibility with employers, means that what is a source of distinctiveness has become instead something that is tolerated. That food and beverage management education has been curriculum driven is reflected in the fact that faculty appointed to teach the subject have first and foremost been operational practitioners often enjoying lower status, rank and remuneration than academic colleagues in the same schools, employed as instructors, technicians, chef lecturers and tutors rather than as lecturers and professors. In other words, if hospitality management has faced problems of status within the academy, then food and beverage management, for so long predicated on a training model, has been captured in a low status trap within hospitality management. In a wider sense this reflects similar problems with the ambiguous position of food and beverage research in the social sciences. For example, sociologists of food and eating have long observed that the wider discipline of sociology sees research into food and eating as trivial, food and eating being a 'taken for granted' aspect of social life even for a discipline with a penchant for researching the trivial (Curtin, 1992; Lupton, 1996).

It is yet again one of the many ironies of the development of hospitality management that the two subjects that lend the field its arguable distinctiveness, the management of food and beverages and of accommodation, remain dramatically under-researched. In his contribution to this *Handbook*, Clayton Barrows (Chapter 19) conveys a sense of not only the scale and diversity of the global food and beverage sector but also of its economic and social significance. Furthermore, by sketching the boundaries of the field, Barrows gives a suggestive sense of the potential for research into this area that could be possible if the negative status attributes of the field were overcome. This potential is illustrated in Wood's critique (Chapter 20) of the earlier referred to sub-literature on food production and service systems. In this chapter, the purpose is not simply to discern the weaknesses of such 'systems' approaches, but to show, by considering parallels in the sociological literature on food and eating, how such weaknesses can be illuminated and perhaps a start made on overcoming them. Similar potential for food and beverage research, though from a radically different perspective, is found in Lashley's overview of the licensed retail sector (Chapter 21). This examines a business model where strategic and operational elements in food and beverage management (and other areas of hospitality administration) combine in an innovative way relatively free of traditional conceptions of hospitality service provision.

CONCLUSION

We have sought to cover a lot of terrain in this Introduction. For the reasons we have outlined, the 'state of the art' in hospitality

management is best encapsulated in one word: 'confused'. The central problems facing the subject at this point in time are (a) an absence of agreement as to the nature of hospitality and hospitality management; (b) limited evidence of reflective practice in conceptual, theoretical and methodological approaches to the subject; and (c) uncertainty about the future of the subject within higher education arising from a combination of avoidable 'home goals' and unreasoned snobbery towards hospitality within the academy.

In the course of this Introduction we have dwelt on the second and third of these points at length and will address our few concluding remarks to the first. The study of 'hospitality' as a generic concept may offer some opportunities for grounding the subject in a wider intellectual framework. Approaches to such study have thus far been somewhat spasmodic commencing with Wood (1994) (see also Brotherton, 1999a; Brotherton and Wood, 2000 and the collections by Lashley and Morrison, 2000 and Cummings, Kwansa and Sussman, 1998). In candor, these efforts have yet to amount to much for two reasons. First, such an approach necessarily removes, at least in the short term, the focus from hospitality *management*. As the subject has grown up very much as a specialized branch of management the utility of a more broadly based theoretical and conceptual redirection of research effort is not widely appealing. Second, because the question as to what hospitality management is has failed to emerge as an issue throughout the period of the term's adoption, there is now a reluctance to raise questions that might significantly challenge existing approaches to the study and practice of the subject. As we observed earlier, one such challenge that has recently emerged is the view that 'hospitality management' should be abandoned as a term in favor of 'hospitality studies' in order to engineer a focus on the concept of hospitality (e.g. Lashley, 2003). We do not, *pace* contributors to these debates, entirely concur with this view. Nor do we wholly agree with those who genuinely have doubts about the validity of this exploratory enterprise (for example, Riley, Chapter 5 in this volume) because it distracts and detracts from dealing with the realities of 'what is'.

Instead, it seems to us that many of the difficulties we have outlined in this Introduction relate to the rather more general problem of how 'management' is essentially construed.

Traditionally it has been a concept reserved for that activity involved in the control and administration of organizations, but management is something that all of us do, everyday, in small ways and focused upon 'small' and frequently personal activities. In arguing thus, we can sense eyebrows being raised at such a weak notion but our point is simply that there is no epistemological or ideological reason for valorizing the knowledge produced as a result of academic research into 'general' management. We earlier noted the remarks of the most recent UK assessment of hospitality research. Their comment that hospitality research 'lags a number of years behind theory development in mainstream management' gives a privileged and, in our view, far from easily justifiable status to such knowledge, which could easily be argued to 'lag' behind that in the natural or even social sciences. In other words, using academic management research and education as a benchmark for research and education in hospitality is a little like using a Hershey bar to benchmark all chocolate. Of course, such comparisons have themselves been invited by the educational community in hospitality because they have looked to 'management' as a means of validating their credibility with the consequences we have already outlined.

This is not to argue that critical reflection upon the meanings of hospitality as a concept should be some form of self-indulgent navel gazing or exercising of a collective angst. It is, perhaps, true that such reflection has more manifested itself as an activity within the UK hospitality education community than elsewhere, possibly because it is here that the academy's ambivalence to hospitality management has been greatest. Nevertheless, there is a real world of hospitality research produced by hospitality researchers of a range and quality, much of it devoid of self-doubt, which represents honest scholarship and merits serious treatment. An excellent flavor of this is seen in the contributions to this volume. It does not seem sensible to advocate a future of extremes. The 'hospitality studies' position with its implied abandonment of management as the focus of attention ignores the history of the field's development without explaining why 'hospitality studies' any more than 'hospitality management' deserves to be regarded as a necessarily independent area of study. Equally, seeking to avoid extensive reflection on the meanings of hospitality and its implications for the development of hospitality management seems to us to be an unnecessarily ostrich-like strategy.

Both positions, and others besides, can be respected. It *is* necessary to deal with the realities of hospitality management education and research as they have emerged in the many specialist schools and programs dedicated to their development and promulgation, and indeed, reflection on the meanings of hospitality is, for the most part, an element of those realities for it is from these schools that the concerns have largely emerged. We also accept the implication of the 'hospitality studies' approach that the management of hospitality is an extension of the study of hospitality but 'hospitality management' as it is currently understood (i.e. as coterminous with the hospitality industry) is only one such form of the management of hospitality (for example, hospitality management can be construed as the study of how hospitality is managed between individuals, between groups and in the home, or in various commercial and non-commercial public contexts – see Brotherton and Wood, 2000). In the wider world of industrial organizations, hospitality management is only one form of general management. The problem with the idea of 'hospitality studies' is that, deep at its heart remains the residual notion that in some way hospitality as a concept is in some way so special, distinct and even unique that it requires a special and distinct field of study to elaborate it. Read our lips: it isn't.

There may be a growing tendency to question the second view but there is little escaping the first. In a recent contribution to this debate Morrison (2006: 4) while acknowledging 'the multiple, complex and diverse ways of knowing hospitality' nevertheless premises such a view on a torturous simile, likening hospitality to a mischievous genie released from a bottle. This genie is '... incredibly infectious (sic) with all its swirling, twirling and intellectual taunts and defiance, exuding a seductive energy that sucks one into its very vortex ...'. While seeking to avoid the personification of hospitality in terms of genies, infectious or otherwise, we do not feel entirely comfortable with the view that definitional enterprises have limited utility. One of the many problems in trying to deal with 'what is' is a danger that we avoid confronting both issues of ideology (effectively moral propositions as to what people claim hospitality management *should* be) and credibility (the presence or absence of which flows directly from success or failure in addressing these essentially moral questions). To avoid definitional controversies completely is to collude in the belief that there are advantages to quite literally not knowing what one is talking about, a policy approach from which we demur.

It is difficult to avoid the tendency to be apocalyptic in speculating on the future of hospitality management as a subject, but we shall try. Certainly, that future will not be an easy one. Hospitality is still a comparatively young subject and at times seems as if it will never reach maturity. There remains, for perfectly sound reasons, a bias towards the practical in hospitality education and there is a suggestion that globally, hospitality as principally a form of vocational education outside of the traditional research/teaching service model of the university is reasserting itself. Within the comparatively small global community of hospitality researchers there is, as we have shown, division, uncertainty, theoretical and methodological weakness and an uneasiness or lack of self-confidence about what should be the intellectual aspirations of the subject and research within the subject – much of this lack of self-confidence engendered by a hostile academy. It would be easy, but facile, to argue that what is required is greater unity of purpose and clearer and publicly articulated statements as to what the educational and research agenda of hospitality management should be – easy, facile, but probably necessary. The difficulty is that this is an idealistic position. From a global academy where once there was at least lip service paid to collaborative and co-operative ideals we have moved to one where (short-term) performance, competitiveness and rankings are the currency of the times. New and young subjects, especially if they cannot quickly establish and legitimize a clear, competent and coherent intellectual presence, are almost inevitably bound to be disadvantaged within such a system. For hospitality management to survive within traditional higher education as anything more than a vocational training spur of more generalized business education, clarity, competence and coherence must be addressed. In compiling this volume, we hope that we have contributed to this process.

REFERENCES

Airey, D. and Tribe, J. (eds) (2005) *An International Handbook of Tourism Education*. Oxford: Elsevier.

Baker, M., Sussmann, S. and Welch, S. (1999) 'Information Technology Management'. In B. Brotherton (ed.) *The Handbook of Contemporary Hospitality Management Research*. Chichester: John Wiley and Sons Ltd. pp. 397–414.

Ball, S. and Roberts, L. (2003) 'Restaurants'. In B. Brotherton (ed.) *The International Hospitality Industry – Structure, Characteristics and Prospects*. Oxford: Butterworth-Heinemann. pp. 30–58.

Barlow, G. (1999) 'Financial management research'. In B. Brotherton (ed.) *The Handbook of Contemporary Hospitality Management Research*. Chichester: John Wiley and Sons Ltd. pp. 513–530.

Barrows, C. W. (1999) 'Introduction to hospitality education'. In C. W. Barrows and R. H. Bosselman (eds) *Hospitality Management Education*. Binghamton: The Haworth Press. pp. 1–20.

Beals, P. and Denton, G. (eds) (2004) *Hotel Asset Management: Principles, and Practices*. Lansing, MI: Educational Institute of the American Hotel and Lodging Association.

Bowen, J. T. and Sparks, B. A. (1998) 'Hospitality marketing research: a content analysis and implications for future research', *International Journal of Hospitality Management*, 17(2): 125–144.

Bowen, J. T. and Ford, R. C. (2004) 'What experts say about managing hospitality service delivery systems', *International Journal of Contemporary Hospitality Management*, 16(7): 394–401.

Brookes, M., Roper, A. and Hampton, A. (1999) 'Interdisciplinary research: The team advantage!' In B. Brotherton (ed.) *The Handbook of Contemporary Hospitality Management Research*. Chichester: John Wiley and Sons Ltd. pp. 61–76.

Brotherton, B. (1989) 'Defining hospitality, tourism and leisure: perspectives, problems and implications', *Proceedings of the IAHMS Autumn Symposium*. Glasgow: The Queen's College.

Brotherton, B. (1998) *The Nature Of Hospitality And Hospitality Management: A Definitive View To Inform Research And Practice For The New Millennium? The Hospitality and Tourism Global Forum (Millennial Retrospective Conference)*, http://www.mcb.co.uk/htgf/current/millenial.htm, MCB Publications.

Brotherton, B. (1999a) 'Towards a definitive view of the nature of hospitality and hospitality management', *International Journal of Contemporary Hospitality Management*, 11(4): 165–173.

Brotherton, B. (1999b) 'Hospitality management research: towards the future?' In B. Brotherton (ed.)

The Handbook of Contemporary Hospitality Management Research. Chichester: John Wiley and Sons Ltd. pp. 531–543.

Brotherton, B. (ed.) (1999c) *The Handbook of Hospitality Management Research*. Chichester: John Wiley and Sons Ltd.

Brotherton, B. (1999d) 'Comparative research'. In B. Brotherton (ed.) *The Handbook of Contemporary Hospitality Management Research: Principles and Practices*. Chichester: John Wiley and Sons Ltd. pp. 143–172.

Brotherton, B. (1999e) 'Case study research'. In B. Brotherton (ed.) *The Handbook of Contemporary Hospitality Management Research: Principles and Practices*. Chichester: John Wiley and Sons Ltd. pp. 115–142.

Brotherton, B. (2002) 'Towards a general theory of hospitality', presented at the Eleventh Annual CHME Hospitality Research Conference, Leeds Metropolitan University.

Brotherton, B. (2003) 'Themes and Prospects'. In B. Brotherton (ed.) *The International Hospitality Industry – Structure, Characteristics and Prospects*. Oxford: Butterworth-Heinemann. pp. 214–230.

Brotherton, B. (2006, forthcoming) 'Some thoughts on a general theory of hospitality', *Tourism Today*.

Brotherton, B. and Wood, R. C. (2000) 'Defining hospitality and hospitality management'. In C. Lashley and A. Morrison (eds) *In Search of Hospitality – Theoretical Perspectives and Debates*. Oxford: Butterworth-Heinemann. pp. 134–156.

Buttle, F. (1996) 'SERVQUAL: review, critique, research agenda', *European Journal of Marketing*, 30(1): 8–32.

Buttle, F. (1999) 'Measurement'. In B. Brotherton (ed.) *The Handbook of Contemporary Hospitality Management Research*. Chichester: John Wiley and Sons Ltd. pp. 233–244.

Cassee, E. H. (1983) 'Introduction'. In E. H. Cassee and R. Reuland (eds) *The Management of Hospitality*. Oxford: Pergamon, pp. xiii–xxii.

Crawford-Welch, S. and McCleary, K. W. (1992) 'An identification of the subject areas and research techniques used in five hospitality-related journals', *International Journal of Hospitality Management*, 11(2): 155–167.

Cummings, P. R., Kwansa, F. A. and Sussman, M. B. (eds) (1998) *The Role of the Hospitality Industry in the Lives of Individuals and Families*. Binghamton: The Haworth Press.

Curtin, D. W. (1992) 'Food/Body/Person'. In D. W. Curtin and L. M. Heldke (eds) *Cooking, Eating, Thinking: Transformative Philosophies of Food*. Bloomington: Indiana University Press, pp. 2–15.

de Bruijn, H., van Wezel, R. and Wood, R. C. (2001) 'Lessons and issues for defining "facilities management" from hospitality management', *Facilities*, 19(13/14): 476–48.

Dittmer, P. R. (2002) *Dimensions of the Hospitality Industry*, (3rd edn). New York: John Wiley and Sons Ltd.

Dutton, C. and Farbrother, C. (2005) 'Responding to change in higher education hospitality provision: two universities' approaches', *LINK*, Issue 12: pp. 10–11, http://www.hlst.heacademy.ac.uk/resources/link12/link12.pdf

Edgar, R. and Umbreit, T. W. (1988) 'Hospitality research: re-assessing our strategy', *Cornell Hotel and Restaurant Administration Quarterly*, 29(2): 51–56.

Ekinci, Y. (2003) 'Which comparison standard should be used for service quality and customer satisfaction?', *Journal of Quality Assurance in Hospitality and Tourism*, 4(3/4): 61–66.

Elsworth, J. D., Yoon, B. J. H. and Bai, B. X. (1999) 'Analysis of papers published in the Hospitality Research Journal: focus and trends of subjects, research designs and statistical techniques'. In K. S. Chon, (ed.) *The Practice of Graduate Research in Hospitality and Tourism*. New York: Haworth Hospitality Press. pp. 163–175.

Evans, M. R. (1992) 'The emerging role of hospitality and tourism research', *Hospitality and Tourism Educator*, 4(4): 57–59.

Frew, A. (2000) 'Hospitality information technology'. In B. Brotherton (ed.) *An Introduction to the UK Hospitality Industry: A Comparative Approach*. Oxford: Butterworth-Heinemann. pp. 188–213.

Fyall, A. and Thomas, R. (1999) 'Quantitative data analysis'. In B. Brotherton (ed.) *The Handbook of Contemporary Hospitality Management Research*, Chichester: John Wiley and Sons Ltd. pp. 263–286.

Gee, D. A. C. (1994) 'The Scottish Hotel School – the first fifty years'. In A. V. Seaton, C. L. Jenkins, R. C. Wood, P. U. C. Dieke, M. M. Bennett, L. R. MacLellan and R. Smith (eds) *Tourism: the State of the Art*. Chichester: John Wiley. pp. xvi–xxiii.

Geller, A. N. (1984) *Executive Information Needs in Hotel Companies*. New York: Peat, Marwick, Michell and Co.

Go, F. (1999) 'Internationalization'. In B. Brotherton (ed.) *The Handbook of Contemporary Hospitality Management Research*. Chichester: John Wiley and Sons Ltd. pp. 477–496.

Gray, W. S. and Ligouri, S. (1980) *Hotel and Motel Management and Operations*. Englewood Cliffs, NJ: Prentice-Hall.

Hamel, G. (1996) 'Strategy as revolution', *Harvard Business Review*, July–August: 69–82.

Hampton, A. (1999) 'Qualitative data analysis'. In B. Brotherton (ed.) *The Handbook of Contemporary Hospitality Management Research*. Chichester: John Wiley and Sons Ltd. pp. 287–304.

Harris, P. J. and Brander-Brown, J. (1998) 'Research and development in hospitality accounting and financial management', *International Journal of Hospitality Management*, 17(2): 161–181.

Haywood, K. and Wilson, G. (2003) 'Contract foodservice'. In B. Brotherton (ed.) *The International Hospitality Industry – Structure, Characteristics and Prospects*. Oxford: Butterworth-Heinemann. pp. 59–85.

Hegarty, J. A. and O'Mahony, G. B. (2001) Gastronomy: a phenomenon of cultural expressionism and an aesthetic for living, *International Journal of Hospitality Management*, 20(1): 3–13.

Hemmington, N. (1999) 'Sampling'. In B. Brotherton (ed.) *The Handbook of Contemporary Hospitality Management Research*. Chichester: John Wiley and Sons Ltd. pp. 245–262.

Higher Education Funding Council for England (HEFCE) (1998) *Review of Hospitality Management*. Bristol: HEFCE.

Jauncey, S. (1999) 'Observational research'. In B. Brotherton (ed.) *The Handbook of Contemporary Hospitality Management Research*. Chichester: John Wiley and Sons Ltd. pp. 191–206.

Johns, N. (1999) 'Quality management'. In B. Brotherton (ed.) *The Handbook of Contemporary Hospitality Management Research*. Chichester: John Wiley and Sons Ltd. pp. 333–350.

Jones, P. (1996) 'Hospitality research – where have we got to?' *International Journal of Hospitality Management*, 15(1): 5–10.

Jones, P. (1998) 'Editorial', *International Journal of Hospitality Management*, 17(2): 105–110.

Jones, P. (1999a) 'Experimental Research'. In B. Brotherton (ed.) *The Handbook of Contemporary Hospitality Management Research*. Chichester: John Wiley and Sons Ltd. pp. 97–114.

Jones, P. (1999b) 'Catering operations management'. In B. Brotherton (ed.) *The Handbook of Contemporary Hospitality Management Research*. Chichester: John Wiley and Sons Ltd. pp. 441–454.

Jones, P. and Lockwood, A. (1998) 'Operations management research in the hospitality industry', *International Journal of Hospitality Management*, 17(2): 183–202.

Jones, P. and Lockwood, A. (1999) 'Hotel operations management'. In B. Brotherton (ed.) *The Handbook of Contemporary Hospitality Management Research*. Chichester: John Wiley and Sons Ltd. pp. 415–439.

King, C. A. (1995) 'What Is hospitality?' *International Journal of Hospitality Management*, 14(3–4): 219–234.

Kirk, D. and Pine, R. (1998) 'Research in hospitality systems and technology', *International Journal of Hospitality Management*, 17(2): 203–217.

Lane, H. E. and Dupre, D. (1997) *Hospitality World: An Introduction*. New York: John Wiley and Sons Ltd.

Lashley, C. (1999) 'Action research'. In B. Brotherton (ed.) *The Handbook of Contemporary Hospitality Management Research*. Chichester: John Wiley and Sons Ltd. pp. 173–190.

Lashley, C. (2000) *Hospitality Retail Management: A Unit Manager's Guide*. Oxford: Butterworth-Heinemann.

Lashley, C. (2003) 'Time for a change of name: in search of hospitality studies', *The Hospitality Review* 5(4): 3–4.

Lashley, C. and Morrison, A. (eds) (2000) *In Search of Hospitality: Historical and Sociological Perspectives*. Oxford: Butterworth-Heinemann.

Lewis, R. (1988) 'Uses and abuses of hospitality research', *Cornell Hotel and Restaurant Administration Quarterly*, 29(3): 11–12.

Litteljohn, D. (1990) 'Hospitality research: philosophies and progress'. In R. Teare, L. Moutinho and N. Morgan (eds), *Managing and Marketing Services in the 1990's*. London: Cassell.

Litteljohn, D. (1999) 'Industry structure and strategic groups'. In B. Brotherton (ed.) *The Handbook of Contemporary Hospitality Management Research*. Chichester: John Wiley and Sons Ltd. pp. 455–476.

Litteljohn, D. (2000) 'Industry structures and competitive environments'. In B. Brotherton (ed.) *An Introduction to the UK Hospitality Industry – A Comparative Approach*. Oxford: Butterworth-Heinemann. pp. 23–45.

Litteljohn, D. (2003) 'Hotels'. In B. Brotherton (ed.) *The International Hospitality Industry – Structure, Characteristics and Prospects*. Oxford: Butterworth-Heinemann. pp. 5–29.

Lockwood, A. and Ingram, H. (1999) 'Hotel operations management'. In B. Brotherton (ed.) *The Handbook of Contemporary Hospitality Management Research*. Chichester: John Wiley and Sons Ltd. pp. 415–440.

Losekoot, E., Verginis, C. and Wood, R. C. (2001) Out for the count: some methodological questions in 'publications counting' literature, *International Journal of Hospitality Management*, 20(3): 233–244.

Lucas, R. (1999) 'Survey research'. In B. Brotherton (ed.) *The Handbook of Contemporary Hospitality Management Research*. Chichester: John Wiley and Sons Ltd. pp. 77–96.

Lundberg, C. C. (1997) 'Widening the conduct of hospitality inquiry: toward appreciating research alternatives', *Journal of Hospitality and Tourism Research*, 21(1): 1–13.

Lupton, D. (1996) *Food, the Body and the Self*. London: Sage.

Lynn, M. (2002) 'The industry needs less descriptive and more causal research', *Cornell Hotel and Restaurant Administration Quarterly*, 43(2): 1.

Mars, G. and Nicod, M. (1984) *The World of Waiters*. London: George Allen and Unwin.

Mars, G., Bryant, D. and Mitchell, P. (1979) *Manpower Problems in the Hotel and Catering Industry*. Farnborough: Gower.

Mazurkiewicz, R. (1983) 'Gender and social consumption', *The Service Industries Journal*, 3(1): 49–62.

Middleton, V. T. (1983) *Marketing In The Hospitality Industry*. In E. H. Cassee and R. Reuland (eds) *The Management of Hospitality*. Oxford: Pergamon. 51–68.

Mintzberg, H. (1994) *The Rise and Fall of Strategic Planning*. Hemel Hempstead: Prentice-Hall International (UK) Limited.

Morrison, A. (2006) 'Who let the genie out?', *The Hospitality Review*, January, 8(1): 3–4.

Nailon, P. (1982) 'Theory in hospitality management', *International Journal of Hospitality Management*, 1(3): 135–143.

Nyheim, P. D., McFadden, F. and Connolly, D. J. (2005) *Technology Strategies for the Hospitality Industry*. Upper Saddle River, NJ: Pearson Prentice-Hall.

O'Connor, P. and Piccoli, G. (2003) 'The impact of information technology'. In B. Brotherton (ed.) *The International Hospitality Industry: Structure, Characteristics and Issues*. Oxford: Butterworth-Heinemann. 110–125.

Olsen, M. D. (1999) 'Macroforces driving change into the new millennium – major challenges for the hospitality professional', *International Journal of Hospitality Management*, 18(4): 371–385.

Olsen, M. (2001) 'Hospitality research and theories: A Review'. In A. Lockwood and S. Medlik (eds) *Tourism and Hospitality in the 21st Century*. Oxford: Butterworth-Heinemann. pp. 94–105.

Olsen, M. D. and Connelly, D. J. (2000) 'Experience-based travel – how technology is changing the hospitality industry', *Cornell Hotel and Restaurant Administration Quarterly*, 41(1): 30–40.

Olsen, M. D. and Roper, A. (1998) 'Research in strategic management in the hospitality industry', *International Journal of Hospitality Management*, 17(2): 111–124.

Olsen, M. D., West, J. J. and Tse, E. C. (1998) *Strategic Management in the Hospitality Industry*, 2nd edn. New York: John Wiley and Sons Inc.

Powers, T. and Barrows, C. W. (1999) *Introduction to Management in the Hospitality Industry*, 6th edn. New York: John Wiley and Sons Ltd.

Riley, M. and Turam, K. (1988) 'The career paths of hotel managers: a development approach', paper given at the International Association of Hotel Management Schools Symposium, Leeds, November.

Roper, A. and Brookes, M. (1999) 'Theory and reality of interdisciplinary research', *International Journal of Contemporary Hospitality Management*, 11(4): 174–179.

Shaw, M. and Nightingale, M. (1995) 'Scholarship reconsidered: implications for hospitality education', *Hospitality Research Journal*, 18/19(3/1): 81–93.

Siguaw, J. A., Enz, C. A. and Namasivayam, K. (2000) 'Adoption of information technology in U.S. hotels: strategically driven objectives', *Journal of Travel Research*, 39, November: 192–201.

Slattery, P. (1983) 'Social scientific methodology and hospitality management', *International Journal of Hospitality Management*, 2(1): 9–14.

Stake, R. E. (1994) 'Case Studies'. In N. K. Denzin and Y. S. Lincoln (eds) *Handbook of Qualitative Research*. Thousand Oaks, CA: Sage Publications. pp. 236–247.

Taylor, S. and Edgar, D. (1996) 'Hospitality research: the emperor's new clothes?', *International Journal of Hospitality Management*, 15(3): 211–227.

Taylor, S. and Edgar, D. (1999) 'Lacuna or lost cause? some reflections on hospitality management research'. In B. Brotherton (ed.) *The Handbook of Contemporary Hospitality Management Research*. Chichester: John Wiley and Sons Ltd. pp. 19–38.

Tse, E. C. and Olsen, M. (1999) 'Strategic management'. In B. Brotherton (ed.) *The Handbook of Contemporary Hospitality Management Research*. Chichester: John Wiley and Sons Ltd. pp. 351–376.

Van Hoof, H. B., McDonald, M. E., Yu, L. and Vallen, G. K. (1996) *A Host of Opportunities: An Introduction to Hospitality Management*. Chicago: Irwin.

Wood, R. C. (1992) *Working in Hotels and Catering*. London: Routledge.

Wood, R. C. (1994a) 'Some theoretical perspectives on hospitality'. In A. V. Seaton et al. (eds) *Tourism: The State of The Art*. Chichester: John Wiley and Sons Ltd. pp. 737–742.

Wood, R. C. (1994b) *Organizational Behavior for Hospitality Management*. Oxford: Butterworth-Heinemann.

Wood, R. C. (1997) *Working in Hotels and Catering*. 2nd edn. London: International Thomson Business Press.

Wood, R. C. (1998) 'New wine in old bottles: critical limitations of the McDonaldization thesis'. In M. Alfino et al. (eds) *McDonaldization Revisited: Critical Essays in Consumer Culture*, Westport, CT: Praeger. pp. 85–104.

Wood, R. C. (1999) 'Traditional and alternative research philosophies'. In B. Brotherton (ed.) *The Handbook of Contemporary Hospitality Management Research*. Chichester: John Wiley and Sons Ltd. pp. 3–18.

Wood, R. C. (ed.) (2000) *Strategic Questions in Food and Beverage Management*. Oxford: Butterworth-Heinemann.

Wood, R. C. (2004a) Hospitality education: they think it's all over … it is now. *The Hospitality Review*, April: 16–18.

Wood, R. C. (2004b) Closing a planning gap? The future of food production and service systems theory, *Tourism and Hospitality Planning and Development*, 1(1): 19–37.

Wood, R. C. (2007) 'The future of food and beverage management research', *Journal of Hospitality and Tourism Management*, 14: 6–16.

Yin, R. K. (1994) *Case Study Research – Design and Methods*. Thousand Oaks, CA: Sage Publications.

PART ONE

Key Themes in Hospitality Management

The Nature and Meanings of 'Hospitality'

Bob Brotherton and Roy C. Wood

1

INTRODUCTION

In a volume such as this, devoted as it is to describing a field in state-of-the-art terms, it would be advantageous to pronounce that debates about the meaning and nature of hospitality are at an advanced and sophisticated stage. Sadly, the very opposite is true. To say that the study of hospitality has received little scholarly attention is to articulate a truism. Conceptual development is limited and indeed, systematic analysis of the phenomenon of hospitality is almost completely absent. The academic literature that does exist is scattered, in terms of disciplinary origin, through time and in terms of loci of publication.

From the point of view of both the theory and practice of 'hospitality management' this is both ironic and intellectually problematic. It is ironic because the term 'hospitality management' has emerged globally, but with little apparent reflection as to meaning, as the preferred means of describing the activities of those who provide and manage the provision of accommodation, food and related services in diverse commercial, non-commercial and voluntary contexts. It has come to replace (though by no means universally) such descriptive labels as 'hotel management', 'catering management', 'restaurant management' and 'institutional management'. The irony lies in the fact that in presenting to the world an idea of 'hospitality management' there is little evident understanding of what hospitality 'is' in historical or philosophical terms and little consistency in its application in terms of the delivery of hospitality services. This irony is compounded by the observation that, in a simple commercial sense, the term 'hospitality' offends against the principles of clarity of mission and vision that have been promulgated as central to modern business ideology and the conduct of management. There is a further

suspicion that the Gadarene rush to adopt the term 'hospitality management' has more to do with efforts to professionalize the activities it is meant to embrace than with any meaningful shift in the practice of those activities. Simply put, 'hospitality management' has a veneer of respectability and 'sexiness' not enjoyed by many of those labels it has supplanted. In an industry that is globally notorious for variably poor or mediocre management and employment practices, the term, whether intentionally or not, performs a 'disguising' function. It should also be added that in education, industry and elsewhere, the term 'hospitality management' has something of the character of a wearily adopted flag of convenience, a generic label for summarizing activities that are difficult to classify. This in part reflects long-standing debate about what activities and enterprises should be included in industry classifications of these types of services, and indeed, parallels similar discussions about the nature of tourism. In a prescient observation predating much of what has come to constitute debates about the nature of hospitality, Bright and Johnson (1985: 27) commented:

> However, despite the widespread adoption of this term [hospitality] and its use to describe the activities of the industry, its meaning is still elusive. Academics have failed to clarify the concept and set it on a firm theoretical base. Meanwhile, industrialists, unconcerned with the finer points of semantics and definition, seek ways in which to operationalize the concept to best advantage.

The intellectual problem attendant on defining the term 'hospitality management' is no obscurantist preoccupation and can be summarized simply: for the most part 'hospitality management' functions without any explicit understanding of the nature of hospitality (Brotherton, 1999a; Brotherton and

Wood, 2000). Within hospitality management itself (that is, the academic infrastructure of the field) there have been occasional efforts at exploring these issues, represented most obviously in collections of papers by Cummings, Kwansa and Sussman (1998) in the USA and Lashley and Morrison (2000) in the UK, but these efforts have not been sustained. The history of ideas is, of course, littered with terms and concepts that are widely used but not clearly defined, and to nobody's particular detriment. Yet in most academic disciplines one encounters at least some reflection on the nature of those subjects which if not consistent over time, or always explicit in the nature of such reflection, mark some serious contribution to the etiological form of the discipline.

At the risk of caricature, it is possible to describe the 'state of the art' in terms of current understandings of hospitality by reference to three mutually inter-related preoccupations. The first of these is the preoccupation with semantic definitions of hospitality, of seeking to simply and unambiguously circumscribe what is being studied (Brotherton and Wood, 2000). Semantic definitions include those favored by various informed commentators, from dictionary compilers to hospitality academics. The second preoccupation is with semantic definitions of 'hospitality management', which largely emanates from within the community of hospitality academics and practitioners. Whilst ostensibly a more rarefied concern, understanding the received wisdom here is critical to forming more productive strategies for investigating and understanding hospitality as a phenomenon more generally. The third preoccupation focuses on evidential definitions of hospitality which Brotherton and Wood (2000) contrast with the semantic approach. Evidential definitions are precisely those that arise from efforts to understand, interpret and utilize existing diverse documentary sources on hospitality to inform definitional processes in terms of theory building, or more precisely in terms of providing theoretical context. The evidential approach is thus rooted in academic literature and seeks to locate and define hospitality within the 'real world' of evidence, although, as we have asserted, without thus far much evidence of synergy. Nevertheless, attempts at the evidential definition of hospitality provide a bridgehead into consideration of the theoretical sources that have thus far come to inform research in the field. Flowing

from these three preoccupations and, in the manner of a systems theoretical process model, feeding back into them, is a series of research questions or puzzles that constitute something approaching a nascent research agenda. In what follows, the first section of this chapter will review the definitional issues we have described, following the structure of these preoccupations in order to chart the territory of the field as it currently stands. The discussion draws extensively on the authors' previous work in this area (e.g. Brotherton, 1999a; Brotherton and Wood, 2000). This section concludes with some attempt to circumscribe a rather simplistic summary of the main themes thus emerging from the 'study' of hospitality. The second part of the chapter deals with the research puzzles and questions that appear to us to be indicated by a review of extant approaches to the understanding of hospitality and offers a commentary on how these may usefully be addressed in the future.

SEMANTIC DEFINITIONS OF HOSPITALITY

As intimated earlier, the absence of definitions of concepts is not always inimical to discussion of the substance to which the concepts refer. In the study of hospitality in general, and hospitality management more specifically, definition is problematic because of the lack of general agreement as to what hospitality 'is'. This issue is exacerbated by problems centering on the degree of fluidity that should be tolerated in differentiating and circumscribing the meanings of hospitality in varying contexts, problems that tend to distill to concerns about the 'authenticity' of hospitality in these contexts.

Semantic definitions include those in dictionaries, thus hospitality is the 'friendly and generous reception and entertainment of guests or strangers' (*Oxford Quick Reference Dictionary,* 1996: 424) or 'kindness in welcoming strangers or guests' (*Collins Concise English Dictionary Plus,* 1989: 604). Variant terms, such as the word 'hospitable' is defined by *The Oxford English Dictionary* (1970: 405) in very similar terms to 'hospitality' as 'offering or affording welcome and entertainment to strangers ... of persons ... of things, feelings, qualities etc. ... Disposed to receive or welcome kindly; open and generous in mind or disposition ... Hence hospitableness, a hospitable quality or character'. As with most dictionary definitions, these all share a prescriptive quality in terms of behavior – they indicate to some degree what one should do in order to extend hospitality or behave hospitably.

Amongst hospitality industry academics and practitioners, similarly simple (and often simplistic) attempts at definition are to be found, frequently couched in terms of crude economics with hospitality rendered in terms of the activities of the hospitality industry. Sometimes, such definitions are so general as to be useless, as is the case with Tideman's (1983: 1) observation that hospitality is 'the method of production by which the needs of the proposed guest are satisfied to the utmost and that means a supply of goods and services in a quantity and quality desired by the guest and at a price that is acceptable to him so that he feels the product is worth the price' – a definition that could be a description of almost any economic activity. Our earlier cited dictionary definitions tend to be simple, pragmatic and behaviorally focused, echoed in Tideman-like definitions where the focus, however, is on the nature of the hospitality (industry) product. Thus, Jones (1996: 1) argues that 'hospitality is made up of two distinct services – the provision of overnight accommodation for people staying away from home, and the provision of sustenance for people eating away from home'. The main problem with this view is that it conflates the definitions of 'hospitality' with the commercial hospitality industry. The hospitality industry may well be an expression of some concepts of hospitality but it is but one form of hospitality – definitions like those of Jones and Tideman tell us little about the generic qualities of hospitality. Other academic writers in the hospitality field have proffered more holistic definitions. For example, Cassee (1983: xiv) sees hospitality as: 'a harmonious mixture of tangible and intangible components – food, beverages, beds, ambience and environment, and behavior of staff', a definition modified by Cassee and Reuland (1983: 144) to 'a harmonious mixture of food, beverage, and/or shelter, a physical environment, and the behavior and attitude of people'. These definitions avoid the problem of conflating definitions of hospitality with the hospitality industry but continue to exhibit the underlying assumption that hospitality is something that is, principally, commercially 'created' for consumption.

DEFINITIONS OF HOSPITALITY MANAGEMENT

Definitions of hospitality management parallel the 'conflation model' outlined above, where 'hospitality' is seen as coterminous with the hospitality industry. In the UK, a 1998 study, *Review of Hospitality Management*, commissioned by a key public body, the Higher Education Funding Council for England (HEFCE, 1998: 2), defined hospitality management as 'having a core which addresses the management of food, beverages and/or accommodation in a service context. Although, as King (1995: 220) points out, 'effective management of hospitality in any type of organization must begin with a clearly understood definition of what hospitality is', 'hospitality management' is a recent term used only to describe the management of industrial hospitality and the associated infrastructure of education and research that supports it. It is perhaps surprising that, following King, it does not seem to have occurred that in seeking to understand what hospitality 'is', a wider interpretation of the term 'hospitality management' could be rather useful in this regard. Freed from its industry context and interpreted more broadly, hospitality management can be construed as the study of how hospitality is managed between individuals, between groups and in the home, or in various commercial and non-commercial public contexts.

Put another way, in terms of the scale and complexity of the provision of hospitality, however defined, approaches to the study of hospitality management that begin with industry contexts are likely to be circular and unlikely to be either analytically profound or complete. As we noted in our Introduction to this volume, there is a semantic circularity at work here: hospitality is what the hospitality industry offers and hospitality management is the management of what is offered, which is hospitality. With regards to the likely absence of analytic depth and completeness in such definitions there are two basic limitations. The first relates to the necessary but reductionist (industry) imperative of defining hospitality and hospitality management purely in terms of products and services and in studying (and delivering) these products and services mechanistically. The dominant model in the analysis of product and service provision in hospitality is characterized by a crude systems orientation reflected in the treatment of human agency, and in particular, human interaction with hospitality products and services as a cipher: people are seen as acted upon by systems but not as contributing to the mutability or operation of those systems (Wood, 2004). Second, applying 'hospitality management' only in the hospitality industry context invites application of an interpretive framework based solely on the repertoire of formal management concepts and techniques to the provision of hospitality products and services. In the wider context of the provision of hospitality such a framework is a blunt instrument that effectively excludes detailed consideration of the social, and indeed sociological/social psychological influences on motivations to provide and receive hospitality. More significantly, the application of management concepts and techniques is viewed as (relatively) intellectually unproblematic as is reflected in periodic attempts to construct theories and 'models' of hospitality management which borrow concepts from 'general' management discourse and seek to adapt these to the hospitality sector (Nailon, 1982).

In summary, as is implied by King's earlier quoted remark, an approach to the study of hospitality management based solely on industry provision and employing the language and concepts of management provides us with an approach that is in essence atheoretical, having no theory of hospitality and, more importantly, offering little prospect of ever developing one.

EVIDENTIAL DEFINITIONS OF HOSPITALITY

Thus far we have considered semantic definitions of hospitality and hospitality management. Those definitions emanating from within the hospitality 'community' are usually narrow and limiting (although there are honorable exceptions, e.g. Burgess, 1982; Reuland et al., 1985; Hepple et al., 1990) and point to a need to consider the nature of hospitality more generically. Evidential definitions of hospitality rooted in an (albeit) limited and dispersed literature offer the potential to do this, not least because the absence of extensive consideration of the phenomenon of hospitality means that the intellectual terrain is relatively easy to map. At the same time however, it must be recalled that the absence of extended theorizing

about, and empirical investigation of, hospitality means that there is little in the way of a coherent theory or theories of hospitality and therefore pronounced limits on potential for generalization.

Most 'broader' discussions of hospitality are to be found in social scientific literature, generated in particular from within the disciplines of philosophy, history, and sociology and range from the highly theoretical and analytic (Finkelstein, 1989; Heal, 1990; Murray, 1990; Mennell et al., 1992; Visser, 1992; Beardsworth and Keil, 1997; and Warde and Martens, 1998) to the largely descriptive in nature, being primarily concerned with tracing the evolution of the type and incidence of hospitality practices over time (Langley-Moore and Langley-Moore, 1936; Watts, 1963; White, 1968; Borer, 1972). From the earliest days of academic consideration of the nature of hospitality, two themes have run throughout this literature – hospitality as a means of social control, especially the control of 'strangers', people who are essentially alien to a particular physical, economic and social environment, and hospitality as a form of social and economic exchange (including hospitality as a 'gift') (Muhlmann, 1932). We shall consider these themes in turn.

Hospitality and the stranger

The concept of the stranger has enjoyed considerable social scientific attention in the last two decades largely because of interest in the work of German sociologist Georg Simmel (1858–1918) (see for example Frisby, 2002). For Simmel, the stranger was a core figure in the newly, nineteenth century, industrialized and urbanized European landscape. As Pickering (2001: 205) puts it: 'Simmel treated the stranger as a social form at the centre of structures of interaction characterized, from a perspective of belonging, by both remote and close at hand, mobile and yet somehow settled, feared and yet desired'. For Pickering (2001: 204) strangers occupy an inherently ambivalent position in society because they are 'neither socially peripheral nor symbolically central but somewhere peculiarly in between'. They also possess power, a power which derives from their very quality of ambivalence, 'of "being strange" but not starkly unfamiliar, of being close and yet distant' (Pickering, 2001: 206).

Pickering (2001) tends to focus on super-ordinate or 'absolute' categories of stranger in terms of ethnicity or those from other countries. In this, he follows a trend established by Bauman (e.g. Bauman, 1990) perhaps the most pre-eminent contemporary sociological commentator on the subject of the stranger. Bauman (1990: 54) asserts that a stranger is not simply someone who is unfamiliar, someone not known well, but, more remarkably, tends to be to a large extent familiar or, put another way, in order to label someone as a stranger we must, generally, know many things about them. What Bauman appears to be arguing is that in order to label someone as a stranger we must be able to draw on contextual knowledge about their differences from other, 'non-strangers', whether these are physical or social. Bauman (1990: 61) comments on the range of possible responses to the ambiguous position of the stranger in society. One such response is to send them back 'where they come from' and Bauman notes that if this is not successful, genocide may follow as an extreme form of restoring order to a social world fractured by the presence of strangers. More often, separation occurs between 'strangers' and the rest of society (as, one presumes, in the creation of ghettoes for example). This said, Bauman (1990: 62–63) then asserts that this kind of separation rarely occurs, because, spatially, our society (by which he means, following Simmel, contemporary urban society) encourages high density living and people travel a lot. The consequence of this is that for (Bauman, 1990: 63):

The world we live in seems to be populated mostly by strangers; it looks like the world of *universal strangerhood*. We live among strangers, among whom we are strangers ourselves. In such a world, strangers cannot be confined or kept at bay. Strangers must be lived with.

Even ignoring the seeming unevenness of Bauman's comments (first strangers are dis-tinguishable from non-strangers, second they are separated from society, then they are not) it is difficult to avoid the conclusion that he is arguing that 'we are all strangers now'. The consequence of the 'we are all strangers now' argument for Bauman is that – echoing Foucault (1979) – societies develop means of controlling strangers – all of us – through diverse means of conducting surveillance and establishing entitlements. Thus are concepts of 'admission' established such that when moving around strangers must identify themselves in order to demonstrate their entitlement to enter a space (Bauman, 1990: 65). He cites security guards and receptionists as typical examples of the occupations that manage such identifications and entitlements. A satisfactory outcome to these processes is that some (but by no means all) of strangers' 'stranger-ness' is removed but we cannot remove all the unsettling aspects of living and dealing with strangers who we constantly encounter in everyday life. At the individual level, Bauman (1990: 66–67) argues, other methods of control exhibit the characteristics of Erving Goffman's concept of 'civil inattention' (Goffman, 1963) whereby in a studied way we do not look at, or listen to, the strangers around us, most commonly evidenced in the avoidance of eye contact.

As might be expected, where the concept of the stranger has been dealt with explicitly in the context of tourism and hospitality, both differences and points of contiguity with the more general social scientific themes caricatured above readily emerge. The most significant conceptual distinction in this literature is that between private and public hospitality and the role of the stranger in each. Authors like Visser (1992: 93) writing from the perspective of the history and sociology of food tend to focus on domestic hospitality:

The laws of hospitality deal firstly with strangers – how to manage their entry into our inner sanctum, how to protect them from our own automatic reaction, which is to fear and exclude the unknown, how to prevent them from attacking and desecrat-ing what we hold dear, or from otherwise behaving in a strange and unpredictably dangerous manner. We remember that we too might one day need a stranger's help. So we behave in the prescribed civilized manner ...

Zeldin (1994: 437), from the perspective of cultural history, elaborates the domestic/public axis of hospitality:

Do people find it more or less easy to speak to strangers than they did in the past? The answer can be found in the history of hospitality. Today in the rich countries, hospitality means, above all entertaining friends or acquaintances in one's home; but once upon a time it meant opening one's house to total strangers, giving a meal to anyone who chose to come, allowing them to stay the night, indeed imploring them to stay, although one knew nothing about them. This kind of open hospitality has been admired and practiced in virtually every civilization that has existed, as though it fulfils a basic human need.

Mary Douglas' work on the social structure of the meal arguably undermines Zeldin's suggestion that *above all*, hospitality means entertaining acquaintances since acquaintances possess many of the characteristics of the stranger, and in terms of domestic hospitality are entitled only to lesser forms of hospitality (see for example Douglas, 1975). This aside, in the quotation above and elsewhere, Zeldin (1994: 438) undoubtedly captures a further dimension to discussions of the private/public divide in hospitality when he talks of the decline of the former which he traces to sixteenth century England:

> As soon as the rich appointed almoners to do their charitable work for them, they lost direct touch with their visitors; as soon as distress was dealt with impersonally by officials, hospitality was never the same again [.] Free hospitality was superseded by the hospitality industry.

Zeldin's remarks reflect assumptions about the decline in hospitality not principally in terms of a diminution in the quantity of domestic hospitality, but in the wider cheapening of the nature of hospitality as it becomes increasingly, and nastily, commercialized. Such assumptions in the literature are therefore reinforced by a tendency to imbue moral virtues to hospitality – the hospitality of archaic and pre-industrial societies (or traditional 'domestic-based' hospitality) is 'good' and industrial and post-industrial hospitality ('commercial' hospitality) is 'bad' (Wood, 1994b). This vulgar Orwellianism was foreshadowed by Mauss (2002) and Muhlmann (1932: 464), the latter writing:

> The germ of the decay of hospitality is inherent in the institution itself, in that it inevitably extends frontiers and the domain of peace and promotes trade; as a result there arise public legal principles, which go beyond the personal and the familiar and take the place of hospitality ... Primitive hospitality was addressed to the public enemy; in the modern world the distinction between friend and enemy in the political sense is irrelevant. The old hospitality was a social or religious obligation; that of modern times rests with the discretion of the individual.

Muhlmann's complaint is, that in essence, the spiritual qualities of 'traditional' domestic-based hospitality have disappeared to be replaced in the public sphere by a formally rational system of impersonal hospitality based on monetary exchange. More importantly perhaps, underpinning most of the commentaries mentioned so far is a somewhat romantic view of what might be termed the 'nobility' of pre-industrial hospitality. This is most emphatically seen in the emphasis placed on notions concerning the protection of strangers through hospitality in pre-industrial societies. For Muhlmann (1932: 463) hospitality 'represents a kind of guarantee of reciprocity – one protects the stranger in order to be protected from him'. Visser (1992: 93) points out that in the control of strangers in our 'inner sanctum' abusing a defenseless stranger is unacceptable. Zeldin offers an entertaining historical insight when he informs us of the Albanian host's obligation to entertain strangers and revenge himself upon anyone who harmed them before they reached their next destination (Zeldin, 1994: 437). Heal (1990) in her seminal study of hospitality in early modern England (c. 1400–1700) locates hospitality as a phenomenon emanating from the home, and contemporary hospitality as something comparatively free of overtones of social duty inherent to hospitality in fifteenth to eighteenth century England.

Although, historically, the protection of strangers may have had a self-serving function, a clear theme in the literature is that this was subordinate to a system of social values that emphasized the proffering of hospitality as a duty and virtue, vestigial elements of which remain in the modern domestic sphere but have been largely expunged from modern forms of public provision of hospitality. Indeed, Heal (1990: 1) begins from this position noting that: 'For modern Western man hospitality is preponderantly a private form of behavior, exercised as a matter of personal preference within a limited circle of friendship and connection'. As we have seen, this is a view subsequently echoed by Zeldin (1994) and others. What, in essence, we are offered here is a two dimensional model of hospitality which proposes a distinction between 'historical' hospitality, rooted in domesticity and premised on duty and virtue and highly personal in conception and delivery, and 'modern' hospitality which is publicly organized and premised on forms of 'rational' – usually monetary – exchange (i.e. is predominantly commercial) and is highly impersonal in conception and delivery. It is not a very persuasive or plausible model. Many of the writers cited mistake the importance of impersonality represented by public hospitality.

If Bauman (1990) is correct (and interpreted correctly) that in modern society 'we are all strangers now', then impersonality constitutes a normative feature of nearly all contemporary public social behavior. If impersonality is a social norm then it makes little sense to analyze contemporary hospitality wholly by reference to a putative (and evidentially unsafe) historical benchmark as to what hospitality 'was', especially when that benchmark contains more than an element of apparently romanticized nostalgia.

To summarize thus far, most treatments of the role of the stranger in the provision of hospitality are rooted in (a) assumptions about the distinctions that exist between the provision of hospitality in domestic and non-domestic, usually public commercial, contexts; and (b) fairly simplistic assertions (economic, historical) about how these forms of provision have changed, by implication, mainly for the worse, over time. Although the stranger is placed at the heart of 'historical domestic hospitality', as the person to whom such hospitality was directed, very little is said in the literature about the role of the stranger in modern public hospitality, an asymmetry which taken with the tendency to moralize and romanticize the qualities of pre-industrial hospitality forces us to turn outwards to the work of those, largely influenced by Simmel, who offer more generalized perspectives on the societal role of the stranger. Even here, clarity is not assured but at least there is a positioning of the stranger in a wider social web, a positioning which, if Bauman (1990) and Pickering (2001), as representatives of this broader approach, are correct, suggest that contemporary social inter-action fundamentally comprises the personal and inter-personal management and control of encounters between strangers, albeit there are varying degrees of 'stranger-ness' in these encounters.

Such an attitude finds resonance, albeit largely unintentional, in the academic field of tourism and hospitality studies. Although largely in ignorance of these issues, a strand of thinking in tourism and hospitality studies has developed the idea of the impersonality of the tourism and hospitality 'experience'. As Ryan (1991) notes, tourists are strangers and bring with them the threat of social, cultural and environmental damage. The tourist is not, however 'simply a stranger, but a *temporary* stranger ... they are a guest, but

an impersonal guest' (Ryan, 1991: 42). The consequences of this impersonality for hotel hospitality have been characterized by Wood (1994c) in terms of the mechanisms that hotels use to control their stranger-guests. For public hospitality more widely however, the problem of the stranger is compounded by the fact that the majority of persons who participate in public hospitality are not tourists but permanent members of their communities who use the public hospitality facilities rooted in those communities. To what extent are regular users of these facilities justifiably classified as strangers? In our own country, the UK, the culture of the public house is instructive in this regard. We refer to the hostelry we most frequently visit as our 'local' and frequent visitors to a particular hostelry are known as 'regulars'. Are regulars strangers? Following Bauman (1990) we can perhaps suggest that by establishing clear traditions of access and entitlements, some strangers are less strange than others, even in a world comprised entirely of strangers. Indeed, if the desire existed to be mischievous one might argue that Bauman's 'we are all strangers now' is a deliberately self-negating argument – if we are all strangers now then can we speak any longer of 'strangers' as a generic category? The point is not wholly trivial, for as we have seen, in many of the accounts of the provision of hospitality considered in this discussion, the 'stranger' effectively disappears at that supposed point in history where morally virtuous private domestic-based hospitality gave way to amoral commercial, publicly provided 'institutional' hospitality. This is a point to which we shall return subsequent to examination of our second major theme here, hospitality as a form of social and economic exchange.

Hospitality as social exchange

It is important to begin this discussion by noting that any attempt to link extant commentaries on the role of social exchange in hospitality to broader sociological debates on exchange theory are bound to be limited because writers on hospitality and social exchange have made few connections to wider debates about 'general' exchange and rational choice theory, the intellectual spadework does not exist. The principle reason for this lies in the indebtedness of such writers to concepts of exchange developed by Marcel Mauss (2002) which emphasizes the role of reciprocity within a system of gift exchange. In contrast, rational exchange theory in its diverse forms emphasizes the workings of the market and, as Shilling and Mellor (2001: 167) observe:

> Utility-maximizing exchanges are guided by rationality, rather than normative factors, and produce social relationships rather than being shaped by them. Patterns of exchange do not derive from the pre-contractual foundations of solidarity, but emerge as individuals seek to maximize their interests. Sociality and solidarity ... are *secondary* phenomena arising from rationally interacting individuals.

Shilling and Mellor (2001: 167) contrast rational exchange theory quite explicitly to the work of Mauss who, they claim, refutes a view of exchange as rationally informed utility maximization. At the heart of Mauss's argument is the notion that the apparently voluntary nature of gift exchange 'disguises how it derives from the creation and sustenance of allegiances between families, clans and tribes' and is in fact predicated on complex rules and obligations. Even in modern society, Shilling and Mellor write, Mauss 'emphasized that the emotional values arising from gift exchange can represent the consolidation and creation of bonds between people'. Shilling and Mellor's point is that Mauss's view of exchange has been effectively excluded from consideration in 'mainstream' rational exchange theory. In an earlier review of the field, Scott (1995: 75) goes a little further, noting:

> The exchange model of interaction has sometimes been compared with an earlier analysis of exchange ... developed by Marcel Mauss ...[.] Mauss presented an account of the exchange of gifts in tribal societies, but he showed that these exchanges involved a norm of 'reciprocity' that was quite distinct from the economic logic of the market. Although many exchange theorists have attempted to build norms of obligation and reciprocity into their work, this has always been a problematic exercise. Economic theorists, the mainstream of exchange theory, and recent 'rational choice' theories have all been more at home with those forms of action that can be assumed to follow a purely rational 'economic' or 'market' orientation.

Both Scott (1995) and Shilling and Mellor (2001) regard such distinctions as sufficient basis for effectively sidelining accounts of

exchange in the tradition of Mauss (although writers like Davis, 1992 take a less dismissive view). This is perhaps, understandable. Debates revolving around the varieties of rational exchange theory on offer reveal themselves to be highly disputatious even by the standards of modern sociology (Ritzer, 2003) largely because they strike at the heart of the sociologist's trade in seeking, crudely put, to explain social structure and behavior in terms of economic imperatives. It is, however, worth noting, that the distinction in the 'stranger literature' between pre-industrial, domestic hospitality and industrial and post-industrial hospitality characterized by commercial imperatives mooted earlier in this discussion finds a peculiar, even bizarre, reflection in this rather dismissive approach. The preferred and somewhat sentimentalized view of the former in that literature effectively demonizes 'commercial' hospitality as a form of exchange and has very little to say on the subject. The position of writers on exchange theory described above, none of them with an interest in 'hospitality', whether commercial or of any other kind, effectively writes out of intellectual history views of exchange represented by writers such as Mauss (2002) because incorporating such views, in Scott's (1995) words, is a 'problematic exercise'. Descriptively this may be accurate, but as a justification for excluding a particular intellectual tradition from consideration it seems somewhat cavalier. Just as in the 'stranger literature' there is a privileging of 'historical' domestic hospitality and an ignoring dismissiveness about the forms and meaning of commercial hospitality, exchange theorists seem content to privilege those forms of exchange that valorize modern industrial societies while marginalizing those that might be supposed to underpin historical and less complex societies, a point effectively demonstrated by Davis (2000) in her essays on the gift in sixteenth-century France, who shows that the Maussian and other social anthropological approaches to exchange will not simply go away.

Such are the lacunae with which commentaries like this must deal in seeking to elucidate the nature of hospitality. In considering hospitality as social exchange, we do not have the luxury of ignoring the Maussian tradition, but nor do we possess the means to assess the role of hospitality in the context of rational exchange theories. The key work of Mauss in question is *The Gift*, first published according to Lechte (1994) as *Essai sur le donne* in

1923–24. *Contra* rational exchange theory (or at least some varieties of it), Mauss does not view social relationships as being determined by processes of economic exchange but rather there is a complex interaction between economic and social factors in such relationships. Put this way it is hard for a lay reader to credit some of the intent of rational exchange theory since such a statement, experientially, seems obvious. In the Maussian tradition, the inter-relationship between economic and social exchange is taken to involve shared values and trust, not simple economic rationality on the part of social actors alone. In the field of hospitality this view has been most obviously developed in an inexplicably neglected paper by Burgess (1982). Burgess (1982) takes the view that the concept of the gift is best used as a *metaphor* for studying hospitality and hospitable behavior. Five important dimensions of this 'hospitality as gift metaphor' are important.

First, though any gift may have symbolic qualities, those who give seek to enhance the value of their gift by transferring some part of the self to the recipient in order to establish bonds which communicate, variously, degrees of formality in relationships, personal warmth and sincerity. Burgess argues that this is evidenced in the *'mein host'* role adopted by many hospitality practitioners (whether proprietors or managers) in an effort to convey something of the 'self' and imprint their own personality on the operation (in the context of small hospitality businesses this has almost become a *sine qua non* for understanding the nature and forms of relationships in these establishments, see, for example, Stringer, 1981, on bed and breakfast providers and, more recently, Lynch, 2000, on the homestay sector).

Second, gifts convey information about and confer identity on those who give, just as the nature of hospitality offered in a particular context establishes the commitment and involvement of the host in hospitality provision. Here, Burgess reflects early (and anticipates subsequent) work in the sociology of food and eating and in particular that part of the field which focuses on domestic dining, which, using Bauman's terms, explores rights and entitlements of 'admission' to particular forms of hospitality within the home (see for example Douglas, 1975). Additionally, the degree of hospitality perceived by guests to be on offer has been the subject of some debate. Stringer (1981) notes that in bed and breakfast establishments

the ambivalence of the 'host' over the degree of access to certain parts of the building, or the availability of certain facilities, can create doubts about the extent to which guests are welcome (see also Wood, 1994c).

Third, Burgess argues that gift exchange and hospitality share a preoccupation with assessing the needs and desires of recipients by givers/providers which tends to be focused on optimization of bonds of trust in the exchange relationship. Perhaps one of the limitations of Burgess's 'metaphor' approach is that in 'industrial hospitality' there is a constant tension between formal corporate proclamations of commitment to customer service (themselves often highly metaphorical in content) and the resources available to realize such commitment and service. Put more obviously, large hotel organizations and corporations must treat customers as an agglomeration whereas customers themselves buy in to the metaphor that they are individuals with individual needs, desires and problems that should be addressed individually (Wood, 1994c). It is when metaphor meets reality that the binds of hospitality are truly tested as is witnessed by the whole actual and parallel academic industry centering on improving customer satisfaction and service.

Fourth, Burgess (1982) suggests that gift exchange and hospitality are both oriented towards establishing an 'interaction order' whereby the character of exchanges is developed according to implicit rules negotiated by parties to the exchange. These rules include, *inter alia,* those concerning mutual respect of public and private areas of hotels (Goffman, 1959), participation in the rituals of the hotel organization (Hayner, 1969 [1936]) and maintenance of prevailing standards of decorum (Wood, 1994c).

Finally, the reciprocity involved in social exchanges, together with the rules that are applied in practicing exchanges, assume a shared responsibility for the outcome of the exchange on the part of givers and providers.

The greatest significance of the general Maussian view of exchange and the role of reciprocity, as well as its more specific applications in Burgess's (1982) essay lies in the fact that, notwithstanding the peculiarities of rational exchange theories alluded to earlier, it raises a so far unanswered case for the role of social exchange and reciprocity in (at least historical) analyses of hospitality that cannot, as it were, be brushed under the intellectual carpet. More importantly, concepts of exchange and reciprocity in the sense outlined here permit us the beginnings of a more even and less romanticized view of the development of hospitality. This is because they clearly suggest that the giving of hospitality, domestically, historically or in pre-modern societies, was never a neutral act, a point somewhat ironically acknowledged by Heal (1990) who otherwise, as we have seen, tends to the rose tinted view of such hospitality. Christian (1979), in possibly the earliest contribution from the perspective of hospitality management to the debates outlined in this essay, additionally notes that, historically, private domestic hospitality might have been offered without charge or monetary expectations but some form of reciprocity *was* expected. One motivation to protect strangers is the desire to control them and in so doing protect one's property, effects and immediate social circle. Another motivation is the possibility of reciprocal benefits that might accrue as a result of such protection, in other words the prospect of some form of exchange benefit inherent to the act of 'giving' hospitality. If this view is accepted then there are further reasons for rejecting the 'nostalgic' view of hospitality, not simply from the viewpoint of the expectation of reciprocal benefits from the proffering of hospitality but also in terms of the seemingly intrinsic 'falseness' that motivates the protection of strangers. Put another way, not only is the integrity of pre-commercial hospitality undermined by the exchange principle but so is the very concept of pre-commercial hospitality promulgated by some writers. This is because the idea of 'protecting the stranger' is, in motivational terms, indivisible from the expectation of some 'return'. This point is reinforced by the philosopher Elizabeth Telfer (1996: 82–87) who in discussing the different meanings of the terms 'hospitableness' and 'hospitality' argues that the former can be motivated by diverse forces including desires for company, the pleasures of entertaining, the desire to please others, and to meet others' needs. Other motives might include a person's allegiance to their perceived duties in matters of hospitality, and even ulterior motives which have nothing to do with a guest's pleasure or welfare. Indeed, Telfer (1996: 82) goes as far as to suggest that 'Being a good host is not even a necessary condition of being hospitable' or, in other words, it is entirely possible to 'achieve' hospitality and hospitableness without being intrinsically motivated by reasons of altruism or duty, a fact to which the modern hospitality industry more than adequately testifies.

TOWARDS A WORKABLE SYNTHESIS

So far in this chapter, we have sought to bring together some of the main themes in the (so far limited) study of the concept of hospitality. Meaningful synthesis is difficult to achieve because of the diversity of perspectives involved and, in the case of the sociological literature at least, because some of the themes and issues are, to put it diplomatically, expressed at a high level of abstraction. Nevertheless, it is possible to create some semblance of coherence from the foregoing discussions. Rather than rehearse the arguments reviewed so far, a number of propositions will instead be advanced as representing a consensus on 'the state of the art'. From here, we will identify and elaborate and comment on related research puzzles and questions that may plausibly form the basis of a future research agenda.

The first of these propositions is the simplest: it is that hospitality is an evolving phenomenon that exhibits multiple qualities and characteristics at all and different points in time. To propose that there is some dividing point in history where the qualities and characteristics of hospitality *fundamentally* change is a proposition requiring investigation, not an immutable fact. This is not to say that the nature of hospitality has *not* varied over time, it has, and continues to do so in different contemporary environments, cultures and countries. This diversity is precisely what requires further study rather than some artificially imposed attempt at closure.

Second, hospitality as a phenomenon is present in multiple social contexts, there is no simple dichotomy between 'domestic' and 'non-domestic' hospitality. Indeed, the very concepts 'domestic' and non-domestic' are problematic, especially when directly linked to notions of fundamental historical change in terms of a move from a form of hospitality based on personal duty centered on or around private residences to a form of hospitality based on commercial provision in public places. This is because the latter represents a too delimited concept of the non-domestic, ignoring for example non-commercial provision of hospitality in public places.

Third, hospitality is provided for diverse motives but always embraces the expectation of reciprocity. This is not the same as saying that all forms of the provision of hospitality actually involve reciprocity although many, and probably almost all do. What it does mean is that the existence of such expectations creates a particular and common form of social relations that are subsequently negotiated according to the context of provision.

Fourth, insofar as hospitality is about the control of strangers, then following Bauman (1990) and Ryan (1991) 'we are all strangers now' and tourists are temporary strangers, but the particular forms that tourism and hospitality encounters assume means that 'strangerness' can hardly be treated as an absolute category or indeed one that is especially exceptional. Indeed, both our major literary themes, 'strangerness' and 'reciprocity' seem, in the light of what has gone before strangely inadequate as a basis for a full investigation of the nature of hospitality although their value as an intellectual orientation cannot be gainsaid.

Fifth here, and following Telfer (1996) hospitality can be provided and experienced without the provision or experience of hospitable behavior. This is a more important point than at first appears, if only because it moves us away from the idea that the concept of hospitality is in some way inseparable from its practice, the assumption that bedevils much of the 'stranger' approach to the topic as we have seen. Further, in pointing to the diverse motivational reasons for providing hospitality, Telfer's view also liberates us from the deterministic ramifications of rational exchange theory whereby social relationships are produced by rational economic actions.

These five propositions are probably all that can be confidently asserted about what we know of the nature of hospitality, anything else is speculation, albeit informed speculation. We could add that all hospitality situations, whether public or private, are imbued with symbolic associations and significance but to do so would be to articulate a commonplace. There can be few social situations that are not characterized by symbolic associations. What remains to be identified and debated are those particular to hospitality. We could also add that hospitality also involves the provision (or at least availability) of physical artifacts in the form of accommodation, food and/or drink. This seems to be a fair operating assumption although it

is theoretically conceivable that hospitality can be experienced as a result of the provision of other kinds of artifacts. What is certain is that these propositions generate a list of questions and puzzles for future research without which there is likely to be little further advance on current forms of discussion. It is to these we turn in the final part of this chapter.

RESEARCH PUZZLES AND QUESTIONS

For convenience, we have consolidated these puzzles and questions into five categories mirroring our five propositions. They are as follows.

First, what can we say about the different forms that hospitality takes through time and in different places and cultures? What are the drivers of these forms and the changes that are wrought by time and culture? Second, in addition to time and culture, what variations in hospitality occur according to place/location? Third, how are different motives to provide hospitality mediated by time, place and location (including social structure and agency) and how are they molded by, or themselves mold, systems of economic, social and power relations? Fourth, how might the behavioral aspects of hospitality be understood in terms of the treatment of would-be recipients of hospitality? How voluntaristic is the 'hospitality relationship' between two or more parties, what are the benefits that accrue to the parties who engage in it in terms of commensality and the mutual enhancement, if any, of these relationships? Finally, what concepts and frameworks beyond those already considered are most useful for understanding the nature of hospitality and its forms?

These five areas are distinct yet interrelated. They are all concerned with either the dichotomous question of whether hospitality is spatially and temporally universal or contingent and/or the challenging of commonly held assumptions regarding the nature of the exchange relationship between providers and receivers of hospitality (Brotherton and Wood, 2000). They also imply a need, as has been previously argued (Brotherton, 1999b; 1999c) for more conceptual and empirical research at macro and meso comparative, and micro, case-specific levels. Furthermore, these puzzles and questions can only be addressed and answered by research effort characterized by much greater conceptual depth and empirical detail.

To illustrate this consider the following observation. The question of whether hospitality remains constant over time or between differing spatial entities has often been considered at a rather superficial level. At this level it is possible to make self-evident statements to demonstrate that specific 'forms' of hospitality, in terms of type of location and format, do evolve and change over time. In short, that the places hospitality was predominantly offered at in the past are no longer the primary locations for this activity today. Similarly, the particular form(s) most commonly accepted as 'the way to provide hospitality' in the past are not those necessarily viewed as the 'norm' today, the conclusion then being that hospitality today is different from hospitality provided in the past.

The same argument applies to spatial and cultural variation. Because the United Kingdom is spatially and culturally different from say China or Japan, or even France or Turkey, it would be tempting to conclude that the different spatial (i.e. resource, and cultural characteristics) of these countries would evolve different, perhaps unique, views of what hospitality is and the practices it should embody. However, once again, this may be a superficial and misleading conclusion. Although it is axiomatic that different economic and socio-cultural antecedents have influenced the present forms of hospitality in different societies and cultures, and that these do embody visible differences, the question is whether these differences are as fundamental as they may appear to be.

In both the temporal and spatial, generic-specific, dichotomies it is, and clearly has been, according to much of the extant literature, easy to fall into the trap of arriving at conclusions based on 'self-evident' evidence that, because certain obvious differences exist then these differences must indicate the presence of significant, if not fundamental, differences in the motives for the provision, the forms of, behaviors embodied within and the predominant locations where hospitality is provided. The problem with this interpretation is that it fails to distinguish between what has been referred to as the generic core, or essence, of hospitality and the more visible, malleable and contingent periphery (Brotherton, 2002, 2004, 2005, 2006).

Brotherton and Wood (2000) and Brotherton (2002, 2004, 2005, 2006) have produced work designed to address this core/periphery issue and develop possible approaches for comparative analysis. One analogy used in this work that may have some further value in relation to the issues discussed above is the distinction between species and varieties, or more specifically between genotypes and phenotypes. Even though a particular species may have a large number of varieties the critical issue is not the extent of the variation but the commonality existing across the varieties belonging to a particular species. This is not to say that the nature of the variations are not important in terms of influencing specific behaviors and manifestations – they clearly are – or that these differences do not have any significance or meaning – they clearly do – but the corollary of this line of thinking would be that there are no universals, or at the very least, that if these did exist they would be subservient to the contingent variations. This would deny the primacy, if not the existence, of general principles and universal laws.

In an attempt to avoid this problem Brotherton (2002, 2006) proposes a more systematic approach to developing a 'general theory of hospitality'. This work presents a conceptual model identifying the parameters (natural and human resources), independent (economic, socio-cultural, politico-legal, technological), intervening (domestic and commercial hospitality behavior) and moderating (future expectations) variables influencing the dependent variable of the nature, incidence and forms of hospitality in any given time period and spatial location. Thus, this model explicitly recognizes and incorporates the variables influencing, or determining, the specific form and volume hospitality takes within any temporal–spatial nexus. By postulating the nature and direction of the relationships between these variables the model moves the debate forward by addressing the generic-specific issue through the application of a consistent theoretical framework. The challenge this presents to other researchers is the empirical testing and refinement of this model and its components to verify, or otherwise, its ability to explain, and possibly predict, the common and different aspects of hospitality.

That said, this model really only deals with the macro and meso levels. Though it may be applied to the manifestation of hospitality in a given time period or country, or perhaps to an inter-sectoral or industry analysis, in this form it lacks a suitable operational definition necessary to explore the detail embodied in apparently different forms of hospitality. If any given manifestation of hospitality is to be compared with another, or others, to discern whether they can be categorized as the same (generic) or different (contingent) then an appropriate basis, or framework, for comparison has to be developed. Without such a common denominator comparison is difficult, if not meaningless.

To address this Brotherton (2002, 2003a, 2006) proposes that hospitality may be conceptualized as comprising four dimensions (spatial, behavioral, temporal, physical) relating to where, why and when hospitality occurs and what is included in it. The spatial dimension is concerned with the where aspect, and therefore facilitates a consideration of the locations and places hospitality occurs. The behavioral dimension focuses on the motives underlying the provision of hospitality and the human processes involved in its delivery. The temporal dimension is concerned with the incidence of hospitality, i.e. hospitality occasions, and finally the physical dimension identifies the physical features and products associated with any given type of hospitality.

In a dual attempt to empirically explore the efficacy of this operational definition and simultaneously address the issue of what hospitality means, or how it is conceived by its commercial recipients (guests and customers), Brotherton's (2003a, 2005) exploratory study produced some interesting findings. This was a multiple case study with two hotels comprising the cases. As hospitality is a multi-dimensional concept and its manifestations, in peoples' experience, are varied, the use of a context, i.e. the hotel, as a reference point, or cognitive anchor, for respondents to relate their responses to was an important consideration. By contrast the data collection instrument and process was somewhat less structured, using metaphors as stimuli to elicit responses through face-to-face interviewing of the hotel guests. Although this is a common approach in new product development and market research in general, it has rarely, if ever, been used within this context to ascertain, in a quite unrestrained manner, the guest or consumer view of what they associate with the concept of hospitality. From the results of 89 interviews conducted in the two hotels cross-tabulation and chi square analysis of the data indicated there were no statistically significant relationships between the categorical variables of age, occupation, ethnicity, repeat

visitation, gender, and reason for stay and the responses recorded to the substantive questions asked.

The words the respondents associated with 'hospitality' were overwhelmingly behavioral in nature with only a minority relating to the physical or temporal dimensions referred to above. The words they associated with the physical and service aspects of hospitality in the hotels were identified as being either impressionistic, in terms of the physical and service deliverer characteristics, or judgements made in relation to the performance of the physical or service part of the hospitality experience they were receiving. When the respondents were asked to consider these physical and service aspects as a color, an animal and a season of the year again it was clear that they used these metaphors as vehicles to express their impressions and judgements in a similar manner. Certain colors, animals and seasons were used consistently to record poor impressions and/or performance, and vice-versa.

In a follow-up, as yet unpublished, study to this conducted by the same author and using the same methodology within fast food restaurants very similar findings were obtained. In this study 200 customers were interviewed in two fast food restaurants, a McDonalds and a Burger King, in the UK. The chi square statistics for this data again were not statistically significant indicating once again that the instrument was robust in relation to respondent characteristics variation or, in short, that age, gender, occupation, and ethnicity do not significantly influence the nature of the words associated with hospitality or the nature of the metaphor chosen to represent their impressionistic or judgemental views of the hospitality being received.

There was also quite a remarkable degree of similarity and consistency in this study's results compared to those in the earlier Brotherton (2003a, 2005) study. In the case of the words associated with 'hospitality' again the majority were behavioral in nature, some were physical or temporal and others were spatial, referring to other types of location or place where hospitality could be expected (see Table 1.1). In this sense the findings not only confirmed the behavioral dimension to be the dominant one in the mind of the guest or customer but also that all four of the dimensions posited by Brotherton (2002) were recognized in these responses.

Again, in common with the earlier study, the words the respondents associated with the physical and service aspects of hospitality in the two

Table 1.1   Words associated with hospitality

Behavioral	Physical	Temporal	Spatial
Pleasantness/politeness/manners/courtesy/helpfulness (82)	Comfort (14)	Travel, Tourism	Hotels (8)
Service – great/good, customer, quality (71)	Cleanliness (12)	and Holidays (3)	Restaurants (3)
Friendliness/warmth (66)			Home (2)
Welcoming (46)			Hospital (2)
Care/attention/being looked after (33)			Bars (2)
Kindness/hospitableness/generosity (23)			

Table 1.2   Words used to describe the physical aspects of hospitality in the restaurants

Impression	Performance
McDonalds	*McDonalds*
Modern/bright/colorful (16)	Very nice/good/excellent (3)
Basic/ functional (12)	Adequate/satisfactory/
Shabby/tacky/plastic/	average/acceptable (6)
unwelcoming/cheap/	
boring (14)	
Clean/tidy (51)	
Pleasant/comfortable/	
welcoming (9)	
Burger King	*Burger King*
Modern/bright/colorful (16)	Very nice/good
Basic/functional (8)	Excellent/appealing (6)
Shabby/tacky/plastic/	Okay/satisfactory/
unwelcoming/cheap/	adequate/
boring (9)	average (7)
American (13)	
Clean (33)	
Pleasant/comfortable/	
welcoming (16)	

Table 1.3   Words used to describe the service aspects of hospitality in the restaurants

Service deliverer behavior/characteristics	Service deliverer performance
McDonalds	*McDonalds*
Friendly/cheerful/welcoming/	Very good/excellent (2)
polite/pleasant/	Good (4)
helpful (52)	Average/reasonable/
Quick/fast/efficient (17)	satisfactory (4)
Slow (3)	Poor/awful (2)
Bored/uninterested/unfriendly/	
unwelcoming/	
unenthusiastic/slow/	
careless/robotic/	
regimented (25)	
Burger King	*Burger King*
Friendly/cheerful/	Good (7)
welcoming/polite/pleasant/	Acceptable/okay/average/
helpful (32)	Adequate (8)
Quick/fast/efficient (21)	Poor/disappointing/not
Slow (7)	good (7)
Bored/uninterested/unfriendly/	
unwelcoming/	
unenthusiastic/slow/	
careless/robotic/	
regimented (24)	

restaurants were clearly of an impressionistic or judgemental nature and were also almost identical to those used in the hotels context (see Tables 1.2 and 1.3). The only differences between the two sets of results in these respects were that there were fewer impressionistic words offered by the fast food respondents to the physical aspects question and more reference to speed, efficiency and regimentation by these respondents in the service aspects responses. However, such variations in the relative volume or specificity of words used may be expected where the physical and service aspects clearly differ. In a hotel the physical environment is more heterogeneous and richer than that evident in a fast food restaurant and, similarly, it is not surprisingly to find much greater reference to speed and so on in an environment where this is expected and known to be one of the operation's keys to success.

The predominant colors, or groups of related colors, chosen by the fast food respondents in relation to the physical aspects of hospitality (see Table 1.4) were virtually identical to those of the hotel guest in the previous study, as were the reasons given for the choices, suggesting that it may be possible in the future to develop a more standardized and parsimonious instrument to elicit, record and analyze this type of data. It would appear that the nature of the color association or connotation for the guest or customer is consistent regardless of the nature of the physical environment. This postulate also

Table 1.4   Words used to describe the physical aspects of hospitality in the restaurants as a color

Color group	n	%	Reasons why
McDonalds			*McDonalds*
Brown	3	3.2	Basic, no frills, indistinct, poor hygiene.
Orange	6	6.4	Bright, cheerful, energizing, fast, pleasant, warm.
Burger King			*Burger King*
Brown/Amber	2	2.0	Stained, needs attention.
Orange	2	2.0	Warm, friendly.
McDonalds			*McDonalds*
Red/Pink/Lilac/Maroon/Cyan	11	11.5	Predominant color, vibrant, lively, warm, in your face color, welcoming, pretty.
Burger King			*Burger King*
Red/Pink	51	51.0	Friendly, bright, comfortable, energetic, exciting, warm, welcoming, happy, vibrant, bold passion, strong, brash, bold, color of chairs, seating, signs, logo and power.
McDonalds			*McDonalds*
Beige/Cream/Peach	13	13.7	Bland, dull, neutral, boring, plain.
McDonalds			*McDonalds*
Green	8	8.4	Predominant color, cool, peaceful, refreshing, calm, relaxing.
Burger King			*Burger King*
Green	2	2.0	Clear, freedom, simplicity, nice.
McDonalds			*McDonalds*
Blue	13	13.7	Calm, peaceful, pleasant, clean, cold, bland, basic.
Burger King			*Burger King*
Blue	14	14.0	Bright, caring, clean, cold, clinical, modern, neutral, depressing.
McDonalds			*McDonalds*
Black/Gray/Silver	20	21.0	Standard, bad, boring, dull, outdated, plain, bland, cold, dark, no individuality, ordinary.
Burger King			*Burger King*
Gray/Silver	11	11.0	Bland, basic, clinical, regimented, uninspiring, old, worn out, uniform, mundane.
McDonalds			*McDonalds*
Yellow/Gold	14	14.7	Bright, cheerful, relaxed, eye catching, fresh, clean, bright, warm, welcoming, color of logo, good quality.
Burger King			*Burger King*
Yellow	11	11.0	Accessible, bright, cheerful, nice, welcoming, alive, happy, pleasant, relaxed, busy.
McDonalds			*McDonalds*
White	6	6.3	Clean, bright, neat, light, plain, open.
Burger King			*Burger King*
White	5	5.0	Clean, clinical, sanitized, sterile, impersonal, little personality, relaxing, quality.

holds for the service aspects of hospitality. Here there was again a remarkable consistency between the colors chosen and the reasons given to explain these choices by the fast food restaurant, and earlier hotel, respondents (see Table 1.5). Although there were some differences and inconsistencies between the two sets of results in terms of whether a color was chosen for negative, neutral or positive reasons there was enough commonality to suggest that certain colors are always, or at the very least generally, used to denote positive, neutral or negative impressions and judgements. Therefore, in common with the colors and physical aspects above, it should also be possible to develop a more parsimonious instrument in this respect in the future.

The range of animals associated with the physical and service aspects by the fast food restaurant customers was somewhat wider than

Table 1.5 Words used to describe the service aspects of hospitality in the restaurants as a color

Color group	n	%	Reasons why
McDonalds			*McDonalds*
Orange/Gold	3	3.0	Bright, colorful, good vibes, good quality.
Brown/Amber	6	6.0	Bad, dull, poor hygiene, unfriendly, robotic, rude.
Burger King			*Burger King*
Brown	1	1.0	Bad service.
McDonalds			*McDonalds*
Blue	10	10.0	Calm, clean, polite, easy going, approachable, uniforms, efficient.
Burger King			*Burger King*
Blue	20	20.0	Calm, caring, relaxed, welcome, clean, cool, friendly, honest, genuine, uniforms, confused, miserable, forgetful.
McDonalds			*McDonalds*
Red/Pink/Purple	26	26.0	Bright, cheerful, pleasant, warm, welcoming, active, quick, enthusiastic, fast, speedy, inviting, synthetic, fake, rushed.
Burger King			*Burger King*
Red/Pink/Purple	18	18.0	Bright, cheerful, rushed, welcoming, friendly, hot, fast, frantic, staff uniforms.
McDonalds			*McDonalds*
Green	4	4.0	Fresh, good, welcoming.
Burger King			*Burger King*
Green	3	3.0	Healthy, safe, hygienic, warm, simple, boring.
McDonalds			*McDonalds*
Cream/Magnolia/Beige	6	6.0	Bland, lacks personality, calm, dull, no frills.
Burger King			*Burger King*
Cream/Magnolia	3	3.0	Background color, unoffensive, bland.
McDonalds			*McDonalds*
Gray/Silver/Black	21	21.0	Robotic, awful, rude, dark, depressed, no smile, unfriendly, bland, banal, regimented, bored, monotonous, dull, lifeless, cold, ordinary, predictable, unenthusiastic.
Burger King			*Burger King*
Gray/Black	15	15.0	Slow, bad communication, dull, boring, disappointing, uninterested, monotonous, drab, not hospitable, no interaction, no enthusiasm, unfriendly.
McDonalds			*McDonalds*
White	6	6.0	Bright, fresh, pleasant, clinical, efficient, quick, good service.
Burger King			*Burger King*
White	12	12.0	Basic, bland, clean, efficient, helpful, not creative, quick, impersonal, plain.

those selected by the hotel guests in the prior study (see Tables 1.6 and 1.7) but there was consistency between the two sets of respondents in terms of the type of animal seen to represent a negative, neutral or negative view of both. Once again this suggests that the same 'reductionist' process referred to above could be applied to this element of the instrument in the future.

Finally, consistency was equally evident between the results from the earlier study and those from the fast food restaurant customers in relation to choosing a season of the year to reflect their impressions and judgements of the

physical and service aspects of hospitality (see Tables 1.8 and 1.9). In short, Spring and Summer were chosen for positive and Autumn and Winter for negative reasons. Moving along a scale from very positive to very negative the arrangement would be – Summer, Spring, Autumn, Winter. Once more this holds out the prospect of using a more standardized form in the future.

Nevertheless more work does need to be done to test these postulates in a wider range of hospitality environments and differing cultures. One issue that could not be resolved in these studies, because of the composition of the samples, was how sensitive the instrument may be

Table 1.6   Words used to describe the physical aspects of hospitality in the restaurants as an animal

Animal	n	%	Reasons why
McDonalds			*McDonalds*
Cat	16	16.0	Calm, relaxing, capable, clean, cuddly, friendly, warm, happy, slow, tame, ordinary, common.
Burger King			*Burger King*
Cat	23	23.0	Calm, clean, tidy, pleasant, warm, welcoming, friendly, relaxed, tame, well groomed.
McDonalds			*McDonalds*
Horse	1	1.0	Reliable, steady.
Burger King			*Burger King*
Horse	2	2.0	Not glamorous, gets the job done, just there to do a job.
McDonalds			*McDonalds*
Bear	5	5.0	Big, clumsy, sturdy, cuddly, enveloping, bright, clean, no fuss, no extras.
McDonalds			*McDonalds*
Elephant	6	6.0	Big, noisy, slow, sturdy, slow.
Burger King			*Burger King*
Elephant	5	6.0	Large, inviting, trustworthy, hardwearing, clumsy.
McDonalds			*McDonalds*
Dog	13	13.0	Friendly, helpful, warm, welcoming, loyal, reliable, comforting, familiar, pleasant, pleased to see you.
Burger King			*Burger King*
Dog	13	13.0	Clean, tidy, comfortable, cute, friendly, convenient, loyal, warm, inviting, soft, cuddly, energetic, scruffy, shaggy, raggy.
McDonalds			*McDonalds*
Bird	4	4.0	Common, nothing special, staff shuffle around the restaurant, nice if well kept.
Burger King			*Burger King*
Bird	14	14.0	Vibrant colors, bright, attractive, colorful, dynamic, American style décor, different colors.
McDonalds			*McDonalds*
Insect	6	6.0	Unclean, dirty, poor service.
Burger King			*Burger King*
Insect	1	1.0	Damp, dirty toilets.
McDonalds			*McDonalds*
Rabbit	5	5.0	Calm, serene, friendly, soft, homely, welcoming, neat, quiet.
McDonalds			*McDonalds*
Fish	8	8.0	Calm, chilled, clean, peaceful, streamlined, well designed, boring.
Burger King			*Burger King*
Fish	4	8.0	Calm, tranquil, appealing, all the same, no difference.
McDonalds			*McDonalds*
Pig	6	6.0	Unhealthy food, unhealthy people, manners.
Burger King			*Burger King*
Pig	2	2.0	Dirty.
McDonalds			*McDonalds*
Cow	1	1.0	Burgers
Burger King			*Burger King*
Cow	7	7.0	Not clever, you take what you want and leave, providing food, beef.
McDonalds			*McDonalds*
Monkey	4	4.0	Appealing to kids, circus atmosphere, fun.
Burger King			*Burger King*
Monkey	3	3.0	Bright, bubbly, helpful, grabs attention, in your face.

(Continued)

Table 1.6   cont'd

Animal	n	%	Reasons why
McDonalds Reptile	2	2.0	*McDonalds* Cold, hard, not lovable, not warm.
Burger King Reptile	4	4.0	*Burger King* Chirpy, fast, physically sound, old, worn out.
McDonalds Rodent	1	1.0	*McDonalds* Unattractive.
Burger King Rodent	3	3.0	*Burger King* Routine, dashing about, doesn't do a lot, not noticed.
McDonalds Other Animals – Sheep (3), Sloth (2), Armadillo (2), Goat (2), Hippo (2), Donkey, Fox, Hyena, Lemming, Panda, Squirrel, Wombat.	18	18.0	*McDonalds* Follows orders, follows the crowd, white and comfortable. Little effort, slow, dull. Hard, uncomfortable. Dull, boring, unwelcoming. Big, fat, tranquil, spacey. Happy meal toys. Pessimistic. Awful music. A bit of a joke, follows what others do. Gentle. Uncomfortable, unapproachable. Filthy.
Burger King Other Animals – Zebra (2), Buffalo, Giraffe, Sloth, Dinosaur, Donkey, Hippo, Panda, Skunk, Wolf.	11	11.0	*Burger King* Black and white floor and tiling. Chaotic but patterned. Two-tone coloring. Lazy, boring. Old retro-feel, cool, not bad. Works for money, alone, no motivation. Adequate. Always eating. Black and white. Loud, aggressive presence felt.

Table 1.7   Words used to describe the service aspects of hospitality in the restaurants as an animal

Animal	n	%	Reasons why
McDonalds Dog	23	23.0	*McDonalds* Caring, friendly, helpful, polite, loyal, obedient, quick, simple, attentive, welcoming, subservient, likes to please.
Burger King Dog	14	14.0	*Burger King* Docile, safe, loyal, eager to please, willing to help, friendly, fast, efficient, obedient, quick, reliable.
McDonalds Cat	17	17.0	*McDonalds* Approachable, clean, reliable, friendly, happy, polite, pleasant, non-threatening.
Burger King Cat	24	24.0	*Burger King* Attractive, beautiful, friendly, helpful, temperamental, harmless, tame, quick, efficient, timid, dependable, free-thinking, subtle.
McDonalds Fish	10	10.0	*McDonalds* Efficient, quick, fast, kind, pleasant, ruthless, friendly, tired, helpless.
Burger King Fish	6	6.0	*Burger King* Cold, efficient, neutral, nothing special, shuffling around, inoffensive.
McDonalds Insect	8	8.0	*McDonalds* Filthy, slow, not organized, not expressive, agitated, likely to snap, all follow the same orders.
Burger King Insect	9	9.0	*Burger King* Annoying, fast, disorientated, many colors, efficient.
McDonalds Sheep	5	5.0	*McDonalds* Follows orders, same standard pattern, no extras, quiet, slow, unexciting.
Burger King Sheep	3	3.0	*Burger King* No difference in personalities, staff stick to the corporate instructions, a lot of staff.

Table 1.7   cont'd

Animal	n	%	Reasons why
McDonalds Reptile	5	5.0	*McDonalds* Doesn't go anywhere, slow, staff are hopping around to serve orders.
Burger King Reptile	6	6.0	*Burger King* Fast, quick, precise, slow, unresponsive.
McDonalds Sloth	3	3.0	*McDonalds* Lazy, incompetent, slow, unenthusiastic.
Burger King Sloth	6	6.0	*Burger King* Lazy, slipshod, slow, laidback, rude.
McDonalds Rodent	4	4.0	*McDonalds* Busy, unhappy, fidgety, no personality, small, indiscriminant.
Burger King Rodent	4	4.0	*Burger King* Doesn't do a lot, expressionless, quiet, quick.
McDonalds Monkey	4	4.0	*McDonalds* Circus atmosphere, fun, funny.
Burger King Monkey	2	2.0	*Burger King* Helpful, not serious.
McDonalds Bird	1	1.0	*McDonalds* Cheerful.
Burger King Bird	4	4.0	*Burger King* Fast, staff run around like headless chickens.
McDonalds Other Animals – Rabbit (3), Donkey (2), Fox (2), Bear, Elephant, Kangaroo, Goat, Pig.	12	12.0	*McDonalds* Calm, serene, friendly, soft, neat, quiet. Hard working, not enjoying their job, doing a good job. Fast, quick, unaware of its motives and morals. Cuddly. Big style. Quick. Only interested in getting food. Grunting, cheerful.
Burger King Other Animals – Horse (3), Elephant (2), Cow (2), Pig (2), Rabbit, Hyena, Mule, Panda.	13	13.0	*Burger King* Fast, friendly, hardworking. Large, inviting, doing what is necessary, no customer interaction. Lazy, providing food. Fatty food, offering to increase meal size. Jump for attention and then back away when approached. Always smiling. Not fast. Kind.

to different cultural perceptions and cognitions of colors, animals and seasons. Because the composition of the samples in these two studies was dominated by White-European respondents the opportunity did not arise to test this particular issue. However, given that both the general literature on comparative, cross-cultural research and Brotherton (1999c, 2000, 2003b) identifies the crucial importance of establishing an appropriate, valid and reliable 'comparative base', this work has initiated a process designed to develop such a basis for comparison and thus has moved the hospitality field closer to a position where both the conceptual basis of hospitality and the ability to systematically

apply a comparative framework to address the generic-specific debate can proceed with greater clarity.

As we noted earlier in this chapter, there is a strong underlying theme in the hospitality literature *per se* that takes the view that participation in any hospitality exchange situation, and associated relationship, is voluntary on the part of the parties entering into this exchange. In many respects this may be true as the vast majority of hospitality situations are non-coercive in the strict sense of the term. People generally participate in hospitality exchanges without being forced to do so. However, to view voluntarism as a universal principle and

Table 1.8 Words used to describe the physical aspects of hospitality in the restaurants as a season

Season	n	%	Reasons why
McDonalds Autumn	32	32.3	McDonalds Dull, past its best, boring, colors are red and brown, drab, not bright but not sunny, décor, interior tables.
Burger King Autumn	19	19.2	Burger King Bland, plain, cool, dull, past its best, predominant colors, not memorable, quiet, sad, unenthusiastic.
McDonalds Winter	21	21.2	McDonalds Bare, minimal, cold, gray, depressing, miserable, uncomfortable, lonely, harsh lighting.
Burger King Winter	20	20.2	Burger King Calm, quiet, cold, colorless, dreary, unwelcoming, dark, gloomy, depressing, nothing exciting.
McDonalds Spring	26	26.3	McDonalds Fresh, clean, warm, bright, airy, exciting, cheerful, color scheme, youthful.
Burger King Spring	21	21.2	Burger King Warm, welcoming, bright, clean, hope, light, optimistic, fresh, lively, colorful, blossoming.
McDonalds Summer	20	20.2	McDonalds Bright, colorful, comfortable, easy going, fresh, sunny, warm, vacation, fun, relaxing.
Burger King Summer	39	39.4	Burger King Alive, vibrant, warm, attractive, pleasant, cheerful, bright, hot, lively, happy, summer colors, refreshing, big.

Table 1.9 Words used to describe the service aspects of hospitality in the restaurants as a season

Season	n	%	Reasons why
McDonalds Autumn	15	15.0	McDonalds Bad, boring, breezy, dull, mediocre, no excitement, no extremes, in between warm and cold, impersonal, not sunny.
Burger King Autumn	22	22.2	Burger King Average, bland, cold, dark, dull, dying, neither good nor bad, sad, unenthusiastic, poor attitude, fake smiles.
McDonalds Winter	31	31.0	McDonalds Miserable, cold, uninviting, depressing, frosty, dull, gloomy, lonely, tired, unaccommodating.
Burger King Winter	23	23.2	Burger King Grimy, cold, colorless, unwelcoming, slow, unhappy staff, miserable, dull, gloomy, disappointing, rushed.
McDonalds Spring	24	24.0	McDonalds Bright, airy, happy, sunny, cheerful, fast, fresh, clean, pleasant, appealing, youthful, warm, inviting, friendly.
Burger King Spring	23	23.2	Burger King Bright, cheerful, busy, clean, fresh, new beginnings, new life, young, friendly, helpful, smiling faces.
McDonalds Summer	30	30.0	McDonalds Bright, attractive, colorful, friendly, easy going, pleasant, happy, hot, pressured, smiling, polite, approachable.
Burger King Summer	31	31.3	Burger King Busy, cheerful, warm, happy, friendly, relaxed, hot, smiling, welcoming, pleasant.

characteristic of hospitality exchanges may be too simplistic and, in some cases, probably incorrect. This issue really revolves around how 'voluntarism' is conceived. If we take an extreme view and see this as the absence of physical coercion then it may well be a valid proposition. However, there are other forms of coercion, for example, psychological, emotional, social, economic, that may have a role to play in making, at least some forms of hospitality less voluntaristic than is widely assumed.

We will explore these issues presently but prior to this it should also be noted that they are closely associated with the 'host-guest' or 'self-other' dichotomy. Much of the literature focusing on these, provider-receiver, issues takes the view that there is a munificent relationship between these two parties, and that the host or provider of hospitality seeks to protect and keep safe the guest or receiver of the hospitality while he/she is within the host's domain. This is closely connected with the welcoming, valuing and protection of the 'stranger' discussed earlier. Indeed the French philosophical tradition (see Jelloun, 1999; Bowlby, 2000) consistently invokes the view that 'true', 'pure' or 'authentic' hospitality is given and received in a totally voluntaristic and selfless manner. The corollary being that any ulterior motive or influence contaminates this action and renders it as contrived, false or inauthentic. If purity is viewed in such a philosophical manner then this may be true but real world behavior invariably is not predicated upon such lofty thought. Most people's behavior, including that associated with hospitality, is driven by more instrumental motives that, in turn, modify not only the motivation and reasoning lying behind the provision of hospitality but also its manifestation.

One of the dominant forms of social connectivity and loyalty, whether for voluntary or more pre-determined reasons, over time has been the 'group'. The group, whether based on tribal kinship, caste, religion, social class, family, economic activity, or other criteria, and regardless of whether it is conceived at macro or micro levels always exhibits one key characteristic; a centripetal force that serves to bind its membership into a cohesive entity. Of course, the strength of this force is variable but where it is stronger it serves to differentiate the group more from other groups by encouraging, if not coercing in varying

ways, its members to see their individual self-interests as synonymous with those of the group as a whole. Conversely, where the centripetal force is weaker the group becomes less cohesive and the interests of its members become more individualistic and self-serving. In short, the very antithesis of a cohesive group, centrifugal forces come into play.

The point of this is that, for the individual, voluntarism is relative, and therefore it is hard to see how hospitality, in the vast majority of its manifestations, can be regarded as pure and authentic when there is always an instrumental referent emanating from the nature of the individual's connectivity within the milieu that he/she exists. This may be something as relatively esoteric as a spiritual belief, i.e. that the person's God wishes them to express their religiosity and faith through engaging in the provision of hospitality to others less fortunate than themselves (see Murray, 1990) or something far more earthly and concrete, for example, because they believe that by providing hospitality to others in a position to assist their economic well being is a rational and sensible thing to do, i.e. corporate hospitality being one instance and political hospitality another (see Hollander, 1981). One of the major underlying issues that is said to transgress all, or nearly all, instrumental hospitality exchanges is the, invariably implicit, expectation of reciprocity as a product of the obligations established between the participants within the act itself. What is rarely, if ever, explored in this context is the nature of the power relations and dynamics established by, and operating within this exchange, and their implications for any future exchanges, a point recognized by Sherry, McGrath and Levy (1993) who, in their exploration of the darker side of gift giving, suggest that these types of exchange can engender high levels of anxiety amongst the participants.

Most societies, both those existing in the past and today, have tended to value the concept and practice of hospitality, albeit in varying forms and to varying degrees, because it tends to have a moderating influence on the tensions inherent within any society that has structural inequalities of one kind or another. Prior to the establishment of propertied, class societies Bell and Henry (2001) argue that the tribal societies pre-dating this change embodied 'the rule of hospitality' which constituted the basis for a universal social relationship within such societies. Under these conditions hospitality – 'the mutual right and obligation to receive and provide subsistence' (Bell and Henry, 2001: 211) – was a kinship duty because of the collective nature of social and economic organization and necessary for the survival of the tribe. This collective equality, and hence other relationships based on it, disappears with the advent of money, debt and private property that, in turn, leads to increasing *commodification* and a desire to establish quantitative equivalence within exchange relationships to reflect relative value within an exchange. Over time this migrates to societies that reflect these changing power relationships, within which power elites and dependents of one kind or another signify the asymmetrical ownership and control over the means and processes of production and survival. As this evolves, the provision of hospitality from those who control these means and processes becomes a political imperative, albeit often dressed in the guise of a social or religious obligation, to moderate any potential revolutionary tendencies within the mass of the population who are dependent on the power elites. So, for example, from feudal times, when the power elites provided hospitality for those less fortunate while simultaneously exploiting them (White, 1968), through ameliorating charitable provision in early industrial societies to more contemporary concepts of welfare provision in advanced societies the establishment of obligations and expectations of reciprocity have served to act as a form of social control. Thus, the particular form that hospitality takes, whether viewed historically or contemporaneously, is bound to vary because of temporal and/or spatial variation in the conditions that give rise to it. On the other hand, the underlying reasons for its provision and, in turn, their basic purpose/s have in essence not changed since the emergence of propertied societies. They have always been, and continue to remain, those designed to primarily protect the interests of the provider, whoever and whatever that may be.

Regardless of whether this is viewed from a societal, or a more macro-perspective, or one closer to most peoples' experience of hospitality, i.e. at a domestic or commercial level, the principles hold. In commercial hospitality provision there are hosts and guests and essentially the same expectations of obligation and reciprocity, although the issues of direct monetary exchange do muddy the waters somewhat. Nevertheless, the provider has its vested interests and seeks to inculcate these in the more explicit 'contractual' obligations pertinent to the exchange rather than these being known as unspoken 'norms' by the receiver. What is different in commercial hospitality provision from that provided on a non-commercial basis is that the basic structure of the situation and process moves from being dyadic to triadic. This complicates matters and leads to competing loyalties, as Mars and Nicod's (1984) *The World of Waiters* study demonstrated. There are now (at least) three groups directly involved in the hospitality exchange; the provider (the company), the guest (the consumer) and the deliverer (the staff) that is, in turn, mediated by monetary exchange.

What is interesting here, and something that has received relatively scant attention in the literature, is that although commercial hospitality exchange environments include rules, roles and rituals, in common with non-commercial environments, these are likely to generate different hospitality 'repertoires' because, at least in part, the assumption of voluntarism cannot be equally applied to the participants in the exchange. Although it would be reasonable to assume that the companies involved in providing hospitality have voluntarily, within competing commercial options, decided to enter into this form of business this cannot be so easily assumed in the case of the other two parties. While, on the one hand, it is probably true to say that, in most cases, the people who work in the hospitality industry have not been coerced into doing this against their will it may be equally fair to comment that, on the other hand, many such employees make this choice on the basis that it provides a job with income but not on the basis that it is their ideal form of employment. Similarly, in the case of the guest or consumer, some do make the choice to stay in a hotel or eat out on a free and voluntary basis. Equally, however, others do not. For example, people traveling on business, whether internationally or domestically, are doing so as an integral part of their job and the necessity of using commercial accommodation and/or eating establishments while engaged in this travel is a forced choice. Under these circumstances, which may be described as quasi-voluntarism at best, where employees may not really wish to be hospitality deliverers and guests may not particularly wish to stay or eat in a hospitality establishment, it is clear that the traditional host–guest view of hospitality, and all that this implies, needs to be modified.

CONCLUSION

In our Introduction to this volume we noted that investigations of the concept and meaning of 'hospitality' have been relatively sporadic and, more recent investigations, principally from within the community of hospitality researchers, have amounted to very little. The two are connected. Recent investigation of the concept of hospitality has been unsystematic, reflecting both the piecemeal tradition in hospitality (management) research as well as reluctance to engage with the range of philosophical and social scientific literature where consideration of the nature of hospitality has taken place. This collection of essays edited by Lashley and Morrison (2000) evidences this. While constituting the major recent resource for debates about the nature of hospitality, the volume consists principally of a disparate, if fascinatingly valuable, collection of fragmented insights into the topic.

Of course, to argue in this way is to court accusations of both inconsistency and 'control freakery'. In respect of consistency, it can be fairly argued that consideration of the nature of hospitality and hospitality management outside the community of hospitality management researchers has itself been piecemeal. Accordingly, for an area of investigation still in its infancy, there is merit in garnering as many perspectives as possible in order to generate insights and opportunities for further investigative refinement. On the 'control freakery' question, an objection might be that there is little to be gained in seeking to generate highly delimited frameworks for 'testing' particular investigative routes as these may embody the possibility that some such routes will be effectively closed off. Neither of these positions really holds much water. There can be no reasonable objection to the generation of as many insights as possible in investigating and refining any phenomenon. However, if this activity studiously avoids both establishing linkages to what has gone before and contributes little to conceptual refinement and understanding, then what is left is a situation best represented by the popular misunderstanding of the meaning of Occam's razor, of multiplying entities beyond necessity. On the question of developing models to 'test', we are well aware of the positivist overtones of such a position. Nevertheless, a reading of that literature which has addressed the meanings of hospitality does suggest profitable avenues of investigation that are in danger of being ignored. Negligence for negligence's sake does not constitute a rational research strategy.

The nature of hospitality is an important topic of research and not only for those engaged with hospitality management. It is, as we have seen, largely neglected in philosophical, economic and sociological research, it is on the periphery of social investigation like other, 'taken for granted' (even by sociologists!) aspects of human behavior such as food and eating (the latter, as we noted in the Introduction to this *Handbook*, a not infrequent complaint of sociologists of food). For hospitality management, the importance of *systematically* extending our understanding of the concept cannot be underestimated. It is not simply a question of 'knowing what we are talking about'. It is about seeking to build a framework that may have conceptual and methodological utility in supporting investigation of the wide range of subject applications applied to 'hospitality management' represented in this volume.

REFERENCES

Bauman, Z. (1990) *Thinking Sociologically.* Oxford: Blackwell.

Beardsworth, A. and Keil, T. (1997) *Sociology on the Menu: An Invitation to the Study of Food and Society.* London: Routledge.

Bell, S. and Henry, J. F. (2001) 'Hospitality versus exchange: the limits of monetary economics', *Review of Social Economy*, 59(2): 203–228.

Borer, M. C. (1972) *The British Hotel through the Ages.* London: Lutterworth Press.

Bowlby, R. (Trans) (2000) *Of Hospitality – Anne Duformantelle invites Jaques Derrida to respond.* California: Stanford University Press.

Bright, S. and Johnson, K. (1985) 'Training for hospitality', *Journal of European Industrial Training*, 9(7): 27–31.

Brotherton, B. (1999a) 'Towards a definitive view of the nature of hospitality and hospitality management', *International Journal of Contemporary Hospitality Management*, 11(4): 165–173.

Brotherton, B. (1999b) 'Case study research'. In B. Brotherton (ed.) *The Handbook of Hospitality Management Research.* Chichester: John Wiley & Sons. pp. 113–141.

Brotherton, B. (1999c) 'Comparative research'. In B. Brotherton (ed.) *The Handbook of Hospitality*

Management Research. Chichester: John Wiley & Sons. pp. 41–172.

Brotherton, B. (2000) 'The comparative approach'. In B. Brotherton (ed.) *An Introduction To The UK Hospitality Industry: A Comparative Approach.* Oxford: Butterworth-Heinemann. pp. 1–22.

Brotherton, B. (2002) 'Towards a general theory of hospitality'. *Presented and Work-in-Progress Abstract published in: Proc. Eleventh Annual CHME Hospitality Research Conference,* Leeds: Leeds Metropolitan University, UK.

Brotherton, B. (2003a) 'The nature of hospitality: hotel guest associations and metaphors'. *Presented and Work-in-Progress Abstract published in: Proceedings of the Twelfth Annual CHME Hospitality Research Conference,* Sheffield: Sheffield Hallam University, UK.

Brotherton, B. (2003b) 'Is your mirror the same as mine? Methodological issues in undertaking and interpreting cross-cultural studies'. *Tourism Today,* 3 (Autumn): 26–37.

Brotherton, B. (2004) 'Critical success factors in UK corporate hotels', *The Services Industry Journal,* 24(3): 19–42.

Brotherton, B. (2005) 'The nature of hospitality: customer perceptions and implications', *Tourism and Hospitality Planning & Development,* 2(3): 139–153.

Brotherton, B. (2006) 'Some thoughts on a general theory of hospitality', *Tourism Today,* Issue 6 (Autumn): 8–19.

Brotherton, B. and Wood, R. C. (2000a) *Conceptualizing Hospitality – The Next Frontier? Work-in-progess paper presented at the Ninth Annual CHME Hospitality Research Conference,* 2000, Huddersfield University, UK (only electronic, CD ROM conference proceedings published).

Brotherton, B. and Wood, R. C. (2000b) 'Hospitality and hospitality management'. In C. Lashley and A. Morrison (eds) *In Search of Hospitality.* Oxford: Butterworth-Heinemann.

Burgess, J. (1982) 'Perspectives on gift exchange and hospitable behavior', *International Journal of Hospitality Management,* 1(1): 49–57.

Cassee, E. H. (1983) 'Introduction'. In E. H. Cassee and R. Reuland (eds) *The Management of Hospitality.* Oxford: Pergamon. pp. xii–xxii.

Cassee, E. H. and Reuland, R. (1983) 'Hospitality in hospitals'. In E. H. Cassee and R. Reuland (eds) *The Management of Hospitality,* Oxford: Pergamon. pp. 143–163.

Christian, V. A. (1979) 'The concept of hospitality: a position paper', Mimeograph, School of Hotel Administration, Cornell University, Ithaca, NY: Cornell University.

Cummings, P. R., Kwansa, F. A. and Sussman, M. B. (eds) (1998) *The Role of the Hospitality Industry in the Lives of Individuals and Families.* New York: The Haworth Press.

Davis, J. (1992) *Exchange.* Milton Keynes: Open University Press.

Davis, N. Z. (2000) *The Gift in Sixteenth Century France.* Oxford: Oxford University Press.

Douglas, M. (1975) 'Deciphering a meal'. In M. Douglas (ed.) *Implicit Meanings.* London: Routledge and Kegan Paul.

Finkelstein, J. (1989) *Dining Out: A Sociology of Modern Manners.* Cambridge: Polity Press; Oxford: Blackwell.

Foucault, M. (1979) *Discipline and Punish: The Birth of the Prison.* Harmondsworth: Penguin Books.

Frisby, D. (2002) *Georg Simmel.* London: Routledge.

Goffman, E. (1959) *The Presentation of Self in Everyday Life.* New York: Doubleday.

Goffman, E. (1963) *Behavior in Public Places.* New York: The Free Press.

Hayner, N. S. (1969) *Hotel Life.* College Park, MA: McGrath Publishing Company (originally published 1936 by the University of North Carolina Press).

Heal, F. (1990) *Hospitality in Early Modern England.* Oxford: Clarendon Press.

Hepple, J., Kipps, M. and Thomson, J. (1990) 'The concept of hospitality and an evaluation of its applicability to the experience of hospital patients', *International Journal of Hospitality Management,* 9(4): 305–317.

Higher Education Funding Council for England (HEFCE) (1998) *Review of Hospitality Management.* Bristol: HEFCE.

Hollander, P. (1981) 'Political hospitality', *Society.* November/December: 66–78.

Jelloun, B. T. (1999) *French Hospitality – Racism and North African Immigrants.* New York: Columbia University Press.

Jones, P. (1996) 'The hospitality industry'. In P. Jones (ed.) *Introduction to Hospitality Operations.* London: Cassell. pp. 1–20.

King, C. A. (1995) 'What is hospitality?', *International Journal of Hospitality Management,* 14(3–4): 219–234.

Langley-Moore, J. and Langley-Moore, D. (1936) *The Pleasure of Your Company.* London: William Chappell.

Lashley, C. and Morrison, A. (eds) (2000) *In Search of Hospitality.* Oxford: Butterworth-Heinemann.

Lechte, J. (1994) *Fifty Key Contemporary Thinkers: From Structuralism to Postmodernity.* London: Routledge.

Lynch, P. A. (2000) 'Host attitudes towards guests in the homestay sector', *International Journal of Tourism and Hospitality Research: The Surrey Quarterly Review,* 1(2): 119–144.

Mars, G. and Nicod, M. (1984) *The World of Waiters*. London: Allen & Unwin.

Mauss, M. (2000) *The Gift*. London: Routledge.

Mennell, S., Murcott, A. and van Otterloo, A. (1992) *The Sociology of Food: Eating, Diet and Culture*. London: Sage.

Muhlmann, W. E. (1932) 'Hospitality'. In E. R. A. Seligmann (ed.) *Encyclopedia of the Social Sciences, Volume 7*, New York: Macmillan. pp. 462–464.

Murray, H. (1990) *Do Not Neglect Hospitality – The Catholic Worker and the Homeless*. Philadelphia: Temple University Press.

Nailon, P. (1982) 'Theory in hospitality management', *International Journal of Hospitality Management*, 1(3): 135–143.

Pickering, M. (2001) *Stereotyping: The Politics of Representation*. Basingstoke: Palgrave.

Reuland, R., Choudry, J. and Fagel, A. (1985) 'Research in the field of hospitality management', *International Journal of Hospitality Management*, 4(4): 141–146.

Ritzer, G. (2003) *Handbook of Social Theory*. London: Sage.

Ryan, C. (1991) *Recreational Tourism: A Social Science Perspective*. London: Routledge.

Scott, J. (1995) *Sociological Theory: Contemporary Debates*. Aldershot: Edward Elgar.

Sherry, J. F., McGrath, M. A. and Levy, S. J. (1993) The dark side of the gift, *Journal of Business Research*, 28: 225–244.

Shilling, C. and Mellor, P. A. (2001) *The Sociological Ambition*. London: Sage.

Stringer, P. F. (1981) 'Hosts and guests: the bed-and-breakfast phenomenon', *Annals of Tourism Research*, 8(3): 357–376.

Telfer, E. (1996) *Food For Thought: Philosophy and Food*. London: Routledge.

Tideman, M. C. (1983) 'External influences on the hospitality industry'. In E. H. Cassee and E. Reuland (eds) *The Management of Hospitality*. Oxford: Pergamon. pp. 1–24.

Visser, M. (1992) *The Rituals of Dinner*. London: Penguin Books.

Warde, A. and Martens, L. (1998) 'Eating out and the commercialization of mental life', *British Food Journal*, 100(3): 147–153.

Watts, S. (1963) *The Ritz*. London: The Bodley Head Ltd.

White, A. (1968) *Palaces of the People: A Social History of Commercial Hospitality*. New York: Taplinger.

Wood, R. C. (1994b) 'Some theoretical perspectives on hospitality'. In A. V. Seaton, et al. (eds) *Tourism: The State of The Art*. Chichester: John Wiley & Sons Ltd. pp. 737–742.

Wood, R. C. (1994c) 'Hotel culture and social control', *Annals of Tourism Research*, 21(1) 65–80.

Wood, R. C. (2004) 'Closing a planning gap? The future of food production and service systems theory', *Tourism and Hospitality Planning and Development*, 1(1): 19–37.

Zeldin, T. (1994) 'How humans become hospitable to each other'. In T. Zeldin, *An Intimate History of Humanity*. London: Minerva. pp. 426–464.

The Structure and Nature of the International Hospitality Industry

Larry Yu

2

INTRODUCTION

The globalization of the world economy has been intensified in recent decades. Policy changes in favor of free markets, institutional reforms in removing trade and travel barriers and technological breakthroughs in communications and transportation have contributed to the acceleration of international trade and travel. The rapid development of capital markets around the world continues to stimulate economic integration as large volumes of capital flow from one part of the world to the other. Regionally, economic integration and cooperation organizations have been established to promote and facilitate international trade and travel in their respective regions and around the world.

The service sector has increasingly become a significant part of international business activities in many countries. Financial, legal, medical, communication, transportation and travel services are now performed without the restrictions of national borders. As an integral part of international service import and export business, the international travel and tourism industry has been the direct beneficiary of the globalized world economy because travel restrictions have been removed to facilitate business and leisure travel by most countries in the world (Hoad, 2003). In addition, revenues from international travel accounts have been one of the major sources of income for many countries that depend on tourism and hospitality businesses. National or federal governments of many countries are actively promoting international tourism to maximize international export receipts in their balance of accounts from international trade (Gee, 1994). International travel and tourism business therefore contributes

significantly to the national economy of countries at the different levels of development stages – developed countries, emerging economy countries and less-developed countries. It is particularly emphasized as a vehicle for poverty reduction in poor nations.

As a major component of the international travel and tourism industry, the hospitality industry has witnessed a phenomenal growth worldwide in the last decade. Such rapid growth has been fueled by marked economic growth in many countries and a steady increase in global travel demands as hospitality developers and operators strive to fill all possible market segment gaps by providing different lodging and dining facilities and unique service experiences in different destinations, ranging from ultra luxury resort to low-profile ecolodge; and from elegant commercial hotels to no-frills budget inns. International hotel corporations have been strategically and aggressively jockeying global hospitality markets to capture the increased international and domestic travel market segments in different parts of the world. Competitive regional and national hospitality organizations have in recent years emerged to compete with long-established global hotel brands in selected global markets. The international hospitality industry therefore faces great opportunities generated by global economic integration as well as critical challenges associated with developing and managing hospitality operations in an international context.

This chapter studies hospitality development and management from an international perspective. The hospitality industry discussed in this chapter encompasses mainly the global and regional hotel organizations and development. It begins by defining the international hospitality industry as an integral part of the global economic integration process and examines the global and regional travel distribution patterns as well as strategic development trends evident within international hospitality organizations. It then focuses on the management functions required to run a profitable hotel in an international market: financial investment, marketing, human resources development, and cross-cultural communications. It concludes with the future prospects and challenges for international hospitality development and management.

DEFINING THE INTERNATIONAL HOSPITALITY INDUSTRY

The international hospitality business is an integral part of international business, which encompasses three principal activities: merchandise import and export, service import and export, and investment. As Figure 2.1 illustrates, merchandise import and export refers to the buying and selling of goods and products between buyers and sellers in different countries. Goods and products are then shipped from the origin of production to the market of consumption. With the increased globalization of the world economy, more products are now made with materials or parts that are manufactured and assembled from many different countries. The distinctive characteristic of merchandise import and export is the tangible movement of goods and products from the origin of production to the market of consumption, which includes materials and food and beverage products used in hotel construction and service, such as furniture, fixture, equipment and wine.

Service import and export refers to international businesses that receive and provide specialized services between clients and managerial/consultative professionals in an international context, such as legal service, financial service, hotel management contract, hotel franchise, medical service and food service. In this case, no tangible movement of goods is involved, only the travel of highly specialized professionals and consultants to the host countries to perform management and operation services in hotels, resorts, restaurants and clubs. Revenues generated by service exports have become a significant part of many countries' export receipts, and some countries rely on a service export surplus to offset international trade deficits accumulated from merchandise imports.

The third component of international business includes investment. Investment activities consist mainly of direct investment and indirect investment. Direct investment refers to equity investment by international companies or individual developers in acquiring assets in the host country. Indirect investment includes investment in global equity and debt markets, including government-issued securities. Such investment is now readily available to both institutional and individual investors. Individual investors can participate in global economic growth by investing in home-based companies doing business in other countries or foreign companies by online trading, through brokers, or through global equity mutual funds managed by financial managers. Indirect investment offers investors an opportunity to participate in international business without leaving your own country. For example, the US net international investment position was a negative $2,484 billion in 2004. Most foreign investors purchased US corporate bonds and US Treasury securities. Foreign acquisitions of assets in the USA totaled $11,537 billion in 2004 while US acquisitions of assets abroad reported at $9,053 billion in the same year (Steward, 2005).

Clearly, the international hospitality industry plays a major role in all aspects of international business activities. It involves merchandise imports when a new hotel project needs to import building materials for construction or the hotel food and beverage department buys foreign wine to serve the guests. It is a service import and export when a management contract or franchise agreement is signed between hotel companies in two different countries. It is engaged in international investment when a global hotel company purchases an existing hotel or builds a new hotel in a foreign country. Obviously, many global hotel companies are directly involved in all three aspects of international business operations. The international hospitality industry therefore contributes in various ways to global economic development and growth. Operationally, it serves international travelers' needs when away from home and raises international standards of guest service. The scope of the international hospitality industry in this text refers primarily to hotel development and operations. It is defined as an integral part of the international business that creates a comfortable and unique lodging environment by designing a physical property

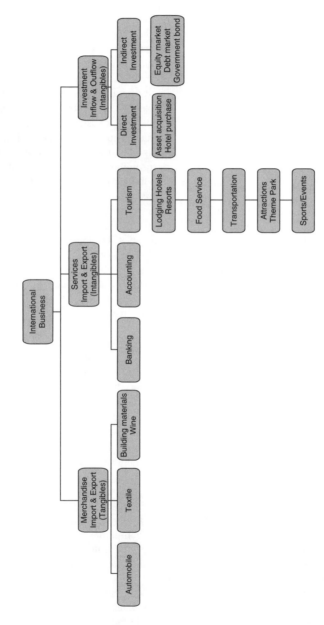

Figure 2.1 Tourism and hospitality as international business with selected sample sectors

that blends into local natural and cultural characteristics and by providing memorable services that manifest the hospitality of the destination.

CHARACTERISTICS OF THE INTERNATIONAL HOSPITALITY INDUSTRY

The international hospitality industry, as an integral part of international business, shares some similar characteristics to other industries, but has some unique characteristics of its own. The typical characteristics of international hotel management are identified as being vulnerable to uncontrollable external events, location-bound, having a capacity constrained by seasonal demand, product intangibility and product perishability. The international hotel business is extremely sensitive to unforeseeable and uncontrollable political instability, economic crisis, natural disasters and epidemics. Many of these events can have a devastating impact on international hotel operations, examples include the 9.11 terrorist attacks on the US in 2001, the SARS epidemics in 2003, the calamitous double whammy of the 9.0 magnitude earthquake and tsunami tidal waves in South Asia and Africa in 2004, the Madrid bombing by terrorists in 2004 and the London bombing by terrorists in 2005. The massive tsunami tidal waves killed tens of thousands of local residents and domestic and international tourists along the coastlines of the most visited tourist resort destinations in 12 South Asian and African countries. The colossal proportions of the loss of human lives and the damage to the tourism economy of these countries was unprecedented and it took considerable time for these destinations to rebuild and recover from this natural disaster. The hotel business is described as location-bound because the physical property is built in a particular geographical location. Unlike other consumer products when goods are produced at the origin of production and then sold at the market of consumption, hotel guests come to the destination, the origin of production, to enjoy the hospitality experience. If the guests are not happy with the services, facilities and amenities, they will complain to the management right away. Therefore, the management is challenged to maintain consistent standards of operations or offer creative and spontaneous solutions to the guests should something go wrong.

Hotel operation is also constrained by its capacity, the number of rooms and the total space for meetings and events. Most tourism destinations experience a seasonal fluctuation of tourism business and therefore the management has to maximize revenues in the peak season and find creative promotion tactics to increase business in the slow season (Duval, 2004). Intangibility is also a typical characteristic of the hotel business since it provides services to visitors who are away from home. The enjoyment of the service occurs in the hotel and the guests have nothing tangible to show after they check out of the hotel. That is why most guests will take photos of the hotel or purchase souvenirs from the hotel to remember their pleasant stay in the property. The hotel management has to create a memorable experience for the guests to enhance guest satisfaction and increase the likelihood of repeat visits and possible word of mouth referral. Perishability in hotel operations refers to the unsold daily room inventory and lost revenues for that day. Hotel management, particularly the marketing and sales managers, face great challenges to increase room sales every day because room inventory has no shelf life compared with other consumer goods such as cameras or shoes. If a room is not sold for that particular day, the sale on that room for that day is lost forever. Hotel management therefore needs to develop creative and effective marketing strategies to augment room sales and implement yield management to maximize the yield on room sales.

INTERNATIONAL HOSPITALITY DEVELOPMENT PARALLELS WORLD TOURISM GROWTH

The development of the international hospitality industry has been influenced by many factors. However, the following four factors have been recognized as the main determinants for international tourism and hospitality development: (1) political facilitation, (2) disposable income, (3) leisure time, and (4) travel motivation.

Political facilitation refers to government policy on international tourism development. Many countries in the world embrace international tourism and hospitality development as a catalyst for the national economy. Therefore, favorable tourism development policies have been enacted to facilitate the rapid growth of tourism and hospitality development projects. Barriers to visitor entry and restrictions on foreign exchange have been removed to encourage the influx of international tourists. Hotels of international service standards are developed to accommodate the increased arrivals of international visitors. On the other hand, a host country can also use the policy leverage to curb international tourism development by issuing restrictive policies on travel visa issuance and prohibiting tourism and hospitality project development in certain destinations. For example, Saudi Arabia used to have a strict policy on permitting Western leisure tourists to visit the country. The Saudi government changed only recently its policy on international tourism development and has formulated a master tourism plan to develop its rich historical, cultural and religious resources for promoting cultural understanding between the Saudis and international visitors.

Disposable income is the income left over after an individual or a household has paid all necessary accounts, such as food, housing, clothing, education and medical expenses. Propensity to international travel is, at least partly, determined by the amount of disposable income a household or individual has. International travel is not a necessity, but a luxury activity to many. Scanning international travel patterns, one can easily discern that most international travel volumes originate in economically advanced regions, such as Europe and North America (Table 2.1). Emerging economies with improved living standards have been steadily gaining international travel market shares, such as China, India and Mexico. Therefore, the level of economic development is a clear indicator for international hospitality companies to examine

Table 2.1 Originating markets for world tourism, 2004

Region	Outbound tourists (million)
Africa	18.2
Americas	127.7
Asia and the Pacific	151.2
Europe	431.3
Middle East	22.0
Origin not specified	12.9
World total	763.3

Source: World Tourism Organization (2005)

when they are contemplating development or expansion decisions.

The amount of leisure time citizens of a particular country enjoy also tends to determine how far or how frequently they can travel overseas. Citizens in Western European countries are known to enjoy longer leisure time each year in a combination of public holidays and paid vacations. Some European countries, such as France, Belgium and Germany, offer its citizens an estimated total of one month's leisure time a year. That is why Europe has dominated the international travel market in travel volumes (Figure 2.2).

Another revealing example of increased outbound travel influenced partly by increased leisure time, is the three one-week holidays instituted by the Chinese government in 1995 to stimulate the tourism economy in China. The institutionalization of the three one-week holidays, May Day (May 1), National Day (October 1) and the Spring Festival (determined by the Chinese lunar calendar, normally occurs in the latter part of January or the first part of February), sent millions of Chinese tourists in motion to various parts of the country as well as many other countries. More than 80 countries have been designated as having Approved Destination Status by the Chinese government and Chinese citizens are allowed to visit these countries in organized outbound tour groups (Figure 2.3a and 2.3b).

Business travelers travel to perform their jobs or to enhance professional development and networking by attending conferences. Therefore, they do not have much choice in determining the destinations to visit. However, travel motivation influences a leisure tourist's selection of an international destination. Some leisure tourists enjoy visiting cities while others like to visit natural wonders. A growing trend now is to visit ecologically developed and managed tourist attractions and stay at eco-resort or eco-lodge. Travel motivations have been shaped by two primary sources: own knowledge of the destination accumulated through years of learning, and promotions by the tourism and hospitality industry (Gunn, 1988).

A decision on travel to an international destination is therefore determined by various forces. Concerns for travel safety and security have been a primary factor for many international tourists after the 9.11 terrorist attacks and frequent bombings of transportation and lodging facilities in the world since 2001. Understanding of

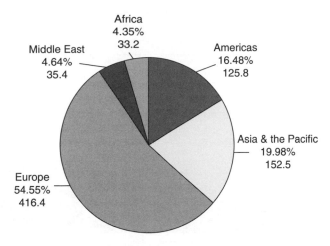

Figure 2.2   International tourist arrivals (mn) 2004
Source: World Tourism Organization (2005)

these major determinants can assist international hospitality developers to research the travel markets in a particular destination and fully understand international tourist perceptions and behaviors for developing appropriate hospitality products and services.

INTERNATIONAL HOSPITALITY DEVELOPMENT

As international travel continues to increase and the pent-up demand for domestic travel in emerging economy countries keeps surging, international hotel companies are aggressively expanding global development and operations to capture the growing global travel businesses. The motivations for global hotel expansion have been identified as (1) sales expansion, (2) geographic diversification, and (3) brand recognition.

International hotel companies are always looking for new opportunities to grow their businesses, either by responding to a new niche market, or a market segment or an entirely new market. When sales at home are

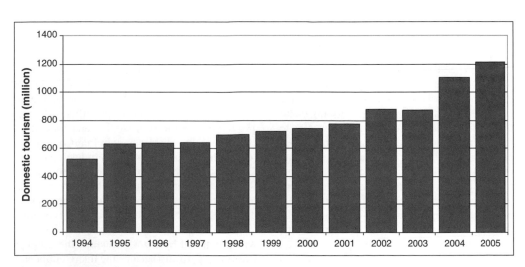

Figure 2.3(a)   Domestic tourism development in China, 1994–2005
Source: China National Tourism Administration (2006)

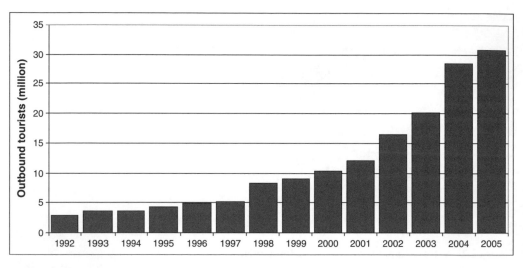

Figure 2.3(b)   China outbound tourism, 1992–2005
Source: China National Tourism Administration (2006)

flat, the pressure will be intense for corporate executives to explore new markets overseas. Therefore, sales expansion in overseas markets is normally a driving force for developing hotels in other countries. Geographic diversification is another major motivation for international hotel companies to develop hotels in other countries. In order to avoid putting all their eggs in one basket, international hotel companies diversify strategically their portfolios into many different tourism destinations. If one destination experiences an uncontrollable catastrophic event, such as the 9.11 terrorist attacks, natural disasters or SARS epidemics, the loss of sales in this destination will be compensated for by profitable operations in other destinations (Scoviak, 2004d). Therefore, geographic diversification can reduce the risk of many unforeseeable events on hotel operations in certain geographic locations. Brand development is a driving factor that motivates international hotel companies to expand into as many countries as possible. When an international hotel company develops and operates a hotel in a foreign country, it wants to serve three primary markets: its own citizens traveling in the host country, other international tourists traveling in this host country and the domestic tourists. If a tourist from the home country or a third country is loyal to a hotel brand, he or she will look for this brand in a foreign country. On the other hand, if a domestic tourist enjoys staying at the international brand

hotel, he or she may want to stay in the same brand when he or she travels overseas. Therefore, hotel brand management is crucial to developing a global loyal guest base for the international brand.

Global expansion of the hotel industry started gradually after World War II when Hilton Hotels International, Sheraton Hotels Corporation, Club Med, InterContinental Hotels, and others began to develop hotel operations in foreign countries, particularly in the Caribbean region (Ingram, 1996; Pine and Go, 1996). The pace of global hotel development has been accelerated since the latter part of the 1980s when acquisitions of major international hotel companies took place, such as the acquisition of Holiday Inns International in 1988 and the remaining Holiday Inn operations in North America in 1990 by UK-based Bass plc, a brewing company founded by William Bass in 1777 in Burton-on-Trent. At the same time, Bass Hotels and Resorts also bought InterContinental in March 1988 and later Southern Pacific Hotels Corporation and UK-based Bristol Hotels and Resorts in January 2000. It therefore became one of the leading global hotel companies in the world and stimulated increasing interest in global acquisitions and expansions. After it was purchased by Six Continents, the original Bass hotel portfolio became the InterContinental Hotels Group. Another major transaction at that time was the acquisition of Motel 6 by Accor,

Table 2.2 The most globalized hotel companies by geographic distributions

Hotel company	Number of countries represented
InterContinental Hotels Group	100
Starwood Hotels & Resorts Worldwide	95
Accor	90
Best Western International	80
Hilton Group plc	80
Carlson Hospitality Worldwide	69
Marriott International	66
Golden Tulip Hotels, Inns and Resorts	47
Wyndham Hotel Group	44
Global Hyatt	43
Choice Hotels International	42
Rezidor SAS Hospitality	41
Club Méditerranée	40
Four Seasons Hotels and Resorts	31
Sol Meliá SA	30

Source: Karyn Strauss and Mary Scoviak (2005). 'Hotels' 325 Giants', *Hotels*, July, p. 33 and company web search to reflect the most current information

a French hotel corporation, as a springboard to enter the North American lodging market. Accor has since become one of the leading global hotel corporations.

The rapid global development and strategic mergers and acquisitions by international hotel corporations have produced some highly diversified international hotel companies, both by brands and geographical distributions. Table 2.2 shows the leading global hotel companies in the world as defined by geographic distributions in most countries. The InterContinental Hotels Group was ranked the most globalized hotel company in the world, with its 3,600 properties represented in 100 countries by some of the most recognized brands in the travel market: Holiday Inn Hotels and Resorts, Holiday Inn Express, Holiday Select, Holiday Inn SunSpree Resort, Holiday Inn Garden Court, Nicklodeon Family Suites by Holiday Inn, Staybridge Suites, Crowne Plaza, Candlewood Suites, Hotel Indigo and InterContinental Hotels and Resorts.

Starwood Hotels and Resorts' rise to the top ranks of international hotel companies can be attributed to its strategic acquisition of Sheraton Hotels and Westin Hotels and Resorts in the mid 1990s and Le Meridien Hotels and Resorts in 2005. As one of the leading global hotel companies, Starwood Hotels and Resorts had 850 properties in its portfolio in 95 countries by 2005. The company owns, manages, franchises, leases hotels globally and operates joint venture hotels. The brands include: the St. Regis Hotels and Resorts, Sheraton Hotels, Fourpoints by Sheraton, Westin Hotels and Resorts, W Hotels, Le Meridien Hotels and Resorts and the Luxury Collection – a collection of 40 luxury hotels under their individually recognized names in many countries, such as the Hacienda Uayamon in Mexico, the L'Amphitrite Palace in Skhirat, Morocco and Hotel Kamp in Helsinki, Finland. Its newest brand, *aloft*, was designed to serve the mid-market segment.

The French hotel company, Accor, pursues a brand and geographic differentiation strategy to cater to every market segment of international travel. It is interesting to note that Accor's budget hotels make up 55% of the company's total portfolio and these properties include: Formula 1, Motel 6, Etap Hotel, Red Roof Inns and Ibis. The mid-market products by Accor are Suitehotel, Mercure and Novotel, accounting for 37% of the company's total hotel inventory. Sofitel is Accor's luxury brand and makes up 8% of the total hotel portfolio. Accor made an aggressive acquisition of a 28.9% stake in Club Med in 2004 and this acquisition greatly enhanced Accor's position in the resort segment and continues to keep its leading global position. As for global sales, the bulk of Accor's business came from Europe and North America: 65% and 22% respectively. The rest of the world contributed 13% of the company's worldwide sales.

Best Western International, based in Phoenix, Arizona, USA, started as an informal referral organization: binding individual hotel operators together to compete with chain hotels by referring business to each other. It has now developed into a global hotel giant with individually owned and operated hotels in over 80 countries. Best Western International began its global expansion in 1964 when referral memberships were sold to Canadian individual hotel operators. A key difference between Best Western International and the other top three global hotel giants is that Best Western International does not own any hotels. It provides member hotels with marketing, reservation and quality management services through its 30 international affiliate offices and property-direct relationships within four regions.

Since the split of the Hilton Hotel Corporation into two entities in 1964, the UK-based Hilton International has been developing branded Hilton hotels worldwide except for North

Table 2.3   Hotel brands by Marriott International

Brand	Service level	Total property	Number of property in other countries
Marriott Hotels and Resorts	Upscale	482	170
JW Marriott Hotels and Resorts	Luxury	20	12
The Ritz-Carlton Hotel	Luxury	57	22
The Ritz-Carlton Club	Luxury private residence in resort destinations	5	1
Renaissance Hotels and Resorts	Upscale	130	66
Courtyard by Marriott	Mid-market	638	55
Residence Inn	Mid-market	454	13
Fairfield Inn	Economy	530	3
Towne Place Suites	Mid-market extended stay	112	–
Spring Hill Suites	Mid-market all-suite	116	1
Marriott Vacation Club International	Luxury vacation ownership resort	52	8
Horizons	Mid-market vacation ownership resort	2	–
Marriott Conference Centers	Small to mid-sized conference facilities	13	–
ExecuStay	Corporate housing	37	–
Executive Apartment	Corporate housing	14	13
Grand Residence Club	Fractional property ownership	2	1

Source: Compiled from published information on the website of Marriott International. Retrieved March 31, 2006, from http://marriott.com/corporateinfo/glance.mi?WT_Ref=mi_left#brand0

America while the Beverly Hills-based Hilton Hotels Corporation has been primarily focusing on development expansion in North America. However, the $5.7 billion acquisition of the Hilton Group plc by Hilton Hotels Corporation in early 2006 reunited these two Hilton companies. The combined Hilton family of hotels greatly enhanced the global expansion of Hilton and Conrad brands and other brands in the portfolio: the mid-market Scandic brand, Doubletree, Embassy Suites Hotels, Hampton Inns and Suites, Hilton Garden Inn and Homewood Suites by Hilton and Hilton International Grand Vacations Club.

Carlson Hospitality Worldwide is a conglomerate of hospitality products and services, which includes lodging, food services (TGI Fridays), travel agency (Carlson Wagonlit Travel), cruises (Seven Sea Cruises), destination marketing services (CDMS) and other marketing and consulting services (Pepper and Rogers Group and Carlson Marketing Group). Its lodging operations include branded properties such as Radisson Hotels and Resorts, Park Inn, Country Inns and Suites, Park Plaza Hotels and Resorts, and Regent International Hotels.

Since its corporate strategic reorganization in the early 1990s, Marriott International has become one of the major global hotel operators in a relatively short period of time. The success of Marriott International could be attributed to the company's strategic vision and prudent acquisition of the Renaissance Hotels and Resorts, Ramada International Hotels and Resorts, and the Ritz-Carlton Hotel Company in the mid 1990s. Marriott International is now one of the most diversified global hotel companies and its tiered product brands clearly reflect market strategy for capturing travel businesses in all market segments (Table 2.3).

Based in Armersfoort, the Netherlands, Golden Tulip Hotels, Inns and Resorts formed strategic alliances with the German Top International Hotels to become the Golden Tulip Top Hospitality Group developing and operating hotels in Europe, the Middle East, Asia and the Pacific, the Americas and Africa. Golden Tulip offers two brands that focus on implementing international standards while maintaining local characteristics: Golden Tulip – upscale business and resort hotels and Tulip Inn – mid-market segment. Golden Tulip is a hospitality franchise company.

Wyndham and Choice Hotels International share two similar characteristics in their global expansion: (1) only through franchise development and (2) focus on mid-market and budget market segments. Wyndham is the largest hotel franchisor controlling 10% of the hotel supply in the USA. Its nine brands include: Wyndham, Ramada, Days Inn, Supper 8 Motel, Windgate Inn, Howard Johnson, Travelodge, AmeriHost

Inn and Knights Inn. The hospitality company franchising these brands is named Wyndham Worldwide to reflect its global expansion strategy. A significant portion of Choice Hotels International's growth in the last few years came from international development, a 56% increase in properties by franchising was attributed to overseas growth since 2000. Choice only franchises four of its nine brands in other countries: Comfort Inn, Quality, Sleep Inn and Clarion (the other five brands are Comfort Suites, Mainstay Suites, Econo Lodge, Rodeway Inn, and Cambria Suites). Clearly, Choice's strategy is to build its global operations around these four brands in the major global travel markets. Its newest brand, Cambria Suites, was developed to capture the low end of the upscale market in the USA.

Other global hotel companies in Table 2.2 are also highly recognized brands in the world. The Paris-based Club Méditerranée (28.9% of the company was acquired by Accor in late 2004), the Chicago-based Global Hyatt and the Toronto-based Four Seasons Hotels and Resorts are all world-class hospitality companies that offer highly personalized services to international travelers (Selwitz, 2002). Club Med primarily targets leisure and vacation tourists while Global Hyatt and Four Seasons attract business travelers as well as leisure tourists. The Rezidor SAS Hospitality, a wholly owned subsidiary of the Scandinavia Airlines System, grew from a regional hotel company to a global giant. It also formed a strategic alliance with Radisson Hotels, the Radisson SAS Hotels and Resorts in Europe. It offers multiple brands and owns, franchises, manages, and leases hotels. Based in Palma de Mallorca, Spain, Sol Meliá SA has been focusing its strategy for global expansion in Spanish-speaking countries. It offers five brands in its portfolio: Meliá Hotels, Sol Hotels, Paradisus Resorts, Tryp Hotels and Hard Rock Hotels. Sol Meliá's entry to the USA was the Hard Rock Hotel Chicago in 2003.

In addition to these leading global hotel companies by geographic distribution, there are also many competitive regional hotel companies and fast growing global companies. The Berlin-based Kempinski Hotels and Resorts is one of the oldest hotel companies in the world and operates hotels in more than 20 countries. The Malta-based Corinthia Hotels International operates international hotels through mainly management contract services. The South Africa-based Sun International is a hotel, resort and casino operator in Africa. It operates both hotels and casinos in several African countries and contributes significantly to the economies of these developing countries. The Hong Kong-based Shangri-La Hotels and Resorts is a well-known brand in Asia and the Pacific and the Middle East. Its first entry into the US lodging market is the Shangri-La Hotel in the Westview Tower in downtown Chicago, a mixed-use complex of luxury condominiums, penthouse residences and hotel condominiums. Another Hong Kong-based growing global hotel company, the Mandarin Oriental Hotel Group, has been aggressively developing hotels in the USA. It has opened three new hotels in the USA (Mandarin Oriental Miami, Mandarin Oriental New York and Mandarin Oriental Washington, DC) in the last few years and has acquired one boutique hotel in New York City, The Mark. New properties have been planned for Boston, Chicago, Las Vegas and Mexico. Dubai-based Jumeirah and India's Taj Hotels, Resorts and Palaces have both developed management contracts in the USA. Alila Hotels and Resorts, Six Senses Hotel, Resorts and Spas (with Soneva and Evason brands), and Banyan Tree Hotels and Resorts are all fast growing regional hotel developers and managers specializing in stylish design and quality personal services.

MARKET ENTRY STRATEGY

As international hotel companies consider overseas development expansion, one of the key decisions they have to make is to determine a market entry strategy for a particular country. Due to the differences in political, economic, social, legal and cultural systems, international hotel companies have to choose the most effective entry mode that can reduce investment risk and augment expected returns on their investment. Market entry choice is defined as an institutional arrangement for organizing and conducting international hospitality management operations in a foreign country. Six market entry choices are identified for expansion into other countries by international hospitality companies:

- sole ownership;
- joint-ventures;
- franchise;

- management contract;
- strategic alliance; and
- consortia.

The selection of a strategic market entry choice has a great impact on the future success of hotel operations in the host country (Roper, Brookes, Price and Hampton, 1999). Each of the six market entry choices has its advantages and disadvantages compared to the host market environment, partners in the host country, international developer/owner's expected returns and the level of their risk tolerance. A comparative analysis of these market entry choices can reveal the pros and cons of each strategy and aid decision making for international expansion.

Sole ownership

Sole ownership refers to the complete (100%) control of the hotel assets and therefore the complete control of management operations. A sole ownership can be acquired by investing the entire equity required for a new hotel project, or by acquiring 100% ownership of an existing hotel property or the entire company in the host country. A sole ownership thus gives the owner complete control of hospitality business decision-making and allows the owner to keep all the profits from operations because there are no other partners to share decision making and split the profits. However, investing in a new hotel project requires a lot of capital for building and furnishing the physical property, and then financing the operations of the hotel in the initial 3–5 years before the hotel turns in any profits. If any unforeseeable or uncontrollable events occur in the host country that have an adverse effect on the hotel industry, such as terrorist attacks or naturalization of foreign assets, the owner of the hotel is thus exposed to the loss of operating revenues for a certain period of time or the confiscation of the assets. Therefore, sole ownership allows the owner to have complete control of management decisions and receive 100% of the profits, but also exposes the owner to any potential political, economic and market risks.

Most international hotel companies do not own many of their overseas properties because of the tremendous outlay of capital investment and the concerns for investment risk in the host country, particularly countries with low political, economic and financial stability ratings.

However, there are a few regional hotel companies that own most of the properties in their portfolios, such as the Mandarin Oriental Hotels and Shangri-La Hotels and Resorts. For instance, of the 47 hotels and resorts operated by Shangri-La, most are owned by the company itself. However, the company has made a paradigm shift to consider management contracts as a new market entry strategy for international expansion to achieve its goal of doubling its current portfolio by 2008 (*Hotels*, 2004).

Joint ventures

Joint ventures are a commonly used market entry choice by international hotel companies to develop hotel business in the host country. A joint venture is a partnership of two or more developers or companies to exchange resources, share risks, and divide rewards from a joint enterprise. In this case, the partners pool their resources to develop the hotel project: the capital and the land. The international partner may commit investment capital and the local partner may contribute the land. Investment risk is therefore shared among all partners and the profits are also proportionally distributed to the partners depending on the stakes each partner has committed. Therefore, the huge outlay of initial investment is shared by all partners and the investment risk is also shouldered by all participating partners in the joint venture. Naturally, the rewards of the hotel operations are also distributed among the partners.

Joint ventures are often perceived as a win/win market entry choice for the international hotel company from a Western developed country and for the local partner in the developing country. For the international hotel company, the partnership with a reputable local hotel operator can assist the company quickly to establish its presence in the host country because the local partner knows well the local market as well as the political and social networks to effectively navigate the bureaucratic and social maze. For the local partner, the international hotel company brings to the table not only investment capital, but also the sophisticated management know-how in all areas of hotel operations. The international partner will effectively train the local managers and staff to enhance their competency in delivering international standard services. A successful joint venture is built on

Table 2.4   Hotel companies with the most franchised hotels, 2004

Company	Total hotels	Franchised hotels	% of total
Cendent Corporation (USA)	6,396	6,396	100%
Choice Hotels International (USA)	4,977	4,977	100%
InterContinental Hotels Group (UK)	3,540	2,971	84%
Hilton Hotels Corporation (USA)[1]	2,259	1,900	84%
Marriott International (USA)	2,632	1,658	63%
Accor (France)	3,973	949	24%
Carlson Hospitality Worldwide (USA)	890	864	97%
Global Hyatt (USA)	818	505	62%
Starwood Hotels and Resorts (USA)[2]	733	310	42%
Worldwide Louvre Hotels (France)	887	307	35%

[1] Data does not include the portfolios of Hilton International acquired in 2006.
[2] Data does not include the portfolios of Le Méridiem acquired in 2005.
Source: Karyn Strauss and Mary Scoviak (2005). 'Hotels' 325 Giants', *Hotels*, July, p. 33

mutual trust, the complement of each other's expertise, risk sharing and a partner in profits. Different countries have specific laws governing the development of joint venture hotel project. Some countries may restrict the international hotel company from taking the controlling stake in the joint venture project in order to protect the national interest, such as the 51%/49% split of stakes in a joint venture. This was true with the financial structure of the Euro Disney complex in France when it was first developed in the early 1990s.

Franchise agreements

Franchising is a quintessential American business idea. Franchising has two types of business models: product franchising and business format franchising (Bradach, 1998). Product franchising only involves the franchisee selling products for the product producers, such as BMW car dealerships, Shell gas stations and Coca-Cola® bottling plants. In business format franchising, the franchisor allows the franchisee to both make and sell the products by using its brand name. Hospitality franchises are defined as business format franchises because the franchisee is granted the right to use hotel or restaurant brand name, prepare the food according to standardized menus, and sell guest rooms and food to the guests. The franchisor receives in return fees for granting the franchisee to use the proven business format for the hotel or restaurant business.

Franchise agreements are now one of the commonly used market entry choices by international hotel companies to expand business operations both domestically and globally. Several large hospitality companies are only devoted to franchise business development. As discussed earlier, Choice Hotels International is one of the leading global companies that only franchises mid-market and economy segments (Table 2.4). As Table 2.4 illustrates, many leading global companies have substantial businesses in franchise development.

Franchising, as a major market entry choice, can be operationalized by deploying different strategies. For instance, Choice Hotels International has been pursuing three different franchise strategies for global growth: (1) multi-unit franchising businesses controlled by Choice; (2) management company partnerships; and (3) open-enrollment. Multi-unit franchising with the franchisor's control refers to the acquired control of a hotel organization in the host country and the transition of its portfolio to Choice-defined brand segmentation. The example is the acquired control of the largest franchisor of mid-market hotel companies, Flag organization, in Australia, in 2003 that was transformed into a revitalized Flag Choice organization. Management company partnership identifies a successful hotel company in the host country and partners with this company to develop Choice brands in the host country. The partnership between Japan's Evergreen Company and Choice in 2003 resulted in the creation of Choice Hotels Japan: a marriage of Japanese management, asset control, and market knowledge with Choice brands. Now the Comfort brand is the largest US mid-market brand in all major Japanese cities. Open enrollment refers to the solicitation of new individual franchisees in the host countries by the country or regional offices of Choice Hotels International (Choice Hotels International, 2004).

The advantage of franchising for the franchisor is the ability to grow its business rapidly without equity investment and minimize investment risk in host countries because franchisors only grant the franchisees the use of hotel brands while the franchisees in the host country have to build the hotels and operate them under each selected brand. The advantage for the franchisee is that the newly built or converted hotels can have instant name recognition in the travel market because the franchised brand has a proven successful track record. In addition, franchisees also receive operational manuals with expected levels of standards for quality services. The franchisee is provided with marketing, reservation, product procurement and continuous training services (Taylor, 2000).

Two major issues facing the franchisee and franchisor are quality control and franchisee/franchisor relationships. Due to the business format of franchised operations, hotel operations are managed by the franchisees. If the franchisees do not follow the franchisor's standards for operations or violate certain operation procedures, such poorly managed operations will affect guest satisfaction and eventually diminish the hotel brand. It is therefore crucial for the franchisors to select the hotel operators with a good track record in quality service and implement a systematic quality control program to ensure quality management and guest satisfaction. One common practice on the part of the franchisor is to establish regional or country offices to work closely with the franchisees to ensure management quality.

The second issue is the friction in franchise relations. Generally speaking, franchisees and franchisors are partners in profits. However, the two may differ on certain operational and development issues such as the impact of new development, termination, purchasing, etc. (Berg, 1999). Therefore, disagreement may occur between the two parties during the course of a franchising agreement contract (Brewer, 2003; Walsh, 2003). Mutual trust between the two parties and a certain flexibility of operations can strengthen the working relationships of the franchisee and franchisor (Bhakta, 2003).

Management contracts

The hotel industry involves two kinds of businesses: real estate investment and hotel operations. Many hotel owners get into the hotel business as investors in real estate properties. These owners have no expertise and experience in managing hotels as a business or even interest in operating the hotels. Therefore they turn to professional hotel management companies for assistance and pay them a share of the operating revenues for their services (Eyster, 1997). The popularity of management contract services has been on the rise in the last decade and most hotel companies offer management contract services to individual or institutional hotel investors (Table 2.5).

As Table 2.5 illustrates, five of the leading global companies were also ranked as hotel companies that managed the most hotels for other owners. It is also interesting to note that some hotel companies only provide management contract services, such as Extended

Table 2.5   Hotel companies that managed the most hotels, 2004

Company	Total hotels	Hotels managed	% of total
Marriott International (USA)	2,632	889	34%
Extended Stay of America (USA)	650	650	100%
Accor (France)	3,973	535	13%
InterContinental Hotels Group (UK)	3,540	403	11%
Tharaldson Enterprises (USA)	360	360	100%
Global Hyatt (USA)	818	316	39%
Interstate Hotels and Resorts (USA)	306	306	100%
Starwood Hotels and Resorts Worldwide (USA)[1]	733	283	39%
Hilton Hotels Corporation (USA)[2]	2,259	206	9%
Worldwide Louvre Hotels (France)	887	227	26%

[1] Data does not include the portfolios of Le Meridien acquired in 2005.
[2] Data does not include the portfolios of Hilton International acquired in 2006.
Source: Karyn Strauss and Mary Scoviak (2005). 'Hotels' 325 Giants', *Hotels*, July, p. 33

Stay of America, Tharaldson Enterprises, and Interstate Hotels and Resorts. Management contract services have been used as a global expansion strategy by most hotel companies. The advantage of developing a management contract service is to expand its global operations rapidly without committing equity investment and reduce business risk in the host country.

The provisions of management contracts vary from company to company. However, the contract length normally lasts from 15 to 25 years. The owner is responsible for financing the operations and the manager is responsible for managing the daily operations. The management fee is 4–6% of the total revenues of sales. To reward good performance by the management, the owner often gives an incentive fee to the management by allocating a small percentage of the income before income taxes and amortization (Scoviak, 2004a). Therefore efficient management performance in revenue generating and cost control is rewarded by the incentive fee.

Owners in the host countries, particularly the developing countries, often consider management contracts as knowledge transfer in the service industry. Hotel management by a team of specialized managers from internationally known hotel companies can improve the competency of the local managers and staff to meet international service standards. In addition, the management team brings with them an established management system, such as cost control, marketing, human resources development and technology applications in hotel operations. The local managers and staff can benefit from systematic training programs and learn from experienced global managers how to operate an international standard hotel.

Strategic alliances

Strategic alliance refers to a partnership between two hotel companies in different countries to jointly market their hotels in each country and respective region, and refer guests to each other's properties. Such strategic partnerships allow hotel companies that do not have immediate resources to develop hotels in other countries and to work with a partner for marketing and reservation cooperation (Chathoth and Olsen, 2003). In 2000, Le Meridien formed a global partnership with Nikko Hotels International for marketing and reservation alliance. Le Meridien has its strategic strength in Europe. However, its presence in Japan and other parts of Asia and the Pacific had not been to the level the company wanted it to be. Therefore, Le Meridien sought Nikko Hotels International to launch the strategic alliance because most of the 40 hotels operated by Nikko Hotels International, a subsidiary of Japan Airlines, are located in Japan and other parts of Asia and the Pacific. This strategic alliance gave Le Meridien's guests immediate access to many destinations in Japan and other parts of Asia by staying at Nikko's properties. On the other hand, Nikko would reciprocate by referring its guests to Le Meridien in Europe. This partnership seems to be a natural one since both started out as a subsidiary of an airline company and both serve luxury and upscale markets. The marriage of European and Asian hospitality greatly enhanced the global competitive advantage of the two companies.

Consortia

Consortia as a form of a hotel organization have developed from the original hotel referral or membership groups. As a referral organization, individual hotels band together to compete with large chain hotels by pooling resources for marketing and guest referral through membership directories and reservation systems. Today consortia organizations have outgrown the original functions of marketing and reservations and encompass organizations that provide hospitality technology, such as Unirez, soft brands such as SRS-WORLDHOTELS, and marketing and representation service providers such as Vantis owned by TravelClick and Pegasus Solution's Utell. Table 2.6 lists the top 20 consortia organizations in 2004.

After a decade of rapid growth, mergers and acquisitions, hotel consortia organizations have now been recognized as an effective provider of sales, reservations and technological applications for small, individual hotel owners and operators. Individual hotel operators are attracted by the flexibility offered by the consortia organizations to receive marketing, reservation and technological assistance while maintaining its own hotel name and autonomy of operations, the key difference between franchising and consortia.

Table 2.6   Top 20 consortia organizations in the world, 2004

Company	Location	Rooms	Hotels	Service
Utell/Unirez-Pegasus Solutions' Rep. Services	Dallas, Texas, USA	1,050,091	7,487	Reservations Marketing Property management systems Commission processing
SynXis Corporation	McLean, Virginia, USA	720,000	6,500	Reservations Marketing Account and revenue management Commission processing
Vantis /TravelClick	Calgary, Alberta, Canada	615,840	5,493	Reservations Marketing Channel management
Supranational Hotels	London, UK	257,000	1,692	Reservations Marketing Representation Technology solutions
InnPoints Worldwide	Albuquerque, New Mexico, USA	145,936	1,066	Reservations Marketing Technology solutions
Hotusa-Eurostars-Familia Hotels	Barcelona, Spain	118,861	1,439	Reservations Marketing
WORLDHOTELS	Frankfurt am Main, Germany	100,000	500	Reservations Marketing Representation
Keytel, SA	Barcelona, Spain	92,000	1,150	Reservations Marketing Representation
Leading Hotels of the World	New York, NY, USA	83,000	420	Reservations Marketing Representation
Logis de France	Paris, France	66,881	3,517	Reservations Marketing Representation
Preferred Hotel Group	Chicago, Illinois, USA	56,726	285	Reservations Marketing Channel management Revenue management
Associated Luxury Hotels	Washington, DC, USA	48,280	86	Reservations Marketing Meeting planning
Historic Hotels of America	Washington, DC, USA	37,745	213	Reservations Marketing Education Community building
AHMI-RES Hotels (Thed International)	Paris, France	34,308	178	Reservations Market analysis Project financing Short-term (3–5 year) management
Sceptre Hospitality Resources (SWAN)	Englewood, Colorado, USA	30,732	140	Reservations Marketing Channel management Revenue management Design
Great Hotels Organization	London, UK	27,252	168	Reservations Marketing Representation

Table 2.6   cont'd

Company	Location	Rooms	Hotels	Service
Minotel International	Lausanne, Switzerland	25,500	591	Reservations Marketing Representation Purchasing
Small Luxury Hotels of the World	Surrey, UK	17,250	329	Reservations Marketing Representation
Selected Hotels for Business, Congresses and Incentives	Marbella, Spain	17,000	62	Reservations Marketing Representation
ILA-Châteaux and Hôtels de Charme	Brussels, Belgium	15,253	325	Reservations Marketing Representation

Source: Karyn Strauss and Mary Scoviak (2005). 'Seminal Times for Consortia', *Hotels*, July, p. 53

Choosing market entry strategy

Appropriate market entry choice is crucial to the success of subsequent operations in the host country. The choice depends on the company's strategic mission in developing global business in the host country or the region. Generally, a hotel company needs to consider three key factors in deciding which entry choice to use: operational control, resource commitment and risk tolerance. If a company wants to have greater control of the operations in the host country it has to commit a greater investment stake and be willing to tolerate a higher level of risk. If it is not willing to do this then sole ownership in building a new property or acquisition of existing properties will not be the right choice. If a company can tolerate a moderate level of risk and is willing to share operational control with a partner or partners, then joint ventures can be an effective entry strategy for sharing the investment risk. If a company wants to have a high degree of operational control for service standards and quality, but is risk averse and unwilling to commit investment equity, franchise agreements and management contracts are the two appropriate market entry choices. Finally, if a company does not want to have any operational control and has a minimum tolerance for financial risk, strategic alliances and/or consortia affiliation may serve as appropriate market entry strategies.

INTERNATIONAL HOTEL MANAGEMENT OPERATIONS

Once a hotel company has established its operations in the host country, it has to deal with a complex environment of political, commercial, legal, and socio-cultural systems in the host country in order to operate a profitable business. Therefore management operation standards cannot be simply transferred from the home office to the host country as some may not apply directly to management operations there. Successful global hotel companies determine how their products and services can best fit the market needs in the host country and then modify the products and services to satisfy guest needs through quality service. Hotel operations in a global environment are analyzed in this section with a focus on the management functions of marketing, human resources development, managing cultural diversity, and hotel financing for international development.

International hotel marketing

International hotel marketing has always been a complex and challenging task for marketing executives. They have to design marketing campaigns that target local, regional and global markets to promote business for each of its brands. Normally, each brand has a marketing team that focuses on enhancing consumer awareness and performance while differentiating each brand from the competition. Most global hotel companies typically perform the following sales and marketing programs to build strong brand loyalty and guest satisfaction:

- global sales and marketing programs;
- global distribution channels;
- global brand standards;
- global loyalty program; and
- global marketing partnership.

Global sales and marketing programs focus on brand recognition and guest satisfaction assurance through advertising and other public relations announcements. For instance, InterContinental Hotels Group employs over 85 marketing professionals worldwide and they promote each different brand within different regions. Such an organizational structure encourages localized sales and marketing programs for the properties. Marketing teams for each brand develop strategic marketing programs for local, regional, national and international promotions and they work in conjunction with the regional sales force to maximize efficiencies while maintaining a focus on strong marketing results. Choice Hotels International promotes '100% Guest Satisfaction Guarantee' and 'Best Choice e-Rate Guarantee' programs to attract international visitors to its properties in different countries. Demographically, more attention has been placed on targeting Generation X, or Gen X, by using engagement marketing – marketing activities that show product authenticity to potential customers, such as having a pajama party to introduce the new beds at Marriott hotels in Malaysia and Australia and distributing branded gloves around Manhattan by Club Med (Strauss and Gale, 2006). Podcast marketing has been recognized by many international hotel companies as an effective marketing medium because of the increasing users of MP3 players and iPods (*Hotels*, 2006). Information on hotel features, services and promotions can be podcast for users to listen at their own convenience.

Global distribution channels are essential for hotels to sell rooms to the end users. Typically, a hotel company utilizes three major forms of distribution systems: (1) own distribution channels such as Central Reservation System (CRS), Internet Distribution System (IDS) through company websites for direct bookings by potential visitors and CRS call centers staffed by multi-lingual reservationists (Murphy, Olaru, Schegg and Frey, 2003); (2) various directories such as Worldwide Hotel Directory, e-Directory, e-Brochure, VIP Directory, Rack Card, etc.; (3) Third-Party Distribution Channels such as Global Distribution Systems (GDS), Alternative Distribution Systems (ADS), General Sales Agents (GSA) network and travel agents (Tse, 2003). All hotel companies now effectively use IDS on company websites that handle room reservations for its properties around the world, and which also has links to its global partners'

IDS (Carroll and Siguaw, 2003). Therefore, Internet savvy guests can book rooms online. Guests who feel comfortable with booking through reservationists can call the reservation centers to reserve rooms, and the call centers are now staffed by multi-lingual staff to assist inquiries and bookings from different countries. In addition, international hotel companies list their hotels in various targeted directories to reach end users, and most hotels increasingly list its products and services through online directories and brochures.

Third-party distribution channels include Global Distribution Systems (GDS), Alternative Distribution Systems (ADS), Global General Sales Agents (GSA), and travel-related websites such as Lastminute.com, Expedia.com, Ctrip, etc. (O'Connor and Frew, 2004). The GDS connects the Central Reservation Systems (CRS) of many hotel organizations and many Internet travel websites for travel agents to make reservations for their clients (O'Connor and Piccoli, 2003). Pegasus Solutions, one of the leading online channel distributors, developed an Online Distribution Database and Internet booking engine in the mid 1990s. Pegasus' GDS now has access to the CRSs of more than 60,000 hotels worldwide with detailed information on individual properties and includes many travel-related Web sites for hotel booking, such as HotelHub, ebookers.com, Lastminute.com, Hotwire and Orbitz, just to name a few. To better serve travel agents in different countries, Pegasus has provided the capability for its member hotels to start loading their hotel content in French, German, Spanish and Italian since June 2002. As the Internet continues to gain wider acceptance as a means to both shop for hotel accommodations and make hotel reservations through access to the Internet via computers, wireless phones and personal digital assistants (PDA), international hotel companies have to be effectively wired to the end users through the third party distribution systems (Frey, Schegg and Murphy, 2003). Alternative Distribution Systems refers to the web-based travel service providers, such as Lastminute.com, Expedia, Travelocity, Orbitz, CarsandHotels, PlacesToStay, HRN, TravelWeb, TravelNow, TravelHero, YahooTravel and many others. They serve as alternative hotel reservation channels for many Internet users (Scoviak, 2004b).

General Sales Agents (GSA) Network refers to specialized hotel sales companies in the host country that market the international hotels in the host country. For example, Pernas Hotel Management (PHM), the manager of Malaysia-based Mutiara Hotels and Resorts appointed two overseas General Sales Agents as an integral part of their worldwide sales network to represent PHM in different countries. The chain has six properties located in key cities and resorts in Malaysia which includes Burau Bay (Langkawi); Johor Bahru (Johor); Kuala Lumpur; Pedu Lake (Kedah); Penang and Taman Negara/National Park (Pahang). Mutiara Hotels and Resorts has been working towards developing an integrated network of sales representatives in global key markets. The company negotiated a mutually beneficial arrangement with a leading UK marketing representative, Five Continents, to represent Mutiara Hotels and Resorts in England, Scotland, Wales and Ireland, and brought Air Marketing Pty. Ltd. into its sales network to represent them in the Australian and New Zealand markets. The company worked with a Japanese GSA, Hotel Japan Networks, to represent and promote its properties in the Japanese markets. Clearly, a partnership with a GSA in an overseas market can be an effective marketing strategy for certain targeted markets.

Another important aspect of global marketing is internal maintenance of brand standards through brand management. Each brand operated by international hotel organizations or individual hotels in the consortia organizations have established high standards of operations and guest services. Hotel guests decide to stay in a particular hotel because they know the brand well and have certain expectations of the facilities, amenities and services. Therefore, global quality assurance programs will enable the management to review the quality of the facilities and services on a regular basis and ensure that the guests are satisfied with their stay and will then share positive word of mouth with their friends and colleagues (Cruz, 2003). Many hotel companies also recognize one property in the entire system or one property in each brand as the international hotel of the year to publicize the high quality service achieved by these individual properties and promote these award-winning properties for public relations.

Global loyalty programs are practiced by all international hotel companies. These programs are designed to reward repeat and frequent guests for staying with a particular brand or company and to strengthen customer relationship management (Geddie, DeFranco and Geddie, 2002). InterContinental Hotels Group established one of the earliest guest loyalty programs – Priority Club Rewards. The club now has over 12 million members worldwide and makes a significant contribution to the hotel's annual occupancy for various brands. Another example is the MaS Program by Sol Meliá. Every time a guest stays in a Sol Meliá hotel, the guest will automatically earn MaS points for the stay. The points are determined by the total room spending in any of the Sol Meliá hotels: each euro or dollar expenditure earns 10 points (excluding value-added tax). Points can later be exchanged for free stay in the Sol Meliá hotel of the guests choice when they reach a specific level. The points can also be redeemed for other benefits such as airline mileages, rental car discounts and membership points of credit card services.

Global marketing partnerships include a broad marketing cooperation with various business organizations that can promote business for the hotel company. These business organizations include Internet companies, merchandisers, airlines, car rental companies and food service establishments, and other strategic partner hotels, such as the sales alliances between Le Meridien and Nikko Hotels International. These marketing alliances can benefit the international hotels to increase sales more effectively through more channels.

International hotel human resources development

Human resources development for international operations is one of the challenging management issues facing global hotel companies (Dwyer, Teal, Kemp and Wah, 2000). As global expansion accelerates, most hotel companies are now operating hotels in many countries with thousands of employees from various cultural backgrounds and religious beliefs. The challenge is to align unit operations with corporate mission and culture through knowledge transfer while maintaining the unique characteristics of each local property (Antonis, 2000; Garcia-Almeida, Bolivar-Cruz and Garcia-Falcón, 2004; Hope, 2004). Two levels of human resources are critical to successful hotel operations in the host countries: management professionals and service employees. This section focuses on the development of these two levels of human resources for international hotel operations.

Every global hotel company has a clear strategy for attracting, developing and keeping managers and service employees. Hotel companies tend to deploy one of two approaches to selecting executive and mid-level managerial positions: the ethnocentric approach and the geocentric approach. The ethnocentric approach is to identify and recruit managers for overseas operations within the hotel organization in the home country. The advantage of this approach is to maintain a unified corporate culture worldwide. However the disadvantage of this approach has been the adaptation ability of the home-country managers in the host countries. Some managers from the home country may not be able to adapt effectively to the local cultural and business environment and their adaptation may directly affect their effective management operations. The geocentric approach is to seek competent managers within and outside its own hotel organization in the home country, the host country and a third country. This approach increases the pool of management talent for international operations and enables the corporate recruiters to find managers who have management experience in the host country. However, one of the major concerns of this approach is that the selected managers, if from other hotel organizations, need to be trained to align local operations with corporate mission and culture.

The development of expatriate managers is therefore an important issue for human resources executives of global hotel companies. Global hotel companies have developed a blended approach in recruiting and training managers for overseas assignment. They have developed systematic selection and training programs for the expatriate managers as well as their spouses. The pre-departure training program emphasizes both management functions and cultural adaptation challenges. Expatriate managers are briefed by their colleagues who have been managing hotels in the target country and are given guidance on effective management in the host country. Great efforts are made to introduce the expatriate managers to the local cultural and business systems so they can familiarize themselves with the local ways of doing business and reduce any cultural shock when they enter the host country (Magnini and Honeycutt, 2003).

Each hotel organization regards its frontline service employees as providers of superior guest service experience. Such superior service can only be performed by well-trained and competent employees who believe in the corporate service culture (Agut, Grau and Perio, 2003). However, many global hotel companies have identified training as one of the major challenges when entering any new market because of cultural differences, language barriers and different attitudes toward service. For instance, when Four Seasons first entered Indonesia in 1992, the company received 10,000 applications for 580 positions in the Bali resort. However, most applicants spoke very little English and had limited knowledge of Western culture and food. The hotel company realized immediately that their corporate training program would not work in developing countries, and a new Self Access Learning Center program was developed to address the training needs in non-Western markets. These Self Access Learning Centers were initially developed for teaching service employees English, but they are now expanded as language and cultural learning centers equipped with books, magazines, computers and videos for employees to study English and Western culture. New employees study at their own pace and progress through five levels of training modules. An award is given to employees who have completed each level of study. Expatriate managers also use the Self Access Learning Center to learn the language and culture of the host country or learn the language of a country whose tourists frequent the hotel. The Self Access Learning Center, is now a mandatory facility for any new Four Seasons property in a non-Western market and plays an effective role in developing service employees' competency of language skills and knowledge of service culture as well as expatriate managers' language skills of the host country.

Many global hotel companies have been transforming their organizations into learning organizations by providing academic education opportunities for different levels of management and service employees (Bayraktaroglu and Kutanis, 2003). The Berlin-based Kempinski Hotels and Resorts has developed through partnerships with universities a series of business education programs for its management professionals. These academic programs include: (1) New Potential Program, (2) Certificate in Business Administration focusing on Global Management and (3) Executive MBA program. The New Potential Program is a partnership between Kempinski and the Reims Management School in France to identify 15 students in the management school annually who show an interest in pursuing a career in international hospitality management. These 15 students are thus selected as potential candidates for professional positions in Kempinski upon graduation. The Certificate in Business Administration (CBA) is also offered by the Reims Management School and the focus is on the Global Manager Program (GMP). The participants are prepared for the managerial responsibilities and challenges of Kempinski's global development. It is based on a three-week program with six learning modules and can be taken as a part-time study. The subjects include service marketing strategies, hotel financial management, information technology, performance development, human resources management and strategic management in the hospitality industry. The objective of the program is to shape its managers to develop an international perspective in hotel management. The program offers the participants a chance to experience the challenges which hotel managers face today: global competition, changing markets, complex social forces and technological changes that have been reshaping today's hospitality business environment through case studies and team work. The highest level of education program offered by Kempinski is the European Executive MBA (EEMBA) program as the company strongly believes that the MBA program is a unique opportunity for its unit executive committee members to enhance their leadership skills, analytical and problem-solving ability. Part of the credits from the CBA program are accepted for the EEMBA program. Through the relevance and efficiency of this program, the executive level managers are able to turn their experiences into transferable knowledge and to develop a clear view of their professional assets. The learning methods of the EEMBA program focus on problem solving, methodology and quality management. The lectures and work sequences challenge the participants to be confronted with critical and realistic situations. This degree enables executive managers to take on higher management responsibilities.

Managing cultural diversity

Managing cultural diversity is a very important function in international hotel operations. Job behaviors and perceptions of managers and service employees are conditioned by their own cultural values and beliefs (Ng and Pine, 2003). Since the hotel business is people-oriented, international hotel managers have to manage, interact, negotiate, and compromise with people of different cultural backgrounds (Sharpley and Forster, 2003; Wood, 2003). They also need to learn and understand the culture of the guests in order to provide superior personal services. Ignorance or misunderstanding of the cultural values of the local managers and staff will negatively affect the effectiveness of international managers' operations or even lead to expatriate failure. However, when mutually understood and sensitively managed, differences in culture can lead to innovations in business practices and sustainable sources of competitive advantage (Yu, 1999).

To understand the culture of a given society and its influence on business decision and management, one needs to first define the concept of culture. Culture refers to the ways of living built up by a group of people in a geographic area and passed on from one generation to another. Clearly, culture is learned after one is born and cultural learning occurs at home, school, religious institutions and in other public or social environment. Culture is shared by members of the same ethnic, social or religious group as they speak the same language and follow the same religious belief. In order to be accepted by the host society, one needs to make a conscious effort to respect and learn the host culture. Different aspects of culture are interrelated in a given society because one aspect of culture can directly affect other aspects of the culture, such as religious belief dictates diet in many cultures.

The essence of a culture is its value system, upon which a society's norms are established and justified (Hill, 1994). Values are the beliefs a society holds in regard to right and wrong, good and bad, ethical or unethical. These beliefs constitute a society's attitudes toward many business management issues such as entrepreneurship, work ethics, loyalty, individualism, honesty, and so forth (Jogaratnam and Tse, 2004). International hotel managers therefore need to understand the host cultural values that influence host managers and employees' perceptions and behaviors in the workplace. These perceptions and behaviors are normally reflected in superior and subordinate relationships, loyalty and mobility, work ethics, individual achievement and team work. A good understanding of these perceptions and behaviors as influenced by the host cultural values will enhance the international hotel manager's cultural sensitivity toward cultural diversity management.

Cross-cultural communications

Effective communications are essential in hotel management operations as managers have to work with employees, guests, suppliers and other contacts on a daily basis. Communication skills in a cross-cultural environment require not only spoken and written language of the host country, but also the silent language, nonverbal and non-written forms such as body language, perception of space, colors and numbers. Expatriate managers who have a command of the spoken and written language of the host country can communicate and interact effectively with the local managers and employees. Local managers and employees will feel closer to the expatriate managers since there is no language barrier between them. Expatriate managers who rely on interpreters to communicate with local managers and employees may feel the lack of spontaneity of interpersonal interaction. In addition, the quality of translation may also affect the mutual understanding between the expatriate managers and their local staff. Therefore, a working knowledge of the host language can enable the expatriate managers to adapt into the local culture environment and manage the operations effectively.

A knowledge of the written language of the host country is also important for expatriate managers to run effective operations. Written language is usually harder to acquire as the writing symbols differ from the phonetic pronunciations in many language systems. Expatriate managers have to ensure the truthful translation of hotel marketing materials, service directory and other collateral materials from the host language to standard English. Mistranslation can cause humorous, offensive, or unexpected situations.

Silent language refers to the transmission of cultural meanings that are not expressed by spoken or written language (Hall, 1973). It encompasses body language, such as eye contact, touching, facial expressions, and hand gestures and motions; and the cultural perceptions of time, personal space, color and numerology. As discussed earlier, these behaviors and perceptions are conditioned by the cultural values of a given society and they are expressed in a subtle manner. However, these body languages and perceptions convey clear cultural meanings and the expatriate managers need to have the cultural knowledge to decipher the hidden cultural meanings embedded in a shy smile, or a nod. The following is a description of some commonly observed body languages and perceptions that convey cultural meanings.

Eye contact is one body language that carries cultural meanings. People in Western culture tend to maintain moderate eye contact when they talk to each other to show interest in the conversation and not appear to be intrusive. However, Arabs in the Middle East keep a direct and intense eye contact with the person they speak to as they believe the eyes are the window of the soul. The Japanese are, to the contrary, taught at a young age to show respect by not looking into the eyes of teachers or elders. Minimal eye contact is a normal behavior in Japan and other countries in East Asia. Clearly, eye contact as body language varies from culture to culture in the world and understanding of such behavior will enable managers to respect the local people.

People in different cultures like to embrace or touch each other to show love, affection or praise for a job done well. In Western culture, it is perfectly normal to pat a colleague on the back for achieving outstanding job performance. However, touching is a sensitive issue in many other cultures as certain parts of the body cannot be touched, such as the head or shoulders. It is impolite to touch Arabs and North Africans with the left hand because the left hand is considered unclean, or the 'toilet hand'. One has to apologize if one's foot or shoe touches an Indian host since the feet are considered dirty. It is generally advised that touching should be minimized when meeting or managing people from different cultures. Inappropriate touching can cause serious misunderstanding that may result in embarrassment or offending the local people.

Facial expressions show people's emotions. However, a smile may not always mean happiness, joy or excitement in different cultures. It can express different emotions in different societies, such as praise, embarrassment or anger. It is also interesting to note that people in some cultures appear to be more expressive and lively, such as the Arabs and Latin Americans, while in others they tend to be more reserved, such as the East Asians. Correct reading of the facial expressions can thus enable the international hotel manager to better understand the cultural meaning of this body language and effectively communicate with the local staff. The motion of the hand also signals hidden cultural meanings in most societies. The gesturing of one's figure or arms may have different cultural meanings to people from different cultures. It is vitally important to avoid using gestures that will cause misunderstanding by people in different cultures.

The perception of time varies from culture to culture and two types of time are generalized in the world: monochromic time and polychromic time (Hall, 1973). The monochromic time concept views time in a linear way: once time passes, it is gone forever. People who value monochromic time organize time into segments and do only one thing at a time. Making an appointment for a business meeting, setting deadlines for project completion, punctuality for scheduled meetings and events are highly valued in a monochromic time culture. The polychromic time concept perceives time in a circle: time travels in a cyclical way and it always comes back as experienced in day and night and the cycle of four seasons. People who use polychromic time tend to do several things at the same time and do not organize time as rigidly as their counterparts do in the monochromic culture.

Personal space refers to the distance between two persons when they speak to each other. People in the Middle East, Latin America and South Europe keep a close distance when they talk to each other. The speaking distance in North America and Western Europe is considered moderate. However, people in East Asia tend to keep a longer distance between two people speaking to each other. Therefore, keeping an appropriate speaking distance can show one's respect for the local culture and make the local person feel comfortable.

People in different cultures have preferences for certain colors and numbers as they signify certain psychological and cultural meanings of happiness, joy, fortune or luck. Since colors and numbers are used in hotel decorations and numbering the floors and rooms, it is essential to know the cultural preference of the colors and numbers in interior decorations, hotel design and room assignment. For instance, the number four is always absent in Japanese

hotels: no fourth floor and no rooms numbered with four. This is because the number four sounds the same as the word 'death' in Japanese, therefore this number is avoided in the Japanese culture because of its negative connotation. In East Asia, particularly in Chinese culture, *feng shui* (geomancy) also has influence on hotel site selection, building orientation and hotel decoration. An ideal location and appropriate orientation are believed to bring prosperity to the hotel. Conversely, if the location and orientation are not perfect, certain corrections in internal design and decorations have to be made to the physical building to reduce the chance of mishaps in operations. The grand opening of the Mandarin Oriental Hotel Washington, DC included a *feng shui* ceremony performed by a local *feng shui* master. Every guest to this hotel receives a little booklet of *Feng Shui, the Art of Living*, when he or she checks into the hotel.

Culture clearly plays a vitally important role in influencing peoples' perceptions and behaviors in work and in everyday life. Attempts have been made to generalize different cultures in the world such as the low-context culture and the high context-culture by Edward Hall (1977). The low-context culture refers to the Western culture which emphasizes explicit communication and written contract in business management. The high-context culture refers to the cultures that value kinship, familial and personal ties, and depend extensively on nonverbal communication cues. Many countries in Asia, the Middle East, Latin America and South Europe are described as high-context culture countries. However, culture is dynamic and is ever-changing. There are also cultural sub-groups in a major cultural region. Therefore, international hotel managers need to know the cultural values and norms of the host society and adapt to the local cultural practice of business management. When international managers demonstrate their efforts in learning the host culture, respecting and appreciating local cultural practices in management operations, he or she can communicate more effectively with the local managers and staff, and develop a successful operation in the host country.

International hotel financial management

International hotel development is a capital intensive business because the building of hotel properties requires tremendous financial resources. Hotel developers also have to compete with other types of development for financial resources, such as residential real estate and office building projects. Therefore, hotel developers and financial lenders have been creative in putting together financial deals for hotel projects around the world. Generally speaking, hotel financing sources can be identified from three geographic areas: the home country, the host country and a third country. Financing from the home country is generally difficult to obtain, particularly if the project is in a developing country with a high risk premium. Finding financial resources for hotel development in the host country can also be a challenging task, especially when the foreign exchange rate of the host country's currency has been strengthening against that of the home currency. The appreciation of euros against the dollars in 2003 and 2004 made investment in Europe by US companies more expensive because more units of dollars were required to acquire the same units of euros. Conversely, the weakening of the dollar against other hard currencies such as the Japanese yen and the Euro made hotel investment in the USA more attractive to international hotel investors. Financing for hotel development can also be secured from a third country even though high lending rates and fluctuating exchange rates may increase the cost of borrowing. However, many successful hotel projects are financed by borrowing equity capital from a third country.

In addition to finding financial resources from different geographic areas, many different financing instruments have been created to fund hotel projects in different countries. The commonly used financial arrangements for hotel development in North America, Europe, the Middle East, Asia and Latin America are discussed in this section. In North America, most major global hotel companies are public companies (except for Global Hyatt) and they are able to raise capital from the equity and debt markets for global expansion. Other potential investment sources include opportunity funds, public and private real estate investment trusts (REITs), multilateral funding agencies such as the International Finance Corporation (IFC), the mezzanine debt market, institutional and private equity investors. Opportunity funds are managed by real estate investment companies and many are looking for investment opportunities in the

hotel sector. For instance, the Los Angeles-based Colonial Capital is one of the leading global opportunity fund companies that invest in hotel properties. Colonial Capital is a principal investment organization with capital asset management capabilities and has a history of optimizing value. Its strategy is designed to consistently achieve attractive risk-adjusted returns by minimizing competition with other capital sources, while maximizing value through intensive post-acquisition management.

Real estate investment trusts (REITs) companies are one of the major hotel investors in North America (Adams, 2004). REITs are passive investment vehicles that raise funds for investment in mortgages and income producing properties through debt and equity gained by selling shares to the public. In the USA, REITs avoid double taxation because they are required by federal tax code to distribute at least 90% of their taxable income to shareholders annually in the form of dividends. The shareholders then in turn must pay income tax on dividends, but are not personally liable should the REIT fall. There are three different types of REITs in the USA, (1) equity REITs which own and operate income-producing real estate; (2) mortgage REITs which lend money directly to real estate owners and their operators, or indirectly through acquisition of loans or mortgage-backed securities; and (3) hybrid REITs which are companies that both own properties and make loans to owners and operators. REIT companies that invest in hotels and resorts in the USA made up 5.5% of all REIT companies in the USA by the end of 2005 (Gering, 2006). Host Marriott is an equity REIT hotel company and other major hotel REIT companies include La Salle Hotel Properties, Highland Hospitality Corporation and Sunstone Hotel Investors. All the above hotel REIT companies are publicly traded companies. There are also many private hotel REIT companies such as Apple Hospitality in the USA.

The International Finance Corporation (IFC), a member of the World Bank Group, provides financing for hotel and resort development by private companies in developing countries. The mission of IFC is to promote sustainable private sector investment in developing countries as a way to reduce poverty and improve people's lives. Therefore it provides financing to hotel and resort projects by international hotel companies as economic development to improve infrastructure and reduce poverty in developing countries. A review of the funded project descriptions on its website revealed hotel developments in many countries: Courtyard by Marriott in Port of Spain in Trinidad and Tobago, Kabul Serena Hotel by Aga Khan Development Network; a UPDC hotel in Nigeria, a six-lodge project by Bhutan Resorts Corporation Limited, safari lodges by Wilderness Safari Limited in South Africa, and so forth. Normally, IFC does not fund 100% of the hotel project but it will assist part of the investment proposed by the private companies.

Another financing vehicle is to use the mezzanine debt market to develop hotel projects. Mezzanine financing (or, perhaps more appropriately, mezzanine capital) fills the gap between the first mortgage financing, which usually has a loan-to-value ratio of between 40% and 75%, and the equity participation of the borrowing principals (which is usually no more than 10% of the cost of the project). Mezzanine financing commonly supplies financing that is equal to 50% to 90% of the cost of the project's capital structure. This type of financing can take several forms. Most commonly, it will involve extending credit to the partners or other equity holders of a borrower and take a pledge of such parties' equity interests (including the right to distributions of income), or else take a preferred equity position that is entitled to distributions (in the form of excess cash flow after debt service) ahead of the borrower's principals (Sisson, 2003). A combination loan structure may also be utilized, which combines a first mortgage loan with mezzanine financing at an aggregate loan-to-value ratio of 90–95% and contains a shared-appreciation and/or contingent feature or requires an exit fee to be paid by the borrower. Mezzanine debt financing bridges the gap between equity and senior debt and it can be a valuable tool for companies that want to boost the performance of individual assets. But it is pricey, with interest rates currently topping out at nearly 20%. It is not the best solution for a company that already has a heavy debt load. Adding mezzanine financing to a deal where money was not being invested in the asset would only serve to increase the cost of debt, which would only exacerbate an already bad situation. Some hotel companies devote 60% to 80% of capital to direct investments and the balance to mezzanine loans.

Other financing providers for hotel and resort projects come from institutional and private equity investors. Large mutual funds, pension funds and other managed financial funds may be interested in hotel and resort properties as a way to diversify their investment portfolios. The same is true with private individual investors who are interested in hotel projects as an investment strategy.

Hotel investment in Europe follows most financing practices in North America. Most major hotel companies are planning to increase their property asset disposals through sales and lease backs and more recently through sale and manage back. The major financial institutions and the private equity funds continue to invest in the hotel sector and the introduction of tax efficient Property Investment Fund structures (PIFs) stimulated investment in the hotel sector. North American hotel companies will continue to develop their brands in Europe. However, since the value of the euro has risen substantially in the first half of the 2000s, it will be too costly for North American hotels to develop new projects in Europe through equity investment and management contracts will be an effective development strategy for Europe.

The gulf region of the Middle East has attracted great interest in hotel development in the last few years. Hotel projects have been financed by individual investors, international hotel groups and government investment in tourism and hotel development. Saudi Prince Walid bin Talal has invested $400 million in Fairmont, Mövenpick and Four Seasons hotels in Lebanon, Egypt and Dubai. Fashion designer Giorgio Armani formed a join venture with Dubai-based Emaar Properties to develop a global chain of Armani luxury hotels and resorts in Dubai and other major world cities. Hilton Hotel Group and InterContinental continue to increase their presence in this region by forming joint ventures and retaining management contract service. Commitment by governments to tourism and hotel investment further assured the confidence of the private developers. Private funds will continue to be invested in mega-projects, such as the Palm in Dubai, the Wave in Muscat, the Pearl of the Gulf in Doha, and the Amwaj and Durrat Al Bahrain in Bahrain.

Financing for hotel project development is still hard to come by in Latin America despite the growing interest in resort development in the region, particularly in Mexico, Costa Rica and Brazil. Many countries in the region have higher lending interest rates and require high percent cash collateral for a maximum five-year amortization. At present, financing opportunities vary from country to country in the region. In Mexico, pension funds are now allowed to make direct investment in real estate properties, a potential source for hotel financing. REITs have been created to finance real estate development. In addition, debt is now available in US-dollar denominated markets such as Mexico City and resort markets (Scoviak, 2004d). Project finance structure, such as completion bonds, are being accepted by the federal government banks in Brazil. In most countries, one development opportunity is to convert private and family owned hotels to branded hotels.

Hotel development in Asia has been fueled by the rapid economic growth in China and India, however the Chinese banks have recently tightened their lending to the hotel sector in an effort to clean up previous bad loans to hotel projects in the last decade (Yu and Gu, 2005). Despite this there has been a growing interest by private Chinese investors and the large domestic hotel companies in hotel development. Most Asian regional hotel companies, such as Shangri-La Hotels and Resorts and Mandarin Oriental Hotel Group, will continue to expand hotel development with their own equity investment. International hotel companies will continue to seek franchise and management contract opportunities in Asia and investment competition will be intensified from resurging regional investment sources.

FUTURE DEVELOPMENTS AND CHALLENGES

International hospitality companies will continue to follow the flow of international travel by creating elegant and comfortable lodging facilities and providing memorable service experience. Future development will be determined by a myriad of factors at global, national and local levels and will be guided by the strategic direction of each global hotel organization (Luiz et al., 1995; Brown and Harris, 1997; Harrison, 2003). Organizationally, there will be continued mergers, acquisitions and strategic alliances by global hotel organizations to expand development, such as the 28.9% acquisition of Club Med by Accor and the acquisition of Hilton International by Hilton Hotel Group. Partnership between a global hotel company and a regional hotel company will be increased as many global hotels consider it as a strategic market entry choice. From a development standpoint, hotel developers will continue to focus on the following four aspects: luxury and design, smaller niche products, condotel and mid-market properties in the emerging market countries and the application of technology in hotel operations.

As global expansion intensifies, luxury hotel and resort companies compete to provide the highest level of luxury and elegance to the wealthy tourists. The Mandarin Oriental Hotel in New York and the Ikal del Mar at Riviera Maya in Mexico are just two of the latest examples. Kempinski is developing the second '7-star' hotel in Abu Dhabi to rival Dubai's Burj El-Arab in offering a luxury experience to international tourists. Clearly, the luxury brands will continue to compete by providing the ultimate luxury and elegant design, amenity and service. The sustainable development concept and strict government regulations on hotel development will influence hotel developers to closely integrate design and architecture with natural and cultural settings (Calveras, 2003). Smaller niche markets will continue to grow, particularly eco-sustainable concepts and the budget hotel sector. Eco-lodge or eco-resort is not simple lodging accommodation any more. Eco-resorts have been developed as segmented upscale brands, such as Banyan Tree and Spain's Riu Hotels and Resorts. Condotel, condo hotel, has been gaining popularity in North America as an investment opportunity for individual investors (Blank, 2004). For instance, the Westin Grand Hotel in downtown Vancouver was built as a condotel and each condominium was sold to an individual investor. Room revenue is put into a rental pool and then distributed among the owners according to a usage formula (Rushmore, 2004). Such development benefits the developers immediately as they can charge a premium for the condo units because they are under a hotel brand and the developers can exit the project once the condo units are sold to the individual investors. Condotel developers will search for potential markets worldwide. Competition for mid-market products has escalated among international hotel companies, particularly in emerging economy countries such as China and Eastern Europe (Scoviak, 2004c). International hotel companies will primarily focus on conversion of local properties through repositioning or re-branding as well as acquisition of profitable properties located in a good market. International hotel companies will continue to apply the latest technology to enhancing branded website bookings, information presentation, business communications and guest room entertainment amenities (Oliva, 2004). Le Meridien has developed a prototype of the Art + Tech hotels to combine state-of-the-art technology with unique designs of local art and culture. These hotels are popular with business travelers because they offer the best technology available for conferences as well as a pleasant environment to hold them.

The international hotel industry also faces many challenges in developing and managing hotels in different countries. These challenges include finding financing resource, managing distribution channel, human resources development, increased competition and risk management (Stafford, Yu and Armoo, 2002; Brotherton, 2003; Holjevac, 2003; Scoviak, 2004c). Finding financing for international hotel development has always been a challenge for hotel executives because of a myriad of considerations such as interest rate, exchange rate, expected rate of return and competition for project financing from other economic sectors (Higley, 2004). A creative approach to finding finance and structuring the investment is crucial to a viable hotel project in a foreign country. As global hotel companies expand to many countries, it is necessary to manage distribution channels effectively by using the host language for booking rooms in the host country and create GDS in the host language for convenient operations by the host travel agents. Staff shortage will continue in many developed countries and the shortage of mid-level managerial and supervisory professionals is evident in many developing countries. Effective training, learning, employee retention programs and attractive expatriate compensation packages will enhance employee competency and increase employee satisfaction. Competition for the international market will continue to intensify as international, regional and local hotel companies compete for international and domestic travel businesses. Companies that truly understand international travelers' needs and offer a product with superior service can succeed in today's competitive environment. Many devastating political, financial and natural crises have occurred since the beginning of this decade, particularly the 9.11 terrorist attacks on the US, the SARS epidemics in Asia and Canada and the unprecedented tsunami tidal waves destroying hundreds of resort properties and killing hundreds of thousands of tourists in South Asia and Africa. These events had a short- to mid-term disruptive effect on hotel operations and hotel management is required to be prepared to manage any crisis of significant magnitude. It normally takes a shorter time for a hotel management with a well-prepared risk management plan to recover from a catastrophic crisis (Yu et al., 2006).

International hotel development will continue to follow the sustained growth of world tourism and will contribute significantly to the host economy and society. The structure and nature of the international hotel industry is complex and encompasses many aspects of the tourism industry. International hotel development and operations are challenging because of the political, economic, cultural and legal differences in the host countries. Successful operations of international hotels depend on a sound understanding of the global travel market, brand management, cultural diversity management in human resources development, creative financing sources and technological applications.

REFERENCES

Adams, B. (2004) 'REIT buying trend expected to continue', *Hotel and Motel Management*, 219(2): 1 and 42.

Agut, S., Grau, R. and Perio, J. M. (2003) 'Competency needs among managers from Spanish hotels and restaurants and their training demands', *International Journal of Hospitality Management*, 22(3): 281–295.

Antonis, K. (2000) 'Empowering hotel worker across national borders', *Tourism, Culture and Communication*, 2(3): 191–199.

Bayraktaroglu, S. and Kutanis, R. O. (2003) 'Transforming hotels into learning organizations: a new strategy for going global', *Tourism Management*, 24(2): 149–154.

Berg, P. (1999) 'Friction in franchise relationships', *Hotels*, March, 58–59.

Bhakta, H. (2003) 'Full disclosure, transparency lead to trust in franchising', *Hotel and Motel Management*, 218(17): 26.

Blank, D. (2004) 'Tracking keeps owner use, rentals in line', *Hotel and Motel Management*, 219(13): 3 and 26.

Bradach, J. L. (1998) *Franchise Organizations*. Boston: Harvard Business School Press.

Brewer, W. A., III (2003) 'Franchises and shareholders: the next wave of hotel litigation', *Cornell Hotel and Restaurant Administration Quarterly*, 44(3): 77–88.

Brotherton, B. (2003) 'Themes and prospects'. In B. Brotherton (ed.), *The International Hospitality Industry: Structure, Characteristics and Issues.* Oxford: Butterworth-Heinemann. pp. 214–230.

Brown, J. B. and Harris, P. (1997) 'Organizational culture and control in a strategic planning context: implications for international hospitality industry'. In R. Teare, B. F. Ganziani and G. Brown (eds), *Global Direction: New Strategies for Hospitality and Tourism.* London: Cassell. pp. 105–132.

Calveras, A. (2003) 'Incentives of international and local hotel chains to invest in environmental quality', *Tourism Economics*, 9(3): 297–306.

Carroll, B. and Siguaw, J. (2003) 'The evolution of electronic distribution: effects on hotels and intermediaries', *Cornell Hotel and Restaurant Administration Quarterly*, 44(4): 38–50.

China National Tourism Administration (2006) *Yearbook of China Tourism Statistics.* Beijing: China Travel and Tourism Press.

Chathoth, P. K. and Olsen, M. D. (2003) 'Strategic alliances: a hospitality industry perspective', *International Journal of Hospitality Management*, 22(4): 419–434.

Choice Hotels International (2004) *Choice Hotels International Annual Report.* Silver Spring, Maryland: Choice Hotels International.

Cruz, T. D. (2003) 'Hotels use many strategies to maintain brand standards', *Hotel and Motel Management*, 218(1): 4 and 54.

Duval, D. T. (2004) "Why buying into the business we know it was seasonal': perceptions of seasonality in central Otago, New Zealand", *International Journal of Tourism Research*, 6(5): 325–337.

Dwyer, L., Teal, G., Kemp, S. and Wah, C. Y. (2000) 'Organizational culture and human resource management in an Indonesian resort hotel', *Tourism, Culture and Communication*, 2(1): 1–12.

Eyster, J. J. (1997) 'Hotel management contracts in the US: the revolution continues', *Cornell Hotel and Restaurant Administration Quarterly*, 38(3): 14–20.

Frey, S., Schegg, R. and Murphy, J. (2003) 'E-mail customer service in the Swiss hotel industry', *Tourism and Hospitality Research*, 4(3): 197–212.

Garcia-Almeida, D.J., Bolivar-Cruz, A.M. and Garcia-Falcón, J.M. (2004) 'Determinants of successful knowledge replication in new units: evidence from the hotel industry'. Paper presented at the British Academy of Management Annual Conference, St. Andrews, August 30–September 1.

Gee, C. (1994) *International Hotels: Development and Management.* East Lansing, MI: Education Institute of American Hotel and Lodging Association.

Geddie, M. W., DeFranco, A. L. and Geddie, M. F. (2002) 'From guanxi to customer relationship marketing: how the constructs of guanxi can strengthen CRM in the hospitality industry', *Journal of Travel and Tourism Marketing*, 13(2): 19–34.

Gering, Art. (2006) Lodging on the mend: less room at the inn. Special Report by National Association of Real Estate Investment Trust, January/February.Retrieved March 31, 2006, from http://www.nareit.com/portfoliomag/06janfeb/sector.shtml

Gunn, C. A. (1988) *Vacationscape: Designing Tourist Regions*, 2nd edn. New York: Van Nostrand Reinhold.

Hall, E. T. (1973) *The Silent Language.* Garden City, NY: Doubleday.

Hall, E. T. (1977) *Beyond Culture.* Garden City, NY: Doubleday.

Harrison, J. S. (2003) 'Strategic analysis for the hotel industry', *Cornell Hotel and Restaurant Administration Quarterly*, 44(2): 139–152.

Higley, J. (2004) 'Asset pricing remains difficult piece of lodging puzzle', *Hotel and Motel Management*, 219(13): 1 and 38.

Hill, C. W. L. (1994) *International Business: Competing in a Global Marketplace.* Burr Ridge, IL: Irwin.

Hoad, D. (2003) 'The general agreement on trade in services and the impact of trade liberalization on tourism and sustainability', *Tourism and Hospitality Research*, 4(3): 213–227.

Holjevac, I. A. (2003) 'A vision of tourism and the hotel industry in the 21st century', *International Journal of Hospitality Management*, 22(2): 129–134.

Hope, C. A. (2004) 'The impact of national culture on the transfer of "best practice operations management" in hotels in St. Lucia', *Tourism Management*, 25(1): 45–59.

Hotels (2004) 'Asia's new tiger: Shangri-La's global aspirations', *Hotels*, 7(3): 14–22.

Hotels (2006) 'Podcast marketing: the next big thing?', *Hotels*, 40(2): 22.

Ingram, P. L. (1996) *The Rise of Hotel Chains in the United States 1896–1980.* New York: Garland Publishing, Inc.

Jogaratnam, G. and Tse, E. C. Y. (2004) 'The entrepreneurial approach to hotel operation: evidence from the Asia-Pacific hotel industry', *Cornell Hotel and Restaurant Administration Quarterly*, 45(3): 248–259.

Luiz, M., DcDonagh, P., Peris, S.M. and Bigné, E. (1995) 'The future development of the hotel sector: an international comparison', *International Journal of Contemporary Hospitality Management*, 7(4): 10–15.

Magnini, V. P. and Honeycutt, E. D., Jr. (2003) 'Learning orientation and the hotel expatriate manager experience', *International Journal of Hospitality Management*, 22(3): 267–280.

Murphy, J., Olaru, D., Schegg, R. and Frey, S. (2003) 'The bandwagon effect: Swiss hotels' website and e-mail management', *Cornell Hotel and Restaurant Administration Quarterly*, 44(1): 71–87.

Ng, C. W. and Pine, R. (2003) 'Women and men in hotel management in Hong Kong: perceptions of gender and career development issues', *International Journal of Hospitality Management*, 22(1): 85–102.

O'Connor, P. and Frew, A. J. (2004) 'An evaluation methodology for hotel electronic channels of distribution', *International Journal of Hospitality Management*, 23(2): 179–199.

O'Connor, P. and Piccoli, G. (2003) 'Marketing hotels using global distribution systems', *Cornell Hotel and Restaurant Administration Quarterly*, 44(5 and 6): 105–114.

Oliva, R. (2004) 'At the crossroad', *Hotels*, 38(6): 49–50, 52, 54 and 56.

Pine, R. and Go, F. (1996) 'Globalization in the hotel industry'. In R. Kotas, R. Teare, J. Logie, C. Jayawardena and J. Bowen (eds), *The International Hospitality Business*. London: Cassell. pp. 96–104.

Roper, A., Brookes, M., Price, L. and Hampton, A. (1999) 'Towards an understanding of centricity: profiling international hotel groups', *Progress in Tourism and Hospitality Research*, 3(3): 199–211.

Rushmore, S. (2004) 'What is a condo-hotel?' *Hotels*, 38(11): 28.

Scoviak, M. (2004a) 'Management companies get flexible', *Hotels*, 38(10): 40–42, 44.

Scoviak, M. (2004b) 'Internet wars', *Hotels*, 38(5): 40–42, 44 and 46.

Scoviak, M. (2004c) 'Asia: back on track', *Hotels*, 38(4): 30–32, 34 and 36.

Scoviak, M. (2004d) 'Latin America: turning point', *Hotels*, 38(9): 50–52, 54 and 56.

Selwitz, R. (2002) 'Hyatt concentrates on international growth', *Hotel and Motel Management*, 217(14): 15.

Sharpley, R. and Forster, G. (2003) 'The implications of hotel employee attitudes for the development of quality tourism: the case of Cyprus', *Tourism Management*, 24(6): 687–697.

Sisson, J. (2003) 'Mezzanine financing helps balance capital needs', *Hotel and Motel Management*, 218(10): 37 and 46.

Stafford, G., Yu, L. and Armoo, A. K. (2002) 'Crisis management and recovery: how Washington, D.C., hotels responded to terrorism', *Cornell Hotel and Restaurant Administration Quarterly*, October: 27–40.

Steward, R. (2005) 'Value of foreign investments in the U.S. rises more than value of U.S. investments abroad in 2004'. Bureau of Economic Analysis, U.S. Department of Commerce, June 30, p. 1. Retrieved March 30, 2006, from http://www.bea.gov/ bea/newsrelarchive/2005/ intinv04_fax.pdf

Strauss, K. and Gale, D. (2006) 'Global update: create Buzz', *Hotels*, 40(2): 12–13.

Strauss, K. and Scoviak, M. (2004) 'Hotels' 325 giants', *Hotels*, 39 (7): 31–33, 53.

Taylor, S. (2000) 'Hotels'. In C. Lashley and A. Morrison (eds), *Franchising Hospitality Services*. Oxford: Butterworth-Heinemann. pp. 170–191.

Tse, A. C. (2003) 'Disintermediation of travel agents in the hotel industry', *International Journal of Hospitality Management*, 22(4): 453–460.

UN World Tourism Organization (2005) *WTO Tourism Highlights*. Madrid: World Tourism Organization.

Walsh, J. P. (2003) 'Lengthy negotiations settles differences between Sheraton franchisees, Starwood', *Hotel and Motel Management*, 218(10): 1 and 68.

Wood, R. C. (2003) 'Diversity management'. In B. Brotherton (ed.), *The International Hospitality Industry: Structure, Characteristics and Issues*. Oxford: Butterworth-Heinemann. pp. 93–109.

Yu, L. (1999) *The International Hospitality Business: Management and Operations*. New York: The Haworth Hospitality Press.

Yu, L. and Gu, H.M. (2005) 'Hotel reform in China: a SWOT analysis', *Cornell Hotel and Restaurant Administration Quarterly*, 46(2): 153–169.

Yu, L., Stafford, G. and Armoo, A.K. (2006) 'A study of crisis management strategies of hotel managers in the Washington, D.C. metro area', *Journal of Travel and Tourism Marketing*, 19(2/3): 91–105.

The Inter-Relationships between Leisure, Recreation, Tourism, and Hospitality

3

Robert Christie Mill

INTRODUCTION

For many people the debate over terminology and definitions is uninteresting, unimportant, unnecessary and/or impossible to agree upon. Therefore, they argue, why bother? There are a number of reasons to pursue such a debate (Mieczkowski, 1990). First, any field that aspires to be scholarly must develop strict criteria that are generally accepted in order that communication between all interested parties can go on. The procedures of scientific method dictate that theory is dependent upon measurement and definition must precede measurement (Franklin, 2003). Second, the establishment of generally accepted standards and definitions is necessary for any longitudinal research. The definition of 'visitor' in Samoa changed when different individuals managed the Office of Tourism (Mieczkowski, 1990). Third, clear definitions are necessary for legal/administrative reasons related to such things as differentiating between different types of tourists.

Finally, how leisure is defined influences how agencies that provide leisure services operate. A qualitative definition – leisure is a state of mind – leads to more concern over such things as leisure education, alternative programming and the mainstreaming of the disabled. A quantitative definition – leisure as the amount of free time – places more attention on such things as accessibility, barriers to leisure, carrying capacity of resources and ability to satisfy demand (Smith and Godbey, 1991). Having said that, it must be noted that we are entering perilous waters as definitions of leisure, tourism and hospitality are not universally agreed upon and, at the same time, are hotly debated. This chapter follows a convention of going from the broadest concept to narrower ones. Leisure is

considered broader than recreation, the activities that take place during leisure, and the inter-relationships between the two terms are then considered. Tourism is regarded as a sub-set of recreation that involves some combination of time and distance. Hospitality is narrower still and is discussed as a concept alone and in relation to tourism.

LEISURE

Contemporary definitions of leisure evolve from the Greeks and the Romans. Mieczkowski quotes Aristotle as writing: 'we labor to have leisure' (Mieczkowski, 1990: 8). There is certainly a value judgement here on the relative importance of leisure compared with work. Indeed, in both the Greek and Latin languages, the word for work emphasizes the absence of leisure by placing a prefix in front of the word leisure to, in essence, be 'unleisure' or 'non-leisure'. The Greek word for leisure is *skhole* while the word for work is *askholia*. Similarly, the respective Latin words are *otium* and *negotium* (Mieczkowski, 1990: 8).

Ideas on leisure have evolved over the centuries. To the Greeks, leisure was one of the three goals of human life – theoretical wisdom, happiness, and leisure (Smith, 1990). Leisure was seen, in an elitist way, as an ideal state of being. To the Romans leisure was time off work to be used to 'combat boredom, to renew energy for work or warfare, and to win political support from the masses through provision of free entertainment' (Smith, 1990: 180). From the Catholic Church we learn that leisure is time free from the obligation of work. People worked for physical survival and as atonement for sin while leisure was for rest and recuperation

(Smith, 1990). Leisure was tied to blocks of time, notably the Sabbath and special holy days that evolved into *holidays*.

As more time and money became available to more people (including clergy) during the Middle Ages excesses in behavior led to calls for reform – the Protestant Reformation. The resulting return to a harsh lifestyle led to a curtailment of the pursuit of leisure and the development of the Protestant Work Ethic – the idea that people should spend most of their time and seek an identity through, work and have minimal leisure for rest. These values were brought to the New World and, in Europe, helped drive the Industrial Revolution (Smith, 1990). Thus a view developed that saw leisure as a symbol of social class (Leitner and Leitner, 1996). A sign of wealth is the possession and use of free time. This perspective is not as relevant as it used to be as more people have more leisure.

Four streams of definitions have developed over the ages (Beatty and Torbert, 2003: 240):

- time-based approach: how much time is available?
- activity-based approach: what do people do?
- intention-based approach: why do people engage in certain activities?
- holistic view: leisure and work cannot be separated.

Time-based approach

The *Oxford English Dictionary* lists 16 definitions of leisure. A time-based definition of leisure is the most commonly used definition today. Time has a value of one and all activities are a fraction of time. Simply put, leisure equals time minus work. Yet as we increasingly see, the boundaries between leisure and work are increasingly blurred. Is the business executive entertaining clients to a sumptuous dinner on a company expense account at 'work'? Is that same executive, socially pressured to get involved in a civic activity, for which he or she is not directly compensated, at 'leisure'?

To many people leisure is viewed as the opposite of work (Beatty and Torbert, 2003). It is the time 'left over' after work and the obligations of life – child rearing, etc. – have been taken care of. This definition is quantitative – how much time is available? There is the feeling that work and other obligations are scheduled first and whatever is left is 'leisure'. To a large extent this definition reflects the industrialized view of the world as, indeed, it was the industrial revolution that set the stage for so many people to have the means and the necessity to have leisure.

However, the idea that residual time is considered to be free time is ambiguous at best (Shaw and Williams, 1994). Free time is usually though of as 'freedom from' such things as work. This is different from the idea of 'freedom to' enjoy such things as leisure. As such it is argued that the idea of free time has no intrinsic meaning because it ignores the quality of time that is available and the resources that are needed to participate in leisure activities (Shaw and Williams, 1994). These contemporary definitions contrast with definitions from the late nineteenth century when people were regarded as 'having the leisure' to do something *before* something else occurred. This is in sharp contrast to the contemporary idea of leisure as coming *after* (Koshar, 2002).

Most definitions stress the idea that leisure is free or unoccupied time – time that individuals can spend as they please. In its simplest form leisure can be defined as 'free or unobligated time during which one is not working or performing other life-sustaining functions' (Leitner and Leitner, 1996: 3). 'Free time' can be defined further in terms of segments of the population or periods of time. In terms of the former, Smith and Godbey note Kaplan's segmentation of leisure as (Smith and Godbey, 1991, 90):

- permanent;
- voluntary leisure of the rich;
- temporary involuntary leisure of the unemployed;
- regularly allocated voluntary leisure of the employed on holidays and vacation;
- temporary incapacity of the employed;
- permanent incapacity of the disabled; and
- voluntary retirement of the aged.

Leisure can also be characterized on the basis of available time slots (Mieczkowski, 1990). It can consist of:

- time available on a daily basis after work;
- a single day/weekend, usually two days;
- long weekend, usually three days;
- vacation of four or more days; and
- retirement.

Seen this way, leisure is viewed objectively. It is quantitative and can be easily measured (Smith and Godbey, 1991).

People think they have less free time yet in time diaries they report that they have more (Godbey, 1998). There is also a discrepancy in the way leisure time is organized. People want large blocks of leisure time as much of what is valued about leisure seems to occur during those large blocks. However, 25 of the average 40 hours of free time a week (over 60%) comes in small, daily increments (Godbey, 1998). There is an obvious link to the technological progress of society. It can be argued that technological advances allow more people to have more free time (Smith and Godbey, 1991). On the other hand advances in communications technologies such as e-mail, voice mail and text messaging have increased expectations on how quickly one is expected to respond to incoming messages. In addition, since it is easy to be in touch 24 hours a day, seven days a week, the distinction between being at work and being away from work is further blurred.

Despite some views to the contrary (Godbey, 1998) leisure must clearly be defined within the context of time (Voss, 1967). To do so gives the definition maximum objectivity. Beyond that there is the difficulty of differentiating between work, non-work, and leisure (Voss, 1967). One way around this is to divide time into three categories (Voss, 1967: 100), work, leisure, and non-discretionary time. Another way is to stress the relationship between time and money. Work is associated with time spent earning a living. Work is paid time (Voss, 1967). Leisure is part of non-work time. Most writers agree that the amount depends upon the degree of freedom one feels in 'spending' it. Thus leisure can be thought of as discretionary time when an individual has no sense of 'economic, legal, moral or social compulsion or obligation nor of physiological necessity' (Voss, 1967: 101). The question is 'Do I have to do what I am doing?' (Voss, 1967: 102).

Moving from 'leisure' to 'free time' is a move from a qualitative to a quantitative concept (Mieczkowski, 1990). 'Leisure' time puts together two contradicting words. Leisure means being free while 'time' puts a constraint on that freedom (De Grazia, 1962). A time-based definition of leisure is objective, value-free, and neutral. However this definition misses the experiential quality of leisure (Beatty and Torbert, 2003). It also limits leisure by counting it only as time not spent at work.

Activity-based approach

Modern theories of leisure continued to rely on the idea of leisure as unobligated time until the 1920s when attention was given to the activities engaged in during leisure time. Post-World War II research included an examination of how leisure activities helped influence a person's identity. This ushered in a variety of writings focusing on the subjective, humanistic and psychological views of leisure (Smith, 1989).

The roots of this movement are seen in the writings of Veblen who considered leisure as the unproductive consumption of time (Esteve et al., 1999) and deGrazia who feel that leisure is the opposite of work and, as such, unproductive (Jensen, 1977). In work there is a narrowing of consciousness while in leisure there is a widening of consciousness (Jensen, 1977). Out of this stream has developed a typology of leisure activities such as watching TV and engaging in various hobbies and sports (Leitner and Leitner, 1996). Dumazedier (1967) sees leisure as the activities an individual can engage in voluntarily after he/she gets free from professional, family and social duties (Dumazedier, 1967).

Leisure as the time when leisure activities occur overlaps with the definition of recreation as the activities undertaken during leisure time (Shaw and Williams, 1994). Leisure as a list of activities is also problematic in that an activity such as gardening can be seen by one individual as leisure and another as an obligation (Shaw and Williams, 1994). If 'leisure' equates to 'activities' then it is synonymous with 'recreation' (Leitner and Leitner, 1996).

Intention-based approach

In response to criticism of the definitions of leisure in terms of residual time or as a list of activities much modern research has viewed leisure as a state of mind (Shaw and Williams, 1994). It is the *perception* of individuals that leisure is enjoyable, gives them a sense of well-being and is personally satisfying (Shaw and Williams, 1994: Poria et al., 2003). It is how the time is used and how meaningful the activity appears. However, society places boundaries on what choices are socially acceptable. As such individual choices have to be seen against the backdrop of what is considered acceptable in society.

The intention-based approach to leisure sees it as an experience. The foundation for this approach is Aristotle who sees leisure as an 'inner attitude of voluntary engagement and inquiry' (Beatty and Torbert, 2003: 241) and having nothing to do with consumption. Leisure is seen in terms of personal development consistent with the Greek belief that the goal of leisure is cultivation of the self. Individuals who act as if they are doing nothing may, in fact, be meaningfully using their leisure time to meditate.

The key is the perception of freedom (Neulinger, 1974). This is noted by Iso-Ahola (1980) as the 'threshold of leisure'. The motivation for leisure is intrinsic and comes from the feeling of satisfaction and fulfillment gained from the experience and not from external rewards. To be leisure the activity itself must be the final goal of the activity. This is sometimes referred to as the classical or traditional view of leisure where leisure is a highly desired state of mind wherein the state of being is realized through participation in intrinsically motivated activities. Leisure must involve a positive state of mind. Unlike the concept of leisure as 'activity', leisure and free time are not synonymous. It is obviously difficult to quantify leisure under this definition (Leitner and Leitner, 1996).

Closely related to this concept is the anti-utilitarian view that sees leisure as a state of mind. Leisure need not serve any purpose and needs no justification. One problem is that this view of leisure makes it difficult to quantify leisure. It can also be used to justify activities detrimental to healthy self-development. By contrast, the social instrument view of leisure views it as a away of promoting self-growth and helping others. This view can lead to a stressful attitude to leisure wherein achievement is overemphasized.

There does seem to be general agreement that the term 'leisure' is derived from the Latin *licere* to be allowed or free and is related to the French *loisir* – to be permitted (Jensen, 1977; Mieczkowski, 1990). In many ways freedom seems to be the essence of leisure whether it be freedom of time (time not spent in making a living or in self-maintenance) and/or freedom of attitude (free will, lack of compulsion, freedom of choice) (Jensen, 1977).

There is a debate in the literature between psychologists, who see leisure as a state of mind, and sociologists, who prefer a behavioral definition within a social context. Social psychologists

agree that a leisure experience involves perceived freedom, intrinsic motivation, enjoyment and relaxation (Smith and Godbey, 1991). One paradigm divided leisure activities on the basis of perceived freedom versus perceived constraint and motivation (intrinsic versus extrinsic) (Neulinger, 1981; Leitner and Leitner, 1996). Intrinsic motivation indicates a willingness to participate in an activity for its own sake while extrinsic motivation refers to the desire to engage in the activity for an external reward. At the two extremes are what might be termed 'Pure Leisure' in which an individual chooses to participate in an activity for its own sake. At the other extreme is 'Pure Job' where the individual feels the need to work for external rewards. In between there is 'Leisure-work': consisting of activities engaged in freely and motivated by a combination of intrinsic and extrinsic rewards. An example would be a sport that is considered enjoyable and also has fitness benefits. 'Leisure-job' consists of activities that are freely engaged in and motivated by extrinsic rewards. Jogging or aerobics undertaken to improve health would be an example of this. 'Pure work' consists of activities that are engaged in under restraint for intrinsic rewards. A professional basketball player must play the game but might get intrinsic satisfaction from his/her ability to perform at a high level. The 'work-job' category can describe a college professor who performs under restraint and receives both intrinsic and extrinsic rewards from the job.

Reisman thought of leisure as a means to personal growth (Esteve et al., 1999) while Kaplan, quoted by Esteve et al. uses words like 'relatively self-determined activity-experience ... psychologically pleasant ... opportunities for recreation, personal growth, and service to others' (Esteve, Martin and Lopez, 1999: 153).

Thus, leisure might be defined as 'The experiential quality of our time when we engage voluntarily and intentionally in awareness-expanding inquiry which in turn generates ongoing, transforming development throughout adulthood' (Beatty and Torbert, 2003: 243). It can rightfully be argued that this definition is elitist. Who is to say that meditating is leisure but watching 'Monday Night Football' on TV is not?

Holistic view

The holistic view of leisure views work and leisure as being so inter-related that they cannot be readily separated (Leitner and Leitner, 1996). Proponents argue that elements of leisure can be found in work, education, and other social spheres (Leitner and Leitner, 1996). Godbey (1998) argues that leisure and work are not opposites. The industrial model of work and leisure is, he says, coming to an end. Neither work nor leisure happens only on weekends; 'work is not fast and leisure slow. Privileged people don't get more leisure (they get slightly less); rather they get the good jobs'.

The 'traditional leisure paradox' links the amounts of time and money available. The paradox suggests that when people have the money to engage in various leisure pursuits, they lack the time. In essence, when one is young there is plenty of time for leisure travel yet this activity is limited by a lack of funds. As work provides the money there are time constraints placed on the individual. Later in life after retirement from the workforce, the pursuit of leisure activities is again restricted by a lack of financial resources. However, one study found that the 'traditional leisure paradox' is not valid (Litvin et al., 2002). The authors note that, with increasing wealth often comes greater control over one's time. Indeed discretionary income more than time correlates with travel frequency.

The key elements of leisure seem to be that it is the antithesis to work as an economic function; involves pleasant expectation and recollection and a minimum of involuntary social role obligations; there is a psychological perception of freedom; it is closely related to the values of the culture; it is a non-compensated activity; and it often, though not necessarily, involves an activity characterized by the spontaneous elements of play (Mieczkowski, 1990).

While many argue the need for one comprehensive, universally-agreed upon definition of leisure, one respected authority (Iso-Ahola, 1980) suggests that the various ways of defining leisure are not in conflict. Facility planners, for example, are interested in how much of various activities people will engage in. Social psychologists, interested in whether or not active leisure users experience less stress, will be interested in how people *feel* when pursuing leisure activities. Thus, from an *external* viewpoint, leisure is defined by the researcher of a particular study. From an *internal* perspective, it may be useful to have leisure defined by the individual. The individual mowing the lawn is the best person to say whether or not that activity is a chore or a relaxing escape from work.

RECREATION

Recreation is derived from the Latin *recreare* meaning to restore or refresh – it refers to refreshment of the strength and spirits after work (Mieczkowski, 1990). The idea is that of 'recreating' human physical and mental resources depleted by working activity; it is a renewal of body, mind and spirit in order to prepare the individual for better performance of work (Mieczkowski, 1990).

According to Marxist doctrine recreation in the capitalistic doctrine exploits the working masses because, as leisure time increases, the 're-created' worker faces more intense work that makes them more tired than before. In the West recreation is increasingly seen as independent from the preparation for work. It contains values for itself, values that help shape human life. Thus we move from recreation as 'non-working activity engaged in for pleasure' (Theodorson and Theodorson, 1969: 15, 337) to '(A)ll those activities that individuals or groups of individuals choose to do during leisure time, with the object of making life more satisfying and more enjoyable' (Ontario, Dept. of Education 1970: 65 quoted in Mieczkowski, 1990: 15). This latter definition stresses the voluntary character of recreation. It says that it is more than the activity but it is also the attitude with which the activity is pursued. This takes into account the fact that what is recreation for one may be work for another. Gardening is only one of many possibilities. When seen as an onerous chore, gardening is not considered recreation. When undertaken for pleasure, it is.

Post-World War II authors say that recreation is purposeful, constructive and positive. These kinds of statements obviously place a value judgement on the activity. A more tolerant attitude indicates that any activity can be considered recreation as long as it is not a threat to public welfare.

Goodale and Godbey identify five concepts of recreation need (Goodale and Godbey, 1988: 121–122):

- expressed need: individuals express their values through the activities they freely select;

- comparative need: suggests government should give priority to those (i.e. the poor) who are most dependent;
- created need: grows out of an individual's choice of activity after being taught the value of the activity;
- normative need: views leisure as a series of activities undertaken during nonwork time to restore and refresh the individual to prepare her/him for work and contribute to his/her well-being. This concept assumes experts can set objective standards to determine the minimum supply needed; and
- felt need: the individual need for leisure is a function of belief, perception and attitude.

Normative and comparative assume a minimum level of recreation is needed as part of the work–recreation–work cycle. Comparative brings in the government to level the playing field of opportunity for those with a higher need for leisure – the poor. The expressed need and felt need concepts have a marketing ring to them: the important things are 'what people say they want to do and what they actually do' (Goodale and Godbey, 1988: 119).

Thus, recreation is seen as activity conducted during leisure time where:

- participation is voluntary;
- the major purposes are enjoyment, fun, personal satisfaction, revitalization;
- it usually involves activity;
- it is usually motivated by internal goals;
- a person's attitude towards the activity is more important than the activity itself;
- it usually benefits a person physically, mentally and/or socially, in addition to being enjoyable;
- recreation services should meet ethical standards and provide a healthy and constructive experience; and
- it remains a very broad concept involving a diverse range of activities.

(Weiskopf, 1982; Leitner and Leitner, 1996: 13–14).

LEISURE AND RECREATION

Mieczkowski (1990) attempts a theoretical framework of tourism. He considers the relationship between leisure, recreation and tourism as falling into one of three areas: 'tourism which

is not leisure, tourism in leisure but in which recreation activity does not take place; and tourism in leisure when recreation activity does take place' (Poria et al., 2003: 27).

Recreation is something that takes place during leisure – but not all leisure is recreation. Recreation is only part of the content of leisure; it is, in its most basic form, any activity pursued during leisure. Thus, if leisure time is available, recreation is one major activity chosen for leisure. According to this view, recreation activities cannot take place during work time. The distinction between 'free time' and 'non-free time' relates to the individual's control over his/her time. An individual might consider some time at work as being 'free'. There are six possible scenarios (Poria et al., 2003: 31–32):

1 An activity not regarded as recreation undertaken in 'free time' not perceived as leisure. An example is given of someone who seeks health treatment during 'free time'. The time is not thought of as leisure and the activity is not considered recreation.
2 An activity, not thought of as recreation occurs during 'free time', that is perceived as leisure. The example is of an individual visiting a museum during leisure time regarded as 'free'. However, since the individual listened to a lecture, the activity is regarded as an education experience rather than recreation.
3 A recreational activity undertaken in 'free time' that is thought of as leisure. The example is a person who plays football (thought of as recreation) during free time regarded as leisure.
4 An activity occurring during 'non-free time' but perceived of as leisure and recreation. People playing basketball during time they think of as 'non-free time' but that they regard as both leisure and recreation.
5 An activity undertaken during 'non-free time' that is thought of as leisure but not thought of as recreation. A conference attendee (non-free time) might, as part of the scheduled activities of the conference, visits a museum (leisure), and engages in an activity not thought of as recreation.
6 An activity, not thought of as leisure or recreation that occurs during time regarded as 'not-free'. The final example given is that a person on a business trip who undertakes activity he/she considers neither leisure nor recreation.

What is the importance of such distinctions? We can use the example of two women on a business trip, one of who has free time at the destination while the other does not. Mieczkowski (1990) would classify both as being in the same segment. However the women can be classified differently, based on the possible use of free time during the business trip. Poria et al. (2003) argue that this would help understand how these two women choose their hotel (near a tourist attraction or closer to a convention center) and their interest in visiting local attractions.

Most writers say that recreation consists of activities but many also include 'inactivities'. This goes against the idea of recreation being conceived of in the generic sense of the word, the 're-making' or 're-creating' of an individual through the use of leisure time in such a fashion as to restore or rebuild what has been depleted or exhausted in his or her makeup and to add to knowledge and abilities with the purpose of a fuller, more satisfying life. Diversion is not recreation.

Some authors argue that recreation is a type of 'conscious enjoyment' that can take place at any time and location (Poria et al., 2003). The deciding factor is whether or not the individual considers it recreation. This contradicts Mieczkowski (1990). Under this concept recreation is defined as 'any activity that an individual associates with enjoyment, this activity is not limited by time or space, and it is up to the individual to decide whether an activity is recreation and whether he/she is participating in such an activity' (Poria et al., 2003: 29). If we accept that 'leisure' and 'recreation' are defined as such based on individual perceptions, then 'tourism' is also a 'subjective dimension of human behavior' (Poria et al., 2003: 29). It also means that it is very difficult to measure how much recreation is occurring without surveying participants to determine whether or not the participants consider themselves as engaging in 'recreation'.

Leisure, it seems, focuses on time while recreation concentrates on content. Jensen and Naylor (1990) offer a modified model of J. B. Nash's hierarchy of recreational quality that expands on this idea. It suggests various qualitative levels of recreational activity undertaken during leisure. The highest level involves 'creativity' and is described as the 'Maker of the Model'. Next are activities that involve active participation and are described as the 'Copy of the Model'. Emotional participation, the next level, involves 'Appreciation'. The next level of amusement and simple entertainment

is no more than an 'antidote to boredom'. All of these activities are described as offering positive experiences. A rating of zero is used to describe the 'Retardation of the Individual's Wholesome Development' as a result of excessive involvement in a low-quality pursuit. A below-zero rating is given to acts performed against society that can result in crime and delinquency.

RECREATION AND TOURISM

The potential for confusion about terms is great. The term 'tourism' in North America is often substituted by 'travel' and 'outdoor recreation' in Europe while in Canada 'tourism' and 'outdoor recreation' are considered synonymous (Mieczkowski, 1990). 'Tourism' and 'recreation' are different. Tourism is associated with free time as well as working time (business tourism) while recreation occurs totally during leisure time. Tourism is always associated with displacement from one's home community, while not all recreation is. The concepts clash on practice in that the purchase of recreational equipment may involve financial conflicts in family budgeting with allocation of funds for tourism. Tourism has commercial connotations while recreation's commercial ties are weaker or non-existent. In many cases recreation may be provided free by the government. Finally, recreation centers on activities which require acquisition of specific skills (Mieczkowski, 1990).

TOURISM AND LEISURE

A starting point to the inter-relationships between leisure and tourism is to say that travel undertaken in relative freedom as a pleasurable, intrinsically rewarding activity falls under leisure (Smith and Godbey, 1991). It becomes difficult to conclude where and under what circumstances tourist experiences become leisure experiences. While tourism fills a part of leisure time, much of leisure time is beyond the scope of tourism. Indeed, part of what is defined as 'tourism' is associated with working time. Attending a convention is considered part of tourism yet, for the attendee, much – if not most – of the activity involves work (Mieczkowski, 1990).

According to Shaw and Williams tourism and leisure intersect at several points (Shaw and Williams, 1994: 6–8):

1 They occur in the same time–space framework. To some extent individuals can vary how much leisure they have by reorganizing the time they spend on other activities. If tourism is defined as involving at least one night away from home, it is obvious that tourism can only occur during some leisure time. Whether and how tourism occurs is also influenced by the level of economic development enjoyed at the point of origin and advances in technology. For example, the development of supersonic aircraft opens the possibility of a round-trip from the USA to Europe, which would cost a lot of money but which could be achieved without spending a night away from home. On a more logical scale, air travel opens up the possibility of long weekend tourism breaks.

2 They compete for the same household budget. When the level of disposable income cannot satisfy the demands for leisure and tourism choices substitutions must be made. To a large extent this is impacted by the motivation of the individual. The desire to explore new cultures cannot be substituted through locally-based leisure activities. On the other hand, the desire to play golf on vacation can be accommodated to a large extent by a round of golf on a local course. The level of costs is also a factor. A holiday may have to be postponed to pay for a leisure good at home.

3 Third, tourism and leisure activities are socially constructed. Tourism elements can be designed for local leisure consumption. Dry ski slopes can be constructed to allow locals to experience some of the joy of a ski vacation. Leisure elements can also influence what occurs on vacations. The proliferation of in-home entertainment systems leads to an expectation that these facilities be available in hotels for the vacationing tourist. The evolution of leisure activities at the local level places pressures on tourism destinations to offer more and better attractions and facilities in order to attract visitors.

There are several topics in the literature of research in leisure that are relevant to tourism (Smith and Godbey, 1991). One such area is that of recreation programming. Recreation programming is equivalent to the idea of hospitality in tourism. The goals of recreation programming are to promote participation, a sense of belonging and the feeling that participants are welcome and respected (Smith and Godbey, 1991). The same can be argued for the idea of 'hospitality'. A second topic is that of optimal arousal. Optimal arousal is the concept of 'mental stimulation at which well-being is maximized' (Smith and Godbey, 1991: 95). Applied to tourism, it can help us understand what motivates an individual to seek a quiet relaxing 'get away from it all' break one weekend and a stimulus-filled city experience the following weekend.

Carrying capacity, the third topic, has historically been applied by leisure researchers. The concept considers the number of people an individual site can handle before the experience for the user is reduced and the resources (usually natural) at the site are diminished. A variety of management techniques can increase carrying capacity without damaging the resource. As increased numbers of people become concerned about 'tourist pollution' this idea can be utilized by communities to help ensure the sustainability of tourist destinations and resources.

The subject of marketing is thought of as the province of the private sector. Indeed many who operate leisure and recreational facilities and resources in the public sector tend to think of marketing in negative terms and believe it should not be used when considering the use of public resources. However, in its broadest term, marketing involves developing and delivering products and services desired by customers, guests, tourists or the clients of a public agency. A number of writers have been able to successfully apply private-sector techniques to the marketing of public services.

Some of these 'principles' are (Smith and Godbey, 1991: 96):

- the quality of leisure or tourism experiences are more important than the quantity;
- developers and programmers serve market segments rather than the entire population;
- these market segments are only partially informed of the opportunities available to them;
- the social status of individuals has a direct impact on the attitudes, desires and activity patterns of these same individuals;
- effective management requires information about how people behave, the structure of the organization and the political and economic environment in which agencies and business operate; and
- the concepts of recreation, leisure and tourism are, in part, defined by an individual's evaluation of the experience.

TOURISM

The term 'tourism' appeared in print shortly after 1800 (Smith, 1990). The various derivations of what we now call 'tourism' revolve around the idea of circular movement. The term comes from the Latin *tornare* to turn or to round off and *tornus* wheel – a circular movement relating to change of residence (Mieczkowski, 1990). The Greek word *torus* describes a tool used to inscribe a circle (Mieczkowski, 1990; Smith, 1990). The French word *tour* suggesting circular tower and circular travel with a return to the point of departure leads to *tourisme* in French, *tourismo* in Italian, *tourismus* in German, the English 'tourism' and the Russian *turizm* (Mieczkowski, 1990: 21).

Various researchers have suggested different types of definition. One suggestion is to offer technical or conceptual definitions (Poria et al., 2003). Another offers economic, technical and holistic options (Leiper, 1979). In this latter case, economic definitions focus exclusively on the supply perspective. Demand-related definitions, although an economic concept, are not included. A better typology might be demand-based definitions, supply-based definitions, and integrated or holistic definitions (Smith, 1990). Demand- and supply-based definitions are both examples of technical definitions. Technical definitions emphasize where individuals are in time and space compared to their normal place of residence. They are useful for measurement purposes but are narrow in scope and do not consider tourism as a social phenomenon (Poria et al., 2003).

There are numerous options for defining tourism in terms of demand. Tourism can be defined in terms of (Mieczkowski, 1990: 37–41):

1 Residence of visitors

   a resident
   b non-resident (out of state)

2 Residence of visitors

   a domestic
   b international

3 Age of visitors

   a youth
   b golden age

4 Duration of the tourist experience

   a excursion
   b weekend
   c vacation

5 Season

   a summer
   b winter

6 Means of transportation

   a auto
   b etc.

7 Mode of movement

   a single stop
   b round trio

8 Organizational pattern (arrangement)

   a individual
   b group

9 Financial status of tourists

   a mass
   b élite

10 Mode of financing

   a commercial
   b closed or restricted

11 Type of accommodation

   a hotels
   b private homes
   c etc.

12 In relation to religion

   a pilgrimage
   b secular

13 Type of activity

   a recreational
   b non-recreational

14 Purpose

   a pleasure
   b visiting friends and relatives
   c personal
   d business

15 Setting

  a urban
  b resort
  c wilderness

16 Location of the destination

  a urban
  b suburban
  c near-urban
  d extra-urban

Early definitions focused on the tourist or visitor rather than on 'tourism'. The Committee of Statistical Experts of the League of Nations recommended in 1936 a definition of 'foreign tourism' adopted by the Tourism Committee of the League of Nations in 1937 as 'any person visiting a country, other than that in which he usually resides for a period of at least 24 hours' (Mieczkowski, 1990: 21). This definition was amended by the Economic Committee of the League of Nations to say that a 'tourist is a person staying in a locality situated outside his place of residence during minimum of 24 hours and maximum of one year' (OECD, 1963: 3).

A joint United Nations/World Tourism Organization definition states that a 'visitor is any person visiting a country other than that in which he has his usual place of residence, for any reason other than following an occupation remunerated from within the country visited' (Mieczkowski, 1990). This definition covers tourists on leisure or business and excursionists (those people on a visit of less than 24 hours). Visitors are classified according to their place of residence, not their nationality. One problem is that some countries have difficulty excluding diplomats and soldiers while other countries include transients, thereby inflating their numbers (Mieczkowski, 1990). In the USA, domestically, definitions vary from state to state. There is a common tendency to regard out-of-state visitors as tourists, intrastate travel is almost always excluded and business and personal travel are only sometimes included (Mieczkowski, 1990).

The most common popular conception of *tourism* involves traveling for pleasure with an overnight stay (Medlik, 2003). However, according to the World Tourism Organization (WTO), tourism involves 'the activities of persons traveling to and staying in places outside their usual environment ... for leisure,

business and other purposes' (Medlik, 2003: vii). A suggested clarification is that tourism

> denotes a temporary short-term movement of people to destinations outside their normal environment and their activities; within this broad concept 'technical' definitions are formulated for particular purposes, to include or exclude particular trips and visits, mainly by reference to purpose, time and distance criteria (Medlik, 2003: vii).

Many define tourism not by what it *is* but by what it is *not*. It is *not* home and *not* work. Thus we get sub-definitions such as the 'non-business tourism' – 'a person who undertakes one or more recreational activities in leisure time, at a location temporarily away from the normal place of residence and at locations at which such recreational activities are normally undertaken' (Franklin, 2003: 27) or that 'business tourism' consists of 'a person who undertakes work related activities at a location temporarily away from their normal place of residence and work' (Franklin, 2003: 27). These definitions 'reduce tourism to acts of leisure and recreation at the end of acts of travel' (Franklin, 2003: 28).

Demand-based definitions emphasize tourism as a human activity (Smith, 1990) such as that used in the US National Tourism Policy Study Final Report (Committee on Commerce, 1978). That report suggests that tourism is 'the action and activities of people taking trips to a place or places outside of their home communities for any purpose except daily commuting to and from work' (Smith, 1990: 325). Although the authors regard 'tourism' and 'travel' as being synonymous, the trend is to regard 'tourism' in terms of the above definition and 'travel' as human movement by vehicle regardless of the purpose of the travel.

Demand-based definitions ignore the supply-side aspects of tourism. While there is agreement that tourism involves people coming in from where they normally live, the facilities for tourism can benefit residents who, engaging in these activities, are not tourists but recreationists or pursuing leisure. There is also the problem of defining 'home community'. This problem is confronted by defining tourism as 'the temporary short-term movement of people to destinations outside the places where they normally live' (Burkhart and Medlik, 1974: 5). A long-term solution is either to impose a minimum distance requirement or to allow individuals to self-report when they have moved from their home community. In the USA, for example, a 'trip' is defined as an individual moving at least 50 miles from home, while in Canada the definition of tourism includes those traveling in Canada 80 kilometers or more from their residence, Canadians traveling outside the country, and non-residents traveling in Canada. Depending on whether or not there is an overnight stay, these travelers are referred to as tourists or same-day visitors (Wilton, 1997). This approach acknowledges that different people define their home community in greater or smaller terms. It does, however, make it difficult to provide objective measurements (Smith, 1990).

We see that traditionally tourism referred to the act or experience of touring. Post-World War II tourism's economic, environmental and social impacts saw tourism applied to the travel industry. This trend was furthered by the involvement of public agencies such as convention and visitor bureaus in the promotion of businesses and regions in efforts to attract tourists (Smith, 1990). Thus, we notice a movement from the demand to the supply aspects of tourism.

Supply-side definitions focus on the production of commodities, not on the demand for those commodities. This approach is consistent with that of other industries to define themselves. As an example we have '(T)he tourist industry consists of all those firms, organizations, and facilities which are intended to serve the specific needs and wants of tourists' (Leiper, 1979: 400). Yet we have businesses like restaurants that serve the needs of tourists as well as local residents. Are restaurants part of the tourism industry? It may make sense conceptually yet most restaurant receipts are derived from residents not tourists (Wilton, 1997). Some definitions recognize this fact yet are vague when attempting to define when a business is part of tourism. Consider the following.

> The tourist sector or the tourism industry … can be broadly conceived as representing the sum of those industrial and commercial activities producing goods and services wholly or mainly consumed by foreign visitors or domestic tourists (Smith, 1989: 31).

> The interrelated amalgamation of businesses, organizations, labor, and governmental agencies which totally or in part provide the means of transport, goods, services, accommodations, and other facilities, programs, and resources for travel and recreation (Smith, 1989: 31).

One solution has been proposed by the Canadian National Task Force on Tourism

Data (1985). Their definition is supply-side: the tourism industry is an 'aggregate of those retail goods and services businesses that serve the needs of people traveling outside their home community' (Smith, 1989: 32). However, it goes one step further. Tourism businesses are divided into two tiers: tier 1 would not exist without travel – hotels, airlines, cruise ships, travel agents; tier 2 would exist without travel but in a diminished form – restaurants, taxis, local attractions. Most tier 2 businesses get between one-fourth and one-third of their income from tourism. Such a distinction, to be workable, must be reasonable and able to overlook minor inconsistencies.

This definition is consistent with the definition of other industries; it permits relatively easy measurement of the size of the industry; it recognizes, in spirit, the distinction between tourists and excursionists. And it does take into account money spent at home in preparation for the trip or vacation. However, there are limitations. They focus on only one aspect of a larger occurrence. Additionally, it is still necessary to define the 'home environment'. The third type, holistic or integrated, combines the supply and demand aspects of tourism. Tourism is seen as comprising various businesses and also as a response to a social need. As such its 'product' includes all of the elements that combine to form the tourism consumers' experiences and that exist to service their needs and expectations.

Smith attempts to bring supply and demand together by defining tourism as:

> (1) The act of travel and set of actions engaged in by people during the trip to places away from the home environment. (2) The aggregate of all businesses that directly provide goods or services to facilitate business, pleasure, and leisure activities away from the home environment. (3) The combination of these two phenomena (Smith, 1990: 323).

In a similar vein, Franklin summarizes various definitions as follows: 'the temporary movement of people to destinations outside their normal places of work and residence, the activities undertaken during their stay in those destinations and the facilities created to cater to their need' (Franklin, 2003: 27–28, after Mathieson and Wall, 1982).

Conceptual definitions are much more holistic as they consider the complex social phenomenon aspects of tourism. This is offset by the fact that it is difficult to use these types of definitions for measurement purposes. One example is that of Cohen, who views a tourist as a 'voluntary, temporary, traveler, traveling in the expectation of pleasure from the novelty and change experience on a relatively long and non-recurrent round trip' (Cohen, 1975: 533). Franklin holistically identifies the characteristics of modern tourism as follows (Franklin, 2003: 26):

- it is derived from the condition and experience of life in modernity and is not an escape from it;
- modernity, in turn, is about the permanence of novelty and not an escape to it;
- it is more than travel – it is about accessing novelty and the modern world;
- it is consumerism;
- the framework for tourism has been influenced by nationalism, nation states and latterly by cities and regions;
- it is more than a visual experience and certainly more than rest, relaxation and pleasure. It exists within a political and moral context; and
- it is a way of accessing the world and, increasingly, our place within it.

Another approach is to consider the various 'stakeholders' that make up what is known as tourism. Goeldner and McIntosh (Goeldner and McIntosh, 1986) identify four different perspectives of tourism. First is the tourist who seeks various psychic and physical experiences and satisfactions; the second part are the businesses that provide tourist goods and services and whose owners see tourism as an opportunity to make a profit by supplying the goods and services the market demands; the third element comprises the governments of the host community or area who see tourism as a wealth factor in their economy. This element includes the income their citizens can earn from these businesses, the foreign exchange receipts as well as the tax receipts collected either directly or indirectly; finally, there are the host communities who see tourism as a cultural and employment factor.

Seen this way, tourism may be defined as 'the sum of the phenomena and relationships arising from the interaction of tourists, business suppliers, host governments, and local communities in the process of attracting and hosting these tourism and other visitors' (Goeldner and McIntosh, 1986: 4).

Seeing tourism in an integrated or holistic fashion leads to a greater variety of definitions.

One definition suggests tourism is 'the sum of the phenomena and relationships arising from the travel and stay of nonresidents, in so far as they do not lead to permanent residence and are not connected to any earning activity' (Burkhart and Medlik, 1974: 40, quoted in Smith, 1990: 325–326). This is the definition adopted by the International Association of Scientific Experts in Tourism. It has since been criticized because 'the phenomenon and relationships' has not been adequately defined.

Jafari (1977: 6) introduces the idea of studying what occurs when he says that '(T)ourism is the study of man away from his usual habitat, of the industry which responds to his needs, and of the impacts that both he and the industry have on the host's socio-cultural, economic, and physical environments'. This definition explicitly recognizes demand, supply to meet that demand, and the impacts that come from both It also acknowledges the idea of flow from origin to destination but does fail to define 'usual habitat'. In addition the motives or purpose of travel is avoided (Smith, 1990).

A comprehensive definition is offered by Leiper (1979: 403–404) when he suggests that tourism is

the system involving the discretionary travel and temporary stay of persons away from their usual residence for one or more nights, excepting tours made for the primary purpose of earning remuneration from points enroute. The elements of the system are tourists, generating regions, transit routes, destination regions, and a tourist industry. The five elements are arranged in spatial and functional connections. Having the characteristics of an open system, the organization of the five elements operates within broader environments: physical, cultural, social, economic, political, technological with which it operates.

However, Smith (1990) argues that the length of the definition works against its widespread use, the five elements and the open system are inadequately defined, as is the idea of a tourist industry. In addition, adoption of an overnight element excludes day trips that can involve significant distances away from home.

Nevertheless, there does seem to be agreement that tourism involves (Sessa, 1983: 16):

- an element of transfer;
- transfer related to a stay in a location outside one's residence;

- the stay must be a temporary one; minimum duration is insignificant; the maximum duration has been variously defined; and
- tourism phenomena composed of the subject [person] and the object [tourism facilities], and direct relationship between the two in that the person must utilize the facilities for there to be tourism consumption [the tourism product].

However, Smith (1990) concludes that no one definition of tourism will be developed because the concept of tourism is too broad for universal agreement. Instead, he suggests that a variety of definitions, each suited to a specific purpose, be accepted.

HOSPITALITY

The Shorter Oxford English Dictionary defines 'hospitality' as 'the act or practice of being hospitable; the reception and entertainment of guests or strangers with liberality and goodwill" (Medlik, 2003: vii). It may be that hospitable behavior was first exhibited in the hunter/gatherer society when a newcomer would offer to share food that he/she had gathered in order to establish a right to share the food of others. Thus would a relationship begin between individuals and groups of people (O'Connor, 2005).

The term *hospitality* is taken from the term 'hospice', meaning a house of rest for pilgrims during medieval times (Grottola, 1988). The term was formalized in Europe in the Middle Ages by monasteries operating 'guest houses' for Christian pilgrims. These guest houses then morphed into roadside inns for travelers (Ingram, 1999). Dictionary definitions from the 1930s on stress a common theme of 'kindness welcoming strangers or guests' (Brotherton, 1999: 166). English hospitality over the last few centuries is identified through five underlying principles (O'Connor, 2005: 268–269):

- the host/guest relationship is a natural one;
- having regard for the scared nature of the guest is an inherent aspect of being a host;
- hospitality is noble;
- selfless giving is an established way of English society; and
- the relationships formed through hospitality are as important as are found in the marketplace.

Lashley (2000) argues for a broad definition that goes beyond the 'commercial' to include a 'social' and a 'private' dimension. The social dimension takes into account the social context within which hospitality activities take place. The importance of hospitality and of being hospitable varies temporally and geographically. Therefore, it is argued, hospitality needs to take into account the surrounding historical, cultural and anthropological perspectives. For example, in earlier Western societies, the duty to provide hospitality to strangers was seen as a moral imperative. Hospitality also played a part in the local political economy, providing social cohesion through the practice of redistributing of food and drink to both neighbors and the poor. Food is a central part of hospitality. It is an integral part of the duty to protect travelers; it symbolizes trust and closeness between host and guest, a distinction that continues today in the business lunch; and it is an act of kindness (Lashley, 2000).

The private domain influences the more-written-about commercial domain of hospitality. Expectations formed in the home shape guest demands outside of the home. The provision of in-room facilities can be seen as satisfying these home-learned expectations. We learn about being a good host and guest from early experiences growing up – entertaining neighbors and friends or on 'sleep-overs' and visiting relatives. It used to be common practice for the family to enjoy the evening meal together. Through maternal admonishments to 'keep elbows off the table' or 'never chew food with the mouth open', children learned how to behave in a commercial setting. Today it is increasingly rare for the family to gather together around the table as many households have both parents working different hours and children are engaged in their own individual activities. Companies now pay for outside consultants to provide etiquette training for their young executives that parents used to provide in the home.

The commercial domain of the hospitality literature is more specific in its definitions. Cassee sees hospitality as 'a harmonious mixture of tangible and intangible components – food, beverages, beds, ambience and environment, and behavior of staff' (Brotherton, 1999: 166). This definition has been since modified to a 'harmonious mixture of food, beverage, and/or shelter, a physical environment, and the behavior and attitude of people' (Brotherton, 1999: 166).

The literature is dominated by supply-side economic, product-oriented, commercial definitions. Examples include 'the provision of overnight accommodation for people staying away from home, and the provision of sustenance for people eating away from home' and 'the method of production by which the needs of the proposed guest are satisfied to the utmost and that means a supply of goods and services in a quantity and quality desired by the guest and at a price that is acceptable to him so that he feels the product is worth the price' and 'hospitality consists of offering food, beverage and lodging, or, in other words, of offering the basic needs for the person away from home' (Brotherton, 1999: 167).

The problem with these definitions is that they suggest that hospitality is a one-way process. Later definitions of hospitality agree that it is a form of exchange rather than a one-sided encounter (Grottola, 1988; Lashley, 2000). A better definition considers three elements: how hospitality is configured; the motives for providing it; and its essential nature (Brotherton, 1999: 168). First, hospitality is closely associated with interactions between humans. It is conferred by a host on a guest who is away from home. The philosopher Max Beerbohm divided society into two classes – hosts and guests – based on the instinct to either offer hospitality or to accept it (O'Connor, 2005: 270).

Second, an exchange takes place that benefits both provider and those for whom the products and service are being provided. It is interactive between provider and receiver. This provides a major problem for those seeking to provide hospitality. The hospitality product can be seen as the sum of satisfactions and dissatisfactions that are the hospitality experience. Guests determine whether or not they are satisfied using their own subjective frames of reference that are both inconsistent and unique to the individual. Thus, it is extremely difficult for the providers of hospitality service – managers and employees alike – to define what hospitality is and to consistently deliver it (Ingram, 1999). Finally, hospitality involves the simultaneous provision and consumption of certain types of products and services.

There is some evidence in the literature that people are born with a certain amount of hospitableness and that, to varying degrees, are able to judge the extent to which one's host is genuinely hospitable. Prehistoric people used hospitable gestures as 'currency' to buy their way into another group or clan. Gestures were disregarded if the potential group member was viewed as having suspect ambitions (O'Connor, 2005).

Hospitality involves a blend of tangible and intangible factors that include the behaviors of employees and provides for the guest's security, psychological and physiological comfort (Brotherton, 1999). This final element emphasizes the importance given to the treatment and protection of strangers. It almost suggests this responsibility as a moral imperative. It can certainly be argued that providing for the security of those away from home has a central place in one's value system. Food is seen as a central piece of this protection. Sharing food can be viewed as the 'foundation of civilized behavior' (Brotherton, 1999: 168).

As such, hospitality can be seen as '… a contemporaneous human exchange, which is voluntarily entered into, and designed to enhance the mutual wellbeing of the parties concerned through the provision of accommodation and food and drink' (Brotherton, 1999: 168). This definition differentiates hospitality from hospitable behavior. Some confuse the concept of hospitable behavior with hospitality. It might be argued that guests do not want to feel at home – a major motive for being away from home is the feeling of being different. Hospitality, it can be said, is intended to make people feel as if they are *not* at home.

This is not, and cannot be, a static definition. The concept of hospitality is subject to a variety of religious, political, social and economic influences over time. This definition focuses on *hospitality* rather than the *hospitality industry*. The 'hospitality industry' is defined as the 'provision of accommodation, food and drink for people away from home for reward' (Medlik, 2003: vii). It is said that the hospitality industry is (Ingram, 1999: 143):

- important but insufficiently researched;
- fragmented but increasingly dominated by smaller players;
- operationally centered but needing a more strategic focus;
- unable to accurately define its product offering;
- traditionally managed by managers with specific competencies;
- known for low productivity but needing higher performance;
- generally unwilling to train staff; and
- unable to use the talents of its employees fully.

Finally, there is the related concept of hospitality management that has a core that deals with the 'management of food, beverages and/or accommodation in a service context' (Brotherton, 1999: 168). The operational characteristics of hospitality include the following (Ingram, 1999: 142):

- service that involves host/guest interaction, is provided and consumed at the same time, and can either please or displease the guest;
- processes that are planned and controlled by management and delivered (often inconsistently) by employees;
- information – inconsistently stored, retrieved and used – about guests, competitors and macro trends affecting the operation;
- work hours that are long, involve shift work and, because they are subject to the shifting demands of business, place stress on employees and management; and
- functional tasks, organized by departments that are often in conflict with each other.

TOURISM AND HOSPITALITY

Is there any relationship between 'tourism' and 'hospitality'? It is common, though incorrect, to use the term *hospitality industry* interchangeably with *tourism* or *tourism industry*. The term is also used to refer to the various types of lodging accommodation that are part of tourism (Grottola, 1988). To many, 'tourism' involves the movement of people while 'hospitality' is concerned with overnight stays (Bushwell and Williams, 2003). On a deeper level, the 'tourist process' can be thought of as consisting of the three elements of travel, accommodation and participation in activities at the destination. Others would add the social, economic and environmental impacts resulting from these elements (Bushwell and Williams, 2003).

Brotherton (2002) has examined whether or not hospitality exists as a separate entity from tourism, travel or leisure. He indicates that hospitality can, in fact, exist without tourism (people enjoying a meal while shopping), travel (friends in a local pub) or leisure (a businessperson taking a client to lunch). Tourism, on the other hand, cannot exist without travel but can without leisure (business tourism). Travel can, however, exist without tourism or leisure (business travel). Leisure can also exist independent of hospitality – reading books at home – tourism and/or travel. Thus, he concludes, hospitality can be distinguished from tourism, travel and leisure. Further, hospitality, leisure and travel are all concepts distinct and discrete from each other. Although travel is seen as a necessary condition for tourism to occur other things – motivation, time, money – are also required.

One way to view this inter-relationship is to examine the way academics have organized tourism and hospitality programs at the university level. There are three primary models that assist in understanding the philosophical bases of tourism and hospitality academic programs (Chen and Groves, 1999). The first views tourism and hospitality as mutually inclusive. In this model both are independent with some areas of overlap. While the identity of each discipline is recognized, the common overlap areas include the pieces that can be transferred from one to the other. Tourism concentrates on the impact of marketing studies, economic, environmental and social impact studies. Hospitality is concerned with service, marketing and management of travel, hotels, commercial recreation and other leisure businesses.

The second views hospitality in a superior position to tourism where hospitality is a 'primary driving force as a service component to other industries' (Chen and Groves, 1999: 38). This model views hospitality as service based (hotels, restaurants, casinos, etc.) and tourism as synonymous with the travel sector. The third model views tourism as superior to hospitality. Tourism is viewed as an important economic activity that expresses some concern for the impact of development on the social, cultural and ecological fabric of a destination. The hospitality industry develops to service tourism because of tourism's great economic importance. Its role is in the development of infrastructure to support tourism.

Within hospitality management education itself there are continuing issues of academic credibility (Lashley and Morrison, 2001). The curriculum for hospitality management education has evolved from a vocational emphasis based on 'an amalgam of craft, ritual and inherited practices' (Morrison and O'Mahoney, 2003: 38). Two decades of research have resulted in broad support for including social sciences in the curriculum to balance the vocational, action-oriented emphasis with one that is liberal and reflective (Morrison and O'Mahoney, 2003).

Others suggest adding the natural sciences perspective to add insight into not only the social but also the physiological needs of guests.

The form of hospitality within a society at a given point in time has been addressed by Brotherton (2002). He postulates that the nature, incidence and forms of hospitality in any given period are a function of natural and human resources, economic, socio-cultural and politico-legal factors, technology and hospitality behavior. The greater the resources in any or all of these areas, the greater the potential for hospitality to exist.

From an operational perspective hospitality can be seen to have four dimensions (Brotherton, 2002):

- spatial – where it takes place;
- behavioral – the motives behind the provision of hospitality;
- temporal – when it is delivered; and
- physical – the physical features and products associated with the provision of hospitality.

A pilot study in two UK hotels finds that individuals primarily considered hospitality in terms of the behavioral dimension (warmth of service, polite, friendliness). However, in addition, words associated with the temporal and physical dimensions were also given (Brotherton, 2005).

As the debate continues it is fair to ask how the subject of hospitality management can be taught in a sound manner when the broad boundaries of the subject are not well defined.

REFERENCES

Beatty, J. E. and Torbert, W. R. (2003) 'The false duality of work and leisure', *Journal of Management Inquiry*, 12(3): 239–252.

Brotherton, B. (1999) 'Towards a definitive view of the nature of hospitality and hospitality management', *International Journal of Contemporary Hospitality Management*, 11/1: 165–173.

Brotherton, B. (2002) Towards a general theory of hospitality'. Presented as a work-in-progress abstract published in: *Proceedings of the Eleventh Annual CHME Hospitality Research Conference*, Leeds Metropolitan University.

Brotherton, B. (2005) 'The nature of hospitality: customer perceptions and implications', *Tourism Hospitality Planning & Development*, 2(3): 139–153.

Burkhart, A. J. and Medlik, S. (1974) *Tourism*. London: Heinemann.

Bushwell, J. and Williams, C. (2003) *Service Quality in Leisure and Tourism*. Wallingford, Oxon, UK; Cambridge, MA: CABI Pub.

Chen, K. C. and Groves, D. (1999) 'The importance of examining philosophical relationships between tourism and hospitality curricula,' *International Journal of Contemporary Hospitality Management*, 11: 37–42.

Cohen, E. (1974) 'Who is a tourist? A conceptual clarification', *Social Review*, 22(4): 533.

Committee on Commerce, Science and Transportation. (1978) *National Tourism Policy Study Final Report*. Washington, DC: US Government Printing Office.

De Grazia, S. (1962) *On Time, Work and Leisure*. New York: Anchor Books.

Dumazedier, J. (1967) *Toward a Society of Leisure*. (S. E. McClure, Trans.). Toronto, Canada: Collier-Macmillan. (Original work published 1962).

Esteve, R., Martin, J. S, and Lopez, A. E. (1999) 'Grasping the meaning of leisure; developing a self-report measurement tool', *Leisure Studies*, 18(2).

Franklin, A. (2003) 'What is tourism?'. In *Tourism: An Introduction*. Thousand Oaks, CA : Sage Publications.

Godbey, G. (1998) 'Toward another century of parks and recreation', *Parks & Recreation*, 33(7): pS28 (6).

Goeldner, C. and McIntosh, R. (1986) *Tourism Principles, Practices, and Philosophies*. New York: John Wiley & Sons.

Goodale, T. and Godbey, G. (1988) *The Evolution of Leisure*. State College, PA: Venture Publishing, Inc.

Grottola, M. (1980) 'The spiritual essence of hospitality practice: seeing the proverbial stranger as a pretext to reading ourselves'. In P. R. Cummings, F. A. Kwansa and M. B. Sussman (eds) (1988) *The Role of the Hospitality Industry in the Lives of Individuals and Families*. New York, NY: The Haworth Press, Inc. pp. 1–22.

Ingram, H. (1999) 'Hospitality: a framework for a millennial review', *International Journal of Contemporary Hospitality Management*, 11(4): 140–147.

Iso-Ahola, S. (1980) *The Social Psychology of Leisure and Recreation*. Dubuque, IA: William C. Brown.

Jafari, J. (1977) 'Editor's page', *Annals of Tourism Research*, 5: 6–11.

Jensen, C. R. (1977) *Leisure and Recreation: Introduction and Overview*. London: Henry Kimpton Publishers.

Jensen, C. R. and Naylor, J. H. (1990) *Opportunities in Recreation and Leisure Careers*. Chicago, IL: VGM Career Horizons.

Koshar, R. (2002) 'Seeing, traveling, and consuming: an introduction'. In R. Koshar (ed.) *Histories of Leisure*. Oxford, UK: Berg.

Lashley, C. (2000) 'In search of hospitality: towards a theoretical framework', *International Journal of Hospitality Management.* Oxford; Boston: Butterworth-Heinemann, 3–15.

Lashley, C. and Morrison A. (eds) (2001) *In Search of Hospitality: Theoretical Perspectives and Debates.* Oxford: Butterworth-Heinemann.

Leiper, N. (1979) 'The framework of tourism', *Annals of Tourism Research,* 6(3): 90–407.

Leitner, M. and Leitner, S. (1996) *Leisure Enhancement.* New York: Haworth Press, Inc.

Litvin, S. W., Woo, I. J. H., Li, F. L. and Lim, K. H. F. (2002) 'The traditional leisure paradox' a valid tourism model?', *Capitalizing on Travel Research for Marketing Success.* Travel and Tourism Research Association 33rd Annual Conference Proceedings.

Mathieson, A. and Wall, G. (1982) *Tourism: Economic, Physical, and Social Impacts.* London: Longman.

Medlik, S. (2003) *Dictionary of Travel, Tourism and Hospitality.* Oxford; Boston: Butterworth-Heinemann.

Mieczkowski, Z. (1990) *World Trends in Tourism and Recreation.* New York: Peter Lang.

Morrison, A. and O'Mahoney, G. B. (2003) 'The liberation of hospitality management education', *International Journal of Contemporary Hospitality Management,* 15/1: 38–44.

Neulinger, J. (1974) *The Psychology of Leisure: Research Approaches to the Study of Leisure.* Springfield, IL: Charles C. Thomas.

Neulinger, J. (1981) *Leisure: An Introduction.* Boston: Allyn & Bacon.

O'Connor, D. (2005) 'Towards a new interpretation of "hospitality"', *International Journal of Contemporary Hospitality Management,* 17(3): 267–271.

OECD (1963) *Tourism Policy and International Tourism in OECD Countries.* Paris: OECD.

Poria, Y., Butler, R. and Airey, D. (2003) 'Revisiting Mieczkowski's conceptualization of tourism', *Tourism Geographies,* 5(1): 26–38.

Sessa, A. (1983) *Elements of Tourism Economics.* Roma: Catal.

Shaw, G. and Williams, A. M. (1994) *Critical Issues in Tourism.* Oxford: Blackwell.

Smith, S. L. J. (1989) *Tourism Analysis.* Essex: Longman Group U.K. Limited.

Smith, S. L. J. (1990) *Dictionary of Concepts in Recreation and Leisure Studies.* New York, NY: Greenwood Press.

Smith, S. L. J. and Godbey, G. C. (1991) 'Leisure, recreation and tourism', *Annals of Tourism Research,* (18), 85–100.

Theodorson, G. A. and Theodorson, A. G. (1969) *A Modern Dictionary of Sociology.* New York: Crowell.

US Department of Commerce. (1977) *Analysis of Travel Definitions, Terminology, and Research Needs among States and Cities.* Washington, DC: US Travel Service.

Voss, J. (1967) 'The definition of leisure', *Journal of Economic Issues,* 1(5): 91–106.

Weisskopf, D. (1982) *Recreation and Leisure: Improving the Quality of Life.* Boston: Allyn & Bacon.

Wilton, D. (1997) *Recent Developments in Tourism, as Revealed by the National Tourism Indicators.* A Report Prepared for the Canadian Tourism Commission from the Department of Economics, University of Waterloo, Ontario.

Women in Hospitality

Judi Brownell and Kate Walsh

4

INTRODUCTION

It is unlikely that there will ever come a time when gender in the workplace will not matter. Regardless of culture, historical context, or social circumstance, men and women view the world – and often each other – through gender-specific lenses (Tannen, 1990; Arliss and Borisoff, 1998). While this element of diversity has the potential to enrich workplace interactions and improve organizational outcomes, it also brings with it issues of power, justice, and identity. Hospitality organizations, in particular, have been the focus of numerous studies as women in service contexts – whether consumers, employees, or leaders – confront gender-linked dilemmas that are particularly complex and acute.

As this chapter unfolds, it will become clear that, while women have made progress toward parity in the workplace, significant issues surrounding women employees in hospitality and the needs of women travelers remain unresolved. After several decades of study, and in spite of growing legislation addressing issues of women and work, women are still poorly represented in the senior management ranks (Abelson, 2001; Brown and Ridge, 2002; Vigil, 2002; Archer, 2003; Rindfleish and Sheridan, 2003). In fact, one report finds that 'both in earnings and promotions, women are worse off than they were six years ago' (Isaacson, 2002: 12). While other researchers remain more optimistic, there is no doubt that serious barriers remain and continue to stall women's career development. In addition, there is little question that hospitality organizations are among the most difficult environments for women seeking career advancement and personal satisfaction (Martin, 2000; Primavera, 2001).

While we explore the subject of women as workers and consumers in hospitality through a North American lens, we hope that the ideas and issues that arise will provide insight to all hospitality professionals. Toward this end, the chapter begins with an historical overview of women's entry into the workplace in the United States. The unique features of the hospitality environment are then delineated as they help to explain the need for special focus on this industry segment. A discussion of women's career development follows. This section reviews the current status of women in hospitality management and explores the multi-faceted subject of organizational leadership. Research findings are presented that help us better understand both gender-related issues as well as the dynamics of women's leadership roles. The subject of salaries and gender equity is also discussed.

The central portion of this chapter presents a review of literature related to four challenges women confront as they seek to reach and succeed in senior leadership positions in the hospitality industry. Topics such as gender stereotyping, work and family balance, overcoming old boy networks, and mentoring are discussed in light of gender-specific concerns. Research gaps are also identified for each theme, and current organizational responses to each of these challenges are then reviewed. Next, we examine the emerging interest in a new and growing market segment, women as business travelers and consumers of hospitality. As women in all industries travel more frequently, their unique needs become an important concern to hospitality professionals. Women's travel preferences are discussed and examples are provided of the ways in which the hospitality industry is addressing this new market segment. Finally, the last section of this chapter moves into the future, suggesting how globalization might affect women's careers and outlining three other topics that will require research in the decades ahead.

A BRIEF HISTORY OF WOMEN AND WORK

In 1943, a set of 'tips' was provided for male supervisors looking to maximize the effectiveness of their female employees (Anonymous, 2003). Among them:

- pick young married women ... they are less likely to be flirtatious;
- older women who have never contacted the public ... are inclined to be cantankerous and fussy;
- 'husky' girls ... are more even-tempered and efficient; and
- women make excellent workers when they have their jobs cut out for them, but they lack initiative in finding work themselves.

While it might be assumed that women have come a long way, progress toward workplace parity has been along a rocky road whose end is not yet in sight. In the United States, most women entered the workforce due to the country's economic and social needs rather than because of individual choice. For instance, women took clerical positions during the Civil War period when there was an increased need for record keeping. This early introduction of women into the office contributed to the feminization of what was later referred to as secretarial activities (Strom, 1989). Even today, office work continues to be gender-linked with nearly 97% of clerical work being handled by women.

It was assumed from the beginning that women would work longer hours and receive less pay than their male counterparts. Due to this attitude, women laborers soon began to organize. Among the earliest collective efforts was The International Ladies Garment Workers' Union. Formed in 1900, these female garment workers held a memorable strike in 1909 often referred to as the 'uprising of 20,000'. Another early organization created to ensure that women's voices were heard was the National Women's Trade Union League, pioneered by Mary O'Sullivan and Leonora O'Reilly (Elman, 2001). While it had been common for single women to work, the needs of a war time economy saw married women leaving their homes for offices and factories. Just when women were becoming accustomed to their new found independence and productivity outside the home, the great depression made jobs scarce. A significant number of US cities and states passed laws prohibiting married women from working. As a consequence, women sought the support of their peers through professional association. In 1919 Lena Phillips founded the National Federation of Business and Professional Women's Clubs which served as an advocacy organization for women who wanted to remain in the workforce. A decade later, the International Federation for Business and Professional Women was founded and remains active today. By affiliating with like-minded colleagues, women's voices could not as readily be ignored.

In addition to a gradual movement of women from the home to the workplace, major changes in the labor markets after World War II included a shift from manufacturing to service industries (Beck, 1998). As previously noted, both the laws and the social norms of the early twentieth century operated to keep most married women at home. One study places the percentage of married working women in 1913 in the neighborhood of 2% (Mouton, 2000). Throughout the early years of the twentieth century it was common for women to become managers only through the early death of their husbands. As post-World War II women began entering the job market in greater numbers, inequities were even more readily apparent. In his history of workplace bathroom practices, for instance, Linder (1997) points to the fact that even the government's early efforts to regulate equality were often misguided. For instance, when the number of men's and women's toilets was specified, the government did not require that companies allow their employees to use them. It is reported that when women began to win seats in Congress, they missed a significant number of votes due to the long hike they were forced to make to use the women's restroom facilities (Walsh, 2000). Such stories create a backdrop upon which we clearly see the emerging picture; working women in America have been treated 'differently'.

The 1950s was an important decade in the history of women and work. New prosperity no longer required women in the factories. A wide range of new products for the home began to change the role of wives and mothers. The mass media was becoming more influential, and promoted an image of family togetherness that solidified the woman's role as center of domestic activity. This culture came to be known

Table 4.1 The family and women's changing roles

1950s – mothers had no destiny, did everything for husband and children
1960s – dramatic split from old roles
1970s – women fading from place in center of family
1980s – female yuppie
1990s – new family unit, mothers one member of a group

Adapted from Valentine, V. (1994). Advertising's happy families, *Campaign*, 26–28.

as the 'feminine mystique', a term coined by Betty Friedan (Powell, 1993). It characterized a framework in which women had no real destiny of their own but rather derived their sense of self and personal satisfaction from service to their families (Valentine, 1994). One element of this perspective was that respectability demanded that mothers control their daughters' actions (Mouton, 2000) and keep girls' attire, interests – and work – distinct from those of boys. Little girls stayed clean, learned to decorate and cook, and never raised their voices. As a result, women coming of age in the 1950s would later find the discomforts of asserting themselves in the workplace to be particularly acute.

The 1960s witnessed a striking departure from the old roles and rules of past decades (Table 4.1). While previously women had been 'drafted' into the workforce due to economic and political conditions, and later kept at home to tend to domestic issues, in the 1960s women began coming back into the workforce voluntarily (Beck, 1998). The shift from manufacturing to service industries was also accelerating and women, as we will discuss in a later section, were in demand as never before. This trend has continued and, as a consequence, the balance of work and family life has been shifted (Gini, 1998). Yet, as studies in the 1970s and 1980s revealed, women working outside the home continued to shoulder nearly all of the responsibility for making sure their homes were clean and their families satisfied.

By 1984, almost two-thirds of women with children between six and eighteen years were in the labor force (Powell, 1993: 36). Still, stereotypes created in earlier periods served to limit the nature of work women could do. One study reports that half of all those in the labor force during the 1980s continued to be in gender-stereotyped occupations. Men were hired for heavy manual labor, jobs that required technical expertise, and managerial positions.

Women, on the other hand, were dominant in service and support roles (Beck, 1998). Work for both men and women continued to be influenced by gender; even now, women continue to fill a much narrower range of occupations than do men. In addition, men in female-dominated workplaces hold a majority of the senior management positions (Brown and Ridge, 2002).

WOMEN IN MANAGEMENT

Today, while woman comprise 47% of management, they hold only 12% of corporate-level positions, 5% of top-management jobs, and half of 1% of the highest positions in corporations (Aguinis and Adams, 1998; Adler, 1999; Oakley, 2000; Isaacson, 2002; Vigil, 2002). They also represent only 4% of the top wage-earners (Appelbaum et al., 2003). These statistics represent only a two to three percentage point gain from 1995 to 2000 (Catalyst, 2001). And, while 25% of men reach executive-level positions, only 9% of women are likely to do so (Schneer and Reitman, 1995). This is not a phenomenon particular to the United States. Women in Europe are no better off than their US colleagues. In Europe, women represent approximately 30% of management, yet hold between 1 and 5% of senior-level managerial roles (Gardiner and Tiggemann, 1999).

Today, researchers are finding that many women seem to remain in what is termed 'the marzipan layer just below the top-executive icing' (*The Economist*: June 28, 2003: 90). In this layer, women, such as those in human resources and sales, are rarely chosen to move to executive-level positions. Instead, the highest position they usually attain in these support positions is the director level. In tournament fashion, women appear to drop out of the running as they move up the executive ladder (Isaacson, 2002). At the current rate of increase, one author suggests that it will be 2466 before women will reach equity in the executive suite (Beck, 1998). Determining why women's career advancement has seemingly been stalled, and the specific obstacles that need to be addressed, is the focus of our later discussion.

There was a time when researchers hypothesized that the numbers of women executives automatically would continue to increase; that simply placing more women into senior positions somehow would make it easier for others to follow. Rindfleish (2003) is among those who have recognized that the future will not unfold quite so seamlessly. He argues that deliberate strategies will be required for women's leadership opportunities to increase. Women will need to take risks to get ahead (Vigil, 2002). On this theme, Hardy-Sellers (2002) reminds us that the glass ceiling has been renamed the concrete ceiling by those who have continued to struggle in their climb to the top. Perhaps this is no where more true than in hospitality organizations where a sexualized workplace contributes to the obstacles women continue to confront.

FEATURES OF THE HOSPITALITY WORKPLACE AND THE NATURE OF WOMEN'S ROLES

The hospitality environment itself is a strong force in shaping the way in which men and women interact. The term 'sexualized' has frequently been used to describe the hospitality workplace (Gutek, 1985; Gutek et al., 1990). Hospitality implies having a good time, doing whatever it takes to satisfy others. Dominant images of the industry include wine glasses, whirlpools, and breakfast trays – symbols of romance, of feeling good, of pampering.

Dimensions of the workplace directly influence employee behavior. Many service providers work in close proximity to one another. Their shifts are long and irregular; men and women work together closely during evening and night-time hours. The duties of the hospitality workplace are likely to take employees into settings traditionally associated with gender-linked behaviors. Job responsibilities frequently require employees to spend time together in bedrooms, bars, and lounges. Restaurant kitchens are an example of one of the strongest male-dominated hospitality cultures. As the former director of the French Culinary Institute once lamented, many chefs are reluctant to hire women graduates. She explains: 'They say, You are going to ruin the spirit of my kitchen if you send me a woman because then the other chefs aren't going to pay attention to their work, they are going to be chasing after her' (Peters, 1988: 118). Contributing to a culture that accentuates

gender differences is the fact that hospitality employees are often hired, at least in part, because of their physical attractiveness. Airline attendants, sales managers, and convention planners all project their organization's image to the public and, in many instances, this image accentuates and perpetuates gender-related stereotyping. Finally, the hospitality industry is one of the most diverse and, while a highly desirable characteristic, this diversity is often accompanied by a set of complex gender-related challenges. Different cultures mix gender and business in different ways (Axtell, 1990). In hospitality, bringing together men and women from different cultures with different gender-related experiences, expectations, and assumptions often creates awkward situations for women managers, employees, and guests. For instance, if a customer's understanding of the requirements of a barmaid includes services the female employee does not feel obligated to provide, problems are likely to result. As Wood (2004) notes, increasing gender and other diversity dimensions is a journey that ultimately will provide hospitality organizations with a talent advantage. Such advantages, however, will be realized only as we learn more about the challenges diversity presents and as we design and implement human resources strategies to address them.

Another characteristic of many hospitality organizations is their emphasis on tradition. Repeat guests, in particular, have firm expectations concerning how they want to be treated and the types of services they want to receive. These customers value a consistent and stable product. Consequently, the industry's journey into the twenty-first century, and its willingness to adopt new policies and implement new technologies, has often been slower than changes that have occurred in other types of industry.

It becomes clear that women in hospitality experience additional challenges as a result of the nature and characteristics of the industry in which they work. As employees respond to the varied 'moments of truth' that arise, both men and women have an opportunity to define and influence organizational practices. Hospitality leaders are gradually learning how best to create cultures in which expectations and professional roles are not inappropriately gender-linked. Achieving this goal will undoubtedly require continued attention and commitment, both from industry leaders and from the women who are reaching for the top.

WOMEN'S CAREER DEVELOPMENT IN HOSPITALITY

Women working in hospitality

Job opportunities in the hospitality industry are continuing to increase. In 2004, the US hospitality industry employed more than 12 million people; women and minorities constitute 57% of this workforce (Wood, 2004). While hospitality has been one of the fastest areas of employment growth, it has been particularly so for women with nearly three-quarters of the recent increase represented by women's jobs. Many of these positions, however, are part-time, low-status and low paid. In fact, gender segmentation has been relatively stable with women horizontally segregated into particular positions and areas of operation and vertically segregated into relatively low status areas (Babin and Boles, 1998).

While the industry heralds some exceptional female CEOs and executives (e.g. Marilyn Carlson Nelson, CEO of Carlson companies; Stephanie Sonnabend, President, Sonesta International Hotels; Charlotte St. Martin, EVP, Loews Hotels and Barbara Talbot, EVP Four Seasons, to name a few), women who hold top-level positions remain the exception rather than the norm (Mann and Seacord, 2003). In the hospitality industry in the USA, women outnumber men in entry-level managerial positions. Yet, less than 44% of managerial positions are held by women and, similar to the situation in other industries, only a small number of women occupy executive-level positions (Knutson and Schmidgall, 1999; Costen et al., 2003).

Similar statistics characterize the food-service industry where women comprise 44% of managers but only 4% of top-level executives (Primavera, 2001). A recent study concluded that women in foodservice hold 14% of corporate office positions and only 4% of board of director seats at the parent companies of the hundred largest foodservice chains (Walkup, 2003). When Catalyst (a US non-profit organization working to advance women in business) studied women's roles in the industry's 100 largest restaurant chains (Table 4.2), they arrived at similar conclusions. While the majority of employees were female, women were grossly under-represented at the senior levels, holding only 8% of the board seats and 4% of the 'highest titles' in these foodservice organizations (Martin, 2000). Another recent Catalyst

Table 4.2 Catalyst study of women in food service

- 56% of employees are women
- 44% of managers are women
- 14% of corporate officers are women
- 8% of board directors are women
- 4% of the 'highest titles' are women

Adapted from Primavera, B. (2001). Women stand tall in the heat of the kitchen but executive prospects are still chilly, *Nation's Restaurant News*, 35(46), 32–34.

study (2002) suggests that at the present rate, it will take 39 years for women to occupy 50% of corporate office positions. It is clear that women are barely visible in the top executive positions in food-service (Wood, 2004).

The situation is identical in the UK and many other European countries where hospitality is one of the fastest growing sectors and, in the UK, represents the nation's second-largest industry (Purcell, 1996). By the early 1990s, British women comprised 47% of the hospitality workforce, but held only 8% of director positions and half of 1% of executive-level positions (Maxwell, 1997). While women account for most of new industry entrants, especially at the managerial level, they still do not hold influential positions. In fact, women in managerial positions often report feeling left out of important decisions that affect their departments and companies (Bates, 2002). In one study, over 15% more women than men reported feeling dissatisfied with their career progress and advancement (Backmon et al., 1997).

Renewed attention by researchers and practitioners alike is required to uncover the reasons why women's movement into senior hospitality positions appears to have stalled. This situation is particularly troublesome in light of women's facilitating and inclusive leadership characteristics, a subject discussed in the following section.

Women as hospitality leaders

The majority of studies indicate that today's successful organizations are team-oriented, agile, flatter, flexible and holistic in their vision and strategy (Appelbaum et al., 2003). As a result, organizational leaders need to be non-coercive, comprehensive thinkers – individuals who are skilled at building work relationships and fostering collaborative teams. These are the traits and behaviors most frequently associated with women's management style (Fletcher, 1998; Colwill and Townsend, 1999; Kolb, 1999; Pounder and Coleman, 2002; Birute and Lewin, 2003).

In addition, women tend to possess transformational leadership characteristics, those traits that enable them to enact dramatic organizational change through providing a vision and inspiring a sense of purpose in others (Bass, 1985; Rosener, 1990; Yammarino et al., 1997). Women also demonstrate characteristics of 'superleadership', a style in which the leader creates self-direction and self-leadership in followers (Sims and Lorenzi, 1992).

In a groundbreaking study that examines gender differences in leadership style, Eagly and Johnson (1990) found that women emphasize both interpersonal relationships and task accomplishment, whereas their male counterparts focus more intently on the task. Women also tend to adopt a more democratic style than men. They are more likely to manage others by offering rewards while their male counterparts are more likely to manage others through punitive measures (Cooper, 1992). It would appear that women typically act in ways that are more participative, consultative and egalitarian than their male counterparts. They also tend to display more effective communication and people-management skills (Brownell, 1994; Ibarra, 1999; Vinnicombe and Singh, 2002). Women who lead in facilitative ways are likely to be accepted and rated highly by both male and female subordinates (Eagly et al., 1992; Vroom and Jago, 1995). And, as a result of these leadership behaviors, individuals who work for women often demonstrate higher levels of performance, job satisfaction, and job commitment (Yammarino et al., 1997).

Yet, research also suggests that women may be caught in a double-bind (Vinnicombe and Singh, 2002). That is, many of the behaviors they demonstrate – such as using consensus in their decision-making, viewing power as relational, building supportive work environments, and promoting diversity – may not be recognized as valuable in more traditional, male-oriented work cultures (Oshagbemi and Gill, 2002). Consequently, when women try to adopt what are traditionally viewed as typically 'male-oriented' behaviors – such as acting in a highly assertive manner or emphasizing task dimensions of

a project – the results can be disastrous, for in addition to increasing their already high stress levels, these women leaders risk facing harsh criticism from both their peers and their supervisors (Colwill and Townsend, 1999; Gardiner and Tiggemann, 1999). Only when women use a combination of what is traditionally viewed as feminine and masculine behavior does their likelihood of success in traditional, male-oriented work cultures increase (Appelbaum et al., 2003).

Given the frustrations many women encounter, increasing numbers of women are taking charge of their own careers in an effort to advance more smoothly (Hall, 1996, 2002). Career-oriented women realize that it is unwise to assume that hard work and the quality of their contributions alone will ensure recognition and timely promotion (Dowling, 1981). Women are searching for ways to drive and reinvent their careers and to assume more responsibility for the paths they take (Mirvis and Hall, 1994). Increasingly, professional women are seeking companies that offer them challenging work, learning-oriented relationships and valued rewards – rewards that are often intrinsic (Hall, 2002). In their search for particular job features, women in hospitality management are increasingly ready to shift both the companies they work for and the type of work they do. Consequently, women's careers are more likely than ever to zigzag, in a non-linear manner, as they move to and from companies and jobs that meet their needs and provide growth opportunities (Bateson, 1994). It is clear that sophisticated women will seek organizations where they have salary equity and where gender-related workplace challenges are being addressed.

Salaries and gender equity

Not surprisingly, in addition to finding limited opportunities to advance, women also experience a pay disparity. On average, women executives earn 68% of the salary that their male counterparts demand for the same work. According to one recent study, this gap has been widening (Seglin, 2002). In 1995 a female manager earned 86 cents for every dollar her male counterpart earned; by 2000, this gap increased to 72 cents. In a similar study, seven out of ten industries that employ over 70% of women saw the pay-gap increase over the past ten years (DeCrow, 2002). In other research that examined executive-level pay, women accounted for 31% of the lowest fifth pay level rank, yet comprised only 15% of a sample of 336 executives (Renner et al., 2002). Indeed, when asked if they believed their compensation to be fair, only 62% of female executives agreed while 72% of men holding similar positions believed this to be true (Bates, 2002).

In the hospitality industry, pay equity findings are very similar. By 1994, women in hospitality management positions were earning close to 18% less than men holding similar positions, and many believe that pay gaps actually widen at executive-levels (Brownell, 1994; Woods and Kavanaugh, 1994). When asked about pay discrepancies, most women agreed they exist and, while women traditionally have been more likely to accept lower salary levels than men (Burgess, 2003), this situation is rapidly changing. While issues of pay equity remain severe in far too many hospitality organizations, we have seen that the most successful women are beginning to assess organizational cultures and practices and are looking to join those companies that are addressing their salary issues and that are seeking to identify and address other career challenges in meaningful ways.

CHALLENGES FOR WOMEN IN HOSPITALITY

A host of factors can impede a woman's career climb and salary levels (Catalyst, 2003). These include organizationally-based stereotypes as well as factors relating to women's decisions about their careers and families. Whether aware of it or not, women managers too frequently are excluded from participation in communication networks, especially the informal networks that shape recruiting decisions and succession plans (Purcell, 1996). In the hospitality and restaurant industries, senior leadership often fails to recognize the need to develop its junior colleagues. As a result, they neglect to provide mentoring opportunities, particularly for their female managers. Research related to each of these four challenges is examined below, and research gaps are addressed.

Gender stereotyping

In hospitality environments stereotyping (Walkup, 2003), treating both men and women

employees in a manner consistent with gender expectations regardless of the person's organizational position (Gutek et al., 1990), constitutes a serious barrier to women's career advancement. For instance, the stereotype of a woman as nurturing may be in sharp contrast to her role requirements on the job; yet, the way she is treated cannot help but influence her subsequent behavior as she receives cues regarding what it means to be a woman in a particular role or position (Smeltzer and Werbel, 1986). Those with decision making responsibilities frequently presume that women are less motivated and loyal than their male counterparts, and are only committed to their careers for the short term. This perception is due in part to the fact that women require greater flexibility with regard to periods of maternity leave and shifting family needs (Hicks, 1990; Traves et al., 1997). These individuals may also hold onto more traditional, masculine-oriented ideas about what makes an effective leader. For example, a 'cowboy mentality' still exists in some organizations that perpetuates the notion that leaders must be pioneering, take-charge individuals who make a decision and then forge ahead (Hogue, Yoder and Ludwig, 2002).

In line with this thinking, female managers have been criticized for not being decisive when managing male employees, for not responding assertively, and for being unable to make the tough decisions (Purcell, 1996). Certainly, women's linguistic style, specifically women's tendency to qualify their assertions, can contribute to misinterpretations of women as weak managers (Brownell, 1994; Oakley, 2000). Even a recent hospitality study found pervasive attitudes towards women as the weaker sex, as well as gendered presumptions about the types of jobs appropriate for women and men (Woods and Viehland, 2000). In looking across industries, a second study found that 40% of women surveyed had been denied a promotion or raise because of their gender-related attributes (Dickerson and Taylor, 2000). Perhaps not surprisingly, as a result of these preconceived notions, women also are likely to short-change their own contributions (Burgess, 2003). Women often fail to promote themselves in ways their male counterparts recognize. They more frequently demonstrate self-limiting behaviors as a result of their lower self-confidence in their ability to perform their job. In addition, women are often willing to accept the 'dirtier', less glamorous, forms of work (Dickerson and Taylor, 2000). Thus, in a culturally imbedded, often unconscious manner, both men and women alike foster gendered stereotypes about feminine and masculine-oriented work. In fact, Fletcher's (1998) study of female engineers indicates important ways both men and women create cultural systems that marginalize feminine-oriented work contributions. The implication of her research is that many of today's organizational reward structures ignore the care-taking functions women often assume. The presumption is that women adopt these roles to fulfill their basic primary needs as nurturers and carers. Such views overlook the contribution these and similar female-linked behaviors make to organizational health and effectiveness.

In terms of research gaps, asking the right questions often assures us that researchers will identify, and inevitably enable us to address, high priority areas of concern. Unfortunately, this is less the case with regard to gender stereotypes. Not only are stereotypes frequently held at a cultural level, they are imbedded in the way men and women think and act on a largely unconscious level. Organizational scientists are not in a position to change the way individuals think, they can only observe behavior and ensure that organizational hold its members accountable for appropriate behavior. To date, research tools and approaches have not sufficiently considered the questions related to stereotypes and their impact on women's careers.

Work/family balance

In addition to stereotypes, women also face difficult personal demands and tradeoffs that impact their ability to advance through the management ranks. More so than men, women often bear responsibility for managing their family lives regardless of their own job requirements. This may include attending to young children and aging parents (Scase and Goffee, 1989; Traves et al., 1997). Such 'dual managerial roles' often leave women feeling exhausted, pulled, and fragmented. Many female managers with families report that they continually have to juggle not a work/family balance but, instead, a work/family tradeoff. The implication is clear, one primary responsibility is often compromised for the sake of the other. In fact, one respondent in a 1994 study wrote, 'The real issue is sacrifice.

Sacrifice is required if you want to stay in the profession – sacrifice of everything non-work related' (Brownell, 1994b: 106).

To meet these challenges, some women try to find supportive help at home; others opt for a reduced work schedule and take themselves out of the running for jobs with greater responsibilities and heavier workloads (McGrath, 1999; Higgins et al., 2000). In addition, some women temporarily leave their careers to take care of family needs, hoping to re-enter the industry some time in the future (Burgess, 2003). Others remain at their jobs, but because of their families and spouses' obligations, are geographically immobile. As a result, they are unable to accept new responsibilities at different operational locations. All of these factors have the potential to dramatically stall a woman's career advancement.

In the hospitality industry, a field legendary for its long and often inflexible work hours as well as its boundaryless crossover between work and non-work life (Purcell, 1996), women have reported responding to their work-family challenges by leaving their positions to pursue more flexible entrepreneurial ventures both within and ancillary to the hospitality industry (Taylor and Walsh, 2004). Simply put, the demands hospitality organizations make of its managers act as strong disincentive to its female managers to remain employed within them. Yet, the decisions women make can hardly be viewed as a 'choice'. In response to their employer's needs and demands, many women have been forced to make changes in the way they work and have subsequently opted out of the corporate and operational tracks in favor of self-employment (Burgess, 2003).

Research gaps in work/family balance are considerable. Many organizations view work/family initiatives as expenses to be minimized rather than investments that provide a return over time. Studies that link work/family human resources practices to the bottom line will be invaluable to hospitality organizations looking for ways to justify their women-friendly policies. It would also be useful to know more about how women who have elected to work part-time or share jobs can be transitioned back into full time positions and, importantly, what effect non-traditional work schedules have on judgements of their readiness or suitability for promotion. Other issues related to work/family initiatives pertain to employees' perceptions of organizational justice and equity.

Do single employees resent the organization's focus on family issues and, importantly, do these feelings have an impact on their loyalty and performance?

Old boy networks

Networks are informal social systems that use friendship and alliances to organize and control power, influence, and rewards within the formal organizational structure. In a reciprocal manner, members support one another's needs and agendas in efforts to preserve the status quo (Oakley, 2000). In hospitality organizations, large numbers of women continue to report that they have been excluded from these informal communication structures, especially those that shape critical organizational practices such as recruiting and succession planning (Purcell, 1996). This research suggests that the old boy network still pervades the industry and serves as a barrier to women seeking opportunities for growth and advancement. In fact, in her study of women's career development, Brownell (1994a) reported that both senior and middle women managers ranked the old boy network and limited access to information as the most significant obstacle to their career development.

Clearly, the most effective way to reduce the negative impact of old boy networks is to increase the number of women ascending to senior-level positions (Oakley, 2000). New entrants, many of whom would have perspectives different from current informal network members, would likely challenge the way decisions are made. Even behavioral norms, such as the use of conversational sports metaphors or happy hours as the setting for deal-making, would be altered substantially (Oakley, 2000). Thus, to preserve their positions (as well as the salaries that accompany them), members of these networks are likely to put female senior management candidates through rigorous competency tests. Tests such as these signal that women have to fight to gain entry to the upper echelon and that if they do gain access, they are not always welcome. Even if women held senior-level positions, they would likely remain excluded from this sort of social bonding and would be on the periphery of decision making activities.

Constituting a major research gap, the study of old boy networks is particularly illusive. To date, little evidence has been offered for how to break into these informal but powerful social links. Efforts to do so require a change in initiative and this literature may provide the best direction for those seeking to better understand this dynamic. The questions that need to be asked include 'What does it mean to break into an old boy network?' and 'How can the influence networks bring to their members be distributed in a more equitable manner?'. While the literature on social networks is robust, much more study is required before we understand fully what these social structures mean for women seeking to move into tighter and more exclusive circles.

Mentoring

In the hospitality and restaurant industries, senior leadership often neglects to provide mentoring opportunities for its female management. As a result, women fail to find and develop their own advice-based networks, as well as individuals that can assist in their career development. Networks such as these are important for women managers who often feel they are 're-creating the wheel' in trying to address the challenges they face both at home and within their organizations. In fact, Brownell (1994) found that women general managers rated mentoring as much less of an important factor than did their lower-status counterparts. One explanation may be that the general managers did not rely on a mentor for their own career advancement while women entering the industry today have higher expectations. Regardless of this, it appears that the stage a woman is at in her career influences her perceptions of the most serious workplace obstacles to career development. Without mentoring and advice from those men and women that have been 'in their shoes', many women simply cope as best they can and plateau in middle-management positions.

In a never-ending loop, organizations that fail to organize and develop mentoring relationships for its female managers often have only a token few holding top-level positions. These few token women face tremendous pressure to survive and thrive in their positions. They face more on-the-job scrutiny than the men holding similar positions and this visibility increases their pressure to perform (Oakley, 2000). As a result of their minority status, they tend to feel isolated and alone in their struggle to succeed. While 'token' executive-level women may be unable to provide the mentoring breadth needed to help develop the sheer volume of women managers stalled in middle-management ranks, other reasons for the lack of mentoring have also been uncovered. First, these women may be uncomfortable sharing the depth of the challenges they faced in rising to their positions. The fact that they hold a 'token role' also may prevent them from being able to provide developmental advice. In addition, one stream of research suggests that relationships among industry women are not always collaborative but can be characterized by jealousy and competition. A number of surveys have revealed that it is too frequently other women, not men, who have made it difficult to advance. Thus, the organizational challenge to develop senior female leadership can be complex.

While an equal number of female and male professionals graduate from management programs and enter the hospitality and restaurant industries with equivalent salaries, female managers quickly begin to lag behind in their career development. When they are unsupported and frustrated, many women simply drop out of the race (Anker, 1997; Burgess, 2003).

When it comes to research gaps, we know that the success of mentoring programs is largely dependent upon the strength of the relationship that is developed between the mentor and mentee. To date, we know relatively little about how to make these matches successful and what characteristics are important and under what circumstances. Intuitively, we recognize that the effectiveness of mentoring is related to the extent to which it is tied to the organization's evaluation and reward system. Additional research is required to better understand the incentives that can be put into place to encourage mentoring, and the specific impact mentoring has on the career development of women managers.

SOLUTIONS FOR SUCCESS: FOSTERING WOMEN'S CAREER DEVELOPMENT IN HOSPITALITY

While the four obstacles just reviewed present significant challenges to professional women pursuing high-level careers in the hospitality industry, solutions are gradually being addressed. The industry can improve its ability to develop and retain current and future women leadership in several significant ways.

Women seeking job satisfaction and career advancement will be looking for organizations that demonstrate the best practices in human resources. Some of these practices are described below as they address the four career challenges previously discussed.

Gender stereotypes

First, hospitality and restaurant companies could benefit from examining their internal processes, especially those that foster implicit gender stereotypes. For example, company decision-makers might ask themselves: Are women expected to work in different ways than their male counterparts? Are women held to different standards of performance? What preconceived assumptions about women – especially women leaders – need to be uncovered and tested? For example, as a society, we conventionally assume that more attractive male leaders – and less attractive female leaders – are more competent than their male and female counterparts (Oakley, 2000). Uncovering and addressing assumptions in structured ways, such as through training sessions and discussion groups, could go far toward lessening their impact. In addition, to promote a transparent performance-based environment, organizational leaders can make job descriptions, work loads, and performance expectations explicit and readily available (Simms, 2003). These leaders should also be clear about potential succession plans and career paths within the organization.

Human resource practices such as these will help ensure that women, as well as men, are fairly and explicitly evaluated on their performance. These practices will also help make clear why specific individuals are selected for promotional opportunities and why others are deemed to be less well prepared. Such policies eventually will dispel the belief that women are evaluated for their performance and men are evaluated for their potential (McCracken, 2000). In addition to fostering a performance-based work environment, these practices also have the potential to close the gender-based pay gap.

Finally, to keep women in promotion pools, organizational leaders can organize forums to discuss the dire need to develop performance-based, female leadership within their organizations. They may come to recognize that women who work on flexible and/or reduced schedules can still be eligible for new opportunities and increased responsibilities. In fact, they may be ready to take on more active roles in their organizations if asked to do so.

Work/family balance

In addition to uncovering and resolving stereotypes about women, human resource initiatives aimed at reducing work/family conflict have been shown to make a significant difference (Konrad and Mangel, 2000). Organized programs such as providing assistance with childcare, days off to care for children, flexible work schedules and parental leaves have reduced absenteeism and turnover for both female and male employees. As an example, KFC works in partnership with the YMCA to offer childcare options, especially during non-traditional work hours (Walkup, 2003). These programs reduce the level of conflict that employees confront. This is especially helpful for women managers who experience the greatest work/family dilemmas – often during their prime years of productivity (Hammer et al., 1997; Greenhaus and Parasuraman, 1999).

An interesting idea that several organizations are experimenting with is bundling their work/family initiatives. In other words, organizations are offering a menu of options and even combining different packages of support to accommodate employees' varying needs. For example, Cisco Inc., the software design company based in Virginia, offers employees and their families on-site schooling, medical care, work-out facilities, a post office, a dry cleaner, and even a golf course. Employees are encouraged to have lunch with their children in one of the on-site restaurants. While extreme in its bundling, Cisco is an example of a company that weaves work/family support seamlessly into its daily working culture. Initiatives such as these send powerful cultural signals that the organization cares about the challenges its employees face and is committed to working with its employees to resolve, if not reduce them.

When the well-being of employees is such an overt organizational value, companies are likely to attract and retain a very dedicated and loyal staff (O'Reilly and Pfeffer, 2000; Perry-Smith and Blum, 2000). Work/family initiatives have been linked with improved recruitment efforts, organizational commitment, use of organization citizenship behaviors and even firm productivity and performance (Osterman, 1995; Tsui, Pearce,

Porter and Tripoli, 1997; Konrad and Mangel, 2000; Perry-Smith and Blum, 2000). Most importantly, the presence of these initiatives has been shown to increase the percentage of senior management positions held by women (Dreher, 2003). While we may applaud these organizational initiatives, Cendent Corporation's Mary Mahoney reminds us that women also need 'strong familial support systems to navigate the winding roads between work and home life' (Mann and Seacord, 2003: 22).

Old boy networks

To weaken the impact of the old boy network, hospitality and restaurant companies encourage women to formally and informally interact with both women and men (Linehan, 2001). These types of networking opportunities help women to forge stronger working relationships. They also tend to help falsify gender-based stereotypes and fears that keep networks such as these from developing. In other words, once men have an opportunity to work with women, their gender-based stereotypes tend to disappear; they begin to view women more as individuals rather than as representatives of their gender (Powell, 1993).

In addition to providing networking opportunities, progressive hospitality leaders also ensure that decision-making processes are explicit and formalized and are held within a context that is appropriate for all managers, men and women alike. Organizations can hold accountable leaders who fail to open their networks and adopt explicit performance-based practices. For example, Marriott now requires its leaders to develop and advance its women management. Leaders who do not develop diversity initiatives or programs to improve the number of higher-ranking females run the risk of losing their bonuses and reducing their overall compensation package (Wells, 2001).

Mentoring

Mentoring and all-women coaching programs are developmental options that have been shown to make a difference in the rate of women's career advancement. Formalized mentoring programs whereby senior executives provide support and coaching to junior colleagues have been linked with an increase in job performance, pay, promotions, career development and employee satisfaction (Fagenson, 1989; Scandura, 1992; Ragins and Scandura, 1994; Dreher and Cox, 1996). Mentoring relationships broaden managers' formal and informal networks. Effective mentors teach apprentices how the organization works. They also serve as role models, as they help socialize apprentices to the organization's norms and values. Most importantly, mentors often act as champions or political sponsors who advocate on their junior manager's behalf when important decisions, such as promotions, are being made (Roemer, 2002). All-women coaching programs and networking opportunities allow women to consider, without penalty, ways they can develop their strengths as leaders as well as discover and address their personal limitations (Vinnicombe and Singh, 2003). So, too, networking opportunities offer ways for women to test ideas, find solutions to common problems, and obtain empathy and support. One such event is the Leadership Development Conference, formed in 1989 by women in the foodservice industry who were searching for ways to ensure that women had the resources to succeed in this competitive environment. The Leadership Development Conference provided such services as workshops, keynote speakers, networking events, and mentoring – all factors that have been shown to be crucial to women's career success. The benefits of these approaches have prompted companies such as Marriott International to organize a series of leadership conferences for its women managers, especially those who work in isolated locations and have limited networking opportunities (Wells, 2001). Working in tandem, these and similar initiatives can help to shatter the barriers keeping women from top-level positions. Most importantly, they have the potential to improve the productivity and, ultimately, the profitability of the hospitality organizations to which they belong.

Given these four areas of concern, hospitality companies benefit from examining their internal human resources processes. With the goal of fostering a meritocratic and transparent performance-based environment, organizations can make job descriptions, work loads, career paths and performance expectations explicit and readily available to all employees (Simms, 2003). Transparent and clearly communicated policies will help to dispel the notion that women are evaluated for their performance and men are evaluated for their potential (McCracken, 2000). Companies can also explore ways to keep women who work on flexible and/or reduced schedules eligible for new and more responsible positions. In addition, they can create informal networking opportunities for both men and women (Linehan, 2001), and provide forums to discuss strategies for developing female-based leadership. Finally, as has been discussed, organizations can hold accountable leaders who fail to open their networks and adopt explicit practices (Dreher, 2003). Increasingly, progressive human resource practices will become essential for organizations to attract and retain women employees (Morrison and Von Glinow, 1990; Powell, 1993; Oakley, 2000).

WOMEN TRAVELERS

In addition to seeking hospitality organizations that address and encourage their career development, women also are consuming hospitality-related services in growing numbers. While our focus has been on women's career development in the hospitality industry and the challenges they confront as hospitality employees and leaders, this section addresses a parallel concern. As women in all businesses move up the career ladder, they are traveling more frequently. In fact, in the United States women are the fastest growing segment of the business travel industry (Scott, 1997; Wlazlowski, 2000; Carbasho, 2002). Because their numbers are increasing, women as consumers of hospitality – particularly those relatively privileged North American executives – have become an important market segment for hotels, restaurants, airlines, and a range of other travel industries.

In 2003, women accounted for more than half of all business travelers – up from 25% in 1991 and 1% approximately 35 years ago. While attention first began to focus on women travelers as a separate market segment during the 1970s, much of the literature during that decade outlined things women could do for themselves to ensure a smooth travel experience (Much, 1977; Wells, 1985). At that time few hospitality organizations recognized women travelers as an important demographic, or considered their responsibility to make travel for women safe and productive. Times have changed. Public relations efforts, advertising, and online partnerships are just a few of the many ways in which the travel industry is recognizing the profit to be made by addressing women's travel needs.

Women's travel behavior

Hospitality organizations increasingly ask 'Do women travelers have different needs from men?'. The vote is in, and it appears to be a resounding 'definitely'. While critics question whether marketers have contributed to the perception of women as a unique niche, a 1997 survey found that women indeed expressed different travel preferences (OAG's *Business Travel Lifestyle Survey*). Not only are women traveling more, they are also traveling differently. D.K. Shifflet and Associates in 1998, for instance, discovered that over half of room nights spent by women were associated with multi-night stays for meetings, conferences, or conventions. Men, on the other hand, were significantly more transient and often had sequential one-night stays for sales or consulting purposes (Shifflet and Bhatia, 1998).

Women's behavior associated with traveling also differs in several important ways from their male counterparts. Women book rooms further in advance and more frequently contact the hotel directly rather than going through a reservations center. A survey of corporate travel managers conducted by Runzheimer International (2000) reported that women follow travel policies more closely than men. They also make fewer after-ticket itinerary changes and travel by coach more frequently than their male counterparts.

In 2001, Embassy Suites commissioned a survey on women business travelers and discovered that while over two-thirds of respondents said they consider themselves extroverts at home and at work, half of that group believed they become introverted when they travel. Marketing professionals believe that this finding suggests that room service and the comfort and convenience of in-room facilities play an important role in securing women's travel business (Sharkey, 2002). Another 2001 survey, for instance, found that over 75% of women order room service at least once a day when they travel compared to 54% of men (Carbasho, 2002).

Women also appear to be more concerned about getting a good night's sleep than their male counterparts (Women and Marketing, 1998). The National Sleep Foundation and Hilton Hotels conducted a joint study and discovered that nearly 20% more women than men are concerned with travel-related sleep issues; 40% more women than men reported having difficulty getting a good night's sleep before their travel.

It appears that women simply take sleep more seriously than do men (women are twice as likely as men to bring their own pillow when they travel). The Sleep Impact study also found that nearly 80% of women surveyed believed that sleep is a valuable use of time, allowing them to enjoy themselves more fully and be more productive while they're conducting business away from home. On the other hand, nearly 30% of men (and only half as many women) saw sleep as 'a waste of time'. Do men pay for their attitude? Apparently so, as nearly two out of every ten men admitted to falling asleep at meetings and conventions (Hamilton, 1999).

Women's travel preferences

John Portman and Associates, an architectural firm specializing in hospitality, conducted a 2001 survey of 'what women want' when they travel (Carbasho, 2002). The results of this study of 13,000 women from Fortune 1,000 companies confirmed what numerous pervious surveys on women travelers' preferences revealed (Rhymer, 1996; Taylor, 2000; Kamberg, 2001; Carbasho, 2002; McCoy-Ullrich, 2002). At the top of the list of women's concerns is security. Women want their room numbers kept private and appreciate a phone call to alert them that room service is on the way. Many hotels deliberately assign female room service personnel to deliver meals to their female guests.

With regard to specific security measures, women travelers seek well lit hallways and lighting in all public areas. Hyatt, for example, uses a special service code to identify single women business travelers so that front desk attendants can assign them to rooms near an elevator (Wlazlowski, 2000). Women also want a hotel close to the event they are attending – preferably one with an on-site fitness center and spa. Free valet parking (Coleman, 2002), to-your-door escorts, and jogging partners are provided at several luxury properties to create a safe environment for their female guests (Swift, 2000). To further promote safety, a number of hotels provide women with information on local restaurants and places of interest. Crowne Plaza offers a mapping service to assist women venturing out of the hotel for dining or recreation. This service is well appreciated, as only about half of all women business travelers research their destination before leaving on a trip and therefore

Table 4.3 Recommended precautions for women travelers

- Request a room with a peephole, dead bolt and chain lock
- Make sure there is no connecting door to another room
- Select hotels that take extra measures to ensure personal security
- Travel light
- Read or work while traveling
- Use crowds to be inconspicuous; stand in a group while waiting for a cab
- Make arrangements to arrive before dark if possible
- Before driving away in a rental car, make sure the gas tank is full and the tires are properly inflated
- Take a cell phone for emergencies
- Use valet parking whenever possible
- Ask for an escort to your car if valet parking is not available
- Never give out your room number
- Keep some money in an outside pocket to avoid fumbling through your purse for tips
- If you are expecting a delivery from outside the hotel, have it left at the front desk
- Ask to have a five minute warning phone call before room service or other deliveries are sent to your room
- When going out, leave the lights on and the closet doors and shower curtain open
- Meet others in a public location such as the lobby
- Make sure friends or family at home have your schedule and hotel information

Adapted from McCoy-Ullrich, Dawn (Feb. 1, 2002). Alone on the road: Travel industry responds to women's security needs, *American Woman Road and Travel*, 3–4.

find it stressful to make their way around in an unfamiliar city (Coleman, 2002). And, while every hotel, restaurant, airline, or other hospitality business has an obligation to protect its customers, there are a wide range of actions women travelers can initiate to ensure that their travel is as safe as possible (Table 4.3).

It has been suggested that women also appreciate up-graded amenities, and hotels have responded by providing makeup mirrors, gender-appropriate reading materials, climate control, flavored coffees and herbal teas. Women travelers were the inspiration for Westin's Heavenly Bed, which features multiple layers of sheets, a down comforter and a pillow-top mattress (Swift, 2000). Larger bathtubs and ample shampoo are also amenities women are thought to appreciate. Westin concluded that its female guests prefer white sleeping room walls over darker wood grains; other surveys have found that women seek large windows and stylish room furnishings.

Wyndham Hotels and Resorts ran a contest among 1,300 frequent female business travelers, nearly 90% of who were executives. They asked what respondents would do to improve business travel if they were CEO of a travel company. The winning suggestions included:

(1) complimentary steaming of suits upon check-in;
(2) providing emergency travel kits just for women upon check-in, with pantyhose and feminine supplies; and
(3) giving guests the option to exercise in-room by supplying videos, weights, steps, and other portable equipment.

Hotels that are meeting women's needs

A number of hotels have been in the forefront in identifying women's needs and responding to what they have discovered. Wyndham is credited with taking much of the initiative to better understand women's travel requirements and preferences. Conducting joint research with New York University, Wyndham Hotels' Women On Their Way program includes an all-female advisory council that makes regular recommendations on how the company can best respond to the growing number of women travelers (Khan, 1999). Another hotel that understands women's needs is the Pan Pacific San Francisco which recently conducted a survey of female guests and responded to findings by taking such measures as adding diffusers for hairdryers. They also upgraded their in-room fax machines with copy capabilities as a result of survey responses (Caldwell, 2002). Three phone lines in each room now make it possible for guests to log on, fax, and retrieve voicemail simultaneously! Expotel, a hotel reservations company, addresses women's concerns by asking customers who use its booking service to rate the hotels in which they have stayed. Those given high marks for catering to women's preferences and requirements are awarded 'Woman Aware' status, allowing travelers to identify and select from this group of hotels when making reservations (Rigby, 1996).

Restaurants are also responding to this new and growing market. To make solo female travelers more comfortable, a number of restaurants, such as those in Loews and Wyndham properties, are offering 'networking tables' designated specifically for women business travelers seeking conversation and companionship while on the road (Swift, 2000; McCoy-Ullrich, 2002).

Women traveling abroad

Efforts to create female-friendly environments are not limited to US properties. Novotel Atlantis Shanghai has a dedicated executive floor catering to the growing number of women travelers. Here, rooms include such amenities as nail clippers, floral arrangements, a garment dryer, and a selection of aromatherapy treatments. Special female security personnel are assigned to the floor, and a curfew is set for visitors. Similarly, Regal Airport Hotel in Hong Kong has developed Feminine Focus Rooms with special amenities that make a woman's stay more comfortable. Among the most notable are sewing kits, pot-pourri, back-lit and full length mirrors, and bath salts. The Park Hotel in Chennai offers babysitting facilities and in-room massages. For its LADY (Luxury Amenities Designed for You) program, the Ritz-Carlton Hong Kong creates female-friendly rooms for a modest supplement. Amenities include luxury toiletries, keepsake silk pajamas, and complimentary pressing. Few hotels, however, can match the accommodations of the Four Seasons Singapore, which include a business suit, matching shores, accessories, and cosmetics for women who have lost their luggage (Manila, 2000).

Web sites for women travelers

Nothing is easier than accessing information online, and an increasing number of hotels and women's organizations have developed web sites targeted to meet the needs of women business travelers. Evelyn Hannon created one of the more highly regarded resources, www.journeywoman.com. In June, 2000, Telecomworldwire launched another successful site at www.m2.com. This site features articles for women covering such topics as foreign travel, tips on traveling alone, parenting while away on business, traveling while pregnant, and work-family balance (Telecomworldwire, 2000). Wyndham's web site, www.womenbusinesstravelers.com, has received praise for its focus on issues and concerns important to women.

www.HERmail.net is an interactive site where women can ask questions and network with their female colleagues (Sharkey, 2002). Worldroom.com is the web arm of I-Quest Corporation, a global provider of Internet services to the hospitality industry which offers extensive information for business travelers. Recently, the company expanded its services to include a new women's web channel, Women's World, which will be available both in the US and Asia. In addition many airlines, like Delta's Executive Women's Travel Network, address the concerns of women traveling alone in the air.

Training employees to meet the needs of women travelers

As they travel more, women are also registering a significantly higher number of complaints about their accommodations and service. They are finding more problems with hotels, restaurants, airlines, and car-rental agencies than their male counterparts. In fact, a poll cited in *USA Today* revealed that well over half of all women business travelers believe they 'routinely' encounter second-class treatment and service – what they describe as poor, inadequate, or unacceptable. Expotel found the situation equally as grim; only 2% of respondents to their survey of women travelers said that they are 'seldom uncomfortable' in hotel bars. Sharkey (2002) warns that airport hotels can be particularly unsatisfactory for single women due to the high percentage of one-night male guests. In addition, as one article explains, service employees often assume that when a man and woman are traveling together that the man holds the higher level position. Yet another frequent act of poor judgement – women are tired of being seated between two men on a plane with little room and no armrest (*Travel Trade Gazette*, 2001).

Given this situation, the hospitality industry would do well to examine its employee training practices more closely. Programs to ensure non-discriminatory and gender-appropriate service delivery would seem particularly relevant. Concierge staff might be prepared to recommend safe dining options for single women travelers and to provide additional local information to make women feel more confident when they venture into the surrounding community. Restaurants, too, might benefit from increased attention as to how employees can best deliver service to single female travelers. Walkup (2000) describes the dining experiences of several business women, emphasizing that servers need to be trained in how to treat single women in restaurants.

The final word on women travelers

In spite of progress on many fronts, it appears that women too often receive different treatment in their leisure as well as their professional activities (Foley, Maxwell and McGillivray, 1999). What do women want? To get the job accomplished efficiently and effectively. Specific services, employee attitudes, and hospitality facilities can either support their efforts or can hinder the woman traveler's ability to work effectively on the road (Taylor, 2004). There appears to be no down side; men nearly always benefit from the incentives hospitality organizations have taken to respond to the needs of women travelers. Additional office equipment in sleeping rooms, business lounges, increased security measures, and even amenities like makeup mirrors have made men's travel easier (Khan, 1999). As women's career development accelerates there undoubtedly will be a growing number of business women in airplanes and hotel rooms. This transition will focus increasing attention on service features that enhance safety, enjoyment, and productivity for all business travelers.

FUTURE DIRECTIONS FOR THE STUDY OF WOMEN IN HOSPITALITY

The future for both women in hospitality management and women travelers will depend in large measure on the nature and quality of information generated by those who relentlessly probe and seek answers to critical questions. It is likely that a variety of approaches and methods will continue to be brought to bear on the subjects of study.

While there are numerous areas that require further exploration, the following four topics represent several of the most promising directions for researchers seeking to contribute to our knowledge of women and hospitality.

Globalization/technology and its effect on women's careers

The shift toward a knowledge economy and the increasingly global nature of the hospitality industry has affected the profile of those most likely to succeed in the business. Today's manager requires not only a strong knowledge base, but the ability to work collaboratively irrespective of spatial, time and cultural differences. Successful managers are those who demonstrate well-developed communication skills and who are continually flexible and creative (Baum, 1990). If this is the case, the future looks particularly bright for women who have repeatedly demonstrated strong communication abilities and a personal style characterized by a focus on building consensus (Gillian, 1997). As we have discussed, women managers have also been shown to demonstrate a facilitating style that fosters teamwork (Shirley, 1995) as well as more effective listening skills (Arliss and Borisoff, 1998). Such well-developed interpersonal competencies will serve them well as diversity increases and multinational companies seek employees who can facilitate global understanding. At this time, however, only 3% of women are international managers and some researchers suggest that unless they belong to formal support networks, it is unlikely that these numbers will increase at a significant rate (Linehan, 2001).

Work and family balance is an issue likely to continue to dominate human resource concerns. Technology makes more options possible as women and men alike set up home workstations and take advantage of flexible shifts. Decision support systems and other communication technologies allow group interaction and facilitate decision making.

Issues of women's wellness

Women are not only working in greater numbers than ever before, they are also working harder as they aim for the tops of corporate ladders. Consequently, an emerging concern that extends issues related to work/family balance is the degree to which women are able to maintain cognitive/emotional as well as physical health, and what interventions might be available to ensure their well being in the hospitality workplace. Those who hold middle-management positions – where most women currently can be found – are more likely to experience stress and burnout than any other managerial level (Buick and Thomas, 2001). As a consequence, the likelihood that these managers eventually will leave the industry is particularly high. Stories from those women who pioneer as leaders in their organizations might reveal insights into how 'token' women have managed stress and isolation.

Chronic physical illness in the workplace – not just acute – has become an area of concern and study for organizational theorists and practitioners alike. What happens when women believe they must hide, or at least minimize, their recurring health problems? How does the actual health issue as well as the climate of mistrust affect the individual's success? Increasing recognition of this concern has encouraged researchers to examine the link between mental and physical well-being and to seek ways in which work can be reconfigured to help individuals perform at their best without sacrificing their personal well-being.

Human resource policies that facilitate the establishment of such supportive practices as work/family balance, mentoring, and informal networking opportunities reduce absenteeism and turnover and increase both women's satisfaction and their performance. Thus, as organizations look after women's cognitive/emotional well being, contributions from these employees increase. Given projected labor pools, retaining employees will become increasingly important for organizational success. Research that ties this improved performance to the organization's bottom line will ensure that such policies become institutionalized and more commonplace.

Women's career development as an organizational change effort

Another future direction for research pertains to the gendered assumptions that surround work for both men and women. While an uncomfortable topic, to be successful organizations will need to identify and implement large-scale change initiatives. The most successful organizations will be those that question current practices and traditional patterns by asking, 'Why are room attendants almost always female?' or 'What can we learn from female chefs?'. Researchers who pose these and similar questions surface information that will inform and prepare the next generation of women leaders.

Further, research that demonstrates the value diversity brings to decision making and organizational effectiveness will become more frequent and more forceful. Women's distinctive ways of viewing dynamic situations and solving problems will be studied more frequently with the goal of better understanding the tangible added value of multiple perspectives.

Expanding our understanding of women travelers

We have just begun to probe the needs of women travelers and the ways in which their increasing numbers are changing the shape of hospitality services and service delivery. As international travel becomes more commonplace, accommodations for women overseas will become ever more important. Researchers may focus on better understanding women's needs as they travel through time zones and within unfamiliar cultures. The lodging and food service sectors have been quick to respond to women as a new and growing market demographic. The coming years will likely see an increase in the attention paid to women travelers by other segments of the hospitality industry. Cruise lines, casinos, airlines, and clubs may all begin to address women's needs in slightly different ways. Studies that provide detailed information on women's concerns, needs, and expectations will prove valuable as women more frequently venture into ships and casinos alone.

CONCLUSION

Those who believed that all women needed was 'time in rank' to be promoted into senior level positions have been largely disappointed with the lack of women's career progress over the past decade. As noted earlier, there is reason to speculate (Isaacson, 2002) that women may be worse off than they were six years ago in the rate of progress they are making toward both earnings and promotions. What many organizational leaders failed to recognize is that career development requires a combination of several factors, including well-defined human resource initiatives. Research being done on women's careers in hospitality has begun to surface some of the strategies that hospitality organizations can implement to assist women in reaching senior level positions. This work, however, has just begun.

If enrollment in hospitality management programs is an indicator of women's potential to impact the industry's future, the decades ahead indeed look bright. The percentage of women in the entering classes of the major US hospitality programs continues to grow (Sigala and Baum, 2003). As women are increasingly focused on achieving senior management positions, the range of available role models will widen and opportunity for success in the industry will become more readily apparent. These women also will be among those who travel more frequently, both for business and pleasure. Through surveys, interviews, and other research efforts, data will be gathered and brought to bear on current practices with the goal of making travel safer and more satisfying for women who increasingly depend upon buses, trains, airplanes, hotels, restaurants, and other service providers to meet their travel needs. A better understanding of women and hospitality, both as employees and consumers, will benefit men and women alike as they work together in the decades ahead to create high-performing and socially responsible service organizations.

REFERENCES

'American woman 2001–2002: Getting to the top'. (2001) *WIN News*, 27(3): 71.

Abelson, R. (2001, July 26) 'A survey of Wall St. finds women disheartened'. *New York Times*, p. C.1.

Adler, N. (1999) 'Global leaders', *Executive Excellence*, 16(12): 15.

Aguinis, H. and Adams, S. (1998) 'Social-role versus structural models of gender and influence use in organizations', *Group and Organization Management*, 23: 414–446.

Anker, R. (1997) 'Theories of occupational segregation by sex: an overview', *International Labour Review*, (136): 315–339.

Anonymous. (1980) 'Survival strategies for the woman on the road: don't be ladylike about your rights', *Canadian Business*, 53(10): 188–190.

Anonymous. (2001, September) 'Female friendly', *Asian Business*, 37(9): 63–64.

Anonymous. (2003) '1943 job standards for hiring women', *Women in Business*, 55(1): 18–19.

Appelbaum, S., Audet, L. and Miller, J. (2003) 'Gender and leadership? Leadership and gender? A journey through the landscape of theories', *Leadership and Organization Development Journal*, 24(1/2): 43–51.

Archer, J. (2003) 'Survey studies barriers to women leaders', *Education Week*, 22(25): 1–3.

Arliss, L. and Borisoff, D. (eds) (2001) *Women and Men Communicating: Challenges and Changes*. New York: Harcourt Brace Jovanovich College.

Axtell, R. E. (1990) 'Culture shock: the "S" word', *Meetings and Conventions*, 25(3): 132.

Babin, B. and Boles, J. (1998) 'Employee behavior in a service environment: a model and test of potential differences between men and women', *Journal of Marketing*, 62(2): 77–92.

Backmon, I., Clark, G. and Weisenfeld, L. (1997) 'Is it really getting better? Race, gender and career advancement in accounting', *The National Public Accountant*, 42: 7–33

Bass, B. M. (1985) *Leadership and Performance Beyond Expectations*. New York: Free Press.

Bates, S. (2002) 'Top female managers see gender gap in salaries', *HR Magazine*, 47(4): 12.

Bateson, M. (1994) *Peripheral Visions: Learning Along the Way*. New York: HarperCollins.

Beck, B. (1998) 'Women and work: a gentle invasion', *The Economist*, 348(Iss 8077): S6–S9.

Brocato, B. (1996) 'Women travelers get their due', *Successful Meetings*, 45(8): 13–14.

Brown, K. and Ridge, S. (2002) 'Moving into management: gender segregation and its effect on managerial attainment', *Women in Management Review*, 17(7/8): 318–327.

Brownell, J. (1994a) 'Personality and career development: a study of gender differences', *The Cornell Restaurant and Hotel Administration Quarterly*, 35(2): 36–42.

Brownell, J. (1994b) 'Women in hospitality management: general managers' perceptions of factors related to career development', *International Journal of Hospitality Management*, 13(2): 101–117.

Brownell, J. (1998) Striking a balance: the future of work and family issues in the hospitality industry, invited chapter in special issue of *Family Studies*, F. Kwansa and P. Cummings (eds). New York: Haworth Press, Inc. pp. 109–123.

Brownell, J. (2001) 'Gender and communication in the hospitality industry'. In L. P. Arliss and D. J. Borisoff (eds) *Women and Men Communicating: Challenges and Changes*. New York: Harcourt Brace Jovanovich College. pp. 193–216.

Buick, I. and Thomas, M. (2001) 'Why do middle managers in hotels burn out?', *International Journal of Contemporary Hospitality Management*, 13(6): 304–309.

Burgess, C. (2003). 'Gender and salaries in hotel financial management: it's still a man's world'.

Women in Management Review, 18(1/2): 50–60.

Burgess, Z. (2003) 'A longitudinal study of women directors in Australia', *Women in Management Review*, 18(7): 359–365.

Caldwell, C. (2002) 'Philadelphia Crowne Plaza Hotel: an ideal place to stay in the heart of America', *American Woman Road and Travel*, 15: 12–13.

Carbasho, T. (2002, September 6) 'Survey offers insight into what female business travelers seek', *Pittsburgh Business Times*, 7: 24.

Catalyst (1998) *Census of Women Corporate Officers and Top Earners*. New York: Catalyst.

Catalyst (2001) *Cracking the Glass Ceiling: Catalyst's Research on Women in Corporate Management, 1995–2000*. New York: Catalyst.

Coleman, A. (2002) 'Should women receive special treatment?, *Director*, 56(5): 45.

Collins, D. and Tisdell, C. (2002) 'Gender and differences in travel life cycles', *Journal of Travel Research*, 41(2): 133–144.

Colwill, J. and Townsend, J. (1999) 'Women, leadership and information technology: the impact of women leaders in organizations and their role in integrating information technology with corporate strategy', *The Journal of Management Development*, 18(3): 207.

Costen, W., Hardigree, C. and Testagrossa, M. (2003) 'Glass ceiling or Saran Wrap (TM)? Women in gaming management', *UNLV Gaming Research and Review Journal*, 7(2): 1.

DeCrow, K. (2002) 'Unequal signs: the wage differentiation between men and women still doesn't add up', *Syracuse New Times*, 1615: 5.

Dickerson, A. and Taylor, M. A. (2000) 'Self-limiting behavior in women; self-esteem and self-efficacy as predictors', *Group and Organization Management*, 25(2): 191–209.

Dowling, C. (1981) *The Cinderella Complex: Women's Hidden Fear of Independency*. New York: Pocket Books Pub.

Dreher, G. (2003) 'Breaking the glass ceiling: the effects of sex ratios and work-life programs on female leadership at the top', *Human Relations*, 56(5): 541.

Dreher, G. and Cox, T. (1996) 'Race, gender and opportunity: a study of compensation attainment and establishment of mentoring relationships', *Journal of Applied Psychology*, 81: 297–308.

Eagly, A. and Johnson, B. (1990) 'Gender and leadership style: a meta-analysis', *Psychological Bulletin*, 108: 233–256.

Eagly, A., Karau, B. and Johnson, B. (1992) 'Gender and leadership style among school principals: a meta-analysis', *Educational Administrative Quarterly*, 28: 76–102.

Fagenson, E. (1989) 'The mentor advantage: perceived career/job experiences of protégés vs. non-protégés', *Journal of Organizational Behavior*, 10: 309–320.

Fletcher, J. (1998) 'Relational practice: a feminist re-construction of work', *Journal of Management Inquiry*, 7: 163–186.

Foley, M., Maxwell, G. and McGillivray, D. (1999) 'Women at leisure and in work – unequal opportunities?', *Equal Opportunities International*, 18(1): 8–19.

Gardiner, M. and Tiggermann, M. (1999) 'Gender differences in leadership style, job stress and mental health in male- and female-dominated industries', *Journal of Occupational and Organizational Psychology*, 72: 301–315.

Gillian, M. A. (1997) 'Hotel general management: view from above the glass ceiling, *International Journal of Contemporary Hospitality Management*, 9(5/6): 230.

Gini, A. (1998) 'Women in the workplace', *Business and Society Review*, Iss. 99: 3–17.

Greenhaus, J. and Parasuraman, S. (1999) 'Research on work, family and gender: current status and future directions'. In G. N. Powell (ed.) *Handbook of Gender and Work*. Thousand Oaks, CA: Sage. pp. 391–412.

Grossman, C. L. (1997, April 22) 'Restaurants catering to dining needs of women traveling solo', *USA Today*, 10.B.

Gutek, B. A. (1985) *Sex and the Workplace: The Impact of Sexual Behavior and Harassment on Women, Men, and Organizations*. San Francisco: Jossey-Bass, Inc.

Gutek, B. A., Cohen, A. G. and Konrad, A. M. (1990) 'Predicting social-sexual behavior at work: a contract hypothesis', *Academy of Management Journal*, 33(3): 560–577.

Hall, D. (ed.) (1996) 'Long live the career: a relational approach'. In D. Hall (ed.) *The Career is Dead – Long Live the Career: A Relational Approach to Careers*. San Francisco: Jossey-Bass. pp. 1–12.

Hall, D. (2002) *Careers In and Out of Organizations*. Thousand Oaks, CA: Sage Publications.

Hamilton, C. (1999) 'You are getting sleepy: do women make better business travellers than men?', *CMA Management*, 73(7): 38.

Hammer, L., Allen, E. and Grigsby, T. (1997) 'Work–family conflict in dual-earner couples: within individual and crossover effects of work and family', *Journal of Vocational Behavior*, 50: 185–203.

Hardy-Sellers, T. (2002) 'The glass may be broken, but the ceiling remains', *Recorder*, 107(35): A1.

Hicks, L. (1990) 'Excluded women: how can this happen in the hotel world?', *Service Industries Journal*, 10: 348–363.

Higgins, C., Duxbury, L. and Johnson, K.L. (2000). 'Part-time work for women: does it really help balance work and family?', *Human Resource Management*, 39(1): 17–32.

Higgins, S. (2004) 'Breaking down barriers', *Hotel and Motel Management*, 219(14): 118–125.

Hogue, M., Yoder, J. and Ludwig, J. (2002) 'Increasing initial leadership effectiveness: assisting both women and men', *Sex Roles*, 46 (11/12): 377–384.

Ibarra, H. (1999) 'Professional selves: experimenting with image and identity in professional adaptation', *Administrative Science Quarterly*, 44: 764–791.

Isaacson, K. (2002) 'Research for today's women', *Women in Business*, 54(3): 16–17.

Kamberg, M. L. (2001) 'Travel industry sets sights on women travelers', *Women in Business*, 53(6): 30–33.

Khan. S. (1999, June 10) 'Aiming to please women business travel industry introduces more services for female customers', *USA Today*, 01.B.

Kolb, J. (1999) 'The effect of gender role, attitude toward leadership and self confidence on leader emergence: implications for leadership development', *Human Resource Development Quarterly*, 10: 305–320.

Konrad, A. and Mangel, R. (2000) 'The impact of work-life programs on firm productivity', *Strategic Management Journal*, 21(12): 1225–1237.

Knutson, B. and Schmidgall, R. (1999) 'Dimensions of the glass ceiling in the hospitality industry', *The Cornell Hotel and Restaurant Quarterly*, 40: 64–75.

Linder, M. (1997) *Void Where Prohibited*. Ithaca, NY: Cornell University Press.

Manila, J. (2000) 'What a girl wants', *Businessworld*, June 16: 1.

Mann, I. and Seacord, S. (2003) 'What glass ceiling?', *Lodging Hospitality*, 59(4): 38–40.

Martin, R. (2000) 'New study quantifies gender disparity in senior positions', *Nation's Restaurant News*, 34(12): 58.

Maxwell, G. (1997) 'Hotel general management: views from above the glass ceiling', *International Journal of Contemporary Hospitality Management*, 9(5/6): 230.

McCoy-Ullrich, D. (2002) 'Alone on the road: travel industry responds to women's security needs', *American Woman Road and Travel*, February 1: 5–7.

McCracken, D. M. (2000) 'Winning the talent war for women: sometimes it takes a revolution', *Harvard Business Review*, November–December.

McGrath, C. (1999) 'Do females want to be the future?', *Hospitality*, 8.

McKee, S. (2003) 'Keep your sanity at 30,000 feet; tips for women business travelers', *American Woman Road and Travel*, May 1: 32–33.

Mirvis, P. and Hall, D. (1996) 'New organizational forms and the new career'. In D. Hall (ed.) *The Career is Dead – Long Live the Career: A Relational Approach to Careers*. San Francisco: Jossey-Bass. pp. 72–101.

Morrison, A. and Von Glinow, M. (1990) 'Women and minorities in management', *American Psychologist*, 45: 200–208.

Mouton, M. (2000) 'The boundaries of women's work: political battles and individual freedoms', *Journal of Women's History*, 11(4): 167.

Much, M. (1977) 'Women cope with being on the road', *Industry Week*, 194(3): 38–41.

Oakley, J. (2000) 'Gender-based barriers to senior management positions: understanding the scarcity of female CEO's', *Journal of Business Ethics*, 27(4): 321–334.

O'Reilly and Pfeffer, (2000) *Hidden Value: How Ordinary Companies Achieve Extraordinary Results*. Boston, MA: Harvard Business School Press.

Oshagbemi, T. and Gill, R. (2003) 'Gender differences and similarities in the leadership styles and behavior of UK managers', *Women in Management Review*, 18(6): 288–298.

Osterman, P. (1995) 'Work/family programs and the employment relationship', *Administrative Science Quarterly*, 40: 681–702.

Perry-Smith, J. and Blum, T. (2000) 'Work–family human resource bundles and perceived organizational performance', *Academy of Management Journal*, 43(6): 1107–1117.

Peters, J. (1988) 'Bridging the gender gap: RB women's council challenges the status quo', *Restaurant Business*, 87(13): 115–131.

Pounder, J. and Coleman, M. (2002) 'Women – better leaders than men? In general and educational management it still "all depends"', *Leadership and Organization Development Journal*, 23(3/4): 122–133.

Powell, G. (1993) *Women and Men in Management*. Newbury Park, CA: Sage.

Primavera, B. (2001) 'Women stand tall in the heat of the kitchen but executive prospects are still chilly', *Nation's Restaurant News*, 35(46): 32–34.

Purcell, K. (1996) 'The relationship between career and job opportunities: women's employment in the hospitality industry as a microcosm of women's employment', *Women in Management Review*, 11(5): 17.

Ragins, B. and Scandura, T. (1994) 'Gender differences in expected outcomes of mentoring relationships', *Academy of Management Journal*, 37(4): 957–971.

Renner, C., Rives, J. and Bowlin, W. (2002) 'The significance of gender in explaining senior executive pay variations: an exploratory study', *Journal of Managerial Issues*, 14(3): 331–345.

Rhymer, R. (1996) 'Feel safe, will travel', *Management Today*, 32, 102–104.

Rigby, R. (1996) 'Feel safe, will travel', *Management Today*, 102–104.

Rindfleish, J. and Sheridan, A. (2003) 'No change from within: senior women managers' response to gendered organizational structures', *Women in Management Review*, 18 (5/6), 299.

Roemer, L. (2002) 'Women CEOs in health care: did they have mentors?', *Health Care Management Review*, 27(4): 57–67.

Rosener, J. (1990) 'Ways women lead', *Harvard Business Review*, November–December: 119–125.

Scase, R. and Goffee, (1989) *Reluctant Managers: Their Work and Lifestyles*. London: Unwin Hyman.

Scandura, T. (1992) 'Mentorship and career mobility: an empirical investigation', *Journal of Organizational Behavior*, 13: 169–174.

Schneer, J. and Reitman, F. (1995) 'The impact of gender as managerial careers unfold', *Journal of Vocational Behavior*, 47: 290–315.

Scott, D. (1997) 'Travel is up for women of all ages, but survey reveals a troubling note', *Telegram and Gazette*, January 26: F.1.

Seglin, J. (2002) 'How to get a company's attention on women's pay', *New York Times*, March 17: 3–4.

Sharkey, J. (1999) 'Journeywoman is a World Wide Web site with a lot of appeal for women on the go', *The New York Times*, August 4: C.11.

Sharkey, J. (2002) 'The hotel industry is increasingly paying attention to the number of women on the road', *The New York Times*, June 7: C.10.

Sharkey, J. (2002) 'Hotel lore from female travelers', *The New York Times*, August 6: C.6.

Shifflet, D. K. and Bhatia, P. (1998) 'Hotels must change to meet needs of female travelers', *Hotel and Motel Management*, 213(16): 32–33.

Shirley, S. (1995) 'Getting the gender issue on the agenda', *Professional Manager*, 12–14.

Sigala, M. and Baum, T. (2003) 'Trends and issues in tourism and hospitality higher education: visioning the future', *Tourism and Hospitality Research*, 4(4): 367.

Sims, H. and Lorenzi, (1992) *The New Leadership Paradigm, Social Learning and Cognition in Organizations*. Newbury Park, CA: Sage Publications.

Simms, J. (2003) 'Business: women at the top – you've got male', *Accountancy*, 131(1313): 62.

Smeltzer, L. R. and Werbel, J. D. (1986) 'Gender differences in managerial communication: fact or folklinguistics?', *Journal of Business Communication*, 23(2): 41–50.

Strom, S. (1989) 'Light manufacturing: the feminization of American office work, 1900–1930', *Industrial and Labor Relations Review*, 43(1): 53–64.

Swift, S. (2000, April 17) 'Hotels, airlines catering to women travelers', *Indianapolis Business Journal*, 21(5): 23–25.

Tannen, D. (1990) *You Just Don't Understand: Women and Men in Conversation*. New York: Ballantine Books, Inc.

Taylor, M. and Walsh, K. (2004) Developing in-house careers and retaining managerial talent: What professionals want from their jobs in hospitality. Unpublished manuscript.

Taylor, L. R. (2004) 'Women on the move', *Government Executive*, 32(2): 72–75.

Telecomworldwire (2000, June 23). New web site to serve female travelers. p. 1.

Traves, J., Brockbank, A. and Tomlinson, F. (1997) 'Careers of women managers in the retail industry', *The Service Industries Journal*, 17(1): 133–154.

Tsui, A., Pearce, J., Porter, L. and Tripoli, (1997) 'Alternative approaches to the employee – organization relationship: does investments in employees pay off?', *Academy of Management Journal*, 40: 1089–1121.

Valentine, V. (1994) 'Advertising's happy families', *Campaign*, 26–28.

Vigil, J. (2002) 'Women in corporate America: does the glass ceiling still exist?', *Diversity Career Opportunities and Insights*, 4(2): 18.

Vinnicombe, S. and Singh, V. (2002) 'Sex role stereotyping and requisites of successful top managers', *Women in Management Review*, 7(3/4): 120–130.

Vinnicombe, S. and Singh, V. (2003) 'Women-only management training: an essential part of women's leadership development', *Journal of Change Management*, 3(4): 294–306.

Vroom, V. and Jago, A. (1995) 'Situation effects and levels of analysis in the study of leader participation', *Leadership Quarterly*, 6: 169–181.

Walkup, C. (2000) 'Service training lapses: dissing of solo women is frequent flaw', *Nation's Restaurant News*, 34(30): 188–191.

Walkup, C. (2003) 'The female factor', *Nation's Restaurant News*, 37(13): 25–30.

Walsh, M. (2000) 'Blue-collar urgency: bathroom rights', *New York Times* (East Coast Late Edition), G1.

Wells, L. (1985) 'Hotels warily woo women travelers', *Advertising Age*, 56(59), 4–5.

Wells, S. (2001) 'Smoothing the way', *HR Magazine*, 46(6): 52–59.

Wlazlowski, T. (2000) 'As women business travelers increase, hospitality industry takes note, adapts', *The Daily Record*, January 29: A.5.

Wood, K. (2004) 'Foodservice execs should reflect melting pot of workers, customers', *Nation's Restaurant News*, 38(24): 28–29.

Woods, R. and Kavanaugh, R. (1994) 'Gender discrimination and sexual harassment as experienced by hospitality-industry managers', *Cornell Hotel and Restaurant Administration Quarterly*, 35: 16–21.

Woods, R. and Viehland, D. (2000) 'Women in hotel management', *Cornell Hotel and Restaurant Administration Quarterly*, 41: 51–54.

Yammarino, F., Dubinsky, A., Comer, L. and Jolson, M. (1997) 'Women and transformational and contingent reward leadership: a multiple-level-of-analysis perspective', *Academy of Management Journal*, 40(1): 205–222.

A Critique of Hospitality Research and its Advocacy of Multi- and Interdisciplinary Approaches: An Alternative Agenda

5

Michael Riley

PROLOGUE

Anyone wishing to advise a researcher who was new to the hospitality and tourism subject field could do worse than to suggest that, before starting out, they look at three particular studies, namely, Robert Lewis's set of articles in the *Cornell Quarterly* on hotel selection, in which a detailed quantitative study is described both as research and as an educative illustration of statistical propriety (Lewis, 1984a, 1984b); Barbara Townley's qualitative look at the perennial problem of commercializing culture in her study of a museum undergoing organizational change (Townley, 2002); and finally Peccei and Rosenthal's exposition of the responses of front line retail workers to normatively driven customer service programmes (Peccei and Rosenthal, 2000). The rationale for recommending these studies is that whilst each is about an important topic, irrespective of the topic, they each tell a different research story which gives us a perspective and, possibly a reason to pause for thought, on the larger issues of doing research in hospitality and tourism.

Lewis's research on why people select particular hotels is an excellent model of how to do an attributional study. The sample is good and everything is defined and measured in line with positivist principles. But, it is to the credit of the researchers that they admit that at the end they are still scratching their heads as to why people select particular hotels: 'idiosyncratic' is their conclusion. The moral is that good research does not always find the answer. Townley's work could not be more different. She looked at an issue which is salient

to tourism development around the globe – the organizational problems caused by the conflict between antiquary conservation and the commercialization of attractions. The particular case under scrutiny was a museum. What is significant about this study is that she used classical Weberian analysis on her data. No interdisciplinary work here. Instead we have a rare example of a single mother discipline, in the form of an 'old theory', being applied directly to a modern problem with illuminating results. This case raises the issue first, of how close hospitality and tourism research is, or should be, to disciplines such as economics, sociology and psychology and second, in the pursuit of interdisciplinary studies is there a danger of overlooking the explanatory power of single theoretical solutions? The last case is a review of how retail workers respond to 'customer service programmes'. In a sense, it addresses an issue that should be of direct relevance to management. The conclusions are interesting but not entirely helpful to the user community, in that the findings suggest that sometimes they work and sometimes they do not, but that an explanation of either case cannot be given. The implication is that explanations lie elsewhere and in individual variables. For management it is both good news and bad news research: on the one hand they know the programmes can, and often do, work but, on the other hand, they do not know why. It could be argued that it is good for end-users of research to realize that sometimes useful research comes up with incomplete answers and that perhaps there are deeper questions to ask. In other words, this study raises the issue of 'level of explanation' which is one which should concern hospitality and tourism research for two reasons: first, because of its place within the notion of 'relevance' which itself sits at the heart of the education–industry relationship and second because the degree to which research using hospitality and tourism can address questions at the generic and theoretical levels depends on the level of explanation expected.

These three examples are selective but they punch home some important points – that attributional studies are only as good as the attributes, single theory can often cut deep into a complex phenomenon, and the answer is not always out there! Other studies could have been evoked to make different points but the three studies selected here have the purpose of illustrating that good methodology and application are not necessarily enough when the phenomenon under investigation is not fully understood, and, even if a phenomenon is conspicuously complex and hard to conceptualize, translating that to mean that there is a need for multidisciplinary and/or interdisciplinary approaches should not be automatic. They also all illustrate that 'level of explanation' is an important issue in the development of research within hospitality and tourism.

INTRODUCTION

This chapter begins by reviewing some of the assumptions and tendencies that appear to influence thinking on research in hospitality. The purpose of such a review is threefold: to highlight areas where a technical rethink might be fruitful; to provide a background for the evaluation of multi- and interdisciplinary methods; and to recognize some of the inherent difficulties in doing research in hospitality. The important practical point made in this review is that, whilst there is nothing wrong or inappropriate about using multidisciplinary and interdisciplinary methods, there is a tendency to make the assumption that they are especially useful to a complex context such as hospitality and this point is contested. The salient strategic point of the review is that hospitality research has a propensity to focus disproportionately on one of its main characteristics – diversity. This, it will be argued, is a questionable approach which leads away from the core task of seeking coherence within a small number of key research areas.

The first part of this chapter is essentially a critique of the thinking, and consequently the approaches, that are current in hospitality research. Its purpose is to suggest that a reappraisal of some of the underlying ideas that govern hospitality research is at least worth considering. In this sense, the critique aims to be helpful to future developments. At the centre of the critique are the appropriateness of multi- and interdisciplinary methods, the inherent problems of concept definition and a sympathetic view of the issues surrounding research into the adoption of generic management practices by the hospitality industry. The second part of the chapter is an undeniably selective and arguably idiosyncratic perspective on possible future directions of hospitality research, based on critique and appraisal of current approaches.

In the interests of clarity it might be helpful, at the outset, for a statement to be made on exactly where the critical arguments are coming from. The critique is structured around three 'positions' which are in themselves a matter of debate. The intention is not to be dogmatic or prescriptive but merely develop arguments from a known starting point. The legitimate criticisms of hospitality research thinking summarized by Brotherton (1999) are not reprised here but extended so as to view them from a different perspective. This alternative perspective does however, on one very important issue, disagree with one of the main conclusions drawn by Brotherton. To be specific, when he argues that progress requires the research community to address the perennial problems of definition and boundary, in other words the 'what is hospitality?' question, the analysis here could not disagree more. The contention in this chapter is that, even if it were worth asking, hospitality simply is not at a stage of development in research terms to provide an appropriate research agenda to answer it. This issue can be 'lived with' as it does not interfere with progress – always asking for fundamental definitions is self-defeating – imagining a start line and constantly returning to it is not doing the subject any favors. That this is in fact the case in hospitality research thinking is one of the main criticisms made here.

The three distinct positions are: first that, in essence, hospitality research, out of a concern for its own legitimacy/maturity and out of a perverse obsession with its own diversity, is showing too much concern for range of methodologies and philosophies and is not expending enough cognitive energy on both defining questions which it can actually address and in rounding up the disciplines that can help it to do so. One possible explanation for this might be a sense of ontological insecurity that makes hospitality often feel uncomfortable in certain academic disciplines. This might be compounded by the unfortunate fact that despite the long-established dependence of any mature hospitality industry on its vocational educational output, the actual scholarship that produced that output is not properly recognized by employers in the industry (Riley, 1993a). As if this were not enough, hospitality compounds the problem by scoring an own goal – that is, getting its own diversity out of proportion. Second, and somewhat subjectively, an argument could be made that hospitality research, like tourism research and to an extent management research, is in denial: it does not feel comfortable in a behavioral science context – yet to a large extent that is what it is. In particular, of all the artifacts of behavioral science it is behavior itself that is most neglected in hospitality. Acknowledging this, it will be argued, is one of the ways that hospitality research can prosper. Hospitality is a vocational context which has lessons for the generic case but without behavioral science there is no way behavior in hospitality that is either unique or shared in common with the generic world can be translated into the generic case. In other words, before it can be moved across different contexts any behavior has to be described in theoretical terms. This particular argument leads to the third position, which is that much hospitality research is management research and consequently researchers have become embroiled not just in the evolving world of management theory, but also in the problems of applying generic techniques that are themselves in a constant state of change. This is inevitable. However, the effect of both is first, to confound the debatable, but commonly held view about, the uniqueness of the industry rather than to clarify it and second, because there is little critical thinking about the veracity of those techniques in the generic world, it reduces debate to descriptions of different contexts. Hospitality research needs to report back to the generic world its difficulties in application which would benefit the generic case but it does not do so. Often it reports back an unconvincing 'perfect fit'.

These three critical positions are not directed at any particular piece of hospitality research

they are aimed at the general picture. They may be unfair but they are at least legitimate interpretations of what goes on and what is missing in hospitality research. To be fair to the subject it has to be said that the academics who conduct the research are distributed across the globe and have to cope with local circumstances. This leads to fragmentation and possibly a lack of a unified voice. The role of journal editors is rarely discussed in relation to research coherence despite it being a subject of debate within management research. Furthermore, horizons may be restricted by the fact that, to a large extent, they are welded to a well-established and largely successful vocational curriculum that reflects functionalism within the industry. This latter point is bound to intervene in the creation of research questions and it cannot be surprising if hospitality research reflects this division of labor.

A CRITIQUE OF HOSPITALITY APPROACHES

Ideas that influence thinking

Whatever philosophies and approaches exist towards research within hospitality they result from the influence of a particular constellation of ideas which appear to work in consort. The most prominent of these ideas are concerned with notions about the nature of the industry and how it works. In this perspective the big picture appears to consist of, on the one hand, the much vaunted uniqueness of the industry and, on the other, an equally hyped concern for its diversity. Accepting that, at least to an extent, both are true – it is unique and diverse – these themes have had a curious effect upon research thinking. The picture is further embroidered by three other major concerns. The first is the perceived need to be relevant to the hospitality industry (the perceived user group), which is an absolutely legitimate perspective. Second, there is a concern for the role of theory in a vocational subject area – this concern is problematic. It also has a sub-category, that of an apparent need for multidisciplinary and interdisciplinary approaches. Finally there is a concern to show a link with generic management. In one way or another these themes form the backdrop to the thinking of most research on any specific hospitality topic.

The international hospitality research community is healthily critical of its own performance and within this community of academics there is continuous debate about the future of hospitality research. This debate is reflective in character in that from time to time a scholar in the area publishes a review of progress. It is also speculative and open-ended in that there is a concern about possibilities for the future. The reflective review normally describes what has been done and then attempts to discern some overall purpose and direction to the subject area from what has been done. This deductive approach does not imply that researchers are not proactive in their pursuits it simply means that the global research community, like the industry, is fragmented and therefore it is difficult for academics to be aware of coherent themes let alone develop them. At a prosaic level, Baloglu and Assante (1999) display and analyze the content of, and methods used, in hospitality research. There appears to be a balance between conceptual and empirical work and a spread of different research methods. The analysis also suggests the influence of functionalism which cannot be too surprising. More important is the fact that whilst some themes are developed in the literature, there is a failure to follow up many good studies. This is a characteristic shared with the tourism literature where there are excellent one-off studies that are not extended. Obvious themes such as 'what hospitality managers do' are regularly researched over the years but such activity is spasmodic so that otherwise good material is prevented from saying anything significant because of the large time gaps in between – the road from Arnaldo (1981) via Nailon (1982) to Hales and Nightingale (1986) to Shortt (1989) to Kim (1994) and to Chareanpunsirikul and Wood (2002) is a broken one despite each study being well researched. This kind of pattern is reflected in the generic management literature but to a much lesser extent. Again, the finger could be pointed at the fragmented research community. However, the issues surrounding labor turnover would be an example of a theme that has been well developed in the literature. A more important consequence of this fragmentation, lack of coherence and failure to extend themes is that it appears to have led some academics to call for, and search for, appropriate paradigms for hospitality research (Littlejohn, 1990), conceptual frameworks within which hospitality research can blossom (Morrison, 2002) and a theory of hospitality (Jones, 1996; Lashley, 2000). In other words, the hunt is on for a unifying theory and methods, and multidisciplinary and interdisciplinary approaches are frequently advocated on the grounds that they are suitable for eliciting theory from complex data. By going down this road hospitality is posing itself questions, such as, 'what is hospitality?' which it may not be able to answer and furthermore believing that achieving the firm basis of a concrete definition will lead to enlightening pathways of research, is, at least to this pair of eyes, doubtful.

Uniqueness: in what way does it matter?

Every business is unique because it has its own markets, its own economic value system and it will operate within both a particular industrial culture as well as in a business culture – which is a way of saying that hospitality can be both unique and generic simultaneously. The real questions are whether the unique parts actually matter and if they do, how do they matter? In response to both these questions it is possible to identify two areas where uniqueness does matter – in the first place those unique elements of an industry define both what has to be learnt and the extent of the knowledge differential with the generic case. In the second place, uniqueness may translate into a particular mindset which has implications both for research and for integration with the generic world. Both these arguments come together with the notion of industry culture.

In the context of arguing a case for uniqueness the notion of particularism is important because in can lead to a mindset. Highlighted by Spender (1989), particularism is concerned with common problems, 'collective learning' and 'industry recipes'. In Spender's arguments independent managers who do not know each other come to define problems and consequent solutions in the same way. Within industry, but not organizational, boundaries, what develops is an industry culture where a 'common sense' exists about 'taken for granted' notions that lie behind intention and action (Golding, 1980). How things work, what will or will not work are all mutually understood by people who are strangers to each other but share the same problems. What is interesting in this analysis is that it applies to strategic thinking and to learning based on a shared vision of how the industry works. Furthermore, these industry assumptions enter the process of strategic formulation at an early stage where identification of opportunities and problems and objectives are created (Dess, Ireland and Hitt, 1990). It is assumed that within the strategic formulation process there is a rationality which is common to the decision makers and that this is founded upon some mutually held assumptions about key aspects of the industry such as competition. The idea of the importance of assumptions draws to the fore the matter of knowledge and the relationship between specific and general knowledge.

'Knowing the business' as distinct from 'knowing business' is common coinage within industrial parlance but, Spender's point is that firm-specific solutions are derived from experiences commonly shared within an industry as well as knowledge of the firm. The really crucial point here is one that the generalist/specialist debate misses, namely that within specific industries, knowledge and information is actually structured and embedded within industrial culture (Phillips, 1996). However, given bounded rationality and the limits of information; what are the limits of hospitality managers' knowledge? Is everything they need to know embedded in the hospitality industry and hospitality education? Doubtful, because exogenous knowledge is necessary and is located within overlapping contexts and exists at various levels of abstraction and detail. Seen in this light, modern ideas such as clustering, knowledge transfer and networking are process artifacts of that knowledge/information structure of which the hospitality industry is simply a part (Spender, 1998). The processes themselves directly improve the structure itself by swelling the capacity of human capital within it. What is being suggested here is that defining hospitality by some specific skills and knowledge cuts out the truth that they exist and always have existed, in a wide range of contexts. The difference today is that that wider context is rapidly changing. However, the suggestion that industrial boundaries may be acting as important information structures by which managers mimic each other to mutual advantage has to be taken seriously, but also qualified. Ideas come into the hospitality industry from outside its boundaries. Innovation does not recognize industrial boundaries and is often inevitable and therefore simply has to be accommodated (Brazeal and Herbert, 1999).

What these arguments suggest is that the place of uniqueness lies in the areas of skills and knowledge where it would be fruitful to pay more consideration to looking at the symmetry or asymmetry of generic and vocational knowledge. In a sense, the degree of symmetry defines the learning gap. Whilst there is evidence from other fields that symmetry between the knowledge of owners/managers and the operational workforce brings benefits to development activities (Madesen et al., 2003) there is strong empirical evidence, particularly in the hospitality industry, that people go into businesses they know nothing about and still manage to learn and prosper (Shaw, 2004). This said, there is pressure from the wider world for hospitality managers to expand their knowledge beyond that which is particular to the industry. This pressure comes from three forces which work in tandem, namely the growth of worldwide businesses (often referred to as globalization), the growth of information access and the pressure to see knowledge as not being contextually specific (genericism). Any attempt to embrace generic business knowledge would require a shift in mindset and this is part of the argument about why uniqueness matters and suggests a research agenda about management knowledge and the structure of management knowledge. Hospitality education not only contains partitions between vocational subjects and generic subjects but within this categorization scheme there are functional partitions. All this may be educationally necessary and sound but the risk is that these categories are taken into industry where they are often reinforced by organizational specialisms. Beck and Young (2005) suggest that knowledge restructuring has a relationship to occupational identities, particularly ideas about professionalism and subject loyalty. Forcing managers to change through global generic expansion may have the beneficial effect of loosening mindsets so that learning can take place without devaluing necessary partitions between knowledge areas. If vocational education does not handle the generic material well then the 'messy' output enters industry and has a knock-on effect for occupational categories.

Diversity: drawing the wrong conclusion

Hospitality is not short of direct texts on research methods applied to the area (see for example Clark et al., 1998; Brotherton, 1999).

Nor is it short of good descriptions of relevant research method papers (see for example Connolly's (2005) excellent evocation of case study approach; the good theoretical/methodological advice given by Christensen Hughes (1997) and Lynn and Mullen (1997); and the informative look at experimentation by Namsivayam (2004)). However, the issue of relating methods to concepts of interest seems to be clouded rather than clarified by a concern for research paradigms. One thing is clear from looking at reviews of hospitality research and that is that the debate over appropriate research paradigms and methods has become intimately intertwined with the continuous debate over the need for a holistic unifying theory of hospitality. What appears to be happening is that everything is driven by an assumption of diversity of the subject. Hospitality research questions are characterized by diversity and are therefore complex and susceptible to diverse perspectives. This view is realistic in the sense that it reflects the real nature of the industry but is actually unhelpful. To make matters worse, at the conceptual level, the phenomenon of hospitality itself eludes definition. These difficulties have led some scholars in two particular directions that are perfectly legitimate but not necessarily fruitful.

The first direction concerns the appropriateness of method to hospitality research problems. In this line of thinking diversity and lack of theory is translated into a need for interdisciplinary approaches, multidisciplinary approaches (Roper and Brookes, 1999) and a hybrid version of both, transdisciplinary approaches (Littlejohn, 2004). There is a tendency in this debate to fudge the boundaries between 'approaches' and actual 'methods' and to confuse collaboration with interdisciplinarity. Working together is a means to something but has no intrinsic value. If more than one discipline is needed to identify and refine a research question that is not the same thing as pursuing the question in an interdisciplinary 'mixed methods' way. There is a lack of clarity as when and how each case is relevant. There is nothing wrong with any of the multi- and interdisciplinary approaches but the argument for their justification in hospitality, if not exactly suspect, is worthy of debate. Notwithstanding the merits of interdisciplinary research it is possible to jump too soon in that direction. That diversity needs diverse methods is a seductive argument: the subject is big, complex and slippery so single disciplines and single techniques are immediately assumed to be at a disadvantage. A sub-branch of this argument substitutes strategy for diversity; strategy is hard to pin down, has future connotations, and is therefore not only diverse but also opaque and therefore in need of mixed method approaches (Pansiri, 2005). The counter argument suggests that 'you should count to ten' before making that assumption. The second line of argument, similar to the first, is also about methods but has a theoretical angle. This argument pushes qualitative methods to the fore and gets to its conclusion by means of a trawl through both critical theory and postmodernist thinking (Filmer, 1998). In these arguments the boundaries between academic disciplines are no longer appropriate. Because the world is becoming borderless, barriers are, if not completely collapsing, becoming fuzzy at the edges, and social distinctions such as class and age no longer matter. In these postmodern circumstances, it is argued, it becomes easier to perceive and measure phenomenon in holistic terms. The central idea is that one can see the whole clearly once the distinctions have evaporated. From this position it is fairly easy to throw a rope bridge between holistic conceptions, qualitative approaches and the development of unifying theory. Given the claim for uniqueness and the difficulties of defining hospitality it appears that hospitality scholars have seen a connection between their conceptual problems and their desire for a unifying theory and postmodernist views of social theory. Not unnaturally, this approach gives rise to the advocacy of a variety of qualitative measures within a multidisciplinary framework.

The premise on which this approach is justified can be, and should be, challenged because, exactly like positivism, it is based on questionable assumptions, two at least which are of particular importance and should be examined. First, what is being assumed here is that loss of boundaries and distinctions makes the desired holistic concept clearer and more visible – but why would this be so? Second, it is being assumed that a measurable holistic concept is a gateway to a theory. A clear holistic picture of a concept leads to a clear explanation of that concept – but again, why should this be so? There is still a way to go and, given any methodological approach, why should a holistic concept be more amenable to measurement and interpretation than a web of smaller causal relationships that have to be woven together piecemeal? When it comes down to practicalities the claim for the superior quality of holistic approaches tends to rest on there being a measurable phenomenon that captures the holistic concept: the 'dispositions' contained within Bourdieu's notion of 'habitus' would be a ready example whereby the identification of dispositions within a group or society is said to be evidence of the larger concept of habitus (Bourdieu and Passeron, 1977; Lane, 2000). Even in these circumstances the researcher is still left with methodological problems. This argument does not deny the existence of holistic concepts nor that individuals can think and make decisions in a holistic way. It accepts fully that methods such as cognitive task analysis exist that capture holistic thinking. This is not a diatribe against qualitative research methods nor an advocacy of quantitative methods. What it is, however, is an argument that suggests that if the spurious connections described above are being made and applied to hospitality research thinking then the researcher is in fact simply changing battle site from the beginning to the end, not solving the problem. In other words, conceptual cognitive effort is not applied to the complexity of a problem at the beginning, but postponed to the end where it becomes synthesis from unstructured data. If there is no representative attitudinal or behavioral measurement then often the 'holistic' has to be described by finding the boundaries and properties of its parts (see Dey, 1999, for an exposition of the innate problems of establishing meaning through categories and properties within ethnographic and grounded theory approaches). In other words, the argument here is that an immediate assumption that diversity can be sidestepped by holistic approaches that leads toward theory is a myth. The case for any methodological approach, be it quantitative or qualitative, is determined by the conceptual clarity that precedes it.

Wrestling with theory

Riley and Szivas (2005) in the case of tourism research, point to the limiting effects of having only a few mother disciplines involved. It is a similar case with hospitality. The exclusion of disciplines means that their central theories and

forms of analysis are not open to hospitality so that the questions they ask are not asked in the subject area. For example, in an area where people are often the subject of research there is little interest in applying well-developed metric tests on occupational issues in hospitality research despite the fact that when specific tests are developed and applied they are often illuminating (Manning et al., 2005).

One of casualties of this diversity/ complexity perspective is that existing theoretical explanations are often overlooked (possibly because of a dislike of old references in publications). Overlooking established theory, however old, is not a luxury a vocational subject area can afford. Socio-technical theory, for example, could easily support various characteristics of uniqueness if called on to do so. If, hospitality and management are conceived as particular cases of general social theory and social psychological theory then the use of established theory seems appropriate. That is a big step and it takes the argument back to the issue of diversity. Viewing hospitality through the eyes of general theory whereby behavior in hospitality or for that matter management behavior is seen merely as a special example can illuminate both hospitality and general theory. Seeing hospitality management in such behavioral terms has the advantage of guarding against being trapped in managerial rhetoric – a problem shared with generic management research; what people do is some kind of protection against being sucked into the rhetoric. Similarly, an immediate adoption of multidisciplinary approaches brings with it multiple theoretical frameworks. There is nothing wrong with this but there is evidence that single theories or a set of single theories applied discretely produce insights that are useful to hospitality and to social theory (see for example Riley, 1984; Ingram and Inman, 1996; Baum and Haveman, 1997). Again it must be emphasized that single theory analysis is not being advocated except as an option.

Revisiting attributes

Attributional research forms a large proportion of empirical studies in hospitality and marketing studies and there is a case for looking again at how we go about these studies. There are two good reasons for looking closely at attributes: that they are always problematic is one but, the other is that the rise of information society has had an impact on the way we perceive the things we desire. We have been doing attribution studies since long before people had wide access to information and maybe it is time to rethink how we approach them. In one respect what hospitality shares in common with marketing, management, organizational behavior and many other disciplines and subject areas is the need to improve its quantitative research where attributes are being used as independent variables. The basic tenets of nearly all research are conceptual clarity, theoretical foundation and unambiguous variable definition. This 'holy trinity' runs easily off the tongue but is very hard to achieve. Getting these matters right at the beginning is the primary task of the researcher whether they are involved in commercial or academic research. Assuming a theoretical foundation, success in the technical, operational sense, is dependent on the concepts of reliability and validity. Can the results be replicated and did the research instrument measure what it was supposed to measure? Commercial research may not demand the former but it certainly wants the latter. These concepts become particularly crucial where the research involves scaling. Notwithstanding mathematical testing, these concepts are themselves dependent on variable definition and the precision with which stimuli capture those definitions. Quantitative research is only as good as its questionnaire statements and they are only as good as the concept clarity which they purport to represent. In other words, reliability and validity involve both descriptive language and numbers, but content validity rules!

In the light of this bold statement it is possible to suggest that hospitality, in this attribute research context, is in need of a new perspective on researching variable definition. The literature of hospitality is littered with good, well-organized quantitative attributional studies on guest satisfaction, perceived quality, perceived value, hotel selection criteria, job satisfaction, organizational commitment – all based on defined attributes (Getty and Thompson, 1994; Gundersen, Heide and Olsson, 1996; Ekinci and Riley, 2001; Ekinci, 2004; Petrick, 2004). In many cases the research has advanced to the stage where modeling is possible. However, whilst in most cases attempts have been made to clarify how subjects understand the definitions of attributional variables, the contention here is

that this type of study will continue to produce the roughly similar results and conclusions it always has, not because of technical research incompetence, but because of the definitions and meanings attributed to the variables have not been secured through other, possibly qualitative means. In other words, what people mean when they say they are satisfied or not with a variable or, what it means to say a variable is important, is open to interpretation and probably constant reinterpretation. This problem is inherent in all types of quantitative attributional studies *but the special difficulty for hospitality is the small range and repetitive nature of product and service attributes*. The world of travel and hospitality continuously grows and over time matures and gets old – tastes change and people find new ways to describe their experiences. How do we know that 'old' words like 'satisfied', 'comfortable', 'friendly' and so on have the same meaning as in the past? The language of expectation needs to be constantly checked and verified. However, the real rationale for emphasizing such an obvious point is that the world has changed and growing access to information, particularly the ability to preview attributes, is bound to have an effect on how attributes are perceived and expectations constructed. At the very least we should assume that the value of the effort involved in the information search and evaluation processes is factored into value judgements be they satisfaction or quality assessments (Grewal, Monroe and Krishnan, 1998; Al-Sabbahy, Ekinci and Riley, 2004). The hospitality research community tends to avoid comparative research but in doing so it misses the opportunity to see the shared and differential vocabulary used in the cases of products and services. The concepts themselves are now deliberately made fuzzy in the interests of branding. How we should get at these new meanings is a worthwhile challenge.

This is, in fact, a general problem and the rise of focus group processes is testament to this deficiency in variable definition. The implication is that quantitative attributional studies need more thorough prior qualitative research or, to put it another way quantitative measuring techniques are running ahead of real meaning. In addition to pure qualitative studies, what is needed is more qualitative focus on the variables used in quantitative studies. There is nothing new in this statement but it has not happened enough. The same comment could be made about the lack of control groups in hospitality research. Although, there is a balance in the literature between conceptual approaches and empirical studies that slightly favors the former, the really important point is that the two rarely meet. The attributional empirical papers rarely display serious evidence of establishing prior meanings. Qualitative and quantitative research are not working for each other. Here is a more precise meaning of multidisciplinary research – multiple methods serving one end: method in series. This is the very opposite of triangulation where the same object is measured by different measures simultaneously then combined by interpretation. The idea of building a research method from other research methods in an architectural way can be applied to a single discipline or in an interdisciplinary context. The logical coupling would put qualitative study first giving rise to quantitative work with good content validity, but the other way around is just as valid. Help is at hand in the form of a bridging method – Q methodology.

In praise of Q methodology

The justification for singling out Q methodology is nothing to do with its intrinsic merit – it is simply that, in advocating that qualitative and quantitative approaches should serve each other it is only proper to highlight an approach which has only that purpose. Q methodology is not an overused technique. It can be argued that the distinction between qualitative and quantitative research is disabling to both but to an extent Q methodology sits in both camps and offers a genuine connection which can be helpful to both. Although ostensibly a qualitative technique it can produce numerically measurable data. Its importance to the arguments used here is that it offers a way in which the problem of attributes described earlier can be approached. What is it about? It is about wrestling with subjectivity through inter-subjectivity.

When the researcher is armed only with a suspicion and a few observations that a social entity, such as an evaluative construct, exists, and when, in addition, they are faced with the complication that even if it were established it could be described in a variety of ways, the technique required is one that can capture subjectivity. In other words, where the topic, even when socially constructed, remains slippery to define, both definition and consensus

can be captured by using a method which works through the process of social constructivism. These are the circumstances that can benefit from Q methodology which, in essence, mimics social construction. Exploratory work where subjective judgements of an indescribable object are the order of the day exactly suits Q methodology and more particularly Q-sort technique (Stephenson, 1953). This methodology is very versatile and though it is often directed at priorities and suspected rank orders (Tractinsky and Jarvenpaa, 1995), it is especially suited to cases where the very existence of concepts have not been established. The concepts such as hospitality, quality, fairness, and commitment come into this category. There is no social consensus on the meaning of them even when there might be an evaluative agreement on a specific example of them.

Q-sort technique addresses problems of this nature but it must be clear from the start that it is not a methodology from which results can be generalized to a population unless, that is, the results of the Q-sort undergo factor analysis. Without confirmatory factor analysis the technique must be seen only as a preliminary methodology to be followed by more empirical approaches (McKeown and Thomas, 1988). The output of a sample of Q-sort tests should be seen as proof of a 'reliable schematic' or a cognitive pattern (Thomas and Baas, 1992). It plays the role of setting up empirical approaches so that theory can be tested (Kerlinger, 1986). Essentially Q-sort is about finding concepts and categories. To this end the researcher generates alternative definitions of the elusive concept and amasses statements that might describe each definition. These statements are then entered into a free sort protocol that allows for rejects. Subjects attempt to match descriptors with definitions. Both descriptors and statements are perishable in this process. The process uses statistical rules that are the equivalent of significance rules in hypothesis testing to allow definitions and stimuli to go forwards into the next methodology. Q methodology goes well beyond the sensible approaches to 'content adequacy assessment' suggested by Hinkin, Tracy and Enz (1997). Q-sort testing shares objectives with approaches such as Repertory Grid methods that were devised from personal construct psychology (Kelly, 1955). However, it is important to note the difference between Q-sort technique and Repertory Grid. Repertory Grid can only be applied when the research is reasonably certain that the object of the research is frequently in the consciousness of the subjects. The uncertainty in Repertory Grid methodology is in finding stimuli which represent that particular world in which the object exists, the existence of the domain is assumed. By contrast, in Q-sort technique, the existence of the domain is not assumed. Q-sort technique is about capturing an entity by finding stimuli which can be clustered to form a description of it. If people can describe it, it *may* exist! It is a 'dimensionless' task in which subjectivity and objectivity grope around to find each other (Coxon and Jones, 1978: 65). Time spent on this technique greatly enhances the construct validity of questions inserted into questionnaire (and it is good for your Cronbach Alpha as well!).

Underestimating and under-researching some conspicuous features

Possibly because of the claim for uniqueness hospitality has ignored exploration of some of its conspicuously important features. Three obvious areas come to mind: the stochastic nature of short-run demand; repeated behavior or repeat business; and the power relationships within the industry structure. There must be more underexplored areas but these three, it is suggested, would open up some of the existing lines of research. It may be going backwards to go forwards but the obvious often has hidden depths. Understanding the micro-level implications of constant variation in consumer demand opens up important areas like productivity where normal measures of productivity explain only the level but not how it was achieved (Riley, 1999). The model by Gronroos and Ojasalo (2004) captures very convincingly the productivity context but the actual relations between the variables remains underexplored (Riley, 2000). In the absence of studies, practitioners make decisions through best guessing, which can often be misleading even when it appears to be common sense. For example, the idea that more employee flexibility leads to greater labor productivity, which is an appealing idea, was qualified by the study by Brusco et al. (1998) who found that the optimum return was not total flexibility: a sub-optimal solution was best. Although devised from a generic source the

principle is directly applicable to hospitality. The advent of process engineering into service systems is fine but it has not fully taken on board the nature of demand in the industry. Its response has been to standardize and customize without acknowledging the productivity consequences of, on the one hand, very short-run stochastic demand and on the other, extended customer choice. In the context of having to cope with ever greater fluctuations in demand the world of manufacturing and other service industries are becoming like the hospitality industry. The hospitality industry with its endemic labor mobility could, for example, teach the world about deregulated labor markets (Riley, 1993b). Further exploration as to what it means to manage in these circumstance is an area where hospitality is a case from which the generic world can learn.

In an excellent review of research in marketing in hospitality Oh, Kim and Shin (2004) lay out the territory that has been and should be covered – but there is little discussion of how customers actually behave. Most studies of customers in hospitality are attitudinal or perceptual which use behavior only as behavioral validation as in 'would you return?'. Here behavior is represented by intention. Using the theory of reasoned action, researchers rate attributes in terms of importance which takes measurement as far as predicting intention but ends before actual behavior. It is actual behavior (beyond mere statistics about visitors and occupancy) which is largely missing from hospitality and tourism research. A special case of this argument is habit. One of the tenets of hospitality is 'the satisfied customer', the rationale being that satisfied customers will return. In truth, there is very little work done on repeat business. Here hospitality shares the same issue as tourism. It is one thing to go into attitudinal studies of loyalty but quite another to explore patterns of behavior that display repetition. Again there is nothing wrong with attitudinal approaches but the nature of habit as applied in hospitality consumption is neglected. The growth of travel implies that people are not only developing experience but also travel habits. People develop habits in relation to any common activity (that includes avoiding it) and travel and hospitality cannot be an exception. Furthermore actual behavior could offer insights into the origins of expectations and motives – knowing more about what people did on holiday might give us a clue to their motives. The third area of underdevelopment is concerned with power and dependence within the structure of which hospitality organizations are a part.

One way of looking at the tourism industry in its widest definition is that it is an integrated industry within a visible value chain yet the converse is also true, that it is a fragmented and interdependent structure. Hospitality lies within this structure. Whatever the perspective, hospitality research appears reluctant to apply theoretical analysis of social forces such as power and conflict to understanding of the industry and its organizations. Submerged within the fragmented whole are fundamental components of the industry: its meaningful structure and driving forces. Packed with different stakeholders, each with their own interests and agendas, rational planning and strategic foresight has to cope with the entrepreneurial ethos and the stochastic nature of demand which drives this economic activity. That there is a degree of interdependence becomes conspicuous whenever a major event such as an act of terrorism or outbreak of disease takes place. The levels of dependence and power become visible. The fundamental components, normally submerged, come to the surface. Suddenly, the degree of interdependence that exists between these stakeholders becomes raw and visible. Luxury hotels, coach companies and agro-tourism operations make strange bedfellows but when things go wrong they realize they are in the same boat. When this occurs a competitive industry looks for consensus, a common solution, and normally also looks to a superordinate authority to provide it. What is important about a crisis is that it acts as a reminder that human activities such as tourism, travel and hospitality are an outcome of, not just economic activity, but of many social forces such as power, authority, common consciousness and influence that form both the structure of the industry and its organizing principles: pricing is not just a market response. Research in these matters is normally the province of economics but other disciplines need to get involved. As hospitality companies become larger and more global in focus their relationship to local industries and local markets changes. Organizational strategies are the outcome of forces that distribute power and dependence/independence, they are not just the inevitable consequence of greater size.

Serving industry is problematic

Not unnaturally in this vocational context, a serious concern is that research should be useful to industry. Sturman (2003) offers a review of industry's likely interest in research. The emphasis on managerial problems and swelling the knowledge base are sensible approaches. It is easy for both educators and industry to take for granted the regular swelling of human capital some of which is caused by research. Taylor and Edgar (1999: 24) recognize this point in their summary of what they see as the purpose of hospitality research. They suggest three principal purposes of hospitality research, as follows:

- 'to uncover and make sense of existing patterns of behavior and phenomena within the hospitality industry' – essentially a positivist approach;
- 'to identify new and better ways of managing within the hospitality industry' – a normative approach; and
- 'to enable hospitality faculty to educate future practitioners'.

These are very laudable ambitions but trying to be relevant to industry is itself full of difficulties which are now further complicated by the need to keep up with the rapid changes in modern business management brought about by globalization and technological change. The hospitality industry is not immune from changes in corporate governance, the rise of strategic thinking and the separation of operational and technical management from business management. The implications are for change and this is an opportunity for hospitality researchers.

In terms of direct relevance, management research offers two useful outcomes to practicing management, namely, helping managers to understand the processes that they are involved in and undertaking the evaluation of managerial activities. However, endeavoring to achieve either of these objectives has its complications. There are three issues here. The first stems from the fragmented nature of the industry itself. If relevant means research simply addressing problems the issue becomes one of 'whose problems?'. Social psychology can speak of industry mindsets but at the institutional level the problem is not easy to address. All organizations have their problems and some of those problems are common to all players – but how does a shared problem enter the common consciousness of decision makers? Who speaks for the industry? In other words, the issue is when does an organization problem (consultancy) become an industry problem (worth empirically sampling)? The research needs of the industry and those of companies and individuals are not the same. Cobanoglu et al. (2004) asked practitioners and educators some direct questions about what research was important and unsurprisingly industry trends features fairly highly as did marketing but awareness of actual 'industry' as against organizational problems and issues did not feature. The problem for the hospitality researcher is that what is seen as an issue for the industry need not be one for a particular organization – for example, the whole issue of skill development and training falls squarely into this little trap. Case research is rarely an adequate substitute for addressing this type of topic.

The second issue, very much related to the first, is the level of evidence that would satisfy the question being asked. Industry wants solutions, not necessarily detailed analysis. 'It is good enough if it works' is pragmatic philosophy that is both a problem, in the sense of management having limited horizons in terms of research, and an opportunity for hospitality research to show what thorough research can do. Evaluative studies, however, could be a major contribution to the academia/industry interface because of the independence of academia. The process, however, presumes a level of critical maturity on behalf of industry. The third issue that of the application of generic practices to the vocational context reinforces the idea that evaluative research would be appropriate to hospitality. Hospitality management has been invaded by the generic ideas born on the back of technological innovation and globalization. This is both good and inevitable but it does present problems of applicability and adaptation. Although changes have been well described the impact of the changes are not a strong feature of hospitality research. The dilemma for hospitality researchers is that to be relevant they have to engage with generic approaches but must do so without the certainty that these approaches are directly relevant to the industry. This speaks volumes for the need for critical evaluative studies of generic applicability and the adaptation processes necessary to implement them. The problem is one of criteria. Comparative studies with other industries require detailed contextual description because every industry is in part unique.

Summary of critique

In brief, the main arguments from the above form into recommendations as follows. First is to view the hospitality industry, however clumsily defined, from the outside. Second, is to make better use of established theory instead of looking for new theory. Third, it is important to be careful in assuming that complexity equals the need for multi- and/or interdisciplinary approaches. In involving a range of disciplines the purpose has to be clear. If multidisciplinary involvement confirms the complexity of a subject, this does not necessarily lead to the requirement for a complex research method. Fourth is to recognize that single theory applications can be enlightening. Fifth, it is important to re-examine attributional studies in the light of growing access to information. Sixth, we should recognize the need for actual behavior to feature as a variable in research design. Seven, research design should itself be seen in terms of architecture where an object is pursued by methods run in series and in this respect the argument is to see that quantitative and qualitative methods are servants of each that can be applied in series rather than as parallel alternatives. Finally, we should give emphasis to evaluative studies because they are useful to practitioners and inevitably involve taking a behavioral approach.

AN ALTERNATE PERSPECTIVE AND AGENDA

New knowledge in old themes

The preceding critique of hospitality research has raised a number of issues in respect of influences on hospitality research thinking and methods. In glib shorthand the advice might be to go easy on yearning for apposite philosophies and paradigms, cut down on interdisciplinary methodologies and to lay off the search for a unifying theory. That said the purpose in this section of the chapter is to outline an agenda for exploring new areas of knowledge that can advance the topic of hospitality as an academic subject but also reiterate those questions which have been asked but still have only fragmented answers. If you ask the same questions you tend to go in a familiar direction even if you ingeniously invent new methodologies. The search for new knowledge, whether about old or new topics, requires new questions to be asked. The creation of new questions is, of course, the remit of both theoretical thinking and the analysis of newly minted data.

The outside world in its economic and political guise tends to ask the same questions of hospitality: does the quality of products and services support tourism expansion; how can a destination be marketed; how do people earn a living in the industry and does it provide jobs? In truth these big questions are only partially answered. Hospitality researchers need to join the quest of marketing and tourism to develop destination marketing through a more advanced consumer behavior framework. It also needs to know why people join and stay in the industry – old chestnuts in a way, but not answered and still important. The suggestion here is that within these themes lie a number of smaller questions which could be addressed. First, the hospitality research community should adopt a strategy of looking closely at some of these old but fundamental themes. Second, in terms of approach, the strategy should be to cut out thoughts of a unifying theory, address the rethink on attributes and concentrate on some areas with the goal of adding to empirical knowledge but to do so without necessarily contributing to theory development.

In pursuit of a lesser God

The reluctance to support the idea of pursuing a theory of hospitality is not based on doubts about theory itself. Such a theory may or may not be developed but the real concerns are that the amount of empirical research and data collected so far is insufficient and too diverse and, more importantly, the question of what follows such a theory has not been seriously considered. What questions will it pose? As an alternative perspective Sutton and Straw (1995) point out that theory development is a very high hurdle to jump over and that there are other worthy data collection goals such as the clear description of social phenomenon. They argue that a preliminary strategy (prior to ideas about theory development) is possible in which the research community builds up descriptive empirical research which identifies and locates key concepts and variables and describes contexts in sufficient detail for them to be differentiated. Here the development of typologies becomes a research goal. This, they argue, is every bit as useful as finding the causal relationships necessary to theory. Data itself is useful and important even if it doesn't support a hypothesis.

They go on to suggest that as entities are rarely static and that looking for the changes, *change stimuli and thresholds* that give clues to possible real change locations and the whereabouts of possible relationships are every bit as vital as the production of theory. In other words, to understand a phenomenon you understand how it is changing rather than how it exists in some static perspective. There are change points, 'tipping points' and thresholds, the identification of which advances knowledge. In terms of general orientation to research this is appropriate to hospitality but it essentially postpones the idea of theory.

The normal way of treating change is as precursor of impacts – nothing wrong with that but change can be used as an indicator or descriptor of the existence of an entity and as an identifier of influences (note that this is not necessarily the same as proving causation). In other words, change can be used to place an entity so that we get a really good view of what kind of typology it stands in and what might influence it before attempting to research actual causation. The consequences of change are always illuminating because they show up and alter a previous pattern of development as well as indicating a future set of consequences. For example, redesign a job and you change its labor market position and alter the history which produced the current level of skill and knowledge and you set in train a new development process – all this from one action. This is the nature of social change. If causal relationships are the aim, they should, in this scenario, be limited, small-scoped studies only partially related to theory. People are coping, adapting, learning, and changing their choice preferences, their references points, their evaluative criteria, their values, changing their behavior habits, their information seeking habits and their identities. We may learn a lot about the forces which cause change simply by accurately describing the effects. We are forever identifying factors which cause levels or magnitudes of a particular variable (satisfaction, perception of quality, perceptual direction, loyalty, image retention) without knowing why they cause a particular level. Capturing points of change instead of levels would be fruitful in this respect. Studies of 'switching' that go beyond 'intentions' would be a good example of this type of approach. Change of importance, change of salience and change of level may be more illustrative than any particular measurement of level. We rarely plunder experience, rarely examine patterns of behavior over time, and in detail, yet these are the materials of change exploration. We often ask what caused 'x' to change and sometimes we ask about the process of change but not *when* did 'x' change. Agents of change such as willpower, vision, power, and previous experience are hard to measure because they can only be interpreted from their effects but searching for points of change is where it starts. What follows is not a specific research agenda but merely a suggestion of the character of future hospitality research. What these ideas have in common is that they are about capturing some effect that indicates that something is moving or changing.

In the context of the adoption of generic policies and techniques by hospitality a behavioral shift (here behavior implies attitudes, perception, mindsets) is implied. The evaluative approach might be – does it fit? However, a generic technique or system assumes certain behaviors. Is such behavior exhibited in hospitality after the implementation? What are the knock-on effects? Case research would capture this if it were time based. The problematic relationship between strategic concepts, actual practices and consequent effects is one in which observation of change can be helpful as a key indicator of the whole relationship. Policies and practices can both contain inner contradictions which may be elicited through the study of the effects of change. Although there is criticism of strategic research for its lack of normal science, the approach that looks at measured effects and interprets backwards carries no such critical luggage. This approach is appropriate to the generic case and would require no alteration at all to be used across the border in hospitality, and is in line with the evaluative emphasis being advocated here.

In the context of hospitality consumption, what changes in individual patterns of consumption, and are such changes in disposable income? In the same area, how does hospitality compete against other forms of consumption and again how does that role change within changing levels of income (Scitowsky, 1986)? The important question of 'with what does hospitality consumption compete?' is rarely asked. When it is, answers, taken from secondary data, are unconvincing simply because they provide a static picture of something which is moving. For example, the sudden growth in eating out in English pubs was well documented in retrospect but still not actually explained in behavioral terms and therefore its eventual recession is also left without explanation. How does 'taste' change and what changes when taste changes? Given the evidence that people shift market in both directions, how sure is the industry that this is purely an economic judgement?

It is possibly in the area of attributional studies that the notion of looking at change has real significance. For example, what is the temporal influence on dimensions of satisfaction, quality, and commitment? Do dimensions change their character, their importance, their salience by time distance from consumption or decision (Trope and Liberman, 2003)? The disjuncture of pre- and post-experience is often applied in studies of quality and satisfaction but what actual change is implied and when does it actually take place? These seem hugely important questions where there is a time gap between choice and consumption.

In the area of decision making we have the rational models and the holistic conceptions but most processes involve interdisciplinary areas, most usually psychology and economics. Buying something has connotations of both: so does choosing a career or an educational course. How do the economic and psychological dimensions of a decision interact? At what point does the relative salience or importance of each type of dimension actually change? (see Ekehammer, 1972 and Riley, 2001 for an example of a methodology that seeks to explore this).

In the area of role proscription and interpretation, hospitality is seen from the outside as suffering from occupational rigidity (by economists anyway). Is this true? Job titles remain the same but has something changed beneath? There is some evidence of functional flexibility and empowerment but have the actual tasks changed? Studies of job satisfaction abound but little consideration is given to conceptions of 'job' in job satisfaction studies. Role perceptions are a matter of interpretation and there will be points of change that effect the evaluation of satisfaction.

In the area of structural approaches to the hospitality industry, we have a *prima facie* case that the institutions of the industry relate to other industries such as leisure, travel, tourism and banking but what exactly is their relationship? In a market environment the currency of the relationship is bound to be about power and dependency, concepts that are very difficult to measure directly. They can however be assessed from their change effects. Agency theory and stakeholder theory seem, at least to this observer, hopelessly inadequate to explain inter-organizational behavior between the hospitality industry and its related industry components. What changes in airline policy, for example, cause effects in the accommodation industry and what kinds of effect are they?

This is a short and highly subjective list but illustrates that finding points of influence are important: a small piece of identification possibly accompanied by a casual relationship is a pointer towards theory. Note that this is not an advocacy of 'systems thinking', far from it – it does not offer the 'desired' causal relationships that often pass for theory in business process engineering. It is a search for entities which ends in clear description and location. The point about changes and thresholds is that they can circumvent the need to describe fundamentals. A reflective view of their role suggests that 'maturity' in terms of research development means growing towards a position where causal theory development is actually possible through the build-up of conceptual identities, variable identities and context typologies. The question as to whether hospitality is at a stage where theory development is possible should be, but has not been directly asked. If it is not at this stage then the suggestion here is that the above approach, in conjunction with the strategy to look again at perennial questions of import, might be a fruitful route for hospitality research. Research in hospitality is always at its best when it is being practical, but the problem is that results do not accumulate. It is plea to be practical and less ambitious but also to focus on what is fundamental and important. Agreement on what that is, is the challenge for leadership in the hospitality research community.

REFERENCES

Al-Sabbahy, H. Z., Ekinci, Y. and Riley, M. (2004) 'An investigation of perceived value dimensions: implications for hospitality research', *Journal of Travel Research*, 42(3): 226–234.

Arnaldo, M. J. (1981) 'Hotel general managers: a profile', *Cornell Hotel and Restaurant Administration Quarterly*, 22: 53–56.

Baloglu, S. and Assente M. L. (1999) 'A content analysis of subject areas and research methods used in five hospitality management Journals', *Journal of Hospitality and Tourism Research*, 23: 53–70.

Baum, J. A. C. and Haveman, H. A. (1997) 'Love thy neighbor? Differentiation in the Manhattan hotel industry 1998–1990', *Administrative Science Quarterly*, 42(2): 304–338.

Beck, J. and Young, M. F. D. (2005) 'The assault on the professions and the restructuring of academia and professional identities: a Bernsteinian analysis', *British Journal of the Sociology of Education*, 26(2): 183–197.

Bourdieu, P. and Passeron, J. C. (1977) *Reproduction in Education, Society and Culture*. Beverly Hills: Sage.

Brazeal, D. V. and Herbert, T. (1999) 'The genesis of entrepreneurship', *Entrepreneurship Theory and Practice*, Spring 23(3): 29–45.

Brotherton, R. (1999) 'Hospitality management research: towards the future'. In R. Brotherton (ed.) *The Handbook of Contemporary Hospitality Management Research*. Chichester: Wiley.

Brusco, M. J., Johns, T. and Reed, J. H. (1998) 'Cross-utilization of a two-skilled workforce', *International Journal of Operations and Production Management*, 18(6): 555–564.

Chareanpunsirikul, S. and Wood, R. C. (2002) 'Mintzberg, managers and methodology: some observations from a study of hotel general managers', *Tourism Management*, 23(5): 551–556.

Christensen Hughes, J. (1997) 'Sociological paradigms and the use of ethnography in hospitality research', *Journal of Hospitality and Tourism Research*, 21(1): 14–27.

Clark, M., Riley, M., Wilkie, E. and Wood, R. C. (1998) *Researching and Writing Dissertations in Hospitality and Tourism Management*. London: International Thomson Publishing.

Cobanoglu, C., Moreo, P. J. and Wood, D. F. (2004) 'Hospitality research: a comparison of industry professionals' and educators' perceptions', *Journal of Hospitality and Tourism Education*, 16(1): 20–30.

Connolly, D. J. (2005) 'Research methods: a guide to using the case study method to explore hospitality information technology phenomena', *Information Technology in Hospitality*, 4(1): 23–46.

Coxon, A. P. and Jones, C. L. (1978) *The Images of Occupational Prestige*. London: Macmillan Publishers.

Dess, G. G., Ireland, R. D. and Hitt, M. A. (1990) 'Industry effects and strategic management research', *Journal of Management*, 16(1): 7–27.

Dey, I. (1999) *Grounding Grounded Theory*. Academic Press: London.

Ekehammer, B. (1972) 'Test of a psychological cost benefit model of career choice', *Journal of Vocational Behavior*, 10(3): 245–260.

Ekinci, Y. (2004) 'An investigation of the determinants of customer satisfaction', *Tourism Analysis*, 8(2–4): 197–203.

Ekinci, Y. and Riley, M. (2001) 'Validating quality dimensions', *Annals of Tourism Research*, 28(1): 202–223.

Filmer, P. (1998) Theory/practice. In C. Jenks (ed.) *Core Sociological Dichotomies*. London: Sage. pp. 299–314.

Getty, J. M. and Thompson, K. N. (1994) 'The relationship between quality, satisfaction, and recommending behavior in lodging decisions', *Journal of Hospitality and Leisure Marketing*, 2(3): 3–21.

Golding, D. (1980) 'Establishing blissful clarity in organizational life: managers', *Sociological Review*, 28(4): 763–782.

Grewal, D., Monroe, K. B. and Krishnan, R. (1998) 'The effect of price-comparison advertising on buyers' perception of acquisition value, transaction value, and behavioral intentions', *Journal of Marketing*, 62 (April): 46–59.

Gronroos, C. and Ojasalo, K. (2004) 'Service productivity. Towards a conceptualization of the transformation of inputs into economic results in services', *Journal of Business Research*, 57(4): 414–423.

Gundersen, M. G., Heide, M. and Olsson, U. H. (1996) 'Hotel guest satisfaction among business travelers: what are the important factors?', *Cornell Hotel and Restaurant Administration Quarterly*, 37(2): 72–79.

Hales, C. and Nightingale, M. (1986) 'What are unit managers supposed to do? A contingent methodology for investigating managerial role requirements', *International Journal of Hospitality Management*, 5(1): 3–11.

Hinkin, T. R., Tracy, B. J. and Enz, C. A. (1997) 'Scale construction: developing reliable and valid measurement instruments', *Journal of Hospitality and Tourism Research*, 21(1): 100–120.

Howey, R. M., Savage, K. S., Verbeeten, M. J. and Van Hoof, H. B. (1999) 'Tourism and hospitality research journals: cross-citations among research communities, *Tourism Management*, 20(5): 133–139.

Ingram, P. and Inman, C. (1996) 'Institutions, intergroup competition, and the evolution of hotel populations around Niagara Falls', *Administrative Science Quarterly*, 41(3): 629–658.

Jones, P. (1996) 'Hospitality research – where have we got to?', *International Journal of Hospitality Management*, 15(1): 5–10.

Kelly, G. A. (1955) *The Psychology of Personal Constructs*, Vols. 1, 2. New York: Norton Pub.

Kerlinger, F. (1986) *Foundations of Behavioral Research*, 3rd edn. New York: Holt Reinhart and Winston.

Kim, S. M. (1994) 'Tourist hotel general managers in Korea: a profile', *International Journal of Hospitality Management*, 13(1): 7–17.

Lane, J. F. (2000) *Pierre Bourdieu. A Critical Introduction*. London: Pluto Press.

Lashley, C. (2000) 'Towards a theoretical understanding'. In: C. Lashley and A. Morrison (eds), *In Search of Hospitality; Theoretical Perspectives and Debates*. Oxford: Butterworth-Heinemann pp. 1–17.

Lewis, R. C. (1984a) 'The basis of hotel selection', *Cornell Quarterly*, May, 54–69.

Lewis, R. C. (1984b) 'Isolating differences in hotel attributes', *Cornell Quarterly*, November, 64–77.

Littlejohn, D. (1990) 'Hospitality research: philosophies and progress'. In R. Teare, L. Moutinho and N. Morgan (eds), *Managing Services in the 1990s*. London: Cassell, pp. 209–232.

Littlejohn, D. (2004) 'The UK Research Assessment Exercise 2001: an analysis of hospitality research', *International Journal of Hospitality Management*, 23(1): 25–38.

Lynn, M. and Mullen, B. (1997) 'The quantitative integration of research: an introduction to meta-analysis', *Journal of Hospitality and Tourism Research*, 21(1): 121–139.

Madesen, H., Neergaard, H. and Ulhei, J. P. (2003) 'Knowledge-intensive entrepreneurship and human capital', *Journal of Small Business and Enterprise Development*, 10(4): 426–434.

McKeown, B. and Thomas, D. (1988) *Q Methodology. University Paper 66*. London: Sage Publications.

Manning, M. L., Davidson, M. and Manning, R. L. (2005) 'Measuring tourism and hospitality employee workplace perception', *International Journal of Hospitality Management*, 24(1): 75–90.

Morrison, A. (2002) 'Hospitality research: a pause for reflection', *International Journal of Tourism Research*, 4(3): 161–169.

Nailon, P. (1982) 'Theory in hospitality management', *International Journal of Hospitality Management*, 1: 135–143.

Namasivayam, K. (2004) 'Repeated measures experimentation in hospitality research: a brief overview',

Journal of Hospitality and Tourism Research, 28(1): 121–129.

Niininen, O., Szivas, E. and Riley, M. (2005) 'Destination loyalty and repeat behaviour: an application of optimum stimulation measurement', *International Journal of Tourism Research*, 7.

Oh, H., Kim, B.-Y. and Shin, J.-H. (2004) 'Hospitality and tourism marketing: recent developments in research and future directions', *International Journal of Hospitality Management*, 23(5): 425–447.

Pansiri, J. (2005) 'Pragmatism: a methodological approach to researching strategic alliances in tourism', *Tourism and Hospitality Planning and Development*, 2(3): 191–206.

Peccei, R. and Rosenthal, P. (2000) 'Front-line responses to customer orientation programmes: a theoretical and empirical analysis', *International Journal of Human Resource Management*, 11(3): 562–590.

Petrick, J. F. (2004) 'The role of quality, value and satisfaction in predicting cruise passenger behavior', *Journal of Travel Research*, 42(4): 397–407.

Phillips, M. E. (1996) 'Industrial mindsets: exploring the culture of two macro-organizational settings'. In J. R. Meindl, C. Stubbart and J. F. Porac (eds), *Cognition Within and Between Organizations*. London: Sage. pp. 475–508.

Riley, M. (1984) 'Hotels and group identity', *International Journal of Tourism Management*, 5(2): 102–109.

Riley, M. (1993a) 'Labor markets and vocational education'. In T. Baum (ed.) *Human Resource Issues in Tourism*, Chapter 4. Oxford: Butterworth-Heinemann. pp. 47–59.

Riley, M. (1993b) 'Back to the future; lessons from free market experience', *Employee Relations*, 15(2): 20–28.

Riley, M. (1999) 'Re-defining the debate on hospitality productivity'. *Tourism and Hospitality Research*, 1(2): 182–186.

Riley, M. (2000) 'How can we better understand operational productivity in food and beverage management? A resource substitution framework. In R. C. Wood (ed.) *Strategic Questions in Food and Beverage Management*. Oxford: Butterworth-Heinemann. pp. 119–128.

Riley, M. and Szivas, E. (2005) 'New knowledge in tourism'. In D. Buhalis and C. Costa (eds), *Tourism Management Dynamics*. Oxford: Elsevier. pp. 78–84.

Riley, M. Niininen O., Szivas, E. and Willis, T. (2001) 'The case for process approaches in loyalty research in tourism', *International Journal of Tourism Research*, 3(1): 23–32.

Roper, A. and Brookes, M. (1999) 'Theory and reality of interdisciplinary research', *International Journal of Contemporary Hospitality Management*, 11(4): 174–179.

Scitowsky, T. (1986) *Human Desire and Economic Satisfaction*. Brighton: Wheatsheaf.

Shaw, G. (2004) 'Entrepreneurial culture in small businesses in tourism'. In A. A. Law, M. Hall and A. M. Williams (eds), *A Companion to Tourism*. Oxford: Blackwell. pp. 122–134.

Shortt, G. (1989) 'Work activities of hotel general managers in Northern Ireland: a Mintzbergian analysis', *International Journal of Hospitality Management*, 8(2): 121–130.

Spender, J. C. (1989) *Industry Recipes*. Oxford: Blackwell. pp. 35–67.

Spender, J. C. (1998) 'The dynamics of individual and organizational knowledge'. In C. Eden and J. C. Spender (eds), *Managerial and Organizational Cognition: Theory Methods and Research*. Sage: London. pp. 13–39.

Stephenson, W. (1953) *The Study of Behavior*. Chicago: University of Chicago Press.

Sturman, M. C. (2003) 'Building a bridge from the other bank', *Cornell Hotel and Restaurant Administration Quarterly*, 9–13.

Sutton, R. I. and Staw, B. M. (1995) 'What theory is not', *Administrative Science Quarterly*, 40(3): 371–384.

Taylor, S. and Edgar, D. (1999) 'Lacuna or lost cause? Some reflections on hospitality management research'. In R. Brotherton (ed.) *The Handbook of Contemporary Hospitality Management Research*. Chichester: John Wiley. pp. 19–38.

Thomas, D. B. and Baas L. R. (1992) 'The issue of generalisation in Q Methodology; reliable schematics revisited', *Operand Subjectivity*, 16(1): 18–36.

Townley, B. (2002) 'The role of competing rationalities in institutional change', *Academy of Management Journal*, 45(1): 163–180.

Tractinsky, N. and Jarvenpaa, S. (1995), 'Information systems design decisions in a global versus domestic context', *Management Information Systems Quarterly* (December): 507–534.

Trope, Y. and Liberman, N. (2003) 'Temporal construal theory of time-dependent preferences', In I. Brocas and J. D. Carrillo (eds), *The Psychology of Economic Decisions*. Oxford: Oxford University Press. 235–252.

Hospitality Management Education

6

Clayton W. Barrows and Novie Johan

Higher education is critical to the social and economic futures of all nations, and more specifically in the case of developed nations. In an age of knowledge in which educated people and their ideas have become the basis for establishing the wealth of nations, the value of university education has never been more important. (Gamage and Mininberg, 2003: 183)

INTRODUCTION

The above quote does an effective job of summarizing the role of education in general, but the authors could just have easily been referring specifically to hospitality management education. This chapter is quite different from the chapters that come before or after it in that it does not focus on a management function or a segment of the industry but instead focuses on hospitality management education and its importance in the success and performance of the hospitality industry. In this chapter then, we discuss the role and purpose of hospitality education; the relationship between education and the hospitality industry; provide examples of hospitality management programmes in different countries; examine curriculum and curriculum-related issues; and identify current issues and trends in hospitality management education.

This chapter will focus primarily upon programmes at the post-secondary level and, specifically, those at universities. This is not to exclude those programmes at other levels but as different international models are explored, a baseline for comparison must be established. Further, it should be mentioned at this point that the chapter will also focus primarily on programmes in English-speaking countries (or countries that are predominantly English-speaking). However, it is important to remember that different countries have different systems

of higher education – although it should be noted that many are increasingly modeling their systems on those of North America and the UK (Gröschl and Barrows, 2003).

Definition of higher education

The international universe of higher education is both exceptionally complex and continuously changing. Hence, perhaps the basis for understanding various types of available education institutions is to understand the basic definition of higher education. Indeed, the definition of higher education itself has been the source of debate for many years, and has changed throughout history. For the purpose of this chapter, we will use the general definition of higher education as follows: 'education beyond the level of a complete secondary education' (Robinson, 1968: 48) which means 'beyond the post-compulsory education' (Carter, 1980: vii). For this reason, it includes university education in its entirety (including teacher training) and adult or 'continuing' education. Nevertheless, it is only a part of 'further education' as some ambiguity remains in the classification of 'adult education'. Accordingly, this designation applies differently according to different countries, e.g. this signifies education after 16 years of age in the British education system but is used to denote 'non-traditional' students (e.g. older students) in other countries.

BUSINESS AND MANAGEMENT STUDIES EDUCATION

Hospitality management education is, in effect, a sub-set of business and management education. The subject areas of business and management are broad and multidisciplinary, with a wide variety of course titles and subject combinations. They cover many different educational levels and qualifications, designed to meet the needs of both experienced practitioners and those without practical experience. These include general courses in business studies, business administration and management, more specialized courses covering specific aspects of business management such as human resources management, marketing and operations management, and courses specializing in particular sectors such as public management, services management and, of course, hotel and catering or hospitality management.

Multiple aims and objectives reflect the diversity of the subject area, the variety of courses available to students, and specific disciplinary and institutional needs and philosophies. Aside from theoretical components, since the 1980s business and management education has been concerned with the 'performance' of students, and this is no less true of hospitality management programmes. Many claim that graduates only 'know' (theoretical) rather than having 'the ability to do' (practical). This has put pressure on business and management schools to produce graduates with the required skills needed by modern organizations. Thus, they now emphasize both cognitive and intellectual skill development in management education as well as growth of a set of personal and interpersonal practical skills, e.g. self-awareness, problem-solving.

AN OVERVIEW OF HOSPITALITY MANAGEMENT EDUCATION

The primary purpose of this section is first, to describe what is meant by hospitality management education, why students choose to study in this particular academic area; and where and how potential students might access hospitality programmes within higher education.

Hospitality management education is a specialized area of study designed to prepare students for management careers in various segments of the hospitality industry. Broadly speaking, it can encompass any structured academic programme that helps to achieve these means. As such, it would be considered one type of professional programme. Hospitality as an academic area evolved out of early European apprenticeship programmes. They began to take

root in universities in the early 1900s in North America, rather later in Europe. Hospitality management programmes generally provide courses/units from several different areas, both within and outside the area of hospitality. In addition to general education courses (e.g. liberal arts courses required in some countries, notably the United States), students typically take a variety of courses in (1) general business management, and (2) more specialized courses focusing on the management of hotels and foodservice operations. These courses might include marketing, financial management and accounting, strategic planning, human resources management and organizational behavior – each as they apply to hospitality management operations. Beyond this, some programmes offer a selection of even more focused courses in the management of other types of (usually more specialized) hospitality operations including casino gaming, private clubs, meeting and convention planning, resorts, vacation ownership and timeshares, bars and nightclubs, and culinary management. In fact, one of the trends in hospitality education is to offer a greater number of specializations which increases the options for students.

Programmes that offer these types of courses were once referred to as Hotel and Catering, Hotel and Food, or Hotel and Restaurant Management. More recently, as programmes have broadened their scope, they have adopted more all-encompassing labels such as Hospitality Management (or in some cases where tourism courses are also offered, Hospitality and Tourism Management) to better reflect their changing missions (for a review of some of the issues related to this, see the Editorial Introduction to this volume). Such programmes can be found at a variety of levels (for example in high schools, the French *lycée*, trade schools, colleges, polytechnics and universities).

One of the first questions that must be asked is why study hospitality education at the post-secondary level? Many factors influence the choice of a university major as discussed by Montmarquette et al. (2002) among others. These factors include quality and amount of information available, family background, the occupation of family members, expected earnings, socioeconomic factors, and availability/accessibility of quality programmes. No matter what particular combination of factors are considered by the individual student though, most understand that a strong hospitality-based curriculum will provide them with an opportunity to study the industry (usually from some combination of theoretical and hands-on experience), provide them with key contacts in the industry, and provide excellent job prospects. It is generally accepted that students are able to learn more during a fixed period in school (typically three or four years) than is possible if they were to spend the same fixed period working in the industry. With that said, it is also generally accepted that success in the industry usually comes from a background that combines both work experience and formal education. Formal education allows students to learn about the industry, in a relatively low risk environment, and learn about both the practical and the more theoretical elements of the industry. However, the ability to relate it to an actual workplace setting is crucial. Indeed, some students decide after finishing school, that the hospitality industry is not for them and that they would prefer to work in another industry sector other than hospitality. One study of graduates of a USA programme found that 29% of graduates (over a 10-year period) were not working in the hospitality industry (Kang and Gould, 2002).

Who are the students that typically study hospitality management? Historically, they have been 'traditional' university aged students looking to enter a specific occupation. Some have reached the age at which many enter university and may have had some practical experience in the hospitality industry and decided that they enjoyed that experience. Many of those same students will have worked during summer breaks at a hotel, restaurant or resort in entry-level service positions (such as server, bartender or cook). As with many things, though, the profile of entering students is changing. It could be argued that there is no longer a 'typical' hospitality student. They now represent a combination of 'traditional' university-aged students (aged 17–22); more mature students seeking a change in careers; nontraditional students (who might not have had the opportunity to study in another era) and hospitality workers looking to upgrade their credentials. As a result of this changing student demographic, many hospitality programmes are also changing to better address the needs of non-traditional students. These changes span everything from entrance requirements (which might focus more on work experience than grades), programme delivery methods, programme duration, scheduling of courses/modules, curriculum mix, and degree of choice within the curriculum. In addition, largely because of the changing student base, there has been a proliferation of post-secondary diploma programmes, certificate programmes, distance programmes and credit provided for 'life' experiences. Further, programmes are now being brought to students where hospitality is thriving. An example of this is the First Nations University of Canada which offers a hospitality specialization at its Regina (Saskatchewan) campus for First Nations students where casino gaming has become an important part of the economy. All of these changes have made hospitality management education more accessible to a broader range of students. As a result, the students that study hospitality management are becoming more reflective of the diverse group of people who work in the industry.

The second question that this section attempts to answer is the 'where' question: that is, where are hospitality programmes offered? This must be answered in two different ways. First, in terms of geography, hospitality management education is offered on almost every continent and in numerous countries. Some have long traditions of hospitality education including the UK, Switzerland, and the USA. It is probably safe to say that a student wanting to study hospitality management in a post-secondary environment would not have to travel too far from home. Many universities offer a hospitality major on multiple campuses as well – a practice that is very common in Australia, for instance, where the same university may offer hospitality courses on three or more widely dispersed campuses (among other reasons, this is because the population is so widely dispersed). Further, the sheer number of programmes (globally) continues to increase, particularly in areas where hospitality (and tourism) industries are thriving. For instance, after a small contraction, the number of four-year programmes in the USA has begun to increase again and is estimated to be approximately 200. Many of the programmes in the USA were established at large 'Land Grant' institutions dating back to the 1800s.

Therefore, the answer to where hospitality programmes are offered is: in many areas throughout the world. However, even this statement somewhat understates the reach of the field. In recent years, numerous higher education institutions have begun offering studies via distance where students can study (and earn a degree) from their homes and offices. When one considers the possibilities of distance education (whether it be via the Internet or more traditional correspondence) and the opportunities that it offers potential students, it becomes clear that exposure to the formal study of the hospitality industry knows few bounds. Distance education is now being used as a platform for post-secondary certificates and diplomas (e.g. University of Guelph in Canada), undergraduate degrees (e.g. University of Massachusetts in the USA); Masters degrees (University of Wisconsin – Stout, US); and PhD degrees (Oklahoma State University which offers a PhD programme partially via distance). In addition, several universities are offering different types of distance programmes where instructors travel to deliver educational programming. For instance, Southern Cross University (in New South Wales, Australia) delivers its Bachelor's degree curriculum in Singapore. Other universities have undertaken similar initiatives. Again, when one considers all of the various 'distribution' points of hospitality education programmes, the choices are many.

COMMON FACTORS ACROSS HOSPITALITY PROGRAMMES

There are three important factors that bind the majority (if not all) of the programmes discussed thus far – the first factor that they have in common is their objective of preparing students for careers in a specific industry. Their entire infrastructure (curriculum, faculty, facilities) are designed to accomplish this. That hospitality management programmes are 'tied' to an industry means the number of stakeholders tends to be greater than is the case for other, especially more traditional, university units. Stakeholders will typically include: governments, industry sectors, professional associations, faculty, administrators, the university, alumni, taxpayers, high schools, students, parents, benefactors, advisory boards, and others. Each of these constituents has influence in a variety of spheres including curriculum funding, research endeavors, service commitments, and new initiatives.

The reasons that this is a salient point include: (1) feedback on performance and outcomes is available from a variety of sources when desired, and (2) decisions are not easily made without seeking consultation from these various groups. In other words, hospitality programmes both benefit from the availability of stakeholders who are usually very willing to provide feedback on various issues (funding, curriculum, marketing and promotion, etc.) but at the same time, remain accountable to these same groups. Perhaps the most visible group of stakeholders is the industry in which an institution is located and which, to varying degrees, advises administrators on issues, serves on boards and committees, assist in teaching classes, recruit and hire students, and provide financial support for programmes. In short, they play a very important role and could be considered partners in education in many cases. Again, for this reason, decisions regarding processes and outcomes that potentially affect the industry (such as new modules, programmes, units or courses) must include the industry in the process. Developing a strong relationship with the industry is crucial in the success of the programme (see Nickason and Barrows, 2005).

The second common element in hospitality programmes is their focus on the management of the hospitality enterprise (although different programmes will approach this objective in different ways). This is what typically distinguishes three- and four-year programmes (in the USA) from two-year programmes and others. The primary focus is on management which encompasses theory and application. This also drives student careers and the point at which they are hired into organizations.

Third, administrators understand that schooling alone (and theory alone) will not create a successful hospitality student. For this reason, virtually every hospitality programme requires students to complete a period of employment in the industry. This assures, among other things, that the student will at least have some exposure to the hospitality workplace before embarking on their career. Internships, if conducted effectively, can encourage applied learning by providing students with exposure to both first line positions and management responsibility that can enhance their understanding of operational management and encourage development of analytical and problem solving skills, as well as inculcating an understanding of the realities of the hospitality workplace.

Together, these factors drive much of what programmes do and how they choose to do it. We might consider the first factor (career preparation) as an overall objective and the second and third factors (focus on management and work experience) as strategies for achieving the objective.

A TYPICAL NORTH AMERICAN B.COMM (BACHELOR OF COMMERCE) PROGRAMME

Before we continue our discussion, it would be advantageous to present a vignette of a 'typical' hospitality school, its conception and offerings. The following is the profile of the School of Hospitality and Tourism Management at the University of Guelph in Ontario, Canada, principally sourced from the 2004–2005 Hospitality and Tourism Management Undergraduate Student Handbook (School of Hospitality and Tourism Management, 2005). The School of Hospitality and Tourism Management is part of the College of Social and Applied Human Sciences, one of six colleges in the University. The School offers two majors: (1) Hotel and Food Administration which also has a Co-op (one-year industry placement) option; and (2) Tourism Management. The Bachelor of Commerce programme is coordinated by the Faculty of Management, an umbrella administrative arm of the College.

The School of Hospitality and Tourism Administration (established as the School of Hotel and Food Administration) at the University of Guelph enrolled its first Bachelor of Commerce students in 1969. The small number of students in this class represented a significant time in the evolution of professional education for the hospitality industry in Canada since it was the first bachelors degree programme in the country. The School was established out of a recognized need for qualified managers in the industry and was made possible with the support of industry leaders. To help establish the School, the hospitality industry provided funds to cover part of the initial capital outlay and operating expenses. To serve this function the Hospitality Industry Founders' Fund was established. Monies from this fund have been used for capital improvements over the years including the most recent addition to the building completed in 2003. This most recent addition includes the Compass Group Culinary Management Facility, and an enlarged dining room in which students run restaurants.

Between 1969 and 1979, the focus of the School was on undergraduate education. The School took a new direction in 1979 when the focus began to include scholarly activity.

This was evidenced by supporting faculty to return to university to earn their doctorates as well as an increased emphasis on published research. In addition, management development programmes for senior executives in the hospitality industry were introduced. Over 1000 executives and managers from leading companies have completed these management development programmes. The School introduced another dimension in 1992 when its Master of Management Studies (MMS) in Hospitality was established at this time. The MMS was later changed to an MBA in Hospitality and Tourism ten years later and a distance version of this course was introduced in 2000. Graduate education has since become an integral part of the programme mission representing an additional service to the industry. Also in 2000, a new tourism major was introduced which included the addition of six new courses (units) focusing exclusively on tourism. Partially, in an effort to recognize the schools expanding focus, the name of the School was changed to the School of Hospitality and Tourism Management.

The growing convergence between business schools, including hospitality schools, and the business world is reflected in the growing tendency for vision and mission statements to encompass a philosophy of the relationship between the institute, the programme and the diverse stakeholders served (see Table 6.1 for some examples). The School of Hospitality and Tourism Management is dedicated to preparing its students for management careers in the hospitality industry. Its mandate is:

> to give students a broad exposure to the basic disciplines and a sound professional management education which prepares graduates for responsible positions in the hospitality and tourism foodservice industries.

The School was not intended to be a training ground for young chefs or front-line hospitality staff. Instead, it aims to produce graduates who will become managers with an understanding of how to capitalize on opportunities, resolve problems and limitations of their facilities, manage service operations, market their facility and services to customers and develop excellent staff relations.

In addition to the University-wide learning objectives which form the basis of a liberal education, the School has identified five other major outcomes for its programmes. A graduate

Table 6.1   Mission statements of selected hospitality schools

Southern Cross University (Australia)
The School of Tourism and Hospitality Management at Southern Cross University aims to be recognized as the leading Australian-based institution serving the Asia-Pacific region. We offer government funded and full-fee-paying education programmes on-campus, by external study, or through our network of education and industry partners to a diverse range of students. We offer industry-relevant research and expertise in the areas of Regional Tourism, Gaming, and Business Events. We also aim to serve our local region, with internationally relevant programmes, research and community linkages.

Florida State University (USA)
To prepare future leaders for the global hospitality industry by delivering excellence through personalized education, research and service.

Hong Kong Polytechnic University (Hong Kong)
The Mission of the School of Hotel and Tourism management is to be globally recognized as Asia's leader in teaching, research, and scholarship in hospitality and tourism management.

University of Guelph (Canada)
The mission of the School of Hospitality and Tourism Management is to empower individuals and organizations with the applied research, professional skills and management education necessary for exceptional performance.

[And] To achieve the above through fostering a school culture based on innovation, strong service and qualified, dedicated people.

Moi University (Kenya)
The overall objective of the BHM programme is to provide students with knowledge, skills and appropriate attitudes in hospitality as an academic discipline and to improve the standards of management in the hospitality industry.

Institute for International Management and Technology (India)
IIMT's mission is to use education and lifelong learning as a means of economic, social and cultural emancipation. We will strive for empowerment through education such that self-actualization is not a mere dream and ensure that no part of the society remains untouched from the forces of positive change.

from the School of Hospitality and Tourism Management should develop:

- an understanding of the economic, legal, technological, social and cultural milieu so as to appreciate the national as well as international environment in which the hospitality and tourism industry operates;
- the substantive professional knowledge necessary for managers to function effectively in this field;
- the necessary management skills and tools with which to apply that professional knowledge;
- a critical mind that can analyze problems, adopt a systematic approach to decision-making and apply sensitivity to inter-personal issues; and
- a professional orientation that supports ethical conduct, professional upgrading and community awareness.

In order to realize these outcomes, the School for its part seeks to provide:

- a culture that truly values learning, promotes independent scholarship and deters mediocrity;
- a well-designed curriculum that integrates liberal and professional studies as well as develops critical thinking;
- effective methods of delivering course material including adequate laboratory facilities, varied teaching methods and appropriate class sizes;
- competent faculty with appropriate academic and professional qualifications who have a manifest commitment to teaching; and
- a network of contacts with individuals, businesses, associations and government agencies that can contribute to the academic and work experiences of students as they progress through the programme.

CONTEMPORARY THEMES IN HOSPITALITY MANAGEMENT EDUCATION

There are many issues facing hospitality education at the current time. In order to try to 'capture' some of the more current ones, the authors reviewed four consecutive years of issues of the *Journal of Hospitality and Tourism Education* (*JHTE*), regarded by many to be the benchmark North American academic publication in this field not least because of its singular focus. Four main themes emerged from this literature review: (1) student perceptions, attitudes, behaviors and knowledge; (2) teaching effectiveness and instructional techniques; (3) curriculum and curriculum development; and (4) distance education and classroom technology.

The greatest number of articles was written on two separate topics: student perceptions, attitudes, behaviors and knowledge, and teaching effectiveness and instructional techniques. The first area included articles which focused primarily upon how students selected hospitality programmes to attend and how they viewed hospitality education programmes were meeting their needs. Other articles focused on student attitudes toward certain issues (such as personal travel after 9/11) and their knowledge level of various subjects including food safety and sanitation (topics which are simultaneously receiving a lot of attention in other hospitality management journals). Some articles examined the views of a specific segment of the student population (such as minority students or international students). In short, articles about students and their views and behaviors continue to be important in gaining a broader understanding of the types of students who study hospitality management, what they think of their educational experiences and how they utilize this knowledge. Past articles have also focused on student perceptions of careers in different segments of the industry. A greater understanding of students can only serve to improve the ability of hospitality programmes to deliver an effective educational experience while accommodating diverse needs. Research of this kind could further benefit from being conducted on a longitudinal basis for comparison purposes over time.

The second area which received an equal amount of attention was teaching effectiveness and instructional techniques. This included articles on how to teach effectively various dimensions of subject areas within the discipline (e.g., food service, lodging, ethics, diversity). These articles also tended to examine effective ways of teaching and learning activities (such as writing) through various instructional techniques, one evident preoccupation being the effectiveness of instructional systems (Feinstein

et al., 2005) and the reflective practice of teaching specific subjects, for example strategic management, an increasingly important subject often taught as a capstone course in hospitality management programmes (Okumus and Wong, 2004). The articles in this category are typical of the dynamism of educational practice in hospitality management education and underscore the importance that academicians place upon these issues.

A third area that figured heavily and reveals the preoccupations of hospitality academics was curriculum and curriculum development. Current areas of interest include the role of industry constituents in inputting curriculum reviews to identify course areas that are under-represented; the problems and opportunities faced by hospitality programmes in specific academic settings (such as business schools); how best programmes can meet the needs of the industry by properly preparing students; and the challenges associated with devising a curriculum which provides a proper balance between general topics and specialization while satisfying various constituents including the hospitality industry.

Fourth, distance education and classroom technology are assuming increasing importance. In this age of changing delivery systems and questions around access as well as the matter of the effectiveness of various technologies (some unproven) this remains an important topic of research. Current issues of interest include copyright law as applied to distance technologies; the challenges involved in teaching distance courses and in the general use of classroom technologies (Sigala and Christou, 2003; Sigala, 2004); and measuring the learning effectiveness of students taking distance courses.

In addition to the four predominant areas discussed above, several other issues currently attract considerable attention from hospitality educators. These include student recruitment and retention; multicultural education (particularly in terms of accommodating students from various backgrounds); student learning styles; performance assessment of students (an area that seems to be attracting increasing attention as in the English-speaking world at least there is a growing emphasis on the importance of learning and teaching); studies examining the importance of perceptions of various constituents including students (mentioned earlier), alumni, faculty and industry representatives of hospitality programmes; educational ethics; and the ranking of hospitality programmes, and of hospitality journals.

It is clear from this review that there is a vibrant interest in the hospitality education community in issues relating to learning and teaching. Two observations in particular cannot be overlooked. First, the major themes that emerged all focused on 'traditional' classroom issues (students, teaching). This serves to underscore the ongoing importance of these issues and the attention that hospitality educators pay to them. The other observation is that many of the broader issues facing education (funding, programme start-ups, internationalization, strategic planning) received scant, if any attention. This would suggest that, from a research perspective, there are numerous opportunities to explore additional worthy topics.

CURRICULUM DEVELOPMENT

It is perhaps unsurprising given the diverse stakeholders in hospitality management education, that, as indicated in the previous section, curriculum dominates much pedagogic discourse. Most institutions offering hospitality management education see themselves as having the responsibility to provide the industry with fully skilled and highly competent hospitality graduates. The curriculum represents the overall teaching plan for an academic unit. Regardless of the diverse interpretations of curriculum in circulation, Longstreet and Shane (1993) suggest the following principles are at the basis of curriculum development:

1 curriculum consists of various contents;
2 curriculum represents collection of learning experiences; and
3 schools need to carefully organize and plan in order to include all the intended contents and capturing the intended learning experiences.

Various factors shape the evolution of hospitality curriculum. In the past three decades, post-industrial societies have been undergoing extensive structural transformation with economies increasingly shaped by the power of knowledge (Castells, 1995; Florida, 1995; Nonaka and Takeuchi, 1995). Hospitality management curricula and delivery systems have not been immune to these changes. Information-literate hospitality graduates are considered

an asset and are required to have critical abilities to (1) recognize a need for information, (2) identify and locate appropriate information sources, (3) know how to gain access to the information contained in those sources, (4) evaluate the quality of information obtained, (5) organize and analyze the information, (6) use the information effectively, and (7) share and disseminate information sources for problem-solving or knowledge-creating activities (Sigala and Baum, 2003).

The hospitality industry has also become a smaller community because of globalization. Merger and acquisition activity in the international hotel industry and increases in international travel have increased interactions between hospitality employees and multicultural guests and fostered demand for multilingual abilities and diversity skills in hospitality graduates. Students are also expected to be multiskilled to allow them to be creative, flexible and adaptable (Baum, 1990).

Dopson and Tas (2004) have suggested that curriculum development in hospitality programmes benefit by focusing on the end competencies that graduates should possess. The hospitality curriculum also needs to be constantly aware of international, national and local trends and their likely effect on the industry, as well as subsequent implications for the curriculum. Major events in the first five years of the millennium have strongly impacted on the development of the hospitality curriculum: the Asian SARS breakout, the events of September 11, 2001, Asian economic turbulence, and the Indonesian tsunami tragedy have been reflected in heightened interest in safety and security management, health management and business ethics courses into the curriculum.

The hospitality industry, as a 'people industry', has operating and human resource characteristics that differentiate it from other industrial sectors. This has a bearing on the way the education system administers the delivery of education and training. The tourism and hospitality industries are undergoing a period of major change the outcomes of which include the consolidation of providers, standardization of service offerings, a movement away from personalized marketing and selling through a network of agents to electronic direct sell, and continued mobility within the tourism and hospitality workforce. With these changes has come another, namely the higher expectations that hospitality practitioners have of hospitality graduates. Lefever and Witham (1998) capture hospitality practitioners' views on the effectiveness of hospitality-education curricula in their study on curriculum review. They found that hospitality-programme graduates are criticized for not having realistic expectations of the industry, especially in their first job. They are also criticized for their lack of financial training, analytic and problem-solving skills, communication skills and understanding of the nature of industry demand.

Traditionally, the hospitality industry is practical and technical in its nature, and this deeply rooted tradition continues to have influence in the educational field (Gillespie and Baum, 2000). However, the changing labor market has imposed new needs as employers in the hospitality industry and other sectors increasingly give priority to social, communication, technological and other 'usable' and 'practical' skills when recruiting employees. Greater emphasis is increasingly given to skills for employment, a key challenge being that although many of these skills can be learned in school, interpersonal abilities need to be practiced in the field. Within the curriculum, one response has been to develop and extend existing approaches to 'real world' skill development with an emphasis on developing students' analytic and problem-solving skills through the use of case studies, 'live' projects and vignettes, normally entailing extensive interactive group work. The demands of employers are not the only pressure for change in respect of the curriculum. Other pressures, such as university financing (which we return to briefly later in this chapter) and emerging approaches to teaching and learning emanating from within the higher education sector itself, have also contributed to the curriculum being viewed as a more fluid entity than has hitherto been the case. In many parts of the world the role of the educator is now changing, with faculty increasingly seen as facilitators of student learning. Increasing emphasis is placed on the formulation and delivery of 'learning outcomes' (Maher, 2003).

For hospitality schools in particular, the growing diversity of the industry and the increasing development of niche markets have also generated a demand for provision within the curriculum to service these new areas. Elective classes and even whole programmes have developed in events management; club management; casino and gaming management; cruise line management; resort management;

and the meetings, incentives, conventions and exhibitions (MICE) sector among others. Thus, in addition to the traditional core hospitality curriculum, students increasingly have the opportunity to become more specialized.

One consequence of these new emphases for hospitality schools is that curricula now tend to be reviewed on a more regular basis, making it a continuous process rather than a fixed outcome, to ensure relevance. A second, at least in the English-speaking world and parts of the world influenced by the Anglo-American education systems, is a growing emphasis on a competency-based approach to education. The competencies approach to management education is not new and can be traced back at least as far as the 1950s. A growing number of tourism and hospitality university courses have taken up the challenge to prepare students by developing and enhancing the management competencies skills needed to operate successfully. Competencies, as defined by Quinn et al. (2003), suggest both the possession of knowledge and behavioral capacity to act appropriately. Competencies are acquired by using knowledge and practicing skills in the field. The core competencies typically prized in management and which have become an increasingly important focus in hospitality management education are generic in nature and include leadership, oral, written and interpersonal communication, entrepreneurial skills, creativity, strategic thinking and decision-making (Buergermeister, 1983; Williams and DeMicco, 1998; Gustin, 2001; Scheule and Sneed, 2001). Brownell and Chung (2001: 139) discussed the role of management competencies that motivated Cornell University to apply these principles to its Master of Management in Hospitality (MMH) programme. The programme uses integrated competency-based aspects that are designed to develop students' communication and leadership/group process skills and involve three types of activities: (1) required benchmarking, (2) individual assessment, and (3) elective mini-courses. The noted benefits of the competency-based management development models included:

1 healthier relationship between members and students as the educator becomes an 'advocate and coach who provides direction and assistance';
2 facilitation in the information sharing between faculty member regarding student outcomes;
3 clear measurement and immediate feedback of programme effectiveness;

4 clear external communication (e.g. to the potential employers); and

5 increased student satisfaction and learning.

Literature on tourism and hospitality education in the USA and Europe (e.g. Knutson and Patton, 1992; Burbidge, 1994; Tesone, 2002) has repeatedly suggested that hospitality management graduates are perceived by employers as not sufficiently competent to manage employees, and lack both 'basic' skills such as the ability to speak effectively in public, and strategic skills, for example an ability to focus on long term planning. Meanwhile in Asia, purchasing, room management and interpersonal communication competencies have all been identified as problematic (Li and Kivela, 1998). A key concern of the competencies approach is to educate students in an awareness of the importance of lifelong learning and development and the practice of competencies in various work and non-work-related activities (for example sporting endeavors). One extension of this approach in UK higher education in recent years has been the emphasis on personal development planning in which students are increasingly encouraged to take responsibility for their own learning and exposed to skills intended to support this process over the life-cycle and in employment and personal contexts (life-long learning).

LINKAGES BETWEEN HOSPITALITY EDUCATION AND INDUSTRY

As has been demonstrated, an ever present concern in hospitality management education is the degree of 'fit' between the curriculum and student development on the one hand, and industry needs on the other. Traditionally, curriculum content and development has been viewed as primarily an internal management issue for institutions of higher education moderated by necessary external influences whether political, or from professional bodies. In management education generally in recent years much greater emphasis has been given to 'meeting industry needs'. This has been an ever present concern in hospitality management because of the aforementioned very specific ties that are perceived to exist between the sector and the industry it serves.

Earlier, we considered some of the distinctive features of hospitality education. This section more fully explores one of those features – the linkages that exist between hospitality programmes and the hospitality industry-a feature common to much professional education, but one that differentiates these from more traditional academic programmes and has a particular salience in hospitality where, in many ways, it would be fair to say (and is often believed in the hospitality community) that the strength of the relationship between a hospitality programme and the industry is an indication of the strength of that programme.

Nickason and Barrows (2005: 3) have suggested that it is in the best interest of hospitality programmes to develop alliances with the industry for multiple reasons including:

- the enhancement of student learning;
- the enhancement of the hospitality programme;
- raising the visibility of the programme in the industry;
- identifying sources of financial support;
- identifying potential job placement opportunities for their students;
- establishing internship opportunities for students;
- providing professional development opportunities for faculty;
- receiving feedback on curricula; and
- research opportunities.

The same authors suggest that the industry seeks these same relationships for the following reasons:

- to recruit students and fulfill their needs for qualified workers;
- to influence curricula decisions;
- to promote the broader industry to students;
- to recruit faculty for consulting and other external activities; and
- to act as guest speakers in classes.

Administrators, faculty and students all stand to benefit from close ties to industry. In the best-case scenario, the industry and hospitality department will develop a mutually beneficial and respectful relationship whereby both parties will benefit. Ideally, industry will help to shape the programme, contribute to the education of the students and provide the students with rewarding careers following graduation. In turn, academic departments will engage in ongoing dialogue with industry representatives with regard to educational objectives, student expectations and provide their own advice (through consulting activities) where appropriate. Foucar-Szocki and Bolsing (1999: 37) highlight three primary ways in which these working relationships manifest themselves in: (1) advisory councils; (2) involvement in professional associations and (3) provision of student internships (experiential learning). Each of these serves to help meet the objectives and outcomes listed above. Advisory councils (made up of industry executives) exist to give industry partners a voice within a formally structured environment. Professional associations (such as hotel associations, foodservice associations) provide a forum for networking, professional development and an ongoing exchange of ideas. In fact, many industry associations make special accommodation for enhancing the interaction between academic and industry representatives. Finally, student internships provide a win/win situation for academic departments, industry and students in allowing students to work in a supervised (and relatively low-risk) environment.

Historically, strong relationships have existed between hospitality programmes and industry – evidence of this exists globally where companies (and individual benefactors) have stepped forward to provide financial support for programmes. The trends in this area seem to suggest that academic units and industry (represented by individuals, individual companies, and associations) are becoming ever more reliant on one another. Three examples of this are very evident. First, where certain segments of the industry are becoming more specialized, the industry has an opportunity to influence programmes to better prepare students for these more specialized career paths (IT as applied to the hospitality environment is one example). Second, where labor shortages exist, the industry is able to rely upon the human resources that hospitality programmes are able to provide. Third, where governments are cutting back their financial support for institutions of higher education, hospitality programmes look more and more to private sector support. There is evidence that these trends are occurring, in varying degrees, in many parts of the world and, as the hospitality industry continues to mature, as it becomes more specialized, as universities rely more on private sector funding and as the need for educated workers continues, then so the need for strong industry/academic relationships is likely to acquire increasing significance.

HOSPITALITY MANAGEMENT EDUCATION IN A GLOBAL CONTEXT

One of the intents of this chapter is to provide as global an overview of hospitality education as is possible. While hospitality management education may have a longer history in some countries than others, while some countries may have more programmes than others, or while some countries may enroll more students, there are some key similarities that exist among programmes around the world. First, different educational systems grew largely in response to the needs of the local, regional, and national hospitality industries. Second, most programmes have grown out of a what was essentially a vocational education structure – Airey and Tribe (2000) have suggested that hospitality education basically grew out of hotel training programmes. Finally, programmes tend to offer studies focusing on foodservice and/or lodging as their primary emphasis. For all of these reasons, programmes from around the world have greater commonality than difference. It would be impossible to profile the nature and structure of hospitality management education of every country – instead this section will discuss some of the differences (and similarities) that exist among programmes in several different countries.

Even though formalized hospitality education has its roots in early programmes established in the early part of the twentieth century, many of the most important changes that have occurred have been within the last 30 years (Hobson, 1999). As Airey and Tribe (2000) and others have noted, hospitality education is at a critical juncture in its development. While in some regions of the world, it seems to be fully entrenched in its vocational roots, it is clearly moving beyond vocational preparation in other regions. The difference seems to be where it is in its development in any particular country or region. Other factors that affect the level of training/education that it provides include the expectations of governing bodies as well as expectations of the local hospitality industry.

Perhaps the single greatest factor affecting programmes around the globe continues to be the growth of the hospitality industry. Industry growth continues to stimulate demand for qualified managers and other employees. In many parts of the world new programmes are opening and existing programmes are increasing in size, enrollment and offerings. Demand in the USA remains strong and there is a growing emphasis on programme specialization. China and India are but two countries which are poised to drastically increase and improve their hospitality management education systems to support their growing hospitality industries.

It is worth re-emphasizing the point that while the history, traditions, and content of different countries, different higher education systems and different hospitality schools give each programme its own uniqueness, in general, similarities far outweigh whatever differences might exist. Historically, programmes have been established for the same reasons, have evolved in much the same ways and even encounter some of the same challenges during their developments. Some key differences that exist among programmes in different parts of the world (aside from terminologies) include programme length and content, extent of work experience required and funding sources.

Programme length and content

In North America (and other regions where similar institutions exist), community colleges play a large role in training students and providing supervisory level employees for the industry. Community colleges are typically two (or sometimes three) years in length and focus more on training or preparing students for immediate (and seamless) entry into the industry (or in some cases, entry into university). In many cases, culinary programmes can be included in this category since many of those are offered through community colleges and are typically two years in length. More generally, most university-level institutions offering hospitality programmes up to and including higher degrees offer three or four year programmes. There are considerable variations across the globe in the balance of programmes, many polytechnics and institute of technology-like establishments providing a more 'practical', hands-on education than universities, although the differences are becoming less distinct. Perhaps the most interesting source of variation is that different countries require different amounts and combinations of general education and hospitality specific courses. In brief, a US hospitality degree will require as much as 75% non-hospitality courses while degree programmes in the UK may require 100% hospitality-related courses

and no outside content. Universities in other countries (such as Canada) may require a blend of courses that fall somewhere between these two extremes outlined above.

Work experience

Among all of the factors that help to discriminate between programmes in different countries, this is perhaps the least significant. That is simply because the majority of programmes now require that students either enter a hospitality course with work experience or exit that course with experience. The primary difference that may exist between programmes is required length and level of experience. Some may require managerial or supervisory experience while others may only require front-line experience. Some programmes (such as the University of Guelph in Canada) may also offer a Co-op option for students which provides an additional year of work experience (resulting in a five-year degree).

Funding sources

Sources of funding for higher education in general and hospitality programmes in particular vary from country to country, and even from system to system. It would be safe to say that most of the countries (and systems and programmes) studied for this chapter are part of a larger, publicly (government) funded system. This is particularly true in countries such as the UK, Australia, Canada and the USA (it should be noted, however, that the USA is a unique example: whereas many universities in the USA are private, the majority of hospitality programmes are offered at public universities). This means that programmes rely upon government funding (in addition to student tuition, donations, and other funding) to support themselves. This, too, is changing, however, and will be discussed further in the final section of the chapter.

CURRENT ISSUES AND TRENDS IN HOSPITALITY EDUCATION

As hospitality education, globally, continues to evolve, it is necessarily affected by changes in society, changes in government, changes in the hospitality workplace and changes in educational institutions. In fact, one could easily argue that the changes affecting universities in the early part of the twenty-first century are greater than those that have occurred in earlier times. This final section will look at some of the trends and issues affecting hospitality programmes and contains preliminary results from ongoing research by the authors in 15 different countries.

Budgetary challenges

First and foremost, hospitality management programmes are greatly affected by governments (which often provide financial support) as well as the larger organizations of which they are part (colleges, universities). For this reason, funding is a constant concern for many programmes that are dependent upon governments and government budgets. It seems that almost without exception, budgets have been reduced over the last decade resulting in programmes having to do 'more with less'. For instance, in the USA, state governments – which often would provide 50% of a university's budget – have reduced their share of funding to less than one-third in many states. This means that universities (and individual programmes) have to rely on other sources of income including increased tuition fees, grants, donations and other outside sources. In fact, when educators were asked to list the top issues facing hospitality education in their respective countries, several identified budgetary challenges (or related issues) as one of the most important.

Reduced budgets often result in over-crowded classrooms, increased faculty work-loads, increased financial burdens on students and an overall decrease in the quality of education. In light of this, programmes have begun looking at other means of generating income to cover expenses. These include providing professional development opportunities to industry professionals (at a cost), increasing the number of international students (who often pay higher fees to attend), and offering entire programmes (or parts thereof) via distance education which is deserving of some additional attention.

Just a few short years ago, distance education was hardly discussed in the context of hospitality education. Now, the number of programmes that are offering distance courses (from a few courses to entire degrees) is increasing rapidly. Distance education provides many benefits for all involved. Sigala and Christou (2003) outline

many of the advantages for both learners and educators. First, it offers a greater degree of flexibility to students (particularly those who are studying part-time due to other life responsibilities). Second, it brings the curriculum to the student (rather than the other way around), and it overcomes many challenges associated with traditional educational delivery methods. The technology that is capable of delivering distance education is becoming increasingly sophisticated and more user-friendly. Finally, as was suggested earlier, it provides additional income for programmes – often times the fees that students pay for distance education programmes are not regulated in the same way that residential programmes are. For this reason they can be quite effective in contributing to the budgetary need of the academic unit. Distance education will likely as not continue to grow and develop, although with the entry of more and more for-profit universities, competition will only increase for traditional universities.

Curriculum issues

Delivery method and curriculum are intertwined and just as there are changes taking place with modes of delivery, there are also changes with respect to curriculum. Perhaps the most significant change to address here is the attempt to internationalize curriculums to the extent that students' exposure is not limited to industries and management practices in their home countries. There has been a significant effort to internationalize curriculums, especially in the USA which has been making tremendous strides in this area (this has largely followed the lead of business schools which were mandated to internationalize their curriculum by accrediting agencies).

Internationalization of a curriculum means that a programme makes the effort to alert students to global business issues, management strategies, global alliances and global opportunities. This can be accomplished in four primary ways: (1) recruiting international faculty; (2) introducing courses with an international perspective; (3) offering international exchanges or work experience modules and/or (4) developing international alliances with other universities. Each of these strategies has proved to be effective under different circumstances. The main objective for internationalization is for programmes to be able to expose their students to global work opportunities, to allow students to work effectively with people of different international backgrounds and different management practices. Hospitality programmes continue to do all of the above on the understanding that hospitality is truly a global industry.

Graduate education

This chapter has so far neglected to mention graduate education but it has become one of the most important developments in hospitality education over the last decade. Bosselman (1999) provides a valuable review of the history of graduate education and how graduate education in hospitality has evolved. Graduate programmes are generally understood to include Master's degrees (MBA, MSc and so on) and doctoral degrees (for example, PhDs, EdDs, DBAs). Most graduate programmes which offer graduate degrees offer the MSc (or the MS in the USA). Some offer an MBA with a hospitality curriculum (such as the University of Guelph) and some offer 'tagged' degrees (such as the MMH at Cornell). Fewer programmes offer a doctorate in hospitality and most of those that do offer a hospitality concentration as part of an interdisciplinary degree. While it is still possible to obtain a faculty position in a hospitality programme with a doctorate in another discipline, more programmes are requiring that candidates possess a doctorate in hospitality.

The reason for the growth of graduate degree offerings is twofold: (1) increases in funding for research have allowed (and encouraged) programmes to expand their offerings and (2) the increased need for credentialed faculty has increased demand. Graduate education generally prepares students for three types of careers: research and consulting, education, or advanced positions in the hospitality industry. Even with the growth of graduate programmes, the need for faculty is still going largely unfilled. In addition, schools in developing countries are now seeking faculty with upgraded credentials. As a result, it is likely that existing PhD programmes will see continued demand and new programmes will appear.

Quality assurance

It has been said that the issue of quality assurance, while always important, receives intermittent attention on a cyclical basis. Currently, it is again gaining attention particularly in

Europe, and specifically in the UK. Bogue and Saunders (1992: 20) define quality in higher education as '… conformance to mission specification and goal achievement – within publicly accepted standards of accountability and integrity'. Barrows and Nickason (2005) have suggested that quality assurance (in hospitality) is a means of ensuring that universities (and smaller academic units) are meeting their objectives, meeting them effectively and in a cost efficient manner. Specific quality assurance issues usually focus on the teaching aspect of the university's role and include development and adherence to standards that result in teaching effectiveness and cost accountability. It is generally accepted that quality assurance programmes must be mission driven – that is, the quality standards will vary according to the type of institution and programmes offered.

Hospitality programmes strive to achieve (and measure) quality via several means (see Fenich, 1999; Robbins, 2005 for reviews). It may be externally mandated (for instance, by governments) or internally motivated (via applying for accreditation). Either way, standards must be established, measured and met. This is true for all aspects of the academic unit including teaching, research and service responsibilities. Teaching quality is measured usually by student evaluations and research and service are measured through peer evaluation. Overall quality is measured in different ways in different university systems, including graduation rates, job placements, and student achievement. But, in the end, the primary question that is asked is whether the programme has met some pre-determined standard which was set by or for the unit. The ultimate objective of a quality assurance initiative is to attain excellence through continuous improvement.

Research and scholarship

The final topic of this section is devoted to a discussion of research and scholarship in hospitality management programmes. Rather than representing a trend, *per se*, it is an area of hospitality management education that is developing, maturing and contributing more and more toward the professionalization of the hospitality industry. Research often results in (and is disseminated through) a variety of means including published articles, books, working papers, conference presentations, monographs and reports. The primary purpose of research is to create knowledge. It may be of the applied type (in which case it attempts to address current issues in the industry) or more theoretical (on which future research may be based). As hospitality management education matures, the role of research plays a larger role – in providing new knowledge to the industry, in enhancing the reputation of the field, and in generating research funds to subsidize educational activities.

Most of the research that is conducted by hospitality academics is either published in academic journals or presented at professional conferences. The number of journals devoted to hospitality is at an all-time peak, as is the number of conference venues. Research efforts by academicians are evaluated and rewarded differently in different countries with the government taking a more active role in some countries than others (for instance in the UK and Australia). In some cases, this involvement influences the amount and type of research that is conducted, as well as where it is disseminated or published. Periodic Research Assessment Exercises (RAE) in the UK over the last 15 years have grown to influence the funding of research activities in universities and other institutions of higher education. Finally, it should be noted that as more and more centers for research develop in hospitality programmes, hospitality research seems to be gaining more respect, is becoming more applied in nature, and is helping to strengthen the links between industry and education. Examples of such centers include those at Southern Cross University (in Australia), Bournemouth University (in England) and the University of New Orleans (in the USA).

Summary of issues and trends

There is no shortage of change taking place in the area of hospitality management education. This section has provided a brief discussion of some of the more current issues affecting how hospitality management education is being managed and delivered. Different regions of the world have different challenges, as supported by comments made by programme administrators contacted for this chapter. In developing countries (including India and Kenya) administrators mentioned concerns about curriculum content, instructors having proper credentials for teaching, and inadequate facilities (presumably budget related). In other markets where the number of hospitality programmes is growing (and in some cases, exceeding the growth of the industry) there were concerns about the job opportunities for graduates. Administrators from a cross-section of countries indicated they were concerned about the lack of respect/prestige for the industry as a career choice. Still others mentioned either lack of communication between the industry and educational programmes or actual lack of understanding.

The field of hospitality management is obviously not without its challenges. As is the case with the industry, it can probably be said that things will continue much the way they are before improvements in funding, prestige and industry support occur. Despite these challenges, though, educators continue to educate students and conduct research and provide services in an effort to improve the outlook for the broader hospitality industry.

CONCLUSION

As noted earlier in this chapter, hospitality management education continues to mature. This is important to keep in mind since changes continue to take place with regard to philosophy, teaching, research and relationships with the industry. New programmes continue to develop, particularly in emerging economies. Specializations (and sub-specializations) continue to be developed and offered. programmes develop international alliances which allow them to provide richer learning experiences for their students. At the same time that educational programmes are maturing, the body of literature focusing on hospitality education also grows. There are journals devoted to the study of hospitality education (e.g. *Journal of Hospitality and Tourism Education*), there are associations for hospitality educators (e.g. *CHRIE International, Council on Hospitality Management Education, Council of Australian University Tourism and Hospitality Education*) and educators are finding means of networking as never before. Demand from students in choosing hospitality management as a major remains buoyant in many parts of the world, scholarship monies are readily available in some countries, and hospitality educators are increasingly becoming terminally qualified. While there are numerous issues to contend with (many of them being budget-related) many hospitality programmes are thriving at this time. Hospitality management programmes would be well advised to continue to focus on delivering high quality education to its students, providing applied research that is of use to the industry, developing even stronger ties to the industry and otherwise doing what it can to help professionalize the industry.

REFERENCES

Airey, D. and Tribe, J. (2000) 'Education for hospitality'. In C. Lashley and A. Morrison (eds) *In Search of Hospitality*. Oxford: Butterworth-Heinemann. pp. 276–292.

Barrows, C. W. and Nickason, S. (2005) An overview of quality assurance in hospitality management education programmes in Ontario. Paper presented at the annual conference of the Council on Hospitality Management Education, Bournemouth, 2005.

Baum, T. (1990) 'Competencies for hotel management: industry expectations of education', *International Journal of Contemporary Hospitality Management*, 2(4): 13–16.

Bogue, E. G. and Saunders, R. L. (1992) *The Evidence of Quality*. San Francisco: Jossey- Bass Publishers.

Bosselman, R. H. (1999) 'Graduate programmes in hospitality management education'. In C. W. Barrows and R. H. Bosselman (eds) *Hospitality Management Education*. Binghamton, NY: The Haworth Press. pp. 239–260.

Brownell, J. and Chung, B. G. (2001) 'The management development programme: a competency-based model for preparing hospitality leaders', *Journal of Management Education*, 25(2): 124–145.

Buergemeister, J. (1983) 'Assessment of the educational skills and competencies needed by beginning hospitality managers', *Hospitality Education and Research Journal*, 8(1): 38–53.

Burbidge, D. (1994) 'Student perception of preparation for success: a view from Europe', *Hospitality and Tourism Educator*, 4(4): 45–50.

Carter, C. (1980) *Higher Education for the Future*. Oxford: Billing and Sons Ltd.

Castells, M. (1995) *The Rise of the Network Society*. Oxford: Blackwell.

Dopson, L. and Tas, R. (2004) 'A practical approach to curriculum development: a case study', *Journal of Hospitality and Tourism Education*, 16(1): 39–46.

Feinstein, A. H., Raab, C. and Stefanelli, J. M. (2005) 'Instructional systems research in the hospitality industry', *Journal of Hospitality and Tourism Education*, 17(3): 34–44.

Fenich, G. (1999) 'Quality and its assurance in hospitality education'. In C. W. Barrows and R. H. Bosselman (eds) *Hospitality Management Education*, Binghamton, NY: The Haworth Press. pp. 67–95.

Florida, R. (1995) 'Towards the learning region', *Futures*, 27(5): 527–536.

Foucar-Szocki and Bolsing, C. (1999) 'Linking hospitality management programmes to industry'. In C. W. Barrows and R. H. Bosselman (eds) *Hospitality Management Education*. Binghamton, NY: The Haworth Press. pp. 37–65.

Gamage, D. and Mininberg, E. (2003) The Australian and American higher education: key issues of the first decade of the 21st century, *Higher Education*, 45(2): 183–202.

Gillespie, C. and Baum, T. (2000) 'Innovation and creativity in professional higher education: development of a CD-Rom to support teaching and learning in food and beverage management', *Scottish Journal of Adult and Continuing Education*, 6(2): 147–165.

Gröschl, S. and Barrows, C. W. (2003) 'A cross-cultural comparison of French and British managers: an examination of the influence of higher education on management style', *Tourism and Hospitality Research: The Surrey Quarterly Review*, 4(3): 228–246.

Gustin, M. (2001) 'Think for yourself: bringing critical thinking skills to the classroom', *Journal of Hospitality and Tourism Education*, 13(1): 41–47.

Hobson, J. S. P. (1999) 'International perspectives'. In C. W. Barrows and R. H. Bosselman (eds) *Hospitality Management Education*. Binghamton, NY: The Haworth Press. pp. 213–238.

Kang, S. K. and Gould, R. (2002) 'Hospitality graduates' employment status and job satisfaction', *Journal of Hospitality and Tourism Education*, 14(4): 11–18.

Knutson, B. and Patton, M. (1992) 'How prepared am I to succeed in the hospitality industry? What students are telling us', *Hospitality and Tourism Educator*, 4(3): 38–43.

Lefever, M. M. and Withiam, G. (1998) 'Curriculum review: how industry views hospitality education', *The Cornell H.R.A. Quarterly*, 39(4): 70–78.

Li, L. and Kivela, J. (1998) 'Different perceptions between hotel managers and students regarding levels of competency demonstrated by hospitality degree graduates', *Australian Journal of Hospitality Management*, 5(2): 47–53.

Longstreet, W. and Shane, H. (1993) *Curriculum for a New Millennium*. Needham Heights, MA: Allyn and Bacon.

Maher, A. (2003) 'Learning outcomes in higher education: implications for curriculum design and student learning', *Journal of Hospitality, Leisure, Sport and Tourism Education*, 3(2): 46–54.

Montmarquette, C., Cannings, K. and Mahseredjian, S. (2002) 'How do young people choose college majors?', *Economics of Education Review*, 21(6): 543–556.

Nickason, S. and Barrows, C. W. (2005) Forming and maintaining linkages between hospitality management programmes and industry. Unpublished manuscript.

Nonaka, I. and Takeuchi, H. (1995) *The knowledge creating company*. New York: Oxford University Press.

Okumus, F. and Wong, K. (2004) 'A critical review and evaluation of teaching methods of strategic management in tourism and hospitality schools', *Journal of Hospitality and Tourism Education*, 16(2): 22–33.

Quinn, R., Faerman, S., Thompson, M. and McGrath, M. (2003) *Becoming a master manager: a competency Framework*, 3rd edn. New York: John Wiley and Sons.

Robbins, D. (2005) 'Quality assurance'. In D. Airey and J. Tribe (eds) *An International Handbook of Tourism Education*. Oxford: Elsevier. pp. 451–468.

Robinson, E. (1968) 'A comprehensive reform of higher education'. In T. Burgess (ed.) *The Shape of Higher Education*. London, UK: Cornmarket Press. p. 48.

Scheule, B. and Sneed, J. (2001) 'Teaching leadership in hospitality management programmes: a model for learning from leaders', *Journal of Hospitality and Tourism Education*, 14(2): 34–37.

School of Hospitality and Tourism Management (2005) *Hospitality and Tourism Management Undergraduate Student Handbook*. Guelph: University of Guelph, Canada.

Sigala, M. (2004) 'Investigating the factors determining e-learning effectiveness in tourism and hospitality education', *Journal of Hospitality and Tourism Education*, 16(2): 11–21.

Sigala, M. and Baum, T. (2003) 'Trends and issues in tourism and hospitality higher education: visioning the future', *Tourism and Hospitality Research*, 4(4): 367–376.

Sigala, M. and Christou, E. (2003) 'Enhancing and complementing the instruction of tourism and hospitality courses through the use of on-line educational tools', *Journal of Hospitality and Tourism Education*, 15(1): 6–15.

Tesone, D. V. (2002) 'Why do some new hospitality college grads lack management skills?', *Journal of Human Resources in Hospitality and Tourism*, 1(4): 33–45.

Williams, J. and DeMicco, F. (1998) 'The challenge of multi-department management for future hospitality graduates', *Journal of Hospitality and Tourism Education*, 10(1): 13–17.

PART TWO

Generic Management Functions in the Hospitality Industry

From the Top Down: Strategic Management in the Hospitality Industry

7

Eliza Ching-Yick Tse and Giri Jogaratnam

INTRODUCTION

Despite the recent slump, international tourism and hospitality have grown by leaps and bounds since the end of World War II. It has become a major economic force in the world in terms of revenue generated and employment created. According to the World Travel Organization the industry accounted for some $463 billion in economic activity, roughly 11% of the planet's gross product. Similarly, the World Travel and Tourism Council reports that approximately 200 million jobs were either directly or indirectly associated with this industry, the equivalent of 8% of world employment, or one in every 12 jobs. It is estimated that there may be a minimum of 20 million enterprises across the globe that provide goods and services as part of this industry. It is a complex industry interwoven into the fabric of a nation through jobs, taxes, infrastructure and overall well-being.

The hospitality industry has experienced many changes in its business environment over the course of its recent history. Fierce competition exists among businesses as evidenced by price manipulations, package deals, introduction of new products and services, and open entry and access to differential marketing promotions to maintain and extend market share. In fact, competition has intensified in response to sharp declines in business. These factors have forced the hospitality industry to focus upon ways to compete in an increasingly volatile and dynamic business environment, one that becomes more acute as a result of terrorist acts worldwide and health-related concerns. Many firms compete at a global level by means that include management contracting, franchising and joint ventures in hopes of gaining greater market share, to maintain their rates of growth and

increase profitability. However, despite its size in aggregate, it is still an industry that experiences an abnormally high rate of failure, often due to a lack of well-defined strategy that could otherwise result in investments that sustain firm life and contribute to economic development. Some of these declining organizations are able to successfully implement a turnaround to prevent the organization from dissolution, whereas others are unable to react and their situation becomes irreversible (Elwood and Tse, 1991).

In terms of industry development and structure, the hospitality industry is characterized as being fragmented. While there are major chains like Holiday Inn, Hilton, Marriott, Sheraton and McDonald's present in the marketplace, a good proportion of hospitality businesses are owned by individual proprietors. In terms of change and dynamism, competition from international hospitality firms is mounting as the world quickly becomes a global economy. The major forces driving change in the industry over the coming decade will include capacity control, safety and security, assets and capital, advancing technology, new management, and environmental concerns (Olsen, 1995). At the same time, there is growing interest among hospitality industry management in the concept of strategy and the practices of strategic management in their efforts to anticipate change and adapt to the challenges they face (Feltenstein, 1992). In other words, strategy as competitive method has become the management tool to survive and sustain growth. According to a survey of firms, over 80% of companies from a variety of industries reported conducting strategic planning (Harrison, 2003). For instance, executives of many major companies have utilized such methods as branding strategy in order to develop balanced and structured portfolios, and frequent guest programs, while investing in greater marketing efforts and computer reservations systems to obtain a competitive advantage.

The notion of strategy and strategic management is essential for the survival and continued success of hospitality and tourism businesses. Adding value for customers, employees, and owners has become a central theme in the strategic management of hospitality businesses. As such, hospitality managers need to understand how their firm can achieve a competitive advantage over their competitors (Kim and Oh, 2004). Research has shown that industry conditions account for approximately 19% of a firm's performance, while developing a sound competitive strategy is responsible for 32% of performance results (McGahan and Porter, 1997). Thus, the purpose of this chapter is to provide an overview of the concept of strategy and strategic management, a review of literature reflecting different perspectives in regard to strategic management, and research studies that have been conducted in the hospitality industry. Finally, problems facing research in strategic management are discussed and future research themes are suggested.

THE RISE AND FALL AND RISE OF STRATEGY AND NEW PERSPECTIVES ON STRATEGY

Strategy has become a buzzword in the business community over the last 30 years. Its roots can be traced back all the way to the Old Testament. The word strategy comes from the Greek word *stratego*, which means to 'plan the destruction of one's enemies through the effective use of available resources' (Bracker, 1980; Cummings, 1993). The concept of strategy has had wide application in the military and political arenas. The work by the Chinese strategist Sun Tze, *Art of the War* (McNeilly, 1996), is still widely read by graduates of the West Point Military Academy in the USA. The adoption of the concept by the business community came after World War II. As business moved from a relatively stable environment into the rapidly changing and competitive environment of today, the need for strategic management has become greater than ever. With the onset of the industrial revolution, and the realization that resources are scarce, business operators realize that one cannot conduct business as usual.

Strategy research has developed rapidly over the past 50 years beginning with views of the organization by Weber (1947), the Aston School (Pugh, 1973), Thompson (1967), Lawrence and Lorcsh (1967) and on through to Mintzberg (1975), Porter (1980), Miles and Snow (1978), and Hamel and Prahalad (1994). Harvard professors Ken Andrews and C. Roland Christensen in the early 1960s articulated the concept of strategy as a tool to link together the functions of a business and assess a company's strengths and weaknesses against competitors.

Many studies emerged after the rapid expansion of formal strategic planning in the 1960s, e.g. Thune and House (1970), Ansoff et al. (1970), Herold (1972), and Rhyne (1986). In explaining financial performance variance, strategic management researchers and industrial organization economists have emphasized industry factors, market share, generic strategy, and strategic group membership. In contrast, organizational contingency theorists have emphasized alignments involving environment and internal structure (Powell, 1992). Porter (1980) defined strategic groups as groups of firms that follow similar strategies within a given industry. Barnett et al. (1994) suggested that the reasons why organizations vary in how well they perform can be due to differences in their strategic positions and to differences in their competitive abilities. They propose an evolutionary model in which there is a trade-off between these two sources of advantage.

By the 1980s, as companies in the United States were challenged by the rise of global competitors, corporate America turned away from strategic planning and began to focus on operational improvement. In the business community, General Electric (GE) emerged as the pioneer in strategic planning. The consulting firm McKinsey and Co. helped the company to come up with the GE 9-cell approach in evaluating the performance of its portfolio. At the same time, the Boston Consulting Group became famous with such concepts as the 'experience curve' and the 'growth and market-share matrix'. As GE was the pioneer in embracing strategy, so was it at the forefront of its demise. In 1983, new GE Chairman, Jack Welch, reduced the corporate planning group. Numerous other companies followed suit as they struggled to improve quality and restructure their organizations. By the late 1980s, corporate America began massive downsizing and re-engineering of operations to increase efficiency and productivity. Executives embraced the teachings of gurus Edwards Deming, father of the total quality movement, and Michael Hammer, who led the re-engineering revolution. In the hospitality industry, ITT Sheraton Corp. used the re-engineering approach to streamline its operations. The typical 300-room Sheraton Hotel had required up to 40 managers and 200 employees. By eliminating narrowly defined jobs and rethinking antiquated procedures, a re-engineered version emerged with 250 suites overseen by 14 managers and 140 employees (Byrne, 1992). Best of all, these changes produced higher customer satisfaction.

In the 1980s, strategic management research on organizational performance was dominated not by the alignment approach, but by Harvard professor Michael Porter's economics based theories. In his seminal work *Competitive Strategy* (1980), Porter introduced the concept of generic strategies, low cost leadership, differentiation, and focus. The generic strategies remain useful to characterize strategic positions at the simplest and broadest level: the base for positioning – varieties, needs, and access. The implicit strategy model of the past decade includes: one ideal competitive position in the industry, benchmarking of all activities and achieving best practice, aggressive outsourcing and partnering to gain efficiencies, advantages resting on a few key success factors, critical resources, core competencies, and flexibility and rapid responses to all competitive and market changes.

Most recently, the resource-based view (RBV) has emerged which goes further into the analysis of the firm (Wernerfelt, 1984). The RBV addresses the unique differences between and among firms and how unique resources that are inimitable are able to create sustainable competitive advantage (Barney, 1991). This view maintains the focus on the firm and its management. This creates many measurement problems as key relationships often represent intangible or perceived variables. Yet, it is perhaps a more realistic acceptance that firm strategy is a unique set of decisions that are often serendipitous and incremental and such, not seen as lending themselves to classifications that have widespread generalizability (Olsen, Sharma, Echeveste and Tse, 2005). As one might expect, most of these practices target productivity and efficiency. Unfortunately, some do not generate a distinctive competitive advantage. In 1994, after ten years of downsizing, companies began to focus on how to grow and strategic planning was seen as making a comeback in the 1990s (Byrne, 1996). At one company after another, from Sears to IBM to Hewlett-Packard to Searle, strategy was again a major focus in the quest for higher revenues and profits. Some companies were even recreating fully fledged strategic planning groups. Many practitioners and academicians agree that business strategy is now the single most important management issue and will remain so for the foreseeable future. While strategy has made a rebound and become a part of the main agenda of many organizations today, companies need to democratize the strategic process by involving line and staff managers from different disciplines and include interaction with key customers and suppliers.

The comeback of strategy witnessed the emergence of a new generation of business strategists. Now, a bevy of new books is out from a new group of strategy gurus who are capturing the attention of corporate executives and redefining the process of strategy creation. Academics Gary Hamel and C. K. Prahalad have become the most influential of a new group of strategists with the publication of *Competing for the Future* (1994). Hamel (1996) claimed that strategy is revolution and everything else is tactics. According to this perspective, strategy should not include incremental change. The authors considered that the time was ripe for industry revolutionaries and more hostile to industry incumbents. The authors pointed out that strategic planning is not strategic. In the vast majority of companies, strategic planning is a calendar-driven ritual, not an exploration of the potential for revolution. The essential problem in organizations today is a failure to distinguish planning from strategizing. They proposed that strategic thinking should be seen as an opportunity to transform a corporation and change the rules of an industry to its advantage, i.e. transformational shift.

As the environment changes and the business community rebounds from a period of downsizing, Porter (1996) offers alternative views of strategy. Strategy is the creation of a unique and valuable position involving a different set of activities. However, choosing a unique position is not enough to guarantee a sustainable advantage. In order to create value, management must possess the knowledge of how to invest in and maintain an organization's core competencies. A valuable position will attract imitation. Thus, a strategic position is not sustainable unless there are tradeoffs with other positions. Positioning tradeoffs are pervasive in competition and essential to strategy. The essence of strategy is making tradeoffs in competing and choosing what not to do. Without tradeoffs, there would be no need for choice and thus no need for strategy (Porter, 1996).

Porter further argued that operational effectiveness is not strategy. He maintained that operational effectiveness and strategy are both essential to superior performance. Operational effectiveness means performing similar activities better than rivals perform them. In contrast, strategic positioning means performing different activities than rivals or performing similar activities in different ways with the aim of delivering a unique mix of value. While operational effectiveness is about achieving excellence in individual activities or functions, strategy is about combining activities. As fit drives both competitive advantage and sustainability, the competitive advantage comes from the way its activities fit and reinforce one another. It is harder for a rival to match an array of interlocked activities than it is merely to imitate a particular activity (Tse and Olsen, 1999). Once there were popular concepts such as value chain, experience curves, stars, and dogs associated with strategic management. These are some of the new concepts: value migration (the movement of growth and profit opportunities from one industry player to another), co-evolution (the notion that by working with direct competitors, customers, and suppliers, a company can create new businesses, markets, and industries), business ecosystems (the creation of networks of relationships with customers, suppliers, and rivals to gain greater competitive advantage), and white-space opportunity (new areas of growth possibilities that fall between the cracks because they do not naturally match the skills of existing business units). Mintzberg et al. (1998) classified previous research on strategy as belonging to different schools of thought: the design school (strategy formation as a process of conception), the planning school (strategy formation as a formal process), the entrepreneurial school (strategy formation as a visionary process), the cognitive school (strategy formation as a mental process), the learning school (strategy formation as an emergent process), the power school (strategy formation as a process of negotiation), the cultural school (strategy formation as a collective process), the environmental school (strategy formation as a reactive process), and the configuration school (strategy formation as a process of transformation).

THE CONCEPT OF STRATEGY AND STRATEGIC MANAGEMENT

Strategic management is a relatively young discipline and has its roots in the disciplines of Business Policy, Organizational Theory, and Organizational Behavior. Because of different perspectives, there is no clear-cut definition of strategy. The first modern authors to relate the concept of strategy to business were Von Neumann and Morgenstern (1947). Various researchers since then have presented different perspectives in their definitions of the concept, but with some common threads. The differences are found in three primary areas: the breadth of the concept of business strategy, the components of strategy, and the inclusiveness of the strategy-formulation process. The similarities include a recognition that business strategy is an environmental or situational analysis used to determine a firm's posture in its field and that the firm's resources are utilized in an appropriate manner to attain its major goals.

Strategy, from the business perspective, is defined as a course of action aimed at ensuring that the organization will achieve its objectives in sustainable advantage over competitors (Henderson, 1989). Thus, strategic management is a continuous process of analyzing the internal and external environments of a firm, investing in competitive methods which are effective, and maximizing the utilization of resources in relation to objectives (Bracker, 1980). Strategic management entails a stream of decisions and actions which lead to the development and implementation of an effective strategy (Mintzberg; 1979; Webster and Hudson, 1991; Olsen et al., 1999). In other words, the practice of strategic management enables the leadership to help their organization adapt continually to its changing environment. The central focus of strategic management relates to the question of how to better deal with the competition. Why do some organizations perform better than others do? Studies have examined the performance consequences of formal strategic planning efforts in achieving competitive advantage (Powell, 1992). These studies provide inconclusive evidence that formalized strategic planning efforts will result in superior financial performance. Certainly, it is clear that a formal strategic planning process will not guarantee a successful formulation and implementation of strategy nor result in a more rewarding financial performance. On the other hand, there are advantages and disadvantages of strategic management and the question remains as to whether the advantages outweigh the disadvantages. Many executives believe that even though it is difficult to judge the cost-effectiveness of strategic management, it is considered worthwhile even if benefits are largely intangible. They believe that explicit strategy is required to reconcile coordinated action and entrepreneurial effort as a company grows (Tiles, 1969). The major importance of strategic management is that it gives organizations a framework for analyzing their own strengths and weaknesses while identifying future opportunities and threats.

THE CO-ALIGNMENT PRINCIPLE AND STRATEGIC MANAGEMENT PROCESS

Strategic management is concerned with the relationship between key variables – environment, organizational structure, culture, life-cycle stage, strategy – and performance. Over the past few decades, there has been increasing academic and practitioner interest in the issue of a fit between a firm and these variables (Lawrence and Lorsch, 1967; Drazin and Van de Ven, 1985; Miller, 1991). In other words, organizational theorists have asserted that there is a connection or alignment between environmental context and organizational capabilities and resources that is critical to organizational effectiveness (Miller, 1988; Venkatraman, 1989; Lamont et al., 1993; Lumpkin and Dess, 1996). Strategic management scholars are generally in agreement that firms that align their strategies with the needs of their environment are more successful than firms that do not realize such alignment (Venkatraman and Prescott, 1990).

Since the emergence and increasing prominence of open systems models of organization, researchers no longer are able to comfortably ignore the effects of environments on organizations (Scott, 1987). In essence, the open systems approach calls for an investigation of the relationship between organizations and their environments. Central to this approach is the recognition that the survival of an organization is dependent on an exchange with outside elements. Aldrich and Pfeffer (1976) have argued that managerial choice may be severely constrained by some environments and that managers must correctly perceive the nature and dictates of those environments. Contingency theorists suggest that successful performance results from the appropriate alignment of endogenous factors such as strategy and structure with exogenous context variables such as competitive environment (Venkatraman, 1989; Dess et al., 1997). Accordingly, it is the 'fit' or internal consistency among environment, strategy, and/or structure that is thought to determine performance (Venkatraman and Prescott, 1990). Hence, the contingency view of environmental determinism generally focuses on the need for flexible strategic responses in order to align the business with its competitive environment (e.g. Venkatraman, 1989; Dess et al., 1997). It is generally believed that without co-alignment between structure, strategy and the environment, organizations may have difficulty in achieving long-term success (Tse and Olsen, 1999). The environment thus establishes the context within which the importance of various organization-performance relationships should be evaluated. Research conducted within the context of the hospitality industries (e.g. Dev, 1989; West, 1990; Tse, 1991; Jogaratnam et al., 1999a; Jogaratnam, 2002) provides preliminary evidence suggesting that achieving a match between strategy and context – whether it is internal or external – has significant performance implications. Contingency theory holds that the task of the manager is essentially one of maintaining co-alignment between the firm and its environment (Bluedorn, 1993).

Researchers adopting the perspective of environmental determinism argue that the environment may influence both the selection of strategies and their viability, and on this basis suggest that there are particularly appropriate strategy-environment combinations. These researchers believe that there is no 'best' strategy, and that a given strategy will not be equally effective under different contextual conditions (Venkatraman and Prescott, 1990; Miller, 1991). It has been found that the environment, strategy, strategy implementation, and performance are all inter-related (Kwock and

Tse, 2002). Thus, when a firm makes a decision, it should consider all of these components in the right combination and within the strategic management process to increase the probability of success.

There are several major components in the strategic management process: strategy formulation (environmental scanning, competitive methods, core competencies), strategy implementation, and evaluation and control. The following sections address each of these components.

STRATEGY FORMULATION PHASE

This is primarily the planning phase of the overall process where organizations develop their strategic plan. The planning phase involves scanning of the business environment, developing a mission statement and long-term objectives for the organization, and selecting the appropriate strategies.

Scanning the business environment

Studies of environmental influences on organizational behavior have generally focused on two conceptions of the environment. One is environmental uncertainty, or the flow of information as perceived by managers (Gerloff et al., 1991; Sharfman and Dean, 1991), and the other views environments as stocks of resources, the level and the terms on which they are available being the critical factor; more or less ignoring the process by which information about the environment is apprehended by decision makers (Castrogiovanni, 1991; Sutcliffe, 1994). Researchers focusing on the hospitality industry have looked at a variety of environmental concepts such as environmental scanning (e.g. West and Anthony, 1990; Costa and Teare, 1994), uncertainty (Dev and Olsen, 1989), risk (Chathoth and Olsen, 2003a), dynamism (Olsen and DeNoble, 1981), and munificence (Jogaratnam, Tse and Olsen, 1999b). Covin and Slevin (1989) argue that environmental hostility poses a significant threat to firm viability and success and according to them (1989:75) 'precarious industry settings, intense competition, harsh, overwhelming business climates, and a relative lack of exploitable opportunities' are characteristics that typify hostile environments. Non-hostile or benign environments, in contrast,

provide a generally safe context for businesses due to their abundant investment and market opportunities as well as their largely munificent settings.

Environmental munificence is defined as the importance of a resource to the organization and the number of sources from which the resource is available (Dess and Beard, 1984; Castrogiovanni, 1991). Environmental munificence has been positively linked with the range of strategy and organizational options available to firms (Sutcliffe, 1994). A highly munificent or resource abundant environment enables a firm to focus less on its primary goal of survival because survival is possible under a variety of alternative goals, strategies, and configurations (cf. Brittain and Freeman, 1980). Such an environment presents minimal competitive pressures, offers maximal strategic options, and relative harmony among organizational constituencies (Castrogiovanni, 1991). Scarce or resource poor environments, however, evidence intensified competition, rigidity of response, and fewer strategic options (Yasai-Ardekani, 1989). There is support for the predominance of efficiency concerns in scarce environments, manifested in the tightening of budgets, increased emphasis on cost cutting, and intensification of efforts to insure accountability (Koberg, 1987). Alternatively, firms may avoid competition in resource-poor environments and resort to legally questionable activities such as unfair market practices or restraints of trade (cf. Staw and Szwajkowski, 1975; Pfeffer and Salancik, 1978).

Before any planning can be undertaken, a firm begins by scanning the business environment in order to identify the threats and opportunities that exist in the environment. This effort is designed to detect both long- and short-term trends affecting the business. The purpose of environmental scanning is to identify and track current and potential trends that afford business opportunities and pose challenges to the continued success of an organization (Auster and Choo, 1993). The process of scanning is the primary means by which managers acquire information about external environmental events that may have an impact on the organization (Hambrick, 1981; Jain, 1984). Environmental scanning is a source of input to the strategic planning process and is viewed as the first step in the process that attempts to link strategy and the external environment (Daft et al., 1988;

Ebrahimi, 2000). Executives' interpretations of environmental forces influence their strategic actions and determine how they manage their companies. Therefore, environmental scanning as well as information acquisition and interpretation play a vital role in organizational effectiveness (West and Olsen, 1989; Kumar et al., 2001).

Whether the scanning systems in place are formal and organized or informal and unscientific, environmental scanning has traditionally been viewed as the domain of top management (Auster and Choo, 1993) who might spend considerable time and effort monitoring the environment (Mintzberg, 1973; Hambrick, 1981). Although managers may have limited time and means for scanning (e.g. Ebrahimi, 2000) and despite the fact that formal or advanced environmental scanning models are not commonly used, top-level decision makers assume the responsibility for environmental scanning, or identifying and evaluating trends within the environment (e.g. Coulter, 2002; Okumus, 2004). An uncertain environment requires that an organization continually evaluate organization-environment alignment. Top-level decision makers of firms facing greater environmental uncertainty are expected to take on greater responsibility for environmental scanning (Daft and Weick, 1984; Yasai-Ardekani and Nystrom, 1996). As top managers find it difficult to comprehend rapidly changing environments they tend to become more involved in scanning those environments (Utterback, 1979). Since very few organizations have dedicated individuals or units conducting environmental scanning many managers resort to informal scanning in their role as strategic decision makers (Keegan, 1974; Jain, 1984). This seems to be the case with managers in the hospitality industry as well (West and Olsen, 1989; Costa and Teare, 1996; Olsen, Tse and West, 1999). Moreover, research has failed to show the benefits associated with the adoption of formal scanning systems (e.g. Lenz and Engledow, 1986).

The traditional view of environmental scanning, as posited by Design School proponents holds that environmental scanning and analysis determine strategy, as opposed to being the product of it (e.g. Mintzberg, 1990). However, Jennings and Lumpkin (1992) have argued that the types of environmental information sought differ according to the competitive strategies in place. In support of their thesis, they found that organizations embracing a differentiation strategy tended to implement scanning activities that placed a greater importance on assessing opportunities for growth and improving customer perceptions. Those espousing a cost leadership strategy, on the other hand, tended to focus on scanning that assessed competitive threats and traced competitors' plans and procedures.

Research evidence suggests that an organization's scanning scope and frequency is also related to its strategy. Yasai-Ardekani and Nystrom (1993) examined the relationship between firms adopting a low-cost leadership strategy and the scope and frequency with which they scanned their environments. They found that among firms espousing low-cost leadership, those with effective scanning systems scanned their environments more frequently and broadly than those with ineffective scanning systems. Hambrick (1982) suggests that organizations adopting different strategies have different predispositions and abilities to act on environmental information. Although Hambrick (1982) found that strategy alone did not appear to affect the amount of scanning conducted, he reported that the industry within which an organization functioned, had a strong influence on the content of what was scanned.

Research has also examined the link between scanning and performance. Subramanian, Fernandes and Harper (1993) found that strategy and scanning were related and that high performance organizations exhibit more advanced scanning systems when compared to low performance firms. They reported that the majority of prospectors exhibited scanning systems that were either reactive or proactive while analyzers were more likely to adopt reactive scanning systems and defenders more likely to adopt *ad hoc* scanning systems. In this regard, both the proactive and reactive approaches are considered to be effective scanning models while an *ad hoc* approach is considered to be ineffective (Jain, 1984). Similarly, Daft, Sormunen and Parks (1988) concluded that executives of high-performing firms scan their environments more frequently and broadly than their counterparts in low-performing firms. Previous hospitality researchers have also claimed that better scanning of the environment leads to improved performance (West and Olsen, 1989; Olsen, Murthy and Teare, 1994). Research also confirms the moderating role played by environmental scanning activities in the strategy/performance relationship (West and Anthony, 1990; Kumar et al., 2001). However, Dev and Olsen (1989) discovered few significant relationships between strategy, environmental uncertainty and performance in the lodging industry. Despite the rigorous research methodologies adopted by these researchers, Olsen and Roper (1998) note that many of these studies have only achieved marginal success in contributing to the body of knowledge due to the realization that strategy is a contingent process.

The strategic management literature also suggests that there is an enduring theoretical tension regarding the idea of particularly appropriate strategy-environment combinations versus the concept of equally viable strategies (Zajac and Shortell, 1989). At the heart of this debate is whether organizational adaptation is environmentally governed or strategically shaped. The population ecology paradigm supports the view that organizational adaptation is environmentally determined and that managerial choice is limited (Aldrich et al., 1984). However, according to the strategic choice paradigm, managers have some degree of influence over their environments and often have considerable choice in making strategic decisions.

It is generally accepted for organization theorists to observe that the environment of organizations is becoming more complex and uncertain over time. Researchers adopting the perspective of environmental determinism argue that the environment may influence both the selection of strategies and their viability, and on this basis suggest that there are particularly appropriate strategy/environment combinations. Moreover, there seems to be general consensus that the hospitality industry is in its mature stages; manifested by characteristics such as increased competition, shortening of concept life cycles, saturated markets, stagnant sales, declining margins, and associated consolidation, as well as high failure rates (e.g. Olsen and Roper, 1998; Tse and Olsen, 1999). Confronted with this increasingly competitive and dynamic environment, it is becoming ever more important for the hospitality manager to understand and accurately gauge the environment in order to develop reasoned, yet distinctive methods of adapting to, and exploiting environmental opportunities. Organizational theorists have

argued that managerial choice may be severely constrained by some environments and that managers must correctly perceive the nature and dictates of those environments (e.g. Aldrich and Pfeffer, 1976; Powell, 1992; Lumpkin and Dess, 1996).

Resource dependence theorists view organizations as actively engaged in exchanges with the environment in order to improve performance and increase the probability of survival (Pfeffer and Salancik, 1978). While this task is a formidable one in itself, it is even more so for the small, independent operator who does not have access to the means and capabilities available to larger corporations and multi-unit chain operations. Moreover, Utterback (1979) has argued that it might be relatively simple to identify environmental changes, but that it is much more difficult to predict the effect of these trends upon the firm and its outcomes.

From an international perspective, scholars have focused primarily upon the behavior of multinationals. The focal point in the early phases was upon direct investment with emphasis on location and control of production facilities (Stopford and Well, 1972). Some of this early work can be characterized as being centered upon the environment of the multinational as it sought to develop strategies for growth through expansion into new international markets (Goodnow and Hansz, 1972; Keegan, 1974; Sethi, 1982; Rosenzweig and Singh, 1991). The constructs of uncertainty and complexity became important components as efforts were made to develop an understanding of the cause and effect relationships of the environment to the firm. While efforts were helpful in explaining the concepts of the environment, little emphasis was directed at research that attempted to identify forces that drive change in a national or global environment and their causal impact upon firms. Little, if any, work linked these impacts to the value adding mandates of stakeholders.

International generic strategies have been a favorite of researchers with most focusing upon the MNE (Levitt, 1983; Kogut, 1985; Sullivan and Bauerschmidt, 1991). Porter (1990) chose to focus on nations in addressing his, now well-known and often controversial four diamond, model (Davies and Ellis, 2000). The model addresses industry wide issues and offers several integrating propositions. Many have challenged its claims as an overarching framework for understanding strategy. While it clearly rests upon Porter's industrial economist views, it is criticized for leaving out important elements with regard to governments' roles in enhancing or limiting the strategies of firms.

There is little doubt that the environment profoundly shapes and influences organizational performance. Most researchers today subscribe to the notion that environments in general pose constraints and opportunities for organizational action and no longer question the importance of the environment as a contingency variable when examining organization – performance relationships. Prescott (1986) suggests that the environment establishes the context within which to evaluate the importance of various relationships between organizational conduct and performance. As a result, organizational members, in the operation of strategic choice, may have to identify meaningful sub-environments or domains in which their firms are to compete (Dess et al., 1990).

Different environmental conditions might require different strategies to achieve acceptable levels of performance (Lawrence and Lorsch, 1967). Research conducted within the context of the hospitality industries (cf. DeNoble and Olsen, 1986; West, 1990) provides preliminary evidence supporting the importance of the task environment and its effect on performance. Hospitality managers facing mature and rapidly changing environmental conditions urgently need to adapt to and accommodate changes in their environments if they are to survive and prosper. To succeed and outlast the competition, restaurateurs must not only have the ability to accurately estimate changes in the environment, but also an appreciation of the impact the external environment may have on the firm.

Most theoretical models of organizational responses to crises, threat, and scarcity emphasize the importance of perceptions in the process of adaptation. Regardless of how environments are modeled, managers' perceptions of environmental conditions lie at the heart of organizational responses and strategic adaptation to environments. An assumption that is implicit within this stream of research is that managers' perceptions of the objective environment are congruent with actual conditions, and that managers develop strategies and core competencies that support their accurate perceptions of the environment. Empirical research evidence indicates that the greater the match between managerial perceptions of environmental characteristics

and actual environmental conditions, the better an organization performs (Bourgeois, 1985).

Organizations respond to what they perceive; unnoticed events do not affect an organization's decisions and actions (Weick, 1969; Miles et al., 1974). As a result, the same objective environmental attributes may be perceived differently by different organizations (Snow, 1976). 'The environment one organization perceives as unpredictable, complex, and evanescent, another organization might see as static, and easily understood' (Starbuck, 1983: 1080). The performance consequences of such differing perceptions was confirmed by Bourgeois (1985) who was able to report that higher performance was associated with firms experiencing a greater degree of congruence between objectively measured volatility and perceived environmental uncertainty. In other words, firms that survey their environments with greater perceptual precision tend to achieve higher than average levels of economic performance.

Developing mission and long-term objectives

The first step in the strategic management process is then followed by the creation and evaluation of the mission statement which defines what business the firm is in, or plans to be in, and the environmental domain in which it will compete. Following development of the mission statement, the firm must then decide upon the competitive methods it will choose in order to take advantage of the opportunities in its domain or environment. The competitive methods are viewed as the primary value producing activities of the business. A close match, or alignment, must be achieved between the opportunities in the environment and the competitive methods chosen. Bourgeois (1980) conceptualizes the relationship between strategy and environment with primary strategy (domain definition) being linked to the general environment and secondary strategy (domain navigation) being linked to the task environment.

Once completed, the firm will then assess its strengths and weaknesses to determine if it has the resources and capabilities to properly implement and execute the chosen methods. This assessment will determine whether or not the firm has the core competencies to realize the overall strategy it has chosen through its selection of competitive methods (Olsen, 2000). Strategy formulation is not a linear process but a continuous process that is regularly evaluated and revised as it is carried out, with each element being interactive and interdependent.

Once the firm has identified its strengths and weaknesses, it is then ready to set long- and short-term objectives. Long-term objectives are considered to be those that apply to a time horizon of one year or more. The objectives should be designed so as to enable the firm to overcome its weaknesses and take full advantage of its strengths. Each objective should be tied directly to a particular competitive method or set of methods. The objective must identify the physical, financial and human resources necessary to implement and execute the chosen strategy. For instance, the Ritz-Carlton hotel chain is known for its excellent service and for providing customers with the experience of a lifetime. The company is dedicated in training its human resources with its special service philosophy (Anonymous, 2002).

Strategic orientation and strategy selection

Strategic orientation or strategic posture refers to the competitive posture, actions and tactics adopted by a firm's decision makers in an ongoing effort to adapt to the environment for a more favorable 'fit' or alignment. There are various levels of strategies that play distinct roles throughout the organization: corporate, business, and functional. These strategies differ in four aspects: focus, specificity, responsibility, and time frame. The strategies at different levels need to be coherent to ensure competitive advantage (Hofer and Schendel, 1978). Strategy coherence is the consistency of strategic choices across business and functional levels of strategy. Nath and Sudharshan (1994) found performance differences using various performance measures between more and less coherent firms.

A corporate strategy is a master game plan for managing and operating an organization. The primary function of a corporate strategy is in deciding the scope or domain of the operation, in other words – what business (es) should we be in? This level of strategy provides the blue print of the business plan in which a functional strategy can be implemented. Corporate strategies, if successfully chosen, implemented and carried out, can lead to a synergistic effect. A firm

chooses a corporate strategy depending upon its mission and the goals and the objectives it wants to accomplish. These strategies can guide a firm's allocation of resources among several business units and/or other ventures the firm may choose. Porter (1986) identified four concepts of corporate strategy that have been put into practice: portfolio management, restructuring, transferring skills, and sharing activities. Every corporate strategy has its costs and benefits, but the main purpose for implementing a corporate strategy is to gain a greater return on investment for all its stakeholders. This can be achieved through the co-alignment principle, which involves finding the perfect corporate strategy, environment, and corporate-structure fit.

Organizational researchers have used several methods to conceptualize and operationally define the construct of strategic orientation in different research settings. Some have used multiple indices obtained from the PIMS (acronym for Profit Impact of Market Strategy) database to measure strategy (e.g. Manu and Sriram, 1996) while others have adopted Miles and Snow's (1978) or Porter's (1980) typologies (e.g. Beal and Yasai-Ardekani, 2000). In terms of business-level strategy, Miles and Snow (1978) proposed a typology of strategic types based on the organization's orientation toward product-market development. They suggested four strategic types: defenders, prospectors, analyzers and reactors. Miles and Snow (1978) view their defender, prospector, and analyzer strategies as being equally effective across differing environments. Hambrick (1983) notes that the generic character of Miles and Snow's typology 'ignores industry and environmental peculiarities' (p. 7). Porter (1980) suggested that there are three potentially successful generic competitive strategies in any industry – overall cost leadership, differentiation, and focus – and a fourth, less successful strategy, stuck in the middle. He implies that his three generic strategies may be applied with equal success in dealing with competitive forces across a broad range of markets and industries. According to the strategic choice perspective, the environmental context is not as important as the proper implementation of a strategy (Miles and Snow, 1978; Manu and Sriram, 1996). Subsequently, there has been a large body of empirical research attempting to operationalize and investigate these two typologies and the sources of sustainable competitive advantage

(Hambrick, 1980; Snow and Hrebiniak, 1980; Segev, 1989; Conant et al., 1990). These studies generally have found support that companies espousing the stable archetypes perform equally well in terms of profitability and outperform reactors or those 'stuck in the middle'.

Given both perspectives, strategy research within the hospitality industry has adopted the Miles and Snow typology (e.g. Dev and Olsen, 1989; Schaffer and Litschert, 1990; Williams and Tse, 1995) as well as Porter's generic strategy archetypes (e.g. West and Anthony, 1990; Tse, 1991) to empirically assess various organization-performance relationships. Schaffer and Litschert (1990) adopted the contingency perspective and studied the internal consistency between strategy and structure in the hotel industry while Tse (1991) assessed the link between strategy and structure in restaurants. Williams and Tse (1995) addressed the relationship between strategy and entrepreneurial type and suggested that type of entrepreneur may influence choice of strategy. West and Anthony (1990) studied the performance effects of strategic group membership and environmental scanning behavior within the foodservice industry. Many of these early studies on the hospitality industry have only achieved marginal success in contributing to the body of knowledge (Olsen and Roper, 1998; Tse and Olsen, 1999), perhaps due to deficiencies in the measurement of generic strategy – nominal variables were used to measure the multidimensional construct of competitive strategy (for an extensive review, see Murthy, 1994). On the other hand, cost competitiveness, mobilizing people and partners, and building a robust service delivery are the top competitive strategies which senior managers of Hong Kong and Singapore hotels and travel agents seem to employ (Wong and Kwan, 2001).

Also popular within the strategic management literature is the characterization of strategic posture along the conservative-to-entrepreneurial dimension (e.g. Covin and Slevin, 1989; Becherer and Maurer, 1997; Miles et al., 2000). Miller (1983) offers one of the earliest operationalizations of the entrepreneurial orientation construct. He describes an entrepreneurial firm as one that 'engages in product market innovation, undertakes somewhat risky ventures, and is first to come up with proactive innovations, beating competitors to the punch' (p. 780). Authors adopting this perspective operationalize strategic posture in terms of the degree to which firms are inclined to

compete aggressively, to take business related-risks, and to support change and innovation in the pursuit of a competitive advantage (Miller and Friesen, 1982; Covin and Slevin, 1989; Miles, et al., 2000). Miller (1983) has argued that innovation, proactiveness, and risk-taking were three components of strategic posture that comprise a basic uni-dimensional strategic orientation:

> In general, theorists would not call a firm entrepreneurial if it changed its technology or product-line simply by directly imitating competitors while refusing to take any risks. Some proactiveness would be essential as well. By the same token, risk-taking firms that are highly leveraged financially are not necessarily entrepreneurial. They also must engage in product-market or technological innovation (Miller, 1983: 780).

Covin and Slevin (1989) observe that this characterization is consistent with the prospector firms conceptualized by Miles and Snow (1978) and entrepreneurial organizations proposed by Mintzberg (1973). Likewise, conservative firms are those with strategic postures that are risk-averse, non-innovative, and reactive. These firms are said to approximate Miles and Snow's (1978) defender firms and Mintzberg's (1973) adaptive organizations (Covin and Slevin, 1989). Such a differentiation is also consistent with the strategic orientation paradigm that suggests that organizational adaptability and organizational rigidity are two modes of achieving competitive advantage. Adaptability is consistent with the entrepreneurial profile and rigidity is compatible with the conservative posture (e.g. Miles and Snow, 1978; Hambrick, 1983).

Although Dess, Lumpkin and Covin (1997) argue that there seems to be a normative bias toward the value of entrepreneurial behavior and the assumption of a positive relationship between an entrepreneurial posture and performance outcomes, Hart (1992) suggests that entrepreneurial behavior is more likely to be associated with poor performance. Miller and Friesen (1982) caution that increasing levels of entrepreneurship beyond a particular threshold may negatively affect a company's financial performance. Moreover, the results of empirical studies considering the link between entrepreneurial orientation and performance have been mixed. Covin and Slevin (1986) initially found that entrepreneurial posture and performance were positively correlated, but subsequently reported that strategic posture was not a significant independent predictor of firm performance. These authors (1989) found that small firms in hostile environments should adopt an entrepreneurial posture to obtain higher financial performance. The authors note that in benign environments the relationship between an entrepreneurial orientation and performance may be weak and possibly negative. Consequently, although an entrepreneurial orientation in a benign environment could very well produce a competitive advantage, such a posture may not be necessary to sustain superior performance. In other words, these researchers argue that while an entrepreneurial posture may be equally effective in a hostile as well as a benign environment, such a posture may not be warranted when faced with a benign environment and could represent an unnecessary risk for small firms (Covin and Slevin, 1989). This argument lends support to the contingency perspective and the view that the best alignment for a hostile environment may be an entrepreneurial posture. Covin, Slevin and Schultz (1994) also found no significant relationship between these constructs. However, Becherer and Maurer (1997), Zahra (1991), Smart and Conant, (1994), Zahra and Covin (1995) and Jogaratnam, Tse and Olsen (1999b) reported positive and significant associations between entrepreneurial orientation and performance. Li and Tse (2005) examined the relationship between strategic planning and entrepreneurial business orientation; while Jogaratnam, Tse, and Olsen (1999c) addressed the match of strategy with performance in restaurant firms. Given the mixed results obtained thus far, Zahra (1991) notes that there is a paucity of empirical evidence relating to the effect of entrepreneurship on financial performance. Moreover, different entrepreneurial postures may influence different measures of performance quite differently as well as at different points in time (Zahra, 1991; Lumpkin and Dess, 1996).

STRATEGIC IMPLEMENTATION PHASE

To assess a firm's strategic position, its managers must collect and interpret data regarding the firm itself, its competitors, its stakeholders, and the industry. Crook, Ketchen and Snow (2003) propose a 'competitive-edge' model to guide the strategic decision-making and data-collection processes so that managers gain an explicit picture of what is happening with their firm, their competitors, and the industry. Once the objectives are finalized and approved and resources allocated, implementation begins. Implementation involves the actual utilization of resources for the successful execution of processes and activities associated with each competitive method. Key variables affecting successful implementation include structure, leadership, and culture. Furthermore, effective communication is a primary requirement of effective implementation (Peng and Litteljohn, 2001).

Success in strategy implementation depends upon appropriate organizational structure as different strategies pose different administrative requirements (Tse and Olsen, 1988). In other words, effective strategy implementation depends partly on whether a firm's strategy is congruent and complementary with its internal configuration. Implementation involves the actual utilization of resources for the successful execution of processes and activities associated with each competitive method. In order to achieve higher performance in the hospitality sector, firms are required to focus attention on achieving internal consistency between structure and strategy. Eccles and Teare (1996) emphasize the importance of alignment at the unit level and suggest that unit managers develop skills in strategic thinking in order to stay competitive. Such a focus calls for an organizational structure that allows the unit to be proactive, generating ideas on how best to alter the unit to meet specified objectives.

Organization structure

All organizations have a structure that influences the flow of information and the nature of human interactions. Structure defines the lines of authority and channels for communication and serves to allocate tasks and resources to promote coordination among organizational units. The fundamental purpose of organization structure is for management to maximize the effectiveness of day-to-day operations of the firm. Corporate structures are the arrangements among people in an organization that provide firms with an orderly system in order to get work done. They provide the fundamental building blocks for the construction of the organization and let persons in the firm know how information will be traveled throughout the organization. Corporate structures determine locus of control and responsibility at every level of the business. The organization structure, in large part, determines the interactions, relationships, and roles to create and apply knowledge that determine competitiveness (Tse, 1992). This competitiveness starts with the organization's ability to adapt to influence its environment (Twomey, 2002).

Chandler (1962) showed how changes in strategy require subsequent alterations in structure. Then Rumelt (1974) demonstrated how the match between strategy and structure influences performance. Galbraith (1977) suggested that strategy implementation requires a 'fit' between strategy and organization design. Miller (1986, 1988) synthesized the relationships between common strategic and structural configurations and their implications for performance in different environments. Combining Porter's generic strategy and Mintzberg's configuration of organization design (1979), Miller proposed that differentiation (niche) strategy should be followed by simple structure, cost leadership strategy matched by machine bureaucracy structure, differentiation (innovative) strategy with organic structure, while conglomeration strategy is seen as being supported by a divisionalized structure. While most of the research on the strategy–structure fit has examined domestic organizations, Habib and Victor (1991) analyzed the strategy–structure fit and its effect on the economic performance of US manufacturing and service multinational corporations. Similarly, Tse and Olsen (1990) and Eccles and Teare (1996) reviewed the interrelationships between business strategy and organizational structure in the hospitality industry. They suggest that unit managers are in better positions than the corporate office to monitor and respond to the local environmental conditions. Therefore, the internal structure can be a source of strength that provides competitive advantage as well as weaknesses for the overall firm. A successful firm not only engages in entrepreneurial managerial behaviors, but also has the appropriate internal mechanisms, especially organizational structure, to support such behaviors (Slevin and Covin, 1990).

Mechanistic versus organic structure

Organization structure can take many forms along a continuum where the structure of an organization can be classified ranging from highly mechanistic to highly organic, according to the technology in place (Burns and Stalker, 1961). The 'mechanistic' structure represents a high degree of specialization, division of labor, vertical communication, centralized authority, and low autonomy. Mechanistic organizations tend to be more traditional, more tightly controlled, more hierarchical, highly formalized, non-participative, and inflexible in their approach. The classical approach to management views organizations as being similar to machines, as a result of its roots in the manufacturing economy. The emphasis is on efficiency, uniformity, control, predictability, and economies of scale. Therefore the structure of the company is based on mechanistic principles and managerial intervention is thought to be necessary to get people to perform. According to this perspective, employees must be managed and controlled and they are viewed in terms of being cogs in machines and expenses to the company. 'Organic' structure, on the other hand is characterized by informality, decentralization of authority, open channels of communication, adaptability, and flexibility (Khandwalla, 1976/1977). The organic structure allows less strict task differentiation, less clear hierarchy, is more consensual, more loosely controlled, and permits a relatively higher degree of autonomy. Organic structures support the systematic discovery of innovative opportunities and foster opportunities through facilitation and motivation (Drucker, 1985; Covin and Slevin, 1990; Slevin and Covin, 1990). These authors maintain that entrepreneurial behaviors can be promoted by organizational structures that are organic and amorphous. Structures that support entrepreneurship foster the right climate or culture (Chung and Gibbons, 1997) and minimize bureaucracy while maximizing adhocracy (Echols and Neck, 1998). The high levels of performance achieved by many entrepreneurial firms with flexible, non-bureaucratic structural attributes suggest that the fit between organization structure and a firm's entrepreneurial orientation may be particularly crucial to the effectiveness of the firm.

Leadership style

Research has shown that a firm's strategy is influenced by a number of variables, including management style, characteristics of the organization's leaders, and stage of the corporate life cycle (Tse and Elwood, 1990). The prevailing leadership style of the organization's top-level managers is believed to be one of the most critical factors in determining organizational strategy. The challenge of developing or reestablishing a clear strategy is often primarily an organizational one and depends on leadership. Thus, the impact of leadership style upon strategy formulation and implementation is considered to be a major explanatory variable in determining financial variability (Buzzell, Gale and Sultan, 1975). General management therefore involves much more than the stewardship of individual functions. At its core lies strategy: defining and communicating the company's unique position, making tradeoffs, and forging fit among activities. Effectiveness of strategy implementation is affected by the quality of people involved in the process. According to the upper-echelon perspective, strategic leadership encompasses a leader's ability to anticipate events, maintain flexibility, and a long-term perspective in order to guide the organization to continued success. This perspective examines the concept of co-alignment between specific attributes of managerial characteristics and the strategic behavior of their firms (Miller et al., 1982; Hambrick and Mason, 1984; Miller and Toulouse, 1986). Typologies and theoretical models have been developed to explain the impact that the fit between top executive characteristics, managerial influence and strategic orientation has on organizational performance (Miles and Snow, 1978; Porter, 1980; Thomas et al., 1991). Bruce and Hinkin (1994) suggested that given the competitive nature of the hospitality industry, most improvements in performance and service quality would have to be made through strong leadership that will in turn result in the better use of resources. Strategic leaders are in charge of setting and changing the culture, strategy, and structure of an organization and motivating employees to implement decisions (Nahavandi and Malekzadeh, 1993). Chathoth and Olsen (2003b) focused on the study of the relationship between the micro and macro perspectives for the leadership construct.

As Leontides (1982) contends: 'Managers make strategy and strategy determines business success or failure'. Jack Welch, the former CEO of General Electric, stated that: 'Strategy follows people; the right person leads to the right strategy' (as quoted in Hinterhuber and Popp, 1992). It is the responsibility of the top management to ensure that the strategic decisions and actions are carried out throughout the various levels of the organization. The leader must provide the discipline to decide which industry changes and customer-needs the company will respond to, while avoiding organizational distractions and maintaining the company's distinctiveness (Porter, 1996). For example, with the arrival of the new chief executive, Antoine Cau in 1998, the Forte Hotel Group embarked on a mission of brand restructuring, a radical culture change program, and a commitment to excellence. These changes had a positive impact on both employee and guest satisfaction (Erstad, 2001). As international markets, suppliers, competitors, technology, and customers are constantly changing, global leaders need a set of context-specific abilities and must have a core cluster of managerial characteristics that foster and promote success. For example, corporate cultures, industry dynamics, and 'country of origin' management practices can permeate a company's worldwide operations and require unique knowledge and skills for successful leadership. Adopting this perspective, general global leadership characteristics may include exhibiting character, embracing duality, and demonstrating savvy. Most important, these leaders consider inquisitiveness as the force underlying these characteristics (Gregersen et al., 1998).

National and organizational culture

Culture exists at three levels: national culture, ethnic or group culture, and organizational culture. National culture is defined as a set of values and beliefs shared by people within a nation. In addition to an overall national culture, different ethnic and religious groups might live within each nation and share national cultural values but have their unique subculture. Countries like Singapore and the USA with different ethnic and religious groups have considerable cultural diversity. Hofstede (1980) and his colleagues developed five basic cultural dimensions along which cultures differ: power distance, uncertainty avoidance, individualism, masculinity, and dynamism. Low power distance facilitates the implementation of a participative management style, for example, the United States tends to be a low to medium power-distance culture. On the other hand, in cultures with high power distance, employees have limited expectations for participation in decision making. For example, many Chinese business leaders who operate from a variety of locations around the Pacific Rim have highly authoritarian-oriented, family controlled organizations. The Chinese value order, hierarchy, and a clear delineation of power (Becker, 2000). Because of national cultural traits Asian staff are more reluctant to accept participative management practices and become empowered when compared to their counterparts in Western societies. Asian cultures do not always encourage risk taking, and social security and freedom of speech are not always common. Therefore, culture and management may be deterrents to the adoption of a participative management style. In the case of China, its political system and business environments are in flux. Business in China is typically done through personal relationships and networks, a system called 'guanxi' and it is virtually impossible for a foreigner to become part of this network. To prosper, international firms will have to appreciate China's political, social, and cultural frameworks, in particular the need to work with local partners who are part of the guanxi network (Pine, 2002).

Moreover, an organizational culture is the set of values, norms, and beliefs shared by members of an organization. Given time, all organizations develop a unique culture and character whereby employees share common values and beliefs about work-related issues. It is through the strong commitment of resources and the fostering of an appropriate organizational culture and reward system that successful strategy implementation is achieved (Tse and Elwood, 1990). It is believed that companies with a strongly developed corporate culture usually sustain an innovative outlook and a commitment to customers and staff members. Woods and Sciarini (1996) have described cultural congruence as the extent to which its members share an organization's culture. Managers do not control their cultures but they do play important roles within them. It becomes a challenge for management to understand and appreciate the unique cultural characteristics of their own organizations and then using this information to facilitate cultural change in all organizational activities.

THE EVALUATION AND CONTROL PHASE

The implementation phase also includes evaluation and control of the strategic process against the corporate mission and long-term objectives to ensure it is functioning properly. While implementation is technically not a direct part of the formulation process, it is the link to strategy evaluation. Evaluation involves the assessment of the success of each competitive method in adding its targeted value to the firm. Results of this evaluation are used to continually cycle through the formulation process.

While the strategy field has evolved dramatically since the 1960s, theoretical models of the relationship between strategy and the control process have evolved little since then. The control system is a process which involves incentives and sanctions for business management as well as an agreement between senior and unit management on the business's objectives, the monitoring of performance against these objectives, and feedback on the results achieved (Goold and Quinn, 1990). Simons (1994) found support for the notion that managers use formal control systems as a means of promoting and implementing business strategy. He identified four types of management control: belief systems (to define, communicate, and reinforce the values and purposes of the organization); boundary systems (to establish explicit limits and rules), diagnostic control systems (to monitor organizational outcomes), and interactive control systems (to involve top managers in the decision activities of subordinates). He indicated that regardless of which type is adopted by top management, these systems appear to be vitally important in building credibility and selling new strategies to constituents. It is also recommended when designing a strategic control system to ensure a balance between strategy and operations, the long term and the short term.

HOSPITALITY RESEARCH AND STUDIES IN STRATEGIC MANAGEMENT

A review of the literature includes both conceptual and empirical studies of strategic management in the hospitality industry.

Conceptual studies

Most of the early and some contemporary work has been conceptual (Olsen and Bellas, 1980; Olsen and DeNoble, 1981; Reid and Olsen, 1981; Canas, 1982; DeNoble and Olsen, 1982; Reichel, 1982 and 1986; Slattery and Boer, 1991; Webster and Hudson, 1991; Tse and West, 1992; Zhao and Merna, 1992) Some of the works were descriptive in nature, while others emphasized the use of a contingency approach for corporate strategic planning. Examples of anecdotal work that focused upon the analysis of specific companies can also be found (Hazard et al., 1992; Langton et al., 1992; Webster, 1994). Nanus and Lundberg (1988) proposed a systemic futures research process that allows executives to examine external future trends and events that have critical implications for the organization's internal strategies and policies. Slattery and Clark (1988) pointed out the need for strategic planning to bridge the gap between the different levels of management throughout the corporation in order to enhance communication flow and to achieve the company mission and objectives. This line of work primarily addressed the application of strategy related models developed in other sectors and applied to the hospitality industry without the actual conduct of empirical investigation (Olsen and Roper, 1998).

Empirical research

The second line of research activity has attempted to apply more empirical approaches to theory building. Success in strategy implementation depends partly on a proper match between strategy and organizational context and this match is expected to have a positive impact on financial performance. Utilizing the underpinnings of the work of Miles and Snow (1978) and Porter (1980), researchers such as Tse and Olsen (1988), West (1988), West and Olsen (1989), Dev and Olsen (1989), Schaffer (1986), and Crawford-Welch (1991) have examined the multi-faceted dimensions of strategy. They examined various hypotheses regarding the relationships between strategy, environmental scanning, firm structure, and the impact on financial performance. Tse (1988) examined the strategic planning activity and the degree of internal strengths and weaknesses analysis performed by restaurant firms. Parsa (1994)

found that implementation plays an important role in determining performance of hospitality franchise systems. Olsen, Murthy and Teare (1994) examined the environmental scanning practices of chief executive officers of multinational hotel chains. Elwood-Williams and Tse (1995) empirically investigated the relationship between strategy and entrepreneurship in the US restaurant sector.

Attempts were made to recognize that strategy is a process that is contingent upon many variables and acknowledge the difficulties of defining strategic typologies using large sample sizes. Researchers recently have begun to use the case study methodology and Delphi methods to assess strategy and its related issues. The issues addressed by these case studies include: co-alignment of human resources management practices and business strategy (Ishak, 1990), exploitation of synergies between hotel brands (Weinberg, 1991), international development and modes of entry into new foreign markets (Zhao, 1992), strategy implementation (Schmelzer, 1992; Schmelzer and Olsen, 1994), and strategic alliances (Dev and Klein, 1993; Monga, 1996). Research that used the Delphi approach include Kim's (1992) study of Asia political environments and Turnbull's (1996) study of hotel projects in the Caribbean region. These investigations have permitted in-depth analysis of several national and multinational hospitality firms. The bulk of this research was exploratory in nature and has resulted in the formulation of propositions encouraging further research and theory building (Olsen and Roper, 1998). In the study conducted by Olsen et al. (1996), the relationships between business environmental forces driving changes in the multinational hotel industry and the competitive methods of its major hotel firms were identified. Burgess, Hampton and Roper (1995) also have looked at the factors underlying the success of international hotel groups.

Most recently strategy research has focused upon the types of competitive methods that firms use. Typologies of competitive methods in the hotel industry have been developed by Murthy (1994) and by Jogaratnam (1996) for the restaurant industry. These studies have focused upon identifying a wide range of competitive methods and some have employed factor analysis to bring about a more parsimonious classification of methods to be used in further research. In these cases the investigations further explored the relationship between these typologies and firm performance. Significant results were obtained between the choice of competitive methods and firm performance.

The latest additions to the literature have focused upon the core competencies that firms have used to seek to obtain competitive advantage. As the use of information technology (IT) has become an essential component within the commercial sector, Cho (1996) has identified it as a core competency in multinational hotel companies. Core competencies in three US casual theme restaurant concepts were studied by de Chabert (1997). Brotherton and Shaw (1996), Brotherton (2004a, 2004b) completed work towards the identification and classification of critical success factors in UK Hotels plc, while Griffin (1994) attempted to ascertain the identity of critical success factors of yield management systems in lodging firms. Rispoli (1997) examined competitive analysis and competence based strategies in the hotel industry. Roberts and Shea (1996) characterized core capabilities in the hotel industry. Overall, the focus here has been to identify what abilities within firms or industry sectors offer competitive advantage. While work has been primarily case study and/or descriptive, little has been done to assess the relationships between these competencies and other constructs of the strategy paradigm (Olsen and Roper, 1998).

PROBLEMS ASSOCIATED WITH SERVICE STRATEGY RESEARCH

The complex nature of the hospitality industry calls for a need to effectively manage the organizations, but the hospitality industry is generally slow to adopt good management practices (Webster and Hudson, 1991). Research in the service industry has lagged behind both in volume and in scope to similar activities in the manufacturing industry. Consequently, service industry executives, along with strategy scholars, have had to rely on manufacturing sector research rather than on their own well-developed body of literature to guide their strategic efforts. Like many other young disciplines that are in the process of defining and cumulating their body of knowledge, study and research in the area of strategic management have exhibited the following problems.

- The concept of strategy is a multidimensional concept that makes conducting research in this field extremely challenging. The extensive number of variables to be studied and the interdependencies among them makes it difficult to encompass all the variables in one study. Studies tend to oversimplify the multidimensionality of archetype constructs. As researchers cannot agree on the definition of strategy, they also cannot agree on operationalizing the constructs of strategy, measures for financial performance, choice of appropriate research design, and overall methodology.

- In the case of strategy research in the hospitality industry, the problem is further confounded by the very fragmented nature of an industry that is characterized by many thousands of business units. These units can be individually owned and/or parts of corporate chains and management companies. This fragmentation, coupled with a wide variety of brands and segments, makes it very difficult to conduct large-scale studies that are designed to contribute important theoretical frameworks to enhance our understanding of this industry (Olsen and Roper, 1998). Furthermore, the impact of strategy is longitudinal and most studies have the constraints of time and resources and thus are cross-sectional in nature.

- As the service sector started to gain momentum in the 1980s, research studies examining the application of strategic management in the hospitality firms began to emerge. The concepts and models tested in these studies have been primarily borrowed from the proven concepts in strategy management that were developed based on the manufacturing industry, which uses product-oriented terms. However, the service industry is fundamentally different from the manufacturing industry with the key elements being that of labor intensity, customer interaction, and service customization. As some researchers have pointed out, the strategy for the service industry is different than those of manufacturing and that the characteristics of services have important implications for strategic planning (Thomas, 1978; Carmen and Langeard, 1980; Schmenner, 1986). Moreover, Habib and Victor (1991) indicated that service multinational corporations (MNCs) appear to be different from manufacturing MNCs in terms of a fit-performance relationship. Thus, the findings of these research studies leave the researchers not certain whether the theories apply. Tse and Olsen (1988) found that 'statistical analysis indicated that findings were inconclusive to validate Porter's model'. This conclusion is shared by other research studies (West, 1988; Dev, 1989). Thus, there is a gap in knowledge between the research studies in the manufacturing and service industries and a lack of theory construction in the area of strategic management.

FUTURE RESEARCH ISSUES

Olsen (2004) stated that 'the field of strategy in hospitality is rich with relationships yet to be investigated'. The following is a sample of issues that warrant further research efforts.

Multidimensional constructs

Much of the research reported here has focused upon traditional constructs of the strategy paradigm such as environmental analysis, strategy formulation, strategic planning, and the strategy–structure–performance relationship. These mostly unidimensional views and research in strategy offer limited perspectives on how strategy really functions in the competitive marketplace. Thus, contemporary strategic management literature attempts to offer a more dynamic viewpoint. It takes into account the fact that organizations tend to prosper in highly changeable environments when they sustain states of instability, contradiction, contention, and creative tension in order to provoke new perspectives and continual learning (Hamel and Prahalad, 1994). It is in this direction that future research into strategy in the hospitality industry should proceed. Pursuing this direction is more complex, requiring less prescriptive fine-grained research and favoring more qualitative methods designed to reach deep into the internal workings of organizations. This will yield a more authentic, real worldview of strategy in the contemporary marketplace (Olsen and Roper, 1998).

Longitudinal studies

There is a need for rigorous research studies and a more speculative approach. Future research should go beyond a simple extrapolation from previous/current work in the field by suggesting alternative perspectives and approaches and propose contemporary issues that may have not been explored in the field. In order to further the understanding of the concept of strategy, other relevant variables and the impact on performance in the service setting, efforts are needed in the area of theory construction.

The aim is to develop new paradigms that would reflect the unique characteristics of the service industry. It is believed that systematic, longitudinal research on strategy and its impact on financial performances as well as a larger sample may show some significant differences in hypothesis testing.

Strategy implementation

Future research is also needed as there has been very little research into strategy implementation in relation to firms in the hospitality industry (Okumus, 2001). Studying strategy implementation in the context of the co-alignment model is one area where hospitality researchers could really contribute to mainstream strategic management literature. It is at the regional/divisional or unit level where strategy is most often operationalized. More research studies are called for to validate Brotherton and Adlers' (1999) 'Strategic Constellation' model, which considers cultural influences and strategic orientations and integrates the alignment concept and resource-based approaches.

International scope

Limited research has been conducted to examine the concept of strategy in the international arena. Research in strategic management has been developed primarily in the context of the developed world and has focused on organizations and corporations that dominate the business environment, especially organizations which have enjoyed large market capitalizations and excellent market share. The forces that drive change in developing countries are many and varied and often differ from a Western perspective. These same organizations, when they have decided to expand internationally, became interesting to those researchers looking at international strategy.

For many decades the international hotel industry has been dominated by large US lodging chains that expanded throughout the world by following a set prescription to cater to the wishes of United States' business executives traveling abroad. However, this trend is changing. Although room supply in the United States has stabilized over the past five years, the hotel industry in China is in an accelerated growth phase with numerous international competitors vying to establish and increase their presence in what is seen as a growth market. In the past 15 years, there has been an emergence of European, Asiatic, and other international ownership. While strategic management is relatively well conceptualized and gaining momentum in hospitality and tourism, the literature focuses largely on the Western world and is built on the body of knowledge developed from the manufacturing sector. Service organizations have different needs, markets, and competitive situations that they are in need of models to help them compete and maintain effectiveness (Olsen, Tse and West, 1999). These unique attributes include: intangibility, simultaneity of production and consumption, heterogeneity, and perishability.

A firm must align its approach to globalization with its strategy. The firm's internal context must be appropriate for its strategy. This means that an international firm's organization design must accommodate the specific challenges that operating across national boundaries pose. These challenges can be grouped into three categories: local responsiveness, global efficiency, and learning in a global context. Although the scale and scope of changes in globalization are obvious, the implications for managers who develop firm strategy are less clear. Thus, strategy research has provided little insight into how globalization will impact the strategies of firms in the developing world. For example, little research is available to explain the impact upon businesses of the convergence of the three Chinas (People's Republic, Taiwan, Hong Kong). The implications for strategic management research are that firms from different countries will vary in their characteristic approaches to strategy. Future hospitality strategic management research needs to investigate firms from other cultural foundations, whose objectives and context might be more complex than the simplicities of profit maximization and perfect markets. In addition, the use of alternative strategic management frameworks will be a necessity.

Strategic management in small firms

Strategic management is vital for large firms' success, but what about small firms? The strategic management process is just as vital for small companies. From their inception, all organizations have a strategy, even if the strategy just evolves from day-to-day operations.

Widespread corporate layoffs have contributed to an explosion in small businesses and new ideas. The lack of strategic management knowledge is a serious obstacle for many small business owners. There is also a lack of both sufficient capital to exploit external opportunities and a day-to-day cognitive frame of reference. As a result, strategic management in small firms is more informal than in large firms, but small firms that engage in strategic management outperform those that do not.

Moreover, small firms are notoriously limited in their efforts at information gathering and formal planning (Pelham, 1999). For instance, Hills and Narayana (1989) found that many small firms do not conduct market research nor value it. Small firms also tend to lack strategic thinking (Sexton and Van Auken, 1982) and a long-term orientation (Gilmore, 1971). Small businesses are also especially susceptible to environmental influences (Covin and Slevin, 1989) and are obliged to compete in a constantly changing and increasingly competitive business environment (Kean et al., 1998). Moreover, the limited resources available to small firms may exacerbate the effect of the competitive environment on performance (Pelham, 1999). Miles et al. (2000) caution that the findings of many empirical studies adopting samples of medium-to-large firms may not be pertinent to the management of small firms. In addition, Prescott (1986) contends that the relationship between environment, strategy and performance needs to be further studied. Covin and Slevin (1989) suggest that such studies should be especially focused on various small businesses and pertain to the use of effective managerial practices in differing environments.

CONCLUSIONS

Organizations are subject to ever-increasing change in the economy, increasingly demanding customers, the ever-changing workforce, rapidly changing technology and communications, as well as a growing volume of new laws and regulations. The hotel industry is extremely dynamic and in a continuous state of change. To succeed and outlast the competition, hoteliers must not only have the ability to accurately estimate changes in the environment, but also an appreciation of the impact the external environment may have on the firm. There is a need for hospitality managers to anticipate and adapt efficiently to changes and respond positively in their efforts to ensure long-term success. Moreover, strategy involves the creation of fit between a company's varied activities. Companies need to focus on their core competencies, what they do best, and on what differentiates them from the competition. They should also search for ways to expand beyond their existing resources through licensing arrangements, strategic alliances, partnerships and supplier relationships. Success is more likely where managerial decisions are theory based, rather than being founded on mere hunch or intuition, and draw on a body of empirically established evidence to make informed business decisions.

REFERENCES

Aldrich, H. and Pfeffer, J. (1976) 'Environments of organizations', *Annual Review of Sociology*, 2: 70–105.

Aldrich, H., McKelvey, B. and Ulrich, D. (1984) 'Design strategy from a population perspective', *Journal of Management*, 10: 67–86.

Anoymous. (2002) 'Drive change or cultivate it?', *Strategic Direction*, 18(6): 17–19.

Ansoff, H., Avner, J., Brandenburg, R., Portner, F. and Radosevich, R. (1970) 'Does planning pay? The effect of planning on success of acquisitions in American firms', *Long Range Planning*, 3: 2–7.

Auster, E. and Choo, C. W. (1993) 'Environmental scanning by CEOs in two Canadian industries', *Journal of the American Society for Information Science*, 44(4): 194–203.

Barnett, W. P., Greve, H. R. and Park, D. Y. (1994) 'An evolutionary model of organizational performance', *Strategic Management Journal*, 15: 11–28.

Barney, J. B. (1991) 'Firm resources and sustained competitive advantage', *Journal of Management*, 17: 99–120.

Beal, R. M. and Yasai-Ardekani, M. (2000) 'Performance implications of aligning CEO financial experiences with competitive strategies', *Journal of Management*, 26 (4): 733–762.

Becherer, R. C. and Maurer, J. G. (1997) 'The moderating effect of environmental variables on the entrepreneurial and marketing orientation of entrepreneur-led firms', *Entrepreneurship Theory and Practice*, 22(1): 47–58.

Becker, C. (2000) 'Service recovery strategies: the impact of cultural differences', *Journal of Hospitality and Tourism Research*, 24(4): 526–538.

Bluedorn, A. C. (1993) 'Pilgrim's progress: trends and convergence in research on organizational size and environments', *Journal of Management*, 19: 163–191.

Bourgeois, L. J. (1980) 'Strategy and environment: a conceptual integration', *Academy of Management Review*. 5 (1): 25–39.

Bourgeois, L. J. (1985) 'Strategic goals, perceived uncertainty, and economic performance in volatile environments', *Academy of Management Journal*, 28: 548–573.

Bracker, J. (1980) 'The historical development of the strategic management concept', *Academy of Management Review*, 5(2): 219–224.

Brittain, J. W. and Freeman, J. (1980) 'Organizational proliferation and density dependent selection'. In J. R. Kimberly and R. Miles (eds). *The Organizational Life Cycle*. San Francisco: Jossey-Bass. pp. 291–338.

Brotherton, B. and Adler, G. (1999) 'An integrative approach to enhancing customer value and corporate performance in the international hotel industry', *International Journal of Hospitality Management*, 18(3): 261–272.

Brotherton, B. and Shaw, J. (1996) 'Towards an identification and classification of critical success factors in UK Hotels Plc', *International Journal of Hospitality Management*, 15(2): 113–135.

Brotherton, B. (2004a) 'Critical success factors in UK corporate hotels', *The Services Industry Journal*, 24(3): 19–42.

Brotherton, B. (2004b) 'Critical success factors in UK budget hotel operations', *International Journal of Operations and Production Management*, 24(9): 944–969.

Bruce, T. and Hinkin, T. (1994) 'Transformational leaders in the hospitality industry', *Cornell Hotel and Restaurant Administration Quarterly*, 35(2): 18–24.

Burgess, C., Hampton, A. and Roper, A. (1995) 'International hotel groups: what makes them successful?', *International Journal of Contemporary Hospitality Management*, 7(2/3): 74–80.

Burns, T. and Stalker, G. M. (1961) *The Management of Innovation*. London: Tavistock.

Buzzell, R. D., Gale B. T. and Sultan, R. G. (1975) 'Market share – a key to profitability', *Harvard Business Review*, February: 97–106.

Byrne, J. (1992) 'Management's new gurus', *Business Week*, August 31: 44–52.

Byrne, J. (1996) 'Strategic planning: it's back!', *Business Week*, August 26: 46–52.

Canas, J. (1982) 'Strategic corporate planning'. In R. C. Lewis, T. J. Beggs, M. Shaw and S. A. Croffoot (eds).

The Practice of Hospitality Management II. Westport, CT: AVI Publishing. pp. 31–36.

Carmen, J. M. and Langeard, E. (1980) 'Growth strategies for service firms', *Strategic Management Journal*, 1: 7–22.

Castrogiovanni, G. J. (1991) 'Environmental munificence: a theoretical assessment', *Academy of Management Review*, 16: 542–565.

Chandler, A. D. (1962) *Strategy and Structure: Chapters in the history of the industrial enterprise*. Cambridge, MA: The MIT Press.

Chathoth, P. K. and Olsen, M. D. (2003a) Testing and developing the environment risk construct in hospitality strategy research, *Proceedings, International CHRIE Conference and Exposition*, pp. 57–62.

Chathoth, P. K. and Olsen, M. D. (2003b) 'Organizational leadership and strategy in the hospitality industry', *Journal of Services Research*, 2(1): 5–30.

Cho, W. (1996) A case study: Creating and sustaining competitive advantage through an information technology application in the lodging industry. Unpublished doctoral dissertation, Virginia Polytechnic Institute and State University, Blacksburg, Virginia.

Chung, L. H. and Gibbons, P. T. (1997) 'Corporate entrepreneurship: the roles of ideology and social capital', *Group and Organization Management*, 22(1): 10–30.

Conant, J. S., Mokwa, M. P. and Varadarajan, P. R. (1990) 'Strategic types, distinctive marketing competencies and organizational performance: a multiple measures-based study', *Strategic Management Journal*, 11: 365–383.

Costa, J. and Teare, R. (1994) 'Environmental scanning: a tool for competitive advantage'. In R. Kotas, R. Teare, J. Logie, C. Jayawardena and J. Bowen (eds) *The International Hospitality Business*. London: Cassell. pp. 12–20.

Coulter, M. K. (2002) *Strategic Management in Action*. Upper Saddle River: NJ: Prentice Hall.

Covin, J. G. and Slevin, D. P. (1986) 'The development and testing of an organization-level entrepreneurship scale'. In R. Ronstadt et al. (eds). *Frontiers of Entrepreneurship Research*. Wellesley, MA: Babson College. pp. 628–639.

Covin, J. G. and Slevin, D. P. (1989) 'Strategic management of small firms in hostile and benign environments', *Strategic Management Journal*, 10: 75–87.

Covin, J. G. and Slevin, D. P. (1990) 'New venture strategic posture, structure, and performance: an industry life cycle analysis', *Journal of Business Venturing*, 5(2): 123–135.

Covin, J. G., Slevin, D. P. and Schultz, R. L. (1994) 'Implementing strategic missions: effective strategic, structural and tactical choices', *Journal of Management Studies*, 31(4): 481–505.

Crawford-Welch, S. (1991) An empirical examination of mature service environments and high-performance strategies within those environments: The case of the lodging and restaurant industries, unpublished doctoral dissertation, Virginia Polytechnic Institute and State University, Blacksburg, Virginia.

Crook, T. R., Ketchen, D. J. Jr. and Snow, C. C. (2003) 'Competitive edge: a strategic management model', *Cornell Hotel and Restaurant Administration Quarterly*, 44(3): 44–53.

Cummings, S. (1993) 'Brief case: the first strategists', *Long Range Planning*, 26(3): 133–135.

Daft, R. L. and Weick, K. E. (1984) 'Toward a model of organizations as interpretation systems', *Academy of Management Review*, 9: 284–295.

Daft, R. L., Sormunen, J. and Parks, D. (1988) 'Chief executive scanning, environmental characteristics, and company performance: an empirical study', *Strategic Management Journal*, 9: 123–139.

Davies, H. and Ellis P. (2000) 'Porter's competitive advantage of nations: time for the final judgment', *Journal of Management Studies*, 37(8): 1189–1213.

de Chabert, J. (1997) Core competencies and competitive advantage in the casual theme restaurant industry: A case study. unpublished doctoral dissertation, Virginia Polytechnic Institute and State University, Blacksburg, Virginia.

DeNoble, A. and Olsen, M. D. (1982) 'The relationship between the strategic planning process and the service delivery system'. In A. Pizam, R. Lewis, and P. Manning (eds). *The Practice of Hospitality Management*. Westport, CT: AVI Publishing. pp. 229–236.

DeNoble, A. F. and Olsen, M.D. (1986) 'The foodservice industry environment: market volatility analysis', *F.I.U. Hospitality Review*, 4(2): 89–100.

Dess, G. G. and Beard, D. W. (1984) 'Dimensions of organizational task environments', *Administrative Science Quarterly*, 29: 52–73.

Dess, G. G., Ireland, D. R. and Hitt, M. A. (1990) 'Industry effects and strategic management research', *Journal of Management*, 16: 7–27.

Dess, G. G., Lumpkin, G. T. and Covin, J. G. (1997) 'Entrepreneurial strategy making and firm performance: tests of contingency and configurational models', *Strategic Management Journal*, 18(9): 677–695.

Dev, C. S. (1989) 'Operating environment and strategy: the profitable connection', *Cornell Hotel and Restaurant Administration Quarterly*, 30: 9–13.

Dev, C. S. and Klein, S. (1993) 'Strategic alliances in the hotel industry', *Cornell Hotel and Restaurant Administration Quarterly*, 34(1): 42–46.

Dev, C. and Olsen, M. D. (1989) 'Environmental uncertainty, business strategy and financial performance: an empirical study of the U.S. lodging industry', *Hospitality Education and Research Journal*, 13(3): 171–180.

Drazin, R. and Van de Ven, A. H. (1985) 'Alternative forms of fit in contingency theory', *Administrative Science Quarterly*, 300: 514–539.

Drucker, P. (1985) *Innovation and Entrepreneurship*. New York: Harper and Row.

Ebrahimi, B. P. (2000) 'Perceived strategic uncertainty and environmental scanning behavior of Hong Kong Chinese executives', *Journal of Business Research*, 49(1): 67–77.

Eccles, G. and Teare, R. (1996) 'Integrating strategy and structure: perspectives and challenges for hospitality managers'. In R. Kotas, R. Teare, J. Logie, C. Jayawardena and J. Bowen (eds). *The International Hospitality Business*. London: Cassell. pp. 42–51.

Echols, A. E. and Neck, C. P. (1998) 'The impact of behaviors and structure on corporate entrepreneurial success', *Journal of Managerial Psychology*, 13(1/2): 38–46.

Elwood, C. M. and Tse, E. C. (1991) 'Strategic implications of organizational decline in the hospitality industry', *SECHRIE Research and Review Journal*, 3(1): 1–14.

Elwood-Williams, C. and Tse, C. Y. (1995) 'The relationship between strategy and entrepreneurship: the U.S. restaurant sector', *International Journal of Contemporary Hospitality Management*, 7(1): 22–26.

Erstad, M. (2001) 'Commitment to excellence at the Forte Hotel Group', *International Journal of Contemporary Hospitality Management*, 13(7): 347–351.

Feltenstein, T. (1992) 'Strategic planning for the 1990s: exploiting the inevitable', *Cornell Hotel and Restaurant Administration Quarterly*, 50–54.

Galbraith, J. R. (1977) *Organization design*. Reading, MA: Addison-Wesley.

Gerloff, E. A., Muir, N. K. and Bodensteiner, W. D. (1991) 'Three components of perceived environmental uncertainty: an exploratory analysis of the effects of aggregation', *Journal of Management*, 17: 749–768.

Gilmore, F. (1971) 'Formulating strategy in small companies', *Harvard Business Review*, 47: 71–83.

Goodnow, J. D. and Hansz, J. E. (1972) 'Environmental determinants of overseas market entry strategies', *Journal of International Business Studies*, 3(1): 33–50.

Goold, M. and Quinn, J. J. (1990) 'The paradox of strategic controls', *Strategic Management Journal*, 11: 43–57.

Gregersen, H. B., Morrison, A. J. and Black, J. S. (1998) 'Developing leaders for the global frontier', *Sloan Management Review*, Fall: 21–32.

Griffin, R. K. (1994) Critical success factors of lodging yield management systems: An empirical study. Unpublished doctoral dissertation, Virginia Polytechnic Institute and State University, Blacksburg, Virginia.

Habib, M. and Victor, B. (1991) 'Strategy, structure and performance of U.S. manufacturing and service MNCs: a comparative analysis', *Strategic Management Journal*, 12: 589–606.

Hambrick, D. C. (1980) 'Operationalizing the concept of business-level strategy in research', *Academy of Management Review*, 5(4): 567–575.

Hambrick, D. C. (1981) 'Specialization of environmental scanning activities among upper level executive', *Journal of Management Studies*, 18: 299–320.

Hambrick, D. C. (1982) 'Environmental scanning and organizational strategy', *Strategic Management Journal*, 3(2): 159–174.

Hambrick, D. C. (1983) 'Some tests of the effectiveness and functional attributes of Miles and Snow's strategic types', *Academy of Management Journal*, 2(1): 5–26.

Hambrick, D. C. and Mason, P. A. (1984) 'Upper echelons: the organization as a reflection of its top managers', *Academy of Management Review*, 9: 193–206.

Hamel, G. (1996) 'Strategy as revolution', *Harvard Business Review*, July–August: 69–82.

Hamel, G. and Prahalad. (1994) *Competing for the Future*. Boston, MA: Harvard Business School Press.

Harrison, J. S. (2003) 'Strategic analysis for the hospitality industry', *Cornell Hotel and Restaurant Administration Quarterly*, 44(2): 139–152.

Hart, S. (1992) 'An integrative framework for strategy-making processes', *Academy of Management Review*, 17: 327–351.

Hazard, R., O'Rourke-Hayes, L. and Olsen, M. D. (1992) 'Going global – acting local: the challenge of Choice International'. In R. Teare and M. D. Olsen (eds). *International Hospitality Management*. London: Pitman Publishing. pp. 91–94.

Henderson, B. D. (1989) 'The origin of strategy', *Harvard Business Review*, 67(6): 139–143.

Herold, D. (1972) 'Long range planning and organizational performance: a cross-validation study', *Academy of Management Journal*, 15: 91–104.

Hills, G. E. and Narayana, C. L. (1989) 'Profile characteristics, success factors, and marketing in highly successful firms'. In R. H. Brockhaus et al. (eds). *Frontiers of Entrepreneurship research: Proceedings of the Babson College Conference on Entrepreneurship*. Boston College: Wellesley, MA.

Hinterhuber, H. H. and Popp, W. (1992) 'Are you a strategist or just a manager?', *Harvard Business Review*, January–February: 105–113.

Hofer, C. W. and Schendel, D. (1978) *Strategy Formulation: Analytical Concepts*. St. Paul, MN: West Publishing.

Hofstede, G. (1980) *Culture's Consequences*. Beverly Hills, CA: Sage Publications.

Ishak, N. (1990) An exploratory study of human resource management and business strategy in multiunit restaurant firms, unpublished doctoral dissertation, Virginia Polytechnic Institute and State University, Blacksburg, Virginia.

Jain, S. C. (1984) 'Environmental scanning in U.S. corporations', *Long Range Planning*, 17: 117–128.

Jennings, D. F. and Lumpkin, J. R. (1992) 'Insights between environmental scanning activities and Porter's generic strategies: an empirical analysis', *Journal of Management*, 18(4): 791–803.

Jogaratnam, G. (1996) Environmental munificence, strategic posture and performance: An empirical survey of independent restaurant, unpublished doctoral dissertation, Virginia Polytechnic Institute and State University, Blacksburg, Virginia.

Jogaratnam, G. (2002) 'Entrepreneurial orientation and environmental hostility: an assessment of small independent restaurant businesses', *Journal of Hospitality and Tourism Research*, 26(3): 258–277.

Jorgaratnam, G. and Tse, E. C. (2004) 'The entrepreneurial approach to hotel operation: evidence from the Asia-Pacific hotel industry', *Cornell Hotel and Restaurant Administrative Quarterly*, 45(3): 248–259.

Jogaratnam, G., Tse, E. C. and Olsen, M. D. (1999a) 'Strategic posture, environmental munificence, and performance: an empirical study of independent restaurants', *Journal of Hospitality and Tourism Research*, 23(2): 118–138.

Jogaratnam, G., Tse, E. C. and Olsen, M. D. (1999b) 'An empirical analysis of entrepreneurship and performance in the restaurant industry', *Journal of Hospitality and Tourism Research*, 23(4): 339–353.

Jogaratnam, G., Tse, E. C. and Olsen, M. D. (1999c) 'Matching strategy with performance: how independent restaurateurs' competitive tactics relate to their success', *Cornell Hotel and Restaurant Administration Quarterly*, 40(4): 91–95.

Kean, R., Gaskill, L., Leistritz, L., Jasper, C., Bastow-Shoop, H., Jolly, L. and Sternquist, B. (1998) 'Effects of community characteristics, business environment and competitive strategies on rural retail business performance', *Journal of Small Business Management*, 36(2): 45–57.

Keegan, W. J. (1974) 'Multinational scanning: a study of the information sources utilized by headquarters' executives in multinational companies', *Administrative Science Quarterly*, 19(September): 411–421.

Khandwalla, P. N. (1976–77) 'Some top management styles, their context and performance', *Organization and Administrative Sciences*, 7(4): 21–51.

Kim, C. Y., (1992) Development of a framework for identification of political environmental issues faced by multinational hotel chains in newly industrialized countries in Asia, unpublished doctoral dissertation, Virginia Polytechnic Institute and State University, Blacksburg, Virginia.

Kim, B. Y. and Oh, H. (2004) 'How do hotels firms obtain a competitive advantage?', *International Journal of Contemporary Hospitality Management*, 16(1): 65–71.

Koberg, C. S. (1987) 'Resource scarcity, environmental uncertainty, and adaptive organizational behavior', *Academy of Management Journal*, 30: 798–807.

Kogut, B. (1985) 'Designing global strategies: profiting from operational flexibility', *Sloan Management Review*, 26(4): 15–28.

Kumar, K., Subramanian, R. and Strandholm, K. (2001) 'Competitive strategy, environmental scanning and performance: a context specific analysis of their relationship', *International Journal of Commerce and Management*, 11(1): 1–33.

Kwock, Y. S. and Tse, E. (2002) 'Strategic management in the lodging and restaurant industry: Environment, strategy implementation and performance', *International Journal of Tourism Sciences*, 2(1): 85–104.

Lamont, B. T., Marlin, D. and Hoffman, J. J. (1993) 'Porter's generic strategies, discontinuous environments and performance: a longitudinal study of changing strategies in the hospital industry', *Health Services Research*, 28(5): 623–640.

Langton, B. D., Bottorff, C. and Olsen, M. D. (1992) 'The strategy, structure, environment co-alignment. In R. Teare and M. D. Olsen (eds). *International Hospitality Management*. London: Pitman Publishing. pp. 31–35.

Lawrence, P. R. and Lorsch, J. W. (1967) *Organization and the environment*. Boston: Division of Research, Graduate School of Business Administration, Harvard University.

Lenz, R. T. and Engledow, J. (1986) 'Environmental analysis units and strategic decision-making: A field study of selected leading-edge corporations', *Strategic Management Journal*, 7: 69–79.

Leontides, M. (1982) 'Choosing the right manager to fit the strategy', *Journal of Business Strategy*, 2: 58–69.

Levitt, R. (1983) 'The globalization of markets', *Harvard Business Review*, May–June: 92–102.

Li, L. and Tse, E. C. (2005) *The Relationship between strategic planning and entrepreneurial business* orientation, *Bridging the Gap: Entrepreneurship in theory and Practice EDGE Conference*, organized by Singapore Management University, Singapore, July 11–13.

Lumpkin, G. T. and Dess, G. G. (1996) 'Clarifying the entrepreneurial orientation construct and linking it to performance', *Academy of Management Review*, 21(1): 135–172.

McNeilly, M. (1996) *Sun Tzu and the Art of Business: Six Strategic Principles for Managers'*. Oxford: Oxford University Press.

McGahan, A. and Porter, M. (1997) 'How much does industry matter, really?' *Strategic Management Journal*, 18, Special issue, Summer: 15–30.

Manu, F. A. and Sriram, V. (1996) 'Innovation, marketing strategy, environment, and performance', *Journal of Business Research*, 35: 79–91.

Miles, R. E. and Snow, C. C. (1978) *Organizational strategy, structure and process*. New York: McGraw-Hill.

Miles, M. P., Covin, J. G. and Heeley, M. B. (2000) 'The relationship between environmental dynamism and small firm structure, strategy and performance', *Journal of Marketing Theory and Practice*, 8(2): 63–78.

Miles, R. E., Snow, C. C. and Pfeffer, J. (1974) 'Organization–environment: Concepts and issues', *Industrial Relations*, 13: 244–264.

Miller, D. (1983) 'The correlates of entrepreneurship in the three types of firms', *Management Science*, 29(7): 770–791.

Miller, D. (1986) 'Configurations of strategy and structure: towards a synthesis', *Strategic Management Journal*, 7: 233–249.

Miller, D. (1988) 'Relating Porter's business strategies to environment and structure: Analysis and performance implications', *Academy of Management Journal*, 31: 280–308.

Miller, D. (1991) 'Stale in the saddle: CEO tenure and the match between organization and environment', *Management Science*, 37: 34–52.

Miller, D. and Friesen, P. H. (1982) 'Strategy-making and environment: the third link', *Strategic Management Journal*, 4(3): 221–235.

Miller, D. and Toulouse, J. M. (1986) 'Chief executive personality and corporate strategy and structure in small firms', *Management Science*, 32: 1389–1409.

Miller, D., Kets de Vries, M. F. R. and Toulouse, J. M. (1982) 'Top executive locus of control and its relationship to strategy making, structure and environment', *Academy of Management Journal*, 25: 237–253.

Mintzberg, H. (1973) 'Strategy-making in three modes', *California Management Review*, 16(2): 44–53.

Mintzberg, H. (1975) 'The manager's job: Folklore and fact', *Harvard Business Review*, July–August: 49–61.

Mintzberg, H. (1979) *The structuring of organizations*. Englewood Cliffs, New Jersen: Prentice-Hall.

Mintzberg, H. (1990) 'The design school: Reconsidering the basic premises of strategic management', *Strategic Management Journal*, 11: 171–195.

Mintzberg, H., Ahlstrand, B. and Lampel, J. (1998) *Strategy safari: A Guided tour through the wilds of strategic management*. New York: Free Press.

Monga, R. (1996) Strategic alliances in the lodging industry: A multi-case study, unpublished doctoral dissertation, Virginia Polytechnic Institute and State University, Blacksburg, Virginia.

Murthy, B. (1994) Measurement of the strategy construct in the lodging industry and the strategy–performance relationship, unpublished doctoral dissertation, Virginia Polytechnic Institute and State University, Blacksburg, Virginia.

Nahavandi, A. and Malekzadeh, A. R. (1993) 'Leadership style in strategy and organizational performance: an integrative framework', *Journal of Management Studies*, 30: 405–425.

Nanus, B. and Lundberg, C. (1988) 'In quest of strategic planning', *Cornell Hotel and Restaurant Administration Quarterly*, August: 18–23.

Nath, D. and Sudharshan, D. (1994) 'Measuring strategy coherence through patterns of strategic choices', *Strategic Management Journal*, 15: 43–61.

Okumus, F. (2001) 'Towards a strategy implementation framework', *International Journal of Contemporary Hospitality Management*, 13(7): 327–339.

Okumus, F. (2004) 'Potential challenges of employing a formal environmental scanning approach in hospitality organizations', *International Journal of Hospitality Management*, 23(2): 123–143.

Olsen, M. D. (2000) 'Strategic formulation'. In J. Jafari and A. Pizam (eds) *Encyclopedia of Tourism*. New York: Routledge. 562.

Olsen, M. D. (2004) 'Literature in strategic management in the hospitality industry', *International Journal of Hospitality Management*, 23: 411–424.

Olsen, M. D. and Bellas, C. J. (1980) 'Managing growth in the 1980s: a blueprint for food service survival', *Cornell Hotel and Restaurant Administration Quarterly*, 21(2): 23–26.

Olsen, M. D. and DeNoble, A. (1981) 'Strategic planning in a dynamic environment', *Cornell Hotel Restaurant and Administration Quarterly*, 21(4): 75–80.

Olsen, M. D. and Roper, A. (1998) 'Research in strategic management in the hospitality industry', *International Journal of Hospitality Management*, 17(2): 111–124.

Olsen, M. D., Murthy, B. and Teare, R. (1994) 'CEO perspectives on scanning the global hotel business environment', *International Journal of Contemporary Hospitality Management*, 6(4): 3–9.

Olsen, M. D., Tse, E. C. and West, J. J. (1999) *Strategic management in the hospitality industry*. New York: John Wiley and Sons.

Olsen, M. D., et al. (1995) *Into the new millennium: A white paper on the global hospitality industry*. Paris: published by the International Hotel Association.

Olsen, M. D., Sharma, A., Echeveste, I. and Tse, E. C. (2005) 'Strategy for hospitality businesses in the developing world – are current concepts relevant in today's complex and dynamic environment?' *Proceedings, International CHRIE Conference and Exposition*, Las Vegas, July 27–31.

Parsa, H. (1994) Exploratory investigation of organization power and its impact on strategy implementation and firm performance: A study of the hospitality franchise systems, unpublished doctoral dissertation, Virginia Polytechnic Institute and State University, Blacksburg, Virginia.

Pelham, A. M. (1999) 'Influence of environment, strategy and market orientation on performance in small manufacturing firms', *Journal of Business Research*, 45: 33–46.

Peng, W. and Litteljohn, D. (2001) 'Organizational communication and strategy implementation – a primary inquiry', *International Journal of Contemporary Hospitality Management*, 13(7): 360–363.

Pfeffer, J. and Salancik, G. (1978) *The External Control of Organizations*. New York: Harper and Row.

Pine, R. (2002) 'China's hotel industry: Serving a massive market', *Cornell Hotel and Restaurant Administration Quarterly*, 43(3): 61–70.

Porter, M. (1980) *Competitive Strategy: Techniques of analyzing industries and competitors*. New York: Free Press.

Porter, M. E. (1987) 'From competitive advantage to corporate strategy', *Harvard Business Review*, 65(3): 43–59.

Porter, M. (1990) *The competitive advantage of nations*. London: The Macmillan Press.

Porter, M. E. (1996) 'What is strategy?', *Harvard Business Review*, November–December: 61–78.

Powell, T. C. (1992) 'Strategic planning as competitive advantage', *Strategic Management Journal*, 13: 551–558.

Prahalad, C. K. and Hamel, G. (1990) 'The core competence of the corporation', *Harvard Business Review*, May–June: 79–91.

Prescott, J. E. (1986) 'Environments as moderators of the relationship between strategy and performance', *Academy of Management Journal*, 29: 329–346.

Pugh, D. S. (1973) 'The measurement of organization structures: Does context determine form?' *Organizational Dynamics*, Spring: 19–34.

Reichel, A. (1982) 'Corporate strategic planning for the hospitality industry: a contingency approach'. In A. Pizam, R. C. Lewis and P. Manning (eds). *The Practice of Hospitality Management*. Westport, CT: AVI Publishing. pp. 49–63.

Reichel, A. (1986) 'Competition and barriers to entry in service industries: The case of the American lodging industry'. In A. Pizam, R. C. Lewis, and P. Manning (eds) *The Practice of Hospitality Management II*. Westport, CT: AVI Publishing. pp. 79–89.

Reid, R. and Olsen, M. D. (1981) 'A strategic planning model for independent food service operators', *Journal of Hospitality Education*, 6(1): 11–24.

Rhyne, L. (1986) 'The relationship of strategic planning to financial performance', *Strategic Management Journal*, 7: 423–436.

Rispoli, M. (1997) 'Competitive analysis and competence based strategies in the hotel industry'. *Dynamics of competence based competition*. In R. Sanchez, A. Heene and H. Thomas (eds). London: Pergamon. pp. 119–137.

Roberts, C. and Shea, L. (1996) 'Core capabilities in the hotel industry', *Hospitality Research Journal*, 19(4): 141–153.

Rosenzweig, P. M. and Singh, J. V. (1991) 'Organizational environments and the multinational enterprise', *Academy of Management Review*, 16(2): 340–361.

Rumelt, R. P. (1974) *Strategy Structure and Economic Performance*. Cambridge, MA: Division of Research, Graduate School of Business Administration, Harvard University.

Schaffer, J. D. (1986) Competitive strategy, organization structure and performance in the lodging industry: An Empirical Assessment of Miles and Snow's (1978) Perspectives of Organizations (Environment), unpublished doctoral dissertation, Virginia Polytechnic Institute and State University, Blacksburg, Virginia.

Schaffer, J. D. and Litschert, R. J. (1990) 'Internal consistency between strategy and structure: performance implications in the lodging industry', *Hospitality Research Journal*, 14(1): 35–53.

Schmelzer, C. D., (1992) A Case study investigation of strategy implementation in three multi-unit restaurant firms, unpublished doctoral dissertation, Virginia Polytechnic Institute and State University.

Schmelzer, C. and Olsen, M. D. (1994) 'A data based strategy implementation framework for companies in the restaurant industry', *International Journal of Hospitality Management*, 13(4): 347–359.

Schmenner, R. W. (1986) 'How can service businesses survive and prosper?', *Sloan Management Review*, Spring: 21–32.

Scott, W. R. (1987) *Organizations: Rational, natural and open systems*, 2nd edn. Englewood Cliffs, NJ: Prentice-Hall.

Segev, E. (1989) 'A systematic comparative analysis and synthesis of two business-level strategic typologies', *Strategic Management Journal*, 10: 487–505.

Sethi, N. K. (1982) 'Strategic planning systems for multinational companies', *Long Range Planning*, 15(3): 80–89.

Sexton, D. L. and Van Auken, P. M. (1982) 'Prevalence of strategic planning in small business', *Journal of Small Business Management*, 20(3): 20–26

Sharfman, M. P. and Dean, J. W. (1991) 'Conceptualizing and measuring the organizational environment: a multidimensional approach', *Journal of Management*, 17: 681–700.

Simons, R. (1994) 'How new top managers use control systems as levers of strategic renewal', *Strategic Management Journal*, 15: 169–189.

Slattery, P. and Boer, A. (1991) 'Strategic developments for the 1990s: implications for hotel companies'. In R. Teare and A. Boer (eds) *Strategic hospitality management: Theory and practice for the 1990s*. London: Cassell Educational Ltd. pp. 161–165.

Slattery, P. and Clark, A. (1988) 'Major variables in the corporate structure of hotel groups', *International Journal of Hospitality Management*, 7(2): 117–130.

Slevin, D. P. and Covin, J. G. (1990) 'Juggling entrepreneurial style and organizational structure – how to get your act together', *Sloan Management Review*, 31(2): 43–53.

Smart, D. T. and Conant, J. S. (1994) 'Entrepreneurial orientation, distinctive marketing competencies and organizational performance', *Journal of Applied Business Research*, 10(3): 28–38.

Snow, C. C. (1976) *The role of managerial perceptions in organizational adaptation: An exploratory study. Working Paper*. University Park, PA: Graduate School of Business, The Pennsylvania State University.

Snow, C. C. and Hrebiniak, L. G. (1980) 'Strategy, distinctive competence, and organizational performance', *Administrative Science Quarterly*, 25: 317–366.

Starbuck, W. H. (1983) 'Organizations and their environments', In M. D. Dunnette (ed). *Handbook of Organizational and Industrial Psychology*. New York: Wiley. pp. 1069–1123.

Staw, B. M. and Szwajkowski, E. (1975) 'The scarcity–munificence component of organizational environments and the commission of illegal acts', *Administrative Science Quarterly*, 20: 345–354.

Stopford, J. M. and Well, L. T. (1972) *Managing the multinational enterprise*. New York, NY: Basic Books Inc.

Subramanian, R., Fernandes, N. and Harper, E. (1993) 'An empirical examination of the relationship between strategy and scanning', *The Mid-Atlantic Journal of Business*, 29(3): 315–330.

Sullivan, D. and Bauerschmidt, A. (1991) 'The basic concepts of international business strategy: A review and reconsideration', *Management International Review*, 31 (special issue): 111–315.

Sutcliffe, K. M. (1994) 'What executives notice: Accurate perceptions in top management teams', *Academy of Management Journal*, 37: 1360–1378.

Thomas, A. S., Litschert, R. J. and Ramaswamy, K. (1991) 'The performance impact of strategy-manager coalignment: an empirical examination', *Strategic Management Journal*, 12: 509–522.

Thomas, D. R. E. (1978) 'Strategy is different in service business', *Harvard Business Review*, July–August, 158–165.

Thompson, J. D. (1967) *Organization in Action*. New York: McGraw-Hill.

Thune, S. and House, R. (1970) 'Where long-range planning pays off'. *Business Horizons*, August: 81–87.

Tiles, S. (1969) 'Making strategy explicit'. In H. I. Ansoff (ed). *Business Strategy*. Harmondsworth: Penguin.

Tse, E. C. (1988) An exploratory study of the impact of strategy and structure on the organizational performance of restaurant firms, unpublished doctoral dissertation, Virginia Polytechnic Institute and State University, Blacksburg, Virginia.

Tse, E. C. (1991) 'An empirical analysis of organizational structure and financial performance in the restaurant industry', *International Journal of Hospitality Management*, 9: 287–299.

Tse, E. C. (1992) 'Organization structure in the hospitality industry'. In M. A. Khan, M. D. Olsen and T. Var (eds). *VNR's Encyclopedia of Hospitality and Tourism*. New York: Van Nostrand Reinhold. pp. 347–353.

Tse, E. C. and Elwood, C. M. (1990) 'Synthesis of the life cycle concept with strategy and management style: a case analysis in the hospitality industry', *International Journal of Hospitality Management*, 9(3): 223–236.

Tse, E. C. and Olsen, M. D. (1988) 'The impact of strategy and structure on the organizational performance of restaurant firms', *Hospitality Education and Research Journal*, 12(2): 57–72.

Tse, E. C. and Olsen, M. D., (1990) 'Business strategy and structure: a case of U.S. restaurant firms', *International Journal of Contemporary Hospitality Management*, 2(3): 17–23.

Tse, E. C. and Olsen, M. D. (1999) 'Strategic Management'. In R. Brotherton (ed). *The Handbook* of Contemporary Hospitality Management. New York: John Wiley and Sons. pp. 351–374.

Tse, E. C. and West, J. (1992) 'Development strategies for international markets'. In R. Teare and M. D. Olsen (eds). International Hospitality Management. London: Pitman Publishing. pp. 118–134.

Turnbull, D. R., (1996) The influence of political risk events on the investment decisions of multinational hotel companies in caribbean hotel projects (Tourism), unpublished doctoral dissertation, Virginia Polytechnic Institute and State University, Blacksburg, Virginia.

Twomey, D. F. (2002) 'Organizational competitiveness: Building performance and learning', Competitiveness Review, 12(2): 1–12.

Uttterback, J. M. (1979) 'Environmental analysis and forecasting'. In D. E. Schendel and C. W. Hofer (eds). Strategic Management: A new view of business policy and planning. Boston, MA: Little and Brown.

Venkatraman, N. (1989) 'The concept of fit in strategy research: Toward verbal and statistical correspondence', Academy of Management Review, 14(3): 423–444.

Venkatraman, N. and Prescott, J. E. (1990) 'Environment-strategy coalignment: An empirical test of its performance implications', Strategic Management Journal, 11: 1–23.

Von Neumann, J. and Morgenstern, O. (1947) Theory of Games and Economic Behavior (2nd edn.). Princeton: Princeton University.

Weber, M. (1947) The Theory of social and economic organization. New York: Free Press.

Webster, M. M. (1994) 'Strategic management in the context at Swallow hotels', International Journal of Contemporary Hospitality Management, 6(5): 3–8.

Webster, M. and Hudson, T. (1991) 'Strategic management: a theoretical overview and its application to the hospitality industry'. In R. Teare and A. Boer (eds). Strategic Hospitality Management: Theory and Practice for the 1990s. London: Cassell Educational Ltd. pp. 9–30.

Weick, K. E. (1979) The social psychology of organizing. 2nd edn. Reading, MA: Addison-Wesley.

Weinberg, L. S. (1991) Synergy among brands of multiproduct hospitality firms, unpublished dissertation, Claremont Graduate School.

Wernerfelt, B. (1984) 'A resource based view of the firm', Strategic Management Journal, 5: 171–180.

West, J. J. (1988) Strategy, environmental scanning and their effect upon firm performance: An exploratory study of the food service industry, unpublished doctoral dissertation, Virginia Polytechnic Institute and State University, Blacksburg, Virginia.

West, J. J. (1990) 'Environmental scanning and firm performance: An integration of content and process in food service industry', Hospitality Research Journal, 14: 87–100.

West, J. and Anthony, W. P. (1990) 'Strategic group membership and environmental scanning: Their relationship to firm performance in the food service industry', International Journal of Hospitality Management, 9(3): 247.

West, J. and Olsen, M. D. (1989) 'Competitive strategies in food service: Are high performers different', Cornell Hotel Restaurant and Administration Quarterly, 31(1): 68–71.

Williams, C. E. and Tse, E. C. (1995) 'The relationship between strategy and entrepreneurship: the US restaurant sector', International Journal of Contemporary Hospitality Management, 7(1): 22–26.

Wong, K. and Kwan, C. (2001) 'An analysis of the competitive strategies of hotels and travel agents in Hong Kong and Singapore', International Journal of Contemporary Hospitality Management, 13(6): 293–303.

Woods, R. H. and Sciarini, M. P. (1996) 'The role of organizational culture in service'. In R. Kotas, R. Teare, J. Logie and C. Jayawardena (eds) The International Hospitality Business. London: Cassell Educational Ltd. pp. 112–121.

Yasai-Ardekani, M. (1989) 'Effects of environmental scarcity and munificence on the relationship of context to organizational structure', Academy of Management Journal, 32: 131–156.

Yasai-Ardekani, M. and Nystrom, P. C. (1996) 'Design for environmental scanning systems: tests of a contingency theory', Management Science, 42(2): 187–204.

Zahra, S. A. (1991) 'Predictors and financial outcomes of corporate entrepreneurship: an exploratory study', Journal of Business Venturing, 6: 259–285.

Zahra, S. A. and Covin, J. G. (1995) 'Contextual influences on the corporate entrepreneurship–performance relationship: A longitudinal analysis', Journal of Business Venturing, 10(1): 43–58.

Zajac, E. J. and Shortell, S. M. (1989) 'Changing generic strategies: likelihood, direction, and performance implications', Strategic Management Journal, 10: 413–430.

Zhao, J. L. (1992) The antecedent factors and entry mode choice of multinational lodging firms: The case of growth strategies into new international markets, unpublished doctoral dissertation, Virginia Polytechnic Institute and State University, Blacksburg, VA.

Zhao, J. L. and Merna, K. (1992) 'Impact analysis and the international environment'. In R. Teare and M. D. Olsen (eds). International Hospitality Management. London: Pitman Publishing. pp. 3–32.

From the Bottom Up: Operations Management in the Hospitality Industry

Peter Jones and Andrew Lockwood

INTRODUCTION

Production and operations management (POM) is the study of how goods get made and service gets delivered. It is founded on studies of how best to organize factories manufacturing automobiles and other consumer goods. As an academic discipline it is highly applied, to the extent that some have argued that it is almost a-theoretical (Schmenner and Swink, 1998). The applied nature of operations management is further illustrated when applied to the hospitality industry. Very rarely are managers assigned job titles as 'Operations Managers'. Rather than this generic title, managers with operations responsibility are given specific roles such as Rooms Division Manager, Food and Beverage Manager, Restaurant Manager and so on.

It can be argued that hospitality has some distinctive features. For instance, Bowen and Ford (2004) conducted an extensive review of literature to see if there was evidence indicating there are differences in the management of hospitality organizations and manufacturing organizations from the perspective of organizing, staffing, and commanding. Their results indicated that there are a number of differences between managing a manufacturing firm and a hospitality firm:

- tasks have to be designed to fit with degree of interaction with the customer;
- the 'servicescape' is important (see below);
- operations must be designed to cope with high degrees of uncertainty;
- employees must be recruited with the right 'service attitude';
- internal marketing may be significant;
- employees may suffer from boundary role stress (role conflict, role ambiguity, etc.);
- customers become 'partial employees'; and
- employee empowerment, especially of front line staff, may be important.

Bowen and Ford (2004) argue this case based on asking hotel executives and managers what they thought. Since most managers think that their industry is unique in some way or another, often because they have no direct experience of any other industry, this may have biased their conclusions.

However, this chapter does not share Bowen and Ford's (2004) view. It acknowledges the importance of all of the factors listed above but argues that they are not inconsistent with operations thinking in general. The chapter deliberately sets out to explore hospitality in the context of generic operations management theory. As we shall see no other review of the research in this field has been analyzed in this way. In most cases, hospitality operations research itself, as well as reviews of this research, have been phenomenological in approach. That is to say they have been grounded in what has been investigated rather than in testing theory. These two issues – lack of theory and specific application in hospitality – leads to the major theme of this chapter, namely that the principles and concepts of operations management are poorly understood and implemented in the field of hospitality.

PRODUCTION AND OPERATIONS MANAGEMENT (POM)

Johnston (1994) defines operations management and the scope and role of operations management within an organization. He states 'operations management … is a body of knowledge, experience and techniques covering such topics as process design, layout, production planning, inventory control, quality management and control, capacity planning and workforce management' (Johnston, 1994: 21).

Until the late 1990s, operations management was a very applied subject, with very little theory. However, based on Schmenner and Swink (1998) and Johnston and Jones (2005), four main theories can be identified:

- the Theory of Swift and Even Flow (applies to all operations);
- the Theory of Materials Processing;
- the Theory of Process Improvement and Superiority (applies to materials processing operations); and
- the Theory of Service Experience (applies to customer processing operations).

Because this theory is relatively new, even in the field of operations management, there has been very little hospitality research that has explicitly investigated the theories and laws outlined. However, where such research has been conducted, it is identified below.

The theory of swift and even flow

'The Theory of Swift and Even Flow holds that the more swift and even the flow of materials through the process, the more productive the process is' (Schmenner and Swink, 1998: 102). There are four laws associated with this Theory of Swift and Even Flow:

- the law of variability 1 – the greater the randomness of the process the lower the productivity;
- the law of variability 2 – the greater the variability of the requirements of the process, the lower the productivity;
- the law of bottlenecks – the greater the difference in the rate of flow through stages in a process, the less productive the process is; and
- the law of prioritization – in operations of inherent instability, the greater the instability the greater the prioritization of orders (Westbrook, 1994).

In the hospitality industry, these laws are applied, but there has been no explicit empirical research of these.

The theory of materials processing

When processing materials productivity is enhanced by applying principles designed to eliminate waste of all kinds. The Japanese guru, Taiichi Ohno, one-time Chief Engineer for Toyota, has identified seven types of waste:

1 doing too much;
2 waiting;
3 transporting;
4 too much inflexible capacity or lack of process flexibility;
5 unnecessary stocks;
6 unnecessary motions; and
7 defects.

By tackling each of these, Japan has achieved global dominance in a wide number of industry sectors such as motorcycles and electronic goods. It can be argued that the McDonalds service delivery system, along with many others derived from this, applied many of the ideas developed by Ohno.

There are a number of laws associated with the Theory of Materials Processing:

- the law of scientific methods – labor productivity is improved by applying scientific management principles;
- the law of quality – productivity improves as quality improves since waste is eliminated. This is a controversial law that may not hold in all cases, although there is widespread anecdotal evidence that it is generally true;
- the law of limited tasks – factories that perform a limited number of tasks will be more productive than similar factories with a broad range of tasks; and
- the law of value added – a process will be more productive if non-value added steps are reduced or eliminated.

These laws, too, have been applied in industry, for instance by Taco Bell in the 1980s in redesigning their concept and units and by Ritz-Carlton in the 1990s when winning the Malcolm Baldridge Award. The Rimmington and Clark (1996) study of hospital catering is an example of research based on this theory, but there has been very little other empirical research.

The theory of process improvement and superiority

Schmenner and Swink (1998) propose a 'theory of performance frontiers' because they use a production function or performance frontier curve to illustrate this theory. However, we suggest that the substance of this theory is concerned with why some processes are more efficient and effective than others. Hence it has been renamed here the theory of process improvement and superiority. Production function methodology maps 'the maximum output that can be produced from any given set of inputs, given technical considerations' (Schmenner and Swink, 1998: 107). They expand this economic model by defining inputs to include all dimensions of manufacturing performance, as well as defining technical considerations as all choices affecting the design and operation of the manufacturing unit. They suggest, consistent with operations management thinking, that a distinction can be drawn between the 'operating frontier,' which represent operational activities within a given set of assets; and the 'asset frontier' which reflects the infrastructural elements or asset utilization of the operations. In effect, the operating frontier models the most effective and efficient use of inputs; and the asset frontier models the best design and configuration of the transformation inputs.

Within this theory there are a number of proposed laws:

- The law of cumulative capabilities – an improvement in one manufacturing capability leads to improvements in others. Schmenner and Swink (1998) suggest that such improvements are made over time. Moreover there may be certain sequences or trajectories of improvement that build one upon the other, for instance quality leads to lower cost, followed by increased speed of delivery.
- The law of diminishing returns – 'as improvement (or betterment) moves a manufacturing plant nearer and nearer to its operating frontier (or asset frontier) more and more resources must be expended in order to achieve each additional incremental benefit' (Schmenner and Swink, 1998: 110).
- The law of diminishing synergy – the law of cumulative capabilities suggest there is synergy between policies and procedures. This synergy diminishes as a plant approaches its asset frontier.

De facto, research in the hospitality field that uses data envelopment analysis is exploring this theory.

The theory of service experience

Customers are different to materials in that they sense and respond to their environment. Hence they interact with the operation and form opinions about their experience. The laws associated with the Theory of Service Experience are:

- The law of adaptive experience – a customer process is more productive when customer feedback adapts the process, both immediately (during the transaction).
- The law of matching expectations – a customer process will be more productive if customer expectations are matched by their perceptions.
- The law of cumulative effect – productive customer processes have a cumulative effect on customer expectations.

Research into the servicescape and service encounter is grounded in this theory.

Hence, there is no general agreement about the theoretical frameworks and key concepts that make up the discipline. Operations Management research and teaching is focused on the issues of process design and layout, capacity and production planning, materials and inventory control, supply chain management, workforce management and quality management (Johnston, 1994; Render and Heizer, 1997).

REVIEWS OF OPERATIONS MANAGEMENT RESEARCH IN HOSPITALITY

Although the hospitality research literature is now quite substantial, and growing rapidly, a relatively small proportion of this literature focuses on the area of operations management. For instance, in a review of research, Teare (1996) provides an overview of 'hospitality operations management' articles published in selected journals from 1989 to 1994, but in his summary of the main themes and sub-themes (sic), hospitality operations is not referred to at all. Ingram (1996: 92) in a similar review of 820 postgraduate research projects in the hospitality and tourism field, comments that in the hospitality area 'most relate to the leisure and hotel sectors while food and catering entries show a marketing or science focus and rarely relate to operational or service issues'.

Jones and Lockwood (1998) specifically explore the nature of hospitality operations management research by reviewing 143 articles from 1970 up to 1997. They divide this literature into five areas, gradually shifting from a macro perspective down to a micro perspective of hospitality operations. They start with a consideration of the industry as a whole, go on to consider research into chain and unit operations, then operating systems in accommodation and food and beverage, and conclude with a review of the operational interface between providers and customers (the so-called 'service encounter'). They draw three conclusions from this analysis. First, 'there is no lack of terminology, but various definitions, few taxonomies and alternative typologies. This can result in researchers using the same term to describe different phenomena' (Jones and Lockwood, 1998: 196). Second, a high proportion of the research is 'conceptual in nature'. Third, much of the research is 'phenomenological'. They state 'it is certainly the case that very little hospitality operations management research is related to the generic discipline of operations management or based on operations research methodologies'.

Drawing on this work, two further analyses of the literature have been published. Lockwood and Ingram (1999) reviewed research in hotel operations management, whilst Jones (1999a) considered catering operations management. Lockwood and Ingram (1999) consider 141 articles that they sub-divide into the topics of strategy and environment, property and asset management, human resources, customers and marketing, profitability and yield management, productivity and performance, service and quality, and operating systems. Jones (1999a) reviews 63 articles and categorizes these into six main areas – classification, systems design and technology, 'operations management', catering managers, menu planning and analysis, and chain development and growth.

Since these reviews of the research literature, the situation with regard to operations management research in hospitality has got worse rather than better, with even less output between 2000 and 2005 than in the preceding five years. This is demonstrated by reference to the bibliography of this chapter that cites only 65 hospitality articles from this millennium, which represents just one third of the total citations. O'Connor and Murphy (2004) reviewed research on information technology in the hospitality industry. Their perspective on its quality mirrors the comments of Jones and Lockwood (1998) made seven years earlier. O'Connor and Murphy (2004: 482) state ... 'too much of this research (in IT) is descriptive ... [and] needs more originality in both the topics addressed and the research methods used'.

Each of these earlier reviews of hospitality operations management research have been unique in terms of their analytical framework. In this chapter hospitality operations research is analyzed by specifically adopting the generic POM framework, i.e. the issues of process design and layout, capacity and production planning, materials and inventory control, supply chain management, productivity and workforce management, quality management and innovation. This approach is adopted for two reasons. First, it identifies the scope of hospitality research and therefore helps to identify the future research agenda. Second, it emphasizes the need for future operations management research to test the theories and 'laws' stated earlier.

PROCESS DESIGN AND LAYOUT

In order to understand a discipline it is usual to classify phenomena into types. The seminal work in production and operations management is that of Hayes and Wheelwright (1979). They proposed five main types of operations process – project, job shop, batch, line assembly and process flow – based on the volume of output being produced and the variety of that output. Projects (such as major construction) have very low volume and high variety, whereas process flow operations (such as brewing) have very high volumes but little or no variety. Hayes and Wheelwright's taxonomy is essentially based on manufacturing. Since this time other authors have proposed a classification of services (Schmenner, 1986) and attempted to integrate both manufacturing and service (Silvestro, Fitzgerald, Johnston and Voss, 1992).

However Morris and Johnston (1988) suggest that most operations are a combination of materials operating processes (MPOs), information processing operations (IPOs), and customer processing operations (CPO). Most manufacturing is an MPO, most financial services are IPOs, and 'consumer services' are generally considered to be CPOs. In reality nearly all operations have some combination of material, information and customer processing. This suggests that the classification schemes discussed above are too simplistic to capture the rich diversity of operations.

Hospitality process types

In hospitality a few attempts to classify operations have been made, but only one has contextualized this in relation to generic operations management theory. Jones (2002a) considered both accommodation and foodservice, developing systems models for them both. He argued that for accommodation there is a *core* system comprising four sub-systems of reservations, reception, overnight stay (housekeeping) and payment (or billing). Besides these, depending on the type of market being served there are ancillary systems that may or may not be offered. These sub-systems include laundry, restaurants, bars, business services and leisure services. Jones does not suggest how many different types of hotel arise from the potential combinations of the core system with ancillary systems, but *de facto* such a typology would resemble quite closely the typical star-rating approach to hotel classification.

In foodservice, Jones (1993, 1996a) and Huelin and Jones (1990) have made a number of attempts to classify foodservice operations based on an analysis of their systems design, technology and configuration. They identify ten sub-systems of foodservice, namely storage, preparation, cooking, holding, transport, regeneration, service, dining, clearing, and dishwash. Jones (1996a) goes on to suggest that these have been configured in a limited number of ways, within three broad categories – integrated foodservice systems, food manufacturing systems and food delivery systems.

Based on Hayes and Wheelwright (1979) and Schmenner (1986), Jones and Lockwood (2000) argue that a classification based on differentiating between 'materials processing' and 'customer processing' based operations is logical. This is also consistent with industry practice, where it is common to think in terms of 'back-of-house' (food production, housekeeping) and 'front-of-house' (restaurant,

bars and reception). It should also be noted that these operations, whether predominantly CPO or MPO, also incorporate information processing. Jones and Lockwood's (2000) classification is shown in Figure 8.1. They propose that if an operation is a hybrid, i.e. it processes customers and materials, then it should be divided into its two constituent parts and each categorized accordingly.

By comparing hospitality operations with generic types, Jones and Lockwood (2000) suggest some key aspects of hospitality operations management can be identified. These are:

1   Hotels are generally more complex than foodservice operations, simply because other than limited service hotels, they provide both lodging and foodservice.
2   Hybrid operations are more complex to manage than non-hybrid operations, because they incorporate both MPO and CPO.
3   Hospitality materials processing operations may be job shops (e.g. à la carte restaurant), batch production (e.g. cook-chill) or mass production (e.g. fast food).
4   Most hospitality customer processing operations are service shops (e.g. table service restaurant) or mass services (e.g. fast food).
5   There is generally a relationship between volume and variety, i.e. the greater the variety the less volume produced.
6   It follows therefore that hybrid operations that are batch production MPOs are typically associated with service shop CPOs, whilst mass production matches mass service.

Trends in hospitality process design

In generic operations theory three key trends have been identified. The first is the so-called 'shift along the diagonal' from job shop (low volume, high variety) towards mass production (high volume, low variety). This has been going on throughout the twentieth century and is epitomized by Henry Ford's development of automobile manufacturing. The second is automation, which is the gradual replacement of a human workforce with machines such as computers and robots. And the third trend is a shift away from the diagonal towards mass customization (high volume *and* high variety) made possible through so-called agile manufacturing, just-in-time techniques and effective supply chain management.

Predominantly CPOs	Predominantly MPOs
Full-service hotel	Cook-chill
Mid-service hotel	Tray serve
Limited service hotel	Home delivery
Hostels	
Long-term residential accommodation	

Hybrid operations

Table service restaurant	A la carte kitchen
	Table d'hôte kitchen
	Call/short order kitchen
Buffet/sandwich bar	Buffet/sandwich bar
Fast food restaurant	Fast food kitchen
Hibachi style restaurant	Hibachi style restaurant
Counter/cafeteria style	Assembly serve

Figure 8.1 CPOs, MPOs and hybrids

In hospitality operations process design, Jones (1988) first identified three key trends: production lining, decoupling, and customer participation. Production-lining refers to the concept of breaking down production activities into simple tasks so that they may be organized on a production-line basis, just as Henry Ford production-lined the motor manufacturing process in the 1920s. It has long been argued (Levitt, 1972) that services in general are moving towards more industrialized processes. Indeed, this has actually been termed the McDonaldization of society (Ritzer, 2000).

Decoupling refers to the idea of separating, both in place and time, back-of-house from front-of-house activity. Often the rationale for doing so is that one or the other (usually back-of-house can be production-lined). For instance, a number of health authorities in the UK have created one large central production kitchen for a number of hospitals and introduced cook-chill, so that the kitchen may produce 5,000 to 6,000 meals for transportation the following day to five or more different hospitals.

Customer participation is otherwise known as self-service. Many hospitality operations now enable their customers to do things for themselves that were previously done for them.

It is possible to check into a hotel by using a swipe card system, select salad items for a self-help salad bar, and check out of a hotel using the in-room television set.

These trends are consistent with what has happened in industry in general. It has not only led to firms moving *towards* the diagonal, but also *along* it, away from high variety/low volume in the direction of lower variety and higher volumes. For instance, à la carte restaurants and full service hotels have been around since the 1880s, whereas Kemmons Wilson only conceived the mid-service hotel, which he called Holiday Inn, in 1952. Fast food only really began when Ray Kroc took over the McDonald's chain when it had 200 outlets in 1961. Cook-chill and *sous-vide* are even more recent innovations.

Jones (2002a) has subsequently identified two further process trends in the industry – the development of so-called micro units and the dual or multi-use of physical infrastructure. Micro units are foodservice outlets of a very small size aimed at serving often limited and/or captive markets. They include outlets in petrol filling stations, cinemas, sports stadia, the workplace and so on. Their growth derives from the fact that more traditional sites are now unavailable and demand for eating out continues to grow. The final trend of dual or multi-use of infrastructure is sometimes a consequence of devising micro units. By enabling a brand to be delivered inside a small 'footprint' it can then be incorporated into an existing outlet.

The final question is the extent to which the hospitality industry will follow other industries towards the notion of mass customization. In this context both high volume and variety are accommodated, using a range of different approaches to achieve this technically difficult task (Brotherton, 1997). This remains the biggest challenge for hospitality operators – how to serve large numbers of customers with high quality food of their choice, at a low price, and at sufficient speed.

A major implication of understanding process type is that each process needs to have a different approach to the planning and control of capacity, inventory, supply chain, productivity, quality and innovation.

CAPACITY AND PRODUCTION PLANNING

This aspect of operation is largely concerned with the rate of flow of inputs into the system. In manufacturing this is especially important in job shop operations, as the flow of materials needs to be optimized in order to maximize the usage of equipment and minimize down time due to set-ups or re-tooling. Likewise in services, due to perishability, ensuring customers utilize the service is fundamental to the success of the business. Brotherton and Coyle (1990, 1991) explore the nature of both instability and variety in the hospitality operation environment.

In hospitality research, limited operations management research into capacity and production planning has been undertaken. Two exceptions are Sill (1994) and Sill and Decker (1999) who explicitly consider capacity management in restaurants. Thompson (2002, 2003) has also conducted studies of table layouts in restaurants to evaluate how this affects capacity.

However, three areas that assist the hospitality operations management team to manage capacity and plan production have been extensively researched. In foodservice, research into menu development has taken place; in lodging there is an extensive literature on yield, or revenue, management; and in a variety of settings there has been research into queuing.

Menu development

Terminology in this area is often confusing. Mooney (1996) resolves this by differentiating between key terms. He defines 'menu planning' as the process for creating the original menu, and 'menu development' as the subsequent process of adapting and changing this menu. 'Menu analysis' is defined as the process that is gone through in order to develop the menu, whilst 'menu engineering' is one specific type of menu analysis.

Most research has focused on menu analysis. Kreck (1984) advocates a technique that compares the menu average versus the guest-check average. Miller (1987) extends this by calculating the frequency distribution of the average-check. Bayou and Bennett (1992) suggest what they call 'profitability analysis'. But most research has investigated alternative approaches to menu engineering, with researchers advocating different variables (Kasavana and Smith, 1982; Pavesic, 1985; Jones and Atkinson, 1994). Hayes and Huffman (1985: 65) however are generally critical of menu engineering because '[such] methods suffer from the common flaw of matrix analysis … some items must fall into the less desirable categories'.

Most of the above research has been conceptual in terms of proposing what might be 'best practice'. Some studies have investigated how menu development is carried out in the industry. Carmin and Norkus (1990) investigated alternative pricing strategies in restaurants. Morrison (1996) studied menu engineering amongst 21 upscale restaurants in Australia. Mifli and Jones (2001) investigated the menu analysis practices of seven UK foodservice chains, whilst Kwong (2005) researched its application in Asian restaurants.

Yield or revenue management

Yield management (YM) is one of the most researched areas in the hospitality field. Yield management is frequently defined as selling the right room, at the right price, to the right customer, at the right time (see for instance Kimes, 1989). Jones (1999b: 1115) argues that this is what hoteliers have always tried to do, and hence this simply defines the advanced reservations process in general. He defines yield management as 'a system for hotel owners to maximize profitability through their senior management in hotels identifying the profitability of market segments, establishing value, setting prices, creating discount and displacement rules for application to the advanced reservations process, and monitoring the effectiveness of these rules and their implementation'. Thus yield management seeks to ensure that the capacity of the property is always fully utilized by adjusting how reservations are taken.

Research interest is mainly focused on particular issues such as the analysis of the YM concept and its development into implementation models (such as Orkin, 1988; Rowe, 1989; Brotherton and Mooney, 1992; Jones and Hamilton, 1992; Donaghy et al., 1995, 1997; Daughy et al., 1997; Jones, 1998b), the development of a YM culture (Jones and Hamilton, 1992), and the adoption, understanding and implementation of YM in the hotel industry (Bradley and Ingold, 1993; Bitran and Mondschein, 1995; Peters and Reilly, 1997; Jarvis et al., 1998; Badinelli, 2000). Savkina and Yakovlev (1997) have researched the application of YM in Russia.

Griffin (1995, 1996, 1997) has focused attention on the critical success factors of a yield management system. The contribution and value of information technology (IT) use for YM implementation is also heavily mentioned in the literature. These highlight the need for systems integration (Kimes, 1989) and on addressing the development of different modules and the information system architecture of computerized YM systems (Gamble, 1990; Jauncey et al., 1995). Sigala et al. (2001) identify the strategic role that IT plays in successful yield management practices. Schwartz and Cohen (2005) found from a study of 57 experienced revenue managers that the interaction between a human revenue manager and a computer screen offering revenue-management data is influenced by certain attributes of the computer interface.

More recently researchers have turned their attention to two issues. The first is the extension of YM principles and techniques either by using more sophisticated analysis of customer spend (Dunn and Brooks, 1990; Noone and Griffin, 1997; Choi and Cho, 2000) or applying it not just to rooms but also banqueting and conference centers (Van Westering, 1994). The second area of research is into issues of concern about YM's long-term effect on customer satisfaction and loyalty, as considered by Kandampully and Suhartanto (2000) and Kimes (2003). Huyton et al. (1997) were concerned with the ethical and legal issues of applying YM.

Queuing and customer perceptions of waiting time

Sasser et al. (1978) documented the management of perceived waiting time, citing anecdotal evidence derived from installing mirrors in elevator wait areas. But it was not until Maister (1985) identified eight 'propositions' relating to what he called the psychology of waiting lines that these ideas were conceptualized. His eight propositions are:

- unoccupied time feels longer than occupied time;
- pre-process waits feel longer than in-process waits;
- anxiety makes waits feel longer;
- uncertain waits seem longer than certain waits;
- unexplained waits seem longer than explained waits;
- unfair waits seem longer than equitable waits;
- more valuable the service, the longer people will wait; and
- solo waiting feels longer than group waiting.

These propositions have been further developed to suggest a number of other variables may also affect perceptions of wait time:

- uncomfortable waits feel longer than comfortable waits (Davis and Heineke, 1998); and
- new or infrequent users feel they wait longer than frequent users (Jones and Peppiatt, 1996).

Other factors that may influence perception of wait time may include:

- length of queue (Nie, 2000; Rafaeli, Barron and Harber, 2002);
- number of people behind person in the queue (Zhou and Soman, 2003);
- level of interest in the activity designed to occupy time (Nie, 2000);
- rate of queue movement (Nie, 2000); and
- attribution of cause of wait in terms of 'locus', 'stability', controllability, and 'legitimacy' (Nie, 2000).

A number of studies have gone on to test some of these propositions. Findings from these studies are contradictory (Katz, Larson and Larson, 1991; Graessel and Zeidler, 1993; Smidts and Pruyn, 1994; Jones and Peppiatt, 1996; Groth and Gilliland, 1998; Pruyn and Smidts, 1998; Luo et al., 2004). Overall the findings suggest that as wait times become longer, the exaggeration of perceived time does not increase proportionally. The level of this exaggeration may (Groth and Gilliland's fast food study, 1998; Luo et al.'s pizza shop study, 2004) or may not (Katz et al., 1991; Smidts and Pruyn, 1994; Jones and Peppiatt, 1996) be reduced if their time is occupied. This time distortion has an impact on people's ability to estimate time and draw more attention to the wait itself and the waiting circumstances (Graessel and Zeidler, 1993; Van Dierdonck, 2003).

Church and Newman (2000) focused on UK fast food retailers and the importance of the service delivery systems in fast food burger outlets. Waiting time and the impact it has on customer perceptions of service quality is considered alongside a typology of customers, based on their waiting characteristics. They assert that the cost-effective maximization of service speed is likely to be the primary consideration for management, and lead to business success. When using conventional research approaches, such as tracking studies and queuing theory, these arguably offer burger restaurant managers a rather simplistic analysis. The research concludes that computer-based simulation packages offer a way of measuring most of the influencing factors.

MATERIALS AND INVENTORY CONTROL

This feature of operations is concerned with ensuring that stock levels are optimized and inventories are kept securely. In hospitality the focus of research has almost exclusively been on security issues – either of the hotel guest, the property or its income. Bach and Pizam (1996) used police records of hotel crime in Florida, as well as surveys of security procedures and devices in order to investigate the link between the incidence of crime and the measures taken to prevent it. Jones and Gronenbaum (2002) investigate the nature of crime in nine central London hotels, whilst Gronenbaum and Jones (2003) look at security in London hotels. Gill et al. (2002) consider both crime and security more generally. Hobson and Ko (1995) identify alternative forms of credit card fraud.

Post 9/11 the whole issue of guest safety and security has become significantly more important as part of a wider concern for tourists in general. Pizam (2002) goes on to provide specific guidance as to policies and procedures for assuring security. Enz and Taylor (2002) devised an inventory for indexing the safety and security features of hotels. Safety equipment includes items such as sprinklers and smoke detectors, while security features include electronic locks and security cameras. Their study of 2,123 US properties found an uneven distribution of these key amenities in various hotel types, with differences relating to such factors as hotel size, age, price segment, hotel type and location. Luxury and upscale hotels recorded the highest scores for safety and security, while economy and mid-price full-service hotels scored lower than most segments on the safety scale – even though a large proportion have sprinklers.

There has also been some limited research on waste management, mainly in public sector foodservice. Ghiselli et al. (1995a, 1995b) researched school foodservice waste in the USA, whilst Hong and Kirk (1995) researched plate waste in UK hospitals. Jones (2004) discusses this issue in relation to flight catering. In general however, there is limited research of environmental issues. Kirk (1995) identifies a framework for understanding the issues, whilst Gustin and Weaver (1996) researched the preparedness of the industry for 'green' consumers.

SUPPLY CHAIN MANAGEMENT AND THE 'SERVICESCAPE'

Whereas in many industries the management of the supply chain is an essential aspect of a firm's competitive strategy, in the hospitality industry this concept is little used and rarely researched. Webster (2001) identifies the scope and structure of the food supply chain in the UK. Jones (2004) discusses the role of the supply chain in the flight catering industry. Of increasing importance is the role that the Internet is playing in support of supply chain management. Kothari et al. (2005) investigated the purchasing managers' views about e-Procurement in hotels in Philadelphia.

In the hospitality industry production and consumption are often simultaneous, so that it can be argued that the customer is part of the supply chain infrastructure. Bitner (1992) identified the importance of physical surroundings on customers and employees in a service environment. She coined the term 'servicescape' to describe this. It is surprising that very little research into this concept has been undertaken in hospitality until recently, given the growth of design led operations such as boutique hotels, the shorter 'life cycle' of theme restaurants, and the importance placed on interior design by industry.

Reimer and Kuehn (2005) researched this in banks and restaurants. They found the servicescape is not only a cue for the expected service quality, but also influences customers' evaluations of other factors determining perceived service quality. Thus, the servicescape has a direct and an indirect effect on perceived service quality, which leads the servicescape to have a high overall effect. The results also show that the servicescape is of greater importance in determining customers' evaluations of the expected service quality in a hedonic service, e.g. restaurant, compared to a utilitarian service, e.g. bank. The servicescape has also been investigated in relation to nightclubs and bars, by Skinner et al. (2005) who were able to rate the relative importance of various elements of the servicescape in influencing customer decisions to enter this type of operation for the first time, and also the relative importance of factors which prompt subsequent visits to a venue. Oakes (2000) conducted a thorough literature review of the role that music plays in many servicescapes, demonstrating that this may link with other aspects of operations such as workforce productivity and customer waiting times. Wels-Lip et al. (1997) looked at six industries, including restaurants, and identified the servicescape as one of seven major areas leading to positive or negative critical incidents in the service experience of customers.

PRODUCTIVITY AND WORKFORCE MANAGEMENT

Roth and Menor (2003) note the ongoing challenges to the management of productivity in services and that further study of the design and delivery of service productivity is warranted. One reason that studying service productivity is challenging is the inherent difficulty in managing such productivity. Johnston and Jones (2004) identify the concept of 'customer productivity', which could be important in the hospitality industry as so much of what the customer experience derives from self-service. They define customer productivity as a function of the ratio of customer inputs, such as time effort and cost, to customer outputs, such as experience, outcome and value. This highlights a major issue that is rarely discussed in relation to productivity, namely from whose perspective productivity is judged. In manufacturing, higher productivity is generally good for both the provider and the customer as it leads to lower costs and prices. In services, higher productivity for the provider could lead to lower productivity (through poorer experience and perceived satisfaction and value for example) for the customer. Ford and Heaton (2001) discuss how customers become 'quasi-employees' of the operation. They suggest the most common functions performed by customers are managers or supervisors and trainers of employees and other guests, quality-control inspectors, consultants, marketers, and co-producers of their own service experience or that of other guests.

The focus of productivity research in hospitality has been on processes inside the firm rather than outside, although few empirical studies have been conducted. Witt and Witt (1989) identified the key characteristics of the hotel industry and suggested these were the reason that productivity in the sector had lagged behind other industries. Hotel productivity has also been found to vary from one country to another by McKinsey (1998), who found that hotels in the UK had 60% of the productivity of hotels in the USA and France. In the mid 1990s, Johns (1996) collated the findings of a number of studies into a single text devoted to productivity.

Productivity is very difficult to research as discussed by Witt and Witt (1989). One approach pioneered by Johns et al. (1997) is to use data envelopment analysis (DEA), which they used to compare the efficiency of 15 hotels in a small chain. Andersson (1996) also adopts this approach in his study of restaurants in Sweden. More recently Sigala, Jones et al. (2004) used DEA to investigate the productivity levels of 97 UK hotels, and to explore the impact of information technology (IT) on productivity levels. This approach has also been adopted to examine the productivity of

Portuguese hotels, by Barros and Mascarenhas (2005).

A number of studies have suggested that information technology (IT) has not been well exploited in the hospitality industry. Cho and Connolly (1996) suggested that managers are reluctant to invest in IT because of the time it takes to see actual results. Jarvis et al. (1998) found a lag of 12 months between implementing a YM system and measurable improvement in hotel performance. Ham, Kim and Jeong (2004) investigated the effect of IT on performance in upscale hotels. More recently a few studies have considered how the Internet may assist hospitality firms to manage their operations (Siguaw and Enz, 1999).

In foodservice, there have been a number of studies designed to compare the relative efficiencies of alternative systems and technologies. Williams and Brand Miller (1993) compared hot holding systems with cook-chill in 30 hospitals in Australia. Manning and Lieux (1995) empirically measured productivity in a commissary with four satellite kitchens. Rimmington and Clark (1996) also studied hospital foodservice systems, comparing the efficiency of alternative approaches. Ball (1996) conducted productivity research in fast food restaurants.

Another key area of research has been in relation to workforce deployment, in particular the issues of employee scheduling and labor flexibility. Lane (1976) and Smith and Giglio (1979) both identified scheduling as a key aspect of hospitality operations. Goodale, Verma and Pullman (2003) consider a specific approach to labor scheduling. Thompson (2004) devised a simulation experiment which showed that increased variability in the customer-arrival rate and high mean customer-arrival rates both work to reduce the ideal length of both data-collection and schedule-development intervals, suggesting scheduling employees at least by the quarter hour is required in hospitality.

A seminal study of labor flexibility in 15 hotel groups was conducted by Guerrier and Lockwood (1989). This work established that numerical flexibility (the employment of a combination of full-time, part-time and casual workers) was commonplace in the industry. Such flexibility enables operations to cope with wide variations in demand, both long term (seasonal) and short term (hourly or daily patterns). Moreover they found that managers believed full-time staff were likely to

be transient, whereas part-time staff recruited locally were more likely to stay longer. Kelliher (1989) also found that numerical flexibility was used extensively in contract foodservice within the health sector.

Guerrier and Lockwood (1989) found little evidence of functional flexibility, or multi-skilling. They suggested that barriers to implementation were strong departmentalization in the hotel chains they studied. Kelliher (1989) suggest this form of flexibility is most needed in smaller businesses and operations, a view supported by Riley et al. (2000).

Riley (1992) argues that there is little incentive for hotels to implement functional flexibility, because they almost always operate in an environment of surplus labor, combined with an increase in qualitative demand from consumers, ensures that it is unlikely to be used, simply because other approaches are easier to implement. Furthermore, as Riley and Lockwood (1997) note, it may be that labor laws present barriers to the implementation of functional flexibility. Nonetheless, Riley et al. (2000) did find examples of multi-skilling and articulated why and how it should be adopted in hospitality. They reported that operators adopt multi-skilling for a number of reasons:

- more efficiently schedule staff, especially during relatively quiet periods of operation. Two organizations reported major labor cost savings of up to 50%;
- increase staff retention, especially amongst part-time employees; and
- improve team working.

Organizations that have adopted multi-skilling have reported additional benefits to those that they expected:

- improved work processes, as multi-skill employees approach their second role with experience of the organization but objective insights towards their new department;
- lower induction training costs, as multi-skilled staff need only be inducted into the organization once; and
- better co-ordination and collaboration between Heads of Department.

Riley et al. (2000) suggest management have a number of choices to make if they are interested in multi-skilling their organizations, in relation to the scheme's breadth (across all or parts of the operation) and depth (level of training in each 'job'), whether staff will be moved between departments within a shift, and who should be allowed to participate in the scheme.

Employee empowerment, often as part of a quality program, has also been extensively researched. Brymer (1991) first identifies the role that empowerment might play in the industry. Lashley (1995a, 1999) develops a framework for understanding the empowerment in hospitality and looks at its application in McDonald's (Lashley, 1995b), Harvester Restaurants (Ashness and Lashley, 1995) and TGI Friday's (Lashley, 2000). Hales and Klidas (1998) question the application of empowerment in hotels. Spinelli and Canavios (2000) found that empowerment led to increased employee satisfaction and customer satisfaction. Nelson and Bowen (2000) reported on a study of the effect employee uniforms had on satisfaction of employees with their work.

QUALITY MANAGEMENT

Quality management is the most researched operations management topic in hospitality. In foodservice most studies have focused on the application of specific techniques. In the 1980s a number of articles advocated the adoption of a quality assurance approach (Wyckoff, 1984). A number of studies have been conducted with respect to the application of hazard analysis and critical control points (HACCP). Jones (1983) and Farkas and Snyder (1991) both identified how this might be applied to catering and O'Donnell (1991) describes its application in a specific firm. Eves and Dervisi (2004) undertook a detailed study of HACCP in seven different types of foodservice outlet, identifying that compliance with regulations was the main motivation for adopting it. Two studies have looked at the application of statistical process control (SPC). Jones and Dent (1993) report on a study in a cafeteria, and Jones and Cheek (1997) compare SPC with mystery shopper programs to assess the efficacy of these two alternatives. Paraskevas (2001) considers the application of the internal service chain to hospitality.

In lodging, a number of studies have considered how the industry has gone about adopting a quality management program. Walker (1986) assessed the impact of the American Hotel and Motel Association sponsored quality assurance (QA) program, finding that hotels with QA had higher employee satisfaction and lower labor costs than hotels without QA. Breiter et al. (1995) investigated how Bergstrom Hotels had implemented their quality program. Lockwood, Baker and Ghillyer (1996) report on quality management in six hotels and Harrington and Akehurst (1996) survey hotel managers to investigate their quality management practices. Baldacchino (1995) reported on an in-depth study of total quality management (TQM) being applied in a single property. Hsieh and Hsieh (2001) research the role that job standardization has in delivering service quality.

The external accreditation of quality has also been researched. Camison (1996) also considers TQM and the application of the European Foundation for Quality Management (EFQM) to hotels and Soriano (1999) look at the application of TQM to hotels in Spain. Breiter and Bloomquist (1998) review TQM in American hotels. Another external accreditation of quality is through ISO 9000, researched by Ingram and Daskalakis (1999) in their study of hotels in Crete.

A number of studies of so-called 'best practice' have been undertaken, often sponsored by national governments. The UK's Department of State for National Heritage (1996) commissioned a study of best practice in small, independent hotels based on a sample of 70 businesses. CERT, the Irish agency for tourism development, undertook a study of international best practice by interviewing hospitality managers in Ireland, UK, Europe and USA. This study identified 21 key processes that needed to be managed well. The study concluded that hospitality has lagged behind other industries in applying new management thinking, in particular with regards to concepts such as just-in-time, business process re-engineering and total quality management. In 2003, the UK's Department of Trade and Industry sponsored research into best practice with hospitality and tourism SMEs, based on a sample of 89 different firms. This research underpinned an initiative called 'Profit through productivity' which was designed to improve the competitiveness of UK SMEs (Jones, 2002b). This research focused on seven areas:

1 partnerships and networks (Jones, Hwang and Warr, 2002);

2 standard setting (Lockwood, Bowen and Ekinci, 2002);
3 internal communication practices (Kyriakidou and Bowen, 2002);
4 employee retention strategies (Bowen, Kyriakidou and Warr, 2003);
5 performance measurement (Louvieris, Phillips, Warr and Bowen, 2003);
6 customer value (Lockwood and Bowen, 2003); and
7 operational planning and control (Jones, Van Westring and Bowen, 2004).

Voss et al. (1997) examined the international competitiveness of the UK service sector based on the International Service Study of 310 UK and US service firms. They concluded with respect to the hotel industry that US performance was 'excellent' and UK performance 'good'. Potential areas for improvement in the UK centered around improved approaches to employee management (training and empowerment) and creating customer value (understanding customer needs and better complaint management). Dube and Renaghan (1999) studied the US lodging industry and identified 115 functional best practices. A key finding from this study is that the development and implementation of best practice was greatly influenced by one individual in an organization, who championed the best practice. Enz and Siguaw (2003) followed up on the 1999 study to see if best practice had been maintained within the companies researched. They suggested that best practice could be lost due to the high mobility of managers in the industry and the high rate of industry consolidation, through mergers and acquisitions.

Another major focus of attention has been on guest perceptions of service quality, typically based on the application of SERVQUAL (Parasuraman et al., 1985). Knutson et al. (1991) measure service quality in hotels using an adapted scale which they call LODGQUAL. Stevens et al. (1995) and Knutson et al. (1995) adopt a similar approach to restaurant quality in their development of DINESERV. Another adaptation of this approach is TANGSERV proposed by Raajpoot (2002). The issue of customer satisfaction has also been researched in other ways. However, this approach to service quality measurement is being questioned, for instance by Ekinci (2002). He argues that the SERVQUAL methodology is inherently flawed. Spinelli and Canavos (2000)

investigate the relationship between customer satisfaction and employee satisfaction. Hartline, Ross-Wooldridge and Jones (2003) identify the role that different groups of employees have in forming guest perceptions of hotel quality. Finally, Lynn (2001) has considered the relationship between service quality and tipping.

Nikolich and Sparks (1995) researched the nature of the service encounter itself, in particular the nature and role of communication between hotel service providers and customers. Their survey of 579 hotel employers and 326 customers identified two key role related topics of conversation. The first topic related to the actual task and process itself, whilst the second they identified as personal topics and 'small talk'.

Service failure and recovery has also been researched in the hospitality context. Hoffman et al. (1995) found eight different service recovery strategies, most commonly used in the restaurant industry. Lockwood and Deng (2004) reviewed 79 critical incidents in order to categorize different types of service failure in the hotel context and the effect of recovery strategies on customer satisfaction. Sundaram et al. (1997) investigated the impact of four types of service recovery efforts in the restaurant context. They found that the scale or 'criticality' of the recovery effort had to match the customers' perceived level of failure. Sparks and Bradley (1997) identified factors that influenced customers' satisfaction ratings and intention to complain. They found that service employees' efforts in the service recovery process were rated highly if they had an accommodating communication style (flexible verbal and non-verbal behaviors) and high discretion (i.e. had been empowered to take action). Sparks and Callan (1996) demonstrated that customers have different expectations about service failure and recovery depending upon whether the failure is perceived to be caused by something internal or external to the business.

Hoffman and Chung (1999) compare the recovery strategies used by hospitality firms with the strategies that customers would prefer. Susskind (2005) investigated the relationship between the extent to which a failure was recovered and intention to return in the restaurant context. The effect of gender on service recovery has also been researched (McColl-Kennedy et al., 2003), as has the issue and importance of assuring 'justice' in the context of service recovery (Collie et al., 2001).

INNOVATION

Research in innovation has focused on two main areas – the process of innovation and its impact on hospitality operations. Jones and Wan (1993) investigated how fast food firms innovate and Jones (1995) conducted a similar study in the flight catering industry. Jones (1996b) reviews innovation in the hospitality industry in general. Ottenbacher and Gnoth (2005) surveyed 184 hotel managers in Germany and identified nine factors that were perceived to influence the success of service innovations. Those factors were tangible quality (service product-related dimension); market selection and market responsiveness (market-related dimensions); employee commitment (process-related dimension); and strategic human resources management, training employees, empowerment, behavior-based evaluation, and marketing synergy (organization-related dimensions).

The impact of new technology on operations has been researched by Decareau (1992) who looks at the application of microwave technology to foodservice and Kasavana (1994) who considers the role of IT in multi-unit operations. There has been little research into creativity, except for Wong and Pang's (2002) study of the factors that motivate managers and employees to be creative.

A FUTURE RESEARCH AGENDA?

A key feature of this review is the extent to which research into operations management topics are actually published in the operations management literature. A fairly high proportion of the citations for this chapter are from marketing journals. This is partly explained by the fact that customer service in hospitality results in marketing and operational activity occurring simultaneously. In particular, research into the servicescape, service encounter, and service failure and recovery tends to be categorized as marketing research. Marketers research these topics however because they are part of a broader research agenda in relation to consumer behavior. Similarly, there is research into empowerment and labor flexibility that

could be considered part of the organizational behavior or human resources literature. But the topics included in this chapter have been selected because quite clearly they occur under the management and control of the operations manager. However this overlap with other disciplines suggests that research in hospitality may need to be conducted with a multi-disciplinary approach.

A second issue is the extent to which there is a commonly accepted typology of different hospitality operations. Almost certainly there is not, as there is not even common terminology and definitions. This largely arises from using common industry terms to describe operations, and such terms vary from one country to another. Most notably there are major differences in terminology between the UK and USA. British terms such as accommodation, catering, fast food are the equivalent of the American terms lodging, foodservice and quick service. Even words that are commonly used, such as hotel, have a range of meaning, often because legislation in different countries has defined a hotel in a specific way.

The third issue for a future research agenda is the need to relate clearly operations research to underlying operations theory. This means designing research studies to test the laws associated with Theory of Swift and Even Flow, the Theory of Materials Processing, the Theory of Process Improvement and Superiority and the Theory of Service Experience.

Finally, hospitality operations research needs to consider carefully methodological issues. The investigation of operations lends itself to experimental research designs, but very few experimental studies have been done, except in the area of service encounter research.

CONCLUSIONS

This chapter has sought to explain operations management theory and to relate hospitality research to this. Most studies to date have not been conducted in this context and it is argued that future operations research needs to be founded on a stronger theoretical base. This review demonstrates that hospitality research is wide ranging in scope, investigating issues that are fundamental to the success of hospitality business – process design, capacity planning, inventory control, the servicescape, productivity, quality, and innovation. Managing these issues is complex because the industry is made up of many types of operation, that are different bundles of customer, materials and information processing, designed to provide products and services to different market segments.

REFERENCES

Andersson, T. D. (1996) 'Traditional key ratio analysis versus data envelopment analysis: a comparison of various measurements of productivity and efficiency in restaurants'. In N. Johns (ed.) *Productivity Management in Hospitality and Tourism.* London: Cassell. pp. 209–226.

Ashness, D. and Lashley, C. (1995) 'Empowering service workers in Harvester Restaurants', *Personnel Review,* 24(8): 17–32.

Bach, S. and Pizam, A. (1996) 'Crimes in hotels', *Journal of Hospitality Tourism Research Journal,* 20(2): 59–76.

Badinelli, R. D. (2000) 'An optimal, dynamic policy for hotel yield management', *European Journal of Operational Research,* 121(3): 476–503.

Baldacchino, G. (1995) 'Total quality management in a luxury hotel: a critique of practice', *International Journal of Hospitality Management,* 14(1): 67–78.

Ball, S. (1996) 'Perceptions and interpretations of productivity within fast food chains: a case study of Wimpy International'. In Johns, N. (ed.) *Productivity Management in Hospitality and Tourism.* Cassell: London. pp. 166–193.

Barros, C. P. and Mascarenhas, M. J. (2005) 'Technical and allocative efficiency in a chain of small hotels', *International Journal of Hospitality Management,* 24(3): 415–436.

Bayou, M. E. and Bennett, L. B. (1992) 'Profitability analysis for table service restaurants', *Cornell Hotel and Restaurant Administration Quarterly,* 33(2): 49–55.

Bitner, M. J. (1992) 'Servicescapes: the impact of physical surroundings on customers and employees', *Journal of Marketing,* 56(2): 57–71.

Bitran, G. R. and Mondschein, S. V. (1995) 'An application of yield management to the hotel industry considering multiple day stays', *Operations Research,* 43(3): 427–443.

Bowen, A., Kyriakidou, O. and Warr, D. (2003) 'Strategies for employee retention in small hospitality businesses', *Hospitality Review,* 5(1): 50–54.

Bowen, J. and Ford R. C. (2004) 'What experts say about managing hospitality service delivery systems',

International Journal of Contemporary Hospitality Management, 16(7): 394–401.

Bradley, A. and Ingold, A. (1993) 'An investigation of yield management in Birmingham hotels', *International Journal of Contemporary Hospitality Management,* 5(2): 13.

Breiter, D. and Bloomquist, P. (1998) 'TQM in American hotels: An Analysis of Application', *Cornell Hotel and Restaurant Administration Quarterly,* 39(1): 26–33.

Breiter, D., Tyink, S. A. and Corey-Tuckwell, S. (1995) 'Bergstrom Hotels: a case study in quality', *International Journal of Contemporary Hospitality Management,* 7(6): 14–18.

Brotherton, B. (1997) 'Modular solutions to the standardization v customization problem in hospitality and tourism operations', *English Tourist Board Insights Journal,* January: A121–A125.

Brotherton, B. and Coyle, M. (1990) 'Managing instability in the hospitality operations environment', *International Journal of Contemporary Hospitality Management,* 2(4): 17–24.

Brotherton, B. and Coyle, M. (1991) 'Managing variety in the hospitality operations environment', *International Journal of Contemporary Hospitality Management,* 3(2): 30–32.

Brotherton, B. and Mooney, S. (1992) 'Yield management – progress and prospects', *International Journal of Hospitality Management,* 11(1): 23–32.

Brymer, R. (1991) 'Employee empowerment: a guest driven leadership strategy', *Cornell Hotel and Restaurant Administration Quarterly,* 32(1): 58–68.

Camison, C. (1996) 'Total quality management in hospitality: an application of the EFQM model', *Tourism Management,* 17(3): 191–201.

Carmin, J. and Norkus, G. X. (1990) 'Pricing strategies for menus: magic or myth?', *Cornell Hotel and Restaurant Administration Quarterly,* 31(3): 45–50.

Cho, W. and Connolly, D. J. (1996) 'The impact of information technology as an enabler in the hospitality industry', *International Journal of Hospitality Management,* 11(1): 3–23.

Choi, T. Y. and Cho, V. (2000) 'Towards a knowledge discovery framework for yield management in the Hong Kong hotel industry', *Hospitality Management,* 19(1): 17–31.

Church, I. and Newman, A. J. (2000) 'Using simulations in the optimization of fast food service delivery', *British Food Journal,* 102(56): 398–405.

Collie, T. A., Sparks, B. A. and Bradley, G. (2000) 'Investigating interactional justice: a study of the fair process effect within a hospitality failure context', *Journal of Hospitality and Tourism Research,* 24(4): 448–472.

Davis, M. M. and Heineke, J. (1998) 'How disconfirmation, perception and actual waiting times impact customer satisfaction in a service operation', *International Journal of Service Industry Management,* 9(1): 64–73.

Decareau (1992) *Microwave Foods: New Product Development.* Connecticut: Food Nutrition Press Inc.

Donaghy, K., McMahon-Beattie, U. and McDowell, D. (1995) 'Yield management: an overview', *International Journal of Hospitality Management,* 14(2): 139–150.

Donaghy K., McMahon-Beattie, U. and McDowell, D. (1997) 'Implementing yield management: lessons from the hotel sector', *International Journal of Contemporary Hospitality Management,* 9(2/3): 50–54.

Dube, L. and Renaghan, L. M. (1999) 'Strategic approaches to lodging excellence: a look at the industry's overall best-practice champions', *Cornell Hotel and Restaurant Administration Quarterly,* 40(6): 16–26.

Dunn, K. D. and Brooks, D. E. (1990) 'Profit analysis: beyond yield management', *Cornell Hotel and Restaurant Administration Quarterly,* 31(3): 80–90.

Ekinci, Y. (2002) 'A review of the theoretical debates on the measurement of service quality: implications for hospitality research', *Journal of Hospitality and Tourism Research,* 26(3): 199–216.

Enz, C. A. and Siguaw, J. A. (2003) 'Revisiting the best of the best: innovations in hotel practice', *Cornell Hotel and Restaurant Administration Quarterly,* 44(5/6): 115–123.

Enz, C. A. and Taylor, M. S. (2002) 'The safety and security of U.S. hotels: a post September 11 Report', *Cornell Hotel and Restaurant Administration Quarterly,* 43(5): 119–136.

Eves, A. and Dervisi, P. (2005) 'Experiences of the implementation and operation of hazard analysis critical control points in the food service sector', *International Journal of Hospitality Management,* 24(1): 3–19.

Farkas, D. F. and Snyder, O. P. (1991) 'How to describe a food process for quality control', *Journal of Foodservice Systems,* 6(3): 147–153.

Ford, R. C. and Heaton, C. P. (2001) 'Managing your guest as a quasi-employee', *Cornell Hotel and Restaurant Administration Quarterly,* 42(2): 46–55.

Gamble, P. R. (1990) 'Building a yield management system – the flip side', *Hospitality Research Journal,* 14(2): 11–22.

Ghiselli, R., Hiemstra, S. J. and Almanza, B. A. (1995a) 'Estimating the amount of solid waste in Indiana School Foodservice operations', *Journal of Hospitality Research Journal,* 19(2): 57–66.

Ghiselli, R., Hiemstra, S. J. and Almanza, B. A. (1995b) 'Reducing school foodservice waste through the choice of serviceware', *Hospitality Research Journal,* 19(1): 3–11.

Gill, M., Moon, C., Seaman, P. and Turbin, V. (2002) 'Security management and crime in hotels', *International Journal of Contemporary Hospitality Management,* 14(2): 58–64.

Goodale, J. C., Verma, R. and Pullman, M. E. (2003) 'A market-utility approach to scheduling employees', *Cornell Hotel and Restaurant Administration Quarterly,* 44(1): 61–69.

Graessel, B. and Zeidler, P. (1993) 'Using quality function deployment to improve customer service', *Quality Progress,* 26(11): 39–63.

Griffin, R. K. (1995) 'A categorization scheme for critical success factors of lodging yield management systems', *International Journal of Hospitality Management,* 14 (3/4): 325–328.

Griffin, R. K. (1996) 'Factors of successful lodging yield management systems', *Hospitality Research Journal,* 19(4): 17–30.

Griffin, R. K. (1997) 'Evaluating the success of lodging yield management systems', *FIU Hospitality Review,* 15(1): 57–71.

Groenenboom, K. and Jones, P. (2003) 'Issues of security in hotels', *International Journal of Contemporary Hospitality Management,* 15(1): 14–19.

Groth, M. and Gilliland, S. W. (2001) 'The role of procedural justice in the delivery of services: a study of customers' reactions to waiting', *Journal of Quality Management,* 6(1): 77–97.

Guerrier, E. and Lockwood, A. (1989) 'Core and peripheral employees in hotel operations', *Personnel Review,* 18(1): 9–15.

Gustin, M. E. and Weaver, P. A. (1996) 'Are hotels prepared for the environmental consumer?', *Hospitality Research Journal,* 20(2): 1–14.

Hales, C. and Klidas, A. (1998) 'Empowerment in five star hotels: choice, voice or rhetoric?' *International Journal of Contemporary Hospitality Management,* 10(3): 88–95.

Ham, S., Kim, W. G. and Jeong, S. (2005) 'Effect of information technology on performance in upscale hotels', *International Journal of Hospitality Management,* 24(2): 281–294.

Harrington, D. and Akehurst, G. (1996) 'An exploratory investigation into managerial perceptions of service quality in UK hotels', *Progress in Tourism and Hospitality Research,* 2(2): 135–150.

Hartline, M. D., Ross-Wooldridge, B. and Jones, K. C. (2003) 'Guest perceptions of hotel quality: determining which employee groups count most', *Cornell Hotel and Restaurant Administration Quarterly,* 44(1): 43–52.

Hayes, D. K. and Huffman, L. M. (1985) 'Menu analysis: a better way', *Cornell Hotel and Restaurant Administration Quarterly,* 25(4): 64–70.

Hayes, R. and Wheelwright, S. (1979) 'Link manufacturing process and product life cycles', *Harvard Business Review*, 57(1): 133–140.

Hobson, J. S. P. and Ko, M. (1995) 'Counterfeit credit cards: how to protect hotel guests', *Cornell Hotel and Restaurant Administration Quarterly*, 36(4): 48–53.

Hoffman, K. D. and Chung, B. G. (1999) 'Hospitality recovery strategies: customer preference versus firm use', *Journal of Hospitality and Tourism Research*, 23(1): 71–84.

Hoffman, K. D., Kelley, S. W. and Rotalsky, H. M. (1995) 'Tracking service failures and employee recovery efforts', *Journal of Services Marketing*, 9(2): 49–61.

Hong, W. and Kirk, D. (1995) 'The analysis of edible plate waste results in 11 hospitals in the UK', *Journal of Foodservice Systems*, 8: 115–123.

Hsieh, Y-M. and Hsieh, A-T. (2001) 'Enhancement of service quality with job standardisation', *Service Industries Journal*, 21(3): 147–166.

Huelin, A. and Jones, P. (1990) 'Thinking about catering systems', *International Journal of Operations and Production Management*, 10(8): 42–52.

Huyton, J., Evans, P. and Ingold, A. (1997) 'The legal and moral issues surrounding the practice of yield management', *International Journal of Contemporary Hospitality Management*, 9(2/3): 84.

Ingram, H. (1996) 'Clusters and gaps in hospitality and tourism academic research', *International Journal of Contemporary Hospitality Management*, 8(7): 91–95.

Ingram, H. and Daskalakis, G. (1999) 'Measuring quality gaps in hotels: the case of Crete', *International Journal of Contemporary Hospitality Management*, 11(1): 24–30.

Jarvis, N., Lindh, A. and Jones, P. (1998) 'An investigation of key criteria affecting the adoption of yield management in UK hotels', *Progress in Hospitality and Tourism Research*, 4(3): 207–216.

Jauncey, S., Mitchell, I. and Slamet, P. (1995) 'The meaning and management of yield in hotels', *International Journal of Contemporary Hospitality Management*, 7(4): 23–26.

Johns, N. (1996) *Productivity Management in Hospitality and Tourism*. London: Cassell.

Johns N., Howcroft B. and Drake L. (1997) 'The use of data envelopment analysis to monitor hotel productivity', *Progress in Tourism and Hospitality Research*, 3(2): 119–127.

Johnston, R. (1994) 'Operations; from factory to service management', *International Journal of Service Industry Management*, 5(1): 49–63.

Johnston, R. and Jones, P. (2004) 'Service productivity: towards understanding the relationship between operational and customer productivity', *International Journal of Productivity and Performance Management*, 53(3): 201–213.

Johnston, R. and Jones, P. (2005) 'On theory in operations management: a critique from a service perspective', *Journal of Operations Management*.

Jones, P. (1983) *Foodservice Operations*. Eastbourne: Holt Rinehart Winston.

Jones, P. (1988) 'The impact of trends in service operations on food service delivery systems', *International Journal of Operations and Production Management*, 8(7): 23–30.

Jones, P. (1995) 'Developing new products and services in flight catering', *International Journal of Contemporary Hospitality Management*, 7(2/3): 24–28.

Jones, P. (1996a) (ed.) *Introduction to Hospitality Operations*. London: Cassell.

Jones, P. (1996b) 'Managing hospitality innovation', *Cornell Hotel and Restaurant Administration Quarterly*, 37(5): 86–95.

Jones, P. (1999a) 'Operational issues and trends in the hospitality industry', *International Journal of Hospitality Management*, 18(4): 427–442.

Jones, P. (1999b) 'Yield management in UK hotels: a systems analysis', *Journal of Operational Research Society*, 50(11): 1111–1119.

Jones, P. (2002a) *Introduction to Hospitality Operations*. London: Thomson Learning.

Jones, P. (2002b) 'Researching profit through productivity', *Hospitality Review*, 4(1): 37–41.

Jones, P. (2004) *Flight Catering*. Oxford: Elsevier.

Jones, P. and Atkinson, H. (1994) 'Menu engineering: managing the foodservice micro-marketing mix', *Journal of Restaurant and Foodservice Marketing*, 1(1): 37–56.

Jones, P. and Cheek, P. (1997) 'Service quality: an evaluation of approaches to measuring actual performance against standards in the foodservice industry', *6th CHME National Research Conference*, Oxford Brookes University.

Jones, P. and Dent, M. (1994) 'Lessons in consistency: statistical process control at Forte PLC', *TQM Magazine* 6(1): 18–23.

Jones, P. and Groenenboom, K. (2002) 'Crime in London hotels', *Tourism and Hospitality Research*, 4(1): 21–36.

Jones, P. and Hamilton, D. (1992) 'Yield management: putting people in the big picture', *Cornell Hotel and Restaurant Administration Quarterly*, 33(1): 88–96.

Jones, P., Hwang, J. and Warr, D. (2002) 'Making the most of partnerships and networks', *Hospitality Review*, 4(2): 45–49.

Jones, P. and Lockwood, A. (1998) 'Hospitality operations management', *International Journal of Hospitality Management*, 17(2): 183–202.

Jones, P. and Lockwood, A. (2000) Operating systems and products. In Brotherton, R. (ed.) *An Introduction to the UK Hospitality Industry: A Comparative Approach.* Oxford: Butterworth-Heinemann. pp. 46–70.

Jones, P. and Peppiatt, E. (1996) 'Managing perceptions of waiting times in service queues', *International Journal of Service Industry Management,* 7(5): 47–61.

Jones, P. and Wan, L. (1993) 'Innovation in the UK foodservice industry', *International Journal of Contemporary Hospitality Management,* 5(2): 32–38.

Jones, P., Van Westering, J. and Bowen, A. (2004) 'Best practice in operational planning and control', *Hospitality Review,* 6(1): 42–47.

Jones, P. A. (1983) 'The restaurant – a place for quality control and product maintenance', *International Journal of Hospitality Management,* 2(2): 93–100.

Kandampully, J. and Suhartanto, D. (2000) 'Customer loyalty in the hotel industry: the role of customer satisfaction and image', *International Journal of Contemporary Hospitality Management,* 12(6): 346–351.

Kasavana, M. L. (1994) 'Computers and multiunit foodservice operations', *Cornell Hotel and Restaurant Administration Quarterly,* 35(3): 72–80.

Kasavana, M. L. and Smith, D. I. (1982) *Menu Engineering: A Practical Guide to Menu Analysis.* Okemus, MI: Hospitality Publications.

Katz, K. L., Larson, B. M. and Larson, R. C. (1991) 'Prescription for the waiting-in-line blues: entertain, enlighten, and engage', *Sloan Management Review,* 32(2): 44–53.

Kelliher, C. (1989) 'Flexibility in employment: developments in the hospitality industry', *International Journal of Hospitality Management,* 8(2): 157–166.

Kimes, S. E. (1989) 'The basics of yield management', *Cornell Hotel and Restaurant Administration Quarterly,* 30(2): 14–19.

Kimes, S. E. (2003) 'Revenue management: a retrospective', *Cornell Hotel and Restaurant Administration Quarterly,* 44(5/6): 131–138.

Kirk, D. (1995) 'Environmental management in hotels', *International Journal of Contemporary Hospitality Management,* 7(6): 3–8.

Kothari, T., Hu, C. and Roehl, W. S. (2005) 'e-Procurement: an emerging tool for the hotel supply chain management', *International Journal of Hospitality Management,* 24(3): 369–389.

Knutson, B., Stevens, P., Wullaert, C., Patton, M. and Yokoyama, F. (1991) 'Lodgserve: a service quality index for the lodging industry', *Hospitality Research Journal,* 14(3): 277–284.

Knutson, B., Stevens, P. and Patton, M. (1995) 'Dineserv: measuring service quality in quick service,

casual/theme and fine dining restaurants', *Journal of Hospitality and Leisure Marketing,* 3(2): 35–44.

Kreck, L. A. (1984) *Menu: Analysis and Planning.* (2nd ed.) New York: Van Nostrand Reinhold.

Kwong, L. Y. L. (2005) 'The application of menu engineering and design in Asian restaurants', *International Journal of Hospitality Management,* 24(1): 91–206.

Kyriakidou, O. and Bowen, A. (2002) 'Effective internal communication for successful small hospitality business', *Hospitality Review,* 4(4): 49–54.

Lane, H. E. (1976) 'The Scanlon plan: a key to productivity and payroll costs', *Cornell Hotel and Restaurant Administration Quarterly,* 17(1): 76–80.

Lashley, C. (1995a) 'Towards understanding employee empowerment in the hospitality industry', *International Journal of Contemporary Hospitality Management,* 7(1): 27–32.

Lashley, C. (1995b) 'Empowerment through delayering: a pilot study at McDonald's restaurants', *International Journal of Contemporary Hospitality Management,* 7(2/3): 29–35.

Lashley, C. (1999) 'Employee empowerment in services: a framework for analysis', *Personnel Review,* 28(3): 169–191.

Lashley, C. (2000) 'Empowerment through involvement: a case study of TGI Friday's restaurants', *Personnel Review,* 29(6): 791–815.

Levitt, T. (1972) 'Production line approach to service'. *Harvard Business Review,* 50(5): 41–52.

Lockwood, A. and Bowen, A. (2003) 'Enhancing customer value for successful small business operations', *Hospitality Review,* 43(4): 46–141.

Lockwood, A. and Deng, N. (2004) Can service recovery help when service failures occur? *Journal of Hospitality and Tourism Management,* 11(2): 149–156.

Lockwood, A. and Guerrier, Y. (1989) Flexible working: current strategies and future potential, *Journal of Contemporary Hospitality Management,* 1(1): 11–16.

Lockwood, A. and Ingram, H. (1999) 'Hotel operations management. In: Brotherton, B. (ed.) *Handbook of Contemporary Hospitality Management Research,* 1st edn. Chichester: J. Wiley & Sons. pp. 415–440.

Lockwood, A., Baker M. and Ghillyer, A. (1996) *Quality Management in Hospitality: Best Practice in Action.* London: Cassell.

Lockwood, A., Bowen, A. and Ekinci, Y. (2002) 'Achieving standards for successful small business operations', *Hospitality Review,* 4(3): 37–43.

Louvieris, P., Phillips, P., Warr, D. and Bowen, A. (2003) 'Balanced scorecards for performance measurement in SMEs', *Hospitality Review,* 5(3): 49–57.

Luo, W., Liberatore, M., Nydick, R. L., Chung, Q. B. and Sloane, E. (2004) 'Impact of process change on customer perception of waiting time: a field study', *Omega: The International Journal of Management Science,* 32(1): 77–83.

Lynn, M. (2001) 'Restaurant tipping and service quality: a tenuous relationship', *Cornell Hotel and Restaurant Administration Quarterly,* 42(1): 14–20.

Maister, D. (1985) 'The psychology of waiting lines'. In J. A. Czepiel, M. Solomon and C. S. Surprenant (eds) *The Service Encounter.* Lexington: Lexington Books, pp. 113–123.

Manning, C. K. and Lieux, E. M. (1995) 'Labour productivity in nutrition programs for the elderly that use a commissary-satellite production system', *Journal of Foodservice Systems,* 8(3): 187–200.

McColl-Kennedy, J. R., Daus, C. S. and Sparks, B. A. (2003) 'Customising service recovery: gender effects of customers and service providers', *Journal of Service Research,* 6(1): 66–82.

McKinsey Global Institute (1998) *Driving Productivity and Growth in the UK Economy.* London: McKinsey Global Institute.

Mifli, M. and Jones, P. (2001) 'Menu analysis in UK foodservice chains', *Tourism and Hospitality Research: the Surrey Quarterly Review,* 3(1): 61–71.

Miller (1987) *Menu Pricing and Strategy.* Boston: CBI Publishing.

Mooney, S. (1996) 'Planning and designing the menu'. In P. Jones with P. Merricks (eds) *The Management of Foodservice Operations.* London: Cassell. pp. 45–58.

Morris, B. and Johnston, R. (1988) 'Dealing with inherent variability: the difference between manufacturing and service?', *International Journal of Operations and Production Management,* 7(4): 13–22.

Morrison, P. (1996) 'Menu engineering in upscale restaurants', *International Journal of Contemporary Hospitality Management,* 8(4): 17–24.

Nelson, K. and Bowen, J. (2000) 'The effect of employee uniforms on employee satisfaction', *Cornell Hotel and Restaurant Administration Quarterly,* 41(2): 86–95.

Nie, W. (2000) 'Waiting: integrating social and psychological perspectives in operations management', *Omega: The International Journal of Management Science,* 28(6): 611–629.

Nikolich, M. A. and Sparks, B. A. (1995) 'The hospitality service encounter: the role of communication', *Hospitality Research Journal,* 19(2): 43–56.

Noone, B. and Griffin, P. (1997) 'Enhancing yield management with customer profitability analysis', *International Journal of Contemporary Hospitality Management,* 9(2): 75–79.

Oakes, S. (2000) 'The influence of the musicscape within service environments', *Journal of Services Marketing,* 14(7): 539–556.

O'Connor, P. and Murphy, J. (2004) 'Research on information technology in the hospitality industry', *International Journal of Hospitality Management,* 23(5): 473–484.

O'Donnell, C. D. (1991) 'Implementation of HACCP at Orval Kent Food Company Inc'. *Journal of Foodservice Systems,* 6: 197–207.

Orkin, E. B. (1988) 'Boosting your bottom line with yield management', *Cornell Hotel and Restaurant Administration Quarterly,* 28(4): 52–56.

Ottenbacher, M. and Gnoth, J. (2005) 'How to develop successful hospitality innovation', *Cornell Hotel and Restaurant Administration Quarterly,* 46(2): 205–222.

Paraskevas, A. (2001) 'Exploring hotel internal service chains: a theoretical approach', *International Journal of Contemporary Hospitality Management,* 13(5): 251–258.

Parasuraman, A., Zeithaml, V. and Berry, L. (1985) 'A conceptual model of service quality and its implications for future research', *Journal of Marketing,* 49(4): 41–50.

Pavesic, D. V. (1985) 'Prime numbers: finding your menu's strengths', *Cornell Hotel and Restaurant Administration Quarterly,* 26(3): 70–77.

Peters, S. and Riley, J. (1997) 'Yield management transition: a case example', *International Journal of Contemporary Hospitality Management,* 9(2/3): 89–91.

Pizam, A. (2002) 'Severity versus frequency of acts of terrorism: which has a larger impact on tourism demand?', *Journal of Travel Research,* 40(3): 337–339.

Pruyn, A. and Smidts, A. (1998) 'Effects of waiting on the satisfaction with the service: beyond objective time measures', *International Journal of Research in Marketing,* 15(4): 321–334.

Raajpoot, N. A. (2002) 'TANGSERV: a multiple item scale for measuring tangible quality in foodservice industry', *Journal of Foodservice Business Research,* 5(2): 109–127.

Rafaeli, A., Barron, G. and Harber, K. (2002) 'The effect of queue structure on attitudes', *Journal of Service Research,* 5(2): 125–139.

Reimer, A. and Kuehn, R. (2005) 'The impact of servicescape on quality perception', *European Journal of Marketing,* 39(7/8): 785–808.

Render, B. and Heizer, J. (1997) *Principles of Operations Management.* Upper Saddle River, NJ: Prentice Hall.

Riley, M. (1992) 'Functional flexibility in hotels – is it feasible?', *Tourism Management,* 13(4): 363–367.

Riley, M. and Lockwood, A. (1997) Strategies and measurement for workplace flexibility: an application of functional flexibility in a service setting, *International Journal of Operations & Production Management*, 17(4): 413–419.

Riley, M., Kelliher, C. and Jones P. (2000) *Multiskilling*. Hospitality Training Foundation, unpublished report.

Rimmington, M. and Clark, J. (1996) Productivity measurement in foodservice systems. In N. Johns (ed.) *Productivity Management in Hospitality and Tourism*. Cassell: London.

Ritzer, (2000) *McDonaldization of Society*, 4th edition. Thousand Islands, Cal: Pine Forge Press.

Roth, A. V. and Menor, L. J. (2003) Insights into service operations management: a research agenda, *Production and Operations Management*, 12(2): 145–163.

Rowe, M. (1989) 'Yield management, lodging hospitality', 45(2): 65–66.

Sasser, W. E., Olsen, P. R. and Wyckoff, D. D. (1978) *Management of Service Operations*. Allyn and Bacon: Boston, MA.

Savkina, R. and Yakovlev, V. (1997) 'Yield management in Russia: characteristics and evaluation', *International Journal of Contemporary Hospitality Management*, 9(2/3): 46–141.

Schmenner, R. W. (1986) 'How can service businesses survive and prosper?', *Sloan Management Review*, 27(3): 21–32.

Schmenner, R. W. and Swink, M. L. (1998) 'On theory in operations management', *Journal of Operations Management*, 17(1): 97–113.

Schwartz, Y. and Cohen, E. (2005) 'Hotel revenue-management forecasting: evidence of expert-judgment bias', *Cornell Hotel and Restaurant Administration Quarterly*, 45(1): 85–98.

Sigala, M., Lockwood, A. and Jones, P. (2001) 'Strategic implementation and IT: gaining competitive advantage from the hotel reservations process', *International Journal of Contemporary Hospitality Management*, 13(7): 364–371.

Sigala, M., Jones, P., Lockwood, A. and Airey, D. (2004) 'Productivity in hotels: a stepwise data envelopment analysis of hotels' rooms division processes', *Service Industries Journal*, 25(1): 61–81.

Siguaw, J. A. and Enz, C. A. (1999) 'Best practices in information technology', *Cornell Hotel and Restaurant Administration Quarterly*, 40(5): 58–71.

Sill, B. (1994) 'Operations engineering: improving multi-unit operations', *Cornell Hotel and Restaurant Administration Quarterly*, 35(3): 64–71.

Sill, B. and Decker, R. (1999) 'Applying capacity management science: the case of Browns Restaurants', *Cornell Hotel and Restaurant Administration Quarterly*, 40(3): 22–30.

Silvestro, R., Fitzgerald, L., Johnston, R. and Voss, C. (1992) 'Towards a classification of service processes', *International Journal of Service Industry Management*, 3(3): 62–75.

Skinner, H., Moss, G. and Parfitt, S. (2005) 'Nightclubs and bars: what do customers really want?', *International Journal of Contemporary Hospitality Management*, 17(2): 114–124.

Smidts, A. and Pruyn, A. (1994) 'How waiting affects customer satisfaction with the service: the role of subjective variables', *Management of Services: a multidisciplinary approach* (3rd Conference), pp. 677–696.

Smith, R. S. and Giglio, R. J. (1979) 'Reducing labour costs in foodservice operations by scheduling'. In G. E. Livingstone and C. M. Chong (eds) *Food Service Systems*. New York: Academic Press. pp. 201–218.

Soriano, D. R. (1999) 'Total quality management: applying the European model of Spain's urban hotels', *Cornell Hotel and Restaurant Administration Quarterly*, 41(6): 54–59.

Sparks, B. A. and Bradley, G. (1997) 'Antecedents and consequences of perceived service provider effort in the hospitality industry', *Hospitality Research Journal*, 20(3): 17–34.

Sparks, B. A. and Callan, V. (1996) 'Service breakdowns and service evaluations: the role of customer attributions', *Journal of Hospitality and Leisure Marketing*, 4(2): 3–24.

Sparks, B. A. and McColl-Kennedy, J. (2001) 'Justice strategy for increased customer satisfaction in a services recovery setting', *Journal of Business Research*, 54(3): 209–218.

Spinelli, M. A. and Canavos, G. C. (2000) 'Investigating the relationship between customer and employee satisfaction', *Cornell Hotel and Restaurant Administration Quarterly*, 41(6): 29–33.

Stevens, P., Knutson, B. and Patton, M. (1995) 'DINESERVE: a tool for measuring service quality in restaurants', *Cornell Hotel and Restaurant Administration Quarterly*, 36(2): 56–60.

Sundaram, D. S., Jurowski, C. and Webster, C. (1997) 'Service failure recovery efforts in restaurant dining: the role of criticality of service consumption', *Hospitality Research Journal*, 20(3): 137–149.

Susskind, A. M. (2005) 'A content analysis of consumer complaints, remedies, and repatronage intentions regarding dissatisfying service experiences', *Journal of Hospitality and Tourism Research*, 29(2): 150–169.

Teare, R. (1996) 'Hospitality operations: patterns in management, service improvement and business performance', *International Journal of Contemporary Hospitality Management*, 8(7); 63–74.

Thompson, G. (2002) 'Optimizing a restaurant's seating capacity: use dedicated or combinable tables?', *Cornell Hotel and Restaurant Administration Quarterly,* 43(4): 48–57.

Thompson, G. (2003) 'Optimizing restaurant table configurations: specifying combinable tables', *Cornell Hotel and Restaurant Administration Quarterly,* 44(1): 53–60.

Thompson, G. M. (2004) 'Planning-interval duration in labor-shift scheduling', *Cornell Hotel and Restaurant Administration Quarterly,* 45(2): 145–157.

Van Dierdonck, R. (2003) 'Capacity management'. In B. van Looy, P. Gemmel and R. Van Dierdonck (eds) *Service Management: An Integrated Approach.* Harlow: Pearson Education Ltd. pp. 277–316.

Van Westering, J. (1994) 'Yield management: the case for food and beverage operations', *Progress in Tourism Recreation and Hospitality Management,* (6): 139.

Voss, C., Blackmon, K., Chase, R., Rose, B. and Roth, A. V. (1997) 'Achieving world class service: an Anglo-American benchmark comparison service practice and performance', Severn Trent Plc: Birmingham.

Walker J. R. (1986) 'The viability of quality assurance in hotels', *Hospitality Education Research Journal,* 12(2): 461–470.

Webster, K. (2001) 'The scope and structure of the food supply chain'. In J. F. Eastham, E. Sharples and S. D. Ball (eds) *Food Supply Chain Management.* Oxford: Butterworth-Heinemann. pp. 37–54.

Wels-Lips, I., van der Ven, M. and Pieters, R. (1998) 'Critical service dimensions: an empirical investigation across six industries', *International Journal of Service Industries Management,* 9(3): 286–309.

Westbrook (1994) 'Priority management: new theory for operations management', *International Journal of Operations and Production Management,* 14(6): 4–24.

Williams, P. G., Ross, H. and Brand Miller, J. C. (1995) 'Ascorbic acid and 5-methyltetrahydrofolate losses in vegetables with cook/chill or cook/hot-hold foodservice systems', *Journal of Food Science,* 60(3): 541–546.

Witt C. A and Witt S. F (1989) 'Why productivity in the hotel sector is low', *International Journal of Contemporary Hospitality Management,* 1(2): 28–34.

Wong, S. and Pang, L. (2003) 'Motivators to creativity in the hotel industry – perspectives of managers and supervisors', *Tourism Management,* 24(5): 555–559.

Wyckoff, D. D. (1984) 'New tools for achieving service quality', *Cornell Hotel and Restaurant Administration Quarterly,* 25(3): 78–91.

Zhou, R. and Soman, D. (2003) 'Looking back: exploring the psychology of queuing and the effect of the number of people behind', *Journal of Consumer Research,* 29(4): 517–530.

Innovation and Entrepreneurship in the Hospitality Industry

9

Cathy A. Enz and Jeffrey S. Harrison

Most hotel companies are in the business of 'selling sleep' to their customers. I teach our staff that we're in the business of 'creating dreams'. (Chip Conley, CEO Joie de Vivre Hotels)

INTRODUCTION

The hospitality industry has undergone tumultuous changes in the last five years. Competitive pressures, shifting consumer preferences and consumption patterns, technological advances, consolidation, price discounting, and new distribution channels are but a few of the changes in the business landscape. Innovation has been championed as a way to cope with these and other changes in the industry. But what exactly is innovation, how has it functioned in the hospitality industry and what are the key ideas to help foster innovation? The purpose of this chapter is to explore hospitality innovation and the related area of entrepreneurship. Innovation and entrepreneurship are connected because the entrepreneurial mindset is essential to founding new businesses as well as rejuvenating existing ones (McGrath and MacMillan, 2000). In this chapter we define innovation and explore how to foster it in hospitality contexts. Entrepreneurship, or the creation of new businesses, is explored in the second portion of this chapter. We focus on the characteristics of entrepreneurs, key issues of concern in start-ups, and franchising as a business form in the hospitality sector. The chapter concludes by offering suggestions for future study of this area. Most of the research referenced in the discussions in this chapter is based on North American conceptualizations of innovation and entrepreneurship and of the activities of North American innovators and entrepreneurs.

INNOVATION

Innovation cannot be separated from a firm's strategy or its competitive environment, which means that what we consider to be innovative is defined by the strategic choices a firm makes and the setting in which the firm operates. Some argue that innovation is the most important component of a firm's strategy because it provides direction for the evolution of a firm (Hamel, 2000; German and Muralidharan, 2001). This view is supported by a variety of studies that have found innovative firms to be higher performers (Grimm and Smith, 1999; Roberts, 1999; Subramaniam and Venkatraman, 1999). Hamel (2000) for example found that CEOs in a wide variety of industries felt that newcomers, not incumbents, had changed their industries primarily by changing the rules. Amit and Zott (2001) find support for this contention in a study of e-businesses in which the introduction of new services and goods (i.e. novelty) was a key driver of value creation.

Other researchers have found that those firms who are first to introduce new goods or services (first movers) are able to gain benefits until competitors imitate (Grimm and Smith, 1999). The concept of the 'Heavenly Bed', first launched by the Westin brand in September of 1999, may be an example of benefit gained by being the first to introduce a product rejuvenation. 'It was inconceivable to me that hotels in the business of selling sleep paid so little attention to their beds', claimed Barry Sternlicht, the then Chairman and CEO of Starwood Hotels and Resorts when he and senior executives first launched the innovation (*Hospitality Design*, 1999). Starwood transformed a basic good into a luxurious object of desire, in the process spawning a new retail enterprise with sales of over $1 million annually and imitators who followed (Sheehan, 2001). Was the new bed really an innovation? If competitors had been providing high quality beds for decades what made this introduction so profitable and innovative? To explore how the industry could consider the offering of a hotel bed as an innovation we first must clarify what innovation means.

What is innovation?

The invention of a new service, product, process, or idea is often called an innovation. For many invention and innovation are synonymous. However innovation also includes existing ideas that are reapplied or deployed in different settings for different customer groups. The early development of innovation theory by Schumpeter (1934) conceived of innovation as a source of value creation in which novel combinations of resources produced new products, production methods, markets or supply sources. Innovations may be a recombination of old ideas or a unique approach that is perceived as new by the individuals involved (Van de Ven et al., 1999). The development of electronic newspapers from around the world delivered to hotel guests on-demand is an example of combining the old idea of providing a copy of a local paper to each guest room with the benefits to be derived from developments in information technology.

Innovation combines invention with commercialization, making it easy to see why innovation and entrepreneurship are so closely linked. Developing a new product or process is not enough; the innovative firm must know how to convert an idea into a service or product that customers want. In many instances the new idea requires the creation of a new business to produce and sell the idea to customers. However, innovation within existing firms is also possible. Returning to the 'Heavenly Bed', as part of the promotional efforts to roll out the new beds *USA Today* ran a story on the front page of its business section (Enz, 2005). On the same day 20 pristine white 'Heavenly Beds' lined Wall Street up to the New York

Stock Exchange in New York City. Inside the Stock Exchange, Sternlicht rang the opening bell and threw out hats proclaiming 'Work like the devil. Sleep like an angel'. Meanwhile, at New York's Grand Central Station 20 more beds graced one of the rotundas, and commuters disembarking the trains were invited to try them out. Similar events were staged that day in 38 locations across the US, tailored to each city. Savannah's event featured a bed floating on a barge down the river, replete with a landing skydiver. Seattle's event took place atop the Space Needle. And to reinforce the message, a concurrent advertising campaign asked: 'Who's the best in bed?' (Sheehan, 2001). In the case of Westin hotels, the commercialization of the innovation was not a new business start-up but a successful marketing and public relations campaign.

Firms innovate in a number of ways, including business models, products, services, processes, and marketing channels with the goal of maintaining or capturing markets, or the desire to reduce costs or prices through greater efficiencies (Harrison and Enz, 2005). Starwood appears to have been as clever at marketing the bed as developing the original 'all white' look of the product, raising the possibility that the real innovation was in marketing the bed. Further, the introduction of the all-white 'Heavenly Bed' with a custom-designed pillow-top mattress, goosedown comforters, five pillows and three crisp sheets ranging in thread count from 180 to 250, was not a radical product innovation.

Types of innovation

To understand innovation it is important to realize that it can be characterized into different types depending on the nature of the change in knowledge. Innovations are often characterized as 'radical' when the knowledge required is different from what exists currently versus 'incremental' when the existing knowledge is built-on to enable a new product, service, process, or marketing channel. The 'Heavenly Bed' was an incremental product innovation. In contrast, expanding worldwide communication via the Internet is more likely to yield radical innovations for the hospitality industry and the establishment of new business enterprises. According to Peter Drucker, 'The explosive emergence of the Internet as a major, perhaps eventually the major, worldwide distribution channel for goods, services, and, surprisingly, for managerial and professional jobs is profoundly changing economies, markets, and industry structures; products and services and their flow; consumer segmentation, consumer values, and consumer behavior; jobs and labor markets' (Drucker, 1999: 47). Firms are using the Internet for e-tailing, exchanging data with other businesses, business-to-business buying and selling, and e-mail communications with a variety of stakeholders. Travel is the most successful commercial sector on the Internet, bringing fundamental and radical changes to both airlines and travel agencies. Airlines in particular were aggressive leaders in using the Internet to bypass their product and service intermediaries. With the advent of electronic ticketing in 1995, airlines were able to reduce distribution costs by combining their established national networks and brand awareness with direct Internet sales. Traditional travel agencies began losing sales not only to airline sites but also to online agencies. According to Sabre® (the Semi-Automatic Business Research Environment, a large global distribution system, was the first real-time business application of computer technology in the travel industry, designed in the 1950s through a partnership between American Airlines and IBM, an innovation that transformed the airline industry from handwritten passenger reservation information to an automated system) 15% of all airline tickets are sold through the Internet, with more than half being sold directly by airline web sites, and the other half from online agencies (National Commission, 2002). Travelers have discovered that they can obtain direct access to information, lower rates, and other benefits (Enz, 2003). Finally, information technologies are changing at such an amazing rate that the Internet is likely to be a source of entrepreneurial ventures for many years to come. In summary, incremental innovations like the 'Heavenly Bed' rely on existing knowledge while the one-stop travel services that permit a customer to complete all travel-related activities by visiting one site, such as Travelocity, rely on radical new technologies, new forms of inter-firm cooperative alliances, sophisticated customer databases and complex revenue management systems.

Another distinction developed in the innovation literature categorizes innovations as product versus process innovations. Product innovations address final goods or services while process innovations address how an organization does

its business. In the first week of Westin's new bed introduction numerous guests called to ask where they could buy the 'Heavenly Bed'. While Westin executives had not anticipated a viable retail business they quickly put order cards with a toll-free number in every room, started placing catalogs by bedsides and desks, and set up a Web site (Guadalupe-Fajardo, 2001). By June of 2004 Westin had sold enough beds on-line to spread the idea throughout Starwood, with the Sheraton (four star), St. Regis (five star) and W (boutique) brands all turning into retailers (Schoenberger, 2004). The use of on-line retailing was a process innovation for getting beds to customers, but also a new product innovation in the form of selling beds and a channel innovation in retailing hotel items. Finally, the 'Heavenly Bed' has spawned new businesses that help hotels run their retail arms. Boxport, a spin-off of San Francisco-based hotel procurer Higgins Purchasing Group, operates Web sites and catalogs for a number of hotel chains (Enz, 2003). In total the simple introduction of a comfortable 'all-white' bed in a hotel chain has illustrated how just one innovation can incorporate incremental, product, process, marketing, and supply chain innovations in order to move from idea to commercialization.

Fostering innovation

Several factors seem to encourage innovation according to a variety of studies. Some of the factors that encourage innovation include: a clear vision and culture that supports innovation and risk taking; top management support; teamwork and collaboration; decentralized approval processes; excellent communications; a learning focused innovation orientation; and rewards for successful managers (Harrison and Enz, 2005). In fact a firm's success may rely more on an overall innovation orientation that produces capabilities for innovation and less on specific innovations. The concept of an organizational innovation system or orientation was developed by Siguaw, Simpson and Enz (2006) and is defined as:

A multidimensional knowledge structure composed of a learning philosophy, strategic direction and trans-functional beliefs that guides and directs all organizational strategies and actions, including those embedded in the formal and informal systems, behaviors, competencies, and processes of the firm.

This orientation promotes innovative thinking and facilitates successful development, evolution, and execution of innovations. Having an orientation toward innovation means developing a pervasive set of understandings about learning, thinking, acquiring, transferring and using knowledge (Siguaw et al., 2006).

In the innovation-orientation framework, strategic direction is the 'way of thinking and leading' that drives the firm over the long run, keeping it innovative, and clear in thought and purpose. The direction is generally articulated through vision and mission statements and objectives. The existing literature suggests that successful innovators tend to have a clear-cut, well-supported vision that includes an emphasis on innovation (Quinn, 1985). Their cultures support this vision by encouraging people to discuss new ideas and take risks. The organization not only tolerates failures, but encourages employees and managers to learn from them (Kuratko and Hodgetts, 2001). The cultures of service firms like Disney, Southwest Airlines, Starbuck's and Ben and Jerry's illustrate the importance of having line-level service workers engaged in creating the experience.

Firms that foster an innovation orientation have designed a unique set of structures and guiding principles that determine activities and behaviors in each functional area. The various functional areas of an innovation-oriented firm are guided by a unique, embedded knowledge structure that encourages and facilitates knowledge transfer across and within sub-units. As Sivadas and Dwyer (2000: 33) state, 'Innovators need some mechanism to connect departmental "thought worlds" so that insights possessed by individual departments can be combined to develop new products that harness the collective wisdom of all involved'.

A culture that supports innovation encourages employees and managers to challenge old ideas by instilling a commitment to continuous learning and strategic change. 'Past wisdom must not be a constraint but something to be challenged. Yesterday's success formula is often today's obsolete dogma.' As J. W. 'Bill' Marriott Jr., the CEO of Marriott characterizes his philosophy, 'Success is never final'. He continually stresses three things in articulating his company's values and culture. The first is the constant need to improve, to always try to get better. Second, is the sharing of best practices across brands. Practices that are invented in one part of the company should be shared with everyone in the company. Third, he notes always be looking for new ideas. Customer needs change and competitors improve (Dube et al., 2001).

Innovation is also more likely to emerge from a company with a culture that values the ideas of every person. Making everyone in an organization responsible for innovation may be one essential way to foster strong innovation cultures according to some experts. As one expert on the topic notes, 'Many companies have succeeded in making everyone responsible for quality. We're going to have to do the same for innovation' (Hamel, 2001: 135). Innovative cultures also promote personal growth in an effort to attract and retain the best people. Joie de Vivre, a small regional hotel company uses a month-long sabbatical program for its salaried employees to reflect and nourish themselves, while Day Hospitality Group provides sabbatical leaves to GMs after five years of service (Conley, 2001; Enz and Siguaw, 2003). The best people also seek ownership, and innovative companies often provide it to them through stock incentives and stock options (Naisbitt and Aburdene, 1985). This is one way to align the interests of the organization with the interests of talented individuals.

Top-management support of innovation is essential, and numerous lodging firms have begun to develop corporate innovation positions or even programs to develop and train employees with regard to innovation and corporate entrepreneurship (Pearce, Kramer and Robbins, 1997). Choice Hotels conducts an annual organization-wide talent review, which includes a mapping of upcoming business initiatives against competency shortfalls by senior executive staff. They use this readiness assessment to determine current leadership capability to pursue new business initiatives (Dube et al., 2001) Because they shape the vision and purpose of the organization, top managers must also serve a disruptive role, making sure that managers and employees don't get too comfortable with the way things are. Richard Branson, CEO of the Virgin Group (including Virgin Airlines), is an excellent example of a CEO that supports innovation. The overall philosophy of the group is to find areas in which Virgin can provide a better service or product to people than they are currently getting (Harrison and Enz, 2005). This philosophy has led the group into a wide variety of hospitality, entertainment, and service businesses.

As top managers support innovation, they also have to be careful not to be too dictatorial in their decision making. Authoritarian management can stifle innovation. This type of management is being replaced by networking, teams and a 'people friendly' style of management (Naisbitt and Aburdene, 1985). At Chowking Food Corporation, an oriental fast-food restaurant, new product development involves almost all key departments, not just the head cooks and the research and development department, 'We are one big team with the president himself heading the product board. All aspects of operations are involved', notes Jojo Ajero the marketing manager (*Business World Online*, 2002).

In addition to top managers, organizational champions are important (Green, Brush and Hart, 1999). A champion is committed to a project and is willing to expend energy to make sure it succeeds. Two champions are needed. The first is a managerial champion, a person with enough authority in the company to gather the resources and push the project through the administrative bureaucracy. The second is a technical champion. This is an expert with the knowledge needed to guide the technical aspects of the project from beginning to end. In a study of best practices in the lodging industry, the importance of an idea champion to foster new practices was revealed in case after case of innovative hotel operators (Dube et al., 2001). The development and successful implementation of hotel level innovations is greatly influenced by just *one* individual in an organization who believes in, is committed to, and champions the idea or practice (Enz and Siguaw, 2003). Unfortunately, many of these champions are unable to sustain the innovations they begin. The lack of time to think, plan, and develop best practices, and insufficient nurturing of innovations with needed resources and top-management support were identified as barriers to the development of innovations in the lodging industry (Dube et al., 2001).

A follow up analysis to a comprehensive Cornell University study of best practices in the US lodging industry found that many of the champions were no longer working for the same company, and many of the practices they initiated had been discontinued. The high mobility of hospitality managers and the escalating rate of consolidation through mergers and acquisitions were the factors that most influenced the longevity of innovations. Enz and Siguaw (2003) report on one innovator whose departure from his hotel resulted in the best practice being discontinued under the new management, although the practice had been responsible for generating a 20% increase in occupancy rates and the highest average daily rate (ADR) of all the same branded peer hotels. As idea champions are transferred, or leave the company altogether, the practice is typically not championed by new management and consequently is no longer utilized, regardless of the documented benefits it previously brought the company. As Ali Kasciki, one industry innovator, observed, 'Unfortunately in this industry short- and medium-term versus long-term strategy is the norm. We go in to turn around a problem and then jump to the next position with a better salary' (Enz and Siguaw, 2003: 116). Hotel companies that are wholly absorbed by another organization appeared unable to sustain their best practices in the wave of sweeping managerial, process, and procedural changes. Further, the acquiring companies often lack the historical knowledge that provides the roots and benefits of the innovation and thus, makes it difficult for the acquiring company to accept and benefit from past best practices. These results provide disquieting insights into how tenuous innovations in the hospitality industry can be.

Rigid bureaucracies can also stifle innovation. They are characterized by rules, policies, and procedures that make it difficult for an individual to vary from normal activities. People who feel as though they cannot or should not vary from established rules are unlikely to be sources of creativity and innovative thought. McDonald's for example has had to reinvent itself to continue market growth by experimenting with a number of product innovations, acquiring new concepts such as Chipotle Mexican Grill and Boston Market (*Restaurant Business*, 2002). To maintain an adaptive, learning atmosphere at all organizational levels, many firms have created self-managed work teams and cross-functional product-development teams, so that multiple perspectives will be brought to problem solving. Teams cut across traditional functional boundaries, so that a single team might include representatives from finance, marketing, information systems, and human resources. These teams are kept small so that they are highly flexible, adaptable, and easy to manage (Quinn, 1985). The management hierarchy in these types of organizations tends to be flat, meaning that there are not a lot of levels in the management hierarchy between the customer and the top manager.

The level at which projects are approved is also a key factor in determining support for innovative activities. Some large corporations require that an idea receive approval from five or more managers before any resources are committed to pursuing it. Innovative organizations allow project teams to form that do not report through the traditional lines of authority. Consequently, their work does not have to pass through multiple levels for approval. The Ritz-Carlton Tysons Corner for example established an innovative program to shift decision making from management to the hourly staff and eliminate by attrition certain management positions. The initiative began with the executive committee of the hotel changing its name to the 'guidance team', to help set the tone for what it hoped to achieve (Walsh et al., 2003). A mission statement was created and signed by all employees, and special attention was given to keeping everyone, especially the hourly workers fully informed and consulted every step of the way. After considerable discussion, the hotel staff identified a number of management tasks for possible transfer to the hourly staff, including forecasting budgets and work scheduling. The results of this initiative were reductions in management costs, lowered employee turnover, increased guest satisfaction, and a more motivated and committed staff (Dube et al., 2001).

Unfortunately, many large companies do not give equal attention to everyone's ideas. They expect senior managers to come up with all of the innovations. Along with an egalitarian culture, excellent communications are found in innovative organizations. They encourage communication by having informal meetings whenever possible, forming teams across functions, and planning the physical layout of the facility so as to encourage frequent interaction (Harrison and Enz, 2005). Higher levels of excellence, competitive advantage, and profitability can only be accomplished when existing innovations are implemented, retained, and improved. Routinization is an important final step in championing new ideas, and true innovators need to be sure that their excellent ideas have staying power. Success in the introduction of a best practice occurs only when the practice becomes incorporated into the

regular activities of the organization and loses its separate identity.

Organizations must commit resources such as people, money, information, equipment, and a physical location for innovations to take hold (Normann, 1971). Giving people time to pursue their ideas is critical, however effective rewards systems can speed the process of change. Innovative firms allow creative people to realize the rewards from their innovative talents without having to leave the company (DeCarolis and Deeds, 1999). Innovation should be rewarded through raises, promotions, awards, perquisites, and public and private recognition. While the upside rewards for innovation should be high, the downside penalties for failed innovation efforts should be minimal.

The findings on innovation in the hospitality industry reinforce the importance of operational integration, and the need to build organizational learning capacity. Hotel companies and individual properties can gain a competitive advantage only if they are able to integrate and apply innovations in day-to-day operations (Enz and Siguaw, 2003). From self-managed housekeeping teams to recycling programs, successful execution of innovations requires top-management support, the involvement of employees, and strong organizational communication. Sadly innovation appears to be one of the casualties of the significant consolidation in the lodging industry. This view is consistent with earlier authors who argued that the standardization built into large hospitality chain operations serves to stifle innovation (Peacock, 1993; Morrison and Thomas, 1999). Not all large organizations lack innovativeness. Corporate entrepreneurship, sometimes called intrapreneurship, corporate venturing, or corporate enterprise involves the creation of new products, processes, and services within existing corporations that enable them to grow (Pinchot, 1985). While there is some debate on the concept of corporate entrepreneurship, it does appear to enhance the performance of large organizations (Pittaway, 2001). For example existing restaurants have begun offering new menu items at an accelerating rate (up 31.6% since the mid 1990s), although competition and the ease of imitation has made these product innovations short-lived (Yee, 2001). Some argue that small companies tend to be better than large companies at innovation. One reason for the difference is that smaller companies are more flexible. They are not subject to the constraints of a rigid bureaucracy that can stifle creative activity. Indeed much of the literature on entrepreneurship has revealed that they possess a greater ability to innovate (Stewart, 1998). In studies within hospitality firms small firm marketing efforts were found to be more dynamic, distinctive, and thus more innovative. Others have found entrepreneurs to be more innovative than managers in large firms (Buttner and Gryskiewicz, 1993). We now turn to a discussion of entrepreneurship to more fully understand this unique group of innovators.

ENTREPRENEURSHIP

Would-be entrepreneurs live in a sea of dreams. Their destinations are private islands – places to build, create, and transform their particular dreams into reality. Being an entrepreneur entails envisioning your island, and, even more important, it means getting in the boat and rowing to your island (Shefsky, 1994: 10).

Entrepreneurial start-ups

The history of the hospitality industry is a story of entrepreneurship. In the broadest sense of the term, entrepreneurship is the creation of new business. It involves opportunity recognition or creation, assembling resources to pursue the opportunity, and managing activities that bring a new venture into existence. Some ventures are complete start-ups, while other ventures are pursued within an existing organization. According to Arnold Cooper, widely acknowledged as a pioneer in the study of entrepreneurship, 'Entrepreneurial ventures, whether independent or within established corporations, might be viewed as experiments. They test to determine the size of particular markets or whether particular technologies or ways of competing are promising. They have good internal communication and enormous commitment from their key people' (McCarthy and Nicholls-Nixon, 2001: 29).

Hundreds of thousands of small firms are created each year. In the United States more than 1 million new jobs across a range of industries are created annually by these firms, while Fortune 500 companies are cutting their workforces. A recent study reported a surge in new business start-ups in the

United States with women, minorities and baby boomers leading the growth in new venture formation. In fact since 1990 the number of entrepreneurs over the age of 50 has increased by 23% to 5.6 million workers according to the American Society of Training and Development (2005). Eating and drinking places in America are mostly small businesses, with more than half being sole proprietorships or partnerships (Milton, 2003). More than half of the private workforce is employed in firms with fewer than 500 employees. These businesses account for about half of the private-sector gross domestic product. Interestingly, two-thirds of new inventions come out of smaller firms (Reynolds et al., 1999). Nevertheless, entrepreneurship is a high-risk activity. Entrepreneurs in nations with highly developed economies often complain about how difficult it is to keep a new business going, and they are right. However, entrepreneurial efforts in less-developed economies such as Russia are even more difficult: 'An unstable government, an undeveloped legal system, overregulation, a virtually unfathomable taxation system, a pervasive mafia, and an inadequate business structure characterize the maze that Russian entrepreneurs must navigate in their attempts to create successful ventures' (Puffer and McCarthy, 2001: 24).

The entrepreneur

Entrepreneurs have been studied for many years, and lists of their characteristics are numerous (Brockhaus, 1980; Gartner, 1989; Hay et al., 1990; Lumpkin and Dess, 1996). Research seeking to identify the specific traits that distinguish entrepreneurs from those who do not start new businesses has been inconclusive; however some evidence exists to suggest that entrepreneurs have a higher need for achievement, a greater risk-taking propensity, and greater internalized locus of control (Wooten et al., 1998). In one study that focused on a battery of personality tests only aggressiveness was a significant predictor of new business starters (Wooten et al., 1998).

Turning to the literature that examines hospitality entrepreneurs, one common characterization used by researchers is the 'craft' versus 'opportunistic' entrepreneur. While 'craft' entrepreneurs are characterized as blue-collar, working-class, with low education and paternalistic management styles, the 'opportunistic' hotelier is defined as middle class with higher levels of education and professional management styles. An early study by Hankinson (1990) found that small hoteliers were just trying to survive, relying on price competition and little marketing, hence more 'craft' like. In contrast more recent work has found that the 'opportunistic' entrepreneur is more likely the case in small hotel proprietors. A close look at entrepreneurs in the small hotel sector in Scotland revealed that those who survive actively pursue rational business objectives and employ marketing strategy to achieve those objectives (Glancey and Pettigrew, 1997). In short, successful entrepreneurs appear to be opportunists, in that they recognize and take advantage of opportunities. Kemmons Wilson founded Holiday Inn in 1952 after a family vacation the previous year in which he became annoyed at the $2-per-child surcharge attached to his bill for each of his five children. He saw the opportunity for a new concept and introduced a chain of hotels that defined the modern hotel era with amenities we now take for granted, such as kids stay for free, air conditioning in every room, free parking, free ice, in-room phones, rates by the room and not the number of people, and high cleanliness standards (Brewster, 2004). Entrepreneurs are also resourceful, creative, visionary, hardworking, and optimistic. Conrad Hilton got his start in the lodging industry by renting out rooms in his home in New Mexico. They are independent thinkers who are willing to take risks and innovate. They also tend to be excellent leaders (Min, 1999). Above all, they are dreamers. Everyone around her thought Debbi Fields would fail when she decided to start selling her delicious cookies. She founded Mrs. Fields' Original Cookies, a company with over $100 million in sales and over 4,000 employees. Unfortunately these common characteristics may seem quaint and the examples simplistic, but they do suggest that there may be several key characteristics that individuals may need to possess in order to succeed in starting their own businesses. More research is needed on the effects of hospitality entrepreneurs' personality in shaping and growing new business startups. Future research should consider whether personality influences entrepreneurship in hospitality and in what ways. A more comprehensive and thoughtful understanding of key characteristics can be

particularly helpful in guiding students to career choices. We now turn to the major activities associated with new business start-ups.

The key entrepreneurial tasks

The primary tasks associated with a new venture are recognition or creation of an opportunity, creation of a business plan, securing start-up capital and actual management of the start-up through its early stages. Entrepreneurship is often envisioned as a discovery process that entails channeling resources toward the fulfill-ment of a market need (Jackobson, 1992). For a start-up to be successful, this often means meeting a need better than other companies Take for example the efforts of Kapil Grove and his father who developed in the early 1980s wines that complemented traditionally spicy Indian cuisine. Grover Vineyards, the business that emerged from this idea was based on experimenting with different types of French grapes and Indian growing conditions and consumer tastes. This business became a joint venture with Veuve Clicquot, a brand of Paris-based luxury goods giant LVMH Moet Hennessy Louis Vuitton SA, only after the Grove family took on the challenge of creating a market where none had previously existed (Parmar, 2002). As this example illustrates, entrepreneurial discovery may be viewed as the intersection of a need and a solution. Entrepreneurial activity occurs anytime an entrepreneur is able to link a need to a solution in such a manner that a new business emerges.

Everything associated with a new venture revolves around a business plan. Creation of the plan forces the entrepreneur to think through the details of the venture and determine whether it really seems reasonable. Investors are also interested in what might be called an 'endgame' strategy. This is a plan for concluding the venture, transferring control to others, or allowing potential investors to exit the venture with a high return on their investments. It may also include contingency plans in the event the venture does not succeed (i.e. alternative uses or sales potential for acquired resources), and an executive-succession plan in case the primary entrepreneur decides to leave the venture. Finally, potential investors will be very interested in the amount of risk found in a venture.

Obtaining start-up capital is probably the most difficult problem facing a potential entrepreneur, and not obtaining sufficient capital is one of the biggest causes of failure. Some of the most common sources of start-up capital include commercial banks, personal contacts, venture capitalists, corporate partnerships, investment groups and business angels. Bank loans result in debt. Personal contacts may be among the most flexible sources of financing because the financiers have a personal interest in the entrepreneur. In the early years of the gaming business in Las Vegas, for example, most of the funding came from the Teamsters' Central States Pension Fund because financial institutions steered away from casino investments (Lalli, 1997). Venture capitalists, corporate partners, investment groups and business angels may provide loans, receive equity, or own part or all of the property in exchange for the capital they provide.

Some entrepreneurs are able to start with their own financial resources. For example, the first of Colonel Sanders' fried-chicken restaurants was financed with his social security (i.e. government retirement) check (Shefsky, 1994). Anne Beiler of Auntie Anne's, Inc. began her first pretzel stand with a $6,000 loan from her in-laws. For larger ventures or once these resources are exhausted, entrepreneurs often turn to a bank. Because of the risks involved, commercial banks do not tend to get very excited about financing entrepreneurial ventures unless substantial secured assets are involved. For example, entrepreneurs often mortgage their homes or offer their automobiles, jewelry, or financial investments as loan security. Banks also consider loans more attractive if a wealthy third party is willing to co-sign, thus taking on the financial obligation if the entrepreneur is unable to pay. Occasionally, a bank will make an unsecured loan based on the reputation or credentials of the entrepreneur or on a personal relationship. Restaurants are often considered a bad investment by bankers who will refuse to finance these ventures because of the low barriers to entry, little collateral value in used restaurant equipment, and the long hours required on-site by owners (Rainsford and Bangs, 1992).

Venture capitalists are another potential source of start-up capital. They are individuals or groups of investors that seek out and provide capital to entrepreneurs with ideas that seem to have the potential for very high returns.

Retail and service businesses began to receive more attention from the venture community in the 1990s, although they typically do not get involved in restaurant investments unless they are larger and more established multi-unit operations. They may seek an annual return as high as 60% or more on 'seed money' for a new venture (Schilit, 1987). In addition, recent research has found that venture capital involvement can have negative consequences for wealth formation of the entrepreneur. In one study founders who rely on high levels of venture capital were worse off financially two years after their businesses engaged in a public offering (IPO) and were more likely to be fired from their firms (Florin, 2005). Financing from a venture capitalist is often combined with capital from other sources such as banks or private investors. In the restaurant industry venture capitalists often wait till later stages in the company's life cycle to provide capital. The most common first disbursement is usually provided to companies that are about to expand (called third-stage or mezzanine financing) rather than to provide start-up financing to develop an initial unit (Hudson, 1999). The House of Blues, a restaurant and nightclub concept used three venture capital firms: Aeneas Group, US Venture Partners, and the Platinum Group to help finance the building of new units and a merchandising operation (Waddell, 2004).

The restaurant industry has many advantages as an investment target including its fragmented nature with good growth potential, low risk of obsolescence in products, and the potential for mass distribution. Considering the use of venture capital can also benefit the entrepreneur because of access to large amounts of capital and the ability to obtain management expertise and advice to refine and sustain the start-up (Hudson, 1999). Entrepreneurs may also turn to corporations to obtain financing. From the entrepreneur's perspective, the chief disadvantage of this form of financing is a partial loss of control and ownership. Large corporations often seek investments in new ventures as a way to obtain new technology, products, or markets. Another potential source of capital is business angels, wealthy individuals who provide start-up capital to entrepreneurs with promise. Many of them were once entrepreneurs themselves. They sometimes seek high returns, but many of them enjoy investing simply for the sake of helping an entrepreneur or advancing the state of technology in an area such as medicine, the arts, or computer technology. Unlike venture capitalists, business angels do not pursue investing full-time.

Why entrepreneurs fail

The early stages of an entrepreneurial start-up are the most difficult (Terpestra and Olson, 1993). Fundamental concerns for entrepreneurs are adequate capital and managing cash flow. Many new ventures fail because of a lack of capitalization. Entrepreneurs often experience cash flow problems because occupancy rates and other cash flows typically take a while to materialize. Low sales can plague a new venture, especially in the first few months after introduction. Many consumers and businesses wait to see if the new restaurant or hotel receives good reviews. They look for a 'track record'. Without sufficient capital, the venture may fail even if the idea was good and the management skills were present. For example, a business may need to be a particular size to generate enough efficiency to make a profit. Or a venture may fail because not enough people know about a product or service due to insufficient advertising. A firm that does not initially have enough financial backing may also assume too much debt too early. Interest payments can divert funds away from more-important uses, and the risk of insolvency from not being able to make timely payments is a constant threat. When entrepreneurs feel high levels of financial risk, their behavior may change. They may be less willing to take other risks that are necessary for the venture to continue to progress.

Even after the process of securing initial financing, the entrepreneur must still set up a system to manage financial flows and keep records necessary to satisfy venture capitalists, creditors, and governmental institutions.

Another common challenge for hospitality entrepreneurs is devising an effective service delivery system. Entrepreneurs seldom get a service exactly right from the outset. Early consumers will very quickly discover flaws, and setting up a system that collects feedback from early customers can help improve service. Theme restaurants, like the once bankrupt Planet Hollywood, suffered from low profitability because of the high wages of their entertainers, inflated prices, stagnant menus and the lack of repeat customers (Campbell, 2000). Continuous improvement is essential because if the product or service is a success, other firms will quickly imitate it, particularly larger firms with more resources. Therefore, it is important to stay one step ahead of the competition in order to enjoy first-mover advantages. It is interesting to note that most entrepreneurs do not feel that competitors are much of a problem. This point attests to the advantages of being small and introducing a new product or service to the market, and the risk-taking characteristic of entrepreneurs.

Even if a venture has sufficient capitalization, and a good service delivery system, it can still fail if market conditions are not favorable. This is a timing issue. An entrepreneur may begin the launch of a new hotel or restaurant right before a downturn in the domestic economy or in a foreign economy upon which the new venture is dependent. Tourism is an industry that is extremely vulnerable to localized recessions and seasonal demand. For example, some expatriate-owned bars and cafés are so focused that they depend on particular nationalities within the already niche tourism market for their success (Blackwood and Mowl, 2000). In these instances sudden and unpredictable changes in consumer demand can be fatal. The language barrier and ignorance of local customs and regulations can also be sources of failure for expatriates running small businesses. From an owners' perspective, a variety of factors appear critical to successful hospitality ventures in mass tourist destinations including: access to sufficient capital, sound planning, effective financial management, management experience, industry experience, business training, use of external advisors, and oversees experience (Blackwood and Mowl, 2000). Management experience may be the most important factor when exploring new venture failure.

According to both entrepreneurs and venture capitalists, the number-one reason new ventures fail is lack of management skill (Zacharakis et al., 1999). Entrepreneurs often have enthusiasm, optimism, and drive, but do not possess the business skills they need to make a venture successful. Management problems are also experienced with inventory control, facilities and equipment, human resources, leadership, organization structure, and accounting systems. The low barriers to entry in the hospitality industry make it possible for inefficient operators lacking skill and experience to enter the industry (English et al., 1996). According to Dun and Bradstreet's 'Business Failure

Record', the retail sector, which includes the restaurant industry, and the service sector, which captures the lodging industry, experiences the highest business failures. In addition, within the retail sector, that includes food stores, and general merchandise stores along with other types of businesses, the eating and drinking places have more business failures than any other single industry (Gu and Gao, 2000). Although experts, executives, and the investment community estimate restaurant failure rates as high as 90% in the United States and West European cities, recent research has found failures to run about 30% in the first year of operations (Hubbard, 2003; Parsa et al., 2005).

For some entrepreneurs the benefit of brand recognition, economies of scale, training, access to a reservation system, and marketing support make franchising a viable approach to business ownership. In addition, chain affiliation often gives hotel developers an edge with lending institutions (Graves, 2003). Of particular concern to many entrepreneurs in recent years are the highly variable reports on the failure rate of franchise operations. The US Federal Trade Commission's consumer protection director notes, 'The most widespread myth is that franchises are a safe investment because they have a much lower failure rate than independent business. In fact, there may be much less of a difference than is commonly thought' (Oleck, 1993: 91). We now turn to a brief discussion of franchising.

Franchising

In the United States, lodging industry franchising is a viable way to start a new venture with around 70% of hotels affiliated with a chain, although this percentage is substantially lower in other parts of the world. Franchising is also popular in the restaurant industry, with the greatest number of franchised concepts being in the fast-food industry (Milton, 2003). Defining new market niches and developing new operating systems are two ways in which franchisors foster innovation (Kaufman and Dant, 1998; Combs et al., 2004). Franchising is when two independent companies form a contractual agreement giving one (the franchisee) the right to operate a business in a given location for a specified period of time under the other firm's (franchisor) brand. Franchisees

agree to give the franchisor a combination of fees and royalties usually in the form of a percentage of unit sales in restaurants or a percentage of room sales in hotels. Also included in these agreements are an advertising contribution paid to the franchisor as a percentage of unit revenues. Hospitality firms engage in what is called business-format franchising, which is when the franchisor sells a way of doing business to its franchisees. This form of franchising is in contrast to traditional franchising in which the franchisor is mostly a manufacturer selling its product through a franchise network such as car dealerships (Lafontaine, 1999).

In addition to helping create new businesses in a home country, franchising has historically been an important tool for international expansion. International franchising is an extremely profitable tool to accomplish branding and growth. In the beginning, the first to export a business-format franchise model to markets outside of the US were fast-food franchise powerhouses such as McDonald's and Kentucky Fried Chicken of parent company YUM! Brands (Polly, 2002). Now these pioneers of international franchising are as common in many other countries as they are in the United States, and they have been joined by other food concepts, hotels and most of the major players in all industries that franchise. However, franchising is a lower return strategy compared with equity investments in hotels abroad (Contractor and Kundu, 1998).

A franchise strategy may be more difficult outside of North America because of the lack of infrastructure in some countries. Finding franchisees with good sites to build on is also a challenge in light of regulations restricting hotel property development in Europe and other parts of the world (Cruz, 1998). A certain level of learning skill or absorptive capacity is required of a franchisee to adopt the business concept in the overseas location; hence studies in hotel franchising have shown that franchising is more likely in developed nations because of the greater likelihood that the global partners possess the needed organizational skills (Contractor and Kundu, 1998). To help deal with the challenges of developing internationally sometimes chains develop master franchisees as partners. Master franchise agreements involve larger franchisees who have the rights to develop in a specific territory. Cendant, for example, continues to expand through master licenses. In contrast,

Marriott does not master franchise as much, and not at all with their Ritz-Carlton brand. Markets dictate whether franchising is used, for example, Marriott relies on franchising in Moscow and has a master franchise agreement with Whitbread in the UK. Often times a master franchise is used in non-strategic or smaller markets.

From the perspective of the franchisee, these business deals are often used to reduce the risks association with new business formation (Combs et al., 2004). Is franchising less risky than going into business on one's own? While conventional wisdom might say yes, current research suggests that joining a new and small franchise may be more risky than starting one's own business because success depends on the capacity of the franchisor and the other few franchisees to make the entire chain work. The likelihood of failure is lower when one joins an established chain with many units such as Subway, Pizza Hut, Applebee's Neighborhood Grill and Bar, Panera Bread Company, or Red Lobster. It is important to understand that franchising is not without risks, with one study showing that less than 25% of companies that offered franchises in the USA in 1983 were still franchising ten years later (Lafontaine, 1999).

An entrepreneur considering franchising as their method of doing business needs to keep in mind that multi-unit franchisee ownership is common in the hospitality industry; for example the average McDonald's franchisee in the USA owns three restaurants. The multi-unit franchisee will have far more bargaining power in their transactions with the franchisor, and hence the new entrepreneur needs to consider their own long-term ownership strategy. Further, a study of quick-service restaurant franchise systems found that growth was faster for chains with a greater proportion of multi-unit franchisees (Kaufman and Dant, 1998). Franchising can be very promising although there will always be opportunities for entrepreneurs who operate independent hotels or restaurant, in which they can reap substantial store-level profits and leverage prime locations and distinctive service features.

CONCLUSION – FUTURE DIRECTIONS

This chapter has examined hospitality innovation and entrepreneurship by defining and exploring how to foster innovation and summarizing the key characteristics of new business formation. In an industry that has historically relied on entrepreneurs and franchising business models, several fruitful areas of future study remain. One promising area for future research is the link between the personal characteristics of the entrepreneur and the strategies they choose. An entrepreneur's past history and personal issues may pervade if not profoundly shape the direction of a new firm and its organizational functioning. A recent study of a family firm found that founder life issues were strongly reflected in strategic priorities (Kisfalvia, 2002). Within the area of franchising, further study of multi-unit franchisees could be a fascinating new area as many firms engage in transnational strategies. In what ways do multi-unit franchisees shape franchisor direction setting and corporate performance? As firms like Starbucks continue their international expansion how do master franchisees help or hinder global expansion?

The troubling findings reported on hotel innovation sustainability and the role of the single idea champion suggests that efforts to craft and sustain an innovation-orientation in the firm may be essential for strategic flexibility and renewal. When idea champions in hotel companies are unable to sustain their innovations it suggests that the industry needs to invest more in the building of a dominant logic that leads to the support of entrepreneurial actions and capabilities. In the complex, uncertain and global world of hospitality successful firms will be those that are able to continuously innovate and encourage entrepreneurship at all levels. There is still much we do not know about innovation and entrepreneurship in hospitality, and hence many promising areas for future study.

REFERENCES

American Society of Training and Development. (1995) 'US Self-Employment rising, says small, business administration,' *Training and Development* 59(9): 19.

Amit, R. and Zott, C. (2001) 'Value creation in E-business,' *Strategic Management Journal*, 22: 493–520.

Blackwood, T. and Mowl, G. (2000) 'Expatriate-owned small businesses: measuring and accounting for success,' *International Small Business Journal*, 18(3): 60–73.

Brewster, M. (2004) 'Kemmons Wilson: America's innkeeper,' *Business Week Online*, 10/13/2004.

Brockhaus, R. (1980) 'Risk taking propensity of entrepreneurs,' *Academy of Management Journal*, 23: 509–520.

Business World. (2002) 'Innovation key to success,' October 31, 2002.

Buttner, E. H. and Gryskiewicz, N. (1993) 'Entrepreneurs' problem-solving styles: an empirical study using the Kirton adaptation/innovation theory,' *Journal of Small Business Management*, 31(1): 22–31.

Campbell, S. (2000) 'Prosperity bodes well for the hospitality industry in the new millennium,' *The Black Collegian*, 30(2): 68–75.

Combs, J., Ketchen, D. and Hoover, V. (2004) 'A strategic groups approach to the franchising-performance relationship,' *Journal of Business Venturing*, 19(6): 877–897.

Conley, C. (2001) *The Rebel Rules: Daring To Be Yourself in Business*. New York: Fireside Book.

Contractor, F. and Kundu, S. (1998) 'Franchising versus company-run operations: modal choice in the global hotel sector,' *Journal of International Marketing*, 28–53.

Cruz, T. (1998) 'Speed to market,' *Hotels*, 32(2): 40.

DeCarolis, D. M. and Deeds, D. L. (1999) 'The impact of stocks and flows of organizational knowledge on firm performance,' *Strategic Management Journal*, 20: 953–968.

Drucker, P. F. (1999) 'Beyond the information revolution,' *Atlantic Monthly*, October: 47–57.

Dubé, L., Enz, C., Renaghan, L. and Siguaw, J. (2001) *American Lodging Excellence: The Keys to Best Practices in the US Lodging Industry*. Washington, DC: American Hotel Foundation.

English, W., Josiam, B., Upschurch, R. and Willems, J. (1996) 'Restaurant attrition: a longitudinal analysis of restaurant failures,' *International Journal of Contemporary Hospitality Management*, 8(2): 17–20.

Enz, C. (2005) 'The heavenly Bed, Could This Be An Innovation? Case Study Prepared for Student Use,' *USA Today*, Fall 2004.

Enz, C. (2003) 'Hotel pricing in a networked world,' *Cornell Hotel and Restaurant Administration Quarterly*, 44(1): 4–5.

Enz, C. and Siguaw, J. (2003) 'Revisiting the best of the best: innovations in hotel practice', *Cornell Hotel and Restaurant Administration Quarterly*, 44(6)

Florin, J. (2005) 'Is venture capital worth it? Effects on firm performance and founder returns,' *Journal of Business Venturing*, 20(1): 113–135.

Gartner, W. (1989) 'Some suggestions for research on entrepreneurial traits and characteristics,' *Entrepreneurship Theory and Practice*, 14: 27–37.

German, R. and Muralidharan, R. (2001) 'The three phases of value creation,' *Strategy and Business*, 22(1): 82–91.

Graves, T. (2003) 'Industry surveys – lodging and gaming,' in *Standard and Poor's*, 16.

Green, P. G., Brush, C. G. and Hart, M. M. (1999) 'The corporate venture champion: a resource-based approach to role and process,' *Entrepreneurship Theory and Practice*, March: 103–122.

Grimm, C. and Smith, K. (1999) *Strategy as Action: Industry Rivalry and Coordination*. Cincinnati, OH: Southwestern.

Gu, Z. and Gao, L. (2000) 'A multivariate model for predicting business failures of hospitality firms,' *Tourism and Hospitality Research*, (2)1: 37–49.

Guadalupe-Figaro, E. (2001) 'Westin And W brands introduce retail catalogue to sell heavenly bed and in-room, trendsetting items,' *Caribbean Business*, 01948326, 2/1/2001, Vol. 29, Issue 4.

Hamel, G. (2000) *Leading the Revolution*. Boston, MA: Harvard Business School Press.

Hamel, G. (2001) 'Is this all you can build with the Net? Think bigger,' *Fortune*, April: 134–138.

Harrison, J. and Enz, C. (2005) *Hospitality Strategic Management: Concepts and Cases*. Hoboken, NJ: John Wiley and Sons, Inc.

Hay, R. T., Kash and Carpenter, K. (1990) 'The role of locus of control in entrepreneurial development and success,' *Journal of Business and Entrepreneurship*, 2: 13–22.

Hospitality Design (1999) 'Sleep study a design wakeup call for Westin,' *Hospitality Design*, Nov/Dec. 1999, Vol. 21, Issue 8.

Hubbard, H. (2003) 'Putting your money where your mouth is restaurants: how to spot a hot investment,' *International Herald Tribune*, January 11: 13.

Hudson, B. (1995) 'Venture capital in the restaurant industry,' *Cornell Hotel and Restaurant Administration Quarterly*, 36: 50–61.

Kaufmann, P. J. and Dant, R P. (1996) 'Multi-unit franchising: growth and management issues,' *Journal of Business Venturing*, 11(6): 343–358.

Kisfalvi, V. (2002) 'The entrepreneur's character, life issues, and strategy making: a field study,' *Journal of Business Venturing*, 17: 489–518.

Kuratko, D. F. and Hodgetts, R. M. (2001) *Entrepreneurship: A Contemporary Approach*, 5th edn. Fort Worth, Texas: Harcourt College Publishers.

Lafontaine, F. (1999) 'Survey—Mastering Strategy: 9 Myths and Strengths of Franchising,' *Financial Times*, November 22: 10.

Lalli, S. (1997) 'A peculiar institution.' In J. Sheehan (ed.) *The Players: The Men Who Made Las Vegas*. Reno/Las Vegas: University of Nevada Press, pp. 1–22.

Lumpkin, G. and Dess, G. (1996) 'Clarifying the entrepreneurial orientation construct and linking it to performance,' *Academy of Management Review*, 21: 135–172.

McCarthy, A. M. and C. L. Nicholls-Nixon (2001) 'Fresh Starts: Arnold Cooper on entrepreneurship and wealth creation,' *Academy of Management Executive* 15: 29.

McGrath, R. and MacMillan, I. C. (2000) *The Entrepreneurial Mindset*. Boston, MA: Harvard Business School Press.

Milton, D. (2003) 'Industry surveys restaurants,' *Standard and Poor's*, May 8, 2003.

Min, S. J. (1999) 'Made not born,' *Entrepreneur of the Year Magazine*, Fall: 80.

Morrison, A. and Thomas, R. (1999) 'The future of small firms in the hospitality industry,' *International Journal of Contemporary Hospitality*, 11(4): 148–146.

Naisbitt and Aburdene (1985) *Re-inventing the Corporation*.

'National Commission to Ensure Consumer Information and Choice in the Airline Industry,' *Upheaval in Travel Distribution: Impact on Consumers and Travel Agents* (November 12, 2002).

Normann, R. (1971) 'Organizational innovativeness: product variation and reorientation,' *Administrative Science Quarterly*, 16: 203–215.

Oleck, J. (1993) 'The numbers game: failure-rate statistics run the gamut, but whose are right?', *Restaurant Business*, 86 (June 10): 91.

Parmar, A. (2002) 'Exposure wins Indian Vintner favor', *Marketing News*, 6. October 28, 2002.

Peacock, M. (1993) 'A question of size,' *International Journal of Contemporary Hospitality*, 5(4): 29–32.

Pearce, J. A., II, Kramer, T. R. and Robbins, D. K. (1997) 'Effects of managers' entrepreneurial behavior on subordinates,' *Journal of Business Venturing*, 12: 147–160.

Pittaway, L. (2001) 'Corporate enterprise: a new reality for hospitality organizations?', *International Journal of Hospitality Management*, 20: 379–393.

Polly, L. (2003) 'International growth patterns remain strong,' *Franchising World*, April.

Puffer, S. M. and McCarthy, D. J. (2001) 'Navigating the Hostile Maze: a framework for Russian entrepreneurship,' *Academy of Management Executive*, November: 24.

Quinn, J. B. (1985) 'Managing innovation: controlled chaos,' *Harvard Business Review*, May/June: 73–84.

Rainsford, P. and Bangs, D. (1992) *The Restaurant Planning Guide: Starting and Managing a Successful Restaurant*. Dover, NH: Upstart Publishing Company.

Restaurant Business (2002): 'McDonalds set to unveil new format,' June: 11.

Reynolds, P. D., Hay, M. and Michael Camp, S. (1999) *Global Entrepreneurship Monitor* (Kauffman Center for Entrepreneurial Leadership).

Roberts, P. (1999) 'Product innovation, product-market competition and persistent profitability in the US pharmaceutical industry,' *Strategic Management Journal*, 20(7): 655–670.

Schilit, W. K. (1987) 'How to obtain venture capital,' *Business Horizons*, May/June, 78.

Schoenberger, C. R. (2004) 'Room for rent – or sale,' *Forbes*, 6/7/2004, Vol. 173(12).

Schumpeter, J. (1934) *The Theory of Economic Development*. Cambridge, MA: Harvard University Press.

Sheehan, P. (2001) 'Back to bed,' *Lodging Hospitality*, 57(4).

Shefsky, L. E. (1994) *Entrepreneurs Are Made Not Born*. New York: McGraw-Hill. p. 10.

Siguaw, J., Simpson, P. and Enz, C. (2006) 'Conceptualizing innovation orientation: a framework for study and integration of innovation research,' *Journal of Product Innovation Management*, 23: 556–574.

Sivadas, E. and Dwyer, F. R. (2000) 'An examination of organizational factors influencing new product success in internal and alliance-based processes', *Journal of Marketing*, 64(1): 31–49.

Subramaniam, M. and Venkatraman, N. (1999) 'The influence of leveraging tacit overseas knowledge for global new product development capability: an empirical examination. In M. Hitt, P. Clifford, R. Nixon and K. Coyne (eds) *Dynamic Strategic Resources*. Chichester: Wiley. pp. 373–401.

Terpestra, D. E. and Olson, P. D. (1993) 'Entrepreneurial start-up and growth: a classification of problems,' *Entrepreneurship Theory and Practice*, 19 (Spring).

Van de Ven, A., Polley, D., Garud, R. and Venkataraman, S. (1999) *The Innovation Journey*. New York: Oxford University Press.

Waddell, R. (2004) 'HOB sets sights on growth armed with fresh funding,' *Billboard*, 116 (14): 10.

Walsh, K., Enz, C. and Siguaw, J. (2003) 'Innovations in hospitality human resources: cases from the US lodging industry.' In Kasluvan, Salih (ed.) *Managing Employee Attitudes and Behaviors in the Tourism and Hospitality Industry*. New York: Nova Science Publisher.

Wooten, K., Timmerman, T.A. and Folger, R. (1998) 'The use of personality and the five-factor model to predict new business ventures: from outplacement to start-up,' *Journal of Vocational Behavior*, 54: 82–101.

Yee, L. (2001) 'Bold new day: top 400 chains keep innovation on the menu,' *Restaurants and Institutions*, July 15, 2001.

Zacharakis, L., Meyer, G. D. and DeCastro, J. (1999) 'Differing perceptions of new venture failure: a matched exploratory study of venture capitalists and entrepreneurs,' *Journal of Small Business Management*, July: 1–14.

10

Financial Management in the Hospitality Industry: Themes and Issues

Helen Atkinson and Tracy Jones

INTRODUCTION

This chapter reviews research in the areas of financial management and management accounting in the hospitality industry, focusing predominantly on research output that has been subjected to peer review through publication in academic articles. It presents a critical review of the state of the art; including an audit of activity, a discussion about where the subject area is going and an identification of key themes and issues for future development. It is based on a review of key academic journals in hospitality and reflects applied literature published since the late 1980s when the last major census of activity was prepared by Harris and Brander Brown (1998). The changes and developments in industry and academe provide a context for a topical review of published research. The literature is reviewed with a subject focus that reflects the range of sub-disciplines in the accounting profession and the topics and issues that have arisen over the last eight years to identify the lacunae in, and the trajectory of, current research. The final section synthesizes the preceding review to make a critical assessment of the state of the art, including a discussion of the links to generic research and makes recommendations for future research directions and approaches to encourage continued development in the field.

Before reviewing the literature it is worthwhile to review the research context, methodology and basis for this chapter. According to Morrison, hospitality research has 'progressed and made significant gains over recent decades' (Morrison, 2002: 167) and much of the research activity is diverse with researchers approaching from many different professional and ontological backgrounds (Guerrier and Roper, 2001). In common with the study by Mason and Cameron (2006), all academic journals in this review display a multidisciplinary approach, covering articles from a range of perspectives including operations management, marketing, human resource management and finance. Based on earlier studies, Baloglu and Assante (1999) identified six functional areas under which publication output could be categorized. These categories were: marketing, finance, administration/strategy, operations, research and development, and human resources. Reviewing the main articles published in five top journals over a seven-year period, they found a total of 1073 articles, of which 29.4% were focused on human resources; 20.2% on operations; marketing and administration/strategy each accounted for 18.9%; and finance a mere 7.8%. The remaining 4.8% of contributions focused on Research and Development. These findings match the authors' experience, which consistently shows that these applied academic journals include relatively few articles focusing on finance and accounting related issues.

In order to ensure that this review captured the bulk of published academic articles in the area of finance, a systemic approach was taken to capturing the extant literature base. Based on the authors' experience and previous literature (Baloglu and Assante, 1999) the following key hospitality journals were audited:

Cornell Hotel and Restaurant Administration Quarterly

International Journal of Contemporary Hospitality Management

International Journal of Hospitality Management

International Journal of Tourism and Hospitality Research (Surrey Quarterly)

Journal of Hospitality and Tourism Research (the journal of ICHRIE)

These journals were selected as they were considered to be the most respected and represented an editorial focus across the UK and Europe, USA and Australasia. These journals were also shown to have provided the majority of refereed output in recent years (Mason and Cameron, 2006).

Following this initial journal search a database of 125 articles was established and analyzed to identify the most prolific authors. An author search was then conducted to find relevant articles in generic journals. Finally a content search was carried out in key generic journals (e.g. *Management Accounting Research*) to find articles focusing on the hospitality industry that were published in mainstream management and accounting journals. As a result of this systematic search process a final database of 187 journal articles was developed which the authors believe captures significant work in the area.

CONTEXT

The hospitality industry has experienced huge change in the past decade, building on insatiable globalization and ever increasing customer expectations. Hospitality companies have evolved into global brands, using a range of strategies to expand and develop in the growing economies of Asia and China amongst others. These markets have massive growth potential and provide the playing field for future strategic competition. Competition is intensifying and customers are more sophisticated, large hotel companies have responded with a portfolio of global brands (Litteljohn, 2003; Olsen et al., 2005) which require standard operating procedures and sophisticated planning and control systems to maintain brand standards in widely distributed areas, and have become highly efficient organizations (Anderson et al., 1999). The increase in large chains and global organizations also applies to the restaurant and contract catering sectors in addition to hotels. The meetings and conventions sector is also growing with increasingly sophisticated management practices and a growing research base (Lee and Back, 2005). These developments have led to changes in approaches to finance related to increasing expansion through management contracts in hotels and an increasing trend to separate ownership from operation.

This trend could lead to diverging interests and needs of hotel operators and hotel investment companies (Guilding, 2003; Sangster, 2003; Beals and Denton, 2005). Investors will follow the best returns (Singh and Schmidgall, 2000) and so the demand for increasing return on investment (ROI) in conjunction with rising costs will lead to increased demand for the sector as a whole to improve productivity. The search for efficiency, considered by many as the managerial 'holy grail' (Ference, 2001), has led to cost saving measures such as outsourcing service departments and centralizing finance functions. These changes also have an impact on performance measurement systems and financial structures in addition to the nature and development of the financial management role.

However, the industry is simultaneously highly diversified with the majority of hotels, restaurants and pubs being small to medium sized enterprises (SMEs). These businesses are in the majority in terms of numbers and volume of business but there is, with a few minor exceptions (Phillips and Louvieris, 2003, 2005), little research on such organizations. The hospitality industry, and in particular the hotel sector, is still hypersensitive to the economic cycle and world events (Felton, 2003); occupancy levels and revenues fluctuate in direct correlation to the economic prosperity of the major economies of the USA, Europe and others. The hospitality industry is also a major contributor to the economies of developed and developing nations, for example in the UK, hospitality, leisure and tourism provide employment for 2 million people and generates a turnover of £76 million (Quest and Needham, 2005).

Hospitality businesses are multifaceted enterprises. Harris (1995) discusses the hotel industry where the product and service elements are complex and interrelated. Harris explains that a hotel product combines three different kinds of businesses in a single operation: (1) pure service (rooms division); (2) the retail (beverage) functions combining stock management and service provision and (3) the production operations of restaurants and food and beverage departments involve all three functions. Each function presents different operational, managerial and financial issues and priorities and thus makes a hotel operation a complex business to manage and an intriguing arena for research.

In addition to the diversity of functions within the hotel operation, hospitality services cannot be stored; the perishability of the product/ service adds another dimension to managing the business. The other features of services also apply, the involvement of the customer in the production process leads to two key characteristics. First, the unique nature of the service encounter (heterogeneity) where every service encounter is different from the last, this has implications for costing and control. Second, services are produced and consumed at the same time (simultaneity) this intensifies the impact of people in the process; the behavior of both employee and customer and the way they interact will have a significant impact on performance and very often leads to a high proportion of associated costs. The high level of intangibles makes customer service and customer satisfaction key issues, thus measuring performance is complex and difficult. Together these characteristics are collectively unique to service operations and present particular demands on management and the financial management systems of such organizations.

The hospitality industry is also populated by many high fixed cost businesses that, according to Kotas (1973), demonstrate a particular business orientation. Harris and Brander Brown (1998) argue that the combination of factors such as, cost structure, demand fluctuation and capital intensiveness, result in a strong market orientation compared to manufacturing companies where the business focus is more cost orientated. This has an impact on accounting systems and costing and has led to calls for the development of new approaches to accounting and reporting systems (Guilding et al., 2001) that are discussed later.

These factors and characteristics combine to make the hospitality industry an interesting and challenging domain in which to engage in financial management research and arguably provide an opportunity for hospitality researchers to contribute new ideas and theory to mainstream research. Within this context we will now continue to review the published research material under six main headings – performance management; planning and control; budgeting; price determination and revenue management; financial management; and finally, the role of financial managers and the hotel Financial Controller. Some of these topics are more diverse and substantive than others but they have been organized this way to try to identify cognate areas of research and provide an effective structure for this review.

PERFORMANCE MANAGEMENT

Measuring business performance is a challenging and ever changing aspect of business management. It is often said that 'what gets measured gets done', so the use of performance measures in business can have profound effects on managerial performance and behaviors. Published results and statistics on different sectors of the hospitality industry can have implications for availability of capital and investors, so this is an important area for hospitality researchers. Performance management can encompass a range of topics so this next section is organized to address the published literature under the following sub-headings: the uniform system of accounts for the lodging industry (Educational Institute of the American Hotel and Motel Association, 1996) and the use of industry statistics; Revenue per Available Room (RevPAR) its uses and alternatives; critical success factors (CSFs) and performance measurement.

Uniform system of accounts for the lodging industry and industry statistics

The hospitality industry, in particular the lodging (hotel) sector, restaurants and clubs, have a long established approach to external benchmarking facilitated by the widespread adoption of a uniform chart of accounts (Harris and Brander Brown, 1998; Chin and Toye, 1999; Kwansa and Schmidgall, 1999). The uniform system of accounts for the lodging industry (USALI) is widely used by hotel companies across the USA and Europe and the growth of US-based chain hotels has led to a worldwide application of this standard. Even where companies are not explicitly operating the USALI, it appears to influence the design of accounting packages, which adopt a departmental accounting system common to USALI (Harris and Mongiello, 2006). The provision of standardized data enables well established consultancy firms such as Pannell Kerr Forster (PKF), Ernst and Young, HVS International and Smith Travel Research, to name but a few, to provide regular reports on operational statistics for sectors, regions and countries to enable companies to externally benchmark performance (Rompf, 1998; Enz et al., 2001) and thus identify realistic and attainable targets and goals at various levels. The benefits of this approach are widely recognized (Enz et al., 2001) but there have been recent debates about USALI regarding the treatment of service charge (gratuities) in the ninth edition (Kwansa and Schmidgall, 1999) and it was suggested by Rompf (1998) that there was a need to reflect industry developments and increasing diversification, for example bed and breakfast inns and timeshare, in industry census and databases. Despite this, the active publication and use of benchmarking data is still a facet of the hotel sector that other sectors and industries would benefit from copying and facilitates longitudinal analysis of industry trends, which in turn facilitates efficiency and performance improvements. Research, such as Enz and Canina's (2002) analysis to better understand the impact of world events on productivity, would probably not be possible in other sectors. However, there are drawbacks to this established benchmarking practice and weaknesses in the accounting data underpinning it. Many critics question the reliability of the statistics produced (Rompf, 1998; Enz et al., 2001). Enz et al. (2001) reviewed 13 years of data and warned against focusing on headline statistics such as the mean without recognizing its weaknesses, they advocated the broad consideration of median and mode and identified the need to carefully choose reference points for effective analysis.

RevPAR, its uses and alternatives

There is an ongoing debate about the appropriateness of the long established measure RevPAR (Brown and Dev, 1999; Douglas, 2000; Slattery, 2002), which like the above statistics, focuses attention on results and is, to a large extent, a product-orientated performance measure in a customer-orientated industry (Krakhmal, 2006). There is arguably an industry wide obsession with RevPAR despite recognition of its well-established weaknesses. Brown and Dev (1999: 33) question whether hotel productivity measures can effectively 'reflect hotels' changing emphasis from a room-only orientation to a full service orientation'. In addition they ask whether a customer-orientated approach should take over from the current product-orientated one; a call later supported by Krakhmal (2006). Slattery (2002) presents three arguments why RevPAR needs reform.

He claims reporting of RevPAR is unreliable, room supply and demand measures are flawed and the variability or lack of links to cash undermines its effectiveness. He also states that 'if reported RevPAR is to regain it credibility' (Slattery, 2002: 148) certain key principles must be accepted:

1 room nights must include total stock and every night of the year;
2 revenue must be cash based, i.e. actual turnover generated from room sales, with no adjustment for complimentary rooms;
3 room revenue should be disaggregated from the hotel package (and the criteria for this made explicit); and
4 all other turnover must be reported separately including non-rooms turnover from all other departments and in-room services.

Slattery (2002) claims that the current situation is unacceptable and that investors and other professionals will demand credible and audited data in the future. Measures such as RevPAC (revenue per available customer), TrevPAR (total revenue per available room) and GOPPAR (gross operating profit per available room) are increasingly being employed (Youres and Kett, 2003; Banker et al., 2005). However RevPAR remains the key measure adopted in a range of research studies such as Brown and Dev (1999) who review the effectiveness of strategic decisions in relation to performance using RevPAR as the key measure performance; Ismail et al. (2002) who review risk and return in hotels, monitoring volatility of RevPAR and Kimes (2001) who found a direct relationship between a reduced RevPar and defects in hotels' facilities. Also, Sin, Tse, Heung and Yim (2005) found that the variety of strategic actions had an impact on performance measured by RevPAR. The perennial difficulty of finding effective productivity measures is recognized by some researchers. For example, Morey and Dittman (2003a, 2003b) have developed approaches to evaluating a general manager's (GM's) performance. Building on work published in 1995, they present and discuss a methodology that endeavors to identify proxies for environmental and local factors thus facilitating meaningful comparison of GM's performance with a view to improving unit performance and identifying best practice (Morey and Dittman, 1995, 2003a, 2003b).

Critical success factors (CSFs)

Another important focus in business performance management are critical success factors (CSFs). However, there is little recent applied work in this area other than that published by Brotherton and others (cited below) who acknowledge that this approach, proposed originally in 1961 by Daniel, has been applied mainly in the Information Systems domain (Brotherton, 2004a). Bullen and Rockart (1981) and Munro and Wheeler (1980) are acknowledged authors on the topic, which also attracts attention from Geller (1985) and Jones (1995), who adopted a CSFs approach to identifying the information needs of managers in hotels. The only recent work is from Brotherton (2004a, 2004b) who builds on his earlier work with Shaw (Brotherton and Shaw, 1996) analyzing research based on a survey questionnaire addressed to the top 50 hotel groups in the UK. In this work quantitative *t*-test analysis revealed 56 CSFs to be statistically significant and confirmed the findings from 1996, that 'the overwhelming majority of CSFs are generic in nature' (Brotherton, 2004a: 36). Importantly, he concluded that the 'high degree of commonality suggests that the nature and focus of hotel management is more generic than contingent' (Brotherton, 2004a: 39); this will be a feature in the discussion about the future of hospitality applied research later in this chapter. In a further article Brotherton (2004b) reviewed CSFs in budget hotels and identified two key dimensions; first, accessibility in terms of location and easy booking and second, performance in terms of accommodation standards, value for money and hygiene and cleanliness. These research findings also challenge the extant literature's dichotomous analysis of CSFs with a more contingent approach and suggests that further research is needed to develop a CSF typology that reflects their multidimensional nature. One of the features of Brotherton's discussion is the operational versus strategic perspectives, which also features in other CSFs studies he has been involved in (see Brotherton and Watson, 2000, 2001), and it is the need to link operations and strategy that leads into the next topic in this review, that of performance management.

Performance measurement

A significant proportion of articles published since 1998 relate to performance measurement. Atkinson (2006) explains that performance measurement is an important area that attracts growing attention from academics and practitioners alike. Building from early work in France on the Tableau du Bord (Epstein and Manzoni, 1997) various models and frameworks have been proposed, the most widely adopted being Kaplan and Norton's Balanced Scorecard (BSC) approach, which integrates performance measures from four perspectives (finance, customer, learning and growth and internal business) to link strategy and operations (Kaplan and Norton, 1992). Since 1998 there have been a series of empirical research projects looking at the implementation of the BSC in the hospitality industry.

Huckestein and Duboff (1999) report on the success at Hilton of implementing a balanced scorecard approach, which was at the center of a review of their business model. This included a review of their value chain and the establishment of a series of integrated initiatives to improve performance by focusing on key value drivers of brand management, revenue maximization, operational effectiveness, and value proposition. Interestingly they identified the need to follow through and the need for this new approach to 'be ingrained in the business culture', Huckestein and Duboff (1999: 38). They also recognized the need for such systems to evolve and acknowledged that as managers 'become more familiar' (1999: 38) they adapt the measures to make the system more effective. These findings are in line with Philips's (1999a: 364) who identifies the need for 'improved techniques for collecting and analyzing data'. Denton and White (2000) provided a detailed account of the implementation of the BSC and the resulting improvement in performance. What was notable about this case study was the ability of the scorecard to mediate and galvanize the differing perspectives and priorities of owners and operators (Sangster, 2003; Beals and Denton, 2005). 'With its alignment of owner and management the balanced scorecard takes a large step toward reversing the lodging industry's longstanding trend that has seen alienation between those interests' (Denton and White, 2000: 107). As this trend is expected to continue the issue of aligning the goals and responsibilities of owners and operators will also continue (Wilson, 2001; Sangster, 2003; Beals and Denton, 2005).

Despite these positive examples from the USA, there is still evidence that progress is slower in the UK and Europe. Atkinson and Brander Brown's empirical study into UK hotels, showed that there was still a 'predominance of financial and past orientated dimensions' (Atkinson and Brander Brown, 2001: 134) and little or no adoption of new frameworks in a comprehensive or systematic way. The reasons cited include 'the influence of corporate ownership, as well as cultural and technological factors' (Atkinson and Brander Brown, 2001: 134). In addition, work by Harris and Mongiello (2001) also identified an emphasis on financial metrics although they identified differences at corporate and unit level. Reviewing practice in European hotel groups they observed a tension between the market orientation of hotels and a reliance on financial metrics and noted the degree of 'balance' between finance, customer, human resources and operations evident in hotel company performance indicators. Some hotel groups showed an imbalance, leaning towards customers and others towards finance.

What is interesting about Harris and Mongiello's research is they found that even where financial indicators are used, these did not dominate the general manager's behavior and actions. They also found that the actions of managers 'suggest that when general managers want to improve their business performance, they initially act on human resources ... then marketing ... and then on operations' (Harris and Mongiello, 2001: 125). Haktanir and Harris (2005) observed, in a separate study of independent hotels, a similar variation between operational managers, who focus on customer satisfaction and senior management, who focused on finance in the independent hotel sector. In addition, Atkinson (2006) noted that a review of recent studies revealed companies with functionally orientated scorecards, which diverge from Kaplan's original notion, thereby losing the essence of innovation, growth and organizational learning in particular.

As part of this ongoing research Atkinson (2006) revealed how performance measurement systems are being used and how they are integrated with other initiatives to deliver improved performance. In one large hotel group, in depth interviews identified an unbalanced scorecard with an emphasis on finance, customer and employees, with little apparent evidence of a focus on the internal business and innovation and learning dimensions. However detailed discussions revealed a series of 'off scorecard'

activities that encouraged innovation through a corporate university, with learning zones in all major units, targets for staff development and continuous improvement initiative teams, which does appear to address this aspect of the scorecard.

The other very interesting pattern emerging in the hotel groups detailed above is the increasing engagement with the scorecard as part of incentive programs, and the move towards the integration of more non-financial metrics (Banker et al., 2005; Atkinson, 2006). Atkinson (2006) states that traditionally incentive schemes have been based on the budgetary system (as identified by Collier and Gregory, 1995b) but in recent years the scorecard has been integrated into the incentive scheme rating system. In one hotel group, each year the scorecard's relative weighting has increased with 25% of the bonus coming from the balanced scorecard scores. This still leaves 75% of the incentive being driven by financial dimensions of performance, but the fact that in the last two years the weighting of the scorecard score has been increased shows growing acceptance and trust in this model. This integration of performance measurement frameworks into management incentives provides an area for interesting research and can build from work such as Arhens and Chapman (2002) who found 'contests of accountability' relating to the use of performance measures in restaurant chains.

Nevertheless, research is still being published that could be interpreted as contradictory. A regional postal survey carried out in the north-east of England by Evans (2005) found a variety of measures being used, thus refuting Atkinson and Brander Brown's earlier work. On the other hand, detailed investigations of the use of management accounting systems in Australia (Mia and Patiar, 2001) found general managers relying heavily on financial measures. This apparent contradiction should be reviewed with caution considering the generalization of small scale findings or it could be argued that this is merely evidence of steady progress over time when viewed in the context of the above literature (Huckestein and Duboff, 1999; Denton and White, 2000; Atkinson and Brander Brown, 2001; Harris and Mongiello, 2001; Haktanir and Harris, 2005) and concurs with Harris and Mongiello's (2001) view that the hospitality industry has evolved.

Although it is argued that performance measurement frameworks and in particular the Balanced Scorecard are becoming widely accepted and widely used, there is however, still a need for further research. Philips (1999a) identified the need for better information systems and data concurring with Harris and Brander Brown (1998) for the need for research with a broader context; Atkinson and Brander Brown (2001) call for research into culture, technology and the role of informal and formal control systems and, along with Evans (2005), they recognize the need to identify up-to-date CSFs. Focusing on another feature, Atkinson and Brander Brown (2003) contend that the balanced scorecard has a key role to play in strategy implementation. The most recent published research confirms the value of understanding the relationship between performance measures and financial performance. Banker et al. (2005) found clear evidence that improvements in simple measures of guest satisfaction were linked to changes (improvements) in profitability when linked to incentive programs. Observing a six-month time lag they noted that there was no need to invest in complex and expensive information systems to create an effective performance measurement system (PMS). In addition, Philips and Louvieris (2005) found an effective PMS operating environment in best practice Tourism and Hospitality SMEs providing an optimistic view of the scorecard's potential for adaptation in the SME context. In a joint publication with Warr and Bowen, they present best practice scorecards integrating key performance indicators (KPIs) and CSFs with a word of caution about the temporal nature of such measures (Louvieris et al., 2003). Although there is a variety of studies in this area research is predominantly focused on the lodging (hotel) sector and based upon small scale qualitative and case study research, this will be a recurring feature in the review and will be discussed later.

PLANNING AND CONTROL

Whilst budgeting is often considered as budgetary 'planning and control', budgeting has been dealt with under a separate heading for a number of reasons. First, alone it accounts for more research articles than all other considerations of planning and control combined. Second, whilst budgets have a planning and control phase they have a broader scope, which is reflected by the variety of research outputs related to budgeting.

Research into the planning and control aspects of accounting lends itself to quantitative research and sophisticated modeling techniques, as shown by Cranage (2003) who tests a simple sales forecasting model for restaurants, which he believes non-accounting specialist managers in restaurants could use to successfully forecast future sales. Using time series software seven years of data was used to predict daily, weekly and monthly sales forecasts. It is argued that short-term forecasting can reduce costs as it allows for better planning of labor and material requirements, adding to more efficiency; however it is also emphasized that managerial judgement is realistically still required and there is no research that identifies the full cost benefit of such systems.

A topic covered by a number of researchers (Enz et al., 1999; Noone and Griffin, 1999; Guilding et al., 2001) is that of the profitability of different market segments and how this can be accounted for and used in business planning. Enz et al.'s (1999) research considered the relationship between the customer mix, products offered and associated costs and thus profitability in hotels. They argue that the idea of increasing the customer base, through serving new market segments could lead to additional costs, as different customer groups may require different products and services. Following their empirical, US-based, research they conclude that offering existing market segments increased products and services does produce higher operating profits, despite the additional costs incurred. However, they conclude increasing the market segments served did not increase financial returns. Their advice is to 'offer more to fewer' (Enz et al., 1999: 62).

Noone and Griffins' (1999) work in Ireland considered 'customer profitability analysis' (CPA) in hotels. As with Enz et al. (1999), they believed profitability varied greatly between customers. The key to implementing CPA is to match individual customer (or customer group) costs to the revenue generated. Using an activity based costing (ABC) system costs and profits are tracked in relation to the customer, not by operating department. Their results showed that high profit contributions were made by some market segments (retail, commercial and UK customers) that generated 137% of total operating profit from 38% of hotel sales whilst only incurring 24% of costs (Noone and Griffin, 1999). In contrast the loss making customers (groups and concessions and non-room customers using bars and food) generated substantial losses and a negative contribution to profits. The implications encompass many aspects of management including, marketing strategy; cost analysis; room contracts, package pricing and services offered in the case study hotel. Whilst different in nature, this research supports that of Enz et al. (1999) in identifying that customer diversity does not always lead to increased profitability.

Guilding et al. (2001) also review the potential use of CPA within the hospitality industry, particularly the implications related to marketing. Within this paper they also consider customer asset accounting (CAA), which they believe to be more radical than CPA. In essence CAA draws upon the concept of intangible assets and views the customer from an intangible marketing asset viewpoint. Guilding et al. (2001) believe this could be used in making marketing based decisions about specific customer groups. They however recognize this would be a radical move and argue that the nature of current management accounting in the hospitality industry does not lend itself to such a marketing-based approach as CAA, although they believe it may be beneficial in the long term.

The opinion that hotels focus on improving operational profit at a unit level, is key to the 'profit planning framework' developed by Graham and Harris (1999). The principle behind this was to fully understand cost behavior and then to apply cost volume profit (CVP) analysis and flexible budgeting to aid the decision-making process. Like other research into hospitality planning and control they recognized the need for organizations to be market orientated, but at the same time the need for such businesses to control associated costs. They also identify, like others, the complexity of product and services in hotels can be challenging in this respect. The productivity consequences of hotel strategies are explored by Brown and Dev (1999). In particular they considered labor and capital productivity measures in hotels. They believe considering these aspects can reduce costs in these areas and may help hotel organizations in running 'optimum' size (200+ rooms) hotels for productivity and may also use such data to consider outsourcing or centralizing

functions currently undertaken in individual units (Brown and Dev, 1999).

As with some other aspects of hospitality accounting and financially applied research, research into planning and control is focused on the hotel sector of the industry. It would appear the complexity of products and services offered to different customer groups leads to specific complexities in this industry sector. The relationship of sales revenue and the associated costs and operating profit generated are not easily considered by market segment. Research has suggested ways in which current management accounting practice can be changed to provide a better link to the needs of decision making in the industry, specifically decision making by operational and marketing managers.

BUDGETING RESEARCH

Whilst there are several journal articles concerning research into hospitality, applied budgeting is not a subject that has been extensively studied, particularly in a European context. This is perhaps surprising when this 'has traditionally been the central plank of most organizations' control mechanisms' (Otley, 1999: 370). Harris and Brander Brown (1998: 166) identified that 'contributions to the area of budgetary planning and control have been relatively diverse'. If anything, the contemporary picture shows even greater diversity since that time. This reflects a vector in generic management accounting research, which has moved from mainly a 'neoclassical economics' base to research that encompasses the broader areas of social sciences, such as the behavioral sciences and organizational theory within research in recent decades (Ryan et al., 2002; Baxter and Chau, 2003).

The work of Collier and Gregory (1995a, 1995b) was included in Harris and Brander Browns (1998) review but is still notable as it represents the first empirical work to cover operational budgeting applied to the UK hospitality industry. Schmidgall joined with new co-authors, a decade after his initial research into hospitality-applied budgeting, to further consider operational budgets in USA hotels. This time the empirical work was extended to draw comparisons with the Scandinavian hotel industry. This work by Schmidgall, Borchgrevink and Zahl-Begnum (1996) recognizes the earlier empirical research by Kosturakis and Eyster (1979) and Schmidgall and Ninemeier (1987), but identifies that these investigations were US-based. The rationale for the 1996 study was that the hotel industry had become more global over the past 20–30 years and therefore research beyond the USA would be useful.

Schmidgall et al. (1996) generally based their hotel industry questionnaire around that previously used by Schmidgall during the 1980s. It does not draw direct comparisons to the previous USA results from the 1980s, but focuses on the comparisons between countries. It identifies a number of similarities between the two countries, but statistically there are a number of differences. For example, whilst they conclude the 'majority' of hotel chains in both samples use a bottom-up approach to budgeting, the statistics show 80% and 64% for USA and Scandinavia respectively. They recognize the limitations of the research, both in sample size and geographical coverage, which does not allow generalizations to be formed from the research results. This article was a benchmark, in that it was the first empirical work reported that specifically focused on hotel operational budgets outside of the USA.

At a similar time, Jones (1997a, 1997b) undertook empirical research investigating hotel budgeting practices, surveying UK based hotel organizations. The results were derived from responses from 43 hotel organizations based in the UK and presented at conferences (Jones, 1997a, 1997b), with the summary results published later (Jones, 1998). This research was the first empirical investigation to focus specifically on budgeting in the UK hospitality industry. It provided many interesting findings and comparisons were drawn to Schmidgall's previous work in the USA. However, the conclusion was reached that although this research provided interesting findings concerning contemporary industry practice more research was required and so Jones continued her research into budgeting within the UK hotel industry employing content analysis to establish, 'budgeting theory', as portrayed in textbooks (Jones, 2003), augmented by a postal survey establishing hotel industry budgetary practice and further in-depth interviews with finance directors in hotel organizations to explore the rationale behind current practice and investigated perceived 'gaps' between theory and practice (Jones, 2006). The findings from

this research have made a valuable contribution to budgeting research in UK hotels.

DeFranco's (1997) USA based study, focused on forecasting and budgeting at the department level in hotels and was based on a survey of hotel based financial controllers. Many questions concerned short-term forecasting, with six questions related to budgeting. The emphasis on the shorter term, forecasting and departmental level issues reflects the view of an industry that is more dynamic and having to react to environmental changes more rapidly than in the past. DeFranco joined forces with Schmidgall a year later to conduct further research into current practice in forecasting and budgeting within US-based hotels (Schmidgall and DeFranco, 1998). These published results had a very different focus from the previous published budgetary research by Schmidgall. The focus of this research was not so much concerned with the process of budgeting, but with the purpose of the budgets and forecasts in the operation. Budgetary control was identified as a key reason for budgeting and much of the paper related to how budgets are used in cost control and the tolerances that are allowed for specific cost items. It does not however identify the process used in budgeting and specific budgetary techniques used.

Since 1998 hospitality applied articles concerning budgeting have related to specific aspects of budgeting and sometimes budgeting is part of a broader research focus. For example, Graham and Harris (1999) consider the development of a profit-planning framework in an international hotel chain. As part of their study they considered the use of flexible budgets specifically.

Brander Brown and Atkinson (2001) considered budgeting in the 'information age'. Their article follows some of the generic management accounting research from the late 1990s into the 2000s concerning alternative approaches to budgeting (better budgeting) and that of 'beyond budgeting'. They review the concerns raised of traditional budgeting systems and whether traditional budgeting is suitable in the twenty-first century. Suggested areas for 'better budgeting', include the use of activity based budgeting (ABB) and zero-based budgeting (ZBB). However, they also recognize that previous empirical work applied to the hospitality industry identifies 'traditional budgeting' as firmly embedded in the hospitality industry. The research of Brander Brown and Atkinson (2001) generally considers budgeting from the perspective of a performance management system (PMS) and how budgeting can be developed alongside fresh approaches to management structures in the hospitality industry. The US- based empirical investigation considers an organization already implementing such management structure changes. They believe that such a re-think of traditional budgeting can lead to a more responsive, empowered and flexible approach, linked to new organizational structures. This was the first article, applied to the hospitality industry, to consider new approaches to budgeting, or 'beyond budgeting'. Within generic management accounting literature there is no agreement over the way forward for budgeting (Hansen et al., 2003). There are those who believe 'traditional budgeting' is not dead and buried, those who believe we must continue to budget but should do so more effectively, whilst others believe we need to move, 'beyond budgeting' (Hope and Frazer, 1997).

Sharma's (2002) detailed paper concerning budgeting systems in hotels is very specific in nature, focusing on the relationship of the budget system characteristics in relation to the perceived environmental uncertainty. The paper acknowledges a lack of previous research into hospitality budgeting. The results, based on 100 Queensland-based hotels, showed that, where perceived environmental uncertainty was low or predictable, budgets were used more frequently than forecasts. However where perceived environmental uncertainty was unpredictable forecasts were more likely to be used. This links to previous research findings that have investigated the role of forecasts, as opposed to budgets, within which traditional budgets are viewed as less flexible than shorter-term forecasts. Part of the 'beyond budgeting' argument relates to the increasing environmental change and the ability of budgets as a tool to respond to such external factors.

Another Australian-based hotel budgeting research project focused on participation in the budgeting process (Subramaniam et al., 2002). These researchers considered the role of budgetary participation in decentralized hotel organizations and postulated that budgetary participation can improve managers' commitment to the organization. Whilst detailed, this research is narrow in focus and does not identify whether participation needs to be a fully 'bottom-up' approach to budgeting, or whether such management commitment can be achieved

through a lower level of participation in the budgetary process. In the same year, Mia and Patiar (2002) studied the relationship between budgetary participation and effective superior-subordinate relationships in hotels in Australia. Their work focused on food and beverage and room managers in large hotels. They concluded that where there are good relationships between these managers and their superiors and there is participation in the budgetary process performance was at its highest. However, they noted performance was not as high when one of these two factors (good relationships and budget participation) was missing. Hence their findings identified that budget participation *per se* did not improve performance; it needs to be coupled with good superior–subordinate relations to increase a manager's performance.

The work by Yuen (2004, 2006) is based on survey work conducted in Macau. Initially his work considered goals and reward systems in relation to managerial propensity to create budgetary slack, where he concluded that the approach to budgeting varied due to the organizational context of the budget. His further research in Macau linked budgetary design with managers' job satisfaction. The work of Yuen is based around the behavioral aspects of budgeting and the relationship of individual managers engaging or interfacing with the budgetary system in their organization. Although there is some valuable work included in the above review, it remains mainly US- and hotel-based.

PRICE DETERMINATION AND REVENUE MANAGEMENT

Harris and Brander Brown (1998) identified the existence of limited literature post 1990 concerning price determination from a financial perspective. Burgess and Bryant (2001) argue that much of the work concerning revenue management has had a marketing or operational management focus. They argue this has led to a focus on maximizing sales revenue but without consideration to costs, therefore the impact on profits is largely ignored in such approaches. They argue that advances in technology now allow the necessary sophisticated costing calculations to be undertaken quickly. In this respect they believe the financial function needs to be more involved in revenue management developments to ensure profit, as opposed to revenue, is maximized.

The series of articles by Quain and Sansbury with LeBruto (1998a, 1998b) consider many aspects of enhancing revenues, both within the lodging sector and in restaurants. These articles provide advice for enhancing revenues and they suggest revenues can be enhanced, whilst at the same time still improving guest satisfaction. DeRoos (1999) suggests that there are 'natural occupancy rates' (NORs), he argues that in each market place there is a NOR, at which point there is little trade-off between occupancy and rates achieved, which impacts upon price setting and average daily rates (ADR) achieved.

DeRoos (1999) believes, in the context of room rate pricing, the NOR regression equation can be calculated and used to judge what price the market is likely to be able to bear and thus this information can assist managers in setting room prices. He does however recognize this potential application needs to be subjected to further study. Gu and Caneen (1998) also applied quantitative techniques to rooms division.

Tso and Law (2005) recognized an expansion in online bookings and specifically focused on the differential in prices offered by key online booking providers, including hotel's own websites in Hong Kong hotels. They identified, that particularly in the three- and four-star market, direct websites generally offered rooms at a higher price than indirect online providers. This study, albeit only a snap shot, highlights the increasing complexity of pricing decisions in an ever-increasing, sophisticated, age of fast-moving technology. Quan (2002) considers the costs associated with taking a booking. He argues that whilst a charge is generally not made to the customer when making a hotel reservation, there is a measurable cost incurred. Option-pricing models are used to determine reservation and cancellation charges for specific groups of customers.

Whilst Pellinen's (2003) study of pricing decisions in Finnish Lapland focused more broadly on tourism enterprises the study included a hotel case study. This identified different pricing strategies for different hotel products. Restaurant pricing was very much a centralized decision, with the hotel having little say in pricing matters. Within rooms pricing the approach was viewed as needing to be made 'holistically'. A revenue management package was used for room pricing, but he emphasized prices could not be merely mechanical calculations and that profits also had to be considered in making room pricing decisions. He concluded that cost is not always considered important in such pricing decisions; market forces take precedence over cost calculations.

As with many aspects of accounting and financial research into the hospitality industry, price determination research has focused around the hotel sector, however there are some exceptions. Chan and Au (1998) consider price determination in their study of profit measurement in Hong Kong-based restaurants. Their research also focuses on the new opportunities offered by newly developed information technology. They argue, with the use of IT, production costs for individual menu items are now feasible and the industry could move away from the gross profit/food cost based traditional pricing. However they also recognize that whilst it may be academically interesting to identify the costs of individual menu items, it may not be as appealing to industry, noting the adoption of loss leaders and competitive pricing in reality.

The above research demonstrates that price determination, whilst having links to financial costing and impacting on profits, also has great implications for operational management, revenue managers and the marketing function alike. This highlights the integrated nature of much research into the hospitality industry. From an accounting and financial researcher perspective such interdisciplinary research needs to be encouraged. Revenue management provides a classical example, with much research focusing on maximizing sales revenue, without consideration of profit generation. A financial perspective to such a topic enhances the body of knowledge and can ensure a broader perspective is maintained.

FINANCIAL MANAGEMENT

In addition to hospitality applied accounting research there is a body of applied research focusing on the financial management of the hospitality industry. Broadly this research can be broken down into that related to financial performance, valuation, investment and financing. Some research focuses at the 'industry' level, assessing the situation across a sector of the industry as a whole, whilst other research focuses more at the organizational level. Much of the research is country or sector specific and does not readily allow for broader implications to be drawn. For the purposes of this review hospitality financial management research has been broken down into six discrete, but not mutually exclusive, areas. These are: financial performance, valuation models, investment analysis tools, hospitality investments, internal asset management, and debt/financing.

Financial performance

The performance of hotel real estate investment trusts (REITs) was investigated by Kim et al. (2002). REITs can be related to property equity, mortgage debt, or both and can be sector specific (Kim et al., 2002). They compared the performance of 183 REITs in different industries over a six-year period, whilst hotel based REITs showed the highest mean returns, they also had the highest standard deviation. They concluded, 'as a portfolio hotel REITs' risk-adjusted performance was similar to that for the overall REIT portfolio' (Kim et al., 2002: 94). The implications of their findings has significance for future strategy directions in the industry property sector as they suggest consolidation, rather than new build, is the correct future growth strategy for hotel REITs. Quan et al. (2002: 81) identify 'increased merger and acquisition activity' in the lodging industry, which supports the findings of Kim et al. (2002) related to REITs. Quan et al. (2002: 89) do however challenge the fact that hotel property 'performs similar to other commercial property'. They also identify that hotel property performs well in inflationary environments.

Beals and Arabia (1998) identify the increased investment in hotel-based REITs over the previous five years, to the extent that they owned 5% of USA hotel room inventory. They identify that the growth of REITs has led to a consolidation of hotel property ownership, which has implications for the industry and is a recurring theme in this review. Today's increase in REITs is compared to the increase in management contracts of the 1970s and Beals and Arabia (1998: 59) believe REITs will attract 'new talent' into the industry, 'vertically integrated REITs that operate multiple brands should appeal to the most competent, ambitious managers'.

Whilst the above research considered the property investment performance of hotels, Pine and Phillips (2005) considered the performance of hotels in China by hotel ownership, size and star rating. They identified hotels funded by groups based in Taiwan, Macau and Hong Kong had the best performance. This was reasoned to be due to such hotels having 'international standards', but also their understanding of the local environment in China. In many respects their categories overlapped, in that larger hotels and those of a higher star rating were also viewed as being higher performers, but such hotels also tended to have funding from foreign partners (Pine and Phillips, 2005). They also identified profits for all overseas-invested properties were higher than domestic invested properties. In a growing market, these findings are interesting, but further research is still required.

Whilst much of this research is focused on hotel properties two research projects focus on restaurants (Gu, 2002; Pratten, 2004; Parsa et al., 2005). Gu (2002) identifies a high risk of bankruptcy for restaurants in the USA and uses a 'multiple discriminant model' to predict those at risk of failure. Using key financial ratios he models the characteristics of bankrupt and non-bankrupt restaurant businesses. He concludes the key features of bankrupt restaurants are that they have 'heavily relied on debt to finance sales growth without proper control of their operating and financing costs' (Gu, 2002: 40). Whilst the majority of financial management based research is quantitative, Parsa et al. (2005) took a qualitative approach to considering the issue of restaurant failure. They argue that bankruptcy is a narrow economic definition of failure and other perspectives, such as marketing or managerial perspectives should also be considered and conclude that restaurant viability is influenced more by internal, rather than external factors.

O'Neill and Lloyd-Jones (2001, 2002) considered hotel values and the strategic implications of 9/11 in the USA. Using automated valuation models that made use of multiple regression analysis they identified economic data that showed the 'down turn' had pre-dated 9/11. From a strategic perspective they believed the evidence identified the need for a 'retrenchment strategy'. Chen et al. (2005) also used regression analysis to consider hotel stock returns, but in Taiwan. They recognize, due to the small number of lodging companies trading in the

Taiwan market, that it is difficult to generalize about their findings. Clearly this is an issue with much of the industry specific financially applied research.

Valuation models

A number of researchers have considered methods or models for the valuation of hotels. It is interesting to note that whilst such research has taken place in a number of countries the consideration of valuation models is focused only on the lodging sector of the industry. Granchev (2000) specifically looks at value drivers, such as growth, RevPAR, market share and profits to build projected cash flow forecasts. He believes that too often investors use an 'accounting-driven' approach, based on the uniform system (USALI) and this can mask what the key drivers are. Nilsson, Harris and Kett (2001) however evaluate different methods of hotel valuation. They conclude that an 'income-based' income capitalization method seems best suited, but believe it can be used alongside a secondary method in order to generate a final valuation for a hotel.

Verginis and Taylor (2004) further considered income capitalization and specifically discounted cash flow (DCF) through their empirically based study. After research conducted with key stakeholders (hotel executives, lenders and valuers) they concluded the general view was that DCF was a superior method for hotel valuation. Some respondents however believed the method needed to be supported by others.

Mitchell and Ingram (2002) reviewed five models of valuation used in retailing for their applicability to hotel valuation. They recognize hotels are often viewed as a 'special case' in terms of valuation, but feel much can be gained from considering best practice in other sectors. Corgel and deRoos (2003a, 2003b) updated their previous work from the early 1990s concerning lodging property prices. They believe the availability of transaction information, alongside better knowledge of the markets developed through the 1990s, has led the lodging industry into a more 'disciplined' approach to hotel pricing. The work of Roubi (2004) with Litteljohn (Roubi and Litteljohn, 2003) added a UK focus to hotel valuation, but drew comparisons to the above work of Corgel and deRoos in the USA. Their hedonic valuation model (HVM) identified a significant

'relationship between hotel property prices and a multiplicity of value drivers' (Roubi and Littlejohn, 2004:180).

Following on from his earlier work with Lloyd-Jones (O'Neill and Lloyd-Jones, 2001, 2002), O'Neill (2004) further considered automated valuation models (AVM) for hotel valuation. He argues this regression analysis, 'captures much of a hotel's value' (O'Neill, 2004: 260), but suggests that splitting the value of the hotel real estate and business operation still remains. He concludes that AVMs are best at valuing a portfolio of properties, as opposed to individual properties. Despite the number of projects in this area, there is agreement that much research work still remains to be undertaken concerning the valuation of hotel properties. It is worth noting the focus of research in this area is specifically lodging industry-based.

Investment analysis tools

Whilst much of the research considered under 'valuation models' relates to valuation to assist in investment decisions its focus remains on the tools used for valuation. Other tools are considered from a more 'financial analysis' perspective. The work of DeRoos (1999) concerning natural occupancy, already discussed from a price determination perspective has wider implications. Natural occupancy rates (NOR) can also be used to determine the investment potential in a given market. Likewise Denton and White's (2000) work concerning the balanced scorecard has implication for asset management and long-term investment enhancement. Similarly, whilst RevPAR can be considered a tool by managers for performance measurement, it can equally be used as a financial management tool. Ismail, Dalbor and Mills (2002) identify that a high RevPAR can signify greater volatility in lodging investment. Breakeven analysis (which is usually associated with costing) is used by Younes and Kett (2004) as a tool to consider investment returns. They extend breakeven analysis to identify the point at which revenues and operating performance cover, not only operating costs, but required equity returns for the hotel (Younes and Kett, 2004). Such research illustrates the arbitrary split made between management and financial accounting techniques, which can often see techniques used as both management and financial accounting tools.

Kim and Arbel (1998) developed a binomial logit analysis model to predict hospitality merger target firms. They identified four key areas that were likely to show a hospitality firm was a potential takeover target. The four areas identified were: a relatively larger firm, mismatch in growth opportunities and liquid resources, high capital expenditure to total assets, and that the firm is undervalued (Kim and Arbel, 1998: 315). Omotayo Brown and Kwansa (1999) use the measurement tools of internal rate of return (IRR) and net present value (NPV) in a novel way to evaluate the societal costs of projects in developing countries. Research into investment analysis tools reflects much of the financial management research, which heavily relies on mathematical modeling and is quantitative in nature.

Hospitality investments

Whilst such research is closely linked with that covered under the 'financial performance' heading, hospitality investment research has an investor, as opposed to industry, perspective. Pernsteiner and Gart (2000) investigated why buyers pay a premium when purchasing hotel properties. Having considered a number of financial aspects and characteristics of purchasers (REITs versus non-REITs for example) they identified that there was little attention paid to many of the financial aspects tested. They concluded that strategic intent, for example market penetration, 'may be a stronger factor in influencing high premiums than are the financial characteristics we studied' (Pernsteiner and Gart, 2000: 77).

Elgonemy (2000) investigated the stock market process of lodging stock to ascertain if they were fairly priced. Whilst identifying the hotel business in real estate terms for investment, he acknowledges that hotels differ from other real estate stock in that they are labor intensive operations, as well as being capital intensive. He argues that 'what counts in the current economy is solid management and proprietary products with large growth opportunities' (Elgonemy, 2000: 23). Oak and Andrew (2003) also focused on the USA real estate market from an investor perspective and found weak forms of market efficiency only.

Singh and Schmidgall (2000) applied the Delphi method to review lodging industry finance and found optimism that different sectors would find suitable finance, but from different sources. For example life insurance companies, pension funds and investment banks would mainly finance upscale luxury hotels, whereas mid-scale and budget hotels were more likely to be financed by local and community bankers and finance companies. Canina (2001) highlights the record number of acquisitions and mergers that took place in the lodging industry during the 1990s. She argues these have generated gains for buyers and sellers alike, 'even though the gains are uneven, the results show that the shareholders of both the acquiring and target firms gain at the time of the merger announcement' (Canina, 2001: 53). This research, as with much financial management based research, is quantitative in nature and the reason why this is the case needs further investigation.

The separation of hotel property ownership from hotel operating was viewed as a US model (Dymock and Clack, 2002; Beals and Denton, 2005), however in more recent times this has increased in Europe. Dymock and Clack (2002: 12) argue that as such models are extended it will lead to 'a more rigorous investment and management process'. Haywood (2003) considers the hotel investment market in Canada as often being viewed in the same light as the USA hotel investment market, but argues Canada has quite a different hotel investment market. Canina and Gibson (2003) considered the issue of 'under pricing' in initial public offering of shares when private firms enter the public markets. Under pricing is calculated as the difference in price at the start and end of the first day's trading. Whilst they identified figures for the hospitality industry were in line with other industries it would appear there has been a significant increase in under pricing during the 1990s.

Mooradian and Yang (2001) considered the dividend policy and performance of REITs in comparison to non-REITs hotel companies. As it is a requirement of a REIT that it 'must distribute 95% of their taxable income (profit) to shareholders in order to maintain their preferential tax status' (Mooradian and Yang, 2001: 80) this has implications. Such a dividend policy means less internal equity funding available, in comparison to non-REITs, which leads REITs to require more external funding for acquisitions (Mooradian and Yang, 2001). Having tested over 30 variables they found some significant difference between the two groups, specifically in asset-adjusted earnings, leverage level, dividend policy and free cash flow levels. Canina et al. (2001) also considered dividend policies in the US hotel industry, but not in relation to REITs. They identified that dividends within the lodging sector were significantly less than other listed stocks on the market. The nature of ownership in the industry, with an increased focus on the separation of property real estate and property management has influenced much of the research work during this period.

Internal asset management

Whilst much of the financial management research considers an industry wide focus there is research focused at the organizational level, specifically related to internal asset management. Guilding and Hargreaves (2003) identify that little is known about capital budgeting within the industry; this is reflected in the lack of research in this area. They considered the use by Australian hoteliers of four key techniques, payback period, net present value (NPV), accounting rate of return, and internal rate of return (IRR). They identified payback was the most commonly used technique, with NPV being second. Although this was true across sub-sections in the study, they found a greater use of more sophisticated techniques in larger companies, but interestingly star-rating did not have an impact.

Denton (1998) considered capital budgeting in the context of the separation of lodging property ownership and property operation. In such situations there needs to be a clear division in responsibility between what one might term 'routine maintenance' (an operator's expense) and 'capital expenditure' (long-term investment) as this can cause tensions. Denton (1998) believes the use of value engineering techniques, which establish a reserve for the replacement schedule by an asset manager can resolve such tensions. The work of Chow, Wright and Haddad (2000) addresses project management and how to ensure costs do not escalate. To 'avoid throwing good money after bad' there have to be sound financial controls in place, but these authors highlight that such controls have additional cost implications so, at the end of the day, the situation becomes a matter of managerial judgement.

Another aspect of financial management not widely researched in the industry is that of equipment leasing. Upneja and Schmidgall (2001) identify a significant growth in hospitality firms leasing, as opposed to purchasing equipment in the last two decades, although the growth was not expected to increase as rapidly in the future. The key reasons cited by respondents for leasing were to avoid equipment obsolescence, tax advantages, and uniform cash flows. The implementation of FRS 15, accounting standards for tangible assets, is a UK specific issue. Whilst Adams (2001) provided guidance on its implementation in the industry, academic research into its subsequent implications needs to take place. Within the broad areas of financial management research, as identified above, little of the research undertaken has really focused on internal asset management issues.

Debt/financing

Singh and Kwansa (1999) made use of the Delphi technique to consider the future of financing in the lodging industry. Their panel consisted of academics, consultants, mortgage bankers, REITs, investment banks, hotel chains, finance and insurance organizations and they discussed debt- and equity-related issues. Whilst raising many different opinions, Singh and Kwansa (1999) concluded operators needed to run efficient operations and achieve consistent margins to encourage debt and equity investors. Further research (Singh and Schmidgall, 2000) considered specific lodging industry segments and how investors had been attracted to different lodging segments, such as motels, full-service, and resort hotels over a period of time. They identify the more recent growth came from gaming related properties (i.e. in Las Vegas), hotel branded timeshares and extended stay development, often associated with all-suite hotels. Their findings are specific to the USA, however the notion of lodging sector segment popularity as investments changing over time has broader implications.

Elgonemy (2002) considers the issue of debt to equity ratio and the pros and cons of debt financing in the lodging sector. Refinancing and restructuring debts are considered and Elgonemy (2002: 21) argues 'the Achilles' heel of real estate is too much debt' and that a balance must be struck. Corgel and

Gibson (2005) further explore the debt/equity balance in the lodging industry, focusing on mortgage rates. By undertaking a time-series simulation over a 17-year period they identified hotels would fare favorably by having variable mortgage rates. Considering this by industry sector, they found this to be particularly true for mid-market, limited-service operations.

Altinay and Altinay (2003) use a case study of a specific organization to consider how hospitality industry growth can be financed. The use of management contracts and franchise arrangements are considered in some detail, but understanding individual 'host country' national markets for such expansion is viewed as key. The issue of estimating hotel financing costs is explored by O'Neill and Rushmore (2000) who use a regression model, linked to corporate bond interest rates, and argue this model works, as it can constantly adjust as the market changes. They believe that hotel mortgage rates are closely linked to corporate bond values, making this a realistic estimate of financing costs in the industry.

Brooker (2002) focused on the finance needs of small hotel enterprises. He suggests the industry needs to look at other 'capital intensive' industries, such as airports, airlines and commercial property to draw comparisons to the hotel industry. Ozer and Yamak (2000) also consider financing for small business, but in the context of Turkey. Empirical investigation with small hotel operators showed the key sources of funds being personal funds and, as the business developed, retained earnings. The use of debt was low as it was not perceived that such financing was unavailable, more that it was not considered desirable.

Only two studies considered financial management in the restaurant sector (Upneja and Dalbor, 2001; Dalbor and Upneja, 2002). In their first study these authors considered short- and long-term debt of publicly traded restaurants in the USA, the second focused specifically on long-term debt. They concluded that restaurant firms with growth opportunities used less long-term debt, whilst there was a positive correlation between size, probability of bankruptcy and a higher long-term debt ratio. Although much of this research focuses on larger-scale US-based lodging organizations, it is clear that many trends and practices can and will travel across to Europe and the rest of the world in due course.

FINANCIAL CONTROLLER AND THE ROLE OF FINANCIAL MANAGERS

The role of the financial controller has evolved over the last seven years but the trends and challenges identified by Harris and Brander Brown (1998) continue, with technology and globalization being issues then and emerging in this later review as catalysts for change. Burgess (2000a) reports the future challenges for hotel financial managers. The findings are based on focus groups, comprised of hotel consultants and controllers, discussing four key issues including changing trends in the industry, technological and environmental issues and the impact of contracting out hotel services. On the basis of this research she suggests that managers need to focus on revenue and cost control to maximize profits; financial managers need to be more customer led and increasingly involved in operations. The need for training and development was also identified to ensure that 'the financial manager is aware of the implications of their actions' (Burgess, 2000a: 8). The need for certification, i.e. a recognized professional qualification in hospitality accounting, was noted in 1998 (Harris and Brander Brown, 1998; citing Geller et al., 1990) and is identified as an important factor in the professional development of the controller role by Potter and Schmidgall (1999) who argue that it is now more important than ever.

Other commentators also recognize key trends in the hospitality industry impacting on the role of financial controllers and managers, including increasing global branding and growth of chains (Atkinson and Brander Brown, 2001; Brotherton, 2003; Littlejohn, 2003; Olsen et al., 2005); the separation of ownership and operation and the resultant tension of stakeholder demands (Denton and White, 2000; Sangster, 2003; Beals and Denton, 2005; Burgess, 2006b). In addition changes in technology and the continued development of revenue management systems, the use of global distribution systems (GDS) and customer relationship marketing (CRM) result in less time taken for basic accounting functions and facilitate more opportunities for data analysis to support optimum business decisions. Graham (2003) identifies best practice of many leading companies, including cost reduction particularly in low value transaction processing. This is achieved through outsourcing (for example payroll) and centralization or clustering of the accounting function; improved quality of information and strategic analysis. These developments require a new approach from financial controllers and Graham (2003) advocates a business partner model, similar to that proposed by Brander Brown and Atkinson (2001), and a future ideal controller who manages technology as a tool and interprets information to facilitate better guest experience. He also advocates a focus on cash 'the right currency in the right bank account at the right time' (Graham, 2003: 8) and personal characteristics of curiosity, creativity and integrity with a team spirit. Gibson (2004) confirms these as traits of the on-property hotel controllers (OPHC) valued by practitioners and recruiters and identifies in addition the need for proactive, problem solving team players with a business minded approach.

Burgess, the main author publishing in this area in the UK, identifies the role of the finance function in revenue management decisions (Burgess and Bryant, 2001). Looking at techniques such as customer profitability analysis (CPA) and activity based accounting (ABC) to identify costs, with Bryant, she calls for the increased involvement in revenue management decisions by the finance area to provide improved financial information to facilitate optimum decision making.

Gibson (2002) concurs with Burgess (2000a) and Graham (2003) that the environment and the role of financial controllers are changing. He builds on his earlier work on decision making (Gibson, 1998), using discourse analysis of interviews to look at the behavioral role of controllers, finding that they are not perceived as 'bean counters' nor 'valued business partner' but rather that they have 'a strong tendency toward characterization of the main role as "company cop" ' (Gibson, 2002: 21). It appears that stereotypes of controllers persist and this applies to gender issues too. Burgess (2000b) found that women generally have lower status jobs and less pay than their male counterparts and Countryman, DeFranco and Venegas (2005) also found pay disparities in clubs and hotels. Burgess (2003, 2004) later noted that although limited improvements are evident, occupational segregation and educational level are key drivers for the continuing discrepancy in achievement of women in financial control. It is suggested that the changes experienced over the last decade have reduced the number of dedicated controllers at unit level particularly in chain-operated hotels (Burgess, 2006b) and increased the demands on financial controllers in the sector (Burgess, 2003; Graham, 2003). In addition, these trends have put more emphasis on the financial skills of general managers and this may become the next critical area in the financial management of hotels. Burgess (2006b) suggests that the controllers are aware that financial skill gaps in management may be leading to sub-optimal decision making and losses.

REVIEW OF HOSPITALITY FINANCIAL MANAGEMENT RESEARCH

In this section we summarize the achievements and characteristics of the published research in each of the topic areas with a view to developing a picture of the state of the art of hospitality accounting research in the final section. A comparison to the generic field will be made where appropriate and suggestions for future research will conclude this chapter.

Review of performance management research

Research in the area of PM demonstrates a practical approach, focusing on the use and effectiveness of industry statistics and performance measures. Research is both critical of (Slattery, 2002) and dependent on (Enz and Canina, 2002; Sin et al., 2005) RevPAR as a measure of performance. The widespread use of benchmarking is acknowledged and criticized and academics continue to explore and debate the efficacy of a wide range of performance measures (Brown and Dev, 1999). Several studies have looked at multidimensional performance measurement frameworks with some in-depth research. Many of these have explored how measures are used for decision making and some have been conceptual papers proposing new or adapted models (Phillips, 1999b; Southern, 1999). In this work a range of methodologies were applied with a predominance of interview and survey techniques, with these often being combined. In this area, in contrast to other topic areas, there were few large-scale quantitative studies. However, in common with other areas of research, and with few notable exceptions, e.g. Arhens and Chapman (2002) and Louvieris et al. (2003), most research takes place in the lodging (hotel) sector.

Many research studies are descriptive; capturing the state of play (Atkinson and Brander Brown, 2001) and identifying benefits (Denton and White, 2000). Others are evaluative providing useful practitioner-orientated outcomes (Harris and Mongiello, 2001; Phillips and Louvieris, 2005) and as such are applied and problem-solving.

Although all these are valuable, there is little evidence of new theory or ideas being generated and thus no evidence to counter the view of the UK Research Assessment Exercise (RAE) 2001 panel that hospitality research 'borrowed mainstream management theory and applied it' (Litteljohn, 2004: 30). Arguably research has not moved on from 1999 and is still often 'isolated and fragmented … with preliminary findings left where they fall rather than providing a basis for further investigation' (Harris and Brander Brown, 1998: 174). CSFs is a case in point; this is an area where there are very few active researchers and yet here, valuable insights into the comparability between the hospitality industry and general business could be further developed and new typologies, which may be applicable beyond the hospitality domain could evolve. However there is no significant coordination within the academic communities and as such work is not developed or replicated, in this respect hospitality research is similar to wider management accounting research (Otley, 2001).

Review of research into planning and control

Research into planning and control has provided some key insights and advice for practitioners. Cranage (2003) reviewed the possibilities of using forecasting tools but warns on drawbacks. Several researchers focus on customer profitability and agree that market orientation is a key feature of the hospitality industry (Brown and Dev, 1999; Guilding et al., 2001). There was significant agreement between researchers of the need to understand different customer segments and that segmentation did not always lead to improved profitability. These studies again add value to our understanding by applying established concepts or methodologies such as activity-based costing and profitability analysis, but were mainly evaluative and informative. Although Guilding et al. (2001) were more radical in proposing a new approach to customer

asset accounting which recognizes current management accounting is not geared to market orientated business environment (Guilding et al., 2001), this is one area where perhaps hospitality research can contribute to generic debates and theory building. Brown and Dev (1999) adopt a more strategic rather than operational focus, looking at how strategic decisions can affect productivity. This research provides useful insights but would benefit from further development and replication as advocated by Otley (2001). It also draws attention to the link between accounting and finance research and development of strategic-orientated research and the potential benefits of multidisciplinary research identified by Otley (2001) and Olsen (2001).

Review of budgeting research

Hospitality-applied budgeting research has continued for almost 30 years, but still, few authors have published findings of more than one research project related to hospitality budgeting. Over the decades Schmidgall is the most prolific researcher into hospitality-applied budgeting. Only five other authors have been identified as having published more than one hospitality-applied budgeting research project: Ninemeier, Rusth (e.g. 1991), DeFranco (e.g. 1997), Jones and Mia; of these five authors, two have published joint research with Schmidgall (Schmidgall and DeFranco, 1988; Schmidgall and Ninemeier, 1986, 1987, 1999), whilst Rusth and Lefever (1988) only briefly mentioned budgeting as part of a wider study. Mia and Jones are therefore the only authors, other than those associated with the work of Schmidgall, to publish research of more than one empirical study into hospitality-applied budgeting.

The USA has been the predominant focus in hospitality-applied budgetary research. Of the empirical based studies identified that had some mention of aspects of budgeting, eight were based on US empirical findings, three in Australia and six in Europe. Of those in Europe this included four in the UK, two of which are by Jones. In terms of hospitality industry sectors hotels have dominated research into budgeting. This is not out of line with the research by Baloglu and Assante (1999) that showed, in general, the lodging sector dominated research into the hospitality industry. Of those papers that focus on a specific sector of the hospitality industry, only one is not applied to the hotel sector.

Harris and Brander Brown (1998: 166) noted that 'contributions to the area of budgetary planning and control have been relatively diverse'. If anything, the picture shows even greater diversity since that time. The continued work by Schmidgall and co-authors remains around the core area of operational budgets, more recently compared to the role of forecasts. Other hospitality-applied budgeting research since the late 1990s has covered specific aspects of budgeting such as; 'better budgeting' (Brander Brown and Atkinson, 2001), risk in corporate governance (Collier and Berry, 2002), environmental uncertainty (Sharma, 2002), and budgetary participation (Mia and Patiar, 2002; Subramaniam et al., 2002). The theoretical perspectives of this research are also varied, but reflect the prominence in generic budgeting research of economic, psychological and sociological perspectives (Covaleski, Evans, Luft and Shields, 2003). As Schmidgall concluded on a number of occasions, the currently published research does not answer all the questions concerning budgeting in the hospitality industry. Empirical research, particularly that focused on the UK, is limited and often this reports what current practice is, without a detailed focus on the rationale for such practice. Potter and Schmidgall (1999: 399) also identify that research into hospitality management accounting also needs to consider other aspects of management to ensure such research 'fits into the overall organizational design and culture of the property'.

Review of research into pricing and revenue management

Although widely researched from a marketing and operations perspective, there are still relatively few research studies published in this area with a financially orientated perspective, a paucity that was reflected by Harris and Brander Brown (1998). The studies included in this review share a common message and support the view that a financial perspective on this topic enhances decision making and can contribute to a useful wider perspective. Research by Burgess and Bryant (2001) argues that the finance function needs to be involved in revenue management to ensure profit is maximized. DeRoos (1999) postulates that there

is a natural occupancy rate (NOR) which affects the efficacy of pricing decisions and calls for further research into this. Isolated investigations into online pricing (Tso and Law, 2005) and the cost of booking (Quan, 2002) provide some insight, but for the industry to benefit, further research is needed to take snapshot findings and generalize them. Chan and Au (1998) advocate that IT can provide detailed cost information to aid restaurant pricing but acknowledge, whilst this is theoretically possible, competition and market forces play a key role in price setting. This area clearly has strong links to other disciplines (operations and marketing) and provides a fertile environment for interdisciplinary research.

Review of financial management research

A number of conclusions can be reached concerning recent applied financial management research. First, it is dominated by research into the US-based lodging sector and it is difficult to draw wider conclusions from this at times. Likewise, research related to other countries can be specific in nature, giving a national, not international focus. Second, the research is generally quantitative in nature, using mathematical models to confirm or predict trends at an industry level, little research is undertaken at the organizational or sub-organizational level. Third, much of the research provides a 'snapshot' in time, which may not be applicable in different market and economic conditions. Fourth, country specific financial regulations considered in some research may have few implications in the international arena.

Given this, what is the heart of hospitality-applied financial research? First, the complexity of lodging ownership is key. Whether this be how you manage both the asset of the property and the operation successfully, or how stakeholders work together when hotel real estate and hotel operation are managed separately. Second is the inter-relationship between the hospitality industry, investment institutions and investment markets. To be adequately financed the industry needs to be attractive to potential investors in an ever changing investment market and hospitality industry. Third, more so than accounting research, financial management research relies heavily on mathematical modeling techniques, with little empirical qualitative research being undertaken.

Review of research into the financial controller

Research into the role and development of financial control is conducted at the forefront of industry developments such as globalization, outsourcing and separation of ownership and operation. The stoic work of a very small number of dedicated researchers (epitomized by Burgess who has published many articles and book chapters in this area) has provided a significant contribution to understanding the changing role of hotel financial controllers (Burgess, 2000a, 2004) and the attitudes towards and perceptions of them (Gibson, 2002). In this area, attempts at longitudinal research address weaknesses identified by Otley (2001) and Harris and Brander Brown (1998), however much of this research was carried out through questionnaires in the UK and thus may have limited applicability to the USA. This area provides an opportunity to follow generic accounting research trends concentrating on 'accounting change and the reconstruction of accounting roles' (Hopper et al., 2001: 282) building on earlier findings to understand the impact on skills in unit based management staff and the effect of changes on decision-making effectiveness.

OVERVIEW OF RESEARCH PROGRESS AND THE STATE OF THE ART

Whilst Harris and Brander Brown (1998) trace hospitality-applied finance research back to the 1970s the history of generic research has a far longer history (Ryan et al., 2002). This is reflected in the volume, scope and maturity of approach in generic research and the development of methodological approaches used. Luft and Shields (2003) map the diverse streams of management accounting literature found in six leading management accounting journals. Their work highlights the diversity of topics and methodological approaches adopted in contemporary research. At a broad level many similarities can be drawn between the spectrum of generic research and that applied to the hospitality industry. At this broad level, this signifies that hospitality-applied research covers generic research areas, but in an applied context. It is at the detailed level that differences can be drawn between the body of generic and hospitality-applied research. For example performance measurement is a topic considered in both generic and applied research, but specific measures, such as RevPAR or TrevPAR are industry specific. Hence hospitality-applied management accounting research can be seen to incorporate both elements of generic research areas in addition to research that is industry specific in focus, but this industry specific aspect tends to be at the 'sub-topic' level.

It is well recognized that management accounting research, up until the 1970s, had a strong neoclassical economic base (Hopper et al., 2001; Ryan et al., 2002; Scapens, 2006). Since that time however, 'new accounting techniques, such as activity based costing, balanced scorecards and strategic management accounting' (Ryan et al., 2002: 91) have developed. Baxter and Chua (2003) focus specifically on the development of alternative approaches to management accounting research in recent times, whilst Covaleski et al. (2003) highlight the use of psychology and sociology in addition to economic-focused research. Much of the applied hospitality research could be said to fit into the broad area of 'traditional' economic based research, with empirical research often being positivistic in nature. Whilst some applied research draws from a broader social sciences perspective this is still limited in the context of applied hospitality research. Ryan et al. (2002: 93) suggest a need for recognition that a range of alternative research approaches are valid, 'and that together they can provide richer insights into the subject'.

Equally within the area of financial based research there is a demonstrable connection between the direction of research in the generic area and that applied to hospitality. In generic research over the last 40 years research has developed through increased financial models and those theoretical models being empirically tested by observation in industry (Ryan et al., 2002). They argue that there has been a clear articulation between observation and theory, particularly in asset pricing research, and that this equally applies to hospitality-applied finance research. As with management accounting research, a picture can be seen that at the broad level the issues and topics are common in generic and hospitality-applied finance-based research. However, the specific characteristics and nature of the hospitality industry can lead to industry specific financial models being developed in hospitality-applied research. For example, new approaches to customer accounting or new theories to mediate hotel owner/operator relationships and tensions.

This review has offered a major census of hospitality-applied financial research since Harris and Brander Brown (1998) and found both a case for optimism and pessimism. First, in terms of volume, there are more research findings being published than ever before. In the 1998 review, the average number of publications per year was nine (based on items included in the bibliography, calculated over the eight years preceding publication), in this review we identified an average of 18 articles published per year (over the eight years preceding this publication). However, it should be noted that this probably does not represent the total robust research output, as anecdotal evidence suggests that much valuable PhD work is not fully published. When we compare with the comments made in 1998, there is still a wide range of topics covered in the literature although the areas of cost control and pricing have attracted relatively less attention from academics in recent years.

There has been little progress in areas highlighted as innovative in 1998, such as 'industry based statistics; business orientation market segment profit analysis' (Harris and Brander Brown, 1998: 174) and there is little evidence of new theories being developed. There is still evidence of 'behind the desk' research with postal surveys and analysis of secondary data (Altinay and Altinay, 2003; Evans, 2005) although there is increasing use of qualitative, in-depth interviews and case-study methods such as Harris and Mongiello (2001), Brander Brown and Atkinson (2001), Jones (2006), Walsh (2003) and Mia and Patiar (2002). Data collected in research centers in the US and UK provides a rich resource for researchers and facilitates larger quantitative studies such as those conducted by Roubi and Litteljohn (2004) and Upneja and Dalbor (2001). However, there is still an ongoing need for more depth in research projects and for academics to follow through on initial or isolated studies.

This is also the case in the generic domain of management accounting research. Otley (2001) discusses the value of replication to increase legitimacy. He also continues to review the tension between rigor and relevance and notes that some mainstream journals have a tendency to prefer large scale generalizable research studies, suggesting that in management accounting research we have perhaps lost sight of what matters: 'It seems that a small effect that is statistically significant is valued more highly than a potentially major effect which, for reasons of sample size or variability does not reach conventional levels of statistical significance' (Otley, 2001: 247). This difficulty is faced by hospitality accounting researchers who, with a few exceptions (Chin and Toye, 1999; Sharma, 2002; Guilding, 2003; Phillips, 2007), do not publish in mainstream journals. It appears that some of the challenges facing generic management accounting research are being experienced in the hospitality-applied finance research domain.

In addition, the majority of academics in the hospitality financial research area are not prolific and produce one or two articles only, those researchers who have published more regularly often work in teams from established US-based research clusters and jointly publish (for example Schmidgall and Enz). Mason and Cameron (2006) observed a link between editorial board membership and research productivity, they also noted regional productivity differences, with Europe achieving the second highest total output behind the North Atlantic Free Trade Area (NAFTA), but when this was calculated relative to the number of universities and academics, the score fell to the bottom of the table behind Australia and New Zealand, Asia and the Middle East. In the UK there is still evidence of a two tier research community; of the two UK universities included in Mason and Cameron's top twenty both were pre-1992 institutions (referred to as 'old' universities), Litteljohn (2004) noted that 70% of submissions to the last research assessment exercise (RAE) in hospitality were from the post-1992 university sector ('new' universities). It could be postulated that the lack of substantial and sustained research output is due to lack of research funding in the 'new' universities, which in turn is responsible for the relatively immature research ethos and lack of economies of scale in research in many UK post-1992 universities. Although criticized for being inward-looking (Olsen, 2001) and relying heavily on theory developed in the generic management fields (Bessant et al., 2003), a feature observed earlier by Ingram (1999), hospitality-applied research has considerable value and it is recognized that there is a place for both applied and theoretical research (Jones and Phillips, 2003; Van Scotter and Culligan, 2003).

Despite this somewhat gloomy picture there is cause for optimism. This comes from increasing self-awareness and maturity in hospitality academics, reflected in recent research debates and self-analysis (Brotherton, 1999a; Lashley and Morrison, 2000; Morrison, 2002; Jones, 2004) and increasing numbers of PhD students engaging in good quality research within the context of a three- or four-year PhD (Otley, 2001). Hospitality financial and accounting researchers should focus on those areas where hospitality is distinctive, where the characteristics and context of the industry could lead to the creation of new ideas and approaches which could be applied to mainstream management research, thereby answering the call for more theoretical research (Van Scotter and Culligan, 2003) and provide an opportunity to contribute to the generic field, thus reversing the observed situation of receiving and applying theoretical frameworks (Litteljohn, 2004). However, Scapens (2006) reflects that generic management accounting research has shifted away from 'what ought to be', theory development research in the 1970s, to research into 'what is' (industry proactive) in the 1980s, to research in the 1990s and 2000s that is more focused on developing an understanding of industry practice and conducting research that can understand and aid practitioners. Whilst some applied hospitality research is descriptive, focusing on 'what is', more reflects the current generic picture, focusing on understanding industry practice to aid practitioners.

Key issues of globalization, technology and empowerment identified by Harris and Brander Brown (1998) remain significant issues for the industry and these provide the context and the driver for changes which make the hospitality industry a rich research arena. We have shown that changing methods of financing hotel companies have led to the increasing use of management contracts (Beals and Denton, 2005; Beals, 2006). These changes will provide opportunities for research in a range of areas, for example, mediating the relationship and duties (Wilson, 2001) of owners and operators, building on the work of Denton and White (2000) relating to performance measurement tools or Beals and Denton's (2005) proposition of détente versus resolution. Also there is an imperative for the continuation of Burgess's work on the role of the financial controller addressing the call from Hopper et al. (2001: 282) to concentrate on 'accounting change and the reconstruction of accounting roles'. Other areas where hospitality industry practice leads the way is in areas such as benchmarking and use of industry statistics, where Chin and Toye (1999) and Harris and Mongiello (2006) call for further research. Also, the strong focus on business orientation could lead to the development of new, more customer-focused, accounting systems (Guilding et al., 2001).

If these rich research opportunities are to be exploited, hospitality financial and accounting researchers should cooperate through collaborative research projects to create research communities of larger size and scale to attract more substantive research projects and funding. Mason and Cameron's (2006) work suggests that clusters of academics interested in similar areas can provide a critical mass of activity and thus foster the development of methodological and philosophical debate and maturity. This review has shown the propensity of this research community to grow and develop demonstrating broad methodological and philosophical engagement and thus providing an optimistic outlook for the future.

REFERENCES

Adams, D. (2001) 'FRS 15 – Friend or foe', *International Journal of Contemporary Hospitality Management*, 13(3): 111–115.

Altinay, L. and Altinay, M. (2003) 'How will growth be financed by the international hotel companies?', *International Journal of Contemporary Hospitality Management*, 15(5): 274–282.

Anderson, R. I., Fish, M., Xia, Y. and Michello, F. (1999) 'Measuring efficiency in the hotel industry: a stochastic frontier approach', *International Journal of Hospitality Management*, 18(1): 45–57.

Arhens, T. and Chapman, C. (2002) 'The structuration of legitimate performance measures and management: day to day contests of accountability in a UK restaurant chain', *Journal of Management Accounting Research*, 13: 151–171.

Atkinson, H. (2006) 'Performance measurement in the international hotel industry'. In P. Harris and M. Mongiello (eds) *Accounting and Financial Management: Developments in the International Hospitality Industry*. Oxford: Butterworth-Heinemann. Chapter 3.

Atkinson, H. and Brander Brown, J. (2001) 'Rethinking performance measures: assessing progress in

UK hotels', *International Journal of Contemporary Hospitality Management*, 13(3): 129–136.

Atkinson, H. and Brander Brown, J. (2003) 'Strategy implementation and the balanced scorecard'. *CHME 12th Annual Research Conference, Trends and Developments in Hospitality Research*, 23–24 April 2003, Sheffield, UK: Hallam University.

Baloglu, S. and Assante, L. M. (1999) 'A content analysis of subject areas and research methods used in five hospitality management journals', *Journal of Hospitality and Tourism Research*, 23(1): 53–70.

Banker, R., Potter, G. and Srinivasan, D. (2005) 'Association of nonfinancial performance measures with the financial performance of a lodging chain', *Cornell Hotel and Restaurant Administration Quarterly*, 46(4): 394–412.

Baxter, J. and Chua, W. F. (2003) 'Alternative management accounting research – whence and whither', *Accounting, Organizations and Society*, 28: 97–126.

Beals, P. (2006) 'Hotel asset management: will a North American phenomenon expand internationally?' In P. Harris and M. Mongiello (eds) *Accounting and Financial Management: Developments in the International Hospitality Industry*. Oxford: Butterworth-Heinemann. Chapter 15.

Beals, P. and Arabia, J. (1998) 'Lodging REITs', *Cornell Hotel and Restaurant Administration Quarterly*, 39(6): 52–59.

Beals, P. and Denton, G. (2005) 'The current balance of power in North American hotel management contracts,' *Journal of Retail and Leisure Property*, 4(2): 129–145.

Bessant, J., Birley, S., Cooper, C., Dawson, S., Gennard, J., Gardiner, M., Gray, A., Jones, P., Mayer, C., McGee, J., Pidd, M., Rowley, G., Saunders, J., Stark, A. (2003) 'The state of the field in UK management research: reflections of the 2001 Research Assessment Exercise (RAE) Panel', *British Journal of Management*, Chichester 14(1): 51–68.

Brander Brown, J. and Atkinson, H. (2001) 'Budgeting in the information age: a fresh approach', *International Journal of Contemporary Hospitality Management*, 13(3): 137–143.

Brooker, D. (2002) 'How to raise finance for a small hotel enterprise – a way forward', *The Hospitality Review*, 4(1): 13–20.

Brotherton, B. (ed.) (1999a) *Handbook of Contemporary Hospitality Management Research*, John Wiley.

Brotherton, B. (1999b) 'Towards a definitive view of the nature of hospitality and hospitality management', *International Journal of Contemporary Hospitality Management*, 11(4): 165–173.

Brotherton, B. (2003) 'Themes and prospects'. In B. Brotherton (ed.) The *International Hospitality Industry: Structure Characteristics and Issues*. Oxford: Butterworth-Heinemann. Chapter 11.

Brotherton, B. (2004a) 'Critical success factors in UK Corporate hotels', *Service Industries Journal*, 24(3): 19–42.

Brotherton, B. (2004b) 'Critical success factors in UK budget hotel operations', *International Journal of Operations and Production Management*, 24(9): 944–969.

Brotherton, B. and Shaw, J. (1996) 'Towards an identification and classification of critical success factors in UK hotels plc', *International Journal of Hospitality Management*, 15(2): 113–135.

Brotherton, B. and Watson, S. (2000) 'Shared priorities and the management development process: a case study of Bass Taverns', *Tourism and Hospitality Research (The Surrey Quarterly Review)*, 2(2): 103–117.

Brotherton, B. and Watson, S. (2001) 'Licensed house management skills in Bass Taverns: a comparative study of senior and house manager views', *Human Resource Development International*, 4(4): 521–542.

Brown, J. and Dev, C. (1999) 'Looking beyond RevPAR', *Cornell Hotel and Restaurant Administration Quarterly*, 40(2): 23–33.

Bullen, C. V. and Rockart, J. F. (1981) 'A primer on critical success factors'. Centre for Systems Research, Sloan Management Centre, MIT Cambridge, Mass. In Brotherton and Shaw (eds) (1996) 'Towards an identification and classification of critical success factors in UK hotels plc', *International Journal of Hospitality Management*, 15(2): 113–135.

Burgess, C. (2000a) 'The hotel financial controller – challenges for the future', *International Journal of Contemporary Hospitality Management*, 12(1): 6–12.

Burgess, C. (2000b) 'Hotel accounts – do men get the best jobs?', *International Journal of Hospitality Management*, 19(4): 345–352.

Burgess, C. (2003) 'Gender and salaries in hotel financial management: it's still a man's world', *Women in Management Review*, 18(1/2): 50–59.

Burgess, C. (2004) 'Planning for the centralization of accounting in chain hotels', *Tourism and Hospitality: Planning and Development*, 1(2): 145–156.

Burgess, C. (2006a) 'Do hotel managers have sufficient financial skills to help them manage their areas?' *CHME 15th Annual Research Conference 2006, Nottingham Trent University*. pp. 55–66.

Burgess, C. (2006b) 'Hotel unit financial management: does it have a future?' In P. Harris and M. Mongiello (eds) *Accounting and Financial Management: Developments in the International Hospitality Industry*. Oxford: Butterworth-Heinemann. Chapter 14.

Burgess, C. and Bryant, K. (2001) 'Revenue management – the contribution of the financial function to profitability', *International Journal of Contemporary Hospitality Management*, 13(3): 144–150.

Canina, L. (2001) 'Acquisitions in the lodging industry: good news for buyers and sellers', *Cornell Hotel and Restaurant Administration Quarterly*, 42(6): 47–54.

Canina, L. and Gibson, S. (2003) 'Understanding first-day returns of hospitality initial public offerings', *Cornell Hotel and Restaurant Administration Quarterly*, 44(4): 17–28.

Canina, L., Advani, R., Greenman, A. and Palimeri, I. (2001) 'Dividend policy on lodging industry', *Journal of Hospitality and Tourism Research*, 25(1): 69–89.

Chan, W. and Au, N. (1998) 'Profit measurement of menu items: in Hong Kong's Chinese Restaurants', *Cornell Hotel and Restaurant Administration Quarterly*, 39(2): 70–75.

Chen, M.-H., Kim, W. G. and Kim, H. J. (2005) 'The impact of macroeconomic and non-macroeconomic forces on hotel stock returns', *International Journal of Hospitality Management*, 24(2): 243–258.

Chin, J. and Toye, P. (1999) 'A five star accounting system for the hotel industry', *Accounting and Business*, Feb: 24–27.

Chow, C., Wright, P. and Haddad, K. (2000) 'Increasing the effectiveness of hotels' investments: how to avoid throwing good money after bad', *Cornell Hotel and Restaurant Administration Quarterly*, 41(6): 49–55.

Collier, P. and Berry, A. (2002) 'Risk in the process of budgeting', *Management Accounting Research*, 13: 273–279.

Collier, P. and Gregory, A. (1995a) 'Strategic management accounting: a UK hotel sector case study', *International Journal of Contemporary Hospitality Management*, 17(1): 16–21.

Collier, P. and Gregory, A. (1995b) 'The practice of management accounting in hotel groups'. In P. Harris (ed.) *Accounting and Finance for the International Hospitality Industry*. Oxford: Butterworth-Heinemann. Chapter 8, pp. 137–160.

Corgel, J. and DeRoos, J. (2003a) 'Buying high and selling low in the lodging-property market', *Cornell Hotel and Restaurant Administration Quarterly*, 44(5/6): 69–75.

Corgel, J. and DeRoos, J. (2003b) 'Buying high and selling low revisited: the "quiet industry"', *Cornell Hotel and Restaurant Administration Quarterly*, 44(5/6): 76–80.

Corgel, J. and Gibson, S. (2005) 'The use of fixed-rate and floating-rate debt for hotels', *Cornell Hotel and Restaurant Administration Quarterly*, 46(4): 413–430.

Countryman, C. C., DeFranco, A. and Venegas, T. (2005) 'Controller: a viable career for hospitality students', *International Journal of Contemporary Hospitality Management*, 17(7): 577–589.

Covaleski, M., Evans, J., Luft, J. and Shields, M. (2003) 'Budgeting research: three theoretical perspectives and criteria for selective integration', *Management Accounting Research (USA)*, 15: 3–49.

Cranage, D. (2003) 'Practical time series forecasting for the hospitality manager', *International Journal of Contemporary Hospitality Management*, 15(3): 86–93.

Dalbor, M. C. and Upneja, A. (2002) 'Factors affecting the longterm debt decision of restaurant firms', *Journal of Hospitality and Tourism Research*, 26(4): 422–432.

Daniel, D. R. (1961) Management information crisis (Harvard Business Review Sept/Oct 111–120). In Brotherton and Shaw (eds) (1996) 'Towards an identification and classification of critical success factors in UK hotels plc', *International Journal of Hospitality Management*, 15(2): 113–135.

DeFranco, A. (1997) 'The importance and use of financial forecasting and budgeting at the departmental level in the hotel industry as perceived by hotel controllers', *Hospitality Research Journal*, 20(3): 99–110.

Denton, P. (1998) 'Managing capital expenditure: using value engineering', *Cornell Hotel and Restaurant Administration Quarterly*, 39(2): 30–37.

Denton, P. and White, B. (2000) 'Implementing a balanced-scorecard approach to managing hotel operations', *Cornell Hotel and Restaurant Administration Quarterly*, 41(1): 94–107.

DeRoos, J. (1999) 'Natural occupancy rates and development gaps: a look at the U.S. lodging industry', *Cornell Hotel and Restaurant Administration Quarterly*, 40(2): 14–22.

Douglas, P. C. (2000) 'Measuring productivity and performance in the hospitality industry', *The National Public Accountant*, 45(5): 15.

Dymock, K. and Clack, V. (2002) 'Investment vehicles and operating companies', *The Hospitality Review*, 4(1): 6–12.

Educational Institute of the American Hotel and Motel Association (1996) *Uniform System of Accounts for the Lodging Industry* (9th edn). Educational Institute of the American Hotel and Motel Association.

Elgonemy, A. (2000) 'The pricing of lodging stocks: a reality check', *Cornell Hotel and Restaurant Administration Quarterly*, 41(6): 18–28.

Elgonemy, A. (2002) 'Debt-financing alternatives: refinancing and restructuring in the lodging industry', *Cornell Hotel and Restaurant Administration Quarterly*, 43(3): 7–21.

Enz, C. and Canina, L. (2002) 'The best of times, the worst of times: differences in hotel performance following 9/11', *Cornell Hotel and Restaurant Administration Quarterly*, 43(5): 41–52.

Enz, C., Canina, L. and Walsh, K. (2001) 'Hotel industry averages: an inaccurate tool for measuring performance', *Cornell Hotel and Restaurant Administration Quarterly*, 42(6): 22–32.

Enz, C., Potter, G. and Siguaw, J. (1999) 'Serving more segments and offering more products: what are the costs and where are the profits?', *Cornell Hotel and Restaurant Administration Quarterly*, 40(6): 54–62.

Epstein and Manzoni, J. F. (1997) 'The balanced scorecard and tableau de bord: translating strategy into action', *Management Accounting*, 79(2): 28–37.

Evans, N. (2005) 'Assessing the balanced scorecard as a management tool for hotels', *International Journal of Contemporary Hospitality Management*, 17(5): 376–390.

Felton, J. (2003) '9/11 or the global recession? Quantifying the impact on the world hotel industry', *The Hospitality Review*, 5(1): 4–11.

Ference, G. (2001) 'Improving organizational performance', *Cornell Hotel and Restaurant Administration Quarterly*, 42(2): 12–27.

Geller, A. N. (1985) 'Tracking critical success factors for hotel companies', *Cornell Hotel and Restaurant Administration Quarterly*, Feb: 76–81.

Geller, A. N., Ilvento, C. L. and Schmidgall, R. S. (1990) 'The hotel controller revisited', *Cornell Hotel and Restaurant Administration Quarterly*, 31(3): 66–70.

Gibson, D. (1998) 'A qualitative research study on perceptions held by Hong Kong financial controllers in decision-making roles', *International Journal of Hospitality Management*, 17(1): 65–81.

Gibson, D. A. (2002) 'On-property hotel financial controllers: a discourse analysis approach to characterizing behavioral roles', *International Journal of Hospitality Management*, 21(1): 5–23.

Gibson, D. A. (2004) 'Hotel controllers in the 21st century – a Hong Kong perspective on desired attributes', *International Journal of Hospitality Management*, 23(5): 485–503.

Graham, I. (2003) 'Hotel controllership (a speech given at the Finance/Sales and Marketing Conference of Kempinski Hotels and Resorts July 2003)', *BAHA Times*, Sept: 5–9.

Graham, I. C. and Harris, P. J. (1999) 'Development of a profit planning framework in an international hotel chain: a case study', *International Journal of Contemporary Hospitality Management*, 11(5): 198–208.

Granchev, O. (2000) 'Applying value drivers to hotel valuation', *Cornell Hotel and Restaurant Administration Quarterly*, 41(5): 78–89.

Gu, Z. (2002) 'Analyzing bankruptcy in the restaurant industry: a multiple discriminate model', *International Journal of Hospitality Management*, 21(1): 25–42.

Gu, Z. and Caneen, G. (1998) 'Quadratic models for yield management in hotel rooms operation', *Progress in Tourism and Hospitality Research*, 4(4): 245–253.

Guilding, C. (2003) 'Hotel owner/operator structures: implications for capital budgeting process', *Management Accounting Research*, 14: 179–199.

Guilding, C. and Hargreaves, B. (2003) 'How hoteliers do their capital budgeting', *The Hospitality Review*, 5(1): 45–49.

Guilding, C., Kennedy, D. and McManus, L. (2001) 'Extending the boundaries of customer accounting: applications in the hotel industry', *Journal of Hospitality and Tourism Research*, 25(2): 173–194.

Haktanir, M. and Harris, P. (2005) 'Performance measurement practice in an independent hotel context: a case study approach', *International Journal of Contemporary Hospitality Management*, 17(1): 39–50.

Hansen, S., Otley, D. and Van der Stede, W. (2003) 'Practice developments in budgeting: an overview and research perspective', *Journal of Management Accounting Research*, 15: 95–116.

Harris, P. (ed.) (1995) *Accounting and Finance for the International Hospitality Industry*, Oxford: Butterworth-Heinemann.

Harris, P. and Brander Brown, J. (1998) 'Research and development in hospitality accounting and financial management', *International Journal of Hospitality Management*, 17(2): 161–182.

Harris, P. and Mongiello, M. (2001) 'Key performance indicators in European hotel properties: general manager's choices and company profiles', *International Journal of Contemporary Hospitality Management*, 13(3): 120–128.

Harris, P. and Mongiello, M. (eds) (2006) *Accounting and Financial Management: Developments in the International Hospitality Industry*. Oxford: Butterworth-Heinemann.

Harris, P. and Mongiello, M. (2006) 'Developing a benchmarking methodology for the hotel industry'. In P. Harris and M. Mongiello (eds) *Accounting and Financial Management: Developments in the International Hospitality Industry*. Oxford: Butterworth-Heinemann. Chapter 6.

Haywood, K. M. (2003) 'Hotel investment in Canada: gaining perspective', *International Journal of Contemporary Hospitality Management*, 15(6): 333–335.

Hope, J. and Frazer, R. (1997) 'Beyond budgeting: breaking through the barrier to the third wave', *Management Accounting*, Dec: 20–23.

Hopper, T., Otley, D. and Scapens, B. (2001) 'British management accounting research: whence and whither: opinions and recollections', *The British Accounting Review*, 33: 263–291.

Huckestein, D. and Duboff, R. (1999) 'Hilton Hotels: a comprehensive approach to delivering value for all stakeholders', *Cornell Hotel and Restaurant Administration Quarterly*, 40(4): 28–38.

Ingram, H. (1999) 'Hospitality: a framework for a millennial review', *International Journal of Contemporary Hospitality Management*, 11(4): 140–148.

Ismail, J., Dalbor, M. and Mills, J. (2002) 'Using RevPAR to analyze lodging-segment variability', *Cornell Hotel and Restaurant Administration Quarterly*, 43(6): 73–80.

Jones, P. (2004) 'Finding the hospitality industry or finding hospitality schools of thought', *Journal of Hospitality, Leisure, Sport and Tourism Education*, 3(1): 33–45.

Jones, P. A. and Phillips, D. (2003) 'What use research anyway? Industry and academe's differing views', *International Journal of Contemporary Hospitality Management*, 15(5): 290–293.

Jones, T. A. (1995) 'Identifying manager's information needs in hotel companies'. In P. Harris (ed.) *Accounting and Finance for the International Hospitality Industry*. Oxford: Butterworth-Heinemann. Chapter 10.

Jones, T. A. (1997a) 'The practice of budgeting in UK hotels (workshop)', at *6th Annual CHME Hospitality Research Conference*. Oxford: April 1997.

Jones, T. A. (1997b) 'UK Hotel operators' use of budgetary procedures', at *EuroCHRIE and IAHMS Conference – Hospitality Business Development*, Sheffield, November 1997.

Jones, T. A. (1998) 'UK hotel operators use of budgetary procedures', *International Journal of Contemporary Hospitality Management*, 10(3): 96–100.

Jones, T. A. (2003) 'What the books say – the use of content analysis to establish textbook "normative theory"', *CHME 12th Annual Research Conference*, Sheffield Hallam University, pp. 156–160.

Jones, T. A. (2006) 'Budgetary practice within hospitality'. In P. Harris and M. Mongiello (eds) *Accounting and Financial Management: Developments in the International Hospitality Industry*. Oxford: Butterworth-Heinemann. Chapter 4.

Kaplan, R. S. and Norton, D. P. (1992) 'The balanced scorecard: measures that drive performance', *Harvard Business Review*, January/February: 71–80.

Kim, H., Mattila, A. and Gu, Z. (2002) 'Performance of hotel real estate investment trusts: a comparative analysis of Jensen indexes', *International Journal of Hospitality Management*, 21(1): 85–97.

Kim, W. G. and Arbel, A. (1998) 'Predicting merger targets of hospitality firms (a Logit model)', *International Journal of Hospitality Management*, 17(3): 303–318.

Kimes, S. (2001) 'How product quality drives profitability: the experience at Holiday Inn', *Cornell Hotel and Restaurant Administration Quarterly*, 42(3): 25–28.

Kosturakis, J. and Eyster, J. (1979) 'Operational budgeting in small hotel companies', *The Cornell Hotel and Restaurant Administration Quarterly*, 19(4): 80–84.

Kotas, R. (1973) 'Market orientation', *Hotel, Catering and Institutional Management Journal*, July: 5–7.

Krakhmal, V. (2006) 'Customer profitability accounting in the context of hotels'. In P. Harris and M. Mongiello (eds) *Accounting and Financial Management: Developments in the International Hospitality Industry*. Oxford: Butterworth-Heinemann. Chapter 10.

Kwansa, F. and Schmidgall, R. (1999) 'The uniform system of accounts for the lodging industry', *Cornell Hotel and Restaurant Administration Quarterly*, 40(6): 88–94.

Lashley, C. and Morrison, A. (eds) (2000) *In Search of Hospitality. Theoretical Perspectives and Debates*. Oxford: Butterworth-Heinemann.

Lee, M. J. and Back, K. J. (2005) 'A review of economic value drivers in convention and meeting management research', *International Journal of Contemporary Hospitality Management*, 17(5): 409–420.

Litteljohn, D. (2003) 'Hotels'. In B. Brotherton (ed.) *The International Hospitality Industry: Structure, Characteristics and Issues*. Oxford: Butterworth-Heinemann. Chapter 1.

Litteljohn, D. (2004) 'The UK Research Assessment Exercise 2001: an analysis for hospitality research', *International Journal of Hospitality Management*, 23(1): 25–38.

Louvieris, P., Phillips, D., Warr, D. and Bowen, A. (2003) 'Balanced scorecards for performance measurement in SMEs', *The Hospitality Review*, 5(3): 49–57.

Luft, J. and Shields, M. (2003) 'Mapping management accounting: graphics and guidelines for theory-consistent empirical research', *Accounting, Organizations and Society*, 28: 169–249.

Mason, D. D. M. and Cameron, A. (2006) 'An analysis of refereed articles in hospitality and the role of editorial board members', *Journal of Hospitality and Tourism Education*, 18(1): 11–18.

Mia, L. and Patiar, A. (2001) 'The use of management accounting systems in hotels: an exploratory study', *International Journal of Hospitality Management*, 20(2): 111–128.

Mia, L. and Patiar, A. (2002) 'The interactive effect of superior–subordinate relationship and budget participation on managerial performance in the hotel industry: an exploratory study', *Journal of Hospitality and Tourism Research*, 26(3): 235–257.

Mitchell, P. and Ingram, H. (2002) 'Space revenue and valuation models in retailing and hotels', *International Journal of Contemporary Hospitality Management*, 14(1): 28–33.

Mooradian, R. M. and Yang, S. X. (2001) 'Dividend policy and firm performance: hotel REITs v non-REIT hotel companies', *Journal of Real Estate Portfolio Management*, 7(1): 79–87.

Morey, R.C. and Ditman, D.A. (1995) 'Evaluating a hotel's GM performance', *Cornell HRS Quarterly*, 36(3): 30–35.

Morey, R. and Dittman, D. (2003a) 'Update and extension to evaluating a hotel GM's performance', *Cornell Hotel and Restaurant Administration Quarterly*, 44(5/6): 60–68.

Morey, R. and Dittman, D. (2003b) 'Evaluating a hotel GM's performance: a case study on benchmarking', *Cornell Hotel and Restaurant Administration Quarterly*, 44(5/6): 53–59.

Morrison, A. (2002) 'Hospitality research: a pause for reflection', *International Journal of Tourism Research*, 4: 161–169.

Munro, M. C. and Wheeler, B. R. (1980) 'Planning critical success factors and management information requirements', *Massachusetts Institute of Science (MIS) Quarterly*, 37(4): 29–33. In Brotherton and Shaw (eds) (1996) 'Towards an identification and classification of critical success factors in UK hotels plc', *International Journal of Hospitality Management*, 15(2): 113–135.

Nilsson, M., Harris, P. J. and Kett, R. (2001) 'Towards a valuation framework for hotels as business entities', *International Journal of Contemporary Hospitality Management*, 13(1): 6–12.

Noone, B. and Griffin, P. (1999) 'Managing the longterm profit yield from market segments in a hotel environment: a case study on the implementation of customer profitability analysis', *International Journal of Hospitality Management*, 18(2): 111–128.

Oak, S. and Andrew, W. P. (2003) 'Evidence for weak-form market efficiency in hotel real estate markets', *Journal of Hospitality and Tourism Research*, 27(4): 436–447.

Olsen, M. (2001) 'Hospitality research and theories: a review'. In A. Lockwood and T. Medlik (eds) *Tourism and Hospitality in the 21st Century*. Oxford: Butterworth-Heinemann. Chapter 8, pp. 94–105.

Olsen, M. D., Chung, Y., Graff, N., Lee, K. and Madanogh, M. (2005) 'Branding: myth and reality in the hotel industry', *Journal of Retail and Leisure Property*, 4(2): 146–162.

Omotayo Brown, D. and Kwansa, F. A. (1999) 'Using IRR and NPV models to evaluate societal costs of tourism project in developing countries', *International Journal of Hospitality Management*, 18(1): 31–43.

O'Neill, J. (2004) 'An automated valuation model for hotels', *Cornell Hotel and Restaurant Administration Quarterly*, 45(3): 260–268.

O'Neill, J. and Lloyd-Jones, A. (2001) 'Hotel values: in the aftermath of September 11, 2001', *Cornell Hotel and Restaurant Administration Quarterly*, 42(6): 10–21.

O'Neill, J. and Lloyd-Jones, A. (2002) 'One year after 9/11: hotel values and strategic implications', *Cornell Hotel and Restaurant Administration Quarterly*, 43(5): 53–64.

O'Neill, J. and Rushmore, S. (2000) 'Refining estimates of hotel-financing costs', *Cornell Hotel and Restaurant Administration Quarterly*, 41(6): 12–17.

Otley, D. (1999) 'Performance management: a framework for management control systems research', *Management Accounting Research*, 1999(10): 363–382.

Otley, D. (2001) 'Extending the boundaries of management accounting research: developing systems for performance management', *The British Accounting Review*, 33: 243–261.

Ozer, B. and Yamak, S. (2000) 'Self-sustaining pattern of finance in small businesses: evidence from Turkey', *International Journal of Hospitality Management*, 19(3): 261–273.

Parsa, H., Self, J., Njite, D. and King, T. (2005) 'Why restaurants fail', *Cornell Hotel and Restaurant Administration Quarterly*, 46(3): 304–322.

Pellinen, J. (2003) 'Making price decisions in tourism enterprises', *International Journal of Hospitality Management*, 22(2): 217–235.

Pernsteiner, C. and Gart, A. (2000) 'Why buyers pay a premium for hotels: variables that influence the decision to bid high', *Cornell Hotel and Restaurant Administration Quarterly*, 41(5): 72–77.

Phillips, P. (1999a) 'Hotel performance and competitive advantage: a contingency approach', *International Journal of Contemporary Hospitality Management*, 11(7): 359–365.

Phillips, P. (1999b) 'Performance measurement systems and hotels: a new conceptual framework', *International Journal of Hospitality Management*, 18(2): 171–182.

Phillips, P. A. (2007). 'The balanced scorecard and strategic control: a hotel case study analysis', *Service Industries Journal*, 27(6): 731–746.

Phillips, P. and Louvieris, P. (2003) 'Performance measurement in the SME UK hospitality, tourism and leisure industry: a balanced scorecard perspective', *CHME 12th Annual Research Conference, Sheffield Hallam University*, pp. 161–177.

Phillips, P. and Louvieris, P. (2005) 'Performance measurement systems in tourism. Hospitality and leisure small medium sized enterprises: a balanced scorecard perspective', *Journal of Travel Research*, 44(2): 201–211.

Pine, R. and Phillips, P. (2005) 'Performance comparisons of hotels in China', *International Journal of Hospitality Management*, 24(1): 57–73.

Potter, G. and Schmidgall, R. S. (1999) 'Hospitality management accounting: current problems and future opportunities', *International Journal of Hospitality Management*, 18(4): 387–400.

Pratten, J. D. (2004) 'Examining possible causes of business failure in British public houses', *International Journal of Contemporary Hospitality Management*, 16(4): 246–252.

Quain, B., Sansbury, M. and LeBruto, S. (1998a) 'Revenue enhancement, Part 1: a straightforward approach for making more money', *Cornell Hotel and Restaurant Administration Quarterly*, 39(5): 41–48.

Quain, B., Sansbury, M. and LeBruto, S. (1998b) ' "Revenue enhancement", Part 2: making more money at your hotel', *Cornell Hotel and Restaurant Administration Quarterly*, 39(6): 71–79.

Quain, B., Sansbury, M. and LeBruto, S. (1999) 'Revenue enhancement, Part 4', *Cornell Hotel and Restaurant Administration Quarterly*, 40(3): 38–47.

Quan, D. (2002) 'The price of a reservation', *Cornell Hotel and Restaurant Administration Quarterly*, 43(3): 77–86.

Quan, D., Li, J. and Sehgal, A. (2002) 'The performance of lodging properties in an investment portfolio', *Cornell Hotel and Restaurant Administration Quarterly*, 43(6): 81–89.

Quest, M. and Needham, D. (2005) *BHA Trends and Statistics 2005*. London: British Hospitality Association.

Rompf, P. (1998) 'Industry operating indices: time for a greater diversity?', *Cornell Hotel and Restaurant Administration Quarterly*, 39(4): 20–27.

Roubi, S. (2004) 'The valuation of intangibles for hotel investments', *Property Management*, 22(5): 410–423.

Roubi, S. and Littlejohn, D. (2003) 'What makes hotel value in the UK? A hedonic valuation model', *CHME 12th Annual Research Conference, Sheffield Hallam University*. pp. 178–189.

Roubi, S. and Littlejohn, D. (2004a) 'What makes hotel values in the UK? A hedonic valuation model', *International Journal of Contemporary Hospitality Management*, 16(3): 175–181.

Rusth, D. (1991) 'Hotel budgeting in a multinational environment: results of a pilot study', *Hospitality Research Journal*, 14(2): 217–222.

Rusth, D. and Lefever, M. (1988) 'International profit planning', *The Cornell Hotel and Restaurant Administration Quarterly*, 29(3): 68–73.

Ryan, B., Scapens, R. and Theobald, M. (2002) *Research Method and Methodology and Accounting*, 2nd edn. London: Thomson.

Sangster, A. (2003) 'Splitting the bricks from the brains under fire', *BAHA Times* (British Association of Hospitality Accountants) 2003 Nov: 1–2.

Scapens, R. W. (2006) 'Understanding management accounting practices: a personal journey', *The British Accounting Review*, 38: 1–30.

Schmidgall, R. and DeFranco, A. (1998) 'Budgeting and forecasting: current practice in the lodging industry', *Cornell Hotel and Restaurant Administration Quarterly*, 39(6): 45–51.

Schmidgall, R. and Ninemeier, J. (1986) 'Food-service budgeting: how the chains do it', *The Cornell Hotel and Restaurant Administration Quarterly*, 26(4): 51–57.

Schmidgall, R. and Ninemeier, J. (1987) 'Budgeting in hotel chains: coordination and control', *The Cornell Hotel and Restaurant Administration Quarterly*, 28(1): 79–84.

Schmidgall, R. and Ninemeier, J. (1989) 'Budgeting practices in lodging and food service chains: an analysis and comparison', *International Journal of Hospitality Management*, 8(1): 35–41.

Schmidgall, R., Borchgrevink, C. and Zahl-Begnum, O. (1996) 'Operations budgeting practices of lodging firms, in the United States and Scandinavia', *International Journal of Hospitality Management*, 15(2): 189–203.

Sharma, D. S. (2002) 'The differential effect of environmental dimensionality, size and structure on budget systems characteristics in hotels', *Management Accounting Research*, 13: 101–103.

Sin, L. Y. M., Tse, A. C. B., Heung, V. C. S. and Yim, F. H. K. (2005) 'An analysis of the relationship between market orientation and business performance in the hotel industry', *International Journal of Hospitality Management*, 24(4): 611–633.

Singh, A. and Schmidgall, R. (2000) 'Financing lodging properties', *Cornell Hotel and Restaurant Administration Quarterly*, 41(4): 39–47.

Singh, A. J. and Kwansa, F. A. (1999) 'Financing the lodging industry in the next millennium – a handbook for managers and researchers', *International Journal of Hospitality Management*, 18(4): 415–425.

Slattery, P. (2002) 'Reported REVPAR: unreliable measures, flawed interpretations and the remedy',

International Journal of Hospitality Management, 21(2): 135–149.

Southern, G. (1999) 'A systems approach to performance measurement in hospitality', *International Journal of Contemporary Hospitality Management,* 11(7): 366–376.

Subramaniam, N., McManus, L. and Mia, L. (2002) 'Enhancing hotel manager's organizational commitment: an investigation of the impact of structure, need for achievement and participative budgeting', *International Journal of Hospitality Management,* 21(4): 301–471.

Tso, A. and Law, R. (2005) 'Analyzing online pricing practices of hotels in Hong Kong', *International Journal of Hospitality Management,* 24(2): 301–307.

Upneja, A. and Dalbor, M. C. (2001) 'An examination of capital structure in the restaurant industry', *International Journal of Contemporary Hospitality Management,* 13(2): 54–59.

Upneja, A. and Schmidgall, R. (2001) 'Equipment leasing in the U.S. lodging industry: what, why, and how much', *Cornell Hotel and Restaurant Administration Quarterly,* 42(2): 56–61.

Van Scotter, J. R. and Culligan, P. E. (2003) 'The value of theoretical research and applied research for the hospitality industry', *Cornell Hotel and Restaurant Administration Quarterly,* 44(2): 14(14).

Verginis, S. C. and Taylor, S. J. (2004) 'Stakeholders' perceptions of the DCF method in hotel valuations', *Property Management,* 22(5): 358–376.

Walsh, K. (2003) 'Qualitative research: advancing the science and practice of hospitality', *Cornell Hotel and Restaurant Administration Quarterly,* 33(2): 66–75.

Wilson, R. H. (2001) 'Agency law, fiduciary duties and hotel management contracts', *Journal of Hospitality and Tourism Research,* 25(2): 147–158.

Younes, E. and Kett, R. (2003) 'Refining the anomalies out of RevPAR', *The Hospitality Review,* 5(2): 16–20.

Younes, E. and Kett, R. (2004) 'Investment driven break-even analysis for hotels', *The Hospitality Review,* 6(1): 10–16.

Yuen, D. C. Y. (2004) 'Goal characteristics, communication and reward systems, and managerial propensity to create budgetary slack', *Managerial Auditing Journal,* 19(4): 517–532.

Yuen, D. C. Y. (2006) 'The impact of budgetary design system: direct and indirect models', *Managerial Auditing Journal,* 21(2): 148–165.

Organization Studies and Hospitality Management

Yvonne Guerrier

INTRODUCTION

In simple terms, organization studies is the academic study of organizations using social scientific methods. But, as the editors of the *Sage Handbook on Organization Studies* argue, the study of organizations is no longer confined to a relatively restricted range of approaches and processes but 'has opened up in ways that might once have seemed unimaginable' (Clegg, Hardy and Nord, 1996: xxi). Even Morgan's (1986) influential book on the different metaphors that various writers use to understand organizational processes hardly encompasses the richness of the approaches now used. I am focusing here on a sub-set of broader organization studies: the attempt specifically to understand hospitality organizations. But hospitality organization studies does not have a simple relationship with organization studies generally because of the way it has historically developed.

There is a long history of research by organizational researchers who just happen to have become interested in some aspect of hospitality. For example there is Whyte's (1948) study of restaurants and hotels in Chicago in the 1940s, Shamir's study (1978) of workplace relations in British hotels and Gabriel's (1988) study of various forms of catering work. But these are relatively rare examples: organization theorists in general have traditionally been much more interested in either factory or office environments as the (then) predominant work environments in developed economies.

The people who were most interested in studying hospitality organizations were academics based in the hotel and catering or hospitality management departments that had developed separately from the business schools or management departments of universities

(especially in the Anglophone world). There have never been any journals that have focused specifically on organization studies within hospitality but the general hospitality journals have a strong history of accepting and encouraging this work, particularly the *International Journal of Hospitality Management*. Some terrific work has emerged from this tradition, strengthened by the very strong links these specialist departments have with the hospitality industry. But at its worst, hospitality organization studies may be characterized as a remote colonial outpost of organization studies – always keen to copy the homeland but never quite able to keep up with the latest fashions or match the same standards, its local heroes ignored and unknown on the mainland.

However, this is changing. In the last 20 years, there has been an increased interest by organizational theorists in service organizations generally. This is partially a reflection of the growing importance of the service sector in developed economies but also reflects how customer focus has become a dominant management rhetoric across all types of organizations (e.g. Du Gay and Salaman, 1992) so that, for example, hospitals, train companies and universities have all been encouraged to think in terms of customers rather than patients, passengers or students (and hospitality organizations in terms of customers not guests). At the same time, and related to this, organization theorists have started paying attention to previously neglected areas of organizational life: emotions (Hochschild, 1983; Fineman, 1993, 2000), the body and aesthetics (Tyler and Abbott, 1998) and sexuality (Hearn and Parkin, 1995). As I will show, hospitality organizations, especially the customer service interaction in these organizations, are an excellent arena to explore these issues.

Where once hospitality organizations were ignored by organizational theorists because they predominantly employed female staff whose main skill lay in being nice to the customer, they are now of interest precisely because that is what they are like.

Hospitality organizations are also changing and it is some of the newer forms of hospitality that have received particular attention, especially the practices of two companies: McDonald's and Disney theme parks. Ritzer's (1996) popular sociological thesis of McDonaldization not only looks at the way that the fast food restaurant offers its consumers, workers and managers efficiency, calculability, predictability and control but also asserts that its influence extends far beyond the fast food sector in the USA. McDonaldization, Ritzer (1996: 3) claims, is the process by which 'the principles of the fast food restaurant are coming to dominate more and more sectors of American society as well as the rest of the world'. Bryman (1999) has proposed a complementary notion to McDonaldization, the process of Disneyization. This is the process by which the principles of the Disney theme parks dominate more and more sectors of society and comprises four aspects: theming, de-differentiation of consumption, merchandising and emotional labour. Whatever the merits of Ritzer's and Bryman's theses, it is difficult to ignore a sector with not just one but two organizations which are held up as archetypes of late modern society.

Finally, the structure of hospitality education has been changing, certainly in the UK. Many of the old specialist hospitality management departments have merged, either into business schools or with leisure and tourism. There has also been pressure to publish in what are regarded as more prestigious general organization studies journals as well as in the specific hospitality ones. So a mapping of organization studies as it relates to the hospitality industry is no longer a matter of merely searching the main hospitality journals for relevant articles and adding a few key texts from elsewhere. Valuable insights into this field are published across a wide range of outlets and by people who may describe their main discipline as organization studies, hospitality, tourism, sociology even geography or anthropology.

This makes it an exciting time to attempt a mapping of the area but it does not make the process an easy one. Maps have to have boundaries. I have had to make decisions in two main areas about where to draw the line. The first dilemma is 'what is a hospitality organization?' Hospitality has been defined as 'a contemporaneous exchange designed to enhance mutuality (well-being) for the parties involved through the provision of food and/or drink, and/or accommodation' (Lashley, 2000a: 3). However, as Bryman (1999) argues in his Disneyization thesis, one characteristic of late modern organizations is the de-differentiation of consumption. For example, having just claimed theme parks for the hospitality sector, it is clear that whilst Disney theme parks contain hospitality operations (hotels and restaurants) they also contain retail operations and leisure attractions, they are not strictly just hospitality. Even hotels, which are normally seen as one of the main components of the hospitality sector, do not just provide hospitality services as defined above. They often also have leisure facilities and shops. So, for example, are hotel entertainers, or leisure club staff, or even tour 'reps', hospitality workers because they work in a hospitality organization (a hotel)? Are air cabin crew, who have been much studied by academics, hospitality workers because they serve food and drink even though an airline is not, in normal terms, a hospitality organization? The boundaries between hospitality, retail, leisure and tourism are particularly contested. I have taken a pragmatic approach and have focused on the main sectors usually included as part of the hospitality industry: hotels, restaurants, licensed retail, contract catering but also leisure and entertainment and welfare services (HEFCE, 2001).

The other dilemma is around what comprises organization studies. Because of the way in which hospitality education has developed, there is a strong tradition of interdisciplinary work. This has been highly productive but causes problems when one tries to put this work back into its disciplinary boxes. Is the excellent work by Roper, Doherty, Brookes and Hampton (2001) on international hotel groups to be classed as work in strategic management, in human resource management or in organization studies? It covers all of these areas. The distinction between organization studies and human resource management is a particularly difficult one. I have avoided discussion of human resource practices such as selection and appraisal but have included discussion of empowerment and flexible working practices, both of which link with a discussion about job design which has long been of concern to organization theorists. Another problematic boundary is between organization studies, as a field of study within management or business, and the study of work by sociologists. Again I have included work where I feel it makes a contribution to our understanding of organizational processes within the hospitality industry without being too concerned about the academic discipline from which it has come.

I will first introduce some general approaches to researching hospitality organizations, particularly looking at hospitality organizations as cultures, then explore the process of leadership and management in hospitality and finally look at the attitudes and work of operative level staff.

WAYS OF LOOKING AT HOSPITALITY ORGANIZATIONS

At one level, hospitality organizations are both universal and timeless. Everywhere on the globe and throughout history, people have found some way of providing accommodation, food and drink to those who are away from home (Selwyn, 2000; Walton, 2000). But the nature of these organizations is incredibly varied. This is the study of everything from the micro-organization, the paying guest in a home setting, to the international hotel company, like Hilton or Intercontinental, managing a network of complex units across the globe. It includes organizations that have grown out of the norms and needs of a specific place and community, like the British pub or the American diner or the French café, and organizations that have been designed to operate in the same way everywhere, like McDonald's. It includes organizations that are associated with leisure and tourism activities, the resort hotel or the cruise liner, as well as operations that are institution based, such as catering within prisons or hospitals. It includes the temporary organization, event catering for a festival or family celebration, or it may include organizations with a history of a 100 years or more, Claridges in London or the Georges V in Paris.

The rationale behind the study of hospitality management is that these very varied organizations have some aspects in common: that some insights will be gained by classifying them together. One key feature of all hospitality operations is they involve both production and service operations. Food is cooked or prepared in some way as well as being served. Rooms are 'made up' as well as being sold. Hospitality operations include both back-of-house work like cooking and cleaning, as well as the front-of-house work of dealing directly with the guests. However, hospitality organizations are commonly defined as a type of service organization (Nailon, 1982; Gabriel, 1988; Korczynski, 2002). Both anthropological and historical accounts of hospitality as well as modern management commentaries emphasize that looking after the guest is crucial to the success of hospitality.

Looking after guests involves a personal interaction of some description; in this sense hospitality is an archetypal 'people industry'. To look after guests appropriately requires not just technical skills but also the appropriate attitude and demeanor: what are now conceptualized as 'emotional' and 'aesthetic' labour. But it is much more difficult to control and manage attitude than it is to manage behaviour. It is made additionally difficult by the ambiguous status of hospitality work which, in developed economies at least, is typically characterized as low-skill, low-paid, feminized work (Lindsay and McQuaid, 2004), the type of work people do on a short-term basis or because they have to rather than as a career of choice (Gabriel, 1988; Lucas and Bailey, 1993; Wood, 1993; Guerrier and Adib, 2000a; Ram et al., 2001). Hospitality's historical link to transgressive activities (Selwyn, 2000; Walton, 2000), the requirement for hospitality workers to work when other people are at leisure and in other people's leisure space (Urry, 1990; Crang, 1994; Adler and Adler, 1999a, 1999b; Guerrier and Adib, 2003) and the link between hospitality work and the traditional women's work of cleaning, cooking and home making (Adkins, 1995; Hunter, Powell and Watson, 2006) all tend to devalue the status of hospitality work. So how do hospitality organizations manage the way staff interact with customers when customer service work cannot be de-skilled and controlled in exactly the same way as factory work, but neither can managers depend on their poorly paid and transient staff's vocational or professional commitment to their work as a mechanism of control?

Managing hospitality workers so they provide appropriate service to guests then becomes a crucial problem for hospitality organizations. The quality of service provides a competitive edge for organizations (Corsun and Enz, 1999) but managing this is by no means simple. So the dilemma of customer service runs like a *leitmotif* through much of the research on hospitality organizations. But it is worth remembering it is not the only possible focus for study. Hospitality organizations, like organizations in other sectors, use technology. They have formal structures. They have managers who exercise leadership in particular ways. They acquire and use knowledge. They employ staff with a diversity of ethnic and national backgrounds and cultures. They are influenced by their history and location. They experiment with different ways of organizing. They survive or they disappear. All of these features can and do form the basis for academic study.

There are a wide range of possibilities here but academics have not explored all of them. Most work has been focused on commercial hospitality organizations, usually leisure based organizations such as hotels and restaurants, in the developed world, particularly the USA, UK and Australia. Approaches and perspectives go in and out of fashion. Whyte's (1948) study of restaurants and hotels had a human relations orientation. Shamir (1978) focused on understanding hotels in terms of level of formality and levels in hierarchies again using the type of methodology which was popular at the time (see Pugh, 1998). Gabriel (1988) looked at different types of catering organization focusing on issues of technology and control, influenced heavily by Braverman's (1974) thesis on technology and de-skilling. More recently there have been studies of hotels taking a population ecology approach and looking, over time, at the ways in which communities of hotels thrive or fail (Baum and Mezias, 1992; Ingram and Inman, 1996).

At the moment, however, the dominant approach to understanding hospitality organizations is to understand them as cultures. Much of this work is extremely recent: indeed a review article less than ten years ago (Guerrier and Deery, 1998) commented on the relative dearth of recent work on hospitality organizations as cultures.

HOSPITALITY ORGANIZATIONS AS CULTURES

The cultural metaphor is an attractive one for hospitality researchers for a number of reasons.

It is an adaptable metaphor. Culture has been studied using a variety of different methods. For example, there are quantitative attempts to use culture to predict some other variable, for example job satisfaction or attitudes to turnover (Iverson and Deery, 1997; Tepeci and Bartlett, 2002). Alternatively, there are more qualitative attempts to uncover the symbols and rituals of culture usually based around a case study or series of case studies. Woods' (1989, 1991) studies of uncovering culture within the restaurant industry are particularly good examples. As Ogbonna and Harris (2002) argue, culture can also be studied from a variety of different theoretical perspectives. The optimists believe that cultural control is both desirable and possible. The pessimists (or culture purists) are simply interested in uncovering culture and not in identifying its practical use for managers. Some of the more critical studies of customer service I will discuss below would fall into this category. Finally, the realists argue that cultural change is possible and can be influenced but not fully controlled by managers. Clearly then, fuller explorations of the process of culture change are necessary. Most of the current studies on culture (Meudell and Gadd, 1994; Watson and D'Annunzio-Green, 1994; Kemp and Dwyer, 2001; Ogbonna and Harris, 2002; D'Annunzio-Green and Francis, 2005) would fall into this 'realist' category and much of the discussion is around the extent to which managers can secure commitment to a shared culture given the nature of a hospitality workforce which is often part-time and temporary.

Studies using this cultural metaphor often tend to focus on organization culture and to ignore or downplay other cultural influences that can affect workplace behaviour. An exception is the interest that has been shown in national culture and the way this determines what organizations are like. Much of this work builds on Hofstede's definitions of national culture (Hofstede, 1980, 1991). These issues are important within the hospitality industry, both because hospitality organizations exist in some form everywhere in the world but also because many hospitality organizations have multi-cultural workforces. Thus Groschl and Doherty (2006) compare the way French and British managers interpret the appraisal system in an international hotel group; Roper et al. (2001) show how Anglo-Saxon cultural values permeate the culture of another international hotel group; and Royle (1995) looks at the way German approaches to labour-market operation affect McDonald's culture in Germany. The conflicts between an essentially US-inspired model of corporate culture and cultural assumptions in other parts of the world are explored by D'Annunzio-Green (2002) in relation to Russian hotels and Mwuara, Sutton and Roberts (1998) in relation to hotels in China. All these studies are useful reminders that people bring with them to work certain assumptions about workplace relations which shape the culture of their organizations.

The studies quoted above are essentially applications of broader organization studies models and debates to the hospitality industry. They address crucial issues for the industry and they are based on competent and interesting research but they are essentially contributions within a well-trodden path. A few authors have strayed outside this approach. Wood (1994) argues that hotels need to be understood as agents of social control, constraining and enabling the actions of guests and their interactions with staff. Wood's notion that we should understand commercial hospitality organizations through an understanding of domestic hospitality, of the 'home', is taken further by Lynch (2005a, 2005b) in his explorations of the commercial home enterprise and the ways is which hosts negotiate having paying guests into their homes. Wood's (1994) work also emphasizes how hospitality organizations are a product of their historical and social milieu affected as much by broader cultural and social trends (class structures, social attitudes towards the role of men and women) as by labour market trends and management practices.

Wood and Lynch are both interested in culture but taking what Ogbonna and Harris (2002) would call a 'cultural purist' position, neither are primarily interested in the way in which managers might change cultures and both emphasize how organizational cultures are not closed societies but need to be understood in a wider societal context. But however culture is conceptualized, the dominant actors in an organization, the leaders and managers, have the most power to affect organizational symbols and values. It is to this group that I will turn next.

MANAGERS AND LEADERS

I have discussed in the previous section the debate about how far managers are able to shape the culture of the organizations in which they work. But if managers shape their organizations, managers' work is also shaped by the organization. As Hales (1993) argues, managers manage through organization and what they do will be related to what they are managing. Within this argument, the work of a manager in the hospitality industry will be different from the work of a manager in a different industry.

Associated with the study of the management role in the hospitality industry is the study of the leadership role. Although Testa (2001: 80) may argue that 'over the past decade "leadership" has replaced "management" as the operative word in hospitality operations', the truth is that the relationship between management and leadership can be defined in a variety of ways (Pittaway, Carmouche and Chell, 1998). The terms 'leadership' and 'management' may be viewed as qualitatively different (as Testa, 2001 implies); or as interchangeable; or leadership may be viewed as one of the roles that managers take (Mintzberg, 1973).

Early studies of hospitality managers' roles often adopted Mintzberg's classical framework of management roles (Ley, 1980; Arnaldo, 1981; Ferguson and Berger, 1984; Shortt, 1989). These studies have been extensively criticized both for methodological and theoretical reasons (Guerrier and Lockwood, 1991; Pittaway et al., 1998). However, as Chareanpunisirikul and Wood (2002) argue, Mintzberg does at least provide a relatively simple framework for collecting data.

In the 1990s a major theme emerged from the discussion about managers' work in hospitality and this was explored from a range of different conceptual positions. This is about the extent to which management style and work in the hospitality industry is changing. In summary, the argument is that industry managers have traditionally focused on the hands-on, operational elements of their work, on 'being there and doing it' (Guerrier and Lockwood, 1989), directly supervising staff and meeting customers. By contrast what they should be doing is focusing on strategic development, empowering and consulting their staff to gain their commitment to change through transformational leadership (Tracey and Hinkin, 1996; see also Brownell, 1992; Ghei and Nebel, 1994; Becker and Olsen, 1995). Chung-Herrara, Enz and Lankau (2003: 24) summarize the new skills required: '(hospitality) leaders of the future will need to possess a strategic orientation and approach towards decision making that permits them both to plan and redesign their organizations. In addition, communicating persuasively, listening and enabling others will be essential skills for managers hoping to reach senior leadership positions'. Whilst there is some evidence of a shift towards a new more consultative and strategic style of management within the hospitality industry, much of that evidence merely demonstrates that managers have espoused the rhetoric of 'new management work' (Anastassova and Purcell, 1995; Gilbert and Guerrier, 1997; Ogbonna and Harris, 2002; Chung-Herrara et al., 2003). Does this mean there is evidence of an actual shift in approach? As Testa (2001) demonstrates in a study of US hospitality organizations, managers' perceptions of the leadership climate in their organizations is often much more positive than the way it is perceived by operative staff. As Hales and Tamangani (1996: 748) argue, the nature of the hospitality environment and the way in which most day-to-day business problems have extremely short time leads inevitably means that 'the pressing needs of the immediate and the recurrent often drive out longer-term considerations'. Ogbonna and Harris (2002) point out that whilst the UK hospitality managers they studied were quite sophisticated in their understanding of culture management, they were dubious about whether this approach could be extended to peripheral part-time and temporary employees (a point also made by Hales, 2000) so made less attempt to consult and gain commitment from them.

Taking a very different theoretical approach, Mutch (2003) gives a different insight into the factors that structure the way hospitality managers work by using Bourdieu's concept of habitus to explore the work of UK public house managers. He explores the ways in which the embodied practice of managers is influenced by their social origins. Traditional pub managers who have moved into the industry as a mid-life career change, often with little or no formal education, understand their work and the skills needed to do it in a very different way from the younger graduates now joining this occupation (see also Smith, 2003). Mutch (2000, 2003) reminds us that the practices of 'new management work' with its emphasis on analysis are another way of colonizing and changing traditional community based hospitality outlets such as pubs. The growth of the 'analytical manager' may give opportunities for those who have traditionally been excluded from occupations such as pub manager (for example single women), but Mutch also points out that traditional managers had tacit skills, such as the ability to prevent violent situations from developing, which the new manager may not. Mutch's analysis may help to explain why there often seems to be a gap between the management skills the hospitality industry expects and the skills and expectations of new hospitality graduates (Raybould and Wilkins, 2005): they lack these tacit skills. Nonetheless, in all sectors of the industry, the graduate manager is becoming more common (Harper, Brown and Irvine, 2005).

Mutch draws attention to the issue of how the manager 'fits' with the culture of the organization, in this case drawing attention to social origins. But in a diverse and multicultural industry the issue of how staff respond to managers and leaders from different national backgrounds is also significant. There is relatively little work that relates to the hospitality industry. Testa (2002) argues from a study in the cruise industry that followers have relatively more positive views of their leaders when they come from similar national backgrounds. Chareanpunsirikul and Wood (2002), in a study of expatriate and indigenous hotel managers in Thailand found they had different ways of defining their roles, with the indigenous managers operating more according to local cultural imperatives than their expatriate colleagues.

HOSPITALITY EMPLOYEES

The nature and attractions of hospitality work are well documented. Hospitality work is, above all, 'convenient' employment (Szivas, Riley and Airey, 2003). Because of the relative lack of formal skills involved and the frequent opportunity to work flexible hours and on a temporary basis (e.g. seasonal work), hospitality work is attractive as a first job and as student work (Lucas and Bailey, 1993; Woods, 1999); as a life-style choice for those looking to travel (Adler and Adler, 1999a, 1999b); as a 'port in the storm' for those affected by decline in other sectors of the economy or forced to migrate to another country (Ram et al., 2001; Szivas et al., 2003); but also as a job of last resort for the marginal and disadvantaged who have no other options (Gabriel, 1988; Lee-Ross and Johns, 1995; Wood, 1997). However, because hospitality work is available to such groups, it can be perceived as *only* for these groups: as 'servile', 'dirty', low-skilled, low-status and low-paid work. One of the key questions which has been addressed by hospitality researchers is whether operative work can ever be more than this: whether it can be a career of choice rather than a 'pass through' or 'port in a storm' job.

It has been argued that the nature of labour markets in the hospitality industry inevitably means that managers are driven to minimize pay costs and have little incentive to develop employee skills and internal promotion opportunities (Riley, 1991). Against this argument, there is some evidence that the low status and skill level of hospitality jobs is particularly an Anglo-Saxon problem and in Continental Europe there has always been more focus on the development of superior skills and attitudes with consequent gains in productivity (Prais, Jarvis and Wagner, 1989; Baum, 1995). Then there is the issue of quality. As Korczynski (2002) argues, all customer-oriented bureaucracies (including hospitality companies) are subject to the dual pressures of, on the one hand, needing to minimize costs and 'process' customers as quickly and easily as possible but, on the other hand, needing to deliver exemplary service. These pressures are not necessarily compatible (Lai and Baum, 2005). The pressure to reduce costs may encourage the use of cheap, low-skilled, numerically flexible staff. Conversely, the pressure to deliver exemplary service encourages the use of well-trained skilled staff imbued with the appropriate cultural values (I have discussed above, in the section on culture, managers' doubts about whether cultural change methods can work when the workforce is predominantly casual).

It is not surprising, therefore, that considerable attention has been paid by organizational researchers to job design in the hospitality industry. There have been numerous critiques of de-skilled work, particularly in the fast food sector; notably Ritzer (1996), but also Leidner (1993), Buergermeister (1988) and Gabriel (1988). At the same time, there is a long history within the hospitality industry of experiments in multi-skilling and employee participation (Wood, 1997). From the early 1990s, the language of 'empowerment' has been frequently used by both practitioners and academics when discussing what, in the 1970s and 1980s, would

have been termed 'job enrichment' (Brymer, 1991; Sternberg, 1992; Wynne, 1993; Sparrowe, 1994; Ashness and Lashley, 1995; Fulford and Enz, 1995; Lashley, 1995a, 1995b, 1997, 2000b; Hales and Klidas, 1998; Corsun and Enz, 1999; Hales, 2000; Hancer and George, 2003).

Lashley has written extensively on empowerment within a variety of different settings and he shows how different initiatives may carry different managerial meanings. Empowerment, in Lashley's terms, may be about participation, or involvement, or commitment or de-layering. It may involve autonomous work groups, or quality circles or team briefings. But although, as he shows, empowerment initiatives carry a variety of meanings, the switch from the language of 'job enrichment' to the language of 'empowerment' carries other resonances. Whilst 'job enrichment' was about employee motivation and satisfaction with consequent effects on performance and productivity, 'empowerment' is more directly linked with customer service. The empowered employees, it is argued, provides better service and quicker solutions to customers' problems (Brymer, 1991; Hancer and George, 2003).

If providing excellent customer service is a crucial challenge for hospitality organizations, the nature of front-line customer service work becomes particularly interesting to study. I will now consider in some depth a selection of, largely critical, studies of front-line hospitality work. They take as a starting point the notion that the skills involved in managing the customer service encounter effectively are by no means simple and unproblematic. It is interesting that in a study of job-seekers in Scotland many men rejected service work because they felt they lacked the 'soft' skills necessary (Lindsay and McQuaid, 2004). Take the 'happy smile', which is axiomatic of good service. Ogbonna and Harris (2002) in their study of cultural change in the hospitality industry, comment on the emphasis placed by managers on ensuring that their customer service staff display the correct emotions and behaviour towards their customers; even compared with managers in other service organizations such as supermarkets. One of the respondents in Ogbonna and Harris' (2002: 42) study, a manager in a five-star hotel group, described it thus:

Happiness, friendliness, smiling: all false cultures ... that's what our customers like to see. Away from the real world, they come here to experience relaxation, leisure and entertainment. We try to create the ambiance so we encourage our staff to perform and generate these feelings in front of customers.

FRONT-LINE CUSTOMER SERVICE WORK

Hochschild's (1983) notion of 'emotional labour' has now become a core theory for researchers trying to understand the service encounter. Based on a study of airline cabin crew, Hochshild argued that customer service staff are paid to manage their emotions. Smiles must seem sincere to the customer: false smiles are counter-productive. But the pressure to keep generating emotions one may not feel is alienating, argues Hochschild. The smiling faces of hospitality workers (in this context) masks the psychologically damaging nature of their work. Hochschild (1983) also emphasizes the gendered nature of emotional labour. Emotional work is regarded as something that women naturally do and therefore not accorded particular status. Women, because of their relatively lower status in the workplace, are also less protected against the abuse from customers than men, so Hochschild argues. There have been a number of studies that have developed the notion of emotional labour specifically within a hospitality setting and which discuss the darker side of working in hospitality, specifically the pressure to keep smiling and being polite to customers no matter how badly they are behaving, for example, Leidner (1993) (on fast food staff), Adkins (1995) (on hotel and leisure park staff), Guerrier and Adib (2000) (on hotel staff), Hall (1993) (in restaurants) and Tracy (2000) (on cruise liner entertainers). Tracy (2000: 16) discusses the dilemmas faced by staff who were:

> ... continually blitzed with the acontextual service credo message, "We never say no". This situation engendered cruise staff confusion about the level of tolerance expected in regard to passenger demands. For example, Cassie did not know how to deal with a man who was grabbing and holding her too close on the dance floor.

It is only in the last ten years or so that researchers have explicitly recognized the extent to which hospitality environments are sexualized environments where a 'job flirt' (Hall, 1993) is part of the performance and, in many cases,

a certain amount of sexual banter and fondling by customers is accepted as being a natural part of the work culture (Guiffre and Williams, 1994; Folgerø and Fjeldstad, 1995; Johnson and Coupe, 1999; Guerrier and Adib, 2000b). Whilst women are particularly subjected to sexual harassment from guests, men can be affected as well and men as well as women are vulnerable to bullying and occasionally physical violence from guests (Guerrier and Adib, 2000b). Given that many hospitality work environments are multi-ethnic, it is surprising that there has been relatively little exploration of racial harassment with the exception of Guiffre and Williams (1994) and Adib and Guerrier (2003). What all the studies in this area demonstrate is that there is often little management or institutional support to help staff deal with this type of abuse: 'any problems belong to the individual, who is given two choices, both equally appalling: take it – or leave' (Folgerø and Fjeldstad, 1995: 311). Guerrier and Adib's (2000b: 703) conclusions are similar to those in other studies:

> Our respondents learned to accept a degree of abuse from customers as "going with the job". Simultaneously, they also developed strategies for coping such as learning to detach, using humor behind the scenes, or expressing their hurt and anger about incidents in the interview or in private.

However, it is important not to overstate the negative features of work in customer service and understate the extent to which employees can exercise control over the customer and enjoy their ability to exercise that control. Whyte (1946: 132–133; see also Goffman, 1959: 22) in his classic work on popular American restaurants in the 1940s poses this question:

> The first question to ask when we look at the customer relationship is, "Does the waitress get the jump on the customer, or does the customer get the jump on the waitress?" The skilled waitress realizes the crucial nature of this question ...

Sosteric (1996: 301) discusses precisely this type of customer management in his study of a Canadian nightclub:

> Experienced servers set up an elaborate customer service hierarchy and system of reward/punishment to hook potential customers and encourage them to return and spend money. This hierarchy was based on two things: the amount that the individuals tipped and their suitability as regular patrons of the nightclub ... A typical newcomer would not even warrant a glance from the server and might

have to wait until all the staff's regulars have been served.

Similar points are made by Crang (1994) in an ethnographic study of work in a theme restaurant. He observes how staff would pretend not to have seen customers, taking pleasure at least in maintaining control over the timing of the interaction. Nevertheless in this power play between employee and customer, customers are normally able to dominate more explicitly and openly, exercising their control through tipping or through feedback or complaints about staff (Crang, 1994; Tracy, 2000) whilst employees normally, as in Crang's example, have to engage in what Goffman (1959: 22) terms 'subtle aggressiveness' to maintain control. In some cases resistance to the control of both customers and management may move employees beyond actions which merely decrease customer satisfaction towards scams and frauds (Mars, 1994; Peacock and Kübler, 2001).

So far this discussion has focused on the direct relationship between customer and customer service staff. But, as many studies have shown, the way in which management controls the customer service staff is also crucial. Korczynski (2002), as I have discussed above, identifies the dual and contradictory pressures that are certainly evident across the hospitality industry of the need to deliver exemplary service whilst at the same time processing customers as quickly and efficiently as possible. He also identified the different perspective taken by management, who tend to think about disembodied customers, from that of the front line service staff presented with actual embodied customers. For managers, for example, the issue is how to shorten the average number of people in a queue. For customer service staff it is how to deal with the people in front of them. As a theme-park attendant quoted by Hales (2000: 508) put it, 'touchy-feely, being friendly to the customer stuff is no use when you have twenty people queuing for a coke'. Alternatively managers may be equally concerned about customer service staff who emphasize individual customer service at the expense of processing customers quickly. Lashley (1997: 122) quotes the following example of an employee of TGI Friday's:

Last week I had a party in from one of the theatres. I didn't rush them. I took time and had a good laugh with them. After the meal one customer asked me for a cigar. We don't sell cigars so I went next door to the tobacconist and bought one for him. He was really grateful. Afterwards they thanked me for a great time and left a £20 tip. Management wanted me to hurry them through so as to bring in more customers. I don't like to rush people.

It is sometimes argued that where managers provide staff with the opportunity to bring their own personalities and styles to the job and to develop their own ways of dealing with customers, they are more likely to retain a positive and committed attitude to their work (Sosteric, 1996; Seymour and Sandiford, 2005). This, of course, links with the debate on empowerment strategies. Indeed, one of the advantages of customer service work in the hospitality industry is that one operates in an environment where customers are having fun and some of this fun may also rub off on the person working. Several studies illustrate situations, especially in bars, clubs, informal restaurants and resorts where staff hardly seem to distinguish between their work and their leisure (Urry, 1990; Crang, 1994; Riley, Lockwood, Powell-Perry and Baker, 1998; Adler and Adler, 1999a, 1999b; Guerrier and Adib, 2003). Their customers are their friends, their workplace the place where they would 'hang out' anyway, and all they need to do is to bring their normal fun-loving selves to work.

One notion, therefore, is that customer staff's sense of identity (as friendly, helpful people) outside work helps them to be disciplined workers at work (O'Doherty and Wilmott, 2000; Guerrier and Adib, 2003). This raises the question of cultural difference: and what may be regarded by different cultural groups as appropriate ways of dealing with customers. Unfortunately, most of the work described here is based on studies in developed countries, largely the USA and the UK. A short article by Taylor (1996) comparing hotel service in Crete, Warsaw and Eilat, argues that the 'happy face' of Cretan hotel workers may reflect a vestige of an ancient code of hospitality (philoxenia) whereas in Eilat and Warsaw the problem is getting someone to change from 'aggressive soldier' to 'polite worker'. Nonetheless, he counsels against simplistic cultural stereotyping: the demands of the company and the customer challenge the natural responses of staff.

As Nickson, Warhurst, Witz and Cullen (2001) demonstrate, the newer popular hospitality chains frequently try to match the profile of their staff, in terms of age, appearance and interests, to the profile of their customers so they naturally empathise with what customers want. Nickson et al. (2001, 2005) have coined the term 'aesthetic labour' to define another 'soft' skill which it is increasingly expected that hospitality customer service staff bring to work: that they 'look good', 'sound right' and are able appropriately to embody the image of the organization. Whilst Nickson et al. (2001, 2005) argue that recruiting staff with the right 'aesthetic' skills offers companies a competitive advantage, the reality is that the crucial customer service staff who can make so much difference to the success of an operation are frequently those staff with some of the worst conditions of service and the least commitment to the organization – part-timers, foreign nationals learning to speak the language, students – effectively 'peripheral' staff (Guerrier and Lockwood, 1989; Hales, 2000; Ogbonna and Harris, 2002). Managers may not trust such staff to demonstrate appropriate attitudes towards customers unless subject to very tight control (Hales, 2000; Ogbonna and Harris, 2002). Within certain parts of the hospitality industry, notably the fast food sector, the process of (literally) McDonaldization, notably the simplification and routinization of the work, has been taken furthest. But it is inevitably fraught with contradictions. Leidner (1993) has written an excellent ethnographic account of work in McDonald's, which demonstrates precisely these tensions. Although, Leidner observes that McDonald's customers are perfectly happy with routinized service, indeed they may regard anything more personal as an intrusion and a waste of time, even in McDonald's there remains the contradiction inherent in Korczynski's customer-oriented bureaucracies. It is summarized by one of the trainers at Hamburger University who explained 'we want to treat each customer as an individual in sixty seconds or less – thirty seconds for drive thru' (Leidner, 1993: 178). Leidner (1993) describes a work environment which is routinized to the extent that decision making has been practically eliminated from the jobs of crew. This does not mean, she argues, that the job is undemanding. Indeed, she comments on how hard the crew work and the physical and emotional stresses of coping with 'unskilled' work. Given the limited rewards for staff in terms of job security, wages and benefits, the question of how McDonald's keeps its staff committed and disciplined is interesting. Leidner (1993: 83) comments that 'socialization into McDonald's

norms, extremely close supervision (both human and electronic), individual and group incentives, peer pressure, and pressure from customers all play their part in getting workers to do things the McDonald's way'.

I have focused in some detail on this critical work on the nature of customer service. Twenty years ago most work on the labour process focused on the manufacturing sector. However, with the switch to a service-led economy in developed economies, much more attention has been paid to the work of front-line service staff, and studies in the hospitality industry have been central to this endeavour. Many of the same issues persist, whether looking at service or manufacturing staff: how staff are controlled, how they resist control, how they relate to their work. But service work is now seen not just as involving the employee's head and hands, but as also requiring emotional and aesthetic labour. The complex ways in which staff negotiate the demands of customers and of management – 'being themselves' whilst making money for the organization (and, through tips, for themselves), working hard whilst looking as if they are having fun, subtly trying to maintain control of customers even when they are making unreasonable demands – resists simple theories. By contrast, Austrin and West (2005), in a study of casino workers, provide a useful corrective to a model of customer service work as being just about the handling of people. They point out that in some front-of-house jobs the handling of things, in their case the rapid and correct handling of cards on the gaming table, is as important as the handling of customers. Whilst theirs is an extreme case, it is easy to overlook the technical mastery involved in other hospitality front-line jobs: for example, by bar staff, waiters and even coffee shop baristas.

BACK-OF-HOUSE STAFF

Whilst excellent work is being done exploring customer service work in the hospitality industry, back-of-house jobs have been relatively neglected. The work of room attendants may be mentioned in other studies (Adkins, 1995; Guerrier and Adib, 2000b) but Hunter Powell and Watson (2006) provide the first qualitative study of such work for some time. Accommodation work is, as they point out, stigmatized as 'dirty work' (Hughes, 1962), low status and low paid. Such jobs are difficult to fill and for this reason hotels increasingly use agency staff (Lai and Baum, 2005). Yet Hunter Powell and Watson (2006) note the pride that their respondents took in their work and also the tacit and unacknowledged skills that the work required. Food production work has also been neglected in recent research. This work includes low status and low skill roles such as kitchen porter (Saunders, 1981; Rowley and Purcell, 2001) where there are problems retaining and recruiting staff. But it also includes the high-skilled work in top hotels and restaurants, which, given the way chefs have become celebrities recently, would seem an interesting area for exploration.

CONCLUSIONS

There is, as has been shown, a rich stream of research within the broad field of organization studies in the hospitality industry. This research takes a variety of different theoretical and methodological perspectives and can hardly be organized into a single coherent body of knowledge. Indeed it is apparent from this review how research can be undertaken with no reference to related work which comes from a slightly different theoretical perspective. A good illustration is the work of Testa (2002, 2004), Weaver (2005) and Tracy (2000). All are interested in the cruise industry: Testa taking an organizational psychology perspective and publishing in hospitality or management journals; Tracy building on sociological work on emotional labour; and Weaver building on tourism research and concept of McDonaldization. None of them references each other's work.

Nonetheless, there are some themes that recur whatever theoretical perspective is taken. These themes are not unique to the hospitality industry but are particularly significant in this industry. One of these is the nature of skill and knowledge and how certain skills are valued or not valued. Hochschild's coining of the term 'emotional labour' has drawn attention to the work that is required just to be consistently 'nice' to customers; work which has traditionally been devalued because it is regarded as what certain lower status sections of the community (women and certain ethnic groups) naturally know how to do. Similarly, the skills involved in cleaning a room are unacknowledged and unrewarded,

when room attendants are recruited who have already learned to clean in the domestic environment. Hospitality organizations obviously make use of the tacit skills that staff bring with them. The traditional publican tacitly knows how to manage a drunken client who comes from the same cultural background as himself (Mutch, 2003) whilst the middle-class student tacitly knows how to dress, speak and interact with young, middle-class customers in a branded bar (Nickson et al., 2005). The skills and knowledge required to do a particular job are, in this analysis, highly contested. Defining the role of a hospitality manager as requiring essentially management rather than technical skills privileges the graduate and disadvantages the operative employee working their way up. Exclusion and inclusion is not just about gender, which has now been well examined, or about ethnic background, which has been less explored, but also about social class (although see, for example, Madsen Camacho, 1996; Adib and Guerrier, 2003). Wood (1994) commented that although assumptions about social class were inherent in many analyses of the hotel (and by extension, hospitality) industry there has been less analysis of the class position of workers. Ram et al. (2001) in a study of independent ethnic restaurants in Birmingham (UK), show how class and ethnic background are interlocked to limit the opportunities of operative staff to use their work experience as a springboard into self-employment. Following on from Mutch and Nickson and Warhurst, more work on tacit skill and knowledge, and on cultural and social capital would be valuable in relation to hospitality work.

A second theme relates to control. There are a number of different relationships here. First, and most obviously, how do managers attempt to exert control over staff? For customer service staff, this is about influencing a complex set of behaviours and attitudes: it is not just about what staff say to customers but also how they say it and what they feel about it. How do you get someone to smile and look as if they mean it (or even how do you get someone to smile and *actually* mean it)? Developing an appropriate organization culture and empowering staff may work with 'core' staff but are such methods also effective in relation to the transient staff who form a major part of the hospitality workforce? But guests are also trying to control staff. The practice of tipping is one of the most common and direct ways in which a guest can exercise control over staff (Shamir, 1980). In the middle are operative staff members trying, themselves, to exercise control over guests and, often, to resist the control of both guests and management. As I have shown, there has been much research looking at the pressures on staff of managing sometimes unreasonable and difficult guests.

A final theme relates to the boundaries between work and leisure/work and home. Commercial hospitality mirrors to some extent domestic hospitality (Lashley, 2000a; Lynch and MacWhannell, 2000). As I have discussed above, the skills involved in work in the hospitality industry are devalued because they are seen as no more than the skills required to function at home (cooking and cleaning). The pleasures of work within the hospitality industry are the pleasure of working in an environment (a bar, a restaurant, a hotel) where one might choose to spend one's leisure with people who are at leisure. Conversely, are people ever able to truly be at leisure when their work and leisure are so closely bound with each other (Foley and McGillivray, 2000)?

Whilst celebrating the richness of research in this field, I will conclude by identifying some of the gaps. The most obvious gap is the lack of attention currently paid to back-of-house operative staff, particularly those in food production and housekeeping. The last major study of chefs and cooks was probably Chivers' (1972) work. Most research is also, not surprisingly, directed at hospitality organizations in developed countries. Given that hospitality organizations do exist across the world, there are wonderful opportunities for comparative work, which have not been fully exploited. Even within developed countries, relatively little attention has been paid to ethnic diversity within hospitality organizations, although many such organizations are as ethnically stratified as they are stratified by gender (Guerrier and Adib, 2000b).

REFERENCES

Adib, A. and Guerrier, Y. (2001) 'The experience of tour reps in maintaining and losing control of holidaymakers', *International Journal of Hospitality Management*, 20: 339–352.

Adib, A. and Guerrier, Y. (2003) 'The interlocking of gender with nationality, race, ethnicity and class: the narratives of women in hotel work', *Gender, Work and Organization*, 10(4): 413–432.

Adkins, L. (1995) *Gendered Work: Sexuality, Family and the Labour Market*. Buckingham: Open University Press.

Adler, P. A. and Adler, P. (1999a) 'Transience and the postmodern self', *The Sociological Quarterly*, 40: 31–58.

Adler, P. A. and Adler, P. (1999b) Resort workers: adaptations in the leisure-work nexus. *Sociological Perspectives*. 42(3): 369–402.

Anastassova, L. and Purcell, K. (1995) 'Human resource management in the Bulgarian hotel industry: from command to empowerment', *International Journal of Hospitality Management*, 14: 171–185.

Arnaldo, M. (1981) 'Hotel general managers: a profile', *Cornell Hotel and Restaurant Administration Quarterly*, November: 53–56.

Ashness, D. and Lashley, C. (1995) 'Empowering service workers in Harvester Restaurants', *Personnel Review*, 24(8): 17–32.

Austrin, T. and West, J. (2005) Skills and surveillance in casino gambling: work, consumption and regulation, *Work, employment and society*, 19(2): 305–326.

Baum, J. and Mezias, S. (1992) 'Localized competition and organizational failure in the Manhattan hotel industry 1898–1990', *Administrative Staff Quarterly*, 37: 580–604.

Baum, T. (1995) *Managing Human Resources in the European Tourism and Hospitality Industry: A Strategic Approach*. London: Chapman and Hall.

Becker, C. and Olsen, M. (1995) 'Exploring the relationship between heterogeneity and generic management trends in hospitality organizations', *International Journal of Hospitality Management*, 14: 39–52.

Braverman, H. (1974) *Labor and Monopoly Capital*. Monthly Review Press.

Brotherton, B. and Wood, R. C. (2000) 'Hospitality and hospitality management'. In C. Lashley and A. Morrison (eds) *In Search of Hospitality*. Oxford: Butterworth-Heinemann. pp. 135–154.

Brownell, J. (1992) 'Hospitality managers' communication practices', *International Journal of Hospitality Management*, 11: 111–128.

Bryman, A. (1999) 'The Disneyization of society', *Sociological Review*, 47: 25–47.

Brymer, R. A. (1991) 'Employee empowerment: a guest driven leadership strategy', *Cornell Hotel and Restaurant Administration Quarterly*, 32(1): 53–68.

Buergermeister, J. (1988) 'Communication in fast food restaurants', *Hospitality and Education Research Journal*, 12: 53–65.

Chareanpunisirikul, S. and Wood, R. C. (2002) 'Mintzberg, managers and methodology: some observations from a study of hotel general managers', *Tourism Management*, 23: 551–556.

Chivers, T. (1972) 'The proletarianization of a service worker', *Sociological Review*, 633–656.

Chung-Herrera, B., Enz, C. and Lankau, M. (2003) 'Grooming future hospitality leaders: a competencies model', *Cornell Hotel and Restaurant Administration Quarterly*, June: 17–25.

Clegg, S., Hardy, C. and Nord, W. (1996) 'Preface'. In S. Clegg, C. Hardy and W. Nord (eds) *Handbook to Organization Studies*. London: Sage. p. xxi.

Corsun, D. L. and Enz, C. A. (1999) 'Predicting psychological empowerment among service workers: the effect of support-based relationships', *Human Relations*, 52, 205–224.

Crang, P. (1994) 'It's showtime: on the workforce display in a restaurant in southeast England', *Environment and Planning D: Society and Space*, 12: 674–704.

D'Annunzio-Green, N. (2002) 'An examination of the organizational and cross-cultural challenges facing international hotel managers in Russia', *International Journal of Contemporary Hospitality Management*, 14(6): 266–273.

D'Annunzio-Green, N. and Francis, H. (2005) 'Tuning into tensions at times of change: the experiences of line and HR managers in a contract catering firm', *International Journal of Contemporary Hospitality Management*, 17(4): 345–358.

Deery, M. and Jago, L. K. (2001) 'Hotel management style: a study of employee perceptions and preferences', *International Journal of Hospitality Management*, 20: 325–338.

Du Gay, P. and Salaman, G. (1992) 'The cult(ure) of the customer', *Journal of Management Studies*, 29(5): 615–632.

Ferguson, D. and Berger, F. (1984) 'Restaurant managers: what do they really do?', *Cornell Hotel and Restaurant Administration Quarterly*, 25: 27–34.

Fineman, S. (1993) 'Organizations as emotional arenas'. In S. Fineman (ed.) *Emotions in Organizations*. London: Sage. pp. 9–35.

Fineman, S. (2000) 'Emotional arenas revisited'. In S. Fineman (ed.) *Emotions in Organizations*, 2nd edn. London: Sage. pp. 1–24.

Foley, M. and McGillivray, D. (2000) 'Absence *from* or absence *of* work in the "leisure industries": free-time or displacement?', *Managing Leisure*, 5(4): 163–180.

Folgerø, I. S. and Fjeldstad, I. H. (1995) 'On duty – off guard: cultural norms and sexual harassment in service organizations', *Organization Studies*, 16(2): 299–313.

Fulford, M. D. and Enz, C. A. (1995) 'The impact of empowerment on service employees', *Journal of Managerial Issues*, 7(2): 161–175.

Gabriel, Y. (1988) *Working Lives in Catering*. London: Routledge and Kegan Paul.

Ghei, A. and Nebel, E. (1994) 'The successful manager and psychological androgyny: a conceptual and empirical investigation of hotel executives', *International Journal of Hospitality Management*, 13: 247–264.

Gilbert, D. and Guerrier, Y. (1997) 'Hospitality managers past and present', *Service Industries Journal*, 17: 115–132.

Goffman, E. (1959) *The Presentation of Self in Everyday Life*. London: Penguin.

Groschl, S. and Doherty, L. (2006) 'The complexity of culture: using the appraisal process to compare French and British managers in a UK-based international hotel organization', *International Journal of Hospitality Management*, 25: 313–334.

Guerrier, Y. (1987) Hotel managers' careers and their impact on hotels in Britain. *International Journal of Hospitality Management*, 6(3): 121–130.

Guerrier, Y. and Adib, A. (2000a) 'Working in the hospitality industry'. In C. Lashley and A. Morrison (eds) *In Search of Hospitality*. Oxford: Butterworth-Heinemann. pp. 255–275.

Guerrier, Y. and Adib, A. (2000b) 'No, we don't provide that service: the harassment of hotel employees by customers', *Work, Employment and Society*, 14: 689–705.

Guerrier, Y. and Adib, A. (2003) 'Work at leisure and leisure at work: a study of the emotional labour of tour reps', *Human Relations*, 56(11): 1399–1417.

Guerrier, Y. and Deery, M. (1998) 'Research in hospitality human resource management and organizational behavior', *International Journal of Hospitality Management*, 17: 145–160.

Guerrier, Y. and Lockwood, A. (1989) 'Developing hotel managers – a reappraisal'. *International Journal of Hospitality Management*, 8(2): 82–89.

Guerrier, Y. and Lockwood, A. (1991) 'Managers in hospitality: a review of current research'. In C. Cooper and A. Lockwood (eds) *Progress in Tourism, Recreation and Hospitality Management, Vol. 2*. London: Belhaven Press. pp. 151–167.

Guiffre, P. and Williams, C. (1994) 'Boundary lines: labeling sexual harassment in restaurants', *Gender and Society*, 8(3): 378–401.

Hales, C. (1993) *Managing through Organization*. London: Routledge.

Hales, C. (2000) 'Management and empowerment programmes', *Work, Employment and Society*, 14(3): 501–519.

Hales, C. and Klidas, A. (1998) 'Empowerment in five-star hotels: choice, voice or rhetoric?', *International Journal of Contemporary Hospitality Management*, 10(3): 88–95.

Hales, C. and Tamangani, Z. (1996) 'An investigation of the relationship between organizational structure, managerial role expectations and managers' work activities', *Journal of Management Studies*, 33(6): 731–756.

Hall, E. (1993) 'Smiling, deferring and flirting: doing gender by giving "good service" ', *Work and Occupations*, 20(4): 452–471.

Hancer, M. and George, R. T. (2003) 'Psychological empowerment of non-supervisory employees working in full-service restaurants', *International Journal of Hospitality Management*, 22: 3–16.

Harper, S., Brown, C. and Irvine, W. (2005) 'Qualifications: a fast-track to hotel general manager?', *International Journal of Contemporary Hospitality Management*, 17(1): 51–64.

Hearn, J. and Parkin, W. (1995) *'Sex' at 'Work': The Power and Paradox of Organization Sexuality*. London: Prentice-Hall.

HEFCE (2001) *Getting Ahead: Graduate Careers in the Hospitality Industry*. Report 01/30, London: Higher Education Funding Council for England.

Hochschild, A. (1983) *The Managed Heart*. Berkeley: University of California Press.

Hofstede, G. (1980) *Culture's Consequences*. Beverley Hills: Sage.

Hofstede, G. (1991) *Cultures in Organizations: Software of the Mind*. London: McGraw-Hill.

Hughes, E. C. (1971) 'Good people and dirty work', *Social Problems*, 10: 3–11.

Hunter Powell, P. and Watson, D. (2006) 'Service unseen: the hotel room attendant at work', *International Journal of Hospitality Management*, 25(2): 297–312.

Ingram, P. and Inman, C. (1996) 'Institutions, intergroup competition and evolution of hotel populations around Niagara Falls', *Administrative Science Quarterly*, 41: 629–658.

Iverson, R. and Deery, M. (1997) 'Turnover culture in the hospitality industry', *Human Resource Management Journal*, 7(4): 71–82.

Johnson, K. and Coupe, V. (1999) 'Sexual harassment: "that'll do nicely sir" ', *Hospitality Review*, 1(2): 36–41.

Jones, C., Taylor, G. and Nickson, D. (1997) 'Whatever it takes? Managing "empowered" employees and the service encounter in an international hotel chain', *Work, Employment and Society*, 11(3): 541–554.

Kay, C. and Russette, J. (2000) 'Hospitality-management competencies', *Cornell Hotel and Restaurant Administration Quarterly*, April: 52–63.

Kemp, S. and Dwyer, L. (2001) 'An examination of organisational culture – the Regent Hotel, Sydney', *International Journal of Hospitality Management*, 20: 77–93.

Korczynski, M. (2002) *Human Resource Management in Service Work*. Basingstoke: Palgrave.

Lai, P.-C. and Baum, T. (2005) 'Just-in-time labour supply in the hotel sector: the role of agencies', *Employee Relations*, 27(1): 86–102.

Lashley, C. (1995a) 'Towards an understanding of employment empowerment in hospitality services', *International Journal of Contemporary Hospitality Management*, 7(1): 27–32.

Lashley, C. (1995b) 'Empowerment through delayering: a pilot study in McDonald's restaurants', *International Journal of Contemporary Hospitality Management*, 7(2/3): 29–35.

Lashley, C. (1997) *Empowering Service Excellence: Beyond the Quick Fix*. London: Cassell.

Lashley, C. (2000a) 'Towards a theoretical understanding'. In C. Lashley and A. Morrison (eds) *In Search of Hospitality*. Oxford: Butterworth-Heinemann. pp. 1–17.

Lashley, C. (2000b) 'Empowerment through involvement: a case study in TGI Fridays', *Personnel Review*, 29: 333–349.

Lee-Ross, D. and Johns, N. (1995) 'Dimensionality of the Job Diagnostic Survey among distinct sub-groups of seasonal hotel workers', *Hospitality Research Journal*, 19: 31–42.

Leidner, R. (1993) *Fast Food, Fast Talk*. Berkeley: University of California Press.

Ley, D. (1980) 'The effective GM: leader or entrepreneur', *Cornell Hotel and Restaurant Administration Quarterly*, November: 66–67.

Lindsay, C. and McQuaid, R. (2004) 'Avoiding the "McJobs": unemployed job seekers and attitudes to service work', *Work, Employment and Society*, 18(2): 297–319.

Lucas, R. and Bailey, G. (1993) 'Youth pay in catering and retailing', *Personnel Review*, 22: 15–29.

Lynch, P. A. (2005a) 'Sociological impressionism in a hospitality context', *Annals of Tourism Research*, 32(3): 527–548.

Lynch, P. A. (2005b) 'The commercial home enterprise and host: a United Kingdom perspective', *International Journal of Hospitality Management*, 24(4): 533–553.

Lynch, P. and MacWhannell, D. (2000) Home and commercialized hospitality. In C. Lashley and A. Morrison (eds) *In Search of Hospitality*. Oxford: Butterworth-Heinemann. pp. 100–114.

Madsen Camacho, M. (1996) 'Dissenting workers and social control: a case study of the hotel industry in Huatulco, Oaxaca', *Human Organization*, 55(1): 33–40.

Mars, G. (1994) *Cheats at Work*, rev. edn. Aldershot: Dartmouth.

Meudell, K. and Gadd, K. (1994) 'Culture and climate in short life organizations: sunny spells or thunderstorms?', *International Journal of Contemporary Hospitality Management*, 6(5): 27–33.

Mintzberg, H. (1973) *The Nature of Managerial Work*. New York: Harper Row.

Morgan, G. (1986) *Images of Organization*. London: Sage.

Mutch, A. (2000) 'Trends and tensions in UK public house management', *International Journal of Hospitality Management*, 19: 361–374.

Mutch, A. (2003). 'Communities of practice and habitus: a critique', *Organization Studies*, 24(3): 383–401.

Mwara, G., Sutton, J. and Roberts, D. (1998) 'Corporate culture and national culture – an irreconcilable dilemma for the hospitality manager?', *International Journal of Contemporary Hospitality Management*, 10(6): 212–220.

Nailon, P. (1982) 'Theory in hospitality management', *International Journal of Hospitality Management*, 1: 135–143.

Nebel, E. (1991) *Managing Hotels Effectively: Lessons from Outstanding General Managers*. New York: Van Nostrand.

Nickson, D., Warhurst, C., Witz, A. and Cullen, A.-M. (2001) The importance of being aesthetic. In A. Sturdy, I. Grugulis and H. Wilmott (eds) *Customer Service: Empowerment and Entrapment*. Basingstoke: Palgrave. pp. 17–190.

Nickson, D., Warhurst, C. and Dutton, E. (2005) 'The importance of attitude and appearance in the service encounter in retail and hospitality', *Managing Service Quality*, 15(2): 195–208.

O'Doherty, D. and Willmott, H. (2000) 'The question of subjectivity and the labour process', *International Studies of Management and Organization*, 30: 112–132.

Ogbonna, E. and Harris, L. C. (2002) 'Managing organizational culture: insights from the hospitality industry', *Human Resource Management Journal*, 12(1): 33–53.

Peacock, M. and Kübler, M. (2001) 'The failure of "control" in the hospitality industry', *International Journal of Hospitality Management*, 20: 353–365.

Pittaway, L., Carmouche, R. and Chell, E. (1998) 'The way forward: leadership research in the hospitality industry', *International Journal of Hospitality Management*, 17: 407–426.

Prais, S. J., Jarvis, V. and Wagner, K. (1989) 'Productivity and vocational skills in services in Britain and Germany: Hotels', *National Institute Economic Review*, November: 52–74.

Pugh D. (ed) (1998) *The Aston Programme, Volume I*. Aldershot: Ashgate.

Ram, M., Abbas, T., Sanghera, B., Barlowm, G. and Jones, T. (2001) ' "Apprentice Entrepreneurs"? Ethnic minority workers in the independent restaurant sector', *Work, Employment and Society*, 15(2): 353–372.

Raybould, M. and Wilkins, H. (2005) 'Over qualified and under experienced: turning graduates into hospitality managers', *International Journal of Contemporary Hospitality Management*, 17(3): 203–216.

Riley, M. (1991) 'An analysis of hotel labour markets'. In C. Cooper (ed.) *Progress in Tourism and Hospitality Research, Vol. 3*. London: Belhaven. pp. 232–246.

Riley, M. and Szivas, E. (2003) 'Pay determination: a socioeconomic framework', *Annals of Tourism Research*, 30(2): 446–464.

Riley, M., Lockwood, A., Powell-Perry, J. and Baker, M. (1998) 'Job satisfaction, organization commitment and occupational culture: a case from the UK pub industry', *Progress in Tourism and Hospitality Research*, 4: 159–168.

Ritzer, G. (1996) *The McDonaldization of Society*, rev. edn. Thousand Oaks, CA: Pine Forge Press.

Royle, T. (1995) 'Corporate versus societal culture: a comparative study of McDonald's in Europe', *International Journal of Contemporary Hospitality Management*, 7(2/3): 52–56.

Roper, A., Doherty, L., Brookes, M. and Hampton, A. (2001) ' "Company Man" meets International Hotel Customer'. In A. Roper and Y. Guerrier (eds) *A Decade of Hospitality Management Research*. Newbury, Berks: Threshold. pp. 14–36.

Rowley, G. and Purcell, K. (2001). ' "As cooks go, she went": is labour churn inevitable?', *International Journal of Hospitality Management*, 20: 163–185.

Saunders, K. (1981) *The Social Stigma of Occupations: The Lower Grade Worker in Service Occupations*. Farnborough: Gower.

Selwyn, T. (2000) 'An anthropology of hospitality'. In C. Lashley and A. Morrison (eds) *In Search of Hospitality*, Oxford: Butterworth-Heinemann. pp. 18–37.

Seymour, D. and Sandiford, P. (2005) 'Learning emotion rules in service organizations: socialization and training in the UK public-house sector', *Work, Employment and Society*, 19(3): 547–564.

Shamir, B. (1978) 'Between bureaucracy and hospitality – some organizational characteristics of hotels', *Journal of Management Studies*, 12: 285–307.

Shamir, B. (1980) 'Between service and servility: role conflict in subordinate service roles', *Human Relations*, 33(10): 741–756.

Shortt, G. (1989) 'Work activities of hotel managers in Northern Ireland: a Mintzbergian analysis', *International Journal of Hospitality Management*, 8: 121–130.

Smith, M. A. (2003) *Sex, Gender and Power: The Enigma of the Public House*. Hebden Bridge: M. A. Smith.

Sosteric, M. (1996) 'Subjectivity and the labour process: a case study in the restaurant industry', *Work, Employment and Society*, 10(2): 297–318.

Sparrowe, R. (1994) 'Empowerment in the hospitality industry: an exploration of antecedents and outcomes', *Hospitality Research Journal*, 17(3): 51–74.

Sternberg, L. E. (1992) 'Empowerment: trust vs.control', *Cornell Hotel and Restaurant Administration*, 33(1): 68–72.

Szivas, E., Riley, M. and Airey, D. (2003) 'Labor mobility into tourism: attraction and satisfaction', *Annals of Tourism Research*, 30(1): 64–76.

Taylor, G. (1996) ' "Put on a happy face". Culture, identity and performanace in the service role'. In M. Robinson, N. Evans and P. Callaghan (eds) *Tourism and Culture: Towards the 21st Century*. Sunderland: Centre for Travel and Tourism.

Tepeci, M. and Bartlett, B. (2002) 'The hospitality industry culture profile: a measure of individual values, organizational culture, and person-organization fit as predictors of job satisfaction and behavioural intentions', *International Journal of Hospitality Management*, 21: 151–170.

Testa, M. R. (2001) 'Hospitality leaders: do they know how their employees feel about them?', *Cornell Hotel and Restaurant Administrative Quarterly*, December: 80–89.

Testa, M. R. (2002) 'Leadership dyads in the cruise industry: the impact of cultural contingency', *International Journal of Hospitality Management*, 21: 425–441.

Testa, M. R. (2004) 'Cultural similarity and service leadership: a look at the cruise industry', *Managing Service Quality*, 14(5): 402–413.

Tracey, B. and Hinkin, T. (1996) 'How transformational managers lead in the hospitality industry', *International Journal of Hospitality Management*, 15(2): 165–176.

Tracy, S. (2000) 'Becoming a character for commerce', *Management Communication Quarterly*, 14: 90–128.

Tyler, M. and Abbott, P. (1998) 'Chocs away: weight watching in the contemporary airline industry', *Sociology*, 32(3): 433–450.

Urry, J. (1990) *The Tourist Gaze*. London: Sage.

Walton, J. (2000) 'The hospitality trades: a social history'. In C. Lashley and A. Morrison (eds) *In Search of Hospitality*, Oxford: Butterworth-Heinemann. pp. 56–76.

Watson, S. and D'Annunzio-Green, N. (1996) 'Implementing cultural change through human resource management: the elusive organisational alchemy?' *International Journal of Contemporary Hospitality Management*, 8(2): 25–30.

Weaver, A. (2005) 'The McDonaldization thesis and cruise tourism', *Annals of Tourism Research*, 32(2): 346–366.

Whyte, W. (1946) 'When workers and customers meet'. In W. Whyte (ed.) *Industry and Society*. New York: McGraw-Hill. pp. 132–133.

Whyte, W. (1948) *Human Relations in the Hospitality Industry*. New York: McGraw-Hill.

Wood, R. C. (1993) 'Status and hotel and catering work: theoretical dimensions and practical implications', *Hospitality Research Journal*, 15: 3–15.

Wood, R.C. (1994). 'Hotel culture and social control', *Annals of Tourism Research*, 21: 65–79.

Wood, R. C. (1997) *Working in Hotels and Catering*, 2nd edn. London: International Thomson Business Press.

Woods, R. H. (1989) 'More alike than different: the culture in the restaurant industry', *Cornell Hotel and Restaurant Administration Quarterly*, 30(2): 82–97.

Woods, R. H. (1991) 'Surfacing culture: the "Northeast Restaurants" case', *International Journal of Hospitality Management*, 10(4): 339–356.

Woods, R. H. (1999) 'Predicting is difficult, especially about the future: human resources in the new millennium', *International Journal of Hospitality Management*, 18: 443–456.

Wynne, J. (1993) 'Power relations and empowerment within hotels', *Employee Relations*, 15: 42–50.

Human Resource Management in the Hospitality Industry

12

Julia Christensen Hughes

INTRODUCTION

Like all of the management functions identified within this text, there is an extensive generic literature in human resource management (HRM) from which researchers in hospitality and tourism have drawn and to some extent contributed to. It is therefore essential within this review to consider the development of the field in general and to compare this development to that which has occurred in the hospitality and tourism HRM literature in specific.

Scholarship on human resource management (HRM) has evolved considerably since its beginnings in the early 1900s, reflecting the development of the field as well as its espoused practice within organizations. Most notably, HRM (and hence the focus of its study) has shifted from being perceived primarily as a technical administrative function (dominated by applied research that sought to maximize worker and organizational productivity through principles of scientific management and control) to a humanistic one (concerned with employee well-being, motivation and the social dynamics of work), to a strategic one, dominated by a literature that has endeavored (to a certain extent, successfully) to demonstrate attitudinal, behavioral and bottom-line effects of bundles of high-commitment HRM practices, particularly when such practices are congruent with the strategic directions and environments of organizations. It is argued here that the time is right for another shift – towards a more critical view of HRM – in terms of both the discipline and its practice within organizations.

Much of the recent generic HRM literature has focused on demonstrating the link between various Human Resource (HR) practices and organizational outcomes and in encouraging the adoption of these 'best practices'. Researchers in hospitality and tourism have been far less involved in the former than their mainstream counterparts, but have enthusiastically encouraged normative models and profiled organizations, often through case studies of large hotel and restaurant multi-national enterprises (MNEs), that have reinforced these perspectives. Mainstream researchers have also sought to establish the extent to which human resource specialists and organizations 'are subscribing to this new and distinctive approach to the management of people (for example, Storey, 1992, 1995)' (Lucas, 2002: 207). Given the demonstrated effects of strategic HRM, the lack of uptake that has been reported has been somewhat surprising. Researchers have criticized the appropriateness of normative HRM models on this basis and some have sought to provide explanations.

Several comprehensive reviews of the generic HRM literature have recently been written (see for example, Bamberger and Meshoulam, 2000; Alcazar, Fernandez and Gardy, 2005; Boselie, Dietz and Boon, 2005; Edgar and Geare, 2005; Paauwe and Boselie, 2005; and Wright and Haggerty, 2005). According to these authors the field remains quite 'young' in the extent to which concepts have been clearly defined and theorizing has occurred (particularly critical theorizing), and the types of research methodologies that have been employed. Consistent with a functionalist perspective, social systems theory, and objectivism (Burrell and Morgan, 1979), the vast majority of research in the field has adopted an objective ontology, positivist epistemology, deterministic assumptions about human behavior, and nomothetic methodologies, combined with a sociology of regulation. From this perspective, most HRM researchers have assumed (either explicitly or implicitly) that organizations along with their goals (e.g. profits, productivity), practices (including human resource management), and concerns (e.g. turnover) are objective, rational and real (as opposed to subjective, irrational social constructions). HRM researchers have primarily sought to serve rather than challenge this reality.

The research emanating from this paradigm has been criticized on several fronts including the choice of variables and their measurement. Within the hospitality and tourism literature, greater distinction is needed between normative and empirically-based accounts of the field; it is at times difficult to ascertain what is being prescribed or evangelized primarily on faith or altruistic principles, what is being generalized from other industries or single hospitality-organization case studies (potentially uncritically and therefore inappropriately), and what is being advocated on the basis of theoretically and empirically sound research that takes into account the unique aspects of service delivery along with employment, organizational, and environmental characteristics particular to the industry. Research on the effects of strategic HRM and its variants is also clearly needed. In order for the field to fully evolve, however, research from outside social systems theory and objectivism is needed. What is most missing in both the generic and hospitality and tourism HRM literatures is the critical analysis of subjective accounts of what is being practiced and experienced from the perspective of employees and managers and critical theorizing about ways in which HRM as a discipline is contributing (positively and negatively) to these experiences. Through such an approach, multiple explanations for the differences between espoused and enacted HRM will be generated and our understanding of human resource practices (their conceptions and effects) will be enhanced.

The purpose of this chapter is to elaborate on these observations and recommendations, beginning with an overview of the importance of addressing these concerns for the hospitality and tourism industry.

THE IMPORTANCE OF HRM FOR HOSPITALITY AND TOURISM

There are many reasons why the study of HRM is particularly important for hospitality

and tourism, including the human resource intensity of the industry and its impact on the world economy. According to the World Travel and Tourism Council (2005), in 2005 the industry was expected to generate US$ 6,201.49 billion of economic activity, 10.6% of total GDP, and 221,568,000 jobs or 8.3% of total employment. Faced with these numbers it is perhaps not surprising that one of the industry's biggest challenges is a continuing shortage of qualified and willing labor (Powell and Wood, 1999; Kusluvan, 2003). Adding to the potential HRM challenges that these numbers suggest is the nature of service industries as well as employment and industry characteristics that are relatively distinct to hospitality and tourism. All of these factors arguably have profound implications for HR theorizing, research and practice.

According to Lashley (2001), characteristics of service industries, such as hospitality and tourism, that may present particular difficulties for the management of human resources, include the intangibility, heterogeneity, and perishability of the service encounter along with the inseparability of production from consumption. These factors lead to 'high labour intensity' and the 'irreplaceable role of personal service in service delivery' (Kusluvan, 2003: 5). This suggests that labor represents a considerable asset as well as a considerable cost. Lawler and Mohrman (2003: 1) state that 'in service organizations, compensation often represents 70 to 80% of the total cost of doing business'. Within the hospitality and tourism industry, this has led to a management culture that has been fixated on the need to control labor costs; 'the link between employee costs and profits still seems to dominate service industry management concerns' (Lashley, 2001: 192). In addition, service industries are characterized by the need for front-line employees to provide 'emotional labour', i.e. 'the management of feeling to create a publicly observable facial and bodily display' (Hochschild, 1983: 7). According to Lashley (2002a: 201), 'the provision of emotional labour has intensified, particularly in the service sector, as firms have recognized that effective competitive strategy via service quality enhancements requires employees to provide more than standardized and scripted interactions with customers'.

General employment characteristics of the hospitality and tourism industry also have implications for HRM. Kusluvan (2003: 4–12) recently provided a comprehensive review of these characteristics. They included: employment instability (e.g. seasonality; Twining-Ward and Baum, 1998) and high levels of labor turnover (e.g. high turnover culture; Iverson and Deery, 1997); the perception and/or predominance of unskilled and semi-skilled jobs (particularly in the developing world) (Baum, 1996; Riley, 1996); weak internal markets (e.g. lack of opportunity for promotion from within) which is related to 'promotion criteria, training opportunities, pay differentials, evaluations of jobs and which jobs are open to the external labor market' (Riley, 1996: 12); the gendered nature of employment within the industry, with between 40 and 75% of employees being women (depending on the country), and with women comprising a larger percentage of those in part-time, temporary, low-paid, and 'mothering', 'glamorized', or 'sexualized' roles (United Nations Environment and Development UK Committee [UNED-UK], 1999); the low status and respect accorded to jobs and people working in the industry (Guerrier, 1999; Pizam, 1999); low levels of unionization, with the highest rates being found in Australia, at 18% for full-time workers (Piso, 1999); high transferability of customer service skills to other industries (Baum, 1995; Riley, 1996; Guerrier, 1999); the industry's penchant for employing marginalized and disadvantaged labor including high proportions of 'young, ethnic minority groups, migrant workers, and "misfits"' (Kusluvan, 2003: 11); and the generally poor conditions of employment including (op cit.: 17):

> monotonous jobs, harassment and bullying, low job security, low promotional opportunity, long and unsocial hours of work, demanding managers and supervisors, poor co-worker attitudes, night and weekend schedules, heavy workload and stress, labor shortages and poor staff, lack of time for family and low quality of life.

Kusluvan (2003: 12) also noted that 'high rates of work related injuries, work-related illness (especially stress), and violence are also reported in the "hotel catering and tourism sector"'.

One additional – and particularly important – characteristic identified by Kusluvan (2003), is the predominance of small and medium sized enterprises (SMEs) in the industry, within both developed and developing counties. This was reported to be the case particularly in the United Kingdom, Ireland and New Zealand (Kusluvan, 2003: 11):

> In the context of the United Kingdom it is estimated that 81 percent of hotels and 94 percent of restaurants and bars have fewer than 25 employees ... Similarly, 79 per cent of all tourism businesses in Ireland and 90 per cent in New Zealand employ less than 15 people.

According to Baum (1999: 4), organizational size can have a significant impact on HRM as 'small businesses in tourism ... do not necessarily have the capacity, capability, resources or commitment to support the human resource development (HRD) function'.

It is important to note, however, that the extent to which the industry is – and may remain – dominated by SMEs varies considerably by country. In the USA, for example, which is where many of today's branded, multi-national hotel and restaurant enterprises originated, the landscape looks somewhat different. For example, Goss-Turner (2002: 120) noted the dominance of multi-site enterprises in the USA and suggested that such a structure could have a profound impact on the HR function, including the 'move towards more systematic procedures and the drive for standardization and consistency' with managers 'attempting to find a balance between a high level of prescription due to branding with the need to encourage a high level of commitment to the values and philosophy of the company' (ibid. 123). Similarly, in Australia, large MNE's are said to dominate the hotel industry (Timo and Davidson, 2002). Taken together, these findings suggest a possible 'bimodal effect', with the industry as a whole being comprised of many very small and many very large, multi-unit enterprises. National differences with respect to organizational size are important factors to consider in theorizing HRM.

Another important industry characteristic pertains to internationalism. Timo and Davidson (2002: 187) observed that 'over the past three decades, tourism has emerged as a significant global industry ... the hotel industry is becoming increasingly internationalized, with a rapid rise in the importance of MNEs and the importance of global branding'. Associated with internationalization of the industry, and globalization in general, is the increasing ethnic diversity of the workforce and customer populations. Mok (2002: 212) argued that 'the globalization of businesses has created a demand for employees who understand their multicultural customers ... As a result, interest and concern in managing workforce diversity has grown steadily over the past decade'. In linking the importance of service, cross-culturalism, and HRM, Millett (2002: 131) observed:

> In international hospitality and tourism, where customer service is critical and the performance of staff is a central management issue across cultural and national boundaries, there is an obvious need to align human resource management in general, and performance management in particular, to the strategic requirements of service-oriented firms.

All of these factors (i.e. the importance of the industry to the global economy; service culture attributes including the importance of human resources for service delivery, management fixation on reducing labor costs, and the important role of emotional labor; a variety of employment characteristics including high turnover and poor working conditions; and industry characteristics including size, internationalization and cross-culturalism), suggest that perhaps in no other industry is it more important to understand the human resource function. The hospitality and tourism industry provides a rich opportunity for researchers to theorize HRM and by doing so to make a substantial contribution to the field.

HISTORICAL DEVELOPMENT OF THE FIELD AND DEFINITIONS (TYPES OF HRM)

One of the challenges in studying HRM has been the elusive definition of the term. Indeed, according to Lucas (2002: 207), satisfactorily defining HRM 'remains an enigma'. In this section the historical development of the field is briefly reviewed (focusing on the administrative, humanistic, and strategic conceptions of HRM) and its various definitions – including personnel management, Soft HRM, Hard HRM, Strategic HRM, HR Strategy (HRS), Espoused HRS, Emergent HRS, International HRM, Universal HRM, Integrative HRM, and Contextual HRM – are presented.

HRM's beginnings as personnel management: an administrative focus

The roots of HRM arguably began in the late 1800s and early 1900s, with the advent of the factory system and mass production. Several notable classical management theorists and industrial/organizational psychologists contributed to the development of the field at this time, applying theoretical constructs to the practical problems of managing human resources and attempting to identify universal principles 'as a guide to managerial action' (Burrell and Morgan, 1979: 165).

One notable pioneer, Frederick Taylor (1947), was the first to bring principles of scientific management to the study of a variety of HR-related issues including job design, reward systems, and employee productivity. Taylor was an advocate for increasing employee productivity through clearly delineated expectations based on the meticulous and detailed analysis of job tasks, task simplification, and performance-based pay structures. In adopting a deterministic stance with respect to human behavior, Taylor represented a type of classical management theorist who sought fundamental or universal laws to predict and control employee behavior; 'the individual and his behaviour at work is seen as being determined by the situation to which he is exposed' (Burrell and Morgan, 1979: 128). The assumption that workers could be motivated almost exclusively through the reward structure figured prominently in this work.

The era of scientific management was shortly followed by the industrial psychology movement. While also interested in organizational effectiveness, industrial psychologists sought to distinguish themselves from scientific management by attending to the experience of employees; 'the movement was at pains to emphasize its humanitarian as well as its managerial interests' (Burrell and Morgan, 1979: 128). According to Burrell and Morgan (1979: 128), industrial psychology 'was a consultancy-oriented concern, supplying advice to industrial managers on problems associated with industrial fatigue, employee selection, individual differences and the like'.

A related stream of research that emerged at about this time became known as the Hawthorne Studies. Originally published in Mayo's (1933) *The Human Problems of an Industrial Civilization* and Roethlisberger and

Dickson's (1939) *Management and the Worker*, these studies attempted 'to identify cause and effect relationships between physical work conditions [e.g. hours of work, rest periods, wage incentives, supervision and social factors] and employee performance and efficiency' (Burrell and Morgan, 1979: 133). These studies concluded that the impact of the social environment (both inside and outside the workplace) was at least equal to or greater than the impact of the physical environment on employee productivity. While the research methods employed in this work have undergone extensive critique and the results have now been largely discounted, through this research, employee feelings and the quality of the social environment became acknowledged as legitimate organizational concerns and subjects of study.

The administration and practice of personnel management during the early 1900s evolved to incorporate these shifting interests. Illustrative of this evolution, the formal association of UK personnel managers was called the Welfare Workers' Association in 1913, became the Industrial Welfare Workers Association in 1924, and the Institute of Labour Management in 1931, before becoming the Institute of Personnel Management in 1946 (Townley, 1994: 15–16). G. R. Moxon's (1943) book, *The Functions of a Personnel Department*, identified six primary areas of focus for personnel managers: 'employment; wages; negotiation and joint consultation; health and safety, welfare (employee services); and education and training' (Moxon, as cited in Townley, 1994: 3). Due to the seemingly disjointed nature of these activities, the field was criticized for being a collection of ad hoc and reactionary activities or 'incidental techniques without much internal cohesion' (Drucker, as cited in Townley, 1994: 3).

A humanistic approach

In part on the basis of the Hawthorne studies, the 1930s, 40s and 50s saw the rise of the Human Relations Movement. Whyte (1948) contributed his seminal book on *Human Relations in the Restaurant Industry*. As part of this movement, attention shifted from studying 'fatigue' and 'monotony' to 'the determinants of "job satisfaction" and its relationship to "work performance"' (Burrell and Morgan, 1979: 143). Studies focused on the interrelationships between a variety of organizational variables including

'promotion opportunities, remuneration, status, job content, working conditions ...' (Burrell and Morgan: 143) and a variety of outcome variables, including job satisfaction, job performance, absenteeism, turnover, accident rates etc. (Burrell and Morgan, 1979). While some correlations were found, no clear relationship could be established, which led to questions about worker motivation and the need to fulfill higher-level needs such as 'recognition, achievement, self-actualization, etc.' (Burrell and Morgan, 1979: 144).

Ultimately, researchers such as Argyris (1952, 1957, 1964), and Herzberg, Mausner, and Snyderman (1959) became interested in improving working conditions for employees and enhancing organizational success through increased employee involvement. They argued (in contrast to Taylor's perspective), that 'the satisfaction of higher-level needs at work is an imperative as far as human growth and development, job satisfaction, and effective work performance are concerned' (Burrell and Morgan, 1979: 174). Like the classical management theorists, these researchers were interested in advancing a universal approach to human resource management, however, in this instance the focus was on satisfying the psychological needs of employees through enriching their work as opposed to tightly controlling their behavior (Burrell and Morgan, 1979: 166).

The 1970s brought focus to issues of job design, including job-enlargement and job-enrichment experiments incorporating such concepts as skill variety, task identity, task significance, autonomy, and feedback (Hackman and Oldham, 1976, 1980). Organizational structures and decision-making processes challenged to include flatter team-based structures, autonomous work teams, quality circles, participative management, joint consultation committees, works councils, and the redefinition of managerial work. Arguably, much of this work laid the foundation for the concept of soft HRM which is momentarily described.

Contingency theory also became prominent in the 1970s. Interestingly, it provided a means to reconcile the two competing 'universal' notions of HRM (i.e. administrative/scientific and humanistic/human relations). First presented by Lawrence and Lorsch (1967), contingency theory introduced the notion that organizational effectiveness is predicated on the 'degree of differentiation and integration compatible with environmental demands' (Burrell and Morgan,

1979: 165). More specifically, it suggested that organizations and their environments are mutually interdependent; that in some environments scientific management principles might be the most appropriate approach to human resource management and in other environments a human relations/quality of working life approach might be best.

During this time the roots of HRM were clearly formed. In Lashley's (2001) seminal work on empowerment in the hospitality industry, he provided a brief review of various conceptions of HRM. In particular, he suggested that while Armstrong (1987) positioned HRM as simply a modern name for personnel management and Legge (1995) suggested that HRM had more in common with personnel management than not, others argued that the two concepts were quite distinct. For example, Storey (1992) and Blyton and Turnbull (1992) suggested HRM represented a variety of employment practices that were popularized in the USA in the mid-1980s. Similarly, Maxwell and Quail (2002: 91) defined HRM as an 'employee-centred approach to management' and suggested that it had much in common with human resource development (HRD).

In adopting the view of Storey (1992) and Blyton and Turnbull (1992), Edgar and Geare (2005) suggested that the term 'Human Resource Management (HRM)' emerged in North America in the mid-1980s, purportedly as an answer to declining American competitiveness and concerns with unionization. In their account of its evolution, Edgar and Geare (2005) cited the book *Human Resource Management: A General Manager's Perspective*, by Beer et al. (1985), as being particularly seminal. Beer et al. (1995: 12–13) argued that all managers have a responsibility for the effective management of human resources, employees should be regarded as 'social capital', and in addition to assessing the outcomes of HR policies and practices with respect to 'the interests of the enterprise', that the 'well-being of the individual employee' and the 'interests of society' were also important considerations in their own right.

This book was developed to accompany the first new course introduced by the Harvard Business School in over 20 years; a course in HRM. According to Beer et al. (1985: x), the course signaled the recognition that due to a number of mounting pressures (e.g. increasing global competition and rates of change, the need for productivity improvements, employment

legislation, the increasing diversity and expectations of the workforce), human resource management was becoming 'an increasingly important competitive factor'. They went on to suggest that due to these pressures, general managers were 'beginning to demand that managing human resources be approached in an integrated, proactive, and strategic way, one relevant to their business and management problems'.

Correspondingly, Beer et al. (1985: 1) defined HRM as 'all management decisions and actions that affect the nature of the relationship between the organization and employees – its human resources'. They also presented a comprehensive model which delineated four key policy areas in which HRM policy decisions are made: employee influence (i.e. the extent to which employees have 'influence' in the organization through such mechanisms as employee ownership, collective bargaining, or employee participation/involvement strategies); human resource flow (i.e. practices related to the flow of employees in, through and out of the organization through such mechanisms as recruitment, selection, orientation, training and development, and performance management); reward systems (i.e. the collection of both extrinsic and intrinsic rewards employees receive for their labor); and work systems (i.e. traditional versus non-traditional work arrangements). The authors suggested that the policy decisions made in each of these four areas should be (1) internally consistent and, (2) influenced by both situational factors (e.g. 'workforce characteristics, business strategy and conditions, management philosophy, labor market conditions, unions, task technology, and laws and societal values and stakeholder interests') and stakeholder interests (e.g. shareholders, management, employee groups, government, the broader community and unions) (Beer et al., 1986: 16).

In terms of outcomes, Beer et al. (1985: 16) suggested that in the short term appropriate HRM policy choices would result in improved employee commitment, competence, and congruence with the goals of the organization, as well as the overall cost-effectiveness of HR practices. In the longer term, these outcomes were suggested to result in improved individual, organizational, and societal well-being.

Now known as the 'Harvard Commitment Model' (Edgar and Geare, 2005) or 'Soft HRM' (Storey, 1992), this approach reflects a 'developmental humanism' (Legge, 1995: 66) and 'emphasizes fostering commitment, improving quality and developing human resources' (Lucas, 2002: 207). As suggested by Edgar and Geare, the core elements of the model include the explicit acknowledgement of multiple stakeholders (Keenoy, 1990) as well as the existence of a relationship between appropriate HRM practices (Guest, 1997) and management style (communication, motivation, and leadership) (Storey, 1987), with the fulfillment of employee needs, positive employee attitudes, increasing employee commitment, and improved organizational performance.

The major criticisms of this model have been for its focus on employee needs and its lack of realism. Citing the work of Guest (1995), Keenoy (1990), Legge (1995) and others, Edgar and Geare (2005: 536) argued that normative models advocating a focus on employee needs were out of touch with the reality in most organizations; 'meeting employee needs has never been an objective in itself, and has simply been the normative view of what Harvard academics would like to see as the employment relationship'. Further, they suggested that research has shown 'even if the rhetoric of HRM is "soft", the reality is almost always "hard", with the interests of the organization prevailing over those of the individual' (Truss, Gratton, Hope-Hailey, McGovern and Styles, as cited in Edgar and Geare, 2005: 536).

At the same time that soft HRM was being advocated at Harvard, academics at the Michigan Business School were advancing a different point of view; one that has become known as 'Hard HRM' (Storey, 1992), and is more closely reflective of what researchers observed in practice. Edgar and Geare (2005: 535) suggested that hard HRM is 'concerned with the effective utilization of employees (Guest, 2002) and emphasizes the quantitative, calculative and business strategic aspects of managing the head count'. It has also been described as encompassing 'utilitarian instrumentalism' (Legge, 1995: 66); as being 'almost uniformly unitarist in orientation and display[ing] a quite singular endorsement of managerial values' (Keenoy, 1990: 368); 'contingent and calculating in its utilization of the human resource' (Lucas, 2002: 207); and stressing 'the management of human resources as factors of production and the need to control' (Lashley, 2001). According to Lashley (2001: 36), 'firms operating in cost-competitive markets, like fast foods operators, are typical of this approach'.

Although the roots of hard HRM arguably go back to the early 1900s and the rise of scientific management, the seminal work explicitly credited with encompassing this perspective was *Strategic Human Resource Management*, edited by Fombrun, Tichy and Devanna (1984) (Edgar and Gearc, 2005). Suggesting a much narrower focus than that proposed by Beer et al. (1985), from this perspective HRM was defined in a way very similar to personnel management, i.e. as encompassing a number of key processes: 'selection/promotion/placement' processes, 'reward' processes, 'development' processes, and 'appraisal processes' (Tichy, Fombrun and Devanna, 1984: 26, as cited in Edgar and Geare, 2005: 535). A recent review of the HRM literature in hospitality and tourism has further delineated these activities as including 'employee resourcing', 'employee development', and 'employee relations' (see for example, D'Annunzio-Green, Maxwell and Watson, 2002a).

Over the last decade, both generic and hospitality HRM researchers have challenged the presentation of these two concepts as being clearly distinct. For example, Legge (1995: 88) referred to HRM as 'tough love'. Lashley (2001: 197) posited that 'the distinction between hard and soft might be two rhetorics at work in the same situation', particularly in service industries where employee discretion is a crucial element of service delivery and standardization is a crucial element of the product offer; 'both control and commitment … are of equal importance, not two ends of a dichotomous scale' Lashley (2001: 178–179). Similarly, Watson (1986) suggested that organizations have simultaneously pursued both hard and soft approaches, with managers alternating their focus on cost control with employee commitment. Finally, Lucas (2002) proposed that both control and commitment are 'variants' of strategic human resource management, a concept that has dominated much of the HRM discourse in recent years.

A strategic approach

The current focus of the literature on Strategic HRM (SHRM) (or contingent HRM) combines elements of both soft and hard HRM and builds on the seminal work of Harvard historian

Alfred Chandler. Chandler studied approximately 100 large US manufacturing firms from 1909 to 1959 and observed that 'a new strategy required a new or at least refashioned structure if the enlarged enterprise was to be operated efficiently ... unless structure follows strategy, inefficiency results' (Chandler, 1962: 15). Chandler (1962: 13) defined strategy as 'the determination of the basic long-term goals and objectives of an enterprise, and the adoption of courses of action and the allocation of resources necessary for carrying out these goals'. He concluded that the particular stage of development of an organization (i.e. whether the organization was in a stage of birth or formation, growth, maturity, or decline) played a key role in the structure that it should optimally have.

The 1970s and 1980s saw the development of several models or typologies that arguably combined contingency theory with the strategy literature, and explicitly linked organizational strategy or competitive positioning with structural considerations. One is Miles and Snow's (1978) typology in which they identified four types of organizations – defenders, prospectors, analyzers, and reactors. Similarly, Porter (1980, 1990) identified two major generic competitive strategies – lower cost and differentiation. Following this work, Miller (1987) proposed an integrative framework consisting of four key dimensions – innovation, marketing differentiation, breadth, and cost control. Schuler and Jackson (1987a, 1987b) and Schuler (1989) built on much of this work, linking organizational strategy and structure explicitly with HRM strategy. They proposed an ideal match between three generic competitive positions (cost reduction, innovation, and quality enhancement) with three HRM philosophies (utilization, facilitation and accumulation). Lashley (1998), Herzenberg, Alic and Wial (1998), and Boxall (2003) have more recently proposed typologies linking market demands to various types of HR practice and work systems in the service industry. Underscoring the importance of such a typology for this industry, Lashley (2001: 19) states:

> The precise nature of the service offered, the importance of tangibles and intangibles, the degree of standardization and customization of the service offered, the amount of contact between the service deliverer and customers, and the level of discretion to be exercised by employees all shape the potential 'best fit' or match between the management of human resources.

During the 1990s much of the Western world experienced enormous financial pressure and upheaval. 'Downsizing', 'outsourcing', 'headcount', 're-engineering', and 'lean and mean' became common management refrains. At the same time, pressure to produce quality products and services increased, with concepts such as total quality management and empowerment being advanced in the literature. According to Lashley (2001: 7), empowerment became a 'key rhetoric of the 1990s' accompanied by a 'burgeoning literature ... mostly written from a "normative" perspective'.

For the last decade and a half, management consultants and applied researchers have been advocating for 'the effective management of human resources as the key to ensuring quality and a critical source of competitive advantage' (Bamberger and Meshoulam, 2000: 2). Human resources have been reframed as human capital, particularly within knowledge or learning economies, where such capital has been acknowledged as 'the foundation of value creation' (Becker, Huselid and Ulrich, 2001: ix). Along with this, organizations have been encouraged to embrace human resource managers as key strategic partners and human resource managers have been challenged to provide hard evidence (or metrics) to demonstrate the 'value added' of their activities. This challenge has been aided by publications such as *The HR Scorecard: Linking People, Strategy and Performance* (Becker et al., 2001); and *The ROI of Human Capital: Measuring the Economic Value of Employee Performance* (Fitz-Enz, 2000). It is within this context that the concepts of strategic HRM, and its variants – SHRM, HR strategy, espoused HRS, enacted HRS, international HRM, universal HRM, integrative HRM, and contextual HRM – have been advanced. Each of these concepts is now defined.

Strategic Human Resource Management suggests that the better the fit (i.e. 'best fit') or alignment between an organization's HRM policies and practices, its overall strategic direction, its organizational variables (size, technology, structure) and its environment (competitive, technological, macroeconomic, and labor context), the more successful the organization will be (Alcazar et al., 2005). 'To have a significant, positive impact on firm performance, HR practices must be aligned with the organization's overall business strategy' (Bamberger and Meshoulam, 2000: 175).

In theorizing SHRM, Bamberger and Meshoulam (2000) questioned whether it should be conceptualized primarily as a process (e.g. 'the process of linking HR practices to business strategy'; Ulrich, 1997: 189) or as an outcome (e.g. 'organizational systems designed to achieve sustainable competitive advantage through people'; Snell, Youndt and Wright, 1996: 62). Consistent with the view of Ulrich (1997), Bamberger and Meshoulam (2000: 6) concluded that SHRM is a process; 'a process by which organizations seek to link the human, social, and intellectual capital of their members to the strategic needs of the firm'.

Bamberger and Meshoulam (2000: 5) further suggested that Human Resource Strategy (HRS) is an outcome. They defined HRS as 'the pattern of decisions regarding the policies and practices associated with the HR system'. Consistent with this view, Ulrich (1997: 190) defined HRS as 'the mission, vision and priorities of the HR function'. This is similar to the notion of 'employment strategy' advocated by Watson (1986) and endorsed by Lashley (2001). Bamberger and Meshoulam (2000: 5) also suggested that 'it is impossible to understand the nature of HR strategy without taking both intraorganizational politics and environmental/institutional contingencies into account'. Lashley (2001: 168) similarly suggested:

> The study of employment strategy does not perforce validate the view that employment policies are arrived at in a rational-mechanistic manner. Employment policies can be said to emerge from internal political processes, and are shaped by managerial perceptions of the contextual factors within a cultural setting... .

Bamberger and Meshoulam (2000: 6) suggested that it is important to differentiate between an organization's 'espoused HRS' or 'the road map that organizational leaders use to secure the link' between HRM and business strategy, and 'emergent HRS' or 'the road actually traveled'. Similarly, Boselie et al. (2005: 70) advocated distinguishing between HRM policies (i.e. the organization's 'stated intentions') and HRM practices (i.e. 'the actual, functioning, observable activities, as experienced by employees').

An important variant of SHRM for multinational organizations is International Human Resource Management (International HRM). According to D'Annunzio-Green et al. (2002a: 2), international HRM is the interplay between 'basic human resource functions', 'different types of employees (e.g. expatriates, local and host country nationals)', and 'the different countries of operation within which subsidiaries operate'. While descriptions of SHRM have explicitly acknowledged the importance of the environment, including the competitive environment, economic environment (e.g. average wage, unemployment rates), and political environment (e.g. employment legislation), the organization's cultural (e.g. religion, values, education, social structure), and physical environments (e.g. climate, geography, labour demographics) also need to be taken into consideration. Reinforcing this perspective, D'Annunzio-Green et al. (op cit.: 5) argued that 'Strategic HRM, in theory at least, has acute relevance in the context of international hospitality and tourism organizations'.

Another variant which has received considerable attention in the literature is Universal HRM (UHRM). Like SHRM, Universal HRM positions HRM as a strategic endeavor, but focuses on achieving competitive advantage through the use of 'best practices' leading to the development of a highly committed, competent and motivated workforce. This work is based in large measure on the 'high-involvement' (Lawler, 1986; Appleby and Mavin, 2000), 'high performance work systems' (Applebaum and Batt, 1994; Huselid, 1995; Applebaum, Bailey, Berg and Kalleberg, 2000), and 'organizational commitment' literatures (March and Simon, 1958; Grusky, 1966, Mowday, Koberg and McArthur, 1984). In comparing these various approaches, Lashley (2001) notes:

> Although there are some subtle variations in the claims and usage of each of these terms, the core assumption is that organizational performance can be improved by the adoption of a cluster of techniques for the management of the organization's employees.

Bamberger and Meshoulam (2000: 170) described the three-pronged mechanism by which the effect of these techniques on organizational performance is theorized to occur and the types of HR practices that arguably would contribute to this mechanism. The first they refer to as the 'human capital base' or the collection of human resources (skills, knowledge, potential), which the organization has to work with. The organization's recruitment, selection, training, and development processes directly are suggested to affect this base. The second is the extent to which the organization is able to motivate their human resources. This is arguably affected by a variety of processes including reward and work systems (Beer et al., 1985). Finally, is the extent to which employees have the opportunity to contribute, which is affected by such things as job design and involvement strategies. From the perspective of the universal approach, organizations should have a strong, highly motivated human capital base, with the opportunity to make a positive contribution to organizational performance.

Guest, Conway and Dewe (2004), used a similar classification to Bamberger and Meshoulam (2000) but added a fourth category: commitment. They suggested that commitment would be affected by internal labor markets, equal opportunity, and family-friendly HR practices, along with the existence of consultative processes. Others have also provided 'best practice' lists (see for example Pfeffer, 1995; Applebaum et al., 2000; Enz and Siguaw, 2000a, 2000b; Huang, 2001; Boxall, 2003). In their review of 'every [104 articles] empirical research article into the linkages between HRM and performance published in pre-eminent international refereed journals between 1994 and 2003' (Boselie et al., 2005: 67), Boselie et al. (op cit.: 73) concluded that there was no one unified list, but that 'training and development, contingent pay and reward schemes, performance management (including appraisal) and careful recruitment and selection' were the most common items. Within the hospitality industry, 'progressive' HR policies are generally assumed to include the centrality of training and development along with 'empowerment, flexible work, team-working and learning organizations' (Maxwell and Quail, 2002: 92). What most distinguishes UHRM from SHRM is that 'researchers adopting a universalistic perspective ... claimed that all organizations, regardless of size, industry, or business strategy, should adopt these so-called "best practices"' (Bamberger and Meshoulam, 2000: 175).

A concept increasingly encompassed in both SHRM and UHRM, has been referred to as Integrative HRM (IHRM). IHRM specifically focuses on 'internal congruency' (Beer et al., 1985) or 'bundling' (MacDuffie, 1995) amongst various HR practices. Alcazar et al. (2005) and Bamberger and Meshoulam (2000) refer to this perspective as the 'configurational approach'.

Bamberger and Meshoulam (2000: 175) wrote:

> Internal coherence among individual HR practices is key and that, assuming that these practices are internally consistent, combinations of HRM practices are likely to have larger effects on organizational outcomes than the sum of the component effects due to individual practices.

IHRM challenges the traditional personnel management notion of treating HR practices as discrete functions.

Finally, Contextual HRM (CHRM), like international HRM, brings added emphasis to the two-way relationship between HRM and the broader social context in which organizations operate (e.g. social, economic, institutional, political, legal, technological and competitive factors). According to Alcazar et al. (2005: 230), 'the contextual perspective re-analyses environmental influences, not as unidirectional pressures ... but integrating human resource strategies into a social macrosystem, which both influences and is influenced by managerial decisions'. The intention of this approach is to develop models of HRM that are appropriate for 'different industrial and geographical contexts' (Alcazar et al., 2005: 230).

Regardless of the distinctions between these various models (SHRM, HRS, International HRM, UHRM, IHRM, CHRM), they are complementary (Alcazar et al., 2005). Further, they share an appreciation for human resource management as a strategic concern, one that is associated with organizational performance and competitive advantage. How this association actually occurs remains a matter of theoretical and empirical debate. Now that the historical development of the field had been described and the core concepts of HRM defined, the chapter turns its attention to a critical review of current research in the field.

CRITICAL REVIEW OF THE CURRENT STATE OF THE ART, INCLUDING OMISSIONS

Several comprehensive reviews of the HRM literature have recently been written, including the work of Alcazar et al. (2005), Boselie et al. (2005), Edgar and Geare (2005), Paauwe and Boselie (2005), and Wright and Haggerty (2005). According to these authors, over the past decade much of the generic HRM research has focused on empirically testing correlations between various HR practices (either as discrete elements or bundles of practices) and hypothesized organizational outcomes, typically within organizations from a cross-section of industries. This research has sought support for various normative HRM models, often pitting proponents of UHRM and SHRM against one another. The search for evidence in support of SHRM and its variants has been described as the discipline's 'Holy Grail' (Boselie et al., 2005: 67), 'one of the most important research questions in the field' (Alcazar et al., 2005: 214); and the 'HRM and performance debate' (Paauwe and Boselie, 2005: 68).

The aforementioned reviews built upon the pioneering work of researchers such as Arthur (1994), Guest and Hoque (1994), Huselid (1995), MacDuffie (1995), Snell and Youndt (1995), Delery and Doty (1996), and Wright, McCormick, Sherman and MacMahan (1999). At the basis of much of this research has been Becker, Huselid, Pickus and Spratt's (1997) linear normative model that suggested that business and strategic initiatives drive the design of the HR system and its practices, which in turn influences employee skills, motivation, job design and work structures. These factors lead to productivity, creativity and discretionary effort which in turn lead to operating performance, profit and growth, and ultimately market value. Wright and Haggerty (2005: 170) observed that of all of these variables 'most research has only focused on two that are quite distal from one another in the causal chain (HR practices and performance)'.

Other normative models have also been proposed. For example, Guest (1997) suggested that choice of HRM strategy (differentiation, focus, or cost), leads to differences in HRM practices (e.g. selection, training, job design, involvement). These practices in turn lead to various degrees of HRM outcomes (e.g. commitment, quality and flexibility), which result in variances in behavioral outcomes (e.g. effort, cooperation, involvement, citizenship), performance outcomes (e.g. productivity, quality, innovation, turnover, conflict, customer complaints) and financial outcomes (profit, ROI). Providing a simpler model, Appelbaum et al. (2000) suggested that high performance work systems (e.g. opportunity to participate,

skills and incentive) lead to effective discretionary effort, which in turn leads to firm performance.

In reviewing the results of studies empirically testing these models, Boselie et al. (2005: 81) concluded that most supported the existence of a link between HRM and organizational performance, particularly for the 'best practices' concept. Paauwe and Boselie (2005) observed that while 'it seems logical to believe in a best fit approach ... the empirical evidence still supports the best practice approach' (Delery and Doty, 1996: 69). Given this conclusion, it is perhaps surprising that in their survey of academics working in the field, Alcazar et al. (2005: 219) observed that 'the universalistic perspective is no longer adopted by many scholars', and that the 'contingent perspective is much more popular' and 'will be of increasing importance in the future' (op cit.: 224).

In an attempt to reconcile the universal and strategic HRM perspectives, Boxall (2003: 6) commented that UHRM had been found to be most 'cost-effective in high-technology or capital intensive manufacturing ... irrespective of whether cost leadership or differentiation is being pursued as a competitive strategy' while in 'labour-intensive ... manufacturing ... Tayloristic work systems and inexpensive HR practices are prevalent ... and are likely to remain so as long as they are cost-effective' (op cit.: 7). Paauwe and Boselie (2005: 70) provided an alternative model for integrating the two concepts, suggesting that 'some basic principles, such as employee development, employee involvement and high rewards, are universally successful, but the actual design of the HR practice depends to some degree on unique [internal and external] organizational context'.

As intriguing as these results and arguments may be, particularly to HRM practitioners and researchers who have been advocating various types of strategic HRM practices, the comprehensive reviews previously cited also suggested that they should be treated with caution. For example, Boselie et al. (2005: 81) observed 'all findings come with serious caveats attached and concessions concerning methodological limitations, either because potentially decisive variables have been omitted or causality cannot be properly inferred, most studies being cross-sectional and confined to correlations'. Boselie et al. (op cit.: 82) concluded 'Ten years on, the "Holy Grail" of decisive proof remains elusive'.

Various criticisms of the research will now be explored in further detail.

Drawing attention to the HR variables used in these studies, Guest et al. (2004: 79) suggested that there is 'little agreement about which practices should be combined to constitute effective HRM. It seems plausible to expect that theory and empirical research might lead us towards some kind of answer. To date, such optimism appears to be misplaced'. The appropriateness of methods used to measure HR variables has also been brought into question. For example, according to Boselie et al. (2005: 74), HRM practice can be measured in three ways:

> By its presence (i.e. a dichotomous scale for whether it is actually in effect "yes" or "no"), by its coverage (i.e. a continuous scale of the proportion of the workforce covered by it) or by its intensity (i.e. a continuous scale for the degree to which an individual employee is exposed to the practice or policy).

Another approach is to measure the extent to which HRM practices are perceived to be effective (Delaney and Huselid, 1996).

Despite these options, in their study Boselie et al. (2005: 74) found that 'the overwhelming majority relied only on measures of presence'. Similarly, Edgar and Geare (2005: 537) observed that 'To date the most common approach for assessing the relationship between HRM practice and employee work-related attitudes is the additive approach'. This approach involves counting the total number of 'yes' responses to statements describing various HRM practices. 'The assumption is that a higher sum indicates better HRM' (op cit.: 537).

Wright and Haggerty (2005) observed that this method assumes no variability with respect to the quality or extent of implementation of HR practices between supervisors, no variation in employee perception of these practices, and no variation in employee behavior (i.e. resulting from affective, cognitive and/or behavioral dispositional differences). In addition, this approach does not address the potential for bundles of HR practices to have substitutable, positive synergistic effects, or negative synergistic effects. Guest et al. (2004) recommended using sequential tree analysis to address this concern, which they found produced several benefits including: 'setting out a priority list' of practices, 'identifying distinctive combinations' and 'identifying middle-range combinations'

with respect to both highest and lowest levels of outcomes.

With respect to outcome measures, Boselie et al. (2005: 74) identified three potential types: financial outcomes (e.g. profits, sales, market share); organizational outcomes (e.g. productivity, quality); and HR-related outcomes ('attitudinal and behavioral impacts among employees, such as satisfaction, commitment and intention to quit'). Criticisms of these measures provided by Boselie et al. included the limited focus on shareholder interests (e.g. profit was the most common measure used); 'persuasive doubts' about the 'causal distance' or 'direct linkage' between HR practices and financial outcomes; the failure to include the increased costs of certain HR practices; and the lack of customer-relevant outcomes (op cit.: 75).

Lashley (2001: 145) also criticized the appropriateness of outcome measures, suggesting that they predominantly reflected a managerial concern and that it is difficult to control for all potential influences on organizational outcomes such as sales and profits:

> There are difficulties in attributing changes in an organization's performance to one (or a cluster) change. The business environment is rarely static, and changes outside of the control of the organization's managers may be more influential on the organization's performance than the internally generated initiative.

Some studies have specifically attempted to control for such influences. Boselie et al. (2005) found that the most common contingency variable controlled for was organizational size (e.g. number of employees). Other contingency variables included organizational age, trade union influence, and type of industry or sector. Citing Arthur (1994), Hoque (1999a) and Huselid (1995) as exceptions, Boselie et al. (2005: 76) commented that surprisingly, 'only a few articles used strategy as a moderator of the relationship between HRM and performance'.

Edgar and Geare (2005: 538) reinforced the importance of measuring HR-related outcomes (which were the least common measures found in Boselie et al.'s, 2005 study). Based on their review of the literature, Edgar and Geare suggested that HR practices that are likely to have the most significant impact on employee attitudes are working conditions (including safety issues), training and development, equal employment opportunities, and equitable recruitment and selection practices.

In addition to these criticisms, Wright and Haggerty (2005) raised concerns about temporal effects, causal direction, and the fact that most research is unitaristic in orientation (focused on gathering self-report data from managers). With respect to temporal effects, they estimated that the expected time lag between when a HR initiative is first designed and implemented, to when employee behavior is altered and organizational performance affected is between 3 and 4 years. Baum (1993: 14) similarly observed that with respect to tourism development, 'effective human resource strategies require considerable lead time' and that if such lead time is not provided, particularly within remote, low density areas, their absence can result in significant threats to 'service quality, customer satisfaction, and ultimately, to profitability'.

Yet, the vast majority of research is 'post-predictive'; the research design involves a single data collection point of both HR practices and firm economic performance. Researchers have been encouraged to consider 'retrospective' designs which ask about past HR practices in comparison to current results, 'contemporaneous' studies which gather HR practice and organizational results over a common but extended period of time (e.g. a year), and 'predictive' studies which gather HR data at one point in time and then gather organizational results at some future point. Wright and Haggerty (2005: 168) concluded, 'Given the increasingly fast pace of environmental and organizational change, the seeming lack of attention to temporal issues with regard to HRM seems short sighted'.

Related to the concept of time, is the nature of the cause and effect relationship (i.e. between HR practices and organizational outcomes). Wright and Haggerty (2005: 169) suggested that 'from a theoretical standpoint, current endeavors to explore the HRM–economic success relationship seldom address the potential for anything other than a one-way causal direction'. Lashley (2001: 145) similarly asked 'does the approach to managing employees cause the improvement in organizational performance, or is it the other way round?'. Wright and Haggerty (2005: 169) suggested that a 'reverse causation hypothesis' is equally credible, whereby successful organizations are able to provide more generous financial rewards and benefits and invest in more

sophisticated HR systems. They concluded, 'future theory development could benefit greatly from a more deliberate approach to addressing cause in the relationship between HRM and economic performance'.

With respect to a unitaristic perspective, Edgar and Geare (2005: 536) criticized HRM researchers for their failure to explore whether or not the relationships advocated by SHRM theorists could be empirically supported through the experience of employees; 'most of the research and reporting on HRM has ignored the views of employees'. Similarly Legge (1988: 14) observed 'when reading accounts of HRM practice in the UK and North America it is noticeable the extent to which the data are (literally) the voices of management'. Guest (2002: 335) similarly offered 'a feature of both advocates and critics of HRM is their neglect of direct evidence about the role and reactions of workers'. Given all of these criticisms, perhaps it is not surprising that reviews of the literature have noted increasing interest in qualitative research methods (see for example, Alcazar et al., 2005).

In addition to investigating the association between HRM practices and organizational outcomes, researchers have also been interested in the practice of HRM including the extent to which normative HRM models have actually been enacted (as briefly reviewed in the preceding section) and the extent to which HR managers have become strategic in their roles, as evidenced, for example, by the time they spend on various activities and their preparedness to use metrics in order to demonstrate the 'value added' of the HR function.

Consistent with other areas of study in HRM much normative and rhetorical writing exists. For example, according to Fulmer (1990: 1):

> A new shift in the role is occurring. This shift is reflected in the increasing number of companies turning to successful general managers to fill key positions in human resources. Increasingly these managers are moving beyond the traditional administrative role of human resources management (HRM) and are developing a more *strategic* role.

Empirical research on the extent to which this shift has actually occurred, however, has been limited. For example, Lawler and Mohrman (2003: 17) observed:

> Although there has been a great deal of normative writing about the role HR should play, there has

been little empirical investigation of whether it is actually playing this role ... [and] what it takes for HR to become a strategic partner.

In response to this challenge Lawler and Mohrman (2003) conducted a series of related studies in 1995, 1998, and 2001 of primarily large (approx. 21,000 employees and approx. 234 HR employees) US companies. The surveys explored the percentage of time HR employees spent on various activities and the extent to which senior HR executives perceived themselves as strategic partners. They found considerable stability in terms of the average percentage of time reported on key roles across the three surveys. Based on these results, Lawler and Mohrman (2003) concluded that there had been little change in the time spent on traditional HR activities despite calls for a more strategic role. Interestingly, despite these results, the percentage of HR executives who perceived they were 'a full partner in the business strategy process' did in fact increase from 29% in 1998 to 41% in 2001.

This type of research has been criticized on the basis of the underlying assumption that organizations are rational entities. Competing explanations suggested by Bamberger and Meshoulam (2000) as to why a particular HRM strategy or HR management role might evolve include: industry norms and characteristics; the degree of managerial discretion to change existing structures; ownership structure – public versus private; market or resource conditions (e.g. when resources are tight or market competition is intense, organizations are more likely to adopt control-oriented HRM approaches); the presence of a union/collective agreement; the presence of an HRM department; organizational size; and culture. With respect to this last point, the work of Hofstede (1984) suggested that cultural differences can be associated with profound differences in how work is organized and controlled. These issues include the nature of supervision, extent of participation, work ethic, ambition, motivation and attitudes toward change.

Boselie et al. (2005: 81) further identified issues of HR 'delivery' as important factors with respect to successful uptake and impact. They suggested that HR delivery processes include 'aligning HR strategy with business strategy', 'convincing line managers of the value of the organization's HR practices', and effective implementation support practices

including 'proper training, coaching and support for immediate line managers'.

In summary, current generic HRM research has largely focused on demonstrating correlations between bundles of HR practices and organizational outcomes. While supporting evidence has been found, this research has been criticized on several grounds including the choice of variables, measurement issues, and issues associated with temporal, causal direction, and unitaristic factors. Research has also brought into question the extent to which these models are reflected in practice. Possible explanations for the differences between espoused and enacted models of HRM have begun to be generated and include many organizational, industry, and environmental factors.

CURRENT RESEARCH AND THE ADOPTION OF HR PRACTICES IN HOSPITALITY AND TOURISM

Much of the literature on HRM in hospitality and tourism has borrowed from the generic HRM literature, providing normative advice on the importance of strategic HRM and its variants (often combined with case study documentation of 'best practices' within exceptional multinational hotel and restaurant chain operations). It has also explored the (lack of) uptake of these practices. Where it has made a unique contribution is through the identification of such concepts as 'emotional labor, emotional intelligence and HRM in service work' which have now been adopted by mainstream researchers (Lucas and Deery, 2004: 459). It has also challenged the quantitative research methodologies used in mainstream research, questioning the appropriateness of overly simplistic cause and effect models and advocating for the use of qualitative research methods. What has largely been absent, with the exception of Lashley's (2001) work on strategic typologies and a special issue of the *International Journal of Contemporary Hospitality Management* edited by D'Annunzio-Green, Maxwell and Watson (2002b), is research that has explored the impact of SHRM practices on organizational outcomes in the industry. This is an important gap that needs to be addressed:

> Comparatively little has been written ... exploring the nature of the impact of strategic HRM on organizational performance in this sector. The relative

lack of research activity currently centered on strategic HRM … is cause of concern.

(D'Annunzio-Green et al., 2002b: 205)

Where research has tried to demonstrate a connection between HR practices and organizational performance, it has been more in keeping with traditional HRM (i.e. the focus has been on relatively discreet HR practices), although variables studied have been of particular interest to the industry. For example, researchers have explored the links between turnover and a number of organizational variables including pay, employee satisfaction, commitment, morale, customer service, and profitability (see for example, Deery and Iverson, 1996; Iverson and Deery, 1997; Deery, 2002).

The impact of training and development has also come under review. Lashley (2002b) conducted a study on the costs and benefits of training at one organization, in order to test the utility of a model for helping identify such outcomes. He noted that despite the fact that a significant proportion of the literature advocates investing in training and development activities, there has been little empirical evidence that doing so will actually lead to increased organizational effectiveness. Further, he acknowledged that generating such evidence is difficult. Invoking some of the conclusions of the Hawthorne studies, Lashley (2002b: 106) observed:

It is difficult to isolate training as the key independent variable in managing a business unit which leads to specific gains in business performance. Is it training which is leading to improvements in productivity, for example, or are changes the result of improved employee motivation because the employee values training? What effect does the employment environment make?

Lashley (2002b: 116) concluded that it was 'not possible to measure precisely any resultant financial benefits associated with expenditure on training' but that benefits such as 'improvements in service quality, staff satisfaction, and functional flexibility' along with improvements in turnover and productivity, could be identified through qualitative means. Lashley (2001) was also tentative with respect to the results of his study on strategic HRM and questioned the extent to which his typology and the three case studies that provided supporting evidence for his ideas

could be generalized. Lashley (2001: 183) cautioned:

The extent to which they represent a consistency generally found in service firms is questionable and whilst it has been possible to demonstrate 'fit' in these three cases, there is no suggestion as to the causal link nor whether the management of employees was strategically designed to match the wider service features. Thus claims that HRM is fundamentally strategic is not necessarily supported by these examples.

Lashley's (2001, 2002b) observations are particularly helpful in light of criticisms of the generic HRM literature. They highlight the need for more innovative and appropriate methodologies for demonstrating the possible impacts of strategic HRM and its variants in the industry. They also suggest the need to be particularly cautious when generalizing from case study research. Lucas and Deery (2004: 470) similarly suggested that researchers 'consider turning their attentions to more richly informed qualitative approaches' and collect data from employees and customers, in addition to managers, providing the opportunity to 'triangulate the results'.

Several books and articles have also recently been written, providing useful summaries of the normative and uptake literatures in the industry. One relatively recent work is *Managing Employee Attitudes and Behaviors in the Tourism and Hospitality Industry*, edited by Kusluvan (2003). In reflecting a normative perspective, Kusluvan (2003: xxvii) advised:

Employees are one of the most, *if not the most*, important resources or assets for tourism and hospitality organizations in their endeavor to provide excellent service, meet and exceed consumer expectations, achieve competitive advantage and exceptional organizational performance.

This advice is in stark contrast to the oft remarked conclusion that although exceptions have been reported (Haynes and Fryer, 1999; Hoque, 1999a, 1999b) in general there has been poor enactment or uptake of HRM practices and that 'the industry could do better' (see for example, Worsfold, 1999; Lucas, 1996, 2002; D'Annunzio-Green et al., 2002a; Maxwell and Quail, 2002). For example, D'Annunzio-Green et al. (2002a: 5) observed that despite the acute relevance of strategic HRM for the industry – particularly in the context of international HRM – there is 'scant evidence that HRM approaches have been adopted'.

Maxwell and Quail (2002: 93) similarly concluded:

> Despite a couple of decades of debate about, and practice in, elements of HRM, the conclusion that HRM ... has largely failed to achieve its potential in industry as a whole and in hospitality and tourism in particular seems inescapable. Where there are exceptions to this general rule, they seem to be in larger organizations.

Drawing further attention to the importance of organizational size in interpreting the uptake literature, Kusluvan (2003: 17) similarly suggested:

> Apart from a handful of large organizations, tourism and hospitality organizations rarely adopt a strategic approach to the management of human resources. Labor is seen as a cost to be minimized and not as an asset (Buick and Muthu, 1997). The industry is characterized by short-termism and reluctance to invest in its employees, accordingly few organizations align and integrate human resource policies and practices with their business strategy.

These tentative observations concerning the implications of organizational size suggest that clearer distinctions are needed between the HRM practices and experiences of employees in SMEs and MNEs. In support of this effort is the work of Lee-Ross (1999) on *International Perspectives on Small to Medium-Sizes Enterprises*. Also addressing industry demographics, Kusluvan (2003) cautioned that much of the research in hospitality and tourism has focused on lodging and foodservice. Similarly, Lucas and Deery (2004: 459) suggested, 'Tourism as an area of HRM research, is less developed than is hospitality research'. Additional research is clearly needed within the tourism sector of the industry with respect to both domestic and international concerns.

Research has also explored HRM topics of most interest to researchers and practitioners in the industry. For example, Lucas and Deery (2004: 459) reported on the results of a study involving 'a review of over 100 papers concerned with human resource management (HRM) in five leading hospitality journals during 2002 and 2003'. Lucas and Deery concluded that 'the research agenda mirrors what is seen in mainstream HR research and theory, focusing around general HRM, employee resourcing, employee development and employee relations' (op cit.: 459). They also noted that the journals varied in terms of dominant research

methodology with, for example, 'quantitative research using the survey method' being the predominant approach in the *International Journal of Hospitality Management* and 'qualitative research methods, including case studies' being the predominant approach in the *International Journal of Contemporary Hospitality Management* (op cit.: 462).

D'Annunzio-Green et al. (2002a: 7) conducted a survey of senior HR practitioners from international hospitality and tourism operations across 32 countries. Issues found to be of highest priority included service quality, training and development, and staff recruitment and selection issues, which they observed was consistent with the priorities of domestic hospitality and tourism operations. Suggesting some degree of perceived congruency between HR priorities and strategic orientation, these issues were reported to be reflected in '60 percent or more of organizations' strategic planning'. In interpreting these results it is important to keep in mind that they provide a unitaristic/ management perspective and there can be considerable differences between espoused and enacted HRM.

D'Annunzio-Green et al. (2002a: 9) also found that cross-cultural issues were perceived as being of 'low priority' and were included in only 31 percent of the organizations' strategic plans. They concluded that 'organizations are still breaking new ground in developing policies, practices, and procedures to support globalization' and that hospitality and tourism organizations are 'failing to address the complexities of IHRM highlighted in the literature'. Suggesting that the hospitality industry has a unique contribution to make to the generic HRM literature in this regard is the observation by Belcourt, Sherman, Bohlander and Snell (1996: 625) that 'the internationalization of corporations has grown at a faster pace than the internationalization of HRM ... the academic community has not been a particularly good source for ready-made answers to international HRM problems'.

In Kusluvan's (2003: 14–19) summary of the literature, he observed that normative HR practices have largely not been implemented in the industry, although some improvements have begun to be noted, once again in larger organizations. For example, Kusluvan found that: recruitment and selection is largely conducted intuitively and unprofessionally (e.g. Hoque, 1999b); orientation and training has largely been neglected for both management and line employees, although this is starting to improve somewhat in larger organizations in which service quality and customer satisfaction have been recognized as important (e.g. Baum, 1995; Watson and D'Annunzio-Green, 1996; Pizam, 1999); there continues to be a lack of opportunity for promotion and career development, although evidence of the use of internal labor markets has begun to be found (e.g. Lucas, 1996; Iverson and Deery, 1997; Guerrier and Deery, 1998; Lee-Ross, 1999); the industry continues to be notorious for its low wages and lack of benefits, particularly at lower organizational levels (e.g. Woods, 1999; Boella, 2000; Hjalager and Andersen, 2001); results of empowerment and employee participation are mixed – with some studies finding increasing rates and others suggesting managers are becoming increasingly hierarchical and autocratic (e.g. Lucas, 1996; Hoque, 1999a); and the industry can be characterized by a poor leadership style with managers largely being described as 'poorly equipped to manage professionally' (Guerrier and Deery, 1998) and as exhibiting 'unbridled individualism', although a more consultative approach has begun to be observed in some chain hotels (Gilbert and Guerrier, 1997; Hoque, 1999a).

Kusluvan's (2003) conclusions concerning empowerment and leadership style are consistent with the recent work of Lucas (2002: 209) who described managerial style within the industry as highly individualized, non-consultative and controlling, 'with managers being highly selective about what they disclose and how they disclose it'. With respect to other HR practices, Lucas concluded that 'Most HR practices can be regarded as poor, in so far as they represent low pay and poor conditions of employment'. She also observed that HR practices in the industry are 'a long way from being "soft."' Rather, HRM 'provides an extreme example of the "retaining control/cost control" approach to management identified by Cully, Woodland, O'Reilly, and Dix (1999) and a graphic illustration of very "hard" HRM in practice' Lucas (2002: 211).

Despite these results, however, Lucas (2002: 211) also found that in comparison to employees in other industries, hospitality industry employees were 'much more content with their lot'. She reported that they 'show a stronger level of endorsement for the way they are managed ... are more likely to be proud to tell people who they work for ...

[and] display an impression of overall job satisfaction' (op cit.: 210–211). Lucas observed that understanding this dichotomy 'appears to be the key research issue to be picked up in qualitative research' (ibid).

Consistent with mainstream HRM research, hospitality and tourism HRM research has also looked at the evolving role of HR managers. Kusluvan (2003: 14) concluded that while earlier studies 'found little evidence of professionalism and strategy' in personnel departments, that more recent studies (see for example, Price, 1994; Lucas, 1995, 1996; Kelliher and Johnson, 1997; Hoque, 1999b) found 'there are more personnel specialists with formal human resource qualifications in the hospitality industry compared to other industries'. However, he also noted that this has been attributed in part to the industry's high turnover rate, which in turn has been associated with a number of the industry characteristics previously described including poor working conditions and poor HRM practices (Kusluvan, 2003).

In summary, research exploring the impact of strategic HRM and its variants on organizational outcomes is largely non-existent in the hospitality and tourism literature, and is very much needed. Evidence of the existence of these models in practice (particularly in SMEs) is also in short supply, with organizations largely adopting hard HRM practices and focusing on labor as a cost to be minimized. What is not clear is why this is the case and why hospitality and tourism employees are more likely to endorse the way they are managed than their non-hospitality counterparts. Focus is also needed with respect to the implications of organizational demographics (size), internationalism and cross-culturalism for HRM research and practice. Finally, additional research within the tourism sector of the industry would also be beneficial.

As suggested at the outset of this chapter, given the unique challenges of service organizations and a variety of employment and industry characteristics, hospitality and tourism HRM researchers have the opportunity for making significant contributions to HRM theorizing, research and practice. Where the hospitality and tourism literature has already made such a contribution is in the introduction of certain topics, such as emotional labor and international HRM, and in challenging the dominant research paradigm of the discipline; questioning the measurement of simplistic causal relationships and advancing qualitative techniques that include employee and customer perspectives. Lucas and Deery (2004: 459) advised that 'hospitality researchers need to reclaim their territory, push forward the boundaries of theory making and propose theory that is hospitality specific, relevant and useful'. The chapter now turns its attention to theorizing that underlies the research just reviewed.

THEORIZING HRM

Research on HRM – and SHRM and its variants – has been widely criticized for lacking a strong theoretical foundation. According to Bamberger and Meshoulam (2000), theory development and testing has suffered from a lack of conceptual clarity. Similarly, Wright and Haggerty (2005: 165) observed that 'much research was at best "borrowing" meta-theories from other disciplines and at worst was almost completely atheoretical'. Relevant meta-theories identified earlier in this chapter included contingency theory and strategic theory.

Wright and Haggerty (2005: 166) suggested that 'the problem with these "meta-theories" … lies with the failure to specifically articulate the process through which the relationship' between HR practices and organizational outcomes occurs. On this basis, they called for the addition of 'middle level process theories' to help explain the nature of the relationship. Similarly Guest (as cited in Boselie et al., 2005: 67) observed that the field still requires 'a theory about HRM, a theory about performance and a theory about how they are linked'. Lashley (2001) made a similar observation with respect to understanding the processes underlying empowerment in the hospitality industry. He suggested that 'much of the more evangelical and normative literature' on empowerment assumes certain benefits will be axiomatic (e.g. improved customer service, improved employee loyalty), without explaining how empowerment will produce these effects through changes to employee feelings, attitudes, and behaviors. In keeping with Kurt Lewin's (1951: 169) advice that 'There is nothing as practical as a good theory', some HRM researchers have begun to turn their attention to this need.

One area that has received focus is theoretical explanations for the growing interest in SHRM amongst researchers and practitioners. Bamberger and Meshoulam (2000: 7), for example, suggested that organizations embrace strategies that are 'likely to provide the organization with the greatest possible return'. Rational choice theories that explain management interest and the possible mechanisms through which the relationship between HRM and improved organizational returns might occur have been suggested to include: resource-based theory (Prahalad and Hamel, 1990; Barney, 1991), which suggests competitive advantage can be achieved through the effective use of unique, inimitable resources such as human resources; behavioral role theory (Katz and Kahn, 1978) which suggests that aligning HR policies and practices with the organization's strategy will help employees to better meet role expectations both within and outside the organization; human capital theory (Becker, 1964), which suggests that employees represent economic value to the organization, through their knowledge, skills and abilities, and like all economic assets need to be managed effectively; transaction cost theories (Williamson, 1981), which suggests that SHRM can result in reduced internal costs by minimizing the need for complex contracts for dealing with employee self interest and opportunism (Jackson and Schuler, 1995); and agency theory (Eisenhardt, 1989) which suggests that organizational benefits, such as increased efficiency, will result from aligning employee and organizational interests.

Bamberger and Meshoulam (2000) also suggested, however, that rather than assuming a rational explanation, 'it is just as likely that HR practitioners and researchers have embraced SHRM out of a constituency-based interest' (p. 8) (i.e. as a means of gaining personal legitimacy or increasing the legitimacy of the field as a whole). Possible theoretical positions underlying this argument include institutional theory (DiMaggio and Powell, 1983; Meyer and Rowan, 1977; Powell and DiMaggio, 1991) and resource dependence theory (Pfeffer and Salancik, 1977). From an institutional theory perspective, interest in SHRM can be explained by either coercive pressures (e.g. legislative pressures), normative pressures (e.g. from the HR profession, management education), or mimetic pressures (e.g. the perceived successful practices of other firms and industries). Resource dependence theory suggests that personal power and influence are increased to the extent that one controls valued resources. From this perspective the adoption of SHRM may therefore be perceived as an approach for enhancing the power of HR researchers and practitioners, by positioning human resources (and associated knowledge) as a valuable asset.

Despite this broad base of possible theoretical positions, in their reviews of the HRM literature, McMahan, Virick and Wright (1999) and Paauwe and Boselie (2005) concluded that resource-based theory had emerged as the predominant meta-theory in use. Wright and Haggerty (2005: 165) explained this was 'largely because of both its popularity in the broader strategy literature, and its ability to articulate why HRM could be linked to the economic success of firms'.

Paauwe and Boselie (2005: 58) challenged the appropriateness of resource-based theory, suggesting that its propositions cannot be empirically tested, and it does not adequately take into account organizational circumstances (e.g. time, country, industry) and social contexts (e.g. traditions, networks, regulatory pressures). Instead they suggested that 'new-institutionalism' (i.e. new institutionalism acknowledges coercive, normative, and mimetic pressures, and 'assumes that organizations conform to contextual expectations in order to gain legitimacy and increase their probability of survival' (op cit.: 59) held much promise for HRM research, particularly for 'crossnational comparative research' (op cit.: 67), and advanced several propositions concerning the homogeneity of HRM practices across organizations on this basis.

In a later review of the literature, Boselie et al. (2005: 82) suggested that contingency theory, the resource-based view, and 'AMO' (where performance is viewed as a function of an employee's ability, motivation, and opportunity to contribute; Applebaum et al., 2000) had become increasingly blended by authors 'into a formative overall theory for HRM'. They also suggested that more micro-OB theories (e.g. expectancy theory, goal-setting theory) could help 'explore in much greater depth employees' actual experience of HRM' (ibid.).

In summary, some progress in theorizing the discipline has been made, but much more is clearly needed. This will be aided by challenging the dominant research paradigm and epistemology of the discipline as explored in the next section.

MAIN EPISTEMOLOGICAL APPROACHES, THEMES AND ISSUES

In *Sociological Paradigms and Organisational Analysis*, Burrell and Morgan (1979) provide a powerful framework for identifying the ontological and epistemological assumptions underlying theorizing and research in the social sciences. In their comprehensive elaboration of this framework, they illustrate how these assumptions, along with assumptions concerning human nature, shape the types of questions researchers ask, the methodologies they employ, and the conclusions they ultimately draw. While this framework has been of enormous benefit to social scientists wishing to more critically examine their disciplines, it has the potential to be particularly useful to those studying HRM, as many of the examples Burrell and Morgan use are drawn from 'industrial sociology, organization theory, organizational psychology and industrial relations' (p. iix). The discussion that follows is therefore structured on the basis of Burrell and Morgan's framework.

According to Burrell and Morgan (1979) assumptions underlying organizational theory include the ontological nature of the subject (i.e. whether it is assumed to be hard and real and exists independently of the mind, or whether it is a social construction); its epistemology (i.e. whether it is positivistic – concerned with the identification of causal relationships, or anti-positivistic – concerned with achieving understanding through the perspective of individuals involved with the subject); assumptions concerning human nature (i.e. whether people are assumed to be primarily deterministic/externally controlled, or voluntaristic/autonomous and free-willed); and whether or not the research methods used to investigate the subject should be nomothetic (i.e. focused on systematic protocol, hypothesis testing, and quantitative methods), or ideographic (i.e. focused on understanding 'the way in which the individual creates, modifies and interprets the world in which he or she finds himself') (Burrell and Morgan, 1979: 3).

The roots of theorizing and the bulk of research that has taken place in the discipline has arguably embraced an objective ontology, positivistic epistemology, deterministic assumptions about human behavior, and nomothetic methodologies. According to Burrell and Morgan (1979) such a position typically reflects a functionalist sociological position and is reflected in social systems theory and objectivism. More subjectivist positions that could provide additional insights for HRM include theories of bureaucratic dysfunctions, the action frame of reference, pluralist theory and interpretive sociology. Each of these theoretical areas will now be reviewed, with the implications for HRM identified.

Social system theory and objectivism

According to Burrell and Morgan (1979: 123) social system theory and objectivism is the most objective and most 'dominant perspective within the field of organization studies'. Within this perspective, organizations are assumed to be real, rational, adaptive and 'purposive, goal-seeking enterprises' (op cit.: 218). Mimicking the natural sciences, research methods have typically involved the exploration of cause and effect relationships between organizational inputs (such as human resource practices) and a variety of organizational outcomes (sales, profitability). According to Burrell and Morgan (1979: 163), 'There is scarcely an organizational variable which has not been measured in some form and even correlated with itself in the objectivist search for "significant" relationships which eventually prove "determinant"'.

Criticisms of theorists from researchers working outside the functionalist paradigm or from more subjectivist regions within it, include an 'extreme commitment to positivism', a 'naïve empiricism', 'a complete disregard to the nature of the phenomena under study', an inappropriate commitment to the 'methods of the natural sciences' and as being 'ideologically biased in favour of a managerial point of view' (Burrell and Morgan, 1979: 218–219). This has led to the view of some that 'social system theorists and objectivists are little more than the handmaidens and functionaries of those in control of organizational life' (Burrell and Morgan, 1979: 219).

In response to these criticisms, theories that provide the opportunity for more subjectivist approaches for studying HRM are now reviewed.

Theories of bureaucratic dysfunction

During the 1960s and 1970s some researchers challenged the concept of bureaucracy and wrote about worker alienation, exploitation and deviant behavior. For example, Merton (1968) wrote about 'dysfunctions of bureaucracy', 'trained incapacity' and 'goal displacement'. He argued that highly bureaucratic organizations prevented people from exercising good judgement and from responding flexibly and effectively to changing environmental conditions. Similarly, Selznick (1966) studied the dysfunctional aspects of delegation and specialization, and observed that through these mechanisms employees could pursue sub-unit goals, potentially at the expense of organizational interests.

Friedman (1977: 78) wrote about the direct control strategies used to manage unskilled workers (i.e. 'coercive threats, close supervision and minimizing individual worker responsibility') and contrasted this with 'responsible autonomy'; a control strategy used to manage skilled workers (i.e. providing status, authority and responsibility and counting on people's work ethic, self-respect and pride). Friedman (op cit.: 106) argued that both direct control and responsible autonomy failed to resolve fundamental tensions or contradictions between employee and organizational needs:

> To treat workers as though they were machines … or to treat workers as though they were not alienated from their labour power by trying to convince them that the aims of top managers are their own; both of these types of strategies involve a contradiction. People do have independent and often hostile wills which cannot be destroyed, and the aim of top managers ultimately is to make steady and high profits, rather than to tend to their workers' needs.

Direct control and responsible autonomy can be seen in some ways to mirror scientific management and human relations respectively, as well as hard and soft HRM. From this perspective while human relations or soft HRM may be effective to some extent at minimizing the dysfunctional effects of bureaucracy, the underlying contradictions of the workplace remain.

Social action theory

According to Burrell and Morgan (1979), the work of Goffman (1959), *The Presentation of Self in Everyday Life*, is illustrative of social action theory. Goffman explored concepts such as the social self and 'impression management' within organizations. Also included is the work of Turner (1971) who focused on the need to challenge 'taken for granted assumptions' such as 'organizational subcultures'. He was interested in how subcultures are created and maintained and suggested that behavior is influenced by the processes through which organizational members are socialized and sanctioned. Finally, the work of Silverman (1970), *The Theory of Organizations*, also characterizes this perspective. Silverman suggested that in contrast to the natural sciences, sociology is focused on understanding 'social action' and identifying 'social meanings' as opposed to 'observing behavior'.

Social action theory has not been well reflected in HRM research. If it was, studies might explore, for example, the social meanings of formal orientation programs and performance management processes, as well as the informal socialization processes and informal sanctions of behavior that occur within organizational subsystems. The 'impression management' activities of HRM researchers, practitioners and employees might also be of interest.

Pluralist theory

Imbedded within theories of bureaucratic dysfunction and social action theory are elements of pluralist theory. In contrast to the unitary view of organizations, which positions organizations as consisting of well integrated teams pursuing clearly delineated goals and common purposes, the pluralist view acknowledges the existence of multiple and often competing interests. From a unitary perspective conflict is assumed to be rare and concepts such as power are ignored in favor of the more managerially acceptable concepts of authority, leadership, and control (Burrell and Morgan, 1979). In contrast, from the pluralist perspective conflict is viewed as inevitable (given multiple and competing interests) and power (along with the processes through which it is negotiated) is viewed as an important concept in understanding employee behavior.

As previously suggested, most HRM research has drawn almost exclusively on management or employer opinion and has therefore adopted a unitary as opposed to a pluralist perspective. Further, within HRM theorizing, the view that organizations consist of a plurality of legitimate interests does not typically hold sway. For example, implicit within human relations theory is the assumption that individual interests can

be met through the achievement of the organization's goals, if the appropriate HR practices are in place. Soft HRM is one exception where both individual and organizational interests have been acknowledged as legitimate in their own right (in fact this acknowledgement has resulted in the most significant criticisms of this model with respect to it not reflecting 'reality'). Additional theorizing from a pluralist perspective is clearly needed.

Interpretive sociology

Interpretive sociology reflects the most subjectivist region in Burrell and Morgan's (1979) typology. It embraces a subjective ontology, an anti-positivistic epistemology, voluntaristic assumptions about human nature, and ideographic methodologies. Largely a twentieth century phenomena, interpretive sociology provides a direct challenge to the functionalist notion that organizations and topics associated with HRM (e.g. employee motivation, productivity, satisfaction, selection, turnover), or even the profession of HRM itself, are 'hard, concrete, and tangible' (Burrell and Morgan, 1979: 260). Rather, it positions them as social constructions, open to critique and multiple understandings. Drawing on the work of Bittner (1965), Burrell and Morgan (1979: 263) argued that organizational concepts such as 'structure, hierarchy and efficiency, are problematic social constructs' that should be the focus of research and not simply taken for granted as inevitable organizational features. Similarly Weick (1979: 5) argued that 'organizations, despite their apparent preoccupation with facts, numbers, objectivity, concreteness and accountability, are in fact saturated with subjectivity, abstraction, guesses, making do, invention and arbitrariness ... just like the rest of us'. From this perspective, the role of social science is to enhance understanding of social situations from the perspective of people acting within it. The role of the researcher is to 'get inside and to understand from within' (Burrell and Morgan, 1979: 253).

One example of interpretive research into a specific HRM practice is the work of Silverman and Jones (1973), in *Getting In: the Management Accomplishments of "Correct" Selection Outcomes*. They reported on the results of an empirical study on selection interviews and demonstrated that such interviews are comprised of multiple realities, a series of verbal and non-verbal exchanges through which attributions are made, and processes that are heavily influenced by the need for accountability (Burrell and Morgan, 1979).

While understanding of virtually any HR practice may be enhanced from an interpretive perspective, emotional labor is one concept that truly reflects such a position, and would benefit from further research from this tradition. Emotional labor has been positioned as both the 'commercial exploitation' of employee emotions (Hochschild, 1983, as cited in Chappel 2002: 229) and as something 'fun; an exquisite drama' within which play and work occur simultaneously (Fineman, 1993, as cited in Chappel, 2002: 230).

Elements of interpretive critique of HRM as a discipline are also evident in some of the comments concerning soft HRM. Emphasizing the potential of hermeneutics and rhetoric for better understanding the discipline, HRM has been described as a 'rhetorical guise to enhance managerial legitimacy where the management of labour has been intensified and commodified' (Lucas, 2002: 207). Drawing on the work of Keenoy and Anthony (1992) Lashley (2001: 170–171) similarly argued that HRM is 'devised to establish and legitimize a unitary perspective of work organizations, and to de-legitimize employee collectives and puralist analysis of organizational priorities'. From an interpretive perspective, a possible explanation for the distinction between espoused and enacted HRM is provided. HRM may be seen as a rhetorical game; a game that researchers and practitioners working exclusively from an objectivist perspective may be (unwittingly) playing.

Critical theory

Like interpretive sociology, critical theory is subjectivist in orientation, but while interpretive theorists are focused on generating understanding of social situations from the people involved in its construction, critical theorists focus on the 'alienated state of man' (Burrell and Morgan, 1979: 279) and processes of liberation in support of human fulfillment. According to Burrell and Morgan (1979: 284), critical theory 'seeks to reveal society for what it is, to unmask its essence and mode of operation and to lay the foundations for human emancipation through deep-seated social change'.

Alienation is seen to be caused by social creations – such as capitalism, consumerism and organizations – which dominate human consciousness and experience. From the perspective of HRM, social creations particularly in need of critique include 'the ideological mechanisms through which the worker is habituated to accept the roles, rules and language of the workplace', and the reification of concepts such as work and profitability (Burrell and Morgan, 1979: 324). According to Burrell and Morgan (1979: 289), ideological mechanisms include: 'the creation and perpetuation of a belief system which stresses the need for order, authority, and discipline'.

HRM from this perspective, may be seen as a mechanism for imposing order, authority and discipline; an instrument of 'ideological hegemony' (Gramsci, 1971) that masks alienation and therefore needs to be challenged. Edgar and Geare (2005: 535), suggested that 'the real motive' behind the introduction of soft HRM may have been 'to undermine unions'. This idea was also supported by Guest (1990: 389) who offered, 'the main impact of HRM in the US may have been to provide a smokescreen behind which management can introduce non-unionism or obtain significant concessions from trade unions' (as cited in Edgar and Geare, 2005: 535–536). Through critical theory, these dynamics could be revealed and human consciousness potentially raised. In adopting critical theory, HR researchers have the potential to become 'changemakers' as opposed to the 'handmaidens' of business (Storey, 1992).

One HRM researcher that has written from this perspective is Townley (1994: 9), in her book *Reframing Human Resource Management: Power, Ethics and the Subject at Work.* She suggests that with the exception of Legge (1978) 'there has been a reluctance to address the issue of power' within HRM and further, that when power has been acknowledged, an 'economistic' model has predominated, in which power has been commodified and assumed to be centralized (e.g. maintained within hierarchical structures). In contrast, Townley suggested that power and knowledge are inherently linked, and that our knowledge of HRM has been constrained through the reification of management principles. Townley (op cit.: 3) suggested that the work of Michael Foucault (1980) would be particularly instructive in helping us understand 'how is HRM constructed? ... To what has our attention been directed and from what has it been averted? What are the limits of the seeable and the sayable within the discourse of HRM?'. She encouraged HRM researchers to focus on understanding HR practices and their effects, 'with the aim of grasping the conditions which make these acceptable at a given moment' (Foucault, as cited in Townley, op cit.: 18).

Work that has applied these concepts to the study of human resource management in the hospitality industry is Sartre's (1966) *Being and Nothingness*, in which he describes the work of a waiter, demonstrating that the waiter is 'playing at a role in a way which implies a fundamental alienation from his true being' (Burrell and Morgan, 1979: 305). Relatedly, the concept of emotional labor has great potential to be viewed from this perspective. Generic HRM researchers have also conducted in-depth case studies of the work experiences of employees within various organizations. This approach may have particular relevance for the hospitality and tourism industry.

FUTURE TOPICS OF INTEREST

Within the preceding review of current HRM research in hospitality and tourism, several areas for future research were identified. This included: the impact of strategic HRM and its variants on organizational outcomes; explanations for the lack of enactment of these practices; explanations for why hospitality and tourism employees are more likely to endorse the way they are managed than their non-hospitality counterparts; and the implications of organizational demographics (size), internationalism, and cross-culturalism on HRM theory and practice. More research in all of these areas is particularly needed within the tourism sector of the industry.

Other suggestions have also been made in the literature. For example, Lucas and Deery (2004: 471) identified a number of areas that would benefit from further attention:

The "ownership" of career development and the boundary-less career; the role of HR in managing the 24/7 work environment and the impact of shift work on health, work and family life; managing the safety and well-being of employees in dangerous environments e.g. outsourced catering companies in middle-eastern countries; [and] the conflict between the culture and values of the owners and managers of large global companies and those of the host community.

A dearth of research has also been specifically acknowledged in the areas of performance management (Millet, 2002), employee relations practice (Timo and Davidson, 2002), and organizational commitment (Cannon, 2002).

Quite apart from these general topics of study, HRM researchers in hospitality and tourism have the opportunity to redefine the field; to follow Lashley's (2001, 1998, 2002a, 2002b) lead in bringing subjective and critical perspectives to pressing research questions and methodologies. It is recommended here that hospitality researchers embrace theories and epistemologies outside of social systems theory and objectivism. Through alternative approaches, issues of time, causation and voice should be addressed, non-rational models of human resource management explored, new understandings of the lack of uptake developed, and the very nature of the discipline redefined.

CONCLUSION

This chapter has reviewed both the generic and hospitality and tourism-specific HRM literatures. It has suggested that understanding HRM is particularly important for the industry, given the unique features of service businesses (including dynamics of service delivery, labor intensity, a traditional focus on minimizing labor costs, and issues of emotional labor); employment and industry characteristics (in particular organizational size), combined with issues of internationalization and cross-culturalism. Future research needs to give more consideration to the impact of these factors.

It has also reviewed the historical development of various conceptions of HRM, including personnel management, soft and hard HRM, strategic HRM, HR strategy, international HRM, universal HRM, integrative HRM, and contingent HRM. It has been suggested that the theorizing underlying these conceptions has predominantly reflected social system theory and objectivism, embedded within Burrell and Morgan's (1979) functionalist paradigm, and the resource-based view of the organization.

From this perspective, HRM has been positioned as a hard and tangible concept, one that can be studied by correlating the existence of various HRM practices against measures of various behavioral, attitudinal and organizational outcomes. This has been the primary contribution of the generic empirical HRM literature which has had some success demonstrating that normative models of HRM (particularly universal HRM) do affect organizational outcomes. Despite this evidence, the uptake of these models has been far less than expected, and researchers (both generic and hospitality and tourism specific) have struggled (using rational models) to explain why this has been the case. Critiques of the research methods employed, however, have been several. In particular, issues of variable choice and their measurement, combined with temporal effects, the direction of causal relationships, and the lack of employee voice have been identified. Future researchers of HRM in hospitality and tourism are encouraged to adopt more subjectivist perspectives, interpretive social theories and qualitative methods in the exploration of the relationship between normative HR practices and individual and organizational outcomes. It is also important that pluralist approaches be used, in order to fully understand the perceptions concerning, and impacts of, these practices from the perspectives of employees, customers and managers. Critical theorizing of the discipline is also needed in order that we may better appreciate the objectives and complexities of this important discipline and its application (or lack thereof) within organizational settings.

REFERENCES

Alcazar, F. M., Fernandez, P. M. R. and Gardey, G. S. (2005) 'Researching on SHRM: an analysis of the debate over the role played by human resources in firm success', *Management Revue*, 16: 213–241.

Applebaum E. and Batt, R. (1994) *The New American Workplace*. Ithaca, NY: ILR Press.

Applebaum, E., Bailey, T., Berg P. and Kalleberg, A. (2000) *Manufacturing Advantage: Why high-performance Systems Pay Off*. Ithaca, NY: Cornell University Press.

Appleby, A. and Mavin, S. (2000) 'Innovation not imitation: human resource strategy and the impact on world-class status', *Total Quality Management*, 11: 554–561.

Argyris, C. (1952) *The Impact of Budgets upon People*. New York: Controllership Foundation.

Argyris, C. (1957) *Personality and Organization*. New York: Harper and Row.

Argyris, C. (1964) *Integrating the Individual and the Organization*. New York: Wiley.

Armstrong, M. (1987) 'Human resource management: a case of the emperor's new clothes?' *Personnel Management*, 19: 30–35.

Arthur, J. B. (1994) 'Effects of human resource systems on manufacturing performance and turnover', *Academy of Management Journal*, 37: 670–687.

Bamberger, P. and Meshoulam, I. (2000) *Human Resource Strategy: Formulation, Implementation, and Impact*. Thousand Oaks, CA: Sage.

Barney J. B. (1991) 'Firm resources and sustained competitive advantage', *Journal of Management*, 17: 99–120.

Baum, T. (1993) *Human Resource Issues in International Tourism*. Oxford: Butterworth-Heinemann.

Baum, T. (1995) *Managing Human Resources in the European Tourism and Hospitality Industry: A Strategic Approach*. London: Chapman and Hall.

Baum, T. (1996) 'Unskilled work and the hospitality industry: myth or reality?' *International Journal of Hospitality Management*, 15: 207–229.

Baum, T. (1999) 'Human resource management in tourism's small business sector: policy dimensions'. In D. Lee-Ross (ed.), *HRM in Tourism and Hospitality: International Perspectives on Small to Medium Sized Enterprises*. London: Cassell. pp. 3–16.

Becker, G. S. (1964) *Human Capital*. New York: Columbia University Press.

Becker, B. E., Huselid, M., Pickus, P. and Spratt, M. (1997) 'HR as a source of shareholder value: research and recommendations'. *Human Resource Management*, 36: 39–47.

Becker, B. E., Huselid, M. A. and Ulrich D. (2001) '*The HR Scorecard: Linking People, Strategy, and Performance*. Boston: Harvard Business School Press.

Beer, M., Spector, B., Lawrence, P. R., Quinn Mills, D. and Walton R. E. (1985) *Human Resource Management*. New York: The Free Press.

Belcourt, M., Sherman A. W., Bohlander, G. W. and Snell, S. A. (1996) *Managing Human Resources: Canadian Edition*. Toronto: Nelson Canada.

Bittner, E. (1965) 'The concept of organization', *Social Research*, 32: 239–55. Reprinted in R. Turner, *Studies in Ethnomethodology*. Baltimore, MD: Penguin.

Blyton, P. and Turnbull, P. (1992) *Reassessing Human Resource Management*. London: Sage.

Boella, M. J. (2000) *Human Resource Management in the Hospitality Industry* (7th edn.). Cheltenham, UK: Stanley Thornes.

Boselie, P., Dietz, G. and Boon, C. (2005) 'Commonalities and contradictions in HRM and performance research', *Human Resource Management Journal*, 15: 67–94.

Boxall, P. (2003) HR strategy and competitive advantage in the service sector, *Human Resource Management Journal*, 13: 5–20.

Buick, I. and Muthu, G. (1997) 'An investigation into the current practices of in-house employee training and development within hotels in Scotland,' *Service Industries Journal*, 17: 652–668.

Burrell, G. and Morgan, G. (1979) *Sociological Paradigms and Organisational Analysis*. London: Heinemann Educational.

Cannon, D. F. (2002) 'Building organizational commitment in international hospitality and tourism organizations'. In N. D'Annunzio-Green, G. A. Maxwell and S. Watson (eds) *Human Resource Management: International Perspectives in Hospitality and Tourism*. London: Continuum. pp. 156–173.

Chandler, A. D. (1962) *Strategy and Structure: Chapters in the History of the Industrial Enterprise*. Cambridge, MA: MIT Press.

Chappel, S. (2002) 'Hospitality and emotional labour in an international context'. In N. D'Annunzio-Green, G. A. Maxwell and S. Watson (eds) *Human Resource Management: International Perspectives in Hospitality and Tourism*. London: Continuum. pp. 225–240.

Cully, M., Woodland, S., O'Reilly, A. and Dix, G. (1999) *Britain at Work*. London: Routledge.

D'Annunzio-Green, N., Maxwell, G. A. and Watson, S. (2002a) *Human Resource Management: International Perspectives in Hospitality and Tourism*. London: Continuum.

D'Annunzio-Green, N., Maxwell, G. A. and Watson, S. (2002b) 'Editorial', *International Journal of Contemporary Hospitality Management*, 14: 205–206.

Deery, M. (2002) 'Labour turnover in international hospitality and tourism'. In N. D'Annunzio-Green, G. A. Maxwell and S. Watson (eds), *Human Resource Management: International Perspectives in Hospitality and Tourism* London: Continuum. pp. 51–63.

Deery, M. and Iverson, R. D. (1996) 'Enhancing productivity: interventions strategies for employee turnover'. In N. Johns (ed.), *Productivity Management in Hospitality and Tourism*. London: Cassell. pp. 68–95.

Delaney, J. T. and Huselid, M. A. (1996) 'The impact of human resource management practices on perceptions of organizational performance', *Academy of Management Journal*, 39: 949–969.

Delery, J. E. and Doty, D. H. (1996) 'Modes of theorizing in strategic human resource management: tests of universalistic, contingency, and configurational performance predictions', *Academy of Management Journal*, 39: 802–835.

DiMaggio, P. J. and Powell, W. W. (1983) 'The iron-cage revisited: institutional isomorphism and collective rationality in organizational fields', *American Sociological Review*, 48: 147–160.

Edgar, K. and Geare, A. (2005) 'HRM practice and employee attitudes: different measures – different results', *Personnel Review*, 34: 534–549.

Enz, C. A. and Siguaw, J. A. (2000a) 'Best practices in human resources', *Cornell Hotel and Restaurant Administration Quarterly*, 41(1): 48–61.

Enz, C. A. and Siguaw, J. A. (2000b) 'Best practices in service quality', *Cornell Hotel and Restaurant Administration Quarterly*, 41(5): 20–29.

Eisenhardt, K. M. (1989) 'Agency theory: an assessment and review', *Academy of Management Review*, 14: 57–74.

Fitz-Enz, J. (2000) *The ROI of Human Capital: Measuring the Economic Value of Employee Performance*. New York: Amacom.

Fombrun, C. J., Tichy, N. M. and Devanna, M. A. (1984) *Strategic Human Resource Management*. New York: Wiley.

Foucault, M. (1980) *Power/knowledge: Selected Interviews and Other Writings, 1972–1977* (C. Gordon, ed.). New York: Pantheon.

Friedman, A. (1977) *Industry and Labour: Class Struggle at Work and Monopoly Capitalism*. London: Macmillan.

Fulmer, W. E. (1990) 'Human resource management: the right hand of strategy implementation', *Human Resource Planning*, 13: 1–11.

Gilbert, D. and Guerrier, Y. (1997) UK hospitality managers past and present, *The Service Industries Journal*, 17: 115–132.

Goffman, E. (1959) *The Presentation of Self in Everyday Life*. New York: Doubleday.

Goss-Turner, S. (2002) 'Multi-site management: HRM implications'. In N. D'Annunzio-Green, G. A. Maxwell and S. Watson (eds), *Human Resource Management: International Perspectives in Hospitality and Tourism*. London: Continuum. pp. 118–163.

Gramsci, A. (1971) *Selections from the Prison Notebooks of Antonio Gramsci* (Q. Hoare and G. Nowell-Smith, eds). London: Lawrence and Wishart.

Grusky, E. (1966) 'Career mobility and organizational commitment', *Administrative Science Quarterly*, 10: 488–503.

Guerrier, Y. (1999) *Organisational Behaviour in Hotels and Restaurants: An International Perspective*. Chichester, UK: Wiley.

Guerrier, Y. and Deery, M. (1998) 'Research in hospitality human resource management and organizational behaviour', *International Journal of Hospitality Management*, 17: 145–160.

Guest, D. E. (1990) 'Human resource management and the American dream', *Journal of Management Studies*, 27: 377–397.

Guest, D. (1995) 'Human resource management, trade unions and industrial relations'. In J. Story (ed.), *HRM: A Critical Text*. London: Routledge.

Guest, D. E. (1997) 'Human resource management and performance: a review and research agenda', *The International Journal of Human Resource Management*, 8: 263–276.

Guest, D. E. (2002) 'Human resource management, corporate performance and employee wellbeing: building the worker into HRM', *Journal of Industrial Relations*, 44: 335–358.

Guest, D. E. and Hoque, K. (1994) 'The good, the bad and the ugly: employment relations in new non-union workplaces', *Human Resource Management Journal*, 5: 1–14.

Guest, D., Conway, N. and Dewe, P. (2004) 'Using sequential tree analysis to search for "bundles" of HR practices', *Human Resource Management Journal*, 14: 79–96.

Hackman, J. R. and Oldham, G. R. (1976) 'Motivation through the design of work: test of a theory', *Organizational Behaviour and Human Performance*, 16: 250–279.

Hackman, J. R. and Oldham, G. R. (1980) *Work Redesign*. Reading, MA: Addison Wesley.

Haynes, P. and Fryer, G. (1999) 'Effectiveness of quality focused human resource management strategies: a hospitality case study', *Proceedings of CHME Hospitality Research Conference*, UK. 1: 238–248.

Herzberg, F., Mausner, B. and Snyderman, B. (1959) *The Motivation to Work*. New York: Wiley.

Herzenberg, S., Alic, J. and Wial, H. (1998) *New Rules for a New Economy: Employment and Opportunity in Postindustrial America*. Ithaca, NY: ILR Press.

Hjalager, A. and Andersen, S. (2001) 'Tourism employment: contingent work or professional career?' *Employee Relations*, 37: 419–443.

Hochschild, A. R. (1983) *The Managed Heart: Commercialization of Human Feeling*. Berkeley, CA: University of California Business Press.

Hofstede, G. (1984) *Culture's Consequences: International Differences in Work-related Values*. Newbury Park, CA: Sage Publications.

Hoque, K. (1999a) 'Human resource management and performance in the UK hotel industry', *British Journal of Industrial Relations*, 31: 419–443.

Hoque, K. (1999b) 'New approaches to HRM in the UK hotel industry', *Human Resource Management Journal*, 9: 64–76.

Huang, T. C. (2001) 'The effects of linkage between business and human resource management strategies', *Personnel Review*, 30: 132–151.

Huselid, M. (1995) 'The impact of human resource management practices on turnover, productivity, and corporate financial performance', *Academy of Management Journal*, 38: 653–672.

Iverson, R. D. and Deery, M. (1997) 'Turnover culture in the hospitality industry', *Human Resource Management Journal*, 7: 71–82.

Jackson, S. E. and Schuler, R. S. (1995) 'The need for understanding human resources management in the context of organizations and their environment', *Annual Review of Psychology*, 46: 237–264.

Katz, E. and Kahn, R. (1978) *The Social Psychology of Organizations*. New York: Wiley.

Keenoy, T. (1990) 'Human resource management: rhetoric, reality and contradiction', *International Journal of Human Resource Management*, 1: 363–384.

Keenoy, T. and Anthony, P. (1992) 'Metaphor, meaning and morality'. In P. Blyton and P. Turnbull (eds) *Reassessing Human Resource Management*. London: Sage.

Kelliher, C. and Johnson, K. (1997) 'Personnel management in hotels – an update: a move to human resource management?' *Progress in Tourism and Hospitality Research*, 3: 321–331.

Kusluvan, S. (2003) *Managing Employee Attitudes and Behaviors in the Tourism and Hospitality Industry*. New York: Nova Science.

Lashley, C. (1998) 'Matching the management of human resources to service operations', *International Journal of Contemporary Hospitality Management*, 10: 24–33.

Lashley, C. (2001) Empowerment: HR Strategies for Service Excellence. Hospitality, Leisure and Tourism Series. Butterworth-Heinemann: Oxford.

Lashley, C. (2002a) 'A feeling for empowerment'. In N. D'Annunzio-Green, G. A. Maxwell and S. Watson (eds) *Human Resource Management: International Perspectives in Hospitality and Tourism*. London: Continuum. pp. 200–211.

Lashley, C. (2002b) 'The benefits of training for business performance'. In N. D'Annunzio-Green, G. A. Maxwell and S. Watson (eds) *Human Resource Management: International Perspectives in Hospitality and Tourism*. London: Continuum. pp. 104–117.

Lawler, E. E. (1986) *High Involvement Management*. New York: Jossey-Bass.

Lawler, E. E. and Mohrman, S. A. (2003) *Creating a Strategic Human Resources Organization: An Assessment of Trends and New Directions*. CA: Stanford Business Books.

Lawrence, P. R. and Lorsch, J. W. (1967) *Organization and Environment.* Cambridge, MA: Harvard Graduate School of Business Administration.

Lee-Ross, D. (ed.). (1999) *HRM in Tourism and Hospitality: International Perspectives on Small to Medium-sized Enterprises.* London: Cassell.

Legge, K. (1995) *Human Resource Management: Rhetoric and Realities.* London: Macmillan.

Legge, K. (1998) 'The morality of HRM'. In C. Mabey, D. Skinner and T. Clark (eds) *Experiencing Human Resource Management.* London: Sage.

Lewin, K. (1951) *Field Theory in Social Science; Selected Theoretical Papers.* D. Cartwright (ed). New York: Harper and Row.

Lucas, R. E. (1995) *Managing Employee Relations in the Hotel and Catering Industry.* London: Cassell.

Lucas, R. E. (1996) 'Industrial relations in hotels and catering: neglect or paradox?', *British Journal of Industrial Relations*, 34: 267–286.

Lucas, R. E. (2002) 'Fragments of HRM in hospitality? Evidence from the 1998 workplace employee relations survey', *International Journal of Contemporary Hospitality Management*, 14: 207–212.

Lucas, R. E. and Deery, M. (2004) 'Significant developments and emerging issues in human resource management', *International Journal of Hospitality Management*, 23: 459–472.

MacDuffie, J. P. (1995) 'Human resource bundles and manufacturing performance: organizational logic and flexible production systems in the world of auto industry', *Industrial and Labor Relations Review*, 48: 197–221.

McMahan, G., Virick, M. and Wright, P. (1999) Alternative theoretical perspectives for SHRM: progress, problems and prospects. In P. Wright, L. Dyer, J. Boudreau and G. Milkovich (eds) *Research in Personnel and Human Resource Management* (Supplement 4, pp. 99–122). Greenwich, CT: JAI Press.

March, J. G. and Simon, H. A. (1958) *Organizations.* New York: Wiley.

Maxwell, B. A. and Quail, S. (2002) 'Human resource strategy and development for quality service in the international hotel sector'. *Human Resource Management: International Perspectives in Hospitality and Tourism.* London: Continuum. pp. 90–103.

Mayo, E. (1933) *The Human Problems of an Industrial Civilisation.* New York: MacMillan.

Merton, R. K. (1968) *Social Theory and Social Structure.* New York: Free Press.

Meyer, J. W. and Rowan, B. (1977) 'Institutionalized organizations: formal structure and myth and ceremony', *American Journal of Sociology*, 83: 340–363.

Miles R. E. and Snow C. C. (1978) *Organizational Strategy, Structure, and Process.* New York: McGraw-Hill.

Miller, D. (1987) 'The structural and environmental correlates of business strategy', *Strategic Management Journal*, 8(1): 55–76.

Millett, B. (2002) 'Performance management in international hospitality and tourism'. In N. D'Annunzio-Green, G. A. Maxwell and S. Watson (eds) *Human Resource Management: International Perspectives in Hospitality and Tourism.* London: Continuum. pp. 131–155.

Mok, C. (2002) 'Managing diversity in hospitality organizations'. In N. D'Annunzio-Green, G. A. Maxwell and S. Watson (eds) *Human Resource Management: International Perspectives in Hospitality and Tourism.* London: Continuum. pp. 212–224.

Mowday, R. T., Koberg, C. S. and McArthur, A. W. (1984) 'The psychology of the withdrawal process: a cross-validation test of Mobely's intermediate linkages model of turnover in two samples', *Academy of Management Journal*, 27: 79–94.

Moxon, G. R. (1943) *The Functions of a Personnel Department.* London: Institute of Personnel Management.

Paauwe J. and Boselie, P. (2005) 'HRM and performance: what next?', *Human Resource Management Journal*, 15: 68–83.

Pfeffer, J. (1995) 'Producing sustainable advantage through the effective management of people', *Academy of Management Executive*, 9(1): 55–69.

Pfeffer, J. and Salancik, G. R. (1977) 'Organizational context and the characteristics and tenure of hospital administrators', *Academy of Management Journal*, 20: 74–88.

Piso, A. (1999) 'Hotel and catering workers: class and unionization', *Employee Relations*, 21: 176–188.

Pizam, A. (1999) 'The state of travel and tourism human resources in Latin America', *Tourism Management*, 20: 575–586.

Porter, M. E. (1980) *Competitive Strategy: Techniques for Analyzing Industries and Competitors.* New York: Free Press.

Porter, M. E. (1990) *The Competitive Advantage of Nations.* New York: Free Press.

Powell, S. and Wood, E. (1999) 'Is recruitment the millennium time bomb for the industry worldwide?', *International Journal of Contemporary Hospitality Management*, 11: 138–139.

Powell, W. and DiMaggio, P. J. (eds) (1991) *The New Institutionalism in Organizational Analysis.* Chicago: University of Chicago Press.

Prahalad, C. K. and Hamel, G. (1990) 'The core competence of the corporation'. *Harvard Business Review*, 68(3): 79–91.

Price, L. (1994) 'Poor personnel practices in the hotel and catering industry: does it Matter?', *Human Resource Management Journal*, 4: 44–62.

Riley, M. (1996) *Human Resource Management in the Hospitality and Tourism Industry*. Oxford: Butterworth Heinemann.

Roethlisberger, F. J. and Dickson, W. J. (1939) *Management and the Worker*. Cambridge, MA: Harvard University Press.

Sartre, J. P. (1966) *Being and Nothingness*. New York: Washington Square Press.

Schuler, R. S. (1989) 'Strategic human resource management and industrial relations', *Human Relations*, 42: 157–184.

Schuler, R. S. and Jackson, S. E. (1987a) 'Linking competitive strategies with human resources management practices', *Academy of Management Executive*, 1(3): 207–219.

Schuler, R. S. and Jackson, S. E. (1987b) 'Organizational strategy and organization levels as determinants of human resource management practice', *Human Resource Planning*, 10: 441–455.

Selznick, P. (1966) *T.V.A. and the Grass Roots*. New York: Harper and Row.

Silverman, D. (1970) *The Theory of Organizations*. London: Heinemann.

Silverman, D. and Jones, J. (1973) 'Getting in: the managed accomplishments of "correct" selection outcomes'. In J. Child (ed.), *Man and Organization: The Search for Explanation and Social Relevance*. London: George Allen and Unwin. pp. 63–106.

Snell, S. A. and Youndt, M. A. (1995) 'Human resource management and firm performance: testing a contingency model of executive controls', *Journal of Management*, 21: 711–737.

Snell, S. A., Youndt, M. A. and Wright, P. M. (1996) 'Establishing a framework for research in strategic human resource management: merging source theory and organizational learning', *Research in Personnel and Human Resources Management*, 14: 61–90.

Storey, J. (1987) 'Developments in the management of human resources: an interim report'. *Warwick Papers in Industrial Relations*, 17. Warwick, UK: Warwick Business School.

Storey, J. (1992) *Developments in the Management of Human Resources: An Analytical Review*. Oxford: Blackwell.

Storey, J. (1995) 'Human resource management: still marching on, or marching out?' In J. Storey (ed.), *Human Resource Management: A Critical Text*. London: Routledge. pp. 3–32.

Taylor, F. W. (1947) *Scientific Management*. New York: Harper.

Tichy, N. M., Fombrun, C. and Devanna, M. (eds) (1984) *The Organizational Context of Human Resource Management. Strategic Human Resource Management*, New York: Wiley.

Timo, N. and Davidson, M. (1999) 'Flexible labour and human resource management practices in small to medium-sized enterprises: the case of the hotel and tourism industry in Australia'. In D. Lee-Ross (ed.) *HRM in Tourism and Hospitality*. London: Cassell. pp. 17–36.

Timo, N. and Davidson, M. (2002) 'The structure of employee relations in multi-national hotels in Australia'. In N. D'Annunzio-Green, G. A. Maxwell and S. Watson (eds) *Human Resource Management: International Perspectives in Hospitality and Tourism*. London: Continuum. pp. 186–199.

Townley, B. (1994) *Reframing Human Resource Management: Power, Ethics and the Subject at Work*. London: Sage.

Turner, B. A. (1971) *Exploring the Industrial Subculture*. London: Macmillan.

Twining-Ward, L. and Baum, T. (1998) 'Dilemmas facing mature island destinations: cases from the Baltic', *Progress in Tourism and Hospitality Research*, 4: 131–140.

Ulrich, D. (1997) 'Measuring human resources: an overview of practice and a prescription for results,' *Human Resource Management*, 36: 303–320.

United Nations Environment and Development, UK Committee (1999) *Gender and Tourism: Women's Employment and Participation in Tourism*. London: UK: UNED.

Watson, T. J. (1986) *Management Organization and Employment Strategy: New Directions in Theory and Practice*. London: Routledge and Kegan Paul.

Watson, W. and D'Annunzio-Green, N. (1996) 'Implementing cultural change through human resources: the elusive organization alchemy', *International Journal of Contemporary Hospitality Management*, 89: 25–30.

Weick, K. (1979) *The Social Psychology of Organizing*. New York: Random House.

Whyte, W. R. (1948) *Human Relations in the Restaurant Industry*. New York: McGraw Hill.

Williamson, O. E. (1981) 'The economics of organization. The transaction cost approach', *American Journal of Sociology*, 87: 548–577.

Woods, R. H. (1999) 'Predicting is difficult, especially about the future: human resources in the new millennium', *International Journal of Hospitality Management*, 18: 443–456.

World Travel and Tourism Council (2005) *Executive Summary, World Travel and Tourism: Sowing the*

Seeds of Growth. The 2005 Travel and Tourism Economic Research.

Worsfold, P. (1999) 'HRM, performance, commitment and service quality in the hotel industry', *International Journal of Contemporary Hospitality Management*, 11: 340–348.

Wright, P. M. and Haggerty, J. J. (2005) 'Missing variables in theories of strategic human resource management: time, cause, and individuals', *Management Revue*, 16: 164–173.

Wright, P. M., Dyer, L. D., Boudreau, J. M. and Milkovich, G. T. (eds) (1999) *Strategic Human Resources Management in the Twenty-first Century.* Stanford, CT: JAI Press.

Wright, P. M., McCormick, B., Sherman, W. S. and McMahan, G. C. (1999) 'The role of human resource practices in petro-chemical refinery performance', *International Journal of Human Resource Management*, 10: 551–571.

Wright, P. M., McMahan, G. C., McCormick, R. and Sherman, W. S. (1998) 'Strategy core competence and HR involvement as determinants of HR effectiveness and refinery performance', *Human Resources Management*, 37: 17–29.

13

Marketing and Consumer Behavior in Hospitality

John Bowen

INTRODUCTION

This chapter provides an overview of the contribution of marketing and consumer behavior to hospitality management. The chapter shows the relationship of hospitality marketing to marketing and services marketing. The unique concepts of hospitality marketing are then discussed, followed by emerging themes in hospitality marketing. The chapter is not intended to be a comprehensive overview of the principles of hospitality marketing, but rather a look at important concepts and emerging trends.

DEFINITION OF MARKETING

What is marketing? Marketing, more than any other business function, deals with customers. Creating customer value and satisfaction are at the heart of hospitality marketing. Many factors contribute to making a business successful. Successful hospitality companies all have one thing in common – they are strongly customer focused and heavily committed to marketing. Accor has become one of the world's largest hotel chains by delivering *L'esprit Accor*, the ability to anticipate and meet the needs of their guests, with genuine attention to detail (Accor, 2001–2002). Ritz-Carlton also promises and delivers truly 'memorable experiences' for its hotels' guests.

From a marketing perspective, the purpose of a business is to create and maintain satisfied, profitable customers (Levitt, 1986). Not only do customers return to the same cruise line, hotel, or restaurant, but they also talk favorably to others about their satisfaction. Some hospitality managers think producing profits is the purpose of a business. This attitude eventually sinks

a firm as it finds fewer repeat customers and faces increasingly negative word of mouth. Successful managers understand that profits are best seen as the result of running a business well rather than as its sole purpose. When a business satisfies its customers, the customers will pay a fair price for the product. A fair price includes a profit for the firm.

In the 1970s, American consulting firms would draw pie charts showing 80% or more of a hotel's profit came from the rooms division with only about 10% coming from food and beverage. Given the difficulty of running a food and beverage department, many American hotels de-emphasized this area, charging high prices and providing uninteresting menus. Unfortunately they discovered that some of their customers were attracted by good restaurants and never came back. Hotels provide a bundle of products. Those hotels that tried to remove food and beverage from their bundles found out that they were lowering the value they created for some of their customers and as a result were losing customers. These hotels focused on maximizing profits rather than customer satisfaction and as a result actually lowered their profits. Marketing is about creating value for customers who will in turn create value for the business through their profits. Today, marketing can be viewed as a social and managerial process through which individuals and groups obtain what they need and want through creating and exchanging products and value with others (Kotler et al., 2006).

CORE MARKETING CONCEPTS

Marketing can be divided into five core concepts: needs, wants and demands; products;

value, satisfaction and quality; exchange, transactions and relationships and markets (Kotler et al., 2006).

Needs, wants and demands

The most basic concept underlying marketing is that of human needs. A human need is a state of perceived deprivation. Included are the basic physical needs for food, clothing, warmth and safety, as well as social needs for belonging, affection, fun and relaxation. There are esteem needs for prestige, recognition and fame and individual needs for knowledge and self-expression. These needs were not invented by marketers but are part of the human makeup (Murray, 1938). Hospitality products satisfy a variety of needs. The basic need of safety is important. Many advertisements for hotels or restaurants promote fun, relaxation or prestige. Understanding needs is a basic requirement of successful marketing.

The second basic concept to marketing is that of human wants, which are the form human needs take as they are shaped by culture and individual personality. Wants are how people communicate their needs. Wants are described in terms of objectives that will satisfy needs. As a society evolves, the wants of its members expand. As people are exposed to more objectives that arouse their interest and desire, hospitality firms try to provide more want-satisfying products and services.

Coca-Cola® partnered with *Hospitality* magazine to gain insight into restaurant customers' selection habits (Anonymous, 2005). One of the findings was that customers selected different restaurants based upon what they wanted from the dining experience. The wants could vary from home-cooked food to a fun night out (Moschis et al., 2003). Wants can also vary by age. For many senior citizens, a restaurant close to where they live is a desired feature (Moschis et al., 2003). In order to create products that will be wanted by the market, marketers must communicate to customers how their products will satisfy needs. For example, spas satisfy the need to relax. When backed by buying power, wants become demands.

Products

Consumers view products as bundles of benefits and choose those that give them the best bundle for their money. Motel 6 and Sleep Inns mean basic accommodations, a low price and convenience. Four Seasons and Kempinski Hotels mean luxury, comfort and status. People choose products with benefits that add up to the most satisfaction, given their personal wants and resources.

A product is anything that can be offered to satisfy a need or want. Suppose that an executive feels the need to reduce the stress of the job in a highly competitive industry. Products that may satisfy this need include a concert, dining at a restaurant, a four-day Caribbean vacation and exercise classes. These products are not equally desirable. The more available and less expensive products, such as a concert and dining at a restaurant, are likely to be purchased first and more often.

The concept of product is not limited to physical objects. Anything capable of satisfying a need can be called a product. More broadly defined, products include experiences, persons, places, organizations, information and ideas.

Value, satisfaction and quality

Customer Value is the difference between the benefits that the customer gains from owning and/or using a product and the costs of obtaining the product. Costs can be both monetary and non-monetary. One of the biggest non-monetary costs for hospitality customers is time. Luxury hotels in Hong Kong, such as The Shangri La, do not expect regular guests to stand in line to register. Instead, they are escorted to their room where hot tea is waiting and the hostess completes the registration for them. Domino's Pizza saves the customer time and provides convenience by delivering pizza to your home. Many limited service hotels give value to the overnight traveler by offering a free continental breakfast. One of the biggest challenges for management is to increase the value of their product for their target market. To do this, managers must know their customers and understand what creates value for them. This is an on-going process as customers and competition change over time.

Customer satisfaction depends on a product's perceived performance in delivering value relative to a buyer's expectations. If the product's performance falls short of the customer's expectations, the buyer is dissatisfied. If performance matches expectations, the buyer is satisfied.

If performance exceeds expectations, the buyer is delighted. Smart companies aim to delight customers by promising only what they can deliver, then delivering more than they promise.

Customer expectations are based on past buying experiences, the opinions of friends and market information. Marketers must be careful to set the right level of expectations. If they set expectations too low, they may satisfy those who buy, but fail to attract new customers. If they raise expectations too high, buyers will be disappointed.

Managers must realize the importance of creating highly satisfied customers, rather than just satisfied customers. On a 7-point scale, with 1 being very satisfied and 7 being very dissatisfied, most managers are happy to receive a score of 2. However, a survey of hotel customers in Boston found that of those who said they were very satisfied, 65% would return. Among those who rated satisfaction a 2 (between highly satisfied and very satisfied) only 25% said they would return (Booms and Bitner, 1982). There is a huge gap between the guest who rates a hotel a 1 and one who rates it a 2. Think of the last time you went to a restaurant and were just satisfied – would you go back? But when you walk out of a restaurant and say 'WOW, that was great!' you will probably return and tell others about your discovery.

Quality has a direct impact on product or service performance. Thus, it is closely linked to customer value and satisfaction. In the narrowest sense, quality can be defined as 'freedom from defects'; however, most customer-centered companies go beyond this narrow definition of quality. Instead, quality is defined in terms of customer satisfaction.

Exchange, transaction and relationships

Exchange marketing occurs when people decide to satisfy needs and wants through exchange. As a means of satisfying needs, exchange has much in its favor. People do not have to prey on others or depend on charity. Nor do they need the skills to produce every necessity for themselves. They can concentrate on making the things that they are good at making and trade them for needed items made by others. Through a division of labor and specialization, people in a society produce much more than with any alternative system.

Whereas exchange is the core concept of marketing, a transaction is marketing's unit of measurement. A transaction consists of a trade of values between two parties. We must be able to say A gives X to B and gets Y in return at a certain time and place and with certain understood conditions. IBM gives $500 to Hilton and obtains the use of a meeting room. This is a classic monetary transaction. Not all transactions involve money. In a barter transaction, the Anchorage Restaurant might provide free meals to WBC radio station in return for free advertising on that station. A transaction involves at least two things of value, a time of agreement and a place of agreement.

Transaction marketing is part of the larger idea of relationship marketing. Increasingly, marketing is shifting from trying to maximize the profit on each individual transaction to maximizing mutually beneficial relationships with consumers and other parties. The operating assumption is the following: build good relationships and profitable transactions will follow.

The importance of relationship marketing will increase in the future. Most companies are finding that they earn a higher return from resources invested in getting repeat sales from current customers than from money spent to attract new customers. In addition, they realize the benefits gained from cross-selling opportunities with current customers. More companies are forming strategic partnerships, making skilled relationship marketing essential. For customers who buy large, complex products, such as facilities for conventions and large meetings, the sale is only the beginning of the relationship. Therefore, although it is not appropriate in all situations, relationship marketing continues to grow in importance.

Markets

The concept of transactions leads to the concept of a market. A market is a set of actual and potential buyers who might transact with a seller. The size of a market depends on the number of persons who exhibit a common need, have the money or other resources that interest others and are willing to offer these resources in exchange for what they want. A key challenge of marketers is to segment a market into distinct groups that want similar products and then target those market segments for which they can provide the most satisfaction.

Services marketing

Hospitality marketing draws on services marketing, which started to evolve in the 1960s and emerged when Lynn Shostack (1977) wrote a seminal article entitled 'Breaking Free From Product Marketing' in the *Journal of Marketing*. Her article legitimized the need for a specialized area of marketing to deal with intangible products. Several years later, in 1981, the American Marketing Association (AMA) held its first conference focused solely on the marketing of services. The proceedings of this conference were titled, *Marketing of Services*. The AMA continued to hold these conferences throughout the eighties. The early conferences produced a number of research papers, which expanded and directed concept development and research in services marketing.

However, over time the registration fees increased, the conferences became more focused on practitioners and then were discontinued. In 1993 Ray Fisk, of the University of New Orleans, formed the American Marketing Association's Special Interest Group in Services. This organization holds research conferences, which attract scholars interested in services marketing, much the same as the original services marketing conferences. Those interested in interacting with others on issues related to services marketing can benefit from participation in the AMA's SERVSIG. The AMA's journals – The *Journal of Marketing,* the *Journal of Services Marketing*, *The Service Industries Journal* and the *Journal of Services Research* – are all good sources of material on the latest thoughts and research relating to services marketing.

In 1993, three pioneers of services marketing, Ray Fisk, Stephen Brown and Mary Jo Bitner, wrote a review of the evolution of marketing literature (Fisk et al., 1993). More recently Ford and Bowen (2002) reviewed marketing and management literature to identify unique marketing and management techniques required for managing service firms when compared with firms producing tangible products. These reviews provide an overview of the major works that shaped the development of services marketing and management. They provide a great starting point for anyone who wants an introduction to services marketing.

MAIN EPISTEMOLOGICAL APPROACHES, THEMES AND ISSUES

Hospitality marketing

Hospitality marketing is a sub-set of services marketing. The characteristics of services, including hospitality products, are intangibility, inseparability, variability and perishability. Unlike physical products, services cannot be seen, tasted, felt, heard or smelled before they are purchased – they are intangible. However, as Zeithaml and Bitner (2003) point out, very few products are either purely tangible or intangible. The food we receive in a restaurant is tangible. The atmosphere of the restaurant and the employees' uniforms help tangibilize the experience.

In most hospitality services, both the service provider and the customer must be present for the transaction to occur. Customer-contact employees are part of the product. The food in a restaurant may be outstanding, but if the service person has a poor attitude or provides inattentive service, customers will rate the overall restaurant experience poorly. They will not be satisfied with their experience. Service inseparability also means that customers are part of the product. A couple may have chosen a restaurant because it is quiet and romantic, but if a group of loud and boisterous conventioneers is seated in the same room, the couple will be disappointed.

Variability or lack of consistency in the product is a major cause of customer disappointment in the hospitality industry. On the other hand, consistency is one of the major reasons for the worldwide success of McDonald's. Services are highly variable. Their quality depends on who provides them and when and where they are provided. There are several causes of service variability. Services are produced and consumed simultaneously, which limits quality control. Fluctuating demand makes it difficult to deliver consistent products during periods of peak demand. The high degree of contact between the service provider and the guest means that product consistency depends on the service provider's skills and performance at the time of the exchange. A guest can receive excellent service one day and mediocre service from the same person the next day. In the case of mediocre service, the service person may not have felt well or perhaps experienced an emotional problem. Lack of communication and heterogeneity of guest expectations also lead to service variability. A restaurant customer ordering a medium steak may expect it to be cooked all the way through, whereas the person working on the broiler may define medium as having a warm, pink center. The guest will be disappointed when he/she cuts into the steak and sees pink meat. Restaurants have solved this cause of variability by developing common definitions of steak doneness and communicating them to the employees and customers.

Services cannot be stored. Because of service perishability, airlines and some hotels charge guests holding guaranteed reservations even when they fail to check into the hotel. Restaurants are also starting to charge a fee to customers who do not show up for a reservation. They, too, realize that if someone does not show up for a reservation, the opportunity to sell that seat may be lost. If hospitality companies are to maximize revenue, they must manage capacity and demand.

Bowen and Sparks (1998) reviewed the marketing articles published in eight major hospitality journals between 1990 and 1997. They categorized their review of literature into consumer behavior, segmentation, product policy, internal marketing, promotion, personal selling database marketing, pricing and distribution. They identified twelve areas for future research and development. Four of those areas still are very relevant today. These areas are as follows:

- research on the use of data mining techniques to identify market segments;
- analyzing database information to aid in the acquisition of new customers;
- research on how pricing strategies affect image and long-term sales; and
- research investigating the linkages between internal marketing and indicators of organizational performance.

Their article provides a good overview of the work on hospitality marketing in the 1990s.

Consumer behavior

The characteristics of services marketing have an effect on the way customers' process information when they make purchase decisions about hospitality products and when they evaluate hospitality products during the service delivery process. In a seminal article, Zeithaml (1981) developed eleven propositions on how consumers process information differently for tangible products than they do for services. One proposition was since intangible products did not have features that could be examined before they were purchased, customers tended to rely more on personal sources of information. Her proposition was later confirmed by Murray (1991), who found that purchasers of services have greater confidence in personal sources of information. An advertisement from a restaurant stating 'we have the best steaks in town' is less motivating because the only way for the customer to find out if the restaurant has excellent steaks is to purchase one. If the restaurant is right, they may have enjoyed a great meal. However, if it was a shallow advertising claim, the customer could waste both their time and money. When purchasing foodservice products, a recommendation from a friend, business associate or front desk clerk can mean a lot more to the prospective customer than an advertisement. Thus, hospitality managers should do everything possible to encourage customers to spread positive word of mouth. Nothing is more powerful than an enthusiastic recommendation from a friend, relative or business associate.

When purchasing hospitality products, customers often use price as an indication of quality. A business executive who has been under a lot of pressure decides to take a three-day vacation now that the project is complete. She wants luxury accommodations and good food service. She is prepared to pay $175 a night for the room. She calls a hotel that offers a special rate of $85. This hotel may be able to satisfy her needs and has simply dropped its rate to encourage business. In this case, the hotel has dropped its rate too low to attract this customer. Since she has never visited the hotel, she will perceive that the hotel is below her standard. When using price to create demand, care must be taken to ensure that one does not create the wrong consumer perceptions about the product's quality.

When customers purchase hospitality and travel products, they often perceive some risk in the purchase. If customers want to impress friends or business associates, they will usually take them to a restaurant they have visited previously. Customers tend to be loyal to restaurants and hotels that have met their needs. A meeting planner is reluctant to change hotels if the hotel has been doing a good job. When selling hospitality products, salespeople need to use testimonial letters, pictures and other items to reduce the risk of the purchaser.

Customers of hospitality and travel products often blame themselves when dissatisfied. A person who orders scampi may be disappointed with the dish but not complain because he blames himself for the bad choice. He loves the way his favorite restaurant fixes scampi, but he should have known that this restaurant would not be able to prepare it the same way. When the waiter asks how everything is, he replies that it was okay. Employees must be aware that dissatisfied customers may not complain. They should try to seek out sources of guest dissatisfaction and resolve them. A waiter noticing someone not eating their food may ask if they could replace it with an alternative dish and suggest some items that could be brought out very quickly.

Three additional 'P's'

The classic four 'P's' of marketing are price, product, place and promotion. These are the variables that marketers control. Bernard Booms and Mary Jo Bitner (1982) published a classic article in the *Cornell Quarterly* entitled 'Marketing Services by Managing the Environment'. In this article, they discussed three differences that distinguish hospitality marketing from the marketing of tangible goods. They added three additional 'P's' for hospitality marketing: participants, physical evidence and process of service assembly.

Participants

Participants have one of the most profound effects on how we market hospitality products. Employees and customers are both part of the product we produce. When people think of marketing, they usually think of efforts directed externally toward the marketplace, but a hotel or restaurant's first marketing efforts should be directed internally to employees. Managers must make sure that employees know their products and believe that they are good value. The employees must be excited about the company that they work for and the products they sell. Otherwise, it will be impossible for the guests to become excited. This is why it is important for all managers to understand

marketing and its customer orientation. External marketing will bring customers, but it does little good if the employees do not perform to the guest's expectations. It is the employees' delivery of the service that brings customers back. As Christine Andrews, Vice President of Human Resources for Hostmark Hospitality states, 'If your people don't perform, your property won't perform' (Walsh, 2004: 14). The concept of internal marketing is that we market to our employees before we market to our customers. Our employees become our internal customers. Everything a service organization does for its customers is first perceived by its employees (Gronroos, 2000).

Richard Normann (1984) of the Service Management Group says that a key ingredient in almost all service companies is some innovative arrangement or formula for mobilizing and focusing human energy. Normann developed the term 'moments of truth', which Jan Carlzon of SAS later popularized. A moment of truth occurs when employees and customers have contact. Normann states that when this occurs, the company no longer directly influences what happens.

Nevertheless, according to Bob Ford of Central Florida University, if employees do not understand the wants of the customers and how the service offering can fulfill these wants, they will not be effective in their interaction with the customers. The customer contact employee can only do their job if they are supported by back of house employees. Thus, the organization must learn to engage everyone in the service mission. Internal marketing includes both the customer contact employee and the many others who support that customer contact person (Ford and Bowen, 2002). This means that the services managers spend considerable effort communicating the service mission and vision to all employees so that those in the back of house, who are 'off stage', know how important their role is in supporting those, who are 'on stage', in the front of house. This concept of internal marketing has been described as a way of managing the organization's human resources based on a marketing philosophy (George and Gronroos, 1991).

Another way to understand the importance of internal marketing is through the Service–Profit Chain, which 'establishes relationships between profitability, customer loyalty, and employee satisfaction, loyalty, and productivity' (Heskett et al., 1994: 164). Essentially, this chain begins with leadership, which drives internal quality, which drives employee satisfaction, which drives employee loyalty, which drives employee productivity, which drives value, which drives customer satisfaction, which drives customer loyalty, which finally drives profitability and growth (Heskett et al., 1994). It is critical to the success of a company to place value on, and sustain each and every, link in this chain.

Physical evidence

Physical evidence that is not managed properly can hurt a business. Negative messages communicated by poorly managed physical evidence include signs that continue to advertise a holiday special two weeks after the holiday has passed, signs with missing letters or burned-out lights, parking lots and grounds that are unkempt and full of trash and employees in dirty uniforms at messy workstations. Such signs send negative messages to customers. Restaurant managers are trained to do a pre-opening inspection of the restaurant. One of the things they look for is that all light bulbs are working. A little thing like a burned-out bulb can give a guest sitting near it an impression that the restaurant does not pay attention to detail. Indeed, the importance of physical surrounding was validated through a recent study by J. D. Powers (Klara, 2005). This study investigated the most important variables for creating customer satisfaction in a restaurant. Environment was mentioned by 24% of the respondents, behind food at 30% and service at 26%.

Physical surroundings should be designed to reinforce the product's position in the customer's mind. The front-desk staff in a luxury hotel should dress in professional apparel wool or wool-blend conservative clothes. The front-desk staff at a tropical resort might wear tropical, Hawaiian-style, Batik or Guayabera shirts. The counter staff at a fast food restaurant might wear a simple polyester uniform.

A firm's communications should also reinforce their positioning. Ronald McDonald is great for McDonald's, but a clown would not be appropriate for a Four Seasons hotel. All said, a service organization should review every piece of tangible evidence to make sure that each delivers the desired organizational image – the way a person or group views an organization – to target customers (Booms and Bitner, 1982).

Process

The service setting can induce desired behavior and attitudes and can be considered as part of the service experience. Thus, a rope barrier not only tells the guest where to stand in line and sends a message that the organization will make the wait for service fair and conflict-free, but also sends a message that the organization recognizes its role in managing this part of the guest experience and is taking good care of it. Perhaps no one has done more work on this than Bitner (Booms and Bitner, 1981, 1982; Bitner, 1990, 1992). As mentioned earlier, Booms and Bitner (1981) developed an additional three 'P's' for services (e.g. Participants, Physical Evidence and Process of Service Assembly) to add to the classic four 'P's' of marketing. These two writers go on to discuss the contribution of the service environment, or setting, in making the intangible service tangible. Bitner (1992) offers the term 'Servicescape' to represent the effect the setting can have on the customer and suggests a model that details its component elements and moderating variables. The point of her work is to expand the consideration of the organization to include the physical aspects of the setting in which the service is experienced. This work has also expanded to include the impact of the environment on the service provider as well.

CRITICAL REVIEW

The following are some emerging areas of hospitality marketing that create opportunities for companies that master these concepts and for researchers who can help managers understand and master these concepts.

Customer co-production

Hospitality products are often labor intensive. One way of reducing labor is to get customers to co-produce the products. New restaurant formats serving quality food have the customers place their own orders at a counter and then deliver the food to them, reducing the need for service personnel. Fast food restaurants have customers serve their own drinks. Schneider and Bowen (1993) identify five categories of benefits customers might gain from co-producing the service. First, they may get lower prices by helping to produce their own service experience.

A restaurant called the Red Run Grill uses technology to allow the customer to place their own order electronically from their table (Liddle, 2004). This reduces their costs and allows them to keep their menu prices competitive.

A second benefit for customer co-production can be saving the customer's time. Restaurants encourage customers to place their take-out orders over the Internet. A third benefit is that customers can gain greater choice through co-production. For example, a self-service buffet provides customers with a variety of different foods.

Fourth, customers may be able to achieve greater satisfaction by producing a highly customized product. Salad bars allow the customer to create a salad that has the ingredients they like in the amounts they want. Slywotsky and Morrison (2001) state that customers are becoming more actively involved in the purchase process and they like to design their products. Co-production allows them to do this. Restaurant menus feature ingredients that are available for omelets, sandwiches and pizza. Customers can select the ingredients they want to use in their omelet, sandwich or pizza, thus creating a product that meets their unique tastes.

Fifth, they may feel higher levels of self-esteem by producing their own experience. Some customers of a Mongolian barbecue restaurant that choose their own bowl of raw ingredients get a sense of pride when the meal they have helped produce tastes great.

Self-service technologies

Technology is providing additional ways to involve the customer in the delivery process. Airlines and hotels get customers to make their own reservations on the Internet. Hotels have self check-in kiosks. Self-service technologies (SST) are a rapidly growing means for increasing customer co-production in the hospitality industry, though not every customer is ready or capable of using SST, especially if it involves computers. One way to differentiate readiness is offered by Parasuraman (2000), who developed a technology readiness index to measure customers' readiness to embrace technology and interact with it. Using a measure similar to the technology readiness index allows companies to see how ready their customers are to embrace technology. Such measures also allow the organization to see if it is possible to segment its customers on their readiness to adopt technology.

Another approach to assessing customer readiness to use SST is offered by Sneath et al. (2002), who developed a scale for measuring the perceived risk associated with self-service. In comparison to having someone else do it for them, they found customers will evaluate the risk associated with providing the service themselves prior to choosing the self-service versus full-service option. These researchers suggest that marketing communications should reduce the risk associated with self-service options. For example, if you order ahead and get caught in traffic, Starbucks will remake your drink if it is no longer hot when you arrive.

Bobbitt and Dabholkar (2001) suggest that managers should identify customers that have unfavorable attitudes toward using SST and seek to understand what caused these unfavorable attitudes. Understanding when and why customers are willing to use SST is important as restaurants are increasingly using the Internet to provide directions, display menus, dispense coupons, take orders and take reservations. Meuter et al. (2005) found that an ability to use the self-service technology and motivation are important factors in a customer choosing to use SST. Consequently, managers must carefully design their website infrastructure to help their customers become more efficient (Xue and Harker, 2002).

One important benefit of SST is perceived control over the experience. Lee and Allaway (2002) found that customers were more likely to adopt an SST when it offered high predictability, high controllability and a highly desirable outcome. Thus, it is important that potential users understand the benefits they will receive before they use the SST. They should know the process requirements for successful self-service before using the SST. They should be able to tailor the interaction to their personal needs, wants and behavior patterns. Meuter et al. (2000) found that the advantages of time savings, accessibility and ease of use were important drivers of satisfaction with an SST. They discovered that the biggest dissatisfier was when customers were prevented from using the service or it did not function according to the customer's expectations. Meuter et al. (2000) determined this was particularly troublesome if the customer assumes the transaction was completed.

For example, a customer thought she had an Internet reservation, but the restaurant had no record because the customer had inadvertently aborted the online reservation process. Like any other part of the customer interaction with the hospitality organization, managers must design SSTs to maximize the benefits guests receive and minimize customer failures if they wish to use SSTs successfully.

Managing capacity and demand

Because services typically involve simultaneous production and consumption, it is impossible to use inventoried products to match capacity with demand or to smooth out capacity utilization by producing for inventory (Sasser, 1976). Once the plane leaves the gate, the unused seat inventory is gone forever; the same is true for telephone lines, power generation capacity, hospital rooms, classroom seats or teller availability to process bank customer transactions. Once the available capacity is unused, it has no future value. If there is too much capacity, then the idle capacity costs will tend to make the firm uncompetitive with organizations that have been more successful in matching their capacity and demand. On the other hand, if there is not enough capacity to meet demand, the firm runs the risk of losing customers. Klassen and Rohleder (2001) pointed out the uncertainty of demand, which can fluctuate on an hour-by-hour basis, making managing capacity and demand in services difficult. Service organizations must find ways to balance capacity with demand without the benefit of the manufacturers' physical inventory buffer or risk losing customers who refuse to wait for service.

Without a buffering inventory to absorb the unevenness between supply and demand, the service production process has to predict the rate of both the customer arrivals and the customer participation in the service experience. Customer participation can create uncertainty in a number of ways. They may not understand the service offering or their role in obtaining the service experience. When this occurs, the employee has to spend more time with the customer, often causing delays for other customers. This variance in a customer's ability to participate, coupled with the high degree of interaction that can occur between the customer and employees, complicates the predictability of time required in the service experience and the

service organization's ability to match capacity and demand (Booms and Bitner, 1981).

Collier (1987) identified several reasons why demand analysis is both quite different and more complicated for services than it is for manufacturing organizations. Some differences are:

- capacity is a surrogate for inventory in a service organization;
- length of the 'cycle of production' is shorter for services;
- customer may be present in the production process;
- service organizations focus on customer processing times rather than product processing times;
- certainty of customer purchase is greater for product orders than it is for customer appointments for an experience; and
- fewer service firms know the cost structure of producing a satisfied guest than manufacturing firms know about costs of products made to quality specifications.

The service firm seeks to manage capacity and/or demand in an attempt to match capacity with demand. Lovelock and Wright (1999) suggested a number of ways service managers can manage capacity: maintenance can be scheduled during periods of low demand, part-time employees can be used to expand labor-constrained capacity and facilities and equipment can be rented. Sasser (1976) mentioned that increasing customer participation can also increase capacity. When telephone reservation systems get backed up, the customer is often referred to self-service over the Internet. These tactics can be used to create a flexible capacity that expands and contracts with demand.

Other strategies for managing demand include: inventorying demand, requiring customers to make reservations and shifting demand. The service organization can also inventory demand by making customers wait in line and finding ways to divert them so they do not leave, abandon the line or feel dissatisfied because they had to wait as part of the service experience (Maister, 1985; Taylor, 1994, 1995). Busy doctors, popular restaurants, financial counselors and other service organizations inventory demand through reservations or appointments. However, service organizations cannot be sure that their perishable capacity reserved by a customer will in fact be used (Danet, 1981). As a result, they seek to guarantee revenues from customers who may not show up at the appointed time (e.g. a music center will charge students for a lesson canceled on the same day as the lesson is scheduled). Finally, demand can sometimes be shifted (Lovelock and Young, 1979). For example, a patient may request an eye exam for September 21, but will accept an appointment on July 28. A meeting planner often has some flexibility in dates and the meeting can be moved to a date when the hotel has more unused capacity. Without a tangible product to inventory, managing capacity and demand is different in services than it is in manufacturing firms.

Revenue management

With the help of computer programs, managers are using price, reservation history and over-booking practices to develop a sophisticated approach to demand management called revenue management. Revenue management is a methodological approach for allocating a perishable and fixed inventory to the most profitable customers. Revenue management grew out of yield management, which was introduced in the 1980s. During the last five years, many large business class and luxury hotels have added full-time revenue managers to their staff. The ability to maximize revenue has become such an important management tool that today corporate revenue managers are being promoted to the corporate vice-president of marketing. A well designed revenue management system bases pricing decisions on data and can increase revenue by 8% or more. One 200-room hotel was able to add $600,000 to its top-line profit after implementing revenue management. Their system was designed to maximize RevPAR (revenue per available room). Revenue management techniques have also been designed for restaurants, where they are designed to maximize revenue per available seat per hour (RevPASH) (Kimes, 2004). In restaurants, seat utilization and off-peak pricing are among the tools used to maximize RevPASH.

Properly designed revenue management systems value the business of repeat customers. Therefore, a customer who stays at a hotel 11 times a year for two nights per stay is treated differently than a one-time convention guest. The frequent/loyal guest's business is valued and some hotel companies have developed corporate rates for these guests that do not fluctuate with the demand for business. They protect these guests. As one can see, the practice of revenue management for a hotel can be very complex. It takes an understanding of forecasting models and the hotel's customer base (Cross, 1997; Strauss and Weinstein, 2003; Choi and Mattila, 2004).

Research in revenue management is now focusing on pricing by segments and loyalty (Shoemaker, 2003; Vinod, 2004). Companies practicing revenue management need to understand that maximizing revenue at the expense of upsetting a regular customer can be a short-term game. Thus, revenue managers must understand both pricing models and customer segments. Revenue managers seem to have well designed computer-forecasting models. The challenge now is to bring in the human aspect to these mathematical models.

Electronic marketing

Today, three out of ten travel sales are booked online, generating over $65 billion (Katz, 2004). Major hotel chains, such as Hilton and Marriott, book millions of dollars worth of rooms over the Web. For example, Hilton books half a billion dollars in hotel rooms per year over the Internet (Adams, 2003). The Internet has become such an important channel that some companies, such as Hyatt Hotels, have created a position of vice-president of electronic distribution.

'All of us are interested in getting on the information superhighway because we know the channels of travel distribution are changing', said Nancy Vaughn, Best Western's director of corporate communications (Western, 1995). Mary Sweenson, managing director of world-wide communications for Best Western, said the Internet allows Best Western to reach the 72% of their customers who do not use a travel agent (Vis, 1995). Sanchez and Satir (2005) found that hotels using an online distribution system had a higher REVPAR (revenue per available room) than those who did not.

One model of distribution on the Internet is called the merchant model. In this model, distributors mark-up discounted net rate hotel rooms. The distributor makes the difference between the net rate and the selling price of the room. Initially, managers saw this model as a channel that would sell off their extra rooms, performing a function similar to wholesalers. Conventional wholesalers packaged the rooms with air travel and ground transportation, creating new markets with their packages. The Internet distributors simply sold the rooms over the Internet in direct competition and often cheaper than the rooms for sale on the hotel's website (Campbell, 2004). As a result, hotel companies have now taken action to gain pricing control over their products. Many companies now guarantee the lowest prices for their rooms will be available on their websites.

InterContinental Hotels Group (IHG) decided to remove its inventory from all-merchant model websites, including Expedia and Hotels.com, except for Travelocity and Travelocity Business. In order to gain IHG's business, Travelocity had to agree not to undercut the chain's best rate guarantee and not identify as being sold out when the web allotment was gone. InterContinental Hotels' vice-president of global distribution said they would be willing to work with other partners if they would agree to IHG's terms. Some hotel chains, such as Marriott, Hilton and Starwood, do not provide reward points for discounted rates purchased by guests through merchant models (Serlen, 2004).

Priceline uses an opaque system where the buyer cannot specify any particular hotel or airline; thus, someone with a brand preference cannot compare prices with specific hotels. Some hotel managers prefer this model because the guest is unable to make direct price comparisons. Persons who purchase from a third party on the Internet pay the third party. Thus, if the hotel wants to capture guests for their database, they need to collect the guests' names and addresses when they register. Hotels selling rooms through third party vendors on the Internet should make their reservationists and desk staff aware that they are doing this and that there may be a delay from the time the guest books the hotel room and when the distributor transfers the information to the hotel. Guests who are new to Internet booking are often anxious and call the hotel to confirm the booking after making the reservation. The hotel may have no record, and the reservationist can spend valuable time trying to sort out the status of the reservation. By simply asking the guest how they made the reservation, the hotel employee can identify those who book with a third party, inform them that the reservation has not been transferred yet and advise them when to check back.

Restaurant companies are also using the Internet as a distribution channel. Pizza Hut and Domino's have on-line ordering systems. TerraNet was developed in Boston for customers wanting home delivery of restaurant meals. The database allows the user to search by restaurant name or type of food. The Internet user then gets information on the menu, including color photos of the dishes. The customer can select either takeout or delivery. After they have made their selection, they see the amount owed, including any delivery charges (Johnson, 1994). There are a number of services that take online reservations for restaurants. The fees for these services range from $180 per year to $2400 a year. For $2400 year and a $1295 set-up fee, the restaurant gets a computer with a guest management platform that allows managers to see their reservations in real time. They also have access to the guest history of persons making their reservations over the system (Durocher, 2003).

Some of the advantages of the Internet are that it never closes, is open twenty-four hours a day, seven days a week, has worldwide coverage and can transmit color pictures. The capability of transmitting color photographs to millions of people across the globe makes the Internet an exciting distribution channel. It allows companies to make their products tangible through the use of color photos and videos. The Grand Aleutian is a remote resort 800 miles southwest of Anchorage. It attracts fishermen and those who want to explore the Aleutian Islands. It only has 112 rooms, yet through an Internet site called Historic Inns of America, it can provide thousands of potential guests with color photos of its rooms and food and beverage facilities and allow them to make inquiries through e-mail. Similarly, the Rutledge Victorian Inn can show color pictures of its exterior and its rooms. Hyatt provides a video tour of the Park Hyatt Tokyo and the Stardust Casino provides a video clip of its show 'Enter the Night'. These examples show how small, independent properties can use the Internet to gain access to travelers across the country and the world.

By using a menu, websites can provide a lot of information while enabling users to quickly access information of interest. Mandalay Bay Resort gives daily rates on their Internet site. The resort has a wide swing in rates based on their convention and meeting business. A customer driving up from Las Vegas uses this information to choose the less expensive days to come to the Mandalay Bay. Providing this information creates a win-win situation because these are also days when the resort needs business. The Hyatt's website provides information on each hotel, an enrollment form for their Gold Passport, a list of discounted rooms, information on golf packages and much more. Yet somebody wanting information on the Hyatt hotels in the Chicago area could go right to the directory and find that information. Although many customers will decide to make a reservation while they are on the Internet, others use the Internet as a source of information, but like to talk to a live person to make their reservation. The reservation for this person is quicker because they already know what they want as the Internet site answered many of their questions.

Visitors to an Internet site have the ability to print hard copies of information provided on the site's pages. Hilton takes advantage of this by providing an interactive map for each of the hotels linked to its home page. The map can be zoomed in and out to provide as much detail as the prospective guest needs. Marriott, Taco Bell and other restaurant and hotel companies have maps as part of their sites or have a link to MapQuest, an Internet-based mapping program. This makes it easier for tourists to find a hotel or a restaurant in an unfamiliar city. Some restaurants are providing coupons that can be printed. The Internet also allows interaction with the guest through e-mail and by phone and mail when the guest provides the appropriate information.

One of the major advantages of the Internet is that it saves labor. The Internet is an excellent example of how service companies can get the customer to be their employee. When making reservations or purchasing products on-line, the customer is acting as a reservation agent. It would take a reservation center with over 100 full-time employees, a building to house them and equipment to serve them to take in an equivalent number of reservations that Marriott takes in on its Internet site.

The Internet is rapidly becoming an important distribution channel with relatively low costs, allowing the independent operator to gain access to world markets. It allows the multiunit operator to give information about all locations, including color brochures and guided tours of the property. This information is valuable to the individual traveler, meeting planner and the travel agent. Hospitality and travel companies are now producing separate sites to meet the information needs of these unique segments.

CONCLUSIONS

Hospitality marketing is based on the theories of marketing and services marketing. It is an applied area of services marketing. It makes use of the principles that have been developed in services marketing. Like services marketing, hospitality marketing has a short history. In the 1950s, hospitality marketing focused mainly on selling. Today, hospitality integrates many disciplines.

Internet marketing draws on the areas of technology and distribution. The design of websites draws on the catalog design literature. Database marketing draws on psychology, math and technology. Since employees are part of the product, marketing draws on the management literature. The use of self-service technologies allows companies to produce better products at a lower cost. Revenue management draws on psychology, math and forecasting. As one can quickly see, today's hospitality marketing is very complex. It requires specialists who understand their unique area. Those who understand revenue management may not be good at leading a sales force. A public relations expert may not be a good database marketer. Marketing is highly specialized and is becoming increasingly complex. It is important that hospitality marketers have a basic understanding of marketing. However, to be a leader, they must choose an area of specialization. The pursuit of the knowledge of marketing is a never-ending journey – a journey in which the pace has picked up from a walk to a run.

REFERENCES

Accor. (2001–2002) *Asia Pacific Hotel Directory*, p.1.

Adams, B. (2003) 'Hilton Hotel Corp. booked a record of more than 450,000 online reservations', *Hotel and Motel Management*, September 1: 24.

Anonymous. (2005) 'Study reveals consumer's restaurant-selection habits', *Nation's Restaurant News*, 39(12): 96.

Bitner, M. J. (1990) 'Evaluating service encounters: the effect of physical surrounding and employee responses', *Journal of Marketing*, 54(2): 69–82.

Bitner, M. J. (1992) 'Servicescapes: The Impact of Physical Surroundings on Customers and Employees,' *Journal of Marketing*, 56(2): 57–71.

Bobbitt, L. M. and Dabholkar, P. (2001) 'Integrating attitudinal theories to understand and predict use of technology-based self-service', *International Journal of Service Industry Management*, 5(12): 423–450.

Booms, B. M. and Bitner, M. J. (1981) 'Marketing strategies and organization structures for service firms in marketing of services. In J. H. Donnelly and W. R. George (eds), *American Marketing Association Proceedings Series*, 47–51.

Booms, B. H. and Bitner, M. J. (1982) 'Marketing services by managing the environment', *Cornell Hotel and Restaurant Administration Quarterly*, 23(1): 35–39.

Bowen, J. and Ford, R. C. (2002) 'Managing service organizations: Does having a thing make a difference?', *Journal of Management*, Volume 28(3): 447–469.

Bowen, J. B. and Shiang-Lih, C. (2001) 'The relationship between customer loyalty and customer satisfaction', *International Journal of Contemporary Hotel Management*, 13(5): 13–17.

Bowen, J. T. and Sparks, B. A. (1998) 'Hospitality marketing research: a content analysis and implications for future research', *International Journal of Hospitality Management*, 17: 125–144.

Campbell, J. (2004, June 21) 'Hotel merchant model gets corp. makeover'. Retrieved November 28, 2004 from World Wide Web: www.btnmag.com.

Choi, S. and Mattila, A. S. (2004) 'Hotel revenue and its impact on customer's perceptions of fairness', *Journal of Revenue and Pricing*, 2(4): 303–314.

Collier, D. A. (1987) *Service Management*. Englewood Cliffs, NJ: Prentice Hall, Inc.

Cross, R. G. (1997) *Revenue Management: Hardcore Tactics for Market Domination*. New York: Broadway Books.

Danet, B. (1981) Client–organization interfaces. In P. C. Nystrom and W. N. Starbuck (eds) *Handbook of Organization Design*, 2. New York: Oxford University Press, p. 384.

Durocher, J. (2003) 'Easy chair', *Restaurant Business*, September 9: 82.

Fisk, R. P., Brown, S. W. and Bitner, M. J. (1993) 'Tracking the evolution of services marketing literature', *Journal of Retailing*, 69(1): 61–103.

Ford, R. C. and Heaton, C. P. (2000) *Managing the Guest Experience in Hospitality*. Albany, NY: Delmar.

Ford, R. C. and Heaton, C. P. (2001) 'Managing the guest as a quasi-employee', *Cornell Hotel and Restaurant Quarterly*, 42(2): 46–55.

George, W. R. and Gronroos, C. (1991) 'Developing customer-conscious employees at every level', *Internal Marketing*. In C. A. Congram (ed.) *The AMA Handbook of Marketing for the Service Industry*. New York: AMACOM. pp. 85–100.

Gronroos, C. (2000) *Service Management and Marketing*. 2nd edn. Chichester, UK: Wiley.

Heskett, J. L. et al. (1994) 'Putting the service-profit chain to work', *Harvard Business Review*, 72(2): 164–170.

Johnson, M. (1994) 'Technically speaking, plugged in', *Boston Globe*, September 9: 87.

Katz, S. L. (2004) 'Travel distribution services: the new intermediary'. In B. Dickinson and A. Vladmia (eds) *The Complete 21st Century Travel and Hospitality Marketing Handbook*. Englewood Cliffs, NJ: Prentice Hall. pp. 479–491.

Kimes, S. E. (2004) 'Restaurant revenue management: implementation at chevys arrowhead', *Cornell Hotel and Restaurant Administration Quarterly*, 45(1): 52–67.

Klara, Robert (2005) 'The way you look', *Restaurant Business*, 104(13): 14–16.

Klassen, K. J. and Rohlender, T. R. (2001) 'Combining operations and marketing to manage capacity and demand in services', *The Service Industries Journal*, 21(2): 1–30.

Kotler, P., Bowen, J. and Makens, J. (2006) *Marketing for Hospitality and Tourism*. Upper Saddle River, NJ: Prentice Hall.

Lee, J. and Allaway, A. (2002) 'Effects of personal control on adoption of self-service technology innovations', *Journal of Services Marketing*, 16(6): 553–572.

Levitt, T. (1986) *Marketing Imagination*. New York: Free Press.

Liddle, A. J. (2004) 'Red run grill project lets diners manage food-ordering process', *Nation's Restaurant News*, 38(24): 103.

Lovelock, C. H. (2000) *Services Marketing*. 4th edn. Upper Saddle River, NJ: Prentice Hall.

Lovelock, C. H. and Wright, L. (1999) *Principles of Service Marketing and Management*. Upper Saddle River, NJ: Prentice Hall.

Lovelock, C. H. and Young, R. F. (1979) 'Look to consumers to increase productivity', *Harvard Business Review*, 57(3): 168–178.

Maister, D. H. (1985) 'The psychology of waiting lines'. In J. A. Czepiel, M. R. Solomon and C. F. Surprenant (eds) *The Service Encounter, Managing Employee/Customer Interaction in Service Businesses*. Massachusetts: D. C. Heath and Company. pp. 113–123.

Meuter, M. L., Bitner, M. J., Ostrom, A. L. and Brown, S. W. (2005) 'Choosing among alternative service delivery modes: an investigation of customer trial of self-service technologies', *Journal of Marketing*, 69(2): 61.

Meuter, M. L., Ostrom, A. L., Roundtree, R. I. and Bitner, M. J. (2000) 'Self-service technologies: understanding customer satisfaction with technology-based service encounters', *Journal of Marketing*, 64: 50–64.

Moschis, G., Curasi, C.F. and Bellenger, D. (2003) 'Restaurant-selection preferences of mature consumers', *Cornell Hotel and Restaurant Administration Quarterly*, 44(4): 51–57.

Murray, H. (1938) *Explorations in Personality*. New York: Oxford University Press.

Murray, K. B. (1991) 'A Test of Services Marketing Theory: Consumer Information Acquisition Activities.' *Journal of Marketing*, 55(1): 10–25.

Normann, R. (1984) *Service Management: Strategy and Leadership in Service Businesses*. New York: Wiley.

Parasuraman, A. (2000) 'Technology readiness index (TRI): a multiple-item scale to measure readiness to embrace new technologies', *Journal of Service Research*, 2(4): 307–320.

Sanchez, J. F. and Satir, A. (2005) 'Hotel yield management using different reservation modes', *International Journal of Contemporary Hospitality Management*, 17(2): 136–146.

Sasser, W. E. (1976) 'Match supply and demand in service industries', *Harvard Business Review*, 54(6): 131–140.

Schneider, B. and Bowen, D. (1993) 'The service organization: human resources management is crucial', *Organizational Dynamics*, Spring: 39–51.

Serlen, B. (2004, June 7) 'Hotels within web points'. Retrieved November 24, 2004 from World Wide Web: www.btnmag.com.

Shoemaker, S. (2003) 'The future of pricing in service', *Journal of Revenue and Pricing Management*, 2(3): 271–279.

Shostack, G. L. (1977) 'Breaking free from product marketing', *Journal of Marketing*, 4(2): 73–80.

Slywotzky, A. and Morrison, D. (2001) 'The rise of the active customer', *Marketing Management*, July/Aug: 22–26.

Sneath, J., Kennett, P. and Megehee, C. (2002) 'The self-versus full-service decision: gender-based differences in assessment of risk', *Journal of Targeting*, 11(1): 56–67.

Strauss, K. and Weinstein, J. (2003) 'Lesson in revenue management', *Hotels*, July: 22.

Taylor, S. (1994) 'Waiting for service: the relationship between delays and evaluations of service', *Journal of Marketing*, 58(2): 56–69.

Taylor, S. (1995) 'The effects of filled waiting time and service provider control over the delay in evaluations of service', *Journal of the Academy of Marketing Science*, 23(1): 38–45.

Thomas, Dan R. E. (1978) 'Strategy is different in service businesses', *Harvard Business Review*, 56(3): 158.

Vinod, B. (2004 Jul) 'Unlocking the value of revenue management in the hotel industry', *Journal of Revenue and Pricing Management*, 3(2): 178–190.

Vis, D. (1995) 'Best Western is latest hotel chain to market properties on internet', *Travel Weekly*, 54(8): 53.

Walsh, J. P. (2004) 'Employee training leads to better service', *Hotel and Motel Management*, January 12: 14.

Western, K. (1995) 'Internet inn: Best Western marketing on network', *Arizona Republic*, January 31: E1.

Xue, M. and Harker P. T. (2002) 'Customer efficiency: concept and its impact on e-business management', *Journal of Service Research*, 4(4): 253–267.

Zeithaml, V. A. (1981) 'How consumer evaluation processes differ between goods and services'. In J. H. Donnelly and W. R. George (eds) *Marketing of Services*. Chicago, IL: American Marketing Association Proceedings Series.

Zeithaml, V. A. and Bitner, M. J. (2003) *Services Marketing: Integrating Customer Focus Across the Firm*. 2nd edn. Boston: Irwin McGraw-Hill.

Service Quality and Hospitality Organizations

14

Yuksel Ekinci

INTRODUCTION

Despite long-term interest in the understanding of service quality, it remains an elusive concept due to a number of theoretical and methodological shortcomings in the hospitality literature. It is claimed that service quality and satisfaction are theoretically distinct, but the conceptual models fail to acknowledge this distinction in the form of the relationship (e.g. Fournier and Mick, 1999). Oliver (1980, 1997) argues that satisfaction moderates changes between two types of attitude formed at the pre-purchasing and post-purchasing point. Also satisfaction is a transaction-specific evaluation that quickly becomes part of the consumer's overall attitude to the service firm at the post-purchasing point. Therefore satisfaction is similar to the consumer's overall attitude to the service firm. In the quality literature, in contrast, Parasuraman et al. (1988) argue that service quality is universal and more enduring than satisfaction, and therefore is a better reflection of the consumer's overall attitude to the service firm.

Although the literature is awash with detailed arguments of this kind, the relationships between service quality, satisfaction, and the consumer's overall attitude to the firm have received little attention. Importantly, it is claimed that service quality is multidimensional, but there is little agreement on the nature and number of these dimensions. Furthermore, several alternative comparison standards for measuring service quality have been introduced, but they have often caused conceptual and measurement problems due to vague conceptualization and misinterpretations. As a result, these debates have generated confusion in researchers and practitioners alike in the hospitality industry.

The aim of this chapter is to review conceptual issues in the service quality literature. The discussion begins with the definitions and dimensions of service quality, and then examines the role of comparison standards for measuring service quality. The final part of this chapter introduces a conceptual framework to address the ongoing debate on the relationship between service quality and consumer satisfaction.

THE ISSUE OF SERVICE QUALITY DIMENSIONS

Definitions and models of service quality

It has been shown that service quality is an elusive concept that is difficult to define and measure. Accordingly, several alternative conceptualizations have been introduced from different perspectives. In early studies, quality is defined as conformance to specifications. If a product is good quality, its attributes should match with the predetermined standards. However, this simple definition is more suitable for goods than for services, because services are difficult to standardize and if certain standards are determined they are defined from the management's perspective rather than that of the consumer (Reeves and Bednar, 1994). To overcome this limitation, three definitions have been introduced to understand the quality of services from the consumer's perspective: (1) quality is excellence; (2) quality is value; and (3) quality is meeting or exceeding expectations.

The first definition of quality displays some inherent weaknesses, because the word 'excellent' is highly subjective and difficult to measure. Thus, tracking changes between two different assessments may be questionable. The second definition of quality implies that perceived quality is the same as perceived value. This approach introduced the concept of price into the definition of quality, but some scholars argue that perceived value and perceived quality are different (Bolton and Drew, 1991). Perceived value is a ratio between what customers get in exchange for what they sacrifice. The sacrifice components of the value are usually monetary costs, whereas the components of value are product benefits. Thus, quality may be the same as product benefits as consumers compare the quality of goods/services against the price paid in order to assess the perceived value. The final approach views quality in relation to whether performance meets or exceeds expectations. The expectations-performance based definition of quality is more generic and consumer-friendly than other definitions, because quality is defined from the consumer's point of view regardless of being specific to a hospitality unit or a consumer segment. Accordingly, quality is measured either by the perceived disconfirmation or by the inferred disconfirmation scale (commonly known as gap scoring) from the consumer's point of view. However, empirical studies show that disconfirmation-based measurements fail to produce a valid score to capture consumers' perception of service quality (Cronin and Taylor, 1992; Teas, 1994), hence, perceived quality is best captured by a performance-only scale. Findings from recent studies have suggested that service quality should be defined as the consumer's subjective assessment of the performance (Cronin and Taylor, 1992; Dabholkar et al., 2000).

Models of quality suggest that service quality is multidimensional. Acting on this assumption, researchers have investigated the number and nature of the service quality dimensions in a variety of service organizations, such as hotels, restaurants, and banks. However, the outcomes from this research are mixed. To date, there has been no clear agreement in service industries on the generic and specific dimensions of service quality. The lack of consensus can largely be attributed to the fact that service quality research has been dominated by two schools of thought – the North American and the Nordic European – that employ different assumptions.

The North American school initially introduced ten service quality dimensions, commonly known as the SERVQUAL dimensions (Parasuraman et al., 1985). Following their second study, the ten service quality dimensions were found to be highly correlated, and were therefore reduced to five dimensions: tangibles, assurance, reliability, empathy, and responsiveness (Parasuraman et al., 1988). However, applications of the five-dimensional SERVQUAL scale in various service firms showed that these dimensions were not distinct (e.g. Carmen, 1990; Parasuraman et al., 1991, 1994). These studies supported the view that service quality should be conceived as either three or four dimensional. To complicate matters even more, applications of the SERVQUAL model using content specific attributes produced new dimensions in different service organizations such as hotels and restaurants (Saleh and Ryan, 1991).

The Nordic European School (e.g. Lehtinen and Lehtinen, 1991) introduced two- and three-dimensional quality models. For example, Grönroos's (1984) model of service quality is based on two dimensions: (1) what consumers obtain from a service firm; and (2) how consumers obtain services. Although his model is simpler and more generic than the SERVQUAL model, it has been criticized for a number of reasons. First, the study sample used to develop this model was biased because it was specific to only North European nationals (Moore, 1994). Second, the Nordic European model used the perceived disconfirmation scale to measure service quality without offering any insight into what kind of consumer expectations should be measured. Although the perceived disconfirmation scale usually produces a better reliability score than the inferred disconfirmation scale when measuring service quality, the outcome of this measurement offers little information for improving the quality. For example, managers would like to know the level of service performance in relation to different types of expectations (e.g. whether performance is below the ideal or below the minimum tolerable expectation). This would enable managers to better diagnose the deficiency of quality in services, and to track changes over time. The final criticism of the Nordic European School in general is that its proponents have produced little empirical evidence to support the validity of their model.

SERVICE QUALITY MEASUREMENTS IN THE HOSPITALITY INDUSTRY

Although consumer behavior studies are heavily focused on the consumer's pre-purchase evaluation and choice behavior (Riley and Perogiannis, 1990; Callan, 1993), in recent years a large number of researchers have focused on consumers' post-purchase evaluation, in particular the measurement of service quality from different perspectives (Riley, 1984; Barrington and Olsen, 1987; Wilensky and Buttle, 1988; Brathwaite, 1992; Wood, 1994). Ingram (1996) notes that the research on service quality is debated energetically in the wider community, and therefore it deserves more attention in the context of hospitality. Oh and Parks (1997) state that, although some studies in the hospitality literature contribute to the understanding of consumer behavior, more rigorous theoretical and methodological treatments are needed, to improve the underdeveloped pedagogy of satisfaction and service quality research.

Lewis (1988) and Yesawitch (1987) comment that the hospitality industry has lagged behind many other industries in terms of the application of rigorous market research techniques, and has tended to rely too much on intuition and past practice to aid its marketing decisions and measurement of consumer satisfaction. Furthermore, Lewis and Pizam (1981) argue that most of the satisfaction surveys and analytical methods used in the industry are methodologically biased, and therefore produce inaccurate information. They recommend that if researchers intend to measure true components of satisfaction and service quality, multivariate techniques should be used.

The measurement of service quality in the hospitality industry varies according to the research methods employed. Research designs have varied along qualitative and quantitative paradigms. Thus, depending on the study objectives, some differences occur in the selection of research techniques. On the one hand, qualitative studies have aimed to identify the antecedents of service quality. On the other, quantitative studies have sought to measure service quality from different perspectives such as employees, managers, and consumers on the basis of the attributes outlined in the exploratory studies. In addition, some researchers have utilized existing scales to test different theories of service quality.

Early service quality scholars in the hospitality industry focused on the understanding and conceptualization of service quality. They therefore mainly used exploratory research methods. Lockwood (1994) applied the critical incident technique to record the success and failure of service quality in hospitality firms. Nightingale (1983) used repertory grid methods with hotel customers to identify the key success factors for hotel operations. He developed a service management model that was similar to the Nordic European models, in which perceived performance was compared against consumers' desired expectations. Nightingale (1983) also recognized the importance of management and employees' commitment to achieving a high quality of service. Oberoi and Hales (1990) attempted to develop a service quality scale in conference hotels through the application of qualitative and quantitative methodology. Martin (1995) investigated the usefulness of 'Importance/Performance Analysis' and the 'Service Gap Technique' for assessing service quality from management and employee perspectives. Several attempts have been made to develop new methods to use existing techniques for measuring and monitoring service quality in the hospitality industry. For example, Johns and Lee-Ross (1995) introduced the 'Profile Accumulation Technique', which generates qualitative and quantitative service profiles. Their approach made it possible to compare service quality between different hospitality operations, events and departments.

In a study of service quality in the UK roadside lodge sector, Senior (1992) developed 'Perceptual Blueprinting', which was a combination of three different methods: the principles of soft system methodology (e.g. repertory grid, interview, questionnaire), service blueprinting, and perceptual gap analysis. Perceptual blueprinting essentially provided a multi-perspective phenomenological systems tool for studying a service delivery system, as perceived by customers and employees. Senior (1992) recommended that the outcome of this survey would assist managers to direct their human resources and re-design the service delivery system, to achieve high quality service.

Saleh and Ryan (1991) used a form of Fishbein's multi-attribute attitude model to assess service performance and its importance. Barsky (1992) introduced the expectancy-disconfirmation paradigm into the hotel industry. He attempted to expand the perceived disconfirmation model by adding attribute-importance weighting. However, Oh and Parks (1997) commented that Barsky's method was deeply biased because there is no standard way of measuring the importance of a service attribute. Referring to similar deficiencies in the attitude literature, it is agreed that the inclusion of importance measurement into service quality measurement continues to remain a significant research issue.

To assess quality, numerous official and semi-official bodies operate restaurant and hotel rating schemes. These assessments are usually conducted by skilled inspectors based on a checklist of subjectively determined quality attributes. However, Callan (1993) questioned the validity of hotel classification schemes. Further, Callan and Lefebve (1997) compared and contrasted the effectiveness of these schemes from customers' and managers' points of view. They found that they were not consumer friendly and furthermore that consumers' choice of hotels was not influenced by these schemes. The findings of their study indicated that the existing criteria should be defined and assessed from the consumers' point of view. Brotherton (2004) explored the nature of critical success factors (CSFs) in UK budget hotel operations to ascertain the relevance and importance of a range of factors referred to as critical in the extant academic and trade literature. His results showed that budget hotel unit managers from the leading brands largely agree with the criticality of the factors stated in the literature.

Lewis (1987) argued that, rather than developing a new service quality model, the generic service quality models should be tested and if necessary, customized to a hospitality firm. Accordingly, the SERVQUAL model was tested and three new service quality gaps were identified in the hotel industry. A similar approach was adopted by Saleh and Ryan (1991) who utilized a content-specific scale, based on the SERVQUAL model, to measure service quality in hotels from consumers' and managers' perspective. Getty and Thompson (1994) examined the applicability of SERVQUAL in the hospitality industry. They found that only two of the SERVQUAL dimensions were generic for evaluation of service quality. Although Oh and Parks (1997) criticized this study due to using a student sample, Getty and Thompson's (1994) approach made an important contribution to the measurement of service quality in the hospitality industry, for a number of reasons. First, the assessment of service quality was defined from the consumer's point of view.

Second, reliability and validity of a service quality instrument was recognized as critical in measuring quality. Third, service quality was seen as a multidimensional construct that was consistent with the developing generic marketing literature on perceived quality.

Having visited the applications of service quality models in the hospitality literature, the following section reviews the recommended criteria for evaluation of service quality in the hospitality industry.

SERVICE QUALITY DIMENSIONS IN THE HOSPITALITY INDUSTRY

Zeithaml, Parasuraman and Berry (1990), argue that, regardless of the type of organization being studied, reliability is the most important dimension, followed by responsiveness, assurance, empathy and tangibles. However, Fick and Ritchie (1991) demonstrated that tangibles and assurance were the two most important service quality dimensions in hotels. Farsad and LeBruto (1994) reported that consumers were usually interested in the physical environment of hotels, the condition of rooms, the degree of caring, and the consistency of attention paid by employees. Nightingale (1983) suggested that the consumers' expectations of physical attributes were key components of service quality in the hospitality industry. Accordingly, he identified five service quality dimensions from the consumers' point of view: spaciousness, efficiency, guest control, ease of use, and availability.

Clow, Garretson and Kurtz (1994) identified that leisure travelers' selection of hotels was mainly based on security and brand name. Although it is difficult to suggest that the same attributes would be used to evaluate service quality after purchasing, security has always been recognized as an important factor before and after purchase evaluation by managers (Duncan, 1993; Wolf, 1993). Zeithaml (1981) stated that the physical aspects of services were utilized before and after purchase evaluation. Saleh and Ryan (1991) found that the esthetics of the interior and exterior significantly contributed to the perception of service quality in hotels. Lewis (1984a, 1984b) analyzed 66 hotel attributes to determine how business and leisure travelers selected hotels and evaluated quality of service after purchasing. This study suggested that the hotel attributes can be classified into 16 factors, based on travelers' post-purchase evaluation: overall feeling, food and beverage service, beverage quality, security, service quality, restaurant quality-price options, amenities and special conveniences, reputation and image, room-bath furnishings and their condition, quiet, building and esthetics, contemporary and modern conveniences, health facilities, VIP treatment and extra luxury, location, price and value, check in and check out process.

Choi and Chu (2001) examined the relative importance of various hotel factors in relation to travelers' overall satisfaction with their hotel stays in Hong Kong, and the likelihood of their returning to the same hotels on subsequent trips. They identified seven factors that were likely to influence customers' intention to return: staff service quality, room qualities, general amenities, business services, value, security, and internal direct dial facilities. Cadotte and Turgeon (1988) categorized the trends of compliments and complaints of hotel services into four categories: satisfiers, dissatisfiers, critical and neutrals. The most frequently mentioned attributes were (1) employee attitudes and knowledge, (2) availability of services, (3) cleanliness and quietness of hotel environment and (4) price. Nikolich and Sparks (1995) found that good communication skills were an essential element of encounter satisfaction.

Lockwood, Gummesson, Hubrecht and Senior (1992) investigated the key criteria of service quality in low-tariff roadside and budgets hotels. They found that value for money, cleanliness, and employee friendliness were the most frequently quoted dimensions of service quality from the consumer's point of view. They recommended that cleanliness of hotel and friendliness of employee should be seen as a generic dimension in the hospitality industry. Oberoi and Hales (1989) showed that, although the service quality attributes of conference hotels were closely related to the five SERVQUAL dimensions (tangibles, understanding, competence, responsiveness, reliability), they were grouped into two dimensions: tangibles and intangibles.

Haywood (1983) suggested that hotels should be designed according to the purpose of the stay. Therefore, hotel service quality should be measured based on Juran's (1979) 'fitness for use' principle, which has three dimensions: availability, reliability and maintainability. Availability is concerned with the timeliness of services and the convenience of location. Reliability refers to the security and the consistency of the delivery process and the maintainability dimension is the ability of providing services according to market needs.

Barsky and Labacgh (1992) commented that customer satisfaction had neither been integrated directly into the business plan nor accepted as a strategic dimension. Their study indicated that customer satisfaction was based on the following quality dimensions: employee attitude, location, room, price, facilities, reception, service, parking, food and beverage. Their findings were supported by similar studies of the hospitality industry (Atkinson, 1988; Knutson, 1988a).

Lewis and Owtram's (1986) study suggested that facilities, location and comfort were the most important contributors to travelers' overall satisfaction. The most successful hoteliers reported that their quality assurance reputation was based on courtesy of employees, physical environment, home-type atmosphere and consistency of service delivery (Carper, 1991). In a study investigating the pattern of frequent travelers' loyalty behavior, Knutson (1988b) identified five important components: cleanliness and convertibility of room, safety and security of establishment, location, friendliness and courtesy of employees and price.

Studies in the hospitality industry have also referred to the SERVQUAL model as a 'skeleton' for measuring service quality. In line with this trend, service quality researchers either adopted the SERVQUAL model (e.g. LODGSERV, LODGQUAL), or developed a content-specific scale for measuring service quality in the hospitality industry (Getty and Thompson, 1994). Lee and Hing (1995) assessed the applicability of SERVQUAL within the fine dining segment of the restaurant industry. Richard and Sundaram (1993) studied 'Gap 5' of service quality. They focused on the home-delivery pizza market and compared Domino against Pizza Hut. In their study, they used the original SERVQUAL scale to measure the difference between the expected and perceived service quality. Brotherton and Booth (1997) applied the SERVQUAL instrument as a vehicle to assess customer perceptions of service quality within a 4 star hotel leisure club environment. Their study suggested that the 'Tangibles' dimension was not a single entity but that leisure club customers view the tangible elements of the product as comprising two distinct dimensions; hygiene/cleanliness and resource appropriateness. Similarly, the same customers also appeared to differentiate between two aspects of the SERVQUAL 'reliability' dimension; reservations and facilities/opening hours. Again this suggested that the homogeneity of this SERVQUAL dimension may not be sustainable in this type of environment.

Ekinci et al. (2003) found that, when the SERVQUAL scale was applied to resort hotels, perceived quality could be captured by two global dimensions: tangibles and intangibles. Thus, the four SERVQUAL dimensions – assurance, reliability, empathy, and responsiveness – were loaded into a dimension called intangibles, while the tangibles dimension remained distinct. Another stream of research developed new scales that were specific to niche markets of the hospitality industry. For instance, Knutson et al. (1990) developed LODGSERV for measuring service quality in the lodging industry. Mackay and Crompton (1990) designed REQUAL for assessing service quality in recreation centers.

Stevens, Knutson and Patton (1995) introduced DINESERV for service quality measurement in restaurants.

In conclusion, the empirical studies have identified or confirmed some generic and unique service quality dimensions in the hospitality industry. In particular, the validity of the two-dimensional model – physical quality and interactive quality – offered by the Nordic school (e.g. Grönroos, 1984; Lehtinen and Lehtinen, 1991) was found to be more generic than the other service quality models (Mells et al., 1997; Ekinci, 2001). In their study, Brady and Cronin (2001) suggested that service quality should be measured with fewer dimensions than were suggested by the North American School. Further, service quality may be split into primary and secondary dimensions, according to two levels of abstraction. Accordingly, the primary dimensions are generic to all hospitality units, whereas the secondary dimensions are specific to a hospitality unit (a restaurant, a café, or a resort hotel) or consumer markets (leisure or business travelers). Figure 14.1 shows the application of this model to hospitality services.

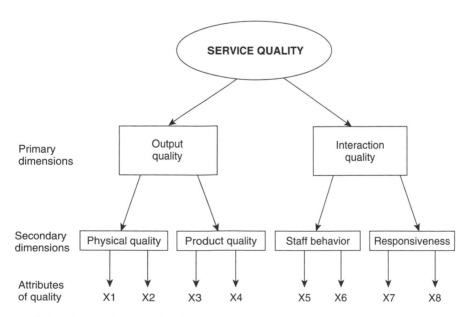

X1, X2 = Clean environment, beautiful décor
X3, X4 = Tasty food, comfortable bed
X4, X5 = Helpful employee, competent employee
X6, X7 = Prompt response, on time delivery

Figure 14.1 A service quality model for hospitality firms

As Figure 14.1 shows, service quality is multi-dimensional and multilevel. Attributes of service quality are grouped into primary and secondary dimensions. In the hospitality industry, the two primary service dimensions are *output quality* and *interactive quality*, because any evaluation of hospitality services concerns assessment of whether or not services meet consumers' goals and how they are received. Based on the complexity of the hospitality unit and its services the two higher-level dimensions can be split into several lower-level sub-dimensions, such as physical quality, product quality, staff behavior, and responsiveness. The dimension of output quality relates to product benefits such as physical quality, whereas the dimension of interaction quality relates to the service delivery process, and is concerned with the quality of the relationship between consumers and service employees. As suggested by Pizam (2004), hospitality and tourism is about the 'experience' that is mainly delivered by service providers. Nevertheless the characteristics of physical quality are evident in such attributes as the beauty of the décor, cleanliness of the environment, appearance of the tangible products, taste of the food, and the sufficiency and comfort of the facilities, whereas the elements of interactive quality are evident in such attributes as the competence and helpfulness of frontline employees, the reliability of Internet services, and on-time delivery of services.

THE ISSUE OF COMPARISON STANDARDS

In the service quality and customer satisfaction literature, several alternative comparison standards (e.g. expectations, equity, experience-based norm, and desires) have been introduced to explain and measure service quality. However, the use of comparison standards has often caused conceptual and methodological problems in empirical studies due to their vague conceptualization and misinterpretation. Measurement problems have occurred when a single comparison standard is expected to operate generically in measuring service quality across multiple service firms. Having recognized the deficiencies of comparison standards in service quality research, the discussion now focuses on the use of expectations, because

expectations is one of the most frequently cited comparison standards in past studies.

Expectations as a comparison standard

Despite the popularity of expectations as a comparison standard, Liljander and Strandvik (1993: 12) argue that a clear definition of expectations is often avoided.

> The term expectations in service quality literature has a different meaning for different authors, and the meaning is not always made clear to the reader, who reads into the word his/her own interpretation. Some research reports do not even mention how expectations were operationalized, thus making it difficult for the reader to draw any conclusion from the results.

LaTour and Peat (1979) argue that consumers may be satisfied even though the product does not meet customer expectations, particularly when the product is better than other products available in the market. Furthermore, additional confusion has occurred when expectations failed to predict service quality in different consumption situations.

The North American school of thought recognized the importance of expectations as a comparison standard. Parasuraman et al. (1988) initially stated that the 'should' type of expectations, which are based on consumers' belief probabilities of what the service should be, must be used to measure service quality. However, in their subsequent study Parasuraman et al. (1991) reported that the 'should' type of expectations was not relevant for measuring service quality, because, when the expectations score (E) was subtracted from the perception score (P), the gap score was usually negative. An increasing number of studies found that the expectations scores were inflated when wording of the expectations were presented in the form of a 'should' statement. Accordingly, Parasuraman et al. (1991: 3–4) changed the expectations statements from 'a company should have …' to 'an excellent company will have …' in order to capture the normative expectations. They stated that an excellent service was the 'ideal' standard, as used in the satisfaction literature. However, Teas (1994) identified a problem in the use of ideal point measurement when the evaluation of service consists of a finite vector attribute such as being 'overfriendly'. Therefore, the real

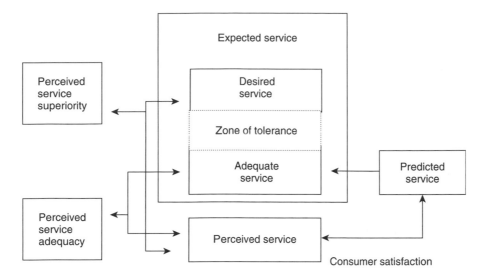

Adapted from Zeithaml et al. (1993)

Figure 14.2   The expectations model

perceived quality may be poor even though the mathematically computed gap score is positive.

Once again the North American scholars changed the meaning and measurement of expectations. Two types of expectations were introduced based on two levels of service performance: *desired service* and *adequate service* (Zeithaml et al., 1993). Figure 14.2 shows the Zeithaml et al. expectations model.

Desired service expectation is the level of service that consumers hope to receive. This is a mixture of what consumers believe the level of performance 'can be' and 'should be'. Therefore, when services are at the desired level, consumers are very satisfied with the quality of service. Adequate services are defined as the lowest level of performance that consumers will accept. Zeithaml et al. (1993) note that this performance level is the same as Miller's minimum tolerable expectations, and it corresponds to consumer satisfaction. An adequate service performance is achieved when the actual service performance is equal to the consumer's minimum tolerable expectations. The area between desired expectations and adequate expectations is called the zone of tolerance (ZOT).

However, Zeithaml et al.'s (1993) definition of desired service is mixed with Miller's (1977) definition of ideal service and deserved expectations. Although Zeithaml et al. argue that the definition of adequate service is

comparable to Miller's minimum tolerable service expectations, Miller (1977) states that this level of performance means merely better than nothing. He argues (1977: 79) that even if the performance is above the minimum tolerable level:

the consumer experiences dissatisfaction. He may attempt to remedy the situation and probably won't purchase that brand (continue patronizing that store) but will switch to another. If no alternative is available, he will probably continue to use the product as long as it 'satisfies' or fills a need.

The above statement suggests that consumers will barely tolerate a level of service performance that is equal to the minimum tolerable expectations. Consumers may tolerate when performance is equal to the *predictive* or *deserved* expectations. A ZOT may occur when the actual performance is below expected (predicted) expectations but above deserved expectations. According to Miller (1977) consumers may be disappointed by this level of performance. Thus, consumers may experience some weak dissatisfaction, but this feeling may better be described as 'unsatisfaction' rather than 'dissatisfaction'. On the contrary, if the actual performance is between minimum tolerable and deserved expectations, consumers will be dissatisfied. Hence, the bottom line for service satisfaction is when the performance is equal to the *deserved expectations*.

Due to the vague conceptualization of expectations as a comparison standard, most studies have used performance-only scales to measure service quality. Even though past studies have found that perceived performance is a reliable measure for service evaluation, the performance level against desired and deserved expectations would add value in deciding what the ideal level of service performance should be from the consumer's point of view. Therefore ideal and deserved expectations may be used as a *benchmark* by which to set the future performance level.

The other comparison standards

In addition to expectations, equity, values (desires), and experience-based norms are also used as a comparison standard in service quality research. Equity postulates that a person involved in a social (or exchange) relationship compares his perceived benefits and sacrifices with the other party's perceived benefits and sacrifices. Thus, equity is a bipolar concept similar to the expectancy-disconfirmation paradigm, but each seems to have different antecedents and consequences (Oliver and Swan, 1989; Oliver, 1997).

The theoretical models suggest that consumer values (desires, needs, or wants) affect human perception and evaluation of service quality (Rokeach, 1973). For instance, the means-end models imply that product attributes are linked to consumer values through perceived benefits (Gutman, 1982; Olshavsky and Spreng, 1989). Past experiences are also used as a comparison standard to evaluate services. Experiences can be accumulated from multiple sources and may eventually become a norm for assessing quality of service. Woodruff et al. (1983) state that the experience-based norm is different from expectations as a comparison standard because it corresponds to the favorite brand experience.

Past studies suggest that no single comparison standard can explain perceived quality and consumer satisfaction (Woodruff et al., 1983). Consumers seem to change the use of comparison standards from single to multiple according to different service firms and consumption situations. Furthermore, consumers seem to apply various combinations of comparison standards before and after purchasing services (Gardial et al., 1994). Therefore the question arose as to which comparison standard would

be the most dominant indicator of service quality and consumer satisfaction. Although past studies have addressed this issue they produced mixed results due to different formulations of comparison standards and poor interpretation of the relationship between service quality and consumer satisfaction.

Cadotte et al. (1987) showed that the best-brand norm and the product-type norm explained consumer satisfaction better than the focal-brand norm. Similarly, predictive expectation was found to be the least useful comparison standard for predicting consumer satisfaction across three service industries. Spreng, MacKenzie and Olshavsky (1996) illustrated that desired congruence had a significant impact on attribute satisfaction, information satisfaction, and overall satisfaction. Tse and Wilton (1988) found that expectations and best-brand norm had an impact on consumer satisfaction, whereas equity had no significant impact. Liljander (1995) showed that *deserved service* had a more significant influence on consumer satisfaction than the other alternatives, such as service excellence, best-brand norm, product-type norm, brand norm, adequate service, predicted service, and equity. Spreng et al. (1996) argue that both expectations and desired congruence had a positive impact on consumer satisfaction. Ekinci (2003) found that hospitality consumers used multiple comparison standards for the evaluation of service quality and satisfaction. In particular, predictive expectations, deserved expectations, desires congruence, and experience-based norm have positive impacts on service quality and consumer satisfaction.

RELATIONSHIP BETWEEN SERVICE QUALITY AND CONSUMER SATISFACTION

There is an ongoing debate as to whether service quality is an antecedent or consequence of consumer satisfaction (e.g. Ekinci and Riley, 1998; Dabholkar et al., 2000). Based on the outcomes of recent conceptual and empirical studies, the direction of the relationship between the two concepts should be from service quality to consumer satisfaction. For example, Oliver (1993) suggests that overall service quality is an antecedent of consumer satisfaction and that both constructs should be positively associated

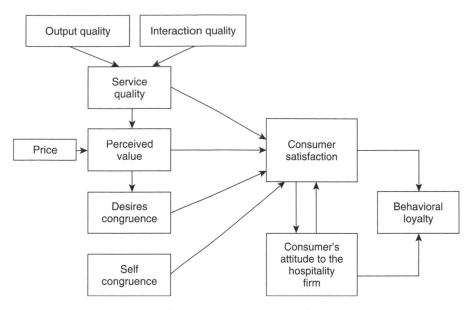

Figure 14.3   A consumer satisfaction model for hospitality firms

with each other. Dabholkar et al. (2000) found support for this notion in non-commercial organizations. In order to address this issue, Figure 14.3 displays a model to outline the relationships between the two concepts for the evaluation of hospitality services.

This model was developed by integrating previous research on self-congruence (Sirgy, 1982), service quality (Brady and Cronin, 2001; Ekinci, 2004), and consumer satisfaction (Oliver, 1997). Accordingly, the model suggests that examination of the relationship between satisfaction and service quality captures the functional aspects of service consumption, whereas examination of the relationship between self-congruence and satisfaction captures the symbolic aspects of service consumption. In line with Dabholkar et al. (2000), the model in Figure 14.3 posits that consumer satisfaction mediates the impact of service quality, desires congruence, and self-congruence on behavioral loyalty, such as the intention to recommend and return. In all cases, the variables are seen as antecedents of consumer satisfaction and they will have a positive impact on consumer satisfaction. Based on the research of Wirtz and Matilla (2001), two paths are specified from the dimensions of service quality to desires congruence that serves as a comparison standard in the hospitality industry.

Moreover, it is important to note that the model proposes a bidirectional relationship between the consumer's overall attitude to the hospitality firm and consumer satisfaction. The consumer's overall attitude to the hospitality service firm is a global image of the entire service organization whereas overall satisfaction is a summary evaluation of the entire service experience for this single experience. Accordingly, the model extends Oliver's (1980) research regarding the theoretical relationship between these two concepts. The recognition of these paths is important, because incorporating the consumer's overall attitude to the hospitality firm into existing models of satisfaction explains one of the logical inconsistencies of the disconfirmation paradigm reported by early scholars (e.g. LaTour and Peat, 1979). Thus the model explains why customers continue to patronize the same service firm when the service performance is below their expectations. By implication, the model posits that satisfaction is not the only indicator of intention to recommend and return behavior. Satisfaction and the consumer's overall attitude to the hospitality firm will have a positive impact on behavioral loyalty.

CONCLUSIONS

A realistic view of the literature dealing with service quality measurement seems to be that, although considerable progress has been made in both the conceptualization and measurement of service quality, some fundamental problems remain. The present study does not change that situation, but it makes a contribution by outlining some of the ongoing debates from the perspective of two schools of thought. The North American School is largely dependent on empirical studies but these studies have produced mixed results. The Nordic European School is mainly theoretical, and has therefore failed to support the validity of its models with empirical studies.

The service quality literature asserts that perceived quality is generic, but empirical testing of the service quality models has produced inconsistent results regarding the validity of the generic dimensions in the hospitality industry. To date, studies have failed to determine the exact nature and number of dimensions. The notions of generic and specific dimensions have important implications for measuring and managing service quality. Basically, generic dimensions help to make comparative analyses across hospitality units. Accordingly, if a dimension is generic it should emerge in a specific hospitality unit. By implication, if physical quality is a generic dimension, it will have an impact on the evaluation of service quality in every hospitality firm. If safety is a secondary and sub-dimension, it may have an impact on the evaluation of service quality in a resort hotel, but not in a fast food restaurant. Thus, a situation-specific dimension can be used as a strategic tool for product positioning in niche hospitality markets (Shocker and Srinivasan, 1979). In summary, primary dimensions are generic and necessary to maintain quality of service across hospitality units, whereas secondary dimensions are valuable for gaining competitive advantage in segmented markets.

In line with the above statement, it is possible to speculate about the SERVQUAL scale and the model's dimensions. The SERVQUAL dimensions may be specific only to a retail sector including specific firms, such as banks and supermarkets: it may therefore not be possible to replicate them in studies of the hospitality industry. A number of researches have demonstrated that the two-dimensional or three-dimensional structure may be more suitable for assessing quality of the hospitality services (Ekinci et al., 1998). In this respect, the service quality models recommended by the Nordic European School of thought (e.g. Grönroos's

model) seems to be more generic than the SERVQUAL model, and therefore may be more suitable for measuring service quality in the hospitality industry.

The issue of comparison standards

It is suggested that the concept of expectations is one of the most important variables for the evaluation of services (Cronin and Taylor, 1992). However, it would be more meaningful to measure consumer expectations after purchasing in order to locate and track the level of service performance. Cote et al. (1989: 504) argue that *current expectations* rather than *prior expectations* should be measured after purchasing because:

> current expectations should be more closely related to current needs and should also account for satisfying decisions ... Our conception of current expectations is most similar to product norm expectations. They are expectations about brands in the current evoked set. Current expectations differ from prior expectations in the timing of the measurement. Rather than assessing expectations at the time of purchase, current expectations assess product norm expectations now (at the time the respondent answers the question).

Predictive and deserved expectations should be seen as thresholds for locating and controlling quality of service and satisfaction from the consumer point of view at the post-purchasing point. Shocker and Srinivasan (1979: 177) argue that 'such a framework provides the analyst with a systematic way of tracking parameter values over time and relating such changes to developments in the marketplace'. However, if desired expectation is employed to track changes in service quality, the measurement of the ideal point can be problematic, depending on whether the service evaluation is based on finite or infinite vector attributes. Thus alternative methods for measuring ideal service performance should be employed (Teas, 1994). For example, Spreng et al. (1996) introduced desires congruence as an alternative method.

In addition to the above conceptual and methodological ramifications, future studies should explore other issues surrounding the use of comparison standards in the hospitality industry. What is the relationship between different types of expectations and other comparison standards? What type of comparison standard is more relevant to service quality and consumer satisfaction? Is there a concept such as ZOT for evaluation of hospitality services? If so, what are the antecedents of the ZOT? Does the ZOT vary according to hospitality units or consumer segments? What is the effect of the ZOT on consumers' post-purchase evaluation (e.g. intention to recommend and intention to visit again)? Can service quality and consumer satisfaction be distinguished by using the ZOT?

The relationship between service quality and consumer satisfaction

One of the conceptual differences proposed between models is that service quality is multidimensional whereas consumer satisfaction is unidimensional. Also, studies in both branches of the literature argue that these two constructs are similar to the consumer's overall attitude to a service firm, but no clear insight is provided into the relationship between service quality, consumer satisfaction and the consumer's overall attitude to the service firm. Consumer satisfaction should be more related to the consumer's overall attitude to the service firm (Oliver, 1980) and service quality should be seen as one of the antecedents of consumer satisfaction. Evaluation of service quality may be related to consumers' goals (Juran, 1979), and specific to the service delivery process. Furthermore both constructs should be seen as multidimensional.

Current satisfaction studies seem to measure satisfaction largely by focusing on service quality dimensions in the hospitality industry. Based on the proposed model, this chapter suggests that such practice is likely to produce inadequate measurement of satisfaction. Due to this deficiency, current satisfaction surveys have already lost their credibility, because they do not contain sufficient potential to improve consumer satisfaction. The proposed model acknowledges the importance of service quality as one of the antecedents of consumer satisfaction. Thus consumer satisfaction studies should take into account other constructs for its measurement. Accordingly, the dimensions of service quality, perceived value, self-congruence, desires congruence and the consumer's overall attitude to the hospitality firm should be taken into account, in order to draw a true picture of consumer satisfaction. This would provide better diagnostic power for managing satisfaction and consumer loyalty in the hospitality industry.

Furthermore, future studies should explore the following issues regarding modeling of service quality and consumer satisfaction in the hospitality industry. What is the relationship between service quality, consumer satisfaction and the consumer's overall attitude to the hospitality firm? How do they influence the consumers' intention to recommend and return? What is the contribution of perceived value to predict intention to return behavior? What is the impact of interaction quality on consumer satisfaction at the service encounter? How do technology and empowerment of service personal affect perceived service quality and consumer satisfaction? Is evaluation of consumer satisfaction emotional, cognitive or both? Does quality of service have a positive impact on the hospitality firms' financial performance?

REFERENCES

Atkinson, A. (1988) 'Answering the eternal question: what does the customer want?', *The Cornell Hotel and Restaurant Administration Quarterly*, 30(2): 12–14.

Barrington, M. N. and Olson, M. D. (1987) 'The concept of service in the hospitality industry', *International Journal of Hospitality Management*, 6(3): 131–138.

Barsky, J. D. (1992) 'Customer satisfaction in the hotel industry: meaning and measurement', *Hospitality Research Journal*, 16(1): 51–73.

Barsky, J. D. and Labacgh, R. (1992) 'A strategy for customer satisfaction', *The Cornell Hotel and Restaurant Administration Quarterly*, 32(October): 32–40.

Bolton, R. N. and Drew, J. H. (1991) 'A multistage model of customers' assessment of service and value', *Journal of Consumer Research*, 17(March): 375–384.

Brady, M. K. and Cronin, J. J. Jr. (2001) 'Some new thoughts on conceptualizing perceived service quality: a hierarchical approach', *Journal of Marketing*, 65(July): 34–39.

Brathwaite, R. (1992) 'Value-chain assessment of the travel experience', *The Cornell Hotel and Restaurant Administration Quarterly*, 32(October): 41–49.

Brotherton, B. (2004) 'Critical success factors in UK budget hotel operations', *International Journal of Operations and Production Management*, 24(9): 944–969.

Brotherton, B. and Booth, W. (1997) 'An application of SERVQUAL to a hotel leisure club environment', *The Proceedings of the EuroCHRIE/IAHMS Autumn*

Conference, ISBN: 086-339-762 X, Sheffield Hallam University, pp. 117–121.

Cadotte, E. R. and Turgeon, U. (1988) 'Dissatisfiers and satisfiers suggestions for consumer complaints and compliments', *Journal of Consumer Satisfaction, Dissatisfaction and Complaining Behavior*, 1: 74–79.

Cadotte, E. R., Woodruff, R. B. and Jenkins, R. L. (1987) 'Expectations and norms in models of consumer satisfaction', *Journal of Marketing Research*, 24: 305–314.

Callan, R. (1993) 'An appraisal of UK hotel quality grading schemes', *International Journal of Contemporary Hospitality Management*, 5(5): 10–18.

Callan, R. and Lefebve, C. (1997) 'Classification and grading of UK lodges: do they adequate to managers' and customers' perception?', *Tourism Management*, 18(7): 417–424.

Carmen, J. M. (1990) 'Consumer perceptions of service quality: an assessment of the SERVQUAL dimensions', *Journal of Retailing*, 66(1): 33–55.

Carper, J. (1991) 'Hoteliers of the world: southern hospitality the right way', *Hotels*, 25(11): 44–45.

Choi, T. Y. and Chu, R. (2001) 'Determinants of hotel guests' satisfaction and repeat patronage in the Hong Kong hotel industry', *International Journal of Hospitality Management*, 20: 277–297.

Clow, K. E., Garretson, J. A. and Kurtz, D. L. (1994) 'An exploratory study into the purchase decision process used by leisure travelers in hotel selection', *Journal of Hospitality and Leisure Marketing*, 2(4): 53–72.

Cote, J. A., Foxman, E. R. and Cutler, B. D. (1989) 'Selecting an appropriate standard of comparison for pros-purchase evaluation', *Advances in Consumer Research*, 16: 502–506.

Cronin, J. J. Jr. and Taylor, S. A. (1992) 'Measuring service quality: a re-examination and extension', *Journal of Marketing*, 56(July): 55–68.

Dabholkar, P. A., Shepherd, D. A. and Thorpe, D. I. (2000) 'A comprehensive framework for service quality: an investigation of critical conceptual and measurement issues through a longitudinal study', *Journal of Retailing*, 76(2): 139–173.

Duncan, V. (1993) 'Fewer chocolates, greater safety', *Lodging Hospitality*, 49(12): 12–13.

Ekinci, Y. (2001) 'The validation of the generic service quality dimensions: an alternative approach', *Journal of Retailing and Consumer Services*, 8(6): 311–324.

Ekinci, Y. (2003) 'Which comparison standard should be used for service quality and customer satisfaction?', *Journal of Quality Assurance in Hospitality and Tourism*, 4(3/4): 61–66.

Ekinci, Y. (2004) 'An investigation of the determinants of customer satisfaction', *Tourism Analysis*, 8(2–4): 197–203.

Ekinci, Y. and Riley, M. (1998) 'A critique of the issues and theoretical assumptions in measuring service quality in the lodging industry: time to move the goal-posts?', *International Journal of Hospitality Management*, 17: 349–362.

Ekinci, Y., Prokopaki, K. and Cobanoglu, C. (2003) 'Service quality in Cretan accommodations: marketing strategies for the UK Holiday Market', *International Journal of Hospitality Management*, 22(1): 47–66.

Ekinci, Y., Riley, M. and Fife-Shaw, C. (1998) 'Which school of thought: the dimensions of resort hotel quality', *The International Journal of Contemporary Hospitality Management*, 10(2/3): 63–68.

Farsad, B. and LeBurto, S. (1994) 'Managing quality in the hospitality industry', *Hospitality Tourism Education*, 6(2): 49–42.

Fick, G. R. and Ritchie, J. R. B. (1991) 'Measuring service quality in the travel and tourism industry', *Journal of Travel Research*, 30(2): 2–9.

Fournier, S. and Mick, D. G. (1999) 'Rediscovering satisfaction', *Journal of Marketing*, 63: 5–23.

Gardial, S. F., Clemons, D. S., Woodruff, R. B., Schumann, D. W. and Burns, M. J. (1994) 'Comparing consumers' recall of prepurchase and postpurchase product evaluation experiences', *Journal of Consumer Research*, 20, 548–560.

Getty, J. M. and Thompson, K. N. (1994) 'A procedure for scaling perceptions of lodging quality', *Hospitality Research Journal*, 18(2): 75–96.

Grönroos, C. (1984) 'A service quality model and its marketing implications', *European Journal of Marketing*, 18: 36–44.

Gutman, J. (1982) 'A means-end chain model based on consumer categorization process', *Journal of Marketing*, 46 (2): 60–72.

Haywood, K. M. (1983) 'Assessing the quality of hospitality services', *International Journal of Hospitality Management*, 2(4): 165–177.

Ingram, H. (1996) 'Clusters and gaps in hospitality and tourism academic research', *International Journal of Contemporary Hospitality Management*, 8(7): 91–95.

Johns, N. and Lee-Ross, D. (1995) 'Profile accumulation: a quality assessment technique for hospitality SMSs'. In R. Teare and C. Armistead (eds) *Service Management: New Directions and Perspectives*. London: Cassell.

Juran, J. M. (1979) *Quality Control Handbook*, 3rd. edn. New York: McGraw-Hill.

Knutson, B. (1988a) 'Ten laws of customer satisfaction', *The Cornell Hotel and Restaurant Administration Quarterly*, 29(3), 14–17.

Knutson, B. (1988b) 'Frequent travelers: making them happy and bringing them back', *The Cornell Hotel and Restaurant Administration Quarterly*, 29(1): 82–87.

Knutson, B., Stevens, P., Wullaert, C. and Yokoyoma, F. (1990) 'LODGSERV: a service quality index for the lodging industry', *Hospitality Research Journal* (Special Issue, Annual CHRIE Conference Proceeding), 14(2): 227–284.

LaTour, S. A. and Peat, N. C. (1979) 'Conceptual and methodological issues in consumer satisfaction research'. In L. W. William (ed.), *Advances In Consumer Research*, Ann Arbor, MI: Association for Consumer Research, pp. 431–437.

Lee Y. L. and Hing, N. (1995) 'Measuring quality in restaurant operations: an application of the SERVQUAL instrument', *International Journal of Hospitality Management*, 14(3/4): 293–310.

Lehtinen, U. and Lehtinen, J. R. (1991) 'Two approaches to service quality dimensions', *The Service Industries Journal*, 11(3): 287–303.

Lewis, B. R. and Owtram, M. (1986) 'Customer satisfaction with the package holidays'. In B. Moores (ed.), *Are They Being Served?*. Oxford: Philip Allan Publisher Limited. pp. 201–213.

Lewis, R. C. (1984a) 'Theoretical and practical considerations in research design', *The Cornell Hotel and Restaurant Administration Quarterly*, 25(1): 25–35.

Lewis, R. C. (1984b) 'Isolating differences in hotel attributes', *The Cornell Hotel and Restaurant Administration Quarterly*, 25(3): 64–77.

Lewis, R. C. (1987) 'The measurement of gaps in the quality of hotel services', *International Hospitality Management*, 6(2): 83–88.

Lewis, R. C. (1988) 'Uses and abuses of hospitality research', *The Cornell Hotel and Restaurant Administration Quarterly*, 29 (November): 11–12.

Lewis, R. C. and Pizam A. (1981) 'Guest survey: a missed opportunity', *The Cornell Hotel and Restaurant Administration Quarterly*, 22(3): 37–44.

Liljander, V. (1995) 'Introducing deserved service and equity into service quality models'. In M. Kleinaltenkamp (ed.), *Dienstleistungsmarketing: Konzeptionen und Anwendungen*, Wiesbadeden (Germany): Betriebswirstshaftlicher Verlag. pp. 143–168.

Liljander, V. and Strandvik, T. (1993) 'Different comparison standard as determinants of service quality', *Journal of Consumer Satisfaction and Dissatisfaction*, 6: 118–132.

Lockwood, A. (1994) 'Using service incidents to identify quality improvement points', *International Journal of Contemporary Hospitality Management*, 6(1/2): 75–80.

Lockwood, A., Gummesson, A., Hubrecht, J. and Senior, M. (1992) 'Developing and maintaining a strategy for service quality'. In R. Teare and M. Olsen (eds) *International Hospitality Management Corporate Strategy in Practice*. London: Pitman Pub., pp. 312–339.

MacKay, K. and Crompton, J. (1990) 'Measuring the quality of recreation services', *Journal of Park Recreation Administration*, 8(3): 47–56.

Martin, D. W. (1995) 'An importance/performance analysis of service providers' perception of service quality service in the hotel industry', *Journal of Hospitality and Leisure Marketing*, 3(1): 5–17.

Mells, G., Boshoff, C. and Deon, N. (1997) 'The dimensions of service quality: the original European perspective revisited', *The Service Industries Journal*, 17(1): 173–189.

Miller, J. A. (1977) 'Studying satisfaction: modifying models, eliciting expectations, posing problems and making meaningful measurements'. In H. K. Hunt (ed.), *Conceptualizations and Measurement of Consumer Satisfaction and Dissatisfaction*. Bloomington: School of Business, Indiana University. pp. 72–91.

Moore, S. A. (1994). *Perceptions of Service Quality: An Empirical Analysis in the Freight Sector*. Unpublished PhD thesis, University of Wales.

Nightingale, M. (1983) *Determination and Control of Quality Standards in Hospitality Services*, Unpublished MPhil. Thesis, Guildford UK: University of Surrey.

Nikolich, M. A. and Sparks, B. A. (1995) 'The hospitality service encounter: the role of communication', *The Hospitality Research Journal*, 19(2): 43–56.

Oberoi, U. and Hales, C. (1990) 'Assessing the quality of the conference hotel service product: towards an empirically based model', *Service Industries Journal*, 10(4): 700–721.

Oh, H. and Parks, S. (1997) 'Customer satisfaction and service quality: critical review of the literature and research implications for the hotel industry', *Hospitality Research Journal*, 20(3): 35–64.

Oliver, R. L. (1980) 'A cognitive model of the antecedents and consequences of satisfaction decisions', *Journal of Marketing Research*, 17(November): 460–469.

Oliver, R. L. (1993) 'A conceptual model of service quality and service satisfaction: compatible goals, different concepts', *Advances in Service Marketing and Management*, 2: 65–85.

Oliver, R. L. (1997) *Satisfaction: A Behavioral Perspective on The Consumer*. London: McGraw-Hill Company.

Oliver, R. L. and Swan, J. E. (1989) 'Equity and disconfirmation perceptions as influences on merchant and product satisfaction', *Journal of Consumer Research*, 16 (December): 372–383.

Olshavsky, R. W. and Spreng, R. A. (1989) 'A "desires as standard" model of consumer satisfaction', *Journal of Consumer Satisfaction, Dissatisfaction and Complaining Behavior*, 2: 49–54.

Parasuraman, A., Berry, L. L. and Zeithaml, V. A. (1991) 'Refinement and reassessment of the SERVQUAL scale', *Journal of Retailing*, 67: 421–450.

Parasuraman, A., Zeithaml, V. A. and Berry, L. L. (1985) 'A conceptual model of service quality and its implications for future research', *Journal of Marketing*, 49(3): 41–50.

Parasuraman, A., Zeithaml, V.A. and Berry, L. L. (1988) 'SERVQUAL a multiple-item scale for measuring consumer perception of service quality', *Journal of Retailing*, 64, 13–40.

Parasuraman, A., Zeithaml, V. A. and Berry, L. L. (1994) 'Alternative scales for measuring service quality: a comparative assessment based on psychometric and diagnostic criteria', *Journal of Retailing*, 70(3): 193–199.

Pizam, A. (2004) 'What happened to the "quality of service revolution?"', *International Journal of Hospitality Management*, 23: 201–202.

Reeves, C. A. and Bednar, D. A. (1994) 'Defining quality: alternatives and implications', *Academy of Management Review*, 19(3): 419–445.

Richard, M. and Sundaram, D. (1993) 'Lodging choice intentions: a casual modeling approach', *Journal of Hospitality and Leisure Marketing*, 1(4): 81–98.

Riley, M. (1984) 'Hotels and group identity', *International Journal of Tourism Management*, 5(2): 102–109.

Riley, M. and Perogiannis, N. (1990) 'The influence of hotel attributes on the selection of a conference venue', *International Journal of Contemporary Hospitality Management*, 2(1): 17–22.

Rokeach, M. (1973) *The Nature of Human Values*. New York: The Free Press.

Saleh, F. and Ryan, C. (1991) 'Utilizing the SERVQUAL model: an analysis of service quality', *The Service Industries Journal*, 11(3): 324–345.

Senior, M. C. (1992) *Managing Service Quality: A Study in The UK Roadside Lodge Sector*, Unpublished PhD thesis. Dorset Institute: University of Bournemouth.

Shocker, A. D. and Srinivasan, V. (1979) 'Multiattribute approaches for product concept evaluation and generation: a critical review', *Journal of Marketing Research*, 16: 159–180.

Sirgy, M. J. (1982) 'Self-concept in consumer behavior: a critical review', *Journal of Consumer Research*, 9(3): 287–300.

Spreng R. A., MacKenzie, S. B. and Olshavsky, R. W. (1996) 'A re-examination of the determinants of consumer satisfaction', *Journal of Marketing*, 60(2): 15–32.

Stevens, P., Knutson, B. and Patton, M. (1995) 'DINESERV: a tool for measuring service quality in restaurants', *The Cornell Hotel and Restaurant Administration Quarterly*, 35(April): 56–60.

Teas, R. K. (1994) 'Expectations as a comparison standard in measuring service quality', *Journal of Marketing*, 58 (1): 132–139.

Tse, D. K. and Wilton, P. C. (1988) 'Models of consumer satisfaction formation: an extension', *Journal of Marketing Research*, 25(May): 204–212.

Wilensky, L. and Buttle, F. (1988) 'A multivariate analysis of hotel benefit bundles and choice trade-offs', *International Journal of Hospitality Management*, 7(1): 29–41.

Wirtz, J. and Matilla, A. (2001) 'Exploring the role of alternative perceived performance measures and needs-congruency in the consumer satisfaction process', *Journal of Consumer Psychology* 11(3): 181–192.

Wolf, C. (1993) 'Setting security', *Lodging Hospitality*, 49(3): 30–32.

Wood, R. C. (1994) 'Hotel culture and social control', *Annals of Tourism Research*, 21(1), 65–80.

Woodruff, R. B., Cadotte, E. R. and Jenkins, R. L. (1983) 'Modeling consumer satisfaction processes using experiences-based norms', *Journal of Marketing Research*, 20: 296–304.

Woodruff, R. B., Clemons, S. D., Schumann, D. W., Gardial, S. F. and Burns, M.J. (1991) 'The standard issue in cs/d research: a historical perspective', *Journal of Consumer Satisfaction, Dissatisfaction and Complaining Behavior*, 4: 103–109.

Yesawitch, P. C. (1987) 'Hospitality marketing for the 90's: effective marketing research', *The Cornell Hotel and Restaurant Administration Quarterly*, 28(May): 49–57.

Zeithaml, V. A. (1981) 'How consumer evaluation processes differ between goods and services'. In J. H. Donnelly and W. R. George (eds) *Marketing Services*. Chicago, IL: American Marketing Association, pp. 186–190.

Zeithaml, V. A., Berry, L. L. and Parasuraman, A. (1993) 'The nature and determinants of consumer expectations of service', *Journal of Academy of Marketing Science*, 24(1): 1–12.

Zeithaml, V. A., Parasuraman, A. and Berry, L. L. (1990) *Delivering Quality Service: Balancing Customer Perceptions and Expectations*. New York: The Free Press.

Information Technology Strategy in the Hospitality Industry

15

Dan Connolly and Mark G. Haley

INTRODUCTION AND OVERVIEW

This chapter looks at the growing strategic importance of technology, specifically information technology (IT) in the hospitality industry. Over the past four decades, the hospitality industry has undergone dramatic changes as a result of technology innovations and developments. One could easily argue that the business has become much more complex, sophisticated, and cost-intensive with the evolution and adoption of technology throughout the industry. Today, it is safe to say that technology and the business are inseparable. Business and technology decisions are inter-related with a co-dependency such that no business or technology-related decision can be made without looking at the complete picture and the long-term implications for the rest of the organization. Consequently, hospitality leaders must have a firm grasp on the competitive dynamics and the critical success factors of the business as well as the roles, capabilities, and limitations of technology. In short, they must be both business- and technology-savvy professionals to succeed.

Since this chapter focuses on IT, it is important to set the stage with a definition of what IT, sometimes referred to as ICT (information and communications technology or technologies) or as IS (information systems), actually is. As Piccoli (2004) notes, IT introduces a variety of acronyms and technical terms to create its own language, which the technical laity find confusing and overwhelming. Unfortunately, the literature does not provide a consensual definition. Piccoli (2004) suggests looking at the entire socio-technical system, which includes four interdependent components: people, processes, computers (hardware, software, and communications networks), and organizational structure.

Weill (1991) and Weill and Olson (1989) suggest using as broad a definition as possible to encompass the many important facets one must consider when thinking about IT. These include people, training, documentation, operating procedures, policies, consulting services, outsourcing, hardware, software, and communications networks. Thus, in this chapter, references to IT will take on a broad meaning to encompass all of its many facets and far-reaching effects.

AN INDUSTRY SLOW TO EMBRACE THE STRATEGIC VALUE OF TECHNOLOGY

To better understand the present state of IT in the hospitality industry, it is helpful to have some historical knowledge of how managerial thinking and IT have evolved. This background provides a context to help explain current mindsets, technology usage, and adoption issues within the hospitality industry today, especially since some of the technologies (often referred to as legacy systems) selected long ago are still in use today (for example, the central reservation systems used by InterContinental Hotels and Resorts and Marriott International are based on airline reservation systems with their cores built on IBM's Transaction Processing Facility, a programming environment popular in the 1960s for processing high volumes of transactions). It is important to note, though, that with time, better training, more advanced technologies, greater experience, increased comfort with technology, more success stories, and the rise of the Internet and electronic commerce, the hospitality industry has made great strides in terms of technology advancement. The good news is that IT is rising to the forefront, gaining respect, and becoming much more strategic than it has been in the past. Nonetheless, the historical perspective discussed below helps to explain some of the factors that have hindered technology adoption and why the industry is not as advanced technically as it could be, particularly when compared to other industries such as banking, financial services, insurance, airlines, and retail.

Over three decades ago, Diehl (1973) noted that the hospitality industry was one of the last major industries to recognize the need for, and use of, computers in its operations. To a large extent, the industry has been playing catch-up ever since, as suggested by industry comparisons of IT spending as a percentage of revenue and per employee (Connolly and Ivey, 2004). To some, the introduction of new technology is welcomed with open arms because of its many promises. These individuals are grateful for the new tools that enable them to be more productive and mobile because they create new ways to transact business and stay abreast of all facets of their businesses. Yet, to others, the introduction of IT is not so welcome because it is perceived as a threat, an infringement on personal space or privacy, or a time for change and uncertainty. To these individuals, the thought of having to learn something as complex as a computer application is overwhelming, frustrating, and a sign that they are not equipped with the skills needed for the future. The information generated by computers can be overpowering at times. People often find themselves being slaves to their computers (namely electronic mail) and inundated with reports that they must try to interpret. There is a sense that they cannot keep up and will always be behind in their work. They need more hours in the work day and more resources to accomplish their work.

In 1985, Michael Porter recognized the potential and value of IT for driving competitive positioning and wrote that technological change was among the most prominent forces driving competition (Porter, 1985). However, it took more than a decade for this same realization to become apparent in the hospitality industry (Cline and Rach, 1996; Olsen, 1996; Cline and Blatt, 1998; Hensdill, 1998). Despite this many hospitality companies still lack a strategic IT focus and should take note of those who have adopted this focus. For example, companies like Harrah's and Ritz-Carlton are aggressively exploiting IT's capabilities

to better know and understand their guests so that they can then personalize each and every interaction (Piccoli, 2004). Wyndham's ByRequest guest profile system, managed by guests through the company's web site (www.wyndham.com), provides another illustrative example of how technology is being used to enable guest services and create wonderful, memorable guest experiences. In yet another example, luxury provider Mandarin Oriental differentiates its product and service offerings by offering a host of in-room digital amenities to enhance its guests' experiences and entertainment (i.e. music, video, and gaming) pleasure during their stays. These are just a few of many examples of innovative technology usage throughout the hotel industry. As these examples demonstrate, IT can and does contribute positively to a firm's strategic objectives, generate value, and lead to competitive advantage. Each moment of truth (Carlzon, 1987) is exceptional, allowing these companies to develop unprecedented loyalty with their guests, which leads to more profitable customers, positive word-of-mouth, and lasting competitive advantage.

Hospitality education, research, and practice have historically placed great emphasis on what can be termed the craft aspects of the business; namely, the art of exemplary guest service, servitude, or personal ministry (Levitt, 1972). For this reason, hospitality practitioners tended to avoid technology advances for fear of de-personalizing services and compromising the value of guest experiences (Geller, 1984). This brought forth great debates between high tech and high touch and the notion that the two were mutually exclusive and could not co-exist without adversely impacting on one another. As a result, technology adoption and usage within the service sector in general and within the hospitality industry in particular has typically lagged that of other industries (e.g. financial, banking, airline, retail) and their manufacturing counterparts (Quinn, 1988).

Heretofore, IT expenditures within the hospitality industry have typically been viewed as discretionary spending and, therefore, subject to intense scrutiny (Antonucci and Tucker, 1998). The traditional paradigm of IT as a support mechanism to help accomplish routine, repetitive tasks prevailed. This thinking influenced IT spending, investment, and usage throughout the industry, placing the primary emphasis, more often than not, on tactical systems that could demonstrate calculable returns on investment rather than on strategic opportunities. Seldom did strategic vision or a pre-emptive strategy drive technology decisions (Cho, 1996). In her study, Cho (1996) found that a tactical or operational focus consistently outweighed strategic pre-emptiveness or competitive advantage when considering IT investment decisions, largely as a result of short-term thinking (namely, addressing immediate needs with solutions that promise short paybacks). A subsequent study by Siguaw and Enz (1999) looking at best practices within the hospitality industry found that the vast majority of the companies evaluated in the study used innovative technology to improve internal operating efficiencies. Most hoteliers tended to view IT as a supporting role rather than a strategic one, but moving forward, investing in technology simply to manage a hotel is insufficient given the competitive nature of the industry and the growing demands from guests (Hensdill, 1998). The focus must shift to that of strategic enablement (Nyheim, McFadden and Connolly, 2005). Other factors contributing to the slow adoption of IT in the hospitality industry include the highly fragmented structure of the industry and the frequent separation of ownership and management, where neither party to the management contract is willing to pay for technology that might benefit the other.

There is often a lag time between technology implementation and the realization of any benefits, but pressures from Wall Street and the investment community create a sense of urgency and drive industry executives to focus more priority on short-term results rather than on projects with long-term potential. When Covey (1997) talks about developing corporate culture, he uses a farming metaphor to illustrate his points. This same metaphor is appropriate when referring to the application of IT in organizations and the subsequent benefits that can result. The introduction, development, and adoption of IT are often part of a long-term process, and seldom are the rewards experienced immediately. Generally, there is some gestation period. Just as in farming, it takes time from initial field cultivation and planting to harvesting crops. To grow, crops require attention, care, and cultivating before they yield bountiful harvests. For this reason, Covey (1997) asserts that organizations must be viewed as organic, not mechanical.

This approach poses great challenges to hospitality and business executives trying to create investment strategies driven by, or dependent upon, IT. Industry executives must make strategic decisions long before any benefits are to be realized and often long before a technology has fully evolved or proven itself. Therefore, they must have an uncanny ability to forecast the future, recognize opportunities, and allocate company resources with sufficient lead-time in order to capitalize on these opportunities. Predicting the future is always a difficult feat, especially in today's complex, ever-changing world. Unanticipated or miscalculated opportunities and threats can result in catastrophic failures (Vitale, 1986). Furthermore this problem is exacerbated by the rapid pace of change with respect to technology, the risks associated with technology investments, and the uncertainties that the selected investments will pay-off and serve the firm's long-term needs.

Shying away from pre-emptive strategies is further reinforced by the continuing trend towards decreasing costs for IT equipment, which encourages deferring technology-related decisions until the technology becomes more affordable (Post, Kagan and Lau, 1995). IT capabilities have also been hampered by the lack of industry-specific applications and proven solutions architected with current technologies and design paradigms. Since many applications were adapted from other industries (e.g. airlines), they are considered inadequate or 'clumsy' because of their poor fit and their inability to address hotel-specific needs (Hensdill, 1998).

Finally, the industry's institutional memory is still fresh with the failure of the Confirm project, a joint venture between AMR (parent company of American Airlines), Marriott, Hilton, and Budget Rent A Car that started in the late 1980s, that was abruptly terminated a few years later and ended with a series of lawsuits between the parties involved. Combined, this illustrious group of industry leaders spent 3.5 years and $125 million (US) on a project that ended in a widely publicized miscarriage (Halper, 1992, 1993; Neelakantan, 1996). The impact of this failure is still felt in many organizations today. In fact, it continues to cast a dark cloud of doubt that overshadows IT projects and investment decisions, with many hospitality executives asking the question: 'How do I know this project will not become the next Confirm?' when an IT-related project is presented in the boardroom.

EXTERNAL FACTORS DRIVE INDUSTRY CHANGE

In extremely competitive environments such as the hospitality industry, the traditional rules for conducting business are no longer valid since there are no sustainable, competitive advantages (Burrus, 1993; D'Aveni, 1994). Companies can no longer be satisfied with their current market share or competitive methods (Tapscott and Caston, 1993). As such, they must continually search for new paradigms, challenge the status quo, and innovate. By looking at service delivery in a new light, hotels can develop new service innovations and apply IT to expand their staff's service repertoires (Barrington and Olsen, 1987). To accomplish this, however, hotel companies need visionary leaders, not mere 'maintenance engineers' (Hamel and Prahalad, 1994b); that is, individuals who are willing to take risks and think creatively.

Increased attention on IT has stemmed largely from market demands (Baumann, 1997). Factors forcing the hospitality industry to embrace technology more so than in the past include the disruptive technologies associated with Internet distribution, consolidation of brands into more-powerful multi-brand franchisors/operators, and certain hotel companies (e.g. Mandarin Oriental, Marriott International, and Starwood, among others) adopting guest-facing technologies as strategic weapons in the marketplace. Additionally, the proliferation of technology in other areas has had significant effects. Since more travelers are trained on technology and accustomed to using it as a result of their schooling or because they are employed in technology-dependent jobs, consumer expectations with respect to technology, technology-related guest amenities, and service levels supported by technology are all on the rise.

As Porter (1985), Quinn (1988), Burrus (1993), D'Aveni (1994), Friedman (2005), and others have astutely observed, IT undermines traditional forms of competition, strategic management, organizational structure, and economic policy making. The resulting environment is one of hypercompetition, where shorter transaction times, non-traditional competitors, volatility, surprise, and new alliances are the norm and must be anticipated. The convergence of powerful computers, intelligent software, and high-speed, global telecommunications networks coupled with the miniaturization and portability of technology is helping to reinvent

how business is conducted, how people interact, and the technology requirements of guests (and increasingly of employees). This Information Age or Digital Economy (Negroponte, 1995; Tapscott, 1996) is creating new opportunities and challenges. As Microsoft's Bill Gates (1999: xxii) so eloquently puts it:

> The successful companies of the next decade will be the ones that use digital tools to reinvent the way they work. These companies will make decisions quickly, act efficiently, and directly touch their customers in positive ways.

In short, there is an entirely new world order being introduced (Friedman, 2005) that is impacting all facets of one's personal and professional life. The fact is, society is in a constant state of transition; therefore, workers and organizations alike must learn to cope and adapt if they want to survive. This new order is challenging all hospitality businesses throughout the world. In order to be successful, companies must become flexible, agile, and aggressive by reducing bureaucracy and formalization within their organizations and by being more open to risk and innovation. Speed, connectivity, and the ability to amass and subsequently employ knowledge are key competitive ingredients. Therefore, companies must embrace change with open arms, foster change, and teach their employees how to thrive in change. Employees, too, will need to be more flexible, willing to learn, and capable of carrying out change. A basic premise that should be instilled in all workers is that everything is subject to change (D'Aveni, 1994), and that traditional thinking is no longer sufficient. Handy's (1989) notion of 'discontinuous, upside-down thinking' must be instilled in every worker so that they question everything and seek to develop better products, services, and efficiencies.

In an information-based economy, knowledge about and access to customers become critical success factors (Cline and Rach, 1996; Cline and Blatt, 1998). However, these critical success factors can only be realized through IT and competent, knowledgeable workers. Only recently has the industry begun to proactively apply IT in areas focused on guest service, a necessity that has resulted from increased competition, consumer demands, and shareholder focus on asset optimization. Traditionally, hotel executives resisted the use of IT for fear of alienating their guests. However, this thinking is outdated as a result of the many technological advancements that have occurred since the first property management system (PMS) was installed at the 2100-room New York Hilton back in 1963 (Alvarez, Ferguson and Dunn, 1983). As Hansen and Owen (1995) note:

> The debate over "high-tech" or "high-touch" is largely a thing of the past in the hospitality industry as emerging technologies drive unprecedented change in the way hotels operate and serve customers. It is clear that investments in technologies can generate greatly improved operating efficiencies, higher hotel revenues and enhanced guest services.

Davis and Botkin (1994) suggest that changing technology is driving the next wave of economic growth. In order to prosper from such growth, they advise that organizations must not only apply new technologies but also new ways of thinking. Segars and Grover (1995) maintain that rapid developments in IT have transformed the role of IT from that of 'organizational overhead' to one of strategic significance. Mills (1986) explains that technology is an important factor in determining organizational structure and its six dimensions: standardization, formalization, specialization, centralization, configuration, and flexibility. In his estimation, technology plays a significant role in determining how people within an organization are organized, how they interact, and what their job responsibilities are. Tapscott and Caston (1993) observe a fundamental change taking place in the nature and application of technology in business. In their estimation, information and IT are leading this revolution. IT is an enabler for faster response times, globalization, transformed business processes, new workgroups, outsourcing, and strategic alliances. Technology of all kinds has made the world a smaller place to conduct business and, to a large extent, changed the way business is conducted. It has created new markets while at the same time introduced new competition. How well prepared an organization is to play in such a dynamic environment will have a great impact on its overall success or failure. Research by Tapscott and Caston (1993) suggests that with the many business and technology-related changes occurring, organizations will be faced with many challenges due to their organizational structures and cultures and the knowledge and skills of their human resources. The ensuing

'paradigm shift' will result in conflict, chaos, and uncertainty and be met with resistance and skepticism.

Ready or not, however, IT will continue to proliferate throughout the hospitality industry to offer such benefits as enhanced guest experiences, better control of operations, improved worker productivity, more timely access to information for improved decision-making, streamlined communications, better security, etc. To achieve these benefits, it is important to recognize that significant changes are required throughout an organization. These changes include structural, procedural (i.e. tasks and business processes), and personnel changes (i.e. new job descriptions, new skill sets, additional training, etc.). Furthermore, IT strategy must be in alignment with the firm's business strategy and vice versa, for they are inseparable (Kantrow, 1980; Benjamin et al., 1984; Neo, 1988; Bacon, 1992; Mahmood and Mann, 1993; Tapscott and Caston, 1993).

IT AS A NECESSARY AND CROSS-DISCIPLINARY RESOURCE

Carr (2003) created an important but polemic debate when he raised the question, 'Does IT matter?' The answer, of course, is a simple and emphatic 'Yes' (Piccoli, 2004). Connolly and Olsen (2001) identify IT as one of the greatest forces driving change within the hospitality industry. Anyone having doubt should just look at how IT has reshaped the hotel distribution landscape, altering the cost structure and balance of power between guests, hotels (suppliers), and third party intermediaries and, in many cases, forcing hotels to be on the defensive (Carroll and Siguaw, 2003; O'Connor and Piccoli, 2003). While there is merit to what Carr (2003) has to say, one should not misinterpret his work or out of convenience, accept under false pretenses that IT can be ignored, completely delegated, or avoided altogether. Nowadays, it would be virtually impossible to try to operate a hospitality business without any technology. Unequivocally, IT does matter, and how it is used or not used can make or break a company.

In the modern hospitality organization, IT plays an important and integral role in the organization's ecosystem (see Figure 15.1).

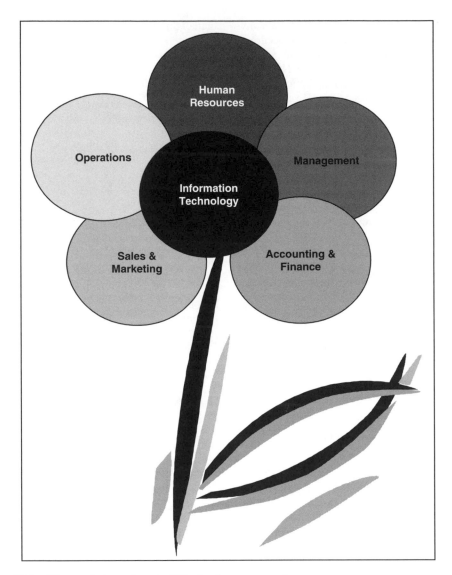

Figure 15.1　IT as an integral part of the business ecosystem

In other words, IT transcends the organization, crossing and blurring all traditional departmental and geographic boundaries (Nyheim et al., 2005). IT often serves as the glue that links everything together within the organization and increasingly between organizations to create a sense of business transparency (Tapscott and Ticoll, 2003). Consequently, given IT's pervasiveness and implications across the firm's value chain (Porter, 1985), leaders must be boundary spanners; that is, possessing knowledge and expertise covering multiple disciplines (Nyheim et al., 2005). Because of a hospitality firm's dependence on IT, all business decisions are likely to involve IT, and all IT-related decisions will likely have a direct impact on the business. Moreover, given the complexities of the business environment, many decisions will likely require input from multiple perspectives within the organization and an enterprise-wide view of the firm to ensure that all dimensions of a decision are completely thought through and that the ensuing ramifications, both positive and negative, are well understood. To support this point, just consider, for example, the various business, technology, and ethical considerations surrounding guest data collection, retention, and usage.

Accordingly, with IT being such an important and capital intensive ingredient in today's business formula, hospitality leaders, if they are to be masters of their own destinies, must possess a firm grasp of technology – not so much the technical aspects but rather its strategic potential – and then assume ownership and responsibility for it in order to ensure its full benefits are realized (Piccoli, 2004). At Marriott, IT is systemically 'intertwined with the business in every way' such that the two are 'indistinguishable' (Pastore, 2005). In fact, according to company president William Shaw, business and IT have 'converged' to a point where in many company meetings, 'IT people are just as likely to respond to questions about the business as they are to a question about technology', and people from the various business disciplines are equally as comfortable fielding questions involving technology as they are addressing business questions germane to their areas of expertise (Pastore, 2005).

A typical full-service hotel (for example, 500-plus rooms) is a complex business with fairly diverse operations (including rooms management, food and beverage operations, meetings and events, retail, and more), numerous stakeholders often having competing needs and interests, and a vast array of technology. The number of variables and employees that must be managed for such a business to be successful is daunting and requires a variety of capable technology applications and a strong IT infrastructure to operate the business, to ensure the right managerial controls are in place, and to report on the business's overall health and financial status.

In any competitive environment, access to timely information is critical. In a hospitality context, this requires getting the right information into the hands of the right people at the right time so that the right decisions can be made and/or the right services can be delivered. To accomplish this awesome goal consistently requires a sophisticated portfolio of IT applications and a very capable IT infrastructure, not to mention good training and good, capable people. As depicted in Figure 15.2, a typical full-service hotel represents an extremely technically complex environment, one that can easily require as many as 100 different computer applications, all of which add to the complexity of the business, the cost intensity of the business, and the competitive stakes, not to mention the knowledge and skills one must

possess to be able to effectively manage such environments. Core applications include a property management system (PMS), a sales and catering system, central reservations (CRS), revenue management (RMS), restaurant and gift shop point-of-sale systems (POS), accounting, inventory, payroll, in-room entertainment, energy management, and more. Generally, the larger a hotel is and the more sophisticated or diverse its operations are (for example, consider those of a resort or casino hotel), the greater will be its reliance on automation, its overall technical complexity (i.e. the number of systems used to manage the business), and its commitment to investing in IT (Van Hoof et al., 1995).

The technical complexity, sophistication, and investment in IT expand significantly when the IT portfolio of a multi-unit or chain hotel company is superimposed on top of that found in an individual hotel, as discussed above. Figure 15.3 provides a conceptual illustration of what a hotel company's IT portfolio looks like. It depicts the many different types of IT applications used to support business functions and stakeholders (e.g. customers, suppliers, employees, and management) across an entire company's operations; including unit, regional, and corporate levels. Technology applications include infrastructural aspects such as the company's communications network (to handle voice, data, and video traffic), intranet, and security; applications to support core business disciplines such as accounting, human resources, sales and marketing, procurement, and operations; analytical tools like data mining, decision support systems (DSS), and executive information systems (EIS) to support business intelligence and enhance decision making; and various enterprise-wide applications like enterprise resource planning (ERP), supply-chain management (SCM), and customer relationship management (CRM) to help leverage and share resources and knowledge across the firm in ways that can create value for the company's shareholders. Needless to say, there are many different systems that must work in unison to enable a company to function efficiently and effectively, use its resources wisely, and consistently deliver outstanding levels of service to all of its guests. Consequently, architectural standards, IT platform considerations, systems integration, and security must be understood by all decision makers to ensure that they will lead their company in a direction it wants to go,

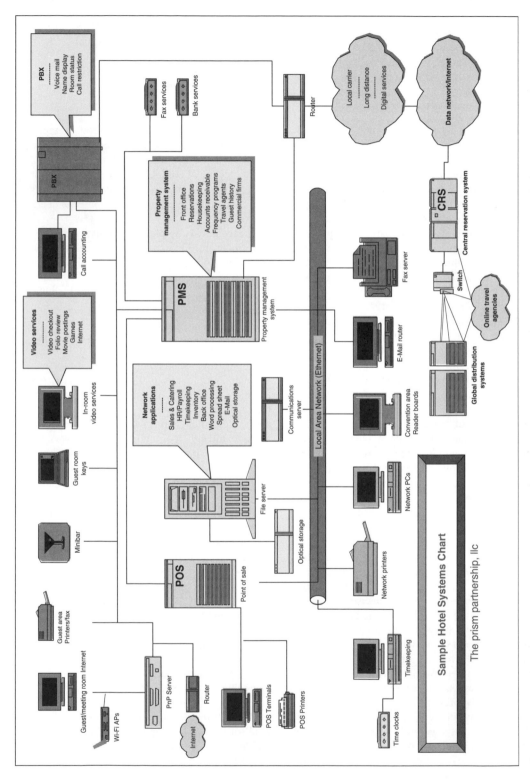

Figure 15.2 The technical complexity of a typical full-service hotel

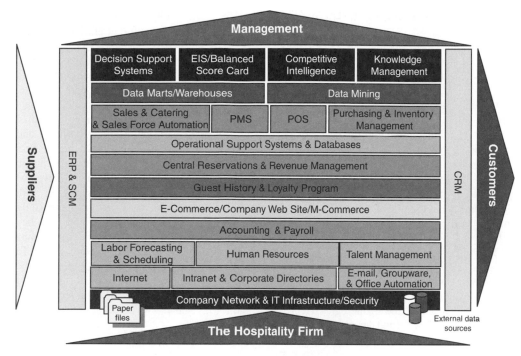

Figure 15.3   IT portfolio for a multi-unit or chain hotel company

provide scalability and interoperability, and not constrain growth or compromise the integrity of its systems, network, or data.

Without question, IT is a necessary component of the competitive equation, but in and of itself, IT is insufficient for providing competitive advantage. To be successful, it must be coupled with people who know how to use the computer applications and the data generated from them and a set of business processes (or tasks) conducive to being automated. Technology requires more advanced skills and a greater knowledge of the operation, often with a cross-functional focus. It helps to remove departmental barriers to provide a more holistic approach to guest service. With more integrated systems, data about a particular guest need only be entered once and then shared throughout the entire hotel (or other hotels within the same chain). Consider, for example, a meeting planner who needs to reserve sleeping rooms for 50 attendees who will be participating in an upcoming corporate retreat. The necessary information (e.g. group room block and rooming list) can be entered by the sales office and subsequently shared with the reservations, front desk, and housekeeping departments to ensure that all of the proper arrangements are made

prior to the group's arrival. From the client and guests' perspectives, there is a continuum of service, not disjointed hand-offs from one service employee to another. This provides the service employee with greater satisfaction as he/she can see a process through from beginning to end. It also eliminates much of the frustration from receiving incomplete work from another department or area. Data can also be shared between properties of the same chain (or its sister or affiliate brands), thereby enabling service consistency and improving one's service repertoire across the entire organization (Barrington and Olsen, 1987). Because the hotel industry is so competitive, product and service differentiation is critical to one's success. The best approach is through more personalized guest service. Information systems can arm hotel employees with important information about guests such as their favorite room, the date of their last stay, or any particular hobbies or allergies. With this information, a hotel employee can then tailor the service delivery process specifically for a particular guest, just like what Harrah's, Ritz-Carlton, and Wyndham are trying to do, as described earlier. It is this customization that will make the service memorable and distinguished from other service providers.

IT–BUSINESS STRATEGY ALIGNMENT

Olsen et al. (1998) define an overarching concept of strategy as the *consistent* allocation of resources to create a well-defined set of competitive methods to achieve a firm's goals and establish a competitive position. Technology strategy refers to a firm's plans, intentions, and policies regarding current and future use of IT, information, and 'softer' IT-related issues such as integration with the firm and its employees (Brady et al., 1992). Porter (1985) defines technology strategy as a firm's approach to the development and use of technology. Because of the pervasive impact of technology on a firm's value chain, this strategy must be broad and far-reaching.

Porter (1985) suggests that technology strategy must include choices regarding the technologies in which a firm should invest, the firm's position with respect to the technologies selected (e.g. leader or follower), and decisions regarding when and how to acquire or license the technologies. A firm's IT strategy guides decisions related to its technological architecture, infrastructure, applications, and services in accordance with that its business strategy and objectives. Yet, in today's context of rapid change and in a marketplace that is inundated with new technology products and offerings (hardware, software, and services), hospitality leaders find it difficult and even daunting to effectively evaluate these technological advancements and assimilate them into their organization's strategy. As a result, they typically maintain short planning horizons. While it is clear they must be judicious as to their investments and select only those that will provide value to the firm, selecting and implementing those technologies are often difficult and risky tasks, since not all of the benefits will be tangible and due to the uncertainties surrounding the technology investment decision (such as the useful life of the technology). Porter (1985) recommends concentrating on those technologies that will lead to the greatest sustainable impact on cost or product/service differentiation, and, subsequently lead to the greatest competitive advantage. Thus, when choosing among technologies in which to invest, hotel executives must base their decisions on a thorough understanding of each technological choice and its impact to the firm's value chain (Porter, 1985).

As things have evolved, IT and business strategy have become inseparable and must,

therefore, be well aligned to be effective (Kantrow, 1980; Benjamin et al., 1984; Bacon, 1992; Mahmood and Mann, 1993; Tapscott and Caston, 1993; Reich and Benbasat, 1996; Gordon, 1999). Achieving this alignment has been a top priority for several years (Pastore, 2005). As Neo (1988) opined, strategy begets IT and vice versa. IT is a business resource and tool that should be used appropriately and wisely; that is as a vehicle to generate firm value and help the firm achieve its strategic vision and goals. Technology should never be deployed for the sake of technology. In such cases, IT decisions may be inappropriately guided by technical elegance and not key business drivers, resulting in technology misfits or overspend (Weill and Broadbent, 1998). To avoid these problems, there should never be a stand-alone technology project but rather business projects that depend upon technology. Technology must always be aligned with the business.

The co-alignment model

The theoretical underpinning of strategic management is the co-alignment principle, which simply stated suggests that if a firm understands the environmental events affecting its business and shaping the future of its industry, plans and develops its strategies so as to exploit these environmental opportunities and minimize any threats, and appropriately allocates and aligns its resources (e.g. people, capital, technology, etc.) through consistent investment to create product and service offerings (i.e. competitive methods), it will outperform industry players and receive competitive advantage (Chandler, 1962; Thompson, 1967; Bourgeois, 1980; Venkatraman and Prescott, 1990; Venkatraman et al., 1993; Murthy, 1994; Olsen et al., 1998).

The co-alignment model (depicted in Figure 15.4) is seemingly quite intuitive, but in reality, it is very complex and complicated to operationalize, as suggested by the number of firms that have found themselves out of alignment, often struggled to get back on course, and sometimes found themselves out of business. The process of achieving this strategic alignment is neither simple nor straightforward due to the lead-time and technical expertise typically required to develop and implement IT solutions (Weill and Broadbent, 1998). Problems can occur as a

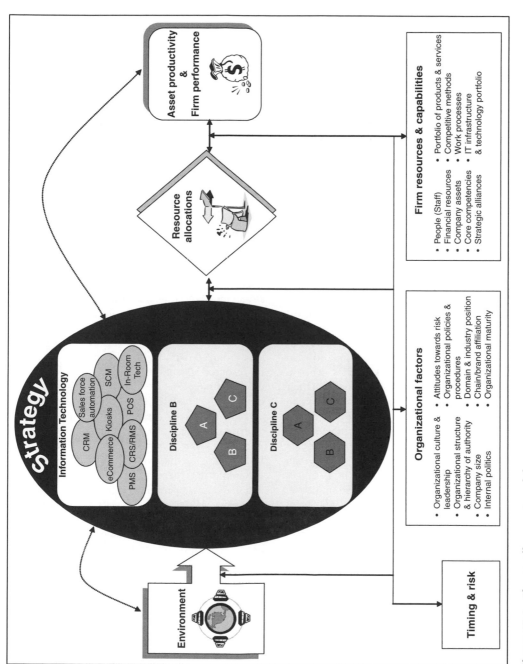

Figure 15.4   The co-alignment model

result of numerous moderating or intervening variables, inadequate evaluation of the external environment or miscalculating the timing and/or impact of environmental events, poor strategy formulation or execution, and inconsistent or misaligned use of resources. Moreover, the decisions regarding where and when to allocate resources to IT can be risky due to the financial, operational, and technical risks involved (Clemons and Weber, 1990). Consequently, Weill and Broadbent (1998) posit that this alignment can never fully be achieved. It is more of an ideal state that can only be expressed in terms of degrees of alignment, particularly when looking at many of the large hospitality conglomerates like Marriott, Hilton, Starwood, Accor, and InterContinental Hotels and Resorts, among others. Each of these companies offers numerous brands targeted at different guests and price points. Consequently, each company must strike delicate balances between corporate standardization and brand individuality (Berinato, 2002).

Monitoring the environment is critical in trying to stay abreast of competitor activities, changes in market conditions, new political or regulatory issues, and technological innovations. Bates (1985) and West and Olsen (1988) note that organizations taking the time to scan the environment and plan strategies tend to outperform those who are less structured in their planning efforts. The key to effective planning is to understand the business environment and the impact of information systems at the macro- and task-levels. Successful planners anticipate new trends so that an appropriate strategy can be formulated and implemented in a timely fashion. To do this, they develop multiple, 'what-if' scenarios for each environmental event that address the probabilities of each event occurring, the timing at which each event may occur, and the likely impact of each event so as to have multiple courses of action to prevent getting trapped in an undesirable or unforeseen situation (Dill, 1958; Child, 1972; Duncan, 1972; Parsons, 1983; Slattery and Olsen, 1984; Bates, 1985; Jackson and Dutton, 1988). Next, the organization must define how it fits into the external environment. This involves a complete understanding of any competitor activity taking place, Porter's five forces (Porter, 1980), the remote environment, the task environment, and the functional environment (Dill, 1958; Duncan, 1972; Bates, 1985; DeNoble and Olsen, 1986; Mills, 1986).

Certainly, the number of technological developments, the array of choices, and the pace of change are overwhelming hotel executives. As the diversity of IT in hotel firms grows, hotel executives must allot an increasing proportion of their time and attention to IT-related issues and to monitoring how IT is evolving both within and outside their competitive arenas. IT is constantly developing, opening new competitive opportunities and altering the overall economics of conducting business. Despite the rapid changes seen in technology and as a result of technology, the fundamental business reasons for applying IT in a firm have ironically remained relatively stable over time: drive revenues, cut costs, gain/retain customers, enhance service, create competitive advantage, achieve efficiencies, improve productivity, build a company's technological infrastructure, establish architectural standards, maximize shareholder returns, and compete globally (Grover et al., 1997).

All strategists stress the need for and importance of well-defined, clearly articulated strategies. Well-aligned firms are posited to outperform firms whose alignment is not optimized or outright misaligned. Alignment implies not only that a firm's strategy is synchronized with its environment and that its resource allocations are consistent with the defined strategies of the firm but also that all of a firm's strategies (i.e. corporate, business and functional) are consistent and in alignment with one another. Corporate strategy provides an umbrella to which business-level and functional-level strategies must relate. To that end, each discipline (e.g. accounting and finance, sales and marketing, operations, management, human resources, IT) typically has its own strategy. If these strategies are not consistent with one another and working in tandem, a firm will not succeed in realizing its full vision and the benefits it expects to achieve. Therefore, these strategies must be complementary in nature with the appropriate level of support.

The co-alignment principle suggests that the strategic context (specified by a firm's strategy) will be defined as the result of opportunities, threats, and constraints posed by a firm's environment. This strategic context will then drive IT strategy, which will subsequently prescribe a firm's IT portfolio. This strategy formulation model implies that effective IT strategy and resource allocations will culminate in well-deployed technologies and applications. In turn, the benefits of these will be reflected by positive firm performance, as measured by profitability and cash flow per share. Better alignment of these constructs is expected to lead to better firm performance, relative to industry competitors.

Alternatively stated, a firm's strategy is comprised of various competitive methods chosen by the firm to capitalize on opportunities available in the task and remote environments while thwarting any potential threats (Dill, 1958; Duncan, 1972; Olsen, 1980; Olsen et al., 1998). IT represents a competitive method or series of competitive methods to help a hospitality firm uniquely differentiate itself, serve its target markets with appropriate value propositions, and contribute to the overarching strategic goals of the firm. This is done through a portfolio of technologies and applications working in unison with one another to enable employees to carry out their roles. In the illustration presented here, some of the more popular components of a hotel firm's IT portfolio are represented. These include, among others, the property management system (PMS), the central reservation system (CRS) and revenue management system (RMS), the point-of-sale (POS) system, electronic commerce applications, kiosks, supply-chain management, customer relationship management (CRM), and sales force automation (SFA). Collectively, these technology solutions should enable the firm contribute to value creation and the achievement of the firm's strategic goals, namely competitive advantage and higher levels of firm performance within its competitive set. In the words of Weill and Broadbent (1998: 41):

In a firm with a well-aligned IT portfolio, the right amount is invested in IT; the mix of investments is appropriate for the firm's strategy; the IT investments are successfully converted into business value; and the IT portfolio facilitates the family of current strategies likely to be implemented within the firm's strategic intent.

Theory notwithstanding, it is important to reiterate a point made earlier – that IT itself is seldom the source of competitive advantage since it can be easily acquired and copied (Carr, 2003). Rather, how IT is implemented and used within a firm drives competitive advantage. IT investment decisions and subsequent implementations must focus on the entire socio-technical system so that the full effects of IT on people, business processes, employee

training, and organizational structure are understood and taken into consideration (Piccoli, 2004). To illustrate this point, Piccoli et al. (2003) describe the challenges of implementing customer relationship management (CRM) in the hospitality industry if it is thought of simply as an information system and not in the greater context it requires. In their view, CRM is a business philosophy enabled and supported by IT. Ergo, the specific competitive advantages derived will be based on how a firm chooses to allocate its resources to implement IT, its overall effectiveness in doing so (e.g. its ability to cost-effectively harness the capabilities provided by the IT tools and applications), and, of course, the portfolio of products and services offered. Hence, IT, coupled with other firm resources and assets, will lead to competitive advantages or disadvantages in the marketplace.

The recursive relationships depicted in the co-alignment model are important but often overlooked in practice. As Farbey et al. (1992) point out, post evaluation is often forgotten, and when this happens, organizational learning fails to take place. This means that flawed assumptions, forecasting errors, and the gap between expected outcomes and actual outcomes or realized strategy versus intended strategy (Mintzberg, 1978) is never fully understood and improved. To avoid these pitfalls from occurring, attention must be called to these reverse linkages. Only then will managers be able to learn from their mistakes, share their experiences, and improve the process for future application.

Argyris and Schön (1978), Argyris (1991, 1993, 1994), and Sink and Tuttle (1989) stress the importance of a feedback loop in any process and the importance to organizational learning. The strategy formulation process is no different in this regard, despite normative thinking that environment drives strategy formulation. The recursive relationship between strategy and environment is suggested by leading contemporary management theorists such as Hamel and Prahalad (1994a) and D'Aveni (1994). In their views, the only way to achieve competitive advantage in today's dynamic, complex, and hypercompetitive marketplace is to alter industry structure. Their thinking suggests that firms can and should change the environments within which they operate, just as environments can stimulate changes within a firm as suggested by systems theory. Thus, their strategies should be developed with the intention of altering the external environment, industry structure, or competitive landscape.

Neo (1988) suggests that the traditional, uni-directional thinking (where IT strategy follows business strategy) is inadequate in explaining how IT strategy development should occur. More importantly, Antonucci and Tucker (1998) report that firm performance does, in fact, drive strategy and resource allocation decisions and underscores the importance of a firm's primary obligation to its shareholders; that is, to create value. While they concede that this may not be the theoretical ideal touted by most scholars, it does, nonetheless, reflect a degree of reality that cannot and should not be overlooked. Positive firm performance will reinforce firm strategies and resource allocations. Conversely, disappointing or negative results will constitute management intervention and prompt action, coming in the form of strategy adjustments and reallocation (most likely reduction) of firm resources.

Moderating variables

To date, causal linkages between IT and firm performance have been difficult to prove due to so many moderating variables. Because no author has been able to successfully refute and subsequently reject the co-alignment principle, the theory must still be considered valid. Accordingly, it is still assumed that effective deployment of IT will lead to positive results in firm performance, albeit empirical studies on this topic provide mixed results (see Weill and Olson, 1989; Weill, 1991; Mahmood and Mann, 1993; Kettinger et al., 1994; Brynjolfsson and Hitt, 1996; Hitt and Brynjolfsson, 1996).

Moderating the linkages depicted in the co-alignment model are several variables; namely, timing and risk, organizational factors, and firm resources and capabilities. Each of these variables is discussed in turn below.

Timing and risk

Much of a firm's strategic alignment has to do with timing, risk (both perceived and actual), and the life-cycle stages (i.e. maturity levels) of both the organization and its technology (including both current and potential technology of the firm). The literature suggests that there must be congruence between technology, the organization, its environment, and the tasks

for which the technology is to be applied if maximum effectiveness and benefits are to be realized. Timing and degree of risk can greatly influence a firm's strategic choices, resource allocations, and, ultimately, firm performance, since all strategies, decisions, and evaluations are relevant in a certain contextual element of time and are determined by many organiza-tional, environmental, and technological factors considered during this given point in time. If executives in an organization feel that timing for a particular strategy or project is wrong or too risky, they will likely defer investing in that strategy or project. Since the environment and competitors do not stand still, all strategic thrusts are relative and moderated by time, risk, conditions and constraints in the firm's external environment, and the moves and counter-moves of competitors – all at the time when decisions are evaluated, made, and executed.

For an example of how time and risk moderate the application of technology, one can study the use of kiosks in the hotel industry for self check-in/out. In the early 1980s, Hyatt and Sheraton were industry pioneers seeking first-mover advantages with their pilot tests of self-service lobby kiosks. Their experiments resulted in abysmal and somewhat embarrassing failures. Both companies took risks and tried to capitalize on a technology long before it was proven in the hospitality industry or accepted by guests. The results were costly investments that were later abandoned. Today, however, these same devices are being deployed by almost every major hotel company with great fanfare, user acceptance, and overall success and guest satisfaction – so much so that Rayport and Jaworski (2005) predict that self-service is the wave of the future and that how well companies can develop user interfaces to create innovative computer-mediated transactions will become a key competitive differentiator.

Why is it that these recent implementations are successful when their predecessor trials were flops? The answer is simple: timing. Timing affects the application of IT and the ensuing value (Hopper, 1990; Post et al., 1995; Grover et al., 1997). Since the earlier trials, banks have aggressively promoted the usage of automated teller machines (ATMs) for money withdrawals, account inquiries, deposits, and more. Today, usage of such devices is commonplace, well accepted with little perceived risk, and often a preferred form of service delivery. Over time, the capabilities of technology have improved while the cost of technology has declined, making the use of self-service technologies more attractive and affordable. Finally, rising costs of labor and shortages in the industry's labor pool create a need for alternatives, thereby driving new opportunities for IT.

In another, more visible case of how time and risk influence strategy and resource allocations, one need only look to American Airline's use, and the subsequent success, of its SABRE reservation system. Hopper (1990) discusses the evolution of SABRE and how its use and strategic value changed with time, the organizational evolution of American Airlines, and the developments of technology. When first introduced, the role of SABRE was to provide relief and efficiencies to the then-arduous tasks associated with taking and processing reservations. At its inception, the primary roles of SABRE were transaction processing and inventory control. Over time, the system's reach, functionality, and strategic purpose changed considerably. The system quickly gained significant market share in travel distribution by locking in travel agents and expanding the system's selling capabilities. Before long, SABRE became a revenue-producing machine, generating more revenue than the airline's primary business, the sale of airline seats. Today, SABRE, is a powerful global distribution system, electronic travel supermarket, and reservations service provider for the travel industry and one of the largest, privately-owned, real-time computer networks in the world.

The instructive point is that when SABRE was first conceived, no one had ever anticipated its strategic importance, the competitive advantage American Airlines came to realize, and the overall potential of the system. American Airlines took a risk in embarking on the SABRE project. With time, the system evolved, adapting to competitive threats and organizational needs, to become the powerhouse that it is today. As the system evolved, its role and ensuing value changed, thus illustrating the importance and significance time can have on strategy, resource allocations, and ultimately, firm performance. Strategies and resource allocations will often depend upon a firm's planning horizon, the window of opportunity in which to act, and the firm's ability to forecast future events and requirements.

Not all firms, though, are as fortunate as American Airlines, and not all technology applications have the impact or provide the

long-lasting competitive advantage as SABRE. For example, early adopters of hotel property management systems (PMS) realized strategic advantage through improved services and guest recognition, better room inventory and financial management controls, and enhanced reporting and analysis. Over time, however, a PMS has become a standard and necessary operating tool for all hotels, big and small alike. Functionality between systems has converged, giving hotel firms relatively little strategic advantage. Today, a PMS is a critical component of a hotel firm's IT infrastructure and required for competitive parity; its emphasis is primarily tactical or transaction-based, not strategic value. As Carr (2003) observes, when IT becomes a commodity, it loses its strategic value. Thus, competitive advantage from IT is not considered to be sustainable.

These are just a few examples to illustrate the moderating affects of time on technology strategy, resource allocations, and implementation. There are many other examples that are equally as illustrative. These include the evolution of the Internet and electronic commerce and their ensuing disruptive (Christensen, 1997) effects on hospitality, particularly in the areas of information search, consumer comparison-shopping, distribution, travel maps and guides, social marketing, and guest feedback; high-speed Internet access (both wired and wireless) in guestrooms and throughout hotels, restaurants, meeting space, lobbies, and other public space; voice-over-IP (VoIP) technologies and their impacts on hotel guest amenities, services, telephone revenues, and organizational structure (for example, VoIP can enable a virtual sales team or home-based reservations agents in lieu of central-based agents); advances in mobile (m-)commerce (i.e. the use of personal digital assistants and cell phones to access the Internet wirelessly to find information, execute business transactions, and take advantage of location-based services). In short, timing, technology maturity, and adoption rates affect the role, value, and appropriateness of technology.

Organizational factors

Organizational factors represent another source of moderating variables. Chandler (1962), Thompson (1967), Venkatraman et al. (1993), and others have long postulated the relationship between strategy and organizational structure.

Normative theory in strategy development suggests that strategy should dictate structure. In practice, however, this is not always the case. At times, firms base their strategies on the constraints and limitations of existing structure. Organizational culture, leadership, size, hierarchy, policies, procedures, and maturity (i.e. life-cycle stages) are all tied to an organization's structure and, in some way, either favorably or unfavorably, impact the strategies chosen or not chosen by the firm. Chain/brand affiliation and industry position also influence firm strategy and play important roles in terms of technology utilization and the creation of service standards. Each of these variables affect how work is carried out within an organization and the priorities set for an organization. They contribute to an organization's priorities, attitudes towards risk and its internal politics, which subsequently influence resource allocation decisions (Weill and Olson, 1989; Clemons and Weber, 1990; Farbey et al., 1992).

Firm resources and capabilities

The final category of moderating variables is firm resources and capabilities. These include visible as well as tacit factors. Clemons and Row (1991), Cho (1996), and Mata et al. (1995) illustrate the importance of a firm's resources, capabilities, and core competencies in determining competitive advantage. These researchers posit that it is a firm's idiosyncratic and tacit resources that lead to inimitability and, hence, a prolonged or sustained advantage over rivals.

It is a firm's resources and capabilities that make it possible for that firm to execute its strategies and realize benefits. Resources include people, capital, and technology, which are combined and often augmented through strategic alliances to create the firm's core competencies, competitive methods, and portfolio of products and services. The skills, capabilities, expertise, reputation (i.e. credibility), and individual and collective experiences of a firm's workforce can impact the strategies undertaken and the corresponding resource allocations, even though cognitive strategic theory suggests that strategy should be defined based on environmental opportunities and threats without regard to a firm's existing resources and capabilities.

Conventional thinking suggests that as part of the implementation and execution of a strategy, a firm should acquire the necessary resources and skills if it does not already have them. However, in practice, this is not always the case. Similarly, a firm's financial resources and access to capital may create or restrict strategic choices. Common considerations will be who will provide the necessary funding, the cost of this funding, and whether or not a firm is financially able to undertake a given strategy, investment decision, or IT project. Finally, a firm's IT portfolio and infrastructure also have bearings on the firm's strategies and resource allocation decisions. Legacy (i.e. dated) systems and technologies, commonly found within the hospitality industry, often constrain a company's strategies because of their lack of flexibility, inadequate functionality and data structures, and their high costs to maintain (which means resources are detracted from other strategic priorities).

IT must create structural differences if it is to provide sustainable competitive advantage (Porter, 1985). These structural differences come in the form of (1) innovations that result from a firm's ability to effectively leverage its unique resources, (2) competitive asymmetry or differences between firms as a result of their unique resources, and (3) the ability to pre-empt competitive responses and thereby maintain technological superiority (Feeny and Ives, 1990; Clemons and Row, 1991; Segars and Grover, 1995; and Cho, 1996). Porter (1985: 171–172) suggests four tests for desirable technological change:

1 The technological change lowers costs or enhances differentiation and provides a sustainable (i.e. inimitable) technological advantage.
2 The technological change shifts cost or uniqueness drivers in favor of a firm.
3 Pioneering the technological change translates into first-mover advantages besides those inherent in the technology itself.
4 The technological change improves overall industry structure.

Undeniably, the IT requirements of today's marketplace are raising the level of investment required to compete successfully. In many cases, the implementation of IT becomes one of strategic necessity (or survival) rather than one of competitive advantage (Clemons and Weber, 1990; Clemons, 1991). Nevertheless, this shift in no way lessens the importance of actively pursuing investments in IT to gain market or cost advantages, to introduce new products or services, or to differentiate product and service offerings from others in the marketplace (Adcock et al., 1993). The focus must be proactive rather than reactive, strategic versus support-oriented.

VALUE CREATION

How and why a technology is implemented are determining factors in the value it provides. Technology can be used in various ways by companies to achieve different goals. Consider, for example, a hand-held restaurant POS. In a casual-themed restaurant, the purpose of this device may be to increase speed of service and the number of table turns, but in a more upscale restaurant setting or country club, this same device may be deployed as a tool to enhance guest service by providing servers with guest information, details about the menu (e.g. how a dish is prepared), and suggestions for complementary items (e.g. side dish or wine). Knowing how, when, and why to apply technologies to business situations (i.e. problems and opportunities) are important skills for hospitality leaders to possess.

Companies must not only be better than their competitors but also capable of identifying and leveraging its competitive advantages to their fullest (Smith, 2006). In an era where goods and services become more like commodities, what consumers will value most is the experience associated with these goods and services (Pine and Gilmore, 1998). So just how can companies create these unique experiences, and, more importantly, how can they convert them to added value for the firm? Table 15.1 presents a series of important and essential questions that should be taken into consideration when evaluating and making decisions regarding IT investment and deployment in a hospitality firm.

Much has been written in the contemporary press about value creation. According to Slywotzky (1996: 4), value stems from a company's business design: 'the entire system for delivering utility to customers and earning a profit from that activity'. As IT continues to permeate the hospitality industry, attention must be given to the role it plays in shaping a firm's business design and in contributing to the ensuing value creation. This value creation must be addressed from two perspectives: (1) the viewpoint of the guest and (2) the vantage point of the investors (shareholders). Traditionally, the hospitality industry has struggled with assessing the benefits of IT. As capital requirements for implementing the IT infrastructure of the future grow, investors and owners will require reliable and valid valuation models. Also, as the pace at which product (hardware and software) upgrades are announced increases, more critical evaluation must be done before authorization and funding will be provided. Absence of such models will likely result in under-investment and, hence, inadequate technology. Since these outcomes are unacceptable when trying to prepare organizations and the industry for the new world, this issue of valuation must be addressed. Without further investigation, the question remains: how should investment decisions in IT be measured and evaluated? Along these lines, one must consider the value and potential of outsourcing. Many companies are turning to outsourcing to fulfill support functions and to control overhead. Questions companies need to answer are what information IT (if any) should be outsourced, and what are the strategic implications? Going forward, what will be the best utilization of resources, and how should these be sourced to fulfill a firm's mission and objectives in the most cost-effective manner possible?

There is no question that the requirements for new, better, and more technology raises the level of capital investment required. This, however, is necessary to survive. There is no escaping IT. It is pervasive and has become a strategic necessity for competing in a complex, dynamic world and should no longer be considered as 'operational overhead' (Segars and Grover, 1995; Grover et al., 1997). While IT offers great potential, it is not always the answer to an organization's woes. As Mathe and Dagi (1996) note, technology alone is not a solution, but rather, an enabler; it must be well integrated, provide synergies, and support the service vision. This implies that the chosen technologies suit the problem at hand, are compatible with the firm's organizational structure, and can be easily maintained (Mathe and Dagi, 1996).

Cline and Blatt (1998) suggest that hotel companies must create a new business model for defining value that accounts for tangible as well as intangible assets, including knowledge, information, and customer relationships.

Table 15.1   Important considerations for evaluating IT usage in a hospitality firm

- Is the proposed IT project aligned with the hospitality firm's business strategy, and is there technology/task congruency?
- Will an IT-driven business strategy create barriers to entry or create lag time effects, making it difficult and more time-consuming for competitors to copy?
- What are the IT project's anticipated benefits, and how will they be measured?
- What are the IT project's critical success factors?
- What risks are associated with the IT project, and how can these be mitigated?
- How can IT be used to change the competitive dynamics and industry structure?
- What position has the competition taken with respect to IT, and what effects should this have on one's own strategy?
- If the IT project is undertaken, how might competitors react (i.e. what might be their likely responses or defense tactics)?
- Can the hospitality firm gain economies of scale using IT and better leverage and use its resources more efficiently?
- Will IT reduce costs and change the hospitality firm's cost structure to provide advantages in the marketplace?
- Can IT create new revenue opportunities, generate new revenue streams, and help the hospitality firm focus on more profitable lines of business?
- Can IT provide access to new markets and new market segments?
- Can IT extend the hospitality firm's reach and, in doing so, lower costs and increase conversion rates?
- Will IT enable the hospitality firm to differentiate itself among its competitors in a demonstrable way that can be easily and effectively communicated to guests?
- Can IT provide business intelligence that will lead to better and more timely decisions and provide knowledge asymmetry that will lead to unparalleled market advantages?
- Will IT improve or enhance guest service, lead to more loyal guests, and allow the hospitality firm to charge rate premiums?
- Will IT increase the revenue generated per guest per visit and allow the hospitality firm to focus on more profitable guests and market segments?
- Will IT positively shift the balance of power away from guests and suppliers in favor of the hospitality firm?
- Will the IT create a more flexible, agile hospitality firm, one that is capable of sensing and responding to changes in the marketplace to capitalize on opportunities and thwart threats quickly?
- Will IT enhance and extend the hospitality firm's core competencies, resources, and capabilities?
- Will IT provide an enabling platform for growth, new functionality, and new business capabilities?
- What are the total costs associated with the IT project, including hardware, software, training, implementation, etc.?
- Do the IT project's benefits outweigh the costs?

Source: Adapted from Nyheim, McFadden and Connolly (2005: 35) and Connolly and Swig (2004: 221).

Figure 15.5 provides one view of how organizational value will be created in the hospitality firm of the future. This model advances many of the concepts espoused by Mills (1986), Barrington and Olsen (1987), Davidow and Malone (1992), and Tapscott (1996). The crux of the model suggests that IT and human resources, armed with intellect derived from knowledge and information literacy, will be the new source of value. Leveraging customer information and the customer relationship to create a memorable, emotional experience will be a leading determinant in firm profitability (Cline and Blatt, 1998).

The base of the model illustrates a grounding in the environment in which a hotel or hotel company competes. In order to successfully compete and prepare for the future, it is essential to understand the environmental events and trends shaping the future, the timing of these events, the causal relationships, and the long-term implications. It is also necessary to have a complete understanding of guests' needs and desires and the ability to anticipate future requirements, even if guests have not already articulated these needs. Finally, it is important to understand the competitive environment; that is the products, services,

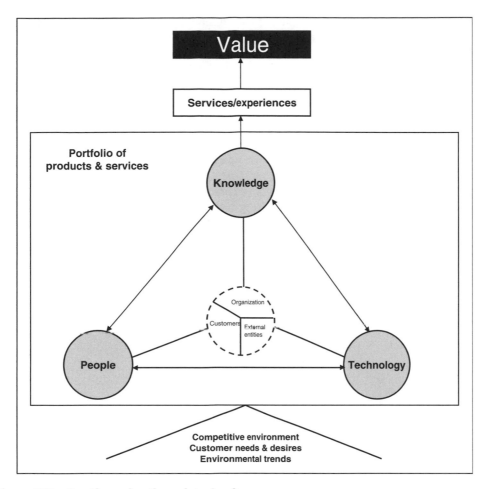

Figure 15.5   Creating value through technology

strategies, and innovations of competing hotels or hotel companies. These three components serve as inputs to the larger model and shape paradigms, products, and services.

The center portion of the model represents the convergence of people, technology, and knowledge. People are the workers and the management of the hotel or hotel company. The technology represents the computer systems (e.g. CRS, PMS, revenue management, CRM, etc.) and communications network. The technology encapsulates the rules, procedures, and knowledge of the organization and distributes it to all those who need access to it in a timely fashion. In today's environment, this goes beyond the organization's workers and the culture of the organization to include the extended enterprise (i.e. strategic partners, outsourced service providers, and participating entities in the global distribution network) and

the customers who actively participate in the service delivery process.

The dyadic interactions between hotel employees, customers, the environment, external entities, and technology applications build knowledge through the exchange of information and help to create a learning organization. It is this knowledge base that allows the organization to build a portfolio of products and services that can be delivered consistently to all guests. The role of technology in this portfolio is strategic and fundamental to achieving consistency and sharing of information necessary to deliver these services.

When a guest shares in these services, he/she has experiences, both positive and negative. These experiences are enriched by the interactions with the hotel organization, its staff, its technology and know-how, and those that represent the organization (i.e. external entities) providing core and peripheral services. It is from these interactions that value will ultimately be judged. If rated favorably, a guest will likely return as well as share his/her experiences with others. This will lead to greater guest loyalty, higher occupancies, more guest spend, increased revenues, and, ultimately, more economic value.

USING TECHNOLOGY TO ENHANCE SERVICE DELIVERY

Long ago, Ives and Learmonth (1984) identified the importance of applying IT to all phases of the customer lifecycle to improve customer service. Roach (1988) posits that IT plays an important role in the production and delivery of services and helps to redefine services and create new ones, especially since information is the raw ingredient of any service. How information is processed will influence the service firm's over-all productivity (Mills and Turk, 1986). Walker (1995) and Barrington and Olsen (1987) define three stages of customer involvement: pre-consumption (anticipatory phase), consumption (the actual experience), and post-consumption (the residue). Each phase builds on the previous one, thus suggesting the need to apply a systems theory perspective to service design and delivery. Sink and Tuttle (1989) recommend diagramming an organization's activities using an input-output model to show the sequential flow of raw materials (i.e. information) and the interdependencies between processes. The model is serial or sequential in its flow, like that of an assembly line, with each stage having profound implications on its successors. Since outputs of one segment become inputs to another, accuracy in each stage is paramount to the integrity of the model. Therefore, the systems theory perspective focuses attention on the importance of collecting complete and accurate information at the beginning stages of the guest life cycle, the reservation, so that all services downstream (e.g. check-in, hotel stay, check-out) will flow smoothly and create positive and lasting guest memories or what Barrington and Olsen (1987) term as the 'residue'. If data collection at each guest touch point is not done well, service failures will result, and the hotel will realize the true meaning of the old adage: 'Garbage in equals garbage out'.

According to Bill Gates (1999: 3), 'The most meaningful way to differentiate your company from your competition ... is to do an outstanding job with information. *How you gather, manage, and use information will determine whether you win or lose*'. To achieve this vision, one must build a knowledge-based enterprise, which is built around the following three core objectives.

1 *Get Data* – Collect high quality information about guests, employees, suppliers, franchisees, etc.
2 *Move the Data* – Share data throughout the organization, transferring it from the point of collection to the point of use via a reliable communications infrastructure.
3 *Use the Data* – Provide users with the tools to quickly and easily access the data, manipulate it, analyze it, infer meaning from it, and make sound business decisions.

Levitt (1972), Chase (1978), and Chase and Erikson (1988) suggest that manufacturing environments can, at times, serve as role models for service organizations when it comes to standardizing offerings and applying technology to deliver these offerings. According to Levitt (1972: 41), quality and efficiency can be improved if less emphasis is placed on service as servitude and more consideration is given to the substitution of 'technology and systems for people and serendipity'. Levitt is not alone in his thinking. Others also suggest applying manufacturing methods to service, and over the years, the service literature has provided various ways to look at services. For example, Thomas (1978) created a continuum anchored by equipment-based at one end and people-based delivery at the other. For Chase (1978), the preferred continuum was based upon the degree (low to high) of contact a customer has with the service provider. Schmenner (1986) attempts to combine these continuums by creating a four-quadrant matrix with one axis representing the degree of labor intensity and the other representing the degrees of personal interaction and customization.

In yet another approach, Mills and Margulies (1980) and Mills (1986) developed a useful typology for classifying service organizations based upon such characteristics like the degree of personal interaction, the amount of information processing, the type of information exchanged during the service transaction, the ease of transferability, and the degree of customer attachment. The unit of analysis is the customer–(client)–organization interface. Paramount to Mills' typology are the respective roles of the service provider (employee) and the customer (a 'partial employee') (Mills et al., 1983). Generally speaking, the employee and the customer must interact with each other in order to complete the service delivery process. The relationship between the service provider and the customer is best characterized as dyadic due to the simultaneous production and consumption of service (Solomon et al., 1985).

Sustainable competitive advantage is dependent upon a firm's ability to provide exemplary and flawless guest service reliably and consistently (Piccoli et al., 2001). Therefore, the approaches cited above to evaluating service prove invaluable when trying to determine which service processes are likely candidates for automation. They help to determine guests' needs that must be fulfilled (i.e. the value proposition), the fit or congruence between technology solutions and tasks (Copeland and McKenney, 1988), an organization's readiness to embrace various technology options, and guests' likelihood to take advantage of these options. By dissecting processes into their guests life-cycle components, organizations can better understand how to use IT and the Internet to offer more and better services, thereby creating enhanced value and building stronger guest relationships at each stage along the way (Piccoli et al., 2001). Business applications represent a series of business logic or rules programmed as a set of instructions to be carried out by computers. Processes that are well-defined, routine in nature, with a standard set of rules can be programmed more easily than those that have exceptions, that must be extensively customized for a situation or person, or that could have multiple acceptable outcomes. Thus, by applying these service frameworks to the various processes of a hospitality operation, one can begin to recognize potential opportunities to apply IT in ways that will be appropriate for the organization, deliver the expected goals, and have a high likelihood of success.

To determine how best to prioritize and incorporate IT in the service delivery process, it is important to differentiate between core services and supplementary support, or peripheral services (Mills, 1986; Lovelock, 1991; Walker, 1995). This can assist with understanding guest expectations, which aspects of service are more

important than others, and where technology usage may be appropriate or inappropriate. From Perrow's (1967) research contributions, one can infer that a person's behavior can be influenced by how well he/she understands a given problem, the corresponding uncertainty, and the actual or perceived risk(s) associated with that problem. The level of understanding and the risk associated with the ensuing transaction (i.e. the search, selection, and booking of hotel accommodations; check-in/out, etc.) will impact the selection of tools or method(s) by which the individual will employ to solve the problem at hand. Operationalizing the problem-solving process will be dependent upon a number of factors including structure, complexity, standardization, routinization, knowledge, degree of control, and perceived risk. From a hotelier's perspective, this knowledge can shed light on how to segment consumer group, what services to offer, and what service delivery methods to use.

What one must understand is how IT can support and, therefore, enhance a service delivery process. Understanding a process is a fundamental first step before one can attempt to automate it since task/technology congruence is a prerequisite to any successful application of IT (Copeland and McKenney, 1988). Shostack (1984) suggests using a service blueprint methodology to map out service delivery processes and identify potential fail points. Hammer and Champy (1993) push to eradicate inefficiencies and to completely transform or re-engineer business processes to make them more effective so that they produce more value for the firm. Using a service blueprint approach can allow for the development of new service delivery options, identification of approaches to reduce service delivery failures, and the development of service recovery strategies. One can look for ways to marry technology with business problems and opportunities to create promising solutions that can build product/service differentiation, drive new revenue opportunities, cut costs, produce exceptional guest experiences, and drive premium pricing.

Research by Champy et al. (1996) suggest that by better understanding the steps a person undertakes when shopping for a product or service, companies can better tailor their delivery methods to meet consumers' needs. While the processes in acquiring a particular product or service can differ from customer to customer, Champy et al. (1996: 60) identify seven fundamental needs shared to varying degrees by all consumers, regardless of distribution/delivery channels used. They are as follows:

1 Knowledge: the search for information and the process of product/price comparisons.
2 Interaction: the need to communicate with the goods or service provider.
3 Networking: the ability to communicate with others who share similar consumption needs or experiences.
4 Sensory Experience: the ability to factor in sensory perceptions such as sight, sound, scent, etc. when making purchasing decisions.
5 Ubiquity: the ability to access the product or service when and where it is needed or wanted (i.e. at the consumer's convenience versus the provider's).
6 Aggregation: the assimilation of a number of related goods and services that address each and every step of the consumer process.
7 Customization: the personalization and individualization of products and services.

The service-profit chain (Heskett et al., 1994) is a theoretical model suggesting that service excellence can be achieved by providing service employees with the proper tools and developing appropriate procedures to ensure internal service quality. IT is one important method for providing employees with the tools necessary to perform their job responsibilities and for systematizing organizational policies and procedures. This, in turn, leads to employee satisfaction, employee loyalty, and service value within the organization. Finally, high service value leads to customer satisfaction and customer loyalty, which, in turn, drive market share and firm profitability (Bhote, 1995; Rust et al., 1995).

Assuming that the linkages between customer satisfaction, loyalty, market share, and profitability are correct, one can focus on the linkage between IT and the technical core (Thompson, 1967). Various methods can be used to test the implications of IT to better understand improvements and repercussions within the service delivery process in terms of reliability (accuracy) of the core service, assurance, etc. and the resulting impact on customer satisfaction. Such techniques include SERVQUAL (Zeithaml et al., 1990), SERVPERF (Cronin and Taylor, 1992; Teas, 1993), and the critical incident technique (Bitner et al., 1990; Keaveney, 1995).

CLOSING COMMENTS

Interestingly, despite the rapid change of technology and the newer capabilities afforded by technology, the principal reasons for implementing IT have remained relatively stable over time (Grover et al., 1997). Despite this stability, there is no one best solution, process, or set of criteria for evaluating IT investment options because the range of circumstances is so broad (Farbey et al., 1992).

The use of IT throughout a firm should reflect the firm's strategic plan. The methods employed should balance short- and long-term needs with appropriate levels of risk and return using a portfolio approach (McFarlan, 1981; Weill and Olson, 1989; Weill, 1991; Applegate et al., 1996; Thorp et al., 1998; Weill and Broadbent, 1998). A firm's IT portfolio includes various types of IT applications, ranging from strategic technologies to operational or transactional (i.e. tactical) systems to technologies that are required as part of infrastructure, for regulatory requirements, or for just plain competitive necessity (Weill and Broadbent, 1998). The administration of these portfolios requires the use of fundamental management practices, business concepts, and strict discipline or focus – with the overall objective focused on creating value for a firm by supporting current strategies and by enabling new ones (Thorp et al., 1998; Weill and Broadbent, 1998). Like any financial investment portfolio, an IT portfolio must be actively managed with continuous monitoring, updating, and suitable investment levels to meet a firm's goals and objectives and to create a balanced set of risk-return profiles. Firms cannot afford to ignore the environment, opportunity costs, and strategic implications of failing to accept a given investment opportunity. Complacency is seldom an option since competitors will most likely quickly capitalize and alter the competitive landscape with their own moves and initiatives, which will force action by sleeping firms and those attempting to avoid taking any action.

Implicitly, all IT investment decisions are designed to improve strategic value, business performance, and return on investment – unless of course, they are made to comply with regulatory, legal, or other government requirements. Realization of the benefits derived from IT applications comes with time, other changes throughout an organization, and complementary resources. IT alone does not generate benefits.

However, the tools and methods for evaluation and IT appraisals to capture IT's contribution to these benefits are ill-defined and lacking, making it difficult to apply the necessary rigor and analysis for objective, fact-based decisions and allocations of firm resources.

There is also consensus in the literature that no single metric can adequately measure or capture the contributions of IT. Assessing the impact of IT should not rely on univariate metrics, but instead, must look at a composite of measures using multiple techniques to provide a more holistic assessment. Multiple measures are almost always preferred to a single measure because of the richness that can be captured. Since a single measure cannot sufficiently assess the impact of IT (e.g. costs, benefits, organizational impact, etc.), King and McAulay (1997) suggest the use of multivariate and multi-method measures to capture the diverse needs of multiple stakeholders, to provide criteria that can be rank-ordered, and to offer a source of triangulation or validation. To that end, a composite of quantitative and qualitative measures should be used to create a balanced scorecard approach (Kaplan and Norton, 1992, 1996; Semich, 1994; Madden, 1998; Shein, 1998). In the words of Weill and Broadbent (1998: 24):

> Managers make decisions about information technology investments based on a *cluster of factors* [italics added], including capabilities required now and in the future, the role of technology in the industry, the level of investment, the clarity with which technology investments are viewed, and the role and history of information technology in the firm.

Bacon (1992) and Farbey et al., (1992) postulate that the criteria used in evaluating and making IT investment decisions are important because they determine which projects are accepted and the level of funding and resources they receive. Ultimately, they become instrumental in determining and measuring the overall success and effectiveness of the decisions. The assumption is that the criteria used will ensure that only the *right* projects are accepted, while all others are rejected. These authors suggest the following significant implications regarding the criteria used.

1 The criteria used (or omitted) and the manner in which it is used (or not used) impact which decisions or projects are funded or rejected (thus, defining the mix of projects adopted) and the pace at which they are adopted.

2 The criteria provide justification and set expectations within the firm for the application, system, or technology.

3 The criteria provide a basis for comparison of multiple projects competing for a finite set of resources.

4 The criteria impact on how a firm attempts to maximize return on investment and any ensuing cost-benefit analysis.

5 The criteria used affect how a firm balances multiple stakeholder requirements and needs.

6 The criteria provide a set of measures so a firm can monitor and control a project and judge its degree of success.

7 Evaluation and subsequent measurement and comparison between actual benefits realized and anticipated benefits as well as any organizational impacts provide critical opportunities for learning, which can then be factored into future evaluation processes.

The convergence of powerful computers, intelligent software, and high-speed, global telecommunications networks coupled with trends towards miniaturization and mobility is creating a new climate for conducting business throughout the world. The new source of competitive advantage will be based on intellect rather than assets and capital. While the latter two resources are necessary, they are no longer sufficient in a dynamic, high-tech world where the customer is king (i.e. more demanding, more informed, and value-conscious). To survive and thrive in the long run, the hospitality firm of the future will be a learning organization, one that must always reinvent itself to create value and provide the ultimate in individualized service. As in the present, knowledge will be the basis of competition in the future. The dichotomy between the 'haves' and the 'have-nots' will be exacerbated by the bipolarization between those who know and those who know not, in what could be categorized as the great digital divide. In other words, it is not sufficient to have the latest in tools and technology. In order to prosper, one must know how to effectively use these tools and technologies and exploit their capabilities in such a way that competitors cannot easily duplicate.

The co-alignment principle (Chandler, 1962; Thompson, 1967; Bourgeois, 1980; Venkatraman and Prescott, 1990; Venkatraman, et al., 1993; Murthy, 1994; Olsen et al., 1998) and the service-profit (value) chain proposed by Heskett et al. (1994) suggest that IT can be applied effectively to enhance service delivery of both peripheral and core services, contribute to guest satisfaction and loyalty, and ultimately lead the firm in gaining competitive advantage through increased profitability and/or market share. How a hospitality firm rises to these new challenges and how it reshapes its business models will continue to be topics of future discussion and industry research. Ultimately, the challenge will be to creatively implement new technologies to effectively and efficiently treat each guest as an individual segment by providing a highly customized, unique experience (even if in a mass-produced way) while simultaneously creating shareholder value. Information and communications technologies will drive these opportunities – but only if the 'right' infrastructure is first established. What is right, of course, will be organization-dependent, but it is clear that the technology architecture in any organization must be flexible and capable of being upgraded to meet changing business needs and take advantage of newer technology innovations. To reach this state, a well-thought strategy must be developed; this can only be done if the events shaping the future are properly identified and understood. Hence, the need to focus on IT and the resulting convergence is not only timely but also essential to the industry's future. IT is a critical strategic asset, and like any asset, requires ongoing management, oversight, and updating. Investing in IT is, in part, investing in the firm's future.

REFERENCES

Adcock, K., Helms, M. M. and Jih, W.-J. K. (1993) 'Information technology: can it provide a sustainable competitive advantage?', *Information Strategy: The Executive's Journal*, Spring: 10–15.

Alvarez, R., Ferguson, D. H. and Dunn, J. (1983) 'How not to automate your front office', *Cornell Hotel and Restaurant Administration Quarterly*, 24(3): 56–62.

Antonucci, Y. L. and Tucker, J. J., III (1998) 'Responding to earnings-related pressure to reduce IT operating and capital expenditures', *Information Strategy: The Executive's Journal*, Spring: 6–14.

Applegate, L. M., McFarlan, F. W. and McKenney, J. L. (1996) *Corporate Information Systems Management: The Issues Facing Senior Executives* (4th edn.). Chicago: Irwin.

Argyris, C. (1991) 'Teaching smart people how to learn', *Harvard Business Review*, May–June: 99–109.

Argyris, C. (1993) 'Education for leading-learning', *Organizational Dynamics*, 21(3): 5–17.

Argyris, C. (1994) 'Good communication that blocks learning', *Harvard Business Review*, July–August: 77–85.

Argyris, C. and Schön, D. A. (1978) *Organizational Learning: A Theory of Action Perspective*. Reading, MA: Addison-Wesley.

Bacon, C. J. (1992) 'The use of decision criteria in selecting information system', *MIS Quarterly*, 16(3): 335–354.

Barrington, M. N. and Olsen, M. D. (1987) 'Concept of service in the hospitality industry', *International Journal of Hospitality Management*, 6(3): 131–138.

Bates, C. S. (1985) 'Mapping the environment: an operational environmental analysis model', *Long Range Planning*, 18(5): 97–107.

Baumann, M. A. (1997) 'Click and drag', *Hotel and Motel Management*, September 1: 28–30.

Benjamin, R. I., Rockart, J. F., Scott, M., Michael S. and Wyman, J. (1984) 'Information technology: a strategic opportunity', *Sloan Management Review*, Spring: 3–10.

Berinato, S. (2002) *Room for two. CIO* [On-line], May 15. Available: http://www.cio.com/archive/0515/02.tow.html.

Bhote, K. R. (1995) '"It's customer loyalty, stupid": nurturing and measuring what really matters', *National Productivity Review*, 14(3): 39–59.

Bitner, M. J., Booms, B. H. and Tetreault, M. S. (1990) 'The service encounter: diagnosing favorable and unfavorable incidents', *Journal of Marketing*, 54(1): 71–84.

Bourgeois, L. J., III (1980) 'Strategy and environment: a conceptual integration', *Academy of Management Review*, 5(1): 25–39.

Brady, T., Cameron, R., Targett, D. and Beaumont, C. (1992) 'Strategic IT issues: the views of some major IT investors', *Journal of Strategic Information Systems*, 1(4): 183–189.

Brynjolfsson, E. and Hitt, L. (1996) 'The customer counts', *InformationWeek*, 48(September 9): 50, 52, 54.

Burrus, D. (with Gittines, R.) (1993) *Technotrends: How to Use Technology and Go Beyond Your Competition*. New York: HarperBusiness.

Carlzon, J. (1987) *Moments of Truth: New Strategies for Today's Customer-Driven Economy*. New York: HarperCollins Publishers.

Carr, N. G. (2003). 'IT doesn't matter', *Harvard Business Review*, 81(5): 41–49.

Carroll, B. and Siguaw, J. (2003) 'The evolution of electronic distribution: effects on hotels and intermediaries', *Cornell Hotel and Restaurant Administration Quarterly*, 44(4): 38–50.

Champy, J., Buday, R. and Nohria, N. (1996) 'Creating the electronic community', *Information-Week*, June 10: 57–62.

Chandler, A. D. (1962) *Strategy and Structure: Chapters in the History of Industrial Enterprise*. Cambridge, MA: MIT Press.

Chase, R. B. (1978) 'Where does the customer fit in a service operation?', *Harvard Business Review*, November–December: 137–142.

Chase, R. B. and Erikson, W. J. (1988) 'The service factory', *The Academy of Management Executive*, 2(3): 191–196.

Child, J. (1972) 'Organizational structure, environment, and performance: the role of strategic choice', *Sociology*, 6: 1–22.

Cho, W. (1996) A Case Study: Creating and Sustaining Competitive Advantage through an Information Technology Application in the Lodging Industry. Unpublished doctoral dissertation, Virginia Polytechnic Institute and State University.

Christensen, C. M. (1997) *The Innovator's Dilemma: When New Technologies Cause Great Firms to Fail*. Boston: Harvard Business School Press.

Clemons, E. K. (1991) 'Evaluation of strategic investments in information technology', *Communications of the ACM*, 34(1): 22–36.

Clemons, E. K. and Row, M. C. (1991) 'Sustaining IT advantage: the role of structural differences', *MIS Quarterly*, 15(3): 275–291.

Clemons, E. K. and Weber, B. W. (1990) 'Strategic information technology investments: guidelines for decision making', *Journal of Management Information Systems*, 7(2): 9–28.

Cline, R. S. and Blatt, L. A. (1998) 'Creating enterprise value around the customer … leveraging the customer asset in today's hospitality industry', *Arthur Andersen Hospitality and Leisure Executive Report*, 5(1): 2–11.

Cline, R. S. and Rach, L. (1996) *Hospitality 2000—a view to the Next Millennium: A Study of the Key Issues Facing the International Hospitality Industry in the Next Millennium*. New York: Arthur Andersen.

Connolly, D. J. and Ivey, E. L. (2004) 'IT budgeting: how to strategize for technology expenditures', *The Bottomline*, 19(4): 22–25.

Connolly, D. J. and Olsen, M. D. (2001) 'An environmental assessment of how technology is reshaping the hospitality industry', *Tourism and Hospitality Research*, 3(1): 73–93.

Connolly, D. J. and Swig, R. (2004) 'The hotel asset manager's guide to information technology'. In

Paul Beals and Greg Denton (eds) *Hotel Asset Management: Principles and Practices*. Lansing, MI: The Educational Institute of the American Hotel and Lodging Association. pp. 215–233.

Copeland, D. G. and McKenney, J. L. (1988) 'Airline reservations systems: lessons from history', *MIS Quarterly*, 12(3): 353–370.

Covey, S. (1997) 'Putting principles first'. In Rowan Gibson (ed.) *Rethinking the Future: Rethinking Business, Principles, Competition, Control, Leadership, Markets and the World*. London: Nicholas Brealey Publishing Limited. pp. 34–46.

Cronin, J. J. and Taylor, S. A. (1992) 'Measuring service quality: a reexamination and extension', *Journal of Marketing*, 56(3): 55–68.

D'Aveni, R. A. (with Gunther, R.) (1994) *Hyper-Competition: Managing the Dynamics of Strategic Maneuvering*. New York: The Free Press.

Davidow, W. H. and Malone, M. S. (1992) *The Virtual Corporation: Structuring and Revitalizing the Corporation for the 21st Century*. New York: HarperBusiness.

Davis, S. and Botkin, J. (1994) 'The coming of knowledge-based business: smart products will turn companies into educators and consumers into lifelong learners', *Harvard Business Review*, September–October: 165–170.

DeNoble, A. F. and Olsen, M. D. (1986) 'The food service industry environment: market volatility analysis', *F.I.U. Hospitality Review*, 4(2): 89–100.

Diehl, T. M. (1973) 'Computers in hotels—1973', *Cornell Hotel and Restaurant Administration Quarterly*, 13(4): 2–23.

Dill, W. R. (1958) 'Environment as an influence on managerial autonomy', *Administrative Science Quarterly*, 2(1): 409–443.

Duncan, R. B. (1972) 'Characteristics of organizational environments and perceived environmental uncertainty', *Administrative Science Quarterly*, 17(3): 313–327.

Farbey, B., Land, F. and Targett, D. (1992) 'Evaluating investments in IT', *Journal of Information Technology*, 7: 109–122.

Feeny, D. F. and Ives, B. (1990) 'In search of sustainability: reaping long-term advantage from investments in information technology', *Journal of Management Information Systems*, 7(1): 27–46.

Friedman, T. L. (2005) *The World is Flat: A Brief History of the Twenty-First Century*. New York: Farrar, Straus and Giroux.

Gates, B. (with Hemingway, C.) (1999) *Business @ the Speed of Thought: Using a Digital Nervous System*. New York: Time Warner Books.

Geller, A. N. (1984) *Executive Information Needs in Hotel Companies*. Peat, Marwick, Mitchell and Co.

Gordon, P. (1999) 'Pilot takes balanced scorecard digital', *InformationWeek*, October 18: 74 and 76.

Grover, V., Fiedler, K. D. and Teng, J. T. C. (1997) 'Corporate strategy and IT investments', *Business and Economic Review*, 43(3): 17–22.

Halper, M. (1992) Outsourcer confirms demise of reservation coalition plan. Compterworld, 20.

Halper, M. (1993) 'AMR calls confirm partners selfish', *Computerworld*, May 24: 4.

Hamel, G. and Prahalad, C. K. (1994a) *Competing for the Future*. Boston: Harvard Business School Press.

Hamel, G. and Prahalad, C. K. (1994b) 'Competing for the future; what drives your company's agenda: your competitor's view of the future or your own?', *Harvard Business Review*, July–August: 122–128.

Hammer, M. and Champy, J. (1993) *Reengineering the Corporation: A Manifesto for Business Revolution*. New York: HarperBusiness.

Handy, C. (1989) *The Age of Unreason*. Boston: Harvard Business School Press.

Hansen, E. L. and Owen, R. M. (1995) 'Evolving technologies to drive competitive advantage in Hospitality Industry'. *Hotel Online* [On-line], Fall. Available: http://www.hotel-online.com:80/Neo/Trends/Andersen/tech.html.

Hensdill, C. (1998) 'Hotels technology survey', *Hotels*, February: 51–76.

Heskett, J. L., Jones, T. O., Loveman, G. W., Sasser, W. E. Jr. and Schlesinger, L. A. (1994) 'Putting the service-profit chain to work', *Harvard Business Review*, March–April: 164–174.

Hitt, L. M. and Brynjolfsson, E. (1996) 'Productivity, business profitability, and consumer surplus: three different measures of information technology value', *MIS Quarterly*, 20(2): 121–143.

Hopper, M. D. (1990) 'Rattling SABRE – new ways to compete on information', *Harvard Business Review*, May–June: 118–125.

Ives, B. and Learmonth, (1984) 'The information system as a competitive weapon', *Communications of the ACM*, 27(12): 1193–1201.

Jackson, S. E. and Dutton, J. E. (1988) 'Discerning threats and opportunities', *Administrative Science Quarterly*, 33(3): 370–387.

Kantrow, A. M. (1980) 'The strategy–technology connection', *Harvard Business Review*, July–August: 6–21.

Kaplan, R. S. and Norton, D. P. (1992) 'The balanced scorecard – measures that drive performance', *Harvard Business Review*, January–February: 71–79.

Kaplan, R. S. and Norton, D. P. (1996) 'Using the balanced scorecard as a strategic management system', *Harvard Business Review*, January–February: 5–85.

Keaveney, S. M. (1995) 'Customer switching behavior in service industries: an exploratory study', *Journal of Marketing*, 59(2): 71–82.

Kettinger, W. J., Grover, V., Guha, S. and Segars, A. H. (1994) 'Strategic information systems revisited: a study in sustainability and performance', *MIS Quarterly*, 18(1): 31–58.

King, M. and McAulay, L. (1997) 'Information technology investment evaluation: evidence and interpretations', *Journal of Information Technology*, 12: 131–143.

Levitt, T. (1972) 'Productionline approach to service', *Harvard Business Review*, September–October: 41–52.

Lovelock, C. H. (1991) *Services Marketing* (2nd edn.). Englewood, NJ: Prentice-Hall.

Madden, J. (1998) 'Vendors help IT measure up with variations on the Balanced Scorecard', *PC Week*, September 28: 76.

Mahmood, M. A. and Mann, G. J. (1993) 'Measuring the organizational impact of information technology investment: an exploratory study', *Journal of Management Information Systems*, 10(1): 97–122.

Mata, F. J., Fuerst, W. L. and Barney, J. B. (1995) 'Information technology and sustained competitive advantage: a resource-based analysis', *MIS Quarterly*, 19(4): 487–505.

Mathe, H. and Dagi, T. F. (1996) 'Harnessing technology in global service businesses', *Long Range Planning*, 29(4): 449–461.

McFarlan, F. W. (1981) 'Portfolio approach to information systems', *Harvard Business Review*, September–October: 142–150.

Mills, P. K. (1986) *Managing Service Industries: Organizational Practices in a Postindustrial Economy*. Cambridge, MA: Ballinger Publishing Company.

Mills, P. K. and Margulies, N. (1980) 'Toward a core typology of service organizations', *Academy of Management Review*, 5(2): 255–265.

Mills, P. K. and Turk, T. (1986) 'A preliminary investigation into the influence of customer-firm interface on information processing and task activities in service organizations', *Journal of Management*, 12(1): 91–104.

Mills, P. K., Chase, R. B. and Margulies, N. (1983) 'Motivating the client/employee system as a service production strategy', *Academy of Management Review*, 8(2): 301–310.

Mintzberg, H. (1978) 'Patterns in strategy formulation', *Management Science*, 24(9): 934–948.

Murthy, B. (1994) *Measurement of the Strategy Construct in the Lodging Industry, and the Strategy-Performance Relationship*. Unpublished doctoral dissertation, Virginia Polytechnic Institute and State University.

Neelakantan, S. (1996) 'Tech goofs', *Forbes*, December 30: 18–20.

Negroponte, N. (1995) *Being Digital*. New York: Vintage Books.

Neo, B. S. (1988) 'Factors facilitating the use of information technology for competitive advantage: an exploratory study', *Information and Management*, 15(4): 191–201.

Nyheim, P. D., McFadden, F. and Connolly, D. J. (with Paiva, A. J.) (2005). *Technology Strategies for the Hospitality Industry* (1st edn.). Upper Saddle River, NJ: Pearson Prentice Hall.

O'Connor, P. and Piccoli, G. (2003) 'Marketing hotels using global distribution systems', *Cornell Hotel and Restaurant Administration Quarterly*, 44(5/6): 105–114.

Olsen, M. D. (1980) 'The importance of the environment to the food service and lodging manager', *The Journal of Hospitality Education*, 4(2): 35–45.

Olsen, M. D. (1996) *Into the New Millennium: A White Paper on the Global Hospitality Industry*. Paris: International Hotel Association.

Olsen, M. D., West, J. J. and Tse, E. C. (1998) *Strategic Management in the Hospitality Industry* (2nd edn.). New York: John Wiley and Sons.

Parsons, G. L. (1983) 'Information technology: a new competitive weapon', *Sloan Management Review*, Fall: 3–14.

Pastore, R. (2005) 'Alignment is dead: long live convergence', *CIO* [On-line], March 15. Available: http://www.cio.com/archive/031505/edit.html.

Perrow, C. (1967) 'A framework for the comparative analysis of organizations', *American Sociological Review*, 32: 194–208.

Piccoli, G. (2004) 'Making IT matter', *CHR Reports*, 4(9): 4–21.

Piccoli, G., O'Connor, P., Capaccioli, C. and Alvarez, R. (2003) 'Customer relationship management: a driver for change in the structure of the U.S. lodging industry', *Cornell Hotel and Restaurant Administration Quarterly*, 44(4): 61–73.

Piccoli, G., Spalding, B. R. and Ives, B. (2001) 'The customer service life cycle: a framework for improving customer service through information technology', *Cornell Hotel and Restaurant Administration Quarterly*, 42(3): 38–45.

Pine, B. J. II and Gilmore, J. H. (1998) 'Welcome to the experience economy', *Harvard Business Review*, July–August: 97–105.

Porter, M. E. (1980) *Competitive Strategy: Techniques for Analyzing Industries and Competitors*. New York: The Free Press.

Porter, M. E. (1985) *Competitive Advantage: Creating and Sustaining Superior Performance*. New York: The Free Press.

Post, G. V., Kagan, A. and Lau, K.-N. (1995) 'A modeling approach to evaluating strategic uses of information technology', *Journal of Management Information Systems*, 12(2): 161–187.

Quinn, J. B. (1988) 'Service technology and manufacturing: cornerstones of the U.S. economy'. In B. R. Guile and J. B. Quinn (eds) *Managing Innovation: Cases from the Service Industries*. Washington, DC: National Academy Press. pp. 9–35.

Rayport, J. F. and Jaworski, B. J. (2005) *Best Face Forward: Why Companies Must Improve Their Service Interfaces with Customers*. Boston: Harvard Business School Press.

Reich, B. H. and Benbasat, I. (1996) 'Measuring the linkage between business and information technology objectives', *MIS Quarterly*, 20(1): 55–81.

Roach, S. S. (1988) 'Technology and the service sector: America's hidden competitive challenge'. In B. R. Guile and J. B. Quinn (eds) *Technology in Services: Policies for Growth, Trade, and Employment*. Washington, DC: The National Academy of Sciences. pp. 118–138.

Rust, R. T., Zahorik, A. J. and Keiningham, T. L. (1995) 'Return on quality (ROQ): making service quality financially accountable', *Journal of Marketing*, 59(2): 58–60.

Schmenner, R. W. (1986) 'How can service businesses survive and prosper?' *Sloan Management Review*, Spring: 21–32.

Segars, A. H. and Grover, V. (1995) 'The industry-level impact of information technology: an empirical analysis of three industries', *Decision Sciences*, 26(3): 337–368.

Semich, J. W. (1994) 'Here's how to quantify IT investment benefits', *Datamation*, January 7: 45–46, 48.

Shein, E. (1998) 'Formula for ROI: IT is gauging project performance to produce tangible results for business', *PC Week*, September 28: 73, 76, 79.

Shostack, G. L. (1984). 'Designing services that deliver', *Harvard Business Review*, January–February: 133–139.

Siguaw, J. A. and Enz, C. A. (1999) 'Best practices in information technology', *Cornell Hotel and Restaurant Administration Quarterly*, 40(5): 58–71.

Sink, D. S. and Tuttle, T. C. (1989) *Planning and Measurement in Your Organization of the Future*. Norcross, GA: Industrial Engineering and Management Press.

Slattery, P. and Olsen, M. D. (1984) 'Hospitality organizations and their environment', *International Journal of Hospitality Management*, 3(3): 55–61.

Slywotzky, A. J. (1996) *Value Migration: How to Think Several Moves Ahead of the Competition*. Boston: Harvard Business School Press.

Smith, J. L. (with Flanagan, W. G.) (2006) *Creating Competitive Advantage: Give Customers a Reason to Choose You Over Your Competitors.* New York: Currency/Doubleday.

Solomon, M. R., Surprenant, C., Czepiel, J. A. and Gutman, E. G. (1985) 'A role theory perspective on dyadic interaction: the service encounter', *Journal of Marketing,* 49(4): 99–111.

Tapscott, D. (1996) *The Digital Economy: Promise and Peril in the Age of Networked Intelligence.* New York: McGraw-Hill.

Tapscott, D. and Caston, A. (1993) *Paradigm Shift: The New Promise of Information Technology.* New York: McGraw-Hill.

Tapscott, D. and Ticoll, D. (2003) *The Naked Corporation: How the Age of Transparency Will Revolutionize Business.* New York: Free Press.

Teas, R. K. (1993) 'Expectations, performance evaluation, and consumers' perceptions of quality', *Journal of Marketing,* 57(4): 18–34.

Thomas, D. R. E. (1978) 'Strategy is different in service businesses', *Harvard Business Review,* July–August: 158–161.

Thompson, J. D. (1967) *Organizations in Action.* New York: McGraw-Hill.

Thorp, J. and DMR's Center for Strategic Leadership. (1998) *The Information Paradox: Realizing the Business Benefits of Information Technology.* Toronto: McGraw-Hill.

Van Hoof, H. B., Collins, G. R., Combrink, T. E. and Verbeeten, M. J. (2005) 'Technology needs and perceptions: an assessment of the U.S. lodging industry', *Cornell Hotel and Restaurant Administration Quarterly,* 36(5): 64–69.

Venkatraman, N. and Prescott, J. E. (1990) 'Environment-strategy coalignment: an empirical test of its performance implications', *Strategic Management Journal,* 11(1): 1–23.

Venkatraman, N., Henderson, J. C. and Oldach, S. (1993) 'Continuous strategic alignment: exploiting information technology capabilities for competitive success', *European Management Journal,* 11(2): 139–149.

Vitale, M. R. (1986) 'The growing risk of information systems success', *MIS Quarterly,* 10(4): 327–334.

Walker, J. L. (1995) 'Service encounter satisfaction: conceptualized', *Journal of Services Marketing,* 9(1): 5–14.

Weill, P. (1991) 'The information technology payoff: implications for investment appraisal', *Australian Accounting Review,* 2–11.

Weill, P. and Broadbent, M. (1998) *Leveraging the New Infrastructure: How Market Leaders Capitalize on Information Technology.* Boston: Harvard Business School Press.

Weill, P. and Olson, M. H. (1989) 'Managing investment in information technology: mini case examples and implications', *MIS Quarterly,* 13(1): 3–18.

West, J. J. and Olson, M. D. (1988) 'Environmental scanning and its effect upon firm performance: an exploratory study of the foodservice industry', *Hospitality Education and Research Journal,* 12(2): 127–136.

Zeithaml, V. A., Parasuraman, A. and Berry, L. L. (1990) *Delivering Quality Service: Balancing Customer Perceptions and Expectations.* New York: The Free Press.

PART THREE

Specialized Management Functions in the Hospitality Industry

Hotel Real Estate Finance and Investments

16

Paul Beals

INTRODUCTION

Viewed from the perspective of the investor, the hotel industry has changed immensely over the last four decades. The era of the owner-operator who stamped his property (or properties) with a family name that heralded consistency (Statler), luxury (Ritz), history (Raffles), or convenience (Hilton) has given way to an era of return driven, opportunistic 'money partners' who own the hotels bearing such brands as Le Méridian, Four Seasons, InterContinental, and Doubletree. From the perspective of the consumer of lodging space, the ineluctable drift from the eponymous and idiosyncratic to chain hotels has been largely reassuring, although experienced travelers almost inevitably guard an affection for a limited number of special, often quirky independent properties that are not to be found in any brand's directory. For investors in hotel property, the bifurcation of the lodging industry into two distinct components – operations and ownership – has provided an opportunity to enjoy returns superior to those achieved by holding shares in publicly traded hotel companies both owning and managing lodging assets.

This transformation of the hotel property market from corporate or individual ownership to what is sometimes called programmatic investing was neither seamless nor painless. The creation (or the resuscitation) of the various vehicles required to facilitate the pooling of capital – limited partnerships, real estate investment trusts (REITs), limited liability companies (LLCs), commercial mortgage backed securities (CMBSs) – required time as investors gained familiarity and eventually comfort with the structures that underpin programmatic investing. At the same time

across the globe owners and operators were slowly coming to a better understanding of how to employ management contracts, franchising, and leases to allocate acceptably the risks and rewards of owning, branding, and managing hotels. While the journey was slow, the destination merited the efforts: today's hotel property investor, whether institutional or entrepreneurial, can hold a diversified portfolio of lodging assets, spread across various property types, markets, and geographic regions.

THE STUDY OF HOTEL REAL ESTATE AND INVESTMENTS

Notwithstanding the proliferation of 'hotel schools' at both undergraduate and graduate levels around the world over the last three decades, there is little emphasis on the study of hotel real estate or hotel investments in the curricula of most of these institutions. The approach to some disciplines (e.g. marketing, information technology, financial management) has become more rigorous in many hospitality management programs, but the emphasis of the teaching remains the formation of property-level managers able to solve the operational problems of individual lodging units. In contrast, the study of hotel real estate looks beyond operational considerations to understand the hotel asset as an investment.

The contrast between the hotel as an operational unit and an investment can be usefully elucidated by comparing the financial mentality of hotel investors versus that of operators. Except as it affects taxes, profit is an abstraction for hotel investors. They count in cash flow and measure outcomes on an absolute basis – after-tax cash inflows versus after-tax cash outflows. Hoteliers count in terms of accounting profit, and measure it on a relative basis at intermediate steps (departmental profit percentage, gross profit percentage, income before fixed charges as a percentage of revenue), emphasizing cost control over revenue generation. Many confrontations between owners and operators reflect this divergence: the owner (and, on occasion, the lender) pleads for cash while the hotelier cites ratios – a 28% food cost, 32% income before fixed charges, etc. – as evidence that s/he has done an adequate job of managing.

Hoteliers and investors also have different perspectives on time. The investor values immediacy (forever asking, as one set-upon hotelier reported to this writer, 'What have you done for me lately?') and discounts future cash flows. Operators are trained to concentrate on outcomes achieved over a longer, more fluid horizon. They value customer service (the more personalized the better), their franchise with consumers, and repeat business. Thus, where investors see frequent-stay programs as discounting, the hotelier sees a made-to-order marketing tactic enabling him or her to achieve numerous important objectives.

The fundamental conflict between investor and hotelier financial perspectives is succinctly summarized by the debate that so often ensues when capital projects are reviewed. Hoteliers insist that an upscale restaurant or a lobby renovation will enhance the hotel's image and yield new business. Investors, to the frustration of operators, seek precision that goes beyond assembling cost estimates to forecasting concrete benefits in terms of net operating income measured over a specific time line. Not surprisingly, operators frequently complain that investors fail to provide adequate capital to realize the full potential of the hotels they manage, and investors accuse hoteliers of misspending capital.

The real estate maxim, 'Don't fall in love with an asset', is regularly practiced by hotel investors, while for hoteliers it is observed by the breech. A possible exception to this generalization is the wealthy investor – typically termed a high-net-worth individual – who purchases a 'trophy' asset (i.e. a distinctive, luxury lodging property) as a status symbol. However, even this breed of investor eventually shifts his or her attention to the cash-flow generation potential of his asset, and will often abide the

notion of selling his prized possession when offered an adequate premium. The hotel investor views the asset in the context of his or her broader holdings and never enters an investment without having identified an exit strategy. In contrast, the objective of the competent operator is continuity – the ongoing improvement of the physical asset, the refinement of the lodging 'product', and the amelioration of service. Thus there are two quite different time horizons for the owner and the operator.

The owner's time horizon may nominally be long-term, as with institutional investors such as insurance companies and pension funds. These investors frequently own hotels for their maturity-matching characteristics – i.e. the regular cash flows from a successful hotel coincide with the institutions' obligations, yielding the streams necessary to pay policy-holders' claims and provide annuitants timely retirement income. But even such classical long-term investors are ultimately opportunistic and will frequently sell their lodging assets at the top of the cycle, harvesting the appreciation component of their returns and reinvesting them in other asset classes perceived to be emerging from a trough in their market cycles. The opportunistic outlook of *all* lodging investors – whether their horizons are nominally long- or short-term – derives from a fundamental economic reality: maximum returns from hotels are realized only by unlocking their appreciated value. Thus owners are traders – 'market timers' seeking the main chance that provides the highest return on their invested capital (Rushmore et al., 2002).

In contrast to this opportunistic time horizon, operators maximize their returns by staying in the management of hotels as long as possible and by protecting their franchise with consumers. Thus, whether the contractual instrument is a franchise agreement or a management contract, the operator seeks the longest term possible and insists on contractual terms that bind owners, requiring them to finance evolving brand standards (Beals and Denton, 2005). An owner entering a franchise or management contract with a strong brand is accepting to maintain his asset's positioning for a period of 20 to 30 years, constraining his ability to exercise strategic options to enhance the value of the property. Similarly, the owner is accepting to make unspecified future improvements and alterations that will be dictated by the brand to protect its franchise with consumers but which may not be aligned with ownership's interests.

The two quite different mentalities sketched above are significantly at odds, making for a tension not only in the commercial world but also in the educational arena. Hotel schools developed historically first as vocational schools teaching the craft of operating multi-faceted lodging enterprises. Although the acknowledged leaders among hotel schools have advanced significantly, developing as true schools of hospitality management, their curricula continue to reflect an operational orientation. The teaching and research at most hotel schools emphasizes the design and control of processes – the procedures by which we plumb the consumer's mind, develop products to meet consumers' needs, train employees to deliver the product and measure our success in achieving unit-level profitability.

The teaching of these operational processes is a worthy endeavor, and critical to the development of a cadre of managers able to deliver hospitality services at necessarily decentralized locations. However, the teaching of these processes does not prepare graduates to understand hotels as investments. Such a preparation requires a larger, more strategic perspective on hotels than is reflected in the curricula of hotel schools. A graduate prepared in hotel real estate and investments must understand the unit-level economics of the lodging industry but he/she must also understand the real estate transactions market and the relative appeal of hotels as an asset class. He/she must understand, like the traditional hotel school graduate, the control mechanisms necessary for efficient hotel operations, while also understanding how capital markets function. He/she must understand the legal, tax, and practical implications of a hotel's entity structure – considerations rarely touched upon in operationally oriented, traditional hospitality management curricula.

Given the history and prevailing culture of hotel schools, it is not surprising that their curricula remain process specific, or that, worldwide, there are only a limited number of hotel-school faculty members teaching and conducting research in hotel real estate and investments. In fairness, the decision of traditional hotel schools to eschew the teaching of hotel real estate and investments may be rooted more in prudence than aversion to change. Notwithstanding the ready flow of capital across international borders that is part of today's globalization, the market for hotel-school graduates well versed in hotel finance and investments is miniscule in comparison to the market for graduates trained in operational processes. Of equal importance is that the supply of candidates with the vision to go beyond operational training to embrace a quite different perspective is limited, making it challenging to recruit students for the study of hotel real estate and investments. If only one hotel school, at Cornell University, has been able to sustain adequately staffed courses in real estate, hotel finance, and investments despite the dramatic change in the industry's structure, it may rightly be perceived as a territory where only fools tread.

Traditional real estate studies vs. hotel-specific real estate studies

While not all business schools regard real estate as an appropriate discipline to include among their offerings, there are a significant number of undergraduate and graduate schools of business that either offer a handful of courses in real estate as electives to complement a traditional business degree or provide students with the opportunity to earn a specialized degree in real estate. As hotels have gained acceptance as a real estate asset class, it might be logical to assume that courses offered in what this writer terms 'generic' real estate programs have been expanded to treat hotels alongside the standard asset classes of office, retail, multi-family, industrial and warehouses. These are the standard property categories whose returns are reported as part of the NCREIF Index, a quarterly report issued by the US National Council of Real Estate Investment Fiduciaries (www.NCREIF.org). Separately, NCREIF also reports returns for hotels, but the number of owners contributing data is limited and thus the returns are probably not representative of the returns achieved across the industry. However, there is little evidence – either through the research emanating from these business schools or from reports of course offerings – that hotels are a subject of much study at generic real estate schools. There are at least three important differences distinguishing hotels and other real estate asset classes that deserve to be understood and which may explain the reluctance of real estate generalists to study hotels more extensively.

The markets for multi-family, retail, office and industrial space are decidedly local, facilitating the study of their potential because users' patterns can be observed more readily. Thus the demand for residential space can be related to its proximity to occupants' workplaces and algorithms developed to express the prices the space will command. In the retail sector, well developed gravity models allow market researchers to deduce the population concentration necessary in a given radius to support an incremental or expanded store (Ling and Archer, 2005).

In contrast, the market researcher attempting to estimate the demand for hotel space is by definition seeking to quantify an external demand and thus faces a more challenging task. The most widely accepted and practiced model uses existing supply as a proxy for demand. The technique, called the build-up approach, requires the analyst to estimate the demand characteristics of competitive hotels in the marketplace and then infer that the subject hotel will capture at least its proportional share of that demand (Rushmore and Baum, 2001). This famous 'fair share' assumption has, in recent years, been supplemented by penetration analysis, which attempts to specify how the subject hotel will surpass or fall short of capturing its fair share of demand because of its individual characteristics (brand, proximity to demand generators, appeal to a specific market segment, etc.). Although competently prepared hotel feasibility studies can be reasonably compelling in their conclusions, their fundamental technique is to infer demand rather than quantifying demand, as can the local developer of, say, an office building.

Not surprisingly, in the face of this challenge, experienced hotel investors have developed their own heuristics for gaining comfort with a lodging property's potential. This ability to 'read markets', while ostensibly not very scientific, is in fact a very important part of the investment-decision process. Even hotel investors who head up large organizations with sufficient subordinates and consultants to perform the market analyses will base their decisions on their own appreciation of the market dynamics of individual acquisitions. However, investors in other commercial real estate asset classes and real estate researchers, habituated to more concrete measures of real estate's potential, appear sufficiently intimidated by the difficulty of estimating

the markets for hotel space to avoid them altogether.

Perhaps one of the least scientific of explanations for an investment decision was related to the writer by Isadore Sharpe, Chief Executive Officer of Four Seasons Hotels. Feasibility authorities from two separate consulting firms had dismissed the potential of the Four Seasons Inn on the Park London, the then fledgling firm's first hotel outside of North America. The feasibility reports were prepared in the aftermath of the 1970s oil shock and a general worldwide economic downturn that impacted London severely. But Sharpe was able to convince his investors to proceed and the Inn on the Park London was ultimately a hugely successful investment that confirmed Four Seasons' credibility as an operator of distinctive luxury properties. Sharpe explained his decision as follows: 'I was in a cab going around the Marble Arch. I saw all this traffic whizzing by me and thought "it simply has to work'".

An equally daunting difference between hotel investments and other real estate asset classes is the length of the lease term. Depending on how well he has calculated the market and his own degree of risk aversion, the developer of an office building or retail complex may have 70 to 100% of his space leased before construction begins. Moreover, he can choose a slightly lower return but reduce his risk significantly by accepting only the most creditworthy tenants and signing them on for longer terms.

In contrast, the hotel lease is for one night's duration and cancelable on short notice. Group contracts, with their guarantees and attrition clauses, are of course more favorable to the hotel investor, but pre-leasing a property under construction (or in the midst of a renovation) is, as any experienced hotel sales manager will attest, challenging. Finally, while an investor in an office building or retail complex can obviate the danger of numerous disruptions by passing the risk to tenants, hotels' short leases leave them vulnerable to weather, natural disasters, air- and ground-transportation capacity fluctuations and security issues.

The upside to hotels' short leases is the ability to change prices readily in response to changing demand. This can provide hotel investors with superior returns in strong markets, but this is the premium to be expected for shouldering the risk of short leases. Moreover, if supply can be readily added, the return premium will quickly evaporate, leaving the hotel investor with an inferior risk-adjusted return. Thus some hotel owners refuse to invest in property types that are readily replicated (e.g. suburban limited service hotels) and all appreciate assets that enjoy high barriers to entry – for example, downtown properties in cities with scarce available land or a beachfront resort property surrounded by a nature preserve.

A lodging property is an operating business housed in real estate. Although appraisers are frequently called upon to separate the real estate value of a hotel asset from its business value (Rushmore and Baum, 2001), this is largely an academic exercise required by local real-estate tax regulations. As consumers have become more sophisticated and hotel brands have channeled their expectations by various segmentation strategies, the lodging product is increasingly an experience and less the sale of fungible space. Thus the value of the lodging asset will depend on the operator's ability to deliver the guest experience. This is a vastly different management challenge from the operation of any other real estate asset class – and rightly a strong deterrent to the entry of inexperienced hotel investors into the sector.

Compare, for example, the operation of an office building to the operation of a hotel. The typical operating budget of an office building will leave some 75% of the rental stream to cover debt service and taxes. In contrast, the heavily management intensive operation of a hotel will absorb some 75% of the property's revenue, leaving 25% to pay debt service and taxes. The risk profile of a hotel is hardly appealing to an outsider used to less risky real estate ventures. The hotel investor's revenue depends not on a fixed lease with a credit-worthy tenant, but on the effectiveness of the operator in selling the property's space and other services. Yet if the cost of the operator's services is disproportionate in relation to the operator's effectiveness in generating revenue, the investor's return is jeopardized.

Current state of the art: hotel real estate studies

As a result of the risks and the unique characteristics of hotels in comparison to other real estate asset classes, the study of hotel real estate has been largely accomplished not by real estate generalists but by a handful of scholars affiliated with hotel schools and a larger group of practitioners. Among the categories

of practitioners contributing to the study of hotel real estate and finance over the last four decades are: consultants, appraisers, investors, asset managers, accountants, tax specialists, lawyers, lenders, operators and government administrators.

As the separation of ownership and operations deepened over the same 40 years, three principal streams of research and commentary developed. A strain of scholarship developed to explore the agency relationships between owners and operators (Eyster, 1988). Most of this scholarship centered on management contracts and franchising, attempting to define the necessary terms to balance appropriately the risks and returns to owners and operators. If the discussions with lodging industry executives in this writer's classroom are any indication, détente has been achieved on some issues in owner-brand relations, but much is still contentious.

Increased understanding of the risks of hotel investments, especially among institutional and publicly traded ownership entities, has led to a second strain of research and commentary into a function now known as asset management (Beals, 2004). Although the asset management function emphasizes heavily creating value through improved operational and marketing techniques, it also gives appropriate weight to the timing of acquisitions and the exit strategy. For a discussion of the various exit strategies employed in the North American lodging industry, see Beals and Arabia (2006). All of the asset manager's functions of course demonstrate the proposition that the risks of lodging investments impose the requirement to strive for commensurate returns.

Finally, as capital markets evolved to meet the demands of investors seeking to replace their individual assets with more liquid and more diverse real estate holdings, a literature describing these entities and structures developed. In North America, the two most common results of these efforts – REITs and CMBSs – are now well established, so study of them has understandably diminished. However, their spread to other parts of the world will bear continuing study.

THEMES AND ISSUES: HOTELS AS INVESTMENTS

In the preceding section describing the 'fit' of hotel real estate studies in the broader field of hospitality management, the differences between hotel investments and investments in other real estate asset classes were illustrated and the risk of hotel investments emphasized. A further, more formal analysis will demonstrate the financial characteristics of lodging investments, evaluate their risks, and suggest the countervailing rewards of hotel ownership.

Operating leverage

Lodging operations are characterized by high fixed costs but low variable costs, potentially yielding a strong upside if an adequate level of sales volume is reached. The effect of operating leverage is best illustrated by considering the sale of the last room of the day in a hotel commanding a 150€ room rate. In a competently managed lodging operation the direct cost of selling a room is approximately 20% of the rooms department's revenue. Although some of the direct costs of the rooms department are fixed (e.g. the salary of the executive housekeeper), our analysis is simplified if we assume the sale of the day's last room entails a full 30€ (150€ × 0.20) of incremental direct cost. The 120€ contribution margin on the transaction is available to pay fixed costs or to provide profit. If we assume further that the sale of all the rooms preceding the sale of the last room of the day precisely covered the fixed costs of the lodging operation – i.e. the hotel was at breakeven before the sale of the incremental room – the entire 120€ 'drops to the bottom line', illustrating the power of operating leverage. (Food and beverage operations have a quite different cost profile and as a result do not enjoy the same level of operating leverage. If, for example, the last sale of the day for a restaurant were an after-hours festive meal for two selling for 150€ and the restaurant had reached breakeven just at closing time, the contribution margin from the incremental meal served would be much less. The 'prime cost' of a restaurant meal – the labor and food costs attendant on serving each meal – run between 60 and 70% of the sale price, diminishing operating leverage. Moreover, the higher levels of variable costs that penalize food and beverage operations in comparison to hotels are not offset by lower levels of fixed costs; successful restaurants typically need to be in the same high cost locations as hotels and feature the same expensive décors. The limited operating leverage provided by food

and beverage operations prejudices the thinking of most hotel investors, who typically view them as a requisite but risky amenity necessary to the sale of rooms.)

On a macro level, the impact of operating leverage is illustrated by the performance of the North American lodging industry in the 1990s. In the early 1990s, the industry went through one of the worst periods in its history, with record foreclosures and an eventual sell-off of assets. As the industry began to recover in 1993 and 1994, average North American occupancy levels reached 63%. The improvement in the industry continued, and in 1999 and 2000 the North American lodging industry posted record profits. Yet during the run-up in performance, the average occupancy percentage for North American hotels increased by less than three points. As demand increased, hoteliers were able to raise rates, benefiting fully from the enhanced contribution margins, whereas improvements in occupancy bring attendant increases in absolute variable costs. Moreover, the period was marked by significant operating cost reductions as new owners acquired underperforming hotels and pushed operators to improve performance. As rates rose and costs declined, contribution margins – or 'flow through' in lodging-industry parlance – increased and the full upside of operating leverage was enjoyed by the industry.

The downside of operating leverage is illustrated on the macro level by developments in the North American lodging industry in the years immediately following the halcyon days of 1999 and 2000. An economic slowdown that began in 2001 was exacerbated by the devastating events of 9/11 and their impact on travel. The industry went from enjoying the upside of operating leverage to feeling dramatically the risk of high fixed costs. Owners and operators moved quickly to cut variable costs, but most also resorted to cutting rates in an effort to generate adequate revenue to cover their fixed costs. Ultimately, a sell-off of assets reminiscent of the early 1990s was avoided because of two factors. Many owners were determined to wait out the industry's distress and refused to sell their assets at depressed prices. Second, overall debt levels on North American lodging assets were lower than in previous 'rough patches', while interest rates were falling. In this environment, many lenders to the hotel industry found forbearance a more rational response than foreclosure, while others agreed to inject capital rather than take back a hotel whose recovery became increasingly distant as the industry struggled through 2002 and 2003.

Financial leverage

Classical finance theory holds that businesses that have a high degree of operating leverage should avoid increasing their fixed costs and risk by limiting their use of debt capital. Except for selected hotel ownership entities (discussed below), most hotel investors perversely turn this logical proposition on its head, arguing that because of the risk of hotel assets they are entitled to a higher return and must achieve this return through liberal doses of cheaper debt capital. Thus hotel investors will strive to turn the 10 to 14% return from an all-equity financed hotel into a 20 to 30% return by the addition of financial leverage.

Obviously, 10 to 14% unlevered returns represent a significant risk premium, especially in an environment where the safest alternative investments – government bonds issued by the largest industrialized nations – yield in the range of 2 to 5% annual return. An observer might reasonably ask therefore if lenders providing the debt financing to the lodging industry are aware of the risk inherent in hotels. Experienced hotel lenders do understand the risks, but they are enticed by the superior yields hotel loans offer.

In addition, lenders will attempt to control their risk exposure by various tactics. Most, for example, will not make loans for hotels that are yet to be built, fearing that the operations will not perform as forecasted or that construction delays and cost overruns will exhaust the equity participant's resources, leaving the project stalled. Instead, hotel lenders seek to make loans on 'seasoned' properties – hotels with stable operating histories, thus limiting the unknowns that might reduce cash flow below the operation's debt service requirement. Lenders also put great store in the track records of the equity participant and, to a lesser extent, the operator. Confidence in the 'sponsorship', as the equity participant and operator are collectively known, is an important reassurance to the lender because their expertise can mitigate the risk of unforeseen developments. Finally, recognizing that 'a rising tide lifts all boats', lenders are more active at the beginning of a lodging industry cycle than at its peak (Bond, 1998).

Not all hotel owners employ high levels of financial leverage. Publicly traded REITs, for example, are typically constrained by their charters to keep debt-to-asset ratios below 40 to 45%. Institutional investors, such as pension funds and insurance companies, are similarly conservative in the debt levels they employ, accepting a lesser return but respecting the fiduciary responsibility they owe to annuitants and policyholders. A large number of other private investors in hotels, however, seek high degrees of financial leverage to boost the returns derived from the particular advantages of hotel investments.

Tax issues

Like all real estate, hotels offer tax-shelter benefits. In the case of hotels, however, their tax-shelter benefits exceed those of other real estate asset classes because a larger percentage of the overall investment consists of furniture, fixtures and equipment, or FF&E. Under the tax codes of most industrialized nations, FF&E enjoys significantly shorter depreciable lives than real property, as well as qualifying for accelerated depreciation schedules. By some estimates, 30 to 35% of a luxury hotel's global asset value is held in FF&E, yielding a significant depreciation deduction that reduces income taxes and improves cash flow.

However, a disadvantage of the nature of FF&E is that economic depreciation corresponds too closely to tax depreciation. Thus, just as the tax accounting depreciation on FF&E – and its tax shelter – are running out it is time for a refurbishment of the hotel. Experienced owners and operators recognize this phenomenon as a mixed blessing. On one hand, a cash reserve – typically termed a reserve for replacement – must be established to fund the refurbishment, reducing ownership's cash flow and return. On the other hand, once spent the reserve for replacement provides a renewed tax shelter as new FF&E is depreciated.

The use of financial leverage adds to the value of depreciation charges, permitting the equity participant to finance assets using inexpensive debt capital while enjoying the tax-shelter the assets provide. Similarly, the interest charges on debt are tax deductible, reducing the cost of debt to the equity participant. The combined effects of the depreciation tax shelter and interest tax shelter make investing in highly leveraged, asset intensive enterprises enjoying high degrees of operating leverage irresistible for certain classes of investors. Moreover, the higher the income-tax rate, the greater is the present value of the tax-shelter benefits provided by depreciation and interest deductibility. Not surprisingly, boom and bust cycles in hotel ownership and construction are often the products of tax-code tinkering by governments intent on accelerating or reining in real estate development.

Reporting issues

Unfortunately, the abundant depreciation charges and high levels of financial leverage sought by the tax-deferring, cash flow oriented private hotel investors are not favored in the public markets. Although the effect of depreciation charges on earnings can be softened by permitting accelerated depreciation schedules for the calculation of tax liability and lengthier depreciation schedules for reporting purposes, ultimately depreciation charges will result in reduced earnings, diminished shareholder equity and under-reported asset values. Although the CEOs and CFOs of numerous public real estate companies, including hotel owner-operators, have argued for years that the appropriate emphasis is on after-tax cash flow and *appreciating* asset values, too many investors evaluate companies in terms of earnings. Since conventional accounting does not capture the tax-shelter benefits or the appreciation potential of hotels, the shares of publicly traded hotel ownership companies have historically traded at prices inferior to their underlying value, rendering capital prohibitively expensive.

Similarly, the high levels of debt attractive to the private investor as a means of improving equity's return increases the cost of capital for a publicly traded hotel ownership entity. Prospective investors in hotel owner-operators may be intrigued by the growth and diver-sification arguments that justify high degrees of financial leverage. If they believe there is adequate upside in the company's growth, they may also be able to accept the risk-reward tradeoff offered by hotels' operating leverage. But high levels of debt increase their downside risk, leaving only a scant asset cushion to protect their equity. Thus, even if they can 'get their arms around' the other components of the risk of hotel owner-operators, they will inevitably be led to

hedge their downside risk by offering less for a stake in the enterprise, driving up the publicly traded hotel company's cost of capital.

As will be demonstrated in the following paragraphs, the various characteristics of hotels as investments discussed above contributed to the separation of ownership and operations, leading the industry to the model that is widespread today.

THEMES AND ISSUES: STRATEGIC AND FINANCIAL CONSIDERATIONS INFORMING THE SEPARATION OF OWNERSHIP AND OPERATIONS

The increasing use of management contracts and franchising as a means to grow revealed to hotel owner-operators the potential to change the underlying paradigm, altering irrevocably the character of lodging companies. Curiously, the potential for management contracts was found only after they were re-imported to North America. Beginning with the Hilton Hotel Corporation, North American hotel companies with international ambitions began employing management contracts to plant their flag in far-flung corners of the world (Eyster, 1988). The distinct advantage of the management contract régime was that it did not require investment on the part of hotel companies, sparing them from raising capital and the risks of deploying that capital in parts of the world often subject to political and economic turmoil. When management contracts were re-imported to North America to accommodate the demands of investors seeking to deploy their capital to the fast growing lodging industry, it is likely that hotel-company executives were merely responding opportunistically and that none grasped in the 1960s and early 1970s their full potential.

Business-model franchising was a thoroughly homegrown concept in North America but its widespread application to lodging had to await Kemmons Wilson and his Holiday Inn chain. For Wilson, franchising presented an oppor-tunity to grow his chain because franchisees employed local capital to finance geographically dispersed units bearing a strong brand identity. Notwithstanding the proliferation of brands and lodging products, Wilson's fundamental model has proven robust and is followed by every successful hotel franchising company operating today.

Although the transition of hotel owner-operators to branded management contract and franchising companies is still underway – and indeed for many companies will never be complete – the benefits are now patent. By shifting their roles from owners to brand purveyors and operators, hotel companies shed assets and reduced depreciation's drag on earnings. Moreover, since they no longer relied on building or buying hotels to increase their earnings base, their appetite for debt declined, reducing the risk of their equity. Today's fee based hotel companies are earnings machines; largely sheltered from the downside of operating leverage they have far less risk in their capital structures and enjoy a lower cost of capital.

Private owners of hotel assets – whether institutional investors such as insurance companies and pension funds or entrepreneurial investors such as private equity funds – have embraced the opportunities offered by hotel companies' retreat from the ownership of lodging assets. As cash-flow, return driven entities they are positioned to benefit from the specialized investment characteristics of hotels, including above all their ample tax shelters. Most private hotel investors are either sophisticated investors in their own right or they gain the requisite expertise by engaging in programmatic investing, often by contributing their capital to private equity funds. For such investors, the use of debt is commonplace (though they of course demand higher returns to bear the risk of financial leverage). Finally, private hotel investors do not have the same conflict when the appropriate time to exit the asset arrives. Whereas a publicly traded hotel owner-operator is foregoing its earnings base when it trades an asset – i.e. shrinking the company – the private investor disposing of an asset is recycling capital, presumably to put it to a better use or to return it to partners in the investment.

Of course the private investor who purchases either a brand or a brand and management competence from one of today's new paradigm hotel companies is concerned that he/she is getting value for the management contract or franchise fees paid (Beals and Denton, 2005). This is a difficult determination to make because the interests of the owner and the brand in a franchise, or the owner and the branded operator in a management contract, are far from perfectly aligned. It is appropriate therefore to

suggest at least some of the conflicts that can develop in the relationships and to explore the efforts to better align the interests of the parties.

THEMES AND ISSUES: OWNER-FRANCHISOR RELATIONS AND OWNER-OPERATOR RELATIONS

The relationship between the owner and the brand may take the form of a franchise agreement, a management contract that includes a brand, or a management contract coupled with a separate franchise agreement. Whatever the document(s) spelling out the relationship, there is a fundamental misalignment between the owner's interests and the interests of the brand. This has many manifestations, as discussed below, but there are three underlying dimensions: financial returns, positioning, and growth. The owner is intent on maximizing the returns from his individual hotel, while the brand's objective is to 'own the top of the mind' of the consumer. A natural conflict develops from these misaligned objectives because the brand is inevitably spending the owner's money to improve the product that captures customers and increases the brand's fees. For the brand, consistency of the lodging product is key to its overall positioning strategy, especially if the same brand name is attached to multiple, carefully differentiated offerings. The owner will always argue that there are brand standards that do not apply to his unique situation, often while also arguing that brand standards for some other service or physical feature should be exceeded. Ultimately, the most contentious issue between owner and brand is the issue of growth. For the brand, the only avenue for revenue growth and improved returns is by adding rooms to its system, or 'increasing distribution'. Obviously, in net terms a brand will not increase its distribution if, while working assiduously to sign up new properties, it also permits room to withdraw from the system. While owners might comprehend this strategy, they find it inconvenient to their own objective, which is to play the cyclicality of the lodging market, selling at the opportune moment and recycling their capital.

Various manifestations of the misalignment between the interests of owners and brands are illustrated below. The two principal relationships, owner-franchisor and owner-operator, are explored. In the discussion of owner-operator relations, the operator is assumed to be a branded operator – i.e. the management contract brings with it the right to market the hotel under the brand's name and access to the brand's reservation system. For each case, the compromises (if any) that have evolved over the years to mitigate the conflicts are suggested.

Owner-franchisor relations

Franchise agreements and the procedures for their promotion and sale are extensively regulated in many industrialized nations. However, all the protections afforded a franchisee by the law cannot change the fact that, on signing, he/she is wagering that the constraints and the costs accepted via the agreement will provide benefits of at least equal value. It is when this relationship is perceived to be out of balance that owners are least satisfied with the 20-year bargain struck with the brand.

For example, to protect their interests and the continuity of their systems, the brands insist that all franchisees share in the basic costs of advertising. Owners of certain types of franchised properties – e.g. airport hotels, hotels located in or near tourist attractions – argue that they gain little from their contributions to the brand's advertising budget since the typical guest makes the booking decision based on the property's location, not its brand or the image of the brand created by advertising. While the brand's representative might listen sympathetically to an owner protesting that the advertising fees exacted from him yield no value, the brand's response – before and after the franchise agreement is signed – will run along the lines of: 'Sorry, company policy. That [contract] term is non-negotiable'.

Virtually every major brand features a frequent guest loyalty program. Most programs operate so that individual hotels in the system are assessed a portion of the program's cost based on the number of points or miles the property issues to member-guests. Since the member-guests are issued points or miles as rewards for choosing the individual hotel, owners typically accept that they are paying their fair share. Similarly, on the redemption side, if a hotel provides a member-guest with a free room-night, the hotel is compensated out of the pool of fees collected across the system,

typically at a negotiated rate approximating the hotel's average daily rate.

Notwithstanding the apparent equity of the preceding arrangement, consider the reaction of the franchisee-owner of a Florida hotel to an advertising campaign mounted by his franchisor. Beginning shortly after the New Year, the brand ran a series of advertisements offering triple points or miles to any loyalty-program member booking three or more consecutive nights in January or February at any of its properties east of the Mississippi River. Undoubtedly, there were numerous owners of properties in the snowy northeast or the hibernating mid-Atlantic states prepared to stand the cost of the guest's rewards if he/she booked three nights' lodging. But the owner of a Florida hotel, located in a major tourist destination, had no need to stimulate business in January and February by offering triple rewards.

In this case, the owner honored the program's offer, distributing triple rewards to member-guests. The owner did receive some compensation for his adherence to brand-initiated programs. Once he discovered his predicament, the owner raised rates for the remaining unsold room nights of the offering period, meeting very little resistance from guests apparently seduced by the triple rewards. He negotiated surcease in other fees paid to the brand as a partial offset to the cost of the unnecessary rewards distributed to member-guests who probably would have chosen his property anyway in the absence of the stimulus of triple rewards.

To protect the integrity of their brand, franchisors must make it a condition of the franchise agreement that the owner will accept future changes in brand standards. Of course, for the owner this is a less-than-reassuring proposition: he/she is agreeing to unspecified new requirements, at an undefined time in the future and at uncertain cost. Moreover, some of the brand standards imposed in the future may seem arbitrary. For example, in 2006 the Hilton Hotels Corporation announced that the company had done extensive research and concluded that the brand's customers were unhappy with the clock radios that are a standard across all of Hilton's various lodging products. Specifically, the research suggested that older guests found the clock radios difficult to read and that the controls were ill adapted to the faltering eyesight of the elderly, making it difficult to adjust the devices. Based on the results of the research, Hilton commissioned a new design for its clock radios (larger readouts, clearer labeling on larger controls located on the front of the devices) and required that all its hotels replace their existing clock radios with the new model. Although the change was probably welcomed by consumers other than the elderly, and the cost to replace all of a property's clock radios was probably not ruinous, one wonders if the new brand standard was not more of a public-relations ploy to appeal to a (growing) demographic than a response to consumer complaints. Surely there are owners wondering if the new brand standard will sway consumers to book at a Hilton-branded property instead of a nearby Marriott product. Perhaps more pertinent: surely owners are asking if the outlay for hundreds of new clock radios will translate into the ability to command a higher rate.

The most all-encompassing and expensive future change that an owner commits to when signing a franchise agreement is the periodic 'product improvement plan', or PIP. The PIP is intended to bring the older properties in a franchise system up to the current brand standards. Thus if Internet connectivity in individual guest rooms has become a standard and the subject hotel is not so equipped, the owner will be obliged to bring his/her property up to the current brand standard. The owner may protest that most of his/her guests do not bring computers to his beachfront hotel or that those who do are happy with the wi-fi connection available in the lobby, but he/she will ultimately be required to honor the contract he/she has signed. It is the accumulation of items in a PIP that rankles owners because the cost can become significant, requiring the owner to look to sources under than the property's cash flow to meet the requirements. If, in addition to 'hard wiring' his guest rooms, the owner must equip his pantry to meet the new brand standard of a cooked breakfast, add an additional lamp to each room because four is now the standard, buy new 1500 watt hairdryers to replace the formerly acceptable 1200 watt model, and purchase new bedding (including the ubiquitous duvets), the cost can be onerous.

PIPs are also required if a property is sold and the new owner assumes the franchise. As a result of this requirement, experienced owners selling franchised properties secure from the brand an estimate of the cost of the PIP required on transition. This provides the seller an advantage in negotiating the sale of his property because the investment required by the new owner, over

and above the acquisition cost, is not subject to debate, allowing the owner to set his asking price accordingly. In addition, the purchaser knows what he/she is engaging to pay to keep the franchise in place. Since the franchisor must approve the purchaser as the property's new franchisee, his willingness to accept the price of the necessary changes can be an important reassurance to the franchisor, thus facilitating the approval process.

Although the above discussion cited some frequently expressed frustrations of franchisees, the relationship is not as one-sided as the examples might suggest. Franchisees have an important recourse in the franchisee councils that are a feature of most successful brands. Franchisee councils typically interact with the brand's highest level managers, who recognize that the best programs are sold to their customers, not imposed. Nevertheless, the fundamental misalignment of interests inherent in the franchise relationship – sketched above in its broader strategic lines and its mundane details – dictates that conflicts will always be present.

Owner-operator relations

A wise visitor to this writer's classroom once observed that franchisee agreements are subject to a great deal of legal scrutiny and government control while management contracts, which bind the owner more conclusively and expose him to more risk, are largely unregulated. The appraisal is accurate and the dismay appropriate because the owner who executes a management contract is giving the operator *carte blanche* to operate his asset, agreeing to fund any operating shortfalls and necessary capital expenditures and accepting to pay the operator a fee, regardless of his level of satisfaction with the property's performance. In exchange, the operator agrees to serve as the owner's agent – i.e. as a fiduciary duty bound to put the owner's interests above his own.

Over the years, the terms of hotel management contracts have moderated somewhat from the preceding stark description, but the underlying nature of the relationship still requires the owner to have great confidence in the operator's commitment to its fiduciary role (Eyster, 1997). But, as with franchise agreements, there remains a misalignment of interests between the owner, who seeks returns and the branded operator whose objectives are to build customer loyalty and increase its inventory of managed rooms. As the following discussion will demonstrate, because of the underlying nature of the contract, owners have had only partial success in ensuring that branded operators are fulfilling unstintingly their fiduciary role.

Save in some jurisdictions where local law overrides convenience and industry practice, the property-level employees of a hotel operated under a management contract are employees of the operator. This is a decided advantage for owners that are not allowed to operate businesses (e.g. pension funds) and for owners such as insurance companies whose work forces have traditionally enjoyed benefits far superior to those offered by the lodging industry. But how will the general manager respond if his/her salary increases, bonuses, and promotion opportunities depend not on the owner of his/her current hotel but on his/her superiors at the branded operator's headquarters? If a directive comes from the branded operator to change operating procedures – say, staffing levels – and these policies are likely to cost the owner significantly, is he/she going to refer the situation to the owner for consideration or follow his/her employer's dictates?

The owner can gain some control over this misalignment of interests through various contract conditions. Incentive fees paid to management companies in addition to base fees calculated as a percentage of total sales are calibrated to reward the operator for achieving operating profit, thus deterring a general manager from letting costs escalate unchecked. Similarly, contract terms providing owners a measure of control over budgets can orient general managers' thinking to owners' concerns. Finally, owners who believe that character and reputation are indicators of a manager's commitment to his/her fiduciary role will negotiate a clause providing some input into the selection of the general manager (and often other key members of the hotel's executive committee). Typically, the clause will give the owner the right to affirm the manager proposed by the operator, but also stipulate that approval cannot be unreasonably withheld (Eyster, 1997).

At first glance, the hotel owner's resolve to secure the right to terminate the management contract on sale may seem misplaced. Presumably, he/she has entered into the negotiation of the management contract because he/she recognizes that he/she needs the operator's expertise and brand. Why is he/she also so determined to be able to rid the property of the operator on sale? It is true that, for a wide swathe of branded properties, the existence of a long-term management contract *adds* value to the property. For these 'routine' properties, the brand is the destination – guests seek them out because they know the product and are reassured by its consistency and features, because they are members of the brand's reward program, because the brand's guaranteed best rate program simplifies their booking, or because their firm has negotiated a corporate rate with the brand. However, for distinctive properties, the presence of a long-term management contract is often a disadvantage and such a property is termed 'encumbered'.

Consider, for example, the prospects of the owner of a 500-room brand-operated hotel in a resort location. If the owner wishes to sell his/her property, the number of prospective purchasers qualified to bid for the asset and able to close the transaction is limited. Moreover, three categories of qualified bidders are eliminated from the pool of potential acquirers if the property is to be conveyed with a management contract in place: other competing brands, hotel investors affiliated with other competing brands, and owners whose property-management subsidiaries operate their hotels. In such circumstances, the owner's flexibility is severely hampered – never a desirable option for an opportunistic investor seeking to trade assets at the most advantageous point in the cycle. More important, the owner relies on the competitive bidding process to achieve the highest price for his/her asset, but he/she is not likely to achieve the best price if the most appropriate purchasers are on the sidelines.

The owner's insistence on the need to terminate the management contract on sale is matched by the branded operator's determination to 'protect the brand'. The best outcome the owner can expect from this standoff is to negotiate the inclusion of a buyout clause in the management contract. Under this contract term, the owner pays the branded operator to take down its flag and remove its management team from the property. The branded operator will win a 'lockout' of at least ten years, thus guaranteeing a minimum duration for the management contract. In addition, the branded operator will be paid a significant fee to walk away from the property. The fee is typically calculated as a multiple of the last year's base management fees but is calibrated to pay the branded operator the present value of (at least) the base fees over the remaining life of the contract.

Although his/her flexibility is still constrained, an owner will often count a buyout clause as a positive element of the management contract he/she ultimately negotiates with the branded operator. He/she knows that he/she will eventually have a window of opportunity to sell his/her asset on terms favorable to him, and he/she knows the price premium he/she must strive to achieve to pay the cost of exercising his/her buyout option.

Indeed, as the present chapter was being prepared in 2006, a situation parallel to that described in the text above developed in North America. In April, Strategic Hotels and Resorts, Inc., a publicly traded hotel REIT, agreed to pay an immediate $5 million to Marriott International to terminate the management contract on the Marriott Rancho Las Palmas Resort, an asset owned by Strategic and located in Tony Rancho Mirage, California. In addition, Strategic agreed to pay an additional $5 million to Marriott in 2009 if the REIT had not entered into a new management agreement with Marriott to operate another of Strategic's properties by 31 December 2008. Strategic also agreed to reimburse Marriott for the severance costs of Marriott's employees at the resort. The estimated present value of Strategic's buyout payment, including the severance costs: $10.4 million. A press release issued by Strategic explained, 'The agreement increases the range of options available to the company with respect to its future plans for the resort including its potential sale'. In May, Strategic announced the sale of the asset to KSL Resorts, a company that (to quote from its press-release tag line) 'owns and operates one-of-a-kind destination resorts'. KSL announced that 'consistent with its strategy [the company] will operate the property as an independent resort'.

Two palliatives

Over the years, the lodging industry has developed structural elements to mitigate the misaligned interests of the owner-franchisor relationship and the owner-operator relationship. These structural elements are: third-party management companies, which remedy some of the imbalances in the relationship between owner-franchisees and franchisors; and the asset management function, which, among other aspects, ameliorates relations between owners and operators. As the following discussion will demonstrate, both structural elements represent a step forward, but the underlying conflicts persist.

Third-party management companies, also called 'second-tier' companies, operate hotels that are branded under a separate franchise agreement with one of the major lodging brands. Many third-party management companies operate hotels that fly different flags, although they tend to specialize in operating hotels bearing one or two brands with which they have longstanding relationships. Often third-party operators began as owner-franchisees and developed an expertise in operating hotels bearing a select brand or brands and then branched out by offering their services to other owners. Most third-party management companies are closely held private companies, although a few of the larger ones are publicly traded.

At first glance, it appears illogical for an owner to pay both a management fee and a franchise fee when he/she could secure the services of the branded operator for a single management fee. But this counterintuitive arrangement is found widely in North America and is spreading to the United Kingdom and continental Europe because the third-party operator adds value in multiple ways. First and foremost, the third-party operator provides an entrée to the franchisor. For the first-time or the one-off owner, securing a franchise is often a prerequisite to arranging the financing of his/her property. But the procedure for securing a franchise requires more than a telephone call and the completion of an application. The stronger the lodging brand, the greater is its interest in welcoming only the most financially sound, capable owner-franchisees. A prospective owner-franchisee presented to the brand by his/her operator, a third-party management company experienced in managing the brand's hotels, is the brand's perfect customer.

The third-party management company may also offer added value by providing financing or by identifying sources of debt for the owner. When the operator provides financing it is often in the form of 'mezzanine debt' – i.e. capital contributed in exchange for returns that are greater than the returns earned by debt and approaching the returns paid to equity. Although more sophisticated hotel investors regularly reject operator capital contributions as too expensive, smaller, less experienced owners often find them attractive, both because they often provide the last slice of financing to 'get the deal done' and because they interpret the contribution as a sign of the operator's commitment to the project.

Finally, perhaps the most important value added by the third-party management company is the strength of its relationships with the brand. As a longstanding customer of the brand, the third-party operator has greater experience and negotiating power than any of the individual owners it serves. Thus if an owner finds himself confronted with a new brand standard that he/she perceives as onerous or unnecessary, he/she can call upon his/her operator to negotiate a compromise. Similarly, when a PIP is in the offing, it is the third-party operator who has the experience to analyze the efficacy of the PIP's components and the clout – because he/she represents multiple owners – to negotiate for concessions from the brand.

Although some North American hotel ownership entities employed personnel to perform duties similar to the asset management function, the activity did not come to the forefront until the hotel industry debâcle of the early 1990s (Beals, 2004). Many asset managers began their careers as turnaround specialists commissioned to improve the operating performance of hotels adequately for the owner to salvage some of his/her equity, or for the lender who was an owner-in-foreclosure to sell the hotel for a value at least in the vicinity of the lender's outstanding note. Some industry pundits predicted that asset managers would fade into desuetude once the period of widespread workouts was past (Feldman, 1995). However, at the same time asset managers were proving their worth to owners, the separation of ownership and operations deepened as investors, sensing that the bottom of the cycle had been reached, began purchasing hotels.

The investors of the period represented two principal categories: private equity – the period's so-called 'opportunity funds' or (less politely) 'vulture funds' – and an entity resurrected from the 1970s, the publicly traded REIT. Both private equity and the lodging REITs had two traits in common: they were run by experienced hotel investors, who had often begun their careers in operations, and they needed separate entities to manage the day-to-day operations of the assets they were acquiring. Recognizing the need to control the operators, who had often negotiated management contracts excessively favorable to their interests during the 1980s boom, private equity and REIT investors began the now widely accepted practice of employing asset managers. As depicted in Figure 16.1, the complete asset management function begins with identifying ownership's objectives, acquiring lodging assets that correspond to those objectives, absorbing them into the owner's portfolio, monitoring the assets' performance and ultimately disposing of the assets (Denton, 2004). Although most asset managers probably find the strategic aspects of their jobs – setting objectives with the owner, 'sourcing' acquisitions, and structuring the exit – more gratifying than the activities described in Step 3 of Figure 16.1, in fact more than fifty% of the time an asset manager devotes to any single asset will be in the performance of the five tasks appearing in the shaded boxes of Figure 16.1.

Management company executives will argue that the operator is the most competent entity to monitor the asset's performance, and therefore asset managers are an excrescence, an unnecessary 'thorn in the side' of property-level management. But in fact because of the misalignment of interests between owners and operators the asset management function is necessary if the owner is to maximize his/her returns. The asset manager's role vis-à-vis the property-level management team is a delicate one. The operator and its employees are authorized to act as the agents of the owner, and in fact are accorded significant latitude in accomplishing their duties. When an asset manager is inserted into this contractual relationship, friction and resentment are to be expected. Successful asset managers acknowledge that, while technical knowledge of the capital and transactions markets are important to the more strategic aspects of the profession, exercising their interpersonal skills and gaining the confidence of property-level management are critical to their success in creating value for the owners they serve.

In a successful asset manager–property management relationship only some of the communications are confrontational. An effective asset manager will necessarily ask hard questions, such as: 'Why is Food and Beverage labor cost over budget?' 'Have you thought of cross-training room-service operators to work the PBX?', 'Where's the internal rate of return analysis to justify the purchase of this equipment?'. But an effective asset manager also acts as a coach and consultant, responding to calls for help from property-level managers confronting new situations. Similarly, asset managers are responsible for conducting analyses outside the understanding of property-level personnel (e.g. real-estate tax appeals, risk management).

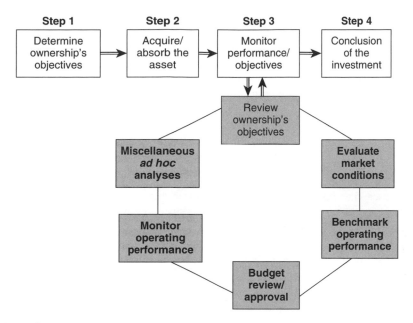

Figure 16.1   The asset management process

For the hotel owner, the compensation paid the asset manager is an agency cost. But increasingly owners are accepting they will incur the cost, apparently concluding that the increase in value achieved by effective asset management outweighs the cost. As the separation of ownership and operations continues, the asset management function is increasingly a feature of the lodging industry across the world (Beals, 2006). To the extent that it alleviates the misalignment of interests between owners and operators, it is a function that will remain a part of the lodging industry's current ownership paradigm.

THE EPISTEMOLOGY OF HOTEL REAL ESTATE: CASH FLOW MODELING

The hotel investor's principal epistemological approach, or way of knowing, is discounted cash flow (DCF) analysis. The basic modeling technique can be quite simple, as in the case of the DCF analysis for a single asset, or more complex, as when the financial results of a portfolio of assets are summarized in a single analysis. Similarly, DCF analysis is employed for modeling transactions that may be quite varied in their structure, from the acquisition of a single asset to sale-leasebacks and combined

stock and cash conveyances. If the entity is publicly traded, the DCF analysis may extend to the transaction's impact on cash flow per share or earnings per share. Finally, while the most common DCF analysis models an acquisition, the same techniques may be used at other points in the life of an asset (e.g. a hold-or-sell analysis) or to analyze the value of an incremental investment in the asset (e.g. a renovation).

A relatively straightforward case study will illustrate the fundamentals of cash flow modeling as practiced in the lodging industry. The 'Maison Cinq' is a hypothetical hotel located in an upscale California community. The hotel will be purchased and renovated (while portions of the property remain open), yielding a 170-room luxury property with a full service restaurant and meeting space accommodating up to 80 persons for private meetings and elegant receptions. The all-in project costs, including acquisition and renovation, are $40.6 million.

As is standard for DCF analyses conducted by hotel investors, an after-tax leveraged return to equity is calculated and the project's future flows are discounted at a relatively high 22%. The equity participant is a partnership, Loop Partners, LLP, whose planned equity contribution to the project will total $13,145,000. The fundamental reasoning of the investors is predicated on the assumption that lodging real estate markets are inefficient – i.e. it is possible to find assets in the marketplace that are mispriced. Thus if the asset can be purchased at a market price that is less than the after-tax value of equity plus the value of the debt placed on the asset, the asset should be acquired.

Table 16.1 presents the operating cash flow projections for the Maison Cinq, a presentation whose bottom line is the after-tax cash throw-off from the operation of the property over a ten-year period. The starting point of the analysis is net operating income, or NOI. This is an accounting figure derived by deducting all cash expenses (i.e. insurance, real estate taxes) after house profit but before management fees, interest, depreciation, and amortization. Although it is an accounting figure, it is used as an approximation of available cash flow from the operation of the hotel. Using the NOI as an estimate of cash flow ignores changes in net working capital. Because accrual items such as current assets and current liabilities are a relatively small percentage of the overall balance-sheet value of a hotel, the industry has long concluded that the cash inflows or outflows resulting from changes in net working capital can be ignored. Moreover, since the entire analysis relies on *projections*, sedulously modeling nominal changes in net working capital would introduce a spurious accuracy into the analysis. Furthermore, the fact that the detailed results of the Maison Cinq's operations are not shown must not be interpreted as a suggestion that the equity participants are unconcerned with them – i.e. that they take for granted that the NOI will be achieved, or that they have reasoned, 'We can leave that to the management company'. Indeed, quite the opposite is true. A great deal more time and debate goes into projecting the property's operating results than into the conversion of those results into estimates of after-tax cash flows. This is because operations are the only engine of returns (save, perhaps, the tax code). Moreover, although the conversion of NOI into after-tax cash flows requires some technical skill, this is relatively easy to develop, whereas the flair necessary to 'read markets', as indicated earlier in this chapter, is one that can only be developed through years of practice.

All after-tax DCF analyses must calculate the cash-flow impact of taxes by presenting a calculation of taxable income. The standard analyses for many other real estate asset classes present the calculation of the taxable income in a separate panel, effectively segregating accounting information from cash-flow information. Traditionally, DCF analyses for hotels incorporate the accounting treatment into the same panel. Thus the top half of the panel shown in Table 16.1 illustrates the calculation of taxable income and presents the tax savings or taxes due, depending on the year's taxable loss or profit. To derive operating cash flow the non-cash expenses deducted in arriving at taxable income (depreciation, amortization of the loan origination fee, amortization of pre-opening costs) are then added back. Next, two non-deductible cash outflows are subtracted from the cash flow available from operations: reserve for replacement and the principal repayments on the Maison Cinq's participating mortgage. The principal repayments are return of capital and therefore not tax deductible, whereas the reserve for replacement will be invested in FF&E – assets that will be capitalized and whose cost will be recovered through depreciation charges over the assets' useful lives.

The line item CFADSRR (standing for cash flow after debt service and reserve for replacement) is a stopping-off point in the analysis because the terms of the management contract call for the management company to receive, beginning in year six of the contract, a percentage of the available cash flow. The incentive fee is paid, however, only if the operator performs adequately, producing enough cash flow to pay the property's debt service and provide an agreed-upon-percentage of revenues as cash set-aside to fund the reserve for replacement. Note that the incentive fee paid is a tax deductible expense that reduces the partnership's tax liability. Accordingly, a tax adjustment is added to the cash flow, effectively reducing the cash impact of the incentive fee to its after-tax cost. The final line of the analysis, called net cash flow to equity, may also be termed, as suggested above, 'cash throw-off', the older 'cash-on-cash return', or the more recent 'coupon'. Note that, while the cash flows occur during the course of a year of operations, all are counted as occurring at the end of the year and the discounting is on an annual basis. This convention, standard to all manner of capital budgeting analyses, provides lesser present values, automatically inserting an element of conservatism into DCF analyses.

The underlying assumption of the equity reversion analysis presented in Table 16.2 is that the hotel will be sold at the end of year ten. It should be noted that this *pro forma* assumption

Table 16.1 Projected annual cash flows: Loop Partners, LLP

	Year 1	Year 2	Year 3	Year 4	Year 5	Year 6	Year 7	Year 8	Year 9	Year 10
Net operating income	3,157	5,582	6,201	6,510	6,818	7,155	7,520	7,885	8,277	8,698
Less:										
Mortgage interest (fixed)	2,601	2,584	2,565	2,545	2,523	2,498	2,472	2,442	2,410	2,374
Interest kicker			354	418	487	511	537	563	591	621
Loan interest	139	138	135	133	131	128	125	122	119	115
Mgmt fee (base)	271	478	532	558	584	613	645	676	710	746
Operating expenses	62	65	67	70	73	76	79	82	85	89
Depreciation	1,415	1,415	1,415	1,415	1,415	1,415	1,415	1,415	1,415	1,415
Origination fee	57	57	57	57	57	57	57	57	57	0
Pre-opening expenses	113	113	113	113	113	113	113	113	0	173
Total expenses	4,658	4,850	5,238	5,309	5,383	5,411	5,443	5,470	5,387	5,533
Total taxable income	−1,501	732	963	1,201	1,435	1,744	2,077	2,415	2,890	3,165
Cumulative losses	−1,501	−769	194							
Less:										
Income tax	0	0	54	336	402	488	582	676	809	886
Net profit loss	−1,501	732	909	865	1,033	1,256	1,495	1,739	2,081	2,279
Plus:										
Depreciation	1,415	1,415	1,415	1,415	1,415	1,415	1,415	1,415	1,415	1,415
Origination fee	57	57	57	57	57	57	57	57	57	0
Pre-opening expenses	113	113	113	113	113	113	113	113	0	173
Total non-cash expenses	1,585	1,585	1,585	1,585	1,585	1,585	1,585	1,585	1,472	1,588
Operating cash flow	84	2,317	2,494	2,450	2,618	2,841	3,080	3,324	3,553	3,867
Less:										
Reserve for replacement	100	150	200	744	779	817	859	901	946	994
Principal repayment mortgage	169	186	205	225	247	272	299	328	361	397
Principal repayment loan	23	24	27	29	32	34	37	40	43	47
Total	292	360	432	998	1,058	1,123	1,195	1,269	1,350	1,438
CFADSRR	−208	1,957	2,062	1,452	1,560	1,718	1,885	2,055	2,203	2,429
Less:										
Mgmt fee (incentive)	0	0	0	0	0	172	189	205	220	243
NCF before tax adjustments	−208	1,957	2,062	1,452	1,560	1,546	1,697	1,849	1,983	2,186
Tax adjustment	0	0	0	0	0	48	53	58	62	68
Net cash flow to equity	−208	1,957	2,062	1,452	1,560	1,594	1,750	1,907	2,044	2,254

Table 16.2 Equity reversion calculation: Loop Partners, LLP

Maison Cinq Hotel

I.	**Net Sales Price**	
	Cash Flow Base (1)	7,318
	Selling multiple	11
	Expected selling price	80,498
	Less:	
	Selling expenses (3%)	2,415
	Net sale proceeds	78,083
II.	**Capital Gains Tax**	
	Net sale proceeds	78,083
	Cost of hotel	40,600
	Additions (2)	6,490
	Total cost basis	47,090
	Less:	
	Accum. depn. & amort. (3)	15,740
	Book value	31,350
	Capital gain	46,733
	Tax on gain (4)	9,347
III.	**Appreciation Interest Kicker**	
	Net sale proceeds	78,083
	Cost of hotel	40,600
	Additions	6,490
	Adjusted basis	47,090
	Appreciation value	30,993
	Interest kicker (5)	5,579
IV.	**Equity Reversion**	
	Net sale proceeds	78,083
	Repayment of mortgage balance	24,767
	Repayment of loan balance	1,413
	Appreciation interest kicker	5,579
	Capital Gain Tax on sale	9,347
	Prepayment penalty fee (6)	557
	Management contract buyout fee (7)	1,119
		35,302
	Income tax (credits) (8)	2,031
	Equity reversion	37,333
V.	**Calculations and Bases**	
	See notes below for calculations and bases indicated by ().	

(1) NOI11 − BASE MGMT FEE − R/R: 9,147 − [0.03 × 26,135] − [0.04 × 26,135] = 7,318
(2) ΣR/R YRS 1–10 = 6,490
(3) ACCUM. DEP. *AND* AMORT: [1,415 × 10] + 900 + 686 = 15,736
(4) 46,729 × 0.20 = 9,346
(5) 30,993 × 0.18 = 5,579
(6) OUTSTANDING BALANCE × 0.0225 : 24,767 × 0.0225 = 557
(7) MOST RECENT YEAR'S BASE × 1.5 = 746 × 1.5 = 1,119
(8) TAX SHELTER EFFECT OF DEDUCTIBLE EXPENDITURES [5,579 + 557 + 1,119] × 0.28 = 2,031

is not a determination of when the hotel will be sold, but merely a means of assigning a terminal value to the hotel. Specifically, the hotel is valued by capitalizing year 11's income stream, but the process of capitalizing one period's stream is a proxy for finding the discounted present value of the property's remaining cash flows. Note that this technique is the appraiser's approach to finding the market value (deRoos and Rushmore, 2003); it requires the appraiser to estimate the cash flow available to the debt and equity participants after the deduction of all cash costs, including base management fees and the deduction of the cash set-aside paid into the reserve for replacement. The cash stream thus derived is divided by the capitalization, or 'cap' rate to estimate the market value in year 10.

The capitalization rate is a blended rate; it reflects debt's return requirement weighted by the percentage of debt financing found in typical hotel capital structures, plus equity's return requirement weighted by the typical percentage of equity financing for hotels. Moreover, it is a risk-adjusted rate. Thus, if the hotel whose value is being estimated enjoys high barriers to entry or some other competitive advantage, the appraiser would adjust the cap rate down, increasing the estimated market value of the property. Finally, cap rates can be expressed as multiples, as in the Maison Cinq case. A multiple is the reciprocal of the cap rate and vice versa. Thus the 'going-out' multiple of 11 used to value the Maison Cinq in year 10 translates to a cap rate of 9% (1/11 = 0.09).

The basic calculation of the equity reversion value can be expressed as follows:

	Selling Price
Less:	Selling Expenses
	Net Sale Proceeds
Less:	Outstanding Debt
Less:	Taxes
	Equity Reversion

The equity reversion calculation for Maison Cinq (Part IV of Table 16.2) is more complex than the basic model outlined above because the participating mortgage calls for the equity participant to pay a portion of the appreciated value of the property as additional interest, as well as a pre-payment penalty if the debt is retired before the end of the mortgage term. In addition, the analysis assumes that the hotel is sold unencumbered by the management contract and that the operator is paid a buyout fee. Note that all three line items – the appreciation

Table 16.3   Net present value analysis: Loop Partners, LLP

Maison Cinq Hotel		IRR (20.38%)		Cash flow description	Cash flow amount	IRR	Discount factor (22%)	Discounted cash flow
Proj. year	TVM year							
SIGNING	0			Equity investment (13,145 × 0.8)	(10,516)		1.00	−10516
SIGNING	0			Organization costs – after tax	(43)		1.00	−43
SIGNING	0			Operator's loan	1,750		1.00	1750
SIGNING	0	Time 0	(9,495)	Origination fee	(686)	(9,495)	1.00	−686
1	1			Equity investment (13,145 × 0.2)	(2,629)		0.8197	−2155
1	1	Time 1	(2,837)	NCF operations	(208)	(2,837)	0.8197	−170
2	2	Time 2	1,957	NCF operations	1,957	1,957	0.6719	1315
3	3	Time 3	2,062	NCF operations	2,062	2,062	0.5507	1136
4	4	Time 4	1,452	NCF operations	1,452	1,452	0.4514	655
5	5	Time 5	1,560	NCF operations	1,560	1,560	0.3700	577
6	6	Time 6	1,594	NCF operations	1,594	1,594	0.3033	483
7	7	Time 7	1,750	NCF operations	1,750	1,750	0.2486	435
8	8	Time 8	1,907	NCF operations	1,907	1,907	0.2038	389
9	9	Time 9	2,044	NCF operations	2,044	2,044	0.1670	341
10	10			NCF operations	2,254		0.1369	309
10	10	Time 10	39,587	Equity reversion	37,333	39,587	0.1369	5111
							NPV Total	− 1069

interest 'kicker', the pre-payment penalty and the management-contract buyout fee – are deductible against ordinary income. Since the analysis is after-tax, the tax-shelter effect of the deductible expenses appears as a tax credit that is calculated as the sum of the three deductions times the ordinary income tax rate (28%).

The calculation of the capital gains tax requires the analyst to first determine the adjusted basis of the asset – i.e. the tax book value of the asset at the end of year 10. The calculation of the adjusted basis follows the formula:

Original Cost + Additions − [Depreciation and Amortization] = Adjusted Basis

A common means to estimate the additions to the property over the ten-year analysis period is to sum the amounts put aside in the reserve for replacement, effectively assuming that the sums are spent immediately and their capitalized cost recovered through depreciation charges. The value for the 'Depreciation and Amortization' element of the formula is the sum of all non-cash deductions taken over the ten-year horizon of the analysis. For the Maison Cinq hotel, this includes the annual depreciation charges, the amortized loan-origination fee, and the amortized pre-opening expenses.

Once the adjusted basis is determined, the calculation of the capital gains realized on sale is straightforward: the adjusted basis is subtracted from the net sale proceeds, yielding the capital gain. Note that, as in the operating-cash-flow analysis, the purpose of the calculation of the capital gain taxes due is to derive the cash outflow that is deducted in calculating the after-tax equity reversion value.

The analysis presented in Table 16.3 is the simplest but the most telling. The estimated after-tax cash inflows from the operating-cash-flow and equity reversion analyses are arrayed and compared to equity's after-tax cash outflows and the net present value (NPV) and internal rate of return (IRR) are calculated. Note that the time line for the Maison Cinq's DCF analysis does not correspond to the standard capital budgeting approach wherein all cash outflows are assumed to occur at time zero, the inception of the project. The model is robust, allowing the flows to be counted on the time line according to when they occur. An analysis for a to-be-built hotel, for example, may begin at a time zero that is two or three years before the property's opening day and the cash outflows may continue in the project's early years of operation. The classic problem of IRR analysis – multiple rates of return – is avoided, however, because hotel projects have only one sign change in their flows (Brealey et al., 2006), as demonstrated in the panel to the far right of Table 16.3.

As the NPV and IRR results in Table 16.3 suggest, the investment, at least under the current deal structure, does not meet the equity participant's 22% hurdle rate. There are numerous approaches equity might take to improve its returns. The most obvious is increasing the leverage used. In the case of the Maison Cinq, equity might look to increasing the operator's loan, effectively 'taking equity off the table' at time zero, thus improving the NPV and IRR by the maximum amount possible. The same result would obtain if equity negotiated a larger mortgage or a reduction in the origination fee. Equity might also negotiate with the management company for a 'ramp-up' of its base management fees, thus saving cash in the early years of the project. Whatever the combination of alternative approaches equity might adopt, two principles hold. The solution is *not* to adjust the hurdle rate; and larger cash flows conserved earlier will always have the most impact on the NPV and IRR.

THE STATE OF THE ART IN HOTEL REAL ESTATE

In the 30 years this writer has been researching hotel real estate, finance and investments, ignorant capital has been replaced by sophisticated, return driven capital. To get to the current state, however, the lodging industry had to pass through various manifestations of its inclination to exploit ignorant capital, including: tax-driven partnerships investing in uneconomic properties, fueling an excess of supply; early REITs that invested in a sector their managements did not understand; 1990s era REITs that besmirched the resurrected REIT concept and disadvantaged their shareholders through self dealing; generalist real estate executives at institutional investors who invested in the lodging sector without regard for its peculiar risks; and of course the branded hotel management companies that, until the advent of the asset management function, exaggerated their value to lodging-industry owners, convincing them that operators deserved a return disproportionate to their risk. From this checkered past has emerged the present situation of intelligent, fast moving capital that seeks returns globally. The current environment has its own risks and today's players are not without their foibles, but overall hotel real estate has evolved to become a more rational, more professional sector of activity. As this trend continues, two positive developments will become apparent, but two lacunae will also surface.

As suggested at the outset of this chapter, the separation of ownership and operations will remain an enduring feature of the lodging industry. But the increasing sophistication of capital will translate into greater demands on the operator to think creatively. In the most positive development, the demands of ownership for returns will cause operators to think less like hoteliers, who typically look back at traditions and custom and more like marketers, who look to their customers for inspiration. We can expect asset managers, as the representatives of ownership, to be instrumental in pushing operators toward a more creative, more customer focused approach to day-to-day management issues, thus creating value at the individual asset level. Similarly, as the flow of capital is facilitated and better targeted, the brands will inevitably grow, replacing not only today's inventory of independent rooms (as is occurring in Europe) but expanding at an even faster pace in Eastern Europe, India, China, and South America. The trend of consolidation of more brands under a single umbrella will continue. The most successful franchise system will present to the consumer (guest) and to the customer (owner) a panoply of choices, from the modest one- or two-star hotel to a luxury offering, as well as branded fractional ownership.

However, a problem is looming for the lodging industry. Notwithstanding occasional protectionist rhetoric from various nations around the world, continued globalization promises to facilitate the flow of goods and financial capital. It is not clear, however, that the flow of human capital will increase at the same pace. Across country after country, there are employee shortages in the lodging industry; these shortages will be exacerbated if current restrictive immigration policies persist. To date, ownership in the lodging industry has left the immigration debate to operators. If the problems are to be addressed effectively, investors must be prepared to bring their influence and capital to bear on governments.

Although there is a vast literature supporting Modern Portfolio Theory (MPT), its potential application to the lodging industry is largely ignored. Currently, even some of the most sophisticated capital sources are opportunistic in their investment decisions and evaluate risk only on an asset-by-asset basis. Theory suggests that, by failing to consider an asset's contribution to the risk of their portfolios, hotel investors are missing an opportunity to reduce volatility and increase their returns (Woods, 2004). Regrettably, the single asset DCF analysis that adjusts for risk only through the discount rate seems the model destined to prevail in the industry for the foreseeable future.

FUTURE TOPICS OF INTEREST

The following areas are likely to draw the future attention of the handful of academic researchers in the field of hotel real estate, as well as the occasional practitioner.

- *The increasing use of REITs and REIT-like structures.* The REIT has proven to be a valid, accepted structure for holding hotels in North America, and has spread to several other countries in Europe and Asia. Individual nations will be drawn to create REITs or their equivalents to prevent the flight of capital from their home markets and to provide their citizens an opportunity to invest in real estate in a transparent, tax efficient manner. Scholarly and practitioner research is needed to influence the structure of hotel REITs to resemble those of North America, where after 30 years of false starts and poor public perception, the industry at last got it right.
- *Expanding the use of MPT.* Academic researchers can influence the development of the hotel real estate field by demonstrating that the application of MPT to hotel real estate can help them build better portfolios. Initial research here is probably best accomplished on a case-study basis – i.e. by analyzing the portfolios of a small number of hotel real estate owners.
- *Hotel returns.* The great disadvantage of real estate as an asset class is that it is not traded in a transparent market, as are financial assets. It takes a significant confidence level for private investors to reveal their returns, and there are measurement issues. But the service would be worth the effort if an academic researcher,

working with the hotel real estate community, developed an index that reported an adequate number of property (or portfolio) returns to provide a representative, reliable estimate of the returns offered by lodging investments.
- *Has securitization made investors more circumspect?* At this writing, much of the capital flowing into hotel real estate is private equity capital (although some private equity funds are floating public offerings to provide smaller investors an opportunity to invest alongside the institutions and high-net-worth individuals who are the traditional investors in private equity funds). Nevertheless, over the last 15 years, a significant amount of hotel debt and equity capital has been securitized, through commercial mortgage-backed securities (CMBSs) (Marre, Gordon and Bonjour, 2005) and REITs (Beals and Arabia, 2003). At the outset of this trend, it was speculated that the greater scrutiny afforded by the public markets and the presence of professional management would reduce the misallocation of capital that characterized the boom-and-bust real estate industry. It would be useful to test this theory, constructing a longitudinal study that tracks hotel real estate cycles since the early 1990s to see if better information leads to more judicious control of capital flows.

CONCLUSIONS

Five trends that will be observed in the years ahead summarize the present chapter, suggest the distance the lodging industry has traveled, and permit this writer to engage in mild punditry. The lodging industry will continue its evolution toward greater professionalism and more acute analysis of investment decisions, but change will come slowly, in fits and starts. Capital will be deployed ever more efficiently and rapidly to sustain the long-term development of the hotel industry, but it will remain a cyclical sector and hotel investors, ever traders, will be for the most part 'market timers'. The separation of ownership and operations will continue to be one of the lodging industry's distinctive features, although there will always be branded hotel operators that will be led to own – and periodically trade – a limited number of strategic assets. As a corollary to the preceding prediction: existing brands will be consolidated into fewer franchise systems, leaving owners an even more acute challenge as they attempt to balance their interests with the brand's interest. Finally, more REITs and REIT-like entities will be created across the globe to provide public-market participants the opportunity to own hotels. Structured correctly, REITs accomplish the objectives of the classical hotel investor, who seeks tax-advantaged operating cash flows and the opportunity to share in the lodging asset's appreciation.

REFERENCES

Beals, P. (2004) 'A history of hotel asset management'. In P. Beals and G. Denton (eds) *Hotel Asset Management: Principles and Practices,* Educational Institute of the American Hotel and Lodging Association. pp. 3–14.

Beals, P. (2006) 'Hotel asset management: will a North American phenomenon expand internationally?' In P. Harris and M. Mongiello (eds) *Accounting and Financial Management: Developments in the International Hospitality Industry.* Oxford: Butterworth-Heinemann. pp. 301–325.

Beals, P. and Arabia, J. V. (2003) 'Lodging REITs'. In L. E. Raleigh and R. J. Roginsky (eds) *Hotel Investments: Issues and Perspectives,* 3rd edn. Educational Institute of the American Hotel and Lodging Association. pp. 167–181.

Beals, P. and Arabia, J. V. (2006) Lodging industry exit strategies. In L. E. Raleigh and R. J. Roginsky (eds) *Hotel Investments: Issues and Perspectives,* 4th edn. Educational Institute of the American Hotel and Lodging Association. pp. 275–299.

Beals, P. and Denton, G. (eds) (2004) *Hotel Asset Management: Principles and Practices.* Educational Institute of the American Hotel and Lodging Association.

Beals, P. and Denton, G. (2005) 'The current balance of power in North American hotel management contracts', *Journal of Retail and Leisure Property,* 4(2): 129–145.

Bond, H. (1998) 'Financing opportunities follow cyclical nature of hospitality industry', *Hotel & Motel Management,* 213(10): 38.

Denton, G. (2004) 'The asset management process'. In P. Beals and G. Denton (eds) *Hotel Asset Management: Principles and Practices.* Educational Institute of the American Hotel and Lodging Association. pp. 15–26.

deRoos, J. and Rushmore, S. (2003) 'Hotel valuation techniques'. In L. E. Raleigh and R. J. Roginsky (ed.) *Hotel Investments: Issues and Perspectives,* 3rd edn. Educational Institute of the American Hotel and Lodging Association. pp. 71–102.

Eyster, J. J. (1988) *The Negotiation and Administration of Hotel and Restaurant Management Contracts,* 3rd edn. Ithaca, NY: The Cornell University School of Hotel Administration.

Eyster, J. J. (1997) *Hotel Management Contracts in the US: The Revolution Continues and Twelve Areas of Concern: A Supplement to the Negotiation and Administration of Hotel and Restaurant Management Contracts.* Ithaca, NY: The Cornell University School of Hotel Administration.

Feldman D. S. (1995) 'Asset management: here to stay', *Cornell Hotel and Restaurant Administration Quarterly,* 36(5): 36–51.

Ling, D. C. and Archer, W. (2005) *Real Estate Principles: A Value Approach,* 1st edn. New York: McGraw-Hill Irwin.

Marre, D. G., Gordon, P. and Bonjour, B. (2005) 'Understanding the commercial mortgage-backed securities market in the hospitality sector', *Journal of Retail and Leisure Property,* 4(2): 105–117.

Rushmore, S., Ciraldo, D. M. and Tarras, J. (2002) *Hotel Investments Handbook – 2002,* The West Group.

Rushmore, S. and Baum, E. (2001) *Hotels and Motels: Valuations and Market Studies.* Chicago: The Appraisal Institute.

Woods, R. (2004) 'Quantitative risk analysis for hotel investments'. In P. Beals and G. Denton (eds) *Hotel Asset Management: Principles and Practices.* Educational Institute of the American Hotel and Lodging Association.

Accommodation and Facilities Management

17

Arnaud Frapin-Beaugé,
Constantinos Verginis and Roy C. Wood

INTRODUCTION AND CONTEXT

We commence this chapter with an assertion: that any sensible discussion of accommodation management in the hospitality sector could usefully benefit from an understanding of developments in a parallel field, namely that of facilities management. Yet, on the hospitality side at least, the area of facilities management is not well understood and the connections between the two subject areas are by no means explicit, either at the theoretical or practical level. Certainly, there have been student textbooks and contributions to textbooks, that talk of facilities management in the hospitality sector and sometimes felicitously combine terms such as 'facilities management' and 'hospitality' (in the first case, see Gee, 1999; in the second Stipanuk and Roffman, 1996) though at the same time, at least one popular (UK) textbook on developing hospitality facilities manages to avoid any mention of the *distinct* area of 'facilities management' (Ransley and Ingram, 2004). Empirical research that focuses on facilities management in hospitality and uses the term as anything more than a descriptor for property and building services is noticeable by its absence (Verginis and Wood, 1999; Losekoot, van Wezel and Wood, 2001). There is considerable uncertainty as to the nature of facilities management, an uncertainty underpinned by debates amongst academics and practitioners of this emerging subject field, many of whom find the very definition of the term an irritation, made all the more irritating, and interesting, by the manifest growth of facilities management practice and international FM organizations dedicated to research and the dissemination of best practice (e.g. the International Facility Management Association; the British Institute of Facilities Management).

In contrast to facilities management, the term 'accommodation management' or 'accommodation studies' (more usually 'lodging management' in the USA) in the context of hospitality management and hospitality management education is easily and clearly circumscribed in terms of two or three core areas – front office, housekeeping and (diminishing in importance except, mainly, in some North American hotel schools) subjects falling under the broad heading 'hotel engineering'. In the UK, the traditional approach to accommodation management education emphasized a soft technical and scientific base, except (until the advent of the computer) in front office management. Thus, housekeeping and hotel engineering teaching utilized diverse concepts from the physical sciences in order to explore equally diverse issues such as lighting, sanitary engineering, chemical treatment of various materials and fabrics, and the operation of ventilation and heating systems. Thirty years ago in the UK one could not pursue a qualification in hospitality management without touching on all these subjects, now it is much less likely. Experts are welcome in the industry, whether they are architects, auditors, interior designers, or lawyers (see Wood, 1999, for further comment in this vein).

While this approach still persists to a greater or lesser degree in hotel education around the world, it is in decline because events in the real world have overtaken it. Growth and application of new technologies, new business models and a (at least superficially) customer, rather than management-centered approach to hospitality service delivery have changed the rules of the game. One rationale for educating prospective industry managers in the scientific mysteries of topics such as those listed above was to provide an elementary counterweight to being hoodwinked by wily specialists. Technique and technical knowledge were emphasized at the expense of 'managerial' knowledge, skill and imperatives. However, many of the operational and financial philosophies and structures of the hospitality (and especially the hotel) industry have changed dramatically in the last 30 years, supported by advances in both hard and soft technologies. Hospitality educators are frequently berated for producing graduates who lack depth of technical knowledge of hospitality operations. It was ever thus: with some irony, changes in hospitality education reflect changes in the industry more accurately than many senior executives would like to admit. In respect of accommodation management, especially in hotels, such change, carefully examined, reveals a tension between what Riley (1984), in a seminal article, called 'touches' and 'things'. Here, Riley's basic thesis was that traditional modes of hotel service based on human delivery were giving way to forms of service centered on various forms of technology to which customers themselves added the human (essentially self-service) element (see also Wood, 1994a for a partial development of this argument). With the benefit of hindsight, the processes to which Riley alluded do not appear to have been uniform either in their application or focus, and indeed, to some extent there has been, at least in the rhetoric of hospitality management, a partial reaction against them, most clearly embodied in a resurgent focus on 'personal' service reflected in stated commitments to 'delight the customer', this last phrase being just one example of management-speak of somewhat dubious meaning which if not at all understood, is readily recognized for its totemic force. This said, there is little doubt that many other aspects of process and procedure in hotel management have become more standardized. Put simply, changes in the language and ideology of management, including hospitality management, has led to many changes in the way management functions are conceived, perceived and practiced, and accommodation management in hotels is no exception, despite the often unthinking persistence of tradition for which the industry is renowned.

Accommodation management in hotels is in essence about the management and protection of physical assets and, in the last quarter century this has arguably become a more systemized process and one therefore easier to control, as a result of the wider development of new technologies; the availability of technologies at a price that makes risk-dissipation available through outsourcing, whether in terms of key accommodation services (for example, laundry) or whole functions (housekeeping); and within hospitality organizations more generally, the evolution of standard operating procedures. At a macro-level, technological change includes developments in building-structural technologies, for example off-the-shelf modular construction packages that allow much greater product homogenization and hence reduced operating costs. At the micro-level there have been small changes in the technology of room cleaning, a task historically defined by its human physicality and the limited scope for technological applications. Ball et al. (2003: 141) state that 'the nature of the work involved and the variety of tasks to be completed in each room mean that introducing technology any more complex than a vacuum cleaner is very difficult'. Nevertheless, progress has been made in some sectors, as for example in the *Formule 1* budget brand owned by the Accor group with their self-cleaning toilets and shower rooms. Although there are limited possibilities for applying the same technology to more upscale properties, the same is not necessarily true of other technological developments, notably those linked to environmental concerns. Protection of the environment is increasingly seen by hotels as both a marketing tool and a means of cost reduction and control although idealists are a little more puritanical, for example Schneider et al. (1999: 272) arguing that concern for the environment 'is more than a marketing buzz word, it is a business-building decision'. Environmental initiatives in hotels typically focus on energy saving procedures, waste recycling, and use of environmentally friendly chemicals following what Schneider et al. (1999: 272) call 'the "reduce, reuse, recycle" credo of the environmental movement'. For instance, in order to reduce wastage of electricity in areas that are not used, sensors or heat detectors can be used and shut down power supply so as to avoid wastage. Computer systems can be programmed to either completely shut down or partially restrict energy usage to areas. One clear example is in guest rooms where air conditioning units may run needlessly while the room is unoccupied. Systems can, when activated, reduce air conditioning unit activity and lighting systems. When linked to entrance security control systems, the energy management programs may reactivate, to guest preferred settings, as the guest re-enters their room or, if installed, as guests activate lifts to return to their floor (for further examples of 'futuristic' control of room environment technology see the website of the technology giant Siemens, www.siemenshotel.com).

In one sense, with developments in technology we can see the hotel or hospitality manager as being liberated from a tyranny of technical micro-management skills and prepared for a re-skilling in other, more strategically oriented competencies. In addition to the manager's role set now emphasizing as a 'prime directive' the satisfaction of the hospitality guest, greater weight has been placed on the importance of financial and budgetary management competencies within managers' skill sets. As these elements have gained ascendancy, so has there been a diminution in the requirement that managers evidence the same degree of scientific/technical *detail* knowledge, as was once the case, at least in the accommodation management area. This situation can be usefully contrasted with the role of food and beverage management in the hotel industry. The mythology of the hotel industry supports the aphorism that in most hotels, it is accommodation (room sales) that account for the major source of revenue, the sale of rooms typically generating over 60% of a four or five star, hotel's revenue and profit, with this percentage in limited service hotels, motels, and other lodging products frequently being even higher. A parallel view is that food and beverage contributes comparatively little to revenue (Riley, 2000) although globally speaking, it would be wise to regard all such generalizations with a due degree of skepticism. The balance of probabilities undoubtedly supports the view that sales of accommodation is in general a hotel's main source of revenue, but operationally, the paradox persists that many educators and older generations of hospitality managers view food and beverage competence and experience as an essential part of any good manager's repertoire of credibility, and food and beverage management remains a core route to promotion in the sector (Wood, 1997; 2007). Food and beverage management is 'sexy', and 'good' hotel management schools are seen as those that continue to place emphasis on practical restaurant and kitchen training and skill acquisition, whereas it has been the

fate of accommodation functions in hospitality management and education to be perceived and experienced by many, especially managers, as necessary and worthy but irretrievably dull. Within the supporting network of hospitality education, compared to other core areas of hospitality management, including food and beverage management, accommodation functions remain starkly under-researched.

Rationale for the objectives and structure of the chapter

The observations thus far in this Introduction have the following consequences for the structure of the discussion that follows. First is consideration of any role that might be played by the emerging field of facilities management in enhancing understanding and analysis of accommodation management in hospitality services. This seems to us entirely appropriate. Although itself a contested area as we shall see, facilities management makes claims that are relevant for understanding multi-service businesses like hotels. There is, in some quarters, a tendency to define 'facilities management' as synonymous with 'building services', an approach generally regarded as limiting by those who propose facilities management as a more distinctive and specialist body of knowledge. The question simply put, then, is does this body of knowledge offer the potential for providing new insights into the hospitality (and particularly hotel) accommodation function? We think it does but, as will be shown, explicit awareness of the philosophical and strategic aspirations of facilities management remains limited in the hospitality industry. Instead, we shall argue that key developments in the management of, specifically hotel, accommodation (in the broadest sense) are 'stumbling' towards a facilities management model, but are unlikely to ever achieve true convergence for reasons relating to deficiencies in the conceptualization of facilities management and, in hotels at least, because of tensions between hotel organization and management on the one side, and a desire to achieve a holistic customer-oriented approach to such organization and management on the other (a holism that as we shall see, is at the heart of concepts of facilities management).

The second element of the ensuing discussion seeks to support this assertion. We have chosen to avoid simply describing accommodation management functions in hotels, because there is limited utility to reviewing the minutiae of front office management, housekeeping operations or hotel engineering as such: the knowledge involved is wholly schematic and operational in focus, and readily accessible in many standard works and commentaries on the subject (for front office see for example Baker et al., 2000; Verginis, 1999; and for housekeeping, Kappa et al., 1997; Schneider et al., 1999). Indeed, we have excluded those topics that fall under the broad heading of 'hospitality engineering' entirely, in so doing choosing to follow the perceived trend of adopting a managerial approach to accommodation management, doubly appropriate given the purpose of this Handbook. In place of this, we attempt to identify those tensions that, we argue, inhibit a full-blooded adoption of a facilities management model in hotel accommodation management, and examine the consequences of these tensions for the current state of the latter in the hotel industry.

FACILITIES MANAGEMENT (FM)

Hospitality management is, like facilities management, a broadly vocational field with its origins in other, more established disciplines in the social science and business fields. In academic terms facilities management has grown out of diverse interests in architecture, building and engineering, and in some views, especially the latter (Jorna, 1999). One of a number of relatively new 'vocational' subjects, there is debate not only over the definition of the subject, but its scope. One way of overcoming this lack of clarity is suggested by Jorna (1999: 44) who asserts that:

> Although there is a common understanding about core competencies of FM, harmonizing educational programmes around them will be neither easy or, perhaps, necessary. The precise balancing of competencies could be a distraction. Facilities management is still very new and still ill defined. This lack of definition is better seen as, not fluidity, but diversity. Perhaps a more productive approach would be to concentrate on understanding the essentials of facilities management. How do they translate into practical skills and individual qualities?

The 'core competencies' to which Jorna alludes are six in number and derived from and developed and disseminated by, various FM associations (Jorna, 1999: 43). They are:

- understanding business organization;
- managing people;
- managing the work environment;
- managing resources;
- managing premises; and
- managing services.

A moment's reflection on the above reveals serious flaws in Jorna's approach. The first of these is that it is not clear that the core competencies on which facilities management experts are apparently agreed are the same as the 'essentials' of facilities management, a problem complicated by the lack of definition of the field. It is a touch difficult to talk meaningfully about 'core competencies' and 'essentials' if facilities management remains impossible to define. The quotation above suggests, and regrettably rather obviously, that Jorna is simply trying to evade an apparently intractable issue among facilities management academics. A second problem here is that the first four core competencies in Jorna's list are entirely generic: only with the management of premises and services is anything distinctive mooted and even here, the competencies described are current in many professional/vocational areas, including hospitality.

Difficulties with the intellectual status and content of facilities management are, however, yet more complex than might be supposed from Jorna's attempts at intellectual sophism. This can be seen from consideration of van Wagenberg's (1997) important paper on this topic. Reviewing various definitions of facilities management he contrasts US and Dutch approaches (the Dutch having played a major role in Europe in promoting the development of facilities management education). Two of the US definitions cited by van Wagenberg (1997: 3–4) are of interest. Facilities management is:

> The practice of co-coordinating the physical workplace with the people and work of the organization; it integrates the principles of business administration, architecture and the behavioral and engineering sciences (Cotts and Lee, 1992: 3, cited in van Wagenberg, 1997: 3)

> … responsible for co-coordinating all efforts related to planning, design and managing buildings and their systems, equipment and furniture to enhance the organization's ability to compete successfully in a rapid changing world (Becker, 1987: 82, cited in van Wagenberg, 1997: 4).

The emphasis of both definitions is on co-coordinating but both definitions imply more than this – specifically that facilities management is an ongoing systems process invoked and implemented at the start of a building project and thereafter constituted as an ongoing concern. If this is so, and facilities management is little more than a classical management co-coordinating function then it is difficult to see the rationale either for facilities management as a distinctive intellectual and vocational activity, or for so much debate as to the circumscription of its intellectual boundaries. Yet, as van Wagenberg (1997) demonstrates, such concerns have only relatively recently become a feature of facilities management practice – in short, historical evidence for facilities management as being concerned with systems throughputs is somewhat lacking.

The underlying issue guiding van Wagenberg (1997: 4) relates to differences in the conception of facilities management in North America and the Netherlands. The main difference emerges in the Dutch (and since, more broadly European) tendency to encompass all services within definitions of facilities management (e.g. reception, catering, security and mail handling). For example, the British Institute of Facilities Management (BIFM) offers a definition that reads:

> Facilities management is the integration of multi-disciplinary activities within the built environment and the management of their impact upon people and the workplace … [.] … Within this fast growing professional discipline, facilities managers have extensive responsibilities for providing, maintaining and developing myriad services. These range from property strategy, space management and communications infrastructure to building maintenance, administration and contract management.

They add that the essence of FM is:

> Integration of the planning and management of a wide range of services both 'hard' (e.g. building fabric) and 'soft' (e.g. catering, cleaning, security, mailroom, and health & safety) to achieve better quality and economies of scale. (http://www.bifm.org.uk/bifm/about/facilities, last accessed 28.12.05).

This moves us from considering a term, facilities management in search of a meaning to defining that term in a manner so all-inclusive that it is nearly meaningless. However, in the case of the American definitions of facilities management recorded by van Wagenberg (1997) above, there is little in the first that would seem to differ from the 'European' approach although the second is, superficially, rather more limited. The efforts by van Wagenberg (1997: 6) to develop a theoretical basis for FM are somewhat confused. He notes that lack of clarity as to the definition and purpose of FM arises because FM draws for the most part on the concepts and literature of other fields and disciplines. FM as a field of study is resultantly lacking in coherence because these concepts relate only to elements of 'a facility' rather than the concept of a facility itself. In an effort to overcome this problem of clarity, and in defining the concept of a facility, van Wagenberg borrows from the language of experimentation. A facility, he suggests, must be established as an independent variable that has effects and outcomes as dependent variables. The concept of a facility is best understood in terms of its functions that are derived from users' expectations. In point of fact it is extremely difficult to understand what is meant here and the independent/dependent variable analogy is virtually meaningless. On the second point, one might observe that since users' expectations are hypothetically infinite it seems unlikely that they could be circumscribed to a level of precision that could provide the basis for a meaningful conceptual clarification of the term 'facility'.

One possible, if small, advance on these opaque discussions is to separate definitions of a 'facility' from 'facilities management'. The whole term 'facility' is problematic. To begin with, its contemporary 'FM' meaning diverges from most dictionary definitions (for example, the *Oxford Minidictionary*, 1991 defines facility as a noun meaning 'ease, absence of difficulty; means for doing something'). Staying with the contemporary form as favored by the facilities management community, it remains difficult to discern any logical imperative that requires us to equate a facility with a building. Whilst a facility is normally construed as a physical structure, not all physical structures are facilities in the 'FM sense'. A facility can normally be separated from other structures by reference to its intended purpose and the manner of its use. In the 'FM sense' a facility is almost invariably a structure that circumscribes or encloses an artificial or constructed physical space. If this is a fair analysis of the meaning of the term 'facility' then it is difficult to see why we should not simply employ the term 'building' as a synonym. This is arguably supported by the observation that the complementary term 'facilities management' is almost universally construed as a set of practices concerned with the management (defined in terms of functional–managerial integration and co-ordination) of buildings and core and ancillary building services. The term 'practices' however cannot be allowed to refer only to management activity, it must also be extended to include the full range of actions that the users of building engage in. In this sense, a facility can be defined as 'a space enclosing physical structure, normally a building, where the space and the structure are acted upon by humans for some purpose or purposes, such actions constituting "facilities management"'. This definition has the advantage of recognizing that a facility is, precisely, a physically and socially constructed phenomenon. The definition of facilities management can be further elaborated as 'the set of actions and practices that different users exert upon buildings'. This allows for the full range of formal and informal management practices that building users employ.

To summarize thus far, the development of facilities management as a distinctive body of academic knowledge and 'real world' skills is beset by internal debates as to what constitute the appropriate definitional and content boundaries of the subject. There is nothing unusual about this, indeed such characteristics are not untypical of many emerging subjects that aspire to intellectual coherence and respectability, including hospitality and hospitality management (see de Bruijn et al., 2001). We should, however, be cautious of the promotional hype that can sometimes obscure rather than clarify the significance of a field, as in the following, somewhat desperate sounding claims made for facilities management on their web site by the British Institute of Facilities Management (BIFM):

> Effective facilities management, combining resources and activities, is vital to the success of any organization. At a corporate level, it contributes to the delivery of strategic and operational objectives. On a day-to-day level, effective facilities management provides a safe and efficient working environment, which is essential to the performance of any business – whatever its size and scope ... [.] ... The facilities management profession has come of age. Its practitioners require skill and knowledge. The sector definition continues to expand to include the management of an increasingly broad range of tangible assets, support services and people skills ... [.] ... Facilities management is a vital strategic discipline

because it 'translates' the high-level, strategic change required by senior decision makers into day-to-day reality for people in their work or living space ... [.] ... Successful organizations in future will approach FM as an integral part of their strategic plan. Those organizations that treat FM as a 'commodity overhead' will be at a significant strategic disadvantage. (http://www.bifm.org.uk/bifm/about/facilities, last accessed 02/11/06)

Such expansive (put kindly) statements, courting in this case the possibility of organizational apocalypse in the absence of systematic facilities management, detract from the simple virtue of facilities management, a reminder of, and a bias towards a holistic model of facilities management that places human behavior at the heart of any understanding of building technology, use and development. This evolving model has useful but largely unexplored implications for understanding hospitality, and especially hotel, accommodation management to which we now turn.

'Facilities management' in hotels

Accommodation management and especially the management of hotel accommodation provide a useful locus for exploring areas of continuity and discontinuity with the concept of facilities management described above. Hospitality organizations, and especially hotels as 'facilities' (buildings), provide a varied range of products *and* services to guests. Conventionally, in hospitality education, rather more emphasis is put on the latter than the former, to the extent that rather too frequently encountered is the over-excited description of the hospitality industry as *the* service industry, a solipsism reflecting much current (and clichéd) management rhetoric, a rhetoric that valorizes the nature, extent and quality of 'service' above all else in the hotel 'offer' while in reality offering guests little more than the opportunity to conform to the operational imperatives and controls of hotels (Wood, 1994a). 'Service' is, of course, important, but the emerging field of facilities management reminds us that hotels are not *only* about services but also about physical products, from hotel buildings to meals provided in hotel restaurants. The rhetorical emphasis on service in the hospitality industry is all too often a means of diverting attention from badly conceived and maintained *products*, it is like saying 'Yes, our rooms are badly designed, they are cold, a draught blows through the window frames and the shower is not powerful enough – but our service is magnificent' (in fact a not unreasonable description, even today, of many 'grand' European hotels!).

Of course, in the hospitality context, as elsewhere, 'service' can be construed in linguistically flexible ways – service as something a person gives and which is the 'possession' of that person (for example a waiter) or service as something that possesses a non-human physical existence (e.g. a swimming pool), the latter that might be more appropriately advertised as a 'facility' of the hotel. Without rehearsing the debates and disputes about the definition and nature of services present in academic thought for over a quarter of a century now (from the tub-thumping theoretical neo-Marxism of Braverman, 1974, who effectively denies any concrete distinction between products and services, to the more prosaic attempts by marketers to define and delimit the nature of services, see for example Gronroos, 2000) we can suggest that the prospect held out by facilities management of managing products *and* services through embracing design skills, processes and practices in a holistic way, from cradle to grave, from the inception of building design, through the construction process and subsequent operational cycle should, in theory, therefore be an attractive one to the hotel industry, where the interaction between the 'physical' and the 'human' is particularly well-marked. Indeed, there is a parallel here between the ambitions of facilities management and services marketing, and particularly that variety of the latter which emphasizes models of service design based on the combination of physical and social elements into 'servicescapes' (see, for example, Lovelock et al., 2004, for an interesting account of these ideas) although in such models, buildings are normally a 'given'.

There are two principal reasons, however, why the widespread adoption of such a holistic 'FM' approach to the management of hotel accommodation remains somewhat uncertain. First, not all, if any, hotel managers (or for that matter facilities managers of other types of building) are blessed with opportunities to become involved with 'new builds' that allow them to plan from the bottom up. In the hospitality industry at least, the fact of rapid career mobility and positional advancement means that it is unlikely that more than a handful of such

managers will, at any point in their career, have more than a passing association with the buildings they manage and few will be involved in wholly new hotel building projects (indeed, anecdotally there is some kudos attached to the status of managers involved in the 'start-up' of newly built operations). By definition, those who come, whatever their job title, to have responsibility for facilities management in hotels and many other types of buildings besides, will, for the most part, be bequeathed the buildings in which they work. A factor present but underplayed in facilities management is serious reflection upon the effects of temporality on the continuity and conception of building management. Buildings not only change their use from one business type to another, but buildings that maintain a specific use over time, for example many hotels, are re-conceptualized, redesigned and refurbished in accordance with a variety of imperatives. To achieve the holism to which facilities management aspires there has to be a significant institutional memory and, in any organization, the development, maintenance and protection of such a memory is an imperfect art, complicating building management because, whatever stage a building is at in its history (new, old, middle aged), the people who operate it nearly always, at first, come to it new. For management there is reliance for information on 'building performance' on historical records (including oral history) that may be incomplete and affected by the fact that a building at the time of its construction may not have benefited from holistic planning, and of course, the use and needs of people, as well as building use itself, may have changed over time.

A second issue is that the management and co-ordination of facilities in hotels has not traditionally been in terms of holism or integration. Instead, the favored operational model of organization in larger hotels is one based on functional departmentalization although it is important to bear in mind that this is hardly an issue for smaller hotel units that constitute the largest part of global provision. Historically, the separation of departments and their functions presents something of a paradox for hospitality researchers as, in one sense, it appears a tried and trusted method of running a hotel business while at the same time it contributes to one of the most widely recognized problems faced by the industry, namely the limitations it places on the integration and reintegration of such functions in terms of communication, efficiency and, most importantly, customer satisfaction (see Shamir, 1978; Wood, 1994a, 1997, 2004). In this rather jaundiced perspective, departmentalization is arguably that force which creates the short-term operational focus that has been identified by some as dominating managerial activity in the sector: instead of integration and the much vaunted 'customer focus' beloved of corporate mission statements, the real managerial focus is the co-ordination of departments and an emphasis, in every sense, on routine maintenance ('keeping the building and business going') and the attainment of integration is in part a result of the subversion of the formal aspects of operational management by front-line staff (Shamir, 1978; Mars and Nicod, 1984). Further, strategic considerations tend to be premised primarily on physical asset protection and real estate investment, an approach that reinforces operational bias in the management of hotel accommodation and may see wider responsibility for the management of the building life-cycle (for example, in terms of refurbishment or physical development of the property) given to higher-level decision makers largely unconnected to any one hotel unit. In short, this second issue needs to be firmly located in the context of an earlier statement of ours: that hotel accommodation management is in essence conceived to be about the management and protection of physical assets. The basic assumption here is that most investors invest money in a hotel with the view to obtaining a financial return whether from long-term investment in real estate, from the operation of the hotel itself, or from both. Hotel accommodation management is, particularly in the light of high modern hotel development costs, realistically defined as the protection and management of the fixed assets of the organization and/or building's owner(s) with a view to generating profit (Schneider et al., 1999).

With such 'hard' approaches, it seems as if the core concepts of facilities management and hotel accommodation management occupy different ends of a continuum, the latter embracing a physicality premised on the routine performance of tasks and skills directed towards the maintenance of fabric alone, the former, as we have already observed, aspiring to a holism that explores the interface between the physical and the human and which, in terms of hotel accommodation management, seems ideally placed as a model for a 'soft link'

between the material assets of the business and customers. In fact, the real world situation has rather more nuance than this. Although direct or explicit awareness of the precepts of facilities management in the hospitality industry appears to be limited, there is evidence from developments over the last 15 to 20 years in the hotel sector at least that indirectly, or implicitly, the sector is stumbling, unsuccessfully as we shall argue, to a largely unarticulated application of facilities management concepts. In this context, by 'unarticulated' we mean that the adoption of facilities management concepts may not be realized or recognized as such and indeed, one of the few empirical studies that supports this notion, though in medium sized rather than large hotels, is Jones (2002). One of the reasons for this is the already alluded to totemic quality of modern concepts of the need to achieve 'guest satisfaction'. Though frequently ill-defined and extremely variable in conception (there are as many *operational* definitions of what 'guest satisfaction' is as there are strategies designed to achieve it) the broad concept of customer (guest) focus has significantly altered the fluidity of structural relationships within hotels, including those relating to the operational management focus engendered by departmentalization. It is not that the management and protection of physical assets, a managerially operational bias or departmentalization have become less important. Rather, it is that however vague, erratic and successful in practice, these elements have increasingly been infused by a bias in favor of holistic notions of customer need that to a greater or lesser extent mirror similar concerns in the emerging subject of facilities management.

Indeed, it is the generalized vagueness of these notions which arguably creates some of the most interesting contemporary organizational tensions in hospitality (see for example Guerrier's contribution to this volume for further fascinating insights on this theme) including that tension at the heart of what we have identified as an implicit but largely unsuccessful 'convergence' of facilities management/accommodation management philosophies which, though far from fully formed, can be illustrated in terms of two key, exemplifying, areas. Our argument here is that these two topics reflect a nascent tension between the traditional departmentalized, short-term and operations-biased model of hotel management and a more holistic approach to hotel accommodation management that reflects something of a facilities management 'approach'. The topics, each of will be examined in turn, are:

- the growth and significance of a single rooms division department to nominally integrate hotel accommodation functions; and
- the development of Standard Operating Procedures (SOPs) and outsourcing.

FACILITIES MANAGEMENT VERSUS ACCOMMODATION MANAGEMENT IN HOTELS

Growth and significance of the Rooms Division Department

If there is indeed a growing, though not always explicit, tendency towards convergence of facilities and hotel accommodation management philosophies it is most evident in the latter in the increasing tendency to unification of front office, housekeeping and other accommodation departments into a single 'rooms division'. The Rooms Division Department (RDD) normally embraces the reservations, front office (front office being a term used to cover the reception, concierge, switchboard, guest relations and reservations functions of a hotel, and not just the 'front desk' – i.e. reception desk), housekeeping and security functions (in some parts of the world, hotel security has become a stand-alone department, sometimes outsourced, as both terrorism and increased hotel-based crime has become a heightened concern for operators and guests) and their sub-functions. The RDD increasingly has its own and (in larger hotels at least) relatively senior manager. Underpinning operation of the Rooms Division Department is the concept of the 'guest cycle', this being the undoubted conceptual contribution of accommodation/lodging management to the wider study of hotel and hospitality administration, which, in its academic codification over the last two to three decades, owes much to a crude application of systems theory.

The guest cycle is a weak systems process model of the various stages of a guest's stay at a hotel depicting the flow of business through a hotel including the service and financial exchanges between guests and hotel employees. It is conceived as having four stages, namely: pre-arrival (reservations); arrival (registration); occupancy (occupancy services); and departure (checkout). The objective of the *pre-arrival* stage is to secure for the hotel a room reservation and the key skill here is that which influences a potential guest to decide to reserve a room at 'this' hotel rather than 'that' hotel. The purpose of the *arrival stage* is effective check-in of the guest through the registration process. In elementary terms, registration is the process that records a guest's arrival, confirms their personal details and satisfies prevailing legal requirements. The desired 'pragmatic' outcomes of the *occupancy stage* are to ensure that customers have a comfortable and enjoyable stay in the hotel, whereas in the *departure stage*, the aim is to provide the guest with a positive final experience of the hotel (as it is normally the last substantial contact with the hotel that a guest has on any particular stay) while ensuring that the hotel secures payment for the guest's stay.

In this rendering then, the guest cycle is a mechanistic but putatively holistic system of processes and procedures concerned to offer a uniform system for dealing with guest procurement and the management of service delivery and hence guest satisfaction. That is, it appeals to holism without disrupting traditional concepts of departmentalization that prevail in the hotel industry. However, this holistic conception of the guest cycle and the edifice that is increasingly built upon it – the Rooms Division Department – is essentially artificial, reflecting the nascent tension between the facilities and hotel management models of accommodation we have outlined. This is because, in the way it underpins the RDD concept, the guest cycle concept is, in reality, undermined by two forces. The first of these is, of course, the realities of the persistence of hotel departmentalization. The essence of the RDD/guest cycle is three components – reservations, reception (receiving) and housekeeping (maintenance) but these elements often have their own departmental structure or sub-structure and managers, the reason being of course that each element has its own priorities, cultural imperatives and distinct tasks and procedures – in other words a separateness that makes a level of co-ordination possible, but genuine holistic integration difficult to achieve.

To illustrate this point clearly, it is necessary to consider a second force at work, namely that of the growing centrality, yet increasing separateness of the first element of the guest cycle, the 'pre-arrival' stage, and thus the reservations sub-division of the front office, from other front office (and by extension other RDD) divisions.

The pre-arrivals, 'procurement' stage of the guest cycle is increasingly pre-eminent within that cycle, even driving it, 'belonging', more often than not to the front office department or sub-department of the RDD although increasingly interfacing, in larger hotels at least, with the sales and marketing functions. The pre-arrivals stage 'reaches out' to the world beyond the hotel on the principle that a 'build it and they will come' philosophy is not a tenable business strategy. In terms of centrality, the procurement of customers in most sizable hotel businesses is necessarily at the core of strategy and is profoundly affected by the variety of media, including the Internet, which customers can use in booking hotel accommodation. Many factors influence customers' purchase decisions but price is always of major importance to customer and hotel because (a) a hotel room is a perishable good (if a hotel room is not sold for a night it is lost revenue, since it cannot be stored and sold the next day) and therefore the price/volume of sales relationship is particularly sensitive; and (b) many hotels operate in markets characterized by the close substitutability of products and services, and price can therefore be a determining factor in customer hotel selection.

Hotel pricing is a complex process and one that is now routinely described in terms of 'yield' (or in the US 'revenue') management defined by Cross (1997: 3) as 'the application of disciplined tactics that predict customer behavior at micro-market level and optimize product availability and price to maximize revenue growth' and by Kimes (1989: 14–19) as 'allocating the right type of capacity to the right kind of customer at the right price so as to maximize revenue or yield'. The word 'maximize' is perhaps misleading in Kimes' remark, as really what is being practiced in (hotel accommodation) yield management is a form of optimization encompassing questions about what percentage of a hotel's total room capacity should be allocated at a particular time to specific market segments in order to 'maximize' revenue (in point of fact, while the field of revenue management has become a highly influential concept in tourism businesses management, its terminology is often problematic and there is little detailed evidence as to the form and extent of its use in the industry – see for example, Ingold et al., 2001). These segments will, in theory, be defined and redefined as a compromise between experiential marketing (for example, the kinds of guests a hotel knows it 'traditionally'

attracts, knowledge and awareness of seasonal trends) and strategic marketing objectives (the kinds of guests a hotel or hotel company wishes to seek to attract) and will be based on any or all of guest characteristics (a typical business hotel, for example, tends to attract expense account business visitors during the week with higher spending power than the 'for leisure' guests who tend to stay during the weekend: thus corporate or business rates are typically higher than weekend rates); and hotel characteristics (grade, size, different room types, location, market position and degree of competition and/or close substitution). Price variations will normally be arrived at as a result of a compromise between these two principal kinds of characteristic and, in addition to the hotel 'rack rate' (the routinely advertised 'normal' price of a room), a variety of other rates will be available for different market segments. These include, *inter alia*, corporate rates, weekend rates, group rates (particularly where hotels have contracts with tour operators and travel agencies that generate a lot of travel business), rates for different numbers of occupants per room, rates according to the characteristics of the room (for example, more for 'a room with a view' or a suite) and conference rates.

The relevance of the foregoing to the argument here is as follows. The guest cycle is a *theoretical* model for dealing in a unified manner with hotel guests: the yield/revenue management driven pre-arrivals stage is a standardized process for dealing with moderate diversity (in markets) as the other stages are similarly standardized processes for managing the guest experience and delivering guest satisfaction within the hotel, and ultimately where appropriate, within a hotel brand more widely. Superficially, this is an appealing notion: for management, a full hotel is a criterion of success – the end justifies the means and, after all, different guests may be paying different prices for their rooms as a result of revenue management practices, but this is unlikely to lead to much variation in guests' (usually high) expectations of entitlements from the hotel. Ignoring the most questionable and important underlying assumption of this view (that an approach which targets different market segments at different prices and at different times can be assumed to have no consequences for the management of guest expectations and satisfaction) the dominance of the guest procurement process within the guest cycle is inimical to holistic integration of accommodation management functions. This is because, *in practice*, the link between customer procurement and customer satisfaction is broken. The other departments – the non-reservations sections of front office and housekeeping – (or in large hotels more accurately, sub-departments) of the Rooms Division are allocated responsibility for the latter, but enjoy both a less equal status not least reflected in the terms, conditions and work experiences of the personnel employed therein (Guerrier and Adib, 2000; Wood, 2003) and less control over the guest cycle process.

Thus, in terms of communication, the front office department is depicted as the dissemination center of the hotel, providing information to the other hotel departments such as guests' requirements, or arrival times. The very term 'front office' suggests to the uninitiated 'front desk', but the two are not synonymous. In modern consumer-speak, the front office department is the communications and impression management 'heart' of a hotel because it typically provides customers with numerous services, normally more than any other department. The front office department is, of course, almost always a *visible* focal point for the guest *because* of the front desk, which is normally the first contact that a guest, or potential guest, has with the establishment ('normally' because increasingly premium service guests staying on executive floors have their own check in facilities and in many deluxe hotels, guests will be taken directly to their room by a member of the guest service team who will register them in their room or otherwise arrange for registration at the front desk without the guest's presence). In some cases, for example in business hotels where guests are often on short trips, arriving late one night and departing early the next morning, it is often the case that the front office might be the *only* department with which guests interact during their entire stay. In these cases, their perception of the level of service provided by the hotel will be based entirely on the level of service provided by the front office. Following on from our comments at the end of the previous paragraph, lower status employment is often associated with 'dirty work' (that is, dirty in the physical sense) but there is also the 'dirty work' that comes from dealing with difficult or dissatisfied customers. The front office (and in reality, often the front desk component) is often depicted as the 'glamor'

end of the rooms' division department, a 'hotel lore' that is greatly exaggerated as its personnel are regularly involved in the dirty work that comes from being a general focus for customer disgruntlement.

As an example, one such source of disgruntlement is overbooking, that is, deliberately accepting more bookings than a hotel's capacity permits (a controversial legal issue in some countries and yet a 'policy' that has penetrated the soul of hotel accommodation management, textbooks directed to students increasingly depicting overbooking as a necessarily *integral* element of yield management approaches to guest procurement, see for example Baker et al., 2000: 277). Yield management approaches to hotel accommodation sales encourage overbooking because opportunities for revenue optimization always contain an element of uncertainty: for example guests who do not have guaranteed reservations, those who have guaranteed reservations but do not materialize (so called 'no shows' who can account for 10% of capacity in some hotels and who are increasingly punished by being charged either part or all of their 'guaranteed' booking). To compensate for such vicissitudes hotels overbook slightly, all very sensible but a source of considerable frustration to those customers who arrive to find no room at the inn and have, in the parlance of the industry, to be 'walked' to other hotels, similar frustrations being faced by guests who arrive at a hotel to find that their room is not ready (it is a matter of some shame to the hotel industry that hotels in destinations that rely on international guests for the bulk of their business still enforce an afternoon check-in).

If working on the front desk of a hotel is not all it is believed to be in terms of status, then the other department responsible for delivering customer satisfaction, housekeeping, is even less glamorous. Housekeeping work is much more physical, conducted largely away from the public eye (at least while cleaning guest bedrooms) and, though operationally vital, goes largely unnoticed. Rawstron (1999: 115–117), himself an industry practitioner suggests that housekeeping staff are the 'unsung heroes within the hotel', rarely tipped by guests and required to perform work that is physically demanding yet viewed as relatively low-skilled. Put simply, it is the housekeeping department that is fundamentally concerned with the maintenance of the hotel's principal product.

The main responsibilities of the housekeeping department lie in the need to 'provide clean and serviced bedrooms on a daily basis to the agreed standards' (Rawstron, 1999: 114). These responsibilities extend to the cleaning of the whole property and are obviously 'critical to the smooth daily operation of any hotel' (Kappa et al., 1997: 3). Schneider et al. (1999: 3) state that 'the one thing every successful lodging establishment must have, regardless of its size, location or industry segment, is clean rooms'. Ball et al. (2003; 135) similarly observe that 'the prime function of the housekeeping system is to provide clean rooms for the hotel to sell to its guests, and to service those rooms for the duration of the guest's stay'. One role of housekeeping is to remove all traces of previous occupants so that incoming guests are psychologically seduced into a sense that they are the room's first occupants. A failure in housekeeping to effectively remove from rooms the traces of previous guests can create an exaggeratedly negative image of (the lack of) service quality. Research demonstrates that the cleanliness of any hotel environment is a clear make or break reason for customers' repeat use of the property as evidenced in the work of Falbo (1999, cited in Ball et al., 2003). A study carried out in 1987 (it is unlikely that results would change dramatically if the research was less 'dated') and reported in Schneider and Tucker (1989) shows that hotel guests cite clean rooms as the most important characteristic in hotels of any star rating. In some hotels, housekeeping services can be required 24 hours a day, depending on the hotel, adding to the stress involved in maintaining standards.

To conclude this lengthy discussion, we can note two main points in summary. First, within hotel accommodation management there is an evident if implicit commitment to holistic management concepts consistent with those advocated in the facilities management literature. This commitment derives from somewhat ill-defined notions of the need to achieve customer satisfaction and is expressed in the concept of the guest cycle. Second, the holistic and integrative qualities of the guest cycle are undermined by both the increasing separation and preeminence of its first stage concerned with guest procurement, and the persistence of hotel departmentalization. The former reflects the rise of the marketing-driven business model that has necessarily come to dominate an expanding and intensely competitive industry. The latter reflects, in a very broad way, the persistence of tradition in the hotel sector but as was observed earlier in the chapter, there is at least a mechanical rationale for departmentalization – it works, and it works specifically (at least in the accommodation area) in its asset maintenance and protection function. We can depict this situation more romantically as the first stage of the guest cycle 'coming of age' in the sense of it reflecting the realities of modern hotel business models, proactive and dynamic, while the other stages of the guest cycle remain firmly reactive and relatively static in their conception and execution, constrained not only by the physical structures with which they must deal, but also with an increasingly constrained guest service concept, a point examined in the following discussion of standard operating procedures.

Standard operating procedures and outsourcing

The very term 'standard operating procedure' (SOP) emphasizes the operational bias of hotel accommodation management and may be seen as one element of the creeping 'McDonaldization' of the hospitality industry (Ritzer, 2004). In its simplest terms an SOP is a written procedure for the execution of a task or tasks in such a way as to meet defined standards. In the hotel accommodation management literature, SOP documents are presented as important both as training and working documents, ideally (and idealistically) defined as 'living' documents, modified as and when procedures, equipment or rooms change. The emphasis on the procedural 'how to do it' aspects of SOPs disguises the fact that in practice, they are not meant to be localized but rather mutually benchmarked throughout the organization to ensure integration and avoid duplication of processes and procedures. Once again therefore, we encounter a putatively integrative device that reflects a weak systems theory approach, and one that should encourage both temperamentally and practically a holistic 'facilities management' approach to hotel accommodation (and indeed wider hotel) management. Though expressively mechanistic in nature, SOPs contribute both towards the definition and practice of standards and reflect an organization's concept of these standards, a concept that however loosely defined is at least meant to be focused on customer satisfaction and essentially holistic in nature. In practice, there are four tensions in both conceptions of, and attempts to operationalize SOPs that tend to thwart their purpose and militate against the ideal of holism.

First, SOPs are often grown through departments and the degree of integration within and between departments is often difficult to attain, especially in large establishments. Second, SOPs by definition are intended to go some way to establishing standards for processes and procedures which may aid in the attainment of customer satisfaction. However, more often than not they become overly-mechanistic expressions of what a hospitality organization thinks the standards should be, imposing a lowest common denominator on the processes and procedures that flow from these standards. This tendency is supported, thirdly, by the fact that the application of SOPs must necessarily be pragmatic and take account of what is possible in terms of the fabric and structure of the buildings to which they apply. Even in hotel 'new builds' where the opportunity exists to thoroughly conceptualize procedures and processes from the outset, the changing requirements of guests, demands on the building and the (financial) necessity of constrained refurbishment cycles, a standard operating procedure that is appropriate today might not be appropriate in the future, leading to necessary *ad hocism*, adaptation, and improvisation in the content and application of SOPs. This third point might be thought to validate the notion that SOPs should be evolving, 'living' documents and undermine the assertion that they are mechanistic and indeed, to some extent this is possibly the case, empirical research is largely silent on the subject. However, it must be kept in mind that adapting processes and procedures to 'keep the building going' still, *out of necessity*, privileges operational imperatives over strategic change (as fundamental aspects of building performance perceived as requiring change are difficult to remedy in the short term) and do not actually detract from the design of those standards that determine the processes and procedures in the first instance. Put another way and to return to a point we touched on earlier, facilities management approaches to building design and management are somewhat naïve in their treatment of temporality and the changing demands placed on buildings. More importantly, in the hotel accommodation context, standards designed as an expression of corporate philosophy may often

not be deliverable in practice and over time: what begins as a desire or commitment to an integrated holism flounders because the realities of maintaining a building intrude.

The fourth point to be considered here is the simpler one of the level and consistency of the delivery of standards, assuming that such standards *are* deliverable through their associated processes and procedures. We are talking here of the role of human variability. As an example, we can note that the use of SOPs in hotel accommodation management is perhaps most obviously found in the housekeeping function. Housekeeping SOPs typically focus on how areas and items are required to be cleaned, highlighting specific areas to which room attendants should pay attention. The key phrase here is 'should pay attention'. One of the appeals of SOPs in any organization is the possibility of eliminating a good deal of human variability in the achievement of standards. The idea is a chimerical one, not least in hotel housekeeping because of the *methods* employed to constrain variability. These usually take the form, as elsewhere, of performance and productivity standards linked to checklists. Thus Rawstron (1999: 120) states that 'in each area of activity and performance in the housekeeping department there should be an agreed target of achievement'. This achievement should consider what should be cleaned in a guestroom and how it should be cleaned (i.e. the performance standard) as well as how many units should be cleaned by a room attendant during a shift (the 'productivity standard'; see Kappa et al., 1997 for further reading on this). In the 'standard view' promulgated by these textbook sources, SOPs should clearly express the standards of cleanliness required. The standard view emphasizes everything that a potential hotel guest might desire to hear, for example that cleanliness has different aspects and that rooms should be clean to the touch as well as hygienically clean; that different room types within the same establishment might have different cleaning requirements (Ismail, 2002); and that SOPs may differ between properties depending on variables such as building fabric, materials used, staffing levels, star rating, location or corporate and consortium affiliation. Further, these sources invariably exhort eternal vigilance in applying housekeeping standards to ensure that rooms will be similarly cleaned leading to consistency and hence to guest satisfaction.

Cleanliness is indeed next to godliness. The point is of course that housekeeping SOPs aim to reduce human variability in standards but to do this they construct surrogates for these standards, simulacra in the form of performance standards, productivity standards and checklists. These restrict the scope for discretion on the part of housekeeping staff as these standards tend to be valorized within the organization to the extent that processes and procedures come to substitute for standards as well as being a key instrument in assessing the performance of staff. The member of the author team writing this sentence is currently in the second week of a stay in one of the flagship hotels (it has been accorded many awards) of what is acknowledged to be one of the world's 'best' hotel groups. Some time ago the housekeeping supervisor called with her checklist and asked to audit the room. After doing this she apologized for the shortcomings of the housekeeping attendant in not arranging the writer's toiletries on hand towels to either side of the sink in the bathroom, announcing that she had now corrected this. When it was explained to her that this alleged delinquency had in fact been in response to a request *not* to so arrange these toiletries, the reply was an apology firmly suffixed with a statement to the effect that nevertheless, this was the hotel's standard and all room attendants were required to adhere to it.

Of course, the anecdote does not prove the case but if one purpose of SOPs is to achieve a holistic approach to standards in a hotel organization or part of that organization through reducing the effects of human variability in order to attain guest satisfaction, it is difficult to see how this is possible by reducing these standards to fragmentary checklists. The point is, in terms of the remarks made at the end of the previous section, that the perceived benefits of reducing human variability are seen as the means of achieving guest satisfaction such that 'the checklist' (or more precisely the checklist approach) *becomes* the guest service concept in most hotels. A notion, the attainment of guest satisfaction, that is perceived as part of a holistic process, the guest cycle, takes operational expression in a set of fragmentary and mechanistic procedures that are reinforced by the fragmentation of departments along lines of functional responsibility.

That hotels are convinced of the efficacy of this approach, at least in their management of accommodation, can be seen in that outsourcing is increasingly becoming a favored approach to handling many hotel departments, including, notably (at least in the West) laundry operations, and of course, housekeeping. In broader terms, outsourcing is depicted by some, for example the British Institute of Facilities Management, as a historical trend that has done much to stimulate the growth of the facilities management profession cast as means of cutting costs by leaving non-essential, non-core services to agencies allowing a business to focus on its core competencies. Housekeeping is frequently the first choice of many hotels for outsourcing, often justified on the grounds of strategic decisions to concentrate on other, core, activities, for example, the desire to focus resources on the marketing and selling of rooms. This begs the rather obvious question as to what such hotels consider their core activities to be if these do not include the provision of good quality, well maintained and clean rooms.

Of course the answer normally posed to this question is in terms of the control of standards, for hotels to ensure that standards are clearly specified and maintained and, in the case of housekeeping, that the quality and range of services is not compromised. Unfortunately, as Gunn (2003) notes, there is a tendency for outsourcing to be seen by hotels as a quick way out of providing a service, a form of risk deferral instead of a partnership where both companies stand together to provide a service (Gunn, 2003). Gunn's idealism is worthy but misses the point that the 'quick way out' has certain advantages to a hotel. Hotel housekeeping departments are no less affected by labor turnover and its concomitant costs than others in a hotel and, often in the hospitality sector, those rates are higher than for other industries (Wood, 1997). Housekeeping departments are often also the largest in hotels, outsourcing the function therefore enables hotels to control costs more effectively (Kappa et al., 1997). Some outsourcing companies have grown to be truly global players, for example Integrated Service Solutions (ISS, www.issworld.com) which is used by many hotels, airports and hospitals all over the world. However, most companies are highly localized, providing support to organizations within a certain area and this may improve symbiosis between a hotel and a service provider and alleviate some of the effects of the abandonment of direct control (though not responsibility) for housekeeping services. The flexibility of outsourcing lies in the varied demands that hotels will make upon contractors in that this demand will change between hotels serviced by one contractor. As Ball et al. (2003: 151) state, 'the scope of the services contracted out can range from simply employing additional contract labor on a short-term basis through an agency or employing the services of a facilities management company that can take over the complete running of the housekeeping department'. Of course, a some-what less sophisticated answer to the question as to why hotels outsource the housekeeping function is a variant of the 'Everest answer' – i.e. because they can (get away with it). In an industry where the average stay of a guest is quite short, it seems plausible to assume that, providing a minimum set of standards is more or less maintained in housekeeping, most guests will not be in a position to experience significant causes for complaint (and of course, if they do, the company providing the outsourced service can always be blamed). Though this may seem cynical and overwrought, it is consistent with the 'maintenance' approach to hotel accommodation management we referred to earlier, the tendency to prioritize operational over strategic considerations in what seems an inevitable consequence of the nature of the hotel business.

CONCLUSION

We began this chapter by noting the intrusion into texts and other discourse on hotel accommodation management of the term 'facilities management'. The latter is a vibrant, emerging and contested field of study with an emphasis on behavioral holism in the management of buildings. Discussions of facilities management in a hotel accommodation context have shown little awareness of these debates despite the likely superficial appeal of the underlying philosophy of facilities management in the context of hotel service environments. However, a review of some of the key features of the management of hotel accommodation reveals that while indistinct concepts of commitment to guest service seem to support a conceptual convergence in facilities and lodging management approaches, this is largely illusory (a possible partial exception to this is the development of standard operating procedures in, and outsourcing of, certain hotel accommodation where there

is adoption of facilities management practice if not philosophy).

The reasons for this are numerous. We observed earlier that the skill sets of hotel managers have changed considerably in recent decades, reflecting wider changes in the nature of hotel management itself. Perhaps the most important of these changes is the growth of hotels as marketing-driven businesses. There is, perhaps, some irony in the observation that as hospitality management has developed conceptually and in practice, notably (in the accommodation field) in terms of adoption of loose but holistic systems' concepts like the 'guest cycle', the adoption of more aggressive business strategies have dislocated and undermined the intended virtues of these systems. In short, the forces for holism, or at least integration, are matched by opposite forces that inhibit such processes. In terms of the 'guest cycle' supporting an integrated rooms division department for example, the centrality yet separateness of the first, guest procurement, stage of the cycle encourages fragmentation through a reassertion of the importance of sub-departmental structures in reception and house-keeping and their subordination to procurement. When combined with the dominance of the 'marketing model' in the hotel industry and its associated rhetoric of guest satisfaction, and the increasing operational difficulties associated with cost and employment of labor, notably in housekeeping, this has led to an increasing marginalization of these services. One indicator of this marginalization is the reductionism inherent to processes and procedures designed to deliver guest satisfaction which show increasing routinization or 'McDonaldization' through the use of standard operating procedures which, as we have argued, substitute for standards of guest satisfaction rather than being the means by which guest satisfaction is achieved.

It is difficult to see how the tension to which we have referred between holism and integration on the one hand and fragmentation on the other can be resolved, or even if it should. The behavioral philosophy at the heart of facilities management certainly courts charges of naïvety and yet in principle, it should be a self-evidently beneficial strategy for many customer service organizations. Arguably, the recent debates about the nature of facilities management are a victim of the temporality they assiduously eschew in their accounts of integrating building services, at least as far as the hotel industry is concerned. The international hotel industry, and in particular international hotel chains, has grown massively in numerical terms in the last 30 to 40 years through such mechanisms as direct investment, joint ventures, franchising and management contracts and in response to the perceptions of many developing countries of tourism and travel as a means of earning foreign currency quickly. Responding to the growth and development of new and traditional markets as well as contributing to that growth and development, a more competitive situation exists in which investment, cost structures and 'traditional' attitudes towards hotel management operation themselves exist in a state of uneasy tension (see Beals, Chapter 16, this volume, for particularly fascinating insights into these and other, similar, relationships). The growing emphasis on standardization across the sector reflects, inter alia, one view of the way in which costs and cost structures can be more easily managed, or perhaps more precisely, contained. It is this, and associated, processes of standardization which are likely to dominate the management of hotel accommodation for the foreseeable future, perpetuating a market offer that if not quite 'take it or leave it' in character, conditions customers to specifically delimited notions of guest service which fall far short of a facilities management philosophy, however vaguely defined.

REFERENCES

Baker, S., Huyton, J. and Bradley, P. (2000) *Principles of Hotel Front Office Operations*. 2nd edn. London: Continuum.

Ball, S., Jones, P., Kirk, D. and Lockwood, A. (2003) *Hospitality Operations: A Systems Approach*. London: Continuum.

Becker, F. (1987) 'Facility management strategies and organizational culture'. In P. Goumain (ed.) *Planning and Managing High Technology Work Environments*. Amsterdam: Elsevier Publishers. pp. 1–11.

Braverman, H. (1974) *Labor and Monopoly Capital*. New York: Monthly Review Press.

Cotts, D. G. and Lee, M. (1992) *Facility Management Handbook*. New York: Amacon.

Cross, R. G. (1997) *Revenue Management: Hard Core Tactics for Profit-making and Market Domination*. New York: Texere Publishing.

de Bruijn, H., van Wezel, R. and Wood, R. C. (2001) 'Lessons and issues for defining "facilities

management" from hospitality management', *Facilities*, 19(13/14): 476–48.

Falbo, B. (1999) 'Room cleanliness remains key to garnering repeat business', *Hotel and Motel Management*, 214(15): 60–61.

Gee, D. (1999) 'Facilities management and design'. In C. S. Verginis and R. C. Wood (eds) *Accommodation Management: Perspectives for the International Hotel Industry*. London: International Thomson Business Press. pp. 172–182.

Gronroos, C. (2000) *Services Management and Marketing: A Customer Relationship Management Approach*. Chichester: John Wiley and Sons.

Guerrier, Y. and Adib, A. S. (2000) ' "No we don't provide that service": the harassment of hotel employees by customers', *Work, Employment and Society*, 14: 689–705.

Gunn, J. (2003) 'Third party politics', *Caterer and Hotelkeeper*, 6th February 2003: 30–32.

Ingold, A., McMahon-Beattie, U. and Yeoman, I. (2001) *Yield Management: Strategies for the Service Industries*, 2nd Revised edn. London: Thomson Learning.

Ismail, A. (2002) *Front Office Operations and Management*. New York: Thomson Delmar.

Jones, C. (2002) 'Facilities management in medium-sized UK hotels', *International Journal of Contemporary Hospitality Management*, 14(2): 72–80.

Jorna, R. (1999) 'Education forum'. In K. Alexander (ed.) *Euro FM Practice: Facilities Management*. Nieuwegein, The Netherlands: Arko Publishers. pp. 43–45.

Kappa, M. M., Nitschke, A. and Schappert, P. B. (1997) *Managing Housekeeping Operations*. Lansing, MI: Educational Institute of the AH&LA, 2nd edn.

Kimes, S. E. (1989) 'The basics of yield management', *Cornell Hotel and Restaurant Administration Quarterly*, 30(3): 14–19.

Losekoot, E., van Wezel, R. and Wood, R. C. (2001) 'Conceptualizing and operationalizing the research interface between facilities management and hospitality management', *Facilities*, 19(7/8): 296–303.

Lovelock, C., Patterson, P. and Walker, R. (2004) *Services Marketing: An Asia-Pacific and Australian Perspective*, 3rd edn. Frenchs Forest, NSW: Pearson Education.

Mars, G. and Nicod, M. (1984) *The World of Waiters*. London: George Allen and Unwin.

Ransley, J. and Ingram, H. (2004) *Developing Hospitality Properties and Facilities*, 2nd edn. Oxford: Butterworth-Heinemann.

Rawstron, C. (1999) 'Housekeeping management in the contemporary hotel industry'. In C. S. Verginis and R. C. Wood (eds) *Accommodation Management: Perspectives for the International Hotel Industry*. London: International Thomson Business Press. pp. 114–127.

Riley, M. (1984) 'Hotels and group identity', *Tourism Management*, 5(2): 102–109.

Riley, M. (2000) 'Can hotel restaurants ever be profitable? Short- and long-run perspectives'. In R. C. Wood (ed.) *Strategic Questions in Food and Beverage Management*. Oxford: Butterworth-Heinemann. pp. 112–118.

Ritzer, G. (2004) *The McDonaldization of Society*. (Revised New Century Edition). Beverley Hills: Sage Publications, Pine Forge Press.

Schneider, M. and Tucker, G. (1989) *The Professional Housekeeper*. 3rd edn. New York: Van Nostrand Reinhold.

Schneider, M., Tucker, G. and Scoviak, M. (1999) *The Professional Housekeeper*, 4th edn. New York: John Wiley and Sons.

Shamir, B. (1978) 'Between bureaucracy and hospitality – some organizational characteristics of hotels', *Journal of Management Studies*, 15: 285–307.

Stipanuk, D. M. and Roffmann, H. (1996) *Facilities Management*. East Lansing, MI: Educational Institute of the American Hotel and Motel Association.

van Wagenberg, A. F. (1997) 'Facility management as a profession and academic field', *International Journal of Facilities Management*, 1(1): 3–10.

Verginis, C. (1999) 'Front office management'. In C. S. Verginis and R. C. Wood (eds) *Accommodation Management: Perspectives for the International Hotel Industry*. London: International Thomson Business Press. pp. 97–113.

Verginis, C. S. and Wood, R. C. (eds) (1999) *Accommodation Management: Perspectives for the International Hotel Industry*. London: Thomson Learning.

Webster, K. (2000) *Environmental Management in the Hospitality Industry: A Guide for Students and Managers*. London: Thomson Learning.

Wood, R. C. (1994a) 'Hotel culture and social control', *Annals of Tourism Research*, 21(1): 65–80.

Wood, R. C. (1994b) *Organizational Behavior for Hospitality Management*. Oxford: Butterworth-Heinemann.

Wood, R. C. (1997) *Working in Hotels and Catering*. 2nd Edition. London: *International Thomson Business Press*.

Wood, R. C. (1999) 'Introduction'. In C. S. Verginis and R. C. Wood (eds) *Accommodation Management: Perspectives for the International Hotel Industry*. London: International Thomson Business Press. pp. 1–9.

Wood, R. C. (2003) 'The status of tourism employment'. In Kusluvan, S. (ed.) *Managing Employee Attitudes and Behaviors in the Tourism and Hospitality Industry*. New York: Nova Science Publishers Inc. pp. 53–65.

Wood, R. C. (2004) 'Closing a planning gap? The future of food production and service systems theory', *Tourism and Hospitality Planning and Development*, 1(1): 19–37.

Wood, R. C. (2007) 'The future of food and beverage management research', *Journal of Hospitality and Tourism Management*, 14(1): 6–16.

The MICE Industry: Meetings, Incentives, Conventions, and Exhibitions

18

Udo A. Schlentrich

INTRODUCTION

MICE is an acronym for four major segments of the group market: meetings, incentives, conventions, and exhibitions. The MICE industry is complex with many parties, such as participants, sponsors, planners, convention and visitor bureaus, meeting venues, accommodations, and suppliers generally being involved in the planning and execution of an event. The group market of the tourism industry has experienced exponential growth fueled by rapid globalization and expansion of service industries, and the continuous evolution of scientific and technological innovations. Although the MICE industry is negatively affected by events occurring in the external environment such as economic and political instability, regional wars, terrorism, environmental disasters, oil prices, crime and health threats, most projections indicate that the industry is expected to continue to grow globally (Coshall, 2003: 4; FutureWatch, 2006).

In this chapter, we will present the most pertinent components of current MICE industry practices and strategies. Because the United States represents the largest market for the MICE industry, a considerable proportion of the data included in this chapter is US derived. However, we also incorporate many examples from around the world. We will close with an examination of global trends that are anticipated to affect the future of the industry. An Appendix (Appendix 1) offers a list of professional resources in support of the discussion contained in the chapter.

HISTORICAL PERSPECTIVE AND EVOLUTION

From the beginning of civilization, people have gathered to exchange goods and to share experiences and knowledge. Early records of the Greek philosopher, Plato, give evidence that meetings were used to communicate information to groups of people gathered to acquire knowledge through the interaction of those present. Fairs and festivals can be traced from the earliest days of human barter and trade (Pizam, 2005: 232). During medieval times, craft and trade guilds were formed to uphold standards and protect their members, much as international associations represent their members today. The Romans expanded geographic boundaries and encouraged the exchange of goods and knowledge of their time by developing a common currency, promoting a common language, and building roads, rest stops and marketplaces.

The need to communicate in order to exchange goods, information, services and know-how accelerated rapidly as a result of the Industrial Revolution that began in Great Britain in the 1760s. The resulting changes in social and economic organizations led to the rapid evolution and growth of trade associations, unions, educational institutions and, ultimately, international trade, each of which required the communication and exchange of information among its members. The Crystal Palace Exhibition that took place in Britain in 1851 is generally considered to be the first modern exhibition (Pizam, 2005: 623). Although many of today's meetings are much larger and more international in nature, they are organized to fulfill the same basic objectives (Schlentrich, 1999).

Beginning in the middle of the twentieth century, industrialized nations underwent a transition from product to service dominated economies. Services now represent the fastest growing sector of the global economy and account for two-thirds of global output, one-third of global employment and nearly 20% of global trade (World Trade Organization, 2006).

As a result of trade liberalization, the economies of industrialized nations have also become more integrated. Cross-border flows of trade, investment and consolidation of companies mean that the world is increasingly becoming a global marketplace. Organizations such as the World Trade Organization (WTO), the North American Free Trade Association (NAFTA), and the Association of South East Asian Nations (ASEAN) have lowered barriers to foreign trade. The aims of such organizations are to accelerate economic growth, social progress, and cultural development of the countries they represent. Virtually all public listed companies and most mid to large size companies pursue international expansion or form strategic alliances in order to promote their products and services in foreign locations. International markets produce and consume approximately 20% of world output and are expected to multiply 12-fold by the year 2030 to more than 80% (Bryan and Fraser, 1999).

In addition to an increase in service-orientation and globalization, the twentieth century has experienced dramatic changes as a result of the impact of technology. Advances in technology and the Internet have caused the cost of communicating to fall rapidly and, as a result, the natural barriers of time and space that have separated different market regions of the world have been steadily decreasing. Financial capital and other traditional factors of production are now considered to be mere commodities, and intellectual capital is widely regarded as the real driver fueling a company's competitive advantage. In such a global knowledge-based economy, companies are challenged to continuously evolve in order to create increased value for customers, employees and shareholders. However, despite these technological advances, participation in meetings, conventions, exhibitions and trade fairs continues to be an essential core strategy for corporations, associations and other public institutions in order to market their products and services, communicate face-to-face, and discover new opportunities for growth.

IMPACT OF THE MICE INDUSTRY

The MICE industry is a significant sub-sector of the tourism industry, which is the world's leading industry. According to an economic research report by the World Travel and Tourism Council (WTTC), the tourism industry is expected to generate more than $4.745 trillion to the global gross domestic product (GDP) in 2005, equivalent to 10.6% of total worldwide GDP (World Travel and Tourism Council, 2005). World travel and tourism is expected to generate $6.25 billion of economic activity in 2005, growing to $10.68 billion by 2015. Travel and tourism demand is expected to grow by 4.6% per annum in real terms from 2006 to 2015. The world travel and tourism industry directly and indirectly accounts for 221,568,000 jobs representing 8.3% of total employment worldwide.

Although there have been several attempts to estimate the size and significance of the MICE industry, inconsistent definitions and measurement practices make such estimates uncertain and difficult to compare (Crouch and Ritchie, 1998). The largest recent growth in the industry has been experienced in the Asia-Pacific region, which grew by 124% between 1980 and 1996 (Hing, McCabe and Leiper, 1998: 264). According to a study by the Convention Industry Council (2005), the economic impact of meetings, incentives, conventions and exhibitions in the USA is estimated at $122.31 billion in total direct spending. Association-sponsored events account for two-thirds, or $81.94 billion, of the direct spending industry total. Corporate-sponsored events account for the remaining third, or $40.37 billion. Thirty-five per cent of the convention and exhibition market is spent in hotels and other facilities. The remainder is widely distributed throughout local economies. The direct employment impact of the MICE industry in the US is 1.7 million full-time equivalent jobs. The direct tax impact is $21.4 billion.

In addition to the primary economic impact of direct spending, the MICE industry creates considerable secondary benefits through indirect spending. The direct economic impact includes the initial convention spending plus subsequent spending by convention-related businesses to pay for wages, supplies, equipment and taxes. For example, in a study on the economic contribution of conventions in Orlando, Florida, it was found that 12 sectors were directly affected by convention spending, with hotels and other lodging and eating and drinking places capturing over 75% of the total direct effects. Convention spending directly added over 45,000 jobs, $269 million in wages, close to $1.2 billion in output, and $17 million in tourist taxes to the regional economy (Braun, 1992: 34).

In order to estimate the economic impact of indirect spending, most economists use a tourism expenditure multiplier. Although economists do not entirely agree on the exact value of the multiplier, research suggests that the multiplier for indirect spending increases the impact of direct spending from 1.5 to 2.5 times (Astroff and Abbey, 2002). In the Orlando study, each direct job in the convention industry led to an additional 0.44 jobs in Orlando, each $1.00 in wages paid directly by the convention industry led to an additional $0.70 of wages in the local economy, and each $1.00 of production in conventions resulted in an additional $0.90 in supporting production from other parts of the economy (Braun, 1992: 34–35). Local municipalities and state governments also benefit indirectly from delegate spending in the host community through additional tax revenues on local purchases. In addition, data suggests that nearly 70% of participants combine leisure with their attendance at a convention, and will often bring guests with them and stay additional days (Lee and Back, 2005; Pizam, 2005: 19). Furthermore, the spending of meeting participants and the people accompanying them is substantially higher than that of any other tourist category (Weber and Ladkin, 2003: 125). Meetings also provide an opportunity for participants to become familiar with the host community. Oftentimes, delegates subsequently revisit the city or speak positively to others about it, thereby accelerating its growth. In short, the total impact of the MICE industry, both direct and indirect, economic and non-economic, is enormous.

SEGMENTS OF THE MICE INDUSTRY

Following is a description of the four major segments of the MICE industry: meetings, incentives, conventions and exhibitions. Meetings and conventions are closely linked segments, whereas incentives and exhibitions are more independent segments.

Meetings

'Meeting' is a generic term used to describe a gathering of people. Meetings vary in size from a few people to several thousand. The purposes of meetings are manifold, for example to communicate, inform, exchange ideas, teach, train or celebrate. Meetings can be held in many different venues, such as corporate offices, hotels, convention centers, universities or sports stadiums. The following are examples of different types of meetings, each of which can be either free-standing or, as is often the case, integrated with other events.

- *Assembly.* This term is used to describe a large formal gathering during which the leadership of an association or corporation addresses its members.
- *Award/Gala Dinner.* Although this can also be a free-standing event, a gala or an award dinner is commonly an integral part of an association's closing ceremony for its annual convention. Its primary function is to socialize and celebrate. It is normally a black-tie affair featuring entertainment, a recognized speaker and a festive setting.
- *Clinic.* A clinic is an educational session where participants learn by doing. It usually involves a small group of people who interact with each other, or it can be led by a teaching staff member.
- *Colloquium.* This is a meeting involving academicians or scientists who deliver lectures followed by a question and answer session.
- *Forum.* This term is used to describe a meeting where experts in a field give short presentations, usually expressing different views, followed by an opportunity for the audience to take part in the discussion and ask questions. A forum may also be called a panel discussion.
- *Lecture.* A lecture is a formal presentation given by a specialist to an audience. Lectures vary greatly in size.
- *Panel Discussion.* A panel discussion involves two or more speakers who offer their viewpoints or areas of expertise. It is open for discussion among the panelists, as well as with the audience. A panel is always guided by a moderator and may be part of a larger meeting format (Astroff and Abbey, 2002: 10).
- *Plenary Session.* A plenary session is attended by all the members of the organization at which time they are normally addressed as a group.
- *Poster Session.* A poster session is part of a major academic conference during which authors are given the opportunity to display abstracts of their papers on notice boards and are able to meet with delegates on a one-to-one basis to discuss the findings of their research.
- *Presentation.* This term is used for meetings in which a speaker describes a product, budget,

or new business strategy in a formal setting. Attendees are usually given handouts of the topic being presented.

- *Retreat.* A retreat is usually a small meeting, typically in a remote location, for the purpose of bonding, intensive planning sessions, or to simply 'get away from it all' (Astroff and Abbey, 2002: 10).
- *Roundtable.* Ten to twelve attendees are placed at round tables throughout the room. A key topic and an expert in that area are assigned to each table and the experts lead the discussion (Pizam, 2005: 424).
- *Seminar.* A seminar is a lecture and discussion period that allows participants to share experiences in a particular field. It is usually guided by an expert discussion leader.
- *Special event.* A special event is a one-time or infrequently occurring occasion outside the normal programs or activities of the sponsoring or organizing body (Van der Wagen and Carlos, 2005: 4). Special events range in scale from mega-events such as the Olympics and World Fairs, to community festivals and programs at parks (Getz, 1989: 125). Governments are often prepared to offer generous funding incentives to attract large special events and to allocate a great amount of capital expenditure to upgrading the facilities needed for such an event (Dwyer, Forsyth and Spurr, 2005: 351). In addition to the direct economic benefits associated with hosting a large special event, a host city usually receives important secondary benefits such as an enhanced image, the attraction of new businesses from outside sources, and the potential for use of the city's improved infrastructure and facilities by future convention delegates and tourists.
- *Symposium.* A symposium is a formal presentation of material by a number of experts on a particular subject. There is generally less give-and-take involvement with the audience than in a forum.
- *Workshop.* Workshops are small groups of 6 to 12 people who meet to discuss a particular problem or assignment in detail. One member of the group is usually designated as the leader or facilitator. A workshop is characterized by intensive face-to-face discussion and is often one component of a larger event.

Incentives

Incentive travel is an important tool used by corporations to motivate, reward, and recognize employees for outstanding performance, service and commitment (Pizam, 2005: 339).

This market segment contributes 5.1% of the total direct spending in the MICE industry in America, or $6.24 billion (Convention Industry Council, 2005). The incentive market is composed of two major sub-sectors: group and individual incentive travel. Group incentive travel provides an excellent opportunity to convey a sense of 'belonging' to the corporation and encourages team spirit and camaraderie (Witt et al., 1992: 277). Individual incentive travel focuses on many of the same objectives as group travel, but is usually attended by about 20 people, whereas group incentives are normally attended by approximately 144 people (Meetings Market Report, 2004). Incentive programs are usually staged at upscale international destinations and include high quality leisure and entertainment experiences. Spouses are normally invited. The largest share of the incentive market is derived from insurance companies and car dealerships (Astroff and Abbey, 2002: 184). Incentive organizers seek venues such as resort hotels, cruise ships and country estates that will provide quality facilities and a memorable experience to participants. Almost all incentive programs involve special entertainment, themed food and beverage functions, and either spectator or participative events. It is not uncommon for larger companies to charter a jet or an entire cruise ship for their incentive program (Schlentrich, 1999). In addition, incentive travel packages normally include exclusive transportation and first-class accommodation (Pizam, 2005: 340). The Society of Incentive and Travel Executives is an international professional association with 1,800 members in 82 countries devoted to the pursuit of excellence in incentive travel. Members represent incentive houses, airlines, hotels and resorts, destination management companies and other industry related organizations (Society of Incentive and Travel Executives, 2006).

Conventions

A convention is an assembly, often periodic, of delegates or representatives of a political or religious group, commercial organization, fraternal society or other organization. The term 'convention' is widely used to describe large meetings ranging from several hundreds to tens of thousands. Conventions usually have a formal structure, extend for a period of several days and include several functions such as board of director meetings, general assemblies, symposiums and workshops. Conventions are normally organized by associations on an annual basis and often include an exhibition component.

A conference is a near-synonym for the term 'convention', usually implying much discussion and participation (Astroff and Abbey, 2002: 9). A conference is an event used by an organization to meet and exchange views, convey a message, open a debate, or give publicity to an area of opinion on a specific subject (Pizam, 2005: 424). Conferences can be large or small. A 'summit' is the term used to describe a conference that is attended by heads of government or high-level officials. The term 'congress' is used in Europe to describe an event that in the USA would be called a convention. Attendance varies greatly.

Exhibitions

Exhibitions and trade shows are a lucrative and fast-growing segment of the MICE industry (Astroff and Abbey, 2002: 475). As is the case in many other areas of the MICE industry, the terms associated with the exhibition segment are often used interchangeably and are not clearly distinguished. In this chapter, we present a model that attempts to distinguish between two major areas of this market segment: exhibitions (expositions) and trade fairs (trade shows) (see Figure 18.1).

Exhibitions (expositions) are events designed to bring together purveyors of products, equipment and services in an environment in which they can display or demonstrate their products or services to

a group of attendees. Exhibitions allow manufacturers and suppliers to reach an audience that would otherwise be difficult and expensive to reach. Exhibitions may be free-standing events, but are usually held in conjunction with the annual meeting of an association and therefore change location from year to year. Most associations include exhibitions in their annual meetings in order to supplement their income, with the fees being paid by exhibitors often literally financing an association's convention (Astroff and Abbey, 2002: 475).

Trade shows or fairs are regularly scheduled events during which suppliers present their products or services in an exhibit format, such as booths or displays. Trade shows are normally independent events that are held in the same location on an annual basis. They are generally not open to the public. However, some of the trade shows that have a wider public appeal (such as travel, food, car and home building) are increasingly open to the general public on specific days. Trade shows are designed to allow companies to meet potential customers face-to-face in a brief period of time inexpensively, and are an important and cost-effective promotional and sales tool. Visitors to trade shows pay an entrance fee and are given the opportunity to inspect products and receive demonstrations and brochures, as well as verbal information from vendors. Trade shows play a key marketing role in most industries and many firms allocate a significant portion of their marketing budgets to participation at these events (Seringhaus and Rosson, 2001: 878). Trade shows play a more important role in the marketing process in Europe than

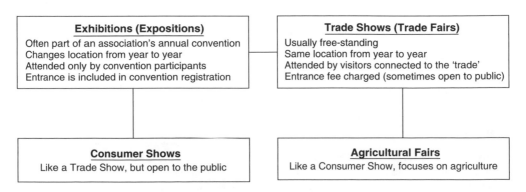

Figure 18.1   Exhibitions and trade shows

they do in America, with about 10% of the business marketing communications budget of US firms being allocated for participation in trade shows and more than 20% of the budget of many European firms (Sandler, 1994). In addition, European trade shows are larger than those held in North America, a higher level of personnel from the company are involved, and many visitors are ready to place orders on the spot (Ponzurick, 1996: 9). According to the Trade Show Bureau, more than 4,300 trade shows were held in the USA in 1994 attracting 85 million visitors (United States Small Business Administration, 2006). Over 2,000 major international trade shows are held each year (Hansen, 1996: 39). Regional, national and international trade shows constitute a multi-billion dollar industry (Hansen, 2002: 1). In recent years, academic researchers have focused their conceptual and empirical attention in several areas, including visitor motivation and interaction with exhibitors, exhibitor management and performance, effectiveness of trade fair expenditure and comparative research on trade fairs across industry sectors and nations (Seringhaus and Rosson, 2004: 152).

In all industries and markets, fairs come and go. Some have a fairly short life, either being cancelled after a few years, or being incorporated into another fair (Trade Show Bureau, 1994). This dynamism of the trade fair industry means that, for any given industry, there are often several changing trade fair alternatives. Some of the largest and most established international trade fairs are as follows.

- *Frankfurt Book Fair.* The world's largest book fair, established in 1949, with more than 7,000 exhibitors from over 100 countries and approximately 285,000 visitors from about 120 countries in 2005 (Frankfurt Book Fair, 2006)
- *International Tourism Bourse.* The world's largest travel trade show, established in 1994 in Berlin, with more than 10,000 exhibitors from 110 countries and approximately 130,000 visitors from 180 countries in 2003 (International Tourism Bourse, 2006)
- *International Motor Show.* The world's largest car fair, established in 1944 in Frankfurt, with over 1,000 exhibitors and 940,000 visitors in 2005 (International Motor Show, 2006)
- *National Association of Broadcasters.* The world's largest electronic media show, hosted in Las Vegas with 1,400 exhibitors from 130 countries and 100,000 visitors in 2005 (National Association of Broadcasters, 2006)
- *Chicago Auto Show.* The largest auto show in North America, established in 1901 (Chicago Auto Show, 2006)
- *National Restaurant Association Restaurant Hotel-Motel Show.* The largest food service event in North America, hosted in Chicago with over 2,000 exhibitors from over 100 countries and 73,000 visitors in 2005 (National Restaurant Association Restaurant Hotel-Motel Show, 2006).

Consumer shows are large scale exhibitions that are open to the public (for example, a home show, a garden show, an auto show or a boat show). A modest admission fee is normally charged. A consumer show is not usually connected with a convention or meeting. According to Tradeshow Week, 26% of the show market are trade shows, 22% are consumer shows, and 52% are combination shows (New Research, 2006).

Agricultural fairs, like consumer shows, are also open to the public and are usually family oriented events. Representatives from the farming, livestock and forestry communities, as well as farming equipment and supply providers, stage elaborate exhibits and demonstrations. Activities such as animal shows, auctions, competitions, rides, games, food concessions and other forms of entertainment are an integral part of these events. Examples of some of the best known agricultural affairs are the Royal Show in the United Kingdom (Royal Agricultural Society of England, 2006) which attracts approximately 150,000 visitors and generates £25 million in direct spending, and the Houston Livestock Show and Rodeo (Houston Livestock Show and Rodeo, 2006) which attracts 1.8 million visitors and generates $179 million in total direct spending. Out of town visitors generate more than 450,000 room night bookings for this event.

THE MEETING PLANNING PROCESS

The different entities associated with planned events are reflected in Figure 18.2. The entities include sponsors, participants, meeting or event planners, destination management organizations, venues with or without accommodation, and other suppliers/services. Although the size

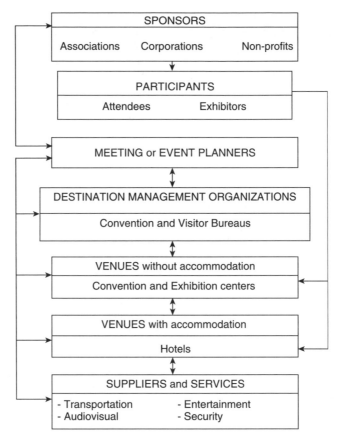

Figure 18.2   MICE industry flow chart

and scope of planned events varies greatly, the general components remain more or less constant.

Sponsors

Sponsors can be broken down into three major categories: associations, corporations and nonprofit organizations. Sponsors initiate the buying process for a particular meeting, convention or exhibition. They define and make the final decisions concerning the objectives, the target audience, the location, the type of facility, and the budget parameters for the event (Schlentrich, 1999). Because sponsors are buyers for an organization rather than for an individual, the decision-making process can be extremely complex, including large groups of participants involved in many functions over an extended period of time. The organizational buying process normally involves a considerable amount of

money, requires professional management and expertise, involves higher risk, and is more formalized than the consumer buying process (Kotler et al., 2003: 234).

Associations are groups of people that find strength in numbers while sharing common interests of industry, profession, charitable activity, hobbies, or philanthropic action (Pizam, 2005). Associations vary greatly in size and scope, from small local organizations to large international ones. Members of associations elect local, regional, national and/or international boards who direct the affairs of the association on a voluntary basis. The elected board members usually serve for a limited period of time (one to three years) since they also hold full-time positions in their respective professions. Almost all larger associations also employ full-time staff at their head office, including a full-time president who reports to the chairman of the board of the association. An association's main board makes the final decision regarding the objectives and location for their annual convention, taking into account the recommendations of the meeting planner and the president of the association. The board also relies heavily on input from its members (Clark et al., 1996).

Associations dominate the MICE industry in America accounting for two-thirds, or $81.94 billion, of the direct spending industry total (Convention Industry Council, 2005). Attendance at association meetings is voluntary, and attendees are responsible for registering, and for making travel and accommodation arrangements. However, attendance at professional association meetings is tax deductible and is often reimbursed by employers.

Association meetings can be divided into two major categories: small regional training or communication meetings, and large annual conventions that usually include educational seminars and workshops, plenary sessions, trade exhibits, award ceremonies, and social functions. Annual association conventions are generally held on a rotating basis in various geographical locations, especially if the membership of the association is widely dispersed (Lee and Back, 2005). As attendance is voluntary, destinations are chosen that have a high level of appeal to the members of the association. Top convention destinations in the USA include cities such as Chicago, Washington DC, Orlando, Atlanta, Los Angeles, New York, Phoenix, Dallas, Las Vegas, and Denver (Fenich, 2005). Annual association conventions generally require a lead time of between 2–5 years, with the largest association conventions being planned 10–15 years in advance (Kotler et al., 2003: 241). Associations invite bids to host future annual conventions from different cities. Given the economic importance of hosting a large annual convention, the preparation of a bid by a host community is extremely important. The preparation of a bid usually involves the support and cooperation of a number of different parties, the most important ones being the local and/or national association chapters, the regional and/or national tourist bureau, the local convention and visitor bureau, the local convention center, local hotel(s), and leaders of the local community (Schlentrich, 1996).

The American Society of Association Executives (ASAE) is the largest organization of association executives and industry suppliers in the world with over 23,000 members.

ASAE also serves as the international secretariat of the Global Forum of Societies of Association Executives, a network for the association management profession worldwide. According to ASAE (2006), over 135,000 trade, professional, and philanthropic associations exist at the local, state, regional and national level in the United States. Ninety-five percent of associations offer education programs for their members, making that service the single most common association function. Conventions, meetings and exhibitions are a prime source of revenue for associations, representing approximately 30% of their annual income (Shure, 2004).

Corporations are for-profit organizations that use events as a means to foster goodwill between employers and management, encourage company support, raise morale, demonstrate leadership, provide training, and express employee and customer appreciation (Pizam, 2005: 114). Whereas attendance at association meetings is voluntary, attendance at corporate meetings is mandatory. The agenda for a corporate meeting is set by one person or an executive committee, whereas the agenda for an association meeting is developed largely in consultation with its membership. The billing for corporate meetings includes transportation, rooms, meals, and company-organized entertainment expenses which are billed to one master account that is paid for by the company. On the other hand, participants at association functions are billed individually for a registration fee that entitles them to take part in the convention. In addition, they must pay for their own travel and accommodation. Lead times for corporate meetings are generally short, and are often governed by unexpected events such as changes in corporate strategy, mergers and acquisitions, or new product or service offerings (Schlentrich, 1996: 332). Some of the most popular American cities for corporate meetings are Chicago, Orlando, Las Vegas, Los Angeles, New York City and Atlanta. The most popular destinations outside America are Europe, Canada, Mexico and the Caribbean (Meetings Market Report, 2004). Corporate-sponsored events account for one-third, or $40.37 billion, of the direct spending industry total in America (Convention Industry Council, 2005).

The 2004 Meetings Market Report by *Meetings and Convention* magazine identified the

Table 18.1   Types of corporate meetings

Type of meeting	Planners involved	Average # planned	Average attendance	Average duration
Sales and Marketing	67%	6.6	118	2.8
Management	66%	8.9	61	2.3
Training and Educational	69%	9.9	95	2.6
Professional and Technical	36%	8.5	111	2.3
Product Introductions	23%	4.8	132	2.2
Individual Incentives	15%	4.9	20	4.5
Group Incentives	26%	3.9	144	4.4
Stockholder	13%	1.7	142	1.9
Other	6%	5.9	136	2.4
Average	100%	17.1	112	2.6

Source: 2004 Meetings Market Report, *Meetings and Convention* magazine.

types of meetings that corporations hold most frequently (see Table 18.1) as follows.

- *Sales and marketing meetings* are held primarily to motivate, familiarize and educate participants about a company's products and services. Meetings often include award ceremonies for high producers, and promotional presentations by advertising or public relations agencies. National marketing meetings often require elaborate audio-visual support. They typically last two to three days and are attended by 100 to 150 participants.
- *Management meetings* typically last two to three days and are attended by 50 to 75 people. Their main purposes are to determine budgets, to develop corporate strategy, and to introduce new policies. Management meetings are also used to form motivational links between management teams. One reason why management holds meetings away from corporate offices is to create a non-threatening, non-hierarchical environment. Such meetings are often held in casual settings, but require state-of-the-art technology and facilities. Recreational and informal 'get togethers' are usually integrated into the meeting agenda. Planned group activities might include outdoor teambuilding activities (such as a cycling tour, a rafting trip, or rappelling) or leisure activities such as golf, clay shooting, or hot-air ballooning. After evening meals, participants often gather into smaller groups for case studies, team projects, or social breaks such as darts, table tennis or snooker.
- *Training and educational seminars* typically last two to three days and are attended by 75 to 100 people. These meetings are very focused and usually involve classroom-style presentations, small teamwork sessions, and individual projects to be completed by participants. Meeting rooms are normally of a high standard, ideally with daylight in a quiet location. Creative meeting breaks are often offered in order to provide a change of pace. In addition, health and fitness facilities are a desirable component, particularly as the people who attend training and education seminars are typically relatively young.
- *Professional and technical meetings* are similar to training and educational seminars, and often involve experimentation and demonstrations. International professional and technical meetings often require sophisticated satellite or videoconferencing support.
- *Product introductions* are traditionally upscale and celebratory in nature. Companies use these events to publicly launch new products and/or brands to the marketplace. National trade and popular press are usually invited to cover these events. Other participants include existing and potential customers, corporate and development executives and staff, and key suppliers. Product launches are often tied in with international auto, information technology, or fashion trade fairs.
- *Individual and group incentives* are a motivational tool used to reward employees for outstanding accomplishment. Individual and group incentives last longer than the average corporate meeting (4.5 and 4.4 days respectively compared with 2.6 days), group incentives are larger than the average corporate meeting (144 people compared to 112), and average upwards of $2,500 per person (Astroff and Abbey, 2002: 183–184; Kotler et al., 2003: 247). Because incentive travel has such a high per person expenditure, it is considered to be one of the primary segments of the MICE industry (as indicated in the previous section on Incentives).
- *Stockholder meetings* are normally annual events to which the financial press, institutional investors, financial analysts and individual shareholders are invited. The size of these events can vary greatly, from 50 to several 100 people, depending on

the size of the corporation. The set up for these meetings requires raised platforms for the board of directors, an excellent sound system, and a staff with wireless mikes to field questions from the floor.

Non-profit organizations represent the third category of sponsors. SMERF is an acronym for one of the non-profit market segments of MICE, consisting of social, military, educational, religious and fraternal groups. Most of these groups are staffed by permanent employees and volunteers, and overseen by a board of directors (Astroff and Abbey, 2002: 170). The majority of functions sponsored by these organizations are individually paid for by the meeting participant, and sometimes the fees are not tax deductible. Involvement in such functions often includes spouse or family members. As meeting participants are normally price conscious, SMERF functions are usually held during off-peak periods. Such functions are regarded by hotels and convention venues as very good 'filler' business.

Another segment of the nonprofit group market is government and political entities. The majority of government meetings are held for training purposes on a strictly controlled per diem basis (Astroff and Abbey, 2002: 180). The national conventions of political parties, government-related summits and conferences of international organizations such as NAFTA, EU, ASEAN, UN and WTO are examples of other types of government and political meetings. These meetings are normally held on a fixed schedule, include a high level of security and are covered extensively by the international press.

Non-government local and international civic organizations (NGOs) such as Rotary, the Boy Scouts and Girl Scouts/Girl Guides and the Red Cross also hold periodic meetings. Other non-profit organizations that regularly hold regional and national meetings are labor unions. Meetings of these organizations normally involve a large plenary session of the representatives who are addressed by feature speakers.

Participants

Despite the important role of attendees in the convention industry, relatively little research has been done on meeting attendees and their participation in the decision-making process (Lee and Back, 2005: 413). Participants at MICE events often include two major categories: attendees (called 'delegates' at a convention) and exhibitors. Whereas attendance at corporate meetings is mandatory, attendance at association meetings is voluntary. Factors that have been shown to positively impact attendance at association conferences include the image of the destination, educational opportunities, and networking, while those that inhibit attendance are lack of funding, time constraints, inaccessibility of the destination and family obligations (Lee and Back, 2005: 413).

Conventions, exhibitions and trade shows are beneficial for exhibitors to attend because they provide a cost-effective means of establishing face-to-face contact with existing and future clients. Such events represent a unique opportunity for exhibitors to meet with prospective clients who have come together from many different regions during a limited time period in order to gather information, make contacts and place orders (Schlentrich, 1999: 165). Some of the primary objectives of exhibitors at such events are to network, personally demonstrate products, express appreciation to existing clients, obtain sales leads and make sales.

Meeting or event planners

The meeting or event planner is an intermediary who is responsible for the planning and supervision of an event (Schlentrich, 1999). A meeting planner is either a part- or full-time member of the organization that is sponsoring an event, or is an externally contracted professional. As a result of the recent trend of outsourcing, both corporations and associations are increasingly contracting their meeting and convention planning needs to independent meeting planners (Toh et al., 2005: 431). The planner acts as an information finder and a liaison between the sponsor and the providers of the various services and facilities. According to a report by Meeting Planners International, 84% of meeting planners were involved in the evaluation and recommendation of vendors and 78% indicated that they were always or often involved in the final purchase decision (FutureWatch, 2006: 9).

Dallas-based Meeting Planners International (MPI) is the leading global association for meeting planners and suppliers, with 18,000 members in 60 countries (Meeting Planners

International, 2004). Another important association is the Professional Convention Management Association (PCMA) with over 4,000 members. According to the PCMA, the most important functions of the meeting planner are site selection, contract negotiation, registration, event promotion and marketing, program and floor management, local tours and transportation, speaker selection and gift selection (Toh et al., 2005: 434). The primary factors associated with the selection of a site are adequacy of the facilities, accessibility of the destination and the site, availability, affordability, destination image and climate, safety and security, and the quality of the facilities and services (Schlentrich, 1999: 154–155; Lee and Back, 2005: 411–412). Some additional tasks that the meeting planner performs are to meet with the sponsor to determine the objectives of the event, review the history of prior meetings, analyze trends and prices, review the policies of the sponsoring organization, identify the meeting format and profile the targeted attendee.

In addition, one of the primary responsibilities of the meeting planner is the meeting budget. Although Return on Investment (ROI) is a focus of the meetings industry, planners report that this term is generally used in reference to cost savings and efficiencies, rather than to the financial impact of achieving strategic goals. Beyond costs and efficiencies, meeting planners are also interested in the development of a measurement model that captures the overall contribution that meetings make in creating value for an organization (FutureWatch, 2006: 3).

Once a meeting planner has finalized negotiations regarding a specific convention with the sales director of a given hotel, the meeting planner will submit the event proposal and budget to the sponsor for final approval and the signing of the contract. At this point, the sales director will normally transfer the account to the Convention Service Manager (CSM) who will work closely with the meeting planner in coordinating all operational and administrative aspects pertaining to the meeting. Under the old organizational structure, the meeting planner often had to deal with up to ten different department heads at a hotel, resulting in considerable inefficiency and communication problems. In order to provide a more reliable and responsive service offering to the meeting market, hotels are increasingly assigning a CSM to coordinate the very complex and diverse requirements of organizing a meeting. The CSM must have an intimate knowledge of the hotel's facilities and how the various operating departments of the hotel function. Typically, the CSM has the authority and responsibility for determining the strategy and the tactical details of a meeting or convention during the time it is in the hotel. Some of these responsibilities include, for example, working with the director of marketing and the director of sales to develop and implement programs, maintaining records of meetings, coordinating with the hotel's department heads to ensure that all plans are followed, checking daily on the event, and scheduling a post-event review session (Montgomery and Rutherford, 1994). Furthermore, the CSM must have the ability to work in a professional and cooperative manner, be detail oriented, be able to handle stress and have the authority to handle last minute changes that will impact the various departments of the hotel (Schlentrich, 2001). Meeting planners feel that the position of Convention Service Manager is extremely important, and the vast majority of full-service hotels where meeting planners book meetings provide such a staff member (Schlentrich, 2001). In case after case, meeting planners state that it is the knowledge and professionalism of the CSM that makes the difference between success and failure (Rutherford and Umbreit, 1993). Unfortunately, although most planners have been working in their position for more than six years with nearly 40% having been in their position for more than ten years, the turnover in the position of CSM is relatively high (Schlentrich, 2001). This is of particular concern as many conventions have a long lead time of between three to six years and require extensive contact between the meeting planner and the hotel. Meeting planners find that this high staff turnover at hotels disrupts the flow of communication and negatively impacts the effectiveness and efficiency of their work.

Destination management organizations

As competition among destinations to host conventions intensifies, destination management organizations face numerous marketing challenges in creating positive destination images (Lee and Back, 2005: 413). Convention and Visitor Bureaus (CVBs) represent the primary destination management organization responsible for creating a positive image for a destination. CVBs are not-for-profit organizations charged with representing a specific destination or region and helping the long-term development of communities through a travel and tourism strategy (International Association of Convention and Visitor Bureau, 2006). CVBs coordinate and promote the diverse interests of city governments, travel suppliers (such as convention centers, hotels, restaurants, transportation companies and local attractions), and trade and civic organizations, acting as information centers and promotional agencies (Schlentrich, 1999: 165). Most CVBs are subsidized through taxes on hotel rooms and dues from local Chamber of Commerce members.

Because the meetings and convention sector of the travel and tourism industry is one of the most competitive and lucrative of their market segments, CVBs devote considerable marketing resources to targeting this important market (Crouch and Louviere, 2004: 118). CVBs can assist meeting planners with a wide range of services such as identifying meeting space and hotel venues, arranging for site inspections, linking planners with suppliers and providing Housing Bureau services for city-wide conventions. Choosing a destination and a venue for a convention is one of the most complex and important tasks for a meeting planner, and the professionalism and image of a destination's CVB can have an important impact on the selection of a destination.

Venues without accommodation

Different types of venues provide facilities for the MICE industry, falling principally into two categories: venues without accommodation, and venues with accommodation. Venues without accommodation include the following.

- Convention and exhibition centers that are able to host exhibitions, tradeshows and conventions.
- Fair grounds and sports stadiums that are normally used for fairs and exhibits that normally do not require any meeting space.
- Theaters and symphony halls that can hold meetings during non-performance periods.

The most important of the venues without accommodation is the convention and exhibition center. Most convention and exhibition centers are owned by governmental authorities and financed through municipal bonds. Their primary objective is to generate local economic activity through the staging of conventions and exhibitions that will attract out of town visitors staying in local hotels, frequenting local restaurants, attending local attractions and spending money in local retail establishments. Convention and exhibition centers vary greatly in size and configuration. Larger centers normally include exhibition halls, ballrooms, meeting rooms, large pre-function foyers, registration areas, a media center, several food and beverage outlets and often a large arena or theater. Some convention and exhibition centers, such as those in Hong Kong, Vancouver, and Glasgow, have attempted to achieve a competitive advantage by means of eye-catching architectural features. During off-peak periods, centers host local events (such as consumer shows, and cultural and sporting events) which are less economically profitable to the community than events that attract out-of-town visitors.

Many cities around the world invest in the construction of large convention and exhibition centers with the dual purpose of improving their image while at the same time generating direct and indirect benefits for the community (Fenich, 1995: 311; Oppermann, 1996). Because the convention and exhibition market injects considerable outside funds into a local economy, many cities – even second tier ones – are eager to compete for a slice of this pie. Unfortunately, however, the majority of convention centers are unable to operate at a profit, especially when the impact of debt service is considered, and are actually planned to operate at a loss which is subsidized through the use of public funds (Fenich, 1998). The findings of a report by the Brookings Institution indicate that public capital spending on convention center construction and expansion in the USA doubled to $2.4 billion in the decade from 1995 to 2005, increasing convention space by over 50% since 1990. In addition, the report found that overall attendance at the top 200 tradeshows had stagnated at 1993 levels (Sanders, 2005: 1). Although industry experts believed that the convention industry would not reach saturation and many consultants advised cities to build new convention centers, there is substantial evidence (such as centers giving away their space in order to attract the convention business) that the increased supply of convention centers is being met with insufficient demand (Sanders, 2005). Debate is therefore growing over the use of public funds to construct large convention hotels (Gilligan, 2005). The issue of whether capital investment of public funds into the building of convention centers and hotels truly generates sufficient economic profit to the wider host community has thus risen to the forefront.

The findings of the Brookings Institution Report – in particular, that there is a glut of convention center space and that the business travel and meetings industry is in eclipse – have been hotly contested by the convention and exhibition industry. The industry seems to agree that many of the projections of the consultants were inflated. However, they argue that the report focused on a time period during which the industry was in decline and that the oversupply in convention space will only be temporary (Hacker, 2005; Lynch, 2005). An additional important issue concerns the validity and reliability of available industry data. The report contends that, although national data on a great many sectors of the economy is readily available in a consistent and relevant form, this is not true for the convention and tradeshow industry (Sanders, 2005: 3). The MICE industry, on the other hand, contends that the report relied on inaccurate data and ignored reliable sources of data that were readily available (Hacker, 2005).

There are some convention and exhibition centers, however, that have been able to be financially viable. An example is the small but internationally recognized Edinburgh International Conference Centre in Scotland. This center has generated steady operating profits since its opening in 1995 (Gerrie, 2005).

Venues with accommodation

Venues with accommodation include, for example, hotels, country estates, dude ranches, retreat centers, cruise ships and universities. The most important of these venues to the meeting market is the full-service hotel. The category of 'hotels' covers a very wide spectrum including, for example, urban, suburban, highway, airport, full-service, limited service, all-suite, boutique, resorts and spas. Virtually all types of hotels host meetings. However, some types of hotels focus specifically on the meeting, convention and exhibition market and offer specialized facilities and services. Resort hotels are the first choice venue for US meeting planners, representing 31% of their total meetings budget, followed

by city hotels which represent 28%. In Europe, city hotels are the first choice venue for meeting planners, representing 32% of their total budget, followed by resort hotels which represent 15% (FutureWatch, 2006: 7).

Convention hotels are usually large properties with between 500 and 3,000 rooms. There are two major types of convention hotels. The first are those that are built adjacent to a convention center and serve as the headquarter property for the center's events. Meeting planners generally prefer to book events at a convention center that has an adjacent convention hotel. However, because some cities have convention centers without adequate nearby accommodation, convention hotels that are financed by local municipalities and/or receive tax abatements are increasingly being built in order to increase the competitiveness of the convention center (Albanese, 2005). The second type of convention hotel is free-standing, and provides both accommodation and its own extensive meeting and exhibition space. Such hotels provide, for example, conference rooms, break-out rooms, pre-function space and exhibit space. In addition, they offer the sophisticated technical and service capabilities that allow them to host large events. These hotels can be destinations in their own right as they usually provide multiple themed restaurants, bars, entertainment, shopping and, often, sports amenities. Examples of such hotels include the MGM Grand Hotel in Las Vegas, the Gaylord Opryland Resort and Convention Center in Nashville, the Hilton Birmingham Metropole in the UK, the Estrell Hotel in Berlin, Germany and the Imperial Hotel in Tokyo.

Conference hotels cater to smaller meetings and provide single-purpose conference spaces, 24-hour meeting rooms, conference services, audio-visual support and Complete Meeting Packages that include guest rooms, three meals per day and continuous refreshment breaks (International Association of Conference Centers, 2006). The International Association of Conference Centers is an association of more than 300 international conference centers, the majority of which include accommodation.

Cruise ships are a growing market with many lines building new ships that have dedicated space for group meetings. Some of the newer ships, such as the Voyager Class, include conference centers that can hold up to 400 people and theaters that can seat 1,300. Cunard Line's Queen Mary II is the largest cruise ship in the world with a total of 20,000 square feet of meeting space in seven rooms. According to Carnival Cruise Lines, groups now account for about 35% of all its passengers (Chapman, 2004).

Other suppliers and services

Convention centers and hotels increasingly outsource many of the critical supplies and services that are not deemed to be core functions, for example audiovisual services, ground transportation, entertainment and security. The setup, furnishing and decoration of exhibition booths are also increasingly being outsourced.

SERVICING THE MICE INDUSTRY

Servicing the MICE industry encompasses multiple parties and functions, all of which can contribute positively or negatively to the overall experience of the attendees. One of the primary responsibilities of the meeting planner is to ensure that the objectives of the sponsor are executed effectively throughout the various stages of an event, from pre-planning, to the hosting of the event, to the post-event process. The position of meeting planners is precarious as they must depend on the reliability of the major suppliers to provide what has been agreed. What makes the service delivery process so complex, especially for larger events, is that these events can include more than 100 functions, each of which is critical in order to have a successful event. In addition, last minute changes and emergencies often arise that need to be effectively communicated and resolved (such as medical situations, special dietary requirements, accidents, changes in guest counts for meal functions, or changes in the weather for outdoor activities). The ultimate goal of a MICE function is to achieve the satisfaction of the attendees and the sponsoring organization, as well as the desired return on investment (ROI). In order to achieve these objectives, it is essential that a positive relationship exists between the sponsor, the meeting planner, the destination, the venue and the attendees of an event (see Figure 18.3).

Given the powerful role of the meeting planner in advising sponsors in the selection of a particular destination and venue, it is important for venues to understand the factors that have the greatest impact in achieving meeting planner satisfaction and commitment. Customer commitment is particularly important since it

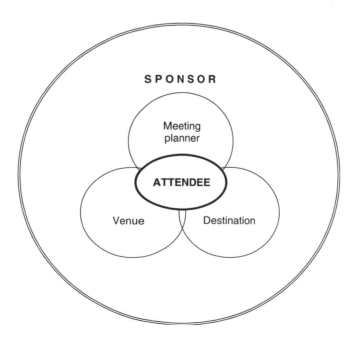

Figure 18.3   MICE industry relationship model

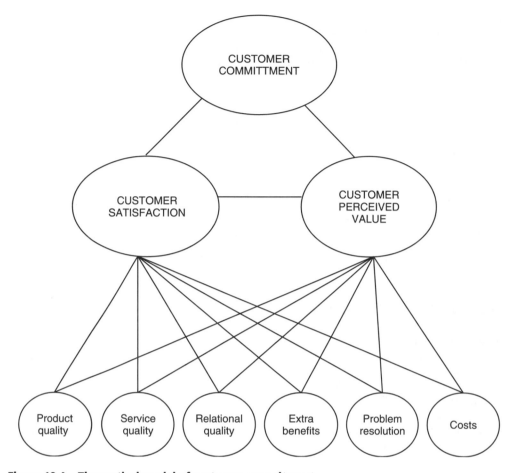

Figure 18.4   Theoretical model of customer commitment

is often little differentiation among hotels and convention centers that serve the same market segment (Bowen and Shoemaker, 2003: 31). A study by Schlentrich (2001) identified the key drivers that have the greatest impact in achieving meeting planner commitment. This theoretical model of customer commitment proposes that meeting planners make a post-consumption assessment based on the following key components: product quality, service quality, relationship quality, extra benefits, problem resolution and costs (see Figure 18.4).

Product quality relates to the setting, design, layout, cleanliness and amenities of the facility. Meeting planners place a high value on facilities that are purpose-built for the meeting market with up-to-date technological equipment. *Service quality* is of particular concern to meeting planners, as service standards can vary greatly. In addition to the quality of the

food and beverage service provided, meeting planners also identify the following staff-related factors as being important: low turnover, responsive, flexible, knowledgeable and professional. *Relationship quality* is a highly valued factor to meeting planners, especially as it relates to the fairness of negotiations, staff reliability, management accessibility and the fulfillment of the agreements that were made. Meeting planners often mention the value to them of the hotel providing an experienced Convention Service Manager. The commitment of meeting planners is oftentimes to the people at the hotel, not to the facility. Good internal communication between the meeting planner and the management of a venue is an essential component of delivering satisfactory service that engenders meeting planner commitment. *Extra benefits*, such as frequent stayer programs, VIP upgrades for attendees, and service customization, are valued highly by meeting planners. However, meeting planners do not like special gifts and privileges being offered to them in order to entice them to choose a specific venue, feeling that this comprises their integrity and professionalism. *Problem resolution* is a very important factor to meeting planners, especially in terms of employees who are empowered to solve problems quickly and effectively, and have a 'can-do' attitude. *Costs* should be seen as reasonable and transparent to meeting planners. Meeting planners do not like 'hidden' costs. In addition, indirect costs such as ambiguity of contract terms, inaccuracy of billings and inefficiency are also important factors to meeting planners.

The outcomes of a meeting planner's assessment of the previous factors are customer perceived value, customer satisfaction and, ultimately, customer commitment (or lack thereof).

- Customer perceived value is defined as an interactive, relativistic, preferential judgement of the benefits and costs of the total consumption experience. Positive value means that benefits outweigh costs.
- Customer satisfaction is defined as a pleasurable feeling of fulfillment resulting from a positive evaluation of the total consumption experience.
- Customer commitment is defined as a positive attitude towards a company's offering. Some of the most important outcomes of commitment are that the hotel is the meeting planner's first choice in the region (95%), that they intend to continue booking meetings at the hotel (95%), that they speak positively to others about the hotel (92%), and that they are willing to pay a premium in order to book meetings at the hotel (42%).

THE ROLE OF TECHNOLOGY

Information technology has a significant influence on the MICE industry and how it is continuing to evolve. Advances in information technology are emerging in multiple forms, providing direct and indirect benefits and challenges to the various segments of the MICE industry. The industry has been greatly affected by the evolution of electronic distribution systems that provide 'real time' information to meeting planners and attendees concerning guest and meeting room availability, meeting room capacities, menu options, audiovisual and other services. However, research on IT applications in the convention and meeting industry has been scant and has focused primarily on yield management applications and forecasting (Kimes, 1999; Kimes and McGuire, 2001).

As a result of the rapid evolution in IT, conference hotels and convention centers find themselves in an 'amorphous' relationship with intermediaries such as global distribution systems, wholesalers, travel agents, travel planners and on-line travel distributors that seek to market and distribute guest room and conference facilities (Carroll and Siguaw, 2003: 38). Conference hotels have adopted computer-based IT capabilities to achieve improved operational efficiency, cost reduction and the enhancement of overall service quality (Law and Jogaratnam, 2005: 170).

The booking, planning, servicing and billing processes involved in organizing conventions and meetings have been greatly facilitated by the development of dedicated software systems that allow conference hotels and convention centers to handle these processes in a more efficient and cost-effective manner. This software reduces the amount of time devoted to managing event logistics by providing a standard electronic template that assists managers in operational planning for an event (Kandampully, 2007: 336).

Newmarket International, a pioneer in the field of such software, launched its first software program in 1985. The primary functions of the early version of the software were removing the paper account files, paper function books and group room control from the sales office. However, the early benefits of sales and catering automation were difficult to justify, as standard office personal computers (PCs) cost upwards of $8,000 per unit. Until the early 1990s, only the innovators in the hospitality industry outfitted their sales offices with automation. Subsequently, the technology expanded to include revenue management, banquet event orders and contracts produced in WordPerfect. During this time period, several property management companies added a sales and catering module or developed a batch file interface with Newmarket's Delphi, the most widely used product during this time. Additional modules were available, such as function room diagram software. However, the entire project cost meant many hotels continued to work in a manual environment.

This all changed in the mid-1990s. The increase in the use of sales and catering technology for hotels was directly related to the reduction in cost of the PC and the Microsoft Windows environment. In addition, the software for hotels became much more sophisticated. Although many hotels took advantage of this IT revolution, it was not until Y2K and industry consolidation that the majority of hotels became automated. The meeting and convention industry was in a positive 'buy cycle', and most properties took this opportunity to install the latest technology. However, despite the fact that the Internet was the buzzword during this period, few software applications took advantage of the Internet for the meetings and convention market.

A general meetings slowdown began in the fall of 2000 with the so-called burst of the Internet bubble, and investment in technology came to a virtual halt in 2000–2001. September 11, 2001 signaled the end of the 'buy cycle' as business travel evaporated. Although 2005 was the beginning of an up-cycle, many hotels continued to use the technology they had purchased in 1999–2000 (Horgan, 2006).

FUTURE TRENDS

The World Travel and Tourism Council projects that spending on international business travel is expected to grow from US$672.5 billion in 2006 to US$1,190.3 billion by the year 2016 (*Travel and Tourism – Climbing to New Heights*, 2006). The MICE industry is also projected to experience growth, largely attributed to the rebounding of the economy in North America and Europe (Future Watch, 2004). In addition, many emerging destinations are experiencing an increase in bookings from the MICE industry. The meeting market has expanded rapidly throughout Southeast Asia and particularly in China. The rapid evolution of the economy in China, particularly in the manufacturing sector, is projected to continue. A shift from manufacturing to the service sector has been taking place in China since their accession to the World Trade Organization in 2001 (*The Economist*, January 14–20, 2006). Since that time, the market has been open for foreign companies to launch wholly owned or majority venture companies in China. With the 2008 Olympics being held in Beijing and the 2010 World Exposition being held in Shanghai, conference and overall tourism travel is expected to experience even further expansion in China (Yu and Huimin, 2005).

Furthermore, in 2004, China eased government regulations for its citizens to travel abroad. In 2005, 28.5 million Chinese tourists traveled overseas compared to just 20 million in 2003. By 2007, China is expected to surpass the United States as the world's largest source of tourists (*The Economist, Special Issue: The World in 2005*: 99).

In addition to Southeast Asian markets, other newly emerging destinations are experiencing an increase in bookings from the MICE industry. The Dubai World Trade Center complex, for example, is undergoing expansion and will provide one of the most technologically advanced facilities in the world (Thomas, 2005). Convention and exhibition centers such as the Nipon Convention Center in Tokyo, the Suntec City Center in Singapore, the Hong Kong Convention and Exhibition Center and the Malaysia Convention and Exhibition Center all offer prime venues and attractions for international meetings and conventions.

As in the past, however, growth in the MICE industry can be negatively impacted by economic and political instability, terrorism and regional wars, crime, oil prices, health scares and natural disasters. The spread of avian flu internationally could have a devastating effect on the industry, much as the reoccurrence of the severe acute respiratory syndrome (SARS) did in 2003 when instant cancellations of conventions occurred in cities such as Toronto and Hong Kong. In some hotels in Hong Kong, for example, occupancy tumbled from 90% to 5%. Similarly, natural disasters such as the 2004 Tsunami in the Indian Ocean region and Hurricane Katrina in New Orleans in 2005 resulted not only in tremendous personal loss, but also in the loss of local infrastructure and billions of dollars of future revenue to the local economy.

At the industry level, the recent trend of mergers, acquisitions and buy-outs that led to consolidation of the leading international hotel brands is expected to continue. Since 1997, 12 of the top 25 hotel groups have changed ownership. Conference and exhibition management companies are also moving into new territory. For example, the Messe Frankfurt Corporate Group, one of the world's leading exhibition corporations, now organizes more than 100 trade fairs worldwide (*We Make Markets Worldwide*, 2006).

The future of technology in the MICE industry is expected to focus in three primary areas: the

Internet, integration of information and global expansion. The Internet has transformed almost every aspect of today's information worker. In order to be competitive, a company must, as a minimum, have a website. However, the best companies are figuring out how to use the Internet to improve revenue, decrease cost and improve customer satisfaction. It is highly unlikely that today's meeting planner would ever book with a hotel without at least one visit to the hotel's website. Even when meeting planners have conducted 20 meetings with a hotel, they know that the end customer will visit the site before attending the meeting, and planners want to be informed about what their customers will see. With this in mind, it is imperative that a hotel's website is easy to navigate and contains the information a planner requires. A second area of note is the group housing market, where group attendees can make their own hotel reservations and receive group rates online. Finally, the Internet will expand as a tool for sending Request for Proposals (RFPs) and booking of meetings. Today, the majority of business is conducted via phone, fax and e-mail. However, hospitality industry groups like the Convention Industry Council's Accepted Practice Exchange (APEX) are working with planners to come up with standard formats to send RFPs via the Internet. This format is already in place on many hoteliers' websites. The format allows hotels to receive their RFPs in a common format, and meeting planners should see a faster and more complete response. It is also quite clear that hotels will move quickly to allow meetings to be booked online, similar to a guestroom reservation. With a confirmed booking, a planner will be able to collaborate on a banquet event order and detail all aspects of booking online from anywhere in the world.

With so many critical systems in hotels and convention centers, information integration will become increasingly essential to a well-run organization. Information workers will require real-time information for everything from customer history and room rates, to today's pricing of menus. The day will come where a booking will automatically trigger, for example, the ordering of food, the scheduling of staff, and the provision of layouts for function rooms – all controlled by Radio Frequency Identification Data (RFID). Additionally, information will be sent automatically to a corporate office from a group of properties so that management can have real-time up-to-the-minute information about

performance and where to provide management assistance, particularly in terms of yield management.

Technology is also expected to expand in order to service the global meeting market. To date, most software vendors have focused the majority of their efforts on North America where there is the greatest concentration of large meeting hotels. With the growth of global commerce, however, software vendors, hotel companies and venue management companies will need to ensure that their technology systems are prepared for global deployment. This preparation encompasses more than hardware and special features, since training and support of the local workforce is essential to achieving a technology ROI. Although the international marketplace will require companies to provide solutions that are tailored to meeting markets outside of North America, companies that will thrive will be those that are capable of providing the same high level of technology, service and support as they do in North America.

APPENDIX 1: PROFESSIONAL RESOURCES

Associations and Organizations

American Hotel and Lodging Association (AHandLA): www.ahla.com

American Society of Association Executives (ASAE): www.asaenet.org

Convention Industry Council (CIC): www.c-I-c.org

European Federation of Conference Towns (EFTC): www.efct.com

Hospitality Sales and Marketing Association International (HSMAI): www.hsmai.org

International Association of Conference Centers (IACC): www.iacconline.org

International Association of Convention and Visitors Bureaus (IACVB): www.iacvb.org (also called: Destination Marketing Association International)

International Association for Exhibition Management (IAEM): www.iaem.org

International Congress and Convention Association: www.iccaworld.com

Meeting Planners International (MPI): www.mpiweb.org

Professional Convention Management Association (PCMA): www.pcma.org

Union of International Associations (UIA): www.uia.org

World Travel and Tourism Council (WTTC): www.wttc.org

World Tourism Organization (WTO): www.world-tourism.org

Trade magazines

Convene: www.pcma.org/resources/convene

Meetings and Conventions: www.meetings-coventions.com

Meeting News: www.meetingnews.com

Successful Meetings: www.successmtgs.com

The Meeting Professional: www.mpiweb.org

Tradeshow Week: www.tradeshowweek.com

Academic journals

Journal of Convention and Exhibition Management

REFERENCES

Albanese, E. (2005) 'San Antonio deal for Hyatt Hotel empowered with tax-exemption', *Bond Buyer*, 352(1): 26 (Issue 32119).

American Society of Association Executives (December 29, 2005) *About Associations.* Accessed on January 29, 2006 from http://www.ASAEnet.org/GeneralDetail.cfm?ItemNumber=7987andsnItemNumber=7393

Astroff, M. T. and Abbey, J. R. (2002) *Convention Sales and Services.* 6th edn. Las Vegas, NV: Waterbury Press.

Bowen, J. T. and Shoemaker, S. (2003) 'Hotel management loyalty: a strategic commitment', *Cornell Hotel and Restaurant Administration Quarterly*, 44(5/6) (Oct–Dec): 31–52.

Braun, B. M. (1992) 'The economic contribution of conventions: the case of Orlando, Florida', *Journal of Travel Research*, (Winter): 32–37.

Bryan, L. L. and Fraser, J. N. (1999) 'Getting to global', *The McKinsey Quarterly*, 4.

Carroll, B. and Siguaw, J. (2003) 'The evolution of electronic distribution: effects on hotels and intermediaries', *Cornell Hotel and Restaurant Administration Quarterly*, Aug: 38–50.

Chapman, B. (2004) 'Hope floats', *Successful Meetings*, 53(11): 62–67.

Chicago Auto Show (2006) Accessed on March 14, 2006 from www.chicagoautoshow.com

Clark, J. D., Price, C. H. and Murrmann, S. K. (1996) 'Buying centers: who chooses convention sites?', *Cornell Hotel and Restaurant Administration Quarterly*, Aug: 72–76.

Convention Industry Council (2005) *The Economic Impact of Meetings, Conventions, Exhibitions and Incentive Travel.* (Sept), McLean, VA.

Coshall, J. T. (2003) 'The threat of terrorism as an intervention on international travel flows', *Journal of Travel Research*, 42(Aug): 4–12.

Crouch, G. and Louviere, J. J. (2004) 'The determinants of convention site selection: a logistical choice model from experimental data', *Journal of Travel Research*, 43(2): 118–130.

Crouch, G. I. and Ritchie, J. R. Brent (1998) 'Convention site selection research: a review, conceptual model, and propositional framework', *Journal of Convention and Exhibition Management*, 1(1): 49–69.

Dwyer, L., Forsyth, P. and Spurr, R. (2005) 'Estimating the impacts of special events on an economy', *Journal of Travel Research*, 43(4): 351–359.

Fenich, G. G. (1995) 'Convention center operation: some questions answered', *International Journal of Hospitality Management*, 14(3/4): 311–324.

Fenich, G. G. (1998) 'Convention center operating characteristics', *Journal of Convention and Exhibition Management*, 1(2/3): 1–25.

Fenich, G. G. (2005) *Meetings, Expositions, Events, and Conventions: An Introduction to the Industry.* Upper Saddle River, NJ: Prentice Hall.

Frankfurt Book Fair (2006) Accessed on March 14 from www.frankfurt-book-fair.com

FutureWatch (2004) *A Comparative Outlook on the Global Business of Meetings* – an Official Supplement of *The Meeting Professional* (Jan), Dallas, TX: Meeting Planners International and American Express.

FutureWatch (2006) *A Comparative Outlook on the Global Business of Meetings* – an Official Supplement of *The Meeting Professional* (Jan), Dallas, TX: Meeting Planners International and American Express.

Gerrie, J. (2005) 'EICC Achieves Best Ever Economic Impact Ahead of Anniversary Year'. Press release from the Edinburgh International Conference Centre on February 26, 2005.

Getz, D. (1989) 'Special events: defining the product', *Tourism Management*, June: 125–137.

Gilligan, E. (2005) 'Visitor attraction: cities lobby for convention hotels', *Commercial Property News*, 19(14): 16.

Hacker, S. (2005) *'The Rhetoric Versus the Facts: What the Brookings Report Fails to Reveal'.* Dallas, TX: International Association for Exhibition Management.

Hansen, K. (1996) 'The dual motives of participants at international trade shows', *International Marketing Review*, 13(2): 39–54.

Hansen, K. (2002) 'Measuring performance at trade shows: scale development and validation', *Journal of Business Research*, 57: 1–13.

Hing, N., McCabe, V., Lewis, P. and Leiper, N. (1998) 'Hospitality trends in the Asia-Pacific: a discussion of five key sectors', *International Journal of Contemporary Hospitality Management*, 10(7): 264–271.

Horgan, L. (2006) *Meeting Technology. Interview by Udo Schlentrich*. Portsmouth, NH: Newmarket International.

Houston Livestock Show and Rodeo (2006) Accessed on March 14 from http://www.hlrs.com

International Association of Conference Centers (2006) Accessed on January 30, 2006 from http://www.iacconline.com

International Association of Convention and Visitor Bureau (2006) Accessed on February 1, 2006 from http://www.iacvb.org

International Motor Show (2006) Accessed on March 14, 2006 from www.iaa.de/index

International Tourism Bourse (2006) Accessed on March 14, 2006 from www.itb-berlin.com

Kandampully, J. A. (2007) *Services Management: The New Paradigm in Hospitality*. Upper Saddle River, NJ: Prentice Hall.

Kimes, S. E. (1999) 'Group forecasting accuracy for hotels', *Journal of Operational Research*, 50(11): 1104–1110.

Kimes, S. E. and McGuire, K. A. (2001) 'Function-space revenue management: a case study from Singapore', *Cornell Hotel and Restaurant Administration Quarterly*, (Dec): 33–46.

Kotler, P., Bowen, J. and Makens, J. (2003) *Marketing for Hospitality and Tourism*, 3rd edn. Upper Saddle River, NJ: Prentice Hall.

Law, R. and Jogaratnam, G. (2005) 'A study of hotel information technology applications', *International Journal of Contemporary Hospitality Management*, 17(2): 170–180.

Lee, M. J. and Back, K.-J. (2005) 'A review of economic value drivers in convention and meeting management research', *International Journal of Contemporary Hospitality Management*, 17(5): 409–420.

Lynch, B. M. (2005) 'Maxed Out?', *Meetings and Conventions*, 40(6): 69–78.

McLaurin, D. and Wykes, T. (2003) *Meetings and Conventions: A Planning Guide*. 2nd edn. Mississauga, Ontario, Canada: MPI Foundation.

Meeting Planners International (2006) Accessed on January 30, 2006 from http://www.mpiweb.org/media/home/factsheet.asp

Meetings Market Report (2004) *Meetings and Convention Magazine*.

Montgomery, R. J. and Rutherford, D. G. (1994) 'A profile of convention service professionals', *The Cornell Hotel and Restaurant Administration Quarterly*, Dec: 47–57.

National Association of Broadcasters (2006) Accessed on March 14, 2006 from www.nabshow.com

National Restaurant Association Restaurant Hotel-Motel Show (2006) Accessed on March 14, 2006 from www.restaurant.org/events

New Research (2006) Accessed on March 15, 2006 from www.tradeshowweek.com

Oppermann, M. (1996) 'Convention cities – images and changing fortunes', *Journal of Tourism Studies*, 7(1): 10–19.

Pizam, A. (ed.) (2005) *International Encyclopedia of Hospitality Management*. Amsterdam: Elsevier Butterworth-Heinemann.

Ponzurick, T. G. (1996) 'International buyers perspective toward trade shows and other promotional methods', *Journal of Marketing Theory and Practice*, 4(1): 9–20.

Powers, T. and Barrows, C. W. (2006) *Introduction to the Hospitality Industry*. 6th edn. Hoboken, NJ: John Wiley and Sons.

Royal Agricultural Society of England (2006) Accessed on March 14, 2006 from http://www.royalshow.org.uk

Rutherford, D. G. and Umbreit, W. T. (1993) 'Improving interactions between meeting planners and hotel employees', *The Cornell Hotel and Restaurant Administration Quarterly*, 34(1): 68–80.

Sanders, H. (2005) *Space Available: The Realities of Convention Centers as Economic Development Strategy*. Washington, DC: The Brookings Institution.

Sandler, G. (1994) 'Fair dealing', *Journal of European Business*, 4(March/April): 46–49.

Schlentrich, U. A. (1996) Business travel marketing. In A. V. Seaton and M. M. Bennett (eds) *Marketing Tourism Products: Concepts, Issues, Cases*. London: International Thomson Business Press. pp. 318–349.

Schlentrich, U. A. (1999) 'Conference and Convention Management', In C. S. Verginis and R. C. Wood (eds) *Accommodation Management: Perspectives for the International Hotel Industry*. London: International Thomson Business Press. pp. 150–171.

Schlentrich, U. A. (2001) A Model of Customer Loyalty: An Empirical Investigation of the Relationship Between Value, Satisfaction and Commitment. Dissertation. Glasgow, Scotland: Strathclyde University.

Seringhaus, F. H. R. and Rosson, P. J. (2001) 'Firm experience and international trade fairs', *Journal of Marketing Management*, 17: 877–901.

Shure, P. (2004) '13th Annual Meeting Market Survey: small signs of recovery', *Convene* (March): 28.

Society of Incentive and Travel Executives (2006) Accessed on March 14 from www.site-intl.org

The ASEAN Secretariat (2006) The ASEAN Vision: 2020. Accessed on March 14, 2006 from http://www.asean.org/1814.htm

The Economist (Jan 14–20, 2006) 'Are You Being Served?' 61–62.

The Economist, Special Issue: The World in 2005.

Thomas, A. (December 5, 2005) HH Sheikh Hamdan Approves AED 16 billion DWTC Masterplan. Accessed on January 31, 2006 from http://www.dwtc.com/Kiosk/news875.htm).

Toh, R. S., DeKay, C. F. and Yates, B. (2005) 'Independent meeting planners: roles, compensation, and potential conflicts', *Cornell Hotel and Restaurant Administration Quarterly*, 46(4): 431–443.

Trade Show Bureau (1994) *A Guide to the US Exposition Industry*.

Travel and Tourism – Climbing to New Heights (2006) Accessed on March 14 from www.wttc.org/2006TSA/pdf/Executive%20Summary%202006.pdf (p. 7).

United States Small Business Administration (2006) *Trade Shows*. Accessed on February 1, 2006 from www.sba.gov/starting_business/marketing/tradeshows.html

Van der Wagen, L. and Carlos, B. R. (2005) *Event Management for Tourism, Cultural, Business, and Sporting Events*. Upper Saddle River, NJ: Prentice Hall.

We Make Markets Worldwide (2006) Accessed on Jan 31, 2006 from www.messefrankfurt.com/corporate/en/

Weber, K. and Ladkin, A. (2003) 'The convention industry in Australia and the United Kingdom: key issues and competitive forces', *Journal of Travel Research*, 42(Nov): 125–132.

Witt, S. F., Gammon, S. and White, J. (1992) 'Incentive travel: overview and case study of Canada as a destination for the UK market', *Tourism Management*, 13(3): 275–287.

World Trade Organization (2006) Services: Rules for Growth and Investment. Accessed on January 30, 2006 from http://www.org/english/thewto_e/whatis_e/tif_e/agrm6_e.htm

World Travel and Tourism Council (2005) *World Travel and Tourism 2005 Economic Research Report*. Oxford, UK: Oxford Economic Forecasting.

Yu, L. and Huimin, G. (2005) 'Hotel reform in China: a SWOT analysis', *Cornell Hotel and Restaurant Administration Quarterly*, May: 153–169.

Food and Beverage Management

19

Clayton W. Barrows

INTRODUCTION

The provision of food and beverage to customers for profit has played a long and important role in society. From the early days of taverns, inns, monasteries and public houses has emerged an industry that is one of the largest in the world with a vast network of providers, suppliers, customers and others associated with the industry. Foodservice providers and services come in all manner of shapes and sizes; from carts and stalls on city streets to upscale dining rooms in restaurants and private clubs. It is truly a large, diverse and internationally dispersed industry. What originally began as a very fragmented, unregulated group of businesses, however, has evolved into a legitimate industry with increasingly fewer international barriers and boundaries. The foodservice industry has developed to the point that there are multinational foodservice companies serving customers in a variety of locations and settings both for profit and not-for-profit. Everyday, in every country, people purchase food while they work, travel and engage in leisure activities. Further, analysts and academics are beginning to study the industry on more of a global level than ever before as the trends that affect it become recognized as a truly global phenomenon.

As one part of the larger service industries, foodservice (used synonymously with food and beverage industry) businesses have much in common with other service providers (the relationship of the foodservice industry to the service sector is depicted in Figure 19.1).

Foodservice operations are essentially accountable to three constituents: (1) their customers; (2) their owners and/or investors and (3) their managers and employees. At times, these three groups (owners, customers and employees) may have separate, and even disparate, objectives. A major challenge of foodservice operators is the challenge of satisfying all three of these constituents. The challenge presented to the individual operator is to meet the needs of all three simultaneously. While on the one hand, customers are being served (and hopefully receiving satisfactory service), on the other, the foodservice industry provides potentially fulfilling careers to motivated employees around the world. Many millions of people work in the industry performing a variety of line-level, supervisory, support and managerial roles and tasks. Multinational companies provide sophisticated training and support to assure that their employees and managers have the necessary skills to both satisfy their customers and to succeed in their careers. On a smaller scale, independent operators are able to offer a more customized, if less progressive, career path.

While the industry provides steady income for small business owners and substantial returns on investment for investors of some of the larger companies, more and more companies, particularly in the Western world are opting to 'go public' as a result of the desire on the part of investors to invest in industries with growth potential. Foodservice companies are traded on

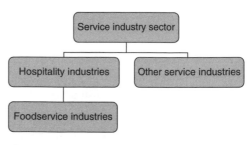

Figure 19.1 Foodservice industry as part of the larger service sector

all of the major stock exchanges across the globe. They also attract investments from individuals and venture capitalist groups.

This chapter will provide an overview of the industry with a specific focus on the management of foodservice operations. The industry has evolved in so many ways – perhaps to a greater degree in the last ten years than in any previous decade. Foodservice businesses continue to find new venues for distribution, develop new methods of marketing, identify new systems of controlling assets, expand internationally, and exploit new niches. All in all, it is a very dynamic time for the industry – as a customer, employee or owner/investor. While the industry has evolved to a certain level of sophistication, however, the basic challenges of providing a meaningful combination of food and beverage and level of service has not changed much over the years. In fact, given the implications that this has for management, productivity, and profit potential, the management of a foodservice operation is as challenging as any industry. This chapter will therefore discuss: (1) the size and scope of the industry on a global basis, (2) food and beverage industry segments; (3) the role and importance of the food and beverage industry as a part of the larger hospitality industry; (4) key elements of the food and beverage experience; (5) marketing and the food and beverage consumer; (6) the management of food and beverage operations; (7) financial control and revenue management; (8) profiles of the industry in five very different countries; (9) current trends affecting the industry and, finally (10) current challenges facing the industry.

SIZE AND SCOPE OF THE INDUSTRY

The international foodservice industry is too large and diverse to adequately discuss within the scope of a single chapter. Instead, certain key countries and regions will be profiled in this chapter, primarily focusing on the industries in North America and Europe. In the USA alone, there are almost 900,000 foodservice outlets generating $440 billion (US) each year; Canada adds another 63,000 units which generate over C$ 43 billion (US $33 billion); and Mexico operates 221,000 units which contribute the equivalent of $12 billion (US). These figures suggest that in North America alone (not including Central America or the Caribbean

region) there are well over 1 million foodservice operations which earn close to half a trillion dollars.

According to Euromonitor (2004) the global restaurant sector generated $1.3 trillion (US) in 2003 suggesting that North American sales represent over one-third of the global industry by sales (this does not include the on-site sector as discussed below or bars that serve alcoholic drinks and do not serve food).

The global foodservice industry

The information in this section has been largely compiled from Euromonitor.com. On a global scale, the foodservice industry is often classified into two primary segments: the 'commercial' (or 'restaurant' or 'profit') segment and the 'on-site' (or 'noncommercial' or 'cost') segment. The former represents most types of foodservice operations with which the average reader would be familiar and would include quick-service, fine-dining, pubs and family restaurants. The on-site segment is comprised of those foodservice outlets that are servicing a larger entity such as a business/industry, university, hospital, correctional facility and so on. The focus of this chapter will be on the commercial (or hereafter, restaurant) segment. The on-site segment will also be mentioned throughout the chapter as it is becoming increasingly difficult to entirely separate the two. In a sense, though, they are often treated as two separate industry sectors with different operating procedures and standards.

The commercial sector will be broken down into its smaller components later in the chapter. Suffice it to say at this point that the commercial sector is the larger and most dominant on both a regional and global scale. On a global scale, it is estimated that the commercial sector is approximately ten times larger than the on-site sector. The commercial portion of the industry has been growing at a steady rate, not only in the more commercially friendly regions of the world but also across the entire globe. Anywhere that people's standard of living is improving they are able to spend more on leisure activities including dining away from home as well as other hospitality services. This is due largely to the fact that foodservice has become such an accepted part of people's lifestyles. Further, the industry is so diversified that when one component declines or otherwise suffers economically, another segment increases its own share of the market or even emerges as a growth leader. For example, when propensity to travel declines and people spend less on hotel dining, they may stay closer to home but will make up for it in local spending in quick-service and casual dining restaurants including pubs. The increasing number of choices has made it possible for consumers to shift their spending in this way.

Overall, the global industry is healthy, especially when one considers all of the hardships that it has encountered so far this decade. As an example of the prosperity of the industry, in the USA, the foodservice industry has experienced decades of real growth – the lone exceptions being during recessionary periods (such as the early 1990s). In recent years, various regions of the world have weathered wars, SARS, BSE, terrorist attacks and food safety scares. In most cases, the industry has come back stronger than ever after these challenges. In the end, the industry continues to reaffirm its resiliency and importance in global markets.

Globally, the industry continues to be strong in most parts of North America, Western Europe and the Asia Pacific region. Further, there are countries where the industry seems poised to explode. These include such emerging markets as India, China and Russia. Indeed, even in countries where the standard of living is not equal to those in the Western world, foodservice is playing an increasingly important role. The sheer size of the global industry is staggering. According to Euromonitor (2004), the 'commercial' industry generated over US $1.3 trillion in 2003 which was in turn generated by some 11 million operational units. Further, Euromonitor analysts expect the growth to sustain itself with the number of units expected to increase by 4% per year into the foreseeable future. Though this growth rate may be modest compared to certain other sectors of the economy, it reflects steady upward consistency over time.

In terms of size and distribution, the Asia Pacific region accounts for almost 40% of global foodservice revenues. This is largely a result of the higher concentration of foodservice operational units. For instance, in China alone, there are over 3.5 million foodservice units – the most in any single country. The high percentage of revenues generated in this region, though, is driven primarily by the high number of units which is offset somewhat by lower than average customer spending; in other words, there are more restaurants selling at a higher volume but at lower average costs. Japan is another large player in this region. Japan represents the second largest foodservice market in the world both in terms of units (second to China) and revenue (second to the USA). The Asia Pacific region is also experiencing the greatest rate of growth in the world largely driven by India and China.

When the Asia Pacific region is contrasted with the North American market, the differences become immediately apparent. The North American market is dominated by the USA which generates the most foodservice revenue of any country in the world with only one-sixth the number of units of China. In other words, revenues are largely generated by higher average checks across segments (and more meal occasions per customer). In terms of the global market, North America as a whole, accounts for just less than 30% of global revenues with only 6% of global units. Average customer spending is among the highest in the world. Somewhat true to the stereotype regarding the 'chaining of America,' there is also a higher penetration of chains than in any other region of the world. While the USA is the dominant country in North America, both Mexico and Canada represent sizable foodservice markets in their own right. Finally, the North American region, in addition to its size, is experiencing above average growth. Much of this is attributed to the development of new concepts, a healthy economy, expansion of foodservice operations into non-traditional sites and the accelerated growth of some emerging companies.

The restaurant industry in Western Europe is almost as imposing with countries such as the UK, Italy, France and Germany (among others) having thriving foodservice industries that are supported by local residents as well as tourists: in the UK, some 178,000 units generated over £24 billion. In total, Western Europe accounts for just over 20% of global revenues – largely driven by the large and thriving industries in Italy, France and the UK (some of these countries will be profiled later). Western Europe is characterized by a lower chain penetration (lower than North America), a larger concentration of bars and cafés serving food, and a higher than average percentage of full-service restaurants, resulting in higher than average customer spending.

Together, the Asia Pacific, North American, and Western European regions account for

Table 19.1   Largest foodservice markets[a]

Country	Sales (in US $millions)	Number of units
1. USA	$365,000	578,558
2. Japan	$180,000	829,576
3. China	$113,000	3,592,242
4. India	$ 98,000	1,040,105
5. Italy	$ 66,000	230,291
6. France	$ 41,000	156,544
7. UK	$ 40,000	177,588
8. South Korea	$ 37,000	708,937
9. Canada	$ 30,000	85,343
10. Germany	$ 29,000	174,735

[a] Information compiled from Euromonitor.com

nearly 90% of global foodservice sales. While other relatively dynamic foodservice markets exist in other parts of the world, these three regions are clearly dominant. Some regions, in fact, are experiencing negative growth, including Latin America and parts of the Middle East. The top 10 foodservice markets are presented in Table 19.1. Despite the prominence of the quick-service industry, one-half of all restaurants in the world are actually full-service restaurants (Euromonitor, 2004). Further, the majority of foodservice units are independently owned and operated despite the prevalence of chains in North America, a point that will be revisited repeatedly.

FOOD AND BEVERAGE INDUSTRY SEGMENTS

The food and beverage industry is so large and diverse that it only makes sense to discuss the industry in terms of its individual operating segments. Each segment has its own standards, benchmarks, customers, operating environment and operating characteristics. To discuss the foodservice industry as a single homogeneous industry is to do an injustice to the many specialized segments that comprise it (Barrows, 2001a). These key segments are discussed in turn (again, the reader should understand that not all conceivable segments will be discussed in full). Different countries and regions of the world have different terms for the types of restaurants that exist (full-service restaurants, quick-service restaurants, cafés, bistros). No matter the region of the world, though, food-service operations are usually classified on the basis of five dimensions: (1) level of service;

(2) extent of their offerings; (3) ownership structure; (4) menu type and (5) price range. Various classification models have been put forth by restaurant associations, governments, consultants, trade journals and industry analysts. Kivela, Reece and Inbakaran (1999) recommended the use of a model segmenting restaurants into four primary types based on a variety of attributes. The model includes four primary segments (Convenience/Fast Food, Theme/Ambience, Family/Popular, and Fine-Dining). This model has been used by other academics in subsequent segmentation strategies and has proven itself as one of the more sensible models available. Among others, Barrows (2001a) has used it to describe the industry. For purposes of even greater simplification, however, restaurants in this chapter will be broken down by service level in an effort to define the individual categories.

Broadly speaking, restaurants may be categorized as full-service or limited-service. Figure 19.2 depicts how these sub-segments appear in relation to the larger foodservice industry. The full-service restaurant category is composed of any operation in which the customer receives complete table service. This category can include dinner houses (including themed restaurants), family restaurants, and fine-dining. The limited-service category is broadly defined as any operation where the customer is an integral part of the service delivery system. This category of operations would include segments such as quick-service, cafeterias and buffets, stalls and kiosks, and pizza restaurants. These are now discussed in greater detail.

Full-service operations

Dinner houses

Dinner houses are an integral part of the full-service category and one of the sectors driving growth in certain markets. These restaurants are sometimes referred to as casual dining restaurants as most tend to be of a more casual nature (at least when compared to fine-dining restaurants). Dinner houses are typically characterized by the following:

* full table-service;
* a casual atmosphere;
* comfortable setting and décor;
* open for multiple meal periods (usually lunch and dinner);

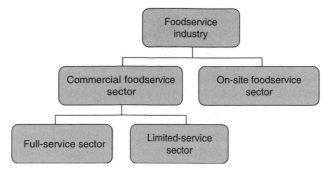

Figure 19.2   The foodservice industry and its sectors

- availability of alcoholic beverages;
- higher check averages (higher than limited-service restaurants and most other full-service restaurants with the exception of fine-dining);
- a diverse menu;
- high unit volume sales (in some); and
- a theme, sometimes (food, entertainment or otherwise).

Dinner houses are most commonly associated with chains – examples include: Mövenpick, Applebees, Bennigans, Kelsey's, the Darden chain of restaurants (including Red Lobster and Olive Garden) and the Brinker chain of restaurants which includes Chili's. This segment would also include so-called theme restaurants such as Hard Rock Café and Rainforest Café. Several of these chains are billion dollar companies and continue to enjoy success. North American chains such as those mentioned above continue to expand into both Europe and Asia.

Family restaurants

Family restaurants represent a slightly smaller segment of the industry but fill an important niche between quick-service restaurants and dinner houses. As the name implies, they are more family-friendly (although more and more restaurant categories are battling for the family share of the foodservice dollar). Family restaurants are typically characterized by:

- family-friendly dining environments with accommodation for young children;
- check averages between dinner houses and quick-service;
- multiple meal periods (usually continuous service from breakfast through dinner);
- a wide range of menu selections;

- widespread use of convenience foods; and
- no alcoholic beverages.

Family dining restaurants are associated with chains as well as being independently owned and operated. They play an important role in meeting the demands of families (often with various needs) dining out. Examples of successful family dining chains include: Denny's, Cracker Barrel and Bob Evans.

Fine-dining

The fine-dining segment is, arguably, the segment of the industry that is responsible for the glamour element of the foodservice industry. It has a long and distinguished history and continues to succeed in areas where discretionary income and tradition support it. Fine-dining (or white tablecloth) restaurants are characterized by their exceptionally high levels of service and superior food products. Additional features and characteristics include:

- high check averages (by definition, the highest in the industry);
- highly trained back-of-the-house and front-of-the-house employees;
- specialized service professionals (such as sommeliers);
- sophisticated wine lists;
- tableside service;
- expensive and comfortable décor; and
- a tendency to be individually owned and operated (as opposed to having chain affiliations).

With the general trend moving toward a preference for casual dining experiences, fine-dining has encountered some challenges in recent years. However, these restaurants still play an important role for business meetings, special occasions, and celebrations.

Other full-service operations

Other full-service foodservice operations exist but beyond the primary categories described above, the segments begin to get 'blurred' as additional segments are defined. Further, categories and their associated definitions tend to change from region to region. Several of these categories that must be mentioned though, would include cafés which are common in much of Europe and parts of South America, and hotel and resort dining. Cafés, as defined here, would serve a balance of food and beverage (alcoholic and non-alcoholic) and would provide full table service. Hotel (and resort) dining is undergoing tremendous changes at the time of writing. While some hotel companies still provide a wide range of offerings to their guests, the trend in recent years has been to outsource foodservice operations to restaurant or catering companies that specialize in this segment. Finally, there are many other specialized types of dining operations that may be further segmented on the basis of location or clientele. These are too numerous to examine here but would include, for example, private clubs and cruise ships.

Limited-service operations

Quick-service

Any discussions of limited-service foodservice must begin and end with quick-service operations. The quick-service segment, formerly referred to as fast-food, is single-handedly changing the way that the world consumes food as the North American quick-service business format continues to expand worldwide. This expansion has been led by such companies as McDonald's (represented in 120 countries), Pizza Hut (84 countries), KFC (80 countries), and Subway (73 countries). A mere 25 years ago, such wide dispersion would have been unthinkable. Whereas it was once news that such restaurant companies were opening outlets in developing markets such as China and Russia, now these same companies are entering these and even newer markets in huge numbers. The segment's appeal globally is due to the same factors that made it a success in the USA – relatively inexpensive fare delivered quickly.

The quick-service segment is defined by:

- relatively inexpensive food (which might include hamburgers, pizza, tacos or fried fish);
- menus that historically have focused on a single menu item (although this is changing);
- fast service (usually accomplished by sophisticated systems to allow for this);
- limited menu choices;
- a large percentage of take-away meals;
- plain décor; and
- a tendency to be chain-affiliated.

Quick-service is an appealing concept to both operators and customers. For operators, the high levels of productivity and ability to utilize unskilled labor generates above average profits. For customers, the appeal of the attractive product/service combination cuts across demographic and income groups. The industry has such broad appeal, and is represented in so many global markets, that a financial index based on the price of a Big Mac (Big Mac Index) (*The Economist*, 2006) is widely used to depict purchasing power parity across international markets. Restaurants in this segment of the industry are often referred to as 'brands' and with good reason. Globally, they are in the same league as Coca-Cola and Levi's as far as name recognition is concerned.

Because of the stature that quick-service holds, a little more discussion is in order. The industry is older than many would believe, but the actual product that the customer purchases is much the same as it was in the early days when menus were largely limited to hamburgers, French fries and soft drinks. The typical quick-service menu is now much longer than it was historically but the actual food product has not changed as much as the surrounding restaurant. To be sure, the segment is maturing, and thus, it is redefining its place in the restaurant landscape. Aside from expansion into international markets, the industry is also targeting non-traditional, on-site locations with smaller prototypes; focusing more on drive-thru business; providing healthier menu options; partnering with other companies or merging with them; and re-evaluating delivery systems. The industry is taking these actions in an effort to combat slowing growth as a result of maturation and threats from other segments of the industry. For example, as menu prices necessarily increase and as baby boomers look for dining alternatives, quick-service finds itself competing more and more with other segments of the industry, such as family dining. In response to this, and in an effort to maintain their core market, the industry has started to offer customers an alternative to the traditional quick-service product – a new emerging segment known as fast-casual.

Fast-casual

This category is comprised of restaurants that offer a slightly increased level of service (albeit customers still place their orders at the counter), a slightly more adventurous menu, and slightly higher check averages. A new and emerging restaurant category is the fast-casual (or quick-casual) segment. The niche that this segment occupies is somewhere between a traditional quick-service restaurant and a family restaurant (or even a dinner house). As the name implies, these restaurants provide 'fast' food in an environment that is slightly more inviting than quick-service and with a slightly higher level of service. Although there is some disagreement over what exactly characterizes this segment (and where it begins and ends), the following are some of the characteristics fairly common throughout the segment:

- higher check averages than quick-service;
- limited service (the customer usually orders at a counter and then the food is delivered to the table);
- food that is made to order; and
- a menu that focuses on specialty food products including soups, salads and sandwiches.

The segment has been so strong and has posed such a threat to traditional quick-service categories that many of the major quick-service companies have either purchased fast-casual chains or begun to experiment with fast-casual elements in traditional quick-service restaurants.

Coffee shops

A few short years ago, coffee shops (something different to the more traditional European style cafés) would not have merited a separate classification. However, with the proliferation of such US-based chains as Starbucks, this segment demands attention. Dubbed 'Specialty Coffee Shops' by Euromonitor (2004), these operations have expanded both in the USA and internationally – some experiencing double-digit growth for several consecutive years.

While Starbucks is the major player in this segment, there are other large operators including Costa Brothers in the UK, Dome in Australia and Doutor Coffee in Japan. Characteristics of this segment that distinguish it from other limited-service foodservice operations include:

- a focus on coffee, and coffee-based drinks, as the primary menu driver;
- coffee is fresh and fresh ground from whole beans;
- some food products are offered, usually limited to baked goods;
- limited seating;
- combination of in-store consumption and take-away;
- continuous service from early morning to late evening;
- a combination of individually owned and operated units, small regional chains and multinationals; and
- no alcoholic beverages.

The growth of this segment continues as a result of the appeal of the product (coffee) and the attributes that the shops have to offer – they have become the meeting places for many-both for social and business purposes and in some markets are replacing bars as the place to meet after work.

Kiosks and stalls

Throughout much of the world, streets are lined with carts, kiosks, stalls, floating river-craft and other small units providing food to passers-by. Individually, they represent the smallest and simplest type of foodservice operation imaginable. Together, though, they represent a very sizable market segment worldwide. They have an especially important presence in the Asia Pacific region as well as parts of Latin America and the Caribbean. Not to be limited to small developing countries, however, certain large restaurant chains have acknowledged the concept as being an effective method of expansion into smaller, more confined spaces such as malls and certain non-traditional locations (such as universities). Chains aside, however, such operations tend to be individually owned and managed and operate on very low cost structures. In fact, according to Euromonitor (2004), this segment is experiencing the greatest growth across segments on a global basis by number of units. As chains continue to utilize carts, kiosks and stalls as a way to penetrate non-traditional sites, this segment of the industry is only likely to continue to grow.

Cafeterias and buffets

Cafeterias and buffet restaurants represent another segment of the industry where segments begin to get blurred. Cafeterias are commercial operations where the guest chooses food items from behind a service counter and is served by an employee. Buffets are commercial operations where the guest is able to help themselves from food buffets in the dining room. These types of operations are deserving of their own classification because of their size and popularity in certain parts of the world. On the other hand, they resemble family dining restaurants in terms of their menu choices and clientele. Further, some full-service restaurants offer buffet service during certain meal periods (for instance during lunch or brunch) and then table service during other meal periods. For this reason, the concept is not as clearly defined as some others although it continues to fill an important niche in the industry. However, these types of operation share some of the following characteristics:

- lower check averages;
- a large number of menu items;
- no alcoholic beverages;
- food prepared from scratch;
- many special deal offers for customers; and
- continuous service through multiple meal periods.

Other limited-service restaurants

Finally, there are a few very important classifications that generally fall under the limited-service sector. These include the following:

1 bakeries, which are common in much of Europe (France, Italy and Germany) and increasingly so in North America, specializing in baked goods (which may constitute a meal or snack) and often serving beverages as well;
2 pubs (public houses) that serve both alcoholic beverages and pub fare; and
3 pizza restaurants, where pizza (and complementary items) are either ordered at a counter for eating in or take-away.

Together, these types of restaurants represent a large segment of certain markets. Pubs, for instance, have a huge presence in the UK and pizza restaurants are present in many parts of the world.

Summary of segments

To many in North America, as well as parts of Europe, it is easy to believe that quick-service (fast-food) dominates the globe but this is far from the truth. Full-service restaurants (representing 56% of overall revenue) still far outnumber fast-food restaurants (22% of overall revenue) on a global scale. In fact, as rapidly as the quick-service chains are penetrating new and emerging markets, they still have a long way to go to come close to reaching the penetration levels that full-service restaurants have achieved. Additionally, while quick-service is the fastest-growing segment (by dollar value), it is the 'stalls and kiosk' segment that is actually growing the fastest in terms of adding new units. Stalls and kiosks are especially prevalent in much of Asia and Latin America.

The proliferation of chains in certain parts of the world also might lead one to believe that chains dominate globally, when in fact they only represent a little over one-fourth of total foodservice dollars generated. This is not to say that chains dominate growth, though, as they continue to increase their market share globally. Continuing our discussion of chains, when it comes to size and scope, North American chains lead the industry. The largest foodservice company in the world, of course, is McDonald's, and it dominates its closest competitors. Overall, 18 of the top 20 commercial foodservice companies in the world are US-based and most fall in the quick-service category. Skylark, based in Japan, is the largest, non-US company in the world.

THE ROLE AND IMPORTANCE OF FOOD AND BEVERAGE IN THE HOSPITALITY INDUSTRY

The hospitality industry is concerned with providing services (accommodation, food, attractions, leisure activities and entertainment) to the public. The hospitality industry is, by definition, the umbrella industry under which the food and beverage (or foodservice) segment operates. The food and beverage industry plays a very important role as one part of the mix of products and services that the hospitality industry offers. When one considers all of the occasions during which a meal, snack or drink is consumed, one realizes the incredibly large number of meal opportunities that occur throughout the day. In most developed countries, residents spend somewhere between 10% and 20% of their income on food. Of this, 40% or more of their 'food dollar' may be spent on prepared food away from home. The amount that consumers spend on 'eating out' has increased over the last several decades and is expected to continue to do so. As lifestyles become more hurried, as income rises and as the foodservice industry continues to offer more choices to customers, both the actual dollars as well as the percentage of the food dollar spent are expected to rise into the foreseeable future. In short, consumers continue to look for 'meal solutions' and growth continues to occur in most segments of the foodservice industry which has relatively unrestricted barriers to entry.

People purchase (or otherwise consume) meals provided by a professional third party for a variety of reasons and in a variety of different venues. It may be as a guest at a catered event; they may be spending the day at a theme park with their families; they may be spending their lunch hour in the employee cafeteria at work or they may be out on a Saturday night at their favorite restaurant with friends or family. In each of these cases, the customer (or, increasingly, guest) is seeking one of two types of experiences: (1) an 'eating' occasion or (2) a 'dining' occasion (Powers and Barrows, 2005). If one accepts the fact that a meal, snack or beverage purchased by a customer from a professional provider consists of some element of 'product' and some element of 'service' along a spectrum, then the notion that meal occasions can be roughly classified into two types becomes clear. The eating occasion occurs when the guest is seeking primarily sustenance (a meal at work, a vending purchase or a quick-service meal). The dining occasion occurs when the guest is seeking something more than just a quick meal – the best example would be a fine-dining experience in which the guest receives much more than just prepared food on a plate. This notion of a restaurant meal as a total experience is an important one and has captured the attention of researchers for many years (Wood's (2000) discussion of the meal experience is a particularly good reference). Both types of experience are of equal importance. In the first, the food product or

service often plays a 'supporting' role. That is, it does not represent the primary reason that the guest is in that place at that time (e.g. at work, at the zoo). The second type of experience (the dining experience) is arguably more of a 'stand-alone' type of experience where the meal experience (including the food) demands to be the center of attraction.

The point here is that the food and beverage may play a greater or lesser role in the overall experience, depending upon the type of guest, the occasion, the setting and other factors. Certainly, however, food and beverage services play an important role, and one that is arguably increasing, in the provision of hospitality services. On the near end of the spectrum (where the product plays a larger role) the food must be reasonably priced, easy to purchase, safe to eat and must taste good. On the other end of the product/service continuum, exaggerated service levels, entertainment and the ability for the guest to relax all come into play. If the eating or dining experience is unable to provide these things then it may leave the guest wanting. This is one of the many challenges of meeting the guests' expectations within either context.

Food and beverage operations come in many shapes and sizes. One way to attempt to understand just how different they can be from one another is to consider that they may be 'free-standing' operations that might represent most 'restaurants' offering the 'dining' experience. They may also be one part of a larger operation such as a place of employment, an attraction or a food court in which case they are more often than not offering the guest an 'eating' experience. Both types of operations are of equal importance in providing much needed products and services to guests. The one type of operation is able to provide the total experience to the guest on its own; the other type is able to contribute to the mission of the larger operation – consider a theme park or sport stadium or hotel without food and beverage provisions (at least close by). In either (or both), the foodservice experience should be able to provide an opportunity for a respite from the daily stresses of modern life.

The role of profit

So far, the discussion has centered on the role of food and beverage in providing an experience for the guest and meeting their foodservice needs, whatever or wherever those may be. At some point, profit (or at least financial concerns) must be considered. For this reason, it would be safe to suggest that food and beverage operations also play an important role in the larger hospitality industry because of their ability to contribute to profitability: to owners, managers, partners or investors in the operation; or to the larger enterprise (casino, hotel, theme park). This ability to make a profit is yet another challenge faced by foodservice operators. Many operations never make a profit and are forced to cease trading. In fact, it has been suggested that restaurants experience a higher than average failure rate (although this is still under some dispute). Over time, it has become clear that there is a strong correlation between an operation's ability to meet guest expectations and its ability to be profitable. Therefore, as Peter Drucker (1973) has noted, attention to the customer must come first and then, and only then, will profit follow. At any rate, food and beverage operations should meet customer expectations and, ultimately, should be able to contribute to the bottom line of an operation. In stand alone operations, this means generating enough sales sufficient to cover all costs and to provide a 'reasonable' return to its owners. In on-site operations (for example, in a healthcare or educational setting) foodservice should be managed in a fiscally responsible manner to meet whatever financial objectives that have been set for it. In summary, foodservice operations must satisfy customers and meet financial objectives in whatever setting in which they operate. One of the key variables driving both the operations and strategy of an organization, though, is the segment in which it is operating (as outlined in the previous section).

KEY ELEMENTS OF THE FOOD AND BEVERAGE EXPERIENCE

This section will focus on the different elements of the foodservice experience that restaurants have to offer. The combination of elements, together, is what differentiates one restaurant from its competitors. Barrows (2001b) has suggested that there are four primary elements of the restaurant 'experience' including: (1) the food (this includes the range of offerings, the diversity of offerings, the quality); (2) the service (this includes the level of service, the abilities

Table 19.2 Key elements in food and beverage

Element	Variables	Management decisions
Food	Range of offerings, diversity of menu	Level of sophistication
Service	Level of service, skill level of staff	Establishing service standards
Ambience	Lighting, décor, furnishings	Ambience as a complementary element
Entertainment	When it is offered, what kind, cost	Whether or not to incorporate entertainment

of the staff, and the personal and technical skills); (3) the 'ambience' (which includes the décor, furnishings and general atmosphere); and (4) entertainment (which might include magic, music, televised events). Table 19.2 presents a list of these four elements along with examples.

Restaurants are challenged to match the combination of various elements with the customer type that they are targeting. Each of these elements will be discussed in turn.

Food

It has been said that the most popular restaurant in the world would be able to offer any customer who walked in the door whatever it was that they might be inclined to order. However, such a restaurant scenario would be impossible to operationalize. In contrast, the most profitable restaurant in the world would offer one very popular item and just that single item. This would create an extraordinarily efficient restaurant but, customers cannot be expected to visit numerous restaurants in an effort to 'build' their meals. The restaurants that we have discussed thus far are to be found somewhere between these two extremes where the operational objective is to offer the customer what they want at a profit to the restaurant. At the risk of oversimplifying, the fewer items that a restaurant has on its menu, the more efficient it becomes and, contrarily, the more items that a restaurant adds to it menu, the more inefficient it becomes. However, the more items that a restaurant has on a menu, the more different types of customers it can appeal to. The challenge for most restaurants is to find the correct balance between popularity and profitability – between a 'large' number of menu items and a 'small' number of menu items. As was clear from previous sections, different types of foodservice operations offer different products and service. From quick-service restaurants offering hamburgers, tacos and the like to fine-dining restaurants offering tableside service, in theory, every potential customer is able to find a foodservice outlet with an appropriate level of service with the product for which they are looking. Food plays an important part in the overall restaurant experience but is only one part of that experience.

Service

Restaurants must also identify the 'correct' level of service to accompany their product choices (menu), image and price structure. Again, there is a range of service levels available across restaurant types. Numerous monographs have been written on this subject alone – it has been argued of late that service is in fact the differentiating factor not only for restaurants but for all service firms. This argument might easily be extended to suggest that it is one of four elements that combine to differentiate a restaurant. Service is generally discussed (and categorized) in terms of its varying levels of customer interaction and its level of customization (Fitzsimmons and Fitzsimmons, 2001). Such service varies from low customization and low interaction (e.g. quick-service) to high interaction and high levels of customization (e.g. fine-dining). There are also obviously various degrees of each between these two extremes. Sometimes restaurants choose to combine different elements of service in the same facility such as is the case when a full-service restaurant offers a buffet during a certain meal period but also allows customers to select from the menu if they desire. Other examples would include offering different levels of service in adjacent dining rooms.

Ambience

Ambience (or atmosphere) is what the physical surroundings have to offer and contribute to the overall guest experience. This encompasses everything from the decorations on the walls to the way that the tables are arranged and set to the furnishings. One would expect a restaurant in an art museum, for instance, to incorporate art (or at least an art theme) into its dining room. The same would apply to theme restaurants that use television, movies, or a particular genre to convey the theme. The ambience has the ability to contribute to (or detract from) the customer experience.

Entertainment

Entertainment is the final element that must be considered. Entertainment and dining have had a long and natural 'marriage' where one has served to enhance the other (McLean, 2003). Indeed, some customers will choose a restaurant on the basis of the entertainment that is available and consider the food and service to be a secondary consideration. Entertainment is not just limited to music but can include live theater, movies, strolling magicians and the like. The decision to offer entertainment must be carefully considered as it carries a financial cost with it, as discussed by Barrows (2005).

A critical factor to keep in mind when making decisions based upon extent of food offerings, service levels, ambience and entertainment is the fact that each of these elements has costs associated with them (food and labor contribute the greatest amount, by percentage, of costs). Each of these elements also has a marketing element associated with it, to which discussion now turns.

MARKETING AND THE FOOD AND BEVERAGE CONSUMER

With the foodservice industry as competitive as it is, marketing plays a key role in terms of creating awareness, attracting and retaining customers, differentiating one restaurant from its competitors, otherwise communicating the desired 'message' and making a profit. One of the challenges of marketing is adequately defining who the customer is, why they choose (or do not choose) a particular restaurant, and what are their likes and dislikes. Marketing helps to match the products and services that a restaurant has to offer with the appropriate customer base.

The four Ps (price, place, promotion and product) all deserve attention in the restaurant environment. Restaurants use a variety of strategies and practices to market themselves to potential customers depending upon the competitive environment, management expertise, industry segment and budgetary considerations. Discounting, couponing, advertising and public relations are all used to varying extents in different segments of the industry. For instance, television advertising is very common with chains operating in the quick-service segment but less common in other segments. Electronic customer newsletters are common with casual upscale and fine-dining restaurants but less so in quick-service. One factor that all marketing activities must consider, however, is the customer. As is true with other management related activities, there are different schools of thought regarding what are the most effective means of identifying, segmenting and marketing to customers because it is difficult, if not impossible to characterize and describe the 'typical' foodservice consumer. The foodservice product is produced and consumed all over the world, at different times of the day at different price points and for different reasons. Customers can be segmented in a variety of ways, however, including by: geography, demographics (including age, income, gender and ethnic origin), by psychographics (the study of attitudes, opinions and interests), by usage (consumers who frequent the restaurant to different extents) and by customer needs (such as dining out for the convenience or for a celebration). Different segmentation strategies may be combined as well – for example combining psychographics with demographics. For instance, a restaurant company might choose to combine knowledge of a segment based on age with one based on lifestyle choice. As an example, it is well documented that the age of the population is drastically changing (the populations of North America and much of Europe are getting older). Further, as individuals age, changes also occur with their levels of disposable income, their lifestyles and their propensity to dine out. Restaurant marketers might choose to focus on this combination of factors as a result. Such are the reasons so much attention is being paid by all service sectors to the older segment. It is also one reason that has been posited for the success of the quick-casual segment – that the baby boomers are aging and looking for alternatives to quick-service which many of them grew up with.

To explore customer changes further, research suggests that their behaviors have changed over time as well. The many consumer changes that have taken place (and continue to take place) include:

- where restaurant meals are purchased (which now includes supermarkets and convenience stores);
- when meals are purchased (increasingly throughout the day as opposed to during discrete meal periods);
- how meals are purchased (for example, the increasing popularity of takeaway);
- demand for quality as well as value (there is evidence that this is occurring at all service levels and in all segments of the industry);
- the rise in influence of consumers who seem to be more outspoken today and, in addition, have been given outlets for voicing their opinions, for example *Zagat's Survey, Restaurants and Institutions' Choice in Chains, PlanetFeedback,* and *Consumer Reports Magazine;*
- the continuing concern for safety (recent concerns have focused on BSE, SARS); and
- changes in overall satisfaction levels, suggesting that overall satisfaction with the restaurant experience is waning.

Customer needs are thus clearly changing – their demands for quality are increasing, they have less time and they have more choices (*Standard and Poor's Survey*, 2004). These changes are not only affecting how restaurants are marketing their businesses but also present operational issues as well. Together, such changes are forcing restaurants to try to understand their customers as they have never done before, a point that will be revisited in subsequent sections of this chapter.

THE MANAGEMENT OF FOOD AND BEVERAGE OPERATIONS

The management of foodservice operations has been researched extensively (see for example, Davis and Lockwood, 1994; Jones and Merricks, 1994). The management of a restaurant (or a chain of restaurants), which include marketing as discussed above, presents many challenges. Barrows (2001a) has suggested that there are four primary challenges associated with the management of foodservice operations: (1) the changing consumer; (2) the increasing turbulence of the external environment; (3) the continuing labor shortages being experienced in certain parts of the world and (4) the increasing complexities associated with the internal foodservice environment. The preceding section focused on the changing consumer, this section focuses on internal management issues.

The challenges associated with the management of a restaurant begin and end with the basic functions and responsibilities of management. As Barrows (1996) argued a decade ago, management responsibilities are changing and increasing in nature and scope. This speaks to the dynamic characteristics of the foodservice industry. Internally, managers must be attentive to such varied areas as the following:

- human resources (including recruiting, hiring, retaining, training and developing employees);
- quality control (including safety and sanitation);
- design and implementation of standards and procedures;
- customer service;
- financial accounting and control;
- internal marketing;
- menu management and new product development;
- information and communications management;
- maintenance of the physical facility;
- providing a safe and secure environment for the health and safety of employees;
- purchasing of food and beverage products (and receiving, proper storage practices and issuing);
- management of alcoholic beverages;
- providing ongoing leadership; and
- protection of physical assets.

These different areas of responsibility challenge a manager to constantly look for new ways of balancing operational efficiency, cash flow, concern for human resources, protection of assets and customer satisfaction. The unique aspects of the foodservice environment are ever-present – the simultaneous occurrence of production and service, the relatively high product and service costs (as a percentage of sales), the exaggerated role of the customer, the perishability of the product, the labor intensiveness, and the relatively low margins. Such varied and intense responsibilities require an individual who has been adequately prepared for the job. In days past, this meant someone who had spent sufficient time in an apprenticeship. More recently, it suggests someone who has taken a management degree from a hospitality program as well as acquired a sufficient amount of experience in different functional areas of the restaurant. Indeed, the management training and development programs of some of the leading restaurant companies may require that a manager in training spend over five years preparing for promotion to general manager.

Restaurants are attempting to accomplish 'more with less' as are many other industry sectors. As operating environments become more complex, they also become more demanding. While it is expected that the core responsibilities of restaurant managers will remain the same into the foreseeable future, it is also expected that managers will need to become more expert in additional areas. One of the critical management responsibilities, financial control, is discussed more fully in the next section.

FINANCIAL CONTROL AND REVENUE MANAGEMENT

One of the leading causes of restaurant failure is undercapitalization and the inability to responsibly manage financial assets. Further, profit margins in the restaurant industry are estimated to be very low – approximately 4% of sales. For this reason, managers must be skilled in cost control and revenue management and must be familiar with some of the key operating ratios in the industry. Restaurants are able to generate revenue from two main sources: sale of food and sale of beverages (alcoholic). In some instances, restaurants are also able to profit from the sale of merchandise (particularly in theme restaurants) and from any extra surcharge charged for entertainment. Food and beverage remain the two primary revenue generators, though. Food typically accounts for the greatest percentage of revenues followed by beverages. The prevailing belief in the industry is that there is an optimum ratio that can be achieved between these two areas in any given environment. Food typically generates a greater dollar profit while beverages typically create a greater profit by percentage. For instance, the sale of a menu item could easily net $10.00 (selling price minus the raw cost of the item). Similarly, the sale of an alcoholic drink (wine, beer or spirit) may net $4.00. Clearly the dollar cost gain of the sale of the menu item is greater (as it usually is). However, when cost is taken into account, the net percentage is typically higher with beverages. This is due to the sole reason that the percentage markup tends to be higher with beverages due to the conventions of the industry. For restaurants to optimize their sales, managers will attempt to sell some effective combination of products in each of these categories. To take this further, for profit sake, managers will encourage the sale of menu (and drink) items with the higher profit potential. Although it is very difficult to estimate averages across the industry, a 'healthy' ratio for many restaurants will typically be a ratio of 4 to 1 (food sales to beverage sales). It should be noted, however, that the author is personally aware of restaurants that have a 1 to 1 food to beverage sales ratio and have proven to be very profitable.

Expenses are incurred from a wide range of areas (as they are in any business) which will include overhead and administrative costs. As was the case with revenues, again, food and beverage are two of the greatest (variable) costs incurred in restaurants. In addition to these two costs, however, we must also add the cost of labor. Together, these costs represent what is referred to as the 'prime' cost and can represent anywhere from 55% to 75% of sales. Restaurants generally try to keep the prime cost at or below 70% and preferably closer to 60%.

Key operating ratios that are used in the industry (at the operational level) focus on both expenses and revenues. Examples include:

- food cost (by percentage) = cost of goods/food sales;
- beverages cost (by percentage) = cost of goods/beverage sales;
- labor cost (by percentage) = cost of labor/sales;
- sales per labor hour = total sales/total labor hours;
- prime cost = cost of food + cost of beverages + cost of labor/total sales;
- average check = total sales/number of customers served;
- seat turnover = number of customers served/number of seats; and
- contribution margin = total sales (expressed as 100%) − total variable costs (expressed as a percentage).

These are but a few of the many performance measures available to restaurant operators. Some caveats must be addressed however. First, standards must be established by the operator. Calculating operating ratios is a meaningless exercise unless there is some standard for comparison. Standards may include industry averages, averages within the chain (from unit to unit) or comparisons over time.

Second, different measures will be used by different types of operations. For instance, while average check may be of interest to most types of operations, sales per labor hour may be of greater use to quick-service restaurants than fine-dining restaurants. It is up to the individual operator which measures to use and how to apply them. Third, whatever measures are used, there should be predetermined time measures. For instance, average check can be calculated for individual meal periods (or day part), on a daily or weekly basis, over time, or in a number of different ways. This is one of the advantages of ratios − the time element. Fourth, once it is determined which measures are to be used, they should be tracked over time so as to show increases or decreases in performance. Again, unless this is done, a historical perspective cannot be constructed. Finally, it is irresponsible to use a single ratio/measure to gauge performance. It is imperative that multiple measures be used to provide a more holistic view of performance.

Controlling food, beverage and labor costs

No matter the size, scale or scope of a foodservice operation, the ability to control these three primary variable costs is directly correlated with financial success of the operation. In recent years, sophisticated systems have been developed (computerized and otherwise) to assist operators in tracking and controlling costs. It remains critical, however, that operators rigorously track these costs and try to minimize them, where possible, without compromising quality.

Revenue management and pricing

The prevailing belief in the restaurant industry is that the menu, and the resulting prices, is a major factor in sales and profits. As a result, much has been written on pricing in the industry (see for example, Lewis and Shoemaker, 1997). Companies are becoming increasingly strategic and sophisticated with their approaches to pricing. However, it remains that many companies continue to rely on three primary methods: (1) cost-based approaches; (2) demand-based approaches and (3) competition-based approaches. Different approaches are appropriate for different operators depending on the clientele, level of competition, operating environment and segment within which they are active. The industry, as a whole, seems to be moving towards more effective pricing methods such as demand-based pricing (Barrows, 1993) and activity-based pricing (Raab and Mayer, 2003). Much of this renewed focus on pricing is the result of restaurants trying to (1) cover a greater proportion of their costs; (2) adjusting for fluctuating (and unpredictable) food prices and (3) gaining a competitive advantage by offering greater flexibility to the customer.

Restaurants are also beginning to experiment more with pricing strategies such as bundling (the grouping of menu items at a reduced price) which has long been a mainstay in certain segments such as quick-service. Otherwise known as the *prix-fixe* in the fine-dining segment, it is also being offered more in the casual dining sector. Bundling offers the restaurant the ability to effectively market a grouping of items in an attractive manner in order to make a profit (see Barth and Rao, 2002, who discuss the application of bundling in the industry at some length). Finally, it should be noted that pricing strategies vary widely across segments of the restaurant industry, suggesting once again, that management practices, in general, tend to be segment-specific.

SOME PROFILES OF INDUSTRIES INTERNATIONALLY

The information presented in this section is based upon the *Euromonitor Global Foodservice Report*, 2004 and provides an overview of the foodservice industry in several different countries. This overview is provided in an effort to reinforce the fact that, even though similarities run through the industry everywhere, substantial differences still exist (across segments and internationally). In many cases, as will become clear, countries, and even regions, are able to retain their cultural (foodservice) identities. Indeed, food, and foodservice conventions are an important part of cultural identity.

The USA and China dominate in terms of units and overall sales. The USA stands out because of its overall spending on foodservice, its large number of chains and multinationals based in that country and the number of new concepts emerging from there. China is notable for its food culture, its overall number of

units, the high percentage of independently owned units, the significant penetration of Western chains and its continued growth. After these top two countries though, there exists a collection of countries that are worth examining. Brief profiles of the industries in Japan, Brazil, the UK, Russia and Germany are presented here.

Japan

In many ways, the Japanese foodservice industry mirrors that of the USA. It is characterized by a high density of firms but relatively slow growth. As is also true in the USA, the greatest growth is occurring in delivery, takeaway and coffee shops. Nationally, the industry is also very competitive. This is where the similarities with the USA end however. The Japanese industry is largely dominated by cafés and bars as well as independently owned and operated units.

Changes that are occurring in Japan include a greater penetration by chains – both US-based and domestic. The largest foodservice company in the country is Skylark which has approximately 20 brands in its portfolio. The slow growth in the industry is attributed not only to the competition but also to recent economic troubles as well as the food scares that have also affected North America and Europe. In a country of only 127 million, the industry generates US$180 billion a year and is expected to continue growing nominally.

Brazil

The industry in Brazil has been affected in recent years by economic difficulties and by the fact that many residents simply cannot afford to eat out. Global chains are not well represented in Brazil and, as a result, the industry is dominated by independently owned and operated restaurants of varying types. This is so much the case that McDonald's has close to a 50% market share of all chains. The food offerings are quite varied with Brazilian barbeque being quite common (a type of cuisine that is now experiencing popularity in other countries including the USA). One of the most unique restaurant concepts in Brazil is the 'kilo' restaurant where customers pay for their food by its weight. Like Japan, the café and bar sector is the largest sector here. Again, most of these are independently owned and operated. The one large and dominant Brazilian chain is Brazil Fast Food although the largest 'non-burger' chain is of Arabic origin. Only 20% of meals are purchased outside of the home but the Home Meal Replacement (HMR) market is growing as consumers look for greater convenience and value.

United Kingdom

The UK has one of the largest and one of the most diverse foodservice industries of any of the countries mentioned in this chapter. Recent years have seen the closing of a large percentage of pubs, still the largest industry sector, which has resulted in a net decrease of units over the last several years. Over 170,000 (profit) units generate approximately US$40 billion annually and sales have been relatively static for several years now. There is a higher concentration of chains in the UK than in other countries discussed (48% of units are chain-affiliated) with a small number of firms controlling a large percentage of the market. Mergers and acquisitions continue to take place as well. Consumers in the UK spend 34% of their 'food dollar' away from home – less than Americans and many other Europeans.

As is the case in other areas, changes are taking place in the industry. Consumers are trading up to higher priced dining options. Just as consumers in the USA are frequenting casual dining restaurants, UK consumers are spending more in 'gastropubs' or pubs with more upscale menu options. Also, delivery and take-away markets are growing, which seems to be a common trend across regions. Even though chain domination has not occurred to the extent that it has in the USA, McDonald's is still the largest player with Gregg's being the second largest brand (sandwiches, baked goods and a large take-away business).

Russia

Russians spend a large proportion of their income on food – 47% according to Euromonitor (2004). Of this, however, they spend a relatively small percentage on food away from home (somewhat less than 15%). This has increased significantly since the late 1990s though and is expected to continue its upward trend. The industry is dominated by street stalls and kiosks (representing almost 40% of total units). A small percentage (less than 4%) of foodservice units are chain-affiliated but the greatest growth that is occurring is in quick-service chains. McDonald's is the largest chain operator but Rustik's (the largest Russian brand) has a respectable market share as well.

Even though dining out is still considered a luxury in Russia, the industry is growing with quick-service chains and full-service chains alike increasing their penetration. Further, Russians continue to spend a greater portion of their food dollar on dining out. As a result, the industry is expected to continue to grow as it becomes an even more important aspect of Russian life and moves from being a luxury purchase.

Germany

One of the few countries (in the West) where the foodservice industry has encountered difficulties over the last few years is Germany. This is due in large part to the poor economy, inflation and high levels of unemployment. Regardless, the industry has some very strong sectors. The country continues to have a high ratio of restaurants per resident (even higher than in the USA) and a high proportion of full-service restaurants. The industry as a whole seems to be following the same trends that are being observed in other countries – a greater variety of different types of restaurants that cater to Germans' increasing demand for speed and convenience. Even though the industry has had a difficult several years, it is expected to rebound eventually.

There are several very large German foodservice companies, the largest of which are Autobahn Tank and Rast followed by Nordsee. Autobahn Tank specializes in cafeterias on the motorways while Nordsee specializes in quick-service (fish). The German foodservice industry is highly diverse though with an exceptionally large percentage of non-German ethnic restaurants represented. There is also a higher than average percentage of independently owned and operated restaurants.

Summary

The industries in the five countries profiled above are provided to give an indication of the different characteristics that exist from country to country. Countries differ greatly with respect to ownership of restaurants, chain penetration, types of cuisine, type of service level, points of distribution, growth potential, and consumer spending. There are other countries whose industries are unique and growing at rates surpassing the average (for example, India) but they cannot all be profiled because of chapter limitations (extensive profiles of 41 countries have been compiled by Euromonitor though and interested readers are encouraged to review their reports for more in-depth coverage). One thing that readers will notice from these profiles, however, is the tendency for common trends occurring in many different countries and these trends affecting the global industry are the subject of the next section of the chapter.

TRENDS IN THE FOOD AND BEVERAGE INDUSTRY

It would be safe to conclude that the foodservice industry is undergoing changes to an extent that have never been experienced before. Overriding factors that are driving many of these changes include fluctuating demographics, the increasing number of dual income families, increasing levels of discretionary income, and changing levels of leisure time.

As the world becomes 'smaller', as people travel further from home to explore different parts of the world and as immigration changes the composition of countries, demand for the internationalization of cuisines only increases. What other explanation could be set forth when one discovers the popularity of Chinese food in the USA, Indian food in the UK and Arabic food in Brazil? Among other things, a large segment of the population seeks new flavors, diversity and a different overall experience when dining out. Cuisines are being 'exported' to a greater extent than ever. Japanese, Thai, Ethiopian and Brazilian barbeque are just some of the cuisines that have been popularized in recent years outside of their home countries. One of the more intriguing studies that has been conducted was a series of documentary films on Chinese immigrants to 13 different countries who opened restaurants in these respective countries. The films begin with a study of the immigrants and their restaurants and then proceed to examine the culture, struggles and communities of the Chinese Diaspora in such varied countries as Trinidad, Israel and Norway (Kwan, 2004). One of the points made in the films is the profound and lasting contribution that the Chinese have made to cultures around the world, at least partially as a result of their cuisine.

Internationalization of the industry does not only occur with the introduction of new restaurants, however. Individual restaurant menus are also beginning to change with the introduction of international items. For instance, in the USA, several dinner-house chains have added Mexican dishes to their menus in an effort to meet the demand for Mexican cuisine. The trend of internationalization and the popularity of international cuisines will no doubt continue as people travel, move, and/or otherwise attempt to experience more of the world around them.

The desire to 'eat healthily' is another trend that is shaping menus in various parts of the world. Healthy cuisine has found its way onto the menus of every type of restaurant – from fine-dining to quick-service to airport-dining. Perhaps the best example of how far this trend has progressed is the Adult Happy Meal recently introduced by McDonald's which comes complete with a pedometer. Much of the desire for healthier food options comes as a result of one's lifecycle stage – baby boomers seem to be driving this particular trend. Restaurants have capitalized upon this trend by building menus and menu options around some of the more popular diets (such as the Atkins diet). It is becoming hard to find a restaurant in certain markets that does not offer at least a couple of 'healthy choices' or even devotes a section of its menu to healthy eating. Since interest in diet and exercise seem to be cyclical, this trend is likely to wax and wane over the next couple of decades.

The overall look of menus has also changed over the last 20 years. This has occurred for a number of reasons – including the reasons noted above. However they have also changed in a very important way, out of necessity. The simple fact is that not all products that were available 10–20 years ago are as plentiful now. Some have disappeared entirely. As a result, restaurants have sought to promote 'under-utilized' species and products in an effort to lower their risk of uncertain supply as well as lowering their overall costs. Recent examples have included under-utilized species of seafood. Seafood continues to be a popular choice in restaurants (note the popularity of such seafood restaurants as Red Lobster). But over time, because of over-fishing, government regulations and other factors, some species have become unavailable. This has happened with cod, haddock, redfish and others. Restaurants then look to other types of seafood or other sources (such as farm-raised species) to meet demand. Unfortunately, as the industry (and the broader consumer market) target 'under-utilized' species, they, too, are at risk of becoming depleted. This is likely to present a challenge to the industry into the foreseeable future. Restaurants are also attempting to introduce other products (aside from seafood) that may appeal to their customers. Efforts to promote under-utilized products are not just limited to seafood though – efforts are being made to promote certain types of meat (emu and ostrich), vegetable and legume products (particularly soy derivatives) among others.

At the same time that menus are changing (becoming more international, more diverse and healthier), customers are also demanding a different type of dining experience. The greatest growth in the industry is in casual dining. Customers are looking for more casual dining experiences where they do not have to spend over a certain amount, where they can dress comfortably and where the surroundings are more relaxed. This has resulted in a general decline in demand for fine-dining as well as the 'creation' of newer, more appealing restaurant segments. High-end fine-dining restaurants run by high-profile chefs are having to seek out new markets rather than the other way around (note the number of fine-dining options in Las Vegas). Some chef/proprietors have either closed their restaurants in recent years or opened more casual counterparts to give their customers greater options. While this trend has been occurring for most of the last decade, there are indications that it, too, is changing. Even though casual dining is at its height of popularity now, fine-dining will almost certainly make a 'comeback' within the next ten years.

A trend that goes hand-in-hand with the increase in casual dining (and the decrease in fine-dining) is the emergence of new restaurant categories. Perhaps the most recent (and most publicized) is the 'new' fast-casual segment discussed earlier in this chapter. The segment is so new that industry analysts are still debating how it should be defined. Fast-casual is generally understood to offer a slightly higher level of service than quick-service, offer a slightly more sophisticated menu and a more comfortable atmosphere. The trend is catching on, particularly in the USA, where one of the fastest growing chains is Panera Bread. This segment is positioned to continue to do well as it takes market share away from established quick-service companies. This has happened to such an extent that McDonald's and others have purchased their own fast-casual chains. This segment will continue to do well as baby boomers look for alternatives to quick-service and as the broader population continues to look for dining alternatives.

Other 'emerging' segments that continue to do well include the coffee shop segment (termed 'specialist coffee shops' which is different than the traditional European café). Led by Starbucks, this segment has saturated the US market and is expanding elsewhere in the world (including Europe and Asia). The segment is not totally monopolized by US based companies however. Companies such as Second Cup (Canada), Doutor's (Japan), Dome (Australia) and Costa Brothers (UK) have been successful domestically. As (on-premises) coffee consumption continues to increase, it remains to be seen how large this segment will grow and how many new companies will enter the market.

Another trend that 'bridges' some of the others identified so far (and, in fact, helps speed their growth) is the proliferation of chains. The largest chain in the world is McDonald's which has been prominently mentioned in this chapter. With over 30,000 restaurants worldwide, McDonald's has achieved this growth primarily through franchising (70% of its restaurants are franchises). The primary advantage to franchising is that it allows a company to grow by providing the systems to franchisees who provide much of the capital. Subway, which is still growing at a phenomenal rate, has over 20,000 restaurants worldwide and has attained this growth through franchising. Franchising (and licensing and partnering) is also a proven method of expanding internationally. It should be noted that not all companies choose franchising as their preferred method of growth. As an example, Starbucks does not franchise and currently has close to 15,000 units.

While some companies choose to expand a single proven concept, others choose to develop multiple concepts (and either develop and expand these concepts or not). Multi-concept operators are becoming an accepted model in the foodservice industry. In fact, it could even be argued that McDonald's is now a multi-concept operator with its acquisition of several other chains in recent years. A notable US example is Brinker International which has conceptualized, developed and grown numerous restaurant concepts including Chili's, Romano's and Corner Bakery among many others. Other companies have fewer concepts but focus more on expansion, such as Darden (Olive Garden, Bahama Breeze, Smokey Bones and Red Lobster). Others have more concepts and less growth such as Lettuce Entertain You Enterprises (LEYE). Some analysts differentiate between larger multi-concept companies (such as Darden) and smaller ones (such as LEYE). For our purposes it would include any single company operating more than one concept (or brand). Adopting a multi-concept strategy allows a company to create (or purchase) new concepts, complement existing concepts with new ones, and, most importantly diversify. This is a trend that will undoubtedly continue.

Finally, consumers continue to express their desire for convenience. This has manifested itself in the variety of ways that the foodservice 'product' is now available to consumers resulting in growth in a variety of areas: take-away, delivery, home meal replacement, and availability of foodservice in non-traditional venues. Some restaurants have specialized in one of these areas – others have tried to offer a variety of additional services. In short though, restaurants have not been able to ignore the necessity of either making the product available where the consumer is – or else bringing it directly to the consumer even if it is at their home. What was once the purview of pizzerias (delivery), Chinese restaurants (take-away) and quick-service (drive-thru) has become a strategic decision that must be made – how and where to offer your product and service. This has resulted in many restaurant products becoming available in supermarkets, entire restaurant units operating in supermarkets (and other retail stores), restaurants preparing entire meals to go, and the opening of specialized take-away units. Some analysts would suggest that this trend has had the greatest impact of any and has been the most far reaching – perhaps of any of the trends discussed in this section, this may be impacting on the industry the greatest as it affects all aspects including planning and layout of the facility, location, menu, staffing, and profit margins among others. As people become more interested in convenience and time-savings this aspect of the foodservice

market will continue to grow. This is evidenced, at least in part, by entire concepts that have emerged from this trend (e.g. Boston Chicken and Eatzi's).

Summary of trends

It bears repeating that the industry is undergoing some major shifts in what it offers, how it is being offered, when it is being offered and where it is being offered. Consumers want different 'experiences' at different times – be it the time of day or the stage of their life. The industry has generally done an effective job of keeping up with their demands, albeit in some cases a while after the demand has manifested itself. One of the challenges that the industry will have to address over the next few years is how long these trends will continue and at what point the cycle is likely to repeat itself, as so often happens. This is but one of the many challenges facing the industry over the next few years – the subject of the next, and final section.

MANAGEMENT CHALLENGES

The fact that the industry is changing as much as it is suggests a range of opportunities on which it should be able to capitalize over the next several years. The downside of this is that there are accompanying challenges which are ever-present. An attempt will be made to address some of the more serious challenges facing the industry although the reader should keep in mind that many of these challenges are segment specific – that is they may be affecting some industry segments but not all.

It is evident that the economy (recent problems in Brazil, Germany and parts of Asia), catastrophic events (such as terrorist activity), health and safety issues in Asia, Europe and North America (BSE, SARS) and natural disasters (hurricanes, earthquakes) affect the foodservice industry and consumer propensity to eat in restaurants. Historically though, consumer confidence tends to return with the passage of time and much returns to 'normal' even though it may be a 'new' normal. Different times bring different challenges – some of them within the control of the industry and some of them clearly outside of that control.

Those areas that are within the control of the industry relate, first, to its maturing. At the time of writing, several segments of the industry are in, or are approaching, maturity. Quick-service has certainly reached the mature stage and companies such as McDonald's have developed appropriate strategies. Others have been slow to respond to this challenge. What is clear is that other segments of the industry will also approach maturity over the next 10–20 years (such as casual dining) and the industry will need to respond in an effective manner or risk the advent of new companies, leaders, and even entire segments.

A second challenge that is not unrelated to the issue of a maturing industry is decline in the number of prime locations available for new operation. Not only are prime locations becoming fewer but the cost of developing sites continues to escalate. This has potentially significant impacts on an industry where the margins tend to be so low to begin with. For larger companies, one of the strategies has been mergers and acquisitions – not always to acquire a company, *per se*, but to acquire its sites. The shortage of locations has also forced some companies to be more creative in site selection and to consider non-traditional sites.

At the same time that the industry is maturing and is having challenges identifying new sites, there is also increasing international competition. The growth opportunities for many companies are outside of their home countries (McDonald's and Starbucks being but two examples). With expansion into new markets, though, come a host of challenges. The industry has proven that forays into new international markets are not always successful. For this reason, it is likely that future expansion will continue to occur but will entail the development of new international partnerships. The industry has always been characterized by low barriers to entry which will only allow further growth and competition on an increasingly global scale.

On a different note, the industry has long been characterized as having certain operational inefficiencies. The fact remains that the industry is a labor-intensive industry and its successes are based on the effective management of its human resources which directly affect its level of efficiencies. Human resources management will continue to be a challenge for managers as labor shortages affect many regions and segments. The industry, as a whole, has not been effective in presenting foodservice as a viable career choice to persons at different

levels of the industry. Recruiting, selection, compensation and training and development are just a few areas of human resources management that will only become more challenging as the industry competes more and more with other service sectors (such as retail and gaming) for employees. Employee turnover also continues to be a challenge as employees leave for other restaurants or other industries. Many studies have suggested that the turnover rate in the restaurant industry far surpasses those of other industries. The industry must continue to offer more attractive working conditions and career opportunities to its employees as well as continuing to pursue other labor markets where appropriate.

The industry is also grappling with increasing levels of government intervention and increased regulations. This obviously varies considerably from region to region and even within a single country. In some cases government regulations have a broad effect on all segments of the industry (such as with the case of fishing restrictions on certain species of fish and the introduction of the Euro). Others affect the industry on a national level (such as with workplace safety laws and laws governing inspection of food products). Still others have local effects such as no-smoking regulations and even minimum wage laws that are sometimes enacted at the local level. One of the most significant issues facing the industry currently is the issue of alcohol consumption, legal blood alcohol limits, responsible server training, alcohol consumption in restaurants (including BYOB laws in which customers are allowed to bring their own alcoholic beverages into an establishment) and the like. For all of these reasons, managers within the industry must learn how to scan the external environment in an effort to (1) anticipate changes in laws and regulations; and (2) manage their operations accordingly.

At both the corporate and the operational levels, restaurants are also grappling with how best to use available technologies without overspending on systems that may soon be obsolete. Restaurants are finding uses for new technologies in every area of the operation – in human resources (recruiting, hiring and training) to purchasing (communicating with suppliers) to customer service (computerized ordering and satisfaction tracking). Cost, economies of scale and purchasing knowledge are factors that either assist restaurants in adopting these new technologies or create barriers. As new technologies only continue to became available and improve, restaurants must develop policies regarding the introduction of these new technologies as well as develop a culture of organizational learning in an effort to properly adopt them.

Summary of challenges

These are but just a few of the challenges that are currently facing the industry. Restaurant operators must continue to identify these challenges, create learning environments, understand their core competencies, and develop benchmarks where necessary to help them adopt appropriate strategies. Barrows (2001a), among others, has suggested that the challenges facing the industry have only become more significant and the last few years have only served to exemplify this. Perhaps this is the one area that best bridges segments, markets and concepts.

The challenges identified above simply reinforce the notion that foodservice businesses must strive to satisfy the needs of customers, employees and investors simultaneously. Some challenges affect one group more than others (such as the maturing of the industry and its effect on investors) while others affect all three groups (such as certain government regulations). The industry must be conscious of the decisions it makes and the strategies it adopts and how they affect each of these three constituents.

CONCLUSION

The foodservice industry is healthy and growing despite having a few challenging years since the beginning of the millennium. The industry offers one of the most desired, universal and far-reaching products and services available to consumers. The industry itself is becoming more dynamic and proactive than ever before. Further, international opportunities continue to present themselves, new products are being developed and new concepts are emerging on a regular basis. As local economies prosper, people look for more choices and greater diversity in restaurant offerings. They also spend a larger share of their food dollar as a result. In short, this is one of the most exciting and interesting times to be associated with the industry. To assure its continued success, however, the industry must understand its history, adopt a long-term view of its business and not lose sight of the basics (such as food quality). Running a restaurant, a successful one at that, will continue to be a challenge but will also continue to attract motivated individuals who will prove themselves to be up to the challenge.

REFERENCES

Barrows, C. W. (1993) 'Pricing and profits: marketing for maximization', *Journal of Restaurant and Foodservice Marketing*, 1(1): 75–88.

Barrows, C. W. (1996) 'Operational issues and trends in the U.S. foodservice industry: implications for managers'. In R. Kotas et al. (eds) *The International Hospitality Business*. London: Cassell Publishing Co.

Barrows, C. W. (2001a) 'The management of foodservice operations: new challenges and opportunities', *PRAXIS – The Journal of Applied Hospitality Management*, 4(1): 54–69.

Barrows, C. W. (2001b) 'Food and beverage trends: applications to private clubs'. Presented at the Annual Conference of the Canadian Society of Club Managers, Ottawa (September, 2001).

Barrows, C. W. and McLean, R. 'Live music in restaurants in Ontario: An examination of the decision making process.' Presented at the annual conference of the Administrative Sciences Association of Canada, Toronto, Canada (May, 2005).

Barth, J. and Rao, V. R. (2002) 'Application of a balanced satiation model to meal bundle utility', *International Journal of Hospitality and Tourism Administration*, 3(4): 25–41.

Davis, B. and Lockwood, A. (eds) (1994) *Food and Beverage Management: A Selection of Readings*. Oxford: Butterworth-Heinemann.

Drucker, P. (1973) *Management: Tasks, Responsibilities, Practices*. New York: Harper & Row.

The Economist (2006) McCurrencies. 379(8479): 74.

EuroMonitor (2004) *Global Foodservice Report*. www.euromonitor.com.

Fitzsimmons, J. A. and Fitzsimmons, M. J. (2001) *Service Management: Operations, Strategy and Information Technology*. Boston: McGraw-Hill.

Jones, P. and Merricks, P. (eds) (1994) *The Management of Foodservice Operations*. London: Cassell.

Kivela, J., Reece, J. and Inbakaran, R. (1999) 'Consumer research in the restaurant environment. Part 2: Research design and analytical methods', *International Journal of Contemporary Hospitality Management*, 11(6): 269–286.

Kwan, C. (2004) *Chinese Restaurants*. 13 part documentary series on Chinese restaurants, Chinese culture and Chinese immigrants. www.chineserestaurants.tv.

Lewis, R. C. and Shoemaker, S. (1997) 'Price-sensitivity measurement: a tool for the hospitality industry', *Cornell Hotel and Restaurant Administration Quarterly*, 38(2): 44–54.

Powers, T. and Barrows, C. W. (2005) *Introduction to Management in the Hospitality Industry*. 7th edn. New York: John Wiley and Sons.

Raab, C. and Mayer, K. (2003) 'Exploring the use of activity based costing in the restaurant industry', *International Journal of Hospitality and Tourism Administration*, 4(2): 79–96.

Standard and Poor's Restaurant Industry Survey (September 30, 2004) www.Standardandpoors.com.

Wood, R. (2000) 'How important is the meal experience?' In R. Wood (ed.) *Strategic Questions in Food and Beverage Management*. London: Butterworth-Heinemann. pp. 28–47.

Food Production and Service Systems Theory*

20

Roy C. Wood

INTRODUCTION

Systems theory constitutes a fascinating, if contested, area of intellectual endeavor and anyone who chooses to write about 'systems' of any kind is asking for trouble. The term is used in most branches of knowledge and though definitions often share similar characteristics, they also, according to usage, emphasize different elements of such definitions. Systems can be large or small; open or closed; focused or diffuse; local or pervasive; simple or complex; specific or generic; and real or imagined. In the hospitality context, systems theory has been most obviously applied in the context of the sub-area of food production and service systems where the emphasis is on the planning of such systems for different styles of food product offering and related service options. Systems approaches to food production and service in the hospitality industry context still excite some interest (e.g. Johns and Jones, 1999a, 1999b, 2000; Kirk, 2000) and there is some small evidence of efforts to extend systems analysis to other areas of hospitality operations (Ball et al., 2003).

This chapter reviews the status of applications of systems theory to food production and service in hospitality. It contends that the level of application of such theory amounts at present to little more than incomplete description, an incompleteness generated by a failure to close a 'gap' between propositions governing the design of food production and service systems in hospitality and the realities of the markets in which these systems are intended to function. The origins of this gap lie, first, in the emphasis placed on production elements at the expense of consumption within hospitality food production and service systems, and second, in the inherent reductionism that lies in any modeling process. On the first of these two points, the argument is that for any analytical progress to be made in the field, a more holistic approach must be taken. Such an approach should place hospitality food production and service systems in a broader cultural context, establishing linkages with wider notions of food systems to generate additional insights into the management of food production and service operations. To this end, the chapter offers a selective analysis of both social scientific literature on food and culture 'systems' and existing literature on food production and service systems in hospitality, to discern a range of features that can be employed in constructing a more holistic approach to food systems. At the same time, and on the second point, it is recognized (and demonstrated) that social scientific modeling is itself an inherently reductionist process, not least in the area of food and culture relationships. Despite this, an understanding of social context can still benefit analysis of hospitality food production and service systems by illuminating the cultural and symbolic significance of food and eating, thereby reducing the gap between the conception of such systems and the contextual influences upon them. Such understanding can both enhance the descriptive utility of systems approaches and provide a more effective basis for conceptual and analytic development.

What this chapter is *not* about is systems theory in general, or for that matter general systems theory – a distinction that those possessing some familiarity with systems theory will appreciate. Indeed, one of the remarkable aspects of many current writings on systems theory (ST) is the extent to which awareness of ST fundamentals is either taken for granted or emerges only as part of investigative discourse. For example,

Dearey (2002) attempts to circumscribe systems theory as no less than a philosophy of management. Following Kirk (2000: 55) writing in a hospitality context, we can note that 'There is an argument that the term "systems" has become so general that its meaning is at best confused and at worst misused'. Kirk (2000) notes that there is some consensus that ST tends towards reductionism. One reason this reductionism occurs, it is suggested here, is because advocates of systems approaches are preoccupied with the technocratic aspects of the 'systems concept'. In other fields of intellectual enquiry, for example sociology and organizational behavior, these tendencies have long been recognized. For example, Hassard (1993) complains of the essentially conservative nature of systems approaches and suggests they constitute an intellectual hegemony in the field of organizational theory. This chapter will follow Dearey's example and rather than focus on ST more generally will approach the issues to be considered through a focus on food production and service systems.

SOCIAL SCIENTIFIC CONCEPTS OF FOOD SYSTEMS

Systems approaches to understanding the social world are characterized by considerable confusion largely centered on conceptual and definitional problems. For example, in much of the literature on food production and service systems, claims are made as to the integrative and holistic nature of systems approaches. Integration and holism also figure in various social scientific contributions to the understanding of food systems particularly at the macrolevel where the term 'food system' is normally construed to mean the totality of production, processing, distribution, retailing, consumption and disposal of food. However, as Beardsworth and Kiel (1997: 32–33) remind us:

> The use of the term 'food system' may conjure up an idea of a formally organized set of links between food production, distribution and consumption which is arranged according to some well-thought-out plan or scheme [.]... such a model is inappropriate and unworkable. However, if we are careful not to assume that there is some underlying plan which informs its organization, the term food system can be a convenient way of drawing attention to the particular character of the complex

of interdependent interrelationships associated with the production and distribution of food...

In short, food systems are not normally mechanistically intentioned: serendipity can play a role in both the form and action of a system. Beardsworth and Kiel add to this the observation that in discussing food systems, there is a tendency to simplistic conceptions of stasis. That is, systems are depicted at a moment in time, with little regard for how they change over time. We can add to this that temporal dimensions to systems should not be viewed in uniform, linear terms, as a journey from 'a' to 'b'. Even in a world of globalized agribusiness, what is taken for granted as 'the' food system in the West need not apply in many societies at different stages of development. Nor need it apply in societies disadvantaged by natural disasters, market disadvantage or outright exploitation (see George, 1976, for the classic study in this vein).

Beardsworth and Kiel (1997: 33) themselves propose a model of food systems that has four 'activities' – production, distribution, consumption and beliefs – and two temporal elements – 'traditional' and 'modern' (food) systems. Each of the activities is thus contrasted 'historically' although the degree of reductionism involved is of questionable utility beyond simple description. In developing this model, these writers acknowledge their debt to Goody (1982) who offers a similar 'unconnected' model of food systems, in this case stripped of temporal elements but relying on a weak correspondence theory between: processes (e.g. growing food); phases (e.g. production); and location (e.g. farm). Again, the value of such a model lies at most in its power of weak description. However, it should be noted that Goody (1982), and by extension in this instance at least, Beardsworth and Kiel (1997) operate in that social anthropological tradition which values 'essence', that is boiling things down, if the pun can be forgiven, to draw attention to the simplest elements of cultural activities. In contrast to such 'unconnected' models of food systems are 'connected' models. Beardsworth and Kiel (1997) highlight an example from Freckleton et al. (1989), instantly recognizable as a 'flow chart', specifying flows and linkages between elements in the food system. Here, the basic elements of the system are depicted not only in terms of processes, phases and logic, but in terms of distinct stages of activity as practiced by various 'specialists' (e.g. processors, wholesalers, retailers) in the food business. This is also a 'closed system', in that little scope is given for feedback or multiple flows within the system: the actions of different parties involved in the food system work upon other parties but the scope for mutual influencing is, generally, not accommodated.

The tension between stasis and temporal change is at the heart of the social scientific analysis of food and, as in the three models just briefly described, there is an inevitable tendency to reductionism in the concern to identify the generic, elemental qualities of 'the' food system. Despite a recent proliferation of commentaries and perspectives on the social scientific (and particularly sociological) aspects of food–culture relationships, the field can still be framed in terms of two broad and competing theoretical frameworks – structuralism and materialism/developmentalism. A consideration of the claims and substance of each is germane not only to elaboration of those studies touched upon briefly above, but also to an adequate conceptualization of the main issues that this chapter addresses in terms of food production and service systems.

STRUCTURALISM

Structuralism does not represent a coherent, unified series of perspectives on the social world but in marketing terms, structuralism is well differentiated into distinctive brands (Sturrock, 1986; Murcott, 1988). In so far as it is possible to distinguish the central tenet of structuralism it is that societies, social institutions and social action can be analyzed in a manner analogous with language and cultural phenomena as elements in systems of signs and symbols. The relationships between these elements, their patterning, are the concern of the structuralist. As Culler (1983: 79) notes, structuralism 'takes from linguistics two cardinal principles: that signifying entities do not have essences [intrinsic meanings] but are defined by networks of relations, both internal and external, and that to account for signifying phenomena is to describe the system of norms that make them possible'.

Undoubtedly the most famous example of structuralist conceptions of food systems is that proffered by social anthropologist Lévi-Strauss (1965) in his concept of the culinary triangle. Briefly, the culinary triangle is based on the proposition that the mentalistic processes of cooking are shared human universals whereby the transformation of raw ingredients into cooked ones represents a cultural transformation of nature. The culinary triangle consists of pairs of 'binary oppositions' such that raw food can be transformed by nature if it is allowed to rot or by human agency if it is cooked. The rotten is a natural transformation of raw and cooked food whereas cooked food is a cultural transformation of the raw. Lévi-Strauss claims that the culinary triangle maps the essential techniques of cooking – i.e. roasting, smoking and boiling – arguing that when food is roasted it (a) requires minimal equipment (cultural objects) and (b) is brought into more or less direct contact with fire, the 'natural' agent of conversion. In terms of process and product, roasting belongs to nature. Smoking too is a natural process but smoked food belongs to culture because smoking preserves food, making it durable and increasing its potential economic value. Smoking requires no cultural apparatus but it does require air. Boiling is a process which reduces food to a state similar to that of rotted food in nature so boiled food belongs to nature, but the process of boiling, requiring a receptacle (cultural object) belongs to nature (see Figure 20.1).

Lévi-Strauss' commentary invites incredulity. Leach (1974: 31) remarks that 'readers might begin to suspect that the whole argument was an elaborate academic joke'. Mennell (1985: 9) suggests that the 'general reader may well consider the culinary triangle a farrago of nonsense'. Harris (1986), more prosaically, is quick to note that no empirical evidence has been forthcoming in support of the concept of the culinary triangle, a regular and largely intuitive criticism of the concept that can be ameliorated somewhat in observing that very little effort has been expended on any such empirical investigation. At the very least the model, or one like it, could assist in developing classifications of hierarchies of food according to methods of cooking and types of ingredient, something attempted in a small way from within the domain of linguistics (Lehrer, 1969). Harris (1986) is on surer logical ground when he points out that even if the culinary triangle reflected some universal mentalistic structure, it still could not explain variations between societies in the selection of some foodstuffs rather than others, as well as preferences for particular types of food preparation. Certainly, Lévi-Strauss' claims are

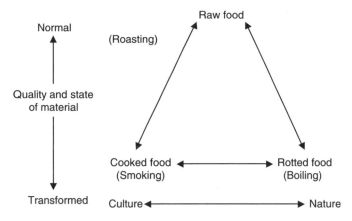

Figure 20.1 Lévi-Strauss' culinary triangle

ambitious, and have not found favor, the culinary triangle languishing in the academic twilight zone as an interesting curiosity. Yet in terms of utility (whether construed as applicability or as a heuristic for further investigation) it is unclear as to how *less* useful the culinary triangle is than any of the other models thus far considered.

The same is true for the work of Lévi-Strauss' compatriot, Roland Barthes (1979 [1961]) who argues that food is a system of communication. To identify the constituents of the system it is necessary to create an inventory of food products, techniques and habits and from this observe patterns of signification, i.e. the cultural meanings of food to those who consume it. Not all varieties of foodstuff are necessarily significant at a collective social level: some are significant only as a reflection of personal taste. Barthes' analytic model is based on Saussure's postulation of a distinction between language and speech. Language is the set of conventions necessary to communication but distinct from the signs and symbols it comprises. Speech is the individual use of language and involves the application of language rules, and the combination of the signs and symbols that make up the language for the purpose of individual expression. According to Barthes, the alimentary language comprises rules of exclusion (e.g. food taboos); signifying oppositions of elements in the culinary language (e.g. between savory and sweet); rituals of association, which work at both the level of the dish and the level of the menu; and rituals of food use. Alimentary 'speech' comprises all the personal, group and national variations of

food selection, preparation and association. For Barthes, the menu is the archetypal expression of the relationship between culinary language and speech. Any menu is constructed with reference to the structure of alimentary language but the structure is filled differently according to the prevailing modes of alimentary speech. What Barthes appears to be arguing (and it is by no means clear) is that alimentary language determines what foods are 'available' for consumption. Availability is to some degree determined by prevailing mores and taboos in respect of what is regarded as edible, what foods may be legitimately associated together, and how these foods are to be prepared. A menu is any given expression of this language.

With a more emphatic focus on the micro-social, Mary Douglas (1975) seeks to model food consumption at the level of the consumer, arguing that there are two contrasted food categories recognized by consumers – meals and drinks. Meals are named events (breakfast, lunch, dinner) whereas drinks are not. Meals are taken against a background of rituals and assumptions (the use of utensils, e.g. forks, spoons, that enter the mouth; sitting at a table, and restrictions on the pursuit of alternative activities, e.g. reading while eating). Drinks are confined to 'mouth touching' utensils and are attended by fewer rituals and assumptions. Meals incorporate a number of contexts – hot/cold; bland/spiced; liquid/semi-liquid – whereas the variety of contrasts incorporated within a drink is fewer and less pronounced. Most important for Douglas is that meals and drinks reflect the quality of social relationships – drinks are widely available in the home to family members, strangers and acquaintances. Drinks are reserved for family members, strangers and acquaintances. Meals are reserved for family members, close friends and honored guests.

For many non-social scientists, the terminology employed by Douglas seems absurdly comparable with the peculiar substance of Lévi-Strauss' arguments. Douglas, however, does establish a 'real world' correspondence between the higher level category 'meals' and the subordinate category of 'drinks' on the one hand, and levels of social intimacy on the other. Douglas (1975: 256) writes that 'Those we know at drinks we also know at meals', or put another way, we reserve the sharing of meals for individuals who are close to us but we are less discriminating about who we share a drink with. Meals and drinks are the two main elements in the food system with the former subsuming the latter in expressions of social intimacy. Thus meals are at one end of the continuum equating to 'greater social intimacy' while drinks are at the other end of the same continuum, equating to 'less social intimacy' (an early observation on this idea in the hospitality context is offered by Mercer, 1977, who specifies relationships between categories of meal consumption and levels of intimacy).

Douglas' work has provided the main impetus to the development of the sociology of food and eating as a distinctive sub-area (see for example Wood, 1995, and Warde and Martens, 2000, for reviews). Of particular note is the extent to which her basic model of meal structures has been adapted and employed heuristically in diverse ways. Wood (1995) for example draws on Douglas' work to explore the provision of meals in the commercial hospitality sector. Of wider importance is the extent to which Douglas' contributions have been harnessed to mainstream sociological concerns in class and gender analysis. Although now a quarter of a century old, Murcott's (1982) study of domestic 'cooked dinners' in South Wales remains one of the best examples of this type of empirical elaboration. Focused on a sample of 37 pregnant women, Murcott charted the content, structural, aesthetic and moral dimensions of meals within what was a predominantly working-class sub-culture. Symbolically and contextually, Murcott's perhaps most significant observation was that in this culture, the overall responsibility for domestic affairs fell to women and this validated their social and economic role in the family and marital context. Women's responsibility for the cooked dinner included deference to the food preferences of the husband or male partner and accommodation of other family likes and dislikes to the extent that Murcott (1982: 693) famously comments:

> If a job defines how a man occupies his time during the working day, to which the wage packet provides regular testimony, proper provision of a cooked dinner testifies that the woman has spent her time in correspondingly suitable fashion … the cooked dinner in the end symbolizes the home itself, a man's relation to that home and a woman's place in it.

Materialism/developmentalism

Murcott's study is but one of a largish number that illustrates the varieties of the structuralist approach to food–culture relationships. In contrast to the relative abstraction of the work of Lévi-Strauss and Barthes, and to some extent even Douglas (although this may perhaps be more accurately described in terms of a commitment to 'essence' noted earlier), Murcott and others have grounded their work in more extensive empirical realities.

All the writers considered thus far seek to describe various elements of food systems although they would probably balk at their work being described in terms of systems theory. However, while they may not be 'systems approaches' in the conventionally understood sense, the 'structuralist school' has attracted criticism precisely for its 'systems qualities', not least from those working within the materialist/developmentalism tradition. Developmentalism is concerned with the historical evolution of food practices and preferences, and premised on the view that contemporary food habits are best understood through the examination of historical trends and data. In the view of developmentalists, structuralists are too concerned with the 'here and now' and underplay the biological, geographical and technological imperatives that influence food supply and consumption, including of course the need to eat to live. In the 1980s, Stephen Mennell (1985) and Marvin Harris (1986, 1987) emerged as the most energetic 'anti-structuralists' and their arguments remain the benchmark in this regard. Harris (1987: 57), for example, terms structuralists 'cultural idealists' and writes:

> In general, cultural idealists explain variations in food preferences and aversions as a consequence of "culture" (by which they mean the learned emic and mental components of social life). This strategy has resulted in three kinds of explanatory propositions: (1) food customs are said to be the consequence of idiographic-historical continuities that regress to an unknown beginning; (2) they are the consequence of arbitrary "taste", chance, or whim; (3) they are the functional symbolic or behavioral correlates or expressions of given systems of values and beliefs. To the extent that none of these varieties of propositions invoke selection principles that can account for specific observed variations in food customs (as well as uniformities) or for the occurrence of the constraining values and beliefs, they constitute a weak form of scientific statement or none at all.

Harris argues that biological, psychological, environmental, technological, political and economic factors *all* influence the foods that can be consumed in a given context, and whilst accepting that foods convey esthetic and symbolic meanings and messages insists that 'Food must nourish the collective stomach before it can feed the collective mind' (Harris, 1986: 15). This leads him to assert that food preferences arise because of a more favorable balance of practical benefits over costs than for those foods that are avoided. These costs and benefits are assessed over a range of criteria, for example, whether or not foods are, in terms of economics and effort, worth producing and preparing; whether or not some foods have cheaper and more nutritious substitutes; and whether or not the cultivation of some foods may be damaging to a particular environment. Harris is particularly skeptical of Douglas' work arguing that her studies of meals are devoid of any consideration of how symbolic values and meanings expressed in food choice and food use relate to economic, nutritional and dietary factors. Harris' assertion, or more accurately reassertion, of his position seems intended to press a position for which he had previously been criticized (and who was to face much subsequent criticism, see for example Murcott, 1988: 19–20) by Douglas (1984: 18) who somewhat grandly writes:

> Marvin Harris' work ... has potentially powerful insights for interpreting long-term changes. But the method is inevitably weak for observing short-term relations between social factors and perceived

needs. Furthermore, it assumes rational economic choice for explaining cultural adaptation, but ... this is precisely the assumption that is challenged in the current thinking about food tastes. The modern consumer has lost credibility as a rational agent in the eyes of food theorists. So this distinctly anthropological approach lacks fine-tuned relevance to the way that the great food problems are posed.

The rationality of human choice behavior remains among the most contentious, enduring and thus unresolved debates in the history of ideas. Douglas' argument that Harris assumes humans to be rational economic actors is, in this sense, no argument at all. One suspects that what makes 'cultural idealists' uncomfortable with Harris is that he poses the most rigorous challenge to our understanding of food systems by focusing on the basic human concept of need – the need to eat to (physically) survive. Western evidenced theories of food and culture relationships not only contain an intrinsic cultural bias but additionally tend to gloss the fact that their application is principally developed in the context of societies with at least a nominal food surplus, or at least where the non-availability of essential foodstuffs has all but been eliminated. The enduring appeal of Harris' brand of developmentalism and its (usually more dilute) variants can be seen, *inter alia*, in Beardsworth and Kiel's (1997) approach to the concept of food systems caricatured earlier. Indeed, there is a marked reluctance to abandon the descriptive power of both connected and unconnected models of food systems, in both social science research and the operations management literature at the heart of studies of food production and service systems in hospitality.

If Harris' developmentalism has its roots in social anthropology, then Stephen Mennell's brand is forged from sociology and history. In other words, Mennell arrives at his critique of structuralism via a different route, most potently expressed in his landmark and magisterial book *All Manners of Food: Eating and Taste in England and France from the Middle Ages to the Present* (1985). He writes that 'structuralist and cultural "explanations" of food preferences really add little to the old argument that "people like what they are used to" – they offer mainly a classificatory scheme, not an explanation' (1985: 13). He adds: 'The structuralist preoccupation with codes and deep structures is a striking example of this [process reduction]: not only are the codes apparently depicted as static and unchanging but so, as often as not, are the patterns of social relations which they are supposed to "express" ' (1985: 14).

Mennell's main intellectual inspiration is the work of Norbert Elias, and in particular Elias' concept of the figuration which is an irreducible 'structure of mutually oriented and dependent people' (Elias, 1978: 261). Figurations both constrain and enable the activities of groups and individuals and are produced and reproduced over time (Rojek, 1985: 160–161). Most importantly, perhaps, is Elias' prescription that figurations are best studied processually. As he puts it: 'structure theories ... embody the spatial dimensions. They have ... the character of three dimensional models. Process theories have the character of four dimensional models ... they do not abstract from either the spatial or the time dimension' (Elias, 1974: 40, quoted in Rojek, 1985: 160–161). Elias' own major illustration of this processual approach is his *The Civilizing Process* (Elias, 1978) the term referring to a supposed set of changes in human personality structure since the Middle Ages involving trends towards much greater levels of self-discipline, self-control and rising standards of shame and embarrassment in interpersonal interaction. In food and eating, he argues, greater refinement can be seen in the ways in which the basic accessories to eating, though changing little in terms of essential form, have been substantially differentiated within their own type. Thus there are many different types of cutlery, crockery, fork, knife and spoon for use in eating different types of food, in different situations, and these reflect a move over time from eating from a common bowl at meals to more individualized, 'dainty' or civilized habits which simultaneously defines the quantity of food available.

Mennell (1985) applies Elias' historical approach with a vengeance. Chronology (in the sense of relating influences on food systems at particular points in time) is not enough, rather 'it is necessary to look carefully at the jumbled historical record to see if it is possible to discern not constants beneath the flux, but an order of a different kind, a sequential order constituting *structured processes of change*' (1985: 15). Applying this method, Mennell's singular contribution to the figurational study of food and eating is to argue that there is evidence over time of 'diminishing contrasts' and 'increasing varieties' between certain food-related habits, attitudes and beliefs.

Contrasts have diminished between seasonal and everyday eating patterns because of advances in technology and transportation that allow more foods and more varieties of food to be available more of the time. They have also diminished between élite professional cookery and everyday cooking as peasant dishes have been absorbed into haute cuisine; cookery guides have disseminated knowledge of 'good' cookery to wider audiences, and the growth of the hotel and restaurant industry has democratized food and eating, diminishing the role of social class in eating out (Mennell, 1985: 326). Increasing variety is seen over time in the proliferation of dishes; the differentiation of public restaurants and private households; the differentiation of many kinds of restaurant; the creation of a competitive market for both domestic and non-domestic foodstuffs; and a decline in the prestige hierarchy of food which places French haute cuisine at its apex.

It is difficult, over 20 years later, to describe adequately the profound influence Mennell's book had on the sociological analysis of food and eating. Almost universally lauded within the field (notwithstanding Murcott's 1988, suggestion that there was a suspicion that Mennell was prey to 'foodie' partisanship) many of his sociological arguments now appear at best naïve, and at worst simply wrong (the historical analysis arguably remains a triumph). Even if there is an irreversible trend towards civility and refinement, figurationalism does little to account either for the varying symbolic significance attached to different types of meals, or foodstuffs, or eating implements in a single culture or for such variance across cultures. This last is important because one of the genuine difficulties with Mennell's work is the culturally privileged position it gives to European gastronomy. However, perhaps the least tenable of Mennell's claims is that the development of the hotel and restaurant industry has encouraged greater culinary democracy. Put kindly, evidence suggests that Mennell overlooked the fact that growth of the industry and participation in dining out has been matched by a growth in the stratification of the sector that focuses social divisions of class, gender and taste (for further examples, see Wood, 1995).

Given the apparent tension between the structuralist and materialist positions, what can be distilled from these debates in terms of common ground that has some theoretical utility? The key word here is 'apparent' as both camps are, in reality, not that distant from one other. First, the social scientific literature on food and eating has, for the most part, an unquestioned bias in favor of *consumption* even though there are differences within and between the structuralist and developmental positions as to the ways in which consumption should be understood. Second, all of the social scientific models examined make at least some claims to applicability in the 'real world' (in the case of developmental perspectives quite significant claims). Third, all can be represented on a scale of ambitiousness in terms of their intended macro- or micro-range and scope. In many ways, this distinction is perhaps of greater significance than that which purports to exist between different theoretical perspectives. Mennell's lauding of the imperative of figurational change is not, in conception, greatly at variance with Lévi-Strauss' desire to identify universalistic mental structures in terms of the development of a grand theory. Fourth, the models examined purport not simply to be descriptions of food consumption realities, but to enable, within reason, an element of prediction about those realities. Thus, the models proposed by writers such as Lévi-Strauss, Barthes and Douglas to a greater or lesser degree all seek to both describe and predict (or at least circumscribe what can be predicted about) consumption behavior. If, for example, we accept what Barthes says about the role of symbolic meaning in human activity, then the structure of the menu is itself a vehicle for selecting and enhancing such meanings. A person on a romantic dinner date may well select foods associated with 'being romantic' in order to give voice to this sentiment. Fifth, as structuralism's critics point out, theorists in this tradition are concerned with the patterning of choices. Patterning is not confined to abstract emotions and values, however, as we have noted. The symbolism of consumption patterns is an expression of socio-economic class (for example, Barthes' fellow countryman, Bourdieu (1984) has argued that the symbolism of consumption patterns is a function of social class); gender (e.g. Murcott, 1982) and household composition (Charles and Kerr, 1988) among other social indicators. Patterning and prediction are at the heart of Lévi-Strauss' undoubtedly simplistic model of the culinary triangle. Similarly, for all its quibbles with structuralism, the developmental approach is essentially complementary in its emphasis on patterning. Mennell's (1985: 15) take on Elias'

figurational approach defaults to examining history for 'structured processes of change' as we have seen. If the concept of 'structure' is utilized here in a manner at variance with that employed by structuralist writers, Mennell fails to establish the nature of that difference in any satisfactory way. Sixth, social scientific models of food systems have a tendency to temporal stasis, all tend to be snapshots in time, even where, following Beardsworth and Kiel's (1997) imprecations, they seek to resist such a tendency. Both structuralist and figurational approaches are biased in favor of temporal stasis. For the root concept in the figurational approach – the civilizing process – to have any analytic value at all beyond a *deux ex machina* explanation of cultural change, it must necessarily demonstrate even in broad terms how food habits have changed over time and this is, in fact, exactly the kind of account that Mennell (1985) provides. Finally, all our models, as models are almost by definition, are reductionist, reducing complex phenomena to their basic elements.

The premise asserted at the beginning of this chapter was that the study of food production and service systems in the hospitality industry emphasizes production elements over the role and contexts of consumption. The question therefore arises as to the utility of the social scientific literature for both illuminating this fact and allowing us to model a closing of the gap between production and consumption in hospitality systems. If this is possible, it should at least allow for the creation of a more useful framework for analyzing such systems. It is to these issues that the discussion now turns.

MODELS OF HOSPITALITY FOOD PRODUCTION AND SERVICE

As already stated, discussion of models of food production and service systems in the hospitality industry tend to eschew questions about the location of such systems in a wider, holistic, schema, distinctly lacking in any focus upon the context of consumption in which these systems operate. They also tend to draw on a much less rich intellectual framework for their conception, due in part to what may be described as a mistaken view of food production and service systems as an essentially artisanal expression of practical need. The consequence of this essentially anti-intellectual approach has been that for the most part, the various social dimensions to food consumption have not been considered relevant to systems planning, save at the crudest level. Thus the role of the consumer in food production and service systems is normally reduced to that of a cipher, expressed in terms of one or both of marketing 'principles' or the required engagement of customers with particular systems in terms of ergonomics, cost and tolerance. In this respect, the treatment of consumption can be usefully compared with 'connected' and 'unconnected' models of the wider food system described earlier in the chapter which find resonance in other areas of applied business scholarship (for example, in food retailing, see Marshall, 1995). We can make explicit the points of contact with the social scientific literature in terms of the seven-item list of features enumerated towards the end of the previous section. So, models of hospitality food production and service are predominantly concerned with applicability – practical solutions to real world problems with a clear focus, however, on the micro- rather than macro- aspects of production (consumption being largely excluded). There is also a claim to utility in terms of the application of an understanding of the development of food systems over time to predicting their future evolution through analysis of the internal patterning of such systems. Similarly, there is a tendency to stasis and reductionism. It is in the other areas, by definition of the problem to which the chapter is addressed, where hospitality food production and service systems theory is deficient – in relegating consumption to a cipher, and in not exploring and barely recognizing the patterning of food choices and their impact upon such systems.

To elaborate these claims, we can begin by noting that in the hospitality business context, foodservice systems are generally accorded a central position. Thus Waller (1996: 261) places generic food service systems within the context of financial and market constraints. Despite asserting that systems are interdependent, Waller's model evidences a relatively isolated character because the externalities which create interdependence in systems are, in essence, caricatured. That is, externalities are taken for granted and this tends to a narrowing of focus. In Waller's case, the production process in food and beverage is almost a black box despite being interdependent with input systems (purchasing)

and output systems (service) (Waller, 1996: 282) (see Figure 20.2).

The criticism here is that in recognizing the interdependency of systems, Waller and other writers on food-service delivery systems rarely follow through on the recognition that externalities are critical to the formation, maintenance and performance of these systems. To illustrate this, we need look no further than the work of Peter Jones, the doyen of hospitality food production and service systems theory. Jones' work has the advantage of both clarity and elegance while simultaneously highlighting the limitations of a narrow systems approach as defined here in terms of the neglect of connections between wider food systems and hospitality food production and service systems.

Jones (see especially 1993, 1994a, 1994b, also Huelin and Jones, 1990; Johns and Jones, 1999a, 1999b, 2000) asserts that there is no widely accepted classification of food service systems. Furthermore, conceptual clarity is impeded by a lack of common definitional frameworks for discussing food service operations. Thus, Jones asks, do we regard cook-chill as a new system or a modification of an existing one? Are central food production systems specific individual systems, even though the separation of one stage of the production process from another may have little impact on the management of the total system (Jones, 1993: 2)? As we noted with Waller (1996) the concept of the service delivery system applied to food and beverage proceeds in the traditional production management model, from changing inputs (foods, capital, labor) through processes (chiefly production and service) into outputs (meals, customer satisfaction, profit). However, with most foodservice systems, production and consumption are usually regarded as simultaneous but this need not be so. Indeed, Jones observes, the challenge for production management models of foodservice systems is the extent to which the participation of consumers in service events can be incorporated into a materials flow model (1993: 4). The essence of Jones' development of models of foodservice systems follows this 'materials flow' approach (Huelin and Jones, 1990; Jones, 1993: 6–7).

He begins by taking the traditional catering service delivery system that has its origins in nineteenth century hotels (what can be termed the 'Escoffierian' model, after the chef Escoffier). Identifying the flow of materials

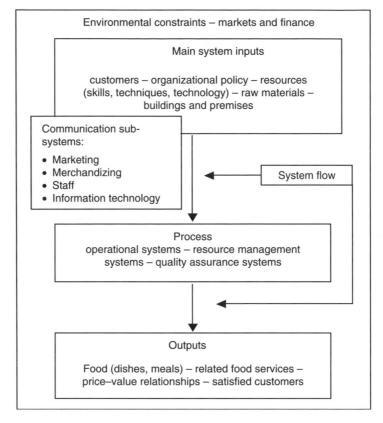

Figure 20.2   Food production and service system after Waller (1996)

through the system, Jones generates eight essential stages, namely: storage; preparation; production (cooking); holding; service; dining; clearing; and dishwash. Many configurations of these stages are possible because of the development of technology, notably regenerative techniques based on food preservation and preparation methods like cook-freeze, cook-chill and sous vide. All of these have increased the period of time that food can be held between production and service stages – the 'holding' stage – and made possible a greater decoupling of production and service in terms of temporal and spatial factors – factors that have given rise to an important 'transportation' stage. With the addition of regeneration and transportation, Jones' eight-stage model is extended to ten stages thus: storage; preparation; production (cooking); holding; transportation; regeneration; service; dining; clearing; and dishwash.

According to Jones, these ten elements can be combined and recombined, omitting some stages and including others to produce generic models

of delivery systems that can be exemplified by reference to real foodservice contexts. Thus the model storage-preparation-cooking-service-dining-clearing-dishwash is operationalized as a conventional à la carte restaurant using fresh commodities cooked to order. In addition to this 'precision' modeling, these and any subsequent models can be classified into three broad types. The first of these is integrated foodservice systems reflecting traditional notions of the restaurant being the locus for both food production and consumption. The second is food manufacturing systems where the production and service of meals is decoupled emphasizing the crucial role of transportation. Finally there are food delivery systems where the operation has little or no food production and focuses primarily on the service of meals: meals are assembled and/or regenerated. The ultimate goal of this type of analysis, Jones (1994a: 142) argues, is to develop further modeling refinements based in the 'real world', mapping generic types to specific contexts in pursuit of 'objective criteria for distinguishing the key features of the catering system'. These criteria would include types of raw materials employed; inventory size; product range; width and depth; capacity; production batch sizes; and flexibility. In addition, Jones is concerned that these models can be used as a basis for investigating variations in management behavior and action depending on the systems in use.

In later work, Johns and Jones (1999a; see also Johns and Jones, 1999b) are simultaneously critical of black-boxism in systems theory while pointing out the heuristic value of not knowing 'what is going on', provided the boundaries, inputs and outputs of a system are known. In both a general and hospitality context, Johns and Jones recognize the problematic iterative nature of systems. The logical conclusion of accepting a systems view of the world is that everything constitutes a system, sub-system or sub-sub-system and so on. They propose that in the hospitality context some measure of order can be imposed on this complexity by employing the concept of systems hierarchy. Conceiving of systems and system derivatives as hierarchical in nature provides procedures for establishing the boundaries of systems and their derivatives and testing whether such boundaries are formal or informal (manufactured or 'naturally' occurring), as well as the degree of interaction between systems and system derivatives. An important limitation of this view is that it requires a high level of conceptual imposition. Who determines what constitutes a system or sub-system? What are the rules of engagement for determining hierarchical structure? Moreover, cast in such terms, the conceptualization of systems persists in eliding the question of interaction with the wider socio-economic systems in which (in this case) business organizations operate. Johns and Jones (2000: 47) appear to appreciate these difficulties in that they suggest:

> In order to understand how a system has developed, how it operates now, and what may cause it to change in the future it is necessary to look at one level at a time. For example, the model is applied at industry, firm or unit level in isolation, although clearly there are relationships between each of these levels.

In this they pay lip service to the role of the wider economic, social and cultural environment while continuing to emphasize the primacy of the systems themselves, of valorizing production at the expense of consumption. The reductionism and technocratic over-descriptiveness inherent in this approach applies not only to 'system inputs' or the contexts in which they operate, but also to the 'outputs', to the *use* of systems in practice. When Jones (1994b: 142) writes, as noted earlier, that a purpose of food production and service systems analysis is the pursuit of 'objective criteria for distinguishing the key features of the catering system', he is perfectly serious. The criteria listed do not include collective human agency as either input or output. Nor do they include those 'objective criteria' that influence the features of 'the' catering system from the wider social system. When Johns and Jones (1999a) talk of knowing the boundaries, inputs and outputs of a system they reveal that, for them, the external environment or (social) 'context' is little more than a cipher.

As we have seen, social scientists (some at least) also pay lip service to the real world 'applicability' of their models while often appearing to indulge in breathtaking levels of theoretical abstraction. Considering the points of contact identified earlier between the two – related – areas it is easy to represent them as opposites, the social scientific overly abstract, the applied systems theory to hospitality production and service too concrete. Yet once again, there is a case for suggesting that areas of difference are much less than areas of similarity. Indeed, at the epistemological level, what these apparently diverse approaches reveal is a marked unity of shared concerns to impose descriptive and analytic order on food systems. Whether dealing with resources (Harris' 'rational' approach), the role of temporal change (Mennell's take on figurationalism), symbolic meaning (the structuralists in all their diversity), or the more prosaic task of designing economic and effective commercial hospitality systems, all such efforts begin by seeking to impose some kind of order on a messy 'real world'. The central – and one suspects unpalatable (sic) – problem for both fields is that neither has progressed very far beyond this point. In other words, the very charge laid against food production and systems service theory in this chapter could be applied to some degree to social scientific research. Indeed, a relatively recent survey of the latter by Ashley, Hollows, Jones and Taylor (2004) from a 'cultural studies' perspective arguably reveals how little progress has been made in social scientific theorizing about food and eating.

While their cultural studies 'twist' is not without interest, theoretically Ashley et al. do little more than rehearse many of the central arguments that have been at the heart of the literature for at least 15 years (see for example Mennell et al., 1992; Wood, 1995; Warde and Martens, 2000).

A notable (but perhaps understandable in light of the rationale of cultural studies approaches) omission in the survey of the field by Ashley et al. is consideration of materialist approaches to food and eating such as those offered by Harris. This is despite having a chapter devoted to the 'contribution of anthropological approaches to the study of food practices' (Ashley et al., 2004: 27). An intellectual opposition to simplistic culturally materialist or more generally objectivist approaches to consumption (including, for example, simplistic notions of establishing the 'objectivity' of catering systems in the manner of Jones, 1994b) should not blind us to what is potentially instructive in the wider materialist case. Clearly at a fully integrated macro-social level, the imposition of descriptive and explanatory models of food systems predicated on 'rational' approaches are, in simple probabilistic terms, unlikely to be very fruitful because of the necessary degree of reductionism involved in constructing them, a point illustrated by consideration of those models proposed by writers such as Goody (1982) and Beardsworth and Kiel (1997). However, *some* elements of food systems (sub-systems if you like) *are*, within the capacity of human reason – more or less – rationally determined, or at least planned. In developed agricultural systems, the choice of what foods to grow, and how and where to grow them, is a planned process. In the retail food industry, distribution and the manner in which food is sold is a planned process. In the hospitality context, for example, the Escoffierian system noted earlier can be seen as representing a planned response to the demands of food production (Mennell, 1985), as can the technology centered processes associated with fast food restaurants (Ritzer, 1996). Indeed, in practice, foodservice organizations of size plan service delivery systems in the context of the business process (strategy, marketing, human resources) and to pretend that rationality is not intended in this process amounts to willful foolishness.

Of course, that something is planned and/or intended as rational does not mean that *what* is planned necessarily 'works' or is rational

in execution or operation. An overemphasis on the supposed evils of analytic reductionism encourages avoidance of dealing with the consequences of human intentionality. Put another way, an unexploited advantage of the application of social scientific knowledge about food and eating to the study of hospitality food production and service systems theory lies in the formers' capacity to explicate the limitations of materialist biases through charting relationships between intention and actuality. The less abstract 'structuralist' literature – for example that of Douglas (1975) and Murcott (1982) – to some extent does this at the micro-level by focusing on the meanings attached to consumption by those doing the consuming. What it does not do is develop beyond the description of those meanings to illustrate what affects this behavior has on other elements in food systems. The real 'black box' at the heart of *both* social scientific approaches to food and eating and the study of hospitality food production and service systems (albeit on rather different scales) is, to borrow a term from systems theory itself, a failure to deal with the nature and impact of any 'feedback loops'. The term is ugly, but is useful shorthand for emphasizing the importance of identifying and analyzing mechanisms of impact on change in food systems (ironically one of the stated – and largely failed because of a distorted emphasis on the importance of a peculiar construal of history – intentions of the figurational approach). The question is, therefore, whether it is possible to develop a meaningful model to guide such analysis, the subject addressed in the final part of this chapter.

FOUR PROPOSITIONS

As originally claimed at the commencement of this chapter, there is an acute limitation in current conceptions of hospitality food production and service systems. This limitation arises from a failure to root models of such systems firmly in the wider social context of food consumption and especially market (consumption) realities and to explore the relationships between hospitality food systems and collective human agency, with what people indirectly or unintentionally contribute to, and 'do' with systems. As a result, the current utility of food production and service systems theory amounts to little more than a mildly interesting description of how technologies may be arranged.

The principle ambition of those who find systems theory in hospitality interesting must surely be to render it useful beyond this mere descriptive felicity. The social scientific literature on food and eating is some help in resolving this situation in terms of widening understanding of patterns of food consumption. However, its integrative power is also acutely limited because it suffers from many of the problems endemic to food production and service systems theory. These include conceptual ambiguity, unrealistic levels of abstraction, poorly elaborated theoretical schema tending to overreach themselves in terms of explanatory claims, a no less distorting tendency to reductionism and a reluctance to explore the role of intentionality in the 'design' and development of food systems. In respect of the last, an acceptance that food production and service systems are planned, or at least have planned elements in the context of available resources – a kind of 'weak materialist' view if you like – may enable better consideration of the motives for, and means and consequences of intentionality in planning. In one sense, such an approach is evident in the critical social scientific literature on work and employment in hospitality services, for example Leidner (1993) and Ritzer (1996).

To develop food production and systems theory in the hospitality context to a more usefully analytic level, four propositions derived from the review of themes discussed in this chapter seem relevant. The first of these is that how food systems are conceived should be a matter for empirical description and analysis rather than *a priori* theorizing – a focus on what 'is' rather than what might be. This necessarily means that we treat with caution remarks such as those by Beardsworth and Kiel (1997: 32–33) to the effect that, provided we do not assume an underlying organizational rationale, conceiving of systems in a large and broad sense can be a useful heuristic, are instructive. Sometimes the bigger picture, the overall context, is useful, but not if it involves the imposition of *a priori* theoretical schema to an understanding of food systems or an avoidance of studying the consequences of human intentionality in the design of food systems.

A second and clearly related proposition concerns analysts' assumptions about the extent to which the structural inter-relationships present in food systems can be synthesized into meaningful analytical principles. By definition, the act of describing systems involves structuring activity and in most descriptions of food systems, the principal form of such structuring activity is the layering of food systems into some kind of hierarchy of influence using macro-/micro- categories. Given the aversion of many social scientists to all forms of determinism there is an irony here. Equating scale with the circumscription and definition of the number, type and level of sub-systems within a single, larger system broadly corresponds to the concept of systems hierarchy in systems theory jargon with the 'layered' structural divisions of food systems treated as the equivalent to 'feedback' mechanisms. Thus, what is produced and how it is produced bears linearly on how it is distributed and consumed, and laterally on how and when it is processed, retailed or consumed. For example, following Beardsworth and Kiel's (1997: 32–33) view, the basic building blocks in this respect are processes and activities, which in the food system case include in the former category production, distribution and consumption, and in the latter, farming, preserving and processing (as a single category), retailing and cooking. The second set of instances is illustrative of the first (and reflects an implicit hierarchy of importance) but again, such an approach involves imposition of *a priori* assumptions about underlying principles of organization which, as we have seen, these authors appear (rightly) keen to avoid. In the hospitality context Johns and Jones (2000) advocate a level-by-level analysis, explicitly articulating a hierarchical view of systems inter-relationships as a model for mapping the complexity of systems inter-relationships. The difficulty with both positions is that the size of a system or sub-system is not necessarily proportional to its influence, even if that influence could be measured, and a hierarchy of influence cannot be assumed. Again, the nature and any 'flow' and 'direction' of influence within a system should as far as possible be established empirically. In the developed world, the contact people have with different parts of the 'wider' food system is limited (principally to those parts of the system concerned with distribution – for example restaurants and food stores). Thus, as a working hypothesis, distribution and consumption systems may be more important than production and processing to understanding patterns of influence and malleability in food systems.

Following this, the third proposition here returns us to the question of the treatment of intentionality in food systems – what a system is supposed to do and what it actually does. A critical wariness of determinism is a positive analytical strategy but in the case of food systems, avoidance of the identification and analysis of deterministic influences is the very approach that has condemned discussions of systems to superficial description. Simply put, elements within food systems and some food systems in their entirety are planned to a greater or lesser extent – hospitality food production and service systems being a good example. To foreclose upon analytical insights into the consequences of such planning (for example upon the operation of food systems) is as poor an intellectual strategy as assuming that such planning is a simple and transparent process. The latter is arguably the principal sin of extant accounts of hospitality food production and service systems, which valorize planning as transparent procedure without acknowledging the tacit knowledge that goes into any planning process; knowledge drawn from wider social contexts. The future study of food production and service systems in hospitality requires exploration of the assumptions underlying planning and design imperatives and, more importantly, how the use and application of systems develop in their interaction with 'environmental' factors, including the impacts of consumer use. For example, the analysis of hospitality supply and distribution chains may allow insights into how these evolve relative to the design intentions of their originators and modifications to such intentions based on operational engagement with consumers.

The final proposition relates to how we study food systems, and particularly hospitality food production and service systems, in terms of integrating different social, managerial and technical perspectives on the subject. Obviously, this is no easy matter. In the literature reviewed here it is easy to become quickly aware of the degree to which disciplinary demarcation excludes study of the range of contributions to a subject: social scientists do not dirty their hands by delving into management literature and vice versa. As a short term device for encouraging greater breadth of consideration in the field, the study of the degree of communicative abstraction in food systems provides an initial conceptual starting point. Communicative abstraction describes the degree to which a system performs either a concrete role (e.g. growing cauliflowers, selling cauliflowers) or abstract role (e.g. determining the appropriateness of cauliflowers to particular types of meal occasion). Communicative abstraction is constituted by system inter-relationships since processes and activities are necessary for communication, and scale and structure is the product of communication which in turn influences the utilization of processes and activities that lead to further communication, a feedback mechanism. Varying types and levels of communicative abstraction are, contextually, dependent on time and culture. Certain types of these relationships will exist at any one point in time, but that point in time is the sum of all previous points in time. That systems are culture bound emphasizes how for any system, modeling can only be a precursor to empirically testing the explanatory power of a model. The difficulty with current positions on food production and service systems is that they begin and end with the model which is usually localized as opposed to contextualized. However, a localized model of food systems reduces or eliminates description and analysis of both the planned and unplanned elements that constitute it. The system inter-relationships that exist between levels of communicative abstraction are essentially, in structuralist terms, relationships between signifiers and what they signify, the signifier being more or less concrete and the signified more or less abstract.

We can seek to illustrate these four themes 'in action' by considering a rather predictable example of their application – the fast food chain McDonald's. This company has been subject to both extensive academic (and 'para-academic') theoretical and empirical study not least in the work of writers on 'McDonaldization' engendered by the work of George Ritzer (1996). Empirically, much is known of McDonald's, satisfying the terms of the first proposition outlined above. In terms of the second proposition, enough is known of the structure, size, scope and range of McDonald's activities to satisfy both those who perceive structured hierarchy as important and the more cautious approach advocated here of focusing on a consumption orientation as a means to evaluating the influence of a food system. In terms of, thirdly, intentionality, little doubt can be cast upon the proactive nature of McDonald's approach in designing, redesigning and reconfiguring elements of its systems to both lead and accommodate changes in fortune or strategic intent. In terms of the first three propositions therefore, we can assert with some confidence that McDonald's is an organization of considerable (global) scale with more or less definable business structures and practices. It has pursued strategies of vertical integration either by direct control of the processes of production or by employing its buying power to secure preferential supplies of materials.

More than this, however, such is its global influence in production, distribution and consumption that the mere fact of its economic power has become secondary to the power of communicative abstraction that McDonald's possesses. With respect to the fourth proposition outlined above, so great is the signifying power of McDonald's that the levels of positive communicative abstraction it professes to embody have been openly challenged and debated in many different forums in recent years (from whence comes the range of empirical data available to us about the company). Such challenges have been to McDonald's manipulation of its principal signifiers. These are, first, to its concrete role as a producer, distributor and consumption-oriented/driven organization and to the allegedly dubious practices it pursues in these regards. Second, challenges have been made to McDonald's abstract role as a perceived representative of what is alleged to be the negative aspects of the Americanization of food and globalization. It is inconceivable that these challenges to McDonald's concrete role would have occurred but for the system inter-relationships between processes/activities and scale/structure that constitute the physical manifestation of McDonald's. At the same time, however, while challenges to McDonald's abstract role(s) have clear roots in the concrete, they have been directed to various perceived signifying and signified forces which may or may not have concrete implications. Most notoriously these include (but are not confined to) the supposedly negative health and lifestyle consequences of consuming McDonald's products. More important, though, has become a wider, and not always more explicit, debate over an even more abstract concept of what McDonald's represents in the modern world in terms of the Americanization and globalization of (American) culture. Such is the level of abstraction involved that McDonald's has been rendered the first true post-modern

hospitality organization, little more than a conceptual receptacle for various circulating signs and symbols imputed and inputted, to it. McDonald's barely exists at any concrete communicative level but has been replaced by a kind of über-McDonald's that co-exists with the 'real' McDonald's that customers use every day.

That customers do continue to use McDonald's in large numbers (despite the concerns periodically raised about the organization and its products) is a useful reminder of the 'ground level' issues with which this chapter is concerned. The technical systems employed by McDonald's (the sum of production and distribution techniques) are in any general sense uninteresting. In McDonald's (and many other fast food firms) it is supposed that the technological form has effects and influences upon personnel in terms of the experience of work, attitudes to work and interventions in the technical system unplanned by management (see Leidner, 1993). It is in the consumption context that McDonald's becomes interesting, not simply for the reasons outlined above but for the continuing motives that people have for consuming McDonald's products. Again, these have been well documented, and are varied. Many relate to the technical systems dimensions of McDonald's and fast food operations more generally, for example the rapid service and consistency of product quality the technology enables. It is the cultural meanings of McDonald's that are important however and these emphatically reside in the wider social and cultural context in which McDonald's operates. Nobody ever visited a fast food restaurant because of the technology it employs, but for what the technology represents in the wider cultural web of consumption.

CONCLUSION

This chapter started from the proposition that current perspectives on food production and service systems in hospitality amount to little more than descriptive frameworks devoid of any contextualization within wider food systems. Although system writers in this tradition recognize that micro-systems such as food production and service operate in a wider systems context, there is little evidence to suggest that this wider context is regarded as anything more than a cipher. Certainly there are no immediately evident discussions in the literature on the role of social context in the operation of food production and service systems.

Social scientific literature on food systems shows a general lack of precision or, if preferred, a higher level of abstraction. Nevertheless a useful fusion can be generated with the 'hospitality' literature and beginning to explore such a fusion has been one of the goals of this chapter, stopping short of previous approaches to 'modeling' food systems. Instead, a list of prescriptions or propositions have been generated as a framework from which future models of food systems may be derived. The emphasis of these propositions is unashamedly empiricist. There is intellectual satisfaction in generating models of phenomenon that serve as heuristics for explaining those phenomena. In the study of food systems, we have yet to come close to such an attainment. Before a modeling process takes place, it is first necessary to do more than simply chart and describe information. Rather, some conceptual framework is required that facilitates meaningful investigation and generates useful ideas and results. It is not claimed that the four propositions outlined here are the only possible strategies for achieving this. However, unless the study of hospitality food production and service systems breaks free of that intellectual straitjacket which restricts it to description of production-oriented processes and instead embraces a consumption-oriented approach, it is unlikely to cover more than the short intellectual distance already achieved. At the same time, we must recognize the limitations of extant social scientific approaches to food 'systems' but nevertheless attempt some broader fusion of these approaches with managerial 'systems' theories in order to widen the horizons of research in the field and offer some hope of progress in our understanding of the meanings of such systems.

NOTE

*This chapter is a revised and extended version of 'Closing a planning gap? The future of food production and service systems theory', first published in *Tourism and Hospitality Planning and Development*, 1, 1: 19–37 (2004). The author is grateful to the journal's publishers, Taylor and Francis (http://www.tandf.co.uk/journals) for permission to re-use the core manuscript here.

REFERENCES

Ashley, B., Hollows, J., Jones, S. and Taylor, B. (2004) *Food and Cultural Studies*. London: Routledge.

Ball, S., Jones, P., Kirk, D. and Lockwood, A. (2003) *Hospitality Operations: A Systems Approach*. London: Continuum.

Barthes, R. (1979 [1961]) 'Towards a psychosociology of contemporary food consumption'. In R. Forster and O. Ranum (eds) *Food and Drink in History*. Baltimore: Johns Hopkins University Press. pp. 166–173.

Beardsworth, A. and Keil, T. (1997) *Sociology on the Menu: An Invitation to the Study of Food and Society*. London: Routledge.

Bourdieu, P. (1984) *Distinction: A Social Critique of the Judgement of Taste*. London: Routledge and Kegan Paul.

Charles, N. and Kerr, M. (1988) *Women, Food and Families*. Manchester: Manchester University Press.

Culler, J. (1983) *Barthes*. Glasgow: Fontana.

Dearey, P. (2002) 'Systems thinking: a philosophy of management', *Reason in Practice*, 2(3): 73–82.

Douglas, M. (1975) 'Deciphering a Meal'. In M. Douglas (ed.) *Implicit Meanings*. London: Routledge and Kegan Paul. pp. 249–275.

Douglas, M. (1984) 'Standard social uses of food'. In M. Douglas (ed.) *Food in the Social Order: Studies of Food and Festivities in Three American Communities*. New York: Russell Sage Foundation. pp. 18–39.

Elias, N. (1978) *The Civilising Process, Volume 1: The History of Manners*. Oxford: Basil Blackwell.

Freckleton, A. M., Gurr, M. I., Richardson, D. P., Rolls, B. A. and Walker, A. F. (1989) 'Public perception and understanding'. In C. R. W. Spedding (ed.) *The Human Food Chain*. London: Elsevier Applied Science Publishers. pp. 17–57.

George, S. (1976) *How the Other Half Die*. Harmondsworth: Penguin.

Goody, J. (1982) *Cooking, Cuisine and Class*. Cambridge: Cambridge University Press.

Harris, M. (1986) *Good to Eat: Riddles of Food and Culture*. London: George Allen and Unwin.

Harris, M. (1987), 'Foodways: historical overview and theoretical prolegomenon'. In M. Harris and E. B. Ross (eds) *Food and Evolution: Towards a Theory of Human Food Habits*. Philadelphia: Temple University Press. pp. 57–90.

Hassard, J. (1993) *Sociology and Organization Theory*. Cambridge: Cambridge University Press.

Huelin, A. and Jones, P. (1990) 'Thinking about catering systems', *International Journal of Operations and Production Management*, 10(8): 42–52.

Johns, N. and Jones, P. (1999a) 'Systems and management: mind over matter', *The Hospitality Review*, July: 43–48.

Johns, N. and Jones, P. (1999b) 'Systems and management: the principles of performance', *The Hospitality Review*, October: 40–44.

Johns, N. and Jones, P. (2000) 'Systems and management: understanding the real world', *The Hospitality Review*, January: 47–52.

Jones, P. (1993) *A Taxonomy of Foodservice Operations*. Paper presented at the 2nd Annual CHME Research Conference, Manchester, April.

Jones, P. (1994a) 'Foodservice operations'. In P. Jones and P. Merricks (eds) *The Management of Foodservice Operations*. London: Cassell. pp. 3–17.

Jones, P. (1994b) 'Catering systems'. In B. Davis and A. Lockwood (eds) *Food and Beverage Management: A Selection of Readings*. Oxford: Butterworth-Heinemann. pp. 131–144.

Kirk, D. (2000) 'The value of systems in hospitality management', *The Hospitality Review*, April: 55–56.

Leach, E. (1974) *Levi-Strauss*. London: Fontana.

Lehrer, A. (1969) 'Semantic cuisine', *Journal of Linguistics*, 5(1): 39–55.

Leidner, R. (1993) *Fast Food, Fast Talk: Service Work and the Rationalisation of Everyday Life*. Berkeley, CA: University of California Press.

Lévi-Strauss, C. (1965) 'The culinary triangle', *Partisan Review*, 33: 586–595.

Marshall, D. (1995) *Food Choice and the Consumer*. London: Blackie.

Mennell, S. (1985) *All Manners of Food: Eating and Taste in England and France from the Middle Ages to the Present*. Oxford: Basil Blackwell.

Mennell, S., Murcott, A. and Van Otterloo, A. (1992) *The Sociology of Food: Eating, Diet and Culture*. London: Sage.

Mercer, K. (1977) Some phenomena and limitations on the understanding of why we eat, *HCIMA Review*, 2(2): 65–75.

Murcott, A. (1982) 'On the social significance of the "cooked dinner" in South Wales', *Social Science Information*, 21(4/5): 677–696.

Murcott, A. (1988) 'Sociological and social anthropological approaches to food and eating', *World Review of Nutrition and Dietetics*, 55: 1–40.

Ritzer, G. (1996) *The McDonaldization of Society*. Thousand Oaks, CA: Pine Forge Press.

Rojek, C. (1985) *Capitalism and Leisure Theory*. London: Tavistock.

Sturrock, J. (1986) *Structuralism*. London: Paladin.

Waller, K. (1996) *Improving Food and Beverage Performance*. Oxford: Butterworth-Heinemann.

Warde, A. and Martens, L. (2000) *Eating Out*. Cambridge: Cambridge University Press.

Wood, R. C. (1995) *The Sociology of the Meal*. Edinburgh: Edinburgh University Press.

Licensed Retail Management

21

Conrad Lashley

INTRODUCTION

The licensed retail industry is fast-moving and dynamic, like few others in Britain. As the name suggests, the sector covers the retailing of alcohol for consumption both on and off the premises, through sites that are both directly managed by large branded corporations, and through non-branded outlets owned and managed by individual retailers. This chapter focuses on the sector where the license to sell alcohol is principally to consume alcohol *on* the premises, because the public house, or pub as it is colloquially known, involves a venue for hospitality and hospitableness. Pubs, bars and inns, as distinct from hotels and restaurants, are mostly operations which specialize in selling alcoholic beverages, though some do offer residential accommodation, and food is increasingly an important part of licensed retail operations.

There are 59,224 pubs in Britain (*The Publican*, 2006). Outlets have to be close to their customers and each pub, bar, café or inn has a manager/licensee who is responsible for the conduct of the pub as well as the development of the business. Those managing pubs, bars and cafés have to be hospitable and responsible for ensuring that guests are entertained, as well as ensuring that product and service quality meet expectations, and that the business is commercially successful. In these highly complex contexts, managers have to be 'reflective practitioners' capable of thinking and doing, of being flexible and adaptable. A sociable and hospitable personality, with good people skills, and business acumen are essential for success in the sector.

Table 21.1 shows a classification of pub ownership in the UK. It can be seen that more than 70% of pubs are owned by a pub group or regional brewer. The pub groups and regional brewers operate pubs as either directly managed, tenanted or leasehold businesses where the pub company owns the premises but the pub is run as an independent business by the tenant or lessee.

There are two broad pathways for managers working in the sector, as a salaried manager, or through some form of self-employment. The increase in size and scale of many retail-oriented pub, bar and café operations means the manager's role is being increasingly professionalized. The opportunities for self-employment are vast. The most dominant form of pub management is through 'tenancy' or 'lease' arrangements and there are many opportunities as pub company tenants or lessees. The second opportunity for self-employment comes via the 'free house' sector. Typically, the pub or bar property is independently owned by the licensee. The building is owned by the licensee and family, and the business is free to buy supplies in the marketplace.

This chapter is structured round a description of the licensed retail sector, exploring some of the sector characteristics, the key players, trends and observations about key management issues and key dynamics facing the sector together with some insights into careers in licensed retail management.

RECENT BACKGROUND

By the late 1980s the major brewers dominated an increasingly concentrated brewing industry.

Table 21.1 Pub ownership, January 2006

Ownership type	Pubs	Market share%
Pub groups (multiple)	33,090	55.9
Free houses	16,450	27.8
Regional brewers	9,684	16.3
Total	59,224	

Source: *The Publican* (2006: 8).

The number of brewers in the UK supplying more than one outlet (that is, excluding micro breweries) had shrunk from 362 companies in 1950 to 141 in 1988, and a handful of firms supplied three out of every four pints of beer drunk in Britain. Furthermore, the major brewers controlled over 53% of pubs, mostly the larger more profitable properties. The key motive for owning pubs was to secure guaranteed outlets for the brewers' beer product. Those pubs owned by the breweries were 'tied' to the particular brewery owner because tied pubs had to buy beer, and other drinks from the brewer that owned them. Clearly, brewers sold their output to other buyers through independent pubs, or hotels, or clubs on the open market, though in competition with other brewers. However, the 'tie' secured a substantial internal market for brewery outputs. The vertical integration of the brewery and pubs, also allowed the major brewers to extract profits at both the production and distribution stages of the process. Given the power of the big six breweries at the time, there was an oligopoly whereby a majority of beer production was in the hands of six companies and these same companies owned a substantial part of the retail end of the chain, in the form of the pub estate.

Against this background the then government enacted legislation that has had a profound effect on the industry and career structures. The 'Beer Orders' resulting from a Monopoly and Mergers Commission (MMC) report set about breaking up a 'complex monopoly' (Williams and Lincoln, 1996) much against the advice of the major companies. This led to a significant and concerted campaign resulting in a watering down of the original recommendations. The key provisions in these regulations were:

- brewers owning over 2,000 licensed premises have to make half the number owned over 2,000 free of the exclusive tie to the brewer;
- brewers were required to allow the tied pubs to stock one 'guest' beer from another brewer; and
- all pubs were free of any tie for the supply of non-beer products including soft drinks, wines and spirits, etc.

Although there is considerable doubt whether the subsequent structure of the industry has increased choice and reduced uncompetitive pricing for customers, the effects of the 'Beer Orders' have been profound (Key Note, 1997). The intention of the free market ideology was

that the brewing and licensed retail industry would subsequently be ordered round smaller brewers and more independent publicans. However, the impact has been different, as Mintel (1998) estimated that a 6% reduction in pub outlets occurred between 1993 and 1998. This represented some 5,000 fewer properties. Similarly, there are now fewer brewers because virtually all national and some regional brewers have sold off their brewing interests to concentrate on retailing activities. Greenall Whitley, Boddingtons, Devenish and Grand Metropolitan are all examples. In the latter case, Grand Metropolitan did a 'pubs for breweries' swap with Courage. Courage subsequently set up Inntrapreneur Estates with Grand Metropolitan's leased pubs. As a consequence of this and other acquisitions, there are now only two major brewing companies in the UK (Coors, and Scottish and Newcastle), though regional brewers like Greene King and Wolverhampton and Dudley are developing an increasingly national profile. The immediate impact of the 'Beer Orders' on pub ownership by the major brewers can be seen in Table 21.2. Change has continued apace, since these changes were charted, Allied Lyons and Grand Metropolitan have ceased to brew altogether, Allied Lyons have divested themselves of all their pubs and the estates of Bass and Whitbread have seen reduced pub holdings (Price, Bleakley and Pennington, 1999). Table 21.3 shows that the current big six pub operators have little in common with these earlier brewer owners.

The MMC recommendations also resulted in different types of companies emerging as owners and operators of pubs. As we have seen, prior to the orders the brewers had been significant owners of pubs. Subsequently, five types of pub operators or licensed retailers emerged as a result of the beer orders:

- national retailer with brewing interests (though none now exists);
- national retailer with no brewing interests (either de-merged or fully independent) – directly managed or indirectly managed through tenancy or leasehold arrangements;
- regional or local retailer with brewing interests;
- regional or local multiple retailer with no brewing interests; and
- totally independent operator or free house.

Significantly, the national brewers have all divested their pub interests and either operate

Table 21.2   Pub ownership by the UK's biggest brewers, 1989–1992

	1989 (pre-MMC rules)			November 1992 (post-MMC rules)				
	Tenanted	Managed	Total	Tenanted	Managed	Leased	Total tied	Total owned
Allied-Lyons	4,458	2,400	6,858	1,900	2,700	1,200	4,600	5,800
Bass	4,285	2,469	6,754	–	3,100	1,400	–	4,500
Courage	4,620	400	5,020	–	–	–	–	–
Grand Metro	3,200	1,580	4,780	2,300	1,650	4,200	–	8,150
Scottish and Newcastle	1,504	850	2,354	1,000	850	–	1,850	
Whitbread	4,600	2,000	6,600	400	1,600	2,300	–	4,300
			31,766					22,750

Source: Williams (1996: 23).

Table 21.3   Pub ownership by the UK's biggest pub operators, January 2006

Pub operator	Pubs with tenancy / leasehold	Pubs managed	Total
Punch Taverns	9,810	–	9,810
Enterprise Inns	8,673	–	8,673
Greene King	1,100	1,300	2,400
Wolverhampton and Dudley	1,290	1,000	2,920
Mitchell and Butlers	–	1,900	1,900
S and N Pub Enterprise	–	1,170	1,170
Total	21,503	5,370	26,873

Source: The Publican (2006: 9).

these as independent companies or have sold their pub estates to other multiple pub operators. Table 21.3 shows that four of the big six pub operators have no brewery linked interests. The two regional brewer/retailers – Greene King and Wolverhampton and Dudley have brewing and pub estates spanning both directly managed and tenanted/leasehold arrangements. Both Mitchell and Butlers and Scottish and Newcastle Pub Enterprises are now licensed retailers with no brewery, though they were formerly owned by Bass and Scottish and Newcastle respectively.

There are significant differences between these categories of retailer in terms of the way they operate their outlets and indeed in the type of outlets they own. In particular, there is a tendency for retailers to want to directly manage the large city- and town-centre sites with high volume sales. The smaller urban and suburban pubs tend to be indirectly managed (or non-managed) in the form of tenancies or leaseholds. The regional brewers tend to have pub interests mostly centred on specific geographical locations. Typically they will have both managed and tenanted properties in their

estates, but again these general principles apply. The higher volume outlets are directly managed whilst more marginal businesses are let out to tenants/leaseholders. Single ownership or free house outlets account for something like 28% of the total pub estate (*The Publican*, 2006). Many of these are in rural or suburban locations and increasingly rely on food sales as the key source of their income. The emergent gastro-pub is often located in these properties run by a chef-owner.

A further consequence of the 'Beer Orders' has been a high level of churn in ownership of pubs as companies have merged and divested pubs in the estate which do not meet the profile of properties which the owners now require. Table 21.4 lists the number of pubs changing hands in corporate deals over the last decade. These figures exclude the churn in ownership of the independently owned 'free houses'. Estimates suggest that this is something in the region of 30% per year (Lashley and Rowson, 2000; 2006), say an additional 4,000–5,000

Table 21.4   A decade of change: corporate pub deals, 1996–2005

Year	Number of pubs changing hands	Deal values (£m)[a]
1996	4,383	910
1997	7,250	1,987
1998	3,202	935
1999	12,173	7,695
2000	5,075	2,841
2001	6,350	4,500
2002	8,269	3,760
2003	6,161	4,430
2004	8,467	3,034
2005	5,646	4,609

[a] Figures exclude undisclosed sums and include other major assets e.g. breweries
Source: The Publican (2006: 10).

independent pub properties changing hands each year.

CONSUMER TRENDS

Pub-going and the profile of typical customers have gone through some dramatic changes over recent years (*The Publican*, 2006). These are having a fundamental effect on the nature of products being offered in the pub, and most importantly on the nature of the management of these businesses. Despite the general growth of other activities, going to the pub still remains the UK's most popular out-of-home leisure activity (Mintel, 1998). However, when compared with the immediate post-war period, pub customers are less overwhelmingly male beer drinkers. Typically, pub customers in the new millennium are likely to include more women, families, youth and older people. They are drinking more soft and low alcohol drinks, wine and coffee and eating breakfasts in pubs. Coffee, soft drinks and the sale of breakfast

are becoming important sources of pub, bar and café profits. More *extra cold*, premium label beers and lagers and packaged drinks are being consumed, and customers are much more likely to eat in pubs (Mintel, 2006). Increasingly pubs offer leisure facilities and games in the pub and these represent major sources of income.

Table 21.5 confirms some important features of consumer demand in the pub sector. As suggested above, pubs are increasingly places where people go to eat. As a whole, more visit a pub to eat rather than just to drink, both in the week and at weekends, though some interesting variations dependent on age, gender and socio-economic group. 25–34 year-olds are most likely to eat out in pubs more at the weekend than during the week, suggesting the presence of children. People in social groups A, B and C eat out more than other groups. Younger people are more likely to go out to pub, bars and cafés to drink than older age groups, as are non-married people and males.

The increased emphasis on retailing and identifying market segments to target tightly

Table 21.5 Eating out and visiting a pub by gender, age, socioeconomic group and marital status

	Eating out, e.g. or pub restaurant		Visiting a pub or club for drinks	
	Weekday (%)	Weekend (%)	Weekday (%)	Weekend (%)
All	39	42	27	32
Gender				
Men	39	42	35	39
Women	39	42	20	25
Age (yrs)				
18–24	39	40	52	58
25–34	38	48	36	43
35–44	36	42	26	33
45–54	37	42	23	26
55–64	42	43	25	28
65+	41	39	13	14
Socioeconomic group				
AB	48	51	26	30
C1	44	51	32	38
C2	38	42	29	34
D	31	33	29	31
E	26	24	16	20
Marital status				
Married	39	44	22	27
Not married	39	40	35	39

Source: Mintel (2006: 55).

defined service offers, among other things, has increased the use of branding in the licensed retailing sector. In particular, branding is focused at demographic groupings and pub-visit occasions, such as, circuit/pre-club, chatting to friends, special meal out, that suggests an array of service attributes, such as service style, ambience, music, food offered, as well as the drinks available.

Since the 1990s, branding in the licensed retailing sector has moved away from the beer product to include the total customer experience. Even in units that are not formally branded, the impact of targeting has been profound. Scottish and Newcastle, for example, make a distinction between branding and 'blueprinting'. In the latter case, the pub is aimed at identified customer types, but is not 'presented' as an identified brand with a common name and signage etc. However, unit management is trained to understand the customer occasions relevant to their pub and the 'critical success factors' in the achievement of customer satisfaction. This approach recognizes the limitations of branding and the application of more sophisticated retailing practices.

The combined impact of these factors has led to dramatic changes in the strategic objectives of businesses and a radical restructuring of the industry sector, as noted earlier. Earlier motives to secure distribution outlets and markets for brewed cask beer through the tie have become increasingly less relevant. Table 21.4 shows that the new millennium has seen the sector going through a period of turbulent change, with mergers and divestment announced on a regular basis. As a consequence, organization forms are in a period of transition with several contradictory tensions. The need to establish consistent brands with uniform operating systems creates pressures for highly centralized procedures and controls, yet at the same time successful units require flexibility and responsiveness to local customers and market needs.

On another level, the shift away from a preoccupation with outlets for beer sales means that skills needed by the manager are different. The management of fast-moving, heavily branded, market-focused businesses, which have significant income streams from an array of sources, requires multi-skilled managers who are far removed from the stereotypical husband and wife publican traditionally described as a 'nice couple who keep a good pint'. In the twenty-first century, unit managers have to be able to understand the food and other income stream

operations as well as the alcohol and drinks operation. They need to analyse the markets and customer segments that use the business and the variety of occasions that trigger a trip to the pub and, based on this analysis, effectively promote their pub to precise customer groups and think strategically about how to grow and develop the business over time. In addition they are required to manage and motivate employees, as well as control service quality and standards, running the unit as an independent business whilst at the same time being constrained by brand operating standards and centralized decision making.

Bearing these changes in mind, it is likely that the sector will increasingly require managers, particularly in the branded sector, who are professionals capable of exercising responsible autonomy. These managers must be able to operate in an entrepreneurial way within the confines and disciplines of the brand. They will be responsible for units that, in themselves, are considerable businesses.

BUSINESS FORMATS

As has been discussed above, the pub, bar and café sector's structure of its recent history, and environment factors such as economic drivers and legislative framework. Indeed these influences are what give the licensed retail sector in the UK a unique profile compared with many other countries internationally. This section of the chapter explores three different formats through which pubs, bars and cafés are owned and managed.

The managed sector

In the past brewers owned pubs but operated them in the form of directly managed properties, or in the form of tenancies. All were typically branded round the brewery and product – Bass; Courage; Tetley; Watney, for example. The customer was not immediately aware whether the pub was being directly managed or whether there was a tenant operating the pub. Frequently the brewers would manage the more profitable pubs, and the less profitable properties would be let out to tenants. Often the same pub would move from tenant to manager and back again as a tenant built up the business and the brewery stepped in take advantage of the extra profit, or

Table 21.6 Top managed estate pub companies, January 2006

Rank	Pub operator	Number of pubs
1	Mitchell and Butlers PLC	1,900
2	Punch Taverns	1,832
3	Greene King Pub Company	900
4	Whitbread Restaurants	670
5	J D Wetherspoon	670
6	Pathfinder Pubs (W and DB)	542
7	Globe Pub Co	470
8	Laurel Pub Co	410
9	London and Edinburgh Inns	300
10	Luminar Leisure	245

Source: The Publican (2006: 15).

let tenants bear the business risk of a pub that was not profitable.

In recent years, as a result of the Monopolies and Mergers Commission's 'Beer Orders', all national brewers have divested themselves of pubs. However, firms have emerged which own and directly manage large estates of pubs. Table 21.6 lists some of the largest companies and some of their brands. Initially the large breweries developed a more retailing focus through the last three decades of the twentieth century. By the late 1980s Allied-Lyons, Bass Courage, Grand Metropolitan, Scottish and Newcastle; and Whitbread directly managed 10,000 pubs. The shake-out caused by the restrictions on ownership introduced by the MMC 'Beer Orders' have meant that none of these major pub companies still continues to trade as a brewer-retailer. Only Scottish and Newcastle Retail and Whitbread exist as trading names. Both have divested their brewery activities and trade under a number of retail brands. Scottish and Newcastle, for example, operates John Barras, as a chain of larger local community pubs, Chef and Brewer and a string of other pubs with a substantial food offer. Whitbread Restaurants have now divested all wet-led pubs and bars and now operate mostly food-led outlets such as TGI Friday's, Brewer's Fayre and Beefeater Restaurants. Although most of these properties now take a large part of total sales in the form of food sales, many still have the persona and ambience associated with a bar or pub.

In addition, firms like J D Wetherspoon have emerged as multi-site retailers operating on a vast scale. Taking average sales per unit as a measure, J D Wetherspoon is now the largest pub retailer in the UK, its 650 pubs individually take

an average £1,500,000 per year. Each manager is, therefore, managing a significant business in its own right. In these circumstances the company is developing a more professional management workforce capable of managing and developing each pub as a unique business unit. Whilst the average sales of a J D Wetherspoon unit is around £30,000 per week and in some cases individual units are taking £80,000 per week, the average for most managed properties is somewhere in the region of £15,000–£20,000 per week. In fact J D Wetherspoon has been a leading player in the new pub format, large space, high footfall, busy locations. Others have emulated the approach but the company's business model has shifted the scale on which the managed pub estate operates. The company has often opened pub and bar premises in former banks and insurance company premises because of their size and location.

The managed pub sector has learnt much from traditional retailing operations. Branding of the name and signifiers of the offer, such as pricing strategies, menu format, service quality, staff performance and appearance are all consistent with establishing brand perceptions in the market place. In the past, branding was largely influenced by the brewery product and range associated with their 'wet' product output. As a consequence pub branding frequently missed out service quality and the quality of hospitality received by the customers. There was a uniformity of mediocrity or in some cases, massive variability of the customer experience in different pubs within the same brand. Now these managed pub operators better understand the service quality experiences required, but still have some difficult tensions to manage.

For example, attempts to manage a consistent customer offer over hundreds, if not thousands, of pubs across the estate is challenging. There are clearly McDonaldizing (Ritzer, 2007) tendencies with these large companies, however customers want some sense of local uniqueness. So some organizations move to a looser brand format which provides a consistent offer in some dimensions, but does not have every unit looking the same in every location. J D Wetherspoon for example, displays the name of the company on the premises, though under the name of the individual pub. The pricing strategy and principles of the service delivery remain the same across the pubs, though décor and the precise product mix in food and drinks menus vary slightly to meet local customer needs.

In other cases, say as with Chef and Brewer, the brand name tends to be more upfront than the immediate pub name. The offer to customers appears to communicate bespoke production and a country pub atmosphere, though in practice it has much consistency across the estate.

In all cases, a management process ensuring consistency, brand standards, management training and development, together with staff training and the management of labour retention are important determinants of successful pub operations in the managed estate. Not all companies have an understanding of the process and priorities needed, and this can contribute to churn in the managed pub estate as individual pubs, and whole pub brands, are successfully managed, or not, as the case may be.

Clearly focused marketing messages aimed at well-defined market segments, women, families, life-cycle position enable pub brands to be more customer focused. Economies of scale enabled through high volume sales, advantageous purchasing and the spread of fixed costs are at the root of the managed house business format, though the skills, motivation and entrepreneurial drive of the immediate unit management are fundamental to success.

Beyond the individual pubs and the immediate unit management personnel, most pub companies will incorporate a multi-unit management hierarchy. Usually, an area manager will be responsible for a cluster of pubs and typically these are organized round a geographical location, though in the case of multi-branded organizations, they may be responsible for a number of pubs in a specific brand. The area manager's role is to ensure brand standards and business performance targets are maintained. They provide support to immediate unit management in their 'patch' and undertake a programme of visits focused on the business in each pub. Clearly, span of control is a significant issue here. Typically an area manager is responsible for about 15–20 pubs in the 'managed house sector'. The more properties each manager is responsible for, the less time that can be spent with each one. In many cases, companies use 'mystery customer' visits and internal quality audits to manage the quality of the service encounter.

The non-managed sector

In the past the major brewer/retailers operated more marginal pubs, in the form of tenancies.

Table 21.7   Top ten tenanted and leased pub companies (non-managed estate)

Rank	Pub operator	Number of pubs
1	Enterprise Inns Plc	8,637
2	Punch Taverns	7,978
3	The Union Pub Co (WandDB)	1,750
4	Greene King Pub Partners	1,500
5	Scottish and Newcastle Pub Enterprises	1,170
6	Wellington Pub Co	839
7	Admiral Taverns Ltd	790
8	London and Edinburgh Inns	590
9	Pubfolio Ltd	545
10	Trust Inns	509

Source: *The Publican* (2006: 17).

Tenancies were linked to the 'brand' in the form of the named brewery, but this had a limited impact on operating systems or business format (Williams and Lincoln, 1996). In this case, the brewers name, e.g. Bass, Tetley's could generate customer loyalty through the brewery product. Tetley's in Yorkshire, for example has a solid loyal customer base because of customer loyalty to the beer brand – similar to other brands in other regions (see Table 21.7).

The relationship between the brewer/property owner and the tenant was generally loose. The tenant had to stock the beer products and purchase all supplies from the pub company. The tenancy was, however, a nominally independent organization, but tied to the bigger firm through property rental and source of supply. The 'tie' meant that the tenant or lessee was tied to buy drinks from the brewery. Frequently properties were 'churned' through periods of being let to tenants and being taken back into the directly managed estate when the tenant had built up the business (Lashley and Rowson, 2000). The tenant had little security of tenure because tenancy agreements were short-lived and the tenancy could not be sold or accrue added value as the business developed.

In many ways, firms operating in the sector followed what Johnston (1989) called 'cost leadership' strategies. In other words they conducted business in a way that minimized costs as a key means of generating profit and competing with other companies. Few companies seemed to be concerned with strategies that gave priority to service quality or service uniqueness, for example. The high levels of staff turnover (Lashley and Rowson, 2000) and generally low levels of training (HtF, 1996) were consistent with firms seeking to minimize labour costs by taking advantage of a large labour market. The 'churning' of the pub estate was also consistent with cost minimization strategies, as it shifted the operating cost for the more marginal properties to the tenant, and when the property became profitable again it was brought back into the directly managed estate.

Over the last decade, and particularly as a result of the changes in ownership patterns, the tenancy arrangement was criticized by pub companies because they believed that tenants had little incentive to grow the business. They were not able to assign the tenancy and thereby gain from capital investment or improved business value (Whitbread Inns, 1995). They could take profits from increased sales and higher volume business activity, but this was not translated into business value. With minimal risk to the brewer and minimal support to the tenant, many tenancies failed to meet their full potential because tenants had limited capital and managerial resources to grow the business. They too suffered from resource scarcity. Increasingly over the last decade, the licensed retail operators have explored leasing arrangements as a way of overcoming the perceived weaknesses of the tenancy (Key Note, 1997).

The leasing arrangement is chiefly focused at changing the financial arrangements between the lessee and the licensed retail organization (Guild, 1996). The aim is to encourage a more entrepreneurial relationship in which the lessee is said to have a financial incentive to invest in the development of the pub as a business opportunity. Typically the lessee pays a more commercial rent, for a property which has some track record as a business (Lincoln, 1996). Table 21.8 lists some of the key differences between tenancy and leasing arrangements.

There are variations in both the levels of restriction placed on the lessee and the levels of support given by the pub company. The branded operations are more likely to require the lessee to conform to brand standards, and provide structured management development and training programmes. Innpartnership, for example, charge all 'franchisees' an annual fee based on 2% of turnover, and this finances a programme of courses to improve the management skills of 'franchisees' (Lashley and Lincoln, 2000).

Though some would disagree (Wormald and Hartley, 1999), in many ways, 'one can view

Table 21.8 Tenancy and lease arrangements in licensed retailing

	Tenancy	Lease
Term	5 years maximum – typically much less	Up to 20 years
Cost	Smaller in-going rent, less than market rate	Full leasehold purchase
		Realistic rent
	Capital investment – shared	Capital investment lessee – responsible
Conditions	Non-assignable	Assignable
	No minimum barrelage	Minimum barrelage penalties
	Usually tied for majority of products	Less wide-ranging tie
	A number of company-imposed constraints	Fewer constraints
Property maintenance	Joint responsibility	Lessee responsibility

Source: Lashley and Lincoln (2000: 205).

pubs owned by chains as well as those operated under long-term leasing as a form of franchising with no up-front fees' (Slade, 1998: 578). Certainly the literature and research on franchising hospitality services (Lashley and Morrison, 2000) can help inform a study of leasehold and tenanted relationships in licensed retailing. Franchising in licensed retailing is almost wholly based on the tenanted/leased agreements, which stem from the 'tie'. The tenant/lessee is, in part, buying access to a business organization that has expertise and a business profile for the venture. As Morrison (2000a) argues in relation to franchising, the owner-manager is minimizing risk by taking on the franchise arrangement. She describes a typical franchisee as being an 'intrapreneur' (Lessem, 1987) rather than an entrepreneur because of the restrictions placed on them by the operating system and the various other requirements to purchase supplies through the franchisor. In some ways, similar restrictions exist for the tenant/lessee in the licensed retail sector. Tenants and lessees have to purchase product through the pub company, the range of services and activities might be defined in the brand or 'blueprint'. That said, the operating standards and systems are generally much less restrictive than in some restaurant and hotel retail brands (Ball, 2000; Lashley, 2000; Taylor, 2000).

Whilst there are many similarities between pub tenancy/lease arrangements and franchising there are, however, some important differences when compared with the more traditional business format franchise. Chiefly, the brand standard applied to the brewer's product, but did not include service standards. Issues like service times, the cleanliness factors, ambience or the range of non-beer services offered are rarely specified in the tenancy or leasehold arrangement (Lashley and Lincoln, 2000).

Without the structure of a rigid business format the monitoring of unit performance tends to be limited to monitoring beer quality and the solidity of the tie are the key concerns during visits by business development managers/operations consultants. Sales volumes, the ability to pay rents and other bills, and conduct an orderly house within the limits of the law are also concerns, but are generally handled only when problems arise (Wormald and Hartley, 1999). Service quality monitoring is minimal, if not non-existent, and support for tenant and lessees management development is equally minimal in many companies. Typically the relationship between the landlord/lessor and the tenant/lessee is much looser than it would be in a 'hard' brand such as McDonald's Restaurants (Price et al., 1999).

In particular, the barriers to entry are usually lower than in a typical franchise arrangement. Pub operators tended to be concerned with the applicant's ability to fund the ingoing (initial tenancy/lease) cost, and secure a license from the licensing authority. Franchisors, like McDonald's require a more substantial up-front fee and require the applicant to work in a restaurant for approximately one year, without a salary, before they are allowed to take on the franchise (Lashley, 2000). They have higher barriers to entry than pub companies, but the business survival rate of McDonald's franchisees is exemplary by comparison.

The relationship between tenants and pub operator's local manager is also much looser than it would be in a 'hard' brand like McDonald's. In the latter case, the operations consultant would work with approximately eight to ten franchised restaurants. Whilst there is an auditing dimension to the relationship because the 'consultant needs to check that the franchisee is working in the "one best way"; there is a considerable consultancy support dimension to the role in the fast food company' (Lashley, 2000). The relationship between tenants and business development managers (BDMs) involves a much greater span of control. Typically each business development manager is responsible for 50–60 pubs. The relationship and support available to the average pub tenant is therefore much lower, and suggests a potential 'fire-fighting' dimension to the BDM's priorities. In other words, most tenants would experience irregular and infrequent visits from the BDM because he/she is likely to be concentrating on the problem pubs.

As was argued above, pubs were turned over to indirect forms of control when the pub was deemed to be marginal as a source of revenue and profits (Slade, 1998). Often the higher volume properties with sales over £10,000 per week are directly managed, properties with sales over £5,000 but under £10,000 per week are let out as leaseholds, and pubs with sales under £5,000 per week are let as tenancies (Lashley and Lincoln, 2000). According to 'agency theory' (Mathewson and Winter, 1985; Brickley and Dark, 1987), the small firm owner has more incentive to grow the business than salaried managers do (Eisenhard, 1989). It is noteworthy that research in other fields has also defined this approach as 'resource scarcity theory' (Oxenfeldt and Kelly, 1969; Norton, 1988; Minkler, 1990). Here the general growth of the property-owning pub company is enhanced by having access to sources of financial capital, labour and managerial talent supplied by the tenant, lessee or franchisee.

The small firm operating a pub as a tenancy, lease or franchise can also be said to be attempting to overcome 'resource scarcity'. As a business venture, the tenant/lessee requires limited capital to take on a pub. The business may also be able to call on the resources and skills of the bigger firm, and in more branded operations is able to benefit from the market position and consumer knowledge of the brand in a way that would not be possible for a truly 'independent' small firm. In the past, the tenant had less access to the resources of the bigger firm but was able to benefit from lower rentals and the brand position of the beer product.

Small firms

The assumption at the root of the decision of many retail operators to change from tenanted to leased arrangement is that the short-run relationship implicit in the typical tenancy acted as a barrier to more entrepreneurial drives by the pub tenant. Many firms hoped that a longer-term relationship, more economic rents, and more entrepreneurial motivations would provide the licensees with growth inspired incentives. Whilst these factors might be important barriers to the entrepreneurial motives of some, the assumption that all small firms are driven by growth and profit maximization objectives is questionable. The Leeds Metropolitan University (Thomas et al., 2000) survey of 1,396 small tourism and hospitality firms showed that only 9% of respondents listed 'to make a lot of money' as a key motivation for owning a small business. 66% identified to 'make a reasonable living', 58% said they 'wanted to be my own boss', and 41% stated that a major reason for owning a small business was 'I enjoy this lifestyle'. These findings are consistent with earlier work on the motives of small-firm owners (Beaver and Lashley, 1998). Owners of these 'micro-firms' with ten or fewer employees, are mostly concerned with a cluster of 'lifestyle' motives for their entrepreneurial activities (Lockyer and Morrison, 1999). Table 21.9 reproduces the responses from the Leeds study. The question asked respondents to identify one or more reasons why they were running their own business.

The values expressed in Table 21.9 lists the total number of respondents who indicated that the statement reflected their objectives for owning the business. These responses give an interesting insight into the motives of people running small firms. In many ways, those operating tenanted, leasehold and the occasional franchised business are in a similar position. Price et al. (1999) have argued that often these businesses are being run at sub-optimal levels partly because the resources used are not charged at a fully economic rate due to family members working in the unit at less

than market rates. Often the pub represents a 'house for free' to the family. The family live above the pub, and many living costs are cross-subsidized by the business. Hence business costs and motives are ameliorated by these more domestic considerations. In effect, pub tenancy or lease provides both a commercial and a domestic setting for the tenant/lessee and there is a need to understand 'lifestyle economics' (Andrews et al., 2000) to better match potential tenants with properties.

The definitions and categories used by Morrison et al. (1999) are helpful because they suggest a number of categories that might apply to the core objectives of those engaged in tenanted or leasehold relationships. In essence they suggest that the term 'lifestyle proprietor' defines an individual who has a multiple set of goals associated with the business. Profitability in the business will only be one of these goals. In addition to the entrepreneurial venture, Beaver et al. (1998: 166) suggest that there are a number of other categories of small firm that may well differ in the nature of their business motives. They suggest that the lifestyle enterprise, the family enterprise, the female enterprise, the ethnic minority enterprise and enterprises where the dominant motives are for self-employment and control are likely to give different priorities to both profitability and their own developmental needs. They say:

> Whilst this is not an exhaustive list of entrepreneurial types, it is sufficient to show that the motives of those setting up and maintaining small hospitality firms are not always compatible with "rationale economic" considerations. Motives associated with personal preferences or which relate to self-image do not automatically lead to levels of self-analysis which suggest that a lack of business skills presents a major threat to their business goals.

In particular, these motives appear to impact on the small-firm owner's motives and interests in personal development. Beaver and Lashley (1998) suggest that lifestyle business objectives represent a barrier to the perception of the need for personal development and growth. Often these firms are economically satisficing. As long as the owner is able to meet the requirements of a reasonable standard of living they will not recognize the need to undertake courses that develop their managerial or entrepreneurial skills (Morrison, 2000b). That said, those running small firms do learn from

Table 21.9 Motivations for owning a small business

Motivation	Value (% of respondents)
To make a reasonable living	926 (66%)
To make a lot of money	125 (9%)
To be my own boss	813 (58%)
I enjoy this lifestyle	576 (41%)
To avoid unemployment	197 (14%)
To live in this location	287 (21%)
It is a form of semi-retirement	125 (9%)
I spotted a market opportunity	246 (18%)

Source: Thomas et al. (2000: 18).

their actions (Kolb, 1988) and Morrison (2000b) suggests that personal networks perform a valuable, if informal, source of education and training.

The relationship between the pub operating company and the tenants/lessees has many similarities with relationships found between franchisors and franchisees. The larger organization is attempting to gain benefits of scale by using the financial and managerial resources provided by the smaller firm. At the same time they aim to gain from the entrepreneurial drives of the tenant/lessee under the assumption that entrepreneurship and personal gain will stimulate extra effort when compared with the performance of salaried managers. From the small firm's perspective, the relationship with the larger firm allows access to the resources and expertise of the larger organization that might be denied to a truly independent enterprise. That said, research into the motives of those running small firms in the sector shows that frequently classically entrepreneurial motives are secondary to other more 'lifestyle' motives for operating the business (Thomas et al., 2000). As a consequence many tenants and lessees are not likely to give the highest priority to business growth and profit maximization. When compared with the formal business format franchising arrangements, the support given to tenants and leaseholds by the operating companies is minimal and may prove to be another factor preventing growth in the small firm.

The foregoing suggests that the selection of tenants and lessees in the licensed retail sector needs to be carefully focused on a realistic understanding of the different needs and motives of the small-firm owner. Only a small proportion will want to grow the business as a way of making a lot of money and they probably need to be carefully recruited and supported by the operating company. The majority are likely to be, to varying degrees, lifestyle entrepreneurs and are likely to be satisficing in business objectives. They, too, need to be carefully selected and recruited into units that are compatible with their needs. In particular, they may require some form of incentive to undertake and develop their personal skills and competencies.

The free house sector

The free house sector describes those pubs, bars and cafés typically owned by private individuals, free of a tie to a brewery or pub company.

The business is not leased from a pub company or brewery, nor is it tied to the company for sources of supply. The licensee is free to buy in supplies from any company and stock a wide array of products. Potentially, the business is able to make more profit because there is no rent to pay, and the operator can shop around for competitive prices for supplies of beer and other drinks. That said, these properties tend to be in the most marginal locations, rural settings, small towns and villages.

The cost of buying a free house is greater than the cost of buying a tenancy or lease, but typically in line with ownership of a large private dwelling. The business and the domestic aspect discussed earlier in relation to the tenanted and leasehold formats also apply here. These small firms are often owned and operated by people whose motives are not primarily entrepreneurial. These 'commercial homes' (Lynch, 2005) involve individuals running a business on the same premises as their domestic home. This has many implications for the management of these pub businesses. Like the tenant/lessee, free house owners frequently buy a pub having had limited experiences of pub management, hospitality management, or even small business management (Lashley and Rowson, 2006).

The term 'free house' has an important double meaning, because not only does it mean a pub that is free of any tie to a brewery or pub company, it also means that the domestic living arrangements are 'free' in relation to the business. For many, the motives involve 'lifestyle' concerns, a desire for more personal control, or living in a particular geographical location, or enjoyment of pub life. The link between small hospitality firms and domestic setting is very powerful in shaping the ambitions and priorities (Thomas et al., 2000), and behaviour of owner-managers (Lashley and Rowson, 2006). Often customers are evaluated on the basis of their match with the owner-manager's friendship set, rather than on more rational market segmentation strategies. Personal antipathy towards certain customer types can result in high-spend customers being turned away, because they are not consistent with the sorts of people the owner-manager would want in their home (Lashley and Rowson, 2007).

The newly emergent trend of 'gastro-pubs' has frequently been located in free house properties. The more marginal properties released by the pub companies are often seen as ideal settings for a food-led offer. From a chef/manager's perspective, pub properties have been available at affordable prices and frequently in locations close to customer market segments, looking for good quality individually cooked food as an antidote to the mass-produced pub food of the branded chain. The lack of a tie to a brewer means that a property can promote a range of products from different brewers, further underlining the more bespoke character of the pub and its offer to customers. The emergence of the gastro-pub has also coincided with increased trends in eating out and in the search for quality food, based on local supplies.

Despite recent innovations introduced by the gastro-pub, the free house sector continues to shrink, as the most marginal businesses operate at sub-economic level. Often the business survives by the use of the 'free labour' of family and friends. In some cases, failing pubs are taken over as domestic dwellings and withdrawn from the pub market, in other cases new owners take over the property. The churn in ownership is difficult to calculate, but research on the tenant/leasehold sector, and ownership of small hotels in Blackpool, suggests that a figure of 20–30% would not be far off. This could mean that 3,000–5,000 properties are changing hands each year (Lashley and Rowson, 2006).

The key problems faced by the free house sector are typically associated with marginal locations in positions where there is minimal pedestrian custom and people are required to drive to the pub. Strict anti-drink/driving legislation, creates a disincentive for most pub goers, hence the growth in the food offer. The lack of expertise in the management of pub business is also a major problem, because people are drawn to pub ownership for a variety of lifestyle reasons which often do not confront the realities of pub life. The link between the domestic and commercial can become blurred, leading individuals to spend money needed for the business. The customer profile may not be to the owner's liking and the business loses because the owner wants a different, more personally acceptable customer profile (Lashley and Rowson, 2006). Ultimately the owners' skills set is the key problem because many do not have even the operational skills, say in cellar management, to operate effectively. Most importantly the business management aspects of the owner/manager often represent 'unreported and latent' skill gaps whereby individuals do not

know what it is they do not know (Lashley et al., 2002).

KEY MANAGEMENT ISSUES

The licensed retail sector faces some challenges and business management issues that overlap with, but differ from, other sectors of the hospitality industry. Recent public concern about the negative health impacts of binge drinking, passive smoking and public order problems have meant that many commentators and industry practitioners have developed an interest in social responsibility and business ethics. The licensed retail sector has a particularly poor record for retaining frontline staff, with many managers, tenants/lessees and owner managers spending significant time and resources recruiting staff to replace leavers. An associated issue relates to the training and development of frontline staff and managers. Too many large and small operators tend to regard training as unnecessary, though it has a key impact on customer satisfaction and service quality. In response to some of the issues emerging from the increasing scale of operations in the contemporary pub sector, many organizations are attempting to professionalize their management as a means of addressing the challenge of a more retailing focus.

Social responsibility and ethical practice

Historically, the pub sector in the UK has been subject to much more regulation than has been the case in many mainland European countries. The narcotic nature of alcohol and its impact on workers' performance can be seen to be a matter of concern to legislators going back hundreds of years in Britain. Until the new licensing legislation which came into effect in recent years in Scotland and then England, Wales and Northern Ireland, the licensing legislation had its origins in the early twentieth century when tight controls limited the sale of alcohol to 'licensed premises'. Licenses were typically controlled by local licensing magistrates and the need to sell beer and other alcoholic drinks through a finite number of premises led the brewers to buy up the pub stock as a way of providing a license for the brewery's product and to exclude the sale of competitor products. Hence the situation, reported earlier in this chapter, that by the late

1980s six major brewers owned half of the pub stock.

Recently, the government has enacted new legislation, ostensibly to loosen the controls on the pub sector, and to move to a more mainland European-style café culture. Ironically the legislation came into effect at the height of public concerns over the impacts on health of passive smoking, and of drinking alcohol to excess, and of children and adults eating mass-produced 'junk' food, activities all associated with pubs, bars and cafés. In addition, there were concerns about perceived public order issues associated with city-centre drinking and well-televised incidents of public disorder problems arising from large numbers of young people engaged in 'circuit' drinking – moving from one venue to another in large numbers.

Renewed attention to the licensed retail sector did expose some industry practices that were interpreted as encouraging drinking to excess and drunkenness. 'Two for one drinks promotions', happy hour price reductions, 'as much as you can drink for £10' are all examples of sales promotions aimed at stimulating the sale of more alcohol. Although only an estimated 26% of British adults smoke tobacco and many workplaces had banned smoking, pubs were places where smoking was usually allowed. Few pubs, bars and cafés had efficient air-conditioning systems and there were loud public health concerns about pub visiting, even for non-smokers. At the time of writing (early 2007), legislation is about to come into force banning smoking in all public buildings including pubs in England, Wales and Northern Ireland. Scotland and Eire introduced smoking bans earlier. Certainly smoking has presented sector management with ethical issues to consider. J D Wetherspoon for example, banned smoking at the bar so as to protect staff health, almost from the time of origination of the chain.

Concerns expressed over healthy eating and the low nutritional value of children's menus have also had an impact on unfavourable perceptions of the pub sector's food menu. High levels of fried and fatty foods together with the use of chemical preservatives have all raised customer awareness of the mass-produced foods that make up much of the pub food menu. Food apart, the sale of alcohol and tobacco in pubs, bars and cafés does involve the sale of harmful toxins which can bring about health problems and death when inappropriately handled. In these circumstances

managers have to have a reasonable under-standing of trading in a legal and sociably responsible manner together with business ethics in general.

In providing an overview of some the ethical issues in business organizations and management, Fisher and Lovell (2003) present a valuable grid devised from two continua. The first dimension relates to the distinction between ethics and morality. In many cases, writers use the terms interchangeably, but understanding licensed retailing issues can be enhanced by seeing these terms as meaning different things. Current industry codes, such as those issued by the British Institute of Innkeeping are concerned with ensuring operators do no harm to clients, are examples of morality. Ethics on the other hand, is more concerned with ensuring good behaviour. 'Ethics is a term that can be thought of as developmental, whereas morality is judgemental' (Fisher and Lovell, 2003: 30). Morality usually involves lists of rules, of codes of what not to do and restrictions on actions that might harm others. Codes opposing some of the drinks promotion strategies discussed earlier are examples of actions by pub companies to limit harm to clients. Ethics are virtues of desirable values that help people to do good actions. Variations along this continuum will be discussed later, but the key point made in this chapter is that licensed retail organizations can gain competitive advantage by being concerned with ethics.

The second dimension in Fisher and Lovells' grid relates to dimensions covering 'good and wrong' and legal and illegal actions. Right and wrong refer to moral or ethical actions, whilst legal and illegal actions relate to actions in relation to the relevant legal codes. They identify four positions on this continuum. These are represented in Figure 21.1 and described below.

Actions that are good and legal, but not a legal obligation

Given the ideology of many corporations which defines their key duty as to increase shareholder value, many licensed retailers may see this as unnecessary. Others might consider that they also have duties to other stakeholders that means that they should, say, limit smoking areas ahead of legislation, promote responsible drinking with low alcohol alternatives, and healthy eating with low calorie menu items.

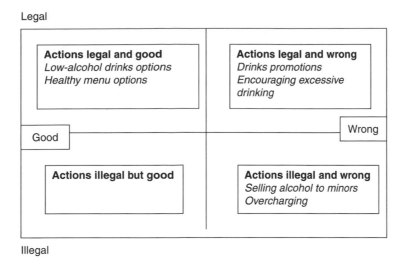

Legal

Actions legal and good
Low-alcohol drinks options
Healthy menu options

Actions legal and wrong
Drinks promotions
Encouraging excessive drinking

Good

Wrong

Actions illegal but good

Actions illegal and wrong
Selling alcohol to minors
Overcharging

Illegal

Figure 21.1   Mapping actions that are legal or illegal, good or bad

Actions that are both wrong and illegal

In some instances high profile cases have included examples of these where managers and employees have served alcohol to people who are under age, or to customers who are already drunk.

Actions that are legal but wrong

This category is the one most likely to involve business and management decisions in licensed retailing, because they relate to these fundamental issues about obligations to shareholders alone, or to a wider set of stakeholder interests – customers – employees – suppliers – communities. In some cases, being 'economical with the truth' that is falling short of telling lies but does either mislead the customer, or cover up useful information. It might also include decisions to pay employees low wages, or to cut back on food quality, or promote excessive drinking.

Actions that are good, but illegal

This category includes actions that may be morally good but illegal. For example, during Apartheid in South Africa, several US and British firms took the view that it was their global duty to adhere to an equal opportunities policy, and broke the South African law by promoting black and coloured workers and providing equal employment rights. Clearly actions in this category lead to some difficult considerations, because organizations are not

free to disobey laws or legal obligations, just because they dislike them. In most countries they are free to lobby and campaign for legislation to be changed, and so decisions to disobey the law are unusual.

The point here is that although licensed retail firms are legally bound to be lawful, they can adopt one of a number of positions in relation to their business practice. As members of one of the trade bodies, they also accept obligations to abide by these associations' codes. Do they exceed these legal obligations and codes in their business practice, or do they abide by the letter of the codes but otherwise adopt practices that break the spirit of them? To some extent, these questions can be better understood through the use of Fisher and Lovell's second dimension relating to ethics and morality. Figure 21.1 is adapted from their grid (2003: 34). Certainly the grid does provide a number of options from which to build a profile as a socially responsible and ethical practitioner. Actions that are legal and good particularly have the potential to build competitive advantage when compared with other firms in the sector.

Labour turnover and staff retention

The retention of well-trained and well-motivated employees is a key issue facing the pub, bar and café sector. The nature of the pub-going experience requires a sense of community

Table 21.10   Staff turnover by unit in one region

Unit	Employees per unit	Recruits over 12 months	Annual staff turnover rate [a]	Cost per unit @ £500	Cost per post £ [a]
1	13	29	224%	£14,500	£1,115
2	18	30	167%	£15,000	£833
3	9	16	178%	£8,000	£889
4	19	17	89%	£8,500	£447
5	11	16	145%	£8,000	£727
6	8	14	175%	£7,000	£875
7	28	45	160%	£22,500	£804
8	17	24	141%	£12,000	£706
9	12	18	150%	£9,000	£750
10	15	26	173%	£13,000	£867
11	10	19	190%	£9,500	£950
12	10	35	350%	£17,500	£1,750
13	22	43	194%	£22,500	£1,023
14	11	16	145%	£8,000	£727
15	11	35	318%	£17,500	£1,591
16	24	69	287%	£34,500	£1,438
17	17	36	211&	£18,000	£1,059
18	8	54	675%	£27,000	£3,375
19	13	18	138%	£9,000	£692
20	6	7	117%	£3,500	£583
21	20	19	95%	£9,500	£475

[a] Rounded to nearest whole number.

belonging and hosts engaging with welcome guests (Lashley et al., 2007). Even amongst circuit drinkers, where groups may use a number of venues, the link between the host and key decision makers in the group is essential for ensuring that the venue remains on the circuit. The transaction between bar staff and management, and regular customers is a fundamental aspect of ensuring customer satisfaction and loyalty. In these circumstances individual employees are an important asset to the business because they develop relationships with customers who become friends (Lashley and Morrison, 2003). In some cases, the aesthetic qualities of the employees can be a considerable draw for customers (Nixon and Warhurst, 2007). Staff turnover can therefore be very damaging to the customer experience and ultimately to the success of the business, yet many pubs, bars and cafés find it difficult to retain staff. One of the few systematic studies of staff turnover in the licensed retail sector, the Lashley and Rowson study (2000), estimated that staff turnover was costing £300 million per year.

A telephone survey of 30 firms revealed an average staff turnover of 188% across the firms. This ranged from 90% in one company to 305% in another. Thirteen of the 30 firms experienced staff turnover in excess of 200%. The standard

deviation (51.4) showed that 95% of the firms had turnover between 134 and 236% per annum. The size of firms appeared to make no difference to the rate of staff turnover. The number of units in the chain, the number of employees and the number of employees per unit showed no significant correlation with staff turnover levels. Table 21.10 reports on the findings from one region for one company.

Several firms had recorded staff turnover levels by brand and managerial area. One company noted staff turnover via manager responsibilities, and this indicated that in an organization with an average turnover of 208%, the rate varied from 118 to 388% in different units in the chain. In another company, one geographical area covering 21 units averaged 200% staff turnover across the region, but this ranged from 89 to 675%.

Costing out the financial implications of staff turnover is rarely undertaken by practitioners but the pub sector research project on staff turnover (Lashley and Rowson, 2000) estimated a tangible cost of at least £500 per replacement. This was based on the researchers' calculation of the costs involved, however it did not take account of some of the more intangible costs such as increased customer dissatisfaction or lost customers. Currently the Chartered Institute of

Personnel and Development (2006) estimates the cost of replacing 'routine unskilled staff' as being £1,000 per head. Table 21.10 shows the cost of staff turnover in each of the pubs in the area manager's patch, though calculated using the £500 estimate of tangible costs. The final column shows these costs averaged out per post. In case 18, for example, the average cost per permanent post is £3,375. The fact that so few licensed retail firms calculate the cost of staff turnover, does not mean that these costs do not exist, they are just not accounted for. It has been suggested by some researchers that one way to tackle labour turnover in hotels is to apportion these costs to the departments responsible for generating the employee leaver.

A number of research projects (Lashley and Rowson, 2000; Eaglen et al., 2001; Lashley, Thomas and Rowson, 2002) suggest a somewhat patchy approach to managing staff turnover. Senior managers generally recognized staff turnover as a problem, but unit managers were rarely appraised against staff turnover targets. In some cases unit mangers seemed unaware that the levels they were experiencing were high, or low. Many expressed the view that, 'this is just the way things are'. Variations amongst manager responses and perceptions confirmed that immediate manager performance was key to managing staff turnover. Frequently unit managers do not perceive high levels of staff 'churn' to be a problem if they are able to easily appoint replacement staff.

Interviews with staff and responses to the employee satisfaction surveys also confirmed the importance of the immediate employment experience in shaping employee decisions to stay or leave. As might have been expected pay was the highest source of dissatisfaction with a significant majority of the respondents (82.1%) of those interviewed in the Lashley and Rowson (2000) study, selecting 'more money' as a potential reason for leaving. A large majority (71.8%) selected 'improved training and development'. Nearly half of the survey respondents (48.7%) said that improved career prospects were important to them. Although the licensed retail industry has a history of the 'long hours culture', 'better hours' only came fourth with (38.5%) of the respondents believing that this would improve their current job. However, this could be because of the high number of part-time employees in the industry working shifts which suited them, although some of the unit staff did complain about night-time working and the very late closing hours of the businesses.

The current debate in the literature, and comments from practitioners, suggests that two camps have formed on the issue of staff turnover in the hospitality industry. One camp considers staff turnover to be a good thing, and the other argues that staff turnover needs to be tightly controlled. The argument of the former group is that staff turnover is a positive factor because it is easier for managers to control staff numbers and is used as a management tool to create numerical flexibility. Furthermore, as long as replacement staff can be recruited high staff turnover is said not to be a problem (Boella, 1996). They argue that some of the positive benefits to uncontrolled staff turnover are that new employees might bring with them more experience, new skills and ideas. This line of thought works best if poor performers leave the organization and if the organization is refreshed by the change of new staff. However, it is not always the poor performers who leave. It is often the better key staff who move on: they easily find alternative jobs. This creates a lower standard of service in the organization. In turn this often leads to more staff leaving because of the added pressure put upon them to cover extra work (Pizam and Ellis, 1999).

Others argue that high staff turnover is a bad thing, and needs to be controlled. Uncontrolled staff turnover can wreck planning, have a disastrous effect on staff morale, represent a considerable extra cost to the business, reduces service quality, and causes customer dissatisfaction (Lashley, 2000). High staff turnover in the hospitality industry is self-perpetuating in that managers are 'firefighting' in just trying to replace staff leaving. Often this leads to recruitment and selection methods being 'bypassed', and new staff are hastily recruited, badly inducted and not properly trained (Lashley and Chaplin, 1999). Hastily recruited employees become dissatisfied and leave which further exacerbates the staff turnover problem. In turn this leads to a vicious downward spiral increasing recruitment and staff turnover leading to ever-greater pressures on the unit manager. The manager then spends increasing amounts of time changing staff rosters to ensure cover in busy periods, and worrying about further recruitment instead of managing and developing the business potential of the unit.

The movement of people into and out of firms is inevitable. Some departures from the company will be because of illness, relocation of a partner, retirement and pregnancy. These are unavoidable reasons for staff turnover. They are a natural consequence of employing people in free labour markets. However units displaying particularly high staff turnover often have problems with staff retention and the reason employees are leaving is not because of 'unavoidable reasons', but more often due to reasons that can be controlled and managed (Pizam and Ellis, 1999). Employees often leave for reasons that are avoidable, despite what they say at exit interviews. Johnson (1986) found that many employees used career advancement as the most common reason for leaving the organization, yet this is frequently a screen for the real reasons for leaving.

In an industry with little, or no, organized trade union, nor independent grievance procedure, employees who are dissatisfied leave the organization as a way of resolving their grievance. Employee dissatisfaction can be managed and staff turnover reduced leading to improved staff retention. Dissatisfaction with wages, the relationship with management, lack of relevant training and so on are issues that lead to employee dissatisfaction. Employees have expectations about how the organization should operate as an employer. As with external customers, managers need to understand and match these expectations (Abelson, 1987). That said, it is rare that a single factor causes an employee to leave an organization. Employees' decisions are usually formed by more than one reason, both in the firm and externally. These can be identified as 'push and pull' factors. Push factors are those experiences within the firm that lead an employee to leave. Pull factors, on the other hand, are the potential attractions of conditions in other competing organizations.

Whilst it is fair to acknowledge some managers' ambivalence about staff turnover, the more retail focus adopted by many firms in the sector does imply the staff leaving the organization in an unplanned manner is ultimately harmful to the business. It raises operating costs, distracts managers from important business building activities, and contributes to customer dissatisfaction and lost custom. The sector cannot build a quality customer experience if there is a constant stream of new faces behind the bar. Licensed retail companies need to manage and cost staff turnover, by making unit managers responsible for it and by accounting for it in unit manager performance measures. The fact that several studies show that labour turnover varies widely between units in the same organizations confirms that staff turnover can be managed and brought down to levels comparable with other industries.

Training and development

Another common issue facing the licensed retail sector relates to the importance and significance given to staff training and management development. The large corporate organizations, such as J D Wetherspoon, Mitchell and Butlers, and Greene King understand the value of training staff and management in their managed estate. Consistent service standards, improved output and sales per employee, improvements in service quality and customer satisfaction are all perceived as benefits to be gained from a programme of formal training for staff and management. The problem for the sector is that many pub outlets are run by tenants/lessees and owner/managers with lifestyle motives which just do not recognize the need to train employees or for their own skill development.

Much of the comment about the skills needs of the sector tends to assume two broadly contradictory positions. The first, flowing from policy makers, assumes that the sector needs to produce more people with hard-edge technical skills which enable them to perform a prescribed list of tasks. The second, flowing from research conducted into the specific needs of the sector, suggests that employers prefer to recruit unskilled employees who are cheap and numerically flexible. Whilst there is truth in both positions, skills needs and skills development in the sector are more complex than these two positions suggest. In part, the problem is rooted in national quantitative surveys, which can miss some of the subtleties revealed by more qualitative local studies.

Lashley, Thomas and Rowson's (2002) report on skills shortages and skills gaps in Greater Manchester suggested that there are broadly three types of skills sets required by the sector. First, there are key specialist jobs where there are limited numbers of well-qualified, skilled people and in which barriers to entry are high, but pay and conditions are perceived as appropriate by recruits. Some of the more skilled jobs in specialist functional areas at head office, along with senior unit and multi-unit manager positions, are sometimes difficult to fill but do attract recruits eventually. Significantly, they usually have a good level of staff retention, so a high level of staff turnover does not exacerbate recruitment problems. Employers are frequently recruiting people who have a vocational education and training in the field, and real careers.

The second group of jobs is typically low-skilled and poorly paid with low barriers to entry. Here there is a potentially high level of supply, often through young people new to the labour market, or students working in part-time, casual or temporary posts. Pay rates are either the national minimum wage or pitched at a point close to the legal minimum wage rate. For younger employees the pay rate is below the adult national minimum wage. Opportunities to find alternative employment on the part of the employee and opportunities to recruit alternative employees on the part of the employer tend to lead to high levels of staff turnover. As we have seen, some employers register levels of staff turnover over 600% per annum. Yet managers do not see staff turnover as a major problem because labour is easily replaced, and it can be a useful means of managing numerical flexibility in the workforce, particularly when there are downturns in demand. Total numbers employed can be reduced simply by not replacing leavers. Some of the best-practice firms, however, pitch their pay and employment conditions above these minimal levels because they are able to pick and choose staff, and labour stability tends to be higher, as is investment in training (Lashley et al., 2002).

Although these jobs are described as low skilled, employers do require certain personal and physical characteristics. Burns (1999) states that 'soft skills' are much more important than hard technical skills for the delivery of this sector's service interactions with its customers. These are defined, primarily, as social and interpersonal skills such as being polite and responsive in service interactions with customers, and displaying work discipline, work readiness, numeracy and literacy. Lashley (2001) indicates the importance of 'emotional displays' and 'emotional labour' in service roles, and suggests that there is a growing body of research on the importance of emotional intelligence for employees delivering high levels of customer service satisfaction. Nixon,

Warhurst and Dutton (2006: 196) point out that recruits are increasingly required to demonstrate these soft skills, but are also required to possess 'aesthetic' skills. Nixon et al. describe these simply as 'looking good and sounding right', and show that in a recent US study involving human resource professionals, 'pride in appearance and good attitude' were the top two criteria for new recruit selection. In the UK, surveys of employers frequently indicate lack of customer-care skills as the most significant skills shortage when searching for suitable recruits and skills gaps amongst existing employees (Lashley et al., 2002; Lashley and Rowson, 2005c).

Training initiatives frequently fail to understand the reality of employment in the sector. Employers are rarely looking for a high level of competence in a wide range of hard technical skills; for a variety of reasons they are aiming to recruit people who possess a range of soft social, emotional and aesthetic skills. In these posts, the harder skills have been simplified so as to require limited on-the-job training. In some cases, as reported earlier, employers feel able to meet business objectives with no investment in the training of this type of employee. Whilst this reflects the reality of employment in many firms, research on the business benefits of training (Eaglen et al., 1999; Eaglen and Lashley, 2001) suggests that there are considerable business benefits to training employees in some of these technical skills. The fact that these benefits remain unrecognized is in itself an indication of a potential latent and unreported skills deficiency of managers.

The third group comprises the relatively small number of jobs in these low-paid sectors that do require skilled employees. In this group, there is competition amongst employers to attract a workforce already equipped with the specialist skills to do the job. Chefs in pubs, bars and cafés tend to be able to command better pay because of the relative rarity of the skills involved and the perceived key significance of their performance to operational success. A recent report (HtF, 2002) claimed that chefs' pay had risen on average by 12%. In part, the rise in chefs' pay has been driven by the competition for their skills, something that has often led one employer to poach staff from another, and plentiful opportunities for a dissatisfied employee to find another job. The skills gap factor is clearly an issue in the case of chefs, since the demand for cooking skills covers a range of competence levels from simple to complex.

At the simple 'snip-and-ping' end, jobs require basic training in health and safety and food hygiene together with the immediate preparation and service standards required. Typically, simple training in the steps required for each dish, together with standard procedures manuals, ensure that job skills sets can be developed in a relatively short time. These jobs are chiefly concerned with product assembly and presentation of foods which are, for the most part, bought in pre-cooked. Potentially, the barriers to entry are low, but work can be monotonous and boring.

At a more intermediate level the skills may be described as 'one-step-cooking'. Goods are taken from a raw to a cooked state, but little is done to the product other than one stage of cooking – typically grilling, griddling, or frying, and assembly and presentation. Skills sets are not complex. Pre-portioned and bought-in foods, together with the use of equipment technology, limit employee discretion and judgement. Again, job training is not overly elaborate and jobs skills sets are typically developed on the job but have to include legal obligations covering health and safety and food handling provisions. Job titles often refer to these occupants as 'chef' and this is in part where some of the confusion reported in several research projects arises (Lashley et al., 2002; Lashley and Rowson, 2006). Employers looking for more complex skills amongst experienced new recruits frequently complain that they are 'not really chefs' (Lashley et al., 2002: 8).

In gastro-pubs, however, the work is often linked to complex operations and an ability to apply a wide range of cooking techniques and skills. It is these more complex cooking jobs that have attracted better rates of pay particularly for qualified and experienced personnel. It is here that there is a long and elaborate training of personnel who will be expected to cook more complex dishes which require the manipulation of materials and equipment. There is a support qualification structure with a long tradition of training prior to full-time employment. The current supply and demand levels for this skills set has led to many firms working closely with colleges to ensure an improved supply of chefs. However, there appear to be drivers in the current shortage of personnel with this skill set. One interviewee in a project for Nottinghamshire STARS (Lashley and Rowson, 2005b) revealed

an insight into the low-level general skill shortage and recent changes in demand for chefs:

> … basically we are looking for 'cheffing' skills. Part of the problem here is the de-skilling that has taken place in the industry. Now most chefs just assemble prepared food. But with the shift back to real cooking there is a problem getting the right craft skills again.

The skill shortages and skill gaps in the pub sector are complex and in need of some subtle interventions. Certainly there is a need to uprate skills in a formal manner, but the dominant approach to training in the sector is a by-product of the latent and under reported skill gaps of managers, tenants/lessees and owner/managers. Corporate organization have opportunities to train and develop their managers as well as monitor and manage the skill development of frontline pub staff, the key problem is in persuading tenants/lessees of the value of their own training and development. Because of the lifestyle motives of many of these small firm operators, they do not recognize the skill gaps that they themselves have. One company, Punch Taverns, has taken steps to alter this by insisting that any tenant or lessee who rents one of their pubs must do a ten-day training programme before they take over the pub. The following reports on the findings from a survey of individuals who had completed the 'X factor' programme, designed to improve business management skills (Lashley and Rowson, 2003).

The impacts of various actions taken by respondents was generally very positive with over 80% of licensed retailers reporting increases in general sales levels (82%), wet sales (82%) and profits (83%). A further 62% reported reductions in costs within the business after the programme and 54% reported increases in food business since the programme. Licensed retailer respondents also reported improvements in 'up selling of wine and food' (50%), 'average sales per staff member' (57%), 'transaction values' (58%) and overall business value (62%).

Licensed retailer respondents also reported some very significant improvements in customer service since the programme. Some 91% of retailers reported increases in levels of service quality since the programme and, as a consequence, customer satisfaction had increased (84%). A significant 74% of retailers reported reductions in customer complaints and 83% reported increases in repeat visits by customers. Furthermore, 71% of retailers reported increases in new customer visits to the pub and 54% reported increases in average spend by customers.

The British Institute of Innkeeping runs an annual training awards scheme for the licensed retail sector in an attempt to improve the intensity of training activity in the sector. This has had the effect of raising the profile of training and management development in the sector and most of the large corporate organizations make entries to the awards each year. Indeed many even sponsor award categories. The key problem for the sector is in raising the profile of training amongst the very large number of small firms that actually operate pubs, bars and cafés as businesses. Punch Taverns, as we have seen, is an example of one large organization that has recognized the importance of tenant and lessee management skills as a means of building its own business. However, their compulsion approach is not without its critics and most other pub companies in the non-managed sector tend to a more voluntaristic approach. As a result most tenants and lessees do not recognize they have a need for training and development, and do not volunteer to attend the programmes on offer. The free house sector has no link to larger organizations, though firms like the major drinks company of Diagio do offer free bar staff training to improve drinks service quality. The owner-managers themselves are typically unlikely to seek out training and development for themselves, and as a consequence the sector is not as professionally managed as it could be.

Graduate careers

There are two broad pathways for graduates working in the sector, as a salaried manager, or through some form of self-employment (see Figure 22.2). The increase in size and scale of many retail-oriented pub, bar and café operations means the manager's role is being increasingly professionalized. The larger organizations in licensed retailing are looking for high quality graduates to manage their sites. Many of these largest pubs, bars and cafés are taking annual sales from drinks, food and other sources exceed £1 million and in some cases £4 million. A bright new graduate could reasonably expect to be in the position of pub, bar or café manager within a few years of leaving university. Rewards are good, often considerably enhanced by bonuses based on performance. Most pub companies also employ graduates in area manager/operations consultant roles. Beyond this multi-unit management role there are also pub company opportunities in regional management and head office management. Most companies also recruit graduates into specialist functional departments in human resource management, operations, training, marketing, finance, purchasing, customer liaison, and public relations. At all levels in the licensed retail sector, graduate salaries are competitively placed, compared with other industries, and hard working, talented persons can be quickly promoted into position of responsibility and authority.

The opportunities for self-employment are vast. The most dominant form of pub management is through 'tenancy' or 'lease' arrangements whereby the property is owned by a pub company but operated as a small business by the tenant or leaseholder. In effect these arrangements are a form of 'franchising' whereby the tenant or leaseholders pays a rental to, and buys supplies from the pub company. Thousands of pubs, bars and cafés are run as small, independent businesses. The immediate landlord/licensee is running a small business, making his or her own decisions and benefiting from the profits earned, once the rental and other costs have been paid. Barriers to entry are low, and it is possible to take on a tenancy or lease for a relatively small capital investment. The opportunity to operate one's own small business is a remarkable feature of the licensed retail sector, and many graduates choose this as their first business venture with a view to building a chain of properties. The second opportunity for self-employment comes via the 'free house' sector. Typically, the pub or bar property is independently owned by the licensee. The building is owned by the licensee and family, and the business is free to buy supplies on the market place. Profits can be greater because the business owner is not tied to a pub company, does not have to pay rent, or buy produce from one source. These types of business are a little more costly to set up than the tenancy or leasehold, but not overly prohibitive compared with the cost of some new business start-ups in other sectors. Often these businesses are located in rural or semi-rural settings and make their restaurant a major attraction to the pub. In recent years, gastro-pubs have been developed by keen young

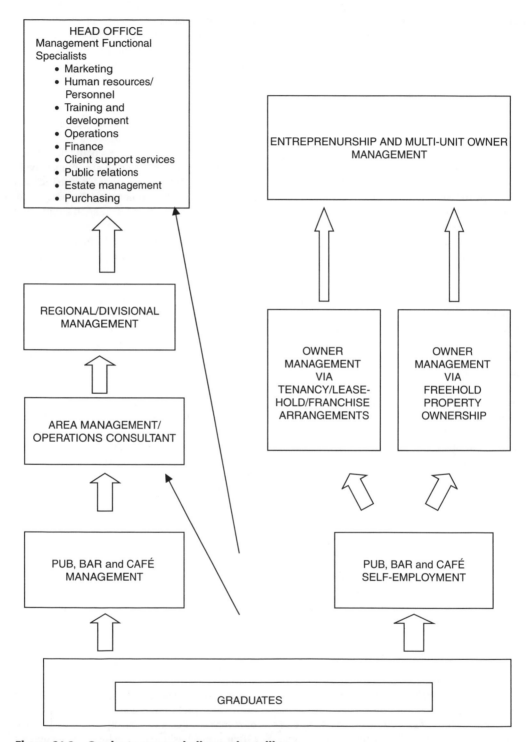

Figure 21.2   Graduate careers in licensed retailing

entrepreneurs with a strong interest in supplying top quality food to patrons.

Licensed retailing offers interesting and rewarding careers to anyone interested in working with people, in an active and dynamic ever changing environment. For graduates interested in a structured career, the corporate pub sector has much to offer, with early promotion and rapid advancement. For graduates interested in entrepreneurship and self-employment the licensed retail sector is unique in presenting low barriers to a business start. There is quite literally, something for everyone!

CONCLUSIONS

The British licensed retail sector has undergone some major changes as a result of the legislative environment and state intervention. The tight licensing environment at the beginning of the twentieth century created a situation where breweries needed to control pubs as outlets for their beer product. As brewery economics moved to take advantage of economies of scale the number of breweries fell throughout the century and ultimately the sector was dominated by six major national brewers with 100 plus regional or local brewers, typically organized round local niche markets. Ownership of the pub estate echoed this concentration of brewery ownership because increased brewing economies of scale required larger numbers of pubs to be 'tied' to the brewery in order to increase the retail volume capacity to match that on the production side. By the late 1980s the big six brewers in the UK owned over 50% of the country's pub estate.

At the end of the 1980s the Beer Orders issued by the Monopolies and Mergers Commission aimed to bring more competition into the market, but this had unforeseen consequences. The link between national brewers and pub estate was broken. None of the big six brewers now own pubs linked to the brewing company. The regional brewers continue to hold pub estates, and some of the bigger regional brewers own a substantial pub estate, however, none is a truly national company in the earlier form. Pub companies have emerged, owning hundreds or thousands of pubs, but none is linked to a brewery. The non-managed estate in particular has grown, the number of pubs directly managed by a branded company has fallen, and there are

a shrinking number of pubs individually owned as a freehouse. Increasingly food is a major source of income for pubs in general, and the gastro-pub has emerged as a means by which the independent freehouse is able to build a competitive advantage.

The licensed retail sector is interesting because it forms a major part of the total commercial hospitality sector. As a result of the move to more of a retailing focus, the sector has had to professionalize its management. The directly managed estate in particular, needs professional managers capable of running individual business units which are substantial businesses in their own right. The need to professionalize management in the non-managed sector throws up some important tensions. The pub companies who own the properties and supply 'wet' products to the pub are dealing with hundreds or thousands of small firms who rent or lease their pubs. The corporate business is dependent on these small firms to grow and develop sales, yet many are run by lifestyle operators whose motivation is not always the same as classic entrepreneurs. In these circumstances it is difficult to engage the tenant or lessee in a programme of self development, and different companies are trying different approaches to intervene with small-firm partner's skill development.

The sector faces some important management issues. The nature of the alcoholic product, together with a cluster of health and public order issues mean that there is concern to ensure that firms operate in a socially responsible manner. At present this is largely concerned with deflecting political attention with codes of practice to avoid direct legislative intervention. However, engagement with more ethical business policies could make a contribution to some firms developing business strategies as ethical companies. Labour turnover continues to be a major problem facing the sector, though this is itself a by-product of the management development profile of the sector. Informally, or untrained, managers are themselves less likely to see the value of formally training staff, or the need to retain staff as a valuable asset to the business. Certainly, the dominance of forms of pub ownership which give predominance to licensees who are mostly lifestyle entrepreneurs does have major implications for the professionalism of the sector's management. Far too many individuals, who have little, or no, formal training in pub or business management are running pubs. That said, there are many opportunities for graduates within both corporate organizations and in various forms of self-employment.

The foregoing highlights a number of research themes that might need to be developed in future research activities. There are some projects which are common across the whole licensed retail sector, such as social responsibility and ethical business practice, the impact of the formal ban on smoking, and trends on consumer tastes. In addition however, there are some projects that have resonance with the management of pubs in directly managed, tenant/leased and free house formats. The managed estate needs to explore some of the service quality and service consistency issues across estates of hundreds, or thousands of properties. The development and retention of employees and the professionalization of managers are key issues that are likely to impact upon business development and growth. The tenanted and leased sector needs to continue research into the relationship between pub companies, tenants and lessees. In addition, the motives and business skills of those running these pubs as small firms is an important research theme which should facilitate a better understanding of business growth potential through these businesses. The free house sector also needs research attention, again there is a need to better understand the motives, aims and skill sets of people who buy a pub property. The survival rates and levels of churn are also important issues which could better inform those buying properties.

REFERENCES

Abelson, M. A. (1987) 'Examination of avoidable and unavoidable turnover', *Journal of Applied Psychology*, 72(3): 382–386.

Andrews, R., Baum, T. and Morrison, A. (2000) *The Lifestyle Economics of Small Tourism Businesses.* Glasgow: Scottish Hotel School.

Ball, S. (2000) 'Catering'. In C. Lashley and A. Morrison (eds) *Franchising Hospitality Services.* Oxford: Butterworth-Heinemann, pp. 145–169.

Beaver, G. and Lashley, C. (1998) 'Barriers to management development in small hospitality firms', *Strategic Change*, 4(4): 223–235.

Beaver, G., Lashley, C. and Stewart, J. (1998) 'Management development'. In R. Thomas (ed.) *The Management of Small Tourism and Hospitality Firms.* London: Cassell, pp. 156–173.

Boella, M. (1996) *Human Resource Management in the Hospitality Industry.* London: Stanley Thornes.

Brinckley, J. and Darke, F. (1987) 'The choice of organisational form: the case of franchising', *Journal of Financial Economics,* 18: 401–420.

Burns, P. (1999) Hard-skills, Soft-skills: Undervaluing Hospitality's 'Service with a Smile'. *Progress in Tourism and Hospitality Research,* 3(3): 239–248.

Chartered Institute of Personnel and Development (CIPD) (2006) *Labour Turnover – 2006 Survey Results.* London: CIPD.

Eaglen, A. and Lashley, C. (2001) *The Impact of Training on Business Performance.* Leeds: Leeds Metropolitan University.

Eaglen, A., Lashley, C. and Thomas, R. (1999) *Benefits and Costs Analysis: the Impact of Training on Business Performance.* Leeds: Leeds Metropolitan University.

Eaglen, A., Lashley, C. and Thomas, R. (2000) 'Modelling the benefits of training to business performance', *Strategic Change,* 9(4): 35–49.

Fisher, C. and Lovell, A. (2003) *Business Ethics and Values.* London: Prentice-Hall.

Guild, S. (1996) 'Lease is more', *Caterer and Hotelkeeper,* 31 October: 76–77.

HtF, (1996) *Who Needs Training Now?* London: Hospitality Training Foundation.

HtF, (2002) *Survey of Employers – 2002.* London: Hospitality Training Foundation.

Johnson, K. (1986) 'Labour turnover in hotels – an update', *Service Industries Journal,* 6(3): 362–380.

Johnston, R. (1989) '"Developing Competitive Strategies" in the service sector'. In P. Jones (ed.) *Management in Service Industries.* Chapter 7. London: Pitman.

Key Note (1997) *Breweries and the Beer Market.* London: Key Note Limited.

Kolb, D. (1984) *Experiential Learning. Experience as the Source of Learning and Development.* Englewood Cliffs, NJ: Prentice-Hall.

Lashley, C. (2000a) *Hospitality Retail Management: A Unit Manager's Handbook.* Oxford: Butterworth-Heinemann.

Lashley, C. (2000b) 'The case of McDonald's Restaurants Limited'. In C. Lashley and A. Morrison (eds) *Franchising Hospitality Services.* Oxford: Butterworth-Heinemann, pp. 244–265.

Lashley, C. (2001) *Empowerment: HR Strategies for Service Excellence.* Oxford: Butterworth-Heinemann.

Lashley, C. and Chaplin, A. (1999) 'Labour turnover: hidden problem, hidden costs', *Hospitality Review,* 1(1): 37–43.

Lashley, C. and Lincoln, G. (2000) 'Franchising in licensed retail operations'. In C. Lashley and

A. Morrison (eds) *Franchising Hospitality Services.* Oxford: Butterworth-Heinemann, pp. 192–218.

Lashley C. and Morrison, A. (eds) (2000) *Franchising Hospitality Services.* Oxford: Butterworth-Heinemann.

Lashley, C. and Morrison, A. (2003) 'Hospitality as a "Commercial Friendship"', *Hospitality Review* 6(3): 31–36.

Lashley, C. and Rowson, B. (2003) *The Benefits of Pub Retailer Training: A Report for the Punch Pub Company.* Nottingham: Nottingham Trent University.

Lashley, C. and Rowson, W. (2000) 'Wasted Millions: Staff Turnover in Licensed Retail Organizations', In Williams, A. (ed.) *Ninth Annual Hospitality Research Conference Proceedings.* University of Huddersfield, pp. 230–242.

Lashley, C. and Rowson, B. (2005) *STARS: The Skills Challenge.* Nottingham: Nottingham Trent University.

Lashley, C. and Rowson, B. (2006) *Developing Management Skills In Blackpool's Small Hotel Sector: A Research Report for England's North West Tourism Skills Network.* Nottingham: Nottingham Trent University.

Lashley, C., Lynch, P. and Morrison, A. (2007) 'Hospitality: an introduction'. In Lashley, C., Lynch, P. and Morrison, A. (eds) *Hospitality: A Social Lens.* Oxford: Elsevier, pp. 1–16.

Lashley, C., Thomas, R. and Rowson, B. (2002) *Employment Practices and Skill Shortages in Greater Manchester's Tourism Sector.* Leeds: Leeds Metropolitan University.

Lessem, R.(1987) *Intrapreneurship.* London: Gower.

Lincoln, G. (1996) 'The need for a new breed of licensee', *International Journal of Wine Marketing*, 6(4): 23–32.

Locker, C. and Morrison, A. (1999) *Scottish Tourism: Structure, Characteristics and Performance.* Glasgow: The Scottish Tourism Unit and Fraser Allen Institute.

Lynch, P. A. (2005) 'Reflections on the home setting in hospitality', *Journal of Hospitality and Tourism Management*, 12(1): 37–49.

Mathewson, G. and Winter, R. (1985) 'The economics of franchise contracts', *Journal of Law and Political Economy*, 28: 503–526.

Minkler, A. (1990) 'An empirical analysis of a firm's decision to franchise', *Economic Letters*, 34(1): 77–82.

Mintel (1998) *Pub Retailing March 1996.* London: Mintel International Group Limited.

Mintel (2006) 'Leisure Time', *Leisure Intelligence, February 2006.* London: Mintel International Group Limited.

Morrison, A. (2000a) 'Entrepreneurs or intrapreneurs?'. In Lashley, C. and Morrison, A. (eds) *Franchising Hospitality Services.* Oxford: Butterworth-Heinemann, pp. 68–91.

Morrison, A. (2000b) *How Do Owner/managers In Small Tourism Firms Learn?* Glasgow: The Scottish Tourism Research Unit.

Morrison, A., Rimmington, M. and Williams, C. (1999) *Entrepreneurship in the Hospitality, Leisure and Tourism Industries.* Oxford: Butterworth-Heinemann.

Nixon, D. and Warhurst, C. (2007) 'Opening Pandora's box: aesthetic labour and hospitality'. In Lashley, C., Lynch, P. and Morrison, A. (eds) *Hospitality: a social lens.* Oxford: Elsevier, pp. 155–172.

Nixon, D., Warhurst, C. and Dutton, E. (2006) 'The importance of attitude and appearance in service encounters in retail and hospitality', *Managing Service Quality*, 15(2): 195–208.

Norton, S. (1988) 'An empirical look at franchising as an organizational form', *Journal of Business*, 16(1): 197–217.

Oxenfeldt, A. and Kelly, A. (1969) 'Will successful franchise systems ultimately become wholly-owned chains?' *Journal of Retailing*, 44(4): 69–83.

Pizam, A. and Ellis, T. (1999) 'Absenteeism and turnover in the hospitality industry'. In Lee-Ross, D. (ed) *HRM in Tourism and Hospitality.* London: Cassell, pp. 109–131.

Price, S., Bleakley, M. and Pennington, J. (1999) *UK Breweries and Pubs: After the Precipice.* London: Credit-Suisse/First Boston.

Ritzer, G. (2007) 'Inhospitable hospitality?'. In Lashley, C., Lynch, P. and Morrison, A. (eds) *Hospitality: a Social Lens.* Oxford: Elsevier, pp. 129–140.

Slade, M. (1998) 'Beer and the tie: did divestment of brewery owned public houses lead to higher beer prices?' *The Economic Journal*, 108(May): 565–602.

Taylor, S. (2000) 'Franchising Organization and Debates'. In Lashley, C. and Morrison, A. (eds) *Franchising Hospitality Services.* Oxford: Butterworth-Heinemann, pp. 1–21.

The Publican (2006) *The Pub Industry Handbook 2006,* 10th edition.

Thomas, R., Lashley, C., Rowson, B., Xie, G., Jameson, A., Eaglen, A., Lincoln, G. and Parsons, T. (2000) *The National Survey of Small Tourism and Hospitality Firms: 2000.* Leeds: Leeds Metropolitan University.

Whitbread Inns (1995) *The Changing Face of the British Pub.* Luton: Whitbread Plc.

Williams, C. and Lincoln, G. (1996) 'New directions for the licensed retail trade: a structural analysis', *International Journal of Wine Marketing*, 8(1).

Wormald, C. and Hartley, D. (1999) *Guide to Franchising in UK Pubs and Restaurants.* London: Martens Information Limited.

Flight Catering Management

22

Peter Jones

INTRODUCTION

Flight catering is probably one of the most complex foodservice operational systems in the world. For instance, Cathay Pacific Catering Services' flight kitchen in Hong Kong produced over 74,000 tray sets in one day in February 2006. Indeed there are over 630 flight kitchens in the world that produce more than a million 'meals', i.e. tray sets, per annum (Momberger and Momberger, 2006). Large international airlines may have more than 1,000 takeoffs and landings every day. A single, long-haul Boeing 747 has over 40,000 items loaded on to it before it flies. All together these items weigh 6 metric tonnes and occupy a space of 60 cubic meters (Jones, 2004b).

These facts and others like them make flight catering unlike any other sector of the hospitality industry. While the way food is served on trays to airline passengers bears some resemblance to service styles in restaurants or cafeterias, the way food is prepared and cooked increasingly resembles a food manufacturing plant (Chang, 2006). The production kitchen in a typical unit is often no more than 10% of the total floor area, with the rest of the space used for bonded stores, tray and trolley assembly, and flight wash-up. There will be relatively few chefs, and many staff employed in tray set-up and aircraft loading. The way food and equipment is stored resembles a freight warehouse, and the way meals and equipment are transported and supplied has a close affinity to military-style logistics and distribution systems. It is therefore not surprising that flight catering is frequently regarded as 80% logistics and 20% cooking.

Despite the scale and complexity of this sector of the hospitality industry, there has been very little research into flight catering. In recognition of this, the International Travel Catering Association (ITCA) – a trade association comprised of airlines, rail and ferry operators, caterers and suppliers – sponsored a textbook on this subject in the mid-1990s and subsequently endowed a chair at the University of Surrey (UK) in 2001. Most of the research reported on in this chapter has been conducted by the Travel Catering Research Centre (TCRC) at the University of Surrey.

In this chapter the size and scale of the flight catering sector of the hospitality industry worldwide will be explored, before examining the role that foodservice plays in the total travel experience. The major stakeholders – airlines, caterers, distributors and manufacturers – and their respective roles are then discussed, and the structure of airline-caterer contracts described. The flight catering system is then examined, along with issues related to supply chain management and logistics, as there have been significant changes in the nature of this supply chain over the last ten years. The chapter concludes with a review of the role and nature of innovation in this sector and an analysis of likely future trends.

SIZE AND SCALE OF FLIGHT CATERING

Flight catering is a very large, global activity. The total market size is estimated to be around 12 billion euros. More than 1 billion passengers are served each year. Although much is made of the global nature of the industry the reality is that there are very few airlines that have a truly global network, and even for these their intercontinental services are a relatively small proportion of their total passenger numbers. Three major markets – North America, Europe, and Asia – account for over 90% of all airline passengers (Jones, 2004a).

The structure of these three main markets is significantly different. In Europe, there are many more airlines, often so-called 'flag' carriers who are the national airline of a country. However,

Table 22.1   Passenger numbers by route (millions) – Europe

Route type	Jan–Mar 2004	Apr–Jun 2004	Jul–Sept 2004	Oct–Dec 2004	Jan–Mar 2005	Apr–Jun 2005	Jul–Sept 2005	Oct–Dec 2005	Jan–Mar 2006	Apr–Jun 2006	Jul–Sept 2006
Domestic	51.3	62.48	66.67	56.68	53.4	65.79	69.26	59.84	54.32	67.2	72.50
Intercontinental	15.3	16.88	18.92	16.41	16.3	17.86	20.00	17.58	17.00	19.01	20.72
Total	66.60	79.36	85.60	73.09	69.7	83.65	89.26	77.42	71.32	86.22	93.21

Source: TCRC (2006: 2).

the number of flag carriers is in decline due to increased competition between them and from low-cost carriers and a shift towards open skies policies. Three countries and airlines dominate the European skies because they have been able to develop their hub airports as hubs for the whole of Europe. These are British Airways in London, Air France (now merged with KLM) in Paris, and Lufthansa in Frankfurt. Half of all passenger demand in Europe originates in these three countries. Domestic routes are more sensitive to seasonality with the summer months as the highest period (respectively 67, 69, and 72 million in 2004, 2005 and 2006) and the winter months as the lowest (respectively 51, 53, and 54 million in 2004, 2005 and 2006). In comparison to domestic routes, the passenger numbers on intercontinental routes are fairly consistent, at around 19 million passengers throughout the year (see Table 22.1). Most of the major growth in Europe has been from the low-cost carriers, in particular Easyjet and Ryanair. In recent years, the former is based at Stanstead in London, whereas Ryanair is based at Dublin in Ireland. However, both are increasing their point-to-point, i.e. not through a hub, route network aggressively.

Although the number of domestic passengers is almost three times the number of intercontinental travellers in this market, this does not represent the demand for in-flight meals. This is because on long-haul flights passengers will be served with more than one meal, whilst on short-haul flights – especially on the low-cost airlines – passengers may have no meal at all. Hence the TCRC estimates that nearly 40% of all meals served are on intercontinental flights (TCRC, 2006).

Unlike other markets, charter airlines are significant in Europe, especially in the UK, Germany and Scandinavia. For instance the three largest package holiday companies in the UK serve nearly 20 million meals per annum. To speed up turn round time, maintain quality, and simplify contracting these meals are all back-catered, i.e. meals are loaded for both the out-bound and the return flight. Until 2004

these meals have also been complimentary, i.e. included in the package price. In the 2004 season some operators unpackaged the in-flight meal from the total package price. Customers were offered a menu to choose from and asked to pay for a meal, if they wanted it. From the airline's point of view this significantly reduced waste, as only meals that were ordered were loaded onboard, and it also created an additional revenue stream. However, this was not continued in 2005 due to the problem of implementing it on board. For instance, passengers who had not ordered meals would claim that they had and seat allocation was unreliable – so the wrong meals were served to the wrong passengers.

In North America there are six main American carriers who operate scheduled services, with a relatively small, but growing low-cost segment. This market is dominated by domestic air travel, which represents 80% of the total passenger numbers (see Table 22.2). The United States has largely deregulated its airline industry and has a so-called 'open skies' policy. While there has not been any significant seasonality impact on intercontinental routes, slight fluctuations have been noted in passenger numbers on domestic routes within North America. The peaks are evident in the third quarter (respectively 165 and 172 million in 2004 and 2005) and low points in the first quarter (respectively 144, 154 and 155 million in 2004, 2005, and 2006). A review of the six major airline websites in January 2005 (TCRC, 2005) identified the following trends.

- Some airlines are promoting branded products, such as Domino's Pizza, others are not.
- One airline is promoting 'buy-at-the-gate', i.e. the purchase of snacks and meals just prior to boarding the aircraft.
- Two airlines have introduced buy onboard.
- All airlines restrict complimentary meal service on flights to reflect the duration of the flight – but they each apply different times.
- All airlines restrict complimentary meal service to designated 'meal' periods of the day.

Table 22.2   Passenger numbers by route (millions) – North America

Route type	Jan–Mar 2004	Apr–Jun 2004	Jul–Sept 2004	Oct–Dec 2004	Jan–Mar 2005	Apr–Jun 2005	Jul–Sept 2005	Oct–Dec 2005	Jan–Mar 2006	Apr–Jun 2006
Domestic	144.24	164.15	165.15	156.2	153.68	171.84	172.34	158.82	155.07	172.66
Intercontinental	31.7	34.96	37.97	38.9	35.16	38.06	44.45	37.55	35.57	39.89
Total	175.94	199.1	203.17	195.1	188.85	209.91	216.79	196.38	190.64	212.55

Source: TCRC (2006: 4).

In the Far East, flag carriers continue to dominate, although a number of countries are moving towards more open skies – India, Korea, Japan and even China. Moreover, low-cost carriers are just entering this market – in India, Thailand and potentially Korea. In this market, short-haul (domestic) and long-haul (intercontinental) markets are equally important. In both 2004 and 2005, the trend in passenger numbers on domestic routes by Asian airlines suggested certain levels of seasonality, varying from 6 million in January to March up to just over 19 million in July to September (see Table 22.3). There is less seasonality on intercontinental routes, which varies from 16 to 21 million. However seasonality was less pronounced in the first quarter of 2006, due possibly to the rapid rise of low-cost air travel in both south-east Asia and Australia.

Passenger numbers in economy class varies from 51 to 71 million per quarter in Europe and are nearly four times of those in business class, which vary from 13 to 19 million. The seasonality patterns between the two seat classes are virtually similar (lowest in the first quarters and highest in the third quarters). Whereas, the trend in passenger numbers in first class is relatively stable at around 3 million. In North America the proportion of the coach class travel is more than ten times that of business class travel, with first class being almost non-existent. In Asia-Pacific, approximately 5% of passengers fly first class, 10% business class and the remainder economy.

In Europe some segments are very stable and predictable and others are not. The long-haul market is relatively stable and is likely to continue to offer complimentary full meal service. However, there are changes in seat class segmentation. The demand for first class is in decline and this seat class is being merged with business class. Also some airlines have developed a seat class that has some features of business class (usually legroom) and some of economy (the onboard service offer) – BA call this 'Economy Plus'. The short-haul segment is the most dynamic. Rising fuel prices and competition from low-cost carriers have led to airlines reducing their costs. Different airlines have adopted different approaches to this, similar to the North American market. Thus it is possible for a passenger to fly out with one carrier and be given a complimentary meal, but to fly back on a co-share flight with another airline and be asked to pay for their meal. This situation is unlikely to be sustainable in the long run and may put pressure on co-share agreements and airline alliances.

The North American market is unstable, if only because a significant proportion of the major airlines are technically bankrupt, having filed for Chapter 11. This explains why many airlines in this market have switched to buy-on-board or buy-at-the-gate rather than providing complimentary meals, and even those that do have free meals restrict when these are served. By contrast, the Asian market has the most 'traditional' model of flight catering. Many airlines such as Singapore Airlines and Cathay Pacific, still operate their own flight kitchens out of their main hub airport, as well as offering full-service, complimentary meals.

Table 22.3   Passenger numbers by route (millions) – Asia

Route type	Jan–Mar 2004	Apr–Jun 2004	Jul–Sept 2004	Oct–Dec 2004	Jan–Mar 2005	Apr–Jun 2005	Jul–Sept 2005	Oct–Dec 2005	Jan–Mar 2006	Apr–Jun 2006	Jul–Sept 2006
Domestic	6.61	16.99	18.49	17.78	5.97	16.63	19.48	17.36	16.23	16.29	19.39
Intercontinental	16.14	18.9	20.69	21.18	16.32	19.59	21.47	21.07	20.69	20.21	21.52
Total	22.75	35.89	39.19	38.36	22.3	36.22	40.95	38.43	36.92	36.5	40.91

Source: TCRC (2006: 7).

It is perhaps because of this that these airlines – Emirates, Cathay Pacific, Singapore Airlines – now dominate the annual recognition awards for onboard service quality. The other key issue in this region is that it is the most rapidly growing market in the world. China is reported to be investing considerable effort in developing airport infrastructure, including many new airports the same size as London Gatwick.

ROLE OF FOOD ONBOARD

How important are food and onboard services to the airlines? Some airlines, such as Emirates, Qantas and Lufthansa, use food as a marketing tool but this only has a limited impact. Surveys over a number of years suggest that passengers appear most concerned about safety, on-time performance, scheduling/ticketing issues, the aircraft's physical surroundings such as seat and leg comfort, and gate check-in and boarding. This means that while food is important, it is unlikely to be the deciding factor in a passenger's airline choice. This is most clearly seen in the USA where deregulation has had a great effect upon competition and fare wars are common. This has led to most US airlines implementing a no-frills policy where no meals are served on board flights within the USA (Lee and Jones, 2005).

One of the problems might be that consumer (and media) perceptions of meal quality in airlines are low. However, a number of factors affect passengers' appetite and behavior whilst flying (Jones and Lumbers, 2003). Sensory abilities such as smell, sight, and taste are affected by the relatively low humidity and air pressure experienced at altitude. This affects taste buds (which may function as much as 30% below par) and mucous membranes in the nose (which blunts the sense of smell). Airline food is often more highly seasoned for these reasons. Likewise, at such a high altitude not all wines retain their subtle aroma and bouquet and this has to be taken into account when wine lists are chosen by the airlines and caterers. Also, as passenger movement and exercise is limited at such high altitude, the meals provided need to be easily digestible. Moreover, the effects of alcohol are more quickly observed in a pressurized cabin and on dehydrated passengers.

Hong (2006) suggests that while food and drink in-flight may not affect pre-purchase decisions, it emerges as a highly significant post-purchase factor. The onboard service and meal is the most remembered aspect of people's travel experience, so the food service offered to passengers is still an important part of the overall service experience. However, as the factors listed above begin to suggest, providing a product that will satisfy the customer is about much more than simply providing a ready meal.

Another feature of in-flight catering is special meals (SPMLs). These may be based on religious belief (kosher, halal), medical needs, (diabetic, low-salt, fat-free) or personal preference (vegan). In total there are 19 types recognized by the International Air Transport Association (IATA). Passengers pick a special meal for a variety of reasons, some of them pertaining to religious and/or health and diet requirements and others pertaining to something else entirely. For instance, British Airways was a pioneer in introducing a vegetarian main course on Concorde in the 1970s, which was then introduced in their first class, and their Club World class. The percentage of special meals is so varied from station to station that it is difficult to ascertain an accurate overall figure to cover its system. Although the numbers are small, the demand is increasing. For example, US Airways serves special meals to around 2.1% of its passengers who take meals, which translates into about 3,000 special meals served per month in first class and 36,000 meals in economy class (Lundstrom, 2001). Overall, the airline estimated that between 5 and 7% of their passengers request some type of special meal.

When passengers place their order through travel agent bookings, direct reservations, at check-in and sometimes at the departure gate, these special meals are generally coded into IATA's four-letter designations (International Air Transport Association, 2001). There has been a trend towards more standardized and uniform special meal types and the use of common ingredients from country to country and airline to airline. As an example, low-fat and low-salt meal options are becoming more commonplace in all meals and in some cases airlines have banned nuts completely from their recipes (Sutton and Gostelow, 1997). The airline expects that by combining the components of several dietary regional meals, SPMLs should save them some money and cut the amount of labor that currently goes into producing each of the meals. Changing the menu and streamlining the way meals are delivered have been important as airlines work across alliances and borders to please an increasingly diverse group of travelers with a myriad of dietary requirements (Lundstrom, 2001).

The common practice is to cook the most frequent special requirements in a separate area of the kitchen according to each airline's specifications. Vegetarian meals, fresh ingredients, seafood, low-fat and low-cholesterol are amongst the most frequently requested meals generally prepared by the flight caterer. The remaining SPMLs would be outsourced to specialist facilities for their preparation especially Kosher, Muslim, and Hindu. A number of religious rituals are involved, particularly with the Jewish faith, involving a rabbi making regular visits to the kitchen, or in some cases being permanently based there. Once completed, special meals are labeled and loaded into designated meal trolleys. All this translates into higher labor costs and higher food wastage. At present nutritional information is not provided to the passenger although some do carry a mark of approval from heart foundations, environmental groups and other institutes. BA, for example, offer a 'well-being selection' of dishes marked with an asterisk (*).

MAJOR STAKEHOLDERS

The in-flight sector of the hospitality industry consists of four major players: the airlines, or their various representatives; the providers, in this case specialized flight caterers; the suppliers, either to the providers or direct to the airlines; and distributors (Jones, 2004b).

The airlines are responsible for the design of onboard service. This is affected by the time of flight, length of flight, point of embarkation and disembarkation, nationality or ethnicity of passengers, seat class (economy, business or first), budget allowed by the airline, price of food, seasonality of food, cost of labor to make a food item, time required to serve the food, number of flight attendants available to serve food, time needed to consume food, ability of meal to be consumed in a small place on a plane, the time and effort needed to clear an item, the needs and desires of the passengers, odors that may penetrate the cabin, the ability of meal to be re-thermalized and the ability of the meal to withstand low humidity and pressures. Given this long list of factors it is not surprising that

the nature of onboard service varies widely from flight to flight and airline to airline.

The caterers have three main roles. First they prepare items not bought in directly from suppliers to a state ready for loading on board. Second they assemble trays and trollies. Finally they transport trollies to the aircraft and load them on board. It is this that is uniquely undertaken by the caterer, as no other stakeholder has the high-lift trucks needed to load aircraft. Flight kitchens are always located near to major airports and are usually used to 'manufacture' consumable food items. There are two main reasons why menu items may be made outside of airport-based flight kitchens: the cost of space and the cost of labor. Airport space is at a premium so often it is not feasible for a flight kitchen to produce all of the meals needed for every seat class. For instance, some flight kitchens or caterers may make their first-class, and in some cases business-class, meals from scratch at the flight kitchen and outsource all other meal production.

The caterer is often in an unusual and sometimes difficult, position. Although they are a customer of the supplier, the products used may not be of their choosing but may have been determined by the airline. When the products used are those purchased directly by the airline, caterers only charge for a handling and storage fee of the product but not the cost of the product. For instance, all liquor products for tax reasons must be purchased by the airlines, either through a pre-paid arrangement with the distributor or through an arrangement whereby the charges are directly invoiced to the airline. However, the caterer is often responsible for keeping and accounting for any such products and these products are usually delivered directly to the caterer's bonded store. The challenge for caterers is that the products are the property of the individual airlines served by the caterer. Products belonging to one airline cannot be used for another, even if the two airlines use identical products.

The suppliers supply the in-flight operation in two main ways. First, based on the planned menus, the supplier receives direct orders from the airlines, although they deliver their goods to flight kitchens operated by the contracted caterers. Airlines buy direct from suppliers because they want to have continuity of supply in all their stations, because they negotiate a discount, or because they want to maintain a particular brand image. Second, the supplier may supply the caterer directly, with products that meet the contract specification.

Likewise suppliers have two approaches to manufacturing their products. Some supply airlines (or their caterers) with their standard products, whereas others make and supply specialist products specifically designed for the in-flight kitchen. In the first instance, the manufacture of these products is likely to take place in a factory or plant producing many other products. The products for in-flight service may be slightly modified for that market. For instance, spirits manufacturers need to bottle their spirits in miniatures rather than 40 oz bottles. In the second case, the manufacturer concentrates on simply producing a cycle of food items, often constituting their sole business, and hence they can produce large amounts of these items to be sold to the flight kitchen as a method of outsourcing. These food manufacturers can make these items in volume at a lower cost than the flight kitchen can. The cost of labor to mass produce meals is obviously cheaper a good distance away from large cities where airports must exist. Historically it was mainly frozen meals, or 'pop-outs' as they are called in the USA, that were outsourced in this way. Today all kinds of specialist food items may be outsourced, such as canapés, ethnic meals, vegetarian items, patisserie, and so on.

The distributors are typically global logistics companies, specializing in moving goods around the world, often in containers. They provide two main services for airlines or caterers. They can distribute materials and meals from vendor/suppliers to both the caterers and the airlines and they can track the numbers, volumes, and brands of the products they distribute. Using a specialized distributor or logistics company allows the airline and caterer to better manage the flow of materials from aircraft to flight kitchen and back again. This applies to both short-term food items and to longer-term recyclable items, including equipment.

THE FLIGHT CATERING SUPPLY CHAIN

Since the 1950s and up to the 1990s there were three basic supply chain models. These can best be described by first of all understanding all the different elements of the supply chain. These are illustrated in Table 22.4. Table 22.4 starts with a need to be clear about the onboard service

Table 22.4 Elements of the flight catering supply 'chain'

Stage in the chain	Element	Qualities
Onboard service strategy	Seat class	
	Rotations	
Design the 'offer'		
Design/select 'items'	Consumables	Fresh
		Retail (ready-for-sale)
	Non-consumables	Rotables
		Disposables
Design/select 'components'		
Galley planning		
Sourcing	Offers	
	Items	
	Components	
	Raw materials	
Storage/warehousing		
Inventory control		
Preparation	Components	
Assembly/packaging	Items	
Tray assembly	Offers	
Trolley assembly		
Aircraft loading		
Aircraft unloading		
Recycling	Rotables	
Waste disposal		
Costing/invoicing		
Storage/warehousing		
Transportation		

strategy, i.e. exactly what each passenger will get. Such strategies depend upon the market segments being served, their respective seat class designations, the route network and aircraft fleet. Once the overall strategy is decided upon, the 'offer' that is to be made to each passenger has to be designed. The 'offer' will be made up of tangible items that will include things such as meals, beverages, onboard entertainment, as well as intangible elements in relation to the service on board. Within the 'offer' there will be a range of different 'items' that can usefully be divided into 'consumables' and 'non-consumables'.

Consumables are those items which are served to the passenger and only used once. These may be 'fresh' items such as meals or 'retail' items that the passenger may take with them when they depart the aircraft such as duty-free goods. In most cases beverages can be considered as retail consumables in the sense that they are pre-packaged in sealed containers and could be removed from the aircraft by the passenger if so wished. Indeed passengers routinely ask for spirit miniatures, which they do not consume on the aircraft. Non-consumables are those items taken off the aircraft by the operator. These can be usefully divided into 'rotables' and 'disposables'. Rotable items are those which are re-used on more than one flight and typically include crockery, cutlery and glassware. Disposable items are those items that can only be used once which typically includes packaging materials of paper, plastic or cardboard.

In some cases, items may be made up of components, most notably meals will be made up of a number of different dishes. Hence it is necessary not only to design and select the item but also to design and select the component. The number of dishes an airline may need in any year can be in the hundreds when taking into account different seat classes, rotations and special meals. Once the onboard service strategy and offer is known, it is then necessary to ensure that this can be effectively loaded onto and stored aboard the aircraft in the fleet. This process is known as galley planning. In airlines with one seat class and one aircraft type this is very straightforward, but for airlines with a mixed fleet and different seat classes and galley configurations, this can be highly complex.

The next element of the supply chain is sourcing, i.e. deciding on who will supply whatever is required. Sourcing can be done at a number of different levels, as identified earlier. That is to say, the offer can be sourced, items can be sourced and components can be sourced. Moreover, if the item is fresh, it may be necessary to source raw materials from which the component will be prepared. Once sourced, items, components and raw materials need to be transported from suppliers to wherever they are to be stored or warehoused. Once in storage, this inventory has to be controlled to ensure it is secure and held in the best conditions. From storage, the 'offer' has to be prepared and assembled. This typically involves four stages. First it may be necessary to prepare components, i.e. meat, fish, vegetables and fruit, either to be served cold or hot. Once prepared these need to be assembled or packaged in some way. For instance, hot dishes are typically assembled into foil containers and sealed with a cardboard top. The next stage is to take all the different items and to put them onto trays. These trays are then loaded into trolleys, on a flight-by-flight basis. This assembly process can be hugely complex.

Once the trollies for each flight have been assembled they then need to be loaded onto high-lift trucks for transportation to the aircraft, and then the aircraft needs to be loaded. At the same time, incoming trollies are unloaded and transported back to the flight kitchen. Incoming trollies then need to be processed. In some cases, items will be recycled, i.e. rotables will be washed ready for re-use. In other cases, items will have to be disposed of as waste – in particular any fresh food items or disposables. At this point, either the costing or invoicing for the above processes can be carried out. Finally, suppliers of raw materials, components or items provide two further elements of the supply chain. They store or warehouse these things prior to delivery; and they transport them from their storage facilities to where they are needed.

As indicated earlier, for around 40 years up to the 1990s, all of the elements in the supply chain were managed by three main stakeholders, namely airlines, caterers and suppliers. During this period there were three basic configurations of the chain. In North America, the basic model was for airlines to take responsibility for determining strategy, designing or selecting offers, items and components, galley planning and sourcing. The airlines then contracted out to caterers – storage, inventory control, preparation, assembly, loading/unloading, recycling and waste disposal. Caterers then purchased from suppliers the raw materials, components and items they needed in order to meet their contractual obligations with the airline.

This 'contracting out model' however, applies only to the supply of fresh items, i.e. meals. There was a different model for the supply of retail items, such as alcoholic beverages, soft drinks and duty-free goods. In this case, airlines tended to negotiate directly with suppliers; whilst the elements of preparation, packaging and tray assembly were unnecessary as these items came in ready for sale. This is the so-called 'retail flight catering supply chain'. It was used not only in North America, but also in Europe. However, the fresh supply chain in Europe was configured differently to North America, as airlines did not have caterers to whom they could outsource. Hence airlines backwardly integrated into flight kitchens creating the 'integrated supply chain'.

Although there have been many innovations in the supply chain from the 1990s onwards, these three basic models – 'contracting out', retail and integrated – continue to the present day. The larger and growing airlines in the Middle East and Asia have tended to adopt the integrated model; whereas the European airlines have tended to divest themselves of their flight catering operations and have adopted the contracting out model. Both in-house and outsourced catering will continue to be adopted in the future, although increasingly this is only likely to be applied to first and business class offers.

This analysis also explains how it is possible for airlines to switch away from complimentary meal service to so-called 'buy on board'. In essence, buy on board is based on the idea that the food items become a retail product. Hence, the retail supply chain can be adopted for this purpose. Low-cost airlines, as part of their business model, adopted the retail approach to the flight catering supply chain from the very beginning.

There are three main ways that the nature of the supply chains outlined above have been changed. First, existing stakeholders have forwardly or backwardly integrated. Second, new stakeholders have taken over some elements of the supply chain and thirdly the supply chain has been re-designed, usually by removing or eliminating some of the elements in it.

One of the first examples of forward integration was in the 1990s when Delta Daily Food, a supplier, forwardly integrated and took over elements of the supply chain normally carried out by the caterer (Jones and Kipps, 1995). This was made possible by the proximity of their food factory to Schipol airport, so that it was possible for them to add packaging, tray and trolley assembly to their existing food manufacturing facility. However, this model is relatively unusual, as it depends on the supplier being located relatively close to airports.

Another way for suppliers to forwardly integrate is to eliminate some elements of the supply chain so that they can supply airports from wherever their factories are located. This typically involves using disposable packaging that eliminates the need for tray, and even trolley, assembly. For instance, Supplair developed a range of retail-style food products and disposable packaging that can be delivered direct to flight kitchens, so that the role of the caterer is reduced to tray and trolley assembly and loading.

A slightly different example of this approach is the Nestlé Sky Tray. This concept consists of the 'Hot Pocket' brand, a hand-held hot snack, being packaged on a thermally resistant service tray. The trays are packaged in boxes that are the same size as aircraft ovens. Hence boxes can be transported by Nestlé to flight kitchens and then loaded directly onto aircraft without any assembly by the caterer. On the aircraft, the trays are unloaded from their container, placed in the oven, reheated and then used to serve the passengers directly from the oven. Not only does the concept eliminate elements of the caterers' part of the supply chain, it also simplifies the airlines' design of meals, requiring them only to select the product they want.

As well as suppliers forwardly integrating, caterers are also able to do this. This means that airlines focus solely on setting the overall service strategy and outsource the specific design of items, components, galley planning and sourcing to the caterer. Airlines have been encouraged to do this by the development of Internet-based systems such as e-gate matrix and e-LSG, which make transparent what is happening at each stage of the supply chain. Alpha Flight Catering have set up a division called In-Flight Service Management (IFSM) which also takes over many of the activities that the airlines in-flight department may previously have carried out. They argue that IFSM, because it manages many airlines, can afford to employ experts in a wide range of areas that individual, smaller, airlines would not be able to employ;

and that such expertise leads to a lower-cost operation.

In summary, it would seem that in addition to the three 'traditional' models of the flight catering supply chain, there are four new models. In fact, these four are simply examples of how different elements of the supply chain are being bundled together in new and original ways. In line with many other industries, it is becoming clear that the concept of the supply chain is somewhat old-fashioned. It is more appropriate to think in terms of a supply network, with all the increased sophistication that a network configuration would suggest. Hence it is possible for a single airline to have adopted a number of different configurations depending on where it flies to, its type of route and so forth.

In addition, this analysis shows that only a few elements of the supply network are always undertaken by the same stakeholder. Airlines are always responsible for their strategy, but may outsource every other element. Likewise caterers are always responsible for loading and unloading aircraft, recycling and waste disposal because no other stakeholder has the infrastructure necessary to perform these tasks. Outside of these areas, it is becoming increasingly blurred as to whether or not it is caterers, suppliers or third parties engaged in the different elements of the supply network.

AIRLINE–CATERER CONTRACTS

The relationship between an airline and caterer is based on service delivery. The airline requires its catering supplier to deliver on certain key variables (Jones, 2004b), such as:

- consistency of food product;
- accuracy of uplift;
- on-time delivery;
- value for money;
- service relationships;
- health, hygiene and safety;
- innovation; and
- overall operational performance.

However in the complex business world of today, all of these things cannot be simply agreed on the basis of a handshake. So in the majority of cases, airlines and caterers enter into a legal relationship based on a contract between them. In most cases, caterers are invited to tender for an airline contract. Such a contract may apply to just one airport, such as Schipol, or apply to all the destinations an airline flies to in a region of the world, such as the Middle East. Rarely does it apply to all the destinations an airline flies to, unless this airline is relatively small. In some cases, caterers do not wait to be invited to tender, they make what is termed a 'pre-emptive bid'. They do this when they know an existing contract is likely to be coming to an end and they believe that this airline's business would be a good 'fit' with the other contracts they have.

Contracts between airlines and caterers may be very long and detailed documents, but they will conform to a fairly standard structure (Jones, 2007), comprising the following elements.

- **Terms of agreement** – this specifies the length of time the contract will be in force. Typically flight catering contracts are for one to three years. The trend is for them to be longer rather than shorter.
- **Definition of services** – each and every element of service being provided will be defined in precise terms. For instance, terms such as 'uplift', 'menu specification' and so on will have definitions if referred to in the contract.
- **Charges and payments** – the prices to be paid for the service rendered will be identified along with any relevant terms and conditions applying to such payments in relation to timing of payment, form of payment, and so on.
- **Title and risk** – as, in most cases, the caterer will be handling equipment belonging to the airline, it is necessary to identify who owns what (title) and who has liability for any loss (risk). Typically the airline has the title, but the caterer bears the risk.
- **Indemnity and liability** – these clauses of the contract limit the ability of either party to the contract to sue the other party.
- **Warranties** – in some cases one of the parties to the contract, usually the caterer, will provide a guarantee, in the form of a warranty, to the other party.
- **Confidentiality** – most contracts contain a clause that ensure that both parties keep the terms and conditions of their contract confidential.
- **Termination** – the contract will specify under what conditions either party can end the contract and how much notice must be given if doing so.
- **Force majeure** – this legal term applies to allowing a suspension of the terms of the contract due to so-called 'acts of God', that is to say if

events outside the control of one of the parties prevents the contract from being honored.

- **Business continuity** – this clause will identify what happens to the contract if one of the parties is taken over by a third party or goes out of business due to insolvency or bankruptcy.
- **Law and jurisdiction** – this clause will specify in which country the two parties agree the contract is signed, so that the laws of contract of this country apply to any legal dispute between the two sides.
- **Waiver** – this clause ensures that neither party is able to change any part of the contract without the agreement of the other party.
- **Invalidity** – this clause ensures that in the event that one clause of the contract is shown to be invalid (i.e. not of legal status), this does not make the whole contract invalid.

In addition to this legal contract, attached to it, or as part of the overall agreement between the airline and caterer, there may be additional documentation such as a service-level agreement, a price list, and standards of performance criteria. A typical service-level agreement would have detailed specifications of how things were to be done, relating to such things as hygiene, punctuality, product specifications, security, equipment control and waste management. It may refer not simply to delivering trolleys to aircraft, but to other operational aspects. For instance, some airlines require their caterers to make quarterly presentations on new menu ideas as part of their agreement. Likewise there will be specific performance targets that caterers will be expected to meet. Such targets might include:

- number of aircraft delays allowed per month (typically no more than 1%);
- number of adverse cabin crew reports permitted;
- number of catering-related passenger letters;
- allowable % of incorrect weights of product;
- number of occasions of incorrect invoicing; and
- hygiene audit scores.

If performance falls outside the allowed tolerances the penalties to pay will be specified. Likewise if performance is particularly good, incentives may be paid.

The range of methods used to price in-flight meals is very wide, from a simple, 'multiply by a factor' to a sophisticated multi-disciplined approach. Some methods are straightforward in that they require the minimum of data collection and manipulation and are therefore attractive for that reason. There is little evidence to suggest that more sophisticated methods are more successful than simple straightforward ones, but they must be based on standard recipes.

However, price is a determinant of demand and therefore pricing is never a simple matter of 'mark-up over cost'. When and how to increase prices is just as critical as the amount of the increase itself. The market for the flight product appears to be becoming ever-more price sensitive and more value conscious, indicating that those flight caterers who wish to survive and increase their profitability in a much more competitive environment will need to concentrate even more on costing and pricing. Successful pricing methods are able to contribute to establishing a 'competitive edge' over very aggressive and increasingly margin-conscious rivals.

In many ground-based catering operations, price is based on raw material cost, with sufficient margin to cover labor and overhead costs. In-flight catering price is often established on the basis of separately calculating each of these elements of cost. This is because the labor cost for a meal item may vary widely according to whether a product is simply handled or significantly processed within the flight production unit. For instance, hot entrées such as casseroles or stews may be outsourced to a food manufacturer (handling costs only) or be prepared from entirely fresh foodstuffs in the flight kitchen (production, processing and handling costs). It is therefore common for separate prices to be established for different aspects of provision, such as stock-handling and warehousing, food production, tray lay-up, transportation, and ware-washing.

FLIGHT CATERING LOGISTICS

Logistics is concerned with adding value and reducing waste across the whole flight catering system. It is particularly concerned with non-consumable or non-disposable stock items (crockery, glassware, trays, etc.), although increasingly it is addressing other types of inventory too (particularly alcoholic beverages and duty free items). In order to use these stocks effectively and efficiently, logistics is concerned with:

- material demand forecasting;
- equipment sector (or shelf) life;
- sourcing of products;

- contracting suppliers;
- managing purchase contracts;
- transportation of stocks;
- warehousing of stocks;
- inventory management of stocks and 'dwell time' (time not in use);
- stock balancing across the network; and
- galley and trolley planning.

The principal objectives of a logistics system are based around getting the *right products/materials* to the *right place(s)* at the *right time* and at *least cost*. The logistics issues of flight catering are affected by a number of important features of the airline industry, the most important being the basic features of the business, the specifics of route scheduling, the impact of actual passenger loadings, and the 'product' mix.

The basic features of the airline industry are that it has global dimensions, is highly competitive and profitability depends largely on maximizing revenue in the face of variable demand. The airline business is increasingly competitive and most airlines in considering their competitive edge take account of the quality of the 'service package' offered to customers. For instance, there are strong pressures in some cases to use quality non-disposable items rather than cheaper disposables, such as china crockery, rather than disposable equivalents. The reinforcement of brand image also causes most to require that several items bear the company livery and logo. This has strong implications for the logistics problem since it could prevent local supply of these items.

Demand can be highly variable both in the shorter cycles (across a week) and longer (across a year). Profitability is very dependent on maximizing revenue for which the technique of yield management was devised. The basic aim of this is to maximize passenger loading while as far as possible ensuring that the average fare paid by customers is also maximized. This may result in a wide variation in the passenger mix. At peak times when seat sales are relatively easy, there may be a high proportion of first-class passengers, while at off-peak times there is a higher proportion of sales in the economy class. Thus, the logistics system must be capable of adapting to variations not only in passenger numbers but also in the mix of passenger service requirements. For instance, outbound flights from London to European destinations will carry a high proportion of business people, especially in the morning, whereas the return flights will have a higher proportion of leisure travelers. Likewise, over the long cycle, flights into e.g. Austria carry a very different mix of business and leisure travelers in the ski season than at other times of the year.

In addition, the drive to maximize seat occupancies sometimes leads to flights having intermediate stops so that tickets may be sold not only for an entire flight but also for parts of it; that is, for one leg of the journey. This may present the additional logistics complication of restocking aircraft at intermediate stops. For instance, although it is technically possible for an aircraft to fly non-stop from Europe to the Far East, many flights have a stop-over in the Middle East or India in order to improve seat occupancy levels.

Long-haul flights present special problems in terms of co-ordinating the logistics function. This is particularly the case where airlines have full traffic rights and seek to maximize revenues from each sector of a multiple-leg flight. For catering uplifts this means that logistical arrangements can be quite varied. For example, long-haul economy meals, as high-volume and relatively standardized products, may be supplied from the place of origin and an intermediate port of call. However, on the same flight, first- or business-class meals offering extensive customer choice and menu flexibility, may be catered throughout from the place of origin. Maintenance of a consistently high standard of service may leave this as the only viable option. Additionally, it may prove advantageous to uplift other items such as liquor elsewhere on the journey (Jones, 2004b).

Passenger factors are major drivers which test the responsiveness of the logistics system on a day-to-day basis. Passenger numbers affect the size of uplifts for meal trays (but not for bars, which are normally stocked to par stock levels). In order that balance is maintained within the system, equipment levels will have to remain relatively constant. For short-haul flights, which fly to a destination and return directly to point of origin, there should be no major problem. If the aircraft flies out with a full set of equipment, it should return with a full set. But even on short-haul, in aircraft with a flexible cabin that allows the size of business class relative to economy to increase or decrease, some equipment imbalance may occur. On long-haul flights, however, especially those with intermediate stop-overs and more than meal service, equipment taken off the aircraft at one point may not automatically be reloaded at the same point. To overcome this problem, airlines have adopted 'dead-heading'. This involves loading aircraft with equipment items sufficient for the maximum number of passengers irrespective of meals required, thereby ensuring that equipment exchanges at intermediate or final destinations can take place without excess stocks developing in some parts of the system and shortages occurring elsewhere. Thus it is a logistics requirement that equipment exchanges take place satisfactorily under conditions where, for example, outward flights may be carrying low occupancy but return legs the opposite. Unless massive stocks were to be held at each catering supply point it is easy to imagine a situation where differences in passenger numbers could lead to much of an airline's equipment ending up in one place. Even for charter business where passenger loadings are less volatile and back catering more common, this type of arrangement tends to hold for equipment items.

Many airlines operate aircraft dedicated to particular routes and with fleets conforming to identical configurations. Therefore, any change of aircraft for whatever reason, such as maintenance overhauls or traffic delays, should have little impact upon the logistics function.

FLIGHT CATERING INFORMATION SYSTEMS

The interface and passage of information between those who provide goods or services and those who receive or use them are important in any business operation. Flight catering is no exception, but the nature and immediacy of the catering product require that the information be both accurate and timely if it is to be of any value in the decision-making process and the continued success of the operation. Information needs to be passed between three major players: the airlines, or their various representatives; flight providers, in this case caterers and other suppliers; and those using the airline's services, that is the fare-paying passengers.

However, the passage and smooth flow of information is not easy and in the airline industry it is compounded not only by the immediacy of the products and services involved but also by the fragmentation and international nature of the business. In addition, it is difficult at times to know who the customer really is; who therefore influences and affects the information being received and processed and, in consequence, the relative importance of these influences in the decision-making process.

The provision of integrated information systems for all aspects of flight catering are still at a relatively early stage of development. This is because it is only recently that the IT industry itself, and software developers, have had common platforms on which to develop their systems. The most obvious common platform that most people are familiar with is the Internet or world-wide-web. But other developments, such as Windows software, have also helped to facilitate the integration of systems that hitherto had been almost impossible to link together.

In the flight catering industry, the scale and scope of such systems often reflects the particular orientation of the IT provider or software developer. Some systems are based on airline reservation systems and have integrated backwards along the supply chain to add on related software programs. Other systems are based on software originally developed by caterers for managing the production processes in in-flight kitchens. In another case, the original software was developed to facilitate galley planning, from which further programs were developed to address issues of forecasting, scheduling, loading and equipment balancing.

Due to the variety of sources of IT solutions, there is no one agreed information systems 'map' or schema which shows *all* the information requirements for flight catering. Indeed there may never be a single such map, as different airlines and/or caterers may have very different needs. Information, and the systems that communicate and analyze this, costs money. There is no point in having a more sophisticated system than the business requires. Hence no-frills or budget airlines are almost certainly going to have a system that looks and behaves in different ways to a system that supports a full-service carrier. Furthermore, the system in use may reflect the age of the firm, or at least the last time a major investment was made in IT systems. Some airlines may have so-called 'legacy' systems, that is to say hardware and software that they are left with, and which are far from state-of-the-art. Nonetheless Table 22.5 attempts to list all the different types of information that might be included in an integrated system.

Table 22.5　Information needs for flight catering

Type of information	Principal source of information
Routes flown and flight schedule	Airline timetable
Aircraft type	
Flight number	Airline timetable
Service provision for each route	
Menus and meal specification for each class	Specification manuals
Dish and recipe specifications	Specification manuals
Raw material requirements	Specification manuals
Menu rotation sequence	Airline policy and/or contract with caterer
Equipment and tray lay-up specifications	Specification manuals
Equipment inventories	Stocktaking and inventory records
Passenger numbers (pax.)	Reservations systems
Classes of passenger	Reservations system
Hot meal production	Pax $\times$ class $\times$ route
Tray assembly data per flight	Pax $\times$ class $\times$ route
Trolley assembly per flight	Pax $\times$ class $\times$ route $\times$ aircraft type
Equipment balancing	
Galley plans	Stowage plans
Aircraft loading	Loading sheet
Budgets	
Actual operating costs	
Invoice reconciliation	

Source: Jones (2004b: 231).

INNOVATION IN IN-FLIGHT CATERING

There are well-established models of how manufacturing firms engage in new product development. More recently innovation in service firms has also been considered. The most comprehensive study of service innovation to date, however, was conducted by Scheuing and Johnson (1989) in which they proposed a model for new service development based on work in financial institutions. The sequence of activities in the proposed model goes beyond existing models on new product development to describe the interplay between the design and the testing functions during the development of a new service.

Two major studies of flight catering innovation have been carried out. Peirce (1994) conducted a survey of 300 firms in the industry with a 40% response rate. The respondents accurately reflected the three main constituent sectors of the industry – food manufacturers/suppliers, flight caterers and airlines. Jones and Bertorello (2001) conducted face-to-face interviews with respondents from 38 different firms within the flight catering sector, from a range of countries including the UK, Germany, USA, Singapore and Australia. The companies ranged from small entrepreneurial businesses up to global companies such as Mars, Qantas and British Airways. The results of both studies are consistent with the findings of other similar surveys in other industries.

In the Peirce (1994) study, all the companies were asked if they had specific long-term objectives or strategies that involved developing new products or services. The majority of companies claimed to have specific company objectives that mention innovating new products and/or services. However, when asked whether their company had developed a new product or service in the past 12 months, very few were able to identify a specific example of any such innovation. Only a small number of companies, around 10%, have a specific department responsible for research and development (R&D). Of those firms that have such departments, these tend to be either food manufacturing companies or large airlines. The department most likely to generate new ideas was the sales and marketing department of firms. In the majority of firms, however, ideas were generated in an *ad hoc* way, either from listening and talking to customers or the brainwave of an individual. This was especially true of all of the smaller firms surveyed. When asked what the most powerful idea sources are for companies, suppliers maintained it was customer feedback. Both airlines and caterers recognized this as important, but in combination with problem-solving, i.e. advantageous modifications to existing products. A somewhat surprising 25% of companies did not actively encourage staff to put forward innovative ideas – but of those that did, 30% claimed that the general company culture promoted the idea of staff contributions through meetings.

With regards to the detailed design of the innovation, most companies chose to carry out concept testing through discussions with customer-contact personnel. New ideas were only formally screened/evaluated in terms of feasibility and profitability by 61% of companies. In the case of most small companies, there was little or no formal business analysis. The number of small companies in the industry also helps to explain why 90% of companies responding stated that one person or department in the company authorized all innovative projects. The majority said this was usually the managing director or the 'committee leader'. The *ad hoc* way in which new ideas are generated is also reflected in how funding is agreed for projects. Research for new services/products is also funded on an *ad hoc* basis by just over half of the firms surveyed. All three sectors found it difficult to identify the number of people specifically involved with innovation development, claiming that it depended on the product or service under development.

All firms agreed that operations personnel need to be involved in testing innovations. But there were some differences between sectors about the need to support innovations with marketing support and personnel training. Suppliers claimed that the products/services they developed required marketing programs; whereas caterers and airlines were less likely to develop a marketing program in support of the innovation. On the other hand, the opposite trend appeared when the different sectors were asked if their innovations required the training of personnel – 91% of airlines claimed they did, 87% of caterers with only 68% of suppliers. Once developed, nearly all companies claimed to carry out pilot runs to test new products/services. At the testing/development stage, the caterers and suppliers tended to rely on internal experience and/or satisfy legal requirements. Only the airlines carried out physical trials as part of the development process. The players tend to evaluate new services/products once on the market in slightly different ways. The majority of airlines use market surveys, whereas caterers and suppliers both rely more on after-sales for

feedback. All companies claimed to monitor customer satisfaction on a constant basis.

With regards to the type of innovation being carried out, all three types of company tend to think about innovation as 'product' innovation. Food manufacturers and suppliers tend to think in terms of changing a food or drink item in such a way as to make it better meet the needs of the flight caterer and/or airline. The small- to medium-size suppliers do not have the financial or human resources needed to support large-scale process or organizational innovation. On the other hand, the larger suppliers may well be engaging in this kind of innovation, but across the whole of their organization, therefore not identifying it as an innovation related solely to the flight catering segment of their activity. Flight catering firms also tend to think in terms of modifying the product, although there is some evidence to show that process innovation is occurring in some cases. It is also likely that organizational innovation is occurring, although the caterers do not think of it as such. This is because many such firms are instituting new approaches to quality management, especially as per official standard BS 5750 in the UK, or ISO 9000 in other parts of Europe. The airlines also tend to think in terms of the product/service bundle. From the survey results, each sector of the industry thought it was the most innovative with regard to the flight catering industry.

Finally, with regards to the level of originality of innovation, there was little evidence of a major research and development activity producing highly original products, processes or organizational forms. Many of the individual innovations cited in the research and reviewed from the IFCA annual Mercury Awards demonstrate that firms tend to adapt or adopt ideas from other firms, either within the industry or from other related industries.

The Jones and Bertorello (2001) study adopted an interview approach which allowed a more detailed picture of innovation to emerge. The 38 firms varied in size from six employees up to several thousand employees. 24% had fewer than 50 employees, 24% were medium sized enterprises (50 to 1000 employees), and 52% had more than 1000 employees. There was a fairly equal split between airlines (38%), caterers (32%) and suppliers (30%). The majority of respondents (80%) were male and two-thirds were employed in the operations or marketing function. Typical job titles of respondents were Managing Director, In-Flight

Service Director and Account Manager. The type of innovation was also almost equally split between food product (36%), non-food product (32%) and service (32%). Examples of the innovations presented for an award were an oxygenated spring water, a multi-function plug for disposable earphones, a hot beverage trolley producing boiling water without electricity, and a new style first-class cabin.

Some 60% of respondents were aware of their company having a mission statement, but many of these were vague as to precisely what it was. Of those that had such a statement only a quarter believe this to make explicit reference to innovation. However, most respondents were clear that their firm did have objectives and a strategy in relation to innovation, even if it was not in the mission. As one said 'there is no explicit reference to innovation … [but] to be the undisputed world leader in the travel market [means] a high degree of innovation must take place …'. Another said '[our mission statement says] providing superior solutions to the food-service operator … [which] has something to do with being innovative I think'.

With regard to organizational structure, respondents were asked if their firms had a research and development (R&D) department. Only 20% had such a department, of which the majority were large firms. In some cases the R&D department was technically based, either with respect to engineering or food production, in other cases it was market research-based, reporting to the Sales or Marketing Director of the company. It was very clear that nearly all the companies, except for the very smallest saw innovation as a team effort. This was always the case amongst the airlines in the sample. In terms of those with specific responsibility, the Managing Director of the firm played an important role in six out of the eleven caterers in the sample, whereas a key role was played by the in-flight service or catering department amongst the airlines. Chefs contributed to innovation in only five cases and ergonomic designers in only two.

Since all respondents were from firms that had innovated, all had experienced the idea generation stage. The most common form of this was through internal consultation and brainstorming, often stimulated by customer feedback. One caterer reported 'We have a weekly forum where everybody gets together to talk'. In five instances, the innovation resulted from the 'inspiration of a single individual'.

One equipment manufacturer stated 'I got the idea from a flight attendant'. In most cases such inspiration was in small firms. Some respondents mentioned that trade shows or traveling led to the idea. One representative from an airline said 'We go to trade shows [or] see some nice things in a restaurant and think maybe we can adapt this to our business'. Only one cited a supplier as providing the original idea.

Just over half (54%) of respondents identified some form of idea screening. The most common approaches to such consultation were with other people within the relevant division or department of the firm and/or with customers. In some cases, the factors taken into account were technical feasibility, practicality, time span and cost. For example, an executive from an airline said 'Each idea is evaluated for its effectiveness – cost, practicality, what regulatory approvals are needed. They go through a series of steps'. However, the nature of the innovation may affect this screening process even within the same firm. Another airline executive identified that 'It depends on the scale of and scope of the ideas. When you talk about a complete new service it's different from a product item … For a large impact idea we go back to the customer and use our frequent flyers as a consumer panel. When it's a smaller idea … we try it out, introduce it for half a year and see if it's OK'.

As the example above illustrates, concept development and testing may be carried out on an *ad hoc* basis. Two-thirds of respondents reported that prior to development, their innovation was externally reviewed in some way. In nearly every case, such a review was conducted by customers. An American airline manager stated 'We work closely with a consumer advocacy group. They are invited at all stages to give their views'. In a very small number of cases, the concept was considered by suppliers and by technical experts. But some firms are reluctant to broaden consultation too widely – 'if ideas were to leak out, our competitors would find out about them. A good idea can be easily copied' (airline representative) and 'it was kept pretty quiet. I didn't talk to anyone until it was patented' (equipment manufacturer).

Most firms (70%), included some form of business analysis in their innovation process. This was usually in the form of a financial appraisal that identified some degree of payback on investment. And 60% had to have project authorization for the innovation to proceed. In small enterprises, this was often not necessary as the person carrying out the innovation was also the owner of the company. In larger firms, approval was often at board level (for major innovations) or at senior executive level, such as Vice-President Foodservice Division or Marketing Director. Once approval has been given for the project to go ahead, the innovation process can vary quite widely both in terms of length of time and complexity. One airline's innovation 'took a couple of months', whilst another's '[took] a long time – about two years from idea to implementation'. This reflects very much the wide range of different innovations that were included in the sample.

In most cases (62%), firms recognized that training of personnel was required. This applied especially to service and process innovations, but even product innovations may have required shop-floor employees to be retrained. But in very few cases (15%) a marketing program was developed in conjunction with the innovation. This is probably because so much of what was done was on a business-to-business basis rather than directly aimed at consumers. The low importance of marketing effort in relation to the innovation, also meant there was very little test marketing. However a very high proportion of firms (82%) engaged in product testing the innovation. One airline 'did some in-flight tests with the prototype'; another reported 'there was a trial period'. For some products the testing was not done with flight caterers or airlines. One drinks manufacturer said 'testing took place in a London hospital'; a wine shipper 'gave samples to customers in supermarkets'; and a food manufacturer has 'a panel of twelve people who taste it on a score chart'.

Firms adopted a wide variety of approaches to the *launch* of the new product, service or process. Some launched it with a press release, others ran an advertisement, yet others exhibited at trade shows. The IFCA trade show was specifically mentioned by 18% of respondents. But in some cases the launch was very low key. One charter airline said 'there was nothing big'. Post-launch review for most firms seems to take place immediately, although it is not at all clear how systematic such reviews are. In effect, most reviews are not specific to the innovation but wrapped up in routine customer feedback. As one airline said 'it comes though from customer comments'; another stated 'we get feedback from the people on the ground, cabin staff and customers too'.

The findings of this study suggest there is a wide variety of practice with regards to innovation. Few firms had explicit statements about innovation in their mission or possessed dedicated R&D departments. Those that did tended to be larger firms from across all types of firm – food suppliers, equipment suppliers, caterers and airlines. However most firms used a variety of means of generating new ideas, in particular using customer feedback, staff feedback, brainstorming and other meetings to come up with new ideas. Individual 'inspiration' was relatively rare, and almost always in the smaller firms.

Idea screening is almost exclusively restricted to discussion in house or with customers, often through focus groups. Concept development and testing is typically carried out on an *ad hoc* basis, also with customers. There is a real concern that ideas may be copied by competitors if they are discussed too openly. The most formal stage of the whole process, and common to most medium and large firms, is in relation to conducting some form of business appraisal of the innovation, along with having the project authorized formally by senior executives of the company.

Most innovation involves some training of personnel, but very little related marketing. The latter is probably due to the nature of in-flight innovation, which is conducted very much on a business-to-business basis. Nearly all innovative products, services or processes were trailed or tested before being fully operationalized. In some cases such testing was out with the in-flight industry. The new products, service and processes examined in this study were launched in a wide variety of ways, with a review of their success being incorporated into routine customer feedback. There was very little specific review of the innovation process itself.

An analysis of the innovation process by type of firm – airline, caterer or supplier – revealed no distinctive pattern. This is because although suppliers tended to be involved in product innovation, and airlines tended to report on service innovation, there was a fair amount of overlap between them. However, a pattern of innovation does emerge when the process is analyzed by type – food, non-food product, or service. It emerges that food products appear to go through an extremely abbreviated innovation process, without even the launch phase being included in the majority of cases. This is surprising. The non-food innovation process is very close to the typical model of innovation described in the innovation literature.

However, there is no evidence from this study that the service process is any more complex than that of products, contrary to what is proposed in the literature. The only three activities which are common to all types of innovation are business analysis, trialing/testing, and using customer feedback to evaluate the success of the innovation.

The role of innovation in the industry was also reflected in a study of chef competencies in in-flight catering. Hayama et al. (2002) compared the job roles and competencies of airline catering chefs with other groups of chefs (i.e. production chefs and research chefs) in the UK, USA and Japan. Only 11 competencies were shared across these three countries, made up of personal attribute competencies and technical proficiency competencies. The 11 competencies were as follows.

1 Skilled at time management
2 Knowledge of culinary fundamentals and production systems, particularly for producing in large volumes, including their limitations
3 Skilled at food presentation
4 Knowledge of culinary uses and applications of products / ingredients functionally
5 Knowledge of kitchen functions and pressures
6 Understanding of food testing
7 Knowledge of quality assurance and food safety
8 Ability to work in multi-task environments
9 Ability to make decisions
10 General communication skills
11 Ability to distinguish levels of quality in food products

A total of 29 competencies were validated in the United States, and likewise there were 20 and 13 competencies identified in Japan and the United Kingdom, respectively. The competencies validated by the United States and Japan tended to stress personal attribute competencies as well as technical proficiency competencies, emphasizing that successful air-line catering chefs need to play an even-greater managerial role in addition to a culinary one. In the United Kingdom in contrast, technical proficiency competencies were the main focus.

FUTURE TRENDS

As airlines continue to demand higher quality in-flight food offerings at lower prices, in-flight caterers and suppliers are continually exploring new, innovative and diverse ways of remaining competitive. Airlines throughout the world are experimenting with different ways of serving meals to passengers. These options include buy-on-board food products, buy-at-the gate options, giveaway-at-the-gate and offering a picnic bag rather than a tray-set. With the external pressures from customers and competitors, it is not surprising that all flight catering firms are seeking to reduce their costs by operating more efficiently. To do this they have turned to the lessons learned in manufacturing and assembly plants – most especially the concepts of lean or agile manufacturing and just-in-time production. The approach being adopted varies from firm to firm, and from plant to plant, but some clear trends are evident as follows.

- Average cycle time, i.e. total processing time, in the industry used to be about 24 hours – some plants have reduced this to 8 hours.
- Reducing cycle time has been achieved by taking 'waste' out of the system – wasted time, wasted movement, too much stock, unnecessary transportation, and etc.
- An industry norm was that each aircraft need 3.5 sets of equipment (one set on the plane, one being cleaned at the point of departure, one ready for loading at the point of arrival, and a half set to cover losses and breakages). By reducing cycle time, global caterers have significantly reduced the total amount of equipment in the system.
- Less equipment frees up space in plants to facilitate revisions to process layouts, simplify inventory control, and generally use space more efficiently.
- Inventory management is switching to the kanban system, i.e. standardized bins of each inventory item.
- Tray assembly is switching from conveyor belts to work stations based on kanbans.
- Non-standard catering, such as for special meals, is being outsourced to specialist suppliers.

Suppliers have also begun to eliminate some elements of the supply chain so that they can supply airlines from wherever their factories are located. This is often in direct competition with airline caterers and typically involves using disposable packaging that eliminates the need for tray, and even trolley, assembly. For instance, as previously stated, Supplair's products can be delivered direct to flight kitchens, reducing the role of the caterer in transportation and loading. Nestlé Sky Tray's 'Hot Pocket' brand, are delivered straight to flight kitchens and then loaded directly onto aircraft without any assembly by the caterer. On the aircraft, the trays can also be used to serve the passengers directly again reducing the role of the traditional flight caterer. Finally with the use of logistics firms such as Kuehne and Nagel, whose global warehousing and transportation capability offer significant economies of scale, elements of the supply chain can become totally removed from traditional stakeholders.

CONCLUSION

As this chapter demonstrates there has been little research conducted into this industry sector. It is only possible to speculate why this is so. It is likely that very few academics with an industry background have worked in this type of operation – most will have hotel or restaurant experience. It is also the case that flight kitchens are relatively rare compared with other industry sectors, being located only at airports. Moreover security and hygiene concerns mean that management are not always keen to provide access to visitors or researchers. The image of airline meals is also very poor, perhaps unfairly so, which may reduce its appeal to the hospitality research community. Another factor that has made it difficult to research this sector is the lack, until a few years ago, of large-scale firms with strong brand recognition. Finally, airline meals are ancillary to the core product of air travel, served to a captive market. It is not surprising therefore that the industry itself had to sponsor research, through the endowment of a professorial chair, in order to promote in-flight catering research.

Although this sector of the hospitality industry has been little researched it has some distinctive features that make it very interesting. Cook-chill technology and systems were originally developed by flight caterers in order to ensure the food safety of transported and reheated meals onboard aircraft. The cabin environment requires sector-specific skills in terms of dish development and the frequency of rotations requires significant levels of menu development. The flight catering supply chain is also specific to this industry, as is logistics. Flight catering kitchens are also some of the largest catering operations in the world producing very large numbers of meals on a daily basis and handling large quantities of beverages. As a result, both managers and chefs that work in this sector have to have skills and competencies quite different to those needed for the hospitality industry in general.

Hence it is worthwhile to conclude by considering what kind of research could or should be conducted in this field. From the flight catering industry's perspective, there continue to be some challenges that remain unresolved. For airlines, these are as follows:

- the attitude of passengers towards food onboard and its significance, both in terms of pre-purchase decision-making and post-consumption satisfaction, with regard to the total travel experience;
- reducing food waste without reducing passenger choice and service;
- cost–benefit analysis of rotable equipment items versus disposable items;
- the adoption of effective and efficient environmentally friendly policies and procedures; and
- efficient and effective logistics with regards to provisioning and equipment.

The caterers also face some different challenges, which include the following:

- significant and sustainable process improvements in order to reduce costs;
- effectively competing with food manufacturers to supply a consistent product at low-cost;
- the role of branding on tray sets; and
- over-capacity of kitchen infrastructure at many major airports around the world.

These industry-specific issues require research but are unlikely to contribute significantly to theory or principles of operations management. However, flight catering is a rich environment for those interested in researching a number of operations management topics particularly process re-engineering, supply chain configuration, the adoption of information technologies in the supply chain and logistics, innovation and quality management – especially since this operation requires the handling and assembly of both perishable (food) items and non-perishable (equipment) items. With an annual production of nearly 1 billion meals, this sector is too large for researchers to ignore.

REFERENCES

Chang, Y.-C. (2006) *Towards Mass Customisation? The Implementation of Modern Manufacturing Concepts in the Flight Catering Industry*. Guildford: University of Surrey, PhD dissertation.

Hayama, M., Simms, R. and Jones, P. (2003) *Flight Catering Chefs in the UK, USA and Japan: Production Workers, Process Managers, or Development Gurus?* TCRC Report No. 1. Guildford: University of Surrey.

Hong, J. (2006) *Passenger Attitudes towards Airline Meals*. Guildford: University of Surrey. Unpublished dissertation.

International Air Transport Association (2001) *In-flight Management Manual*, 1st edn. International Air Transport Association, Montreal.

Jones, P. and Kipps, M. (eds) (1995) *Flight Catering*. Longman: Oxford.

Jones, P. (2004a) *How Big is the Airline Catering Industry?* Aircraft Interiors Expo, 31 March, Hamburg, Germany.

Jones, P. (2004b) *Flight Catering*. Elsevier: Oxford.

Jones, P. (2005) 'Flight catering in the spotlight', *Hospitality Review*, October 2005: 5–13.

Jones, P. (2007) 'Flight-Catering Industry'. In H. Becker and U. Grothues (eds) *Catering-Management: Portrait einer Wachstumsbranche in Theorie und Praxis*. Behrs Verlag: Hamburg, 39–56.

Jones, P. and Bertorello, V. (2001) *The Process of Innovation in-Flight Catering*, 10th CHME National Research Conference, 19–21 April, London.

Jones, P. and Lumbers, M. (2003) 'Appetite and in-flight Catering'. In R. Bors (ed.) *Passenger Behavior*. Ashgate: Aldershot, 261–275.

Lee, S. and Jones, P. (2005) *The Importance of Food Onboard: Attitudes Among Air Travelers In North-East Asia*. TCRC Report No. 3, Guildford: University of Surrey.

Lundstrom, R. (2001) 'For a Special Group: US Airways Revamps SPML Lineup', *PAX International*, 5(5): 40–42.

Momberger, M. and Momberger, K. (2006) *Flight Kitchen Directory*. Momberger Airport Information: Rutesheim.

Peirce, A.-M., (1994) *Innovation in-Flight Catering*. Unpublished dissertation: University of Brighton.

Scheuing E. E. and Johnson E. M. (1989) 'A proposed model for new service development', *The Journal of Services Marketing*, 3(2): 25–34.

Sutton, A. and Gostelow, M. (1997) 'Special meal appeal', *Hospitality Industry International*, 17: 14–16.

TCRC (2005) *Demand for Airline Meals 2005*. Guildford: Travel Catering Research Centre, University of Surrey.

TCRC (2006) *Demand for Airline Meals 2006*. Guildford: Travel Catering Research Centre, University of Surrey.

Resort Management

23

Robert Christie Mill

INTRODUCTION

This chapter begins by defining the resort industry in one of three ways. Resorts can be differentiated in terms of the closeness to the primary market, the type of amenities present at the facility and the types of residential and lodging properties available. Increasingly, resorts are being seen as an entity consisting of various real estate products rather than as an operational property. Three types of real estate product are found in resorts – hotels; timeshares and other vacation ownership entities that require a one-time investment and weekly maintenance fee, and, third, second-home purchases. Resorts are a combination of three elements: recreational attractions that draw guests to the facility; housing and food and beverage services that cater to people away from home; and activities to occupy guests during their stay.

There is a relationship between the natural resource base and the recreational facilities that are developed from that base. The belief is that it is both environmentally conscious and business-smart to develop facilities in such a way that the integrity of the natural base is maintained. This is, after all, the major reason why guests visit. Management is doing nothing more than protecting its competitive differential advantage.

Operating a resort is, indeed, different from operating a traditional hotel and it is important to explore the features that are unique as well as concentrating on the elements of economic feasibility. A brief overview of the principles involved in managing operations is presented followed by in-depth discussions of the challenges unique to resorts for the important functional areas. In particular, guest activity programming is crucial to producing satisfied guests. Good programming does not just happen; it is carefully planned for, thought about, and managed.

The focus is on developing revenue-producing and guest-satisfying activities that are based on knowledge of the demographic, psychographic and physical ability profiles of the guest.

RESORT CATEGORIES

There are a number of ways to characterize resorts. A respected authority – the US Urban Land Institute – differentiates them in terms of the proximity to the primary market, the setting and primary amenities present at the facility and the mix of residential and lodging properties available (Urban Land Institute, 1997). In terms of their proximity to the primary market, resorts are either destination resorts or non-destination resorts. The difference depends on how far the resort is from its primary market; how visitors reach the resort; the patterns of stay – how many times a guest visits and how long the stay is, and the quality of the setting. Within these generalities, it should be mentioned that a resort may fit into both categories. Colorado resorts, for example, draw visitors from Denver several times over the season while also attracting people from Europe for a once-a-season experience.

Visitors categorize resorts by their location and amenities. Defined thus, resorts can be either ocean resorts, lake/river resorts, mountain/ski resorts, or golf resorts (Urban Land Institute, 1997). Ocean resorts depend on the quality and extent of their beaches, views, climate, and water-sports activities. Lake/river resorts obviously rely on water but rely even more on the recreational activities that are water-oriented than do ocean resorts. Mountain/ski resorts have, in recent years, moved away from their traditional reliance on the winter season to become four-season resorts. Capitalizing on their spa heritage, many are using health as the basis for their theme.

The increased popularity of golf has helped spawn an increase in the number of resort properties themed around this activity. Growth is also a function of supply. As the number of waterfront locations expanded, fewer sites associated with water were available. They are also popular in desert settings that, lacking water, rely on scenery, climate, and golf to attract visitors. Other resorts rely on specialized amenities. Examples include resorts developed around tennis, equestrian, ranches, health, natural attractions, sporting expeditions, and entertainment.

Real estate people like to categorize resorts based on the type and mix of residential lodging facilities. This makes sense for the developer as lodging is the major revenue source for the resort, accommodation planning takes a great deal of time, and housing plays a major part in defining the character of the resort.

REAL ESTATE PRODUCTS

Three types of real estate product are found in resorts (Urban Land Institute, 1997). First, there are hotels that require, in relative terms, modest financial investment. Resort hotels are the most common form of resort development. The resort guest visits the development for relaxation. A growing number of resort hotels, however, are seeking to attract the businessperson, usually as part of a conference or meeting. Holding a business meeting in a self-contained resort setting keeps the outside distractions of a city to a minimum, while allowing the company to utilize the recuperative effects of recreation to improve business productivity.

Second, there are timeshares and other vacation ownership that require a one-time investment and weekly maintenance fee. Timesharing began in France in the late 1960s and was first seen in the United States in the 1970s (American Resort Development Association, 1997). The term 'timeshare' is also referred to as 'vacation ownership' and/or 'vacation clubs'. Timesharing is defined as 'the right to accommodations at a vacation development for a specified period each year, for a specified number of years or for perpetuity' (American Resort Development Association, 1997: 5). Owners pay a lump sum up front, either paid in full or financed

over a seven- to ten-year period, in addition to an annual maintenance, management, and operations fee. After the purchase the owner pays an annual maintenance fee that covers the cost of management and maintenance of the resort. Timeshare owners can exchange weeks through membership in exchange companies such as Interval International or Resort Condominium International.

Several timeshare options are possible (Sparks and Smith, 1999). The *fixed week option* allows consumers to buy a specific week – for example the first week in August. Under the *floating weeks option* consumers buy a week within a given period. Consumers may buy one week within weeks six through twelve. A *combination* allows weeks in high demand periods to be fixed and those in low demand periods to float. School holidays, for example, might be fixed while, during other times of the year, people buy the right to use the resort for a week during specific times of the year.

Recently resorts have introduced *points-based memberships* giving members points that can be used to 'buy' resort stays. Periods of high demand would require more points than weeks in times of low demand. Guests can bank, borrow or split up how and when they use their points. Many properties are finding that they can cut back on marketing expenses because they sell the points program to a captive audience. It is, however, initially confusing for the guest and, as such, is more complex operationally for the operating company. Because of the nature of a points program, it makes more sense for a company that has multiple sites. To work effectively there have to be choices available for the customer and multiple sites allow for this. Finally, the *club concept* does not involve any ownership of real estate. Instead, consumers buy shares or points in the club that are exchanged for accommodation or travel.

Timeshare options available have evolved in recent years. They started with traditional fixed units in a set week, moved to a floating week option and, most recently, to the flexible points option (Baumann, 1999a). Increased numbers of resorts are utilizing mixed-use developments that feature a time-share component (Baumann, 1999b). It used to be that developers built a property then created demand for it. Nowadays, the demand for timeshare products dictates production. A major reason for mixed-use developments is the high cost of amenities. Because high-quality amenities cost a great deal of money, being able to spread out the use and cost of these facilities makes it cheaper for everyone. In addition to the cross-utilization of amenities, hotel guests are exposed to timeshare products and may well be induced to buy. In this way, timeshare operators can reduce their marketing costs. The timeshare component brings a steady stream of revenue into the resort – everyone benefits. It does, however, take an experienced staff to meet the differing needs of timeshare owners and hotel guests.

Because of the unique nature of timeshare financing, specialized timeshare lenders have come to the fore. The financing of a timeshare property is different from that of a traditional hotel. Most hotel mortgages are long-term deals wherein the payback comes from the hotel's cash flow generated from daily operations. Timeshare loans, on the other hand, are shorter-term loans based on the developer's ability to market and sell interest in the timeshare (Baumann, 1999c). In addition, the lending process is more complex because of the regulatory issues involved in timeshare. In many respects timeshare financing is simpler and more predictable than the financing of hotels. Both revenue and expenses are more foreseeable for timeshares. Once the timeshare unit is sold, revenue is accounted for, whereas a hotel room has to be re-sold each and every night with no guarantee that it will produce revenue. Hotels incur many costs whether they are full or empty while timeshare costs are easier to predict. High customer satisfaction with, and solid growth of, timeshares – together with the financial characteristics noted above – means fewer timeshare defaults compared to hotels.

Finally a resort can contain second-home purchases. A second-home development consists of a project that consists primarily of second homes and does not include a resort hotel. A second home is 'a home that is owned by an individual or family that also owns or rents another home as a primary residence' (Urban Land Institute, 1997: 11). While second homes are not necessarily found in resort areas, second-home developments are. They consist of a variety of types of properties – detached, attached, and/or multi-family – and can be a combination of various uses.

Developments are one of four types (Urban Land Institute, 1997). Resort condominiums are usually high-rises located on ocean-fronts. Small, low-density residential communities are typically located close to a beach or lake. Single-family developments incorporate a golf club and/or clubhouse. Finally, there are large planned communities that include a variety of housing types as well as a number of amenities. Compared with primary homes, secondary homes place more emphasis on outdoor areas, they are developed at lower densities, and their design is less formal. They are managed under a long-term arrangement by a community association rather than by a developer or resort operator. However, the latter may be involved in the management of a principal amenity such as a golf course.

A multi-use resort community combines two or more of the above categories of facilities. As such they tend to be larger than any of the other types noted. By offering more than one type of ownership and use pattern, they can appeal to a larger variety of markets. Their amenity package is more extensive and usually consists of at least two major amenities such as beaches and golf courses or ski slopes and golf courses in a four-season format. As the needs of the resort user change, the development offers appropriate units for rent or purchase. A resort guest may end up buying a second home for eventual retirement. The diversity of property types requires more sophisticated management.

ELEMENTS OF A RESORT

Resorts are a combination of three elements. First, there are the recreational amenities that draw guests to the facility. Once guests are on property they require housing, food and beverage and retail services that cater to people away from home. Finally, there are activities to occupy guests during their stay.

Recreational amenities

The recreational amenities are a significant part of the character of any planned community. The decision to include or exclude a specific recreational amenity should be based on a number of factors (Phillips, 1986). It is important to consider what is being offered in similar local projects; the future residents/users for whom these amenities are being planned; how much money is available for amenities and whether the costs are justified; how the amenity fits in with the total project physically, economically, and as part of its image; what quantity of the amenity should be provided and what the climate will allow; and what the marketing benefits will be.

An amenity is 'a rather broad concept that can encompass virtually any feature that is attractive to a given market and thus adds value to land' (Phillips, 1986: 4). There are two basic reasons for including amenities in a recreational development (Phillips, 1986). First, amenities increase the value of the real estate. The up-front cost of adding a golf course to a development, for example, can be recovered through the sale of premium lots that front the fairways. Amenities may be developed with the idea that they will form the basis for a profitable operation. The latter is the motivation behind resort developments while the former is more true of primary- or second-home communities.

The second reason for the inclusion of amenities within a development is to get marketing leverage. A well-designed recreational attraction adds credibility to the development and the developer and can assist in attracting guests to a property or customers to a development. The downside is that substantial costs are involved in providing, what is often, a seasonal attraction. The key is to achieve a balance between the cost of providing the amenity with the sales generated because of its presence. Timing is of the essence. Plans must also be made to transfer ownership and management of the amenity to an appropriate group or body after it has achieved its purpose of bringing in guests or customers.

An amenity strategy is a 'clear understanding of the role of recreational facilities within an overall project' (Phillips, 1986: 15). While every project is unique there are certain principles that are accepted as appropriate for any recreational development (Phillips, 1986). For a recreational development to be successful, it is critical that it be developed, designed, and managed to meet the needs of the customer. This means certain things (Phillips, 1986). The package of amenities should be a function of the overall project. As a project progresses from single-family home to multi-family units to a resort hotel, more and better amenities become appropriate. Next, a first preference should be given to natural over built features. Early golf courses in Scotland, for example, relied on the natural features of the coastline. Development was less costly, impact on the environment was minimized and it was more difficult for a competitor to copy because the course was truly unique to the area. These advantages – lower costs, unique design, and less intrusion on the environment – will occur wherever natural resources can be used as the basis for amenities.

Recognizing the risk of being dependent on one season of the year, resorts have sought to reduce their investment risk by converting amenities to off-season use. Many golf courses rope off their greens and promote cross-country skiing in the winter. Ski areas market mountain biking down their ski runs during the summer. A final principle is that facilities should be sufficient to meet the needs of the expected numbers of people who will be attracted to the development.

The developer and the user of the amenity can be in conflict relative to the type and amount of amenities developed. Developers build certain facilities because of their marketing appeal – they will help sell real estate – or because they will be heavily used, thereby becoming a valuable amenity. A championship golf course may help sell real estate but it may be costly to maintain and difficult to play for retired residents. Meeting the needs of the residents by providing an easier course to play might not attract the publicity necessary to sell the project. An operational plan is needed that identifies 'who will develop, own, and operate the facilities and for how long; who will use the facilities and on what terms; and precisely what the expected relationship will be between real estate and recreational amenities, in both the short term and over the long run' (Phillips, 1986: 16).

Development must be timed such that the cost of constructing the amenities is balanced by the revenue generated by their presence. The rule of thumb has been that recreational amenities should be developed up front and used as a draw to stimulate guests or real estate sales. Because of the heavy cost involved, this strategy increases the developer's risk and produces an initial low rate of return on the project. There are several ways to reduce this risk (Phillips, 1986). If recreational developments already exist in an area, it may be possible to negotiate cooperative agreements whereby residents of the newer project can use the facilities of the existing project. In this way the recreational facilities at the newer project can be phased in gradually and their development cost spread out over a number of years. Another strategy is to open up amenities for use by non-residents. Revenue is generated while prospective buyers are exposed to the project. However, this requires careful management because residents may resent having outsiders use 'their' facilities while it may be difficult to phase out the outside members when the project is more fully developed.

It is generally accepted that the developer should continue to control building, operation and maintenance of the amenity package as the development is being built out. If the amenities are not under the control of the developer they may be poorly managed and maintained. This, in turn, could adversely affect future real estate sales. The developer, of course, assumes the operational burden and must have, or hire, the expertise necessary. The rule of thumb is that the developer retains control until at least 50% of the project is completed. Residents will probably want a role in the management of the facilities prior to this point. An advisory committee of residents can be useful in giving input and pave the way towards the eventual transfer of control.

If recreational areas are making money, there is no need for the developer to transfer their management to a third party. This is true of resort hotels and ski areas, for example. However, in residential developments, once the recreational amenity has served its primary purpose of selling real estate, its value to the developer declines while the carrying costs increase. The amenity is then either given away or sold to the residents of the project, who are usually represented by a property-owner's association. The developer has already received a return on the investment by charging premium prices on certain real-estate units based on their proximity to the amenity.

The developer has little or no leverage at the end of the build-out phase of a development. He/she is incurring the costs involved in running the amenity and all the real estate has been sold. It is, therefore, a good idea for the developer to negotiate at the beginning of the project how and when the recreational amenities will be transferred to a residents' group.

Managing the recreational amenity

The management of recreational amenities has become more sophisticated over the years. A variety of organizational structures are possible. When resort operators, particularly ski areas, choose to own and operate amenities themselves, they are typically structured in one of four ways (Shwanke, 1977). They can take the form of an equity club, a right-to-use club, a convertible club, or association membership.

Developers can transfer ownership of the recreational facilities to a separate non-profit corporation while still retaining the right to operate the facilities until most of the residential property has been sold. This protects the developer by ensuring that the amenities will not be operated in a way that adversely affects the sale of the remaining real estate units. The developer contributes the recreational amenities in return for the right to sell equity memberships to real estate owners. Once all the real estate has been sold the club is owned and controlled by the members and run by a duly elected board of directors. Club members pay annual dues for the right to use the facilities. They also benefit from any increase in the value of the amenities. In some cases it is possible for property purchasers to 'inherit' the equity membership of owners. This, obviously, increases the value of the equity membership. If all memberships are sold, new owners must wait for one to become available for them to participate in the amenity program.

In a right-to-use club, the developer retains ownership and control of the facilities. Members buy the right to use the amenities rather than having an ownership interest as above. An initial payment together with annual dues is common. The developer decides the initiation payment in the form of a fee or a deposit. Under the initiation fee program a member who resigns from the club may receive all, some or none of the deposit back. How much, if any, is returned depends on whether or not the membership is reissued to a new member. The initiation fee is treated as taxable income to the developer and as a deductible business expense when refunded to a member who resigns. Under an initiation deposit program, members receive the full initiation fee when they resign but not until a period of 20 to 30 years after their acceptance into the program. The deposit might, thus, be characterized as a loan to the recreational amenities that is not taxable income.

When a developer feels that a market exists for an equity club, but is unsure as to when the club can be turned over to members, a convertible club is a viable option. The program begins as a right-to-use club but members are made aware up front of the intention to turn it into an equity club. The one-time initiation fee or deposit is refundable. When members pay this fee they are told the likely timing of the switch to an equity club together with the purchase price to be paid by the members for the facilities, as well as any likely additional costs to be incurred in the transition. The initiation fee or deposit may be applied to the equity club membership. Lastly, the developer may turn over the recreational facilities to a homeowners' association that is set up to represent the surrounding property units. Association members do not buy memberships but can pay off the debt through assessments and user fees. Memberships may be sold to those owners who want preferential treatment.

The developer recovers the cost of building the recreational amenities through means other than from the sale of real estate. In this way the return on investment for the project may increase because the profit on real estate sales does not have to take into account the construction costs of the recreational amenities. It is crucial that an association pays off the debt and maintains the facilities while keeping assessments reasonable.

The four options discussed above can be compared on a number of criteria (Shwanke, 1977). The option chosen should be based on the criteria that are most important to the developer and the development. The up-front cost is highest for the equity club. However, upon conversion, the membership price on an initial right-to-use club is even higher. The cost, however, is reduced by the original initiation fee. There is no up-front cost for the association ownership unless annual memberships are sold. Even then, the annual cost is relatively low. Gross proceeds from the membership program are greatest with the right-to-use club although the income is dependent upon the selling of memberships. While the income is less in an equity club, there is a greater guarantee that the money will be realized. The convertible program produces less gross income while association management produces none unless annual memberships are sold.

The initial operational cash flow is low with both association management and an equity club and moderate with the other two options. On the other hand, the sell-out operational cash flow is greatest in an equity club, slightly less in a right-to-use club, and lower in the other two options. Because association members own and operate the recreational facilities, a greater sense of community exists among the members. It remains good in an equity club, less so in a right-to-use club because of the loss of owner control and uncertainty over the amenities, and even less so in a convertible

program because owners have no control over the facilities.

The developer has the greatest flexibility under a convertible club program and none with association ownership. In the other two cases, the degree of flexibility is dependent upon terms of the membership plan. Litigation risk to the developer is low in both an equity club and association membership, moderate to low in a right-to-use club, and greatest when a developer sells the amenities in a convertible club program. The convertible club program is the best option where non-owner access to club facilities is important. In an equity club access is limited to available memberships until a cap is reached. In a right-to-use club access is good until conversion takes place. It varies in association ownership depending upon the regulations set down by the members themselves.

Membership structures

Memberships can be structured differently within each of the structures noted above. The type of membership structure is dependent upon the development concept and the type of owner or guest. For example, in a development consisting of primary residences, long-term membership options that do not expire until the member sells are made available to owners. In communities where second-home owners stay for shorter time periods, they are given the option of making changes to the service package they have.

A tiered membership structure offers a variety of options to members. The more services, access and flexibility that are given, the greater the price that is charged. For example full golf membership might allow an owner to make a tee reservation up to 30 days in advance while a less expensive category of membership might restrict reservations to five days in advance. By limiting the number of memberships in each category, owners are enticed into purchasing the more expensive options. This makes their property more valuable in the event they wish to sell. This may, in turn, create a greater than normal demand for higher priced memberships than would occur under a different membership structure. If owners buy the membership as an investment it is conceivable that golf memberships may be sold out but that the golf course is under-utilized because owners are not using their privileges fully. This system works best in residential communities where the number of memberships available is approximately equal to the number of units. A rule of thumb, for example, is 350 golfclub members per 18-hole course (Phillips, 1986). Another structure may become necessary when the number of residential units surpasses the capacity of the amenity.

Under a unitary membership structure all members pay a membership price and receive the same interest in the amenities. Each year members select the type of category they wish. One year a member may purchase the social category that allows access to the dining facilities while the following year the same person can select a category – at a greater expense – that allows access to all the amenities. The member is assured that, if he or she sells, the next owner will also have an annual choice of category. A unitary membership works when the recreational amenities are insufficient to meet the demands of the residents. Unlike the tiered membership described above, artificial demand is not created for a particular level of membership. Members select, on an annual basis, the type of program that meets their needs. Imbalances in demand for specific categories of membership can be handled by adjusting the type and price of memberships available.

Convertible or add-on memberships are a combination of the above two categories. All members purchase a social membership then are free to buy add-ons depending upon the additional access they want. This type of structure works best when the developer is unsure about the level of demand for the recreational amenities.

Developers tend to mix and match organizational and membership structures to accommodate both their needs and those of the members. An equity club may be organized that offers full golf membership to equity members as well as social memberships to others. In settings that have both residents and resort hotels a club may be developed for residents while offering access to hotel guests. There are several advantages for both resident and hotel guest (Shwanke, 1977). Both receive higher-quality services than if two lesser-quality facilities were built for each. Club members get access to hotel services such as concierge and room service. Hotel guests add life to the facility in the early stages of real estate development. Hotel guests can be targeted as future owners. However, residents tend to favor exclusivity while hotel guests desire access when *they* want it. Conflicts can be minimized by a reservation system that protects the rights of use for each group. As an example, a members-only lounge can be created. In resorts with several golf courses, a different course each day can be for the exclusive use of members. Members can be given a longer lead-time than guests in signing up for tee times.

RESORT MANAGEMENT

Management differences

According to Gee managing a resort is different from managing a commercial hotel in a variety of ways (Gee, 1988). No matter how different one resort is from another, they seek to please guests seeking to satisfy three fundamental needs (Urban Land Institute, 1977: 3):

1 desire for a change of pace, getting away from the familiar;
2 desire to satisfy recreational interests while being entertained and stimulated; and
3 desire to travel to interesting and attractive places.

Resorts certainly attract conventions and group business. However, the scheduling of business meetings must be coordinated with recreational activities. Because the average length of stay at a resort is longer than that at a hotel the number and type of facilities are different. Rooms, in general are larger. More closet space is needed. Large amounts of land are required for recreational facilities. Guests are looking to take part in a variety of activities as part of their total resort experience.

Guests are attracted to many resorts because of their remote location. Many guests travel to resorts to 'get away from it all'. In other cases the resort attraction may be an area of natural beauty. This means that these properties must be self-contained. Support services such as laundry and maintenance must be provided. Transportation may need to be provided for employees. Similarly, a shuttle service to and from the nearest airport may have to be provided for guests.

A resort, by definition, is where people go for recreation. Most specialize in one recreational activity, be it beach, skiing, tennis etc. However, it is economic folly to rely on one season of the year. One bad year of snow, for example, can ruin the entire season. To combat this, resorts have attempted to become year-round attractions. In the Colorado mountains, for example, ski lifts are used to bring mountain bikes up the mountain in the summer.

While commercial hotels operate year-round, many resorts are seasonal. Notwithstanding attempts to develop business year-round, some resorts – by virtue of their location – are precluded from doing so. Seasonality produces particular problems. Each season a new group of employees must be hired, trained and motivated. Inventory management, particularly perishables, becomes a problem as the season comes to an end. When the resort is closed up security and maintenance are particular headaches. A season of 90 to 120 days places tremendous pressure on management to cover fixed costs for the year, variable costs for the season and still make a profit.

The resort guest in a vacation setting has extremely high expectations relative to service. He/she expects to be pampered. In vacation ownership resorts, where units are actually bought, the guests are owners who like to be treated as such. This places great pressure on employees to perform at a high level. The resort calls for knowledge that managers of commercial properties do not need. While all managers need to know about rooms, food and beverage, marketing and human resources management, there are two areas in which resort managers must have additional knowledge. These relate to the natural resource base upon which the resort has been developed and guest activity programming. The success of the resort is based upon the natural resource that forms the basis for the attraction. A manager of a ski resort has to know something about the mountain. A resort specializing in golf must be managed by someone who knows the relationship between golf course layout and profitability.

Resort guests, as noted above, expect to participate in a number of activities. When guests are on the property for several days or weeks a well-designed guest-activity program is required to satisfy them. This means much more than having a sleigh ride next Tuesday. Implementing a guest-activity program involves specialized knowledge regarding leisure, recreation, and play. Programs must be developed taking into account the demographic, psychographic and physical backgrounds of guests. Information about these two areas is something that most managers of commercial properties do not have.

Because many resorts are large and located in remote areas they are a major, if not the major, piece of the economy. As such, management takes on a certain responsibility to the community that goes beyond the responsibility of a hotel in a metropolitan area. The community may be totally dependent on the resort for its economic future. Management has to take this into account when making decisions on laying off employees during the off-season. The remote location of certain properties means that the resort may have to provide housing for its employees. This raises issues of employee privacy and access to services required by the staff. Employees at resorts tend to rotate into different jobs both during the season and in the off-season. If there is no snow at a ski area, employees may find themselves working in maintenance. This is especially true in the off-season where having a job means being flexible and having additional skills. Commercial hotel jobs tend to be more specialized and static throughout the year.

Commercial resorts derive most of their revenue from rooms and food and beverage, with additional revenue coming from various minor operating departments. Other departments take on greater importance in a resort. Retail sales are more important as is revenue from recreational activities. Some properties derive a great deal of revenue from land sales. Accordingly, accounting statements are more complex in a resort than in a commercial hotel. Every recreational activity and retail outlet is a potential profit center with separate profit and loss statements. The fact that land and fixed-asset investment is greater in a resort than in a conventional hotel changes the look of the balance sheet. The large amount of land means the resort has few alternate commercial uses. The payback period – the number of years needed to repay the original investment – is longer for resorts because of the large investment in land and other fixed assets.

Traditions are also more important for resorts than for other types of hotels. Many resorts cater to repeat guests who are attracted by annual festivals and theme weekends. They come back to enjoy the experience year after year.

Economic feasibility

There are four critical variables that will determine whether or not a resort will make a profit (Farwell, 1993). These are the capacity, the length of the season, the amount of capital investment, and the amount of revenue per visit. A ski area will be used as an exemplar. However, the principles involved are true for any resort property. While certain guidelines are given relative to ski area capacity, the number of variables that go into determining a range of figures is so great that a certain amount of subjectivity is unavoidable. It is quite common for a developer to identify the number of skiers required to break-even and make a specified return on investment and make development and design decisions in order to achieve that financial result.

There are a number of ways to look at capacity. Physical and ecological capacity takes into account the physical/ecological limitations of the site. Social or normal capacity is when the majority of skiers do not consider the area overcrowded. Maximum capacity is when no more visitors can be served. The upper limit for safety can occur when a single element is at maximum use. For example, the amount of parking available limits the number of people who have access to the ski area. Comfortable carrying capacity is 'the maximum number of participants who can utilize the facility at any one time without excessive crowding and without damaging the quality of the environment' (Phillips, 1986: 126).

Ski area capacity is, therefore, a measure of three things (Farwell, 1993) – the capacity of the terrain, the uphill capacity, and the capacity of the supporting facilities. Terrain capacity is impacted by such things as the steepness of the slope, the way the trail is designed, the amount and quality of the snow cover, the way the slopes are groomed, and the skill levels of the skiers (Farwell, 1993). The skill level of the skiers in turn impacts the safety of the slope for all. Because more advanced skiers prefer fewer other skiers on the slopes, density decreases as slope, speed, and ability increases. Uphill capacity is a measure of the number of vertical transport feet per hour needed. Skiers have a finite capacity for skiing per day. That capacity is based on their physical condition and their ability level. It might, for example, be assumed that beginners will ski for five hours a day and more advanced skiers will ski for six hours a day. Thus, an area that is targeted for the more advanced skier will need more uphill capacity per hour than will one that targets beginners. Finally, capacity is

a measure of the capacity of the supporting facilities. Facilities in a ski area base lodge comprise such things as:

- foodservice;
- restrooms;
- first aid;
- ski school;
- retail sales;
- rental shop;
- lockers;
- ticket sales;
- employee lockers;
- bar/lounge;
- nursery; and
- storage.

For ski areas the main determinants of the length of the season are weather and climate (Farwell, 1993). Ski areas measure the length of the season in terms of skiing periods. One period is equivalent to seven hours. Thus a resort that is open from nine in the morning until eleven at night will include two skiing periods – one day and one night. A growing number of ski areas now use machine snow in an attempt to lengthen the season. Ski area capacity multiplied by the length of the ski season is equal to capacity skier visits – the maximum number of skier visits the resort can handle.

The third critical variable is the amount of capital investment needed to develop the ski area. The capital budget is highly design- and site-specific. The major cost elements that go into a ski resort are (Farwell, 1993: 6):

- ski lifts;
- ski slope and trail construction;
- snow maintenance equipment;
- snowmaking equipment;
- day-use lodge building;
- furniture and fixtures;
- maintenance center;
- base area equipment;
- parking;
- power and slope lighting;
- water and sewer systems;
- site development;
- planning;
- financing;
- land; and
- access roads.

The final variable is the amount of revenue generated from each skier-visit. Totaling all revenue and dividing it by the number of skier-visits determine this figure. Revenue is generated from ski-lift tickets and revenue from supporting services. How well the resort does in maximizing these four variables will ultimately determine how economically successful it will be.

GUEST ACTIVITY PROGRAMMING

Planning the program

A major differentiating factor between resorts and other lodging properties is that the resort guest stays for a lengthier period of time. Guests expect the facility to cater to their need for something to do during their time of leisure. In resorts the programs are referred to as 'guest activity programs'. The activities should be fun, something the guest chooses to do, and of some benefit to the guest. If these conditions are not adhered to guests will not fully enjoy the activity and their stay will be less than it could be. For a guest to truly leave the resort satisfied with the visit it is imperative that the guest-activity director takes an active role in planning the various guest activities to ensure that they provide the benefits noted above.

Guest activity programming involves five steps (Farrell and Lundegren, 1991). Guest needs are assessed and objectives are then defined that will meet guest needs. Cluster or activity analysis is performed to fulfill the objectives. There is the activity itself. Finally, the experience is evaluated relative to its success in meeting guest needs.

Planning a guest activity program could be much more meaningful for the guests if the guest activity director knew what guests expected from the program. Needs assessment is 'a systematic inquiry about needs, attitudes, behaviors, and patterns of both participants and non-participants' (DeGraff et al., 1999: 258). The purpose is to identify what is important to guests in order to better design and deliver guest activity programs that will leave guests satisfied with the program and, consequently, the resort. However, some constraints should be noted. First, needs are infinite. There is no way that a resort can totally satisfy the needs of every guest. Second, there will inevitably be conflicts between different segments of the market. Teens will want different things than

will seniors. On the slopes, there are differences between skiers and snowboarders. The ability of the resort staff to satisfy various segments of the market without encroaching on the satisfaction of others is a major task. Nevertheless, it is a task that needs to be done if we believe in the marketing or customer concept.

In this model needs assessment becomes the first step in the provision of services and programs to meet the stated and implied needs and wants of existing and future guests. The goals and objectives of the guest activity programs nest within those set for the resort itself. Goals are broad, general, final outcomes. The overall goal of the resort might be to produce profits by satisfying the guest. Within this framework the guest activity goal might be to provide satisfying experiences for the guest during their stay; aid in skill development; increase guest health and well-being; and/or encourage social interaction among guests.

Objectives are much more specific and short-term. The resort might set objectives relative to occupancy, rate, percentage of guests who return etc. Again, within this framework, the guest activity director might set specific objectives in terms of the number of people who participate in various activities, targets for guest satisfaction with various programs etc. Objectives should be set for the overall guest activity program as well as for even more specific objectives for every program and activity offered. Program objectives should be set prior to starting an activity. A program will have the guest perform or behave in a certain way, learn something and/or receive instruction (Farrell and Lundegren, 1991). For the guest-activity program to be meaningful (and, therefore, satisfying, to the guest) it is important that the programmer develop some idea of what the outcome of the program should be for that guest and design activities (the next step in the process) to help ensure the objectives are met. Refusing to set objectives reduces the chance that guest needs, identified above, will be met.

Cluster analysis clusters activities that yield similar benefits. Each activity becomes a variable, the correlation between participation in two variables is computed and the resultant cluster is based on the correlation that results. Typically, clusters are determined on the basis of the degree of skill required, the level of activity, the nature of the group needed, the amount of risk or danger and/or whether or not any special facilities are needed (Farrell and Lundegren, 1991).

There are obvious implications for the resort. From existing levels of participation staff can identify which complementary activities might be popular. A guest activity director will match up activities in the format structure desired and design activity programs that are appropriate to the life cycle of the guest. At various stages in the individual's life certain leisure activities are more appropriate than at other times. For example, the primary tasks for school age children are to increase their skills and knowledge while learning about the rules of, and their role in, society. Skills can be developed through such things as advanced arts and crafts, sport clinics, the making of models and the playing of musical instruments. There are certain board games, such as *Life*, that help participants learn about roles in society.

As people approach old age they attempt to come to terms with who they are, where they have been and what they have (and have not) accomplished. Physical and mental faculties require stimulation and social connections must be maintained especially after a spouse dies. There is a desire to 'bring it all together' and pass knowledge onto a younger generation. Walking, dancing and exercise clubs help promote physical activity while bridge clubs, pot luck events and concerts assist with social connections. Current event lectures and card playing help maintain cognitive abilities while classes on yoga and guest speakers on religious topics help with spiritual connections. Finally, journal writing, intergenerational programs and video remembrances allow individuals to pass on accumulated knowledge to those generations that follow (Powers, 1991).

There are seven possible formats that activities can fall into. Activities can be instructional where the intent is to learn a new skill or to further develop or refine an existing one. Competitions can be set up that are either intrinsic (competing against oneself) or extrinsic (looking good in front of others). The activity might be social because of the need to be with people. Trips, either a day or an overnight trip, can be organized. Drop-ins can be developed for those who want self-directed programs. Special events can be planned such as festivals, banquets, shows or exhibitions. Finally, there are activities targeted to spectators looking for playing tips or for those whose active participation (but not their interest) is over (Farrell and Lundgren, 1991; DeGraff et al., 1999).

Designing the program

Designing a guest activity program involves selecting a leadership team, establishing a budget, scheduling the activities, finding suitable facilities and promoting the program (Farrell and Lundgren, 1991). Described by many as the most important factor in determining the success of a program, selection of the appropriate leadership is certainly crucial. First, the tasks involved in the job must be identified. An analysis of the job identifies the various job functions that must be carried out together with the skill level at which they need to be performed. This will result in a job description for the position. From the job description will come the knowledge, skills and abilities necessary to perform the job. This is called a job specification and is the second step in the process. Finally, with a job specification in hand, suitable candidates for the job can be recruited (Farrell and Lundgren, 1991).

The process of setting a price for a guest activity program involves several steps (Farrell and Lundgren, 1991). Costs must be determined, the proportion of costs to be covered is set, the appropriateness of differential pricing is considered and an initial price is set. There are two types of costs that a guest activity will incur – indirect and direct. Indirect costs are those costs that cannot be directly associated with a particular program yet are incurred in operating the guest services program. For example, there is a director and staff involved in running the entire operation whose salaries must be accounted for. Staff salaries must be paid and offices must be heated whether programs operate or not. Resorts have to decide how to allocate the indirect costs of running the guest activity department to the various programs that are offered. There are several possibilities (Farrell and Lundgren, 1991). The equal share method involves each program being assigned an equal share of the indirect costs involved in running the department. Under the percentage of budget method, each program is charged with a percentage of indirect expenses equal to its percentage of the overall department budget. Indirect expenses can be charged based on the amount of time spent on the program after a time-budget study. Finally, indirect costs can be allocated to programs based on the actual costs used by each program.

The objective is to determine the full cost of planning, operating and evaluating a program.

Indirect costs should be allocated in an equitable manner indicating how much of an indirect cost a program actually uses. Direct costs, on the other hand, are specific expenses related to a single item. For example, a program on fly-fishing might include the costs of an instructor and promotional flyers. They may be fixed or variable. Fixed costs stay constant during a specified time – the salary of an instructor. The cost may be fixed within a particular range. For example, if a standard is set of 16 guests per instructor, within the range of one to 16 guests, the instructor's salary is fixed. However, beyond 16 participants, there is a need to hire someone else. Thus, costs are fixed within a specific range. Variable costs vary proportionately with volume. Suppose each guest who participates in an activity receives a souvenir of the occasion. The cost of providing the souvenirs is a variable cost.

The key issue in scheduling is to offer programs that meet the time needs of resort guests (Farrell and Lundgren, 1991). There are three patterns involved in scheduling activities. The first consideration is a seasonal one. Certain activities are season-specific. A full list of programs can be developed for each season taking into account the constraints and appropriateness of each time of the year. A winter program, for example, would focus on activities involving snow – sleigh rides, ski lessons etc. – while tapping trees for syrup and leaf tours would work in the fall.

A second aspect to schedules involves a weekly or monthly focus. The time span would be related to the average length of stay. If most people stay for two weeks, for example, a varied 14-day schedule of activities must be developed so that the second week is not a repeat of the first. Finally, resorts plan a daily time-schedule. Depending on the pattern of activity of the guests, activities might be scheduled in the morning, early afternoon, afternoon activity at a lower level, late afternoon, early evening and/or late evening.

It is important when scheduling activities to consider when regular maintenance can be done. The best time for maintenance is when demand for participation in the program is low. For ski areas, for example, most maintenance takes place in the so-called 'mud season' after the ski season ends. Facilities need to be convenient and accessible to the guest. They must be attractive places in which to undertake the activity while taking into account guest safety (Farrell and Lundgren, 1991).

Modern marketing calls for more than developing a good product, pricing it attractively, and making it available to target guests. Management communicates with customers – both existing and potential – through what is known as the promotional mix. The end goal of promotion is behavior modification: We want to initiate or change the behavior of guests such that they will take the guest activity with us. Specifically, promotion seeks to inform, persuade, and remind.

There is agreement that the aims of program evaluation are two fold – to determine whether or not the program has value and to determine whether or not the program objectives are being met (Farrell and Lundgren, 1991). Thus, to evaluate the program, there must be objectives to measure actual results against. Quantitative and qualitative data is collected in either/or a subjective or objective manner and compared to the preset objective.

Programs can be evaluated in a variety of ways – by the extent to which objectives are met, by the extent to which standards are met, and by the effect on guests (Farrell and Lundgren, 1991). A determination can first be made as to how appropriate the objectives are – both the broad program objectives and the specific behavioral objectives for the guests. If the objectives are appropriate the program is successful if they are met. A standard is defined as 'a degree or level of requirement, excellence, or attainment' (Farrell and Lundgren, 1991: 242). To the extent that a standard can be determined for an activity, the extent to which it is met can also be measured. While this method is easy to administer, it tends to measure things that can be counted rather than the impact of the activity on people. The final method of evaluation is to measure the effectiveness of the program by looking at the impact on the guests who participate in the program. Since the end result of a guest-activity program is somehow related to guest satisfaction, this method would seem to be more appropriate than the other methods described above.

RESORT MANAGEMENT RESEARCH

A considerable amount of research is available concerning resorts. A variety of activity-specific associations issue annual reports on the size and scope of their particular segment. In the

US the National Golf Foundation, for example, produces research on such things as:

- frequent golf travelers: attitudes and behaviors;
- the spending report; and
- the US golf market.

Similar work is published by the American Resort Development Association, the National Ski Area Association, the Association of Marina Industries and the International Spa Association (NGF, ARDA, NSAA, AMI, ISA).

Most of these reports are operationally based. However, several themes in other research are emerging. The economic impact of the different sectors is being documented. For example, the impact of timeshares is a strong focus (Gose, 2003; Simon, 2004). It is noted that timeshare divisions of hospitality companies will account for an increasing percentage of the companies' profits. Much of the research focuses on changing demographics – in particular the growing number of baby boomers who are looking for a second home without the burden of year-round ownership and the potential of the non-white market that, as a whole, has a more positive opinion of, and a higher degree of interest in, purchasing timeshare.

A second theme relates to the increased importance of spas in general and the emergence of men as a viable market segment in particular (Monteson and Singer, 2002; Licata, 2003). The presence of a spa is an important factor in the selection of a resort. Indeed one in three guests spend more on spa treatments than on hotel dining. They are also becoming increasingly popular with men who represent as much as 30% of the clientele at a spa.

A third theme that cuts across all types of resorts is an increased awareness of environmental issues. The issue has been addressed as it relates to sandy beaches (Finkl and Krupa, 2003), the cruise industry (Sweeting and Wayne, undated) and the ski industry's sustainable slopes project (NSAAa, 2004). The overall conclusions from a variety of sources are that much remains to be done to protect the natural resource base for use by future generations.

THE FUTURE OF RESORTS*

Fifty years ago, the modern resort industry, still in its infancy, provided an experience very different than today. Travel to remote resort regions via train, automobile and the still-novel flight provided as much of the exotic allure as the grandeur of the resort hotel lobbies and restaurants. Resort activities focused on soaks in mineral springs, golf, skiing and socializing. The few, generally upper-class guests were pampered by exceptional service, which was a trademark of this era. Today, travelers spend less time considering how the resort will be reached, regardless of the location, and more time deciding on the type and number of activities they are able to fit in within a few days between a busy work schedule. Professional service training is revisited by resort management as a rare commodity used to differentiate otherwise similar resorts. Travelers have high expectations of the overall experience and return to those able to meet the increasingly high standards.

The arena within which today's resorts operate reflects a highly competitive environment. The high price of entrance into today's mature resort industry, combined with seemingly limitless day-to-day operational costs has led to very few new, large-scale resorts being built. A few key players in the industry own many of the established resorts. The few remaining independent resorts are forced to compete against these large conglomerates' powerful network of advertising strength and capital resources. Independent resorts need to prove they offer a unique experience not available at large corporate owned resorts. Conversely, the resorts owned by large corporations need to prove they are capable of individual treatment as well as mass marketing.

As time replaces money as the currency of the twenty-first century, resorts must consider how their location and systems interact with the time value of their guests. Guests are seeking highly amenitized, shorter vacation stays with excellent but transparent service. Leisure is now built around long weekend getaways and consumers expect a maximum return on their vacation minutes. Packaging will be the key to providing guests with the optimum mix of activities within the limited amount of time. Guests will arrive with little or no understanding of the types of activities available for them to enjoy. Guests will need to have the opportunities presented and priced according to an appropriate value system. The guests need to perceive that the value of the activities is greater than the price or expectations will not be met.

Changing demographics will have a significant impact on future resort amenities and programs. Between 2000 and 2010 American Demographics projects that the number of US householders aged 35 to 44 years will decline by four million, or 17%. Currently, there are more older (over 60) Americans than ever before. Six thousand people are retiring every day. In 2006, the first of the baby boomers started turning 60, and for the succeeding 15 or 20 years there will be a large increase of retirees. This shift will have a tremendous impact on both the ski and the golf industry. Baby boomers will become the foundation of the golf industry. Due to increased free time and disposable income it is anticipated that frequency will grow at nearly twice the rate of participation. The aging baby boomers are healthier and more active than any previous generation. In their 40s and 50s they think of themselves as in their mid-30s. They must be accommodated based on their actual age but they must be marketed to on their perceived age. The meaning of 'middle aged' has changed considerably over the last several decades, and the generation of baby boomers raised on the glory of a youth culture is still in denial and a state of 'arrested adolescence'.

With new destinations and cushier, innovative wilderness trips, no one is left out of the action. Adventure travel is growing up and slowing down. Though expeditions that push the endurance envelope remain plentiful, the new century brings a burst of active vacations that are amiably inclusive. People are working more than ever before – at least that is what they say. Work may seem longer now because of longer commutes, increased pace and anxiety levels and the fact that people have more duties both at work and at home. For couples, travel planning must now be scheduled around both partners' work schedules. The sense of time compression is a driving force in vacation decisions. With fewer perceived hours to relax and recreate, vacationers will increasingly cram more activity into the hours they have set aside as non-working hours.

Resorts and technology however, will provide an oasis for the seemingly longer workweeks. With the dramatic increase in the number of telecommuters, the availability of videoconferencing and portable wired offices, business travel will become increasing more discretionary. Workers have more options available for their location of work, whether it be a resort or the home patio. Providing for temporary offices by the pool, in the ski lodge or near the greens will allow vacationing workers to extend their stay while staying in touch with the demands at work.

Tomorrow's leisure travelers will increasingly prefer activity-based vacations that typically include sporting activities, as opposed to traditional relax-by-the-pool vacations (Zimmermann, 1996). Visitors will look for different types of things to do and multiple activities in one trip – there will be more fracturing. Visitors are looking for unique experiences and something to tell their friends about. As a result, resorts will be a place to try out the 'latest and greatest'. Activities such as snowmobiling and unique spa related activities such as herbal wraps and detoxifying treatments are gaining in popularity.

Vacationers will expect a seamless experience, i.e. all activities, lodging, eating, and purchases on one bill with all options easily accessed through the Internet. Accordingly, vacation packaging at all price levels will continue to gain in popularity. Visitors will have the option of having an adventure or spending their trip without hard decisions, problems, or trauma. 'Easy', 'Friendly', and 'Convenient' will be the operative words in the future. Visitor expectations for incredible customer service will become more important than ever before. Many resorts already have personal assistants; staff dedicated to assisting with luggage, booking activities, running errands, and taking care of any type of problem that the visitor is faced with. A future challenge is created because the foundation of the tourism industry is hospitality, yet one of the most pervasive challenges in the hospitality industry is retaining employees with great service skills, and many establishments are unwilling or able to provide the training necessary.

Regardless of the location, image, or reputation of the resort, it must provide a perceived value to the visitor. Meeting or exceeding the guests' expectations is the goal when attempting to construct value, but the future will prove that these expectations are a moving target. Whether vacationing on a budget or spending at will, visitors will expect that they 'got a bargain' for the money they spent. Women today are increasingly making vacation decisions and this will continue to be true in the future.

The future of the modern resort is predicated on satisfying the entire family. Highly organized and integrated children's programs will be important. Parents want to bring their family on vacation but they don't want to do 'kid's stuff' all day (and vice versa). Virtually all ski areas today understand that their future depends on their wise response to issues of environmental protection and impact mitigation. People want to vacation in beautiful places and the natural environment is the resort's most potent attraction. Visitors will have the expectation that the environment is not being destroyed in the name of tourism development.

Successful resorts will understand the fantasy of the resort experience and the interplay of the natural environment, history, regional culture, architecture, art, food, recreation, leisure, housekeeping, romance, and group and family memories. People go to resorts to create something that is missing from their lives. The total resort will have a great entry and arrival, recognizable icons, gathering places, great retail, art and culture, memorable architecture, diverse activities, and the ability to experience the natural environment. Visitor expectations regarding their vacation experience will continue to rise.

NOTES

* This section is contributed by the associates of Design Associates, a Denver-based resort design and planning company.

REFERENCES

American Resort Development Association. www.arda.org

American Resort Development Association. (1997) *The United States Timeshare Industry: Overview and Economic Impact Analysis.* Washington, DC: American Resort Development Association.

Association of Marina Industries. www.marinaassociation.org

Baumann, M. A. (1999a) 'New points system points industry in right direction', *Hotel and Motel Management*, May 17: 22.

Baumann, M. A. (1999b) 'Mixed-use projects possess right ingredients', *Hotel and Motel Management*, September 20: 10.

Baumann, M. A. (1999c) 'Specialized lenders cater to timeshares', *Hotel and Motel Management*, June 3: 20.

DeGraff, D. G., Jordan, D. J. and DeGraff, K. H. (1999) *Programming for Parks, Recreation, and Leisure Services: A Servant Leadership Approach.* State College, PA: Venture Publishing, Inc.

Farrell, P. and Lundegren, H. M. (1991) *The Process of Recreation Programming: Theory and Technique*, 3rd edn. State College, PA: Venture Publishing, Inc.

Farwell, T. (1993) *A Manual for Preparing Break-Even Analyses.* Boulder, CO: Ted Farwell and Associates.

Finkl, C. W. and Krupa, S. L. (2003) 'Environmental impacts of coastal-plain activities on sandy beach systems: hazards, perception and mitigation', *Journal of Coastal Research* (SI 35: 132–150).

Gee, C. Y. (1977) *Resort Development and Management.* 2nd edn. East Lansing, MI: The Educational Institute of the American Hotel and Motel Association.

Gose, J. (2003) 'Capitalizing on timeshare', *National Real Estate Developer*, March 1,

International Spa Association. www.experienceispa.com

Licata, P. G. (2003) 'Men are discovering the salon and spa', *The New York Times*, October 5, http://www.paulalicata.com/men-n-spas.htm, accessed February 17, 2006.

Monteson, P. A. and Singer, J. L. (2002) 'Planning and operating a spa-based spa', *Journal of Leisure Property*, December 2002.

National Golf Foundation. www.ngf.org

National Ski Area Association. www.nsaa.org

National Ski Area Association a. (2004) *Sustainable Slopes*, http://www.nsaa.org/nsaa/environment/sustainable_slopes/sustainable_slopes_annualreport_2004.pdf

Phillips, P. L. (1986) *Developing with Recreational Amenities: Golf, Tennis, Skiing, Marinas.* Washington, DC: Urban Land Institute.

Powers, P. (1991) *The Activity Gourmet.* State College, PA: Venture Publishing.

Shwanke, D. et al. (1977) *Resort Development Handbook.* Washington, DC: Urban Land Institute.

Simon, E. Y. (2004) 'Timeshare study shows $66-billion industry impact', *Hotel and Motel Management*, June 21, http:www.findarticles.com/p/articles/mi m3073/is 1 220/ai n9538915, accessed February 16, 2006.

Sparks, B. and Smith, J. A. (1999) 'Development of timeshare resort management: educational opportunities', *Journal of Hospitality and Tourism Education*, 11(2/3): 54–59.

Sweeting, J. E. N. and Scott W. L. (undated) *A Shifting Tide: Environmental Challenges and Cruise Line Responses.* Washington, DC: The Center for Environmental Leadership in Business.

Urban Land Institute. (1997) *Resort Development Handbook.* Washington, DC: Urban Land Institute.

Zimmermann, R. (1996) *Shoeshoe Resort Market Research and Analysis.* Denver, CO: Design Workshop.

Event Design and Management

24

Donald Getz

INTRODUCTION

In this chapter we explore the nexus between hospitality and event management, with emphasis on event design. 'Event Management' is a generic term to describe the emerging profession that designs, produces and manages all types of planned events. Events are staples within the hospitality and tourism industries, leading to the widespread use of the acronym MICE (i.e. Meetings, Incentives, Conventions and Exhibitions – see Chapter 18). But event management encompasses all planned events including celebrations such as carnivals and festivals, recreation and sports events, trade and commerce (including meetings, fairs and exhibitions), private functions and civic or governmental events. Many practitioners in the hospitality sector already have experience in producing events, but the next generation of professionals will have a college or university specialization. Currently both undergraduate and masters degrees are available in a number of countries, and this academic subject is spreading rapidly. As it develops academically, 'Event Studies' will become an accepted field, providing an interdisciplinary foundation of theory and methodology for increasing knowledge about events.

'Event Studies' (see Figure 24.1) has as its core phenomenon the planned event experience, and meanings attached to it (personal, societal and economic). Managing events is obviously one key element in event studies, as are the antecedents to attendance/participation, the outcomes of events, and dynamic elements including the temporal (history and future studies), the spatial (geography of events), policy and knowledge creation. Professional 'Event Managers' must possess a range of knowledge and skills that are creative and technical, managerial, methodological, theoretical (e.g. how to predict

impacts), and philosophical (ethics, esthetics, and understanding event experiences). Below the level of 'professional' the field requires many trades and suppliers, and in addition event management requires a strong creative or artistic component. Indeed, obtaining a balance between management, or a business approach on the one hand, and the artistic/creative inputs on the other, presents a real challenge for this field.

An additional consideration is the important economic and tourism-related roles of events. 'Event Tourism' can be defined as the planning, development and marketing of events for tourism, economic development and place-marketing purposes, with a specific concern for attracting event tourists. Event tourism is not so much a professional field as it is a market for events and an application of tourism marketing and development. However, there are a number of specialty career paths such as event bidding, event servicing, and strategic event tourism planning that are emerging within destination marketing/management organizations (DMOs).

'Hospitality', as a related professional field, figures prominently in event management, event tourism and event studies – both contributing to, and benefiting from, developments in these newer fields. Many of the facilities or venues events need are within the domain of hospitality management, from convention centers and hotels/resorts to restaurants and even wineries. Hospitality services are essential for events, especially food and beverage. The 'spirit of hospitality', and the meaning of hosts and guests at the venue and destination levels, is important to the events sector, as are the standard hospitality management practices devoted to product and service quality, marketing and communications, and other operational subjects. In return, hospitality will benefit greatly from improvements

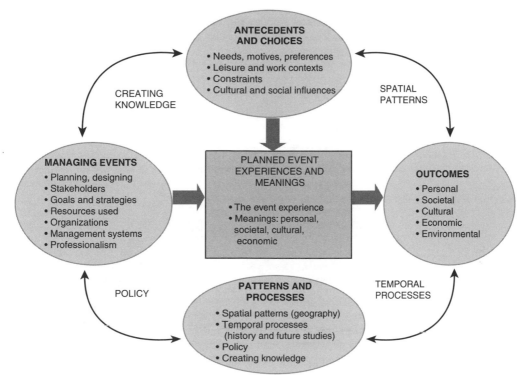

Figure 24.1 Event studies: core phenomenon and major themes
Source: Getz (2007: 10).

in professional event management and increased understanding gained through event studies. The most important contribution will be a better understanding of the planned event experience and its meanings, in concert with improved effectiveness in designing events as unique, memorable and transforming experiences. In many venues 'events' are largely viewed as a sales function (the aim being to fill our facilities and rooms) and a catering function (delivering meals); working with event or meeting planners is part of this traditional hospitality business. Hospitality managers can expect to gain new and crucial insights into what clients need and want from events, why people attend or do not, how to design or facilitate desired event experiences, and to evaluate the outcomes.

A logical question arises whenever a new field is established – do we really need it? Events are already part and parcel of hospitality, tourism, recreation and leisure, sports and arts management, and other closely related professional and academic fields. Yet in none of these are planned events and event experiences

the core phenomenon; they are variously dealt with as a market segment for venues, a type of tourist attraction, a leisure outlet, a mechanism for delivering sport competitions, or a form of art. The emergence of event management and event studies reflects the global importance of events and the fact that they are too important, not to mention risky, to leave to amateurs. Increasingly, hospitality firms, event venues, and tourism organizations will have to employ professional event managers to do what is now an incidental or part-time job.

HISTORICAL DEVELOPMENT OF THE FIELD

Similar to hospitality, tourism, leisure and other management-based academic fields, event management first became established as a profession, then received recognition and formal program development at colleges and universities. Without a substantial base of practitioners

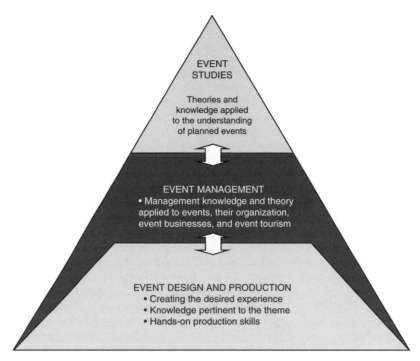

Figure 24.2   Three levels of event education
Source: Getz (2007: 4).

and a clearly identified need for professional education programs, management-based degree programs would not be justified. As well, it takes many years for the teachers and researchers in a new academic area like event management to develop the literature, research journals, conferences, and theory that lead to recognition of a new field of 'studies'.

Figure 24.2 illustrates three levels of event education, and the base consists of 'event design and production'. This is the realm of hands-on tradecraft, technical/artistic design, and the supply of hospitality services to events. Certain events by their theme or form do require some specialized knowledge, such as the registration systems needed for conventions or the entertainment component of concerts and festivals. This level can be taught adequately within hospitality or business programs, but is not in itself professional education. The second level, 'event management', does constitute professional preparation and has to embody some knowledge of design and production. Managers must understand the event itself, as well as what it takes to organize, finance,

manage and sustain the production team, society or firm. At the top of this conceptual pyramid is 'event studies', which cannot exist without the underlying trades and professional fields.

A review of the main professional associations covering events reveals a fundamental problem, namely the fractionalization of current practice into streams that are specific to event types. In 1885, the International Association of Fairs and Expositions (IAFE) began with a half dozen fairs and a commitment to service for all of its members. The International Association for Exhibition Management was organized in 1928 as the National Association of Exposition Managers to represent the interests of tradeshow and exposition managers. The International Festivals and Events Association celebrated its 50th year in 2005, and its orientation appeals to community festivals and other celebrations. Established in 1972, Meeting Professionals International (MPI) is the leading global community committed to shaping and defining the future of the meeting and event industry. The International Special Events Society (ISES) was founded in 1987 and embraces both event designers/producers and their numerous suppliers. As well, there are associations for carnivals, and many arts and sports-specific associations that deal with events, and they organize at local, national and international levels.

Evolving from specializations based on type of event (or the venues, target markets, or functions) to a generic 'event manager' profession will be difficult, as established professional associations will continue to compete for members and prestige. However, this essential process will be facilitated by educational institutions that produce generic event management graduates, and by employers who will increasingly want adaptable professionals.

Historically, there were few if any academic programs in event management prior to the 1990s. Tourism, hospitality and recreation/leisure grew rapidly in the 1970s and 1980s, both as a response to, and an agent shaping, globalization, particularly coinciding with increased disposable incomes, leisure and entertainment, travel for all purposes, and commerce in general. 'Events' in general were barely mentioned in hospitality and tourism texts in the 1970s (they were viewed as a type of tourist attraction, and were given some prominence in the 1980s in both texts and tourism research journals). Conventions and meetings have a somewhat more established academic history. Since 1990 the literature on events and event management has exploded, accompanying a global move to establish diploma and degree programs. There are a growing number of Master's programs in event management, and numerous individual courses offered in tourism, leisure, sport and hospitality programs. Several research journals are devoted to this field, starting with *Festival Management and Event Tourism* in 1993, later renamed *Event Management. Convention and Exhibition Management* was recently renamed *Convention and Event Tourism*, and an online journal of event management research has been established.

The future undoubtedly will see event management gain global recognition and permanence alongside its closely related professional fields, including tourism and hospitality. No doubt its evolution will display a similar growth period (which should cover this and the next decade), followed by a leveling of demand from students and a rationalization of academic programs. It is reasonable to suggest that those event management programs seeking sustainability within the university community will have to establish a solid brand based on quality, innovation, specializations, and outstanding research and publication records – not just great teaching. Inevitably, this means increasing emphasis on event studies as an interdisciplinary field.

EVENT DESIGN AND MANAGEMENT APPLIED TO HOSPITALITY

The event studies and management field is too expansive to cover in its entirety. Rather, a detailed examination of event design provides the best connection to hospitality. It is in the realm of design that venue managers and hospitality service providers will find immediate and significant applications, whereas the broader event management topics are very similar to traditional business management.

Figure 24.3 illustrates core themes in the 'event management body of knowledge' (EMBOK). EMBOK is directed at professional education, whereas the event studies model (Figure 24.1) constitutes the larger field of studies that incorporates management of events. EMBOK is an ongoing process devoted to advancing the event management field, leading to higher standards of education and professional practice, and possibly becoming the basis for certification of event managers.

'Design' is simultaneously a creative and technical process aimed at solving real-world problems. In the case of event design the goal is to produce events that meet specified goals, yet event experiences are highly personal constructs that depend as much on the guest/customer/participant as they do on the event managers and designers. Before examining the scope of event design we need to more carefully define the experiential side of events.

THE PLANNED EVENT EXPERIENCE

This is the phenomenological core of event studies, and what makes event management unique as an area of professional practice.

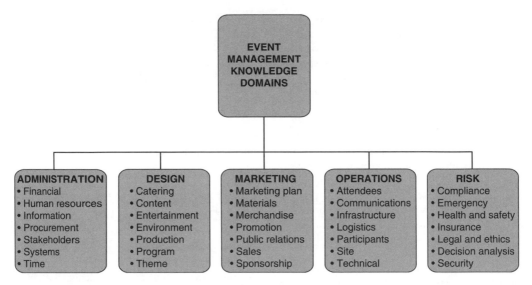

Figure 24.3   EMBOK (Event Management Body of Knowledge)
Source: Silvers, Bowdin, O'Toole, and Nelson (2006: 194).

Event managers have to know how to facilitate desired experiences, confined by time and setting, to meet the purposes of clients, audiences, guests, and other stakeholders. This is in part a technical and in part a creative design process.

It is now almost a cliché to say that tourism and hospitality are key players in the 'experience economy' popularized by Pine and Gilmore (1999). Theorists, drawing from psychology, direct us to examine experience in terms of behavior (the conative dimension), emotion or attitude (the affective dimension), and cognition (awareness, perception, understanding). Accordingly, we want to understand the event experience holistically, from the needs, motivations, attitudes and expectations brought to the event, through the actual living experience (the 'doing', or 'being there') all the way to reflections on the event including meanings attached to it and influences on future behavior. The range of potential event experiences is quite broad, from the fun and revelry of entertainment, carnival and party, to the solemn spirituality of religious pilgrimage and ritual. Many events are all about learning, while others foster commerce; sport for participants is all about challenge, yet sport events encompass feeling of community and sub-culture identity as well as nostalgia on the part of fans.

Li and Petrick (2006) reviewed the literature pertaining to festival and event motivations and concluded from many studies that the

seeking and escaping theory (Iso-Ahola, 1980, 1983) is largely confirmed. These are 'intrinsic motivators', with the event being a desired leisure pursuit. Researchers have demonstrated that escapism leads people to events for the generic benefits of entertainment and diversion, socializing, learning and doing something new, i.e. novelty seeking, and just plain getting away from it all.

The pull or seeking factors apply more to those with special interests who want a specific set of benefits offered by the event. For example, highly involved runners need events to compete in (McGehee et al., 2003) and professionals have to attend certain conferences because of their educational content or the unique networking possibilities (Severt et al., 2006). The exact balance between generic (escapist) and specific (seeking) benefits obtained at any given event will depend on many personal factors including motives, expectations, mood and the experiences obtained. Nicholson and Pearce (2001) studied motivations to attend four quite different events in New Zealand; an air show; an award ceremony; a wild food festival, and a wine, food and music festival. They concluded that multiple motivations were the norm, and that while socialization was common to them all, it varied in its nature. Event-specific reasons were tied to the novelty or uniqueness of each event.

But not all event experiences fall under the heading of leisure. 'Extrinsic' motivators are those related to work, doing business, social obligations, or peer pressure to attend or participate in events. While social psychologists and leisure/tourism researchers have frequently studied festival and sport-event motivators, much less effort has been devoted to the motivations and experiences of those attending events because their job or business requires it, or they feel obligated in some way. It is also necessary to consider the entire range of stakeholder groups that have some experience related to events, even if it is just a temporary negative impact on them through increased noise or traffic. There are staff and volunteers, officials and regulators, sponsors and suppliers, and so on. Event managers cannot afford to be concerned only about guests, customers and participants. Of these other stakeholder groups, the event volunteer has been studied most, including research on motivations, training, experiences, satisfaction and commitment. Ralston et al. (2005) reviewed the literature on event volunteers, covering motivation, profiles, and satisfaction studies and theory. Their own research in Manchester employed focus groups and a survey of Commonwealth Games volunteers. Results on why they volunteered clearly pertain to the experiences they sought, including: excitement, uniqueness (the chance of a lifetime), meeting interesting people, and being part of a team. Meanings attached to the experience included: supporting sport, doing something useful for the community, helping the city, region and country, and using their skills.

Experiences cannot be created or guaranteed, as they are highly individual 'personal constructs'. But event designers have a number of realms in which they can operate with the aim of suggesting, facilitating or constraining experiences. Each of these is illustrated in Figure 24.4 and discussed in the ensuing sections. The figure shows four realms of event design, the first of which is the setting. This is closely related to the concepts of 'servicescape' and 'atmospherics', and draws heavily on cognitive and environmental psychology, sociology, and the theater. Patrons seldom come for the setting, but it is a vital factor in achieving a satisfying, memorable experience. Many elements of the setting and of service delivery are hygiene factors, or potential dissatisfiers – they do not attract but can, if poorly provided, dissatisfy the guest or customer.

The theme and program, however, are really the core product that attract people to most events. They come for the activities, entertainment and various personal and social experiences that the program seeks to provide. In some cases the 'consumables' are the core product, as in food and wine-themed events, but in many events they are secondary design elements. The 'goals' column indicates a number of major goals within each of the four design realms, and each is discussed below. Key theoretical foundations are also listed and discussed, along with specific design tools that can be used in hospitality settings.

DESIGNING THE SETTING

The 'setting' for events is highly variable, ranging from a room or hall (suitably laid out and decorated for a function) to a special-purpose event venue (e.g. a convention center), an open space (e.g. park or street) all the way to an entire community or region (as in hosting a mega-event). Each setting has to be viewed as an experience setting.

Philip Pearce in the book *Tourist Behaviour: Themes and Conceptual Schemas* (2005: 136) conceptualized tourist space from an experiential perspective. Pearce labeled three intersecting circles as: (1) 'activities available on-site for visitors'; (2) 'the physical or cultural setting or resource', and (3) 'the meanings and understandings brought to or influenced by or negotiated at the site'. At the core of Pearce's approach is the notion that a setting likely to promote positive on-site experiences should offer '... clear conceptions of what the place is about, the activities available are understood and accessible, and the physical elements that constitute the setting are distinctive and aesthetically pleasing' (Pearce, 2005: 136). Emphasis should be placed on understanding the guests, their expectations and involvement, and how they are transformed. Certainly these principles also apply to event settings in general.

Event settings, first of all, are places that have to be defined as 'special' for the duration of the 'time out of time' (Falassi, 1987) that constitutes a planned event. The main initial considerations are location (e.g. centrality and accessibility), site characteristics (is it suitable for the event?),

REALMS OF EVENT DESIGN	GOALS	THEORETICAL FOUNDATIONS	SPECIFIC DESIGN TOOLS
THE SETTING –décor and room layout –entire venues/facilities –larger sites (indoor/outdoor)	–create a special place, valorized for the event –maximize accessibility and efficient flow –enable smooth logistics –achieve the wow! response –prevent crowding and other problems	–behavioral settings –arousal and stressors –setting affordances and constraints –setting preferences –affective qualities –cognitive mapping and wayfaring –attraction gradients –personal space	–layout (e.g. to facilitate flow or social interaction –queuing and other crowd management techniques –design capacity From theater: –staging and art –sensory stimulation (lighting, sound, etc.) and other special effects –props, costumes –scale, shape and focus
THEME AND PROGRAM –themes defined in terms of esthetics, the object of celebration, or an intellectual concept –programmic elements of style	–create a unique, memorable or transforming event –establish a sense of 'time out of time' (i.e., escapism) –foster 'communitas' –preserve authenticity –meet the event's particular experiential objectives (e.g. celebrating, entertaining, learning, selling, competitive or recreational, etc.)	–liminal and liminoid (special times) –communitas (a social phenomenon) –valorization and sacralization –authenticity –involvement –engagement	–emotional stimulation –ritual and symbolism –games, competition, humor and surprise –hospitality –commerce –social facilitation –exhibition, education and thematic interpretation –art and entertainment; performance of all kinds (scripting; choreography) –scheduling, 'timing' and 'build'
SERVICE –staff as service providers and 'cast members' –management systems to ensure service quality	–ensure the guests, customers, participants and other stakeholders achieve their goals, without problems –deliver all services to the highest standard	–expectation–confirmation (SERVQUAL) –performance –symbolic interaction	–service mapping and blueprinting –logistics –role playing and critical incident training
CONSUMABLES –gastronomy/catering –beverages –gifts	–ensure that food, beverages and other consumables/gifts are of the highest standard –create themes/events with gastronomy as the core attraction	–taste –esthetics –health/safety –culture	–design of table settings and food/beverage products –theater (applied to preparation and service

Figure 24.4   Four realms of event design applied to hospitality

and the social-cultural context (has it historic and cultural meaning?). Infrastructure and management systems then have to be developed or modified, including basic services, theme and program, amenities and guest services, security and controls. Both site planning and esthetic design are important. Settings and management systems will interact with the people dimension (staff, volunteers, participants, performers, other guests and customers) in shaping the event experiences. There are unlimited ways to combine setting, management and people, yielding great opportunities for creative event design. However, each setting poses its own challenges and opportunities, some of which are identified in the ensuing discussion of generic event settings.

Conventions, concerts, festivals, and spectator sports – any event bringing together large numbers of people – require settings that provide for sitting, viewing and listening. The event manager can often rent 'assembly' venues that have their own management systems, including convention centers, hotel ballrooms, exposition halls, concert halls, auditoria and arenas. Major design challenges include the fact that many venues are either halls or arenas with no inherent esthetics, or require substantial modification on technical or creative grounds to suit the event. This negative factor might be compensated for adequately by the presence of staff and systems to facilitate events. Opportunities for using unique and even strange venues abound. Meeting planners seek out venues in special places with inspiring or provocative features. Advice on meeting and convention venue design can be found in Meeting Professionals International (2003) *Meetings and Conventions: A Planning Guide*. Party design is covered by Bailey (2002), and Lena Malouf's (2002) *Parties and Special Events: Planning and Design*.

Parades, flotillas, cavalcades, marches and other similar events are linear, mobile forms of entertainment, spectacle or ritual with special design and management requirements. The audience might be standing, seated, or moving along with the procession. The most common linear setting, however, is a street with a static audience along the route. Some processions pass through seating areas and even stadia, where they take on the form of theater. The logistics for such events are challenging, such as getting everyone in a parade or race mobilized for proper sequencing, the likelihood of causing traffic disruption and congestion, and the fact that most streets are unsuited for spectating. Gregson (1992) gave advice on using sidewalks, streets and buildings to stage events, noting that architects generally fail to take account of seasonal changes and the needs of public gatherings. The reader is also referred to the International Festivals and Events Association's publication, *Parades* (2000).

Many sport events involve races or other linear forms of activity, including long-distance running and auto racing, which combine procession with nodes of activity. Usually the audience congregates at the nodes, such as start, finish and transition points. The event designer will often have to provide live video feeds from the linear portions to the places where fans congregate. Service points for athletes and vehicles are also needed.

Frequently, events make use of parks, plazas and closed-off streets. Free movement is a feature of these settings, but they usually also contain sub-areas for assembly, procession and exhibition/sales. European cities seemed to have the advantage in terms of beautiful, culturally significant squares for events, while North American cities tend to have more space, such as waterfronts and natural parks to use for large public gatherings (Getz, 2001). Environmental concerns are important in parks, while potential damage to buildings is a concern in urban plazas.

Purpose-built exhibition and convention centers are the best suited for trade and consumer shows, although any event can incorporate areas for food and beverage or other merchandise sales and demonstrations. These settings are designed to entice entry and circulation, browsing and sales. Sometimes the audience merely views the exhibits, at others sales are made. Since the purpose of these events is usually commerce, a number of principles from environmental psychology have to be applied to the design in order to ensure that interpersonal contacts are facilitated. Good circulation is necessary, but it is also desirable to have people linger and talk. See *The Art of the Show* (Morrow, 1997) for details on exhibition design.

There is ample scope for the event designer to draw upon theatrical production to enhance event settings and experiences. 'Experience Design' according to Haahti and Komppula (2006) draws heavily on 'dramaturgy', which is part of theater and performance studies. They provide examples in which high-contact, high-involvement tourists co-create experiences with professional 'stagers' or facilitators. Ideas for 'manuscripts' and 'staged experiences' have to be generated with the needs and expectations of guests in mind, embodying myths, stories and history from the place or event. 'This enables the creation of a place and a space for being together and the development of a group identity in experiencing' (Haahti and Komppula, 2006: 103). In this approach, the 'stage' is whatever venue the experience takes place in, but it has to be appropriate to the design.

This is the most fundamental theatrical concept, based on the fact that plays and many other performances are usually produced in a specific (assembly) venue with a stage and an audience. 'Staging' or 'stagecraft' applies to both the layout of this type of setting and to what is done on the stage (or within the entire performance space, whatever it is) to facilitate the performance and enhance the audience's experience. The basic components are:

- scenery and other artistic design elements, including curtains;
- lighting and related special effects (e.g. lasers);
- sound systems, musicians, orchestras;
- props (short for 'theatrical properties') such as furnishings and hand-held items;
- costumes and makeup; and
- direction, and other management or control systems.

Brown and James (2004) discussed five specific theatrical applications to events. 'Scale', 'shape' and 'focus' apply to the setting, whereas 'timing' and 'build' come under the heading of scripting or programming. It is important to match the scale of the event or activity to the venue, in part to ensure the audience can see and understand what is happening. This principle will affect decisions on whether to stress the visual over the aural, and three-dimensional over two-dimensional. The audience needs enclosure, but does not want to feel restricted. Drawing from environmental psychology, knowledge of how an audience relates to and moves within an environment, is essential. Removing visual and tangible clutter or distractions, and keeping things simple and legible are important design principles for event settings. The use of blocking techniques from theater and film direction ensures that the audience focuses on what the designer/programmer wants them to concentrate on. Consider how lighting, color, movement, and shape affect people. 'Timing', or scheduling,

has to consider the audience's attention span and responses to stimuli, keeping in mind that '... event time is different from real time and audiences respond differently to it'. In general, Brown and James (2004: 61) recommended programming 'tightly' and accurately to maintain 'flow' and contact with the audience. 'Build' is the use of time and programming, including ebbs and peaks of intensity, to maximize impact on the audience. There is a skill in using limited resources to achieve great emotional or intellectual stimulation.

There is both art and science in the following specific design elements. Environmental psychology provides the theoretical foundation for researchers who want to know to what extent these variables can affect the event experience.

Experiments have shown that lower levels of light result in greater interpersonal intimacy and quieter or reduced conversation. So event designers reduce lighting just before the curtain rises or the speakers take the stage in order to quiet the audience. On the other hand, soft lighting during a banquet will likely encourage conversation. Lighting also impacts on functionality. If the event purpose is to discuss important topics, dim lighting will be counter-productive. If it requires audience attention on a stage or person, then dim ambient lights plus a spotlight are effective. Light shows, often including lasers, provide a lot of mental stimulation and generate emotional arousal. Too much light stimulation can be counter-productive if the audience is expected to calm down immediately afterwards. Light stimulation generates a lot of brain activity that is difficult to turn off, hence you are wise to avoid watching television before sleep time, and do not want to have a strobe-light effect just before listening to a speaker.

People have color preferences, and colors affect mood. Color can be manipulated through lighting or other design features. Perceived spaciousness can be influenced by colors and lighting, helping to reduce feelings of crowding. 'Color theory' relates to how specific media affect color appearance (i.e. the effects of context on color appearance) whereas 'color psychology' considers the effects of colors on feelings and behavior (e.g. will a pink room really calm prisoners and a red room increase tension? Does blue make people feel calm and cool?). 'Color symbolism' is culturally defined, as in whether red suggests heat, anger or danger. Art, color, light, and decoration, all have esthetic effects. We either like some art and designs or we do not. Esthetic stimulation might lead to conversation, intellectual appreciation, quiet contemplation – or be ignored. Esthetic design elements might also hold symbolic meaning, and this can be manipulated by event designers. For example, certain colors, design features (like expensive art) and shapes or patterns are associated with political ideologies, royalty, lifestyles, social class, or other potentially unifying or controversial themes. Being in a pleasant setting can also impact on people's willingness to help each other, but it might prove to be a distraction if serious business discussion is required. Loud noise is universally shunned, as it both physically hurts and gets in the way of desired conversations or other interactions. Quiet, ambient music has been found to be relaxing, although many people are rather sick of the elevator music we are too often subjected to.

Foodservice professionals know that their best advertisement is often the smell of cooking. The wrong smells can make people physically ill. Indeed, the military has experimented with smell as a weapon! Similarly, while taste is obviously the critical factor in dining experiences, and at food festivals, taste can be manipulated in other event environments to stimulate emotional and behavioral responses.

The well-known phenomenon of 'museum fatigue' has to be understood by event designers. Whatever is on display, or in learning situations, people only devote so much attention before becoming mentally fatigued. In a museum, visitors eventually start passing by many exhibits without stopping or even looking, because they have already absorbed enough. The same kind of mental fatigue can result in conventioneers skipping sessions, students falling asleep in class (boredom might also be a factor there), or visitors to art exhibits merely glancing at outstanding works of art. Event designers can plan their setting to focus attention quickly on the primary exhibits or other features, to reach visitors prior to fatigue setting in. Lecturers can hit the highlights first, then go on to the mundane details.

When designing for pedestrian flow, ask what is in the event or its design that will most attract people? Exhibition planners know that the best sites are right at the entrance, facing those entering the hall. After that, there is a gradient of desirable locations based on visitor movements (often towards the center, or to the exits, or the food, or the washrooms), although

the movement can be influenced by both overall design and individual exhibit design. Exhibit designers also understand that involvement with displays is better than mere visual stimulation. Getting people to touch and try is one key step towards learning, or buying. Harvey et al. (1998) discovered they could more than double the time visitors spent at exhibits by making them interactive and multi-sensory, along with better lighting and easier-to-read lettering. Visitors felt more immersed in the overall museum experience.

The Kaplan (1987: 8–11) model helps predict people's preferences for various types of environment:

- 'coherence': the scene is organized, everything hangs together;
- 'legibility': we can categorize or understand the setting, everything is clear to us;
- 'complexity': a measure of the number and variety of elements in the setting; and
- 'mystery': hidden information is present and we are drawn into the setting to learn more.

Too much complexity or mystery, however, can be a bad thing. Too much mystery can be incompatible with legibility, and can become frightening. If the event designer provides light and dark contrasts, the viewer might be drawn in, whereas too dark a room can be scary and might discourage entry. Also, consider an empty room versus one in which people are present. Are we normally inclined to enter a space in which no other people are present? What appeals to people for meetings, trade shows and learning seminars might be quite different from settings for sports, public celebrations and private parties. We know that coherence and legibility are important when it comes to environmental preferences, so how do we translate that into event design, and how does it impact on event experiences? Bateson (1989) said that 'legibility' is crucial in all 'servicescapes', because customers arrive with expectations of how the site will function. These are, of course, social constructs, such as the notion that festival sites should always have a main stage and a food/beverage area.

Kevin Lynch (1960: 49) provided the classic approach to cognitive mapping in cities, with implications for event settings. His key principles should be applied to event-site planning so that people can easily understand the layout and efficiently navigate within it. The larger, more complex the site, the more important it is to strive for coherence and legibility. Lynch stressed the following features for wayfaring:

- 'nodes': activity places (provide a central stage and entertainment area within a park; arrange the venue to have multiple, easily located focal points);
- 'paths': routes people follow (direction and flow within an event venue has to be controlled; use signs and edges);
- 'landmarks': shapes, signs or symbols that everyone can see and refer to (e.g. every World Fair builds a monument, usually in the center);
- 'districts': neighborhoods, shopping centers and other themed areas (group compatible activities together); and
- 'edges': perceptual or real barriers between districts (people should recognize where they are in relation to other districts).

Lynch also found age and gender differences in how people wayfind, and probably there are many cultural differences as well. This suggests a research project for application to a variety of event sites.

Barker's (1968: 19) behavior settings can be adapted to fit different circumstances and goals. The three generic means of control pertain to:

- 'access' (who gets in, or under what schedule);
- 'design capacity' (i.e., the numbers allowed; consider peak and average attendance); and
- 'flow' (time spent on site; turnover rates).

It is necessary to also consider accessibility for persons with physical and other disabilities or special needs (see Fleck, 1996). Darcy and Harris (2003) showed how to do an accessibility plan for events that provides for all needs. Traffic management in and around events presents serious challenges, and practical advice is available from a number of sources. The UK National Outdoor Events Association has a manual on traffic (see www.noea.org.uk), and from New South Wales, Australia there is Traffic Management for Special Events (www.rta.nsw.gov.au).

A model produced by Russell and Lanius (1984: 120–121), called 'adaptation level and the affective appraisal of environments' seems very applicable to events. The basic premise is that emotional reactions to environments can be described in words along two continua: from pleasant to unpleasant, from arousing to sleepy. Forty descriptors were developed through research, falling into the four quadrants:

1 highly arousing and highly pleasant (e.g. exciting, exhilarating, interesting);
2 highly arousing and unpleasant (e.g. distressing, frenzied, tense, hectic);
3 unarousing and unpleasant (e.g. dull, dreary, unstimulating); and
4 unarousing but pleasant (e.g. serene, tranquil, peaceful, restful).

Is quadrant 1 close to the 'wow!' factor desired by many event designers? Note that the descriptors are not specifically experiences, only reactions to stimuli. Russell and Lanius also determined through experimentation that the same stimulus (they used photographs) can generate widely different affective appraisals. In other words, setting designers cannot be certain their work will elicit the intended emotional response. One major reason is that people adapt to the environment and particular stimuli, so they react differently the next time.

Interpersonal and environmental stimuli cause responses, both physiological and psychological, triggering behavioral responses. Sometimes event designers want to increase arousal, as in fostering celebration or revelry, and at other times they decrease stimulation in order to foster reverence or attentiveness. People have a limited capacity for dealing with a lot of stimulation and can become over-stimulated. When this happens it can trigger a response such as withdrawal or anxiety, and it will usually result in a filtering of stimuli to focus on the necessary or desirable inputs. Another strategy frequently employed by people is to attempt to eliminate or adjust the stimulus, such as by screening information, turning down noise and light levels, or engaging in conversation in order to mask an annoying or boring speaker. People have their own ways of finding optimal arousal levels, and this can be accomplished through escaping or seeking of stimulation. This is at the core of leisure and travel theory, based on the notion that motivation or need for leisure and travel is a result of simultaneously seeking and escaping. Continuous exposure to simulation can result in 'adaptation', such as people in cities adapting to higher levels of noise or crowding. Loss of perceived control is the first step in the behavioral constraints model.

It leads to discomfort and 'reactance' – that is, we try to regain control. Even the anticipation of loss of control, or another threat, can trigger reactance. If people are constantly told they cannot do something a possible consequence is 'learned helplessness'. People are likely to give up trying to make changes after a while, and that can apply to any consumer of any product or service.

What causes us stress? Certainly when things feel out of control, beyond our ability to cope, we feel stress. But environmental factors can also cause stress, such as event settings or programs that generate sensory overload, over-crowding, nasty surprises, bad behavior on the part of other guests, or poorly managed environmental systems leading to bad air. Fear causes stress, and a lack of knowledge about what is happening can generate fear. What is the difference between intimacy, personal distance, social distance, and public distance? We want intimacy with lovers and family, but not strangers. We tolerate crowds and even seek them out when a certain atmosphere is desired. At meetings, we might feel uncomfortable if the seats are too close.

Hall (1966) identified the four spatial zones, with 'intimate distance' being 0 to 1.5 feet (touching and feeling distance, with lots of contact and various sensory exchanges). 'Personal distance' is 1.5 to 4 feet (mostly verbal and visual contacts; contacts with friends and regular acquaintances). 'Social distance' is 4 to 12 feet (impersonal and businesslike eye and voice contacts, no touching, normal voice levels). Fourth, 'public distance' is over 12 feet (formality, as in students' relationship to a lecturer in a classroom; the need exists for technical assistance or raising one's voice). Environmental psychologists have also studied personal space in various settings, using laboratory experiments and simulations or field methods. For event researchers, field observations and tests will yield the best results. Remember that cultural factors are likely to be important, and that age and gender have to be considered.

'Personal space' can be used by event designers to help achieve goals. For example, it is well known and easily observed that communication effectiveness diminishes with distance from the speaker. That is why classrooms are designed as amphitheaters and not long halls. There have been studies of optimal spacing in learning environments, for professional interaction, and for facilitating group processes. 'Sociopetal' distance brings people together, such as the circular or opposite layout of chairs in one's living room, while 'sociofugal' spacing diminishes interaction (e.g. rows of chairs). A related concept is 'territoriality', which refers to a tendency for similar groups to stick together and apart from other groups. Within and between-group interactions are easy to observe in most social settings, such as the little cliques that form at parties. If you want people to join in, leave an obvious opening, as in a crescent, but if you feel exclusionary, form a tight little knot with everyone facing inwards. Another form of territoriality occurs when people protect space for themselves or their group, like reserving seats or claiming tables at a banquet. Is this a good or bad thing? 'Density' is an objective measure of how many people there are in a given area, but 'crowding' is how people feel about the situation. Studies have shown that in wilderness settings even the sight of a few other canoeists is crowding. Although a potential problem at events, people often expect crowds and they can even add to our enjoyment (Lee et al., 1997; Wickham and Kerstetter, 2000; Mowen et al., 2003).

Some of our reaction to the presence of others is related to the size of the group and our personal space – this is 'social density' (Bell et al., 2001), whereas some of it depends on how much space there is – that is 'spatial density'. It is the difference between too many people to interact with, versus not enough space. Freedom to move, perceived control and risks can also be factors. For example, what would happen in a panic – can we escape? Certainly the context also influences our judgement of what is crowding. Researchers have found that males and females are equally affected by high social density, but males suffer more from high spatial density. Friends and social support mitigate stress or anxiety caused by crowding. Evidence linking crowding with aggression or other anti-social behavior is not clear, especially within event settings.

Bell et al. (2001) compared various theoretical models pertaining to crowding. Critical causes of crowding (not of density, but the resultant feeling) have been attributed to excessive social contact and social stimulation, reduced freedom (e.g. to move about), scarcity of resources (bathrooms?), violations of personal space, unwanted contacts (groping?), interference with desired behavior, and lack of privacy. Possible coping mechanisms to crowding include withdrawal, attempts to reduce stimulation/arousal, escape, aggressive behavior, territoriality and other attempts to maintain freedom, control or privacy. Some of these coping mechanisms might be desirable even if the crowding is considered to be, overall, unavoidable or fun. Cutting across most of these models is the notion of perceived control. If we believe we can take control of the situation, the negative impacts will be diminished.

Freedman's (1975) 'density-intensity model' appears to have great relevance to events, although it has been controversial. His model suggests that density intensifies reactions that would otherwise occur given the particular situation, so that high density heightens the importance of other people and magnifies our reactions to them. High density therefore intensifies the pleasantness of positive situations (e.g. a party or celebration) and intensifies the negativity of situations we would rather avoid. Accordingly, your expectations, desires and mood upon entering an event setting will directly impact on your reaction to density – whether or not you feel crowded. Mowen et al. (2003) found that crowding at events is more likely to be a positive factor at the entertainment stage, and negative at food and beverage outlets; it varies by zone and activity.

'Stressors' at events can also lead to problems. These include: excessive waiting; overcrowding; excessive sensory stimulation; overwhelming security, regulation or threats; fencing that prevents escape (people feel trapped), and other restrictions on movement. Berlonghi (1990) concluded that panic at events is likely to stem from real or perceived threats, and he discussed eight crowd characteristics to help managers or security identify crowd problems and security threats. Freedman (1975) also experimented with 'contagion', which is the rapid spread of emotions or behavior through a group or crowd. This phenomenon obviously has a direct bearing on events, as in some cases we want to foster positive contagion (especially celebration and humor) and in others it is very bad (fear and fighting).

'Crowd management' has to be integrated throughout the design process and management systems. The purpose is to both prevent problems and facilitate good experiences. 'Crowd control', on the other hand, involves security and other measures that only become necessary when there is a problem and should be handled by experts (Rutley, n.d.). Setting a firm site capacity (or 'design capacity'), in

terms of the number of people invited or permitted, is one way to prevent overcrowding and related problems. Similarly, managers can try to regulate the flow and turnover of patrons. Other capacity and crowd management techniques include advance and group ticketing (to avoid bottlenecks), physical barriers and activity spacing, information provision, and the management of queues (Mowen, Vogelsong and Graefe, 2003). See also Ammon and Fried (1998) for advice on event crowd management.

THEMING AND THEMATIC INTERPRETATION

A 'theme' is a unifying idea or concept that gives meaning to the event, or is the object of celebration or commemoration. It can be a visual or sensory theme, in the realms of decorators and chefs, an activity theme (styles of sport, play, recreation), a fantasy theme (usually combining décor and entertainment), an emotional theme (such as a celebration of something of value), or it can be intellectual in nature (such as the conference topic or workshop problem). Derived from cognitive psychology, 'thematic interpretation' is based on a key premise: that people remember themes far easier than they remember facts. If event designers tap into universal belief systems they can more easily communicate with audiences, and audiences both need and want meaningful experiences as opposed to simple entertainment. Thematic interpretation aims to create visitor experiences that have lasting impact, translating into higher levels of satisfaction, positive word of mouth, sales, and repeat visits. It is best described as strategic communication.

Professor Sam Ham of the University of Idaho is most closely associated with developing and applying thematic interpretation within parks, heritage and tourism. Dr. Ham, Anna Housego and Betty Weiler together authored the *Tasmanian Thematic Interpretation Planning Manual* (May 2005: available online at www.tourismtasmania.com), as part of that Australian state's innovative Experience Strategy. We can adapt their planning process to events, so let's start with their definition and explanation of theme:

A theme is a take-home message; it's the moral of the story or main conclusion a visitor takes away … (p. 3).

A theme is a whole idea ... is the way you express the essence of the message you and others in your organisation want to impart to visitors; it is not necessarily the set of words you would use in direct communication to visitors ... when a moral to the story really matters to the visitor then it touches them in lots of ways, and that's when it really sticks ... (p. 13).

If an event theme is thought of merely in terms of decoration or entertainment, which is appropriate at many events, then interpretation is not really required. But at cultural celebrations, religious ceremonies, arts festivals, and many other planned events, we want the visitor to be emotionally and cognitively affected; we want a memorable, even transforming experience. While event guests and customers might not remember all the activities or information provided, they should be provoked into reflection and involvement by the main theme so they can make their own meanings from, and about the event, the place, and the time they spent there. Using both tangible and intangible elements (such as symbols and emotional engagement) in interpretation makes for more powerful theming.

Ideally, the theme and various interpretive media (or tools) are targeted to various audiences depending on their levels of interest, extent and nature of their participation, and how managers want to influence them, thereby requiring a fairly sophisticated research and evaluation process. Higher levels of effectiveness can probably be achieved through greater investment in planning and research. Evaluation of results will have to include measures of actual behavior at the event and afterwards, questions about more intangible emotional and cognitive outcomes, and effects on other people through word of mouth.

Interpretation of, and at, events can include the following tools. They can be thought of as different 'media', each with their own application depending on audiences and situations.

- Guides who interpret the setting, performances, food and beverages, as to their cultural significance.
- Signage: not just directional, but explanatory; impressive entry statements.
- Printed information: programs and souvenir material.
- Websites (informing and preparing potential visitors; before and after augmentation of the event experience).
- School-oriented programs, integrating events with the academic curriculum.

- Audio-visual presentations (slide shows, videos, sound).
- Interactive displays: hands on exhibits, computer simulations, talking robots.
- 'Live interpretation', including performances and storytelling.
- Direct involvement by guests or experiential learning (learn by doing).

PROGRAMMING AND THE ELEMENTS OF STYLE

A program is the scheduled or 'scripted' activities for the audience and other participants. A concert program can be quite simple, consisting of the order of artists or musical pieces. A festival program might be complex, involving multiple days and venues with numerous activities and performances. Sport events have scheduled times for competitions and award ceremonies. Meetings and conventions typically operate with tight agendas to make sure the program of speakers, plenary and breakout sessions, meals, coffee breaks and social events keeps to the schedule.

Program 'portfolios' consist of all the different activities and services provided at events. They have to meet multiple objectives, appeal to diverse audiences, and ideally be sustainable. To evaluate feasibility, desirability and continuance requires measures that reflect underlying goals and values. For example, commercial events have to monitor economic demand and profits, while public festivals might be focused on fulfilling social aims, like awareness building or providing cultural opportunities to specific groups in the community. Other possible values and measures include image; tradition; stakeholder desires; market potential and share; and growth potential.

'Style' is also an important design concept, as every event should be unique in some ways, yet reflect the style (maybe the branding) of the event producers or venue. 'Style' means a characteristic way of doing things, excellence of artistic expression (a measure of product or program quality), or fashion (which always changes). Style is largely subjective and therefore subject to widely different interpretations. Each 'programmic element of style' has a creative and a technical component. Elements can be combined in unlimited combinations to design a unique event program. Generally the elements have to be designed in concert with the setting and implemented through physical development and all the management systems.

Some programmic elements of style are 'hallmarks' of particular types of event. That is, the event form requires it by definition, or as a social construct this element is closely associated with it. For example, business and trade events like fairs and trade shows involve commerce by nature. Festivals are celebrations so they have to incorporate belonging and sharing, emotional stimulation, rituals and symbolism. Sports and recreation must involve games or competition. But standing alone, one element of style looks bare and will generate a rather narrow range of experiences. Sports are packaged as festivals for a good reason, to expand their appeal and generate additional benefits. Business events are serious, but they almost always base part of their appeal on social and touristic opportunities. One way to specify programmic elements of style is to list the actions a programmer or designer can include, or the activities that participants and guests are to engage in. These are the main activity elements subject to design, but keep in mind that each one can have varying cognitive and affective outcomes:

- teach, interpret, inform; engage people in discourse or problem solving;
- play and compete (games; mental and physical activity);
- amuse (use of humor and surprise);
- entertain (including spectacle, performances);
- engage in rites and rituals (including symbolism and protocol; cultural authenticity must be considered);
- exhibit (art; goods and services for marketing purposes);
- buy, sell, trade (commerce);
- mix and mingle (socializing, partying, group discussion);
- sensory stimulation (sight, sound, touch, taste, hearing); and
- hospitality (welcoming, guiding, services, satisfying basic needs such as eating, drinking, resting, toilets).

We have already examined the main programmic elements that constitute sensory stimulation, so here we need to add a list of ways to stimulate emotions. Just about any combination of activities and sensory stimulation can provoke emotional and cognitive responses, but these elements are tried and true in the context of politics, patriotism, religion and affinity groups:

- ritual and symbolism that reflects or suggests cultural and social identity; the display of scared or respected artifacts;
- direct verbal appeals to loyalty, pride, community or faith (i.e. preaching and propaganda);
- celebrity endorsements and the charisma of speakers, especially from recognized leaders; and
- selected information and interpretation (as social marketing and propaganda).

For event designers and programmers there can be a fine line between emotional or cognitive stimulation and exploitation, between facilitating a powerful, transforming experience and provoking a negative, even violent response. 'Playing with emotions' should always be undertaken with the benefit of research and evaluation, and this has sadly, often been ignored.

PROGRAM (OR 'PRODUCT') QUALITY

Getz and Carlsen (2006) discussed the main dimensions of event quality. Quality begins with the organization: its mandate and vision, philosophy and customer orientation; competence of its staff and volunteers; its governance, and effectiveness of its management. Program (or product) quality is experiential and subject to qualitative evaluation by all the stakeholders. Customers evaluate quality by expressing their level of satisfaction with the event overall, or with the quality of what is being presented to them in the form of sport competition, the musical performance, the speakers at a convention, art at an exhibit, food at a banquet, etc. Product quality can also be assessed through benchmarking against other events, the opinions of expert judges, or through experiential research.

Love and Crompton (1996) tested the hypothesis, based on the works of Herzberg (1966) that some event elements are 'dissatisfiers' which can undermine the visitor experience, while others are 'satisfiers' which provide benefits. 'Dissatisfiers' are like Herzberg's 'maintenance' factors – they must be provided to expected levels of quality, but in themselves do not satisfy visitors. The researchers argued that most of the physical factors at events, such as parking, rest rooms, and information, are dissatisfiers, while ambience, fantasy, excitement, relaxation, escape and social involvement are satisfiers. High-quality events must meet expectations in both categories, but they are non-compensatory in that a single or small number of attributes can determine perception of overall quality. Tentative support for this model was confirmed, and the researchers believed that certain attributes were perceived to be of so poor or high quality that visitors disregarded or discounted other attributes in giving their overall appraisal.

Baker and Crompton (2000) determined that generic and entertainment features of an event are more likely to generate increased satisfaction and motivate return visits or positive word-of-mouth recommendations. Saleh and Ryan (1993) found that quality of the music program is the most important service factor in attracting people to jazz festivals. Overall satisfaction levels affected the intention for repeat visits. Similarly, Thrane (2002) explored the link between satisfaction and future intentions of festival-goers. The most important conclusion from his study in Norway was that event managers must try to improve program quality (in this case music) and be concerned with other factors that shape overall satisfaction.

Ryan and Lockyer (2002) studied satisfaction levels of participants in the South Pacific Masters games in New Zealand – a friendly, multi-sport event for older athletes. The results showed that sport event managers need to pay particular attention to improving items of high importance but low satisfaction. In this sample the prime motivators – seeking challenge and fun – were found to be satisfied by the event. A factor analysis was also used to identify five components of importance to participants, namely: social (social events plus meeting people); registration (good communications); challenge; after-event communication, and that the competition is both fun and serious.

Researchers have demonstrated that event satisfaction is primarily dependent upon the core elements of the program, whether this is music or sport competition, and that is exactly what theme and program design seeks to accomplish. In this context, the setting, service delivery, and consumables are supporting factors. An exception is for food and beverage events where consumables are the core, or commerce events where people purchase tangible products. Nevertheless, service delivery is important,

as bad service easily displeases people. It is a design process because good service is both technical (e.g. no errors made, everything is done on time) and creative/qualitative (staff are friendly and helpful; staff as part of the experience).

There is a huge body of literature on service marketing, quality, and delivery, especially for the tourism and hospitality sectors (see, for example, Prideaux et al., 2006). Applied to event design, the basic principle is that all management systems as well as staff and volunteer actions, directly affect the customer's perceptions of quality and therefore their level of satisfaction with the event experience.

Drummond and Anderson (2004) discussed the meaning of quality and how service management impacts on events. They explained what has to be done to create a satisfying 'service experience' before, during and after the event. They argued that service enables the guest or customer to more fully enjoy the product or experience. Wicks and Fesenmaier (1993) studied differences between visitors and vendors in their perceptions of service quality at an event. A comparison of alternative approaches to evaluating event quality was undertaken by Crompton and Love (1995).

SERVICE BLUEPRINTING AND SERVICE MAPPING

'Blueprinting' is a tool with value in all the services, but its application to planned events has been minimal (see: Getz et al., 2001). The idea is to create a chart or 'blueprint' based on the flow of intended visitor activities and experiences, and to show how the experiences are facilitated by the setting (or 'servicescape'), all the management systems, and human contacts. The service 'map' is a diagnostic or evaluation tool that can precede blueprinting, or test its effectiveness.

The blueprint anticipates the flow of customer actions, starting with approach to the site and ending with departure. If there are many activity options or venues it will be necessary to have multiple blueprints, some in great detail and one for the overall process. Although the blueprint specifies actions in settings, it should consider the intended customer or guest experience. For example, 'viewing art in gallery' can be expanded into 'the guest will enjoy a quiet, esthetic experience, aided by interactive information about the artists and their displays'. This experiential elaboration will greatly assist in planning the 'physical evidence' and staff-guest interactions. When doing a service-mapping exercise, as evaluation, multiple observers (engaged in direct and participant observation) will be needed to plot the actual flow and activities of guests and to summarize the experiential dimensions.

Above the customer-actions flow chart, the blueprint specifies all the physical evidence of quality, such as entertainment, the competition, exhibits, facilities, signs, equipment, and audio-visual effects. It is necessary to include the hygiene factors like toilets and soap, water and comfort stations, and anticipate everything the guest will need or desire and specify the quality standards. In the case of evaluations, one should describe gaps and flaws in tangible evidence, such as crowding, unanticipated behavior, safety and health hazards, obvious customer confusion, inadequate signage or direction, and also describe program or product quality as experienced by observers. 'Hygiene factors' have been found to be extremely important at events, not in motivating people to attend or affecting their assessment of overall program quality, but in terms of causing dissatisfaction (these include security, cleanliness, comfort). Event quality can also be assessed by reference to its impacts, through measuring the attainment of positive goals and avoidance or amelioration of negative outcomes.

For each customer action, or experience setting, the blueprint has to specify staff or volunteer support that will, or could involve staff–guest interaction. These also define potential 'critical incidents' where service failure could occur. This line, under the flow chart, also quantifies human resource needs, in terms of staffing levels, duties, and necessary training. Viewed as 'cast members', staff and volunteers have both technical roles to play in delivering essential services, and an experiential role to play in facilitating desired experiences. Their appearance and demeanor are important to theming as well as service. In terms of service marketing theory (i.e. SERVQUAL, developed by Parasuraman et al., 1988), staff and volunteers have to exhibit 'responsiveness' a willingness to help; promptness), 'assurance' (knowledge and courtesy; convey trust and inspire confidence), 'empathy' (caring;

providing individual service), and 'reliability' (ability and dependability).

The usual practice is to draw a line under the 'visible staff contacts' and in this bottom space on the blueprint to indicate the management systems that have to be in place to support the entire service process (which, at events, inevitably means the program as well). In evaluations, the observers can work backwards from obvious failures or problems to determine what was missing or flawed in these hidden systems (for example: police should have regulated the approach road).

In an alternative approach Ralston et al. (2006) developed an 'experience factor model' for event design which combines experiential and service quality elements. The 'experience factors' consist of themed experiences, targeted impressions, reducing negative cues, engaging multiple senses, providing a mix in memorabilia, customizing to the individual, getting into and staying in character, and performing to appropriate form. The service factors are those of SERVQUAL: tangibles, reliability, responsiveness, empathy, assurance, recovery, competence, courtesy, security, access/welcome and communications.

Their model can be used as a diagnostic tool, using a type of SWOT analysis, which includes independent assessment of critical incidents, to assess an event's or attraction's 'experience quotient' and 'service quotient'. Service quality has to be high in order to achieve a high 'experience quotient' (i.e. to achieve memorable and transforming experiences), so the model encompasses an 'experience threshold'. This zone separates displeasure from enjoyment.

DESIGNING CONSUMABLES

At many events the food and beverage service is incidental to the main theme and program, but at others it is experientially paramount. This is true at food and wine festivals, gala dinners, and other events that stress cultural authenticity. Tellstrom et al. (2006: 130) stressed that 'Food and meals are a central field in the communication of culture'. In terms of quality and design, this is the realm of the chef and banquet manager, who are in turn dependent on suppliers for quality. Eating at many events is nothing more than a basic service, but it should be an experience. Lashley et al.

(2004) defined the dimensions of this eating experience: the occasion; the company one dines with; atmosphere; food; service, and setting.

Gustafsson et al. (2006: 89–90) noted that the meal product consists of visual effect, taste/expectation compliance, reflection of style, and standard of service and said '… the whole product process requires both craftsmanship, science and esthetical/ethical knowledge in order to produce good meals and result in the optimum experience for the guest/diner …'. All the senses have to be stimulated, '… and in harmony to create agreement that it was a good meal experience …'.

Gift-giving is also important at some events, including those in which sponsors provide samples to take home, or when employers reward their staff. In these cases the tangibles are a key part of the event experience, so their inherent (or perceived) quality, and how they are presented, are critical. To marketers, each gift is a branding exercise – sponsors want guests to go away with favorable and enduring perceptions of their brand. To employers rewarding staff, the symbolic value of the gift is usually more important.

RESEARCH PROGRESS AND NEEDS

General event management textbooks have been increasing in number, with the emphasis being placed on application of management principles and methods to events and the organizations producing them (Hall, 1992; Watt, 1998; Tassiopoulos, 2000; Shone and Parry, 2001; Allen et al., 2002; Rutherford and Goldblatt, 2003; Goldblatt, 2004; Silvers, 2004; Van der Wagen, 2004; Yeoman et al., 2004; Getz, 2005 and Bowdin et al., 2006). In addition there are numerous practitioner-written and oriented books and manuals, such as Allen (2000, 2002), and Wiersma and Strolberg (2003). These texts have found a rapidly growing market in both event management diploma and degree programs and in closely related professional fields.

Publishers, especially Wiley and Elsevier, have substantial event management book series, resulting in more and more specialized topics. These include a focus on both types of event, and on event management functions. In terms of event types, the coverage includes sports (Graham et al., 1995; Solomon, 2002; Masterman, 2004; Supovitz and Goldblatt, 2004), meetings and conventions (Meeting Professionals International, 2003; Davidson and Cope, 2003; McCabe et al., 2003; Rogers, 2003; Fenich, 2005; Rogers and Davidson, 2006), exhibitions (Morrow, 1997), parties (Malouf, 2002) and even weddings (Daniels and Loveless, 2007).

Festivals, carnivals and other cultural celebrations have received a lot of attention. This is no doubt in large part because of their long-standing interest to anthropologists and their importance within the arts and cultural studies (see, for example: Picard and Robinson, 2006). However, the vast majority of papers and books on festivals and carnivals are not management-oriented. Olympics-related literature is huge, fuelled by Olympic research centers around the world, and there have been many books devoted to the Olympics, world fairs, and other 'mega-events' (e.g. Teigland, 1996; Andersson et al., 1999; Roche, 2000; Toohey and Veal, 2007). Numerous themes are covered in the Olympics literature, including their design and management, but the application of lessons from the Olympics and other mega-events to other types of event and to less capital-intensive (or less political) event circumstances cannot be assumed.

Regarding event management functions, the following specialty books are available: marketing and communications (Hoyle, 2002; Masterman and Wood, 2006), project planning (O'Toole and Mikolaitis, 2002), feasibility (O'Toole, 2007), operations (Tum et al. 2006), risk management (Berlonghi, 1990; Tarlow, 2002), human resources (Van der Wagen, 2006), evaluation and impact assessment (Jago and Dwyer, 2006; Mossberg, 2006), and sponsorship (Skinner and Rukavina (2003).

Sports, meetings and conventions are well explored, and have been the subject of specialist curricula and books longer than event management in general. Professional associations have provided a lot of literature, usually in the form of practitioner-oriented manuals aimed at single types of events but often covering the same material. For example, all event associations seem to provide advice on sponsorship. The global professional situation is clearly marked by this event-specific specialization, which is clearly being challenged by development of generic event management material and curricula – although some schools provide for event-specific or function-specific specialization. The future will probably see the emergence of Event Management as the single, accepted professional standard.

Design, as discussed in this article, has only recently been afforded serious academic attention, as distinct from practical applications. One book has been devoted to design and the event experience (Berridge, 2006), while Getz (2007) treats these topics in a more theoretical manner. A related, fast-developing line of research and literature is that of sport tourism, which incorporates substantial attention to sport events (e.g., Higham, 2005; Gibson, 2006).

Several research journals are devoted to this field: *Event Management* (formerly *Festival Management and Event Tourism*), *Convention and Event Tourism*, the online journal *International Journal of Event Management Research*, and the new *World Journal of Managing Events*. Journals from closely related fields cover event-related topics, especially those in leisure, tourism, hospitality and sport.

Previous overviews of research in the event management field have been undertaken by Formica (1998), Getz (2000), Harris et al. (2001) and Jago and Harris (2003). Formica identified economics or financial impacts of events as the most frequent topic in the journal *Festival Management and Event Tourism* plus three leading tourism journals, followed by marketing, profiles of events, sponsorship, management and trends/forecasts. The Getz overview in 2000, from a detailed analysis of articles only in *Festival Management and Event Tourism* (which changed its name to *Event Management*), concluded that the most frequently studied themes were economic development and impacts (mostly the tourism domain), sponsorship and event marketing from the corporate perspective, other management topics, then general marketing including motivation and segmentation. Design had not yet entered the event management literature as a specific topic, and it still remains rare seven years later.

Formica argued that the emerging event management field needed more theoretical development, and hence more sophisticated and multiple research methods. This admonition remains just as pertinent today. A broad range of methodologies and methods are appropriate and necessary for advancing event management and design. The positivistic approaches standard to management, economics and other social sciences will continue to be useful, but it is necessary to employ both qualitative and quantitative

methods. In particular, the experiential nature of events requires phenomenological approaches, including hermeneutics (the interpretation of texts, which can be the event itself), direct and participant observation, in-depth interviews, and experiential sampling. Consumer experiments are likely to be valuable in exploring the influence of various design and management tools.

MAKING RESEARCH RELEVANT

Harris et al. (2001) examined academic, practitioner and government perspectives on research needs related to events. Practitioners emphasized research on sponsorship, the needs and motives of attendees, market segmentation, and determining why events fail. Government officials wanted research on event failure and risks, as well as the development of standard research tools and methods. Perhaps surprisingly, academics selected risk management strategy formulation as their priority, followed by valuing events and reasons for failure.

Jago and Harris (2003), based in part on discussions at events conferences in Australia, concluded that academics and practitioners did not communicate very well. Both thought the other group had to do more, and the truth was probably somewhere in between. Practitioners always seem to think that academics do not conduct relevant research, or do not communicate research findings to meet their needs, but of course that has never been a particular aim of most academics. If that is true at the level of event design, production and management, it is likely to be even more substantial a gap at the level of event studies.

Jago and Harris concluded that more partnerships should be developed between research suppliers and providers, although this appears to be an easier task in Australia where there has been in place for some time a large source of research grants for sustainable tourism (including events) that is explicitly tied to industry relevance. Elsewhere, it is probable that closing this gap will require direct intervention by professional associations in seeking research and training partnerships with academic institutions that specialize in event management.

Disciplinary approaches will remain very important to development of event design and management, and event studies in general, but probably a greater and quicker advancement will come from partnering with closely related fields, including hospitality, tourism, leisure, sport, theater, performance studies, arts and cultural management. That is because these professional fields already understand and value events, from multiple perspectives, and can deliver relevant theory and methodology that has already been tested.

KEY RESEARCH ISSUES AND RELATED METHODS

In terms of furthering the nexus between event management/design and hospitality, a number of important theoretical gaps should be closed. These are based on the event studies framework:

- examine how people describe, explain and assign meaning to various event experiences within each of these dimensions: conative (behavior); affective (emotional) and cognitive (thinking and problem-solving);
- the nature of the experience as a host and as a guest (i.e. the spirit of hospitality and delivery of service);
- what people need and expect in terms of hospitality at all types of events and settings;
- event outcomes measured in terms of customer and client satisfaction and future behavior; related business outcomes for hospitality service and venue providers;
- hospitality perspectives on the design of event setting, services, and consumables;
- how personal and social constructs are formed regarding event experiences;
- how the level of engagement with an event, or ego-involvement related to lifestyle in general, affects the event experience;
- what exactly makes event experiences memorable and transforming;
- is there a measurable 'wow!' factor? (is it merely surprise, or a fleeting emotional reaction to stimulation?);
- the potential effects of various sensory and emotional stimulations at events;
- how theory from environmental psychology can improve event design, logistics and crowd management; and
- what are the main determinants of customer satisfaction at events?

The development of event management and event design as a professional field, and of event studies as a theory-based, interdisciplinary field, will have substantial benefits for hospitality researchers and practitioners. Improved understanding of the planned event experience, considering the needs, motivations, experiences and meanings attached to events by all stakeholders, will help venue managers and service providers in their marketing, event operations, and overall effectiveness in satisfying clients, guests and customers.

CONCLUSIONS

Event management is a rapidly growing professional field that embodies event tourism and event design. Its development has considerable implications for hospitality management in terms of contributing knowledge about planned event experiences and their design. In turn, hospitality informs event managers in terms of host–guest theory, and especially about practices and issues relating to event settings and services.

It has been argued that planned event experiences are highly personal and cannot be created, only suggested, facilitated and constrained through design processes. Event designers can operate within four realms to affect the setting, themes and program; service delivery; and consumables, all of which are related closely to hospitality. Each of these areas of design application require their own research and progress with respect to concepts, underlying theories, goals, and design tools.

Hospitality and event management are closely interrelated. While event managers and policy makers should understand the roles of events in tourism, economic and arts/cultural development, they absolutely need to know many of the theoretical, methodological, and practical lessons offered by hospitality. Events are hospitality occasions, sometimes fostering host and guest interaction, sometimes stressing corporate hospitality, but always aiming to create a satisfying, memorable experience for guests, consumers and clients.

REFERENCES

Allen, J. (2000) *Event Planning: The Ultimate Guide to Successful Meetings, Corporate Events, Fundraising Galas, Conferences, Conventions, Incentives and Other Special Events.* Toronto: Wiley.

Allen, J. (2002) *The Business of Event Planning: Behind-the-Scenes Secrets of Successful Special Events.* Toronto: Wiley.

Allen, J., O'Toole, W., McDonnell, I. and Harris, R. (2002) *Festival and Special Event Management* (2nd edn). Brisbane: Wiley Australia.

Ammon, R. and Fried, G. (1998) 'Crowd management practices', *Journal of Convention and Exhibition Management*, 1(2/3): 119–150.

Andersson, T., Persson, C., Sahlberg, B. and Strom, L. (eds) (1999) *The Impact of Mega Events.* Ostersund, Sweden: European Tourism Research Institute.

Bailey, P. (2002) *Design for Entertaining: Inspiration for Creating the Party of Your Dreams.* Weimar, TX: Culinary and Hospitality Industry Publications Services.

Baker, D. and Crompton, J. (2000) 'Quality, satisfaction and behavioral intentions', *Annals of Tourism Research*, 27(2): 785–804.

Barker, R. (1968) *Ecological Psychology: Concepts and Methods for Studying the Environment Of Human Behavior.* Stanford CA: Stanford University Press.

Bateson, J. (1989) *Managing Services Marketing: Text and Readings.* Chicago: The Dryden Press.

Bell, P., Greene, T., Fisher, J. and Baum, A. (2001) *Environmental Psychology* (5th edn). Belmont CA: Thomson Wadsworth.

Berlonghi, A. (1990) *The Special Event Risk Management Manual.* Self-published.

Berridge, G. (2006) *Event Design and Experience.* Oxford: Elsevier.

Bowdin, G., Allen, J., O'Toole, W., Harris, R. and McDonnell, I. (2006) *Events Management* (2nd edn). Oxford: Elsevier.

Brown, S. and James, J. (2004) 'Event design and management: ritual sacrifice?' In I. Yeoman et al. (eds) *Festivals and Events Management.* Oxford: Elsevier. pp. 53–64.

Crompton, J. and Love, L. (1995) 'The predictive validity of alternative approaches to evaluating quality of a festival', *Journal of Travel Research*, 34(1): 11–24.

Daniels, M. and Loveless, C. (2007) *Wedding Planning and Management: Consultancy for Diverse Clients.* Oxford: Elsevier.

Darcy, S. and Harris, R. (2003) 'Inclusive and accessible special event planning: an Australian perspective', *Event Management*, 8(1): 39–47.

Davidson, R. and Cope, B. (2003) *Business Travel: Conferences, Incentive Travel, Exhibitions, Corporate Hospitality and Corporate Travel.* Harlow: Longman.

Drummond, S. and Anderson, H. (2004) 'Service quality and managing your people'. In I. Yeoman et al. (eds) *Festival and Events Management.* Oxford: Elsevier. pp. 80–96.

Falassi, A. (ed.) (1987) *Time Out of Time: Essays on the Festival.* Albuquerque: University of New Mexico Press.

Fenich, G. (2005) *Meetings, Expositions, Events, and Conventions: An Introduction to the Industry.* Upper Saddle River NJ: Pearson/Prentice Hall.

Fleck, S. (1996) 'Events without barriers: customer service is a key in complying with the Americans With Disabilities Act', *Festivals*, March: 34–35. (International Festivals and Events Association.)

Formica, S. (1998) 'The development of festivals and special events studies', *Festival Management and Event Tourism*, 5(3): 131–137.

Freedman, J. (1975) *Crowding and Behavior.* San Francisco: Freeman.

Getz, D. (2000) 'Developing a research agenda for the event management field'. In J. Allen, R. Harris, L. Jago and A. J. Veal (eds) *Events Beyond 2000: Setting the Agenda, Proceedings of Conference on Event Evaluation, Research and Education.* Sydney: Australian Centre for Event Management, University of Technology, Sydney. pp. 10–21.

Getz, D. (2001) 'Festival places: a comparison of Europe and North America', *Tourism*, 49(1): 3–18.

Getz, D. (2005) *Event Management and Event Tourism.* New York: Cognizant.

Getz, D. (2007) *Event Studies: Theory, Research and Policy for Planned Events.* Oxford: Elsevier.

Getz, D. and Carlsen, J. (2006) 'Quality management for events'. In B. Prideaux, G. Moscardo and E. Laws (eds) *Managing Tourism and Hospitality Services.* Wallingford: CABI. pp. 145–155.

Getz, D., O'Neill, M. and Carlsen, J. (2001) 'Service quality evaluation at events through service mapping', *Journal of Travel Research*, 39(4): 380–390.

Gibson, H. (ed.) (2006) *Sport Tourism: Concepts and Theories.* London: Routledge.

Goldblatt, J. (2004) *Special Events: Event Leadership for a New World.* New York: Wiley.

Graham, S., Goldblatt, J. and Delpy, L. (1995) *The Ultimate Guide to Sport Event Management and Marketing.* Chicago: Irwin.

Gregson, B. (1992) *Reinventing Celebration: The Art of Planning Public Events.* Orange, Connecticut: Shannon Press.

Gustafsson, I., Ostrom, A., Johansson, J. and Mossberg, L. (2006) 'The five aspects of meal model: a tool for developing meal services in restaurants', *Journal of Foodservice*, 17: 84–93.

Haahti, A. and Komppula, R. (2006) 'Experience design in tourism', In D. Buhalis and C. Costa (eds) *Tourism Business Frontiers: Consumers, Products and Industry.* Oxford: Elsevier. pp. 101–110.

Hall, E. (1966) *The Hidden Dimension.* New York: Doubleday.

Hall, M. (1992) *Hallmark Tourist Events: Impacts, Management and Planning*. London: Belhaven.

Ham, S., Housego, A. and Weiler, B. (2005) *Tasmanian Thematic Interpretation Planning Manual* (available online at www.tourismtasmania.com).

Harris, V. (2004) 'Event management: a new profession', *Event Management*, 9(1/2):103–109.

Harris, R., Jago, L., Allen, J. and Huyskens, M. (2001) 'Towards an Australian event research agenda: first steps', *Event Management*, 6(4): 213–221.

Harvey, M., Loomis, R, Bell, R. and Marino, M. (1998) 'The influence of museum exhibit design on immersion and psychological flow', *Environment and Behavior*, 30: 601–627.

Herzberg, F. (1966) *Work and the Nature of Man*. Cleveland: World Publishing Co.

Higham, J. (ed.) (2005) *Sport Tourism Destinations: Issues, Opportunities and Analysis*. Oxford: Elsevier.

Hoyle, L. (2002) *Event Marketing: How to Successfully Promote Events, Festivals, Conventions, and Expositions*. New York: Wiley.

International Festivals and Events Association (2000) *Parades*. Port Angeles WA.

Iso-Ahola, S. (1980) *The Social Psychology of Leisure and Recreation*. Dubuque, Iowa: Brown.

Iso-Ahola, S. (1983) 'Towards a social psychology of recreational travel', *Leisure Studies*, 2(1): 45–57.

Jago, L. and R. Harris (2003) 'Introduction', *Event Management*, 8(1): 1–2.

Jago, L. and Dwyer, L. (2006) *Economic Evaluation of Special Events: A Practitioner's Guide*. Gold Coast Australia: Cooperative Research Centre for Sustainable Tourism.

Kaplan, S. (1987) 'Aesthetics, affect, and cognition: environmental preference from an evolutionary perspective', *Environment and Behavior*, 1: 3–32.

Lashley, C., Morrisson, A. and Randall, S. (2004) 'My most memorable meal ever! Hospitality as an emotional experience'. In D. Sloan (ed.) *Culinary Taste, Consumer Behaviour in the International Restaurant Sector*. Oxford: Butterworth-Heinemann. pp. 165–184.

Lee, H., Kerstetter, D., Graefe, A. and Confer, J. (1997) 'Crowding at an arts festival: a replication and extension of the outdoor recreation crowding model'. In W. Kuentzel (ed.) *Proceedings of the 1966 Northeastern Recreation Research Symposium* (USDA Forest Service Ge. Tech. Rep. NE-232, pp. 198–204). Radnor, PA: Northeastern Forest Experiment Station.

Li, R. and Petrick, J. (2006) 'A review of festival and event motivation studies', *Event Management*, 9(4): 239–245.

Love, L. and J. Crompton (1996) 'A conceptualization of the relative roles of festival attributes in determining perceptions of overall festival quality',

Paper presented to the Research Symposium, Annual Conference of the International Festivals and Events Association.

Lynch, K. (1960) *The Image of the City*. Cambridge, MA: MIT Press.

Malouf, L. (2002) *Parties and Special Events: Planning and Design*. Weimar, TX: Culinary and Hospitality Industry Publications Services.

Masterman, G. (2004) *Strategic Sports Event Management: An International Approach*. Oxford: Elsevier.

Masterman, G. and Wood, E. (2006) *Innovative Marketing Communications: Strategies for the Events Industry*. Oxford: Elsevier.

McCabe, V., Poole, I., Weeks, P. and Leiper, N. (2000) *The Business and Management of Conventions*. Brisbane: Wiley Australia.

McGehee, N., Yoon, Y. and Cardenas, D. (2003) 'Involvement and travel for recreational runners in North Carolina', *Journal of Sport Management*, 17(3): 305–324.

Meeting Professionals International (2003) *Meetings and Conventions: A Planning Guide*. Mississauga: MPI.

Morrow, S. (1997) *The Art of the Show: An Introduction to the Study of Exhibition Management*. Dallas: International Association for Exhibition Management.

Mossberg, L. (ed.) (2006) *Evaluation of Events: Scandinavian Experiences*. New York: Cognizant Communication Corp.

Mowen, A., Vogelsong, H. and Graefe, A. (2003) 'Perceived crowding and its relationship to crowd management practices at park and recreation events', *Event Management*, 8(2): 63–72.

New South Wales. *Traffic Management for Special Events* (www.rta.nsw.gov.au).

Nicholson, R. and Pearce, D. (2001) 'Why do people attend events: a comparative analysis of visitor motivations at four South Island events', *Journal of Travel Research*, 39: 449–460.

O'Toole, W. (2007) *Event Feasibility: The Business Case for Events and Festivals*. Oxford: Elsevier.

O'Toole, W. and Mikolaitis, P. (2002) *Corporate Event Project Management*. New York: Wiley.

Parasuraman, A., Berry, L. and Zeithaml, V. (1988) 'SERVQUAL: a multiple-item scale for measuring consumer perceptions of service quality', *Journal of Retailing*, 64(1): 12–40.

Pearce, P. (2005) *Tourist Behaviour: Themes and Conceptual Schemas*. Clevedon: Channel View.

Picard, D. and Robinson. M. (eds) (2006) *Festivals, Tourism and Social Change: Remaking Worlds*. Clevedon: Channel View.

Pine, B. and Gilmore, J. (1999) *The Experience Economy: Work is Theatre and Every Business a Stage*. Boston: Harvard Business School Press.

Prideaux, B., Moscardo, G. and Laws, E. (eds) (2006) *Managing Tourism and Hospitality Services: Theory and International Applications*. Wallingford: CABI.

Ralston, L., Ellis, D., Compton, D. and Lee, J. (2006) 'Staging memorable events and festivals: an integrated model of service and experience factors'. In C. Arcodia, M. Whitford, and C. Dickson (eds) *Global Events Congress Proceedings*. Brisbane: University of Queensland. pp. 268–285.

Ralston, R., Lumsdon, L. and Downward, P. (2005) 'The third force in events tourism: volunteers at the XVII Commonwealth Games', *Journal of Sustainable Tourism*, 13(5): 504–519.

Roche, M. (2000) *Mega-Events and Modernity: Olympics and Expos in the Growth of Global Culture*. London: Routledge.

Rogers, T. (2003) *Conferences and Conventions: A Global Industry*. Oxford: Butterworth-Heinemann.

Rogers, T. and Davidson, R. (2006) *Marketing Destinations and Venues for Conferences, Conventions and Business Events*. Oxford: Elsevier.

Russell, J. and Lanius, U. (1984) 'Adaptation level and the affective appraisal of environments', *Journal of Environmental Psychology*, 4: 119–135.

Rutherford, J. and Goldblatt, J. (2003) *Professional Event Coordination*. New York: Wiley.

Rutley, J. (n.d.) 'Security'. In *Event Operations*. Port Angeles: International Festivals and Events Association. pp. 75–83.

Ryan, C. and Lockyer, T. (2002) 'Masters' Games – the nature of competitors' involvement and requirements', *Event Management*, 7(4): 259–270.

Saleh, F. and Ryan, C. (1993) 'Jazz and knitwear: factors that attract tourists to festivals', *Tourism Management*, 14(4): 289–297.

Severt, D., Wang, Y., Chen, P. and Breiter, D. (2007) 'Examining the motivation, perceived performance, and behavioral intentions of convention attendees: evidence from a regional conference', *Tourism Management*, 28(2): 399–408.

Shone, A. and Parry B. (2001) *Successful Event Management*. London: Continuum.

Silvers, J. (2004) *Professional Event Coordination*. New York: Wiley.

Silvers, J., Bowdin, G., O'Toole, W. and Nelson, K. (2006) 'Towards an international event management body of knowledge (EMBOK)', *Event Management*, 9(4): 185–198.

Skinner, B. and Rukavina, V. (2003) *Event Sponsorship*. New York: Wiley.

Solomon, J. (2002) *An Insider's Guide to Managing Sporting Events*. Champaign IL: Human Kinetics.

Supovitz, F. and Goldblatt, J. (2004) *The Sports Event Management and Marketing Handbook*. New York: Wiley.

Tarlow, P. (2002) *Event Risk Management and Safety*. New York: Wiley.

Tassiopoulos, D. (ed.) (2000) *Event Management: A Professional and Developmental Approach*. Lansdowne SA: Juta Education.

Teigland, J. (1996) *Impacts on Tourism From Mega-Events: The Case of Winter Olympic Games*. Sogndal: Western Norway Research Institute.

Tellstrom, R., Gustafsson, I. and Mossberg, L. (2006) 'Consuming heritage: the use of local food culture in branding', *Place Branding*, 2(2): 130–143.

Thrane, C. (2002) 'Music quality, satisfaction, and behavioral intentions within a jazz festival context', *Event Management*, 7(3): 143–150.

Toohey, K. and Veal, T. (2007) *The Olympic Games: A Social Science Perspective*. Wallingford: CABI.

Tum, J., Norton, P. and Wright, J. (2006) *Management of Event Operations*. Oxford: Elsevier.

UK National Outdoor Events Association (www.noea.org.uk).

Van der Wagen, L. (2004) *Event Management for Tourism, Cultural, Business and Sporting Events* (2nd edn). Frenchs Forest, NSW: Pearson Education Australia.

Van der Wagen, L. (2006) *Human Resource Management for Events: Managing the Event Workforce*. Oxford: Elsevier.

Watt, D. (1998) *Event Management in Leisure and Tourism*. Harlow: Addison Wesley Longman.

Wickham, T. and Kerstetter, D. (2000) 'The relationship between place attachment and crowding in an event setting', *Event Management*, 6(3): 167–174.

Wicks, B. and Fesenmaier, D. (1993) 'A comparison of visitor and vendor perceptions of service quality at a special event', *Festival Management and Event Tourism*, 1(1): 19–26.

Wiersma, B. and Strolberg, K. (2003) *Exceptional Events: Concept to Completion* (2nd edn). Weimar, TX: Culinary and Hospitality Industry Publications Services.

Yeoman I., Robertson, M., Ali-Knight, J., Drummond, S. and McMahon-Beattie, U. (2004) *Festival and Events Management: An International Arts and Culture Perspective*. Oxford: Elsevier.

Index

(Page numbers in italic denote figures and tables)